Handbook of Latin American Studies: No. 40

A SELECTIVE AND ANNOTATED GUIDE TO RECENT PUBLICATIONS

IN ART, FILM, HISTORY, LANGUAGE, LITERATURE,

MUSIC, AND PHILOSOPHY

•

VOLUME 41 WILL BE DEVOTED TO THE SOCIAL SCIENCES (ANTHROPOLOGY, ECONOMICS, EDUCATION, GEOGRAPHY, GOVERNMENT AND POLITICS, INTERNATIONAL RELATIONS, AND SOCIOLOGY)

EDITORIAL NOTE

Comments concerning the *Handbook of Latin American Studies* should be sent directly to the Editor, *Handbook of Latin American Studies*, Hispanic Division, Library of Congress, Washington, D.C. 20540.

Advisory Board

Charles Gibson, *University of Michigan*, CHAIRMAN
Cole Blasier, *University of Pittsburgh*
Pauline P. Collins, *University of Massachusetts*
Frank N. Dauster, *Rutgers University, New Brunswick*
William P. Glade, Jr., *University of Texas, Austin*
Joseph Grunwald, *The Brookings Institution*
Javier Malagón, *Embassy of Spain, Washington, D.C.*
Betty J. Meggers, *Smithsonian Institution*
James R. Scobie, *University of California, San Diego*
Kempton E. Webb, *Columbia University*
Bryce Wood, *Friday Harbor, Washington*

Administrative Officers • Library of Congress

Daniel J. Boorstin, *The Librarian of Congress*
Donald C. Curran, *Acting Assistant Librarian for Research Services*
Frank M. McGowan, *Acting Director for Area Studies*
John R. Hébert, *Acting Chief, Hispanic Division*

Representative of the University of Florida

Phillip L. Martin, *Director, University Presses of Florida*

Handbook Editorial Staff

Senior Assistants to the Editor
  Alfredda H. Payne
  Janice M. Herd
Editorial Assistants
  Kim B. Wallace
  Monserrat Alayón

HANDBOOK OF LATIN AMERICAN STUDIES
No. 40

Prepared by

A NUMBER OF SCHOLARS

for

the Hispanic Division

of

The Library of Congress

Edited by

DOLORES MOYANO MARTIN

HUMANITIES

University Presses Of Florida
Gainesville

1978

L. C. Card Number: 36-32633

ISBN 0-8130-0637-6

A University Of Florida Book

COPYRIGHT © 1979 BY THE BOARD OF REGENTS

OF THE STATE OF FLORIDA

TYPOGRAPHY BY CANON GRAPHICS

PRINTED BY ROSE PRINTING CO.

TALLAHASSEE, FLORIDA

Contributing Editors

Earl M. Aldrich, Jr., *University of Wisconsin, Madison*, LITERATURE
*Fuat Andic, *University of Puerto Rico, Río Piedras*, ECONOMICS
*Suphan Andic, *University of Puerto Rico, Rio Piedras*, ECONOMICS
Jean A. Barman, *University of British Columbia*, HISTORY
Roderick J. Barman, *University of British Columbia*, HISTORY
*Robert L. Bennett, *University of Maryland, College Park*, ECONOMICS
*R. Albert Berry, *University of Toronto*, ECONOMICS
*Leslie Ann Brownrigg, *Feura Bush, New York*, ANTHROPOLOGY
Juan Bruce-Novoa, *Yale University*, LITERATURE
Julianne Burton, *University of California, Santa Cruz*, FILM
David Bushnell, *University of Florida*, HISTORY
Edward E. Calnek, *University of Rochester*, HISTORY
D. Lincoln Canfield, *Southern Illinois University at Carbondale*, LANGUAGES
Donald E. Chipman, *North Texas State University, Denton*, HISTORY
Don M. Coerver, *Texas Christian University*, HISTORY
*Lambros Comitas, *Columbia University*, ANTHROPOLOGY
*Cynthia A. Cone, *University of Minnesota*, ANTHROPOLOGY
*Michael L. Cook, *Texas A&M University*, ECONOMICS
Edith B. Couturier, *The Newberry Library*, HISTORY
*José Fabio Barbosa Dasilva, *University of Notre Dame*, SOCIOLOGY
Frank Dauster, *Rutgers University, New Brunswick*, LITERATURE
Maria Angélica Lopes Guimarães Dean, *University of Wisconsin, Parkside*, LITERATURE
*David W. Dent, *Towson State College*, GOVERNMENT AND POLITICS
Ralph E. Dimmick, *General Secretariat, Organization of American States*, LITERATURE
*Clinton R. Edwards, *University of Wisconsin, Milwaukee*, GEOGRAPHY
*Robert C. Eidt, *University of Wisconsin, Milwaukee*, GEOGRAPHY
*Gary S. Elbow, *Texas Technical University*, GEOGRAPHY
*Clifford Evans, *Smithsonian Institution*, ANTHROPOLOGY
*Yale H. Ferguson, *Rutgers University, Newark*, INTERNATIONAL RELATIONS
Rubén A. Gamboa, *Mills College*, LITERATURE
*William R. Garner, *Southern Illinois University*, GOVERNMENT AND POLITICS
Naomi M. Garrett, *West Virginia State College*, LITERATURE
*Marion H. Gillim, *Eastern Kentucky University*, ECONOMICS
Cedomil Goić, *The University of Michigan*, LITERATURE
Roberto González Echevarría, *Yale University*, LITERATURE
Richard E. Greenleaf, *Tulane University*, HISTORY
Oscar Hahn, *University of Iowa*, LITERATURE
*Robert A. Halberstein, *University of Miami*, ANTHROPOLOGY
Michael T. Hamerly, *Pacific Northwest Bibliographic Center, Seattle*, HISTORY
*Norman Hammond, *Rutgers University*, ANTHROPOLOGY
John R. Hébert, *Library of Congress*, BIBLIOGRAPHY AND GENERAL WORKS
*Pedro F. Hernández, *Loyola University*, SOCIOLOGY
*Mario Hiraoka, *Millersville State College*, GEOGRAPHY
Carlos R. Hortas, *Yale University*, LITERATURE
*John M. Hunter, *Michigan State University*, ECONOMICS
*John M. Ingham, *University of Minnesota*, ANTHROPOLOGY
Thomas B. Irving, *University of Tennessee*, LITERATURE
*Quentin Jenkins, *Louisiana State University*, SOCIOLOGY

*Contributing editors to *HLAS* no. 41 (Social Sciences), scheduled for publication in the fall of 1979.

Contributing Editors

Harvey L. Johnson, *University of Houston*, LITERATURE
Djelal Kadir, *Purdue University*, LITERATURE
*W. Jerald Kennedy, *Florida Atlantic University*, ANTHROPOLOGY
Franklin W. Knight, *Johns Hopkins University*, HISTORY
*Peter T. Knight, *International Bank for Reconstruction and Development*, ECONOMICS
Pedro Lastra, *State University of New York at Stony Brook*, LITERATURE
Asunción Lavrin, *Howard University*, HISTORY
*Seth Leacock, *University of Connecticut*, ANTHROPOLOGY
James B. Lynch, Jr., *University of Maryland, College Park*, ART
Alfred J. MacAdam, *University of Virginia*, LITERATURE
Colin MacLachlan, *Tulane University*, HISTORY
Murdo J. MacLeod, *University of Pittsburgh*, HISTORY
*Markos Mamalakis, *University of Wisconsin, Milwaukee*, ECONOMICS
Wilson Martins, *New York University*, LITERATURE
*Tom L. Martinson, *Ball State University*, GEOGRAPHY
Corina Mathieu-Higginbotham, *University of Nevada*, LITERATURE
*Betty J. Meggers, *Smithsonian Institution*, ANTHROPOLOGY
*Frank C. Miller, *University of Minnesota*, ANTHROPOLOGY
*Andrew M. Modelski, *Library of Congress*, GEOGRAPHY
Carolyn Morrow, *University of Utah*, LITERATURE
Gerald M. Moser, *Pennsylvania State University*, LITERATURE
Robert J. Mullen, *University of Texas, San Antonio*, ART
John V. Murra, *Cornell University*, HISTORY
José Neistein, *Brazilian American Cultural Institute, Washington*, ART
Betty T. Osiek, *Southern Illinois University at Edwardsville*, LITERATURE
José Miguel Oviedo, *Indiana University*, LITERATURE
Margaret S. Peden, *University of Missouri*, LITERATURE
Vincent C. Peloso, *Howard University*, HISTORY
Esther Pereyra-Suárez, *San Jose State University*, LITERATURE
*Lisandro Pérez, *Louisiana State University*, SOCIOLOGY
*Jorge F. Pérez-López, *U.S. Department of Labor*, ECONOMICS
Humberto M. Rasi, *Andrews University*, LITERATURE
Daniel R. Reedy, *University of Kentucky*, LITERATURE
Eliana Rivero, *The University of Arizona*, LITERATURE
*C. Neale Ronning, *New School for Social Research*, INTERNATIONAL RELATIONS
*Gordon C. Ruscoe, *University of Louisville*, EDUCATION
*Jorge Salazar-Carrillo, *Brookings Institution*, ECONOMICS
Alexandrino E. Severino, *Vanderbilt University*, LITERATURE
Merle E. Simmons, *Indiana University*, FOLKLORE
Hobart A. Spalding, Jr., *Brooklyn College*, HISTORY
Robert Stevenson, *University of California, Los Angeles*, MUSIC
*Andrés Suárez, *University of Florida*, GOVERNMENT AND POLITICS
*Philip B. Taylor, Jr., *University of Houston*, GOVERNMENT AND POLITICS
Juan Carlos Torchia-Estrada, *General Secretariat, Organization of American States*, PHILOSOPHY
*Agnes E. Toward, *Southwest Educational Development Laboratory, Austin, Texas*, EDUCATION
*Nelson P. Valdés, *University of New Mexico, Albuquerque*, SOCIOLOGY
*Carlos H. Waisman, *University of California, San Diego*, SOCIOLOGY
*Alan C. Wares, *Summer Institute of Linguistics, Dallas*, ANTHROPOLOGY
John Hoyt Williams, *Indiana State University*, HISTORY

---

*Contributing editors to *HLAS* no. 41 (Social Sciences) scheduled for publication in the fall of 1979.

*Hasso von Winning, *Southwest Museum, Los Angeles*, ANTHROPOLOGY
*Jan Peter Wogart, *International Bank for Reconstruction and Development*, ECONOMICS
Benjamin M. Woodbridge, Jr., *University of California, Berkeley*, LITERATURE
Thomas C. Wright, *University of Nevada*, HISTORY
Winthrop R. Wright, *University of Maryland, College Park*, HISTORY

Foreign Corresponding Editors

Marcello Carmagnani, *Università di Torino, Italy*, ITALIAN LANGUAGE
Lino Gómez-Canedo, *Franciscan Academy, Washington*, COLONIAL HISTORY
*Wolf Grabendorff, *Lateinamerikareferat, Stiftung, Wissenschaft und Politik, Ebenhauser/Isar, Federal Republic of Germany*, GERMAN SOCIAL SCIENCE MATERIAL
*Manfred Kossok, *Karl-Marx-Universitaet, Leipzig, German Democratic Republic*, GERMAN SOCIAL SCIENCE MATERIAL
Magnus Mörner, *Latinamerika-institutet i Stockholm, Sweden*, SCANDINAVIAN LANGUAGES
Wilhelm Stegmann, *Ibero-Amerikanisches Institut, Berlin-Lankwich, Federal Republic of Germany*, GERMAN LANGUAGE

Special Contributing Editors

Robert V. Allen, *Library of Congress*, RUSSIAN LANGUAGE
G. Joyce Darilek, *Library of Congress*, DUTCH LANGUAGE
Georgette M. Dorn, *Library of Congress*, GERMAN AND HUNGARIAN LANGUAGES
George J. Kovtun, *Library of Congress*, CZECH LANGUAGE
Maurice A. Lubin, *Howard University*, HAITIAN MATERIAL
Renata V. Shaw, *Library of Congress*, SCANDINAVIAN AND GERMAN LANGUAGES

---

*Contributing editors to *HLAS* no. 41 (Social Sciences) scheduled for publication in the fall of 1979.

Contents

	PAGE
EDITOR'S NOTE	xi
BIBLIOGRAPHY AND GENERAL WORKS .... John R. Hébert	3
Journal Abbreviations: Bibliography & General Works	21

ART

SPANISH AMERICA
COLONIAL ..... Robert J. Mullen	23
19TH AND 20TH CENTURIES ..... James B. Lynch, Jr.	30
BRAZIL ..... José Neistein	41

Journal Abbreviations: Art 54

FILM ..... Julianne Burton 57

Journal Abbreviations: Film 67

HISTORY

ETHNOHISTORY
MESOAMERICA ..... Edward E. Calnek	69
SOUTH AMERICA ..... John V. Murra	77

GENERAL
GENERAL ..... Donald E. Chipman	90
COLONIAL ..... Donald E. Chipman	104
INDEPENDENCE AND 19TH CENTURY ..... Donald E. Chipman	114
20TH CENTURY ..... Donald E. Chipman	118

MEXICO
GENERAL ..... Asunción Lavrin	123
COLONIAL ..... and Edith B. Couturier	128
19TH CENTURY ..... Richard E. Greenleaf and	148
REVOLUTION AND POST-REVOLUTION ..... Don M. Coerver	158

CENTRAL AMERICA .... *Murdo J. MacLeod*		170
THE CARIBBEAN AND THE GUIANAS ..... *Franklin W. Knight*		184

SPANISH SOUTH AMERICA

GENERAL .... *Michael T. Hamerly*		201
COLONIAL .... *Michael T. Hamerly*		204
INDEPENDENCE .... *David Bushnell*		231

19TH AND 20TH CENTURIES

COLOMBIA AND VENEZUELA .... *Winthrop R. Wright*		242
ECUADOR AND PERU .... *Vincent C. Peloso*		249
BOLIVIA AND CHILE .... *Thomas C. Wright*		268
ARGENTINA, PARAGUAY, AND URUGUAY .... *Hobart A. Spalding, Jr.*		280

BRAZIL .... *Colin MacLachlan, Jean A. Barman, and Roderick J. Barman*		309
Journal Abbreviations: History		333

LANGUAGE .... *D. Lincoln Canfield*   341

Journal Abbreviations: Language 359

LITERATURE

SPANISH AMERICA

COLONIAL .... *Daniel R. Reedy*		361

19TH AND 20TH CENTURIES

GENERAL .... *Harvey L. Johnson*		368

PROSE FICTION

MEXICO .... *Juan Bruce-Novoa*		379
CENTRAL AMERICA .... *Thomas B. Irving*		386
HISPANIC CARIBBEAN .... *Roberto González-Echevarría and Carlos R. Hortas*		393

ANDEAN COUNTRIES
BOLIVIA, COLOMBIA, ECUADOR, PERU,

VENEZUELA .... *José Miguel Oviedo and Djelal Kadir*		401
CHILE .... *Cedomil Goić*		416
ARGENTINA, PARAGUAY, URUGUAY .... *Earl M. Aldrich, Jr. and Alfred J. MacAdam*		421

POETRY .... Humberto M. Rasi   433
Rubén A. Gamboa
Oscar Hahn
Pedro Lastra
Corina Mathieu-Higginbotham
Carolyn Morrow
Betty T. Osiek
Esther Pereyra-Suárez
and Eliana Rivero

DRAMA .... Frank Dauster   457

BRAZIL
   NOVELS .... Alexandrino E. Severino   472
   SHORT STORIES .... Maria Angélica   475
                                  Guimarães Lopes Dean
   CRÔNICAS .... Gerald M. Moser   480
   POETRY .... Ralph E. Dimmick   484
   DRAMA .... Benjamin M. Woodbridge, Jr.   494
   LITERARY CRITICISM AND HISTORY .... Wilson Martins   500

FRENCH AND ENGLISH WEST INDIES
   AND THE GUIANAS .... Naomi M. Garrett   510

TRANSLATIONS .... Margaret Sayers Peden   517

Journal Abbreviations: Literature   532

MUSIC .... Robert Stevenson   535

Journal Abbreviations: Music   554

PHILOSOPHY .... Juan Carlos Torchia-Estrada   557

Journal Abbreviations: Philosophy   594

INDEXES:

   ABBREVIATIONS AND ACRONYMS   599
   TITLE LIST OF JOURNALS INDEXED   607
   SUBJECT INDEX   621
   AUTHOR INDEX   661

EDITOR'S NOTE

GENERAL TRENDS

Social themes dominate much of the history section of this volume. Scholarly contributions in social history have appeared on colonial Mexico, the Caribbean, Colombia, Venezuela, Peru, Brazil, and Argentina. In these last two countries many studies of European immigration have been published while European scholars, in turn, have begun to examine the same phenomenon from a European perspective (p. 90). There is a growing interest in the economic history of Venezuela, particularly of the modern period, a trend largely due to the country's noteworthy boom in economic studies (see *HLAS 39*, p. 319-320). In Colombia, however, it is the colonial rather than the modern period that seems to generate the greatest interest among social historians (p. 204). In Brazil, on the other hand, there is a decline of interest in colonial times and a keen concentration on the national period, particularly the Old Republic and the Vargas era as well as on themes of crisis, confrontation, and disequilibrium (p. 309). The development of a sophisticated, interdisciplinary history that employs various methodologies is most notable in Peru where a number of excellent works have appeared (p. 249). Another trend noted in Peru as well as in Chile and Argentina is the growing interest in regional studies, many of which have been published in the last two years.

In literature, however, one notes the opposing tendencies, a movement away from regionalism, especially in Brazilian literature (p. 475) as well as a decline in social concerns. This is particularly true for Mexican fiction and poetry (p. 379 and p. 433). The obvious exceptions to this trend are Cuba, where literature is perceived as an integral part of the socialist experiment, and Chile, where the trauma of the Allende years and the military coup continue to haunt most poetry and fiction (p. 416 and p. 433).

The interaction between events and their portrayal by either historian or artist is discussed in this volume as is a related theme, the conflict between both interpretations or the dialectic between history and literature (p. 401).

SPECIFIC DEVELOPMENTS

As the level of sophistication of Latin American scholarship rises so does the interest of Europeans and other extrahemispheric scholars in the region. An example of this is the SALALM meeting held in July 1978 in London where a number of European scholars reviewed Latin American studies at European universities. Likewise, the Japanese and the French have made a number of significant contributions to Andean ethnohistory. This extrahemispheric interest has been stimulated partly by the publication and microfilming of otherwise elusive and/or inaccessible source material as is being done by a number of countries (e.g., Mexico, Venezuela, Panama, Peru, Colombia, Brazil, Bolivia, and Uruguay).

Research into and exhibiting of Latin American art are receiving increasing financial assistance from official as well as from private sources. As to cinema, Mexico, Cuba, and Brazil apparently continue their leadership in film production.

In March 1977, the Advisory Board of the *HLAS* met at the Library of Congress and made a number of recommendations that have been adopted. Beginning with this volume 40, appointments of contributing editors have been placed on a more formal basis. All appointments and renewals are made for only one volume and by the Librarian of Congress upon the recommendation of the Editor and with the concurrence of Library officials and members of the Advisory Board.

The Board also recommended that the practice of listing tables of contents be curtailed and that English be used as much as possible. The Board, however, recognized that literature is a special case and that the United States is now moving toward recognition of Spanish as the second language of the country. And finally, it was the consensus of members that new guidelines be issued to contributing editors giving details of these and other recommendations concerning content and format of the *HLAS*. Most of their recommendations are incorporated in this volume and noted by contributing editors in their introductions.

CHANGES IN VOLUME 40

Art: Robert J. Mullen (University of Texas, San Antonio) prepared the section on Colonial Art.

Film and/or Folklore: Because of severe space limitations, it has been decided to alternate the Film and Folklore sections in the humanities volume. Julianne Burton (University of California, Santa Cruz) annotated the material on the Latin American cinema for this volume. Volume 42, scheduled for publication in the winter of 1980, will carry a section on Folklore, and volume 44, scheduled for publication in 1982, will carry the next section on Film.

History: Murdo J. MacLeod (University of Pittsburgh), reviewed materials on Central America. Franklin W. Knight (The Johns Hopkins University) prepared the section on the Caribbean and The Guianas. Thomas C. Wright (University of Nevada) annotated the literature on Chile and Bolivia. Roderick J. Barman and Jean A. Barman (University of British Columbia) collaborated with Colin MacLachlan in preparing the section on Brazil.

Literature: Harvey L. Johnson (University of Houston) reviewed materials for the General section. Juan Bruce-Novoa (Yale University) annotated materials on Mexican prose fiction. And for the Caribbean section, Carlos R. Hortas (Yale University) reviewed the prose fiction of Puerto Rico. Djelal Kadir (Purdue University) annotated the prose fiction of Bolivia, Colombia, Ecuador, Peru, and Venezuela. There are six additional new contributors to the Poetry section: Rubén A. Gamboa (Mills College) for Central America; Oscar Hahn (University of Iowa) for Chile; Pedro Lastra (State University of New York at Stony Brook) for Ecuador, Peru, and Bolivia; Corina Mathieu-Higginbotham (University of Nevada) for Argentina; Esther Pereyra-Suárez (San José State University) for Uruguay and Paraguay; and Eliana Rivero (University of Arizona) for the Caribbean.

Subject Index: The subject index headings are the result of an effort to extract major terms from the subject indexes of previous *HLAS* humanities volumes. To facilitate the user's search for a subject, bold face print is used for major terms. Names of countries and regions of Latin America have been introduced as major geographic subject headings. They are broken down by the disciplines presented in this volume. It is hoped that increased use of cross-referencing will aid the user. History and Literature have been broken down into subdisciplines with references to related subjects.

Numbering: As noted in *HLAS 39* (p. xii) a standardized numbering system has been established for all disciplines covered by the *HLAS*. This system expedites publication by allowing the staff to number and index each discipline separately, regardless of its order in the volume, and mail the copy to the press as soon as it is complete. As of *HLAS* no. 40, the block numbers for the humanities are:

```
BIBLIOGRAPHY AND GENERAL WORKS .......(   1–250  )
ART .............................................(  251–950  )
FILM or FOLKLORE ............................(  951–1950)
HISTORY ........................................(1951–6000)
LANGUAGE ......................................(6001–6400)
LITERATURE ....................................(6401–9000)
MUSIC ..........................................  (9001–9400)
PHILOSOPHY ....................................(9401–9900)
```

Changes in the editorial staff of the *HLAS*, the administrative officers of the Library of Congress, and the Advisory Board are indicated in the front matter for the present volume.

Dolores Moyano Martin

Washington
December 1978

Handbook of Latin American Studies

BIBLIOGRAPHY AND GENERAL WORKS

JOHN R. HÉBERT

Hispanic Division
Library of Congress

DURING THIS PAST YEAR A NUMBER of useful bibliographies, collection guides and general works have appeared. The more worthwhile of these publications will be mentioned in these introductory remarks. The heterogeneity of the literature annotated in this section precludes easy categorization of developments in research. Nevertheless, a number of extremely well conceived and presented publications have been noted and researchers in most disciplines will find them of use.

The development of national bibliographies mentioned in *HLAS 39* (p. 3-4) continues this year with the publication of those from Ecuador, Venezuela and Barbados, a trend which will allow scholars improved access to more comprehensive national production information in Latin America.

General bibliographies, including Abeillard Barreto's impressive *Bibliografia sulriograndense* (item 1), Lambros Comitas' exhaustive *The complete Caribbeana, 1900-1975* in four volumes (item 6), and Curtis Wilgus' updated *Latin America, Spain and Portugal* (item 12) will satisfy multiple interests. Undoubtedly, the most impressive of all three works is Comitas' four volume effort which contains over 17,000 references to publications on the Caribbean region; only works on Haiti, Cuba, Dominican Republic and Puerto Rico do not appear because of the availability of existing bibliographies on them.

Indicative of the quality of works published on a wide variety of topics are these subject bibliographies: the English translation of Bruno Basseches' *Uma bibliografia das bibliografias brasileiras* (item 14); Cornelius and Kemper's urban studies bibliography (item 18); the *Bibliografía de bibliografías cubanas, 1859-1972* (item 23); James Cortada's guide to Spanish diplomatic history (item 21); and Hans Zotter's *Bibliographie Faksimilierter Handschriften* (item 29).

A number of valuable contributions to collection catalogs are: Arze Quiroga's listing of Cochabamba papers in the Argentine national archives (item 61); the 1976 printing of the first part of Vázquez Machicado's previously unprinted catalog of the Bolivian (Audiencia de Charcas) materials in the Archivo General de Indias (AGI) (item 87); Lewis Hanke's listing of Mexican and Peruvian vicergal papers to 1700 in the AGI (item 2293); and David Szewczyk's calendar of Latin American manuscripts, especially Peruvian, in the Philip H. & A.S.W. Rosenbach Foundation (item 80) furnish the colonial historian with a number of practical guides. Among the G.K. Hall publications which provide ready access to collections of world-wide institutions are: the subject catalog of the Ibero-Amerikanischen Institut (Berlin, FRG) in 30 volumes (item 69); the catalog of the Cuban and Caribbean library of the Univ. of Miami, Fla., in six volumes (item 85); and the classed bibliography of the Joint Bank-Fund Library (item 70). G.K. Hall also plans to publish the card catalog of the Peruvian National Library in 1979.

For anyone wno has searched for the elusive issue of an obscure journal, the union lists of periodical publications for Mexico and for Costa Rica are welcome additions. The Mexican list contains over 30,000 titles, with holdings, while the Costa Rican publication culled information of periodical holdings from 58 Costa Rican libraries.

Carl Deal's updated listing of Latin American dissertations available through Univ. Microfilms International identifies 7200 titles by discipline (item 67). In the area of microfilm, the announcement of the establishment of Centromidca (Centro Taller Regional de Restauración y Microfilmación de Documentos para el Caribe y Centroamérica) in Santo Domingo suggests that an improved program for the restoration and microfilming of historic documents from the Caribbean and Central America has begun. This *HLAS* section will note future developments in this important sphere.

The interest of Europeans in Latin American studies, on the rise in the past two decades, is evident from the latest edition (1976) of *Latinoamericanistas en Europa*, which provides biographical information on 518 European specialists involved in the study of the region. A related item is R.A. Humphrey's autobiographical sketch of Latin American studies in Great Britain (item 125). Moreover, the 1978 Seminar on the Acquisition of Latin American Library Materials (SALALM), held in July 1978 in London, was devoted to a review of Latin American studies in Europe. The publication of this meeting's proceedings should be of considerable interest.

Among the general works that appeared in the past year are the Puerto Rican and the Cuban encyclopedias edited by Vicente Báez (items 116-117). The work on Cuba is the second edition of the publication. Both items provide useful biographical and historical information, are profusely illustrated and contain wide-ranging and interesting information for the generalist and, in some cases, for the specialist. Two other publications worthy of notice as research tools are the Consejo Episcopal Latinoamericano's (CELAM) ecclesiastical guide to the Church's administrative activities in the region (item 95) and Petriella's and Miatello's Italo-Argentine biographical dictionary (item 106).

Finally, one should note the several catalogs and bibliographies annotated below that will facilitate research. The practice of publishing card catalogs of major Latin American collections continues as do attempts to microfilm documents. Also beneficial to scholars are the development of union list of serials and the increase of periodical indexing. The continued development of these tools and other types of guides and bibliographies will serve to encourage and facilitate the expansion and refinement of research on Latin America.

GENERAL BIBLIOGRAPHY

1. Barreto, Abeillard *comp*. Bibliografía sulriograndense: a contribuição portuguesa e estrangeira para o conhecimento e a integração do Rio Grande do Sul. v. 1, A-J. v. 2, K-Z. Rio, Conselho Federal de Cultura, 1973-1976. 2 v. (1556 p.) (Continuous pagination) facsims., map, plate.

Impressive compilation of printed and manuscript works with references to history of Rio Grande do Sul. Includes books, atlases, maps, etc. Works appear in alphabetical order by author including brief biographical identifications. Also furnishes library location of unique items and separate subject and geographic indexes. Outstanding publication of great value to research.

2. *Boletim Bibliográfico da Biblioteca Nacional*. Ministério da Educação e Cultura, Depto. de Assuntos Culturais, Biblioteca Nacional. Vol. 21, No. 4, 1976- . Rio.

Brazilian publications for part of 1976 received through legal deposit by National Library. Approximately 2400 entries appear in Dewey Decimal Classification order. Includes author index.

3. ———. ———, ———, ———. Vol. 21, No. 4, 4. trimestre, 1976- Rio.

Contains same type of information as in later works that have been described elsewhere. Also includes separate sections on maps, iconography, pamphlets and other ephemeral material, music, periodicals received in 1976 (with addresses) and list of publishers.

4. ———. ———, ———, ———. Vol. 22, No. 1, 1. trimestre, 1977- Rio.

Contains cataloguing information on recently acquired works, both monographs and theses, that were published or issued in Brazil. Classified in Dewey Decimal System.

5. ———. ———, ———, ———. Vol. 22, No. 2, 2. trimestre, 1977- Rio.

Lists Brazilian publications for part of 1976 received through legal deposit by National Library. Includes approximately 2400 entries in Dewey Decimal Classification order. Author index.

6. **Comitas, Lambros** comp. The complete Caribbeana, 1900-1975: a bibliographic guide to the scholarly literature. v. 1, People; v. 2, Institutions; v. 3, Resources; v. 4, Indexes. Millwood, N.Y., KTO Press, 1977. 4 v. (2193 p.) (Continuous pagination)

Listing of over 17,000 complete references to publications, including monographs, dissertations and theses, articles, proceedings, and reports, organized in 63 topical chapters (rather than in geographical arrangement), pertaining to mainland and insular possessions or former possessions of U.K., France, Netherlands and US in the Caribbean region. Does not include publications on Haiti, Cuba, Puerto Rico and Dominican Republic since considerable body of bibliographic literature already exists. Only items actually seen plus their physical location appear in bibliography. Updates author's 1968 publication, *Caribbeana 1900-1965*. Includes author and geographical indexes. Valuable bibliographic achievement.

7. **Mendonça, Rubens de.** Bibliografia matogrossense. Cuiabá, Brazil, Edições Univ. Federal de Mato Grosso (UFMT) [and] Secretaria de Educação e Cultura, Brasília?, 1975. 126 p., illus. (Col. Esboços e levantamento, 13)

Listing of works of 422 authors who have written on subjects relevant to Mato Grosso. Selected biographical information on key writers is included. No subject arrangement is employed.

8. **Universidad de Puerto Rico,** *Río Piedras.* **Centro de Investigaciones Sociales.** Bibliografía puertorriqueña de ciencias sociales. t. 1. 1931-1954; t. 2, 1954-1960. Presentación de José María Bulnes Aldunate y Emilio González Díaz. Río Piedras, P.R., Editorial Universitaria, 1977. 2 v. in 1 (600 p.)

This ambitious compilation of Centro de Investigaciones Sociales of Univ. of Puerto Rico, Río Piedras, presents unannotated listing of publications appearing between 1931-60 on Puerto Rico. Work is divided into two volumes (in one book) with pre- and post-1954 publications in separate volumes. Each volume has its own separate table of contents. Listings include general works and maps, and publications on natural setting, cities and regions, society and culture since discovery (including works on political parties, government and its administration, folklore, religion, labor union development, economy), and social sciences (including history, philosophy and agriculture). Works on law, legislation, natural sciences, and literature do not appear. Contains no index. Important addition to the study of the Island.

9. **University of the West Indies,** *Cave Hill, Barbados.* **Institute of Social and Economic Research** (Eastern Caribbean). A bibliography of the Caribbean. Cave Hill, Barbados, 1974. 167 p. (Occasional bibliography series, 1)

Provides titles of primarily English language publications on Caribbean islands, Belize and Venezuela contained in the collections of Institute of Social and Economic Research (Eastern Caribbean). Separate sections are devoted to each territory; all material is listed by author only.

10. **Uruguay. Poder Legislativo. Biblioteca. Departamento Selección y Registro de Material Bibliográfico. Sección Bibliografía Uruguaya y Depósito Legal.** Bibliografía uruguaya: años 1969-1972 inclusive. v. 1/2. Montevideo, 1977. 2 v. (408 p.) (Continuous pagination)

Publications are presented in alphabetical order by author. The list includes works by Uruguayans published outside of the country. Separate title, subject, pseudonym, publisher, printer, and classification (by Dewey Decimal System) indexes are included. Contains only works within dates 1969-1972.

11. **Villasana, Angel Raúl** comp. Ensayo de un repertorio bibliográfico venezolano: años 1808-1950. t. 1, A-Björkmann; t. 2, Blanco-Churion; t. 3, D-Gornés; t. 4, Borrochotegui-Llovera Solano; t. 5, M-P. Caracas, Banco Central de Venezuela (BCV), 1969-1976. 5 v. (376, 490, 431, 404, 629 p.) bibl., (Col. Cuatricentenario de Caracas, 8)

First five volumes of impressive listing of books and pamphlets by Venezuelans or on Venezuela published 1808-1950. Bibliography contains publications on literature, history and general works; official publications and scientific, technical or didactic works are not included. Library location of each item cited is given. Entries are presented in alphabetical order by author or title. All works by single author appear in one place.

12. Wilgus, A. Curtis comp. Latin America, Spain and Portugal: a selected and annotated bibliographical guide to books published in the United States; 1954-1974. Metuchen, N.J., The Scarecrow Press, 1977. 910 p.

Contains several thousand annotated entries of selected works published in US since 1954. Work is arranged into regional subdivisions, except for two sections on adult fiction and children's literature, and is divided into disciplines in each subdivision. Includes author index. Valuable guide for researchers and acquisition librarians. See also item 2247.

SUBJECT BIBLIOGRAPHY

13. Amaral, Raúl. Las generaciones en la cultura paraguaya: ensayo de investigación bibliográfica. Asunción, Centro Paraguayo de Estudios Sociológicos, Centro Paraguayo de Documentación Social, 1976. 19 p.

Selected bibliography of key works relevant to Paraguayan generations and cultural periods from Romantic (mid-19th century) through Modernist (pre-1930).

Anderson, Teresa J. comp. Agrarian reform in Latin America: an annotated bibliography. See item 2126.

Barceló Sifontes, Lyll. Contribución a la bibliografía sobre el Congreso Anfictiónico de Panamá. See item 2346.

14. Basseches, Bruno. A bibliography of Brazilian bibliographies (Uma bibliografia das bibliografias brasileiras). With a foreword by José Honório Rodrigues. Detroit, Mich. Blaine Ethridge Books, 1978. 185 p.

Contains 2480 entries including works on subject published outside Brazil. Includes general index (author and subject). Titles are presented in alphabetical order by subject or title. Useful work by proven bibliographer.

15. Beeson, Margaret E. and others. Hispanic writers in French journals: an annotated bibliography. n.p., Society of Spanish and Spanish-American Studies, 1978. 155 p.

Work cites writings on Hispanic literature appearing in 18 selected French periodicals published between 1890 and 1930s. Includes works or reviews on or by Darío, Asturias, Miró, Mistral and Neruda, among many others. Provides author index.

16. Bibliografía sobre la frontera entre Venezuela y Colombia (UCAB/M, 5, 1976, p. 1131-1143)

Selected bibliography of works from 1827 to present. Includes atlases, official reports, bibliographies or catalogues, monographs and journal articles. Lists works from both countries.

17. Bibliografía teológica comentada del área iberoamericana. v. 1, Año 1973; v. 2, Año 1974. Presentación de Juan H. Mallau. Introducción general de J. Severino Croatto. B.A., Asociación Interconfesional de Estudios Teológicos (AIDET), Instituto Superior Evangélico de Estudios Teológicos (ISEDET), 1975. 2 y. in 1 (634 p.)

Lists for two-year period nearly 6,000 publications that contribute to theological thought in Latin America. Sections devoted to history of churches, Bible, practical theology, and relevance of social sciences are further subdivided into refined categories. Each subsection is introduced by essay on theme. Includes subject and author indexes.

18. Bibliography: recent urban studies on Latin America, 1974-1976 (in Cornelius, Wayne E. and Robert V. Kemper eds. Metropolitan Latin America: the challenge and the response. Beverly Hills, Calif., Sage Publications, 1978, p. 279-341)

Lists 1185 titles relating to urban studies of Latin America in general and of its individual countries. Major cities in each country appear in separate sections. Impressive compilation considering limited period of coverage, i.e., publications appearing between 1974-76.

Burton, Julianne. The new Latin American cinema: an annotated bibliography of English language sources: 1960-1976. See item 956.

19. Cardozo, Lubio. Bibliografía de bibliografías extranjeras que informan de literatura venezolana (VANH/B, 59:236, oct./dic. 1976. p. 713-739)

Annotated bibliography provides useful list of non-Venezuelan bibliographies in which references to country appear. Includes separate title and chronological listings. Preceded by useful bibliographical essay.

20. ———. Bibliografía de las bibliografías humanísticas sobre Latinoamérica (VANH/B, 60:237, enero/marzo 1977, p. 101-110)

Useful compilation of 104 selected bibliographies. Works are arranged in four sections: Classic non-Latin American, Classic Latin American, Modern non-Latin American and Modern Latin American sources. Classic period extends to 1898. Notes facsimile editions of out-of-print works.

21. **Cortada, James W.** *comp.* A bibliographic guide to Spanish diplomatic history: 1460-1977. Westport, Conn., Greenwood Press, 1977. 390 p.

Selected bibliography containing wealth of listings relevant to study of Latin America's relations with Spain during indicated period. Sections cover particular political regime. Uses various subjects and geographic headings within section in order to classify works. Includes author index.

Costa de la Torre, Arturo. Bibliografía de la Revolución del 16 de julio de 1809. See item 3384.

22. **Couceiro, Solange Martins.** Bibliografia sobre o negro brasileiro. 2. ed. São Paulo, Univ. de São Paulo, Centro de Estudos Africanos, Coordenadoria de Atividades Culturais (CODAC), 1974. 64 p.

Unannotated list of 857 works on subject which originally appeared as part of social science thesis.

Dias, Cicero. Catálogo de documentos referentes ao Brasil. See item 4028.

Dobyns, Henry F. *comp.* Native American historical demography: a critical bibliography. See item 2154.

23. **Fernández Robaina, Tomás** *comp.* Bibliografía de bibliografías cubanas: 1859-1972. La Habana, Biblioteca Nacional José Martí, 1973. 340 p.

Partially annotated listing of over 1300 entries divided into 19th- and 20th-century works. Variety of indexes appear including one to journal entries. Nearly 75 supplementary entries (post-1972 works) have been appended. Informative essay on Cuban bibliography precedes listing. Very useful publication.

Bibliography and General Works / 7

Flores, Angel *comp.* Bibliografía de escritores hispanoamericanos (A bibliography of Spanish-American writers): 1609-1974. See item 6493.

Gomes, Celuta Moreira. O conto brasileiro e sua crítica: bibliografía, 1841-1974. See item 7715.

Gonçalves, Alice Ramos and others *comps.* Bibliografía sobre teatro paulista. See item 7654.

24. **González, Esther B.** *comp.* Annotated bibliography on Cubans in the United States: 1960-1976. Miami, Florida International Univ. Foundation, 1977. 69 p.

Annotated inter-disciplinary inventory of material in Cuban American studies for Castro period. Periodical literature, reports, theses and dissertations, and monographic works appear in separate alphabetical listings. Includes author index. Bulk of work devoted to immigration themes.

Gutiérrez, Laura and others. Bibliografía histórica peruana: 1968-1970. See item 3524.

Johnson, Harvey L. Literature. See item 6503.

Larrazabal Henríquez, Osvaldo; Amaya Llebot; and **Gustavo Luis Carrera** *comps.* Bibliografía del cuento venezolano. See item 6852.

Lastra, Pedro. Registro bibliográfico de antologías del cuento chileno: 1876-1976. See item 6880.

Leal, Juan Felipe and **José Woldenberg** *comps.* Orígenes y desarrollo del artesanado y del proletariado industrial en México: 1867-1914, bibliografía comentada. See item 2739.

25. **Lovera de Sola, R.J.** Contribución a la bibliografía histórica venezolana: 1969-1972 (EEHA/HBA, 17:1/2, marzo/julio 1973, p. 1-47)

Presents works related to Venezuelan history published anywhere between dates given. Works are divided, within year of publication by subject (e.g., according to historical period or to prominent national figure). Because of format, subjects are repeated at least four times. Lacks indexes. See also item 3080.

Lyday, Leon F. and George W. Woodyard comps. A bibliography of Latin American theater criticism: 1940-1974. See item 7353.

Martínez P., Marcos comp. Para la iconografía dominicana: índices de fotografías de personajes históricos en revistas dominicanas. See item 2945.

Mitry, Jean comp. Bibliographie internationale du cinéma et de la télevision. See item 962.

Organization of American States. General Secretariat. Bibliografia filosófica brasileira: período contemporâneo; 1931-1971. See item 9479.

Pintos Carbajal, Mireya comp. Bibliografía y fuentes relativas al año 1825. See item 3946.

26. **Pollak-Eltz, Angelina.** Bibliografía afrovenezolana (UCAB/M, 5, 1976, p. 1023-1047)

Valuable addition to study of subject. Work is enhanced by keyed subject index which covers 14 broad themes and valuable introductory article on state of art. Lists 357 works.

Porras Collantes, Ernesto comp. Bibliografía de la novela en Colombia. See item 6820.

Redmond, Walter Bernard. Bibliography of the philosophy in the Iberian colonies of America. See item 9482.

Reinecke, John E. and others. A bibliography of pidgin and creole languages. See item 6131.

Retamal Avila, Julio. Bibliografía de historia eclesiástica chilena: revistas chilenas, 1843-1973. See item 3084.

Simmons, Merle E. U.S. Political ideas in Spanish America before 1830: a bibliographical study. See item 2374.

Storni, Hugo. Documentación y bibliografía sobre los beatos mártires ríoplatenses. See item 3303.

Teschner, Richard V.; Garland D. Bills; and Jerry R. Craddock eds. Spanish and English of the United States Hispanos: a critical, annotated, linguistic bibliography. See item 6013.

27. **United Nations. Food and Agriculture Organization (FAO).** Bibliography on land settlement (Bibliographie sur colonisation agraire; Bibliografía sobre colonización de tierras). Roma, 1976. 146 p.

Land settlement is defined as planned movement of populations to areas of under-utilized agricultural potential. This work includes references to projects for settlement of nomads, refugees, youth, pensioners, and for persons displaced by construction of dams and by natural disasters. Also lists literature on settlement policy, land administration, land consolidation, village modernization and improvement of rural infrastructure. Notes works published between 1958-75; Latin American section appears p. 91-117.

28. **Vargas, Jorge A.** comp. Repertorio bibliográfico: América Latina y la soberanía sobre sus recursos oceánicos: contiene una selección de obras sobre: derecho del mar, documentos oficiales, organismos internacionales y trabajos científico-técnicos. México, Consejo Nacional de Ciencia y Tecnología (CONACYT), Aprovechamiento de los Recursos Marinos, 1976. 384 p.

Selected multidisciplinary bibliography of over 2500 entries (including laws, official documents, international organization publications, scientific and technical works and periodical articles) on several themes related to the sea and use of its resources in Latin America. Includes separate author, subject, and country indexes.

Woodbridge, Hensley C. Fourteen Chicano bibliographies: 1971-9175. See item 6014.

29. **Zotter, Hans.** Bibliographie Faksimilierter Handschriften. Graz, Austria, Akademische Druck u. Verlagsanstalt, 1976. 285 p.

Useful selective listing of codices and modern facsimiles of them. Includes Mexican and Central American pieces.

30. Zuvekas, Clarence, Jr. An annotated bibliography of agricultural development in Haiti. Washington, Dept. of Agriculture, Economic Research Service, Foreign Development Division, Sector Analysis Internationalization Group, 1976. 106 p. (Working document series: Haiti)

Listing of 550 items, in alphabetical order, on agricultural development in Haiti, published since 1950. Bibliography does not concern scientific agriculture, but rather contains works on credit, marketing, nutrition, technology and income distribution.

COLLECTIVE AND PERSONAL BIBLIOGRAPHIES

31. Arze Aguirre, René and César Gutiérrez Muñoz. Bibliografía paleográfica del Profesor Tanodi (IRA/B, 9, 1972/1974, p. 184-187)

Lists 22 publications devoted to subject of Iberoamerican paleography prepared by Aurelio Tanodi, Director of Centro Inter-americano de Formación de Archiveros in Córdoba, Arg.

32. Bibliografía de y sobre Gabriel García Moreno. (Bibliografía Ecuatoriana [Quito] 7, abril 1977, p. 80-95)

Listing of more than 180 writings by and on Ecuadorian statesman.

Feliú Cruz, Guillermo *comp.* Bio-bibliografía de Eugenio Pereira Salas. See *HLAS 40:3631*.

Grases, Pedro *comp.* Contribución a la bibliografía de Antonio José de Sucre, Gran Mariscal de Ayacucho: 1795-1830. See item 3320.

33. Introducción histórico-social a la obra de Icaza (Bibliografía Ecuatoriana [Quito] 7, abril 1977, p. 96-146)

Listing of monographs and articles related to individual and his works. Introductory essay on work of Icaza precedes bibliography.

Kantor, Harry. Bibliography of José Figueres. See item 2891.

Laurencio, Angel Aparicio. Bibliografía de José María Heredia. See item 7233.

34. Lemus, Juan de Luigi. Don Justo Abel Rosales, archivero y bibliógrafo (Revista de Historia [Univ. de Concepción, Instituto de Antropología, Historia y Geografía, Chile] 2:2, 1977, p. 55-66, bibl.)

Brief record of life and literary output of Justo Rosales (1855-96) noted Chilean archivist and bibliographer.

Maidique Patricio, Hilda; Virgen Gutiérrez Mesa; and Elena Rodríguez Pérez *comps.* Camilo Cienfuegos: estudio bibliográfico. See item 3014.

35. Millares Carlo, Agustin. *Intervolumina*: treinta y seis reseñas de archivología y archivos, bibliografía e historia. Caracas, Asociación de Escritores Venezolanos, 1973. 279 p. (Cuadernos literarios, 134)

Contains selection of book reviews (36) prepared by Millares Carlo during his 11-year residence in Venezuela. Shows his wide interest in archives, history and biography.

36. Subero, Efraín. Contribución a la bibliografía de Enrique Bernardo Núñez: 1895-1964. Caracas, Univ. Católica Andrés Bello, Facultad de Humanidades y Educación, Escuela de Letras, Seminario de Literatura Venezolana, 1970. 203 p. (Col. Bibliografías, 6)

Lists over 950 publications by and about noted Venezuelan essayist and diplomat. Sixth in series of personal bibliographies published by Seminario de Literatura Venezolana. Contains listings of author's major and minor works by and critical and biographical works about him.

37. Sullivan, William M. Bibliografía comentada de la era de Cipriano Castro: 1899-1908. Traducción directa del inglés por Xuan Tomás García Tamayo. Preliminar de Pedro Grases. Caracas, Presidencia de la República [and] Asamblea Legislativa del Estado Táchira [and] Dirección de Educación y Cultura, San Cristóbal, Ven., 1977. 276 p. (Biblioteca de autores y temas tachirenses, 70)

Annotated listing of 1501 entries of publications on Cipriano Castro and Venezuela during his period of rule. Describes archival, library and private collections containing primary materials and volumes of related monographs, articles, dissertations and theses that have appeared. Work has no table of contents or index. Useful compilation for early 20th-century Venezuelan political and social history.

Uruguay. Ministerio de Educación y Cultura. Biblioteca Nacional. Florencio Sánchez: centenario de su nacimiento, 1875-1975; bibliografía. See item 7405.

38. ———. ———. ———. Joaquín Torres-García: centenario de su nacimiento, 1874 -28 de julio- 1974; bibliografía. Montevideo, 1974. 83 p., facsims., illus.

Comprehensive listing of written works by and about Uruguayan artist and his exhibitions. Letters of correspondence with José Enrique Rodó appear in appendix. Issued on occasion of exhibition sponsored by Uruguay's Biblioteca Nacional.

NATIONAL BIBLIOGRAPHY

39. *Bibliografía Ecuatoriana.* Univ. Central del Ecuador, Biblioteca General, No. 7, 1976- . Quito.

Comprehensive listing of current Ecuadorian publications presented in order by Dewey Decimal Classification. Includes separate indexes to authors, institutions, titles and subjects. Special bibliographies of and about Gabriel García Moreno and Jorge Icaza have been added (see items 32-33). Armin Schönberger-Rosero contributes valuable additional introductory article to special bibliography. Also offers short reviews of recently published Ecuadorian titles.

Guttentag Tichauer, Werner. Bibliografía boliviana del año 1972. See item 9040.

40. *The National Bibliography of Barbados.* Public Library. Jan./March 1977- . Bridgetown, Barbados.

Quarterly listing of new works published in Barbados or authored by Barbadians. Excludes periodicals (except first issues) and certain government publications. Includes addresses of publishers/printers.

41. Rossi, Iris. La Argentina y su bibliografía nacional (Documentación Bibliotecológica [Univ. Nacional del Sur, Centro de Documentación Bibliotecológica, Bahía Blanca, Arg.] 6, 1976, p. 14-24, bibl.)

Brief article documents development of *Boletín Bibliográfico Argentino* (initiated 1937) and recent interest in a national bibliography.

42. Venezuela. Biblioteca Nacional. Centro Bibliográfico Venezolano. Anuario bibliográfico venezolano, 1975. Caracas, 1977. 390 p.

Lists publications in three separate sections: 1) books and pamphlets; 2) periodical publications (Venezuela), and 3) publications related to Venezuela published elsewhere. Includes bibliographic sources, biographical information on deceased writers and combined author-title-subject index. Earlier annuals—for 1955 to 1974—and more current annuals are promised in future bibliographical efforts. Noteworthy resurrection.

LIBRARY SCIENCE AND SERVICES

43. Annual Conference of the Association of Caribbean University and Research Libraries (ACURIL), *IV, San Juan, P.R., 1972.* The management of library personnel in the Caribbean: official documents. San Juan, P.R., Association of Caribbean Univ. and Research Libraries, 1975. 92 p.

Contains some working papers and committee reports given at annual meeting held in San Juan, P.R., 1972. Among items appearing is report on Caribbean serial-title indexing performed in several libraries throughout region.

44. Arbulú, Ricardo. La Biblioteca Nacional y la universidad peruana: algunos datos retrospectivos (UP/A, 3:6, 1977, p. 83-87, bibl.)

Provides information on key dates and periods in development of Peru's National Library from official establishment in 1821. Includes references to colonial predecessors.

Biblioteca Nacional, Rio. Divisão de Publicações e Divulgação. Vinte e cinco anos de enriquecimento do acervo: 1950-1975. See item 528.

45. Buonocore, Domingo. Diccionario de bibliotecología: términos relativos a la bibliología, bibliografía, bibliofilia, biblioteconomía, archivología, documentología, tipografía y materias afines. 2. ed. aumentada. Nota para la presente edición de Roberto Couture de Troismonts. B.A., Ediciones Marymar, 1976. 452 p., bibl. (Col. Bibliotecología y documentación)

Second ed. of Buonocore's valuable work contains extensive array of definitions, clarifications, modifications and amplifications of terms relevant to librarian and archivist. Also provides short identifications of publishers, printers, book dealers and librarians. Includes author's working bibliography.

46. Ferreira, Gilda Pires. A biblioteca universitaria em perspectiva sistêmica. Recife, Brazil, Univ. Federal de Pernambuco, Biblioteca Central [and] Ministério da Educação e Cultura, 1977. 39 p.

Library model designed to adjust to trends affecting modern Brazilian university; model is presented in outline. Introductory work.

47. Guerra, José Augusto. Dos incunábulos á microfilmagem e ao computador: um monumento de tradução e cultura (MEC/C, 6:22, julho/set. 1976, p. 67-82, plates)

Interview with Jannice Monte-Mór, Director of Brazilian National Library in which Brazilian national bibliography, automation, legal deposit, and microfilming programs are discussed. Also describes especially timely project to microfilm library's large number of 19th- and 20th-century newspapers and other serials, an ambitious undertaking.

48. Hernández de Alba, Guillermo and **Juan Carrasquilla Botero.** Historia de la Biblioteca Nacional de Colombia. Presentación de Pilar Moreno de Angel. Bogotá, Instituto Caro y Cuervo, 1977. 447 p., facsims., plates (Publicacion, 38)

Superb chronological history of National Library prepared in commemoration of its 200th anniversary in 1977. Individual chapters are devoted to contributions made by each National Librarian. Final chapter describes special collections. Useful record.

49. Kahler, Mary Ellis. Nettie Lee Benson and the Latin American Collection (LARR, 13:1, 1978, p. 173-175)

Glowing description of outstanding US Latin Americanist. Benson was responsible for development of outstanding Latin American research collection at Univ. of Texas and for many programs aimed at enriching study of Latin America in US and abroad.

Kellenbenz, Hermann. Neue Archivführer für Lateinamerikaforscher. See item 2186.

50. Meurer, Carmen Torelly. A Library of Congress e a aquisição de publicações oficiais brasileiras (Revista de Biblioteconomia de Brasília [Associação dos Bibliotecários do Distrito Federal and Univ. de Brasília, Faculdade de Estudos Sociais Aplicados, Depto. de Biblioteconomia, Brasília] 4:2, julho/dez. 1976, p. 201-212, bibl., tables)

Provides first-hand knowledge of one phase of Library of Congress' comprehensive acquisition program in Rio, begun in 1966.

51. Monte-Mór, Jannice and **H.E. Gomes.** ISBD application to Latin American national bibliographies (UNESCO/BL, 31:4, July/Aug. 1977, p. 233-239, bibl., tables)

Assessment of current national bibliographic efforts in Latin America. Lack of effective legal deposit laws in most countries severely hamper development of adequate bibliographic control in region. Calls for greater cooperation among region's national libraries.

52. Newton, Velma. The role of libraries in developing countries: focus on libraries in Barbados and Jamaica (Bulletin of Eastern Caribbean Affairs [Institute of Social & Economic Research—Eastern Caribbean—Univ. of the West Indies, Cave Hill, Barbados] 2:12, Feb. 1977, p. 1-7, bibl.)

Brief description of adequacy of libraries in both countries; a number of depositories are singled out for more descriptive coverage.

53. Peru. Consejo Nacional de la Universidad Peruana (CONUP). Dirección de Evaluación de Universidades. Oficina de Evaluación. Guía de bibliotecas del sistema nacional de la universidad peruana: 1974. Lima, 1975. 97 p. (Serie: Informaciones bibliotecológicas, 1)

Provides pertinent information on 91 libraries in Peru's university system. Provides basic information on each library, e.g., director, address, hours of service, volumes, special collections and availability of reproduction machines. Useful publication for Peruvian and foreign scholars.

54. Rébula, Angela María Amaral. A biblioteca nos programas de alfabetização de adultos. Río, Fundação Movimento Brasileiro de Alfabetização (MOBRAL), 1975. 21 p.

This work describes programs of MOBRAL directed toward increased adult literacy.

55. Reunión de Estudio Centro Catalográfico Centroamericano, *San José, 1976.* Informe final. San José, Univ. de Costa Rica [and] Organization of American States, Washington, 1976. 2 v. (Various pagings) tables.

Contains 15 papers read at June 1976 meeting of Univ. of Costa Rica devoted to development of a centralized catalog for Central America. Costa Rica, Nicaragua and Panamá participated in this initial meeting of the OAS—supported project. Also considers degree of cooperation in cataloguing new publications.

56. Ruz Menéndez, Rodolfo. La Asociación de Bibliotecarios de Enseñanza Superior y de Investigación: A.B.I.E.S.I. (UY/R, 19:111, mayo/junio 1977, p. 127-130)

Resumé of 20 years of activities (since 1957) of Mexico's national association of research librarians.

57. Universidad Nacional del Sur, *Bahía Blanca, Arg.* **Centro de Investigación Bibliotecológica.** Guía de las bibliotecas universitarias argentinas. 3. ed. B.A., Casa Pardo, 1976. 207 p.

This third ed. provides information on 189 libraries in 26 universities. Also indicates size of collections (monographic and serial), location, directors, special collections, and hours of service.

58. Venezuela. Biblioteca Nacional. Informe anual, 1975: presentado por la Directora Virginia Betancourt a la Presidencia del Consejo Nacional de la Cultura (CONAC). Caracas, 1976. 134 p., facsim., map, plates, tables.

Progress report of wide-ranging objectives of library re-development in Venezuela under National Librarian Virginia Betancourt. Describes some 15 goals designed to improve both the National Library and country's library systems.

59. Virgin Islands of the United States. Bureau of Libraries, Museums and Archaeological Services. Virgin Islands Information & Referral Service. Library resources in the Virgin Islands of the United States. St. Thomas, 1977. 28 p.

Useful guide to special library and information services available in US Virgin Islands. Lists and describes 30 libraries and seven library associations. Contains chronology of library development.

ACQUISITIONS, COLLECTIONS AND CATALOGS

60. Andrade, Diva and **Alba Costa Maciel.** Dissertações e teses defendidas nos Departamentos de Filosofia e Ciências Sociais. São Paulo, Univ. de São Paulo, Faculdade de Filosofia, Letras e Ciências Humanas, Deptos. de Filosofia e Ciências Sociais, Biblioteca, 1976. 39 p.

Preliminary listing, by dept. of dissertations and theses defended by students in Faculty of Philosophy, Letters and Human Sciences of university. Notes works completed before 1976. Lacks index.

61. Arze Quiroga, Eduardo. Papeles de Cochabamba en el Archivo General de la Nación Argentina. La Paz, Banco Hipotecario Nacional, 1975. 81 p.

Published in honor of sesquicentennial of Bolivian independence, work serves as guide to papers in legajos Cochabamba 1762-86 and to Cochabamba papers 1810-11 in Argentina's Archivo General de la Nacion. Dates and describes documents appearing in chronological order. Also includes general index to activities in Charcas by patriotic troops against peninsular forces (1810-15).

62. Canedo, Lino Gómez. Spain (*in* Thomas, Daniel H. and Lynn M. Case *eds.* The new guide to the diplomatic archives of Western Europe. Philadelphia, Univ. of Pennsylvania Press, 1975, p. 275-313, bibl.)

Provides brief histories and organizational information of diplomatic collections of Simancas, Archivo Histórico Nacional, Archivo General de Indias, Archivo del Ministerio de Asuntos Exteriores, and Archivo de la Corona de Aragón and briefer statements on 21 other sources. Enhanced by bibliography of guides and other references to Spanish archival collections.

63. Castro Nevares, Federico. El Archivo de la Confederación (Revista del Archivo General de la Nación [B.A.] 5:5, 1976, p. 49-79)

Article serves to locate parts of "long-lost" Archive of Argentine Confederation (1853-61) in Archivo General de la Nación, Ministerio de Relaciones Exteriores, Congreso de la Nación, and other public repositories.

64. *Centromidca.* Centro Taller Regional de Restauración y Microfilmación de Documentos para el Caribe y Centroamérica. Año 1, Vol. 1, Oct. 1977- . Santo Domingo.

Reports on efforts and progress of new center for preservation and restoration of historical documents based in National Archives, Santo Domingo. Center's work will encompass Caribbean and Central American areas.

65. Colombia. Banco de la República. Biblioteca Luis Angel Arango. Catálogo general. v. 6/9. Bogotá, 1972. 4 v. (232, 193, 165, 264 p.) (Suplemento, 1)

This supplement to general catalogue covers Dewey Decimal classes 640 (Domestic Economy) to 997 (History of Oceania) contained in important Colombian library. Each volume of supplement has onomastic index.

66. Consejo Nacional de Ciencia y Tecnología, *México*. **Departamento de Sistemas de Información.** Catálogo colectivo de publicaciones periódicas existentes en bibliotecas de la República Mexicana. 2. ed. México, 1976. 861 p.

This augmented ed. of 1973 list provides holdings information on serials contained in 157 participating Mexican libraries. Over 30,000 titles appear, an addition of 10,558 since previous ed. of work. Valuable research tool.

67. Deal, Carl W. *ed.* Latin America and the Caribbean: a dissertation bibliography. Ann Arbor, Mich., Univ. Microfilms International, 1978. 164 p.

Lists 7,200 dissertation titles published by Univ. Microfilms through 1977 and supersedes their 1974 catalogue. Arranged by country or region within each discipline; cross-listings have been used to facilitate searches. Author index appears. Publication may be obtained without charge from Univ. Microfilms, Ann Arbor, Mich.

Dower, Catherine A. Libraries with music collections in the Caribbean Islands. See item 9065.

68. Gacharná G., Gladys M. Catálogo de las publicaciones de la Universidad Nacional de Colombia. Bogotá, Univ. Nacional de Colombia, Depto. de Bibliotecas, Biblioteca Central, 1976. 198 p., bibl.

Valuable listing of National Univ.'s publications since its founding in 1867 includes reports and other publications of Rectors, Vice-Rectors, faculty and depts. in Bogotá and in branches in Manizales, Medellín and Palmira. Works appear under responsible administrative or academic unit. Includes list of rectors for period and separate author, title and subject indexes. Brief history of institution enhances publication.

Hanke, Lewis and **Celso Rodríguez.** Guía de las fuentes en el Archivo General de Indias para el estudio de la administración virreinal española en México y en el Perú: 1535-1700. See item 2293.

Hanson, Carl A. *comp.* Dissertations on Iberian and Latin American history. See item 2173.

69. Ibero-Amerikanisches Institut, *Berlin, FRG.* Schlagwortkatalog des Ibero-Amerikanisches Institut: Preussischer Kulturbesitz in Berlin (Subject catalog of the Ibero-American Institute: Prussian Cultural Heritage Foundation in Berlin). v. 1/19, General section; v. 20/23, Geographical section; v. 24, Places; v. 25/29, Persons; v. 29/30, Persons index. Boston, Mass., G.K. Hall, 1977. 30 v. (v. 1:795 p. [to] v. 30:859 p.)

This subject catalog provides access to the more than half a million monographs and periodicals in fields of Latin American and Iberian studies in collections of Latin American Institute in Berlin. Books and articles in over 2000 periodicals are arranged by subjects, with headings in German, English and Spanish language equivalency terms appear in the index. Especially valuable for information on elusive European publications related to field.

70. International Monetary Fund (IMF) [and] International Bank for Reconstruction and Development (IBRD), *Washington.* **Joint Bank-Fund Library.** The developing areas: a classed bibliography of the Joint Bank-Fund Library, Washington, D.C. v. 1, Latin America and the Caribbean. Foreword by Charles Olsen. Boston, Mass., G.K. Hall, 1976. 548 p.

Vol. 1 lists materials dealing with conditions in region; entries are arranged in Dewey Decimal Classification order within region, in general, and within each country. Notes holdings of individual issues of journal. Strength of collection lies in post-World War II publications on statistics and economic conditions.

70a. Jackson, William V. *comp.* Catalog of Brazilian acquisitions of the Library of Congress: 1964-1974 (Catálogo de aquisições brasileiras da Library of Congress: 1964-1974). Boston, Mass., G.K. Hall, 1977. 751 p.

Useful and complete listing of publications acquired and catalogued by Library of Congress on or from Brazil 1964-74. Nearly 15,000 entries are arranged by LC call number; access is enhanced by separate author and subject indexes. Collection is particularly strong in history, literature, and the social sciences. Jackson's effort complements Library of Congress' *Accessions List: Brazil* (1:1, Jan. 1975). Important reference and acquisitions tool.

71. Juárez A., Bárbara. Archivos microfilmados por la Biblioteca de Antropología e Historia: inventario comentado. México, INAH, Biblioteca Nacional de Antropología e Historia, 1977. 17 1. (Cuadernos de la biblioteca. Serie Microfilm)

Annotated listing of 71 INAH archives microfilmed. Includes nearly four million documents covering prehispanic to 20th-century items.

72. Matijevic, Nicolás. Centro de Documentación Patagónica. Bahía Blanca, Arg., Univ. Nacional del Sur, Depto. de Ciencias Sociales, Centro de Documentación Patagónica, 1976. 9 p.

Brief description of Centro's program and resources in Bahía Blanca. Primary emphasis is on research related to Patagonia and Tierras Australes.

73. Moraes, Rubens Borba de. O bibliófilo aprendiz. 2. ed. São Paulo, Companhia Editora Nacional, 1975. 187 p.

New augmented ed. of lively account intended to serve as guide to neophyte rare-book collector. Contains specific chapters devoted to Brazilian out-of-print and/or rare books.

74. Pérez, Louis A., Jr. Cuban materials in the Bureau of Insular Affairs Library (LARR, 13:1, 1978, p. 182-188)

Listing of Cuban materials (monographs, pamphlets, and periodicals) for period ca. 1870-1920 located in Bureau of Insular Affairs Library at US National Archives. Especially rich in official publications.

75. Pontificia Universidade Católica, *Rio*. Vice-Reitoria para Assuntos Acadêmicos. A pós-graduação na PUC/RJ: dez anos de teses; 1965-1975. Rio, 1976. 172 p.

Contains brief abstracts of theses presented by Univ. Center and Dept. Includes author index.

76. Rangel, Leyla Castello Branco. Publicações oficiais do Senado Federal. Brasília?, n.p., 1975. 35 l.

Article provides review of publishing and information services rendered by Federal Senate since its move to Brasília. Describes development of *Revista de Informação Legislativa* (first issued in 1964) and other Senate publications.

Revista del Archivo Nacional. See item 3084.

77. *Revista do Instituto do Ceará*. Instituto do Ceará. No. especial, 1977- . Fortaleza, Brazil.

Issue commemorates 90th anniversary of Institute in Fortaleza. Brief sketches appear on its establishment, collections, presidents, and local research conducted in various fields (especially history, geography and anthropology).

78. Ribeiro, Antonia Mota de Castro Memória. Esquematização do Cátalogo de Publicações oficiais Brasileiras (Revista de Biblioteconomia de Brasília [Associação dos Bibliotecários do Distrito Federal [and] Univ. de Brasília, Faculdade de Estudos Sociais Aplicados, Depto. de Biblioteconomia] 4:2, julho/dez. 1976, p. 287-324, bibl.)

Article is intended to consider library control of official publications, however, it contains many references to bibliographic works for Brazilian government publications (see especially p. 303-311).

Rípoda Ardanaz, Daisy. Bibliografías privadas de funcionarios de la Real Audiencia de Charcas. See item 3241.

Smith, Peter Seaborn. The Góes Monteiro papers. See item 4174.

79. Suárez Molina, Víctor M. Los libreros de Mérida en el siglo XIX y algunos más del siglo XX (RY/R, 19:111, mayo/junio 1977, p. 78-101)

Valuable survey-history of book dealers in 19th- and 20th-century Mérida, Mex., from earliest dealer in 1820. Includes information on titles of monographs and serials published by book dealers.

80. Szewczyk, David M. *ed*. A calendar of Peruvian and other South American manuscripts in the Philip H. & A.S.W. Rosenbach Foundation, 1536-1914. Philadelphia, Pa., The Philip H. & A.S.W. Rosenbach Foundation, 1977. 190 p.

Provides useful information on little-known manuscript collection. Includes legal and official documents, letters, marginal notation and descriptive manuscripts. Presents entries in chronological order including documents relating to first years of Spanish rule in Perú, the Tupac-Amaru rebellion, and late period of colonial rule. Provides subject/names index.

Ulibarri, George S. and **John P. Harrison.** Guide to materials on Latin

Bibliography and General Works / 15

America in the National Archives of the United States. See item 2240.

81. United Nations Educational, Scientific, and Cultural Organization (UNESCO), N.Y. Oficina Regional de Cultura para América Latina y el Caribe. Comisión Nacional Cubana de la UNESCO. Breve repertorio cultural de La Habana. 2. ed. La Habana, 1974. 35 p.

As of 1974, provides list of directors, location, and other pertinent data on the following Havana institutions: principal museums, libraries, documentation centers, universities, literary and media institutes, and the National Academy of Sciences.

82. Universidad de Costa Rica, *San José.* **Servicios de Biblioteca, Documentación e Información.** Catálogo colectivo de publicaciones periódicas existentes en Costa Rica. San José, Consejo Nacional de Investigaciones, Científicas y Tecnológicas (CONICIT), 1976. 479 p., bibl.

This union list of serials constitutes impressive addition to literature on research resources. Provides location and holdings of serial titles. Work records information gathered from 58 Costa Rican libraries.

83. Universidad de Oriente, *Cumaná, Ven.* **Biiblioteca Central. Núcleo de Sucre.** Catálogo de tesis de grado ingresadas a la Biblioteca Central desde enero 1975 hasta julio 1976. Cumaná, Ven., 1976. 100 p. (Suplemento, 1)

Supplement to 1975 publication. Includes titles of theses, post-graduate theses and works for faculty promotion that are on file in Central Library. Provides author index.

84. Universidad Nacional del Sur, *Bahía Blanca, Arg.* Catálogo de publicaciones: 1948-1974. Bahía Blanca, Arg., 1976. 260 p., tables.

Provides titles, by dept. or institute, of nearly 1900 publications, i.e., monographs, articles, theses, prepared by faculty attached to Univ. between 1948-74. Over 65 percent of works appeared between 1967-74. Only includes author index.

85. University of Miami, *Coral Gables, Fla.* **Library.** Catalog of the Cuban and Caribbean Library: University of Miami, Coral Gables, Florida. v. 1, A-Cer; v. 2, Ces-D; v. 3, E-I; v. 4, J-M; v. 5, N-Sea; v. 6, Seb-Z. Boston, Mass., G.K. Hall, 1977. 6 v. (847, 813, 884, 855, 836, 812 p.)

Alphabetical listing, by author, subject, title, of publications in Univ.'s general collections relating to Caribbean countries and nations facing sea (i.e., Mexico, Central América, excepting El Salvador, Colombia, Venezuela and the Guianas). Only catalogued items appear. Periodicals, US government publications, and similar works by Pan American Union/OAS, UN and International Monetary Fund do not appear. Especially useful for recent Cuban materials, from island and from exile groups.

86. Valentino Ramírez, Pablo. Bibliografía mexicana de la Universidad de California en San Diego. México, INAH, Depto. de Investigaciones Históricas, 1976. 167 p. (Cuadernos de la Biblioteca Manuel Orozco y Berra)

Separate listings of various Mexican collections (e.g., Baja California, Hispanic, Hill, José Miranda and Armando de María y Campos, etc.) in Special Collections of Univ. library. Includes general index.

Vasco de Escudero, Grecia. Los archivos quiteños. See item 3189.

87. Vázquez Machicado, José. Catálogo descriptivo del material del Archivo General de Indias referente a la historia de Bolivia. v. 1, pts. 1/2, Audiencia de Charcas. La Paz, Univ. Mayor de San Andrés, Instituto de Investigaciones Históricas [and] Archivo de La Paz, 1976. 379 p.

Registry of 1857 documents from 1540 into 18th century relating to Charcas. Although compilation was completed in 1933, it was only published recently. Vol. 1 contains no index; additional volumes should appear.

REFERENCE WORKS AND RESEARCH

88. Academia de Ciências do Estado de São Paulo, *São Paulo.* Quem é quem em ciência de tecnologia no Estado de São Paulo. v. 1, Ciências exatas e naturais. São Paulo, 1976. 475 p.

Provides descriptions of 900 scientists in following fields: astronomy and meteorology; biological sciences; physics; geosciences; mathematics and statistics; oceanography; and chemistry. Arranged in sections by discipline.

89. Agrupación de Bibliotecas para la Integración de la Información Socio-Económica (ABIISE), *Lima.* Catálogo colectivo de publicaciones periódicas en desarrollo económico y social. 2. ed. rev. Lima, 1976. 319 p.

Revised ed. of catalogue of periodicals in socioeconomic field compiled from holdings in 47 Peruvian Institutional libraries. Titles appear only in alphabetical order. Lacks index and subject access to entries. Includes list of acronyms.

90. *Ausgewählte neuere Literatur.* Institut für Iberoamerika-Kunde, Dokumentations-Leitstelle Lateinamerika. No. 3, 1976- . Hamburg, FRG.

Trimestral publication contains selected information on new articles in journals and edited works. Appendix lists libraries and journals consulted in the FRG. Includes author, subject and geographic indexes. Important and useful compilation.

Bandecchi, Brasil and others. Dicionário de história do Brasil: moral e civismo. See item 3960.

91. Barceló Sifontes, Lyll. Indice de repertorios hemerográficos venezolanos. t. 1, Siglo XX. Caracas, Univ. Católica Andrés Bello, 1977. 118 p., bibl., illus. (Col. Manoa, 7)

Provides brief descriptions, tables of content, author-subject indexes and selected bibliographies for three short lived Venezuelan literary journals: *La Alborada* (1909), *Cultura* (1912), and *Válvula* (1928).

Becker, Félix and **Horst Pietschmann.** Indice del *Jahrbuch für Geschichte von Staat, Wirtschaft und Gessellschaft Lateinamerikas.* See item 2135.

92. Bibliographie: les travaux de recherches a l'Université d'Etat d'Haiti (IFH/C, 133, mars/avril 1977, p. 94-100)

Information on research work (theses) completed in Haiti by students at Institut National d'Administration, de Gestion, et des Hautes Etudes Internationales and of the Faculty of Ethnology. Future issues of Journal will list other theses. Includes works since 1960.

93. Brazil. Câmara dos Deputados. Centro de Documentação e Informação. Coordenação de Biblioteca. Catálogo dos editores oficiais brasileiros: área federal. 2. ed. Brasília, 1977. 123 p.

Lists official editors by institution and ministry.

94. *CLASE: Citas Latinoamericanas en Sociología y Economía.* UNAM, Centro de Información Científica y Humanística. Nos. 1/2, enero/junio 1976- . México.

Computer-generated index to articles appearing in single issues of 20 Latin American journals from seven countries (Argentina, Brazil, Colombia, Cuba, Ecuador, Mexico, and Venezuela) and in fields of sociology and economics. Provides access by author, key word and institution. Analysis of table of contents of each issue serves as key to index.

95. Consejo Episcopal Latinoamericano (CELAM), *Bogotá.* **Secretariado General.** Guía eclesiástica latinoamericana 1977. Bogotá, CELAM, Servicio de Información, Documentación, Estadística y Asesoría Técnica (SIDEAT), 1977. 173 p.

Lists executive officers of main CELAM committees (e.g., liturgy, social action, national representatives of Episcopal Conferences, and Papal Nuncios). Also gives names of Church's hierarchy in each country. Series of statistical tables provide comparative information on number of priests, other religious orders, parishes, baptized and unbaptized individuals.

96. Ferreira, Aurelio Buarque de Holanda. Novo dicionário da língua portuguesa. Rio, Editora Nova Fronteira, 1975. 1517 p.

Latest dictionary on renovation in Portuguese language with separate orthographic section describing changes in usage. Includes agreement between Academia Brasileira de Letras and Lisbon Academy of Sciences in 1971, designed to eliminate variation in language so agreed upon in 1943. Provides extensive bibliography consulted by author to compile this impressive work.

97. García Carranza, Araceli. Indice analítico de *Gaceta de Cuba.* La Habana, Instituto Cubano del Libro, 1974. 363 p.

Includes separate author, title and subject indexes to Cuban literary journal, *Gaceta de Cuba,* covering issues Nos. 1 through 62 (April 1962-Dec./Jan. 1968).

98. ———— comp. Indice de la *Revista de la Biblioteca Nacional José Martí*: 1909-1969. La Habana, Instituto Cubano del Libro, 1975. 365 p., bibl.

Serves to monitor publication's progress over Cuba's 20th century political history. Arranged by author, title and subject indexes. Includes useful introductory essay on National Library.

99. González, Alfonso. Indice de *La Cultura en México*: 1961-1972. Ann Arbor, Mich., Univ. Microfilms International, 1978. 452 p. (Sponsor series)

Contains separate numbered author and general indexes to leading Mexican cultural and literary publication over ten-year period. Brief historical description of *La Cultura* precedes indexes.

Guerra M., Margarita. Documentos sobre tema peruano existentes en el Archivo Nacional de París: 1831-1841. See item 3523.

Ingham, Kenneth E. comp. Sources of Jamaican history, 1655-1838: a bibliographical survey with particular reference to manuscript sources. See item 2939.

Instituto Bibliográfico Antonio Zinny, *Buenos Aires.* Indice historiográfico argéntino: 1970. See item 3784.

100. Instituto Italo-Latinoamericano: Roma, 1966-1976. Rome Tipolitografía B. Cruciani, 1976. 75 p., plates, tables.

Review of first ten years of Institute's activities. Provides chronology of exhibits, visits, conferences and other activities.

101. Inter-American Development Bank (IDB), *Washington.* Office of the Controller. Management Services Office. Reports Management Section. Glossary of terms and acronyms: preliminary edition. Washington, 1976. 59 p., bibl.

Contains definitions of selected terms used in IDB documents as well as acronyms of various national and international institutions which commonly appear in Bank's correspondence. In English only. Includes especially valuable, extensive list of acronyms and selected bibliography.

Komissaroc, Boris N. Russkiie istochniki po istorii Brasilii pervoi treti XIX veka (Russian sources for Brazilian history on first third of 19th century). See item 3988.

Lapa, José Roberto do Amaral. A história em questão: historiografía brasileira contemporânea. See item 3989.

102. Latin American area specialists at Texas colleges and universities. 2. ed. Revised by Alma Castillón and Egla Castillo. Introduction by William Glade. Austin, Univ. of Texas, Institute of Latin American Studies (ILAS), 1976. 84 p. (Special publication)

Bibliography and General Works / 17

Second ed. identifies 350 Latin Americanists teaching in Texas' academic institutions. Includes subject and regional specialties but omits specialists in "Latin American Spanish language and the literature of that region." Indexes specialists by geographical interests.

103. *Latin American Index.* Latin Research Group. Vol. 1, No. 1, Jan. 1973 [through] Vol. 4, No. 24, Dec. 1976- . Washington.

Semimonthly publication which provides brief analyses of major events throughout Latin America in two week period. Primary concerns are economics and politics.

104. Lins, Maria Inês de Bessa. Diários oficiais dos Estados Brasileiros (Revista de Biblioteconomia de Brasília [Asociação dos Bibliotecários do Distrito Federal (and) Univ. de Brasília, Faculdade de Estudos Sociais Aplicados, Depto. de Biblioteconomia] 4:1, jan./junho 1976, p. 23-47, bibl., table)

Intended to suggest ways to improve format and distribution of state gazettes in Brazil, this article provides useful data on origins of each gazette, title variations, publishers and addresses, numbers of copies printed, average length, cost, available indexing, contents, and locations of reference collections.

Matos, Odilon Nogueira de. Afonso de Taunay, historiador de São Paulo e do Brasil: perfil biográfico e ensaio bibliográfico. See item 3997.

105. Ortega Ricaurte, Carmen. Dibujantes y grabadores del *Papel Periódico Ilustrado* y *Colombia Ilustrado.* Bogotá, Instituto Colombiano de Cultura, 1973. 224 p., bibl., illus. (Col. De autores nacionales)

Biographical sketches of illustrators for two 19th-century Colombian journals, *Papel Periódico Ilustrado* (1880-88) and *Colombia Ilustrada* (1889-92) edited by Alberto Urdaneta and later José T. Gaibrois. Over 700 illustrations are listed by artist, among them Antonio Rodríguez, Alfredo Greñas and Eustacio Barreto. List of illustrations by volume of *Papel Periódico Ilustrado* appears in index.

106. Petriella, Dionisio and **Sara Sosa Miatello.** Diccionario biográfico italoargentino. B.A., Asociación Dante Alighieri, 1976. 771 p.

Publication filled with useful information which serves as historical record of contribution made by Italians to Argentine society. In addition to nativeborn Italians, it includes only noteworthy first-generation Argentines of Italian parentage. Publisher, Asociación Dante Alighieri, plans to publish collection of monographs on great Italo-Argentines. This biographical work includes bibliography and index by profession.

107. Ríos Velazco de Caldi, Ramona Luisa. Diccionario de la mujer guaraní. B.A.?, Editorial Siglo XXI, 1977. 327 p.

Biographical dictionary which provides brief sketches on Paraguayan women from past and present. Contains useful data in addition to many prosaic passages.

108. Sampaio, Dorian *ed.* Anuário do Ceará. Fortaleza, Brazil, Stylus, 1976. 785 p., illus., tables.

Valuable compendium of diverse information on history, culture, politics and economy of state. Also includes descriptions of municipios, review of monthly activities in Ceará, brief biographical sketches of important figures, descriptions of state agencies and their directors, private industry and administrators of business and university faculty and programs.

109. Sandoval, Armando M. Centro de Información Científica y Humanística: a University Information Centre in the Third World (UNESCO/BL, 32:1, jan./feb. 1978, p. 42-48)

Author describes two valuable bibliographies, ALERTA and CLASE, produced at Mexico's National University (UNAM). Former provides information on currently published publications every two weeks; latter is quarterly listing of articles on Latin-American economic and sociologic themes culled from over 300 regional journals. Both publications are thoroughly indexed.

Spain. Ministerio de Educación y Ciencia. Dirección General del Patrimonio Artístico y Cultural. Comisaría Nacional de Archivos. Secretaría General Técnica. Centro de Proceso de Datos. Guía de investigadores en los Archivos Españoles, Rama de Humanidades: año 1975. See item 2237.

110. Universidad de Antioquia, *Medellín, Colombia*. **Centro de Investigaciones Económicas.** Indice del periódico *El Colombiano*: aspectos socio-económicos y políticos; No. 1, enero/abril 1977. Medellín, Colombia, 1977. 136 p.

Provides access to subjects of economic and sociopolitical interest; personal names are not indexed. Listing of each article selected for indexing (by day of publication) precedes index.

111. Universidade de São Paulo. Escola Superior de Agricultura Luis de Queiroz. Departamento de Ciências Sociais Aplicadas. [no title?] v. 4, pts. 1/3. Apresentação de Joaquim Jose de Camargo Engler. São Paulo, 1976. 1 v. (Various pagings) (Série estudos e didática)

A series of abstracts of the research projects, studies and theses in the social sciences prepared by students or staff of the department. Not indexed. Availability of the works noted.

————. **Faculdade de Arquitetura e Urbanismo. Biblioteca.** Indice de arquitetura brasileira, 1967-1969: biblioteca. See item 503.

112. Valverde y Téllez, Emeterio. Bio-bibliografía eclesiástica del estado de México. Edición preparada por Mario Colín. México, Biblioteca Enciclopédica del Estado de México, 1976. 241 p., plates.

Provides brief sketches of selected priests in state; mainly information on 19th- and 20th-century individuals although colonial figures also appear. Includes literary output of priest where available. Table of contents lists each individual described.

113. van Oss, Adrian. Latinoamericanistas en Europa: registro bio-bibliográfico de 1976. Amsterdam, Centro de Estudios y Documentación Latinoamericanos (CEDLA), 1976. 100 p.

New addition of this valuable publication. Lists 518 European specialists involved in study of Latin America, defined as that area in which Spanish and Portuguese languages remain in common use. Excludes researchers of Guianas and many of Caribbean islands. Includes researchers in sciences and humanities and separate indexes by country and disciplines.

Williams, John Hoyt. Paraguay's historical resources: pt. 1, Paraguay's National Archives. See item 3091.

GENERAL WORKS

114. Aprile-Gniset, Jacques. Colombie. Paris, Éditions du Seuil, 1977. 190 p., illus., plates (Col. Microcosme. Petite Planète, 42)

Frenchman's introduction to Colombia based primarily on his four-year residence there. History and

Bibliography and General Works / 19

current events are mixed together in accounts of geographical regions, government, economy and international relations.

115. Arroyo Cabello, Mary. El libro español en Iberoamérica (MH, 349, abril 1977, p. 36-38, plates)

Review of market for Spanish publications in Spanish-speaking Latin America, where over 70 percent of Spain's exportable publications are destined. As is obvious, national markets are noted for their diversity. Three key problems affect book exports: transportation, censorship and monetary devaluation.

116. Báez, Vicente *ed.* La enciclopedia de Cuba. 2. ed. San Juan, P.R., n.p., 1975-1977. 14 v.

Well illustrated work containing information on all facets of Cuban society. Encyclopedia was compiled by a corps of more than 40 contributors under general direction of Vicente Báez. Volumes are devoted to particular subjects: literature, history, government, municipios, art and architecture, and reflect interests of individual contributors. Includes indexes and bibliographies.

117. ——— *ed.* La gran enciclopedia de Puerto Rico. Madrid, C. Corredera, 1976. 14 v. [v. 1:326 p. (to) v. 14:432 p.] bibl., facsims., illus., maps, plates.

Heavily illustrated work with separate volumes devoted to history, politics, poetry, short stories, the novel, theater, music, art, architecture, law, education, flora and fauna, economy, sports, folklore, municipios, and biography. Sections of each volume were compiled by individual specialists. Includes bibliographies and indexes.

118. Black, Jan Knippers; Howard I. Blutstein; Kathryn Therese Johnston; and David S. McMorris *eds.* Area handbook for Trinidad and Tobago. Washington, The American Univ., Foreign Area Studies, 1976. 304 p., bibl., plates, tables (DA PAM 550-178)

First treatment of country in area-handbook series has chapters devoted to: geography, history, social system, living conditions, education, mass communications, politics, economics, and defense. Includes selected bibliography, glossary and index.

119. Blutstein, Howard I. and others. Area handbook for Colombia. 3. ed. Washington, The American Univ., Foreign Area Studies, 1976. 508 p., bibl., maps, tables (DA-PAM 550-26)

Most recent ed. of Colombian handbook presents concise information on social, political and economic characteristics of society. Includes selected bibliography, index and glossary. Supersedes 1970 ed.

120. Brazil. Serviço Nacional de Aprendizagem Industrial (SENAI). Departamento Regional do Maranhão. Serviço de Pesquisa e Avaliação (SPA). Pesquisa sobre a indústria editorial e gráfica em São Luis. São Luis, Brazil, 1974. 52 p., tables.

Report on survey of printing and publishing industry provides data on size of companies, types of equipment available, salary scales and categories of occupations in trade.

121. Briceño Romero, Gabriel. Personajes y temas falconianos en los 450 años de Coro: 26 de julio 1527-1977. Caracas, Artegráfica, 1976. 359 p., illus.

Work was written in honor of 450th anniversary of Coro's founding. Contains biographical sketches of prominent natives of Falcón state and brief accounts of various themes, e.g. medical association and college, Coro Municipal Council, university, and Coro's history. Useful local history.

122. Carranza, María Mercedes *comp.* Estravagario: revista cultural de *El Pueblo*. Presentación de Fernando Garavito. Bogotá, Instituto Colombiano de Cultura, Subdirección de Comunicaciones Culturales, División de Publicaciones, 1976. 409 p., bibl. (Biblioteca colombiana de cultura. Col. popular, 8)

This potpourri of essays, selected from material that appeared in 1975 in *Estravagario* (cultural review of Cali newspaper *El Pueblo*) provides insights into Colombian literary and cultural society. Interesting reading.

Frota, Francisco Marialva Mont'Alverne. Sousandrade: o último périplo. See item 7742.

Grigulevich, Iosif. Latin American studies. See item 2171.

123. Guyana handbook: 1976, industry, tourism, commerce. Georgetown, Guyana Manufacturers' Association [and] Univ. of Guyana, Faculty of Education, 1976. 255 p.

Sixth ed. of guide includes selected information on Guyana's history, topography, educational and governmental systems, government corporations, and commercial opportunities.

124. Humbert, Marc. La Mexique. Paris, Presses Univ. de France (PUF), 1976. 126 p., bibl., map, tables (Que sais-je?)

Brief but useful overview of Mexican society. Half of work is devoted to current trends in social and economic development.

125. Humphrey, Robin A. Latin American studies in Great Britain: an autobiographical fragment. London, Univ. of London, Institute of Latin American Studies, 1978. 54 p.

Readable personal account of development of Latin American studies in England in this century by one of most distinguished scholars in the field.

126. Kelsey, Vera and **Lilly de Jongh Osborne.** Four keys to Guatemala. 2. rev. ed. Revised by Larry Handel. N.Y., Funk & Wagnalls, 1978. 255 p., plates.

Up-dated rendering of classic work intended for tourist use. Provides excellent descriptions of places to see in Guatemala along with smattering of history, culture and geography.

127. Lacombe, Robert. La République d'Haïti (FDD/NED, 4436/4437, 29 nov. 1977, p. 1-96, bibl., maps, tables)

General overview of history and economic development of Haiti. Illustrated with thematic maps, charts and tables. Useful introductory work.

128. *Latin American Yearly Review.* American College in Paris. Vol. 3, 1975 [i.e. 1977]- . Paris.

Issue of *Review* provides brief assessments of political and economic happenings in Latin America during 1974 gleaned from number of world-wide newspapers and periodicals. Includes sections for each country or geographical region. Preface contains more recent information (1977) in general summary of events.

129. Mantilla, Gabriel *ed.* Who's who among Latin Americans in Washington. Bicentennial ed. Introduction by Herminio Portell-Vilá. Kensington, Md., Gama Enterprises, 1976. 352 p., plates, tables.

Contrary to title, this biographical reference work lists Latin American nationals as well as US citizens with Luso-Hispanic surnames who reside in Washington, D.C. Those selected for inclusion are cited for accomplishments in public and private endeavors. [D.E. Chipman]

Millones, Luis *comp.* La religión andina: estudios y estudiosos de una difícil pregunta. See item 2076.

130. Monbeig, Pierre. Le Brésil. 4. ed. refondue. Paris, Presses Univ. de France (PUF), 1976. 127 p., maps, tables (Que sais-je?)

Introduction to Brazilian society with brief sketches of country's geography, history, economy, and culture. Up-dates previous issues. Provides current economic and demographic assessments.

131. Pilotto, Osvaldo. Cem anos de imprensa no Paraná: 1854-1954. Curitiba, Instituto Histórico Geográfico e Etnográfico Paranaense, 1976. 74 p. (Estante paranista, 1)

Excellent essay is intended to facilitate study of Paraná. Work covers 100 years from first year of printing (1854) in Curitiba and appearance of *O Dezenove de Dezembro* on 1 April 1854.

132. Podestá, Bruno. Revistas peruanas de este siglo (UP/A, 3:6, 1977, p. 69-74)

Brief review of selected cultural, literary and social science journals, e.g. *Amauta, Las Moradas, Amaru, Historia,* and *Mar del Sur.* Attempts to answer questions concerning reasons for existence of a journal and ideological stand, if any, adopted by each.

133. Rosario, Rubén del; Esther Melón de Díaz; and **Edgar Martínez Masdeu.** Breve enciclopedia de la cultura puertorriqueña. With the collaboration of Marcelino J. Canino and others. San Juan, P.R., Editorial Cordillera, 1976. 447 p., plates, tables.

Concisely written introduction to Puerto Rican culture through biographical sketches of current and historical persons, descriptions of cities and towns and brief essays on broad themes and localisms.

134. Sodré, Nelson Werneck. O que se deve ler para conhecer o Brasil. 5. ed. Rio, Civilização Brasileira, 1976. 377 p. (Col. Retratos do Brasil, 54)

Popular work follows same format as in previous editions, i.e., three major sections devoted to historical development, special studies, and Brazilian culture. Each section is divided into number of chapters dealing with related themes. New chapter on Church was added. Provides list of sources for each theme. Useful summary of Brazilian society.

United States. Department of State. Countries of the world and their leaders. See item 2241.

Van Steenberghe de Dourmont, Roberto. Ensayo sobre la encuadernación en Córdoba. See item 3877.

Von Hagen, Victor Wolfgang. The Germanic people in America. See item 2244.

Weiss, Judith A. *Casa de las Américas*: an intellectual review of the Cuban Revolution. See item 3018.

JOURNAL ABBREVIATIONS

EEHA/HBA	Historiografía y Bibliografía Americanista. Escuela de Estudios Hispano-Americanos de Sevilla. Sevilla.
FDD/NED	Notes et Études Documentaires. Direction de la Documentation. Paris.
IFH/C	Conjonction. Institut Français d'Haïti. Port-au-Prince.
IRA/B	Boletín del Instituto Riva-Agüero. Pontificia Univ. Católica del Perú. Lima.
LARR	Latin American Research Review. Univ. of North Carolina Press *for the* Latin American Studies Association. Chapel Hill.
MEC/C	Cultura. Ministério da Educação e Cultura, Diretoria de Documentação e Divulgação. Brasília.
MH	Mundo Hispánico. Madrid.
UCAB/M	Montalbán. Univ. Católica Andrés Bello, Facultad de Humanidades y Educación, Institutos Humanísticos de Investigación. Caracas.
UNESCO/BL	UNESCO Bulletin for Libraries. United Nations Educational, Scientific and Cultural Organization. Paris.
UP/A	Apuntes. Univ. del Pacífico, Centro de Investigación. Lima.
UY/R.	Revista de la Universidad de Yucatán. Mérida, Mex.
VANH/B	Boletín de la Academia Nacional de la Historia. Caracas.

ART

SPANISH AMERICA
COLONIAL

ROBERT J. MULLEN

Assistant Professor of Art History
University of Texas, San Antonio

SCHOLARS LONG AGO LEARNED THE INESTIMABLE value of *A guide to the art of Latin America* published in 1949 by the Hispanic Foundation of the Library of Congress. The co-author of that monumental work, Elizabeth Wilder Weismann, has now written a significant sequel, "The History of Art in Latin America, 1500-1800: Some Trends and Challenges in the Last Decade" published in the *Latin American Research Review* (10:1, Spring 1975, p. 7-50, bibl., plates). Although briefly annotated in *HLAS 38:266* and *2346*, this essay is unique in its portrayal of the state of research for the art historian. With uncommon insight and sensitivity, Weismann offers a systematic analysis of 561 works pertaining to the colonial art of Latin America and published since 1963. She concludes wistfully that a comprehensive history of art for the Latin American countries still does not exist; challenges art historians to consider Latin American art for itself; pleads for greater publication of documents, inventories, photographic catalogues and painstaking field work. On the positive side she notes the excellent topical and area studies and a flood of arguments pro and con on Baroque style; takes a serious look at folk art and sees a shift from stylistic analysis towards sociological relationships. A dearth of monographs on individual artists and almost nothing on iconography is offset by many architectural conservation measures taken in Latin America. We agree with many of Weismann's comments, particularly her shrewd observations that "It may be that for the Americas 'styles' are unsuitable criteria, especially styles described in Europe."

With regard to works by other authors included in this section, we note that official inventories are beginning to appear particularly of countries about which too little has been known: Argentina, Colombia, Costa Rica, Uruguay (see items 255, 266, 269-271 and 302). Preservation is receiving much attention in Mexico and Santo Domingo (see item 263). Most interesting are several architectural "discoveries" in remote areas of Colombia (item 272), Chile (item 268), Peru (item 299), and Paraguay (items 293 and 294). An extensive regional study of architecture in Oaxaca (item 286) adds to our basic knowledge of 16th-century architecture in Mexico provided earlier by Kubler and McAndrew. Of 13 studies of individual sites, it is heartening to note that eight are in countries other than Mexico. Particularly successful among the 13 are Cocóspera (in Sonora, Mex., see item 280) and Santa Catalina (in Arequipa,

Peru, see item 297). We are impressed with the attention given to civil architecture, most notably three articles on defensive fortifications in the Caribbean region (see items 262, 267 and 275).

Painting in Latin America is receiving renewed, professional attention. Basic studies on painting in colonial Venezuela and the Andean region are items 258, 296 and 304. Among the most handsome illustrations of 17th- and 18th-century painting in Latin America is a catalogue printed in Germany for an exhibition (1977) of Andean painters—with scholarly texts (item 251). Monographs on painters and sculptors of merit rescue several from undeserved obscurity (items 282, 295, 300 and 303). The one discussion of the Baroque in Latin America considers the subject from the viewpoint of dialectic analysis rather than style (item 260). We reviewed good articles and books on folk art, that on crafts of Guatemala and El Salvador deserving special mention (item 309). In this volume, the subsection on "Folk Art" appears at the end, after Venezuela.

We are impressed with the professional work of the "new breed" of colonial art historians, themselves citizens of various Latin American countries.

It may be something of a precedent to mention institutional matters, but then so too is the event. A Research Center for the Arts (Univ. of Texas, San Antonio) was established in 1977 whose primary focus will be on the visual and performing arts (studio art, architecture and music) of Spain, Portugal and the Americas. To quote from the announcements:

In the next several years, the Center will compile and disseminate information on current research, scholars working in the field, sources of funding for research, university programs awarding degrees for the study of these arts, and learned societies that have sponsored symposia, papers, or publications concerning these arts. At a future date, the Center will compile bibliographies dealing with Iberian and Interamerican arts and will identify those private and public collections in which these arts are represented . . . The Center plans to organize a series of conferences that will establish the states of the disciplines of art history and musicology . . . pertaining to Iberia and Interamerica.

Another item of particular significance to the art historian is the first official role given to art history as a discipline at the 1977 annual meeting of the Latin American Studies Association (Houston, Tex., Nov. 1977). Papers on prehispanic, colonial and modern subjects were presented as *art history* topics.

Unique to the whole of the US are two prestigious official Mexican institutions located in San Antonio—a branch campus of the Univ. Nacional Autónoma de México and the Instituto Cultural Mexicano. The latter concentrates on the visual and performing arts; its permanent collection is one of the finest assemblies of folk art outside of Mexico.

GENERAL

251. Barocke Malerei aus den Anden: Gemälde des 17. und 18. Jahrhunderts aus Bolivien, Ecuador, Kolumbien und Peru. v. 1/2. Düsseldorf, FRG, Städtische Kunsthalle, 1977. 2 v. (103, 89 p.) bibl., plates.

Two handsome volumes printed for exhibition of 17th- and 18th-century paintings from Andes. Vol. 1: Peru, Bolivia, Ecuador, Colombia with scholarly texts by art historians on each country. Works of European artists are in b/w, those of Latin American artists in color (good but not highest quality). Vol. 2: iconography, including European derivative prints. Many illustrations, all b/w. Excellent introduction by Pál Kelemen. Exceptional work, going well beyond normal catalogue.

252. Goss, Robert C. The churches of San Xavier, Arizona and Caborca, Sonora: a comparative analysis (AAHS/K, 40:3, Spring 1975, p. 165-179, bibl., map, plates, table)

Precise nature of relationships investigated. Kinship is compelling even if identity of architects (brothers) remains uncertain. Conclusion: San Xavier was model for Caborca. Illustrations, plans, dimensions.

253. ———. The San Xavier Altarpiece. Tucson, Univ. of Arizona Press, 1974. 94 p., bibl., plates.

Mission San Xavier del Bac possesses rare example

of 18th-century retablo in the U.S. still in its original condition. Thorough technical analysis, detailed examination of organization, simbolism and iconography. Excellent illustrations (b/w).

254. Polzer, Charles W. Rules and precepts of the Jesuit missions of northwestern New Spain. Tucson, Univ. of Arizona Press, 1976. 141 p., bibl., plates.

Focuses on the administration of the mission system, its inner workings, the more important methods employed and a comparison with Franciscan methods. Section on terminology will be a revelation to many. A *sine qua non* for anyone delving into "missions" in the Americas.

ARGENTINA

255. Universidad de Buenos Aires, *Arg.* **Facultad de Filosofía y Letras. Instituto de Historia del Arte.** Cronología artística: síntesis de lo creado en el campo del arte, en el actual territorio argentino, en los siglos XVI-XVIII. B.A., 1971. 84 p. (Biblioteca de historia del arte. Serie Argentina, 4)

Chronology of events significant to the arts in Argentina from 1527 to 1800. Names, places, works, monuments indexed. Bibliography. An unusual and irreplaceable reference.

256. Varini, César M. Orígenes de Santa Ana. Chajari, Arg., n.p., 1975. 24 p., illus., maps, tables.

History of Santa Ana, small colonial village on Río Uruguay. Present chapel dedicated in 1901. Maps, statistics, a few (average) illustrations.

BOLIVIA

257. Alexander, María Teresa. Teresa Gisbert: guardián del arte (MH, 27:318, sept. 1974, p. 54-55, plates)

Architect and art historian, Gisbert answers questions of Spanish correspondent on arts of her native Bolivia.

258. Mesa, José de and **Teresa Gisbert.** Pintura virreinal en Bolivia (MH, 27:318, sept. 1974, p. 40-45, plates)

General account of painting in Bolivia from early 17th century to 1780. Artists, their works and "school" identified, especially Cuzco. Article based on 35 works sent to Spain for exhibition, of which 15 are illustrated. Five museums in Bolivia holding art works of viceregency are identified.

259. ——— and ———. Pinacoteca de San Francisco. La Paz, Univ. Mayor de San Andrés, División de Extensión Universitaria, Instituto de Estudios Bolivianos, 1973. 58 p., plates.

Brief history of convento from founding in 1548. Pinacoteca is next to National Museum in importance in La Paz by reason of its paintings, sculptures and religious objects. Analyzes paintings by stylistic periods: Renaissance, Mannerism, Baroque, School of Cuzco, Neo-classic, Eclectic. Includes 99 works catalogued by artist (when known), date, topic, medium, size. Includes 30 b/w illustrations (fair-good quality). Another fine contribution by Mesa and Gisbert.

CARIBBEAN

260. Acosta, Leonardo. El barroco de Indias y la ideología colonialista (CYC, 2, 1974, p. 125-157)

Dialectic analysis of culture being used as ideological tool of domination in Latin America with particular attention to Cuba. Baroque art and literature exist but as a style imported by Spanish monarchy and as a cultural constraint tied to imperialist ideologies. More polemical than definitive. Concludes a native Baroque resulted from indigenous artistic forces seeking expression of their concept of world.

261. Canedo, Lino Gómez. La iglesia de San Francisco en Santo Domingo (UNPHU/A, 3:10/11, julio/dic. 1974, p. 114-128)

Using AGI sources author gives detailed historic account of church and convento from founding (1508-14) through various reconstructions until 1795. Not a technical account. Inventory of furnishings and their costs; other financial matters.

262. Caro Alvarez, José A. Las murallas de Santo Domingo. Madrid, Gráficas Martin, 1975. 31 p., fold. table.

Document (dated 1816 discovered in 1973 by engineer corps) describes fully 11 fortifications of Santo Domingo. No plans or illustrations.

263. Sanz-Pastor, Consuelo. Museo de las Casas Reales: Santo Domingo (MH, 27:313, abril 1974, p. 28-34, plates)

Two former 16th-century palacios restored as museum. Photos show work in progress. Plans (two floors). Good description of completed museum and contents.

Vila Vilar, Enriqueta. Algunas consideraciones en torno a las fortificaciones de Puerto Rico. See *HLAS 39:629*.

CENTRAL AMERICA

264. Frison, Bruno. Pahula: estudio histórico pastoral sobre la Parroquia de San Cristóbal Totonicapán desde su origen hasta nuestros días. Guatemala, Instituto Teológico Salesiano, 1975. 184 p., plates (Col. Histórica, 1)

San Cristobal founded by Franciscans in 16th-century. Building programs for two churches and convento. Contents of parish archives (since 1674). Names of pastors. Documentary monograph: descriptive, little analysis. Few photos: quality poor.

265. La Orden Miracle, Ernesto *padre*. La misión franciscana de Orosi: joya artística de Costa Rica (MH, 27:313, abril 1974, p. 16-21, plates)

Church (San José) constructed 1753-66 after mission was transferred from Talamanca to Orosi. Dimensions, contents of church, description of convento. Being restored. Includes 10 photos, good quality.

266. Molina de Lines, María and **Jorge A. Lines.** Costa Rica: monumentos históricos y arqueológicos. San José, Instituto Panamericano de Geografía e Historia, 1974. 221 p., plates (IPGH publicación, 229. Comisión de historia, 91. Monumentos históricos y arqueológicos de América, 13)

Cites legislation and organizations concerned with patrimony and its preservation. Sculptures, ceramics and metalworks of three pre-hispanic cultures are described. Architecture of the colonial period is carefully identified. Brief account of independence and its memorials. Illustrations (b/w, fair quality) of all three epochs. Map. Extensive bibliography. A basic reference.

267. Zapatero, Juan Manuel. La plaza fortificada de Panamá (IAA, 2:3, 1976, p. 227-256, bibl., maps, plates)

Masterful analysis of Panamá's defense works from 1586 to 1818 (author is military historian and restorer). These fortifications present unique continuing case history in development of maritime defense works. Documented. Considerable detail. Excellent maps (four), sketches (three), view (one).

CHILE

268. Universidad de Chile, *Santiago.* Facultad de Arquitectura y Urbanismo. Arquitectura de Chiloé. Santiago, 1976. 70 p., bibl., illus., plates.

Several villages in Chiloé, a region in extreme south of Chile, gives witness to distinct form of architecture in wood. Oldest standing structures date from mid-18th century. Unique vernacular architecture. Maps, drawings, photos (professional). Brief history since Spanish settlement in 16th century. Remarkable work; significant contribution.

COLOMBIA

269. Alvarez Díaz, Enrique. Herencia colonial en la vida rural colombiana. pts. 1/2. Bogotá, Banco Cafetero y de Almadelco, El Fondo Cultural Cafetero, 1974. 2 v. (Unpaged) plates.

Historic, economic and aesthetic analysis of 40 haciendas presented as key to understanding rural Colombia. Succinct texts accompanied by scores of fine photos (mostly b/w, some color). Vol. 1 concentrates on architectural, sculptural, decorative elements; Vol. 2 on economic bases. All aspects illustrated; chapels noteworthy. An outstanding accomplishment. Of unique value to several disciplines.

270. Bogotá: museos/museums. Bogotá, Ediciones Cima, n.d. 160 p., facsims., illus.

More than 20 museums in city identified by locations, hours and lengthy account of holdings. A few illustrations. Excellent reference.

271. Dussan de Reichel, Alicia. Guía de los museos de Colombia. Bogotá, Ministerio de Educación Nacional, Instituto Colombiano de Cultura, División de Museos y Restauración, 1973. 141 p., tables.

Alphabetical listing of 106 museums in Bolivia: address, hours, administration, collection, library. Appendices arrange them by Departamento and types of collections. Statistical tables: size, expenditure, visitors. Invaluable to traveler and scholar.

272. Goslinga, Cornelius Christiaan. Templos doctrineros neogranadinos. Cali, Colombia, Univ. del Valle, Facultad de Filosofía, Letras e Historia, 1972? 51 p., bibl., illus. (Col. Cuadernos del Valle, 5)

Templos doctrineros are village churches of New Granada. Makes comparative analysis of several (Boyacá, Cucaíta, Iza, Chivatá, Sora, Oicatá, Tunja, Tenjo, Sutatausa, Tópaga, and others) in terms of plans, facades, furnishings, decoration, techniques. Atrios (in Colombia) were not walled but had posas. Asks for restoration of several. Believes these churches give evidence of a Latin America Baroque with a "regional expression." Extensive bibliography. Incisive, imaginative, substantial.

273. Lemaitre, Eduardo. Cartagena colonial. Bogotá, Instituto Colombiano de Cultura, 1973. 176 p., bibl., illus.

(Biblioteca colombiana de cultura. Col. Popular, 108)

Strictly historical account, with emphasis on events (Documents) leading to independence.

274. Téllez, Germán. L'architecture de l'époque colonial à aujourd'hui (OEIL, 252/253, juillet/août 1976, p. 34-36, plates)

Mostly about contemporary architects in Colombia. Sketchy review of colonial heritage; symbolic and charming architecture of 19th century.

275. Zapatero, Juan Manuel. Cartagena de Indias: la mejor plaza fortificada de América (MH, 343, oct. 1976, p. 43-47, plates)

Detailed historic account of town and factors which led to construction of this immense fortification (restored by author). Disappointingly no technical nor engineering details are provided.

ECUADOR

276. Moreno Proaño, Agustín. Caspicara. Quito, Ediciones Paralelo Cero, 1976. 160 p., bibl., plates (Artistas ecuatorianos, 1)

The value of this work lies in its nearly 100 folio size, including several double spread, magnificent color plates of the exquisite sculpture of the late 18th century Indian artist Manuel Chili, better known as Caspicara. The accompanying text, however, is disappointing. Moreno offers neither new data on the enigmatic Caspicara nor an explanation of the techniques employed by this consumate artist. [M.T. Hamerly]

MEXICO

277. *Anales del Instituto de Investigaciones Estéticas.* UNAM. Vol. 12, No. 44, 1975- . México.

Under new director, Jorge Alberto Manrique, *Anales* continues tradition of excellence. This issue contains following works: Toussaint's excellent study (1948 heretofore unpublished) of Cathedral in Zacatecas with notes and good b/w illustrations; article on another Zacatecas church which studies the side portal of San Agustín, new dating, fine photos b/w; two additional pieces on architecture are followed by several on painting: impact of Zurbarán's "Home in Nazareth" and works of Luis Berrueco (1717-50). Issue also includes articles on baroque organs; influence of Serlio on cathedrals in Guatemala and Ciudad Real de Chiapas; mannerist painter Rosso Fiorentino, etc.

278. Arthur, Don; Julia Costello; and **Brian Fagan.** A preliminary account of Majolica sherds from the chapel site, Royal Spanish Presidio, Santa Barbara, California (AAHS/K, 41:2, 1975, p. 207-214, bibl., illus.)

Mostly a history of Majolica ware and characteristics of various types made in Mexico. Breakdown of 129 sherds among these types is made. Excellent example of historical archaeology, confirming presence of Spanish at Santa Barbara in 19th century.

279. Carrillo y Gariel, Abelardo. Fachadas vestidas y revestidas (INAH/B, 2:15 [2. época] oct./dic. 1975, p. 23-34, plates)

Using 16th-century document, author cites wealthy citizens (vecinos nobles) then resident in Mexico City. Traces their present location and transformation. Focuses on 18th-century palacios and increasing use of *tezontle* (red volcanic stone) as primary building material. Fascinating insights into America's largest and wealthiest city in 1750.

280. Davis, Natalie Y. and **Robert C. Goss.** Cocóspera: lonely sentinel of resurrection (SAR/P, 83:2, Summer 1977, p. 25-43, bibl., illus., map, plates, tables)

Final (and presently ruined) Franciscan mission church (Sonora, Mex.) dated to late 1780s by documentary evidence and analysis of architectural and decorative styles. Careful analysis of construction (plan, section, details), retablo and facade. Well illustrated. Thorough, professional.

281. Díaz, Marco. Arquitectura religiosa en Atlixco. Presentación de Elisa Vargas Lugo. México, UNAM, Instituto de Investigaciones Estéticas, 1974. 126 p., plates (Col. Cuadernos de historia del arte, 4)

Thoroughly describes eight churches in Atlixco, dating from 16th to 18th centuries, including paintings and furnishings. Some documentation, but no new sources. Comparative analysis of stucco Baroque of province with that of nearby metropole, Puebla. Brief account of pre-hispanic Atlixco. A substantial contribution. Photos are crisp, plentiful (49, mostly by author).

282. García Saiz, María del Carmen and **Luis J. Ramos.** Obras de José de Páez en el Museo de América de Madrid (CH, 103:308, feb. 1976, p. 51-66, plates)

Museo has large collection of colonial paintings especially 18th-century. Seven works by José de Páez (dated 1753-90) are described in detail. Comparative style analysis made of these and his larger works in Mexico. Analysis of signatures. Substantial contribution.

283. Jara Hantke, Alvaro. Plata y pulque en el siglo XVIII mexicano (*in* Siete studies: homenaje de la Facultad de Ciencias Humanas a Eugenio Pereira Salas. Santiago, Univ. de Chile, 1975, p. 163-190, tables)

Comparative economic analysis of production of silver with that of pulque (consumption) and maquey (agriculture).

284. Maza, Francisco de la. El oratorio de San Felipe Neri (FAH/N, 258 [3. época] 1974, p. 27-29, plates)

Describes origins of Oratorio in San Miguel el Grande (completion date of church, 1714) stylistic changes since then, especially in the interior. Possesses 33 oils by Cabrera (life of San Felipe) and one large work by Juan Rodríguez Juárez (the Virgin). Many fine statues "de madera estofada." Convento modified into apartments. Facade (photo) is good example of early 18th-century work.

285. Montejano y Aguiñaga, Rafael. El Palacio de Gobierno de San Luis Potosí. San Luis Potosí, Mex., Academia de Historia Potosina, 1973. 126 p., plates (Biblioteca de historia potosina. Serie estudios, 10)

Monograph of Palacio (1798-1827 and modifications) and several other major buildings around Plaza. Compendium of many sources. Few technical details. Illustrations (fair quality) from 1810 to present. Short history of city.

286. Mullen, Robert J. Dominican architecture in sixteenth century Oaxaca. Phoenix, Arizona State Univ., Center for Latin American Studies, 1975. 260 p., bibl., plates, tables.

Full-length study of 70 plus church/convento complexes established by Dominican religious order. Founding dates documented; churches grouped under four architectural styles; case history (Cuilapan) of building techniques; tentative identification of architects; special role of Rodrigo Gil de Hontañon. Summary description of 60 establishments; chronological listing by founding dates; listing by nations. Selected bibliography, especially of unpublished documents.

287. Nickel, Herbert J. Notas marginales sobre la arquitectura colonial de algunas haciendas e iglesias en la región de Puebla-Tlaxcala: Las "figuritas" de los albañiles (FAIC/CPPT, 12, 1975, p. 23-26, illus., plates)

Graffito-like outline drawings set with interspersed stones. Seen as local artistic expression in defiance of professional mural design and paintings. Good illustrations.

288. Obregón, Gonzalo. Datos sobre algunas obras de arte de Tepotzotlán (INAH/B, 2:11 [2. época] oct./dic. 1974, p. 43-46, plates)

Based on records of costs, offers interesting analysis of additions made by Jesuits between 1757-63 such as new facade, tower, commissioned paintings. Documentary evidence solidifies dating of this very significant work of 18th-century architecture in Mexico.

289. Programa de trabajo de la Dirección del Patrimonio Cultural y Artístico del Estado de México: documentos. Toluca, Mex., Talleres Graficos de México, 1976. 66 p., plates.

Definitive statement on cultural preservation in State of Mexico citing objectives in three main areas: preservation, interpretation and participation by students. Implements law of 12 Jan. 1976 calling for preservation of all forms of artistic expression.

290. Romero Quiroz, Javier. El Convento Hospital de Nuestra Señora de Guadalupe e del Señor San José: recolección de Nuestro Padre San Juan de Dios de Toluca. El Teatro de los Hospitalarios. México, Editorial Libros de México, 1976. 100 p., bibl., facsims, illus., plates (Serie Chimalphain. Col. De divulgación histórica)

First half details life of Juan de Dios (1495-1550), his canonization and founding of hospitals in Nueva España. Second half details the 19th-century theater in Toluca hospital. Plans, sketches, photos (b/w, good quality). Speculates on types of plays.

291. ———. La pila bautismal de barro de Zinacantepec (UAEM/H, 1:1, enero/marzo 1976, p. 42-59, plates)

Lengthy account of rite of baptism followed by description of baptismal font. Dimensions; attribution (16th-century, Franciscan), six illustrations.

292. Yurrieta Valdés, José. La capilla abierta de Zinacantepec (UAEM/H, 1:1, enero/marzo 1976, p. 31-41, plates)

Origin (1569) of Franciscan convento (near Toluca). Plan and illustrations of open-air chapel. Well preserved. Condition of retablo and murals. Detailed descriptions.

PARAGUAY

293. Brugada Guanes, Alejandro. Paracuaria: obras arquitectónicas de la era jesuítica en el Paraguay. Asunción,

Offset Comuneros, 1975. 89 p., bibl., illus., plates.

Non-polemic account of Jesuit missions (30) founded among Guaraní in Paraguay (Paracuaria) from early 1600s to expulsion in 1767. Social structure, arts, architecture. Maps, plans, drawings, photos (b/w, many color, good quality). Extensive bibliography. Conservation program. Rare contribution.

294. Plá, Josefina. Barroco hispano-Guaraní (OAS/AM, 28 [11]:12, nov./dic. 1976, p.s-1—s-16, plates)

Rare and full account of 17th-century missions (13) in Guairá, Par. History of evangelization of Guaraní; method of teaching arts; indigenous arts, artisans. Term "barroco hispano-guaraní" applied mostly to objects. Relatively little on architecture.

PERU

295. Bernales Ballesteros, Jorge. Dos menas en Lima (EEHA/AEA, 31, 1974, p. 79-89, plates)

Two sculptured pieces, an Ecce Homo and Dolorosa, now part of a retablo in Jesuit church San Pedro, Lima, attributed to Pedro de Mena y Medrano (1628-88).

296. Macera, Pablo. El arte mural cuzqueño, siglos XVI-XX (UP/A, 2:4, 1975, p. 59-113, plates)

Quite a number of murals are analyzed by 10 style periods. Key artists identified (e.g., Zapata, Escalante). Social conditions examined. Virtual book-length study with brief outline of ancient mural tradition and extent of previous study. Of many designations, prefers "cultura andina colonial." Includes 30 illustrations.

297. Maldonado, José Luis. Santa Catalina, Arequipa. Lima, S. Valverde, n.d. 14 p., plates.

Santa Catalina, convent for women, founded 1579 and opened to public in 1971, occupies 20,000 square m. Non-technical description of entrance, sections, rooms, "calles," museum (109 paintings). Plan, quality photos, many colored. Unusual monograph.

298. Mariátegui Oliva, Ricardo. Santa Clara de Ayacucho: plateresco y mudejarismo de los siglos XVI y XVII en el Perú. Lima, Industrialgráfica, 1974. 28 p., bibl., plates.

Edifying account of convent for women, established 1563. Includes 16 illustrations.

299. Mesa, José de and **Teresa Gisbert.** La exteriorización del culto: capillas abiertas y atrios en el Perú (EEHA/AEA, 31, 1974, p. 973-1003, illus., plates)

Earlier discovery of at least 27 churches with "atrios and posas" in Bolivia led to discovery of four such in Perú plus three instances of open-air chapels: Triunfo del Cuzco, La Merced de Ayacucho, Guadalupe. Built in 17th century, their function differs from those of 16th-century Mexico. Well illustrated; plans.

300. ——— and ———. El pintor Mateo Pérez de Alesio. La Paz, Univ. Mayor de San Andrés, Univ. Boliviana, Instituto de Estudios Bolivianos, División de Extensión Universitaria, 1972. 130 p., plates (Col. Cuadernos de arte y arqueología, 2)

Biography of artist: birth and education in Italy; sojourn in Spain; paintings in Upper and Lower Peru, especially in Santo Domingo, Lima. Extensively researched. Illustrations (b/w) of fair quality. Significant monograph.

301. Vargas Ugarte, Rubén. La Casa de Jarava o de Pilatos. Lima, Ministerio de Educación, Casa de la Cultura del Perú, 1971. 10 p., plates.

More about its inhabitants than the house. Because so little is known of early Lima, author attempts to trace origins of house to early 17th century. One illustration (poor) of inner court.

URUGUAY

302. Castellanos, Alfredo Raúl. Uruguay: monumentos históricos y arqueológicos. México, Instituto Panamericano de Geografía e Historia, 1974. 1 v. (Various pagings) bibl., plates (IPGH publication, 337. Monumentos históricos y arqueológicos de América, 16)

Official "handbook" of Uruguay's historic monuments. Pre-hispanic cultures and structural types identified. Hispanic period gives history and architecture (military, religious, public, private. The 19th century covers wide range of buildings and monuments. Preservation laws and designated patrimonial sites. Includes 43 representative illustrations (b/w, good to fair). Reliable, definitive. A unique compendium.

VENEZUELA

303. Duarte, Carlos F. El orfebre Pedro Ignacio Ramos. Introducción de Graziano Gasparini. Caracas, Equinoccio Ediciones [and] Univ. Simón Bolívar, 1974. 128 p., bibl., plates.

Masterful account of recently "discovered" 18th-century Venezuelan silver/goldsmith. Graziano Gasparini, in his introduction, says author has portrayed Ramos well both as person and artist. Biography and full catalog of works arranged chronologically. Includes 39 plates, some color, all excellent quality. Outstanding work.

304. ———. Visión de las artes durante el Período colonial venezolano (FJB/BH, 39, sept. 1975, p. 353-382)

Development of arts in Venezuela differed from other countries since there were few prohibitions or rules. The 16th and 17th centuries were formative to florescence of 18th. Includes names of 64 artists (mostly painters, sculptors) and their works.

305. Martínez Salas, Rafael. La Guaira histórica: cronista de La Guaira. Presentación de Diego Arria. Caracas, Gobernación del Distrito Federal, Dirección de Cultura, 1975. 29 p., illus.

Brief history of Venezuelan coastal city, founded 1589. Major buildings described. Present cathedral consecrated 1857. Quality photos (29) except for "soft" printing.

306. Otaduy, Ernesto. Iglesias de la antigua Caracas. Caracas, Imprenta Municipal de Caracas, 1974. 168 p., bibl., illus., plates.

Detailed account of 11 churches and two convents (women) in Caracas from founding in colonial times to present. Reprint of earlier articles. Quantities of facts from many but uncertain sources. Extensive bibliography. No developmental theme nor stylistic analysis. Sparsely illustrated; poor quality.

FOLK ART

307. Coke, Van Deren. Clay figurines of Ocumicho (SAR/P, 82:1, March 1976, 17-21, plates)

Delightful folk art from village near Patzcuaro, Mex. Work in clay goes back only two-three generations but traditions are ancient. Many made just for Day of the Dead.

308. Goodman, Frances Schaill. The embroidery of Mexico and Guatemala. N.Y., Charles Scribner's Sons, 1976. 81 p., illus., plates.

Focusing on embroidery, every form of stitch is identified along with garments. This "dying" folk art is beautifully presented with superb color plates (34) and many fine b/w photos.

309. Osborne, Lilly and Jongh Osborne. Indian crafts of Guatemala and El Salvador. Foreword by J. Eric S. Thompson. Paintings by Julia Ayau de López Escobar. 2. ed. Norman, Univ. of Oklahoma Press, 1975. 385 p., bibl., illus., maps, plates (Series civilization of the American Indian, 79)

Two-thirds treats of textiles: materials, dyes, looms, kinds of weaving, designs and symbols, men's and women's garments. Last third describes fiber products, ceramics, gourds. Conclusion: industrialization is usurping crafts. Thorough, knowledgeable, well illustrated (mostly b/w).

19TH AND 20TH CENTURIES

JAMES B. LYNCH, JR.

Professor of Art
University of Maryland

BEFORE INITIATING OUR BIENNIAL SURVEY let us note, with dismay and sorrow, the deaths of two distinguished Latin American artists since the publication of *HLAS 38*. They are Raúl Carlos Villanueva of Venezuela and Hector Basaldúa of Argentina.

Villanueva was an architect of international prestige. Undoubtedly his masterpiece was University City, Caracas, one of the most intelligently designed and aesthetically satisfying campuses in the world. Villanueva's El Silencio should have been a pilot plan for subsequent Venezuelan housing projects: instead it survived as a standard of excellence against which one measures such failed colossi as Cerro Piloto and Veintitrés de Enero. At his death he was planning a new building for the

Museo de Bellas Artes (see item 399).

Basaldúa was of course a pillar of Argentine figurative painting in the 20th century. In 1933 he was appointed Director Escenográfico of the Teatro Colón, B.A. He was well known also for illustrations of books by Borges and Mujica Láinez.

Among general entries we must cite "What's Latin American in Latin American Art" (item 312), a dynamic symposium with four participating artists.

"Recent Latin American Drawings" (item 313) is of interest. Along with Atilio Palacio's "Cuaderno de Apuntes . . ." of Miguel Carlos Victorica, it attests to a new and growing interest in Latin American drawings.

Mexico has several entries which we recommend. For example, there is the unusual "El Artesano en Mexico" (item 315). Cardozo y Aragón contributes a good essay on Siqueiros (item 317). Teresa del Conde's work on Ruelas (item 319), as well as Fausto Ramírez' on Saturnino Herrán (item 330), puts two turn-of-the-century Mexican painters into accurate perspective.

As of Central America, the most important entry is Vera Blinn Reber's "Art as a Source for the Study of Central America" (item 334). This gem of scholarship, aided by a superb bibliography, will enhance Central American studies considerably. Another valuable entry for the area is *Pintores de Costa Rica* (item 338).

Turning toward the Caribbean, let us mention a rare entry from Trinidad: "Arquitectura de la primera mitad del siglo XIX" (item 336). There is little on Cuba except for Fouchet's new biography *Wifredo Lam* with stunning plates (item 338).

With regard to South America, we note these entries: "La Pintura Argentina del Siglo XX . . ." (item 344) a welcome article, considering the neglect of the study of art after World War II: the monographs from Krass Artes Plásticas (items 352 and 360); and those from Ediciones Dead Weight, ably written by Rafael Squirrú. The Krass books, in particular, have excellent color reproductions.

Chile provides us with at least one outstanding entry: *Arquitectura de Chiloé* (item 366) concerning the striking wood architecture of the archipelago of Chiloé in southern Chile. Oddly enough, it invites comparisons with Finnish architecture.

Of Colombia's contributions the best by far is *Juan Antonio Roda: grabados 1971-1976* (item 372), the first in a series of contemporary Colombian art. One waits impatiently for the others!

Finally, Venezuela. A delightful book on the primitives of Venezuela/*Pintores venezolanos del común* (item 392) heads the entries for this country, closely followed by a fine monograph on Boggio (item 397) sponsored by the Tabacería Nacional. This sponsorship, incidentally, is a token of the significant aid being given Latin American art by banks, commercial institutions, universities, government bureaus, and other institutions in recent years. One last note: readers especially interested in Venezuelan art, are advised to look up the issue of *The Art Gallery* entirely devoted to Venezuela (item 393).

In *HLAS 36* we should have corrected—and unaccountably did not—a foolish error that appeared in the introduction to our section (p. 28). Siqueiros was not of course a "General" in the Spanish Civil War, as we implied. Commanding a batallion of troops on behalf of the Republic, he was at best a *Coronelazo*.

GENERAL

310. Bayón, Damián. El artista latinoamericano y su identidad. Caracas, Monte Avila Editores, 1977. 150 p., bibl., plates (Col. Estudios)

Edited tape of symposium held at the Univ. of Texas, Austin, Oct. 1975. Five themes for debate were submitted to large group of Latin American and North American critics and writers and to a small but distinguished group of Latin American artists.

311. ——— *comp*. América Latina en sus artes. Paris, UNESCO, 1974. 237 p., bibl. (Serie América Latina en su cultura)

Fifteen Latin American scholars collaborated to produce these essays under three main divisions: "El Arte Latinoamericano en el Mundo de Hoy,"

"Raíces, Asimilaciones, y Conflictos," y "Arte y Sociedad." "Las Formas de la Crítica y la Respuesta del Público," by Fermín Febre and "¿Un Arte Mestizo?," by Francisco Stastny, are particularly interesting. Includes helpful chronological table and an excellent bibliography.

312. Halasz, Piri. What's Latin American in Latin American art? (Art News [N.Y.] 74:10, Dec. 1975, p. 95-98)

Consists of 26 works by 22 Latin American artists exhibited at the New Jersey State Museum. Symposium held on occasion dealt with question posed in title. Four artists participated: Alejandro Obregón, José Luis Cuevas, Arnold Belken, and Leonel Góngora. Their repartee is worth reading.

313. Recent Latin American drawings, 1969-1976: lines of vision. Essays by Barbara Duncan and Damián Bayón. Catalogue entries by Ana M. Casciero. Washington, International Exhibitions Foundation, 1977. 79 p., plates.

Intelligently and sensitively chosen cross-sections of 100 drawings. For instance, such well known masters as Tamayo, Lam, and Matta were excluded to make room for "less-exposed talents." A comprehensive exhibition of current Latin American draughts-manship such as this has long been needed. The reproductions are generally adequate.

MEXICO

314. Artistas plásticas, Mexico 75. México, Ediciones Culturales GDA, 1975. 192 p., plates.

A "Who's Who" of Mexican art, book provides complete data on contemporary painters, sculptors, engravers, and photographers, complete with current prices of their works. Also listed are art critics and galleries. It may be added that in the case of young and lesser known artists telephone numbers are provided. In spite of its commercial approach this book may be of use.

315. Bravo Ramírez, Francisco J. El artesano en México. México, Editorial Porrúa, 1976. 103 p., bibl., plates.

Author defines craftsman, distinguished from the artist, as one who, through his hands and his intelligence, creates utilitarian objects. Traces briefly history of craftsman, examines his chief problems, socioeconomic realities confronting him today, and solutions.

316. Camp, Roderic Ai. Artists and politics in Mexico (LARR, 10:2, Summer 1975, p. 225-227)

Two cassettes discussed are interviews with Siqueiros and Octavio Paz, latter conducted by late Howard Cline. Considering hostility between Siqueiros and Tamayo, it is ironical that interviewer's minor theme is a comparison between works of both. His major theme: theme versus style.

317. Cardozo y Aragón, Luis. Alfaro Siqueiros: 23 notas marginales (CAM, 193:2, marzo/abril 1974, p. 81-90)

Thoughtful essay on Siqueiros and his relationship to Rivera and Orozco. As author's ideas pass from Chapultepec Castle to Spanish Civil War through Cimabue and Cézanne, his swift impressions glitter and illuminate.

318. Celorio, Gonzalo. El surrealismo y lo real maravilloso americano. México, Secretaría de Educación Pública, 1976. 175 p., plates, bibl. (SepSetentas 302)

Author's thesis, "una confrontación entre el surrealismo y la literatura de lo real maravilloso americano"—especially between Remedios Vara and García Márquez' Remedios la Bella of *Cien años de soledad* is developed persuasively by and large. Noteworthy bibliography.

319. Conde, Teresa del. Julio Ruelas. México, UNAM, Instituto de Investigaciones Estéticas, 1976. 115 p., bibl., plates (Estudios y fuentes del arte en México, 34)

Key to author's interpretation is Conde's statement: "Simbolismo y art-nouveau son las corrientes que mayormente definen el lenguaje artístico de Ruelas, quien al igual que Klimt en Alemania Tooroppen Holanda, o Beardsley en Inglaterra, plasma sus imágenes decadentes en el floreciente estilo modernista . . ." She views Ruelas as alien to his Mexican contemporaries (e.g., Velasco, Parra, Rebull, etc.) in his passion for fantasy. A glance at the illustrations, however, refutes this postulated rootlessness. Nevertheless, a provocative and rewarding monograph.

320. ———. Vida de Frida Kahlo. México, UNAM, Instituto de Investigaciones Estéticas, 1976. 65 p., plates.

More useful for plentiful biographical information than for insights into Kahlo's art.

321. Crespo de la Serna, J. Lo estético en Siqueiros (CAM, 193:2, marzo/abril 1974, p. 73-80, plates)

Coming from a scholar of rank, this is a disappointment. One looks in vain for a meaningful examination of "lo estético en Siqueiros." Instead the reader is treated to a biography of the artist. Of use only to beginners.

322. Foppa, Alaíde. Confesiones de José Luis Cuevas. México, Fondo de Cultura Económica, 1975. 216 p., illus.

"Confessions," "sin orden y sin ritmo constante," based on series of interviews (March 1973-Sept. 1974) while Cuevas was recuperating from heart attack. They throw much light on Cuevas' personality and his art.

323. Frías y Soto, Hilarión and others. Los mexicanos pintados por sí mismo. Reproducción facsimilar de la edición de 1855. México, Librería de Manuel Porrúa, 1975. 290 p., plates.

Descriptions of national customs and types by six prominent *costumbristas* of the 19th century provide portraits of picturesque persons no longer existing: water carrier, coachman, *la china*, muleteer, street writer, midwife, etc. Attractive book. [H.L. Johnson].

324. García Ponce, Juan. Felguérez. México, UNAM, Dirección General de Publicaciones, 1976. 42 p., bibl., plates (Col. de arte, 30)

Titled "Dialogue between Matter and Spirit," Ponce's introduction is of considerable help in understanding Felguerez' enigmatic art whose sculptures owe much to Jean Tinguely. Satisfactory color illustrations but uneven b/w.

325. Guillén, Pedro. Siqueiros y la política (CAM, 193:2, marzo/abril 1974, p. 63-71)

Interesting political apoligia and photographs. They range from Siqueiros' youthful service in the Revolution (1916) to portraits together with Junio Antonio Mella (1926), journalist Elvira Vargas (1937), Diego Rivera (1952), Nicolás Guillén (1954), Chou En-Lai in Peking (1956); and Siqueiros' release from jail in 1964.

326. Marqués Rodiles, Ignacio. El muralismo en la Ciudad de México. México, Depto. del Distrito Federal, Secretaría de Obras y Servicios, 1975. 103 p., plates (Col. Popular Ciudad de México, 30)

Mediocre or poor illustrations but text is useful to students of mural movement. Author emphasizes economic and social factors and traces development of mural painting from early times to present century. Chapter on 19th century art is lively and informative.

327. Nelken, Margarita and others. Un mundo etereo: la pintura de Lucinda Urrusti. México, Secretaría de Educación Pública, 1976. 158 p., illus. (SepSetentas, 275)

In Urrusti Mexico has benefitted from yet another refugee of the Spanish Civil War. Includes essays by 13 writers (Nelken, Gual, García Ponce, Crespo de la Serna, and Neuvillate) of uneven quality. Illustrations reproduce still lifes, drawings and nudes.

328. Neuvillate-Ortíz, Alfonso de. 10 [i.e. Diez] pintores mexicanos: Rufino Tamayo, David Alfaro Siqueiros, Carlos Mérida, Jesús Guerrero Galván, Carlos Orozco Romero, Ricardo Martínez, Guillermo Meza, Raymundo Martínez, Jaime Saldívar, Ernesto Icaza. México, Ediciones Galería de Arte Misrachi, 1974. 60 p., plates.

Criteria for selection of artists is not spelled out by author or publisher. Why, for instance, were Rivera, Orozco, and Cuevas omitted and Saldívar and Icaza included? Although Mérida is a splendid artist, why should he be included among "10 pintores mexicanos? Color reproductions are adequate.

329. O'Gorman, Juan. A propósito de conservación: un ensayo de arquitectura orgánica (Arquitectura México [México] 112, nov./dec. 1976, p. 92-99, plates)

Concerns O'Gorman's home in Pedregal district, Mexico City. Author explains how, influenced by Frank Lloyd Wright, he tried to harmonize his cave-house with fluid rolling contours of Pedregal lava fields, and how he aspired to integrate architecture, sculpture, and painting.

330. Ramírez, Fausto. Saturnino Herrán. México, UNAM, Dirección General de Publicaciones, 1976. 59 p., plates (Col. de arte, 27)

Ramírez finds artistic roots of Herrán in Fabrés and Gedovius. He analyzes his art, however, within a much broader turn-of-the-century context which includes Gustave Moreau, "femme fatale" theme, Klimt, Symbolism, etc. Ramírez also includes analysis of nearly 30 major works, plus stylistic and critical evaluation.

CENTRAL AMERICA

331. González-Goyri, Roberto. Rodolfo Abularach (RCPC, 31:152, julio/sept. 1976, p. 117-120)

This work contains biographical information about the precocious Guatemalan artist, whose first exhibition took place when he was little more than 14. See also item 333.

332. Orden Miracle, Ernesto la. Historia del arte en Nicaragua (BNBD, 7, sept./oct. 1975, p. 51-59, plate)

Virtually impossible attempt to compress history of Nicaraguan art from precolumbian to modern times in nine pages. Still, enough is offered to tempt the un-initiated into further readings.

333. Pizarro, Agueda. Rodolfo Abularach: ojos primordiales (RCPC, 31:152, julio/sept. 1976, p. 120-133, plates)

Chiaroscuro and curve are Abularach's artistic ingredients: "Hay una ambiguedad en la forma donde la imagen se convierte en otra: pájaro, molusco, pez, esfera, concha, caracol, perla." Very short but nonetheless sensitive and illuminating essay.

334. Reber, Vera Blinn. Art as a source for the study of Central America: 1945-1975, an exploratory essay (LARR, 13:1, 1978, p. 39-64, bibl., plates)

Most significant contribution to study area generally neglected by outside scholars. Reber's purpose: "To show how art represents a unique and collaborating source for understanding the history of people and the development of nations;" her theme: contemporary paintings and prints of Costa Rica, El Salvador, Guatemala, Honduras, and Nicaragua. Even more valuable, than Reber's essay is her remarkably voluminous bibliography.

335. Ulloa Barrenechea, Ricardo. Pintores de Costa Rica. San José, Editorial Costa Rica, 1975. 217 p., plates.

Pintores follows *La escultura en Costa Rica* published by same firm 1973 (see HLAS 38:394). Although author modestly disclaims an "estudio metódico basado en la estricta investigación histórica," nevertheless his book is a storehouse of information about Costa Rican pianting from 1897 on.

THE CARIBBEAN AND THE GUIANAS
(Except CUBA)

336. García Santana, Alicia. Trinidad: arquitectura de la primera mitad del siglo XIX (UCLV/I, 42, mayo/agosto 1972, p. 151-216, bibl., illus., plates)

Thorough, scholarly study of epoch in architectural history of Trinidad which is unusually rich in important examples. Her examination of earlier architecture is useful in itself. Includes list of local landmarks with informative data.

337. The official release of the 1763 monument (NHAC/K, 14, July 1976, p. 36-47, plates)

Sculpted by the Guyanese artist Philip Moore, monument commemorates slave revolt of 1763, led by Cuffy. Both Cuffy's figure and five plaques below are ornamented with revolutionary symbols, which author explains. Includes biographical notice about sculpture and short essay on background of the revolt. Although somewhat polemical in tone, article provides glimpse into national consciousness of one of newest and smallest of Latin American countries.

Otterbein, Keith. Changing house types in Long Bay Cays: the evolution of folk housing in an Out Island Bahamian community. See *HLAS 39:1247*.

CUBA

Documentos del Primer Congreso del Partido Comunista de Cuba sobre la Cultura Artística y Literaria: tesis, resolución. See item 6708.

338. Fouchet, Max-Pol. Wifredo Lam. N.Y., Rizzoli International Publications, 1976. 266 p., bibl., illus., plates.

Most comprehensive monograph on Lam to date. Author examines Cuban, Spanish, Parisian, African, and Haitian elements in his art. Material on childhood fascinating. In addition to excellent color and b/w reproductions there is a rich store of photographic material of a biographical nature. Finally, a catalog and a bibliography, both extensive, cap this splendid volume.

339. González, Juan R. Plástica en *Revista de Avance* (UCLV/I, 51, mayo/agosto 1975, p. 153-180, illus.)

Revista de Avance (1926-30) opened its pages to avant garde in their struggle against official academic art. Not only such native artists as Víctor Manuel, Eduardo Abela, Carlos Enríquez, etc. found a forum there, but also foreign painters including Picasso, Matisse, Orozco, and Carlos Mérida. For the study of modern Cuban artists this article introduces student to primary source.

340. González Jiménez, José Miguel. La casa de vivienda de Osma (BNJM/R, 15:3 [3. Epoca] sept./dic. 1973, p. 125-136, illus.)

Dwellings under discussion were architectural phenomenon of 19th century: native rural quintas of a simple character, well planned, with rubble walls, stone floors, and wooden roofs with native tiles. Ground plans, enhance text of this scholarly article.

341. Moreno, Dennys. La vivienda de embarro en la zona del Escambray (UCLV/I, 49, sept./dic. 1975, p. 147-186, maps, plates, tables)

Scholarly investigation into clay dwellings which still exist in areas of Oriente and Las Villas provinces. Author traces architectural roots of such houses,

342. Sánchez Martínez, Guillermo. Domingo Ramos, pintor del campo de Cuba (BNJM/R, 18:1, enero/abril 1976, p. 143-162)

In his dedication to landscape and his career as academist, Ramos resembles great Mexican landscapist Velasco. Ramos, however, studied and worked for long periods in Europe as well as in Cuba. Both were inspired by special sites: Velasco's Valley of Mexico, Ramos' Valley of Viñales. Author reproduces important documents in appendices.

343. Torriente, Loló de la. Arte cubano y revolución (CAM, 203:6, nov./dic. 1975, p. 189-193, plates)

Inspired by a large retrospective of 1975, Torriente's essay is a rather rambling but thoughtful appraisal of Mariano Rodríguez, from his early contacts with Mexican painters (Rodríguez Lozano, Guerrero Galván, and others) and his study of Cézanne and Matisse.

Trujillo, Marisol. El cartel: lo útil y lo bello. See *HLAS 39:5073*.

SOUTH AMERICA
ARGENTINA

344. Arean, Carlos. La pintura argentina del siglo XX: importación de formas y asunción de la actualidad (CH, 317, nov. 1976, p. 253-279, plates)

Very fine essay, readable and convincing. Author knows subject thoroughly, deals more than adequately with Sívori, Victorica, Pettoruti, Gómez Cornet, Xul Soler, Spilimbergo, etc., and younger Argentine artists. Indispensable for study of modern Argentine painting, but only up until World War II.

345. Atilio Palacio, Rubén *ed.* Miguel Carlos Victorica, 1844-1955: su cuaderno de apuntes, dibujos de Argentina y Europa, manuscritos, poesías. Prólogo de Manuel Mújica Laínez. B.A., Ediciones Palacio, 1974. 1 v. (Unpaged) bibl., plates.

Nudes are dryly academic, but Mar del Plata sketches sparkle with vitality. For growing number of students and connoisseurs of modern Latin American drawings, this sketchbook is recommended.

346. Córdova Iturburu, C. La pintura de Emilio Pettoruti (Anuario [Academia Nacional de Bellas Artes, B.A.] 1, 1973, p. 6-12, plates)

More scholarly and insightful study of Pettoruti than most. It will repay the student of this key figure of modern Argentine painting. Some of the reproductions are fresh and unfamiliar.

347. Curi, Marcos *ed.* Premio Marcelo de Ridder, 1974: julio/agosto 1974. B.A., Museo Nacional de Bellas Artes, 1974. 38 p.

In 1974, for second time, Museo Nacional de Bellas Artes instituted Premio Marcelo de Ridder, reserved for Argentine artists of less than 35 years. Drawings outnumber paintings, and there are virtually no non-figural works in either category. Since almost all the artists selected were born in B.A., this exhibition is of young contemporary artists.

348. De Grande, Eugenia. Mi idilio con Emilio: apuntes biográficos y anecdóticos de la vida del pintor argentino Emilio Alejandro Grande. B.A., The Author, 1974. 67 p., bibl., illus.

More useful information, perhaps, can be found in the bibliography than in these reminiscences, which are uncritical and of course sentimental.

349. Haber, Abraham and others. La pintura argentina. B.A., Centro Editora de América Latina, 1975. 96 p., plates (Pueblos, hombres y formas en el arte)

Handy guide book to modern Argentine painting. Emphasizes three aspects: "Vanguardia y Tradición," "Las Vanguardias al Día," and "La Crisis de las Vanguardias." Color reproductions adequate, b/w poor.

350. Jorge de la Vega, 1930-1971. B.A., Museo de Bellas Artes, 1976. 74 p., bibl., plates.

His roots in "la nueva figuración," Vega has been badly served by compilers of this catalogue. They reproduce all paintings in b/w cruelly weakening extraordinary vitality and imagination of his images.

351. Lo Celso, Angel T. 50 [i.e. Cincuenta] años de arte plástico en Córdoba, desde el año 1920 al 1970, con un apéndice por los años 1971 y 1972. Con 185 ilustraciones en negro y 9 en color. Córdoba, Arg., Banco de la Provincia de Córdoba, 1973. 881 p., plates.

Invaluable guide to artistic activities past and present. Chapter is devoted to chronological development of art in Córdoba; another long chapter has extensive biographical material. In this exhaustive (ca. 900 p.) volume, there is of course much information of use only to the most inquisitive scholar.

352. Pintores de Rosario: Benvenuto, Cochet. Musto, Ouvrard, Schiavoni, Vanzo. Rosario, Arg., Krass Artes Plásticas, 1974. 1 v. (Unpaged) plates (Col. Pintores argentinos: carpeta, 3)

Paintings reproduced represent six works from vast collection of Rosario's principal collector, Dr. Isidoro Slullitel. The six painters "... represent significant periods in the painting of Rosario. They were the disciples of the first Italian teachers who taught here..." Like item 360 also published by Krass, plates are uncommonly good.

353. Sibellino, Antonio. Antonio Sibellino. Text by Abelardo Arias. Traducción al inglés de Nora Wright. Traducción al francés de M.A. de Remy. Lomas de Zamora, Arg., M. Laguna y Orús de Sibellino, 1976. 136 p., plates.

Sibellino studied abroad in France and Italy. Initially his sculpture reflected influence of Bourdelle and Rodin, then a slight touch of Cubism. Plates are barely adequate.

354. Squirrú, Rafael F. Albino Fernández: estudio crítico-biográfico. B.A., Editorial Losada, 1975. 32 p., plates (Ediciones dead weight)

Vol. 3 in Ediciones Dead Weight series (see item 355). Fernández had good teachers: Antonio Berni, Torres García, Spilimbergo, etc. As printmaker he receives good treatment from Squirrú's pen. Includes good color reproductions of some paintings.

355. ———. Berni: estudio crítico-biográfico. B.A., Editorial Losada, 1975. 32 p., plates (Ediciones dead weight)

In the case of an artist as varied as Berni it is often difficult to be judiciously selective in the choice of works to accompany the text. Squirrú, as usual, has chosen intelligently so as to provide as rounded a visual portrait as possible of this important artist.

356. ———. Claves del arte actual. B.A., Ediciones Troquel, 1976. 155 p., plates.

Astute and witty critic, Squirrú has arbitrarily divided modern art into eight categories: 1) "Lo Grotesco;" 2) "La Probidad;" 3) "El Mentalismo;" 4) "Surrealismo;" 5) "Pintura Mágica;" 6) Pintura del Absurdo;" 7) "El Misticismo;" and 8) "La Ironía." In each classification he examines two to four artists in particular, such as Braque, Picasso, Juan Gris, Pettoruti under "El Mentalismo." The title is ambiguous, if not misleading, since he ventures as far from contemporary art as Poussin, Hogarth, and Goya; nevertheless, this is well worth reading.

357. ———. Luis Seoane: estudio crítico-biográfico. B.A., Editorial Losada, 1976. 32 p., bibl., plates (Col. La barca gráfica. Ediciones dead weight)

Squirrú finds antecedents for Seoane's pictures in Romanesque as well as modern European art. Author's methodology can be best summed up by this declaration: "Incursionar, pues, en el mundo de Seoane con miras a cierto grado de aproximación supone aceptar estas complejas reglas de juego, impuestas a partir de su compleja personalidad: un pantallazo por aquí, otro por allá, y así hasta tener la esperanza que el lector pueda ir armando el rompecabezas como mejor pueda en el alambique de su propia inteligencia."

358. ———. Pintura, pintura: siete valores argentinos en el arte actual. B.A., Ediciones Arte y Crítica, 1976? 101 p., plates (Col. Ensayos)

Squirrú introduces seven young artists, whose ages range from 27 to 37. In addition to his introduction, author includes biographical and exhibition information plus brief but cogent critique for each artist.

359. Traba, Marta. Borges bajo los focos (VME/R, 226, agosto/sept. 1976. p. 129-144, plates)

Rambling, tortured, occasionally brilliant, frequently exasperating—Traba's central idea is the quasitheatricality of Borges' paintings. Analyzing several key works, she links them with Endsor, De Kooning, and Bacon.

360. Uriarte, Carlos Enrique. Uriarte. Rosario, Arg., Krass Artes Plásticas, 1973. 1 v. (Unpaged) plates (Col. Pintores argentinos: carpeta, 1)

Brief biographical data are followed by "Una Charla con Carlos E. Uriarte y Algo Más," an interview conducted by Siguart Blum. Outstanding color plates.

361. Vanzo, Julio. Martín Fierro: 24 zinco-grafías de Julio Vanzo. Texto de Attilio Dabini. Rosario, Arg., Krass Artes Plásticas, 1974. 1 v. (Unpaged) plates (Col. Pintores argentinos: carpeta, 2)

As to be expected from Krass, reproductions are stunning. Written in 1952, Dabini's text is illuminating.

CHILE

362. "Los Diez" en el arte chileno del siglo XX. Santiago, Instituto Cultural de Providencia and *El Mercurio*, 1976. 83 p., plates (Ediciones de filosofía, arte y literatura)

Group known as "Los Diez" first exhibited in June/July 1916. It included writers, painters, sculptors, musicians, and architects. Several writers have contributed thoughtful essays to this book. A bibliography would have been a welcome addition.

363. **Galaz C., Gaspar** and **Milan Ivelic.** La pintura en Chile: desde José Gil de Castro hasta Juan Francisco González. Santiago, Univ. de Chile, Ediciones Extensión Universitaria, 1975. 233 p., bibl., plates.

If understood that terminus of this work is 1925, student of Chilean art, may find book useful, particularly as history of academic painting since 1850s.

364. **Granier Chirveches, Juan.** Eugenia Huici Arguedas: boliviana que lanzó a la fama a Picasso (Visión Boliviana [La Paz] 2:7, abril/mayo 1973, p. 27-28, plates)

Forced for political reasons to flee their native Bolivia, progenitors of Eugenia Huici Arguedas settled in Chile. In the early 1900s she and her husband spent time in Europe, where she knew well artists such as John Singer Sargent and Picasso. As wealthy patron Huici Arguedas befriended and assisted the latter in his early days before success and wealth. As such, she provides an interesting, if minor, footnote to Picasso's career.

365. **Marcelo, Carmen.** Por nuestra América: dibujos de Lea Grundig (UCLV/I, 51, mayo/agosto 1975, p. 17-29., illus.)

Includes six drawings by Grundig of East Germany entitled "La *solidaridad ayuda a combatir* and dedicated to the struggle against the ruling junta. Illustrated also are two engravings from Grundig's *Communist Manifesto* series. For those interested in Marxist art these works, along with author's text, are worth perusal.

366. **Montecinos, Hernán B.** and others. Arquitectura de Chiloé: estudio realizado en Chiloé durante el mes de febrero de 1976. Informe preliminar. Santiago, Univ. de Chile, Facultad de Arquitectura y Urbanismo, 1976. 68 p., illus.

Archipelago of Chiloé in extreme south of Chile had produced an extraordinary architecture of wood. Oldest religious structures, with their picturesque central steeples, date from second half of 18th century; secular buildings, with their patterned shingles, from middle of 19th. In spite of technical innovations of present century, old forms still persist. For student of modern Latin American architecture this book is a "must."

Mostny, Grete. Los museos de Chile. See *HLAS 39:835*.

COLOMBIA

367. **Angel, Félix.** Nosotros: un trabajo sobre los artistas antioqueños. Medellín, Colombia, Museo del Castillo, 1976. 220 p., plates

Serves as introduction to ten young artists working in Medellín: Félix Angel, Rodrigo Callejas, John Castles, Oscar Jaramillo, Alvaro Marín, Dora Ramírez, Juan Camilo Uribe, Francisco Valderrama, Aníbal Vallejo, and Marta Helena Vélez. Each artist is treated in terms of a "biografía," "comentarios," "entrevista," and a representative work of art. Recommended to those interested in developing artists since 1970 in an important intellectual and industrial center.

368. **Carbonell, Galaor.** Negret: las etapas creativas. Medellín, Colombia, Fondo Cultural Cafetero, 1976. 1 v. (Unpaged) plates.

Verbal and pictorial record of some 30 years of Edgar Negret's artistic activity. Author is particularly concerned with Negret's "concepto de la piel continua," his adaptation of new materials in N.Y. (1948-50), his French and Spanish period (1950-54) and contact with the art of Gaudí, etc. Carbonell claims this is first significant monograph on Negret and cites lack of bibliographical material.

369. **Colección** *Banco Cafetero*. Bogotá, Museo de Arte Moderno, 1976. 1 v. (Unpaged) plates.

Small but interesting collection. Includes charming colonial painting of St. Theresa and polychromed sculpture of St. Barbara as well as choice modern works by Gómez Jaramillo, Noé León, Obregón, and others. No text but good plates.

370. **Lucena, Clemencia.** Anotaciones políticas sobre la pintura colombiana. Bogotá, Editorial Bandera Roja, 1975. 117 p., plates.

Tendentious Marxist approach, but worth reading because of Lucena's treatment of Obregón and Botero.

371. **Rivero, Mario.** Rayo. Bogotá, Italgraf, 1975. 74 p., bibl., plates.

Rivero's text, embellished with frequent quotations from Omar Rayo, traces and sums up achievements of an artist who is talented, witty, and inventive.

372. Roda, Juan Antonio. Juan Antonio Roda: grabados, 1971-1976. Roda, un barroco subversivo [de] J.G. Cobo Borda. Bogotá, Seguros Bolívar, 1976. 138 p., plates (Arte contemporáneo colombiano, 1)

Seguros Bolívar, a firm, presents most impressive artist in elegant edition, intended as vol. 1 in series devoted to contemporary art. Roda emerges in exemplary reproductions as outstanding printmaker of our time. Prints are centered around several themes (e.g., "Retrato de un Desconocido," "Delirio de Monjas Muertas," etc.) Thoughtful exegetic essays preface each theme. An extraordinary book.

373. Serrano, Eduardo. L'art colombien contemporain (OEIL, 252/253, juillet/août 1976, p. 30-33, plates)

Serrano's thesis—not at all new—is that most contemporary Colombian art is an amalgam of native and foreign influence. He sums up briefly but deftly artistic character of these Colombians: Alvaro Barrios, Luis Caballero, John Castles, Santiago Cárdenas, Hernando del Villar, Ramiro Gómez, Beatriz González, Alfredo Guerrero, Ana Mercedes Hoyos, Darío Morales, Javier Restrepo, Miguel Angel Rojas, Carlos Rojas, Ned Truss, and Manolo Vellojín.

374. ———. Un lustro visual: ensayos sobre arte contemporáneo colombiano. Bogotá, Ediciones Tercer Mundo [and] Museo de Arte Moderno, 1976. 282 p., plates.

Potpourri of art criticism on local artists published 1970-75 in various periodicals, reviews, and catalogues. While perceptive, essays are too brief in most cases to give rounded view; nevertheless, they offer student of Colombian art varied cross-section of recent productions. Among better known artists are Botero, Negret, Roda, and Rayo.

375. ———. Paisaje, 1900-1975: exposición, Museo de Arte Moderno, Bogotá, 1975. Bogotá, Salvat Editores Colombiana, 1975. 1 v. (Unpaged) bibl., plates.

Includes 70 artists represented in this comprehensive exhibition. Some works can with difficulty be construed as landscapes, but in general exhibits offer excellent opportunity for study of landscape development in Colombia during the 20th century.

Téllez, Germán. L'architecture de l'époque colonial à aujourd'hui. See item 274.

376. Traba, Marta. Mirar en Bogotá. Bogotá, Instituto Colombiano de Cultura, Subdirección de Comunicaciones Culturales, 1976. 415 p., plates (Biblioteca básica colombiana)

Selection of articles published in *La Nueva Prensa* (April 1961-Sept. 1965) by one of most respected Latin American art critics. Brief but perceptive, her essays provide especially revealing glimpses of Colombian art during early 1960s, but also refer to wider interests.

PARAGUAY

377. Gutiérrez Z., Ramón. Evolución urbanística y arquitectónica del Paraguay, 1537-1911. Corrientes, Arg., Univ. Nacional del Nordeste, Depto. de Historia, n.d. 412 p., illus., plates.

Invaluable guide to representative monuments. Author introduces relevant and significant political, social and economic factors as they bear on architectural evolution. Includes copious ground plans of many monuments.

378. Pla, Josefina. Historia y catálogo del Museo de Bellas Artes. 2. ed., corregida y ampliada. Asunción, Casa América, 1975. 157 p.

Historical section largely devoted to praise of Juan Silvano Godoy, museum's wealthy and generous benefactor. Although not distinguished, collection may be evaluated through catalogue, which lists self-portrait by Tintoretto; *Venus with a mirror* by Velázquez; a landscape by Courbet; plus a plethora of very minor artists of Europe and Latin America.

PERU

379. Cisneros Sánchez, Manuel. Pancho Fierro y la Lima del 800. Lima, Importadora, Exportadora y Librería García Ribeyra, 1975. 255 p., plates.

A *costumbrista*, Fierro left a memorable artistic legacy of 19th-century Lima's culture during his very long career. Water colors and drawings reproduced here are testaments of a critical but loving eye. Indispensable for study of Lima and limeños.

380. Lauer, Mirko. Introducción a la pintura peruana del siglo XX. Lima, Mosca Azul Editores, 1976. 214 p., bibl.

In spite of major flaw (no illustrations) this is an important work for student of modern Peruvian painting, if only for extensive bibliography. Among more stimulating chapters are those on "El Indio en la Plástica," "Crisis del Indigenismo," "La Teoría de las Raíces," and "Szyszlo como Conciliador."

381. Sabogal, José. Del arte en el Perú y otros ensayos. Lima, Instituto Nacional de Cultura Editorial, 1975. 159 p.

Students of modern Latin American art may find useful data in last portion: "Técnicas Pictóricas Recopiladas por Sabogal." For much of which Sabogal is indebted to such Mexican artists as Siqueiros, Orozco, Pablo O'Higgins (whose name he badly misspells), etc.

382. Szyszlo. Indagación y collage de Mirko Lauer con ensayos de Javier Sologureny y E.A. Westphalen. Lima, Mosca Azul Editores, 1975. 103 p., illus.

Attempts to raise scholarly level and cultural horizons of Peruvian art criticism, and it succeeds. Fourth essay, "Poesía Quechua y Pintura Abstracta," by Westphalen, is especially interesting.

URUGUAY

383. Argul, José Pedro. Proceso de las artes plásticas del Uruguay desde la época indígena al momento contemporáneo. 3. ed. Montevideo, Barreiro y Ramos, 1975. 364 p., plates.

Serviceable introduction to Uruguayan art. Author covers much ground in chapters on: "Primera Producción," "Juan Manuel Blanes" "La Academia," "La Epoca Impressionista," and "La Irrupción de Joaquín Torres García en su País." There is special section on sculpture and its evolution. Book suffers, however, from lack of a bibliography. (First ed. 1958, 2. ed. 1966).

384. Castillo, Guido. *Primer Manifiesto del Constructivismo* por Joaquín Torres García. 2. ed. Madrid, Ediciones de Cultura Hispánica, 1976. 29 p., illus.

This is more a series of reminiscences (Castillo first met Torres García in 1942) than a critical study. Title, incidentally, is misleading. Tucked away in flap of jacket is best part of this volume: a number of delightful drawings by the master.

385. Gómez Rifas, José. Aliseris. Montevideo, Biblioteca Nacional, 1975. 62 p., illus., bibl.

Works of Aliseris are widely scattered among public and private collections in Europe and Latin America. His dream world is a fantastic bestiary of which examples are adequately reproduced here. Extraordinarily extensive bibliography concludes brief text.

386. Laroche, W.E. Juan Manuel Ferrari, 1874-1916, en el centenario de su nacimiento. Montevideo, Museo y Archivo Ernesto Laroche, 1975. 44 p., plates.

Short text is packed with information, much of it footnoted. Murky photographs, however, scarcely do justice to Ferarri's sculpture.

387. Verdaguer, María Graciela. El monumento al Ejército de los Andes (JEHM/R, 2:8, 1975, p. 893-902, bibl., plates)

In 1914 a bronze monument honoring the Army of the Andes, led by Gen. San Martín, was erected in Mendoza, Arg. This article offers information regarding the choice of Mendoza; the life and career of Uruguayan sculptor (Juan Manuel Ferrari) who cast it and other relevant data.

VENEZUELA

388. Adelaida de Juan: Venezuela en su pintura (CDLA, 16:94, ene./feb. 1976, p. 141-148, illus., plates)

In Nov./Dec. 1975 Casa de las Américas (Havana) hosted an exhibition of Venezuelan painting covering a century and a quarter. Juan's review deals knowledgeably and thoughtfully with wide range of artists from old masters such as Tovar y Tovar, Michelena, Borges, and Reveron to those of today. She examines landscapes, impact of foreign influences and local socioeconomic factors, and various strata of the contemporary scene. Highly recommended.

389. Alejandro Otero (VME/R, 34:216/218, nov./dic. 1974, p. 46-60, plates)

Brief text consists of letter from Pablo Neruda to Oscar Niemeyer in which former discusses impact upon him of Otero's sculpture when first seen in Venezuela, plus mini-essay on Otero's art.

390. Artes y letras de Mérida (VME/R, 34:2218, julio/sept. 1975, p. 79-117, plates)

For those interested in regional art in Venezuela outside Caracas, color reproductions are useful. Includes artists of Mérida (northwestern province of the country) namely Carlos Contremaestre, Omar Granados, Homero Nava, Lucrecia Chaves, and Rafael Chirinos.

391. Boulton, Alfredo. La obra de Armando Reveron. Prólogo de Guillermo Maneses. Caracas, Ediciones de la Fundación Neumann, 1976. 189 p., plates.

Maneses' lucid introduction traces development of Reveron; a more leisurely treatment of the artist's works follows in Boulton's text. Useful bibliography at end. Reproductions are perhaps first to do justice to Reveron's ethereal canvases which pose extraordinary problems for color photography.

392. Calzadilla, Juan *ed.* Pintores venezolanos del común. Fotografías de Godogredo Romero. Caracas, Compañía Anónima Nacional Teléfonos de Venezuela, 1975. 119 p., plates.

"Primitivism" in contemporary Latin American painting is associated almost exclusively with Haiti. That this notion must be broadened is affirmed by Calzadilla's book. Includes excellent color plates of charming vignettes of rural and village life. Among the artists: Feliciano Carvallo, Apolinor, Carlos Galindo, Malu, Crisanto Gómez, etc.

393. Caracas/Venezuela (The Art Gallery [The international magazine of art and culture, Hollycroft, Ivoryton, Conn.] 20:5, June/July 1977, p. 85-144)

Special issue devoted to Venezuelan art not to be missed by students of subject. Except for Boulton's studies, there are no better articles—at least in English—on the topic than these included in this issue (e.g., Juan Calzadilla, María Elena Ramos, Alfredo Boulton, Stanton Catlin, Roberto Guevara, Diego Arria, and Pablo Antillano.)

394. Gonzales, Olga. Mezzotintas de Aliria Palacios (CONAC/RNC, 34/224, abril/mayo 1976, p. 121-136, plates)

Educated professionally in Venezuela, this graphic artist has done postgraduate study in China and Poland. Nevertheless, her work is imaginative and poetic rather than polemical. China was her "most beautiful" experience, but her roots are in her native land.

395. Grabados de Carmelo González (UCLV/I, 36, mayo/agosto, p. 12-24, plates)

González has won prizes from sources as disparate as Portugal, the Soviet Union, and the Library of Congress. Besides work of a polemical nature there is also, judging from the illustrations, an element unusual in socialist art: eroticism.

396. Gramajo Gutiérrez, Alfredo. Por nuestra América (UCLV/I, 48, 1975, p. 123-141, plates)

Although he lived until 1961, Gramajo Gutiérrez ignored contemporary trends and continued to paint rural themes—many in the bygone tradition of diptychs and triptychs—in a naturalistic style. A number of them are listed here, including a description of two of the triptychs.

397. Junyent, Albert. Boggio. Caracas, Italgráfica, 1970. 125 p., bibl., plates.

Well written monograph on important artist. Junyent recreates authentically Venezuelan and European milieu of late 19th century from which Boggio evolved. Impeccable illustrations and typography. Valuable bibliography.

398. El Museo de Bellas Artes de Caracas y algunas de sus obras. Prólogo, comentarios e historia de las colecciones de Miguel G. Arroyo C. Fotografías de Petre Maxim. Breve historia del Museo de Rafael Lozano. Caracas, Cromotip, 1975. 248 p., plates.

Uneven but interesting collection ranges from Luis Tristán to Andy Warhol. Well reproduced and handsomely bound. Works of art of special interest to Latin American specialist are paintings by Jacobo Borges, Rogelio Polesello, Manabu Mabe, Roberto Matta, Carlos Mérida, Alejandro Otero, etc.

399. Nuevo edificio del Museo de Bellas Artes de Caracas (Punto [Caracas] 14:53, dic. 1974, p. 17-29, plates)

Last important design by Villanueva before his death in 1975. Striking building with wedge-like volumes interlocking with a central core of soaring verticals—one of the most expressive of his buildings. Indifferent quality of photographs, however.

400. Rengifo, César. Retrospectiva: 1931-1974. Caracas, Pro-Venezuela, 1974. 79 p., plates.

Rengifo's career has been devoted to theater and journalism as well as art. His paintings reveal what is essentially an illustrator confined to the rearguard of Venezuelan art who is nevertheless rather charming at times. Exhibition held May-June 1974 at the Palacio de las Industrias, Caracas.

401. Reverón, Armando. 10 [i.e. Diez] ensayos. Caracas, Consejo Municipal del Distrito Federal, 1975. 162 p., plates.

Growing interest in Reveron is reflected by publication of this and Boulton's monograph (see item 391) within a year of each other. Incidentally, one of ten essayists is Boulton. Two essays might be considered of special interest: "Tras la experiencia de Armando Reverón," by Liscano, and "Aspectos psicopalológicos de Reverón," by Feldman.

402. Ros, Rafael G. Alberto Dutary: descripción de su pintura (INC/RNC, 1:1, oct./dic. 1975, p. 23-31, bibl., plates)

Various stages of Dutary's oeuvre are examined in chronological order, from his *Santos* to his present

Realismo. If reader is willing to plunge into verbal jungle of misty conceits, he may be rewarded by discovery of artist of considerable appeal. Dutary, however, is known to "insiders" through his exhibitions in the US and elsewhere.

403. Salazar, Braulio. Retrospectiva, 1928-1975. Introduccion de Rafael Pineda. Caracas, Pro-Venezuela, 1975. 77 p., bibl., plates.

Pineda informally sketches Salazar's career. Rather good quality plates reveal stylistic transformation of Salazar's art. Lists works exhibited in retrospective, along with dates, measurements, ownership.

404. Sistema de prefabricaciones de viviendas en Venezuela (Punto [Caracas] 15:54, Mayo 1975, p. 9-20, plates)

Rather technical introduction but photographs speak for themselves. Describes prefabrication techniques that parallel those of Castro's Cuba.

BRAZIL

JOSE NEISTEIN

Director
Brazilian-American Cultural Institute
Washington

THIS BIENNIUM, THE SECTION ON BRAZILIAN ART includes more items than in previous volumes as well as new features and some new subdivisions for easier reference. Even so, the works reviewed herein represent only a fraction of the vast literature on the subject, most of which is published in Brazil.

The subsection entitled *Miscellaneous* became so voluminous that we have drawn from it to create a new subsection, *Cartoons and Comic Strips*, a field which has greatly developed in scope and significance in Brazil these last few years, particularly at the creative level (see items 515, 517, 519 and 523-525). There is moreover, an interpretative work on the subject which appears in the subsection entitled *Reference and Theoretical Works* (item 412).

Film and photography, which were more numerous in *HLAS 36* and *HLAS 38*, feature only one title each (included in *Miscellaneous*). This is not due to a decrease in Brazilian publications on these topics but rather to delayed receipts in the US. Publications on these topics will be reviewed in the forthcoming *HLAS 42*.

The proportion of works on the colonial and 20th-century periods remains comparable to previous years, an index of the permanence and continuity of these two areas of bibliography, the richest in the field. Other periods and topics are also the subject of study, as witnessed by the growing number of monographs on, for example, Brazilian 19th-century art. Likewise, urbanism, architecture and landscaping, formerly the province of specialists or professional and technical publications, are now discussed in publications available to the lay reader with a general interest in the arts.

Folk art, on the other hand, is now the subject of rigorous, interpretative study as evidenced by items 506 and 507. Works of equal merit are being published on Afro-Brazilian traditions in art (items 511-512 and 514).

We also welcome new editions of basic works such as Mario Pedrosas' essays (item 418), drawn from his newspaper articles; and Sylvio de Vasconcellos' *Vila Rica* (item 440). Among monographs on 20th-century topics, Aracy Amaral's two-volume work *Tarsila: sua obra e seu tempo* (item 452) deserves special mention for the wealth of material contained and new interpretive vistas offered.

REFERENCE AND THEORETICAL WORKS

405. Almeida, Paulo Mendes de. De Anita ao museu. São Paulo, Editora Perspectiva, 1976. 241 p., facsims., illus. (Col. Debates, 133)

Painstaking documentation of the history of modern art in Brazil, from the role played by Anita Malfati at and after the "Semana de Arte Moderna, 1922" starting with her exhibition in 1917 to the creation of the Museum of Modern Art of São Paulo, in 1948. Basic documents are used and discussed. No bibliography.

406. *Anais da Biblioteca Nacional.* Vol. 96, 1976- . Rio.

Half of volume is devoted to "Escola Brasileira de Gravura," historical introduction on print-making in Brazil by Floriano Bicudo Teixeira and catalogue of original Brazilian prints at Biblioteca Nacional's collection organized by Eunice de Manso Cabral and Cecília Duprat de Britto Pereira. Best part concerns 20th century.

407. Arte brasileira. 2. ed. Brasília, Abril Cultural *em convênio com o* Ministério da Educação e Cultura (MEC), Instituto Nacional do Livro (INL), 1976. 128 p., bibl., fold. table, illus., map, music, plates.

Introduction to Brazilian art in various media, including music and literature. Of special interest are the many color reproductions of Brazilian art from early colonial days to early 1970s. Includes historical introduction and short explanatory texts of plates.

408. Barros, Manoel Souza. Um movimento de renovação cultural. Prefácio de Walderley de Gusmão. Rio, Livraria Editora Cátedra, 1975. 167 p., facsims., illus.

Pt. 2 is devoted to Pernambuco's visual arts in 1920s and 1930s, esthetic trends and social implications. Poor illustrations and no bibliography.

409. Bazin, Germain. L'art baroque (RFEE, 260, jan. 1973, p. 40-45, plates)

Resumé of representative variations of Baroque and Rococo in Pernambuco, Bahia, Rio and Minas Gerais. Comparison is made with sources in Portugal.

410. Cavalcanti, Carlos. Dicionário brasileiro de artistas plásticos: arquitetura, escultura, pintura, desenho, gravura, artes aplicadas. v. 2, D a L. Brasília, Ministerio da Educação e Cultura (MEC), Instituto Nacional do Livro (INL), 1974. 513 p., plates (Col. Dicionários especializados, 5)

Vol. 2 of four. Although somewhat outdated by publication date, they are the most complete reference works on subject.

411. Coelho, Ceres Pisani. Subsídios para o estudo da arte brasileira contemporânea: seleção de textos. Salvador, Brazil, Univ. Federal de Bahia, Escola de Belas Artes, 1972. 242 p., bibl. (Núcleo de recursos didáticos, 44)

Texts on tendencies and history of modern art in Brazil by Flávio de Aquino, Aracy Amaral, Roberto Pontual, Waldemar Cordeiro, Ferreira Gullar, Mário Pedrosa, Ceres Franco, Mário Chamie, Hélio Oiticica, Márcio Sampaio, Rubens Gerchman, Frederico Morais, Décio Pignatari, Eduardo Ângelo, P.M. Bardi, Paulo Francis, Clarival Valladares, Bernardo Cid, Harold Rosemberg, Romano Galeffi, and Theon Spanudis.

412. Fernandes, Anchieta. Literatura e quadrinhos: do verbal ao iconográfico (VOZES, 70:6, agosto 1976, p. 29-48, illus.)

Theoretical study of social implications of comic strips in general and of Brazil's in particular. Also discusses literary affiliations, with comparative conclusions.

413. Ferraz, Geraldo. Retrospectiva: figuras, raízes e problemas de arte contemporânea. São Paulo, Editora Cultrix, 1975. 222 p., illus.

Varied anthology of critic's essays, interviews and articles published in *O Estado de S. Paulo*, from the late 1950s to late 1960s. Covers major figures of 20th-century art and few classics of modern Brazilian art. More illustrations would have enriched an otherwise good edition.

414. Martins, Judith. Dicionário de artistas e artífices dos séculos XVIII e XIX em Minas Gerias. v. 1/2. Rio, Ministerio da Educação e Cultura (MEC), Depto. de Assuntos Culturais, Instituto do Patrimônio Histórico e Artistico Nacional (IPHAN), 1974. 2 v. (407, 335 p.) bibl. (Publicações, 27)

A very valuable tool for research on colonial art in Brazil, this dictionary presents artists and craftsmen according to their specialties. Many original documents are transcribed.

415. Motta, Flavio L. Textos informes. 2. ed. ampliada. São Paulo, Univ. de São

Paulo, Faculdade de Arquitetura e Urbanismo, 1973. 67 p., illus.

Artist, art historian, theoretician and Professor, Flavio Motta put together some of his texts on art in general and on art and artists in Brazil in particular.

416. **Museu Nacional de Belas Artes,** *Rio*. Sintese da pintura no Brazil (no acerva do MNBA): catálogo. Rio, Tijuca Tênis Clube, Depto. de Relações Públicas, 1973. 1 v. (Unpaged) illus.

Unique in Brazil, this collection covers the main periods and tendencies of Brazilian painting, from colonial times to current trends, as well as canvases by European artists who lived in Brazil from the 17th to the 19th centuries. Texts by Maria Elisa Carrazzoni, Clarival do Prado Valladares and Hugo Ramos Filho. This catalogue is comprehensive but not complete.

417. **Oliveira, Luiz Carlos de.** Anotações para a história de uma época. São Paulo, Livraria Pioneira Editora, 1976. 93 p., table (Biblioteca Pioneira de estudos brasileiros)

The change of social habits in São Paulo, in the 1940s and 1950s seen through the visual arts and the art institutions that registered the change, and even helped the change to take place.

418. **Pedrosa, Mário.** Mundo, homem, arte em crise. Organização de Aracy Amaral. São Paulo, Editora Perspectiva, 1975. 321 p. (Col. Debates, 106)

Selection of articles and essays published by Dean of Brazilian art critics in 1960s mainly in *Jornal do Brasil* and *Correio da Manhã* (Rio). Pt. 1 discusses theoretical problems related to 20th-century art history and aesthetics from a social and political perspective; pt. 2 concerns modern art and art institutions in Brazil. Provocative and polemic, a vivid book. Includes author's biography and sources.

419. **Pereira, Uilcon Jóia.** Escritema e figuralidade nas artes plásticas contemporâneas. Assis, Brazil, Faculdade de Filosofia, Ciências e Letras de Assis, 1976. 83 p., plates.

Theoretical contribution to the study and esthetics of the printed and painted word. Author discusses works by Mark Tobey, Isidore Isou, Robert Indiana, Mira Schendel, Giuseppe Capogrossi, Chryssa, Rubens Gerchman, Andy Warhol and Wallace Berman.

420. **Prado, João Fernandes de Almeida.** A grande semana de arte moderna: depoimento e subsídios para a cultura brasileira. São Paulo, EDART, 1976. 139 p.

Personal impression and interpretation of "Semana de Arte Moderna, São Paulo, 1922" by eyewitness and friend of its key personalities.

421. **Silva, Orlando da.** A arte maior da gravura. Prefácio de Paulo de Tarso Santos. Apresentação de Jacob Klintowitz. Participação gráfica de Marcelo Grassmann. São Paulo, Edição Espade, 1976. 125 p., illus., plates.

Historical introduction to print-making, with special chapter on Brazil, represented by Marcelo Grassmann. Book printed with care and expertise.

COLONIAL PERIOD

422. **Alves, Marieta.** Folhas mortas que ressuscitam. Apresentação de Elyette Guimarães de Magalhães. Salvador, Brazil, Prefeitura Municipal do Salvador, Secretaria Municipal da Educação e Cultura (SMEC), Depto. de Cultura, 1975. 142 p., illus.

Although these personal reminiscences are not scholarly, they include much information on painters, sculptors and master masons of colonial Bahia.

423. Arte sacra em Minas Gerais no século XVIII: acervo Geraldo Parreiras. Belo Horizonte, Brazil, Palácio das Artes, 1972. 1 v. (Unpaged) illus.

Reproduces and describes main items in the show, but says very little about collection itself.

424. **Bardi, P.M.** Artistas e artífices do Brasil: séculos XVI, XVII, XVIII. São Paulo, Museu de Arte de São Paulo Assis Chateaubriand, 1977. 114 p., plates.

Catalogue of show on many techniques and media. Very good reproductions (b/w and color) of ca. 300 examples of furnishings, carvings, paintings and silver from 71 private collections in São Paulo. Catalogue is a valuable reference.

425. **Cruz, Ernesto Horácio da.** Casas e Palácio do governo, residências do capitães-mores, governadores e capitães-generais e presidentes da província do Pará, 1616-1974. Apresentação de Fernando José de Leão Guilhon. Belém, Brazil, Governo do Estado do Pará, 1976. 297 p., facsims., illus.

Discusses neoclassical architecture in Pará, its most representative style. Also includes good selection of reproductions, documents, etc.

426. Flores, Moacyr. A carroça colonial (PUC/V, 21:83, set. 1976, p. 259-270, illus., plates)

Technical monograph about the carriage in colonial Brazil. Illustrations and photographs.

427. Fonseca, Fernando L. O convento de São Francisco do Conde. Salvador, Brazil, Museo do Recôncavo Wanderley Pinho, 1975. 49 p., bibl., plates (A Bahia e o recôncavo, 4. Série arte e monumentos)

Representative church of Recôncavo área, Bahia (inaugurated 1722). Includes historical background and description of main features. Bibliography and photographs.

428. ———. Santo Antônio do Paraguaçú. Salvador, Brazil, Museu do Recôncavo Wanderley Pinho, 1973. 43 p., bibl., plates (A Bahia e o recôncavo, 1. Série arte e monumentos)

Now in ruins, this Franciscan church and convent were examples of its kind. Text devotes more attention to history than architecture. Bibliography and photographs.

429. Knoff, Udo. Azulejos do Pelourinho. Salvador, Brazil, Fundação do Patrimonio Artistico e Cultural da Bahia, n.d. 1 v. (Unpaged) plates.

Handsome reproductions, mostly actual size, of Portuguese and Dutch tiles found in Pelourinho area of Salvador, Bahia. Includes brief but basic information (from 1570 to ca. 1820) behind each plate.

430. Lamego, Alberto and others. Arquitetura civil III: mobiliário e alfaias. São Paulo, Ministério da Educação e Cultura (MEC), Instituto de Patrimônio Histórico e Artístico Nacional (IPHAN) [and] Univ. de São Paulo, Faculdade de Arquitetura (FAUUSP), 1975. 194 p., illus., plates.

Ten Brazilian scholars discuss representative buildings of colonial Brazil, and furnishings, jewels, fashion and ornaments. Fine compilation with appropriate illustrations, both drawings and photographs.

431. Mello Júnior, Donato. Antônic José Landi, arquiteto de Belém: precussor da arquitetura neoclássica no Brasil. Apresentação de Clóvis Silva de Morais Rêgo. Belém, Brazil, Governo do Estado do Pará, 1974. 322 p., facsims., illus.

Monograph on great 18th-century architect who built Pará's Governor's Palace in Italian classic style and other elegant buildings in the tropics. Many photographs and plans. Bibliography.

432. Moura, Carlos Francisco. As artes plásticas em Mato Grosso nos séculos XVIII e XIX. Cuiabá, Brazil, Fundação Cultura de Mato Grosso [and] Univ. Federal de Mato Grosso, Museu de Arte e de Cultura Popular, 1976. 93 p., bibl., illus.

Mato Grosso, less known than other areas of colonial art in Brazil, deserves the special attention devoted by this study.

433. Pio, Fernando. A Igreja Matriz do Santíssimo Sacramento do bairro de Santo Antônio e sua história. Recife, Brazil, Univ. Federal de Pernambuco, Editora Universitária, 1973. 103 p., bibl., tables.

History of late 18th-century church, its artists, inventory of paintings and carvings, bibliography and documents.

434. *Revista do Instituto Histórico e Geográfico.* Instituto Histórico e Geográfico, Guarujá/Bertioga. Ano 4, No. 8, 1973- . São Paulo.

Of interest in this issue: "As artes no Brasil-Holandês" by Joaquim de Souza Leão; "Considerações sobre Estilos e Influências no Mobiliário Brasileiro" by Maria Afonsina Furtado Rodrigues; "Arte Religiosa Colonial no Brasil" by Pedro de Oliveira Ribeiro Neto; "Uma Jóia Setecentista" by Maria Helena Brancante; "Algumas Notas sobre o Mobiliário Paulista do Tempo dos Bandeirantes" by Ernani Silva Bruno.

435. Ribeiro Neto, Pedro Antônio de Oliveira. A arte colonial paulista (IHGSP/R, 70, 1973, p. 215-221)

São Paulo was most likely first place in Brazil where religious sculpture was consistently produced in 16th and 17th centuries. Terracota was typical medium, often polychromed. Best examples come from Itanhaém, São Vicente, Taubaté, Embú and Itú.

436. ———. Museu de Arte Sacra de São Paulo. São Paulo, Gráficos Brunner, 1973. 58 p., plates (Col. Cultural mercator, 2)

Most valuable collections of Brazilian colonial art are housed in Museum of Sacred Art of Bahia and São Paulo. The latter is a restored 18th-century convent. Text in Portuguese and English by museum's director.

437. **Rocha, Carlos Eduardo da.** O mobiliário antigo na Bahia. 2. ed. Salvador, Brazil, Museu do Recôncavo Wanderley Pinho, 1973. 67 p., bibl., plates (A Bahia e o recôncavo, 2. Série arte e monumentos)

Brief history of furniture in 18th-century Bahia. Describes and illustrates 24 outstanding examples. Bibliography.

438. **Smith, Robert S.** O Mosteiro Beneditino do Rio de Janeiro e sua fazenda da vargem no século XVIII (IHGB/R, 304, julho/set. 1974, p. 158-200, plate)

Thoroughly documented history of one of the chief examples of Benedictine architecture in Brazil, by late American art historian and leading scholar in field of 17th- and 18th-century Portuguese and Brazilian art.

439. **Souza, Sara Regina Silveira de.** Estudo sobre o barroco: tendências artísticas da América colonial. Apresentação de João David Ferreira Lima. Florianópolis, Brazil, Univ. Federal de Santa Catarina (UFSC), 1973. 79 p., bibl., illus., plates.

Main topics: Baroque in Latin America; Baroque in Brazil; Jesuits missions and colonial architecture at "Sete Povos." Bibliography, photographs.

440. **Vasconcellos, Sylvio de.** Vila Rica. 2. ed. São Paulo, Editora Perspectiva, 1977. 214 p., plates.

This 2. ed. of work published by Ministério da Educação e Cultura in Rio, 30 years ago and out of print, is long overdue. Outstanding monograph devoted to Vila Rica de Ouro Preto deals with architecture and city planning of unique town in colonial Minas Gerais. Traces discovery of this rich area, its origins and administration, social structure and geographical conditions. Studies its architecture in detail, from façade to interior, with special attention to building materials. Plans and drawings by author. Poorly printed photographs.

19TH CENTURY

441. **Banco de Desenvolvimento do Paraná (BADEP),** *Curitiba, Brazil.* Dos precursores à Escola Andersen: Salão de Exposições do BADEP de 25 de setembro a 15 de outubro de 1975. Curitiba, Brazil, BADEP, 1975. 36 p., bibl., illus., plates (Panorama de arte no Paraná, 1)

Discusses Paraná painters who preceded Andersen, from 1840s-80s and b. in Italy, Germany, Paraná, from Frederico Guilherme Virmond to Frederico Lange de Morretes. Biographies. Photographs.

442. **Barata, Mário.** Achegas ao estudo de Debret (IHGB/R, 304, julho/set. 1974, p. 201-205, plates)

Barata suggests possible approaches to study of French artist Debret who illustrated Brazilian life in first half of 19th century in drawings, watercolors and paintings. Important contribution to Braziliana.

443. **Bruand, Yves.** A fundação do ensino acadêmico e o néo-classicismo no Brasil (IHGB/R, 311, abril/junho 1976, p. 101-121, illus., plates)

Study of Brazil's academic training in art, as established by French Artistic Mission, invited by D. João VI. Special attention given to Marcos and Zeferino Ferrez, Rio's French sculptors of first half of 19th century.

444. **Carneiro, Newton I. da Silva.** As artes gráficas em Curitiba. Curitiba, Brazil, Edições Paiol, 1976. 73 p., facsims., illus.

History of printed images and printed word in 19th-century Curitiba. Special attention given to lithographs, most popular medium, at the time.

445. **Cunha, Lygia da Fonseca Fernandes da.** Imagens do Rio de Janeiro na época da Regência (IHGB/R, 307, abril/junho 1975, p. 109-123, bibl.)

Slide presentation illustrates romantic portrayal of Brazilian landscape by foreign and Brazilian artists and amateurs (1831-40).

446. **Debret, Jean Baptiste.** Debret. v. 1. Belo Horizonte, Brazil, Estado de Minas Gerais, Imprensa Oficial, 1976? 1 v. (Unpaged) plates (Col. Jean Boghici)

Catalogue of exhibition of the Jean Boghici Collection, acquired from descendants of Jean Baptiste Debret. Brief texts by Carlos Drummond de Andrade and Afonso Arinos de Melo Franco. Poor reproductions.

447. **Florence, Hercules.** Viagem fluvial do Tietê ao Amazonas, pelas províncias brasileiras de São Paulo, Mato Grosso e Grão-Pará: 1825-1829. Prefácio de P.M. Bardi. Apresentação de Alvarez Machado e Florence Vasconcellos. São Paulo, Museu de Arte de São Paulo Assis Chateaubriand, 1977. 154 p., plates.

Hercules Florence came to Brazil in 1824, became artist of Langsdorff Expedition, and eventually discoverer of "Photographie," in Campinas, 1832, where he was established. This book was translated from the French (manuscript belongs to artist's great-great-grandson, Arnaldo Machado Florence). Reproduces drawings and watercolors for first time, all in b/w, alas. Welcome addition to Braziliana.

448. França, Dirceu Pinho. Manuel de Araújo Porto Alegre e o quadro de sua autoria Coroação de Dom Pedro II, restaurado no Museu Histórico Nacional (BMHN/A, 26, 1975, p. 39-54, bibl., plates)

Discusses restoration of historically important canvas and contribution of Araújo Porto Alegre to Brazilian painting, from neoclassicism to romanticism.

449. Ribeyrolles, Charles. Brasil pitoresco: história, descrições, viagens, colonização, instituições. v. 1/2. 2. ed. Acompanhado de um álbum de vistas, panoramas, paisagens, costumes, etc. por Victor Frond. Prefácio de Afonso d'E. Taunay. São Paulo, Livraria Martins Editora *em convênio com o* Ministério da Educação e Cultura (MEC), Instituto Nacional do Livro (INL), Brasília, 1976. 2 v. (241, 188 p.) plates, tables (Biblioteca histórica brasileira)

An opponent of Napoleon III, Ribeyrolles went into exile in Brazil, where he died in 1860. Originally published in French and Portuguese, this reedition of his Brazilian chronicles are reprinted in Portuguese translation with notes by Gastão Penalva. Includes original photographs and lithographs by Ribeyrolles' contemporary and co-author Victor Frond. Rare and welcome item of Braziliana.

450. Salvador (city), *Brazil.* **Secretaria Municipal de Educação.** Departamento de Cultura. Monumentos da independência. Apresentação de Elyette Guimarães de Magalhães. Salvador, Brazil, Prefeitura Municipal do Salvador, 1973. 88 p., facsims., map, music, plates.

Descriptions and photographs of chief monuments to Brazilian Independence (1822) which exist in Salvador, Bahia, most of them from 1830s to early 1900s.

451. Santos, Célia Regina Ferreira. Um documento sobre a Casa da Câmara e Cadeia Pública da Villa de San Miguel das Arêias no século XIX (USP/RH, 55:109, 1977, p. 271-274, illus.)

Monograph about important example of Brazilian civil architecture of late 1830s. Arêias is in the Paraíba Valley, in São Paulo state.

20TH CENTURY

452. Amaral, Aracy A. Tarsila: sua obra e seu tempo. v. 1/2. São Paulo, Editora Perspectiva [and] Editora da Univ. de São Paulo, 1975. 2 v. (498, 153 p.) bibl., facsims., illus., plates (Col. Estudos, 33)

As of now, the definitive work on Tarsila do Amaral. In vol. 1, author discusses historical background of "Semana de Arte Moderna de 1922," then discusses major contribution of Tarsila (*Pau-Brasil* and *Antropofagia* periods) to Brazilian visual expression, and her role in country's intellectual life in 1920s and 1930s. Great wealth of letters, accounts of poets and composers, iconography, press references and bibliography are brought together to present broad view of artist, her generation, and their search for identity vis-á-vis European influences. Vol. 2 is a "catalogue raisonné" of Tarsila's output, covering painting, sculpture, drawings and prints, with many illustrations and bibliography. Most comprehensive list available.

453. Os artistas e a Olivetti: Exposição, 15 de abril a 15 de maio 1976. São Paulo, Museu de Arte de São Paulo, 1976. 1 v. (Unpaged) plates.

Overall view of Olivetti's international collection, where works by three Brazilian artists are reproduced: Alfredo Volpi, Franz Weissmann and Francisco Stockinger, introduced by P.M. Bardi. Deluxe edition.

454. Assumpção, Clovis. Arte do Grupo de Bagé: história. Canoas, Brazil, Tipografia e Editora La Salle, 1975. 68 p.

Synthesis of scope and achievements of artists that integrated the Bagé group, Rio Grande do Sul, from late 1940s to mid 1950s, painters, printmakers and illustrators. Danúbio Villamil Gonçalves, Glauco Rodrigues and Glênio Bianchetti are studied more in depth.

455. ———. Paulo Osório Flores: monografia crítica. Canoas, Brazil, Tipografia e Editora La Salle, 1976. 49 p., bibl., illus., plates.

Paulo Osório Flores (1926-56), a pioneer of abstract painting in Brazil, was also draftsman, illustrator and poet. Monograph discusses various facets but none in depth. Poor illustrations of his works.

456. Banco de Desenvolvimento do Paraná (BADEP), *Curitiba, Brazil.* Discípulos de Andersen & artistas independentes:

Salão de Exposições do BADEP de 17 de agôsto a 5 de setembro de 1976. Curitiba, Brazil, 1976. 28 p., illus., tables (Panorama de arte no Paraná, 2)

Andersen, Norwegian artist established in Curitiba at turn of century had many disciples of Italian, Polish, German and Hungarian origins, some still active. Special chapter on history of visual arts in Brazil (1880-1960).

457. **Brazil. Ministério da Educação e Cultura** (MEC). **Departamento de Assuntos Culturais.** Arte gaucho/74: exposição. Texto introductório de Walmir Ayala. Rio, 1975? 97 p., plates.

With introductory text by Walmir Ayala, this catalogue brings reproductions of works by 23 artists from Rio Grande do Sul whose show traveled through 14 states in Brazil (1975-76).

458. **Caldas Júnior, Waltércio.** A natureza dos jogos. São Paulo, Museu de Arte de São Paulo Assis Chateaubriand, 1975. 16 p., plates.

Catalogue of avant-garde show with essay by Ronaldo Brito on Waltércio Caldas, Jr.'s drawings, "labels," objects, boxes, and *Silent Readings*.

459. **Camargo, Sergio.** Sergio Camargo: relevos e esculturas, 1963-1975; Museu de Arte Moderna do Rio de Janeiro, 15 maio-15 junho 1975. Rio, Museu de Arte Moderna, 1975? 37 p., illus.

Catalogue of retrospective with Portuguese and English texts by Mario Pedrosa and Ronaldo Brito. Biography and bibliography of artist. Reproductions in b/w.

460. *Cultura.* Ministério da Educação e Cultura. Ano 25, No. 25, abril/junho 1977- . Brasília.

Of special interest: "Guido Viaro: um Artista Paranaense" by Luiz Antônio Alves; "Retrospectiva de Djanira" by Ana Maria Furke; "Cinema Novo: Joaquim Pedro de Andrade, a Câmara da Aurora" by Alberto Silva; "Cerâmica Marúbo" by Delvair Mongner Mellati.

461. **Di Cavalcanti, Emiliano.** Di Cavalcanti: pintura, Galeria Ágora, Galeria da Praça, 13 a 30 de setembro de 1976. Rio, Colorama, 1976? 1 v. (Unpaged) plates.

Catalogue of Di Cavalcanti's show (Rio, 1976) almost entirely devoted to painter's favorite subject: portrait of black and mulatto girls. Reproduces 19 canvases and includes portrait of artist as old man.

462. **Djanira.** Djanira: outubro/dezembro de 1976. Recife, Brazil, Ministério da Educação e Cultura (MEC), Fundação Nacional de Arte, Museu Nacional de Belas Artes, 1976. 1 v. (Unpaged) illus.

Retrospective catalogue with texts by Clarival Valladares, Flavio de Aquino and Maria Elisa Carrazzoni. Biography and bibliography of artist. Many reproductions; a few good ones in color.

463. **Encuentro de Tapicería Uruguayo Brasileño,** *I, Montevideo, 1975.* Primer encuentro de tapicería uruguayo brasileño. Montevideo, Imprenta Municipal, 1975. 1 v. (Unpaged) plates.

Brazilian and Uruguayan tapestry artists met in first group show in Montevideo organized by Instituto de Cultura Uruguayo-Brasileña. Short biographical data and reproductions of some items.

464. **Fonseca, José Paulo Moreira da.** José Paulo Moreira da Fonseca: o pintor e o poeta (the painter and the poet). Tradução de Kerry Shawn Keys and Kern Krapohl. São Paulo, Spala Editora, n.d. 213 p., bibl., illus., plates.

Artistic autobiography draws together literary and pictorial itinerary of José Paulo in past 30 years. Poetry in Portuguese and English. Plush ed. with very good quality reproductions.

465. **Fundação Bienal de São Paulo.** Mostra da gravura brasileira. Apresentação de Francisco Matarazzo Sobrinho. São Paulo, 1974. 144 p., tables.

Texts on history of printmaking in Brazil by Mario Barata, José Roberto Teixeira Leite, Jayme Maurício, Frederico de Morais. Statements by several major Brazilian living printmakers. Index of Brazilian prints in collection of "Casa das Criancas de Olinda," Pernambuco. Chronology and glossary of printmaking's technical terms.

466. **Gonçalves, Danúbio.** Desenho, gravura, pintura, 1964-1976. Porto Alegre, Museu de Arte do Rio Grande do Sul, 1976. 1 v. (Unpaged) plates.

Catalogue of the retrospective of Danúbio, painter from Rio Grande do Sul (1964-76) brings texts by Luiz Inácio Medeiros, Quirino Campofiorito, Diego Rivera, Érico Veríssimo, Jorge Amado, Carlos Scliar, Clóvis Assunção, Carlos Scarinci and Francisco Stockinger.

467. Graciano, Clóvis. Clóvis Graciano. São Paulo, M.A. Marcondes and M. Fittipaldi, 1975. 117 p., illus., plates.

Includes essays by Mário de Andrade and José Roberto Teixeira Leite and 40 reproductions in color, 15 in b/w, selected by Delmiro Gonçalves, José Roberto Teixeira Leite and Marcos Antonio Marcondes. Ed. numbered and signed by artist, 511 copies.

468. Grassmann, Marcelo. Dez desenhos. Apresentação de Marcelo Corção. São Paulo, Editora Cultrix, 1976? 1 v. (Unpaged) plates.

Good reproductions of 10 drawings by one of most fascinating living Brazilian artists: Marcelo Grassmann, who blends late medieval, Flemish Renaissance and modern expressionistic tendencies into a very personal style.

469. Guilhermina, Maria. Exposição individual da escultura, 8 de abril a 4 de maio, Museu de Arte Moderna de São Paulo. São Paulo, Secretaria de Educação e Cultura, 1975. 1 v. (Unpaged) plates.

Catalogue of individual show organized by São Paulo's Museum of Modern Art. Outdoor sculpture includes mostly abstract pieces, some of which have figurative elements. Plush edition.

470. Ianelli, Thomaz. Capitanias de mar e serra: alguns registros. Explicação de Luiz Seráphico São Paulo, Rhodia Indústrias Químicas e Texteis, 1976. 1 v. (Unpaged) bibl., plates.

Deluxe ed. includes 22 beautiful watercolors by Ianelli superbly reproduced and never shown. Impressions of Portuguese Captaincies in colonial Brazil (São Paulo state). Nature and traditional architecture are captured with freshness.

471. Magalhães, Solange. Solange Magalhães. Brasília, Ministério da Educação e Cultura (MEC), Fundação Cultural do Distrito Federal (FUNDARTE), 1977. 16 p., plates.

Catalogue of paintings, with texts by Clarice Lispector, Vera Pedrosa, Clarival Valladares, José Cláudio, and Ruy Sampaio.

472. Morais, Frederico. Guignard. São Paulo, Centro de Artes Novo Mundo, 1974. 97 p., facsims., illus.

Study for Guignard retrospective at Rio's Museum of Modern Art, 1974. Text includes statements by late artist, chronology and analytical approach to his paintings and drawings. No bibliography; only indirect references.

473. Murta, Genesco. Genesco Murta: 1885-1967. Belo Horizonte, Brazil, Univ. Federal de Minas Gerais (UFMG), Conselho de Extensão, Serviço de Documentação das Artes, 1973. 27 p., illus.

Views of Ouro Preto and Brazilian seascapes by post-impressionist artist from Minas Gerais. Also discusses his vast European experience, mostly in France and Germany.

474. Museu de Arte Moderna da Bahia. Acervo MAMB: pintura, escultura, cerâmica, tapeçaria, pastel. Salvador, Brazil, Governo do Estado da Bahia, Secretaria de Educação e Cultura, Fundação Cultural, 1976. 1 v. (Unpaged)

Silvio Robatto and Roberto Pontual introduce more than 200 assorted items of Brazilian art (and crafts) from Bahia's Museum of Modern Art collections.

475. Museu de Arte Moderna de Prefeitura de Belo Horizonte. Roberto Burle Marx. Belo Horizonte, Brazil, 1973. 1 v. (Unpaged) illus., plates.

Catalogue of Burle Marx's major show in Belo Horizonte, with texts by Marc Berkowitz, Flavio Motta, Lucio Costa, Carlos Leão, Gonçalvo Ribeiro Teles, Mario Barata and Roger Caillois. Bibliography on and by the landscape architect, painter and draftsman.

476. Nemirovsky, José. José Nemirovsky: 20 anos de pintura. São Paulo, Museu de Arte de São Paulo, 1976. 1 v. (Unpaged) plates.

Catalogue of 55 paintings (1945-76) by disciple of Joan Ponç, also strongly influenced by Volpi, yet personal in his statement as a "peintre de Dimanche." Good quality plates.

477. The original and its reproduction: a Melhoramentos project. Text by José Neistein. São Paulo, n.p., 1977. 16 p., plates.

Catalogue for show assembled to travel in US, where originals could be compared to their reproductions on notebook covers. Prints and drawings by 12 Brazilian artists working in various styles and media.

478. Paço das Artes, *São Paulo*. Temática brasileira. São Paulo, Estado de São Paulo, Secretaria de Cultura, Esportes e Turismo, Conselho Estadual de Cultura, 1972. 1 v. (Unpaged) illus., plates.

Themes by Brazilian painters, draftsmen and printmakers of several generations, active in 1940s, 1950s and 1960s. Short critical text introduces each artist. Poor reproductions.

479. **Salão Global de Inverno,** *V, Belo Horizonte, Brazil.* 5 [i.e. Quinto] Salão Global de Inverno. Belo Horizonte, Brazil, 1977. 22 p., plates.

The Fifth "Global" Winter Salon displayed works by Álvaro Apocalypse, Antonio Maia, Frans Krajcberg, G.T.O., Glauco Rodrigues, Iberê Camargo, Jacques Douches, Norberto Nicola, Luiz Gregório, Luiz Paulo Baravelli, Marcelo Grassmann, Millôr Fernandes, Osmar Dillon, Paulo Roberto Leal, Roberto Magalhães, Rubens Gerchman, and six new authors of media works. Every artist introduced by different art critic. Good quality reproductions.

480. **São Paulo** (state), *Brazil.* **Secretaria da Cultura, Ciência e Tecnologia. Pinacoteca do Estado.** O desenho jovem nos anos 40: 11 de novembro de 1976. São Paulo, 1977? 1 v. (Unpaged) illus., plates.

Catalogue of show of leading Brazilian draftsmen of 1940s, with texts by Aracy Amaral and Geraldo Ferraz. Includes short biography of each artist and reproduction of one drawing.

481. **Sarubi, Valdir.** Valdir Sarubi: este rio é minha rua. Brasília, Ministério da Educação e Cultura (MEC), Fundação Cultural do Distrito Federal (FUNARTE), Galeria A, 1977. 4 p., plates.

Catalogue of prints and drawings show by Pará artist, with essay on him by Hugo Auler.

482. **Takaoka, Yoshiya.** Cavalos: dez desenhos de Y. Takaoka. Texto de Matias Arrudão. São Paulo, Editora Cultrix, 1975. 1 v. (Unpaged) plates.

Yoshiya Takaoka (b. Japan, 1909) came to Brazil as young man, and became an artist. To Brazil he transplanted his original culture, creating brush drawings in Chinese and Japanese tradition. Horse drawings reproduced on loose plates reveal his very high quality.

483. **Telles, Sérgio.** Porto Seguro recriada. Compiled by Jorge Amado. Rio, Bolsa de Arte do Rio de Janeiro [and] Galeria Wildenstein de Buenos Aires, 1976? 63 p., illus., plates.

Deluxe ed. of reproductions of paintings and drawings by Sérgio Telles of Porto Seguro, Bahia, among oldest historical sites in Brazil, first approached by Portuguese, beginning of 16th century.

484. **Visconti, Eliseu.** Eliseu Visconti. Bahia, Brazil, Museu de Arte Moderna da Bahia, 1978. 18 p., plates.

Catalogue of show of one of best representatives of post-Impressionism in Brazil. Introduced by Mario Barata. Canvases of major periods assembled and reproduced.

485. **Volpi, Alfredo.** Retrospectiva: outubro 1975. Organização de Diná Lopes Coelho. São Paulo, Museu de Arte Moderna de São Paulo, 1975? 1 v. (Unpaged) plates.

Catalogue of retrospective of 60 years of paintings by Volpi, now generally accepted as most important living Brazilian painter. Almost 400 works assembled. Nearly 100 reproduced in color. Excellent printing quality. Texts by Mario Schenberg, Aracy Amaral, Mario Pedrosa, Maria Eugênia Franco and Clarival do Prado Valladares.

486. **Zanini, Mário.** Mário Zanini, 1907-1971: catálogo de exposição, 11 de novembro a 12 de dezembro 1976. Organizada por Walter Zanini. São Paulo, Univ. de São Paulo, Museu de Arte Contemporânea, 1976. 31 p., illus.

Retrospective of paintings, drawings, prints and ceramics of one of representative artists of the "Família Artística Paulista:" Mário Zanini (1907-71). 205 items selected and discussed by Walter Zanini.

**CITY PLANNING, ARCHITECTURE,
AND LANDSCAPE ARCHITECTURE**

487. **Arquitetura civil II.** São Paulo, Ministério da Educação e Cultura (MEC), Instituto do Patrimonio Histórico e Artístico Nacional (IPHAN) [and] Univ. de São Paulo, Faculdade de Arquitetura e Urbanismo (FAUUSP), 1975. 260 p., bibl., illus., plates.

Five scholars' essays on rural and urban architecture and city planning in colonial Brazil, and its documentation: Joaquim Cardoso, Estevão Pinto, Lúcio Costa, Sylvio de Vasconcellos and Augusto C. de Silva Telles. Includes photographs, drawings, plans and bibliography.

488. **Bahia** (state), *Brazil.* **Coordenação de Fomento ao Turismo.** Proposta de valorização de tres monumentos baianos. Apresentação de Fernando Talma Sampaio. Salvador, Brazil, Secretaria da Indústria e Comércio, 1974. 1 v. (Unpaged) bibl., illus., maps, plates.

Renovation and new uses for three major buildings from 18th and 19th centuries in Salvador: Quinta do Tanque, Paço da Associação Comercial da Bahia and the so called "Banheiro dos Jesuítas." Plans, photographs and bibliography.

489. Ballario Yoshida, Celia and others. Henrique Ephim Mindlin: o homem e o arquiteto. Apresentação de Theobaldo de Nigris. São Paulo, Instituto Roberto Simonsen, 1975. 225 p., bibl., plates.

Team awarded "Arquiteto Henrique Mindlin" Prize (1972) wrote monograph on the man, the architect and his contribution. Includes Mindlin's own texts and lectures. Bibliographical notes.

490. Braga, Genesino. Restauração do Teatro Amazonas. Manaus, Brazil, Imprensa Oficial, 1973. 28 p.

Manaus' Opera House, a unique and important building, deserves better than this.

491. Bruand, Yves. L'architecture contemporaine au Brésil (INHA, 17:2, mars/abril 1972, p. 71-74, plates)

Outline of main historical monuments and buildings. Special attention given to blend of traditional and contemporary elements in Brazilian architecture. A few hasty generalizations.

492. ———. L'évolution de l'urbanisme de Olinda à Brasília (RFEE, 260, janvier 1973, p. 57-63, maps, plates)

Discusses variety of urban planning in Brazil, according to historic economic and political needs. Focuses on Olinda, Salvador, Ouro Preto, Rio de Janeiro, São Paulo, Belo Horizonte and Brasília.

493. Bruna, Paulo J.V. Arquitetura, industrialização e desenvolvimento. Prefácio de Nestor Goulart Reis Filho. São Paulo, Editora Perspectiva [and] Editora da Univ. de São Paulo, 1976. 312 p., bibl., illus. (Col. Debates, 135)

Study of relationship between architecture and the Industrial Revolution with specific examination of Brazil. Vast international bibliography.

494. Costa, Lúcio. A arquitetura dos Jesuitas no Brasil. São Paulo, Univ de São Paulo, Faculdade de Arquitetura e Urbanismo, Laboratório de Artes Gráficas, 1973. 14 l., illus.

Historical and technical study of Jesuits' contribution to architecture in Brazil with explanatory drawings related to structures and ornaments.

495. Katinsky, Julio Roberto. Casas bandeiristas: nascimento e reconhecimento da arte em São Paulo. São Paulo, Univ. de São Paulo, Instituto de Geografia, 1976. 183 p., bibl., illus., plates (Série teses e monografias, 26)

In-depth monograph subdivided as follows: 1) "Localização e Identificação das Casas;" 2) "Descrição das Casas e Situação Atual;" 3) "Técnica e Arte;" 4) "O Ambiente Histórico;" 5) Bibliography. Refers to 12 houses built in the surroundings of São Paulo in 17th and 18th centuries.

496. Lemos, Carlos Alberto Cerqueim. Cozinhas, etc.: um estudo sobre as zonas de serviço de Casa Paulista. São Paulo, Editora Perspectiva, 1976. 226 p., bibl., illus., plates, tables (Col. Debates, 94)

In-depth discussion of kitchen architecture in São Paulo, from 18th to 20th century, from houses of rural aristocracy to those of urban working class as well as utensils and cuisine they were designed for. Climate, history and social structure were important determinants.

497. Mello, Eduardo Kneese de. A herança mourisca da arquitetura no Brasil. São Paulo, Univ. de São Paulo, Faculdade de Arquitetura e Urbanismo, Laboratório de Programação Gráfica, 1974? 85 p., bibl., illus.

Monograph on Moorish influence in Brazilian architecture, both religious and civilian, public and private, from 17th to 20th century. Many illustrations comparing details. Exhaustive bibliography.

498. Módulo. Revista de arquitetura, urbanismo e artes. Avenir Editora. Ano 11, No. 42, março/maio 1976 [through] Ano 11, No. 46, julho/set. 1977- . Rio.

Good journal which includes valuable articles on contemporary Brazilian architecture, city planning as well as painting and sculpture (e.g., issue 11:42: articles by Italo Campofiorito, Carlos Lemos, Vilanova Artigas, etc.; 11:43: essays by Oscar Niemeyer, Fausto Cupertino; articles on Di Cavalcanti and Ceschiatti, etc.).

499. Penna, J.O. de Meira. Brasília, fifteen years later (ICPHS/D, 91, Fall 1975, p. 57-69)

Discussion of effects of transfer of Brazil's capital. Examines how Brasília confronts nation's economic problems exemplified by proximity of *Sertão*. City planning vs. history.

500. **Rocha, Carlos Eduardo da.** Museu do Recôncavo Wanderley Pinho: o engenho freguesia. 2. ed. Ilustrações de Floriano Teixeira. Salvador, Brazil, Editora Itapuã em convênio com o Governo do Estado da Bahia, Secretaria de Educação e Cultura, 1973. 43 p., bibl., illus.

Architecture, collections and furnishings of this museum depict history of sugar-cane plantations in Brazil. "Recôncavo" area is discussed and illustrated in detail. Bibliography.

501. **Rodrigues, José Wasth** and others. Arquitetura civil I/II. Introdução de Gilberto Freyre. São Paulo, Ministério da Educação e Cultura (MEC), Instituto do Patrimônio Histórico e Artístico Nacional (IPHAN) [and] Univ. de São Paulo, Faculdade de Arquitetura e Urbanismo (FAUUSP) *com a colaboração da* Secretaria da Cultura, Ciência e Tecnologia do Estado de São Paulo, 1975. 2 v., (318, 247 p.) bibl., illus., maps, plates, tables.

Five art and architecture historians present civil architecture in Brazil in the Colonial period: "Casas de Residência no Brasil" by L.L. Vauthier, with an introduction by Gilberto Freyre; "Arquitetura Civil no Período Colonial" by Robert C. Smith; "O Piauí e a sua Arquitetura" by Paulo T. Barreto; "Notas sobre a Arquitetura Rural Paulista do Segundo Século" by Luis Saia; and "A Casa de Moradia no Brasil Antigo" by José Wasth Rodrigues. Great variety of photographs and plans.

502. **Saia, Luis.** Notas preliminares sobre a fazenda Pau d'Alho: história, restauração e projeto de aproveitamento (USP/RH, 51[26]:102, abril/junho 1975, p. 581-630)

Minute description of early coffee plantation in São Paulo, including architecture and furnishings. Plantation now belongs to Brazilian Coffee Institute. Discusses plans to convert it into National Coffee Museum.

503. **Universidade de São Paulo. Faculdade de Arquitetura e Urbanismo. Biblioteca.** Índice de arquitetura brasileira, 1967-1969: biblioteca. São Paulo, 1970. 168 l.

A very precarious edition of a very important index of Brazilian architects, buildings, projects and scholarly monographs.

FOLK ART

504. **Cedran, Lourdes** *ed.* Santeiros imaginários. São Paulo, Paço das Artes, 1976. 1 v. (Unpaged) plates.

Catalogue of show of paintings, carvings and ceramics by "santeiros" throughout Brazil, from 18th century to present. Concentrates on popular rather than scholarly aspects.

505. O espírito criador do povo brasileiro, através da coleção da Abelardo Rodrigues do Recife: exposição, Palácio do Itamaraty, Brasília, julho e agosto 1972. São Paulo, Fundação Visconde do Cabo Frio, n.d. 1 v. (Unpaged) plates.

Collection of late Abelardo Rodrigues from Recife reflects best of Brazilian creativity in arts of several periods and of Northeastern folk art. Memorable show. Catalogue reproduces best samples.

506. **Frota, Lélia Coelho.** Mitopoética de 9 artistas brasileiros: vida, verdade e obra. Apresentação de Clarival do Prado Valladares. Fotografias de Pedro Oswaldo Cruz and Christina Oswaldo Cruz. Rio, Editora Fontana, 1975. 117 p., plates.

Critic analyzes world and forms of nine Brazilian naive painters and sculptors, using their own myths and poetic style as common denominator.

507. **Magalhães, Gisela** and **Irma Arestizábal** *eds.* 7 [i.e. Sete] brasileiros e seu universo: artes, oficios, origens, permanências. Apresentação de Renato Soeiro. Brasília, Depto. de Documentação e Divulgação, 1974. 215 p., bibl., illus., plates.

One of a kind, this book gathers essays by seven Brazilian art critics and art historians on folk and popular art in Brazil, as represented by seven of the country's best artists in that direction. Many illustrations, biographies, bibliography. Portraits of the artists also.

508. **Piló, Conceição.** Arte e história do Culto ao Divino nas Minas Gerais. Belo Horizonte, Brazil, Museu de Arte da Prefeitura, 1977. 110 p., plates.

Comprehensive catalogue of show about one of most popular and old religious festivals in Brazil, of medieval Portuguese origin. Text describes variations of cult and folk artifacts used therein. Unfortunately, photos did not reproduce well on yellowish paper selected for catalogue.

509. Rodman, Selden. Genius in the backlands: popular artists of Brazil. Photographs by Manu Sassoonian, William Negron and Marilyn Bridges. Old Greenwich, Conn., Devin-Adair, 1977. 148 p., plates.

Study of original contribution of naive artists to Brazilian art. Many photographs and reproductions, some in color.

510. Santos, José Martins dos and others. Xilogravuras populares alagoanas. Maceió, Brazil, Univ. Federal de Alagoas, Museu de Antropologia e Folclore, 1973? 50 p. (Col. Theo Brandão)

Reproduction of 50 folk woodcuts from Alagoas, most illustrations for chap books of Northeastern "string literature." Often woodcuts and texts are by same author: folk printmaker-poet.

AFRO-BRAZILIAN AND INDIAN TRADITIONS

511. Carise, Iracy. Arte negra na cultura brasileira: máscaras africanas. Tradução e apresentação de Nilda Scotti. Fotografia de Guaraciaba Abrahão Calil, Carlos Gomes Faria and Masaomi Mochizuki. Rio, Artenova, 1975? 159 p., bibl., illus., maps, tables.

Study of influence of African black cultures, mainly Nagôs and Bantos on Brazilian culture (art, religion, language, cuisine, fashion and miscegenation). Sections on African cultures and maps of peoples and nations therein.

512. Carybé [pseud. for **Héctor Júlio Páride Bernabo**]. As sete portas da Bahia. Prefácio de Jorge Amado. 4. ed. rev. e ampliada. Rio, Editora Record, 1976. 346 p., illus.

Fourth ed. enriched by new drawings of Bahia's "orixás," religious dances and street life, with larger glossary of Afro-Brazilian religious terminology, musical instruments and cult objects.

513. Exposição-Feira de Artesanato do Pará, Belem, Brazil. Arte popular do Pará. Belém, Brazil, Instituto do Desenvolvimento Econômico do Pará (IDESP), 1973. 180 p., bibl., map, plates.

Describes ceramics and other crafts by Indian tribes in Marajó, Santarém and Maracá. Photographs.

514. Instituto Histórico e Geográfico de Alagoas, Maceió, Brazil. Museu, Catalogo ilustrado da Coleção Perseverança. Maceió, Brazil, Secretaria de Educação e Cultura de Alagoas, Depto. de Assuntos Culturais em convênio com o Ministério de Educação e Cultura (MEC), Depto. de Assuntos Culturais, 1974. 1 v. (Unpaged) bibl., illus., table.

Catalogue of comprehensive collection of Afro-Brazilian artifacts, mostly religious, introduced by several scholarly texts.

CARTOONS AND COMIC STRIPS

Anselmo, Zilda Augusta. Historias em quadrinhos. See *HLAS 39:9292*.

515. Caco [pseud. for **Luiz Carlos Biso**] and others. 14 [i.e. Quatorze] bis. Porto Alegre?, Brazil, Editora Garatuja, 1977? 184, p., illus. (Col. Guaipeca, 2)

Discusses 14 cartoonists of new generation from Rio Grande do Sul, including few older ones. Shows individual styles poking fun at modern life. Includes texts by poet Mário Quintana and biographies.

516. Geandré. A ovelha negra de Geandré: cartuns. Arte de Darlon. Montagem de Marina Pontual. Diagramação de Luiz Alves Junior. São Paulo, Global Editora, 1975. 1 v. (Unpaged) illus.

Young cartoonist from Santos (São Paulo state) tackles with fine wit a variety of themes, from everyday life to morals, politics and ecology.

517. ISSO. Pré Estréia. Aconselhável para maiores de 16 anos. Revista de quadrinhos. Ano 1, No. 1, dez. 1972-   . Porto Alegre, Brazil.

Satirical, critical and aware, these 20th-century cartoons are the counterparts of the old "folhetins picarescos."

518. Klintowitz, Jacob. Zélio Alves Pinto. São Paulo, Museu de Arte de São Paulo Assis Chateaubriand, 1977. 92 p., plates.

First major comprehensive show of cartoonist from Minas Gerais gathered from regular Sunday strips to cartoons of social criticism from newspapers and others for commercials. His approach to life and society is rather optimistic even when critical.

519. Pereira, Ruy. Benvindo. São Paulo, Brazil, Massao Ohno Edita, 1977? 1 v. (Unpaged) illus.

Ruy Pereira's sharp cartoons mock man and his condition as well as life in the megalopolis.

520. Santiago. Humor macanudo. Porto Alegre, Brazil, L. & P.M. Editores, 1976. 1 v. (Unpaged) illus.

Cartoons on contemporary urban life in Brazil, and on "gaúcho" life in Rio Grande do Sul.

521. Soares, Luiz Eduardo. Super-heróis: o poder elevado ao quadradinho (VOZES, 70:1, 1976, p. 33-40)

Semiotic and linguistic analysis of Batman and Robin lead to psychological, sociological and ideological observations about the super-hero.

522. Távora, Araken. Pedri II a través da caricatura. Rio, Bloch Editores *em convênio com o* Ministério da Educação e Cultura (MEC), Instituto Nacional do Livro (INL) *em colaboração com o* Depto. de Assuntos Culturais, Programa de Ação Cultural, 1975. 155 p., bibl., plates.

Good selection and study of the man and emperor as seen by 19th-century Brazilian cartoonists in relation to political parties, his own regime and ministers. Includes chronology of caricature in 19th-century Brazil and parallel list of political events.

523. Vasques, Edgar. Rango: todos os desenhos incluídos neste trabalho, foram publicados pelo jornal *Folha da Manhã*, orgão de Companhia Jornalistica Caldas Junior. v. 1/4. Prefaciado por Érico Veríssimo. 2. ed. Porto Alegre, Brazil, L. & P.M. Editores, 1975/1976. 4 v. (Unpaged) illus.

Reprint of Rango cartoons, character created by Edgar Vasques to represent average Brazilian confronted with country's problems. Dialogues are sometimes more relevant than drawings.

524. Veríssimo, Luis Fernando. As cobras. Porto Alegre?, Brazil, Editora Milha, 1975. 1 v. (Unpaged) illus.

Cartoons involving social criticism, public life, institutions. Personal style. Plain but vivid drawings.

525. Zélio. Sem saída Zélio. São Paulo, Vertente Editora, 1974? 1 v. (Unpaged) illus.

Zélio's cartoons range from understated self-deprecation through social criticism to surrealism. Has fine observations to the point.

MISCELLANEOUS

526. Affonso, João. Três séculos de modas: a propósito do tricentenário da fundação da cidade de Santa Maria de Belém, capital do estado do Grão-Pará. 2. ed. Apresentação de Maria Annunciada Chaves. Belém, Brazil, Conselho Estadual de Cultura, 1976. 226 p., bibl., plates (Col. Cultura paraense. Série Ignácio Moura)

History of fashion in Grão-Pará, Brazil (1616-1916). Description but no interpretation.

527. Almeida, Fernando Azevedo de. O Franciscano Ciccillo. Prefácio de Paulo Nathanael Pereira de Souza. São Paulo, Livraria Pioneira Editora, 1976. 282 p., bibl., facsims., illus., plates (Col. Novos umbrais)

Biographical study in journalistic style but thoroughly documented, of Francisco Matarazzo Sobrinho or Ciccillo (as he was known). This great Maecenas, a unique if controversial personality who died recently, founded and presided over the "Bienal Internacional de São Paulo."

528. Biblioteca Nacional, Rio. Divisão de Publicações e Divulgação. Vinte e cinco anos de enriquecimento do acervo: 1950-1975. Rio, 1975. 52 p.

Includes 403 annotated items in bibliography of art both Brazilian and foreign, acquired by Biblioteca Nacional. Special sections on prints and maps.

529. Carneiro, Newton I. da Silva. O Paraná e a caricatura. Prefácio de Alvarus. Curitiba, Brazil, Univ. Federal do Paraná *em colaboração com a* Fundação Teatro Guaíra, 1975. 73 p., facsims., illus., plates (Col. Memória cultural do Paraná, 1)

Study covers caricature in Paraná from beginning of 19th century to early 1970s. Special attention given to Mário de Barros, outstanding Paraná cartoonist.

530. Dantas, Antonio Arruda. Dona Olivia: Olivia Guedes Penteado. São Paulo, Sociedade Impressora Pannartz, 1975. 103 p., bibl., plate.

One of most innovative and broad-minded members of her generation, this lady played crucial role in setting up São Paulo's "Week of Modern Art-1922" as well as in launching Brazilian modern art.

531. Ferreira, Orlando da Costa. Imagem e letra, introdução à bibliologia brasileira: imagem gravada. São Paulo,

Edições Melhoramentos *com a colaboração da* Editora da Univ. de São Paulo [and] Governo do Estado do São Paulo, Secretaria da Cultura, Ciência e Tecnologia, 1976. 279 p., illus.

Reproduces prints and drawings by Brazilian artists of 19th and the 20th centuries.

532. Grande São Paulo/76: exposição. São Paulo?, n.p., 1976? 1 v. (Unpaged) plates.

Catalogue of show of ca. 60 photographers of one theme: Greater São Paulo. Portfolio includes nearly 40 prints. Varied and fascinating show.

533. **Museu de Arte Moderna da Bahia,** *Salvador, Brazil*. **Comissão do Sesquicentenário da Independência da Bahía.** 150 [i.e. Centocinqüenta] anos de pintura na Bahia. Apresentação de Renato Ferraz. Salvador, Brazil, Artes Gráficas, 1973. 1 v. (Unpaged) illus.

Valentin Calderón's text is a survey of Bahian painting from end of Colonial period to World War II. Antonio Celestino's article covers modern painting in Bahia, for catalogue of exhibition celebrating 150th anniversary of Brazil's Independence.

534. Navilouca: almanaque dos aqualoucos. Editor responsável: Lucio Urubatan de Abreu. Organização e coordenação editorial: Torquato Neto, Waly Sailormoon. Programação visual: Oscar Ramos, Luciano Figueiredo. Trabalhos de Augusto de Campos and others. Fotos de Alexandre Koester and others. Rio, Edições Gernasa e Artes Gráficas, n.d. 1 v. (Unpaged) illus., plates.

Photographic, graphic and literary works by Brazilian artists who experiment in most diverse areas (e.g., Caetano Veloso, Augusto de Campos, Lygia Clark, Haroldo de Campos, Hélio Oiticica, etc.).

535. Santos, José de Almeida. Manual do colecionador de antiguidades. São Paulo, Propag Publicidade, n.d. 308 p., bibl., illus., tables.

Of special interest are chapters devoted to Brazilian antiques: religious and secular art and "objets d'art."

536. Suassuna, Ariano. O movimento armorial. Recife, Brazil, Univ. Federal de Pernambuco, Depto. de Extensão Cultural, Pró-Reitoria para Assuntos Comunitários, Editora Universitária, 1974. 73 p., illus.

Deals with problems of literature, music and visual arts of "Armorial Movement" in Pernambuco, a contemporary creative group representative of a distinct cultural area in Brazil. Texts by several critics. Summaries in English and French.

JOURNAL ABBREVIATIONS

AAHS/K	The Kiva. Arizona Archaeological and Historical Society. Tucson.
BMHN/A	Anais do Museu Histórico Nacional. Ministério da Educação e Cultura. Rio.
BNBD	Boletín Nicaragüense de Bibliografía y Documentación. Banco Central de Nicaragua, Biblioteca. Managua.
BNJM/R	Revista de la Biblioteca Nacional José Martí. La Habana.
CAM	Cuadernos Americanos. México.
CDLA	Casa de las Américas. Instituto Cubano del Libro. La Habana.
CH	Cuadernos Hispanoamericanos. Instituto de Cultura Hispánica. Madrid.
CONAC/RNC	Revista Nacional de Cultura. Consejo Nacional de Cultura. Caracas. See VME/R.
CYC	Comunicación y Cultura. La comunicación masiva en el proceso político latinoamericano. Editorial Galerna. B.A. y Santiago.
EEHA/AEA	Anuario de Estudios Americanos. Consejo Superior de Investigaciones Científicas [and] Univ. de Sevilla, Escuela de Estudios Hispano-Americanos. Sevilla.
FAH/N	Norte. Revista hispano-americana. Frente de Afirmación Hispanista. México.
FAIC/CPPT	Comunicaciones Proyecto Puebla-Tlaxcala. Fundación Alemana para la Investigación Científica. Puebla, Mex.
FJB/BH	Boletín Histórico. Fundación John Boulton. Caracas.
IAA	Ibero-Amerikanisches Archiv. Ibero-Amerikanisches Institut. Berlin, FRG.

IHGB/R	Revista do Instituto Histórico e Geográfico Brasileiro. Rio.
IHGSP/R	Revista do Instituto Histórico e Geográfico. Instituto Histórico e Geográfico, Guarujá/Bertioga. São Paulo.
INAH/B	Boletín del Instituto Nacional de Antropología e Historia. Secretaría de Educación Pública. México.
INC/RNC	Revista Nacional de Cultura. Instituto Nacional de Cultura. Panama.
INHA	L'Information d'Histoire de l'Art. J.B. Bailliere et fils. Paris.
JEHM/R	Revista de la Junta de Estudios Históricos de Mendoza. Mendoza, Arg.
LARR	Latin American Research Review. Univ. of North Carolina Press *for the* Latin American Studies Association. Chapel Hill.
MH	Mundo Hispánico. Madrid.
NHAC/K	Kaie. National History and Arts Council of Guyana. Georgetown.
OAS/AM	Américas. Organization of American States. Washington.
QEIL	L'Oeil. Revue d'art mensuelle. Novelle Sedo. Lausanne, Switzerland.
PUC/V	Veritas. Pontificia Univ. Católica do Rio Grande do Sul. Porto Alegre, Brazil.
RCPC	Revista del Pensamiento Centroamericano. Centro de Investigaciones y Actividades Culturales. Managua.
RFEE	Revue Francaise de l'Élite Européenne. Paris.
SAR/P	El Palacio. School of American Research; Museum of New Mexico; [and] Archaeological Society of New Mexico. Santa Fe, N. Mex.
UAEM/H	Histórica. Univ. Autónoma del Estado de México, Instituto de Investigaciones Históricas. México.
UCLV/I	Islas. Univ. Central de las Villas. Santa Clara, Cuba.
UNPHU/A	Aula. Univ. Nacional Pedro Henríquez Ureña. Santo Domingo.
UP/A	Apuntes. Univ. del Pacífico, Centro de Investigación. Lima.
USP/RH	Revista de História. Univ. de São Paulo, Faculdade de Filosofia, Ciências e Letras, Depto. de História [and] Sociedade de Estudos Históricos. São Paulo.
VME/R	Revista Nacional de Cultura. Ministerio de Educación, Instituto Nacional de Cultura y Bellas Artes. Caracas. *See* CONAC/RNC.
VOZES	Vozes. Revista de cultura. Editora Vozes. Petrópolis, Brazil.

FILM

JULIANNE BURTON

Assistant Professor of Literature
University of California, Santa Cruz

THIS SECOND GENERAL *HLAS* SECTION on Latin American cinema has the dual purpose of assembling the most recent publications available on the topic while simultaneously offering a retrospective selection of essential background material in a field still quite new to many Latin Americanists. In combination with the first *Handbook* film section (see *HLAS 38*, p. 59-69), this listing provides as complete a survey of existing material on the historical situation and thematic and stylistic evolution of Latin American filmmaking as can be offered within the limited scope of this kind of bibliography, Professor E. Bradford Burns' original bibliography contains references for eight film-producing countries—Argentina, Brazil, Mexico, Cuba, Colombia, Chile, Bolivia and Uruguay—as well as general references to publications on related films produced in the U.S. Each of these countries is again represented in the following section, as are in addition Panama, Venezuela, Peru and Puerto Rico. After an initial general section, the present bibliography is organized by country on the assumption that this will enhance the utility of the list for those readers whose interest lies with a particular country or countries. Every effort has been made to avoid duplication of items cited earlier by Professor Burns and to achieve a balance between comprehensiveness and selectivity. I would like to extend my gratitude to Randal Johnson of Rutgers Univ. and Carl Mora of the Univ. of New Mexico Press for providing references and annotations for parts of the sections on Brazil and Mexico, respectively.

The current decade, and particularly the last few years, have witnessed many changes on the Latin American film scene. Production in Chile and Argentina, at a high point five years ago, is now virtually nonexistent following the exile of many leading directors, actors, and technicians, and the institution of harsh censorship. But many of these filmmakers have settled elsewhere in Latin America and are helping to promote film activity in less cinematically developed parts of the continent. As exiled Argentine filmmaker Octavio Getino observed from his current residence in Peru (item 1039) "Latin American cinema has reason to feel somewhat comforted, because the grave situation which many countries are going through has begun to be at least partially offset by the appearance of new centers of production principally located in the Andean region: Venezuela and Peru and, to a lesser extent, Colombia." There is also a marked increase in film activity in Panama and Puerto Rico. Finally, the major film-producing countries—Brazil, Mexico and Cuba—are generating enough film production and scholarly activity to merit particular attention in *HLAS*. The quantity and importance of available material on post-revolutionary Cuban filmmaking motivated the special section in volume 39 on "Revolutionary Cuban Cinema" by this same editor (see *HLAS 39*, p. 425-434). It is hoped that parallel representation in future *HLAS* bibliographies will be accorded Brazil and Mexico.

There has been a marked rise in the number of book-length studies published in various countries: Peter Schumann's *Kino und Kampf in Latein-Amerika* in West Germany (item 964); Guy Hennebelle's *Quinze ans du cinéma mondial* (item 960) and his forthcoming *Los cines de América Latina* to appear first in Spain and subsequently in France; Michael Chanan's *Chilean cinema* published by the British Film Institute (item 1002) and Francesco Bolzoni's *El cine de Allende* (item 1000), published first in Italy and later in Spain; and several promising books on Brazilian cinema, which include Maria Rita Eliezer Galvão's *Crônica do cinema paulistano* (item 989), Raquel Gerber's *Glauber Rocha* (item 990), and Paulo Emilio Salles Gomes' *Humberto Mauro, Cataguases, "Cinearte"* (item 991). These and other titles continue to reflect a tendency toward compilation, largely because of the vastness of the field and the dispersion of available materials.

Venezuela hosted its third *Encuentro de Cineastas Latinoamericanos* in April of 1977, and the *Federation Internationale des Archives du Film* (FIAF), meeting in Mexico the preceding year, made the New Latin American Cinema the topic of its symposium, inviting presentations from several leading Latin American filmmakers.

Latin American film journals continue to appear intermittently. Panama's *Formato 16*, which began publication in 1977 and has currently put out four issues, is a new arrival on the scene, *Cinemateca*, a joint project of the Cinemateca Argentina and the Cinemateca Uruguaya, also began publication in 1977. *Film/Historia*, published in Bolivia, appeared in 1978. Two Mexican journals (*Otrocine* and *Octubre*) appear to have ceased publication, as has the Peruvian *Cinematógrafo* and perhaps also the Colombian *Ojo al Cine* due to the death in 1977 of one of its founders and co-editors, Andrés Caicedo. *Hablemos de Cine*, also from Peru, and the Venezuelan journal *Cine al Día* continue to make sporadic but always worthwhile appearances, as does *Cine y Medios* from Ecuador's Univ. Central. Brazil's Ministry of Education and Culture dedicated issue no. 24 of its magazine *Cultura* to an outstanding anthology of articles on national cinema (item 986). Finally, *Cine Cubano* resumed publication in the spring of 1978 after a hiatus of four years.

Coverage of Latin American filmmaking in US journals has increased in recent years, and the trend may be expected to continue in the immediate future. One journal, *Jump/Cut: A Review of Contemporary Cinema*, is planning special supplements on filmmaking in Cuba and in Brazil during the coming months. In addition, a number of university presses are considering books in this area, an initiative which is to be welcomed given the dearth of serious studies in English.

GENERAL

951. Beceyro, Raúl. Cine y política. Caracas, Gobernación del Distrito Federal, Dirección General de Cultura, 1976. 115 p. (Cuadernos de difusión, 11)

A sophisticated, if somewhat over-ambitious and loosely connected, look at some major issues in contemporary film studies: the relationship of film to ideology; the nature of the photographic image; the semiology of film; and, particularly important for an understanding of Latin American cinema, an evaluation of Italian neorealism.

952. Biskind, Peter. In Latin America, they shoot filmmakers (Sight & Sound [London] 45, Summer 1976, p. 160-161)

On official repression against filmmakers in Chile, Bolivia and Argentina.

953. Burton, Julianne. The camera as gun: two decades of film and resistance in Latin America (LAP, 5[16]:1, Winter 1978, p. 49-76)

An evaluation of the New Latin American cinema movements in Brazil, Argentina, Bolivia, Colombia, Peru and Chile as a form of political and cultural resistance.

954. ———. The hour of the embers: on the current situation of Latin American cinema (Film Quarterly [Univ. of California Press, Berkeley] 3:1, Fall 1976, p. 33-44)

An informative look into what is happening in the South American cinema in the mid-1970s. It is not a happy report, although some freedom of expression and creativity can still be found in Colombia and Venezuela. The essay contains much data which is difficult or impossible to find elsewhere. [E. Bradford Burns]

955. ———. Learning to write at the movies: film and the fiction writer in Latin America (The Texas Quarterly [Austin] 27:1, Spring 1975, p. 92-103)

Argues that the formation of the contemporary Latin American writer, once the result of primarily literary influences, is now increasingly cinematic. Discusses the cases of Guillermo Cabrera Infante, Carlos Fuentes, Manuel Puig and Gabriel García Márquez in particular.

956. ———. The new Latin American cinema: an annotated bibliography of English language sources, 1960-1976. N.Y., Cineaste, 1976. 29 p. (Cineaste pamphlet, 4)

This pamphlet is an indispensable bibliographical tool, a well annotated guide to the essential material, mostly in English, on the progressive Latin American cinema and those who make it. [E. Bradford Burns]

957. Cine latinoamericano y lucha revolucionaria, hoy (Octubre [México] 2/3, enero 1975, p. 3-36)

A far-ranging conversation between three leading Latin American filmmakers: Carlos Alvarez (Colombia), Julio García Espinosa (Cuba), and Miguel Littin (Mexico).

958. Cyr, Helen W. A filmography of the Third Wold: an annotated list of 16mm films. Metuchen, N.J., Scarecrow Press, 1976. 319 p.

The listings—by region and country—are far from complete, but useful nonetheless. Includes a directory of distributors.

959. Filmografía (Octubre [México] 2/3, enero 1975, p. 52-55)

Lists directors and countries of origin for the most important films of the New Latin American cinema movement from 1955 through 1974.

960. Hennebelle, Guy. Quinze ans de cinéma mondial: 1960-75. Paris, Editions du Cerf, 1975. 425 p.

A somewhat polemical collection of essays concerning the development of alternative cinema, especially in the Third World. The section on Latin America (p. 187-215) contains brief accounts of filmmaking activity in Argentina, Bolivia, Colombia, Peru, Uruguay, Mexico and Chile, and slightly longer essays on Cuba and Brazil. Spanish version: *Los cines nacionales contra Hollywood* (Valencia, Spain, Fernando Torres, 1977).

961. Martinez Torres, Augusto and Manuel Pérez Estremera. Nuevo cine latinoamericano. Barcelona, Editorial Anagrama, 1973. 226 p.

A useful if at times inaccurate history of the development of film production in nine Latin American countries: Argentina, Bolivia, Brazil, Chile, Colombia, Cuba, Mexico, Peru and Venezuela. Contains schematic filmographies, but no index or bibliography.

962. Mitry, Jean *comp.* Bibliographie internationale du cinéma et de la télevision. v. 3, Espagne, Portugal et pays de langue espagnole ou portugaise. Paris, Institut des Hautes Études Cinématographiques (IDHEC), 1968. 163 p.

An annotated bibliography of book-length sources in Spanish and Portuguese, organized in six sections: bibliography, history of the cinema, aesthetics, technique, festivals and biography.

963. Murialdo Laport, Hugo. El concepto marxista de ideología y su aplicación al fenómeno cinematográfico latinoamericano (UNAM/RMCP, 21:79, enero/marzo 1975, p. 27-35, bibl.)

A mechanical overview of Marx, Engels, Lefebvre, Fischer, Sánchez Vázquez and Lebel on ideology followed by a superficial discussion of filmmaking in Brazil, people's Chile and Cuba.

964. Schumann, Peter. Kino und Kampf in Latein-Amerika: Zur Theorie und Praxis des Politischen Kinos. Munchen, FRG, Carl Hanser Verlag, 1976. 264 p.

An excellent collection which reprints such widely read essays as Solanas' and Getino's "Towards a Third Cinema" and García Espinosa's "For an Imperfect Cinema" as well as original essays which include the editor's "For a Political Cinema," and several essays by Latin American directors and film historians. Includes a comprehensive bibliography.

965. Smith, Hubert. A filmmaker's journal: Bolivia. Hanover, N.H., American Universities Field Staff, 1976. 25 p., plates (West Coast South America series, 23:2)

An absorbing account of the filming of six ethnographic documentaries on Bolivia's Aymara Indians. The author discusses in detail his unconventional methodology which challenges traditional filmed anthropology because of its emphasis on human relations and passive observation. Shares many philosophical, experiential and methodological points with Latin American political and ethnographic filmmakers.

966. Vega, Pastor. El nuevo cine latinoamericano: algunas características de su estilo (ICAIC/CC, 73/75, 1972, p. 27-39)

A leading Cuban documentarist discusses the style of several important examples of the New Latin American cinema.

967. Xavier, Ismail. O discurso cinematográfico: a opacidade e a transparência. Rio, Paz e Terra, 1977. 151 p., bibl. (Col. Cinema, 4)

A critical presentation of the most significant aesthetic and ideological theories of cinema during the first 60 years of the medium, centering around the relationship of sound and image to external reality. Ranges from early theoreticians to contemporary thinkers like Metz, Comolli and Lebel.

ARGENTINA

968. Cine militante en Argentina: entrevista con Gerardo Vallejo, Grupo Cine Liberación (Octubre [México] 2/3, enero 1975, p. 37-45)

Documentarist Gerardo Vallejo discusses his career from his early training at the Escuela Documental de Santa Fe under Fernando Birri, through his affiliation with Fernando Solanas and Octavio Getino (*The hour of the furnaces*), the making of *El camino hacia la muerte del Viejo Reales* in Vallejo's native Tucumán, and his experience there making weekly *testimonios* for television.

969. Giudici, Alberto. El cine argentino, Hollywood: del esplendor al ocaso. B.A., 'Ediciones Acción, 1976? 80 p., plates (Ediciones acción, 2)

The first section in this double book provides a 25-p. "summary chronology" of Argentine cinema from its origins through the release of *La Patagonia rebelde* in 1973 to the almost total paralysis of the industry in 1975.

970. Mahieu, José Agustín. Breve historia del cine argentino. B.A., EUDEBA, 1966. 78 p., facsim., illus., plates (Serie del siglo y medio, E9)

A brief history of Argentine cinema from 1896 through the short-lived Argentine "New Wave" of the mid-1960s, including a chronology of key events. (not to be confused with Agustín Mahieu's *Breve historia del cine nacional, 1896-1974*.)

971. Martín, Jorge Abel. Cine argentino '76. B.A., Ediciones Metrocop, 1977. 87 p.

A chronological summary of Argentine film production and legislation during 1976, followed by production credits for each film and directors' filmographies.

972. Petit de Murat, Ulises and **Homero Manzi.** Pampa bárbara. B.A., Conjunta Editores, 1976. 230 p. (Col. Guión)

The screenplay of this now-classic 1945 feature on gaucho life directed by Lucas Demaré and Hugo Fregonese. With an introduction ("Cuando Rosas y Lavalle eran amigos") by Homero Manzi.

973. Suber, Howard. Jorge Preloran: an interview (Film Comment [N.Y.] Spring 1971, p. 43-51)

This prolific ethnographic documentarist discusses his method and his films.

BOLIVIA

974. Entretien avec Jorge Sanjinés (Interview with Jorge Sanjinés) (Cahiers du Cinéma [Paris] 253, 1974, p. 6-21)

Sanjinés describes the evolution of his career from its inception through the filming of *The principal enemy* (1974).

975. Keel, Erich. From militant cinema to neorealism: the example of *Pueblo Chico* (Film Quarterly [Univ. of California Press, Berkeley] 19:4, Summer 1976, p. 17-24)

A description and analysis of the first feature film made jointly by Antonio Equino and Oscar Soria, former members of Jorge Sanjinés' *Grupo Ukamau*, after they chose to remain in Bolivia despite the 1971 coup which made Sanjinés a *de facto* exile.

MacLeod, Murdo J. The Aymara of the Bolivian Andes: a review of six films. See *HLAS 39:1512*.

976. Maillat, Philippe. Jorge Sanjinés: un cinéaste bolivien exemplaire (CJN, 157, mars 1975, p. 37-39)

An overview of Sanjinés' filmmaking career which recounts in some detail the plots of *Ukamau, Blood of the condor, The courage of the people* and *The principal enemy*.

977. Mesa G., Carlos D. El cine en Bolivia. La Paz, Editorial Don Bosco de La Paz, 1976. 1 v. (Unpaged) bibl., plates (Cinemática de La Paza: inauguración, 1)

Contains a brief history of Bolivian filmmaking, with primary emphasis on the *Grupo Ukamau*, followed by a schematic chronology and filmography.

978. Sanjinés, Jorge. La búsqueda de un cine popular (ICAIC/CC, 86/88, 1974, p. 60-64)

Sanjinés outlines his ideas on popular culture and collective participation, as practiced in the making of *The principal enemy*.

979. ——. Problemas de la forma y del contenido en el cine revolucionario (Ojo al Cine [Cali, Colombia] 5, 1976, p. 5-10)

Sanjinés discusses the evolution of his film method and the increasing popular participation in the determination of both the narrative content and the form of his films, presenting his approach as a model for revolutionary filmmaking.

Smith, Hubert. A filmmaker's journal: Bolivia. See item 965.

BRAZIL

980. Araújo, Vicente de Paula. A bela época do cinema brasileiro. São Paulo, Perspectiva, 1976. 414 p. (Col. Debates, 116)

A non-analytical chronicle of the development and dissemination of Brazilian cinema and other forms of mass entertainment in Rio from the late 1800s through 1912, when foreign filmmaking began to dominate the national market. Important for its historical documentation.

981. Avellar, José Carlos. A pornochanchada: uma solução típica e natural (VOZES, 70:4, maio 1976, p. 25-32)

On the genesis and evolution of the *pornochanchada* and the successful adaptation of these inexpensive, off-color comedies to the contemporary Brazilian cultural milieu in both content and form.

982. Beirão, Nirlando. Glauber Rocha: profeta? visionario? (Isto É [São Paulo] 5 nov. 1977, p. 29-34)

An account of Rocha's activities and declarations since returning to Brazil on 23 June 1976 which attempts to discern a "method" behind his "madness."

983. Bernardet, Jean-Claude. Brasil em tempo de cinema: ensaio sobre o cinema brasileiro de 1958 a 1966. 2. ed. Rio, Paz e Terra, 1977. 190 p. (Col. Cinema, 3)

Important re-edition of a seminal work on modern Brazilian cinema, originally published in 1967, which analyzes Cinema Novo as essentially a middle-class movement dealing with middle-class problems.

984. Brazil. Universidade de São Paulo. Museu de Arte Contemporânea. O nascimento do cinema: exposição em colaboração com a Fundação Cinemateca Brasileira de 20.3 a 20.4 de 1975. Introdução de Ana Carolina Macedo and Salma Buzzar. Estudo de Paulo Emílio Salles Gomes. São Paulo, 1975. 10 p., illus.

A mostra apresentou placas de vidro coloridas a mão das lanternas mágicas, filmes pintados a mão, fotografias em vidro, máquinas que precedram o cinematógrafo, os experimentos de Muybridge, painéis fotográficos mostrando as principais fases, etc. [J. Neistein]

985. Burns, Bradford; Fred Estevez; Peter L. Reich; and Anne Fleck. History of the Brazilian cinema (Luso-Brazilian Review [Univ. of Wisconsin Press, Madison] 14:1, Summer 1977, p. 49-59)

Three thoughtful essays on themes of dependency, cultural resistance and historical continuity in Brazilian history as seen through four films. *Burn, The guns, Plantation boy,* and *Ganga Zumba*.

986. Cultura. Ministério da Educação e Cultura, Departamento de Documentação e Divulgação. 1977- Brasília.

Special issue devoted to Brazilian film that is beautifully designed and lavishly illustrated. Consists of overview of filmmaking in Brazil from its origins to the present. Also contains articles by several prominent figures on film history, aesthetics, music, producers, market conditions, Cinema Novo and the documentary.

987. Estéve, Michel *ed.* Le cinema nôvo bresilien. Paris, Minard, 1972. 160 p., bibl., filmography (Lettres modernes)

Includes interviews with Nelson Pereira dos Santos and Ruy Guerra, critiques of films by both directors, and two general articles on the Cinema Novo. Originally, these articles appeared in *Études Cinématographiques* (93/96).

988. Ewald Filho, Rubens. Dicionário de cineastas. Revisão por João Evangelista Franco and Dina de Deus.

São Paulo, Global Editora e Distribuidora, 1977. 469 p., plates.

Modeled after the book by French film historian Georges Sadoul, *Dictionnaire des cinéastes*, this useful guide lists the works of the major national and foreign filmmakers and producers whose work has been screened in São Paulo from the silent era through 1976. An appendix lists annual prizes awarded at the world's leading film competitions.

989. Galvão, Maria Rita Eliezer. Crônica do cinema paulistano. São Paulo, Atica, 1975. 333 p., filmography (Ensaios, 15)

Traces the development of cinema in São Paulo from its inception through 1930, arguing that this regional cinema was initially a proletarian form of expression, having grown out of the working class theater of Italian immigrants. A major portion of the book consists of interviews with 15 major figures from the period.

990. Gerber, Raquel *ed.* Glauber Rocha. Rio, Paz e Terra, 1977. 169 p. (Col. Cinema)

Anthology of studies on the leading Cinema Novo director, ranging from an excellent overview of Rocha's role in the movement (Gerber) to a structuralist study of his films (Rene Gardies) to detailed analyses of two sequences from *Land in anguish*. (Three of the four studies are translated from the French).

991. Gomes, Paulo Emílio Salles. Humberto Mauro, Cataguases, *Cinearte*. São Paulo, Editora Perspectiva [and] Univ. de São Paulo, 1974. 475 p., bibl. (Col. Estudos, 22)

A detailed critical biography of one of the principal pioneers of Brazilian cinema. Traces the influences of the social environment on the young filmmaker, analyzes his most important films in depth, and discusses the role of the magazine *Cinearte* in the development of Brazilian film.

992. Leal, Wills. Escritores brasileiros no cinema. João Pessoa, Brazil, The Author, 1969. 85 p., illus.

O livro tanto trata da transposição de obras da ficção brasileira para o cinema nacional, como também dos próprios autores como temas de filmes. Dentre os principais: Machado de Assis, Guimarães Rosa, José Lins do Rego, Vinícius de Moraes, Sousândrade, Gilberto Freyre, Vicente de Carvalho, Manuel Bandeira, Castro Alves e Lima Barreto. [J. Neistein]

993. Micciché, Lino *ed.* Il cinema novo brasiliano. v. 1, Testi e documenti; v. 2, I registi e i film. Roma, n.p., 1975.

2 v. (223, 190 p.) (Quaderno informativo, 64/65)

Publication of the XI Mostra Internazionale del Nuovo Cinema which took place in Pesaro, Italy. Vol. 1 brings together 27 essays on or by members of the Cinema Novo movement; vol. 2 contains separate interviews with 20 Cinema Novo directors. Available from: Mostra Internazionale del Nuovo Cinema, Via della Stelletta 23, 00186 Roma, Italy.

994. Molotnik, J.R. *Macunaíma*: revenge of the jungle freaks (Jump/Cut: A Review of Contemporary Cinema [Chicago, Ill.] 12/13, 30 dec. 1976, p. 22-24)

An analysis of Joaquim Pedro de Andrade's *Macunaíma* which situates the film in its historical, political and social context within Brazil.

995. Perdigão, Paulo. Ficção científica no cinema: a moral da era atômica (VOZES, 66:5, junho/julho 1972, p. 29-36)

"Se o cinema é, como já foi dito, uma lanterna mágica capaz de corporificar o imaginário, a ficção científica deveria ser o mais cinematográfico dos gêneros." O estudo baseia-se nesse pressuposto, e dá filmografia essencial, subdividida em: a conquista do espaço, os visitantes do outro mundo, as radiações provenientes do espaço cósmico, a biologia da era atômica, a vida no futuro e o fim do mundo. [J. Neistein]

996. Santos, Francisco Alves dos. Cinema brasileiro 1975: entrevistas com cineastas brasileiros. Curitiba, Brazil, Edições Paiol, 1975. 72 p., illus.

Short interviews with seven young Brazilian filmmakers: André Luiz Oliveira, Guido Araujo, João Batista de Andrade, Olney São Paulo, Osvaldo Caldeira, Ozualdo Candeias, and Sílvio Back.

997. Silva, Alberto. Cinema e humanismo. Rio, Pallas, 1975. 128 p., bibl.

A rather superficial collection of articles on Brazilian and foreign cinema, from the *chanchada* to Glauber Rocha to Ingmar Bergman. Informed by a vague leftist ideology which rejects the "decadence" of much modern European cinema in favor of films which deal with "the people" and "the great human questions."

998. Souza, José Ignacio de Melo. Retrospectiva do cinema brasileiro, 1975. São Paulo, Kronos Grafica e Editora, 1975? 94 p., bibl.

A catalogue of the Brazilian films screened in São Paulo between Jan. and Dec. 1975, with notes on market conditions, censorship, etc. and a bibliography of related publications.

999. Ventura, Zuenir. Independência ou morte: entre-vista com Nelson Pereira dos Santos (Veja [São Paulo] 27 julho 1977, p. 3-4, 6)

Brazil's most prolific Cinema Novo director discusses his recent *Tent of miracles*, censorship, Brazilian politics and Cinema Novo.

Xavier, Ismail. O discurso cinematográfico: a opacidade e a transparência. See item 967.

CHILE

1000. Bolzoni, Francesco. El cine de Allende. Valencia, Spain, Fernando Torres, 1974. 163 p.

An overview of filmmaking under Allende which reprints interviews with Miguel Littín, Raúl Ruíz, Aldo Francia and Helvio Soto, supplementing them with first-hand exchanges with the editor.

1001. Burton, Julianne. Politics and the documentary in people's Chile: an interview with Patricio Guzmán on *The battle of Chile* (Socialist Review [Oakland, Calif.] 35, Sept./Oct. 1977, p. 36-68)

A thorough discussion of the genesis of this extraordinary three-part documentary in the context of the ideological struggle taking place in the Chilean media and in all sectors of Chilean society at the time of the filming (1972-73), with a detailed look at the methodology, style and content of the film. Reprinted in pamphlet form by the New England Free Press, Sommerville, Mass.

1002. Chanan, Michael. Chilean cinema. London, British Film Institute, 1976. 102 p.

Interviews reprinted from *Cahiers du Cinéma* and other European sources with directors Raúl Ruíz, Helvio Soto and Miguel Littín and communications theorist Armand Mattelart are followed by reprints of several brief articles in the British, US and Chilean press, a filmography and bibliography. The selection is an interesting one, and the editor's excellent introduction places the entire volume in a necessarily broad perspective.

1003. Cinema chilien: entretien avec Helvio Soto (Cahiers du Cinéma [Paris] 249, fev./mars 1974, p. 5-16)

Chilean filmmaker Helvio Soto discusses the politics of the media in Chile during the Allende years and his own feature film, *Metamorphosis of a police chief*, which was never released in Chile.

Film: Colombia / 63

1004. Le cinéma de l'Unité Populaire; bilan d'une expérience: interview with Patricio Guzmán, Miguel Littín, R. Ruiz, H. Soto (Ecran [Paris] 22, 1974, p. 13-20)

Leading Chilean documentary and feature filmmakers evaluate the accomplishments and failures of cinematic activity during the Allende years.

1005. Godoy Quesada, Mario. Historia del cine chileno. Santiago, n.p., 1966. 173 p.

A virtually year-by-year account of Chilean film production from 1902 through 1966.

1006. Guzmán, Patricio. La insurrección de la burguesía. Caracas, Rocinante, 1975. 70 p.

Contains the full text of the first part of Guzmán's three-part documentary, *The battle of Chile*, an over-all plan of the complete film (three parts, four and a half hours), a glossary of *chilenismos* and two reviews of the film.

1007. Santana, Alberto. Grandezas y miserias del cine chileno: 1910-1957. Santiago, Editorial Misión, 1958? 64 p.

A summary account of the course of filmmaking in Chile, containing valuable film production chronologies and statistical data.

COLOMBIA

1008. Alvarez, Carlos. Una historia que está comenzando: Colombia (Cine al Día [Caracas] 10, mayo 1970, p. 3-10)

Pt. 1 of this article is the report on Colombia presented at the IV International Film Festival in Pesaro, Italy in 1968, which suggests that film societies were the only viable vehicle for producing noncommercial filmmakers. Pt. 2 written almost two years later, concedes the failure of that concept in practice and summarizes the most recent developments in independent filmmaking.

1009. Entrevista con Jorge Silva y Marta Rodríguez (Ojo al Cine [Cali, Colombia] 1, 1974, p. 35-43)

Two of Colombia's most important ethnographic filmmakers discuss the genesis of their films—*Chircales* (The brickmakers) and *Planas: testimonio de un etnicidio*—as well as the problems of making independent films in Colombia.

1010. Mayolo, Carlos and **Ramiro Arbeláez.** Secuencia crítica del cine colombiano (Ojo al Cine [Cali, Colombia] 1, 1974, p. 17-34, filmography)

A detailed history of Colombia history from its origins through 1973, including a three-page national filmography.

1011. Mora, Orlando. Presencia actual del cine colombiano (UA/U, 50:194, abril/junio 1975, p. 169-175)

A fine overview of the development of Colombian filmmaking, with emphasis on the period from 1960 to the present, including summaries of relevant national legislation.

CUBA

NOTE: For a complete bibliography on Cuban films, see HLAS 39, p. 425-434.

Carpentier, Alejo and others. Sobre el cine y la literatura. See *HLAS 39:5017.*

1012. Cinemateca de Cuba, *La Habana.* Sección de Cine Cubano. El cine cubano en la prensa nacional y extranjera: 1960-1977. La Havana, Banco Nacional de Cuba, Museo Numismático, 1977. 107 p.

A chronological selection of quotes from the national and foreign press on Cuban films and related activities (posters, archives, etc.) prepared to accompany an exhibition of the international trophies and awards which the Cuban Film Institute has won over the years.

1013. Díaz Rodríguez, Rolando and **Lázaro Buria Pérez.** Un caso de colonización cinematográfica (El Caimán Barbudo [La Habana] 85, dic. 1975, p. 6-7; 86, enero 1976, p. 10)

A detailed study of conflicting European, North American, and national interests in Cuban film activity from 1897 through 1922.

1014. García Espinosa, Julio. Los cuatro medios de comunicación son tres: cine y TV (CDLA, 16:100, enero/feb. 1977, p. 19-32)

A leading Cuban filmmaker and theorist ("For an Imperfect Cinema," 1970), pursuing lines of inquiry established by members of the Frankfurt School (Benjamin, Horkheimer, Adorno) considers the impact of the communications revolution on the concept of universal art with particular attention to the television medium.

1015. Silva, Jorge. La crítica cinematográfica en Cuba: conversación con Enrique Colina (Ojo al Cine [Cali, Colombia] 5, 1976, p. 2-4)

The master-of-ceremonies of a popular Cuban television show on film discusses the philosophy and practice of film criticism in contemporary Cuba.

1016. El tercer cine: el actor en la revolución (Cine al Dia [Caracas] 20, feb. 1976, p. 5-9)

Interviews with two Cuban actresses, Daisy Granados (*Memories of underdevelopment*) and Eslinda Núñez (*Memories of underdevelopment, Lucía*), and with actor Sergio Corrieri (*Memories of underdevelopment, The man from Maisinicú*).

MEXICO

1017. Ayala Blanco, Jorge. La búsqueda del cine mexicano: 1968-1972. v. 1/2. Mexico, UNAM, 1974. 2 v. (292, 272 p.) (Cuadernos de cine, 22)

A continuation of his earlier *La aventura del cine mexicano*. Includes a discussion of President Luis Echeverría's attempt to stimulate the industry.

1018. Cinéma mexicain (La Revue du Cinema: Image et Son [Paris] 295, avril 1975, p. 20-28)

A survey history of Mexican films from the beginning of the sound era.

1019. Contreras Torres, Miguel. El libro negro del cine mexicano. México, Editora Hispano-Continental Films, 1960. 450 p.

One of Mexico's most prolific producer-directors denounces the monopoly over production and exhibition of William O. Jenkins and his associates. A fascinating insider's view of the Mexican film industry.

1020. Galindo, Alejandro. ¿Qué es el cine? México, Editorial Nuestro Tiempo, 1975. 149 p.

A leading Mexican director discusses filmmaking in general and Mexico's in particular in a series of essays.

1021. García Riera, Emilio. El cine mexicano. México, Ediciones Era, 1963. 238 p.

A short, useful history of Mexican filmmaking from its inception through the early 1960s by Mexico's foremost film historian.

1022. ——. Historia documental del cine mexicano. v. 1, 1926-1940; v. 2, 1941;1944; v. 3, 1945-1948; v. 4, 1949-1951; v. 5, 1952-1954; v. 6, 1955-1957; v. 7, 1958-1960; v. 8,

1961-1963. México, Ediciones Era, 1969/1974. 8 v. (309, 324, 370, 431, 377, 385, 499, 475 p.) illus.

Indispensable reference for serious students of Mexican filmmaking; provides complete credits, production details, synopses and critical commentary on virtually every Mexican film ever made. Profusely illustrated. Eight volumes to date.

1023. Heuer, Federico. La industria cinematográfica mexicana. México, The Author, 1964. 435 p.

Economic and structural study of the Mexican film industry by a former director of the *Banco Nacional Cinematográfica*.

1024. Luna, Andrés de and **Susana Chaurand.** Los independientes: entrevista a Eduardo Maldonado (Otrocine [México] abril/junio 1976, p. 29-32)

The director of two important independent documentaries, *Atencingo* and *Una y otra vez*, discusses the genesis of each film and the goals of the Grupo de Cine Testimonio of which he is a member.

1025. Marcorelles, Louis. Le renouveau mexicain (La Revue du Cinema: Image et Son [Paris] 280, Jan. 1974, p. 72-90)

An analysis of the "new" Mexican cinema from 1970 through 1973.

1026. Meyer, Eugenia comp. Cuadernos de la Cineteca Nacional: testimonios para la historia del cine mexicano. v. 1/7. México, Secretaría de la Gobernación, Dirección de Cinematografía, 1976. 7 v. (107, 130, 132, 123, 149, 154, 153 p.)

Oral history project with major veterans of the Mexican film industry—performers, directors, producers. Illustrated with many rare stills.

1027. Noyola, Antonio. Retrospectiva del cine mexicano no industrial (Otrocine [México] 6, abril/junio 1976, p. 49-57)

Synopses of the nine independent feature films and 11 documentaries all shown at a Cineteca retrospective in the spring of 1975.

1028. *Revista de la Universidad de México.* Vol. 25, No. 10, junio 1972- . México.

Consists of articles devoted to the Mexican film industry:
Aurelio de los Reyes "El Cine en México hacen 75 años: Vicios y Virtudes" p. 2-4

Tomás Pérez Turrent "Buñel ante el Cine Mexicano" p. 5-9
Emilio García Riera "Cuando el Cine Mexicano se Hizo Industria" p. 10-14
David Ramón "Aves sin Nido . . ." p. 15-20
José de la Colina "Situación de los Nuevos Cineastas" p. 21-24
Arturo Garmendia "1968: el Movimiento Estudiantil y el Cine" p. 25-32. [F. Dauster]

1029. Reyes, Aurelio de los. Los orígenes del cine en México: 1896-1900. México, UNAM, Dirección General de Difusión Cultural, 1973. 196 p. (Cuadernos de cine, 21)

A history of the earliest years of Mexican film history.

1030. ———; David Ramon; María Luisa Amador; and Rodolfo Rivera. 80 [i.e. Ochenta] años de cine en México. México, UNAM, Dirección General de Difusión Cultural, 1977. 142 p. (Serie imágenes, 2)

A brief, readable survey of Mexican cinema, based on a 1976 program at the Cineteca Nacional.

PANAMA

1031. Calloni, Stella. El GECU: una cinematografía nacional que comienza a proyectarse (Formato 16 [Panamá] 1/2, 1977, p. 85-94)

An account of the activities of the Experimental University Film Group.

1032. Pitty, Dimas L. Entrevista a Pedro Rivera (Formato 16 [Panamá] 1/2, 1977, p. 44-51)

An interview with a leading Panamanian documentarist and founder of GECU (University Experimental Film Group).

1033. Rivera, Pedro. Apuntes para una historia del cine en Panamá (Formato 16 [Panamá] 3, 1977, p. 16-20)

The leading Panamanian filmmaker lists the handful of films made in Panama prior to the organization of the Grupo Experimental de Cine Universitario in 1972 and goes on to discuss the formation of the Panamanian film public.

PERU

1034. Chambi, Manuel. No se puede hablar de un cine nacional, en tanto se siga improvisando en la temática: habla Manuel Chambi (Cinematógrafo:

Revista de Cultura Cinematográfica [Lima] 2, nov. 1974, p. 3-6)

One of Peru's foremost ethnographic filmmakers, a pioneer of the Cuzco School, discusses his own work and current prospects for a national cinema in Peru.

1035. Cine nacional: encuesta (Cinematógrafo: Revista de Cultura Cinematográfica [Lima] 3, mayo 1975, p. 4-6)

Brief interviews with young Peruvian filmmakers: Nora Izcue, Francisco José Lombardi, Nelson García Miranda, and the Grupo Liberación Sin Rodeos.

1036. Cine peruano: ¿Borrón y cuenta nueva? (Hablemos de Cine [Lima] 11:67, 1975, p. 13-41)

This special issue on current filmmaking in Peru contains an introductory note, a colloquium between the members of the magazine's editorial board on the achievements and prospects of Peruvian cinema, and hard-hitting interviews with four young filmmakers: Nelson García, Francisco Lombardi, Arturo Sinclair, and Nora de Izcue.

1037. Cortometrajes y cine nacional, balance y perspectivas (Cinematógrafo: Revista de Cultura Cinematográfica [Lima] 3, mayo 1975, p. 7-10)

A summary of recent 16mm short film production in Peru, and a strategic appraisal of future prospects.

1038. Frias, Isaac León. Hacia una historia del cine peruano (Hablemos de Cine [Lima] 50/51, 1970, p. 43-53)

By the author's own description, a pioneering and "provisional" history from the turn of the century through 1969.

1039. Getino, Octavio. La nueva cinematografía peruana (Formato 16 [Panamá] 3, 1977, p. 12-15)

A leading Argentine documentarist, co-director of *The hour of the furnaces*, describes recent cinematic developments in Peru, where he now lives in exile.

PUERTO RICO

1040. Núñez, Armindo. Por un cine de lucha (Formato 16 [Panamá] 3, 1977, p. 26-27)

Brief account of the work of two young documentarists, José García y Linda Burk García, whose 14 films include *Puerto Rico: destino manifiesto* and *Puerto Rico: Paraíso invadido*.

1041. Trelles Plazaola, Luis. La carrera de Juano Hernández en el cine norteamericano (ICP/R, 14:50, enero/ marzo 1971, p. 10-13, plate)

Brief discussion and filmography of a distinguished Puerto Rican actor (1897?-1970) who specialized in roles of black Americans. [F. Dauster]

1042. ———. El cine visto en Puerto Rico: 1962-1973. Hato Rey, Univ. de Puerto Rico, 1975. 279 p. (Col. Uprex)

This collection of newspaper articles represents the first attempt to provide an overview of the growth in Puerto Rican film culture over the past decade, stimulated mainly by university film societies. A large portion of the book is made up of reviews of foreign films. There is no discussion of incipient Puerto Rican film activity.

URUGUAY

1043. Martínez, Fernando. Entrevista con Mario Handler (Formato 16 [Panamá] 3, 1977, p. 32-37)

A leading Uruguayan filmmaker, now in exile in Venezuela, describes the details of his career.

VENEZUELA

1044. Capriles, Oswaldo; Peran Erminy; and Rodolfo Izaguirre. La censura cinematográfica en Venezuela (Cine al Día [Caracas] 18, junio 1974, p. 4-9)

A study of the mechanisms and motivations of film censorship in Venezuela.

1045. Cine con la película debajo del brazo (Cine al Día [Caracas] 9, marzo 1970, p. 4-11)

On the work of the Centro de Cine Documental at the Univ. de los Andes in Venezuela. Contains an interview with documentarists Carlos Rebolledo and Ugo Ulive, and an appraisal of several films.

1046. Izaguirre, Rodolfo. El cine en Venezuela. Caracas, Oficina Central de Información, n.d. 25 p. (Temas culturales venezolanos. Serie 1:3)

A brief history of filmmaking in Venezuela from its origins in 1909 through the mid-1960s.

1047. Roffe, Ambretta and **Alfredo Roffe.** Situación de la distribución y exhibición cinematográfica (Cine al Día [Caracas] 18, junio 1974, p. 12-19)

An analysis of domestic and foreign, commercial and independent distribution in Venezuela with statistical data.

1048. Una encuesta: cineastas frente al tercer cine (Cine al Día [Caracas] 14, nov. 1971, p. 4-9)

Nine independent Venezuelan filmmakers characterize conditions of filmmaking in Venezuela in comparison to "Third Cinema" as practiced elsewhere.

JOURNAL ABBREVIATIONS

CDLA	Casa de las Américas. Instituto Cubano del Libro. La Habana.
CJN	Croissance des Jeunes Nations. Paris.
ICAIC/CC	Cine Cubano. Instituto Cubano del Arte e Industria Cinematográfica. La Habana.
ICP/R	Revista del Instituto de Cultura Puertorriqueña. San Juan.
LAP	Latin American Perspectives. Univ. of California. Riverside.
UA/U	Universidad. Univ. de Antioquia. Medellín, Colombia.
UNAM/RMCP	Revista Mexicana de Ciencia Política. UNAM, Facultad de Ciencias Políticas y Sociales. México.
VOZES	Vozes. Revista de cultura. Editora Vozes. Petrópolis, Brazil.

HISTORY

ETHNOHISTORY: MESOAMERICA

EDWARD E. CALNEK

Associate Professor of Anthropology
The University of Rochester

IN MESOAMERICAN STUDIES, ethnohistory has until recently served more often as a kind of "handmaiden to archaeology" than the reverse, but as indicated by current reviews there has been a major change of direction during the past few years. Books and articles dealing with the investigation of documentary sources and written by specialists who have opted for ethnohistory as their *primary* specialization rather than as an adjunct to some other field, predominate now and overwhelmingly so. At the same time, there has been a marked reduction in contributions by archaeologists, geographers, botanists, and others, in which ethnohistorical data has been used to clarify or resolve problems of interest to other disciplines.

The effect of these and related changes on the professional quality of ethnohistorical research—at least, in the opinion of this reviewer—has been one of marked improvement. On the other hand, such refinements in historiographic technique tend to result in a (hopefully temporary) narrowing of focus. We begin to learn much more about, for example, number and directional symbolisms, the structure of myth, religious iconography, and so forth, but without any clear indication of how these contribute to a deeper understanding of the societies and civilizations from which they derive.

One important change in the content of the ETHNOHISTORY: MESOAMERICA section of this volume of the *Handbook* should be noted. As the field of Mayan epigraphy has grown in scope and complexity, that previous practice of distributing reviews between the archaeology and ethnohistory sections no longer applies. In the future, publications on this subject will be listed in the subsection entitled "Native Sources" of the ARCHAEOLOGY: MESOAMERICA section. Therefore, the only publications on Maya epigraphy that will be annotated here are those in which decipherment of a text is so far advanced that the actual content can be independently recognized as an ethnohistorical source.

1951. Ades, Dawn and Gordon Brotherston. Mesoamerican description of space I: myths; stars and maps; and architecture (IAA, 1, 1975, p. 279-305, bibl., illus., tables)

Maintains that well-developed concept of world directions linked with cardinal points was lacking in prehispanic understanding of spatial relationships, and that apparent examples from the native literature reflect European influence.

1952. Anawalt, Patricia. The Xicolli: an analysis of a ritual garment (*in* International Congress of Americanists, XLI, Mexico, 1974. Actas [see *HLAS 39:259*] v. 2, p. 223-235, bibl., illus.)

Detailed survey of textual references and pictorial representations of the *xicolli* to determine appearance, probable contexts in which used, and association with other articles of dress and adornment in specific types of religious and civil observance.

1953. Anderson, Arthur J.O.; Frances Berdan; and James Lockhart. Beyond the codices: the Nahua view of colonial Mexico. Berkeley, Univ. of California Press, 1976. 235 p., bibl., illus.

Includes transcriptions and English translations of 35 Nahuatl language texts with 16th and 17th-century dates. Introduction and appendices discuss special problems arising from these and similar colonial period texts, and outline areas where further analysis and research will be especially fruitful. Volume includes short essay entitled "Linguistic Significance of the Texts" by Ronald W. Langacker.

1954. Anguiano, Marina and Matilde Chapa. Estratificación social en Tlaxcala durante el siglo XVI (*in* Carrasco, Pedro and others. Estratificación social [see item 1966] p. 118-156, bibl., illus., maps, tables)

Quantitative presentation of mid-16th century census data in which percent of total population of individual communities classed as nobles (*pipiltin*) or commoners (*macehualtin*), or according to other Nahuatl terms denoting rank or office, can be determined. Also includes detailed survey of documentary evidence useful for interpreting status terminology.

1955. Arjona Santos, Angel. Quetzalcoatl: la historia y el mito (CH, 104:310, abril 1976, p. 94-123)

Attempts to reconcile and synthesize texts which present Quetzalcoatl as a historical personage with those in which he appears as one of the principal Mesoamerican deities.

1956. Barthel, Thomas S. Zur Frage der altmexicanischen Tageszeichen (DGV/ZE, 100:1/2, 1975, p. 195-223, bibl., tables)

Interesting but highly speculative discussion of numerological significance of calendrical system of Mesoamerica based on claimed close relationship to southeast Asian systems.

1957. Berdan, Frances Frei. A comparative analysis of Aztec tribute documents (*in* International Congress of Americanists, XLI, Mexico, 1974. Actas [see *HLAS 39:259*] v. 2, p. 131-142, bibl., table)

Notes similarities and differences in the tribute sections of the *Codex Mendoza, Matrícula de Tributos* and the *Información de 1554*; tabulates variations in quantities represented in each of these documents; and comments on probable significance of the most notable discrepancies between these critically important sources for the study of the Aztec tribute system.

1958. Biedermann, Hans. The pictographic manuscripts of ancient Mexico (Graphis [Zürich, Switzerland] 181, 1975/1976, p. 476-485, illus., plates)

Brief descriptions of types of pictorial manuscripts now in museum or library collections with illustrations taken from some of the most notable examples.

1959. Broda, Johanna. Los estamentos en el ceremonial mexica (*in* Carrasco, Pedro and others. Estratificación social [see item 1966] p. 37-66, bibl., illus.)

Reviews evidence showing that organization of religious ceremonies in Aztec society reflected social stratification and occupational differentiation.

1960. Calnek, Edward E. The internal structure of Tenochtitlan (*in* Wolf, Eric R. *ed.* The Valley of Mexico: studies in prehispanic ecology and society [see *HLAS 39:372*] p. 287-302, bibl., illus., map)

Discusses social composition and territorial organization of Tenochtitlan-Tlatelolco, emphasizing features potentially recognizable in non-historical archaeological contexts.

1961. ———. Organización de los sistemas de abastecimiento urbano de alimentos: el caso de Tenochtitlán (*in* Hardoy, Jorge E. and Richard P. Schaedel *eds.* Las ciudades de América Latina y sus áreas de influencia a través de la historia [see item 2175] p. 41-60, bibl.)

Traces economic development of Aztec capital, emphasizing primacy of market institutions in provisioning the city; also discusses role of tributes and of rents-in-kind from rural landholdings controlled or owned by urban elites.

1962. Carmack, Robert M. La estratificación quicheana prehispánica (*in* Carrasco, Pedro and others. Estratificación social [see item 1966] p. 245-277, bibl.)

Particularly interesting theoretical discussion emphasizing similarity between Quiché politico-economic system and feudal society in Spain. Analyzes ideological correlates of social differentiation, and emphasizes dynamic qualities inherent in the status system when viewed in historical perspective.

1963. Carrasco, Pedro. Estratificación social indígena en Morelos durante el siglo XVI (*in* Carrasco, Pedro and others. Estratificación social [see item 1966] p. 102-117, bibl.)

Analysis of census records and related texts which include data relating to status terminology, political organization, land tenure, and related characteristics of Indian communities in early decades of postconquest period.

1964. ———. The joint family in ancient Mexico: the case of Molotla (*in* Nutini, Hugo G.; Pedro Carrasco; and James M. Taggart *eds*. Essays on Mexican kinship. Pittsburgh, Univ. of Pittsburgh Press, 1976, p. 45-64, bibl., tables)

Analysis of census data from barrio (*calpulli*) of Molotla, probably a subdivision of Yautepec, Morelos, emphasizing family and household compositions, economic organization, and land tenure arrangements.

1965. ———. Los linajes nobles del México antiguo (*in* Carrasco, Pedro and others. Estratificación social [see item 1966] p. 19-36, bibl.)

Important study of structural principles involved in organization of noble lineages throughout late prehispanic Central Mexico, and their role in politicoterritorial organization. Reexamines and rejects traditional definition of the *calpulli* as a type of clan, suggesting instead that it was a political and administrative unit with no significant relation to the idea of kinship or descent.

1966. ——— and others. Estratificación social en la Mesoamérica prehispánica. México, INAH, Centro de Investigaciones Superiores, 1976. 300 p., bibl., illus., maps, tables (SEP/INAH)

Important group of papers presenting new evidence and theoretical interpretations of late postclassic societies of Central Mexico and other regions in Mesoamerica. For individual reviews of these articles see items 1954, 1959, 1962-1963, 1965, 1968, 1972, 1981, 1984, 1986, 2001 and 2013.

1967. Cook de Leonard, Carmen. Reconstrucción geográfico-política del reino de Cozcatlan (*in* International Congress of Americanists, XLI, Mexico, 1974. Actas [see *HLAS 39:259*] v. 2, p. 117-130, bibl., illus.)

Valuable analysis of 16th-century map and *relación* which permit determination of boundaries, principal towns, and territorial subdivisions of Cozcatlan in late preconquest and early colonial times.

1968. Corona Sánchez, Eduardo. La estratificación social en el Acolhuacan (*in* Carrasco, Pedro and others. Estratificación social [see item 1966] p. 88-101, bibl.)

Emphasizes social, cultural, ethnic, and ecological diversity of northeastern sector of Valley of Mexico in relation to system of social stratification.

1969. Davies, Nigel. The Toltecs, until the fall of Tula. Norman, Univ. of Oklahoma Press, 1977. 533 p., bibl., maps, plates, tables (The civilization of the American Indian series, 144)

Comprehensive study of historical and archaeological data bearing on the "Toltec-problem" in Mesoamerica. Best available synthesis of primary sources in the literature to date, despite sometimes speculative nature of Davies' interpretations.

1970. Dobkin de Rios, Marlene. The influence of psychotropic flora and fauna on Maya religion (UC/CA, 15:2, June 1974, p. 147-164, bibl.)

Provocative but highly controversial analysis of Maya art and iconography suggesting that the hallucinogenic properties of mushrooms, certain toads, and water-lilies powerfully influenced religious symbolism. Should be read together with detailed and sometimes highly critical comments by 15 specialists which follow this paper.

1971. Durand-Forest, Jacqueline de. Description de divinités d'après les textes en Nahuatl et leur représentation dans les códices (SA/J, 64, 1977, p. 9-17)

Important study of divergence between descriptions of prehispanic deities given in texts written in Nahuatl and their representations in pictorial manuscripts, with illustrative material drawn from the Sahagun texts (written and pictorial) and pictorial manuscripts in the Proto-Magliabechiano group (*Codex-Ixtlilxochitl* and *Codex Magliabechiano*).

1972. Dyckerhoff, Úrsula and Hanns J. Prem. La estratificación social en Huexotzinco (*in* Carrasco, Pedro and others. Estratificación social [see item 1966] p. 157-180, bibl., map, tables)

Dyckerhoff presents statistical analysis of census data from the *Matrícula de Huexotzinco* with emphasis on status differentiation, and including comparison of types of organization associated with different levels of community organization. Prem adds short note dealing with rural property forms as an indicator of social stratification.

1973. Elzey, Wayne. The Nahua myth of the suns: history and cosmology in prehispanic Mexican religions (IAHR/N, 23:2, Aug. 1976, p. 114-135)

Argues that the myth of the five suns functioned as a "uniquely 'Mexican'" structural paradigm which served to organize and integrate the religious and

72 / Handbook of Latin American Studies

cosmological belief systems of the Nahua speaking peoples of prehispanic Mesoamerica.

1974. Erdheim, Mario. Prestige and kulturwandel eine studie zum Verhältnis subjektiver und objektiver Faktoren des kulturellen Wandels zur Kalssengesselschaft bei den Azteken. Weisbaden, FRG, Focus-Verlag, 1972. 122 p., bibl. (Kultur-Anthropologische Studien zur Geschichte, 2)

Important theoretical study of prestige and power in historical development of Aztec state.

1975. Eschmann, Anncharlott. Das Religiöse Geschichtsbild der Azteken. Berlin, FRG, Mann Verlag, 1976. 371 p., illus., tables (Indiana, 4)

Examines relationship between Aztec historical writing and religious thought.

1976. Feldman, Lawrence H. Names and deities in early Guatemala (*in* International Congress of Americanists, XLI, Mexico, 1974. Actas [see *HLAS 39:259*] v. 2, p. 236-242, bibl., tables)

Documents occurrence of Nahua loan words used especially as personal surnames, calendrical daynames or in Nahua associated religious contexts among Maya of 16th-century Guatemala.

1977. ——. Papers of Escuintla and Guazacapan: a contribution to the history and ethnography of south-eastern Guatemala. Greeley, Univ. of Northern Colorado, Museum of Anthopology, 1974. 105 p., bibl., facsims., maps, table (Occasional publications in Mesoamerican anthropology, 7)

Inventory of documents relating to previously unstudied section of Guatemala; the more important texts are reproduced in this volume.

1978. France, Bibliothèque Nationale. Aztlan, terre des Aztèques, images d'un nouveau monde. Paris, 1976. 113 p., illus.

Illustrated catalogue of the manuscript holdings of the Collection Mexicaine of the Bibliothèque Nationale in Paris, with brief descriptions of individual items.

1979. Frank, Karl Anton. Durch Guatemala ritt der Tod der Zug des Pedro de Alvarado 1524 durch Mittelamerikanach seinen eigenen und anderen spanischen Berichten sowie den Chroniken der Hochland-Maya. Düsseldorf, FRG, Hoch-Verlag, 1973. 224 p., illus.. maps.

Describes Alvarado's bloody campaigns against still unconquered Indian states in Tehuantepec and Highland Guatemala in 1524.

1980. Garcés Contreras, Guillermo. Los códices mayas. México, Secretaría de Educación Pública, Dirección General de Divulgación, 1975. 167 p., illus. (SepSetentas, 210)

Accurately written introduction to Maya culture with brief descriptions of pictorial manuscripts and literary texts.

1981. García Alcaraz, Agustín. Estratificación social entre los tarascos prehispánicos (*in* Carrasco, Pedro and others. Estratificación social [see item 1966] p. 221-244, bibl.)

Traces historical development and internal organization of the powerful Tarascan state up to the Spanish conquest. Useful discussion of documentary evidence available for studying this still poorly known region.

1982. Gilonne, Michel. L'avifaune dans le Codex Borbonicus (SA/J, 64, 1977, p. 29-42, bibl., illus.)

Meticulous study of variations in color and appearance of the 12 birds which appear as "companions" of deities associated with the 260-day ritual calendar (*tonalpoualli*).

1983. Gollob, Hedwig. Die Interkontinentale Mayareligion und die Forschungsmethoden des modernen Rationalismus. Wien, Eigenverlag, 1974. 23 p., illus.

Argues that Maya religion derives ultimately from an *archaic* and widely diffused religious system originally developed in the Old World.

1984. González Torres, Yolotl. La esclavitud entre los mexica (*in* Carrasco, Pedro and others. Estratificación social [see item 1966] p. 78-87, bibl.)

Critical review of previous attempts to define nature of *siavery* as understood in Aztec society.

1985. Hartig, Pauline and Berthold Riese. The Chilam Balam of Kaua: report of the project of a critical edition and first results (*in* International Congress of Americanists, XLI, Mexico, 1974. Actas [see *HLAS 39:259*] v. 2, p. 147-163, bibl.)

Brief description of content of text characterized as "the most comprehensive single document of the Chilam Balam type," and of procedures utilized in preparation of published facsimile reproduction, transcription and translation.

1986. Hicks, Frederick. *Mayeque y calpuleque* en el sistema de clases del México antiguo (*in* Carrasco, Pedro and others. Estratificación social [see item 1966] p. 67-77, bibl.)

Discusses social, legal, and economic position of peasant farmers holding land by virtue of *calpulli* membership (*calpuleque*) as contrasted with those classed as tenant-farmers (*mayeque*).

1987. Ixtlilxóchitl, Fernando de Alva. *Obras históricas* incluyen el texto completo de las llamadas *Relaciones e historia de la Nación Chichimeca* en una nueva versión establecida con el cotejo de los manuscritos más antiguos que se conocen. t. 1. 3. ed. Edición, estudio introductorio y un apéndice documental por Edmundo O'Gorman. México, UNAM, Instituto de Investigaciones Históricas, 1975. 566 p., tables (Serie de historiadores y cronistas de Indias, 4)

Particularly valuable for preliminary studies of Ixtlilxochitl's life, the original sources used in his work, chronological data appearing in the various histories, and other information indispensable for critical historiographic research, together with a new, reorganized version of the *Obras históricas*.

1988. Jiménez S., Tomás E. Los indios de las tierras bajas de la América Central antes de la conquista (III/AI, 36:1, enero/marzo 1976, p. 39-59, bibl.)

Reviews scanty historical and ethnographic documentation available for groups strongly influenced by South American cultural patterns, as well as by the Mesoamerican cultures to the north.

1989. Katz, Friedrich. Comparación entre algunos aspectos de la evolución del Cuzco y de Tenochtitlán (*in* Hardoy, Jorge E. and Richard P. Schaedel *eds.* Las ciudades de América Latina y sus areas de influencia a través de la historia [see item 2175] p. 27-40, bibl.)

Compares historical background, demographic organization, and political structure of Aztec and Inca societies.

1990. Le Clézio, J.M.G. *ed.* Les prophéties du Chilam Balam. Paris, Editions Gallimard, 1976. 201 p., illus. (Col. Le chemin)

French version of Chilam Balam manuscripts of Yucatan based primarily on earlier translations by Roys, Barrera Vázquez, Morley, Rendon and Makemson.

1991. López Austin, Alfredo. Textos de medicina Náhuatl. México, UNAM, Instituto de Investigaciones Históricas, 1975. 230 p., bibl., illus., map (Serie de cultura Náhuatl. Monografías, 19)

Presents series of important texts dealing with medical practice among Nahua groups in Central Mexico from prehispanic to recent times, with detailed and useful introductory discussions by an outstanding student of these materials.

1992. Majewski, Teresita. Ethnohistoric and ethnographic inference for determining precolumbian social structure (*in* International Congress of Americanists, XLI, Mexico, 1974. Actas [see *HLAS 39:259*] v. 2, p. 156-163, bibl.)

Reviews ethnohistoric evidence useful for interpreting archaeological data for lime production at Chalcatzingo in eastern Morelos.

1993. Marcus, Joyce. Territorial organization of the lowland classic Maya (AAAS/S, 180:4086, June 1973, p. 911-916, bibl., illus.)

Uses glyphic and archaeological evidence to identify four primary regional capitals in lowland Maya region; attempts to show that spatial patterning is in close agreement with hexagonal lattices of type predicted in Central-Place Theory.

1994. Martínez Marín, Carlos. La ethnohistoria: un intento de explicación (UNAM/AA, 13, 1976, p. 161-184, bibl.)

Reviews historical development of ethnohistorical studies, and discusses application to indigenous societies of Mesoamerican region.

1995. Melgarejo Vivanco, José Luis. Los lienzos de Tuxpan: códices de tierras. Fotografía de Manuel Alvarez Bravo. México, Editorial La Estampa Mexicana, 1970. 211 p., bibl., fold. maps, fold. plates, fold. table, illus., plates.

Useful descriptive study of three pictorial *maps* believed based on late 15th-century prototypes, with additional documentary material dealing with same region in colonial times.

1996. Menéndez, Elisabeth. Maïs et divinités du maïs d'après les sources anciennes (SA/J, 64, 1977, p. 19-27)

Comparative analysis of closely related Nahuatl and Spanish texts dealing with maize and maize gods indicating that the former often includes important data omitted or given in distorted form in the latter.

1997. Nelson, Ralph ed. and trans. *Popol Vuh*: the great mythological book of the ancient Maya. With drawings from the Códices Mayas. Boston, Mass., Houghton Mifflin, 1976. 86 p., illus.

Introduction provides perceptive study of world view expressed in early sections of *Popol Vuh*. The "new translation" is from Andrian Recinos Spanish version, and not the original Quiche text. For linguist's comment, see *HLAS 39:1711*.

1998. Neumann, Frank J. The Flayed God and his rattle-stick: a shamanic element in prehispanic Mesoamerican religion (UC/HR, 15:3, Feb. 1976, p. 251-263)

Revised version of Neumann's 1974 article (see item 1999).

1999. ———. The rattle-stick of Xipe Totec: a shamanic element in prehispanic Mesoamerican religion (*in* International Congress of Americanists, XLI, Mexico, 1974. Actas [see *HLAS 39:259*] v. 2, p. 2, p. 243-251, bibl., illus.)

Argues that persistent association of the Flayed God, Xipe Totec, with drum and rattle-stick indicate origin in or close association with shamanistic practices. For revised version of this article, see item 1998.

2000. Nowotny, Karl A. El fragmento de Nochistlan. Hamburg, FRG, Hamburgisches Museum für Völkerkunde [and] Klaus Renner Verlag, München, FRG, 1975. 13 p., illus. (Beiträge zur mittelamerikanischen Völkerkunde, 13)

Brief descriptive study of Mixtec style pictorial manuscript closely resembling the *Codex Philipp J. Becker II*.

2001. Olivera, Mercedes. El despotismo tributario en la región de Cuauhtinchan-Tepeaca (*in* Carrasco, Pedro and others. Estratificación social [see item 1966] p. 181-206, bibl., illus., map)

Descriptive study of changing characteristics of status system from 12th century until Spanish conquest.

Ortiz de Montellano, Bernard. Empirical Aztec medicine. See *HLAS 39:2020*.

2002. Piho, Virve. Esquema provisional de la organización militar mexica (*in* International Congress of Americanists, XLI, Mexico, 1974. Actas [see *HLAS 39:259*] v. 2, p. 169-178, bibl.)

Preliminary study of military ranks and titles based primarily on types of dress, ornament, and hair-style represented in pictorial manuscripts or described in written texts.

2003. Prem, Hanns J. Los afluentes del Río Xopanac: estudio histórico de un sistema de riego (FAIC/CPPT, 12, 1975, p. 27-40, map, plates)

Detailed study of archival records and other sources of value in determining structure of irrigation systems and patterns of water use in early colonial period.

2004. Quezada, Noemí. Amor y magia amorosa entre los aztecas: supervivencia en el México colonial. México, UNAM, Instituto de Investigaciones Antropológicas, 1975. 162 p., bibl., fold. illus., fold. tables, illus., tables (Serie antropológica, 17)

Excellent critical survey of prehispanic and colonial texts dealing with magical and religious aspects of love and sexuality.

2005. ———. El valle del Mezquital en el siglo XVI (UNAM/AA, 13, 1976, p. 185-197, bibl., map, tables)

Attempts to show that political and economic changes affecting indigenous communities in early colonial times resulted almost entirely from demands for labor services for Spanish owned mines and cattle ranches.

2006. Rasmussen, Jørgen Nybo. Bruder Jakob der däne OFM: als verteidiger der religiösen gleichberechtigung der Indianer in Mexiko im XVI. Jahrhundert. Wiesbaden, FRG, Franz Steiner Verlag, 1974. 117 p., bibl. (Institut für Europäische Geschichte Mainz, 58)

Outlines main points in debate among Spanish ecclesiastics in Mexico which ended with exclusion of Indians from the priesthood. Brother Jacob was perhaps the strongest opponent of the position taken by the Catholic church.

2007. Rendón, Silvia P. Crónica de la fundación de México-Tenochtitlan.

México, Secretaría de Obras y Servicios, Depto. del Distrito Federal, 1975. 144 p., bibl., illus. (Col. Popular ciudad de México)

Brief introductory study followed by translation of several historical accounts written in Nahuatl which deal with the founding of the Aztec capital.

2008. **Rodríguez Losa, Salvador.** El henequen en la época prehispánica (UY/R, 18:108, nov./dic. 1976, p. 78-93)

Reviews linguistic, historical, and epigraphic data relating to origin, cultivation, and use of henequen in Maya region.

2009. **Romero Galván, José Rubén.** Las fuentes de las diferentes historias originales del Chimalpahin (SA/J, 64, 1977, p. 51-56)

Summarizes information bearing on historical sources and informants used by Chimalpahin, available mainly in the recently translated *Octava relación*.

2010. **Roys, Ralph Loveland.** The ethnobotany of the Maya. With a new introduction and supplemental bibliography by Sheila Cosminsky. Philadelphia, Pa., Institute for the Study of Human Issues (ISHI), 1976. 380 p., bibl. (ISHI reprints on Latin America and the Caribbean)

Reissue of classic study dealing with medicinal plants and ailments described in colonial period of Yucatan. Reprint of Tulane Univ.'s Middle American research series, No. 2.

2011. **Sahagún, Bernardino de.** *Florentine Codex*: general history of the things of New Spain. Book 12, pt. 13, The conquest of Mexico. Translated from the Aztec into English, with notes and illustrations by Arthur J.O. Anderson and Charles E. Dibble. 2. ed. rev. Santa Fe, N. Mex., The School of American Research [and] The Univ. of Utah, Salt Lake City, 1975. 126 p., illus., maps (Monographs of the School of American Research, 14:13)

Significantly improved translation from Nahuatl marks this new edition of a basic source giving the Aztec version of the conquest of Mexico.

2012. **Sánchez, Jean-Pierre.** Le *Codex de Florence*: un manuscrit négligé de l'*Historia general de las cosas de Nueva España* de Fray Bernardino de Sahagún (UHB/EHA, 10, 1975, p. 49-62, tables)

Short discussion of bibliographic history and relationship of the *Florentine Codex* to other versions of Sahagun's work.

Satterthwaite, Linton. The form, dating and probable use of Landa's Christian-Maya year table See *HLAS 39:561*.

2013. **Spores, Ronald.** La estratificación social en la antigua sociedad mixteca (*in* Carrasco, Pedro and others. Estratificación social [see item 1966] p. 207-220, bibl.)

Broad survey of evidence relating to organization of the three principal social groups—rulers, nobles and commoners—as represented in early colonial archival records and other documentary sources.

2014. **Spranz, Bodo.** Untersuchungen zur vorspanischen Geschichte von Puebla und Tlaxcala, Mexiko (JGSWGL, 11, 1974, p. 1-11, maps)

Considers possible relationships between Toltec "folk wanderings" described in *Historia tolteca chichimeca* and archaeological cultures of Puebla-Tlaxcala region.

2015. **Starr, Frederick.** The *Mapa de Cuauhtlantzinco* or *Códice Campos*. Spanish inscriptions translated from the original Náhuatl text by José Vicente Campos. N.Y., AMS Press, 1976. 38 p., table.

Reprint of 1898 ed. published by Univ. of Chicago, which was issued as *Bulletin no. 3* of Univ. of Chicago, Dept. of Anthropology. Reproduced from an original in the collections of the Bancroft Library, Univ. of Calif., Berkeley.

2016. **Stenzel, Werner.** The military and religious orders of ancient Mexico (*in* International Congress of Americanists, XLI, Mexico, 1974. Actas [see *HLAS 39:259*] v. 2, p. 179-187, bibl.)

Argues that psychological character of military preparation, including a "vision quest" and other types of ritual activity, while more elaborately developed in prehispanic Mesoamerica, was actually closely similar to the military culture of the Pueblo and Plains Indians and other North American groups.

2017. **Sullivan, Thelma D.** The mask of Itztlacoliuhqui (*in* International Congress of Americanists, XLI, Mexico,

1974. Actas [see *HLAS 39:259*] v. 2, p. 252-262, bibl., illus.)

Intricately structured discussion of attributes and associations of an important but poorly understood deity.

2018. Thouvenot, Marc. Chalchihuitl: emplois métaphoriques du et symbolisme (SA/J, 64, 1977, p. 43-50, bibl.)

Describes literary contexts and symbolic meanings associated with the word *chalchihuitl* (jade) in literary sources—especially the Sahagun texts—prepared in early colonial times, but preserving prehispanic understandings.

2019. Vrhel, František. *Popol Vuh* y la cosmología maya (UCP/IAP, 8, 1974, p. 171-174)

Emphasizes literary and aesthetic characteristics of the *Popol Vuh*, with brief references to Maya cosmology as represented in this text.

2020. Whitecotton, Joseph W. The Zapotecs princes, priests, and peasants. Norman, Univ. of Oklahoma Press, 1977. 338 p., bibl., illus., maps, tables (The civilization of the American Indian series)

Good introduction to archaeology, ethnohistory and contemporary ethnography of Zapotec region from earliest times to present.

2021. Wicke, Charles R. Once more around the Tizoc Stone: a reconsideration (*in* International Congress of Americanists, XLI, Mexico, 1974. Actas [see *HLAS 39:259*] v. 2, p. 209-222, bibl., illus., tables)

Reanalyzes figures and symbols shown on the Tizoc stone as "symbolic both of Tenochtitlan and its war god, Huitzilopochtli," and suggests that relief figures are principal deities of peoples conquered up to the time of Tizoc's reign.

2022. Wiercinski, Andrzej. The dark and light side of the Aztec stone calendar and their symbolical significance (*in* International Congress of Americanists, XLI, Mexico, 1974. Actas [see *HLAS 39:259*] v. 2, p. 275-278, bibl.)

Discusses mythic and conceptual oppositions embodied in deities and other symbols represented on the calendar stone.

2023. Willey, Gordon R. Mesoamerican civilization and the idea of transcendence (AT/A, 50:199/200, Dec. 1976, p. 205-215, bibl.)

Discusses historical and archaeological evidence which suggest that "the story of the Toltec priest-king, Topiltzin Quetzalcoatl documents a Precolumbian example of a transcendent religious philosophy" closely analogous to those which in the Old World were associated with the appearance of Judaism, Zoroastrianism, Buddhism and other major religious movements.

2024. Zantwijk, R. van. La organización social de la Mexico-Tenochtitlan Naciente: una interpretación de la primera pintura—folio 2r—del *Códice Mendocino* (*in* International Congress of Americanists, XLI, Mexico, 1974. Actas [see *HLAS 39:259*] v. 2, p. 188-208, bibl., illus.)

Stimulating analysis of pictorial and written texts which shed light on possible relationships between early social organization, territorial organization and religious ideology involved in the founding of the Aztec capital, Tenochtitlan.

ETHNOHISTORY: SOUTH AMERICA

JOHN V. MURRA

Professor of Anthropology
Cornell University

THE PROLIFERATION OF JOURNALS favorable to ethnohistory, noted in *HLAS 38*, continues. A group of younger investigators in La Paz, most of them trained as historians, have brought out the first issue of *Avances* (revista boliviana de estudios históricos y sociales) devoted this time to "caciques, comunidad y estado." Ambitiously, they promise two more issues in 1978. Their casilla number in La Paz is 6599. In Lima, Franklin Pease, at the Univ. Católica, is preparing the third issue of *Histórica*, which defines its task as bringing together historians with anthropologists of a diachronic persuasion. The first two issues appeared since *HLAS 38* and are annotated below.

Alas, the proliferation occurs just when some of the older journals have suffered delays: *Revista del Museo Nacional* (Lima) has not yet published vol. 42, devoted to Inca studies, and ready since 1976. Moreover, the editors of *Chungara* (Arica, Chile) have put together a bulky No. 6/7, which has been at the printers for a year. The *Anales Científicos* (Univ. del Centro, Huancayo, Perú) which in each of its four numbers had included previously unpublished materials selected by Waldemar Espinoza is also threatened.

In *HLAS 38*, we announced forthcoming collections of recent articles by María Rostworowski and Franklin Pease. Both have since appeared in the series Historia Andina, published by the Instituto de Estudios Peruanos. Rostworowski's impressive record of rescuing coastal data, neglected until she decided in 1970 to spend most of her time on them, includes a forthcoming volume dealing specifically with the Andean side of early Lima history. She has also scored a notable coup, finding in Spain several sections of the first *visita general* of 1549 and some of these are reviewed below (see items 2108 and 2112). Most of Pease's essays are new, particularly one long attempt to fathom the early organization of the Inka state (item 2095). Next in this series is a collection of demographic studies by Nicolás Sánchez-Albornoz, which appeared in March 1978 (item 2114).

Archaeologists have long been familiar with Japanese research into the Formative period in the Andes. Less well-known is the Americanist seminar at the Univ. of Tokyo and the group at the new ethnographic museum at Osaka. Under the direction of Prof. Masuda, the seminar at Tokyo is planning both ethnographic and documentary research in Peru. They have tabulated for computer use and analyzed all the households enumerated in Iñigo Ortiz's *visita* to the Huallaga valley (see *HLAS 29:2179*). A reader with translations of both Meso-American and Andean ethnohistoric articles appeared in late 1977.

Ethno-historical developments in France include the centenary meeting, in 1976, of the International Congress of Americanists, in Paris (see *HLAS 39:259*). For the occasion, the Société des Américanistes printed a special issue of its *Journal*, most of it devoted to textual analysis of Andean materials, put together by Pierre Duviols (item 2045). Coming out too late for review in this *HLAS* is a special issue of *Annales*, concerned with "historical anthropology" of the Andes. Among the articles will be a reevaluation, based on much new material, of what we know about the Uru, by Wachtel, very new considerations of the political and economic organization of the Northern Andes by Frank Salomon and reports on advances in South Andean ethnohistory by Thiérry Saignes and Thérèse Bouysse.

Note has been made before of the publishing activities of the Seminar für Völkerkunde at the Univ. of Bonn, directed by Udo Oberem and Roswith Hartmann. Recently there have appeared a number of theses, most of them dealing with Ecuadorian problems (see, for example, the one by Albert Meyers noted below, item 2075).

Finally a major development in the collaboration between ethnohistory and astronomy. R. Tom Zuidema's long standing interest in Andean calendars is beginning to bear very important results (item 2124).

2025. Ampuero B., Gonzalo and **Jorge Hidalgo L.** Estructura y proceso en la prehistoria y protohistoria del Norte Chico de Chile (Chungara [Univ. del Norte, Depto. de Antropología, Arica, Chile] 5, 1975, p. 87-124, bibl., map)

Good summary of archaeology of Coquimbo and Atacama is followed by ethnohistoric considerations about the Diaguita ethnic groups. Degree of incorporation into the Inca state is debated, again using both archaeological and historic references (see *HLAS 34:1179*).

Arcila Vélez, Graciliano. Arqueología del Valle de Aburrá. See *HLAS 39:866*

2026. Arguedas, José María *trans*. Dioses y hombres de Huarochiri. 2. ed. Prepared by Angel Rama. México, Siglo XXI Editores, 1975. 175 p.

Since the original 1966 ed. of this translation (see *HLAS 29:2137b*) has long been out of print, Angel Rama has brought out a mutilated version. The Quechua originals are gone but the biobibliographic essay by Pierre Duviols has survived the pruning.

2027. Bouysse-Cassagne, Thérèse and **Thomas Gómez.** Sociétés indigènes et structures de colonisation (CDAL, 13/14, 1976, p. 3-32, bibl., maps)

Comparison of political organization of the Qolla of the Andean altiplano with the Muisca of Colombia. Exchanges in the latter area were of a commercial type and there was intense political rivalry Gómez manages to deal with the topic without quoting Reichel-Dolmatoff's seminal 1961 work. In colonial times destructuration took place in both areas but was slower in the rich, populated area of the Collao.

2028. Bravo Guerreira, Marie Concepción. Los matrimonios de Huayna Capac: su sucesión, según diversas fuentes (*in* International Congress of Americanists, XLI, Mexico, 1974. Actas [see *HLAS 39:249*] v. 2, p. 107-116, bibl.)

Dynastic oral tradition in the Andes is available to us in many versions, most of them unreliable, particularly where matters of legitimacy and succession are concerned. Fratricidal wars at the death of each king were structural. Many years ago M. Rostworowski suggested that royal incest was introduced in an effort to cut down on "legitimate" candidates. Bravo has charted what most of the sources have to say, as a background to the war which ended with the European invasion.

2029. Browning, David G. and **David J. Robinson.** The origins and comparability of Peruvian population data: 1776-1815. Syracuse, N.Y., Syracuse Univ., Dept. of Geography, 1976. 31 p., illus., maps, tables (Discussion paper, 23)

About the time of Tupac Amaru's rebellion of 1780, there was growing interest in better population figures. This led to improvement of both ecclesiastic and tribute lists. In so far as the Andean population is concerned, the authors reveal a probable increase in the central highlands, but detailed checks for regions where information was more copious indicate that "summary population tables should be treated with great caution . . ."

2030. Burkett, Elinor. La mujer durante la conquista y la primera época colonial (UP/EA, 12, 1976, p. 1-35)

Focuses on fate of Andean women whose experiences during this early period are very different from those of men. Many left as widows, many more taken by Europeans to the cities, and very far from home; many became market traders in the mining centers. They appear in archival sources extending powers of attorney, filing wills and testaments, providing for their frequently mestizo children. The contrast between their condition and that of the few European women is notable.

Casassas Cantó, José María. La arqueología histórica en el Norte Grande chileno. See *HLAS 39:805*.

2031. Chávez Velásquez, Nancy. La materia médica en el incanato. Lima, Juan Mejía Baca, 1977. 426 p., bibl., illus.

Raw materials for this study derive from 16th-century sources some of which are used here for the first time. They have been placed in alphabetical order, scientific identifications of most plants are supplied. Also includes list of illnesses and complaints with medications prescribed.

2032. Choque Canqui, Roberto. Pedro Chipana: cacique comerciante de Calamarca (Avances [Revista boliviana de estudios históricos y sociales, La Paz] 1, 1978, p. 28-32, bibl.)

Potosí offered opportunities for many Andean ethnic leaders to use their traditional authority for commercial purposes. In 1680 one such lord in Sicasica province traded coastal wine to the miners. Mortgage papers quoted indicate he also had access to pastures, coca leaf and other distant resources.

2033. Civrieux, Marc de. Los caribes y la conquista de la Guayana española: etnohistoria kari'ña (UCAB/M, 5, 1976, p. 875-1021, bibl.)

After brief introduction locating the Carib, author has organized his information year by year, in true annals fashion. Most of it deals with European settlement in the lowlands of Venezuela. Contains gazeteer of Carib placenames and of missions; index of Carib personalities in colonial times.

2034. Cock C., Guillermo. Los kurakas de los collaguas: poder político y poder económico (PMNH/HC, 10, 1976/1977, p. 95-118, bibl., illus., map)

Ethnic lords of this region were subjects of Inca, whose presence in Cabana Conde was confirmed archaeologically. Some lords were in charge of artisan ayllus; others had wider, political attributions. Cock follows careers of two lords who gradually rose in system at turn of 17th century, when Inca decimal system could still be traced. Settlements controlled by these lords are being located in various ecological zones in ways inadequately described by Murra. Cock stresses need to redefine territoriality in Andes.

2035. Collapiña, Supno and others. Relación de la descendencia, gobierno y conquista. Edited by Juan José de la Vega. Lima, The Author, 1975? 1 v. (Unpaged)

One of earliest attempts to formally record dynastic oral tradition in Cuzco took place in 1542, 10 years after the fall of the Inca. Usually this account is listed under Vaca de Castro, governor who ordered record collected. Vega adds essay evaluating material.

2036. Condarco Morales, Ramiro. Reflexiones acerca del eco-sistema vertical andino (Avances [Revista boliviana de estudios históricos y sociales, La Paz] 1, 1978, p. 65-74, bibl.)

Outlines steps followed by author as he independently figured out several Andean macro-adaptations before and after Inca period. Beginning with "zonas transversales de complementación," Andean states were able eventually to bring them together "en sentido de dirección longitudinal." Compares this with Murra's "archipiélago."

2037. Cook, Noble David. Les indiens immigrés à Lima au début du XVIIe siècle (CDAL, 13/14, 1976, p. 35-50, bibl., illus., map)

Earliest 17th-century censuses reveal that Andean population was no more than a tenth of 14,000 who inhabited Lima. Europeans were just below 40 percent and blacks a few above that figure. Most of Andean population were remnants of local central coastal groups. Others came from the northern highlands and a few hundred from the north coast. But there were also some from Chile and Argentina and one Mexican. Some of the men were traders and artisans; many of the women domestic workers. The mortality of Andean migrants was higher than that of any other ethnic group.

2038. ———. La población de la Parroquia de Yanahuara, 1738-1947: un modelo para el estudio de las parroquias coloniales peruanas (in Pease G.Y., Franklin ed. Collaguas I [see item 2098] p. 13-34)

As early as the dates covered by this study, Arequipa attracted many migrants from the countryside, in this case Collaguas province. As close as Yanahuara was to the city, it was overwhelmingly an indigenous community; some of its inhabitants in 1740 were from as far away as Cuzco and Puno.

2039. ———. La visita de Conchucos por Cristóbal Ponce de León: 1543 (PMNH/HC, 10, 1976/1977, p. 23-45, bibl., map)

Some of earliest visitas were those ordered by Vaca de Castro, soon after Francisco Pizzaro's death, to help reassign encomiendas which had become vacant. Since this event took place long before reducciones of Toledo, it permitted location of 77 settlements, many of them depopulated by viceroy. Cook notes that individual towns housed populations belonging to as many as three ethnic groups, which European administrators, following at first Andean criteria, entrusted to separate encomenderos. Actual inspection was conducted by local Andean lords assigned to ethnic groups not their own. Stress of information is demographic, with cultural details.

2040. Crespo, Juan Carlos. Los collaguas en la visita de Alonso Fernández de Bonilla (in Pease G.Y., Franklin ed. Collaguas I [see item 2098] p. 53-91, bibl.)

In post-Toledan times a general inspection of the Peruvian viceroyalty was carried out in 1588-94. The population here was high and rich in herds, which began attracting merchants since the zone was not too far from the mining country though not directly involved in the *mita* to Potosí. The commercial activities of royal functionaries and private entrepreneurs are recorded. Good information on camelid herding and trading.

2041. Cuadros, Juan José. Informe etnográfico de Collaguas: 1974-1975 (*in* Pease G.Y., Franklin *ed.* Collaguas I [see item 2098] p. 35-53, bibl.)

Aboriginal pattern of zonal complementarity has endured until our time in the Collaguas region. Cuadros surveys rights maintained until today both in pastures and lower lying areas, including the coast.

2042. Dumézil, Georges and **Pierre Duviols.** Sumaq T'ika: la princesse du village sans eau (SA/J, 63, 1974/1975, p. 15-198)

There is an old tradition in the Cuzco area: using Quechua for sermons or dramatic representation. Some 25 years ago Dumézil collected such texts during his stay in Cuzco and he offers here a catalogue he compiled at the time. One play, written by Nicanor Jara is reproduced in full with inter-linear translation; it is supposed to deal with events before the European invasion. Where possible songs, speeches and texts have been traced to sources Jara borrowed them from. All this to p. 153. Includes textual translation from the Quechua.

2043. Duviols, Pierre. Une petite chronique retrouvée: *Errores, ritos, supersticiones y ceremonias de los yndios de la provincia de Chinchaycocha y otras del Piru* (SA/J, 63, 1974/1976, p. 275-297, bibl.)

Texts collected early in the 17th century in a region near Lake Chinchaycocha, dept. of Pasco, found by Duviols in Jesuit archives at the Vatican. Details on herding, the cultivation of *maca* and rituals connected with these activities.

2044. ———. Punchao: ídolo mayor del Coricancha, historia y tipologíia (Antropología Andina [Cuzco, Perú] 1/2, 1976, p. 156-183, bibl., illus.)

Detailed comparison of what many sources dealing with solar cult of Incas had to say about Sun's image kept at Coricancha, in Cuzco. Caution is particularly needed when dealing with 17th-century works by Andean authors who had reason to manipulate not only the oral tradition about ancient religion but also written works that came their way. The image was taken by resisting Incas to their refuge in Vilcabamba and was captured along with resisters in 1572. Duviols reconstructs the image from sources he trusts: it was golden and shared many features with known figures in Andean iconography. Duviols wonders about changes in such "idols" perpetrated in each Inca reign.

2045. ———. Quelques caractères actuels de l'ethno-histoire andine (SA/J, 63, 1974/1976, p. 11-13)

In preparing the centenary meeting of the International Congress of Americanists held in Paris, 1976, the *Journal de la Société des Americanistes* (vol. 63) prepared a special issue most of which deals with Andean religion both ancient and contemporary. In this introduction Duviols points to frequent neglect of philologic and other "internal" dimensions in our use of 16th and 17th-century European sources.

2046. ———. Sumaq T'ika ou la dialectique de la dependence (SA/J, 63, 1974/1976, p. 153-198)

Compares in several sources themes of water shortage and competition between several suitors to provide irrigation to Sumaq T'ika's village. Duviols relates such legends to the dynastic shift in Inca history when it is assumed that the lower, agricultural moiety supplanted the pastoral one. Using the state's ability to mobilize energies, irrigation works are sponsored throughout highlands. Relation between high puna herders who also had ample water but were willing to bargain over some of it in exchange for land, and particularly maize lands, with the cultivators, is examined in illuminating detail.

2047. Espinoza Soriano, Waldemar. Los cuatro suyos del Cuzco: siglo XV y XVI (IFEA/B, 6:3/4, 1977, p. 109-122, bibl., maps)

In 1577, descendants of royal lineages in Cuzco region petitioned to regain rights threatened by viceroy Toledo's policies. In passing, this provides new listing of settlements in each of four *suyu* within a 55-km radius of Inca capital and includes "Incas de privilegio." This listing contradicts previous assignment of particular towns to one or another *suyu*. It also suggests that name of Inca state was Taguansuyo, not Tawantinsuyu. Espinoza accepts this amendment but does not indicate his reasons.

2048. ———. Ichoc Huanuco y el Señorío del Curaca Huanca en el Reino de Huánuco: siglos XV y XVI (UNCP/AC, 4, 1975, p. 7-70, bibl., maps)

Starting with an unpublished *visita* of 1549, author brings together materials suggesting existence of Yaro, a pre-Inca state, centered on camelid herding and of Aymara of *llacuaz* hegemony. Revises errors of ethnic identification committed by Murra; condemns use of terms like "pisos ecológicos" and proposes instead an Andean terminology which one wishes were true.

2049. ———. Los mitmas de Nasca en Ocoña, Vitor y Camaná, siglos XV y XVI: una tasa inédita de 1580 para la etnohistoria andina (IFEA/B, 5:1/2, 1976, p. 85-95, bibl., tables)

Continuing his studies of populations displaced by the Inca, Espinoza reproduces brief *tasa* of Viceroy Toledo showing that people from Nasca had been resettled to the south, in the valleys of Arequipa. Unfortunately the text does not state their functions in either context.

2050. ———. La pachaca de Pariamarca en el reino de Caxamarca: siglos XV-XVIII (PMNH/HC, 10, 1976/1977, p. 135-180, bibl.)

Decimal nomenclature survived in this northern part of Perú until 19th century. This long period allows us to follow political and ethnic realignments. Espinoza also suggests that this decimal system was pre-Incaic in this region, and was adapted by Cuzco to their own ends. Primary sources reproduced deal with litigation over subdivision in colonial times.

2051. Falchetti, Anna María and Clemencia Plazas de Nieto. El territorio de los muiscas a la llegada de los españoles. Bogotá, Univ. de los Andes, Comité de Publicaciones, 1973. 65 p., fold. map (Cuadernos de antropología, 1)

Uses archival, toponymic and archaeological data in an effort to delimit territories of peoples called "Chibcha" in the literature. Most of them were included in two *señoríos* but some had managed to maintain independence. Interesting methodologically. Also published in *Razón y Fábula* (Univ. de los Andes, Bogotá, No. 30, sept./dic. 1972, p. 39-65).

2052. Fuenzalida Vollmar, Fernando. El mundo de los gentiles y las tres eras de la creación (Revista de la Universidad Católica [Lima] 2, 1977, p. 59-84, bibl.)

Syncretic myth about pre-Christian population, prevalent in various parts of Andes, is related to both European and Andean antecedents. Europeans live in time of the Son, gentiles in that of Father, when weaving and agriculture were introduced. Since they were incestuous, gentiles were punished. Third era is still to come. Fuenzalida traces two historical traditions which were joined in the Andes.

2053. Galdós Rodríguez, Guillermo. Visita a Atico y Caravelí (PEAGN/R, 4/5, 1975/1976, p. 55-80)

Ever since Marie Helmer published text of an inspection of the Chupaychu of Huánuco in 1955, fragments of this visita have been located in various repositories. This is first text located for populations south of Lima. These inhabitants of the coast had been in touch with sea traffic in *spondylus* from the warm waters to the north; they were also linked as metal workers to the Inca state. Visita's text is unfortunately brief: seven p.

2054. Garcia, Albert. La découverte et la conquête du Pérou, d'après les sources originales. Paris, Klincksieck, 1975. 778 p.

2055. Gentile Lafaille, Margarita E. Los Yauyos de Chaclla pueblos y ayllus: siglo XVIII (IFEA/B, 6:3/4, 1977, p. 85-107, bibl., illus., map)

One advantage of reproducing 16th-century *visitas* and litigation records is that these precipitate finding and use of other, sometimes lesser sources, which might otherwise escape detailed scrutiny. The Yauyu, living in mountains above Lima were object to unusual interest at first (see *HLAS* 29:2137b). Later, it waned as numbers shrank. However, later changes in political and economic structure deserve notice. Gentile used records of disputes over irrigation to trace fate of various ayllu and other ethnic subdivisions.

2056. Golte, Jürgen. Bauern in Peru. Berlin, FRG, Ibero-Amerikanisches Institut, 1973. 325 p., bibl., illus., maps, plates (Indiana, 1)

Major effort to encompass peasant life in the Andes from Inca times to present. Pre-European part is based on both published and primary sources. Review of demographic data throughout four centuries. Ethnographic material based on author's own fieldwork.

2057. ———. Modo de producción asiático y el estado inca (Nueva Antropología [México] 1:3, 1976, p. 71-84, bibl., illus., tables)

One of achievements of Inca times is fuller and more thorough utilization of all ecologic tiers. Another was grouping of agricultural tasks according to state calender which resulted in movement of large groups of people according to Cuzco's needs. Golte distinguishes several kinds of reciprocity, involving local ethnic and state adaptations of this principle. Important segments of population were transferred to full time state activities. The combination of such village self-sufficiency with an active state qualify the Inca economy for the "Asiatic" label. Still, Golte wonders if the state's continual intervention in local economic production did not change village self-sufficiency to the point where the Asiatic notion no longer applied. Surplus was produced and directed at Cuzco. Golte surveys ideas of Metraux and Godelier, who thought Marx's Asiatic classification was appropriate, and concludes that "el origen de la sociedad clasista inca se encuentra en el desarrollo particular de las fuerzas productivas en las sociedades andinas y no en la expansión militar." Hence, the concept does not fit well. Important analytic piece.

2058. Gómez, Tomás. Un aspect de l'exploitation du travail indigène en Nouvelle Grande au XVI siècle: le portage (SA/J, 64, 1977, p. 89-106, bibl., map)

Describes use of native Americans as bearers in colony's early period. Author notes mortality ensuing from the practice and royal attempts to prohibit it but tells us little about its effect on the social organization of the peoples of Nueva Granada.

2059. Grohs, Waltraud. Los indios del Alto Amazonas del siglo XVI al siglo XVIII. Bonn, FRG, Univ. Bonn, Seminar für Volkerkunde, 1974. 133 p., bibl., maps (Bonner Amerikanistische Studien, 2)

Study based primarily on missionary sources. Grohs tries to locate the ethnic groups of Maynas, such as the Cocama, Omagua and or the Mayoruna and emphasizes their fate in *reducciones*, and mission stations. Demographic data available are tabulated up to the expulsion of the Jesuits.

2060. Guillén Guillén, Edmundo. Documentos inéditos para la historia de los incas de Vilcabamba: la capitulación del gobierno español con Titu Cusi Yupanqui (PMNH/HC, 10, 1976/1977, p. 47-93, bibl., illus.)

Following up on his analysis of reasons why European victory was so easy (see *HLAS 36:1405*), Guillén accumulates evidence on internal factionalism. Hauscar faction of Cuzco royal house was interested in Atahuallpa's death; later they yielded control of capital to establish a "neo-Inca" regime in exile, in eastern lowlands. For next three decades they tried to organize resistance, using both diplomacy and adaptation of European weapons. Primary materials reproduced document a moment in diplomatic negotiations.

2061. Hamilton, Roland C. Americanismos en las obras del padre Bernabé Cobo. Madrid, The Author, 1976. 41 p., maps.

Authorized precis of doctoral dissertation clarifying, from dictionaries and other printed sources, meaning of Quechua and other Amerindian words in Cobo's classic.

2062. Huertas Vallejo, Lorenzo. La revista de los Chocorbos de 1683. With archaeological appendix by Enrique González Carré. Ayacucho, Peru, Univ. Nacional de San Cristóbal de Huamanga, 1976. 157 p.

The Duke of La Palata was a viceroy eager to learn more about his domain and ready to implement fundamental changes in the tribute system by changing the definition of the *tributario* (see *HLAS 36:1439*). In this document his order to determine who was liable to work in the mines of Huancavélica leads to detailed inspection. Most revealing data is on the decomposition of the encomienda system. People from as far away as Cuzco and Castrovirreina are enumerated.

2063. Jijón y Caamaño, Jacinto. Las culturas andinas de Colombia. Bogotá, Biblioteca Banco Popular, 1974. 307 p. (Publicación, 60)

Published posthumously in Quito, 1956, most of this work deals with archaeological matters. But since Jijón was a strong advocate of the Chibcha affiliations of the population of his own country, Ecuador, he had a better knowledge than most of Colombian ethnohistory. Ch. 6, the most relevant here, was obviously put together from Jijón's reading notes on primary sources. Those familiar with his work on Ecuador will find the same care and erudition here.

2064. Lara, Jesús. El Tawantinsuyu. 2. ed. rev. Cochabamba, Bolivia, Los Amigos del Libro, 1973. 399 p.

Second ed., somewhat revised of *HLAS 29:2164*.

2065. Larraín Barros, Horacio. Apuntes para un estudio de la población del corregimiento de Otavalo a fines del siglo XVI (Sarance [Instituto Otavaleño de Antropología, Otavalo, Ecua.] 3:1, 1977, p. 63-82, illus., maps)

Based on published source, an effort is made to calculate the population, late in the 16th century. Here, as elsewhere in the Andes, depopulation was severe. Includes convenient listing of encomiendas, who granted them and population recorded.

2066. ———. La población indígena de Tarapacá entre 1538 y 1581 (UCC/NG, 1:3/4, 1975, p. 269-300, bibl., maps)

Utilizing encomienda grants made by Pizarro to his nephew and to Martínez Vegaso in the Arequipa region (as Europeans called the Kuntisuyu quarter of the Inca state) Larraín tries to estimate the population of the area. Fishermen, desert agriculturists, highland and oasis dwellers were granted together. Evidence is provided for considerable movement of populations in both pre- and post-European times.

Llagostera Martínez, Agustín. Hipótesis sobre la expansión incaica en la vertiente occidental de los Andes meridionales.

See *HLAS 39:831*.

2067. Lohmann Villena, Guillermo. El Licenciado Francisco Falcón: 1521-87; vida, escritor y actuación en el Perú de un procurador de indios (EEHA/AEA, 27, 1970, p. 131-194, bibl.)

Somehow this important reevaluation of Falcón's work escaped earlier notice and was not included in

HLAS. Main conclusion: the well-known *Representación de los daños y molestias que se hacen a los indios* was written not for the third Concilio in Lima (1583), but almost 20 years earlier, for the second gathering. Falcón tried to attend it but was denied entry. Lesser known works are also considered, along with biographical detail. A critic of Indian policy, Falcón challenged veracity of authors like Polo and wisdom of viceroy Toledo. Appendix includes several letters to Philip II, on Andean religion and treatment of aboriginal population.

2068. Lorenzi, Mónica de and **Pío P. Díaz.** La influencia incaica en el noroeste argentino: sector norte (Estudios de Arqueología [Salta, Arg.] 2, 1977, p. 45-57, bibl.)

While most of this report is a site catalogue, some field notes on Inca roads crossing this area are included. Notes how some settlements continued into Inca times about where they had always been while others were created and affected by the Inca highways. The museum at Cachi has published separately maps of the area, indicating some of the roads.

2069. Lucena Salmoral, Manuel. El indofeudalismo chibcha, como explicación de la fácil conquista quesadista: consecuencias de una penetración por el Magdalena hasta la provincia de Metha (*in* Jornadas Americanistas, III, Valladolid, Spain, 1974. Estudios sobre política indigenista en América [see item 2298] v. 1, p. 111-160, plates)

Having reached the stage of "tribal confederation," the Muisca were much easier to defeat than less centralized folk. "Feudalism" when used in this context refers to vocabulary of Jiménez de Quesada and other early observers who saw some local leaders subjected and giving tribute to others. Makes ample use of Broadbent (see *HLAS 29:2141*).

2070. Macera, Pablo. El indio visto por los criollos y españoles (*in* Macera, Pablo. Trabajos de historia. Lima, Instituto Nacional de la Cultura, 1977, v. 2, p. 317-324)

Whereas earlier centuries stressed justice toward and conversion of the Andean population, in the 18th there appeared persons who advocated radical reform of status of Andean population, even if they were convinced that society was ethnically dual. Only with independence approaching does a group proclaim "no esperemos su desesperación..."

2071. ———. El indio y sus intérpretes, peruanos del siglo XVIII (*in* Macera, Pablo. Trabajos de historia. Lima, Instituto Nacional de Cultura, 1977, v. 2, p. 303-316)

Originally published in 1964, this reprint lists foreign and criollo observers of Andean archaeology, languages and the arts. Bishop Martínez de Compañón of Trujillo and Pedro Nolasco Crespo of La Paz, the journal *Mercurio Peruano*, and several derivative historians of the Inca characterize this period, before independence.

2072. Málaga Medina, Alejandro. Los collaguas en la historia de Arequipa en el siglo XVI (*in* Pease G.Y., Franklin ed. Collaguas I [see item 2098] p. 93-129, bibl.)

Rich in herds, the Collaguas were divided early among several encomenderos, including Gonzalo Pizarro. Later shifts included their resettlement, utilization of many as *mitimaes* in the city of Arequipa and in the mines. Early colonial history is traced in some detail, with good, first-hand references. Eventually region of Collaguas was separated from Arequipa and administered by own corregidores.

2073. Marzal, Manuel M. Una hipótesis sobre la aculturación religiosa andina (Revista de la Universidad Católica [Lima] 2, 1977, p. 95-131, bibl.)

Was prompt baptism of Andean population after 1532 just superficial accommodation or more profound phenomenon? Various opinions are surveyed, including modern ones as well as those of participants in process, particularly those undertaking "extirpación de las idolatrías" in 17th century. Marzal offers periodization of conversion process, with stress on post-1650 events, when pre-European past was far enough away. Primary sources used throughout.

2074. Mendoza, Angela. Indianische Bauern in Zentralkolumbien, Gutavita-Tuá (AI/A, 71:5/6, 1976, p. 768-805, bibl., maps, tables)

The Pijao were a Carib-speaking group, known to have given trouble to the colonial administration. Their descendants, living in the state of Tolima, are almost completely acculturated to Colombian peasant status. Settlement pattern, farming and alcoholic beverages were the only activities in which Mendoza could discern continuities with ethnohistoric accounts.

2075. Meyers, Albert. Die Inka in Ekuador. Bonn, FRG, Univ. Bonn, Seminar für Volkerkunde, 1976. 200 p., illus., maps (Bonner Amerikanistische Studien, 6)

While most of the study deals with material remains, Meyers is familiar with ethnohistorical materials from the northern periphery of the Inca state. The azuay "Knot" was a serious ecological and cultural barrier to Cuzco's spread northwards. Tumipampa was a much greater administrative center than Quito. On the basis of the material culture, an attempt is made to chronologize the southern occupation and the known resistance of local groups. Brings together much dispersed and inaccessible material.

2076. Millones, Luis comp. La religión andina: estudios y estudiosos de una difícil pregunta (Revista de la Universidad Católica [Lima] 2, 1977, p. 5-24, bibl.)

Annotated bibliography.

2077. Mörner, Magnus. Continuidad y cambio en una provincia del Cuzco: Calca y Lares desde los años 1680 hasta los 1790 (PMNH/HC, 9, 1975 [i.e. 1977] p. 79-117, bibl., map)

Late in the colonial regime the Bourbon administration collected abundant detail about Andean matters, distinguishing peasant from hacienda data. Mörner thought this a good starting point for a study of a micro-region near Cuzco, in the century before the Tupac Amaru rebellion. During this period, demographic change was favorable, despite epidemics; prices for a variety of crops were comparable; there was ample food; and haciendas flourished. The background for later, major changes is indicated.

Mora Mérida, José Luis. La población indígena paraguaya no reducida. See item 3291.

Moraes, Agueda Vilhena de. A ocupação humana na região Pedro Leopoldo e Lagoa Santa, Minas Gerais: prehistória, etnologia e colonização. See HLAS 39:787.

2079. Morales, Adolfo de. Reparto de tierras por el Inca Huayna Capac. Commentary by Geraldine B. de Caballero. Cochabamba, Bolivia, Univ. de San Simón, Museo de Arqueología, 1977. 18 p., bibl., map.

In the course of reorganizing the municipal archives, Morales came across a brief but exceptional account of how the aboriginal population of this rich valley was deported by the Inca. The valley was then divided into quadrants and each of these into 16 *suyu* planted to maize. No one was resettled into valley but many altiplano groups sent people down on rotation to cultivate the state's grain, which was deposited in Paria administrative center. The find of the year.

2080. Moreno, Fulgencio R. Geografía etnográfica del Chaco. Asunción, Instituto Colorado de Cultura, 1975. 302 p., illus.

Author (b. 1872, d. 1933) left us his impressions of the Chaco in the early part of this century and before the war with Bolivia. Historical observations about the inhabitants are sandwiched throughout.

2081. Moreno Cebrián, Alfredo. El Corregidor de Indios y la economía peruana en el siglo XVIII. Madrid, Instituto Gonzalo Fernández de Oviedo, 1977. 801 p., bibl., illus., tables.

The forced distribution of consumer goods by the *corregidores* among the Andean population is re-examined in great detail. Role of Lima wholesalers who supplied the goods and that of the Andean lords who enforced distribution at local level are stressed. Even abolition of *corregidor*'s job after Tupac Amaru's rebellion did not end the forced *reparto*. Good use of primary quantitative sources.

2082. ———. El intento de reinstaurar los repartos de mercancías a los indios del Perú: Don Jorge de Escovedo y Alarcón (PMNH/HC, 10, 1976/1977, p. 119-134, bibl.)

Mountjoy, Joseph B. Cultural change, archaeology and inference: an Inca example. See HLAS 39:963.

2083. Muro Romero, Fernando. El *Tocuyrico* en los pueblos de indios del Perú según Juan de Matienzo (in Jornadas Americanistas, III, Valladolid, Spain, 1974. Estudios sobre política indigenista española en América [see item 2298] v. 1, p. 305-312)

Analysis of suggestion made by Matienzo (see HLAS 29:2165b) that colonial administration call some of its Andean officials by Inca name. Suggestions did not prosper.

2084. Murra, John V. La correspondencia entre un "Capitán de la Mita" y su apoderado en Potosí (PMNH/HC, 3, 1978, p. 45-58, bibl.)

Early in 18th century lords from Andean altiplano had extensive investments in mines where they frequently transacted business. Successfully completing mita was only one aspect of their work. This correspondence documents commercial transactions in which they availed themselves of their privileges in Andean economic system to obtain commercial participation and advantages. Based on primary materials in Sucre's National Archives.

2085. ———. Los límites y las limitaciones del archipiélago vertical en los Andes (in Niemeyer, Hans ed. Homenaje al Dr. Gustavo Le Paige. Antofagasta, Chile, Univ. del Norte, 1976, p. 141-146)

Concerned with use made by both archaeologists and ethnologists of his "archipiélago" hypothesis (see *HLAS 34:1195*), author attempts to show its probable geographical limits and structural limitations.

2086. ———. La organización económica del estado Inca. México, Siglo XXI Editores, 1978. 270 p., bibl. (Serie América nuestra, 11)

Spanish translation of a thesis defended in 1955 at the Univ. of Chicago.

2087. ——— and **Craig Morris.** Dynastic oral tradition, administrative records, and archaeology in the Andes (World Archaeology [London] 7:3, 1976, p. 269-279, bibl., illus., maps)

Contrasts different archaeological techniques to be used when information analyzed is part of local or of dynastic oral tradition. With examples from authors' own research.

2088. **Mustapha, Monique.** Encore le *Parecer de Yucay*: essai d'attribution (IAA, 3:2, 1977, p. 215-229, bibl.)

The "Toledan" view of Inca statecraft as recent and illegal, hence "tyrannical" and not comparable to legitimate governments is well known. The viceroy thought this point inadequately understood at the highest levels in Spain because of Las-Casist propaganda. A long-familiar document, the *Parecer de Yucay*, offered this argument in detail; its author was unknown (see *HLAS 29:2137c*). Mustapha has located a letter of the viceroy which identifies the writer as his first cousin, the Dominican García de Toledo.

Myazaki, Nobue. Arqueo-etno-história no Brasil. See *HLAS 39:788*.

2089. **Oberem, Udo.** Los cañaris y la conquista española de la sierra ecuatoriana: otro capítulo de las relaciones interétnicas en el siglo XVI (SA/J, 63, 1976/1975, p. 263-274, bibl.)

Among ethnic groups backing the European invasion against the Inca, were the Cañari, inhabitants of what is today southern Ecuador. They contacted Pizarro personally and later helped in the invasion of the north. They also helped break sieges of Cuzco and Lima by the Inca armies. As years passed, they lost privileged status of allies to become another group of "Indians." Oberem traces the change from fervent allies of the invaders to participants in some of the early rebellions against Spanish rule.

2090. **Ossio, Juan.** Las 5 [i.e. cinco] edades del mundo según Felipe Guaman Poma (Revista de la Universidad Católica [Lima] 2, 1977, p. 43-58, bibl., tables)

Wonders if four of five "ages" into which Guaman Poma and other sources divided Andean history is autochtonous or imported. Since there is evidence for both a cyclical and a lineal conception of history, Ossio suggests that there were two models for measuring time: one cosmological, another genealogical. Ossio then relates four-fold division of history to quadripartite organization of Inca state, all of which tends to support notion that Guaman Poma's classification is of Andean origin.

2091. ———. Guaman Poma y la historiografía indianista de los siglos XVI y XVII (PMNH/HC, 10, 1976/1977, p. 181-206, bibl.)

Relates "chronicles" by Europeans about Andes to peninsular tradition of recording the past. It was not enough to be edifying; New World's ways of life had to fit into accurate record of events and individual exploits. Guaman Poma was familiar with such works as well as dictionaries and catechisms published during first century of European rule. He thought of his own work as *new* account, because he stressed pre-Inca events and institutions. He regarded Inca rule as tyrannical and illegitimate, and in this Ossio thinks Poma was reflecting European administrative arguments.

2092. ———. Myth and history: the seventeenth-century chronicle of Guaman Poma de Ayala (*in* Jain, Ravindra K. *ed.* Text and context: the social anthropology of tradition. Philadelphia, Pa., Institute for the Study of Human Issues, 1977, p. 51-93, bibl., illus.)

Difficulties encountered by today's historian who wishes to interpret oral traditions conveyed in Guaman Poma's work are similar to those he faced in interpreting European chronologies and events. Historiographic traditions converging in his *Nueva coronica* were too dissimilar. Ossio suggests that a better title would be *Carta al Rey*, since it was first Philip II and later the III who were the readers Guaman Poma had in mind.

2093. **Paz Ballivián, Danilo.** Ocho hipótesis de José Antonio Arze sobre el Incario (Avances [Revista boliviana de estudios históricos y sociales, La Paz] 1, 1978, p. 81-90, bibl.)

In the 1930s, Arze began studying the Inca state from the perspective of historical materialism. His conclusions were published in *Sociografía del Incario* (1952), where he determined that the Cuzco regime was at the stage of middle barbarism. Article offers a detailed paraphrase of Arze as well as an analysis of his "mistakes."

2094. Pease G.Y., Franklin. Collaguas: una etnía del siglo XVI: problemas iniciales (*in* Pease G.Y., Franklin *ed.* Collaguas I [see item 2098] p. 131-167, bibl.)

Lead article of compilation explaining how study was organized around presence of 1591 *visita* of the Collaguas, found in the Museum of History while Pease was its director. Material for the second half of the 16th century is abundant: population decreased but there were plenty of hands and much wealth in herds, terraces, local mines and coastal holdings. Article examines evidence for complementary access to several micro-climates, early religious syncretism and contacts with ethnic groups and their lords in the Titicaca area.

2095. ———. Del Tawantinsuyu a la historia del Perú. Introduction by Heraclio Bonilla. Lima, Instituto de Estudios Peruanos, 1978. 245 p., bibl. (Serie historia andina, 5)

Collection of four articles, two reprinted and noted earlier (see *HLAS 36:1425* and item 2094) and two new ones, especially prepared for this volume. First one attempts major reevaluation of what we know or guess about formation and expansion of the Inca state. It uses classical sources and charts four of them for comparative purposes; it takes into serious account administrative sources, seen by some as irrelevant for understanding the state. But Pease's specialty has been and still is the ideological component, such as the solar cult sponsored by Cuzco and its role in state formation and management. Final article, "Derroteros Andinos," raises the issue of the Andean dimension in the writing of Peruvian history. Emphasis is placed on changes in population density and growth of cities in first decade of European rule; shifts and adaptations in colonial policy to growing poverty of countryside and mines; background to great rebellions of the 18th century; and Andean participation in the wars of Independence.

2096. ———. Etno-historia andina: un estado de la cuestión (PMNH/HC, 10, 1976/1977, p. 207-228, bibl.)

Although chroniclers were used to writing about men and events, an ethno-history does not appear in Peru until Tello and Valcárcel tried to connect written sources with archaeology. Pease surveys later efforts of Rowe, Rostworowski, Espinoza, Zuidema, Guillén and his own, in providing both new data and interpretations. Read at Mexican gathering, article provides useful introduction to the field.

2097. ———. Las versiones del mito de Inkarri (Revista de la Universidad Católica [Lima], 2, 1977, p. 25-41, bibl.)

In 1950s Arguedas and other fieldworkers began recording a message from remote past and rephrasing it for our times. Old lords and old gods had been defeated but some thought they might return in a new guise. Pease hopes to use these various versions to gain an insight into the past. While all versions begin with Atahuallpa's death, texts can differ in their emphasis on messianic or nostalgic elements. Pease stresses their affiliation with ethnic groups identifiable both before and after fall of Inca state.

2098. ——— *ed.* Collaguas I. Lima, Univ. Católica, 1977. 487 p., bibl., maps.

Collection of texts and commentaries all dealing with the Collagua, an ethnic group inhabiting the Colca river valley, and covering most of the first century after the invasion, though some population figures are for later times. Most of the studies in the volume are based on a primary document found by Pease (see item 2094): *Visita de Yanquecollaguas* (Urinsaya, 1591) and transcribed in its entirety (p. 191-452, map). A major new source.

2099. Platt, Tristan. Acerca del sistema tributario pretoledano en el Alto Perú (Avances [Revista boliviana de estudios históricos y sociales, La Paz] 1, 1978, p. 33-46, bibl., tables)

Although viceroy Toledo systematized forms and extent of tribute after 1572, before his arrival the Andean population had extensive experience with the demands of the European administration. Platt compares two tribute lists from the 1950s concerning the same population and compares them with taxation imposed on neighboring groups. Also analyzes use of ethnic lords as "mecanismos de transferencia de los excedentes producidos dentro del regimen comunitario a los mercados coloniales."

2100. ——— and **Silvia Rivera Cusicanqui.** El impacto colonial sobre un pueblo pakaxa: la crisis del cacicazgo en Caquingora, Urinsaya, durante el siglo XVI (Avance [Revista boliviana de estudios históricos y sociales, La Paz] 1, 1978, p. 7-27)

Succession disputes provide rich source material on Andean political authority. Article offers evidence for fraternal, patrilateral and patrilineal succession but it is not easy to unravel how if any of the customs are pre-Incaic or Cuzco-influenced. Most important is the new access to family archives.

Polia, Mario. Investigaciones arqueológicas en la sierra de Piura. See *HLAS 39:972*.

2101. Ponce Sanginés, Carlos. Apuntes para el estudio de la demografía histórica de Tiwanaku durante el período colonial. La Paz, Instituto de Arqueología, 1975. 62 p., bibl., tables (Nueva serie, 9)

2102. ———. La cultura nativa en Bolivia, su entronque y sus rasgos principales (Illimani [La Paz] 8/9, 1976. p. 11-49, bibl.)

Ambitious attempt to go from earliest archaeological times to present. Aim: "señalar la problemática básica ... dejando del lado el pintoresquismo que empantana a los investigadores estranjeros."

2103. ———. La República Federal de los inkas: los protocolos de 1880. La Paz, Casa Municipal de la Cultura Franz Tamayo, 1975. 163 p. (Biblioteca paceña. Nueva serie)

Reprint of *protocolos* published in 1880.

Puigbó, Raúl. Los aborígenes argentinos: su aporte étnico y sociocultural. See *HLAS 39:1544*.

2104. **Rabell, Cecilia A.** and **Carlos Sempat Assadourian.** Self-regulating mechanisms of the population in a precolumbian society: the case of the Inca empire (*in* International Population Conference, Mexico, n.p., 1977, p. 25-42, bibl.)

Precolumbian population dispute does not take into account productive capacity of Andean societies. *Mit'a*'s rotating labor obligations to state are seen as limiting productivity by channeling it into public works, and other status chores. Wars are seen as serious limiting factors, forgetting fact that Inka army was made up of both women and men; but of course casualties did affect populations. Authors stress war as quick way to obtain new producers and reproducers. Provocative, extremely useful paper.

2105. **Real Cuesta, Javier.** Política lingüística en el Nuevo Reino de Granada durante los siglos XVI y XVII (*in* Jornadas Americanistas, III, Valladolid, Spain, 1974. Estudios sobre política indigenista española en América [see item 2298] v. 1, p. 279-302)

While literacy for sons of the local lords was favored early as part of conversion, most of it meant teaching in Spanish. At times suggestions for the use of local languages were made and Muisca was taught at one of the seminaries. Eventually arrival of Jesuits strengthened this point of view.

2106. **Rénique C., José Luis** and **Efraín Trelles A.** Aproximación demográfica: Yanque-Collaguas 1591 (*in* Pease G.Y., Franklin *ed.* Collaguas I [see item 2098] p. 169-189, bibl., tables)

Reviews problems affecting demographic studies of 16th century population; e.g., ages were counted differently in the Andes than in Europe; effect of depopulation whether as a result of epidemics or exactions; how to determine who were counted as widows or single; etc.

Rivera, Mario A. Una hipótesis sobre movimientos poblacionales altiplánicos y transaltiplánicos a las costas del norte de Chile. See *HLAS 39:849*.

2107. **Rivera Cusicanqui, Silvia.** El *mallku* y la sociedad colonial en el siglo XVII: el caso de Jesús de Machaca (Avances [Revista boliviana de estudios históricos y sociales, La Paz] 1, 1978, p. 7-27)

Last will and testament drawn up in 1673 by an Aymara lord indicates he was active and prosperous participant in colonial trading, not only executor of European orders. Some of his lands and herds were acquired by purchase, others were traditionally still tied to his office; he extended credit to both Aymara and Europeans. While not neglecting personal interest he also defended Aymara rights.

2108. **Rostworowski de Diez Canseco, María.** Algunos comentarios a las ordenanzas del Dr. Cuenca (PMNH/HC, 9, 1975 [i.e. 1977] p. 119-154, bibl.)

Early coastal sources are very few. Records of inspection conducted by Gregorio González de Cuenca in 1566-67 have not yet been located although a fragmentary fiscal summary was circulated in the North coast. In a brief introduction Rostworoski compares these ordenanzas with the later, better known edicts of Toledo. Much of the primary text consists of instructions about traditional authorities, succession, irrigation rights as well as men wearing their hair long or keeping edible dogs.

2109. ———. La estratificación social y el *hatun curaca* en el mundo andino (PUCP/H, 1:2, 1977, p. 249-286)

Discusses ethnic lords, their privileges, rules governing succession and their relation to both the Inca state and the colonial regime. Earliest dictionaries are carefully combed for all expressions relating to authority and servility. They reveal considerably more social complexity than usually assumed. A case in point are the lords of the Ica valley about whom author has found interesting new material. She compares it with information about some highland lords from Cajamarca. Author stresses many characteristics of political leadership which are pan-Andean.

2110. ———. Etnía y sociedad: costa peruana prehispánica. Lima, Instituto de Estudios Peruanos, 1977. 293 p., bibl. (Serie historia andina, 4)

Notable collection of six articles, all written since 1970 that convey author's concern with coastal Andean ethnic groups. Virtually all are based on primary sources located in Spanish and Peruvian repositories. Author stresses independence of coastal cultural development, long-distance coastwise traffic, social and occupational stratification. A major work.

2111. ———. El Señorío de Changuco, Costa Norte (IFEA/B, 5:1/2, 1976, p. 97-147, bibl., maps)

Primary sources on the North Coast are still so few that this record of a lawsuit over a small *señorío*, near Chanchán is notable and provides exceptionally useful data on ethnic lords and their privileges, the calendar, relations to highland populations, the craft organization of hamac carriers. A possible archaeological identification is discussed by Elías Mujica Barreda.

2112. ———. La "visita" a Chinchacocha de 1549 (UNCP/AC, 4, 1975, p. 73-88, bibl., map)

For a long time we had only a fragment (out of 72) of the inspection reports submitted to La Gasca in the 17th year of European rule. Population inspected lived in one of the highest parts of the Andes, near present-day Cerro de Pasco. They controlled not only herd and tubers near their settlements but also lands in the warm valley of Paucartambo. Rostworowski brings out importance of *maca* cultivation, a tuber grown almost nowhere else and a reputed aphrodisiac. Rostworowski promises additional data from its inspection.

2113. Ruiz Rivera, Julián. Las visitas a la tierra en el siglo XVII como fuente de historia social (*in* Jornadas Americanistas, III, Valladolid, Spain, 1974. Estudios sobre política indigenista en América [see item 2298] v. 1, p. 197-214)

Surveys utility of inspection records compiled in Colombia for demographic and social history. Verdict is favorable.

2114. Sánchez Albornoz, Nicolás. The population of Latin America: a history. Translated by W.A.R. Richardson. Berkeley, Univ. of California Press, 1974. 299 p., bibl., illus.

Efficient, thorough review of evidence beginning with estimates of pre-European times, through the prestatistical (1555-1774) and onto modern days. Various figures suggested in the past (A. L. Kroeber, Rosenblatt, Dobyns) are examined and supplemented with more local data (N.D. Cook, J. Friede, G. Colmenares). When discussing depopulation also previews effects of warfare, mines, loss of agricultural lands, epidemics and, finally, "the loss of the will to survive." See also *HLAS 38:2236*.

2115. Sharon, Douglas. The Inca *warachikuy* initiations (*in* Wilbert, Johannes *ed*. Enculturation in Latin America. An anthology. Los Angeles, Univ. of California, Latin American Center Publications, 1976, p. 359-375, bibl.)

Careful summary and comparison of Molina and Cobo's descriptions of ceremonies accompanying initiation of royal adolescents. For a whole month youths re-enacted events from dynastic tradition and were tested for hardy, military participation. Textiles were also exchanged and the crops encouraged as part of the ritual.

2116. Shea, Daniel E. A defense of small population estimates for the Central Andes in 1520 (*in* Denevan, William M. *ed*. The native population of the Americas in 1492 [see item 2279] p. 157-180, maps, tables)

Attempts to calculate Central Andean populations in 1520. Materials used are not best available and figure of less than two million is most likely too low.

2117. Solano, Francisco de. Política de concentración de la población indígena: objetivos, proceso, problemas, resultados (IGFO/RI, 36:145/146, 1976, p. 7-29)

As early as 1503 efforts were made to resettle the aboriginal Caribbean population. On the mainland, this effort to "destructurar" indigenous organization continued. *Pueblos de indios* were created. While most of the material deals with Mesoamerica, references are also given for the Andes.

2118. Taylor, Gerald. *Camay, camac* et *camasca* dans le manuscript quechua de Huarochiri (SA/J, 63, 1974/1976, p. 231-244, bibl.)

Previous commentators of this most important Quechua text in existence have assumed they knew the dialect it was written in. Taylor differs with earlier translators (see *HLAS 29:2137b, HLAS 32:1120*, and *HLAS 34:1204*) believing the language is an extinct Aymara-type language. Philologic comparisons required to gain access to text's real meaning is illustrated through analysis of root *cama-*, poorly understood by Spanish preaches. They interpreted *Camac* as the creator whereas in Quechua the word stands for the spirit (soul) which animates all things: animals, plants, individuals, each one had its prototype *camac* which imparted each being with its essence. Taylor suggests that "to create, to do" is one translation of verb *camay*. Garcilaso's rendering of it as: "to transmit vital forces, to protect a person or the thing which receives this force," is more accurate.

2119. Urton, Gary. Orientation in Quechua and Incaic astronomy (UP/E, 17:2, 1978, p. 157-167, bibl., maps, tables)

Following in the Zuidema tradition, Urton has inquired of contemporary informants and of 16th-century sources about representation of the heavens. Constellations were grouped around the Milky Way, seen as a river. The observatory was at the temple of the Sun, where two rivers met and where the four *suyu* into which the Andean world was divided into gathered. The Milky Way was also used to calculate solsitices.

2120. Villamarín, Juan A. Kinship and inheritance among the Sabana de Bogotá Chibcha at the time of Spanish Conquest (UP/E, 14:2, 1975, p. 173-179)

Chibcha were matrilineal. They married and lived virilocally until the husband's death when widow and children returned to her settlement. Land was inherited matrilineally and so was office. Study based on both primary and published data.

2121. Wankar [*pseud. for* Ramiro Reynaga Burgoa]. Tawantinsuyu: cinco siglos de guerra qheswaymara contra España. La Paz, Centro de Coordinación y Promoción Campesina Mink'a, 1977. 557 p., bibl., illus.

The past, present and future of Andean peoples. "No es secreción retocada de bibliotecas ni quiero matiz indigenista en debates intelectuales. No está dirigida a la minoría blancoide dueña exclusiva y tradicional de toda comunicación escrita. Ya bastantes hermanos qheswas y aymaras estan alfabetizados. Lo he escrito para ellos."

2122. Zevallos Quiñones, Jorge. La visita del pueblo de Ferreñafe—Lamba-

yeque—en 1568 (PMNH/HC, 9, 1975 [i.e. 1977] p. 155-178)

Ethnohistoric research on the coast expands, materials hidden or ignored begin to appear. This is a brief inquest mostly concerned with post-European phenomena: succession squabbles (at the time when population had diminished to a point of no return) and persistence of Andean cults or of artisans. A bonus is a list of personal names in the local, coastal language.

2123. Zuidema, R.T. La imagen del Sol y la Huaca de Susurpuquio en el sistema astronómico de los incas en el Cuzco (SA/J, 63, 1974/1976, p. 199-230, bibl., illus., maps)

Part of continuing study of Andean calendars, particularly those which were part of state solar cult. Shrine of Susurpuquio was related to June solstice and to harvest, being stored at that time. Here was where King Pachacuti met the "true Sun," believed to integrate in his being many of the classificatory contradictions of Inca cosmology.

2124. ———. The Inca calendar (*in* Aveni, A. *ed*. Native American astronomy. Austin, Univ. of Texas, 1977, p. 219-259, bibl.)

Why do we know so much less about Andean than Mesoamerican calendars? Zuidema thinks the reason may be that in Cuzco they were recorded on *quipus* "in terms of an abstract theory of political organization," the *ceque* system (see *HLAS 29:2206-2207*). Also, whereas in other areas calendrical records were graven in stone, in Andes they were frequently woven into textiles. Author urges us to distinguish a wide range of calendars, particularly agricultural, local ones from state, solar methods of reckoning. Astronomical time was measured from pillars that fitted into *ceque* shrine system. Ethnographic fieldwork by Zuidema and his students helped locate many of these shrines and observatories. They offer a basis for numerical analysis of textile calendars and their relation to *ceques*. Provocative paper; its utility to others has already been demonstrated.

HISTORY: GENERAL

DONALD E. CHIPMAN

Professor of History
North Texas State University

THE QUINCENTENNIAL OF BARTOLOMÉ DE LAS CASAS' birth has passed, and the extraordinary number of quality publications devoted to the Age of Exploration and Discovery has not been duplicated in materials examined for this biennium. In my estimation, the overall quality of items in this section suffers by comparison with those issued in the previous two-year period (see *HLAS 38*, p.118-151). I will however, single out two or three works of exceptional quality by any standard in each of the four subsections. At the suggestion of the *HLAS* Advisory Board, I have discontinued the long-established practice of listing tables of contents for multi-authored, edited works. Collected works have been annotated in a manner which will hopefully lead students and scholars to consult the complete compilation. I will conclude the introduction with comments on an especially noteworthy conference and on publications of an unusual nature.

In the first subsection entitled "General" and following this essay, Lester Langley (item 2190) presents a fine analysis of American-European competition in the Gulf-Caribbean from the American Revolution to the early 20th century; a visually attractive book by Hugh Honour (item 2177), complemented by astute observations and interpretations, examines European images of America; and a well-researched synthesis of the rise and decline of feudal systems in Mexico, Argentina, and Chile is the work of the distinguished economic historian, Marcello Carmagnani (item 2145).

Required reading and listed in the subsection entitled "Colonial" is a study by Burkholder and Chandler (item 2265) of royal practices in the selection of judges who served on American Audiencias in the late colonial era. Two works of extraordinary quality on exploration and discovery have appeared in this biennium. Louis-André Vigneras (item 2339) has done a great deal toward illuminating the "minor" Andalusian voyages at the turn of the 16th century which were a brief and unique free enterprise venture by Sevillan financiers and merchants. Particularly exciting is the recent discovery of the original manuscript of Thomas Cavendish, first published three and a half centuries ago. A first-rate introduction by David B. Quinn enhances this revealing account of Cavendish's second and fatal attempt to circumnavigate the globe (item 2319). Also a high merit is an excellent synthesis of the 18th century by Luis Navarro García (item 2307).

Likewise in the category of required reading in the subsection entitled "Independence and the 19th Century" is Timothy Anna's outstanding essay on the last viceroys of New Spain and Peru (item 2344). Anna is among the vanguard of current revisionism which argues persuasively that independence resulted from far more subtle and complex forces than counterrevolution. His article and forthcoming book by the Univ. of Nebraska Press and Doris Ladd's prize-winning *The Mexican nobility at Independence: 1780-1826* (which will be annotated in *HLAS 42*) are likely to become landmark studies.

The past two years have witnessed the premature death of Kalman Silvert. His *Essays in understanding Latin America* (item 2405) are more than required reading among the 20th-century materials. Written between 1966-76, they stand as a monument to a sensitive, scholar-gentlemen and are filled with accumulated wisdom. Also worthy of special note are Cole Blasier's examination of US responses to social revolutions in Mexico, Bolivia, Guatemala, and Cuba (item 2382), and Mark Gilderhus' study of US-Mexican relations under Presidents Woodrow Wilson and Venustiano Carranza (item 2390).

The outstanding edited work in the entire section is *The native population of the Americas in 1492* (item 2279). Articles by contributors are annotated in several sections of *HLAS*. Special attention is directed to a conference held in Germany, the IV Renunión de Americanistas Europeos (Oct. 1975). which examined European emigration to Latin America. The best of the published papers are by Annino (item 2128); Everaert (item 2160); Kellenbenz (item 2187); and Stang (item 2238). For exceptional research effort, recognition is accorded to Karst and Rosen (item 2183) and to the prodigious undertaking of Sister Agueda Rodríguez Cruz (item 2323). For a superb piece of writing and analysis, see Needler's *An introduction to Latin American politics* (item 2396).

I again wish to acknowledge continued support from the Faculty Research Committee of North Texas State Univ. Funds allocated by the Committee have provided me with the aid of Ms. Linda Purcell (1976) and the highly professional assistance of Ms. Michelle Mannering (1977).

GENERAL

2125. Acevedo, Oscar. Fray Bartolomé de las Casas en la interpretación de Carlos Pereyra (EEHA/AEA, 31, 1974, p. 1-32)

Author analyzes treatment of Las Casas in writings of Carlos Pereyra from 1920-45. Concludes that Pereyra presented more balanced view of bishop than is generally accepted, and that it is an injustice to categorize Pereyra as an antilascasian scholar.

2126. Anderson, Teresa J. *comp.* Agrarian reform in Latin America: an annotated bibliography. Madison, Univ. of Wisconsin Press, 1974. 667 p.

All materials listed in this bibliography are held by the Univ. of Wisconsin library system and are available for consultation on the Madison campus. Compilation was a staff project of university's Land Tenure Center Library.

2127. André-Vincent, Philippe. Derecho de los indios y desarrollo en Hispanoamérica. Traducción de Francisco Ortiz Chaparro. Madrid, Ediciones Cultura Hispánica, 1975. 186 p., bibl.

Rather impassioned study of rights of Indians as defined in Spanish and Portuguese law and of Christian missionaries in their capacity as protectors of native rights.

2128. Annino, Antonio. El debate sobre la emigración y la expansión a la América Latina en los orígenes de la ideología imperialista en Italia: 1861-1911 (JGSWGL, 13, 1976, p. 189-215)

Article focuses on political, ideological, and economic developments as they related to expansionism in post-unified Italy. Belief that Italian penetration of Latin America, especially La Plata, could be furthered by emigrants settling there lost favor because of inherent weaknesses in the Italian economy. This strengthened advocates of outright colonialism, secured by military presence, and reoriented Italian interest toward Africa.

2129. Arciniegas, Germán. América en Europa. B.A., Editorial Sudamericana, 1975. 335 p., bibl., facsims., plates, table.

Prolific Latin American historian offers a perspective glance at the impact of America on Europe, not the reverse. Arciniegas finds varied examples of American influences that range from the contagious phenomenon of independence, to utopias and Romanticism, to firsthand experiences of men such as Garibaldi and Tadeo Kosciuszko.

2130. ———. Este pueblo de América. México, Secretaría de Educación Pública, 1974. 195 p. (Col. SepSetentas, 142)

Not previously cited in *HLAS*, this broadly impressionistic portrait of the people of Latin America was originally published in 1562 under the title, *Cosas del pueblo*.

2131. ———. Historia verdadera del buen salvaje (VME/R, 32:209/211, agosto/oct. 1972, p. 104-116, illus.)

Author sees the "American" of all colors representing a romanticized view, as reflected in writings from Montaigne to Diderot and beyond, of the "buen salvaje" or "free man." Cuauhtémoc, Simón Bolívar, Benjamin Franklin, and Benito Juárez are seen as prototypes of the "Good Savage" in America.

2132. Ardao, Arturo. La idea de la Magna Colombia: de Miranda a Hostos (CELRG/A, 1975. p. 11-30)

Traces usage of "Colombia" as term applied to all Spanish (or in some cases Latin) America and implying strong sense of cultural and even political solidarity. Coined by Miranda in 1780s it gained wide currency in independence period, reappeared sporadically after demise of "Gran" Colombia. [D. Bushnell]

2133. Astesano, Eduardo B. Historia socialista de América. B.A., Editorial Relevo, 1973. 178 p., bibl., maps, table (Col. Praxis y liberación)

Brief synthesis, directed principally toward young adults, which portrays socialism as an economic system best suited for Third World nations. Also argues for including the history of Latin America's class struggles in broader works on world socialism.

2134. Bartley, Russell H. Masas y revolución en las colonias iberoamericanas: aproximación a un problema de historiografía moderna (UCP/IAP, 8, 1974, p. 85-110)

Wide range of writings in Russian, Spanish, and English is assessed by author. Bartley urges careful reexamination of generalizations about movements for Latin American independence. He further suggests research by Marxist historians, emphasizing socioeconomic factors as potentially fruitful if rigid formulas employed in the past are discarded.

2135. Becker, Félix and Horst Pietschmann. Indice del *Jahrbuch für Geschichte von Staat, Wirtschaft und Gessellschaft Lateinamerikas*: v. 1/11, 1964/1974 (EEHA/HBA, 18:2/3, julio/dic. 1974, p. 307-333)

Convenient guide to the contents of the *Jahrbuch* (i.e., *Year-book for the History of the State, Economy and Society of Latin America*) through vol. 11, especially for those whose German is limited. [M.T. Hamerly]

2137. Burns, E. Bradford. Latin America: a concise interpretive history. 2. ed. Englewood Cliffs, N.J., Prentice-Hall, 1977. 307 p., bibl., maps, plates, tables.

Revised and slightly expanded version of 1972 ed. (see *HLAS 34:1250*). Burns acknowledges that it incorporates changes in his views and interpretations which have evolved over the past five years.

2138. ———; **Eduardo Hernández;** and **Mary Karasch** eds. Teaching Latin American history. Los Angeles, Univ. of California, Office of Learning Resources, 1977. 65 p. (mimeo.) illus., plates.

Contains examples of successful, innovative teaching of Latin American history courses as well as essays on bibliography, historiography, and media.

2139. Buttrey, Theodore V., Jr. Coinage of the Americas. N.Y., The American Numismatic Society, 1973. 139 p., map, plates.

Narrative traces Western Hemisphere issuances of coins, primarily in the Spanish, British, and US traditions (though including brief accounts of Portuguese, Dutch, Swedish, Danish, and French mintings). Illustrated by hundreds of excellent plates.

2140. Calderón Quijano, José Antonio. Vigencia del término *Hispanoamérica*: discurso de apertura pronunciado en Sevilla el día 12 de octubre de 1973. Madrid, Consejo Superior de Investigaciones Científicas, Patronato José María Quadrado, 1974. 29 p., bibl.

Brief discussion of the concepts incorporated in the words *Indoamerica, Latinoamérica*, and *Hispanoamérica*. Author explains his preference for the latter.

2141. Capela, José. Escravatura: a empresa de saque o abolicionismo; 1810-1875. n.p., Edições Afrontamento, 1974. 305 p., bibl., illus. (Col. As armas e os varões, 3)

Attempt to set straight (after the Salazar era propaganda) the Portuguese role in African slave trade and slavery. Pleasantly abrasive and direct, if based on limited sources and not very theoretical. Does bring out the central role of slavery in the economy of the Portuguese colonies. [R.J. Barman]

2142. Cardoso, Ciro Flamarion S. and **Héctor Pérez Brignoli.** Dependencia y metodología de la historia en América Latina (UNCR/R, 1:2, 2. semestre 1976, p. 1-16)

Originally presented as paper at I Meeting of Latin American Historians in Mexico (1974), authors call for creation of formal organization to promote contacts and sharing of data and methodology among Latin American scholars investigating dependency.

2143. ——— and ———. Los métodos de la historia: introducción a los problemas, métodos y técnicas de la historia demográfica, económica y social. Presentación de Josef Fontana. Barcelona, Editorial Crítica, 1976. 433 p., tables.

This is neither a translation nor a general text, but an original manual by two Latin American researchers on how to quantify the demographic, economic and social history of Latin America. What Cardoso and Pérez Brignoli have done is to apply European, especially French and English, and North American methodologies and techniques to Latin American sources, emphasizing differences and similarities with countries which pioneered quantifying the past. Excellent discussion of sources and perceptive analysis of the lacunae in the literature. Also includes chapters on recent developments in history, comparative history and problems of synthesis as well as several helpful technical appendices. In brief, the kind of work book for Latin America which has long been needed. [M.T. Hamerly]

2144. Cardozo, Manoel da Silvera Soares *ed*. The Portuguese in America 590 B.C.-1974. Dobbs Ferry, N.Y., Oceana Publications, 1976. 154 p., bibl. (Ethnic chronology series, 22)

Curious handbook of chronology, brief studies, and two statistical charts relating to, with the exclusion of Brazil, the Portuguese in America. Publisher's carelessness resulted in pages being bound upside down and in reverse order.

2145. Carmagnani, Marcello. Formación y crisis de un sistema feudal: América Latina del siglo XVI a nuestros días. México, Siglo XXI Editores, 1976. 284 p., bibl., tables.

Well-researched synthesis by distinguished economic historian. Carmagnani analyzes the rise and decline of feudal systems in Latin America with case studies centering on Mexico, Argentina, and Chile. Bibliography is especially impressive, reflecting author's familiarity with a wide range of scholarly works in several languages. Includes 34 statistical charts which enhance the work.

2146. Carpizo, Jorge. Federalismo en Latino-américa. México, UNAM, Instituto de Investigaciones Jurídicas, 1973. 84 p., bibl., fold. table (Serie B, estudios comparativos. Derecho latinoamericano, 1)

Scholarly discussion of development of federalism in Argentina, Brazil, Mexico, and Venezuela. Author also compares aspects of federalism as reflected in the constitutional laws of those nations.

2146a. Carrocera, Buenaventura de. Proyecto de una historia general de la iglesia en América Latina (ISTM/MH, 31:92, p. 239-250)

Challenges professional integrity of Enrique Dussel's *Historia de la Iglesia en América Latina* (1972), and the project of CELAM's Comisión de Estudios de Historia de la Iglesia Latinoamericana. Disputes that it has undertaken a full, documented, scientific, general history of the role of the Catholic Church in Latin America.

2147. Castelo, Julio. The insurance market in Latin America, Portugal, and Spain. Translated by Hernán Troncoso Rojas; Sara Daniel de Wahr; Sue Carolie Hough; and Graham Bourne. Foreword by Ignacio H. de Larramendi. Athens, Univ. of Georgia Press, 1976. 159 p., tables.

Study provides statistical information primarily for South America and Mexico on insurance and their operations. Surveying each country, chapters contain lists of insurance institutions, brief histories of growth, guides to laws, taxes, investments, and corporate structure, and descriptions of overseas expansion.

2148. Chevalier, François. L'Amérique Latine: de l'indépendance à nos jours. Paris, Presses Universitaires de France, 1977. 548 p., bibl., maps, tables (Nouvelle Clio. L'histoire et ses problèmes, 44)

Though a survey of the republican era, this compact work departs from the humdrum approach in significant ways. Divided into three sections: 1) discusses major archival and bibliographic sources for entire region as well as topical and country-by-country bibliography for all save English-speaking or less well studied states (e.g., Surinam, Guyana, and Netherlands Antilles); 2) presents overview of essential geographic and resource information plus chronological table of important events that link Europe, US and Latin America and Caribbean, followed by tables that illustrate demographic, commercial, and production trends; and 3) is organized by problems: interpretations and perspectives are discussed first, including Marxist views, followed by sections on problems of economic growth, tradition and social evolution, and on the level of discussion within the region and its policy implications. At the end discusses Mexican Revolution briefly as model for area and asks if Cárdenas period was a synthesis. Also refers to complex inter-relationships Chevalier finds so central to Latin America, between impact of Church and demands of economic development. Provocative synthesis for graduate students. [V.C. Peloso]

2149. Clementi, Hebe. La abolición de la esclavitud en América Latina. B.A., Editorial La Pléyade, 1974. 219 p., bibl., tables.

Impressive research and synthesis mark this study of the abolition of slavery in 11 areas of Latin America. While acknowledging Brazil and Cuba as exceptions, Clementi postulates that emancipation in each area was a revealing indicator of social and economic conditions; that slaves were no more than 10 percent of the total population; and that slavery was not of great productive value.

2150. Cortés Conde, Roberto. Hispanoamérica: la apertura al comercio mundial, 1850-1930. B.A., Editorial Paidós, 1974. 204 p., tables (Col. Biblioteca América Latina, 18)

Excellent study of economic development (1850-1930) in Peru, Cuba, Chile, Mexico, and Argentina. Author examines demands (in more advanced countries) for silver, copper, nitrates, guano, sugar, tallow, hides, etc.; improvements in transportation; and the local stimulus of export economies. In Mexico, he also studies the influx of foreign capital during the Porfiriato. Useful tables.

2151. Darnell, Donald G. Wilham Hickling Prescott. Boston, Mass., Twayne Publishers, 1975. 140 p., bibl., (Twayne's United States authors series)

Brief account of Prescott's life. Contains extensive quotes from and superficial analysis of his major historical works.

2152. Delpar, Helen ed. Encyclopedia of Latin America. N.Y., McGraw-Hill, 1974. 651 p., maps, plates, tables.

Valuable reference tool for Spanish-speaking republics, Puerto Rico, Brazil, and Haiti. Entries are arranged alphabetically and cover many aspects of countries under consideration. Entries which are weighted toward post-Independence, are signed by contributors. The information is generally up-to-date and useful to students and academicians. For musicologist's comment, see *HLAS 38:9005*.

2153. Denis, Dohou Codjo. Influences brásiliennes a Ouidah (UFB/AA, 12, junho 1976, p. 193-209, plates)

Rather haphazard discussion of Brazilian influences in Ouidah/Wydah, Dahomey, showing that Luso-Brazilian culture was sufficiently assimilated by the slave-freedman community to be retained and propagated after a return to Africa in first half of 19th century. [R.J. Barman]

2154. Dobyns, Henry F. comp. Native American historical demography: a critical bibliography. Bloomington, Indiana Univ. Press *for* The Newberry Library, 1976. 95 p. (The Newberry Library Center for the history of the American Indian bibliographical series)

Useful albeit incomplete, annotated guide to historical demographic literature on Indians of Canada, the US and Mexico. Does not include some studies and sources. Nonetheless, a basic primer. [M.T. Hamerly]

2155. Douglas, William A. and Jon Bilbao. Amerikanuak: Basques in the New World. Reno, Univ. of Nevada Press, 1975. 519 p., bibl., maps, plates, tables.

Based on massive research, work begins with third century and traces role of Basques in the colonization of New World. Although main emphasis is on Basques in American West, their experiences in Latin America and development of Spanish California receive attention. Comparison of Basques in Latin America and those in the US completes the study.

2156. Duncan, Kenneth; Ian Rutledge; and Colin Harding eds. Land and labour in Latin America: essays on the development of agrarian capitalism in the nineteenth and twentieth centuries. Cambridge, UK, Cambridge Univ. Press, 1977. 535 p., bibl., maps, tables (Cambridge Latin American studies, 26)

Gathers representative efforts of a number of scholars in various fields whose efforts to merge several social sciences has resulted in far clearer understanding than heretofore of agrarian society in Latin America since end of 18th century. Essays are contributions to symposium on landlords and peasants held at Cambridge, England (Dec. 1972) organized to highlight historical patterns of agrarian capitalism in region. Pt. 1 contains explorations of transition from traditional, pre-capitalist haciendas to capitalist estates in Mexico, Chile, Peru and Costa Rica. Pt. 2 is concerned with recruitment of labor from highland peasant communities for labor in coastal plantations in Argentina, Peru and Colombia. Pt. 3 deals with immigrant labor and agricultural change in Argentina and Brazil. Pt. 4 examines transition from slave to capitalist agriculture in Brazil, Colombia and Trinidad. One study researches back into 18th-century Mexico while remainder concentrates on 1850-1970. Unifying thread is response of rural social order to demands for increased productivity—usually for export—in epoch of increased technology. Public agricultural materials and private accounts of estates are used to great extent throughout, and each section contains its own introductory essay. Final chapter draws on the vision of Magnus Mörner, who cautions that meaning of "landlord" and "peasant" may be more plural than has been thought. Also comments on the traditional hacienda and tries to draw comparisons among developments in different areas. Mörner poses number of significant questions that should guide further study of Latin American and Caribbean rural history in republican era. Specialists will welcome these studies, several of which are annotated separately in this volume. [V.C. Peloso]

2157. Dussel, Enrique. Caminos de liberación latinoamericana: pt. 1, Interpretación histórico-teológica de nuestro continente latinoamericano. Seis conferencias. 2. ed. B.A., Latinoamérica Libros, 1973. 175 p.

First of projected series devoted to multitude of crises which, in author's opinion, Roman Catholic Church faces in world-wide cultures and specifically within Latin America. Dussel is a prolific writer. For comments on his major work, see *HLAS 38:9412*.

2158. Eckstein, Susan. The impact of revolution: a comparative analysis of Mexico and Bolivia. Beverly Hills, Calif., Sage Publications, 1976. 53 p., bibl. (Contemporary political sociology series)

By analyzing economic and political results of Latin American revolutions within the context of two capitalist societies, author compares economic redistribution and growth and the accumulation and use of political power. She emphasizes that international forces can influence post-revolutionary development more than tensions producing revolt or reforms achieved by new policies. For political scientist's comment, see *HLAS 39:7119*.

2159. Ermolaiev, V.I. La historiografía nacional de los países de América Latina a fines del siglo XIX y principios del XX: Argentina, Brasil, México y Chile (UCLV/I, 51, mayo/agosto 1975, p. 31-57)

Historiographical essays on these countries cover old ground and are too general to be of much use to specialists.

2160. Everaert, John. El movimiento emigratorio desde Amberes a América Latina durante el siglo XIX: 1830-1914; una estadística provisoria (JGSWGL, 13, 1976, 331-360, tables)

Impressive archival research and statistical data contribute to this excellent article on emigration through Antwerp port. Author concentrates on Belgium from its independence to the Great War. He delineates three major phases in emigration: sporadic emigration to 1843; directed emigration to Guatemala (1843-45); and the era of free emigration (1846-1914), emphasizing entry of Belgian nationals into Argentina and Brazil.

2161. Ferguson, Yale H. Through glasses darkly: an assessment of various theoretical approaches to interamerican relations (UM/JIAS, 19:1, Feb. 1977, p. 3-34, bibl.)

In a review of recent literature on inter-American diplomatic theory, author summarizes prevalent syntheses. After extensive study of concepts of dependency and integration, he concludes that analyses based upon particular diplomatic problems remain most effective for sound research and interpretations. For political scientist's comment, see *HLAS 39:8545*.

2162. Fitzgibbon, Russell H. Latin American constitutions: textual citations. Tempe, Arizona State Univ., Center for Latin American Studies, 1974. 18 p., bibl.

Useful research and reference guide to the 247 constitutions promulgated by 20 Latin American nations between their independence and Aug. 1973. Textual citations are arranged by country and the year of the constitution's issuance, and are keyed to 44 published sources listed in bibliography.

2163. Foxley, Alejandro ed. Income distribution in Latin America. Introduction by . . . N.Y., Cambridge Univ. Press, 1976. 244 p., tables.

Concluding that poverty constitutes worst impediment for Latin American development, study suggests new methods for alleviating economic class divisions. Four essays describe recent effects of industrialization on income and spending. Remaining seven propose economic and political programs to achieve effective redistribution without sacrificing economic progress. For economists' comment see *HLAS 39:2808*.

2164. Frank, André Gunder; Rodolfo Puiggrós; and **Ernesto Laclau.** América Latina: ¿feudalismo o capitalismo? Bogotá, Editorial La Oveja Negra, 1972. 162 p. (Col. Cuadernos de la oveja negra, 4)

Bulk of this volume is devoted to continuing dialogue between Frank and Puiggrós over the nature of the economies of Latin America. Theme of capitalism vs. capitalism-feudalism is no longer new, and viewpoints, including those of Laclau, have been expressed in previous publications.

2165. Fulvi, Fulvio. Il contributo degli italiani alla conoscenza dell'America Latina (IGM/U, 55:4, luglio/agosto 1975, p. 705-720, bibl., maps, tables)

Summarizes contributions of Italian travelers from early 16th through early 20th century, to Western knowledge of Latin America. Some of the bibliographic particulars are hard to come by elsewhere. [M.T. Hamerly]

2166. Furtado, Celso. Economic development of Latin America: historical background and contemporary problems. Translated by Suzette Macedo. 2 ed. Cambridge, UK, Cambridge Univ. Press, 1976. 317 p., bibl., maps, tables (Cambridge Latin American studies, 8)

Updated and slightly enlarged ed. of work first published 1970 (for comments on first ed. see HLAS 34:1261). Chapter headings and subtopics remain unchanged. Bibliography includes recent scholarship, and some tables are new.

2167. Geithman, David T. ed. Fiscal policy for industrialization and development in Latin America. Gainesville, The Univ. Presses of Florida, 1974. 370 p., tables.

Volume evolved from the XXI Annual Latin American Conference held at Univ. of Florida, 1971. Conference focused on interaction of fiscal problems, tools, and systems in industrial economies of Latin America. Includes nine original papers, 19 comment papers, and edited remarks by economists and social scientists who participated in conference.

2168. Gibson, Charles; Marcello Carmagnani; and Juan Oddone. L'America Latina. Torino, Italy, U.T.E.T., 1976. 733 p., bibl., plates.

El volumen presenta la historia de América Latina desde la conquista ibérica hasta hoy. La parte colonial reproduce el excelente estudio de Gibson *Spain in America*. La independencia y la formación de los estados nacionales son analizados por Juan Oddone. El período 1880-1970 es analizado por Marcello Carmagnani. [M. Carmagnani]

2169. Glinkin, Anatoli. El proceso histórico mundial y América Latina (UCLV/I, 49, sept./dic. 1975, p. 113-134)

Soviet author presents doctrinaire, cursory review of struggles in individual Latin American countries to resist foreign capitalist imperialism and foster social revolution.

2170. Goytia, Victor F. Anales de hispanidad. V. 1, Crónicas breves. Panamá, Instituto Panameño de Cultura Hispánica [and] Univ. Santa María La Antigua, 1972. 326 p.

Series of thoughtful essays on Hispanic world in general by Panamanian man of letters. Topics covered include the Indian, Spain and *hispanidad*, folklore of Cuba, Chile and the Río de la Plata, heroes of Latin American independence, and history of Panama. [M.J. McLeod]

2171. Grigulevich, Iosif. Latin American studies (USSR/SS, 6:2[20] 1975, p. 187-196)

Annotated bibliography of more than 70 books dealing with Latin American studies published by Soviet authors between 1970-73. For political scientist's comment, see *HLAS 39:8566*.

2172. Hahner, June E. ed. Women in Latin American history: their lives and views. Los Angeles, Univ. of California, 1976. 181 p.

Consists of 17 readings: three from colonial period, four from 19th century, and 10 from the 20th century. Drawn from letters, diaries, and poems. Selections are brief and generalized case studies which may be useful for courses on women in history.

2173. Hanson, Carl A. comp. Dissertations on Iberian and Latin American history. Troy, N.Y., Whitston, 1975. 400 p., plates.

Compilation of some 3500 titles of doctoral dissertations completed in US, Canadian, British, and Irish universities and colleges from 1892-1969. Despite title, listing also includes social science topics and a few from physical sciences.

2174. Harding, Timothy F. Dependency, nationalism and the state in Latin America (LAP, 3[11]:4, Fall 1976, p. 3-11, bibl.)

Introductory article to this issue of *Latin American Perspectives* adequately summarizes development of dependency theory through early 1976.

2175. Hardoy, Jorge E. and Richard P. Schaedel eds. Las ciudades de América Latina y sus áreas de influencia a través de la historia. B.A., Ediciones Sociedad Interamericana de Palnificación, 1975. 451 p., map, plates, tables.

Complete texts of papers presented at the XL Congreso Internacional de Americanistas (Rome, 1972, see *HLAS 37:513*) on the theme of the process of urbanization in Latin America from its origins to present. Contributors include: René Millon, Friedrich Katz, Edward Calnek, Barbara Price, Jorge Hardoy, Woodrow Borah and Sherburne Cook, Francisco de Colano, Sidney Markman, Paul Singer, Edelberto Torres-Rivas, Richard Morse, Richard Schaedel, Anthony Leeds, David Preston, Hans

Buechler, Robert Kemper, Alejandro Rofman, Harley Browning, and Markos Mamalakis. Their articles are annotated separately and entered under author's name in this *HLAS*. Important contribution to the literature of Latin American urban history.

2176. Hellman, Ronald G. and H. Jon Rosenbaum eds. Latin America: the search for a new international role. N.Y., John Wiley and Sons, 1975. 297 p., tables.

Vol. 1 in Latin American International Affairs series sponsored by CUNY's Center for Inter-American Relations. Collection of 13 essays by specialists for years 1972-74 explores these topics: domestic factors of inter-American foreign policy-making, intra-Latin American relations, inter-American relations, and Latin America and the world. For political scientist's comment, see *HLAS 39:8572*.

2177. Honour, Hugh. The new golden land: European images of America from the discoveries to the present time. N.Y., Pantheon Books, 1975. 299 p., bibl., plates, tables.

Superb illustrations, originally assembled by the author as a Bicentennial project of the Cleveland Museum of Art with support from the National Gallery of ARt, are complemented by astute analysis and interpretation. Honour, a noted British art historian, places his work in the genre of Edmundo O'Gorman's *The invention of America*. That is, America was perceived not as a "New World" but from the conceptual framework of European reality. See also *HLAS 38:279*.

2178. Humphreys, R.A. Latin American history: a guide to the literature in English. 2. ed. Westport, Conn., Greenwood Press, 1977. 197 p.

Somehow first ed. of this work escaped mention in *HLAS*. While obviously dated, this reprint makes available a useful and convenient guide to historical literature in English published prior to 1958.

2179. Iglesias, Francisco. A historiografia da América Latina (PAIGH/H, 75/76, enero/dic. 1973, p. 57-73)

Though information in this article is exclusively Brazilian, Iglesias argues reasonably that Brazilian historiography reflects the Latin American mode. After identifying traditional historiography of regimes and personalities and lamenting the state of archival resources, Iglesias argues for the use by historians of methodologies of the social sciences. Concludes with summaries of areas of investigation which might best repay the interdisciplinary researcher. [L. Huddleston]

2180. Ilg, Karl. Die österreichische Emigration nach Südamerika (OLI/ZLW, 11, 1976, p. 100-112)

Author presents firsthand information, gathered from travel and interviews extending over a dozen years, on Austrian and German speaking immigration to South America. Impetus for migration is traced to the Empress Leopoldina of Brazil. Includes Spanish abstract. Chronological coverage extends to the post World War II era.

2181. Irwin, Graham W. Africans abroad: a documentary history of the black diaspora in Asia, Latin America, and the Caribbean during the age of slavery. N.Y., Columbia Univ. Press, 1977. 408 p., bibl., tables.

Author evaluates black captivity in areas previously slighted by historians. Brazil, Cuba, and West Indies receive extensive analysis. Describes plantations, rebellions, slave trade, and lifestyles of free blacks and slaves in Latin America. Also includes discussion of blacks in India, China, and Middle East.

2182. Jaulin, Robert ed. El etnocidio a través de las Américas: textos y documentos reunidos. Traducción de María Dolores de la Peña. México, Siglo XXI Editores, 1976. 365 p. (Col. Antropología)

Originally published in French under title *Le livre blanc de l'ethnocide en Amérique* (1972), this translation contains 18 essays written by contributors ranging from militant Indian leaders in North America (Shirley Keith) to distinguished historian (Jean Meyer) and anthropologist (Gerardo Reichel-Dolmatoff). Papers were originally presented at colloquia in Paris (1970) and Lima (1970). General tenor of papers is consistent with title.

2183. Karst, Kenneth L. and Keith S. Rosen. Law and development in Latin America: a case book. Berkeley, Univ. of California Press, 1975. 738 p., tables (UCLA Latin American studies series, 28)

Impressive and scholarly volume by two professors of law designed to explore "the interaction of the legal process and the process of development." Essays, documentation, court decisions, and case studies are brought to bear on four themes: security, legitimacy, community, and inequality. Valuable reference work for several disciplines, but the historic introduction to law in Latin America, while brief, is especially useful to historians. For political scientist's comment, see *HLAS 39:7045*.

2184. Kay, Cristóbal. Desarrollo comparativo del sistema señorial europeo y del sistema de haciendas latinoamericano (EEHA/AEA, 31, 1974, p. 681-723)

Author's comparative analysis of hacienda systems leads him to conclude that political conditions in

Latin America—especially absence of conflict between landlords and middle class, and inability of peasants to ally with wage earners—inhibited dissolution of latifundia. Article first appeared in English in *The Journal of Peasant Studies* (Oct. 1974).

2185. Keith, Robert G. *ed.* Haciendas and plantations in Latin American history. N.Y., Holmes and Meier, 1977. 200 p., bibl., tables.

Collection of 19 articles and excerpts from books which examine rise of haciendas in several Latin American countries and conditions which encouraged their success and expansion. All materials within this volume were published 1941-71.

2186. Kellenbenz, Hermann. Neue Archivführer für Lateinamerikaforscher (JGSWGL, 11, 1974, p. 352-382)

Author reviews recent archival guides to Latin American materials in European collections. Although these guides were sponsored by *Conseil International des Archives* they are not uniform in their approach. Review covers: West and East Germany, Sweden, Denmark, Great Britain, Scotland, Ireland, the Netherlands, Belgium and France. The British guide is the most outstanding. [R.V. Shaw]

2187. ——— and **Jürgen Schneider.** La emigración alemana a América Latina: 1821-1931 (JGSWGL, 13, 1976, p. 386-403, illus., tables)

Impressive statistics and careful analysis distinguish this article on German emigration to Latin America. Authors point out important problems in study of this nature: collecting data before creation of German Reich in 1870, official US clandestine emigration, and inability to correlate German and Latin American statistics on migration.

2188. Korolev, Nicolai. Emigración de Rusia a América Latina a fines del siglo XIX, comienzos del siglo XX (JGSWGL, 13, 1976, p. 31-37)

Brief article which summarizes conditions in Russia (1861-1917) that prompted emigration and circumstances, mostly bad, which Russian immigrants faced in Argentina and Brazil.

2189. Kovanda, Jan. Latinská Amerika: kontinent v pohybu (Latin America: a continent on the move). Praha, n.p., 1976. 326 p., illus., plates, tables.

Assessment by Czech author of historical developments and present political situation in Latin America from Marxist view-point. Based primarily on works of Soviet and Marxist authors. No biographical index. [F.J. Kovtun]

2190. Langley, Lester D. Struggle for the American Mediterranean: United States-European rivalry in the Gulf-Caribbean, 1776-1904. Athens, Univ. of Georgia Press, 1976. 226 p., bibl., maps.

After analyzing American-European competition in Latin America from the American Revolution to the supervision of customs in the Dominican Republic, author characterizes American policy as a combination of morality and practicality. Other chapters discuss Monroe Doctrine, Texas independence, and French in Mexico.

2191. Lateinamerika: Die Entwicklung der Unterentwicklung. München, FRG, Beck, 1975. 168 p., bibl. (Beck'sche Schwarze Reihe, 135)

Introductory treatment of historical origins of Latin American underdevelopment with specific reference to problems of agrarian and industrial development seen from viewpoint of dependency theory. [W. Grabendorff]

2192. Lavrov, Nikolái. Estudios de la historia de América Latina en la URSS (URSS/AL, 1, 1975, p. 45-58)

Reviews development in study of Latin American history in USSR, which has, not surprisingly, emphasized the Marxist-Leninist approach and working-class history. Conceding that it is a young discipline and that Marxist-Leninist interpretations of conquest, colonization, inter alia are still needed, author nevertheless renders an optimistic assessment of Soviet achievements thus far: "bourgeois historians recognize that they cannot study the history of Latin America without looking at the work of Soviet historians."

2193. LeBlanc, Lawrence J. Economic, social, and cultural rights and the inter-American system (UM/JIAS, 19:1, Feb. 1977, p. 61-82, bibl.)

After analyzing debates on adoption of the American Declaration of the Rights and Duties of Man and the American Convention on Human Rights, author examines implementation of economic and social rights by the OAS. Concludes that policies on human rights fail because they demand broad governmental intervention.

2194. Liebman, Seymour B. Exploring the Latin American mind. Chicago, Ill., Nelson-Hall, 1976. 192 p., bibl., table.

Liebman's study of the Latin American mind is not intellectual history, rather he seeks to broaden understanding of customs, mores, languages, etc., and to explode myths and misconceptions. Intended for students and travelers, the approach seems well studied for courses on Latin American culture.

2195. Llosa, Jorge Guillermo. La dificultad de ser latinoamericano. Ensayos. Prólogo de Jorge Basadre. La Paz, Univ. Nacional Mayor de San Andrés, 1976. 137 p.

Collection of impressionistic essays which examines the uniqueness of the Latin American experience from primitive times to present. Also examines circumstances such as geographic isolation, inconsistencies in political institutions, and religious traditions that have contributed to the difficulty of being a Latin American.

2196. McCullough, David. The path between the seas: the creation of the Panama Canal, 1870-1914. N.Y., Simon and Schuster, 1977. 698 p., bibl., maps, plates.

Significant addition to previous works on subject. Author recounts contribution of West Indians using interviews conducted with canal workers. Also explores French involvement in project and introduces new details on canal's construction. Focuses on myriad personalities and talents responsible for its completion.

2197. Manning, Diana H. Society and food: the Third World. Boston, Mass., Butterworth Publishers, 1977. 60 p., bibl., tables (Science in a social context)

In an introductory sketch of food shortages in developing nations author analyzes political and economic factors that influence food distribution. Specific chapters discuss food production in underdeveloped countries, impact of foreign aid, and world food trade.

2198. Mauro, Frédéric. América Latina oriental e América Latina ocidental: uma oposição histórica (FFCLM/EH, 13/14, 1975, p. 157-169)

Omitting Mexico, Mauro divides Latin America into a West (Central America and the Andean countries) and an East. He finds support for this division in geography, ethnicity, and economics, and he gives broad regional significance to Jacques Lambert's dualism. Admission that Mexico partakes of both East and West does not affect the argument. [L. Huddleston]

2199. Mendes, Candido. Beyond populism. Translated by L. Gray Cowan. Albany, State Univ. of New York Press, 1977. 112 p., tables.

Using Brazil and Argentina as models, author contends that contemporary Latin American political regimes differ from traditional patterns of revolution and authoritarianism. Suggests that present dictatorships are the end result of modernization and concludes that their failure to utilize political opposition as a vehicle for social progress erodes democratic development.

2200. Mörner, Magnus. El estudio actual de la historia latinoamericana (CSUCA/ESC, 4:10, enero/abril 1975, p. 107-123)

Mörner assesses research on Latin American history in US, Western Europe and Latin America. Finds efforts of individual scholars parochial and counsels in favor of team efforts as well as multi-national involvement. Also regards translation of significant research into Spanish and Portuguese as moral obligation of non-Iberoamerican historians. For more on subject, see *HLAS 33:158*.

2201. ———. Slavery and race in the evolution of Latin American societies: some recent contributions to the debate (JLAS, 8:1, May 1976, p. 127-135)

Review article discusses 10 books published 1973-75. Includes specific monographs on Santo Domingo, Peru, Mexico, Barbados, Cuba, and Brazil as well as three general studies of the Americas. Mörner adds a plea for the study of post-abolition conditions as well as slavery, important for understanding existing race relations in the Americas.

2202. Morales, Francisco. Las Casas y la Leyenda Negra (MH, 28:322, enero 1975, p. 51-54, plates)

Author summarizes broad impact of Las Casas and his writings from 16th century to present. He sees propagandistic indictment of fellow Spaniards by Las Casas as nurturing Black Legend historiography and anti-Spanish prejudices prevalent in 20th century. Also suggests ways of correcting these erroneous impressions.

2203. Morón, Guillermo. Historia contemporánea de América Latina. Caracas, Equinoccio, Ediciones de la Univ. Simón Bolívar, 1975. 225 p., tables (Col. Parametros)

Broad approach to the history of contemporary Latin America in which author attempts to chart unified historical developments that transcend national and regional particularisms. Emphasis is placed on political, sociological, economic and cultural dimensions of the collective Latin American experience.

2204. Natella, Arthur A., Jr. *ed.* The Spanish in America, 1513-1974: a chronology and fact book. Dobbs Ferry, N.Y., Oceana Publications, 1975. 139 p., bibl., facsims., tables.

Compilation of contributions made by Hispanic Americans (ranging from Ponce de León to golfer

Lee Trevino) to the history of the US. Also includes selection of generally accessible documents.

2205. Nehemkis, Peter. Latin America: myth and reality. 2. ed. Westport, Conn., Greenwood Press, 1977. 300 p.

Reprint of 1964 ed. For comments on original, see *HLAS 27:1763*.

2206. Ogelsby, J.C.M. Gringos from the far north: essays in the history of Canadian-Latin American relations, 1866-1968. Toronto, Canada, Macmillan, 1976. 346 p., bibl., maps, tables.

Author narrates Canadian diplomatic and commercial relations with Latin America and predominantly Catholic and Baptist missionary work. Concludes that Canadians maintained investment interest in region but produced no coherent policy on Latin America. Study provides empirical basis for further research in a relatively unexplored area of inter-American relations.

2207. Ortega Díaz, Pedro. El Congreso de Panamá y la unidad latinoamericana. Prólogo de Eduardo Gallegos Mancera. Caracas, Editora San José, 1976. 109 p., bibl., facsims.

On occasion of Panama Congress sesquicentennial this long-time Venezuelan Communist leader assails notion that Bolívar was adherent of "Pan Americanism" (as expressed, e.g., in item which he refutes). Nothing new, but a strong case clearly presented. He then goes on to call for a correct contemporary version of Bolívar's *latinoamericanismo*. [D. Bushnell]

2208. Ortega y Medina, Juan A. Otra vez Humboldt, ese controvertido personaje (CM/HM, 25:3, enero/marzo 1976, p. 423-454)

Reserved out pointed criticism of Jaime Labastida's work in the SepSetentas series entitled *Humboldt, ese desconocido* (1975). Author cites both errors in interpretation by Labastida and his failure to appreciate properly subtleties and breadth of Humboldt's scientific observations made within a limited amount of time.

2209. Padgug, Robert A. Problems in the theory of slavery and slave society (SS, 40:1, Spring 1976, p. 3-27)

Seeking a structured concept of slavery and its significance in social systems, author analyzes slavery within historical societies. Believes that only Greco-Roman period witnessed true slave culture, and this period should be the beginning of a comprehensive study of slavery. Author's conclusions suggest areas for further research.

2210. Peralta, José. La esclavitud de la América Latina (UC/A, 30:3/4, julio/dic. 1974, p. 145-215)

This eloquent, if demagogic and rambling, indictment of US imperialism by noted sociologist, focuses on "enslavement" of Panama, Nicaragua, Peru, and in less detail, most other Latin American countries. It is difficult to believe that it was written in 1927.

2211. Pereña, Luciano. Fray Bartolomé de las Casas, profeta de la liberación (ARBOR, 89:347, nov. 1974, p. 21-34)

Las Casas is placed in context of 25th anniversary of Declaration of Human Rights and in vanguard of long struggle to establish sovereignty of people over their natural resources, right of self determination, and equality of all citizens.

2212. Pérez Brignoli, Héctor. ¿Historia política o historia del poder? Reflexiones sobre un libro reciente de Tulio Halperin D. (CSUCA/ESC, 4:10, enero/abril 1975, p. 125-139)

Review article characterizes Tulio Halperín Donghi's *Historia contemporánea de América Latina* (1969) and his *Revolución y guerra* (1972), see *HLAS 36:2770*) as milestones in the emergence of a new style of Latin American political history, one which will halt the decline of political history in the face of increasingly popular social and economic methodologies.

2213. Pescatello, Ann M. Power and pawn: the female in Iberian families, societies, and cultures. Westport, Conn., Greenwood Press, 1976. 281 p., bibl. (Contributions in intercultural and comparative studies, 1)

Emphasizing Latin America, author examines areas of power controlled by women in Iberian societies. Stresses study of broad concepts of authority in addition to more visible power usually wielded by men. Since women's influence often remains within the family, she calls for further research on family groups as a major source of women's historical influence.

2214. ———. ed. Old roots in new lands: historical and anthropological perspectives in black experiences in the Americas. Westport, Conn., Greenwood Press, 1977. 301 p., bibl., maps, tables (Contribution in Afro-American and African studies, 31)

This collection of 10 interdisciplinary essays concerns the preservation of African cultural traits among blacks in the Americas. Four essays discuss black experience in Brazil, Costa Rica, Nicaragua, and Honduras. Other essays explore African folklore, West Indian literature, slave life in Colombia and Ecuador, and an oral history project on black slavery.

2215. Peterson, Harold F. Diplomat of the Americas: a biography of William I. Buchanan, 1852-1909. Albany, State Univ. of New York Press, 1977. 458 p., bibl., plates.

Author records Buchanan's bipartisan diplomatic appointments from 1894 to 1909, especially his work on the Panama Canal treaty, Buffalo's Pan American Exposition, and his service as delegate to early Pan American conferences. Credits Buchanan with establishing inter-American harmony and considers him an early promoter of American commercial expansion. For political scientist's comment, see *HLAS 39:8620*.

2216. Phillips, David Atlee. The night watch. N.Y., Atheneum, 1977. 309 p.

Former director of Western Hemisphere Division of the Central Intelligence Agency, author recounts his service as an agent in Latin America from 1950-75. Filled with personal anecdotes, chapters of special interest cover his CIA activities on the Bay of Pigs and in Chile, Cuba, and Mexico.

2217. Polišenský, Josef. La emigración checoslovaca a América, 1649-1945: problemas y fuentes (JGSWGL, 13, 1976, p. 56-72, tables)

Author points out topics for potential research on Czech and Slavic migration to Latin America and sources of untapped information. While isolated examples of early immigration are cited, e.g., Jesuit missionaries, statistical data are confined to 20th century, confirming impact of US immigration quotas as well as indicating Argentina as major recipient of Czech nationals since 1920s.

2218. Portes, Alejandro and **Harley L. Browning** *eds.* Current perspectives in Latin American urban research. Austin, Univ. of Texas Press, 1976. 179 p., bibl. (Special publication of the Institute of Latin American Studies)

Outgrowth of seminar at Univ. of Texas, 1974, this collection of seven essays probes new directions for urban research, particularly studies of the city within context of national growth patterns. Essays discuss influence of modernization and dependency on urban studies and city's role in the retardation or enrichment of rural Latin America.

2219. Rama, Carlos M. Historia del movimiento obrero y social latinoamericano contemporáneo. 3. ed. rev. Barcelona, Editorial Laia, 1976. 174 p.

Useful book based on archival and newspaper research. Chapters cover: historical overview; popular classes in independence movements; 19th-century social movements, Latin America and First International, social movements from 1900-61, social and labor movements in austral-America, and Latin American "New Left." For 1967 German 1. ed., see *HLAS 32:1182*. [H.A. Spalding]

2220. Rasco y Bermúdez, José Ignacio. Integración cultural de América Latina: panorama histórico. Medellín, Colombia, Editorial Bedout, 1975. 188 p., bibl.

Volume contains transcript of four lectures delivered by Prof. Pasco (Sept. 1974) and sponsored by IDB. Approach is broad and interpretative with three lectures devoted to each century of colonial era and final one to Latin American independence.

2221. Ribeiro, Darcy. Configuraciones histórico-culturales americanas. Montevideo, Centro de Estudios Latinoamericanos, 1972. 139 p., bibl., fold. table.

Revised Spanish ed. of essay which first appeared in English in 1970 (see *HLAS 33:1623*).

2222. Rippy, J. Fred. British investments in Latin America: 1822-1949. N.Y., Arno Press, 1977. 249 p., maps, tables.

Reprint of work first published 1959 (see *HLAS 23:1698*).

2223. Rodríguez, Mario. The impact of the American Revolution on the Spanish and Portuguese speaking world (*in* The Impact of the American Revolution Abroad. Washington, D.C., Library of Congress, 1976, p. 101-125)

Wide-ranging and suggestive essay, that also served as introduction to item 2224. [D. Bushnell]

2224. ———. La revolución americana de 1776 y el mundo hispánico: ensayos y documentos. Madrid, Editorial Tecnos, 1976. 222 p., bibl.

Selected reading tied together by essays that provide further background and analysis. Main subdivisions are devoted to "anti-colonialist" responses to American Revolution (including Spanish proposals for political revolution in America); Spanish diplomatic and military involvement in American Revolution; and image of the revolution and of early US in Spanish press and Miranda's diary. [D. Bushnell]

2225. Romano Ruggiero *ed.* America Indiana: storia, cultura, situaziones degli indios. Torino, Italy, Giulio Einaudi

Editore, 1976. 321 p., bibl.

Interesante antología, precedida de una excelente introducción crítica de Romano, que recoge algunos estudios significativos relativos a la población amerindia. Los estudios provienen de: Alfonso Caso, Laurette Sejourné, Jorge Mencias, José Carlos Mariátegui, Alejandro Lipschutz y André Gunder Frank. [M. Carmagnani]

2226. **Rouse, John E.** The *criollo*: Spanish cattle in the Americas. Norman, Univ. of Oklahoma Press, 1977. 303 p., bibl., facsims., maps, plates, tables.

Attractive volume enhanced by more than 100 photographs. Rouse is probably the foremost bovine authority, having published three volumes on world cattle (1970-73). In this work he traces introduction of "native" Spanish cattle by Columbus and spread of the *criollo* throughout the Americas. Concludes that the unimproved breed is an endangered species.

2227. **Rout, Leslie B., Jr.** The African experience in Spanish America: 1502 to the present day. Cambridge, UK, Cambridge Univ. Press, 1976. 404 p., bibl., maps, tables (Cambridge Latin American studies, 23)

Broad approach to the African experience in Spanish-speaking America. Rout's intent is to present a basic primer or holistic survey ranging through topics which include: slave trade, slave rebellions, blacks in wars for independence, and current status of Negroid in 15 Latin American republics (for editor's comment, see *HLAS 38:13*).

2228. **Russell, D.E.H.** Rebellion, revolution, and armed forces: a comparative study of fifteen countries with special emphasis on Cuba and South Africa. N.Y., Academic Press, 1974. 210 p., bibl., tables (Studies in social discontinuity)

Concentrating on military's role, author studies 14 20th-century revolutions including those in Bolivia, Brazil, Mexico, Colombia and Honduras. With a comparison of Cuba and South Africa, he questions idea that repression is a direct cause of revolution and concludes that army support secures existing governments. For political scientist's comment, see *HLAS 37:9679*.

2229. **Sachs, Ignacy.** The discovery of the Third World. Translated by Michael Fineberg. Cambridge, Mass., The MIT Press, 1976. 287 p., illus., tables.

Exploring ideas of cultural superiority in past societies, author concludes that discovery of the Americas gave Europe an enduring ethnocentrism. Since Third World nations still follow European dictates for social development, he calls for an end to European intellectual domination with financial aid designed to meet priorities and needs of developing nations. For political scientist's comment, see *HLAS 39:8630*.

2230. **Sagrera, Martín.** Los racismos en América Latina. B.A., Ediciones La Bastilla, 1974. 518 p., bibl. (Serie campo minado)

Lengthy and rambling comparisons are drawn between racism in South and North America from precolumbian times to present. Author cites wide range of world literature to buttress his attacks on racial injustice and "racial imperialism."

2231. **Sánchez-Albornoz, Nicolás.** La población de América Latina desde los tiempos precolombinos del año 2000. 2. ed. Madrid, Alianza Univ., 1977. 321 p., bibl., maps, tables.

Revised and augmented ed. of basic text (see *HLAS 38:2235*). Substantially rewritten to accommodate recent studies. Has much fuller bibliography and is indexed. [M.T. Hamerly]

2232. **Sandoval Rodríguez, Isaac.** Las crisis políticas latinoamericanas y el militarismo. México, Siglo XXI Editores, 1976. 195 p. (Col. Sociología y política)

Author examines wide range of circumstances which have contributed to repeated *golpes de estado* in Latin American politics. Perceives military interventions "to save the nation" not as an isolated phenomenon but as a complex process involving pressures from internal groups as well as foreign powers.

2233. **Sanz, Carlos.** Novísimo conocimiento de la historia considerada como entidad sustantiva y no solo como relato (USP/RH, 50:100, 1974, p. 163-185)

Brief essay on the nature of universal history and obligation of historians to relate their independent research on branches of historical experience to the trunk of knowledge. Case in point is how Columbus' letter (1493) has been misused by historians.

2234. **Sempat Assadourian, Carlos** and others. Modos de producción en América Latina. 3. ed. B.A., Cuadernos de Pasado y Presente, 1975. 242 p. (Pasado y presente, 40)

New ed. of work first published 1973. Three of the essays have been reprinted in Portuguese (see item 2328). See also *HLAS 36:2207, 3002* and item 2327.

2235. Sinclair, John H. comp. Protestantism in Latin America: a bibliographical guide, an annotated bibliography of selected references mainly in English, Spanish and Portuguese and useful bibliographical aids to assist the student and researcher in the general field of Latin American studies. South Pasadena, Calif., William Carey Library, 1976. 414 p.

Reissue of 1967 ed. (see HLAS 30:84) is combined in one volume with 1976 ed. which contains additional annotated entries (No. 2046 through No. 3115).

2236. Soeiro, Susan A. Recent work on Latin American women: a review essay (UM/JIAS, 17:4, Nov. 1975, p. 497-566, bibl.)

Author reviews traditional problems in studies of women and argues that inadequate methodology and ingrained misconceptions distort diversity and significance of women's roles in Latin American society. Suggests several new areas of investigations: women's social and political organizations and use of church, legal, and notary records. Analyzing new works in the field, concludes that reexamination of women in their domestic environment remains the foundation of an effective revision.

2237. Spain. Ministerio de Educación y Ciencia. Dirección General del Patrimonio Artístico y Cultural. Comisaría Nacional de Archivos. Secretaría General Técnica. Centro de Proceso de Datos. Guía de Investigadores en los Archivos Españoles, Rama de Humanidades: año 1975. Madrid, 1977. 2 v. (214, 307 p.)

Vol. 1 lists by name, and vol. 2 by research topic the 1509 individuals who used Spanish archives in 1975. Includes introduction by Vicenta Cortés Alonso and onomastic index. Useful guide of research and researchers. [M.T. Hamerly]

2238. Stang, Gumund. La emigración escandinava a la América Latina: 1800-1940 (JGSWGL, 13, 1976, p. 293-330, illus., tables)

Well-researched article with impressive statistical data from Scandanavian archives. Author notes that 19th-century emigrants were primarily from agrarian and marginally industrialized sectors of population; that percentage of emigrants vis-à-vis total population was second only to Ireland and Italy, and that only a small percent of all emigrants settled in Latin America.

2239. Tancer, Shoshana B. Economic nationalism in Latin America: the quest for economic independence. N.Y., Praeger, 1976. 251 p., tables (Praeger special studies in international economics and development)

Emphasizing Latin America's production of vital raw materials, author discusses ways to weaken domination by industrial powers and foster Latin American nationalism and collective bargaining. Specific chapters explore evolution of dependency, push for industrialization, and Latin America's role in world trade. For political scientist's comment, see HLAS 39:8650.

2240. Ulibarri, George S. and **John P. Harrison.** Guide to materials on Latin America in the National Archives of the United States. Washington, National Archives and Records Service, 1974. 489 p.

Supersedes Harrison's 1961 Guide. In fact, more complete and useful tool. Complemented by appendices on microfilm publications, diplomatic and consular post records, and a fine index. Many scholars will be surprised by the variety and wealth of materials on Latin America to be found in the National Archives. Part of the International Council on Archives and UNESCO series of national guides on archival materials relating to Latin American countries. [M.T. Hamerly]

2241. United States. Department of State. Countries of the world and their leaders. 3. ed. Detroit, Mich., Gale Research Co., 1977. 1141 p., maps, plates, tables.

Useful reference work on 166 countries. Includes US Dept. of State's report on status of world's nations, contemporary political and economic conditions, political parties, press, radio, TV, etc. Also includes lists of heads of states and cabinet members as of July 1977.

2242. Urbanski, Edmund Stephen. Los negros: su idiosincrasia, costumbres y vida en las dos Américas. León, Mex., Univ. Autónoma de Nuevo León, 1975. 1 v. (Continuous pagination) (Col. Sobretiro de Humanitas, 16)

Author offers general comments about introduction of blacks into North and South America as well as life and customs. Examines relation of slavery to colonial economies and selectively surveys work of writers and activists in black history.

2243. Viel, Benjamin. The demographic explosion: the Latin American experience. Translated by James Walls. N.Y., Irvington Publishers, 1976. 249 p., bibl., illus., tables (Irvington population and demography series)

First book-length study of Latin American demography by distinguished Chilean physician. Author is pioneer advocate of family planning and controlled fertility as well as critic of illegal and dangerous abortions. Inaccuracies arise when author ventures into historical background, but his chapters on Family Planning are sound medical and social history. For anthropologist's comment, see HLAS 39:1856a.

2244. **Von Hagen, Victor Wolfgang.** The Germanic people in America. Norman, Univ. of Oklahoma Press, 1976. 404 p., bibl., facsims., maps, plates.

Who's who of Germans, from Martin Waldsee Müller to late Werner von Braun, and their contributions to the history of the Americas. Volume based on author's work entitled *Der Ruf der Neuen Welt: Deutsche bauen America* (1970, not previously cited in *HLAS*).

2245. **Weaver, Frederick Stirton.** Capitalist development, empire, and Latin American underdevelopment: an interpretive essay on historical change (LAP, 3[11]:4, Fall 1976, p. 17-53, bibl.)

Broad brush economic history asserts that Latin American underdevelopment springs not from the drain on economic resources caused by economic imperialism from the 16th to the 20th centuries, but rather from the formation, through foreign economic penetration, of "domestic classes and class relationships inimical to dynamic economic growth."

2246. **Whitaker, Arthur P.** The American idea and the Western Hemisphere: yesterday, today, and tomorrow (FPRI/O, 20:1, Spring 1976, p. 161-177)

On the occasion of the US bicentennial, Whitaker revisits in brief the "Western Hemisphere Idea" from the Washington viewpoint, with the same conclusion that today the notion has become "an archaic adornment to a global policy with which it is logically irreconcilable."

2247. **Wilgus, A. Curtis** *comp.* Latin America, Spain, and Portugal: a selected and annotated bibliographical guide to books published in the United States, 1954-1974. Metuchen, N.J., Scarecrow Press, 1977. 910 p.

Title is descriptive of this useful, one-volume bibliographical aid. Books are geographically and topically arranged.

2248. **Wilkie, James W.** *ed.* Money and politics in Latin America. Los Angeles, Univ. of Calif., Latin American Center Publications, 1977. 91 p., tables (Statistical abstract of Latin America supplement, 7)

Enrique Baloyra's study of expenditures for political policy and political influences on budgeting, examines Cuba's record, as an authoritarian regime implementing social programs. James Hanson explores accumulation of presidential power in Mexico's economy. And David Eiteman studies the national government's role in encouraging Argentine corporate growth.

2249. **Yepes, J.M.** Del Congreso de Panamá a la conferencia de Caracas. Caracas, Gobierno de Venezuelaa, Oficina Central de Información (OCI), 1976. 467 p., bibl. (Serie del Sesquicentenario del Congreso de Panamá)

This traditional account by Colombian author of the rise of Pan Americanism, claiming Bolívar as its intellectual author, is now reprinted by the same government whose *Sistema económico latinoamericano* is a good bit closer to Bolívar's thought than is the OAS. Even so, Yepes' survey is useful. [D. Bushnell]

COLONIAL

2250. **Acosta, Evalina.** Perspectiva histórica de la génesis y evolución del derecho español en Indias (UASD/R, 2:4, julio/dic. 1972, p. 5-40, bibl.)

Rather superficial survey of major legal codes and institutions as well as their application and functions, respectively, in the colonial era. Bibliography cites standard works on Hispanic laws and institutions by Hanke, Zavala, Otz y Capdequí, etc.

2251. **Actualidad de Bartolomé de las Casas.** México, Fomento Cultural Banamex, 1975. 72 p., illus., plates.

In observance of the quincentennial of Las Casas' birth, experts from Spanish and Mexican universities gathered in two sessions (Aug. 1974) and their comments were moderated by Miguel León-Portilla. The 16 participants addressed broad topics relating to the work and influence of Las Casas and their comments constitute the text of this publication.

2252. **Alden, Dauril.** The significance of cacao production in the Amazon region during the late colonial period: an essay in comparative history (APS/P, 120:2, April 1976, p. 103-135, tables)

Quantitative study of cacao production in Pará and export from Belém between 1730 and 1822, and comparative study of cacao production and trade in the British and French West Indies, Surinam, Venezuela and Quito (i.e., Guayaquil). Valuable not only because of new data on the history of cacao in Brazil, but also because it summarizes existing knowledge on this basic staple throughout the

Americas, at least for the colonial period, underscoring how much remains to be ascertained. For Portuguese version see *HLAS 38:3935*. [M.T. Hamerly]

2253. Alurralde, Nicanor. El descubrimiento del cuarto continente. B.A., Caporaletti Hermanos, 1974. 278 p., illus., maps.

Author, Argentine engineer by profession, analyzes evidence of voyages of Vespucci to South America—the fourth continent. Using extensive mathematical formulae to convert degrees, leagues, miles, etc., into meters, he attempts to substantiate Vespucci's exploration of much of the continent.

2254. Alvarado Garaicoa, Teodoro. El derecho indiano en las colonias de la América Hispana. Guayaquil, Ecua., Univ. de Guayaquil, Depto. de Publicaciones, 1971. 28 p., facsims.

Brief summary of contents and importance of the *Recopilación de leyes de los reinos de las Indias* presented by distinguished Ecuadorian jurist on the occasion of his induction into the Centro de Investigaciones Históricas de Guayaquil in 1971.

2255. Avelino, Yvone Dias. A naturalização de mercadores-banqueiros portugueses para o exercício do comércio na América dos Áustrias: pts. 1/3 (USP/RH, 42:86, abril/junho 1971, p. 389-414, map; 44:90, abril/junho 1972, p. 469-493; 45:91, julho/set. 1972, p. 79-97, bibl.)

Three-part article based on thesis from Univ. of São Paulo devotes a third of text to summary of Spanish history from Pre-Roman times to 1700 with special emphasis on economic policy. There follows an account of Spanish attempts to monopolize the trade of its Empire. Lacking domestic capacity to maintain such a monopoly, Crown resorted to issuance of letters of naturalization which allowed foreign merchants, especially Portuguese, to conduct trade with the Empire.

2256. Barrett, Ward J. and **Stuart B. Schwartz.** Comparación entre dos economías azucareras coloniales: Morelos, México y Bahia, Brasil (*in* Florescano, Enrique *ed.* Haciendas, latifundios y plantaciones en América Latina [see *HLAS 38:2190*] p. 532-572, maps, tables)

Well-written and researched comparisons between sugar mill operations founded by Cortés in Morelos, Mexico and Mem de Sá in Bahia, Brazil. Comparative data are used for years 1600, 1700, and 1800. Similarities are noted in processing, technology, and organization; differences, in labor (free in Mexico and slave in Brazil) as well as the need for irrigation in Morelia. For contents of entire volume, see *HLAS 38:2190*.

2257. Bitar Letayf, Marcelo. Los economistas españoles del siglo XVIII y sus ideas sobre el comercio con las Indias. México, Instituto Mexicano de Comercio Exterior, 1975. 322 p., bibl., tables. (Serie historia del comercio exterior de México)

First ed. of this work (not cited in *HLAS*), was issued in Madrid, Ediciones Cultura Hispánica, 1968. Author surveys changing views of Spanish economists toward commerce throughout 18th century. Economic prostration at the Peace of Utrecht nurtured diversity of opinion. By the reign of Carlos III, economic liberalism, as espoused by Jovellanos and Adam Smith, while not endorsed totally by Spanish economists, had prevailed over mercantilism in commercial policy.

2258. Borah, Woodrow. The historical demography of aboriginal and colonial America: an attempt at perspective (*in* Denevan, William M. *ed*. The native population of the Americas in 1492 [see item 2279] p. 13-34)

Previously unpublished essay presented at XXXVII International Congress of Americanists in Argentina (Sept. 1966). Minor changes in the text and a brief addendum update this excellent essay on historical demography. Borah defends the high population calculations in regional studies by him and the late S.F. Cook, noting that recent application of aerial photography, chemical analysis of soils, and examination of colloidal clays lend support to their research.

2259. Borges, Analola. Una Real Instrucción de 1714: primer intento reformista de los jueces visitadores en Indias y posible precedente del sistema de intendencias (*in* Congreso Venezolano de Historia, II, Caracas, 1974. Memoria [see item] v. 1, p. 109-149, bibl.)

Important essay on one of the all but forgotten reform efforts of the early Bourbons, Phillip V. In this study, Borges examines and speculates on extent to which a 1714 instruction issued to two *visitadores*, one of whom amounted to quasi intendant of the Royal Exchequer in Caracas, foreshadowed the later overhaul of the administration of the colonies. [M.T. Hamerly]

2260. Boxer, C.R. Some remarks on the social and professional status of physicians and surgeons in the Iberian world: 16th-18th centuries (USP/RH, 50:100, 1974, p. 197-215)

Author examines medical profession in 16th-18th-century Spain and Portugal with emphasis on Portuguese colonies. Sketches social discrimination that crippled advancement in the profession, especially discrimination against Jews, foreign doctors, and native healers. Also describes certification procedures and educational facilities.

2261. Boyd-Bowman, Peter. Patterns of Spanish emigration to the Indies until 1600 (HAHR, 56:4, Nov. 1976, p. 580-604, maps, tables)

Prof. Boyd-Bowman has provided a valuable service to the academic community by summarizing the major conclusions derived from a five-volume compilation of 54,881 Spanish emigrants to America from 1493 to 1600. His work, centered at SUNY (Buffalo) is pregnant for historians and linguists alike. Patterns of emigration, e.g., merchants and women, rather than volume, are emphasized. Also includes statistical data for cities and provinces (see *HLAS 28:1522* and *HLAS 30:2536a* for comments on vols. 1/2).

2262. Brundage, Bun Cartwright. Two earths, two heavens; an essay contrasting the Aztec and the Incas. Albuquerque, Univ. of New Mexico Press, 1975. 128 p., bibl., tables.

Brief essay by author of previous works on Incas and Aztecs. Style is lively and content of potential value to students seeking comparative and contrasting facets of the two great Andean and Mesoamerican cultures.

2263. Bunster, Enrique. Oro y sangre. Santiago, Editorial del Pacífico, 1974. 338 p., plates (Col. Alta mar)

Popularized and undocumented treatment of Spanish conquistadors in North and South America.

2264. Burkholder, Mark A. The Council of the Indies in the late eighteenth century: a new perspective (HAHR, 56:3, Aug. 1976, p. 404-423)

Well-researched article suggesting major revisions in historians' views of the Council of the Indies in late colonial era. Author maintains that a 1773 decree elevating Council to equality with Council of Castile, increased appointment of ministers with experience in America, and expansion of councilors from six to 14 point to increasing, rather than decreasing as commonly assumed, importance of the Council.

2265. ———— and D.S. Chandler. From impotence to authority: the Spanish Crown and the American Audiencias, 1687-1808. Columbia, Univ. of Missouri Press, 1977. 253 p., bibl., tables.

This significant work, based primarily on extensive archival research, examines background and qualifications of 693 men appointed to Royal Audiencias between 1687-1821. Conclusions are posited regarding the sale of audiencia appointments and attitude of Crown toward creole participation in *audiencias*. Functioning of American courts is not examined; rather composite trends in membership are emphasized over 134 years. The 10 appendices contain impressive statistical information heretofore not available on American *oidores*.

2266. Cañete y Domínguez, Pedro Vicente. Syntagma de las resoluciones prácticas cotidianas del derecho del Real Patronazgo de las Indias. Edición y estudio preliminar de José M. Mariluz Urquijo. B.A., Mundial, 1973. 373 p.

Lenghty preliminary study details the life and career of 18th-century Paraguayan scholar and royal official, Pedro Vicente Cañete y Domínguez. Cañete studied application and misapplication of the Patronato Real to a specific area of the Indies, the viceroyalty of the Río de la Plata. His work, regarded by Mariluz Urquijo as the most important juridical scholarship in the viceroyalty, flowed from Cañete's interest in law and his conflicts with the ecclesiastical *cabildo* of Asunción.

2267. Carew, Jan. The origins of racism in the Americas (JBA, 4, Dec. 1976, p. 3-25)

Spanish and Portuguese abuse of Jews and Africans taught Columbus new racial ideologies which he introduced into the Americas. Capitalism defined Indias as tools in the search for gold. Catholic theology defended slavery, enabling Columbus to justify brutality. Author concludes that Spanish-Indian relations established American racism and slavery.

2268. Carletti, Francesco. Razonamientos de mi viaje alrededor del mundo. Estudio preliminar, traducción y notas de Francisca Perujo. México, UNAM Instituto de Investigaciones Bibliográficas, 1976. 281 p.

Primera edición en español de los *Ragionamenti* de Francisco Carletti, un comerciante y negrero florentino que del 1591 a 1606 visitó varias partes de la América española y del Extremo Oriente, en especial sus grandes centros comerciales, sobre los que da informes muy interesantes. En América conoció los de Cartagena de Indias, Lima, México y Acapulco, entre otros. La obra de Carletti no fué publicada hasta 1701, en Florencia, y al parecer con graves mutilaciones; pero se conocen cuatro copias manuscritas del original. Uno de estos manuscritos—el de la Biblioteca Angélica de Roma—ha servido para la presente edición. La editora ha realizado una magnífica labor. Además del estudio preliminar—que es muy bueno—el texto de Carletti ha sido enriquecido con notas abundantes y verdaderamente ilustrativas. Lo que resulta difícil de aquilatar en estos narradores de viajes es el grado de fantasía

History: General, Colonial / 107

con que pueden adornar algunos episodios, lo mismo que la ignorancia o prejuicios que posiblemente influyeron en sus juicios. [L. Gómez-Canedo]

2269. Casas, Bartolomé de las. Brevísima relacion de la destrucción de las Indias. Barcelona, Editorial Fontamara, 1974. 199 p. (Col. De la naturaleza de las cosas. Series, 2)

Contains the text of the *Brevísima relación* and a brief account of the life of Las Casas by J.A. Llorente.

2270. ———. La larga marcha de Las Casas. Selección y presentación de textos de Juan B. Lessègue. Lima, Centro de Estudios y Publicaciones, 1974. 418 p., illus., tables (Col. De centro de estudios y publicaciones, 11)

Compendium of materials illustrating 12 stages or periods in the life of Las Casas. Each *etapa* contains brief introduction by Juan Lessègue followed by selected excerpts from published works and documentation.

2271. Castillo Mathieu, Nicolás del. El segundo viaje de Colón. Bogotá, Ministerio de Educación, Instituto Colombiano de Cultura, 1974. p., bibl. (Biblioteca colombiana de cultura. Col. Popular. Serie, 148)

Popularized account of the second voyage of Columbus. Despite title, book's second half examines in similar manner Pedrarias Dávila's expedition to Tierra Firme.

2272. Castro Seoane, José and **Ricardo Sanlés Martínez.** Aviamiento y catálogo de misiones y misioneros de la Merced de Castilla a las Indias, durante el siglo XVI, según los libros de la contratación (ISTM/MH, 32:94, enero/abril 1975, p. 5-55)

Another segment of work now in progress for several years. This one, in part the efforts of R. Sanlés Martínez, incorporates years 1575-89. For most recent reference to this compilation see *HLAS 32:1214*.

2273. Cervo, Amado Luiz. Contato entre civilizações: a conquista da América como serviço de Deus de Sua Majestade, 1442-1548. São Paulo, Editora McGraw-Hill do Brasil, 1975. 146 p., bibl.

Subtle attack on the Black Legend cast in form of extensive review of concept and use of "service to God and King" during the conquest. Half the book concerns background of idea and incidence of its use. Remainder treats varying concepts of it. [L. Huddleston]

2274. Céspedes, Guillermo. América Latina colonial hasta 1650. México, Secretaría de Educación Pública, 1976. 206 p., maps, tables (Col. SepSetentas. Serie, 260)

Slightly revised ed. in Spanish of vol. first published in English in 1974 (see *HLAS 38:2264*).

2275. Cevallos García, Gabriel. América: Ecua., Casa de la Cultura Ecuatoriana, Núcleo del Azuay, 1975. 228 p. (Col. Libros para el pueblo, 1)

Interpretive account of the discovery of America by distinguished Ecuadorian historian. Author examines science and technology which made the Columbian voyages possible as well as ideological, legal, and philosophical implications of the existence of the New World and its inhabitants for Renaissance Europe.

2276. Chiappelli, Fredi; Michael J.B. Allen; and **Robert L. Benson** eds. First images of America: the impact of the New World on the Old. Berkeley, Univ. of California Press, 1976. 2 v. (957 p.) (Continuous pagination) bibl., maps, plates, tables.

The 56 essays in this two-volume work were selected from papers originally presented at an international Congress (1975) held at UCLA. While contributors are distinguished specialists in their fields, many of the essays which were revised for publication are brief and seem intended for non-professional readers. Illustrations, some in color, make these volumes unusually attractive.

2277. Colóquio Luso-Espanhol de História Ultramarina, *II, Lisboa, 1973.* **Centro de Estudos de Cartografia Antiga.** A viagem de Fernão de Magalhães e a questão das Molucas: actas. Edição organizada por A. Teixeira da Mota. Lisboa, Junta de Investigações Científicas do Ultramar, 1975. 764 p., fold. map, plate, tables (Col. Secção de Lisboa, 16)

Concerns I meeting of Colóquio Luso-Español de Historia Ultramarina which examined origins and wideranging impact of the Treaty of Tordesillas (see *HLAS 36:1557*). At II meeting in Lisbon (1973), multiple facets of Ferdinand Magellan's voyage and its historic significance were examined by 26 scholars and later published in this substantial tome.

2278. Comas, Juan. Fray Bartolomé, la esclavitud y el racismo (CAM, 205:2, marzo/abril 1976, p. 145-152, bibl.)

Author contends, as others have, that Las Casas was far from being a racist or advocate of slavery despite his proposal to substitute Negro slaves for Indians.

2279. Denevan, William M. *ed.* The native population of the Americas in 1492. Madison, The Univ. of Wisconsin Press, 1976. 353 p., bibl., illus., maps, tables.

Volume divided into five parts: 1) Estimating the unknown; 2) the Caribbean, Central America, and Yucatan; 3) Mexico; 4) South America; and 5) North America. It seeks to answer a question long mired in controversy. What was the native population of the Americas in 1492? The last word (?) on this subject may come from geographers and anthropologists, for the prospect of discovery of substantial new historical documentation on the subject is remote. Bulk of contributors to this superbly edited work are significantly geographers and anthropologists: Woodrow Borah (see item 2258); Angel Rosenblat; David R. Radell; William T. Sanders; Daniel E. Shea; James Pyle; and William M. Denevan.

2280. Domínguez Compañy, Francisco. Obligaciones militares de los vecinos hispanoamericanos en el siglo XVI: según se desprende de las Actas Capitulares (PAIGH/H, 79, enero/junio 1975, p. 37-61, bibl.)

Author, making extensive use of cabildo records, concludes that the *milieia concejil* never constituted an effective or permanent force; military obligations, however, specifically decreed by acts of cabildos were more stringent. Significantly, *encomenderos,* who by law were obligated to perform military responsibilities, seem not to have been distinguished from other citizens.

2281. Donoso-Barros, Roberto. Expediciones españolas del primer cuarto del siglo XVI y su contribución a la ciencia (UC/AT, 429/430, 1974, p. 225-263, illus., plates)

Scientific observations of Antonio de Pigafetta on the Magellan-Elcano expedition are analyzed by author. Donoso-Barros identifies several species of birds, fish, reptiles, and mammals which were unknown to Europeans until the 16th century. He similarly examines scientific data collected during García de Loaisa's expedition.

2282. Ezquerra, Ramón. Los asentamientos de población en América (ARBOR, 90:352, abril 1975, p. 25-50)

Founders and founding dates of many towns and cities in the Spanish colonies are listed to year 1570. Generalized and rather obvious comments about location of towns and their importance to Spanish colonization are included.

2283. Ferrer Benimeli, José Antonio. Masonería e Inquisición en Latinoamericana durante el siglo XVIII. Caracas, Univ. Católica Andrés Bello, Instituto de Investigaciones Históricas, 1973. 158 p.

Good study based on extensive archival research. Brief text and lengthy appendices containing Inquisition proceedings in Lima and Mexico confirm, by indirect evidence, that masonry was not of significant concern to the inquisitors. Further, specific *procesos* against Masons invariably contain additional charges of theological and moral transgressions of greater magnitude.

2284. Flórez-Tascón, Francisco José. Enfermedades de los conquistadores (MH, 27:311, feb. 1974, p. 63-67, illus.)

This brief article recounts illness of prominent explorers and conquistadores resulting from food shortages, vitamin deficiencies, and digestive problems. Author also speculates about specific diseases which shortened lives of important colonial persons.

2285. Gandía, Enrique de. La conquista de América (ANH/B, 475, 1974, p. 317-343)

Very generalized narrative which recounts impact of Spanish arms and institutions on America. Gandía argues that the New World, contrary to popular belief, failed to enrich the Old. He does agree that the two worlds had reciprocal influence, resulting in profound changes for both.

2286. ———. Los viajes fracasados de Vespucci a Cattigara, Taprobana y Malaca (USP/RH, 50:100, 1974, p. 87-116)

This analysis of Américo Vespucci's *El Mundo Nuevo* concludes that the controversial explorer actually made voyages to the Orient rather than to South and North America. Evidence of the "lost voyages" rests primarily on the etymological roots of words used by Vespucci which Roberto Levillier identified as indigenous to the Americas, but according to Gandía the roots are related to Chinese.

2287. García-Gallo, Alfonso. Las audiencias de Indias: su origen y caracteres (*in* Congreso Venezolano de Historia, II, Caracas, 1974. Memoria [see item 3094] v. 1, p. 359-432)

Solid up-to-date review of peninsular origins and nature of the American audiencias as an institution.

Notes, which take up more than half this study, are rich in detail and references. [M.T. Hamerly]

2288. Gil-Bermejo García, Juana. Pasajeros a Indias (EEHA/AEA, 31, 1974, p. 323-384, tables)

General analysis of varying circumstances which apparently dictated issuance of licenses for emigration in early 1600s; and detailed analysis of names, sex, place of origin in Spain, and destination in Indies for 1290 emigrants who departed Spain in 1608.

2289. Gliozzi, Giuliano. Adamo e il Nuovo Mondo: la nascita dellantropologia come ideologia coloniale; dalle genealogie bibliche alle teorie razziali, 1500-1700. Firenze, Italy, La Nuova Italia Editrice, n.d. 635 p., bibl.

Es sabido que la polémica sobre el origen de los amerindios, tema de esta obra, servía de pretexto para encubrir objetivos económicos, sociales y políticos. En base a una copiosa bibliografía y documentación, el autor analiza inteligentemente la evolución de este debate entre los siglos XVI y XVII. Demuestra como la polémica encubre una polarización de fuerzas a nivel no solo europeo sino también americano pues en ambas áreas existían fuerzas que defendían una serie de intereses tradicionales y otras que reflejaban los intereses de nuevas fuerzas emergentes. Al evolucionar en el siglo XVI y XVII, estas fuerzas liberan gradualmente la imagen del indio de su originaria vinculación con la Biblia. El mismo será percibido y juzgado en base a consideraciones económicas y sociales, dando lugar al desarrollo de prejuicios raciales diferentes. [M. Carmagnani]

2290. Gómez Canedo, Lino. Evangelización y política indigenista: ideas y actitudes franciscanas en el siglo XVI. Valladolid, Spain, Univ. de Valladolid, Seminario de Historia de América, 1976. 26 p., illus.

Broad approach to Franciscan missionary enterprises in 16th century. Gómez Canedo, a Franciscan and noted historian, emphasizes that the New World endeavors of the Order were flexible and rooted in practical experience that varied in time and place. He characterizes official political influence of the Franciscans as difficult to discern and lacking in theoretical bases. Paper delivered at the simposio Hispanoamericano de Indigenismo Histórico during the III Jornadas Americanistas sponsored by the Univ. of Valladolid, Spain (see item 2298).

2291. Góngora, Mario. El Nuevo Mundo en el pensamiento escatológico de Tomás Campanella (EEHA/AEA, 31, 1974, p. 385-408)

Author examines references (in several works by unorthodox, 17th-century Italian theologian, Thomas Campanella) to New World and Spanish Empire. Two in particular relate to Columbus' role in Christianization of Indians and to Black Legend.

2292. González González, Alfonso. Las audiencias indianas y el mando militar: siglos XVI, XVII, y XVIII (*in* Congreso Venezolano de Historia, II, Caracas, 1974. Memoria [see item 3094] v. 1, p. 487-518)

Highly informative examination replete with examples of a critical issue, to what extent the Audiencia, particularly the *audiencias togadas*, had military attributes. [M.T. Hamerly]

2293. Hanke, Lewis and Celso Rodríguez. Guía de las fuentes en el Archivo General de Indias para el estudio de la administración virreinal española en México y en el Perú: 1535-1700. Köln, FRG, Böhlan Verlag, 1977. 3 v. (398, 340, 386 p.) bibl. (Lateinamerikanische Forschunger, 7)

Major guide to sources in AGI on 16th and 17th-century viceroys of New Spain and Peru and their administrations. Vol. 1 consists of brief biographies of and lists of studies and sources on individual viceroys. Vols. 2 and 3 list vicegeral correspondence and related documents for New Spain and Peru respectively, first those manuscript materials which have been ordered and microfilmed, and then those which have not. Vol. 1 also includes a resumé of vicegeral materials available from the Centro Nacional de Microfilm in Madrid. Although not complete, the work is a monumental, very useful and highly welcome guide to several of the most important source groups for research on Spanish America from aftermath of conquest through advent of Bourbons. [M.T. Hamerly]

2294. Hauben, Paul J. White legend against black: nationalism and enlightenment in a Spanish context (AAFH/TAM, 34:1, July 1977, p. 1-19)

Reviewing the argument in 18th-century Spain over Spanish behavior in Americas, author chooses Juan Nuix de Perpiñá, an exiled Jesuit, as most significant defender of Spanish colonialism. Summarizes and analyzes Nuix's work and includes critique of recent studies on topic.

2295. Hussey, Roland Dennis. The Caracas company: 1728-1784, a study in the history of Spanish monopolistic trade. N.Y., Arno Press, 1977. 358 p., bibl., tables (Harvard historical studies, 37)

Reprint of 1934 work. Hussey, in pioneering study, explained absence of Spanish overseas companies until 18th century, and traced success and failure (mostly latter) of first monopolistic company in Indies.

2296. Ibero-Amerikanisches Archiv. Ibero-Amerikanische Institut. Neue Folge, Jahrgang 3, Heft 2, 1977- Berlin, FRG.

Entire issue devoted to Las Casas consists of eight essays in French, Spanish, and Italian which examine topics such as: first decade of Las Casas' life in the New World; philosophical implications of his thought; unknown episode in his career; and recent publications on the Great Debate.

2298. Jornadas Americanistas, III, Valladolid, Spain, 1974. Estudios sobre política indigenista española en América: simposio conmemorativo del V centenario del Padre Las Casas. v. 1, Iniciación, pugna de ocupación, demografía, lingüística, sedentarización, condición jurídica del indio. Valladolid, Spain, Univ. de Valladolid, Seminario de Historia de América, 1975. 391 p., bibl., illus., maps, plates, tables.

Title is descriptive of major topics examined by Spanish and Latin American specialists at conference held in Valladolid (May 1974). Related conference in Sevilla (March 1974) examined biographical and ideological approaches to Las Casas. Those proceedings presumably will constitute contents of vol. 2. The articles contained in this vol. are annotated separately in this *HLAS* and entered under each author's name.

Julian, Amadeo. Bibliografía de Fray Bartolomé de las Casas. See *HLAS 39:591*.

2299. Lockhart, James and Enrique Otte eds. Letters and people of the Spanish Indies: sixteenth century. Cambridge, UK, Cambridge Univ. Press, 1976. 267 p., plates (Cambridge Latin American studies, 22)

Editors, both distinguished colonial specialists, have translated an unusual collection of letters. Correspondence between officials and agencies of church and state in New World and Spain exists in abundance in Spanish and American archives. Uniqueness of these letters lies in fact that they offer insight into a broad spectrum of colonial society. Accordingly, they constitute an important contribution to social history of colonial Spanish America. The three categories of letters included: "Conquest," "The variety of life in the Indies," and "Officials and clerics."

2300. Marx, Robert F. The capture of the treasure fleet: the story of Piet Heyn. N.Y., David McKay Co., 1977. 276 p., illus., maps.

Besides account of Piet Heyn's capture of 1628 New Spain Flota, author includes chapters on growth of flota system, port cities, English and Dutch raids on Spanish shipping, and Dutch struggles for independence. Contends that Heyn's exploits hastened Dutch independence and Spain's decline.

2301. Mathes, W. Michael. Sebastián Vizcaíno y la expansión española en el Océano Pacífico: 1580-1630. Traducción de Ignacio del Río. México, UNAM, Instituto de Investigaciones Históricas, 1973. 143 p., bibl., maps, plate (Serie historia novo-hispana, 23)

Spanish ed. of volume published 1968 (for comments on English ed., see *HLAS 32:1573*).

2302. Mechoulan, Henri. L'antihumanisme de G.J. de Sepúlveda: étude critique du *Democrates Primus*. Paris, Mouton, 1974. 185 p.

Valioso análisis de las ideas fundamentales de Sepúlveda, enraizadas profundamente en la doctrina de Aristóteles, de quien fue el español un fervoroso y penetrante comentador. El conocimiento del *Democrates Primus* es casi indispensable para entender lo que su autor expuso en el *Democrates Secundus* sobre las justas causas de la guerra a los indios de América, motivo de su enfrentamiento con las Casas. [L. Gómez-Canedo]

2303. Mòrner, Magnus. La hacienda hispanoamericana: examen de las investigaciones y debates recientes (*in* Florescano, Enrique ed. Haciendas, latifundios y plantaciones en América Latina [see *HLAS 38:2190*] p. 15-48, tables)

Spanish translation of article published in *Hispanic American Historical Review* (May 1973, see *HLAS 36:1508*). For contents of Florescano's volume, see *HLAS 38:2190*.

2304. ———. Raza y estratificación social de Hispanoamérica hacia 1800 (LI/IA, 4:2, 1974, p. 17-29)

Brief comments on race mixture and society made by author at session on Latin American history (1974) held at Karl Marx Univ. in Leipzig, GDR.

2305. Muñoz, Juan Bautista. Historia del Nuevo Mundo. Introducción y notas de José Alcina Franch. México, Aguilar, 1975. 323 p., bibl., map (Biblioteca Americana, 1)

Welcome reedition of Muñoz' never before reprinted *Historia del Nuevo Mundo* (1793), still a basic source on Columbus' voyages. Muñoz (1745-99) laid bases for modern historiography in Spain with this, regrettably unfinished work, was responsible for the foundation and initial organization of the Archivo General de Indias, and left still another legacy, the rich Muñoz Collection in the Biblioteca de la Real Academia de la Historia in Madrid. [M.T. Hamerly]

2306. Muratore, Joseph R. The remains of Christopher Columbus: a revealing, documented narrative about Columbus' remains (Los restos de Cristobal Colón: una narración reveladora y documentada sobre los restos de Colón). Published in English and Spanish in one edition. Warwick, R.I. Muratore Agency, 1972. 89 p., plates.

Interesting bilingual narrative of controversy surrounding location of Columbus' remains, i.e., do they repose in Seville or in Santo Domingo? Author, amateur historian, professes certainty about validity of Santo Domingo's claim.

2307. Navarro García, Luis. Hispanoamérica en el siglo XVIII. Sevilla, Spain, Univ. de Sevilla, 1975. 320 p., bibl., fold. maps.

Central theme of this excellent synthesis is expansion of Spanish and Portuguese American empires in 18th century. Navarro García assesses Iberian world in 1700, discusses dynastic crisis in Spain, analyzes Bourbon reforms, and outlines course of international wars in Americas. Chapters are devoted to Caribbean, Mexico, Peru, Chile, Río de la Plata, and Brazil. Highly recommended.

2308. Nemby, Eric. The Rand McNally world atlas of exploration. Introduction by Sir Vivian Fuchs. N.Y., Rand McNally, 1975. 288 p., bibl., illus., maps, plates, tables.

Despite title, this is not an atlas but a concise history of exploration. It is chronologically arranged with respect to geographic areas. Maps depict routes of various explorers. Includes extensive bibliography and appendix of 600 explorers and their routes.

2309. Oliva de Coll, Josefina. La resistencia indígena ante la conquista. México, Siglo XXI Editores, 1974. 281 p., bibl., maps (Col. Historia)

Author maintains that Indians in Hispanic America who fought to protect their lands and liberty are too frequently slighted or forgotten in traditional accounts of conquest. She documents Indian resistance from West Indies to Baja California and from New Mexico to southern Chile.

2310. Parish, Helen Rand and Harold E. Weidman. The correct birthdate of Bartolomé de las Casas (HAHR, 56:3, Aug. 1976, p. 385-403, plates)

Based on Las Casas' testimony from legal transcript in Archives of Indies in Seville, authors believe 11 Nov. 1484 is his correct birthdate. They trace erroneous acceptance of 1474 and refute recent revisions, while analyzing significance of correct date for Las Casas' life.

2311. Peterson, Mendel L. The funnel of gold. Boston, Mass., Little, Brown, 1975. 481 p., bibl., illus., facsims., maps, plates.

In rather exuberant style, author presents panorama of New World discoveries and conquests which funneled bullion, most of it silver, into Western Europe. Some generalizations are suspect and there is little analysis.

2312. Phelan, John L. El reino milenario de los Franciscanos en el Nuevo Mundo. Traducción al español de Josefina Vázquez de Knauth. México, UNAM, Instituto de Investigaciones Históricas, 1972. 188 p., bibl. (Serie historia novohispana, 22)

Spanish translation of late John Leddy Phelan's classic work in intellectual history (for comments regarding first English ed. see *HLAS* 20:2541a).

2313. Pohl, Frederick J. Prince Henry Sinclair: his expedition to the New World in 1398. N.Y., Clarkston N. Potter, 1974. 230 p., bibl., maps.

Volume by Frederick Pohl is yet another example of his passion for precolumbian voyages to America. Pohl proceeds from two premises: Zeno Narrative of late 14th century is authentic and Sir Henry Sinclair is the Prince Zichmni whose exploits are recounted in the Narrative. If premises, which are suspect, are indeed correct, resulting research and clear exposition by author are impressive.

2314. Polišenský, Josef and Ludomír Vebr. Un poco de polémica sobre las actividades de Miguel Sabel (UCP/IAP, 8, 1974, p. 194-197)

Brief note which again challenges Analda Borges' assessment of Miguel Sabel as an agent of Charles II (see *HLAS* 28:865b). For related item on Sabel and his activities, see *HLAS* 36:2521.

2315. Pollak, Michael. The ethnic background of Columbus: inferences from a Genoese-Jewish source, 1553-1557 (PAIGH/H, 80, julio/dic. 1975, p. 147-164)

Author examines New World histories of Joseph ben Joshua ben Meir Ha-Kohen, great 16th century Genoese-Jewish scholar. Ha-Kohen describes Christopher Columbus as a Genoan but never as a Jew, and author considers Ha-Kohen's ignorance of Columbus' Jewish origins as strong evidence against any Jewish ancestry. Author believes Ha-Kohen's works contain new clues to Columbus' personal history.

2316. Pompa y Pompa, Antonio. El cronista Las Casas, humanista y político (UNL/H, 16, 1975, p. 657-665, bibl.)

Author, Director of the Instituto Nacional de Antropología e Historia, offers opinion that Las Casas as humanist and *político* served to bridge worlds of Spaniard and Indian, creating new and ultimately universal human community—the Mexican.

2317. Powell, Philip Wayne. Soldiers, Indians, and silver: North America's first frontier war. Tempe, Arizona State Univ., 1975. 317 p., bibl., maps.

Reprint of 1952 ed. (see *HLAS 18:1725a*).

2318. Proctor, Samuel *ed.* Eighteenth-century Florida and the Caribbean. Gainesville, Univ. Presses of Florida, 1976. 103 p., tables.

Consists of papers and commentary presented at the II Florida Bicentennial Symposia. Participants addressed themselves to commercial ties of two regions, slavery, sugar economy, and historical archaeology.

2319. Quinn, David B. *ed.* The last voyage of Thomas Cavendish 1591-1592: the autograph manuscript of his own account of the voyage, written shortly before his death. From the collection of Paul Mellon. Chicago, Ill., The Univ. of Chicago Press, 1975. 165 p., maps, plates, tables (Studies in the history of discoveries)

Excellent introduction by renowned scholar and historian of Elizabethan exploration is combined with the holography manuscript account of Cavendish's last voyage and his testament. Initially published in 1625, the original manuscript disappeared until discovered some two decades ago in Phillips Collection. This exceptionally handsome volume, with reproductions of Cavendish maps of South Atlantic and Pacific coasts of America, will be sought by both scholars and book collectors.

2320. Quiñonero Gálvez, Juan. El padre Las Casas según su rostro (MH, 28:322, enero 1975, p. 55-58, plates)

In analyzing Las Casas' physiognomy, author concludes that padre's features reflect many of the qualities for which he is famous.

2321. Ramos Pérez, Demetrio. El negocio negrero de los Welser y sus habilidades monopolistas (PAIGH/H, 81, enero/junio 1976, p. 7-81)

Monographic study of second asiento, that issued to the House of Welser in 1528. Major step forward in our knowledge of early, non-Spanish entrepreneurial activities in the Indies. [M.T. Hamerly]

Redmon, Walter Bernard. Bibliography of the philosophy in the Iberian colonies of America. See item 9482.

2322. Roche, Marcel. Early history of science in Spanish America (AAAS/S, 194, 19 Nov. 1976, p. 806-810)

Brief but well-written article outlining early history of science in Spanish America. Conclusions are that scientific pursuits were more practical than theoretical; were discontinuous, peaking in 16th and 18th centuries; and were of significance in amalgamation of metals, agronomy, and especially botany.

2323. Rodríguez Cruz, Agueda María. Historia de las universidades hispanoamericanas: período hispánico. t. 1/2. Bogotá, Instituto Caro y Cuervo, 1973. 2 v. (559, 661 p.), bibl., facsims., illus., plates.

These massive volumes are product of research for doctoral dissertation begun in 1956 by Sister Agueda. Author explores projected impact of Univ. of Salamanca on formation of Hispanic universities in the colonial era. Evidence of research in Spanish, Vatican, and Latin American archives and the utilization of 538 published works gives new dimension to the word "exhaustive." Initially, Sister Agueda's work details the legal and historic foundations of the Hispanic American university. Separate chapters are devoted to universities founded from 1538 to 1812. Lengthy and useful appendices contain references to specific documentation, papal briefs, and royal decrees.

2324. Rosebury, Theodor. Columbus and the Indians (MR, 25:11, April 1974, p. 13-22, bibl.)

Tightly written brief by renowned bacteriologist who persuasively argues that weight of evidence over past 40 years lies against New World origins of syphilis.

2325. Sánchez Bella, Ismael. Visitas a Indias: siglos XVI-XVII (*in* Congreso Venezolano de Historia, II, Caracas, 1974. Memoria [see item 3094] v. 3, p. 165-208)

Detailed, documented review of general *visitas* (i.e., of vice-royalties and/or *audiencias*) of 16th and 17th centuries, of which there were at least 45, and most of which as well as the data generated thereby await research. [M.T. Hamerly]

2326. Sanders, G. Earl. Counter-contraband in Spanish America: handicaps of the governors in the Indies (AAFH/TAM, 34:1, July 1977, p. 59-80)

Author disputes that dishonesty and inefficiency among Spanish governors contributed to smuggling in the Americas. Discusses Indian complicity, insufficient funds for defense, and restraints ordered by Crown and concludes that these factors undermined official efforts to stop illegal trade.

2327. Santana Cardoso, Ciro Flamarion. Los modos de producción coloniales: estado de la cuestión y perspectiva teórica (CSUCA/ESC, 4:10, enero/abril 1975, p. 87-105)

Originally presented as part of symposium on "Methods of Production in Latin America" at the XLI International Congress of Americanists (1974), author seeks to clarify and define precisely concepts such as pre-capitalism, slavery, and feudalism. Also points to significant regional variants within economic patterns of European colonies in Americas.

2328. Santiago, Théo Araujo *comp*. América colonial: ensaios. Rio, Pallas, 1975. 178 p., bibl. (Col. América, economia & sociedade)

Small volume contains six essays written in early 1970s and previously published in either French or Spanish. Translated here into Portuguese, they examine aspects of colonial economies within Marxist framework.

2329. Savelle, Max. Voltaire: historian of America (PAIGH/H, 79, enero/junio 1975, p. 99-141)

Author sketches Voltaire's interpretations of European colonization of America. Presents Voltaire as historian primarily concerned with social and cultural ramifications of major historical events and as one who saw history as a series of human achievements and judged discovery of America on that premise. Nonetheless, Voltaire believed that increased European demand for colonial products would create intense competition for trade, forging new alliances and causing more European wars.

2330. Scenna, Miguel Angel. Antes de Colón. B.A., EUDEBA, 1974. 157 p., bibl. (Col. Biblioteca de América. Serie libros del tiempo nuevo)

Brief study, based on dated sources, which traces precolumbian contacts (both legendary and verified) with America. Author stresses role of Columbus as effective discoverer of New World.

2331. Solano, Francisco de. Introducción al estudio del abastecimiento de la ciudad colonial (*in* Hardoy, Jorge E. and Richard P. Schaedel *eds*. Las ciudades de América Latina y sus áreas de influencia a través de la historia [see item 2175] p. 133-163)

Excellent introduction to theme in need of basic research, especially in local records as Solano correctly stresses, problem of provisioning cities. Notes constitute a useful guide to existing and related literature. [M.T. Hamerly]

2332. Suárez, Santiago Gerardo. Para una bibliografía de las Reales Audiencias (*in* Congreso Venezolano de Historía, II, Caracas, 1974. Memoria [see item 3094] v. 3, p. 209-233)

Useful listing of studies and published sources on and relating to audiencias in Colonial Spanish America. [M.T. Hamerly]

2333. Tanzi, Héctor José. La crítica histórica sobre la conquista de América en el siglo XVIII (FJB/BH, 35, mayo 1974, p. 181-198)

Criticism of Spain's conquest of Indies in 16th century was work of native Spaniards, notably Las Casas, whose point of reference was that Europe was Catholic Spain. Foreign writers in 18th century, with exception of William Robertson, were influenced by Spain's importance within the European balance of power; and, not surprisingly, repudiated Spanish fanaticism, superstition, and violence in conquest out of both philosophical and pragmatic considerations.

2334. Torquemada, Juan de. Monarquía Indiana de los viente y un libros rituales y Monarquía Indiana, con el origen y guerras de los Indios Occidentales, de sus poblazones, descubrimiento, conquista, conversión y otras cosas maravillosas de la mesma tierra [sic]. v. 1/2. 3. ed. México, UNAM, Instituto de Investigaciones Históricas, 1975. 2 v. (1068 p.) (Continuous pagination) illus., map (Col. Historiadores y cronistas de Indias, 5)

Handsome new ed. of Torquemada prepared by Seminario "para el estudio de fuentes de tradición indígena" under the direction of Miguel León-Portilla.

2335. Traboulay, David M. Bartolomé de las Casas and the Crusade of Peace (ZMR, 61:2, April 1977, p. 128-136)

2336. Uslar-Pietri, Arturo. Crucible of races (OAS/AM, 27:3, March 1975, p. 28-35, plates)

New World was considered as such because Spaniards encountered different human community in different historical setting. Result was emergence of cultural *mestizaje* as well as concepts of utopian societies which are worthy of respect in their own right. Also see Uslar-Pietri's related article, item 2337.

2337. ———. The world the Europeans called new (OAS/AM, 28:4, April 1976, p. 9-16, plates)

Uslar-Pietri maintains that identity of Latin America is based on encounter of two different civilizations that had nothing in common. Consequently of this creative encounter revolutionized Western thought which in turn was deeply influenced by American myths of the goodness and natural equality of man. Unique collection of illustrations accompanies article. Also see the author's related article, item 2336.

Vannini de Gerulewicz, Marisa. El mar de los descubridores: documentos y relatos inéditos o poco conocidos sobre el descubrimiento y la exploración de los mares, islas y tierras del Nuevo Mundo: siglos XV-XVI. See *HLAS 39:5267*.

2338. Veitia Linaje, Joseph de. The Spanish rule of trade to the West Indies. Translated by John Stevens. N.Y., AMS Press, 1977. 376 p., facsim.

Nicely bound facsimile reprint of Captain John Stevens' 1702 English translation of José de Veitia Linaje's *Norte de la contratación de las Indias Occidentales*.

2339. Vigneras, Louis-André. The discovery of South America and the Andalusian voyages. Chicago, Ill., Univ. of Chicago Press, 1976. 170 p., bibl., maps, tables (Studies in the history of discoveries)

Author deserves accolades for his publications based on archival research, especially in the Archivo de Protocolos de Sevilla (see *HLAS 36:1631*). In this significant work, Vigneras illumines the Andalusian "minor" voyages to South America in 1490s and early 1500s. He has discovered voyages previously unknown and again demonstrates the important role played by Seville merchants in financing and supplying voyages.

2340. Villamarin, Juan A. and Judith E. Villamarin. Indian labor in mainland colonial Spanish America. Newark, Univ. of Delaware, Latin American Studies Program, 1975. 175 p., bibl., maps, tables (Occasional papers and monographs, 1)

Examines institutional forms of Indian labor, i.e., slavery, encomienda, forced labor for wages, and free labor as well as factors which produced variant patterns of development in Mexico, the Andean region, Colombia, Venezuela, Chile and Paraguay.

2341. Woodbridge, Hensley C. and Lawrence A. Thompson. Printing in colonial Spanish America. Troy, N.Y., Whitston Publishing, 1976. 172 p., bibl., plates, tables.

Revision and enlargement by Woodbridge of Thompson's original work (see *HLAS 28:92*). Includes histories of printing in Mexico, several kingdoms of South America, Central America, and Antilles.

2342. Zapata Olivella, Manuel. Opresión y explotación del africano en la colonización de América Latina (UM/R, 22, julio/sept. 1976, p. 89-107)

Author, folklore specialist, suggests new approaches to study of blacks in Latin America which would emphasize transcultural influences and creative contributions of Africans to religion, dances, musical instruments, customs, etc., in colonial society.

Zavala, Silvio. Aspectos formales de la controversia entre Sepúlveda y Las Casas en Valladolid, a mediados del siglo XVI. See item 6437.

INDEPENDENCE AND 19TH CENTURY

2343. Anderle, Adam. La emigración húngara a América Latina después de la derrota de la revolución de 1848-1849 (JGSWGL, 13, 1976, p. 73-83)

Well-written article which analyzes political (national independence) and economic (land reform) motives that led to the revolution of 1848-49 in Hungary. Failure of the revolt resulted in a disparate and undetermined number of emigrants who settled primarily in Cuba, El Salvador, Mexico, Argentina, and Brazil.

2344. Anna, Timothy E. The last viceroys of New Spain and Peru: an appraisal (AHA/R, 81:1, Feb. 1976, p. 38-65, plates)

Outstanding essay that is suggestive both of research potential in biographical studies of late Spanish viceroys in Mexico and Peru as well as current revisionist trends in historiography of Spanish American independence. Author persuasively argues that last viceroys were inordinately competent. Independence resulted not from counterrevolutionary forces, rather from increasing realization in America of Spain's inability to rule and of weakening of ethos underpinning imperialism.

2345. Arboleda, José Rafael. El abate Domingo de Pradt y el Congreso de Panamá (ACH/BHA, 63:712, enero/marzo 1976, p. 3-32, bibl.)

Good synthesis of career of Abbé de Pradt, self-appointed spokesman for Spanish American cause, with special reference to his proposal that Congress of Panama seek degree of autonomy from Rome in church affairs. The idea fell on receptive ears, though nothing came of it. [D. Bushnell]

2346. Barceló Sifontes, Lyll. Contribución a la bibliografía sobre el Congreso Anfictiónico de Panamá. Caracas, Oficina Central de Información (OCI), 1976. 72 p. (Serie del sesquicentenario del congreso de Panamá)

Lists much that is marginal and not all that is important, but still a point of departure for study of Panama Congress and related themes. [D. Bushnell]

2347. Bateman, Alfredo D. Fernández Madrid en Cuba (ACH/BHA, 62:709, abril/junio 1975, p. 225-246)

Relates medical, literary, and journalistic-political activities of Colombian patriot José Fernández Madrid during period of exile in Cuba 1816-25. Undocumented but carefully researched, and contains full listing of his publications in Cuban interval. [D. Bushnell]

2348. Burke, William. Additional reasons, for our immediately emancipating Spanish America: deduced, from the new and extraordinary circumstances, of the present crises: and containing valuable information, respecting the late important events, both at Buenos Ayres, and in the Caraccas (sic): as well as with respect to the present disposition and views of the Spanish Americans: being intended as a supplement to "South American Independence." 2. ed. N.Y., AMS Press, 1976. 91 p.

Reprint of 1808 ed.

2349. Candido, Salvatore. La emigración política italiana a la América Latina: 1820-1870 (JGSWGL, 13, 1976, p. 216-238, bibl.)

Well-researched article which documents specific examples of Italians who entered and departed Latin America (1820-70). Migrants were generally young, upper class political activists who sought temporary refuge in America to escape prison or the scaffold rather than to find improved social and economic conditions. The ebb and flow is of course related to vicissitudes of Italian politics in a turbulent era.

2350. Castillero Reyes, Ernesto de Jesús. Bolívar en Panamá: génesis y realidad del "Pacto Americano:" las Actas extraviadas del Congreso de Bolívar de 1826. Panamá, Editora de la Nación, 1976. 187 p., bibl., facsims., plates.

Less pretentious than some other publications marking Panama Congress sesquicentennial, but one more useful for reference purposes. Has minutes of sessions, texts of agreements adopted, certain related documents, and connecting commentary by Castillero. [D. Bushnell]

2351. Cruz Hermosilla, Emilio de la. Hispanoamérica en las Cortes de Cádiz (MH, 27:311, feb. 1974, p. 42-43, plates)

Very brief article which points out most illustrious delegates from Hispanic America to Cortes of Cádiz (1810). Lists 100 delegates, 21 of whom were creoles, as well as cities and regions they represented.

2352. Echeverría, Juan María. Las ideas escolásticas y el inicio de la Revolución hispanoamericana (UCAB/M, 5, 1976, p. 279-338, bibl.)

Repeats argument for Francisco Suárez and scholasticism as ideological inspiration in beginning (not necessarily later) phases of Spanish American revolution. Concise summary of changing fashions in interpretation of this question and extensive bibliography are perhaps most valuable portions of article; central argument is presented in systematic fashion, but brings no major new insights. [D. Bushnell]

2353. Fernández de Avila, Rafael Camon. La emancipación y el comercio catalán con América (IGFO/RI, 35:139/142, enero/dic. 1975, p. 229-260)

Good discussion of impact of Spanish American revolution, from 1808 to 1820s, largely as seen through correspondence of Catalan merchants. Data suggestive of changes in quantity, composition, direction of Spanish trade with America. Documentary appendix. [D. Bushnell]

2354. Flórez Estrada, Alvaro. Examen imparcial de las disensiones de la América con la España, de los medios de su recíproco interés y de la utilidad de los aliados de la España. Caracas,

Consejo Municipal del Distrito Federal, 1974. 406 p.

Reedition of work first published London 1811, by Spanish liberal who felt he knew how to satisfy both the just aspirations of Spanish Americans and British commercial interests. Useful prologue by Manuel Alfredo Rodríguez shows among other things Flórez Estrada's impact in Venezuela. [D. Bushnell]

Hale, Charles A. The reconstruction of nineteenth-century politics in Spanish America: a case for the history of ideas. See item 9506.

2355. Heredia, Edmundo A. Las "Cartas al Abate de Pradt, por un Indígena de la América del Sud" (CEHA/NH, 7:13, dic. 1974, p. 16-25)

Research note on curious and quite ineffective example of loyalist propaganda: "Letters" to De Pradt, by Spanish consul in Amsterdam, published in French for edification of European diplomats and officials of Spanish government itself. [D. Bushnell]

2356. ———. Los intereses británicos y los intentos de reconquista de Hispanoamerica (IRA/B, 9, 1972/1974, p. 68-82)

This good article, based on research in diplomatic archives, examines documentary evidence for belief held by Cádiz government that Britain, its ally in the Peninsular War, constituted greater threat to integrity of Spanish Empire than its enemy, France.

2357. Hernández García, Julio. Algunos aspectos de la emigración de las Islas Canarias a Hispanoamerica en la segunda mitad del siglo XIX: 1840-1895 (JGSWGL, 13, 1976, p. 132-150)

Author raises multitude of questions that requires research before synthesis of Canary Island emigration be written. Calls for analysis of Spanish legislation restricting emigration; new methodological studies to correct contradictory statistics; correlation between drought and crop failures and emigration; rural population increases and attendant problems of minifundio, etc.

2358. Hersch, Robert. The transfer of modern weapons and expertise (SECOLAS/A, 8, March 1977, p. 38-47)

Provocative examination of almost forgotten but important theme: impact of introduction of modern arms into late 19th-century Latin America, especially but not exclusively Argentina, Brazil, and Chile. Study based on almost forgotten but no less important source group, reports of War Ministries (Ministerio de Guerra y Marina). Among other things, Hersch argues that increasing reliance on modern weapons stimulated incipient industrialization in more "advanced" countries. [M.T. Hamerly]

2359. Kleinmann, Hans-Otto. Die besonderen Bedingungen der Komerziellen Präsenz Österreichs in Lateinamerika im 19. Jhdt (OLI/ZLW, 11, 1976, p. 68-89)

Examines two conditions—lack of exclusion by major industrialized nations and complementary nature of Austro-Latin American resources and economies—which encouraged development of Austrian commercial ventures in Argentina, Chile, and Brazil. Includes Spanish abstract.

2360. Kossok, Manfred. Character und historischer Ort der Unabhängigkeitskriege Lateinamerikas (*in* Akademien der Wissenschaften sozialistischer Länder. Probleme der Geschichte und der sozialökonomischen Struktur der Länder Lateinamerikas. Leipzig, GDR, 1976, p. 937-960, bibl.)

East German historian analyzes character of Latin American independence movements in 19th and 20th centuries. Concludes there are four different ideologies: 1) radical-democratic; 2) republican-liberal; 3) moderate-liberal; and 4) conservative. Regards most Latin American countries as captive bourgeois entities still on their way to "independencia." [R.V. Shaw]

2361. Langley, Lester D. The Jacksonians and the origins of inter-American distrust (IAMEA, 30:3, Winter 1976, p. 3-21)

Author sketches Andrew Jackson's little known policies in Cuba, Colombia, Ecuador, Venezuela, Peru, and Chile. Outlines Argentine hostility to foreign influence that led to 10-year severence of diplomatic relations between Argentina and US. Only Brazil offered an opportunity for American economic and political growth. With policies directed toward increasing American trade and decreasing European, especially British influence, author concludes that Jacksonian diplomacy fostered much of later suspicion and hostility that developed between US and new republics.

2362. León Tello, Pilar; Concepción Menéndez; and Carmen Herrero *comps.* Documentos relativos a la independencia de Norteamérica existentes en archivos españoles. v. 3, pt. 1, Archivo Histórico Nacional correspondencia diplomática: años 1801-1820. Madrid, Ministerio de Asuntos Exteriores, Dirección Relaciones Culturales, 1976. 666 p.

History: General, Independence and 19th Century / 117

Summaries of correspondence from Spanish legation in US to home government, 1801 through 1816 (*not* 1820). Though all aspects of US-Spanish relations are covered, Anglo-American pressure on Spanish borderlands and real or alleged aid to Spanish American revolutionists loom largest. [D. Bushnell]

2363. Liss, Peggy K. The significance of the American revolution for United States-Spanish American relations (FPRI/O, 20:1, Spring 1976, p. 147-159)

Author briefly examines impact of American Revolution on Spanish America through models and contacts.

2364. Mejía Lequerica, José. Discurso en las Cortes de Cádiz. Guayaquil, Ecua., Publicaciones Educativas Ariel, n.d. 190 p.

Not one *discurso* but compilation of remarks in many different debates of 1812 Cortes by *quiteño* who served as American representative. Biographical introduction by Hernán Rodríguez Castelo. [D. Bushnell]

2365. Mörner, Magnus. Problemas que presenta el estudio histórico de la sociedad hispano-americana del siglo XIX (CDAL, 9/10, 1974, p. 1-10)

Though still the stepchild of Latin American historians, the 19th century is attracting increasing interest, especially from social historians. Mörner notes particular difficulties, as well as few advantages, in working on this period.

2366. Morón, Guillermo. La destrucción de la unidad hispanoamericana (PAIGH/H, 79, enero/junio 1975, p. 11-35)

Interesting article follows three lectures by author outlining process of centralization in Indies. Here analyzes circumstances in 18th century that operated to destroy unity of Spain's New World empire at very time the mother country was taking steps to consolidate that unity.

2367. Pletcher, David M. Inter-American trade in the early 1870s: a State Department survey (AAFH/TAM, 33:4, April 1977, p. 593-612, tables)

Using trade reports sent to State Dept. by American ministers in Latin America, author analyzes European domination of 19th century inter-American trade. Outlining proposals for government encouragement of American commerce, he contends that reports signal change in American policy from territorial aggression to economic colonialism.

2368. Pradt, Dominique Georges Frédéric de Riom de Prolhiac de Fourt de. Congrès de Panamá (Congreso de Panamá). Nota preliminar por Gonzalo Barrios. Caracas, Edición Homenaje del Congreso de Venezuela, 1976. 95 p.

Comments on American affairs, praise of Bolívar, and discreet proposal of ecclesiastical schism, by European sympathizer with Latin American cause. Reprint of 1825 ed., Paris. [D. Bushnell]

2369. Ramos Pérez, Demetrio. Fases de la emigración española a Hispanoamérica en el siglo XIX (JGSWGL, 13, 1976, p. 151-173)

Emigration of Spaniards to Latin America is examined in light of developments in Spanish history. Phases of migration, for example, are produced by restoration of Ferdinand VII, antiliberal purges of 1820s, Carlist wars, etc. Transmigration of political exiles from one Latin American nation to another is also examined.

2370. *El Repertorio Americano*: Londres, 1826-1827. Prólogo e índices por Pedro Grases. Caracas, Talleres de Cromotip, 1973. 4 v. (320, 350, 413, 343 p.)

Facsimile reproduction of journal published by Andrés Bello in London, devoted to American affairs. The "indices" cover only authors and titles of articles but prologue by Grases is, as always, a good one. [D. Bushnell]

2371. Romero, José Luis. La independencia de Hispanoamérica y el modelo político norteamericano (RIB, 26:4, oct./dic. 1976, p. 429-455)

One of best of many essays that appeared concerning relationship between US and Latin American independence during US bicentennial year. Poses good questions as to reasons for and nature of US model's appeal; Romero's answers are suggestive though scarcely final. [D. Bushnell]

2372. Rubio Mañé, J. Ignacio. Fuentes documentales para la historia de la independencia de América. t. 2, Estudio preliminar y panorama europeo. Caracas, Comité Orígenes de la Emancipación, 1976. 591 p. (Publicación, 20)

Inventory of materials contained in Public Record Office, various Spanish archives, and Italian, Austrian and French repositories, all relating to antecedents and preliminaries of independence struggle. This vol. is collection of miscellaneous data of European history, going back to Middle Ages (for t. 3, see *HLAS 38:2373*). [D. Bushnell]

2373. Shur, Leonid Avelevich. El pintor viajero Mijail Tijanov (URSS/AL, 1, 1975, p. 153-175, plates)

Biographical sketch of Russian painter who sailed on V. Golovnin expedition's circumnavigation of the earth in 1817-19 and analysis of some of his drawings made in North and South America, 43 of which are extant. For more on these Russian travelers in Latin America, see *HLAS 34:1295* and *HLAS 36:1970*.

2374. Simmons, Merle E. U.S. political ideas in Spanish America before 1830: a bibliographical study. Bloomington, Indiana Univ., Dept. of Spanish and Portuguese, 1977. 86 p. (Hispanic literary studies, 2)

Excellent survey of works published in both Spanish and French which served, or at least *could* have served, to publicize US political model in Latin America. Generally does not pretend to assess circulation or impact of specific items. In *Santiago F. Puglia: an early Philadelphia propagandist for Spanish-American independence* (Chapel Hill, Univ. of North Carolina Press, 1977, 73 p., bibl. [North Carolina studies in the Romance languages and literatures, 195]) Simmons takes a more detailed look at one of the works in question, *El desengaño del hombre* (printed 1794), its Italian-born author, and some aspects of Philadelphia's role as a disseminating point for revolutionary propaganda. [D. Bushnell]

2375. Soler, Ricaurte. Clase y nación en Hispanoamerica: siglo XIX. Panamá, Ediciones de la *Revista Tareas*, 1975. 68 p., bibl., facsims.

From Frank's lumpenbourgeoisie we now move to "lumpen-naciones." This short study is a neo-marxist examination of the Conservatives and Liberals of 19th-century Latin America, and of how their actions and beliefs gave rise to the region's modern dependency. [M.J. McLeod]

2376. Stegmaier Rodríguez, Juan L. Lord Tomás Alejandro Cochrane: cronología (SCHG/R, 144, 1976, p. 146-166, bibl.)

Modest but useful reference. [D. Bushnell]

2377. Suárez, Diego. Twilight of an empire. N.Y., Transbook, 1976. 124 p., facsims., maps.

This sparsely-documented, 100-p. account of independence movements of Latin America is by Colombian architect/diplomat whose only apparent claim to authority is direct kinship with Santander. Includes 40 p. of facsimiles and English transcripts of letters from era's famous figures to Santander.

2378. Tanzi, Héctor José. El poder político y la independencia argentina.

Prólogo de Demetrio Ramos Pérez. B.A., Ediciones Cervantes, 1975. 305 p., bibl.

Coherent, well-argued statement of conservative Hispanist interpretation of intellectual origins of independence: i.e., that long-term ideological influences could mainly be found in traditional Spanish thought (Suárez, *et al.*), short-term influences in Spanish *juntismo* of 1808; also that, with apparent exception of La Paz, American juntas really were loyal at first to Ferdinand. Over half is background, from medieval thought to Spanish events of 1808; once junta movement appears in America, there is special but not exclusive emphasis on Río de la Plata. [D. Bushnell]

2379. Tello, Pilar León. Archivo histórico nacional: correspondencia diplomática: años 1801-1820. Madrid, Ministerio de Asuntos Exteriores, 1976. 666 p. (Documentos relativos a la independencia de Norteamérica existentes en archivos españoles, 3)

Contains summaries of diplomatic dispatches, housed in the Archivo Histórico Nacional (Madrid), which were sent from Spanish Legation in US, in 1801-16. While a valuable guide to researchers in diplomatic history, volume's usefulness would have been increased by inclusion of index of proper names appearing in documentation.

20TH CENTURY

2380. Alexander, Robert J. Agrarian reform in Latin America. N.Y., Macmillan, 1974. 118 p., plates, table.

Not previously cited in *HLAS*, this is a rather superficial treatment of land reform that is well short of the caliber of work associated with the author.

2381. Baily, Samuel L. The United States and the development of South America, 1945-1975. N.Y., New Viewpoints, 1976. 240 p., bibl., maps, tables.

Poignant critique of a US policy that has contributed to underdevelopment and poverty in Latin America. Individual chapters on Brazil and Chile. Author proposes alternative US policies with some new slants.

2382. Blasier, Cole. The hovering giant: U.S. responses to revolutionary change in Latin America. Pittsburgh, Pa., Univ. of Pittsburgh Press, 1976. 315 p., plates, tables (Pitt Latin American series)

Impressive research underpins this excellent examination of US responses to social revolutions in four countries: Mexico, Bolivia, Guatemala, and

Cuba. Blasier concludes that American reactions were complex and shifting as revolutions progressed, and he emphasizes importance of control over military as well as existence of one-party systems to successful and sustained social revolutions. For political scientist's comment, see *HLAS 39:8514*.

2383. Brathwaite, Edward Kamau. The contribution of M.J. Herskovits to Afro-American studies (ASAWI/B, 5, Dec. 1972, p. 85-94)

Explores impact upon our knowledge of African diaspora of studies by Melville Herskovits in 1920s and 1930s, as ethnographer concerned with roots of the blending of African, Caribbean and North American cultures. Stimulating introductory essay for undergraduates interested in Haiti. [V.C. Peloso]

2384. Burden, William A.M. The struggle for airways in Latin America. N.Y., Arno Press, 1977. 245 p., bibl., maps, plates, tables.

Reprint of 1943 work (see *HLAS 9:116*).

2385. Cornelius, Wayne A. and **Felicity M. Trueblood** eds. Urbanization and inequality: the political economy of urban and rural development in Latin America. Beverly Hills, Calif., Sage, 1975. 316 p., maps, tables, (Latin American urban research, 5)

Vol. 5 in series devoted to Latin American urban research. As title suggests, contributors examine topics related to urbanization and its impact on distribution of wealth. Overall, their findings point to increase in poverty among rural sectors as well as among lower-class urbanites and even greater disparity in wealth and power. Sub-topics include: Urbanization and Uneven Development; Urban-Rural Interface; Political Economy of Urban Poverty; Public Policies as Determinants of Urban Growth and Rural-Urban Inequalities; and Regional Development Programs and Rural-Urban Inequalities. For sociologist's comment, see *HLAS 39:9016*.

2386. Cortés Conde, Roberto and **Stanley J. Stein** eds. Latin America: a guide to economic history, 1830-1930. Berkeley, Univ. of California Press, 1977. 685 p.

Editors agree that century under examination can be divided into two periods, indicating strong conjuncture of forces at about 1880. They also identify pressing historical problems common to region. Precise, provocative judgements make these essays attractive. Work divided into several sections: 1) contains General and Reference Works, including references and statistics, archival sources, economic/social histories, materials on economic, social and geographic conditions and reviews of research problems; 2) concerns Demography, Manpower and Living Conditions; 3) Structures and Institutions; 4) Macroeconomic Growth and Fluctuations; 5) Foreign Trade and Investment materials; 6) Introductory resources on Agriculture and Ranching, Industry: Factory and Artisan, Extractive Industry, and Transport, Public Utilities and Services. Basic economic history materials for each country are introduced by its own editor(s): "Argentina" by Tulio Halperín Donghi; "Brazil" by Nicia Villela Luz; "Chile" by Carmen Ariola and Osvaldo Sunkel; "Colombia" by William P. McGreevey; "Mexico" by Enrique Florescano, and "Peru" by Pablo Macera and Shane Hunt. A thorough, comprehensive tool of wide utility for students of the countries represented and others as well. A model for further such efforts. [V.C. Peloso]

2387. Davis, Harold Eugene and **Larman C. Wilson** eds. Latin American foreign policies: an analysis. Baltimore, Md., The Johns Hopkins Univ. Press, 1975. 470 p., bibl., tables.

Country by country analysis of foreign policies of Latin American nations among themselves and with other nations of the world. The 18 contributors are generally well-established scholars. Discussions of individual countries are often well done, but analysis is lacking. Conclusions, where offered by the editors, are sketchy and inadequate. For political scientist's comment, see *HLAS 39:8531*.

2388. Duff, Ernest A.; John F. McCamant; and **Waltraud Q. Morales.** Violence and repression in Latin America: a quantitative and historical analysis. N.Y., The Free Press, 1976. 322 p., bibl., tables.

Variations in patterns of violence and repression are analyzed and quantified in this pioneer work on 20 Latin American nations during 1950s and 1960s. Examines topics such as social cohesion and lack thereof; variables and deviant cases; and specific examples of several countries which illustrate patterns of revolution (Cuba and Bolivia), declining cohesion (Brazil and Chile), and stability (Costa Rica and Mexico). For political scientist's comment, see *HLAS 39:7024*.

2389. Fatemi, Nasrollah S.; Gail W. Williams; and **Thibault de Saint-Phalle.** Multinational corporations: the problems and the prospects. 2. ed. Introduction by Fairleigh S. Dickinson, Jr. N.Y., A.S. Barnes, 1976. 332 p., bibl., tables.

Since multinational corporations generate continuing controversy and hostility, authors examine their power and address major criticisms of them. Although authors' analysis concentrates on effect of multinationals on US, Latin America serves as example that governmental control can succeed.

2390. Gilderhus, Mark T. Diplomacy and revolution: U.S.-Mexican relations under Wilson and Carranza. Tucson, Univ. of Arizona Press, 1977. 159 p., bibl., maps, plates, tables.

Excellent study that has plumbed archival sources in Mexico and the US as well as an impressive range of literature in Spanish and English. Gilderhus traces difficult and ultimately unsuccessful attempt of Wilson to reconcile his commitment to Mexican self-determination and need to protect US investments after adoption of Mexican Constitution of 1917.

2391. Grieb, Kenneth J. The Latin American policy of Warren G. Harding. Ft. Worth, The Texas Christian Univ. Press, 1976. 223 p., bibl. (Monographs in history and culture, 13)

Revisionist study of the Harding administration, suggesting that its policies toward Latin America were more responsible than traditional views have maintained. Author examines eight incidents which he feels illustrate greater degree of conciliation and understanding under Harding's leadership than forceful and interventionist policies of Woodrow Wilson. For political scientist's comment, see *HLAS 39:8565*.

Karst, Kenneth L. and **Keith S. Rosen.** Law and development in Latin America: a case book. See *HLAS 39:7045*.

2392. Knaster, Meri. Women in Latin America: the state of research, 1975 (LARR, 11:1, 1977, p. 3-74, bibl.)

Essay is detailed, annotated description of work in field of women in Latin America. Article divided into six broad categories of current research. Appendix of research in progress as well as extensive bibliography provided invaluable aids to scholars.

2393. Lerner, Nathan. Jewish organization in Latin America. Tel Aviv, Israel, Tel Aviv Univ., the David Horoqitz Institute for the Research of Developing Countries, 1974. 71 p. (Col. Research report, 4)

With emphasis on Argentina, Chile, Brazil and Uruguay, author sketches membership, financial support, goals, and contributions of Jewish groups in Latin America. Definitive analyses depend on more research and individual case studies.

2394. Lowenthal, Abraham F. *ed.* Armies and politics in Latin America. N.Y., Holmes and Meiers Publishers, 1976. 356 p., tables.

Consists of 12 essays that analyze recent military overthrows of constitutionally elected governments in Latin America. Also examines outside influences whose origins lie in US, USSR, and multinational corporations. Elaborately constructed models, backed by statistical data, which are designed to predict circumstances that will precipitate future *golpes* are of questionable value. For political scientist's comment, see *HLAS 39:7052*.

2395. Meyer, Lorenzo. Mexico and the United States in the oil controversy: 1917-1942. 2. ed. Translated by Muriel Vasconcellos. Austin, Univ. of Texas Press, 1977. 367 p., bibl., tables.

English translation of 1968 work (see *HLAS 31:3301*).

2396. Needler, Martin C. An introduction to Latin American politics: the structure of conflict. Englewood Cliffs, N.J., Prentice-Hall, 1977. 358 p., bibl., maps, tables.

Extremely well-written analysis of bases of political cleavage and structure of conflict in Latin America. Initially, Needler examines variables such as demography, social structure, interest groups, the political role of the military, and types of regimes: pt. 2 outlines specific examples of conflict in individual countries and groups of countries. His treatment of US presence in Latin America is required reading. Highly recommended. For political scientist's comment, see *HLAS 39:7063*.

2397. O'Brien, Dennis J. Petróleo e intervención: relaciones entre los Estados Unidos y México, 1917-1918 (CM/HM, 27:1, julio/sept. 1977, p. 103-140, bibl., tables)

This well-researched article emphasizes importance of Mexican petroleum to US and her allies in the Great War. Interruption of flow of oil, if not avoided by fortuitous circumstances and effective diplomacy, might have required abandonment of Woodrow Wilson's rhetorical commitment to non-interference and non-intervention in Mexican politics.

2398. Pearse, Andrew. The Latin American peasant. London, Frank Cass, 1975. 289 p., bibl., illus., tables (Library of peasant studies, 1)

Bulk of volume is devoted to selected case studies of peasants in 1950s and 1960s. Pearse maintains that conditions for rural folk have been affected adversely by physical expansion of national governments and influence of international markets into countryside. Unfortunately, displaced peasants have been offered severely limited opportunities in new and rapidly changing societies. For sociologist's comment, see *HLAS 39:9057*.

2399. Pommerin, Reiner. Das Dritte Reich und Lateinamerika: Die deutsche Politik gegenüber Süd- und Mittelamerika, 1939-1942. Düsseldorf, FRG, Droste, 1977. 380 p., bibl.

Most complete and balanced study of relations between Third Reich and Latin America. Formal diplomatic relations, trade relations and political impact of different organizations of German immigrants in various Latin American countries have been carefully researched and documented through extensive use of archive materials. Author argues convincingly that German concern was very mild in this period because Hitler showed no interest in Latin America. Based on author's dissertation. [W. Grabendorff]

2400. Puhle, Hans-Jürgen ed. Lateinamerika: Historische Realität und Dependencia Theorien. Hamburg, FRG, Hoffmann und Campe, 1977. 240 p. (Historische Perspektiven, 6)

Papers from a seminar held June 1975 at Univ. of Bielefeld. Consist of critical assessment of dependence theories from historical viewpoint and reach general conclusion that these theories require much more differentiation to serve as an analytic instrument to understand historical reality. Though uneven in quality, a very useful volume. Includes articles by: Hans-Jürgen Puhle; Philip J. O'Brien; Hermann Sautter; Reinhard Liehr; Horst Pietschmann; Konrad Stenzel; and Klaus Lindenberg. [W. Grabendorff]

2401. Schaefer, Jürgen. Deutsche Militärhilfe an Südamerika. Düsseldorf, FRG, Bertelsmann Universitätsverlag, 1974. 311 p.

Author discusses German military influence in Argentina, Bolivia, and Chile, emphasizing years 1880-1914. Based on archival documents in Europe and South America (bibliography, p. 289-300). Author traces German efforts at winning new markets for their industries in the three countries as well as German influence in these nations' armies. [R.V. Shaw]

2402. Schmidt, Steffen W. Political participation and development: the role of women in Latin America (CU/JIA, 30:2, Fall/Winter 1976/1977, p. 243-260, tables)

Analyzing recent studies of women, author concludes that education remains a primary factor in providing political and occupational progress for women in Latin America. He calls for further research, especially in conjunction with polls, to distinguish between professed loyalty to traditional values and actual power held by Latin American women.

2403. *Science and Society*. Independent journal of Marxism. John Jay College, City Univ. of New York, Vol. 39, No. 1, Spring 1975- . N.Y.

Issue devoted entirely to "Latin America: Aspects of Labor History." Discusses Cuba, Chile, Bolivia and Peru. All articles except one, were annotated separately in *HLAS 38* (see item number after title). Contents: Cristobal Kay "Chile: the Making of a Coup d'Etat" p. 1-25. Steven S. Volk "Class, Union, Party: the Development of a Revolutionary Union Movement in Bolivia: 1905-1952" (see *HLAS 38:3554*). Adrian DeWind "From Peasants to Miners: the Background to Strikes in the Mines of Peru" (see *HLAS 38:3463*); Fabio Grobart "The Cuban Working Class Movement: from 1925 to 1933" (see *HLAS 38:2843*); and Louis A. Pérez Jr. "Women in the Cuban Revolutionary War: 1953-1958: a Bibliography" (see *HLAS 38:2851*). [Ed.]

2404. Shaw, R. Paul. Land tenure and the rural exodus in Chile, Colombia, Costa Rica, and Peru. Gainesville, The Univ. Presses of Florida, 1976. 180 p., bibl., tables (Latin American monographs, 19)

This study presents theoretical models of migration from rural areas of four Latin American nations, principally during decade of 1950s. Concludes that economic opportunities for rural-agricultural population were systematically stifled by rigidities within the minifundio-latifundio complex, resulting in high rates of rural emigration.

2405. Silvert, Kalman H. Essays in understanding Latin America. Foreword by Joel M. Jutkowitz. Philadelphia, Pa. Institute for the Study of Human Issues, 1977. 240 p., tables.

Final work by one of the most sensitive, intelligent, and widely experienced Latin American scholars, the late Kalman Silvert. While essays were written between 1966-76, they are arranged out of chronology to illustrate development of Silvert's thoughts on a variety of topics over past decade. Especially poignant is the essay, perhaps his last, entitled "Coming Home." His views on the status of "democracy" and "freedom" in the Hemisphere are required reading.

2406. Smith, T. Lynn. The race between population and food supply in Latin America. Albuquerque, Univ. of New Mexico Press, 1976. 194 p., maps, tables.

Posthumous publication of last book written by one of the most renowned sociologists, T. Lynn Smith. Much of the material in this volume has appeared elsewhere; accordingly, the information within is often dated on this topic. As one would expect, the strongest features of the book are the data on Brazil. For sociologist's comment, see *HLAS 39:9215*.

2407. Sobel, Lester A. *ed.* Latin America 1976. N.Y., Facts on File, 1977. 213 p., tables.

Facts on File format for 1976. Includes individual chapters on 14 major Latin American nations and Puerto Rico. Summaries of events in other nations are condensed into one chapter. Also contains information on international meetings dealing with Latin America.

2408. Spalding, Hobart A., Jr. Organized labor in Latin America: historical case studies of workers in dependent societies. N.Y., Harper & Row, 1977. 297 p., tables.

Interpretive synthesis of historical labor movement, far surpassing other works on subject. Sets emergence of labor movement in context of struggle between ruling and working classes in capitalist world economy. Six chapters define features of stages through which movement has passed and illustrates them with events in Mexico, Argentina and Brazil, where populism and labor were interwoven, and events in Bolivia and Cuba, where drive to organize labor merged with revolutionary movements. Final chapter assesses influence of US labor movement upon trajectory of Latin American labor. Altogether provocative, effectively written reinterpretation based on wide variety of sources and well-focused analytical standpoint. Valuable for advanced undergraduates and graduate students, this essay points way for further research in this wide-open field. [V.C. Peloso]

2409. Stols, Eddy. Penetração econômica, assistência técnica e "brain drain:" aspectos da emigração Belga para a América Latina por volta de 1900 (JGSWGL, 13, 1976, p. 361-385)

Latin American hostility to Anglos and availability of surplus of well-educated Belgians with few domestic opportunities led Latin Americans to encourage and receive Belgian immigrants. Though few, they held important economic and technical positions. [L. Huddleston]

2410. Street, James H. The internal frontier and technological progress in Latin America (LARR, 12:3, 1977, p. 25-56, tables)

Sober and depressing treatment of historic, economic, and demographic factors, all greatly worsened by OPEC oil crisis of 1973, that are viewed as having a potentially apocalyptic impact on Latin America by year 2000. Both short-term crises in balance-of-payment deficits, rising living costs, economic growth rate, and disparate income distribution and long-term consequences of high rate population growth and staggering urban expansion are frightening.

2411. Szekely, Alberto. Latin America and the development of the law of the sea: regional documents and national legislation. v. 1. Dobbs Ferry, N.Y., Oceana, 1976. 361 p., bibl., tables (Oceana transnational services)

First of projected two vol. work. Vol. 1 analyzes contributions of Latin American countries to development of international law of the sea since 1945, especially the Continental Shelf doctrine. Unilateral, bilateral, multilateral, regional, and sub-regional approaches are examined. Vol. 2 will consist of national legislation enacted on the law of the sea by each country. For extensive bibliography on subject compiled by this author, see *HLAS 39:8648*.

2412. Tulchin, Joseph S. *ed.* Latin America in the year 2000. Translated by Paul Hazen. Reading, Mass., Addison-Wesley, 1975. 391 p., tables (Addison-Wesley series in history)

Interamerican Planning Society (SIAP) held its VII congress in Lima, Oct. 1968, where 33 papers were presented. This volume consists of 17 edited papers from meeting, representing divergent range of opinions concerning what can be expected to happen in next 30 years and proposals to improve Third World status of Latin America.

2413. Vangelista, Chiara. Immigrazione, struttura produttiva e mercato del lavoro in Argentina e in Brasile: 1876-1914 (Annali della Fondazione Luigi Einaudi [Fondazione Luigi Einaudi, Torino, Italy] 9, 1975, p. 197-216, bibl., tables)

Utilizando las técnicas de la historia económica cuantitativa, la autora analiza las diferencias entre la inmigración europea e italiana a la Argentina y al Brasil en cuanto al aumento de la producción exportable y la formación de un mercado nacional de la mano de obra. [M. Carmagnani]

2414. Welch, Claude E., Jr. *ed.* Civilian control of the military: theory and cases from developing countries. Albany, State Univ. of New York Press, 1976. 337 p., tables.

The 11 essays in this compilation examine alternatives to military control of Third World nations. Mexico and Chile are the only Latin American countries reviewed. Editor's concluding essay encourages limitation of military authority and establishment of political systems with broad popular support.

2415. Wilkie, James W. and Edna Monzón de Wilkie. Dimensions of elitelore: an oral history questionnaire

(UCLA/JLAL, 1:1, Summer 1975, p. 79-101)

Suggests questions for oral history interviews with elites but cautions that in application interviewers must maintain flexibility and adapt each interview to each personage.

2416. —— and **Paul Turovsky** eds. Statistical abstract of Latin America. v. 17, 1976. Los Angeles, Univ. of California, Latin American Center Publications, 1976. 395 p., tables.

Substantially revised in content and format from previous editions, vol. 17 provides convenient, single-volume reference for statistical information on 20 Latin American countries. Also serves as guide to additional sources containing statistical data. Where feasible, comparative figures are included for US.

2417. Wolf, Eric R. and **Sidney W. Mintz.** Haciendas y plantaciones en Mesoamérica y las Antillas (*in* Florescano, Enrique ed. Haciendas, latifundios y plantaciones en América Latina [see *HLAS 38:2190*] p. 493-531, bibl.)

Thoughtful and well-written analysis of technology, class stratification, marketing, capital investment, etc., which underpin haciendas and plantations in Puerto Rico, Jamaica, and Mexico. Authors note common patterns as well as exceptions in their study. Their findings are not projected elsewhere in Latin America, much less the world. (For contents of Florescano's volume, see *HLAS 38:2190*.)

MEXICO

GENERAL

ASUNCION LAVRIN
Associate Professor of History
Howard University

EDITH B. COUTURIER
Scholar-in-Residence
The Newberry Library

GENERAL

2418. Aguilar Camín, Héctor and others. En torno a la cultura nacional. México, Secretaría de Educación Pública (SEP) [and] Instituto Indígenista, 1976. 221 p., bibl. (SEP/INI, 51)

Collection of essays presented in a symposium sponsored by the Dept. of Historical Research of the National Institute of Anthropology and History in Mexico City. Theme of symposium was search for a national identity or national culture. Contributions by: José Emilio Pacheco "La Patria Perdida: Notas sobre Clavijero y la 'Cultura Nacional'" (p. 15-50); Nicole Giron "La Idea de la 'Cultura Nacional' en el Siglo XIX: Altamirano y Ramírez" (p. 51-84); José Joaquín Blanco "El Proyecto Educativo de José Vasconcelos como Programa Político" (p. 86-94); Héctor Aguilar Camín "Nociones Presidenciales de 'Cultura Nacional': de Alvaro Obregón a Gustavo Díaz Ordaz" (p. 95-134); Stefano Varese "Una Dialéctica Negada: Notas sobre la Multietnicidad Mexicana" (p. 135-158); Carlos Monsiváis "La Nación de unos Cuantos y las Esperanzas Románticas: Notas sobre la Historia del Término 'Cultura Nacional'" (p. 159-219). Some of these contributions are annotated separately and entered under author's name.

2419. Brading, David A. The capital structure of Mexican haciendas: León, 1700-1850 (IAA, 1, 1975 p. 151-182, bibl., tables)

Using available land titles and inventories of six estates in Bajío, Brading tests usefulness of both sources for reconstruction of history of properties and, more importantly, related issues of production, prices of commodities, and outlay of capital required from owners to run properties. Finds upward move in price of corn and land during period under examination. Brading sees correlation between growth of population in 18th century and afterwards, and increased demand for agricultural products. As unclaimed empty land diminished and labor supply expanded, land and its products became more expensive while labor became cheaper. Includes several useful Appendices with inventories and appraised value of commodities. Brading makes excellent use of his sources.

2420. ——. Estructura de la producción agrícola en el bajío: 1700-1850 (*in* Florescano, Enrique ed. Haciendas, latifundios y plantaciones en América [see *HLAS 38:2190*] p. 105-131, tables)

Analyzes the agrarian history of Bajío through survey of development of seven haciendas. Also describes internal organization of several other large properties. With imaginative use of census and other primary materials, Brading concludes that Bajío differs radically from both north and center and south because of presence of a middle class of ranchers and proprietors, and working class which migrated between rural and urban employment.

2421. ———. *Hacienda* profits and tenant farming in the Mexican Bajío: 1700-1860 (*in* Duncan, Kenneth; Ian Rutledge; and Colin Hardings *eds*. Land and labour in Latin America [see item 2156] p. 23-58, maps, tables)

Brading seeks to explore new angle in labor structure and land profitability in Bajío area by focusing on tenant farming. In early 18th century labor was expansive and land was cheap. Large landowners encouraged tenant farming to survive. The situation was reversed at the end of the century when labor was cheap and land values increased. Landowners sought to hike rents and restrict tenants' rights. The devastating effects of the wars of independence changed everything and forced landowners to consider breaking up their estates. The Reforma laws allowed the completion of that process. Brading uses several haciendas as case studies in this interesting and well-written article.

2422. Cabrera y Piña de Corsi, Matilde. La Casa de Cabrera en San Luis Potosí. San Luis Potosí, Mex., Editorial Universitaria Potosina, 1975. 207 p., facsims., illus., plates.

Genealogical study of the Cabrera family beginning in 18th century and continuing through present.

2423. Castañeda García, Carmen. El Colegio de Guadalajara (*in* La Compañía de Jesús en México: cuatro siglos de labor cultural, 1572-1972 [see item 2424] p. 53-76)

Panoramic account of foundation and development of educational institutions of Jesuits in city of Guadalajara. Study based on archival data and secondary sources.

2424. La Compañía de Jesús en México: cuatro siglos de labor cultural, 1572-1972. México, Editorial Jus, 1975. 635 p., facsims, plates.

Collection of scholarly papers on history of Society of Jesus in Mexico, written for the commemoration of 400th anniversary of Society's arrival in New Spain (1572-1972). Contributors to this volume are listed below. Those whose articles are annotated separately in this *HLAS* have item number after name: Ernest J. Burrus (item 2550); Xavier Cacho Vázquez (item 2482); Carmen Castañeda García (item 2423); J. Jesús Gómez Fregoso; Luis González Rodríguez (item 2559); José Gutiérrez Casillas; Thomas Hanrahan; Miguel León-Portilla (item 2468); Luis Medina Ascensio (item 2508); Eugenio Noriega Robles; Gonzalo Obregón; Humberto Ochoa Granados (item 2471); José Ignacio Palencia; Manuel Ignacio Pérez Alonso; Charles W. Polzer; Alberto Francisco Pradeau; Klaus Schreiber; Germán Somolinos d'Ardois; Alberto Valenzuela Rodarte; and Feliz Zubillaga.

2425. Cook, Sherburne F. The conflict between the California Indian and white civilization. Berkeley, Univ. of California Press, 1976. 522 p., tables.

Re-issue of six works by Berkeley demographer on California Indians (published 1949, see *HLAS 9:2771*). Essays include analysis of mission Indians which evaluates disease, nutrition, forced labor and cultural factors as contributors to the declining population, and comparative essay on non-mission Indians. Other articles deal with period after 1848.

2426. Cosío Villegas, Daniel *ed*. Historia general de México. t. 1/4. México, El Colegio de México, Centro de Estudios Históricos, 1976. 4 v. (288, 446, 337, 476 p.) bibl., illus., maps, plates.

Obra preparada por el Centro de Estudios Históricos de El Colegio de México y escrita en su mayor parte por profesores del mismo. Destinada a lectores de cierta madurez intelectual, pero no "cultos" o "ilustrados," como advierte su coordinador, don Daniel Cosío Villegas. Por ello se llamó "general:" por ser completa, en cuanto abarca desde la llegada del hombre al continente americano hasta nuestros días, y por estar dirigida al lector general, "o sea al que no tiene una preparación especial para leerla y apreciarla." Se notan en la obra algunas lagunas y ciertas repeticiones. Se trata más bien de una serie de cuadros que comprenden los principales temas de la historia mexicana. Hay también diferencias de esperarse entre distintos autores, en cuanto a penetración, prejuicios, etc. Todo esto no impide, sin embargo, que esta obra, escrita por competentes especialistas con la finalidad ya explicada, cumpla sus propósitos mucho mejor que ninguna de las existentes hasta el presente. El vol. 1 consiste de los siguientes artículos:

Daniel Cosío Villegas "Advertencia Preliminar" p. 1-4
Bernardo García Martínez "Consideraciones Orográficas" p. 5-82
José Luis Lorenzo "Los Orígenes Mexicanos" p. 83-124
Ignacio Bernal "Formación y Desarrollo de Mesoamérica" p. 125-164
Pedro Carrasco "La Sociedad Mexicana antes de la Conquista" p. 165-288. El vol. 2 contiene:
Alejandra Moreno Toscano "El Siglo de la Conquista" p. 1-82
Andrés Lira and Luis Muro "El Siglo de la Integración" p. 83-182
Enrique Florescano and Isabel Gil Sánchez "La Epoca de las Reformas Borbónicas y el Crecimiento Económico, 1750-1808" p. 183-302
Luis Villoro "La Revolución de Independencia" p. 303-356

Jorge Alberto Manrique "Del Barroco a la Ilustración" p. 357-446. El vol. 3 contiene: Josefina Zoraida Vázquez "Los Primeros Tropiezos" p. 1-84 Lilia Díaz "El Liberalismo Militante" p. 85-162 Luis González "El Liberalismo Triunfante" p. 163-282 José Luis Martínez "México en Busca de su Expresión" p. 283-337 El vol. 4 contiene: Berta Ulloa "La Lucha Armada, 1911-1920" p. 1-110 Lorenzo Meyer "El Primer Tramo del Camino" p. 111-200 Lorenzo Meyer "La Encrucijada" p. 201-284 Jorge Alberto Manrique "El Proceso de las Artes, 1910-1970" p. 285-476. [L. Gómez Canedo]

2427. Costeloe, Michael P. Mexico state papers: 1744-1843; a descriptive catalogue of the G.R.G. Conway Collection in the Institute of Historical Research, University of London. London, The Athlone Press, 1976. 153 p.

Catalogue of seven vols. (1209 items) of original and mostly printed documents on Mexican history from 1744 through 1847. Bulk of documents belong to period 1824-28 although collection is at its strongest between 1815-47. Royal decrees on trade, political proclamations, republican legislation and implementation of laws on fiscal and administrative matters form large part of this collection which covers one of most hectic and fascinating periods of Mexico's history.

2428. Couturier, Edith Boorstein. La hacienda de Hueyapan: 1550-1936. Traducción de Carlos E. Guerrero. México, Secretaría de Educación Pública, 1976. 196 p., map (SepSetentas, 301)

In this study of origins and development of colonial hacienda, Couturier stresses importance of capital and labor as factors determining manner of growth and expansion of this particular hacienda which are also relevant to others. Notes importance of substantially different approaches to landownership of two families who owned this property: Reglas and Landeros. Former represent more orthodox and cautious exploitation, while latter, under influence of rapidly changing social and economic circumstances, were more adventurous in land management. Long time span covered by this study makes it very useful for long-view of hacienda history.

2429. Dysart, Jane. Mexican women in San Antonio, 1830-1860: the assimilation process (WHQ, 7:4, Oct. 1976, p. 365-375)

Preliminary study based on cursory view of baptismal and census records of San Antonio confirms importance of both concubinage and marriage in relations between Mexicans and Anglos. Notes that wealthy Mexican families often married one of their daughters to a capable Anglo migrant.

2430. González Ponce, Enrique B. Catálogo del Ramo de Cofradías y Archicofradías. México, Archivo General de la Nación, 1977. 53 p. (mimeo) (Serie guías y catálogos, 4)

Useful catalogue of 19 volumes of section on confraternities and archconfraternities of Nation's General Archives. Includes complete description of documents contained in each volume. Cataloguer has written a brief but helpful introduction explaining character and functions of confraternities.

2431. Harris, Charles H. The "overmighty family:" the case of the Sánchez Navarros (*in* International Congress of Mexican History, IV, Santa Monica, Calif., 1973. Contemporary Mexico [see item 2730] p. 47-61)

Traces the history of Sánchez Navarro's 16.5 million acre latifundia in northern Mexico from its inception in mid-18th century through 1867 which marked end of individual estates. For complete story of this hacienda, see author's book (*HLAS 38:2440*).

2432. Kessell, John L. Friars, soldiers and reformers: Hispanic Arizona and the Sonora mission frontier, 1767-1856. Tucson, Univ. of Arizona Press, 1976. 346 p., bibl., illus., maps.

Popularly written and profusely illustrated history of region around Tumacacori mission between expulsion of Jesuits and establishment of territory. Based on primary sources, this study is especially rich in biographical information on friars and ethnographic materials.

2433. León-Portilla, Miguel. Culturas en peligro. México, Alianza Editorial Mexicana, 1976. 227 p., bibl., maps (Biblioteca iberoamericana, 2)

Collection of essays by well-known anthropologist on the theme of defeated or subjected groups undergoing a cultural identity crisis as they confront the danger and suffering resulting from assimilation by stronger groups. León Portilla establishes a conceptual framework in first essay and discusses variety of historical circumstances such as the acculturation of Chichimecs in prehispanic times, influence of spiritual conquest on indigenous groups, etc. Very stimulating collection of essays on a novel topic.

2434. Metzgar, Joseph V. The Atrisco Land Grant: 1692-1977 (UNM/NMHR, 52:4, Oct. 1977, p. 269-296)

Factual delineation, based on secondary materials, of history of late 17th-century land grant which still remains in possession of descendants of original recipients.

2435. Moch de Martínez Mezquida, Raquel. La mujer en la legislación mexicana (UY/R, 17:102, nov./dic. 1975, p. 34-51)

Taking 1870 as a starting point for the study of the evolution of the legal status of women in Mexico, the author describes the process whereby women gained civil rights and equality with men before the law. She ends with the 1973 legislation on planned parenthood, which she considers a great gain for women's social equality. This article focuses on legislation only and it is more a personal statement of faith in the progress of women's legal and social status than a scholarly survey.

2436. Moreno Toscano, Alejandra and Enrique Florescano. El sector externo y la organización espacial y regional de México, 1521-1910 (*in* International Congress of Mexican History, IV, Santa Monica, Calif., 1973. Contemporary Mexico [see item 2730] p. 62-96)

Interpretive essay aimed at establishing a new basis for study of development of regions in Mexico and their relations with the capital. Authors underscore need to look into historical background of regions and nation as a whole in order to understand role of center and parts. They contend that during colonial period external trade gave cohesion to Viceroyalty and established pattern of dependency of capital on Spain and Europe and of provinces on capital. Mexico City assumed role of metropolis of provinces. After independence, period of crisis ruralization and desarticulation during Federation was eventually superceded by restoration of strong central government during the Porfiriato. Suggestive and coherently developed paper with well argued thesis.

2437. Moyano, Ángela. Nuevo México y los viajeros norteamericanos (UNAM/A, 6, 1973, p. 31-37)

Utilizing travel accounts of Zebulon Pike, Josiah Gregg, and Susan Shelby Magoffin's descriptions, author notes that North American tactics of conquest included infiltration of settlers and traders.

2438. Neri, Michael C. Narcisco Durán and the secularization of the California missions (AAFH/TAM, 33:3, Jan. 1977, p. 411-429)

Indian policy in California between 1805 and 1846 described from viewpoint of friar working in missions.

2439. Prieto, Alejandro. Historia, geografía y estadística del estado de Tamaulipas. Reproducción facsimilar de la edición de 1873. México, Librería de Manual Porrúa, 1975. 361 p., plates.

Republication of 1873 collection of brief articles on history and geography of Tamaulipas. Includes materials on Indians, conquest, colonial and 19th-century events.

2440. Randall, Laura. A comparative economic history of Latin America: 1500-1914. v. 1, México. Ann Arbor, Mich., Univ. Microfilms International (UMI), 1977. 292 p., bibl., map, tables.

Work of synthesis which draws from studies printed up to 1968. Since that date a number of excellent original contributions have been made in this field. It is therefore unfortunate that this volume suffers from a 10-year bibliographical lag. Nevertheless, work offers readable, compact history of most important economic structures and trends in Mexico since precolumbian times to 1910.

2441. Rees, Peter W. Transportes y comercio entre México y Veracruz: 1519-1910. Traducción de Ana Elena Lara Zúñiga. México, Secretaría de Educación Pública, 1976. 191 p. (Sep-Setentas, 304)

Interesting survey of development of roads as arteries for communication, external and internal trade, agricultural development and urban settlement. Work deals with Mexico-Veracruz area only. Section on republican period stresses development of railroad net between Veracruz and Mexico and role played by state and private entrepreneurs in that process. Author concludes that railroads failed to open new routes or promote important structural changes in area's economy, which retained much of its colonial communications pattern and character.

2442. Río, Ignacio del. A guide to the Archivo Franciscano of the National Library of Mexico. v. 1. With an introduction by Lino Gómez Canedo. Advertencia de Ernesto de la Torre Villar. México, UNAM, Instituto de Investigaciones Bibliográficas [and] Academy of American Franciscan History, Washington, 1975. 499 p., facsims. (Biblioteca Nacional de México. Serie guías, 3)

Vol. 1 of projected three of general guide to Franciscan manuscripts available at National Library of Mexico City and National Institute of Anthropology and History. Vol. 1 covers material existing in 50 boxes, Franciscan and non-Franciscan documents. General introduction by Lino Gómez Canedo, O.F.M., describes contents of both repositories.

Non-Franciscan manuscripts are important for the history of Mexico's northwest.

2443. Salgado, José Eusebio. Historia del dominio mexicano sobre la Baja California y el mar de Cortés (PPO, 14:56, dic. 1973, p. 457-472)

Contribution to diplomatic history which traces Mexico's control over the "Sea of Cortés" (i.e., Gulf of California) from 1524 to 1970s. Based primarily upon published materials, it summarizes both modern and colonial materials on the economic and political development of Baja California.

2444. Sánchez Gómez, María del Pilar. Catálogo de fuentes de la historia de Tamaulipas. pt. 2. Ciudad Victoria, Mex., Univ. Autónoma de Tamaulipas, 1976. 113 p.

Catalogue to manuscripts available in National Library of Mexico City on history of present-day Tamaulipas. Collection contains limited number of 17th-century documents of Franciscan missionary activities in Tamaulipas, Nuevo Santander and Provincias Internas. Strength of collection lies on 19th-century political manuscripts of Liberal leaders.

2445. Semo, Enrique and others. Siete ensayos sobre la hacienda mexicana: 1780-1880. México, INAH, Depto. de Investigaciones Históricas, 1977. 271 p., illus., maps, tables (Col Científica, 55. Historia)

Interesting studies on records and other materials from Agrarian Department archives pertaining to 19th-century hacienda history. They include analyses of history and operation of three different haciendas: Chapingo, near Texcoco; Doña Rosa in Oaxaca; and San Antonio Tenextepec in Veracruz. There are also two general studies of groups of haciendas in Chalco and Acolmán. Jorge Basave Kunhardt contributes a particularly original study of 19th-century agricultural technology, and there is a useful description of weights and measures and their changes in period between 1780-1880. Semo's introduction lucidly describes some of the principle issues in modern hacienda studies. Reproduction of hacienda plans, maps, and photos are another noteworthy aspect of this book.

2446. Sepúlveda, César. La frontera norte de México: historia, conflictos, 1762-1975. México, Editorial Porrúa, 1976. 171 p., bibl., fold. maps.

General study of Mexico's northern frontier starting with acquisition of Louisiana (1763) and concluding with latest frontier adjustments between Mexico and US (1970). Informative work of synthesis but for general reader rather than scholar. Includes useful maps illustrating changes in location of frontier.

2447. Torre, Toribio de la and others. Historia general de Tamaulipas. Presentación de Juan Fidel Zorrilla. Prólogo de Candelari Reyes Flores. Tamaulipas, Mex., Univ. Autónoma de Tamaulipas, Instituto de Investigaciones Históricas, 1975. 248 p.

History of Tamaulipas written in 1843, which includes geographical data, details on conquest, early 19th-century political history, and biographical material about author.

2448. Wilkinsin, J.B. Laredo and the Rio Grande frontier: a narrative. Austin, Tex., Jenkins Publishing, 1975. 456 p., bibl., plates.

General history of Laredo region beginning with José de Escandón and continuing through Carranza administration in 1920. Based principally on secondary material, book informs us about many events, but contains little new interpretation.

2449. Zorrilla, Juan Fidel. La mujer en Tamaulipas. Ciudad Victoria, Mex., Univ. Autónoma de Tamaulipas, Instituto de Investigaciones Históricas, 1976. 67 p., illus.

Biographical sketches, of a number of Mexican women born in Tamaulipas originally published in a newspaper column. Brief and superficial, with scant meaningful information. Only merit of this slim volume is to underline need for better studies on topic.

COLONIAL PERIOD

ASUNCION LAVRIN

Associate Professor of History
Howard University

EDITH B. COUTURIER

Scholar-in-Residence
The Newberry Library

THE SUBDIVISIONS OF THIS SECTION have been revised for greater clarity. Under the subsection entitled "General" (see items 2418-2449) we have placed titles that cover the whole span of Mexican history, from precolumbian or colonial times to the 19th and 20th centuries. The subsection "Colonial General" contains surveys of the colonial period, historiography, bibliographies, guides to archives, comparative studies and others which cannot be said to belong to a particular region of Mexico. The subsection "Central and South" will apply to studies geographically confined between Zacatecas in the north and Yucatan-Chiapas in the South. And finally, the subsection "North and Borderlands" will comprise works on the far northern provinces of Mexico and those areas which are today part of the southwestern and southeastern U.S.

Social and economic history continue to be the most cultivated areas of colonial Mexican historiography. Research on specific social groups seem to be the strongest trend. The nobility at the end of the colonial period, the military, merchants, blacks, and Indians have been the object of several noteworthy studies by Archer (item 2475); Hoberman (item 2499); Ladd (item 2465); and Palmer (item 2513). A significant number of studies focused on Indians. The Seminario de Historia de América de Valladolid (Spain) published two volumes of monographs on Indian groups throughout Spanish America. Although the scope of the contributions is often narrow, in their totality they constitute a substantial contribution to our knowledge of Indians vis-à-vis Spaniards during the colonial period. See for example, item 2505; Anderson (item 1953). Indian policy also received considerable attention in the borderlands area. The reprint of Cook's demographic study of the California Indians (item 2425); articles by Archer (item 2545); Moorhead (item 2565); and Neri (item 2438) explore new aspects of Indian-Spanish relations. The interrelations of groups within colonial society was successfully dealt with by John K. Chance in a study of Oaxacan society (item 2486) and in his work with Taylor (item 2487).

A group of monographs on specific regions—although not quite microhistory—form an interesting new trend tying social and economic history in a dynamic relationship. Under study are areas with a distinctive economic unity, or regions where there was a clear integration between an urban center and its surrounding countryside. Examples of this kind of new approach are those in Altman and Lockhart's multi-essay volume (item 2451). More restricted in range, but equally aiming at strengthening and enlarging the historical literature on colonial regions are some of the monographs produced in Mexico, especially those published by the Dept. of Historical Studies of the National Institute of Anthropology and History. See for example, Hurtado López's book entitled *Dolores Hidalgo* (item 2500).

After a slow start following the publication of François Chevalier's work on 16th and 17th-century haciendas (published in France in 1952, and translated into Spanish in 1956) the subject of hacienda history has generated so many studies that the field is fast becoming crowded. Six of the studies in the work on haciendas and plantations edited by Enrique Florescano (see *HLAS 38:2190*) deal with colonial Mexico and enlarge greatly the literature on the agrarian organization of five regions of New Spain. See for example, Tovar Pinzón (item 2537); Michael Riley (item 2522); Taylor (see *HLAS 36:1993*); Brading (item 2420); James D. Riley (see *HLAS 36:1846*);

López Sarrelangue (item 2504). The contributions to the Altman-Lockhart volume (item 2451) have also analyzed the growth of large agricultural units in their regions. The Jesuit haciendas of the Puebla area are dealt with by Ursula Ewald (item 2491). Additional works by Patch (item 2515); Couturier (item 2428); and Beltrán (item 2479) encompass a variety of regions and time periods. This rich collection of monographs describes and analyzes but does not draw any comparisons or tries to interrelate available material. A work of synthesis will soon be necessary.

An unexpected windfall in Church history was the publication of a voluminous book with 16 articles on the role of the Jesuits in colonial Mexico (item 2424) on the 400th anniversary of their arrival in New Spain. The general character of recent publications on the Church is traditional in approach and content, dealing with the histories of religious orders, the foundation and growth of schools, or Church personalities. A departure from this line—although not strictly Church history—is a provocative study by S. Behocaray Albero (item 2452) correlating the rate of criminality and unstable economic periods, having used as a source the records of the Inquisition. In this instance, a traditional source has been used for a non-traditional research topic. This suggests that ecclesiastical sources are potentially rich in socio-economic data which have remained relatively untapped and that could be used for interesting monographs.

Although demographic studies were on the wane, there was an important contribution by William T. Sanders (item 2525) which challenged the results of the Berkeley School's population estimates in Central Mexico prior to and after the conquest. Debate on this topic is thus likely to continue. Finally, although there were several distinguished contributions to 16th and 17th-century historiography, the late 18th century was the period most intensely studied during this biennium.

In the history of the North and Borderlands the vast microfilming of local and parish archives of those areas has resulted in the increased use of census and other demographic materials. Thus, there was a rise in the numbers of works on social history which may lead to new interpretations of the northern regions of New Spain. Good examples of this new type of works are Dobyn's census material for Tucson (item 2555) and Campbell's work on the soldiers of the presidio (item 2552). Other historians such as Dysart (item 2429) and Timmons (item 2578) have used these data in less ambitious ways.

The appearance of a number of biographies or shorter studies reevaluating significant events in the lives of frontier personalities are also abundant this biennium. Illustrative of this type of work are Albert Stagg on the first Bishop of Sonora (item 2574); Kessel's work on the Franciscan friars (item 2432); the work on Velázquez de León in Baja California (item 2556); and on Pedro de Fages by Joseph P. Sánchez (item 2572). Also very good are John P. Moore's study of revolt in Louisiana (item 2564) which underlines the role of Antonio de Ulloa in the Louisiana rebellion, and María del Carmen Velázquez's work on the borderland activities of the Marquis of Altamira (item 2580). While no new general interpretations have appeared which would modify accepted views of the borderlands in the colonial period, perhaps the slow accretion of monographs on population, the army, the new biographies and the new perspectives on social history will provide a basis for a future synthesis of the history of the region north of Zacatecas.

GENERAL

2450. Aguilar, Francisco de, *Fray*. Relación breve de la conquista de la Nueva España. Preliminary study by Jorge Gurría Lacroix. México, UNAM, Instituto de Investigaciones Históricas, 1977. 225 p., bibl.

Eyewitness of conquest of Mexico, Fray Francisco de Aguilar wrote account of this event when he was over 80, ca. 1560-65. First printed in 1892, this is 7. ed. since then. In preliminary study, Gurría Lacroix explains concept of history of Spanish conquistador and provides helpful analysis of Aguilar's style and contents of his narrative. This ed. has both 16th-century and modern ortography and list of archaisms to assist reader.

2451. Altman, Ida and **James Lockhart** eds. Provinces of Mexico: variants of Spanish American regional evolution. Los Angeles, Univ. of California, 1976. 291 p., bibl., maps, tables (UCLA Latin American Center publications)

Collection of regional studies of colonial Mexico by ten authors. Introduction by James Lockhart (see item 2502) discusses such themes as behavioral patterns of ethnic groups, labor and landed estates and interrelation of capital and provinces. Articles in this volume are reviewed separately and entered under author's name, i.e.: Marta Espejo-Ponce Hunt (see item 2490); William B. Taylor (see item 2533); James Lockhart (see item 2502); Leslie Lewis (see item 2501); David M. Szewczyk (see item 2531); Ward Barrett (see item 2478); John M. Tutino (see item 2539); P.J. Bakewell (see item 2477); John C. Super (see item 2530); and Ida Altman (see item 2544).

2452. Behocaray Albero, Solange. Indices económicos e Inquisición en la Nueva España: siglos XVI y XVII (CDAL, 9/10, 1976, p. 247-64, tables)

Essay attempts new interpretation of information on delictive activities provided by inquisitorial records. Author's thesis is that stable economic situations generated fewer crimes than periods of economic changes or crisis situations. However, stresses that economic crisis did not necessarily lead to increase in crime. It was economic *instability* that triggered increases in criminality. Based on quantitative analysis of data for Zacatecas, Puebla and Veracruz, this article established interesting theory which should be developed in greater detail. Nevertheless, it succeeds in using available data imaginatively and in opening new interpretive possibilities.

2453. Borah, Woodrow. Legacies of the past: colonial (*in* International Congress of Mexican History, IV, Santa Monica, Calif., 1973. Contemporary Mexico: papers [see item 2730] p. 29-36)

Brief but interesting essay in which Prof. Borah stresses continuities in Mexican history. Underscores number of cultural values and social usages such as legal and educational systems, village government, family structure, prestige attached to landownership, political caciquism and many others. Obviously, legacies of past are many, and subtle observation reveals traditional links with colonial period.

2454. Boyer, Richard. Mexico and the seventeenth century: transition of a colonial society (HAHR, 57:3, Aug. 1977, p. 455-478)

Reassesses role of Mexico City and other regions of Viceroyalty in 17th century, as well as previous interpretations of relations between Spain and New Spain. After considering such factors as trade patterns, role of merchants, population changes and agricultural production, Boyer concludes that 17th century was not one of depression but of "transition to capitalism, economic development and vigorous regional economies . . ." Interesting interpretive essay synthesizing latest revisionist opinions on the 17th century."

2455. Florescano, Enrique. Las visiones imperiales de la época colonial: 1500-1811 (CM/HM, 26 [106]:2, oct./dic. 1977, p. 195-230)

Survey of major historians of New Spain during colonial period. Stresses Spaniard's own vision of their role in New World and world history, and their relations with Indians. Great attention is paid to historians of late 18th century. Useful survey.

2456. Frost, Elsa Cecilia. El milenarismo franciscano en México y el profeta Daniel (CM/HM, 26[101]:1, julio/sept. 1976, p. 3-28, bibl.)

Allegory of statue with clay feet and coming of kingdom of the true God from Book of Daniel serves author to trace millenarian inclinations in thoughts of Fray Toribio de Motolinía, Fray Jerónimo Mendieta and Fray Juan de Torquemada. Authors' eschatological allusions are veiled but present nonetheless. Intriguing interpretive essay offers some interesting nuances concerning Franciscans' writers vision of New World, its people and their place in history.

2457. García Saiz, Concepción. La formación artística del indígena en Nueva España (*in* Jornadas Americanistas, III, Valladolid, Spain, 1974. Estudios sobre política indigenista española en América [see item 2298] v. 3, p. 321-343, plates)

Explores circumstances under which Indians could learn and practice arts of painting, sculpturing and architecture in colonial New Spain. Guilds and Academy (founded in late 18th century) barred Indians since mid-17th century. More open attitude towards Indian had existed in 16th century. Whether the Church, as patron of arts, could have influenced this situation remains moot point.

2458. Garrido Aranda, Antonio. La educación de moriscos y mexicas como factor de asimilación cultural (*in* Jornadas Americanistas, III, Valladolid, Spain, 1974. Estudios sobre política indigenista española en América [see item 2298] v. 2, p. 9-19, illus.)

Study of different methods adopted by Spaniards for education of Granada's Moslem and Mexico's Aztec youth, two experiments which ran parallel in time. In both instances, although for different reasons, they failed. Unwillingness of late 16th-century religious orders to continue indoctrinating Mexicans needs stressing.

2459. Gemelli Careri, Giovanni Francesco. Viaje a la Nueva España. Estudio preliminar, traducción y notas de Francisca Perujo. México, UNAM, Dirección General de Publicaciones, 1976. 214 p., bibl., fold. map, illus., map (Nueva biblioteca mexicana, 29)

El viajero italiano Gemelli Careri incluyó en su voluminosa obra *Giro del mondo* (Nápoli, 1699-1700; 6 vols.) un relato del viaje hecho por él desde el puerto de Acapulco en Filipinas hasta el puerto de Acapulco en Nueva España, y de sus experiencias y observaciones en este último país. Todas las ediciones previas han sido ampliamente superadas por la presente de Francisca Perujo. Primera que ofrece un estudio bien documentado, crítico y completo de la persona y obra de Gemelli, y en especial de sus noticias acerca de la Nueva España. Deja bien sentado que Gemelli Careri estuvo en México, cuales fueron las fuentes adicionales que utilizó y que crédito merece, en conjunto, su *Viaje a la Nueva España*. Perujo ha realizado un trabajo excepcional, cuya consulta es indispensable para quien desee conocer la verdad sobre Gemelli Careri. [L. Gómez Canedo]

2460. Gurría Lacroix, Jorge. Historiografía sobre la muerte de Cuauhtémoc. México, UNAM, Instituto de Investigaciones Históricas, Dirección General de Publicaciones, 1976. 73 p., illus. (Cuadernos. Serie histórica, 16)

Exhaustive study of 18 accounts of execution of Cuauhtémoc written in 16th and early 17th centuries. Sources are quoted and then analyzed in order to find areas of agreement on events of 1525. Chart summarizes disputed points. Author concludes that Cortes' fears led him to believe in the existence of a conspiracy.

2461. Hanke, Lewis and Celso Rodríguez eds. Los virreyes españoles en América durante el gobierno de la Casa de Austria. t. 3, México. Madrid, Biblioteca de Autores Españoles, 1977. 336 p. (Col. Rivadeneira)

Vol. 3 in collection concerning all Spanish Viceroys of America during Habsburgh period. Covers following Viceroys of New Spain: Luis de Velasco hijo (1607-11); Francisco García Guerra (1611-12); Diego Fernández de Córdova, Marqués de Guadalcazar (1612-21); Diego Carillo de Mendoza y Pimentel, Marqués de Gelves (1621-24); and Rodrigo Pacheco y Osorio, Marqués de Cerralvo (1624-1635). Brief historical introduction precedes transcription of several documents pertaining to each Viceroy, such as their Instructions, Relations of their administration, sentences of Council of Indies, etc. Very useful Appendix to each Viceroy contains all documents referring to him and now available at Archives of Seville and Mexico. Excellent research and reference tool.

2462. Heredia Herrera, Antonio and José Joaquín Real Díaz. Las cartas de los virreyes de Nueva España a la Corona española en el siglo XVI: características diplomáticas, indices cronológico y de materias (EEHA/AEA, 31, 1974, p. 441-596)

Study of style of viceregal correspondence to King and Council of Indies precedes exhaustive catalogue of all known letters written between 1535-1600. Letters are ordered chronologically and topically. Useful tool for research and reference.

2463. Huerta, María Teresa and Patricia Palacios eds. Rebeliones indígenas de la época colonial. México, INAH, Depto. de Investigaciones Históricas, Seminario de Historiografía Social, 1976. 336 p., maps.

Selection of accounts of 30 Indian rebellions between 1531-1740 divided in two sections: Center-South and North. Extracted from contemporary chronicles and military reports and few secondary studies, works also include bibliography, introductory paragraphs explaining context of events and annotations.

Ixtlilxóchitl, Fernando de Alva. *Obras históricas* incluyen el texto completo de las llamadas *Relaciones e historia de la Nación Chichimeca* en una nueva versión establecida con el cotejo de los manuscritos más antiguos que se conocen. See item 1987.

2464. Jansen, André. Charles et Theodore de Croix: Deux Gardes Wallons. Vice-Rois de l'Amérique espagnole au XVIII siécle. Paris, Gembloux, 1977. 84 p., illus. (Serie Wallonie, art et histoire)

Brief biographies of Charles and Theodore de Croix, written by a Belgian historian and based principally on published works, although some primary sources from the Croix family archives in Franc-Waret were also used. Book has material on early lives and military training of the two Croix, as well as information on their ties to Charles III, to José de Gálvez and to each other.

2465. Ladd, Doris M. The Mexican nobility at independence: 1780-1826. Austin, Univ. of Texas, Institute of Latin American Studies, 1976. 316 p., bibl., tables (Latin American monographs, 40)

Excellent study of Mexican colonial elites at three different levels: economic, social and political. Ladd provides wealth of data on titled nobility's properties, investments, social connections and their political stand throughout independence period. Defines titled nobility as plutocrats and patriarchs who retained those roles even after independence. Suggests further studies of family connections and family itself as socioeconomic unit. Contends future studies of colonial period should be carried out at least until 1821, since 1810 means nothing in social history. Several very useful appendices offer personal information on all nobles of Mexico. Most commendable synthesis study of social group in colonial period.

2466. Lafaye, Jacques. Conciencia nacional y conciencia étnica en la Nueva España: un problema semántico (*in* International Congress of Mexican History, IV, Santa Monica, Calif., 1973. Contemporary Mexico [see item 2730] p. 38-46)

Explores meaning of words such as *nación, patria, mexicano,* etc. as they were used in literary and historical sources throughout colonial period, in order to help determine development of consciousness of separate nationality—despite ethnic differences—among all Mexican-born members of society. Lafaye points to Guadalupan cult as common heritage to all pre-independent social groups. Perceptive exercise in *mentalité* studies.

2467. ———. Quetzalcóatl and Guadalupe: the formation of Mexican national consciousness, 1531-1813. Foreword by Octavio Paz. Translated by Benjamin Keen. Chicago, Ill., The Univ. of Chicago Press, 1976. 336 p., illus.

Excellent English translation of controversial but creative study of development of a Mexican collective identity through analysis of religious sources. A contribution to both intellectual history and study of popular culture. (For previous reviews of French editions, see *HLAS 36:1316* and *HLAS 36:1818*.)

2468. León-Portilla, Miguel. La aportación de Miguel del Barco, 1706-1790, a la historia de Baja California. (*in* La Compañía de Jesús en México: cuatro siglos de labor cultural: 1572-1972 [see item 2424] p. 241-252)

Study of unpublished work of Miguel del Barco whose writings on Baja California provide excellent information on natural history, ethnology and linguistics. León-Portilla considers him one of the primary sources of information for that region.

2469. Mendieta, Gerónimo de, *Fray.* Historia eclesiástica indiana. v. 1/2. Estudio preliminar y edición de Francisco Solano y Pérez-Lila. Madrid, Ediciones Atlas, 1973. 2 v. (219, 313 p.) (Biblioteca de autores españoles, 260/261)

Primera reedición verdadera, con amplia y novedosa introducción y apéndice importante. Este reedita otra obra de Mendieta: "Descripción de la Relación de la Provincia del Santo Evangelio," de México. La presente reedición de la *Historia* reproduce el texto publicado por Icazbalceta; del único manuscrito conocido—hoy en la Colección Latinoamericana de la Univ. de Texas, Austin—sólo fueron tomados los grabados, cuya serie completa nos da el nuevo editor. [L. Gómez-Canedo]

2470. Moreno, Roberto. El indigenismo de Clavijero y Alzate (*in* Jornadas Americanistas, III, Valladolid, Spain, 1974. Estudios sobre política indigenista española en América [see item 2298] v. 3, p. 43-52)

Surveys Clavijero's and Alzate's ideas on Indians and their civilization. While Clavijero concentrated on indigenous heritage and past, neglecting period's population, Alzate was mostly interested in contemporary Indians of late 18th century and their unfortunate situation.

2471. Ochoa Granados, Humberto. Los jesuitas y la filosofía en la época colonial (*in* La Compañía de Jesús en México: cuatro siglos de labor cultural, 1572-1972 [see item 2424] p. 351-378)

General survey of activities of Jesuit philosophers in New Spain, their influence on curriculum of studies in colony, their relations with the university and their intellectual contribution to the colony.

2471a. Pacheco, José Emilio. La patria perdida: notas sobre Clavijero y la cultura nacional (*in* Aguilar Camín, Héctor and others. En torno a la cultura nacional [see item 2418] p. 15-50)

Defines concept of national culture in 18th century as *criollo* product enhanced by indigenous traditions. Clavijero is regarded as definer of national culture in that century. Despite his ardent defense of indigenous cultures, Clavijero is perceived as spokesman for his ethnic group and founder of *criollo* feeling of nationality best expressed by his "anticolonial" attitude which dismissed Europe as center of culture. Pacheco feels that this marked beginning of a national intellectual liberation. This work is a synthesis of Clavijero's own ideas and well-known interpretations of his work.

2472. Parry, J.H. Juan de Tovar and the history of the Indians (APS/P, 121:4, Aug. 1977, p. 316-319)

Brief but pithy essay which convincingly suggests a number of reasons why some histories of indigenous Mexican civilizations were never published despite their merits. Parry points to Council of Indies' concern on spread of "wrong" notions on origins of the Indians, identity of Quetazacoatl and importance of Cortés in the conquest. Author stresses Tovar's significance and contributions to writing an officially acceptable history of Indies not only through his own *Historia* but as reliable source of information for José de Acosta.

Sahagún, Bernardino de. *Florentine Codex*: general history of the things of New Spain. See item 2011.

Sánchez, Jean Pierre. Le *Cordex de Florence*: un manuscrit négligé de l'*Historia general de las cosas de Nueva España* de fray Bernardino de Sahagún. See item 2012.

2473. Semo, Enrique. Historia del capitalismo en México: los orígenes, 1521-1763. México, Ediciones Era, 1973. 281 p., bibl., illus., maps, plates (Col. El hombre y su tiempo)

Examines major components of economic structure of colonial Mexico such as labor, taxation, trade, mining, money accumulation and flow, landownership, etc. Concludes that existence of commercial capital in Mexico did not mean existence of capitalist system during period under study. New Spain only had embrionic capitalist system. There was primitive accumulation of capital in colonies but effects were enjoyed in Europe. Interesting attempt at general analysis and interpretation of colonial Mexico's economic development.

CENTRAL AND SOUTH

2474. Alanís Boyso, José Luis. Introducción al estudio de los corregidores y alcaldes mayores del Marquesado del Valle: títulos de 1590 a 1810 (MAGN/B, 13, Serie 2, 1972/1976, p. 5-185, bibl.)

Article's documentary appendix lists *corregidores* and *alcaldes mayores* of towns belonging to Marquesado del Valle (succesors of Cortés) from 1590 to 1810. Introductory study deals with qualifications required for appointment, terms of service, salaries, provisions for interim occupancy, etc.

Anderson, Arthur O.J.; Frances Berdan; and **James Lockhart** eds. Beyond the Codices: the Nahua view of colonial Mexico. See item 1953.

2475. Archer, Christon I. The army in Bourbon Mexico: 1760-1810. Albuquerque, Univ. of New Mexico Press, 1977. 365 p., illus., tables.

Major study of military in New Spain, towards end of colonial period, which successfully mixes institutional and socioeconomic data. Policies for reorganization and government of military under several Viceroys are well documented to show significant changes and their consequences (with such interesting revelations as shocking state of neglect of regular army in century's last decade). Chapters on the cabildo, merchant class, and army manpower shift book's emphasis to social aspects of military. Backed by extensive archival research, this highly commendable study provides clear picture of mechanisms that helped shape one of the most influential social groups in Mexico.

2476. Báez Macías, Eduardo. Los santos desiertos de los Carmelitas Descalzos en la Nueva España (UAEM/H, 1:1, enero/marzo 1976. p. 15-30, illus., map)

Santos desiertos of Carmelite Order were special kind of convents peculiar to this order in which monks lived partly in the community and partly as hermits in retirement cells physically separated from the community building. Study traces history of these communities in Spain and their transplant to Mexico. Stresses architectural layout of *desiertos* but historian will find enough material on process of foundation, acquisition of land and relations with the state.

2477. Bakewell, Peter J. Zacatecas: an economic and social outline of a silver mining district: 1547-1700 (*in* Altman, Ida and James Lockhart eds. Provinces of early Mexico [see item 2451] p. 199-229)

Lucid exposition of Zacatecas position in New Spain's economy and many socioeconomic factors which contributed to its growth as core of key mining region. Examines techniques of mining and output of silver, patterns of mine and land ownership, role of miners and merchants in economy and as interest groups, and role of mercury on silver production. Bakewell stresses subtle but important relationship between Zacatecas and economy of New Spain, describing how they interlocked. Well written and useful synthesis.

2478. Barrett, Ward. Morelos and its sugar industry in the late eighteenth century (*in* Altman, Ida and James

Lockhart eds. Provinces of Mexico: variants of Spanish American regional evolution [see item 2451] p. 155-175)

Studies general characteristics of Morelos as sugar-producing region. Author's thesis is that sugar haciendas formed system of mutually interrelated units in production and marketing. Also adds that area haciendas were not autonomous isolated feudal or semifeudal estates. Barrett develops his topic by focusing on costs of production and labor and industry's financing. Concludes with assessment of relationship between towns and sugar haciendas. Well organized study with valuable data and conclusions.

2479. Beltrán, Ulises. La hacienda de San Pedro Jorullo, Michoacán: 1585-1795 (CM/HM, 26:4, abril/junio 1977, p. 540-574, maps, tables)

Traces origins and physical growth of hacienda in Michoacan's border with tropical lowlands (*tierra caliente*). Based on legal titles, study illustrates hacienda's expansion, litigations and changes in ownership from early 17th through the mid-18th century. There are many similarities between this hacienda's growth and others in different areas. Useful material for comparative purposes.

2480. Brading, David A. Noticias sobre la economía de Querétaro y de su Corregidor Don Miguel Domínguez, 1802-1811 (MAGN/B, 11:3/4, July/Dec. 1970, p. 275-278)

Growth of bureaucracy under Boubons and employment of many creoles produced heretofore unappreciated wealth of manuscript commentary on political, social and economic issues "as important for the historians as that of Manuel Abad y Queipo" (p. 275). Brading publishes five Domínguez documents dealing with *obrajes* and their owners, agricultural labor, the *consolidación* of 1804, and economic consequences of the violence of 1810. [R.E. Greenleaf]

2481. Brown, Thomas A. La Academia de San Carlos de la Nueva España. v. 1, Fundación y organización. v. 2, La Academia de 1792 a 1810. Traducción de María Emilia Martínez Negrete Deffis. México, Secretaría de Educación Pública, Dirección General de Divulgación, 1976. 2 v. (175, 190 p.) illus., plates (SepSetentas, 299/300)

Foundation of Royal Academy of San Carlos in New Spain is one of best examples of acceptance of Enlightenment in that arca. By 1784, when it received royal approval, Academy had already been organized and secured support of numerous persons and corporations from capital and several other cities. Work traces foundation and subsequent growth of the Academy through 1809. Author has unearthed wealth of archival data which refer not only to institution but to artists who taught or were trained in it. Illustrated with numerous plates, this paperback is a pleasant discovery for cultural historian and historian of art.

2482. Cacho Vázquez, Xavier. Dos *Relaciones* sobre la fundación de la Compañía de Jesús en México (*in* La Compañía de Jesús en México: cuatro siglos de labor cultural, 1572-1972 [see item 2424] p. 27-52)

Analysis of character of two of earliest histories of Compañía in Mexico: anonymous *Relación* of 1602 and *Relación* by Juan Sánchez Baquero, an original founder. Cacho Vázquez underscores driving themes of Jesuits as historians and as missionaries. Interesting contribution to ecclesiastical historiography.

2483. Canedo, Lino Gómez. Fray Lorenzo de Bienvenida y los orígenes de las misiones en Yucatán: 1537-1564 (UY/R, 18:108, nov./dic. 1976, p. 46-68)

Using printed sources and newly discovered archival documents, author clarifies certain obscure points in history of establishment of Franciscan missionary net in Yucatán. Determines that Franciscans did not settle permanently until late 1544 or early 1545. Adds some interesting data on Fray Lorenzo de Bienvenida, one of early founders. Two previously unknown letters of his shed light on process of fitting missionary expedition and goals of Franciscans in Yucatán.

2484. ———. Sierra Gorda: un típico enclave misional en el centro de México: siglos XVII-XVIII. Pachuca, Mex., Centro Hidalguense de Investigaciones Históricas, 1976. 244 p., map, plates (Col. Ortega-Falkowska, 2)

Following introduction on early missionary efforts in Sierra Gorda, study concentrates on period between 1733 and 1769-70, when Franciscans were replaced by secular clergy. New missionary techniques were developed in this region, both Fathers Serra and Palou had their first training here. Also includes material on José de Escandón, and describes relations between civil, military and religious colonizers. Annotated documentary appendices, slightly less than half of book, include significant reports, censuses, and letters.

2485. Carroll, Patrick J. Mandinga: the evolution of a Mexican runaway slave community, 1735-1827 (CSSH, 19:4, Oct. 1977, p. 488-505, map, table)

Studies Mandinga, runaway slave community that survived and became legally recognized town in 1769. Carroll examines reasons for its survival. Accommodation and even connivance of authorities and other interested parties contributed greatly. Study underscores social, demographic and economic changes undergone by this community through 1827, when it had 148 inhabitants. Carroll suggests that Mandinga is possible model of other runaway communities which survived. Valuable contribution to nuances of slavery in colonial Mexico.

2486. Chance, John K. Race and class in colonial Oaxaca. Stanford, Calif., Stanford Univ. Press, 1978. 250 p., bibl., maps, tables.

Mode of interaction among several ethnic groups in colonial Oaxaca is topic of this interesting study. Author analyzes role of Spaniards, Indians, and growing number of *castas* in city's economy and society. Contents of this well written and well organized study are broader than title indicates and there is much information on economy, labor, demographic patterns, etc. Author stresses how changing character of economy and increasingly multiracial society contributed to development of different concepts of power and status throughout time. Book's conclusions (that wealth became very important criterion of status and that system of *castas* was becoming obsolete towards end of 18th century) refine previous generalizations on race and status in colonial Mexico. Important contribution to colonial social history.

2487. ———— and **William B. Taylor.** Estate and class in a colonial city: Oaxaca in 1792 (CSSH, 19:4, Oct. 1977, p. 454-487, bibl., tables)

Suggestive essay on challenging topic: revision of concepts of social, economic and racial status in city of Antequera, Oaxaca, in late 18th century. Census and parochial data are imaginatively analyzed by authors in order to clarify relationships between race, occupation and social rank. While developing essay, authors shed light on topic of racial classification and conclude that caste or estate system was undermined by frequency of intermarriage and that economic considerations of rank were increasingly important: "In the interplay between racial and economic criteria of rank in Antequera the latter was definitely in the upswing in 1792." Work successfully questions old assumptions on race and status and offers new meaningful insights into colonial society.

2488. Cruz, Francisco Santiago. Breve historia del Colegio de la Compañía de Jesús de Ciudad Real de Chiapas: 1681-1767. México, Editorial Tradición, 1977. 80 p., bibl., plates.

Account of foundation of Jesuit College of Chiapas based on manuscript written by Joaquín Antonio Villalobos, S.J., in 1698 and available at National Archives in Mexico (see *Misiones,* Vol. 26, folio 339-360).

2489. Díaz, Lilia. El Jardín Botánico de Nueva España y la obra de Sessé según documentos mexicanos (CM/ HM, 27:1, julio/sept. 1977, p. 49-78)

Detailed description of establishment of botanical garden in Mexico and travels of Martin Sessee in New Spain.

Edmonson, Munro S. *ed.* The work of Sahagún. See item 6417.

2490. Espejo-Ponce Hunt, Marta. The processes of the development of Yucatán: 1600-1700 (*in* Altman, Ida and James Lockhart *eds*. Provinces of Mexico: variants of Spanish American regional evolution [see item 2451] p. 33-62)

Seventeenth-century Yucatán shares characteristics with other remote areas of Spanish empire in continuation of encomienda and partial government autonomy. Governors exercised authority only by patronage, while real power rested with familial networks of encomenderos, clergy and merchants. Indian tribute in the form of cotton cloth, was chief export. Blacks were earliest urban artisans but Indian apprentices were used by end of century. Cycles of economic growth were independent of Indian population decline. Valuable contribution to both regional history and knowledge of 17th-century crises.

2491. Ewald, Ursula. Estudios sobre la hacienda colonial en México: las propiedades rurales del Colegio Espíritu Santo en Puebla. Wiesbaden, FRG, Franz Steiner Verlag, 1976. 190 p., bibl., plates, tables (Das Mexiko-Projekt der Deutschen Forschungsgemeinschaft, 9)

Significant contribution to study of haciendas as well as to history of Puebla region. Begins with description of Jesuit College, its physical plant, sources of urban and banking income before delineating four major groups of agricultural enterprises. There is outline of history of land acquisition for each group, description of character of land, production, buildings, labor force and conclusion on fate of enterprises after expulsion. General chapter includes materials on slavery, wage labor, debt peonage and administrative personnel's compensation. In valuable analysis of Jesuits as scientific farmers, author finds that their agricultural practices were conservative and that their success depended upon good organization and entrepreneurial skills. Includes documentary appendix on local transportation costs. A model regional economic history.

2492. Florescano, Enrique and **Isabel Gil** *comps*. Descripciones económicas regionales de Nueva España: provincias del centro, sudeste y sur, 1766-1827. México, INAH, Depto. de Investigaciones Históricas, Seminario de Historia Económica, 1976. 326 p., tables (Fuentes para la historia económica, 3)

Vol. 3 in economic history series contains statistical news on Guanajuato (1788, 1803); Querétaro (1791); Veracruz (1803); Guadalajara (1803); Valladolid (1803, 1822, 1823); Michoacán (1822); Puebla (1804); Yucatán and Campeche (1766, 1789, 1790); Tabasco (1794); and Oaxaca (1826, 1827). Like preceding volumes, this compilation is excellent work tool for graduate students and researchers.

2493. García Bernal, Manuela Cristina. Los servicios personales de Yucatán durante el siglo XVI (UY/R, 19:110, marzo/abril 1977, p. 73-87)

Surveys personal services rendered by Indians to Spaniards in 16th-century Yucatán, despite legal prohibition. García Bernal provides interesting data on women's labor as maids, cooks and wet-nurses. Poverty of land made black slavery prohibitive leaving Indian labor as only option for menial work in Yucatán.

2494. Gerhard, Peter. Congregaciones de indios en Nueva España antes de 1570 (CM/HM, 26:3, enero/marzo 1977, p. 347-395)

Revises notion that first successful Indian congregations (*reducciones*) took place 1593-1605. Gerhard shows that between 1550-64 Indian communities all over Mexico were relocated into new settlements. Also points out numerous social and economic implications of this reshuffling of population at mid-century. Detailed and informative study based on archival research contributes much to our knowledge of early patterns of resettlement, urbanization and handling of Indian population.

2495. González-Polo, Ignacio. La ciudad de México a fines del siglo XVIII: disquisiciones sobre un manuscrito anónimo (CM/HM, 26:1, julio/sept. 1976, p. 29-47, bibl., plate)

On Nov. 1788, *oidor* Baltasar Ladrón de Guevara, Regent and General Assesor of Mexico City, wrote description of city with suggestions for its physical and administrative improvement. This manuscript remained anonymous until Prof. González-Polo located it in Ayuntamiento of Mexico's archives in 1970. Article partially describes author's character and work, as well as manuscript's contents and interest as source for social and urban history. Writer promises forthcoming annotated publication of entire document.

2496. Hamnett, Brian R. Mercantile rivalry and peninsular division: the consulados of New Spain and the impact of the Bourbon reforms, 1789-1824 (IAA, 2:4, 1976, p. 273-305, bibl.)

Follows vicissitudes in relations of Consulado of Mexico and those of Veracruz and Guadalajara from 1790s through 1820s. Bitter opposition of Mexico City merchants to creation of rival consulados was superseded by accommodation and reconciliation by 1808-10, based on similar attitudes toward defense of Spain and Hidalgo revolt. However, Veracruz supported Liberals in Cortes of Cádiz while Mexico City remained conservative. Peninsular wars, foreign competition, and internal rivalries prevented any long-term significant contribution of Consulados to economic improvement of New Spain's trade. Hamnett summarizes situation by stating that "the intentions behind the formation of the new consulados were far-reaching; the obstacles immense." Based on primary sources, this study gives useful insight into the rifts and internal struggles of one of most important economic interest groups of colonial Mexico.

2497. Hers, Marie-Areti. Los coras en la época de la expulsión jesuita (CM/HM, 27:1, julio/sept. 1977, p. 17-48)

Raises question of our lack of knowledge of Coras of Nayarit after their military conquest in 1722. Using as source an inquest on Coras' religious beliefs in 1768, author provides much information on group's religious life and ceremonies. Article also deals with attitudes held at the time concerning evangelization and assimilation of northwest Mexico to Hispanized world.

2498. Hoberman, Louisa Schell. The colonial urban legacy reexamined: the politics of flood control in 17-century Mexico City (PCCLAS/P, 5, 1976, p. 69-75)

Interesting reexamination of city's role as power center over hinterland. Seeks to substantiate present-day theories regarding nature of this relation. Hoberman uses example of Mexico City during 1629 flood, scrutinizing actions and reactions of ruling bureaucracy and public. Findings point out to a city not entirely able to impose its will over surrounding area but retaining nevertheless significant amount of power over periphery. City terms predominated in their reciprocal relationship.

2499. ———. Merchants in seventeenth-century Mexico City: a preliminary portrait (HAHR, 57:3, Aug. 1977, p. 469-503, tables)

Work aimed at clarifying political, economic and social standing of Mexico City merchants in mid-17th century. Concludes that although ties with government's officials gave merchants power at local level they lacked it to alter major royal policies.

Merchants had achieved measure of social cohesiveness by that period. Nevertheless, they needed constant circulation and replenishment of membership since they were as liable as other groups to loss of fortunes and status. Offers valuable insights into importance of Manila trade with Mexico and role of Judaizer merchants in New Spain. Very good work which answers some important questions about merchant community in 17th century.

2500. Hurtado López, Flor de María. Dolores Hidalgo: estudio económico, 1740-1790. México, INAH, Depto. de Investigaciones Históricas, 1974. 128 p., facsims., maps, tables (Col. Científica, 11. Historia)

Study of economic structure of Bajío town of Dolores Hidalgo based on returns of tithes for second half of 18th century. Hurtado López establishes cycle for prices of corn, wheat, beans, and cattle and its products. Price (and economic) cycles of Dolores are similar to those of Mexico City though slightly shorter and more intense in times of crises. Author also offers good characterization of region's basic agricultural structure and its changes, as well as patterns of landownership. Merit of work lies on fact that it proves that tithes are viable sources and tools for research in economic history.

Jara Hantke, Alvaro. Plata y pulque en el siglo XVIII mexicano. See item 283.

2501. Lewis, Leslie. In Mexico City's shadow: some aspects of economic activity and social process in Texcoco, 1570-1620 (*in* Altman, Ida and James Lockhart *eds*. Provinces of Mexico: variants of Spanish American regional evolution [see item 2451] p. 125-136)

Biographies of Indian principals and Hispanic Texcocan families illustrate town's dependence upon Mexico City, as well as variety of economic activities. Many residents functioned as intermediaries in long-distance trade in cacao, textiles, wine, wool and cotton cloth, while buying corn from Mexico City. Symptomatic of town's marginal position were low land prices and house rents and few large estates.

2502. Lockhart, James. Capital and province, Spaniard and Indian: the example of late sixteenth-century Toluca (*in* Altman, Ida and James Lockhart *eds*. Provinces of Mexico: variants of Spanish American regional evolution [see item 2451] p. 99-124)

Characterizes Toluca as "incomplete and markedly humble sub-society" because of its proximity to Mexico City. No independent artisans developed, alcalde mayor often resided in Mexico City, and no Indian government was formed. On basis of notarial records and linguistic analysis, Lockhart bridges preconquest and 16th century concluding with survey of end of colonial period. He finds that earlier conditions in Toluca were replicated in outlying regions as Toluca had become more prosperous and that Spanish estates moved from cattle to maize production. Also includes family biographies.

2503. López Miramontes, Alvaro *ed*. Las minas de Nueva España en 1753. México, INAH, 1975. 108 p., illus. (Col. Científica, 29. Fuentes historia económica)

Source volume contains informes prepared by mine owners in 1753, as requested by Spanish Crown in 1752. These previously unpublished reports concern mines of Bolaños, Taxco, Tetela del Río, Tetela de Xonatla, Cadereita, Mezquital del Oro, Santa Eulalia and San Felipe del Real (Chihuahua). Editor has written short but helpful introduction to reports on each mine. Valuable source for all aspects of mining in mid-18th century.

2504. López Sarrelangue, Delfina. La hacienda en San José de Coapa (*in* Florescano, Enrique *ed*. Haciendas, latifundios y plantaciones en América Latina [see *HLAS 38:2190*] p. 223-241)

Descriptive study of development of medium-size hacienda south of Mexico City from mid-16th century to early 19th century. A religious order, an Indian cacicazgo and criollo titled families shared in history of this land. Based on archival records, study is useful contribution to growing literature on hacienda history.

2505. Lorenzo Sanz, Eufemio. Los indios de Nueva España y su pugna con las pretensiones encomenderas en la época de los comisarios (*in* Jornadas Americanistas, III, Valladolid, Spain, 1974. Estudios sobre política indigenista española en América [see item 2298] v. 2, p. 471-499, illus.)

Studies encomenderos' efforts to obtain perpetuity in their grants and opposition of Indians and missionaries to such expectation. After surveying Peruvian case, author examines two *memoriales* available in Simancas (1563) which illuminate feelings of Indians of New Spain on topic of perpetuity and King and Council's response. Indians offered large *servicio* in cash and perpetual annexation of encomiendas to Crown. Although concerned about potential civil disorders, Crown was open to idea. Exchanges, however, did not lead to abrogation of encomienda. These documents add an important dimension to our knowledge of it as an institution.

2506. MacNutt, Francis Augustus *ed*. Fernando Cortés: his five letters of relation to the Emperor Charles V. v.

1/2. With a biographical introduction and notes compiled from original sources. Introductory essay by John Greenway. Glorieta. N. Mex., The Rio Grande Press, 1977. 2 v. (354, 374 p.) maps (A Rio Grande classic)

Reissue of 1908 translation of Cortés letters by Francis A. MacNutt. Includes introduction by John Greenway, prof. of anthropology at Univ. of Colorado (Boulder) which dwells on character of conquered and conqueror, and process of cultural exchange between Spaniards and Indians.

2507. Mandeville, Peter B. La jurisdicción de la villa de Santiago de los Valles en 1700-1800. San Luis Potosí, Mex., Academia de Historia Potosina, 1976. 122 p., bibl. (Biblioteca de historia potosina. Serie documentos, 3)

Seeks to rectify previous mistakes in location of towns in jurisdiction of Villa de Valles, 1700-1800, by using archival data and modern mathematical estimates. Includes useful demographic information on this area and transcription of two archival sources describing it in 1743 and 1792.

2508. Medina Ascensio, Luis. El Colegio de San Ignacio y el Seminario de San Javier de Querétaro: 1625-1767 (*in* La Compañía de Jesús en México: cuatro siglos de labor cultural, 1572-1972 [see item 2424] p. 253-325)

Detailed account of these educational institutions, with emphasis on their curricula, teachers and financial situation. Article also covers 19th-century efforts to reopen Jesuit educational center. Documentary appendix includes useful inventory of school papers.

2509. Munch G., Guido. El cacicazgo de San Juan Teotihuacan durante la colonia: 1521-1821. México, INAH, Centro de Investigaciones Superiores, 1976. 79 p., bibl., illus., maps, plates (Col. Científica, 32. Historia)

Using example of San Juan Teotihuacán, one of most important cacicazgos of Mexico, author defines seigneural character of prehispanic cacicazgos and explains how their nature changed throughout colonial period. After conquest, Spaniards stressed link to land but cut down caciques' political power. By 18th century, owners of cacicazgos considered their land as their most important asset and behaved like Spanish landowners. Although this study is brief, documents in Appendix are useful and help to understand status of colonial Indian elite.

2510. Navarro García, Luis. El Arzobispo Virrey Ortega y Montañés y los indios de Colotlan (*in* Jornadas Americanistas, III, Valladolid, Spain, 1974. Estudios sobre la política indigenista española en América [see item 2298] v. 3, p. 29-42)

Studies conciliating means used by Archbishop Ortega y Montañés during uprising of Colotlan Indians in 1702 (Colotlan is on the road from Guadalajara to Zacatecas). Archbishop opted for general pardon which conceded Indians' rightfulness and obtained pacification of area. It is implied that Indians never forgot their legal victory.

2511. Nunn, Charles F. Naturalization in New Spain, 1700 to 1760: the case of Jean Malibran (SECOLAS/A, 8, March 1977, p. 61-71)

Using example of French merchant, long-time resident of Veracruz, Nunn explains process of naturalization in Spanish colonies. Most of those affected were wealthy merchants. Majority of applications for naturalization were granted by Council of Indies, which thus antagonized Consulado's interests.

2512. Olaechea, R. Algunas precisiones en torno al venerable Juan de Palafox (UCAB/M, 5, 1976, p. 1053-1130)

Polemic writing in which Jesuit historian Olaechea defends himself against critique raised by historian F. Sánchez-Castaner. This long article contains many small historical details on unsuccessful process of beatification of Bishop Juan Palafox. Centers chiefly on decision taken in Spanish court and Rome but includes information on Mexican interests in this affair.

2513. Palmer, Colin A. Slaves of the White God: blacks in Mexico, 1570-1650. Cambridge, Mass., Harvard Univ. Press, 1976. 234 p., bibl., tables.

Studies several important aspects of slavery in central colonial Mexico such as slaves' general status in society, their contribution to labor pool. Church's attitude towards slavery, slaves' own religious practices, and process of manumission in relation to slaves themselves and as contributing factor toward creation of free colored population. Qualitative rather than quantitative study which relies on strength of numerous examples of slave life found in archives consulted. Readable text and sound treatment of subject should further studies of topic.

2514. Pastor, Rodolfo. La alcabala como fuente para la historia económica y social de la Nueva España (CM/HM, 27:1, julio/sept. 1977, p. 1-16, tables)

Study illustrates how to use *alcabala* records as source for study of internal trade in New Spain. After qualifying meaning of word *alcabala*, Pastor traces changes in collection and yields through 17th and 18th centuries. Author shows potential wealth of information for historians by analyzing one archival example. Commendable beginning for graduate student exercise in historiography.

2515. Patch, Robert. La formación de estancias y haciendas en Yucatán durante la colonia (UY/R, 18:106, julio/sept. 1976, p. 95-132, maps)

Solid study of agrarian structures in Yucatán. Author maintains that encomiendas and cattle haciendas were most important agrarian units in Yucatán in 16th and 18th centuries. Agricultural haciendas developed in 18th century as result of population growth and increasing demand for staple food: corn. Indianpopulation which up to then had cultivated corn was unable to meet growing demand and white landowners took over production. Growing indigenous population supplied labor to haciendas. Patch also suggests how haciendas further developed in 19th century as result of rise of export agriculture. Important piece of research based on archival sources.

2516. Pietschmann, Horst. El comercio de repartimientos de los alcaldes mayores y corregidores en la región de Puebla-Tlaxcala en el siglo XVII (*in* Jornadas Americanistas, III, Valladolid, Spain, 1974. Estudios sobre política indigenista española en América [see item 2298] v. 3, p. 147-153, map, tables)

Deals with the *repartimiento* or purchase and sale of merchandise to Indians by Puebla's *tenientes de corregidor*. Describes type of merchandise sold to (mostly cattle) and bought from Indians as well as prices and profits involved. While value of merchandise sold to Indians was worth around 250,000 pesos (ca. 1785) agricultural products bought from them were worth a mere 65,000 to 70,000 pesos. In this relation between local and large city market, imbalance against Indian was great. Interesting contribution.

2517. Rabell Romero, Cecilia Andrea. Evaluación del subregistro de defunciones infantiles: una crítica a los Registros Parroquiales de San Luis de La Paz, México, 1735-1799 (UNAM/RMS, 38:1, enero/marzo, 1976, p. 171-185, tables)

Author proposes that data furnished by parochial registers should be subjected to careful and critical examination in order to avoid hasty conclusions in historical demography. Applying Bourgeois-Pichet method for statistical evaluation to parochial records of San Luis de La Paz, she demonstrates some inconsistencies in data. However, she is able to determine three periods of high infant mortality among legitimate children under one year of age: 1735-39, 1760-69 and 1779. Data in need of further explanation by social historian.

2518. Ramos Gómez, Luis J. and Concepción Blasco. En torno al origen del tributo indígena en la Nueva España y su evolución en la primera mitad del siglo XVI: según el testimonio del *Códice de Coyoacán* de Simancas (*in* Jornadas Americanistas, III, Valladolid, Spain, 1974. Estudios sobre política indigenista española en América [see item 2298] v. 2, p. 357-391, facsims., illus.)

Traces roots of tribute in New Spain to three sources: 1) medieval Castilian *parias*; 2) prehispanic Aztec practices; and 3) seignorial aspirations of conquistadors themselves. Latter is linked to origin of encomienda. After considering concept of "moderation" in raising of tribute (applied in 1530s) authors reinterpret evidence offered by *Codice de Coyoacán*, available in Simancas, which contains information on tributaries of Cortés. Study's most significant contribution is this reinterpretation which establishes reduction in tributes by mid-century and persistence of personal tributes in Coyoacán up to 1548.

2519. Riley, James D. Hacendados jesuitas en México: El Colegio Máximo de San Pedro y Pablo, 1685-1767. México, Secretaría de Educación Pública, 1976. 245 p., maps, tables (SepSetentas, 296)

In-depth study based on extensive archival research of origin, growth, labor force and production of haciendas belonging to Jesuit Colegio Máximo. Although much information concerns hacienda of Santa Lucía, there is also data on other Jesuit haciendas of central Mexico. Study of haciendas preceded by author's analysis of Jesuit economic and administrative policies which places data on hacienda management into broader perspective. Informative and sound study.

2520. ———. Santa Lucía: desarrollo y administración de una hacienda jesuita en el siglo XVIII (*in* Florescano, Enrique ed. Haciendas, latifundios y plantaciones en América Latina [see *HLAS 38:2190*] p. 242-272)

Detailed study of one of Jesuits most productive properties. Riley underscores careful practices of acquisition of property and investment of Society's capital, suggesting that they had outlook of modern corporation. Also includes interesting data on legal conflicts with Indian communities and hacienda's labor relations to support conclusion that 18th-century hacienda differed significantly from its 19th-century counterpart.

2521. ———. The wealth of the Jesuits in Mexico: 1670-1767 (AAFH/TAM, 33:2, Oct. 1976, p. 226-266, tables)

This study challenges traditional assumption that Jesuits had superior managerial abilities which enabled them to amass great wealth. During 17th and 18th centuries many Jesuit Colleges passed through rather severe financial crises or survived under economic duress. Although some of these problems reflected general economic conditions others were due to ill-management. After weighing all problems facing Jesuits as property owners and managers, author concludes that success of some of their colleges was due to continuous concern for efficiency and sustained investment through long periods of time. Numerous charts provide useful information on income and expenses of Jesuit Colleges and there is an evaluation of their properties in New Spain in 1760s. Very good study of Jesuit policies and investment priorities.

2522. Riley, Michael. El prototipo de la hacienda en el centro de México: un caso del siglo XVI (*in* Florescano, Enrique *ed.* Haciendas, latifundios y plantaciones en América Latina [see *HLAS 38:2190*] p. 49-70)

Cortés and two other encomenderos in Morelos created incipient hacienda system between 1522-50. Their economic activities included acquisition of small quantities of land and slaves and heavy use of encomienda and salaried Indian labor. Analyzes data on kinds of products, costs and profits. Largest quantities of money to Cortes' estates came from sale of woven cotton cloth received as tribute, and largest source of labor derived from encomienda. Hence, author finds that this "prototype" of hacienda began to develop within the encomienda.

2523. Rodríguez Vallejo, José. Ixcatl, el algodón mexicano. México, Fondo de Cultura Económica, 1976. 95 p., bibl., illus., maps, tables (Sección de obras de antropología)

Including extensive quotes from sources, identifies and maps regions and towns which produced cotton both before and after conquest. Evaluates documents and contains information on costumes.

2524. Sánchez Flores, Ramón *comp.* José Ignacio Bartolache: el sabio humanista a través de sus bienes, sus libros e instrumentos de trabajo (MAGN/B, 13, Serie 2, 1972/1976, p. 187-216)

Transcription of lists of house furnishings and books belonging to one of New Spain's most brilliant scientists. Having died without a formal will, and as government employee, Bartolache's belongings were confiscated and sold out in public auction. Lists will be of value to those interested in material culture and intellectual history.

2525. Sanders, William T. The population of the Central Mexican symbiotic region, the Basin of Mexico, and the Teotihuacán Valley in the sixteenth century (*in* Denevan, William M. *ed.* The native population of the Americas in 1492 [see item 2279] p. 85-150, map, tables)

William Sanders challenges Cook's, Simpson's and Borah's estimates of indigenous population in central Mexico prior and subsequent to conquest. Underlines inaccuracies in censuses and tax assessment data. After careful examination of all data available, concludes that population of precolumbian Mexico was about half of that estimated by Borah, Cook and Simpson. Debate over demographic data will, undoubtedly continue.

2526. Sauer, Carl Ortwin. Colima of New Spain in the sixteenth century. Westport, Conn., Greenwood Press, 1976. 104 p., bibl. (Ibero-Americana, 29)

Reprint of 1948 ed. (see *HLAS 14:186*).

2527. Serrera, Ramón María. Guadalajara ganadera: estudio regional novohispano, 1760-1805. Sevilla, Spain. Escuela de Estudios Hispano-Americanos, 1977. 458 p., maps, plates, tables.

Thorough study of cattle industry in New Galicia. Based on extensive archival documentation, this work packs much information on what was economic pillar of extensive area of Mexico's west and northwest. Serrera covers all aspects of horse, sheep and mule raising and marketing, and special topic of cattle-raising among Indian communities. Aptly underscores importance of cattle industry in regional economy of New Galicia and its impact on rest of New Spain. Given scant attention paid to this topic in Mexico's economic history, this is a worthwhile contribution to colonial historiography.

2528. Solano y Pérez Lila, Francisco de. Autoridades municipales indígenas de Yucatán: 1657-1677. Mérida, Mex., Univ. de Yucatán, 1976. 70 p., fold. map.

List of indigenous authorities occupying municipal posts in Yucatán constitutes useful tool for researching mechanisms of provision of posts in Indian towns and their social implications. In brief introduction to document, author discusses municipality's role as vehicle for Hispanization, urbanization and acculturation. Also points out social prestige and value of municipal posts noting that cabildo posts gave non-noble Indians certain degree of social mobility although indigenous elite did not lose its power and influence.

2529. Sugawara H., Masae *ed.* La deuda pública de España y la economía novohispaña: 1804-1809. México, INAH, 1976. 135 p., bibl. (Col. Científica, 28. Fuentes historia económica)

Author has diligently compiled in this volume number of key documents related to controversial law of *Consolidación de vales reales*. Law allowed forced sale of clerical property and transfer of capital of pious deeds to Crown. Sugawara's brief prologue explains law's origin and puts each document into historical context. Very useful study makes available to historians very important documentary sources in their original format.

2530. Super, John C. The agricultural near north: Querétaro in the seventeenth century (*in* Altman, Ida and James Lockhart *eds*. Provinces of Mexico: variants of Spanish American regional evolution [see item 2451] p. 231-252)

Overview of Querétaro's colonial history, of particular interest because of description of three commercial networks, established by mid-17th century, which tied city to region, northern towns and Mexico City. Describes increasing economic complexity developed by mid-18th century with growing numbers of textile mills, tanneries and tobacco factory. Valuable delineation of process of acculturation in Indian communities supplements analysis of social mobility, occupation, family structure among Hispanized sections of population. Sheds new light on old issues of elite circulation, Bajío economic development, and social stratification.

2531. Szewczyk, David M. New elements in the society of Tlaxcala: 1519-1618 (*in* Altman, Ida and James Lockhart *eds*. Provinces of Mexico: variants of Spanish American regional evolution [see item 2451] p. 137-154)

Beginning with view of preconquest society, and observing continued strength of some Indian institutions, Szewczyk observes that Hispanic population "infiltrated and drained, rather than overwhelmed" Indian society. Europeans settled in countryside first; then moved into city as merchants, and traded in woolen cloth, cacao, and indigo, while renting their stores from Indian *principales*. Indians continued as merchants, butchers, sheep ranchers and farmers. By 1618, there were 20 *obrajes* in the province, producing woolens of all qualities, owned by Indians, mestizos and Hispanics, and employing free labor. Concludes with sample biographies of notaries, barbers, governors, interpreters and women.

2532. Taylor, William B. Haciendas coloniales en el valle de Oaxaca (*in* Florescano, Enrique *ed*. Haciendas, latifundios y plantaciones en América Latina [see *HLAS 38:2190*] p. 71-104, map, tables)

Haciendas and "labores" in Oaxaca developed after end of 16th century, and even at end of colonial period constituted only third of valley's productive land. Inventories revealed that haciendas appraised their value in livestock, money advanced to workers and agricultural land, rather than in buildings and capital investments. "Labores" which equalled ranchos in their small size were exploited intensively with hired workers, and were principally located within seven kilometers of capital city. Both "labores" and haciendas suffered rapid turnover of ownership apparently attributable to heavy labor costs. Analysis of production, sales and profits of one hacienda at end of 18th century indicates reasons why hacienda owners lived in "dignified penury."

2533. ———. Town and country in the Valley of Oaxaca: 1750-1812 (*in* Altman, Ida and James Lockhart *eds*. Provinces of Mexico: variants of Spanish American regional evolution [see item 2451] p. 63-95)

Independent Indian villages dominated 18th and early 19th-century Oaxaca, while low profit margins, heavily mortgaged haciendas and frequent turnover of owners, characterized hacienda system. Cochineal dye trade stimulated by industrial revolution in England caused increased urbanization and tied region to Mexico-Veracruz marketing system. It also created basis for disaffection against Spanish rule, and increasing conflict between Spanish and Indian mores. Creole discontent at many levels eased Insurgents' capture of city in 1812. Article contains wealth of ethnohistorical, political, employment and population data.

2534. Tena Ramírez, Felipe. Vasco de Quiroga y sus pueblos de Santa Fé en los siglos XVIII y XIX. México: Editorial Porrúa, 1977. 225 p.

Work focuses on activities of ecclesiastical cabildo of Morelia's cathedral as patron and protector of pueblo-hospitales, role especially assigned to this body by Vasco de Quiroga himself. Author stresses great degree of autonomy from civil authority enjoyed by pueblos in 18th century. Implies that such freedom was preserved through 19th century until pueblos' extinction. Study based on documents recently discovered in archives of Morelia cathedral. Appendix includes several.

2535. Te Paske, John J. *ed*. La Real Hacienda de Nueva España: la Real Caja de México; 1576-1816. México, INAH, 1976. 1 v. (Unpaged)

Volume contains summaries of Mexico City's *cartas cuentas* or records of income and expenses of Spanish colonial government in overseas possessions. Book consists of straight reprint of computerized figures obtained after searching in hundreds of archival volumes of accounts. Introduction explains structure of fiscal system and evaluates its usefulness in interpreting New Spain's economic trends.

Volume is part of broader long-term project in collaboration with Prof. Herbert Klein which will include other royal *Cajas*. Since analysis of economic patterns and fiscal policies is one of weakest points in colonial studies, this work constitutes important aid to economic historians. However, they must be prepared to analyze data by themselves.

Terán Mata, Juan Manuel. El pensamiento filosófico en la ciudad de México: épocas precortesiana y colonial. See item 9488.

2536. Torre Villar, Ernesto de la. Fray Pedro de Gante: maestro y civilizador de América. México, Seminario de Cultura, 1973. 143 p., bibl., facsim., plates.

Well written brief biography of Fray Pedro de Gante stressing his missionary activities in New Spain. Study's greatest merits are beautiful printing and illustrations and documentary appendix containing text of several letters by friar and his first biography, written by Fray Jerónimo Mendieta.

2537. Tovar Pinzón, Hermes. Elementos constitutivos de la empresa agraria jesuita en la segunda mitad del siglo XVIII en México (*in* Florescano, Enrique ed. Haciendas, latifundios y plantaciones en América Latina [see *HLAS 38:2190*] p. 132-222, tables)

Detailed study of Jesuit haciendas in Mexico, with special emphasis on five years before expropriation, and following period. Rich in comparative material, presented in tables as well as text, author has cumulated data on size of each hacienda organized by region and institution, relative value of livestock and agricultural production, harvest yields in selected enterprises, labor, percentage of income from various activities, rents in relation to hacienda value, and production and income both before and after expropriation. While based largely on archival material in Chile, author also explores Colombian and Mexican sources. Valuable contribution to economic history of 18th-century Mexico.

2538. Trautmann, Wolfgang. Kolonialzeitliche Einflüsse von Staat und Gesellschaft auf die Agrarlandschaft des mexikanischen Hochlandes (DG/TW, 40, Mai 1975, p. 373-378, Illus.)

Changes in colonial Indian agrarian society in Mexican highlands were caused by joint action involving Indian nobility, local administrators, and Spanish Crown. [T.L. Martinson]

2539. Tutino John M. Provincial Spaniards, Indian towns, and haciendas: interrelated agrarian sectors in the valleys of Mexico and Toluca, 1750-1810 (*in* Altman, Ida and James Lockhart eds. Provinces of Mexico: variants of Spanish American regional evolution [see item 2451] p. 177-194)

Increasing Indian population in valleys of Toluca and Mexico in late colonial period provided economic and social opportunities for elite. Small Spanish group located in provincial towns of Chalco, Otumba, Tetepango and Texcoco used their positions as merchants, tax collectors, clergy and estate renters to gain access to larger opportunities in Mexico City. Tutino finds Indian towns were highly stratified, with entrenched upper class. Includes particularly valuable study of hacienda labor force as it affected all levels of local society. Hispanized population often owned or rented ranchos, worked as muleteers, while their sons enjoyed higher paying positions on large haciendas.

2540. Ulloa, Daniel. Los predicadores divididos: los Dominicos en la Nueva España, siglo XVI. México, El Colegio de México, 1977. 329 p.

Tesis doctoral escrita por un joven dominico mexicano. Dividida en tres partes: 1) Los dominicos en el Nuevo Mundo (1509-1526) o sea los antecedentes españoles, establecimiento en las Antillas y primeros ensayos de misión en Tierra Firme (Cumaná); 2) Los dominicos en la Nueva España (1526-1540) o sea la formación y consolidación de la Provincia dominicana de Santiago de México; 3) Los dominicos en la Nueva España y sus actas capitulares del siglo XVI. Sólo esta parte abarca todo el siglo XVI. Más que una historia de la obra misional—que apenas se toca—y ministerial—que se toca muy ligeramente—es una disquisición sobre las diferencias que hubo entre los primeros dominicos respecto de la orientación que debía darse a dichas—especialmente en la tercer parte—pero ha sido elaborado a partir de prejuicios muy definidos acerca de lo que debía y debe ser la Orden de Predicadores y esto influye negativamente, a mi parecer, en los juicios del autor. Además, la información bibliográfica y documental, lo mismo que su crítica, presentan algunas fallas notables, sobre todo en la primera parte. [L. Gómez-Canedo]

2541. Villarino, Ciro. Encuentros culturales y transculturación en la obra de Bernal Díaz del Castillo: historia verdadera de la conquista de la Nueva España (BBAA, 38:47, 1976, p. 83-100)

Studies early process of acculturation which took place in New Spain as reflected in Bernal Díaz' work. Soon after their first confrontation Spaniards and Indians started to exchange cultural traits in warfare techniques, language, religion, transportation, etc. Author distinguishes between forced and voluntary, personal and social acculturation. Interesting essay.

2542. Warren, J. Benedict. La conquista de Michoacán: 1521-1530. Morelia, Mex. Fimax Publicistas, 1977. 487 p., illus., tables.

Detailed account of conquest and first decade of history of Michoacán backed by extensive archival research. Work is packed with carefully verified information on all events and historical actors of that formative period, which mostly revolved around tragic fate of indigenous ruler (Cazonci) and struggle for power and material rewards among Spaniards. Chapters on encomienda, treating political, administrative and economic aspects of the early grants are particularly useful. Figures of Nuño de Guzmán and the Cazonci receive revisionist treatment which makes of latter less the innocent victim often portrayed in traditional accounts and former a lesser villain under circumstances. In sum, an informative and important study.

NORTH AND BORDERLANDS

2543. Adams, Eleanor B. Fray Francisco Atanasio Domínguez and Fray Silvestre Vélez de Escalante (Utah Historical Quarterly [Utah State Historical Society, Salt Lake City] 44:1, Winter 1976, p. 40-58, illus., map)

Popular biographies of Domínguez and Vélez de Escalante both before, during and after their 1776 expedition. Largely based on author's previous publications but including some new archival material.

2544. Altman, Ida. A family and region in the northern fringe lands: the Marqueses de Aguayo of Nuevo León and Coahuila (*in* Altman, Ida and James Lockhart eds. Provinces of Mexico: variants of Spanish American regional evolution [see item 2451] p. 253-272)

Traces history of one of oldest and wealthiest ennobled families of New Spain founded by Basque immigrant, Francisco de Urdiñola, in distant north. Having received title of Marqueses de San Miguel de Aguayo in 1682, family prospered through late 17th and 18th centuries but was bankrupt by 1820, following chronological cycle of colonial period itself. Study devotes special attention to process of land acquisition, management of family's properties and wealth and patterns of social mobility. Using Aguayos as model, author proposes that all colonial elite was basically similar in attitudes, regardless of their economic or geographical power base.

2545. Archer, Christon I. The making of Spanish Indian policy on the Northwest Coast (UNM/NMHR, 52:1, Jan. 1977, p. 45-69, illus.)

Peaceful trading and scientific investigation rather than aggressive missionary activity usually characterized Spanish policy toward Indians on Northwest Coast between 1774-95.

2546. Archibald, Robert R. Cañon de Carnué: settlement of a grant (UNM/NMHR, 51:4, Oct. 1976, p. 313-328, map)

Area east of Albuquerque was first settled in 1763 and abandoned in 1772 because of Apache attacks. After a 25-year Spanish offensive against Indians finally succeeded, second settlement was established in 1819. Based on primary materials, article contains details on land distribution, production, settlers and Indian policy.

2547. ————. Price regulation in Hispanic California (AAFH/TAM, 33:4, April 1977, p. 613-629)

Additional reason for conflict between soldier and missionary is explored in this study of Upper California between 1781-1810. Through analysis of price regulation, author notes that *presidios* expected missions to supply cheap food and hides to soldiers in order to augment low wages. Missions, small subsidies, demanded higher prices in order to support friars' work, pay Indian laborers, and buy commodities. Difficulties and expense of supplying missions from San Blas and Mexico compounded church-army conflict.

2548. Baker, Maury and Margaret Bissler Haas eds. Bernardo de Gálvez's combat diary for the battle of Pensacola: 1781 (FHS/FIIQ, 56:2, Oct. 1977, p. 176-199, tables)

Manuscript combat diary of battle of Pensacola written by Estevan Miró and found by Louis Baumgartner in Guatemala. Consists of short version of diary later published by Gálvez. Translated and with introduction by editors.

2549. Balseiro, José Agustín ed. The Hispanic presence in Florida. Miami, Florida, E.A. Seemann, 1976. 160 p., tables.

Popular account of aspects of Florida history. Articles of possible interest to borderlands historians are: William M. Straight "Medicine in Spanish Florida" (p. 77-93) which uses primary sources; Charles W. Arnade "Florida during the Revolutionary War" (p. 95-122) which summarizes issues.

2550. Burrus, Ernest J. Influencia de antiguos jesuitas mexicanos en la geografía y cartografía universal (*in* La Compañía de Jesús en México: cuatro siglos de labor cultural, 1572-1972 [see item 2424] p. 1-26, maps)

Extolls truly admirable work of geographical description and cartography undertaken by Jesuits in Mexico's northwest, giving brief biographical information on those who excelled in these endeavors.

2551. Busto Duthurburu, José Antonio del. La navegación atlántica de Hernando de Soto la vez que fue a la Conquista de la Florida (PUCP/CSH, 8:10, enero 1970/dic. 1972, p. 15-20, bibl.)

Comparison of six different chroniclers' accounts of Hernando de Soto's voyage, from April 7 to June 11, 1538 and which began at Barra de San Lúcar and ended in Santiago de Cuba. Uses Garcilaso, Oviedo, Gómara, Herrera, Fidalgo de Elvas and Las Casas.

2552. Campbell, Leon G. The Spanish presidio in Alta California during the mission period: 1769-1785 (JW, 16:4, Oct. 1977, p. 63-77, facsim., maps, plates)

Interpretative article based partly on presidial records and other materials suggests that designation of "mission period" to describe years 1769-84 fails to consider important role of soldiers. Until 1776, military governors were weak and subject to Father Serra's authority. But with establishment of interior provinces and Neve's appointment as Governor, military began to assert power and influence. Preliminary examination of social origins and records of presidio troops indicates that most were experienced soldiers and not criminals. Surveys conflicts between friars and soldiers and describes trial records.

2553. Canedo, Lino Gómez. La Sierra Gorda a fines del siglo XVIII: diario de un viaje de inspección a sus milicias (CM/HM, 26:1, julio/sept. 1976, p. 132-149, bibl.)

Annotated first publication of diary of unknown traveler in Mexico's northwest. Author located manuscript in Archives of Franciscan Province, Celaya. Diary starts Dec. 1789 and ends March 1790. Traveler passed through Cadereyta, Zimapa, Xocala, Saucillo, and other towns and places within Sierra Gorda. Speculates that author of this travelogue was brigadier Don Pedro Ruiz Dávalos. This is a minor account, not comparable to those of Bishop Tamarón y Romeral or Fray Agustín de Morfi.

2554. Chipman, Donald. The Oñate-Moctezuma-Zaldívar families of northern New Spain (UNM/NMHR, 52:4, Oct. 1977, p. 297-310, table)

Author traces complicated but fascinating genealogical history of one of Cortés' illegitimate daughters and her descendants' connections with two of northern Mexico's most influential families in 16th century. Includes useful data on subject of marriage and endogamy as bases for social status and family consolidation.

2555. Dobyns, Henry F. Spanish colonial Tucson: a demographic history. Tucson, The Univ. of Arizona Press, 1976. 246 p., bibl., map, tables.

History of missions, presidio, and population of Tucson are recounted in separate sections with long quotations from documents. Includes tables on native American population.

2556. Engstrand, Iris Wilson. Royal Officer in Baja California, 1768-1770: Joaquín Velázquez de León. Los Angeles, Calif., Dawson's Book Shop, 1976. 133 p., bibl., fold. map, plates (Baja California travel series)

Annotated translation of promotional letters and other material written by scientist Joaquín Velázquez de León when he accompanied José de Gálvez on his inspection of Lower California. Work includes information on life of Velázquez de León, description of physical area and regional soil conditions, as well as some notes on history of science in Mexico, as Velázquez de León traced transit of Venus in 1769.

2557. Fernández, José B. Opposing views of "La Florida: Alvar Núñez Cabeza de Vaca and El Inca Garcilaso de la Vega (FHS/FHQ, 55:2, Oct. 1976, p. 170-180)

Comparison of two 16th-century accounts of exploration of Florida which contrasts views of Cabeza de Vaca and Garcilaso on such issues as geography, economic possibilities and Indians. Cabeza de Vaca based his account on experience whereas Garcilaso wrote a romanticized version in order to convince Crown to colonize.

2558. Florescano, Enrique and Isabel Gil comps. Descripciones económicas regionales de Nueva España: provincias del norte, 1790-1814. México, INAH, Depto. de Investigaciones Históricas, Seminario de Historia Económica, 1976. 359 p., tables (Fuentes para la historia económica, 2)

Vol. 2 of documentary series on economic history and sources in colonial New Spain (see HLAS 38:2432). This volume contains statistical information on missions and *presidios* of California (1790-1803); Zacatecas (1804-06); Sinaloa (1805); Coahuila (1811); New Mexico (1812); and San Luis de Potosí (1814).

2559. González Rodríguez, Luis. Itinerario del destierro de los misioneros de Sonora y Sinaloa según los diarios de los arrieros y el epistolario oficial (*in* La Compañía de Jesús en México: cuatro siglos de labor cultural, 1572-1972 [see item 2424] p. 101-194)

Detailed account of process of expulsion of Jesuits from Sonora and Sinaloa. Diaries which recorded expenses of transportation of outcast Jesuits contain lists of prices for food which could be useful for a larger price reconstruction project.

2560. Hammond, George Peter and **Agapito Rey.** Narratives of the Coronado expedition: 1540-1542. Albuquerque, Univ. of New Mexico Press, 1977. 413 p.

Reprint of 1940 ed. (see *HLAS 6:2859*).

2561. Killea, Lucy. The true origins of Spanish colonial officials and missionaries (SDHS/J, 23:1, Winter 1977, p. 55-63, bibl., illus., map)

Most officials and friars in San Diego region between 1768-1810 came from peripheral regions of Spain, especially Catalonia, Majorca and Basque country. Article based on secondary sources and written as part of bicentennial project.

2562. Kraemer, Paul M. New Mexico's ancient salt trade (SAR/P, 82:1, March 1976, p. 22-30, maps, plates)

Popular article on history of New Mexico's salt lakes in Estancia Valley. Discovered in 1581, salt was used for livestock and leather curing. Additional use was silver refining and caravans supplied salt to mines of Parral, 700 m. away. Abandoned sometime after 1672, they were re-opened only in Mexican period.

2563. Mirafuentes Galván, José Luis. Movimientos de resistencia y rebeliones indígenas en el norte de México: 1680-1821. v. 1, Guía documental. México, Archivo General de la Nación, Archivo Histórico de Hacienda, 1975. 201 p., fold. map (Col. Documental, 3)

Titles of 586 documents in Mexico's Archivo General de la Nación and Archivo Histórico de Hacienda from *ramos* of Provincias Internas, Historia, General de Parte, and Cárceles y Presidios, Indian rebellion of 1680 to 1821 revolt of Opatas in Sonora and Sinaloa. Materials are organized by regions, then chronologically and notations include identification of author, classification of document, its destination and summary of content.

2564. Moore, John Preston. Revolt in Louisiana: the Spanish occupation, 1766-1770. Baton Rouge, Louisiana State Univ. Press, 1976. 246 p., bibl., illus., map, plates.

Interestingly written and thoroughly researched account of rebellion against Spain and Spanish governor, Antonio de Ulloa. Contribution to diplomatic history.

2565. Moorhead, Max L. Spanish deportation of hostile Apaches: the policy and the practice (UA/AW, 17:3, Autumn 1975, p. 205-220)

Another chapter in 18th-century Indian policy history. Describes deportation rules under which several hundred Apaches captured in war or raids were sent to Mexico City to remove threatening group from frontier area. Despite careful regulations for good treatment on trip south, many Indians died. Casualties were also heavy in Mexico City. This careful review of both legislation and experience of deportation based on records of journeys, concludes by noting that most Apache prisoners were exchanged or received amnesty.

2566. Nasatir, Abraham F. Borderland in retreat: from Spanish Louisiana to the far southwest. Albuquerque, Univ. of New Mexico Press, 1976. 175 p., bibl., maps.

Summation of some of author's previous publications on northern frontiers, emphasizing political and diplomatic events in period between 1750 and 1820.

2567. Patrick, Elizabeth Nelson. Land grants during the administration of Spanish colonial governor Pedro Fermín de Mendinueta (UNM/NMHR, 51:1, Jan. 1976, p. 5-18)

Between 1767-78, when Mendinueta was governor of New Mexico, great deal of land was alienated into private ownership. Article outlines some procedures used in obtaining land grants, protection of settled Indian villages, and details of some important transactions.

2568. Piñera Ramírez, David. The beginning of secular colonization in Baja California (SDHS/J, 23:1, Winter 1977, p. 80-88, bibl., illus., tables)

Permanent agricultural colonization (the work of naturalized mestizo citizens) gradually replaced mission system after 1768. Article contains list of recipients of land grants in Baja California between 1768-70, along with biographical information, location and quantity of lands distributed.

Polzer, Charles William. Rules and precepts of the Jesuit missions of northwestern New Spain. See item 254.

2569. ———; Thomas C. Barnes; and **Thomas H. Naylor** *comps.* The documentary relations of the Southwest: project manual. Tucson, Univ. of Arizona, Arizona State Museum, 1977. 160 p., tables.

Ingenious manual for researcher of Spanish colonial period in American Southwest (Mexico's borderlands). Contains information on how data are stored by computer (for non-technical minds), tables with conversions of weights and measures, ethnic names, officials in royal government, etc. Manual should be useful to student as well as professional.

2570. Quatrefages, René. La participación militar de Francia en la toma de Pensacola (SHM/RHM, 21:42, 1977, p. 7-30, illus., maps, tables)

Using military and diplomatic archives, author recounts story of rare military collaboration between France and Spain during War of American Revolution. Describes some of difficulties and events of battle. Appendix includes charts with account of costs incurred in these actions. Almost no secondary material has been used in this study.

2571. San Antonio Bicentennial Heritage Committee, *San Antonio, Texas*. San Antonio in the eighteenth century. San Antonio, Tex., Clarke Printing, 1976. 154 p., bibl., illus., tables.

Model popular bicentennial history, collectively produced and well-written. Includes sections on Indians, describes annual cycle of life in missions, as well as demographic history based on parish records. Discusses material culture through wills, inventories and illustrations. Covers both political and economic events as well as account of occurrences of 1776. Authors place settlement of San Antonio within framework of Spanish imperial history.

2572. Sánchez, Joseph P. Pedro Fages in Sonora: 1767-1768 & 1777-1782 (UNM/NMHR, 51:4, Oct. 1976, p. 281-294)

Author claims that Pedro Fages' terms of military service in Sonora, as a leader of Catalan volunteers, deserves greater emphasis. He first experienced Indian warfare there, and then went on to serve in California. His second tour of duty in Sonora made him an experienced frontier officer. Study is contribution to Fages' biography and to history of military organization.

2573. Sánchez-Fabrés Mirat, Elena. Situación histórica de las Floridas en la segunda mitad del siglo XVIII: 1783-1819, los problemas de una región de frontera. Madrid, Ministerio de Asuntos Exteriores, Dirección General de Relaciones Culturales, 1977. 330 p.

Estudio bien escrito y bien documentado, a base principalmente de documentación conservada en el Archivo Histórico Nacional, de Madrid. España recuperó en 1783 sus viejas posesiones de Florida, que había debido ceder a Inglaterra en 1763, pero esto le trajo más problemas que beneficios y hubo de ceder aquellos territorios al expansionismo de sus vecinos norteamericanos. [L. Gómez-Canedo]

2574. Stagg, Albert. The first Bishop of Sonora: Antonio de los Reyes, O.F.M. Tucson, The Univ. of Arizona Press, 1976. 109 p., bibl., maps, plates.

Brief biography of "ambitious, contentious" friar and defender of Indians who worked as missionary in Sonora after Jesuit expulsion, and then achieved high position in hierarchy. Through his alliance with Gálvez, he became first Bishop of Sonora. Includes extensive quotations from his letters and reports.

2575. Suárez Altamirano, Modesto. La hacienda mexicana: una comparación entre el latifundio de los Sánches Navarro y la hacienda de Guadalupe de Cieneguilla (UIA/C, 12:59, feb. 1977, p. 10-37, illus., plates)

Comparative study of two northern haciendas based on research of Charles H. Harris and José Ignacio Urquiola. Sánchez Altamirano compares administration, production, labor, etc., in both haciendas. While this article serves to disseminate work of Harris and Urquiola it adds little to what they did. Suárez Altamirano contends that comparison of different forms of haciendas will help understand how they adapted to varying geographical and historical circumstances.

2576. Thompson, Gerald *comp*. New Mexico history in *New Mexico Magazine*: an annotated bibliography; pt. 1 (UA/AW, 17:3, Autumn 1976, p. 245-278, plates)

Lists historical articles which appeared in *New Mexico Magazine* between 1924 and 1948. Includes some colonial materials.

2577. Thomson, Buchanan Parker. Spain: forgotten ally of the American Revolution. North Quincy, Mass., The Christopher Publishing House, 1976. 250 p., maps.

Written by amateur historian, book concentrates on borderlands and Spanish diplomacy. Based on primary sources and with little evidence of knowledge of secondary ones.

2578. Timmons. W.H. The population of the El Paso area: a census of 1784 (UNM/NMHR, 52:4, Oct. 1977, p. 311-316, tables)

Observations on detailed census of El Paso region shows that population had almost quadrupled since 1692. However, population had declined between 1760s and 1780s because of Indian warfare. Additional aspects of this and other census are briefly noted.

2579. Velázquez, María del Carmen. La Comandancia General de las Provincias Internas (CM/HM, 27:2, oct./dic. 1977, p. 163-176)

Describes establishment of General Command of Provinces Internas beginning with visita of Marqués de Rubí in 1766-68 until its abolition in 1818. Chart summarizes various permutations in organization and personnel. Principal administrative problem was jurisdictional conflict between General Commander and Viceroy.

2580. ———. El Marqués de Altamira y las provincias internas de Nueva España. México, El Colegio de México, Centro de Estudios Históricos, 1976. 207 p. (Jornadas, 81)

Collection of opinions and administrative investigation written between 1747-51 by Juan Rodríguez Albuerne, Marqués de Altamira. Drawing from various archives, author has assembled documents dealing with Sierra Gorda, mission boundaries, presidios, population and costs of settlement. Albuerne was oidor who served as general superintendent of the Reales Azogues and Auditor General of War. Also includes biographical and genealogical material on Sánchez de Tagle family into which Albuerne married in 1730.

2581. Vélez de Escalante, Silvestre. The Domínguez-Escalante journal: their expedition through Colorado, Utah, Arizona, and New Mexico in 1776. Translated by Fray Angélico Chávez. Edited by Ted J. Warner. Provo, Utah, The Brigham Young Univ. Press, 1976. 203 p., bibl., plates.

New English translation of Domínguez-Escalante Journal, based on earliest of three known manuscripts of 1776 expedition. Groups of scholars retraced trail of expedition and identified current place names. Includes some additional annotations and Spanish text of Ayer-Newberry manuscript.

2582. Waciuma, Wanjohi. Intervention in Spanish Floridas 1801-1813: a study in Jeffersonian foreign policy. Boston, Mass., Branden Press, 1976. 371 p.

In this study of background of annexation of Florida, from Louisiana Purchase to War of 1812, author asserts that US consistently claimed hegemony over both North and South America. Based on examination of US diplomatic sources, author notes that US claimed that Louisiana purchase included West Florida, revealing "a premature adoption of the strategy of the 'big stick diplomacy'."

2583. Weber, David J. ed. El México perdido; ensayos escogidos sobre el antiguo norte de México, 1540-1821. Antología. México, Secretaría de la Educación Pública, 1976. 166 p., map (SepSetentas, 265)

Collection and translation of essays or sections of books which have appeared in North America on borderlands. Includes general view of region's history by Weber; Bolton's essay on missions; Faulk on presidio; Simmons on plans of New Mexico's towns and villages; Webb on failure of Spaniards as colonizers of Great Plains; Dozier on Spanish impact on Pueblo Indians; Servín on role of mestizos in colonization of California; Scholes on New Mexican society in 17th century; Hutchinson on Mexican settlement of California; the latter is contrasted with Zavala's views on northern frontier of New Spain. There is introduction to each selection pointing to its historiographical importance. Overall, an admirable work, which succeeds in weaving a coherent story from a variety of disparate sources.

2584. Weber, Francis J. The writings of Francisco García Diego y Moreno: Obispo de ambas Californias. Los Angeles, Calif., n.p., 1976. 192 p.

Edita en traducción inglesa 197 escritos (principalmente cartas y representaciones, 1820-46) del franciscano mexicano García Diego. Después de haber desarrollado importante labor en su Colegio de Guadalupe (Zacatecas) pasó a la Alta California en 1832, al frente de un grupo de misioneros. Sus escritos son importantes no sólo para la historia de California sino para la de México, en un período particularmente difícil. La edición va precedida de buen bosquejo biográfico. [L. Gómez-Canedo]

2585. White, David H. A view of Spanish west Florida: selected letters of Governor Juan Vicente Folch (FHS/FHQ, 56:2, Oct. 1977, p. 138-147)

Spanish West Florida and its problems as seen by its Governor in letters written in 1790s and filed in AGI. Topics range from runaway slaves to cuckolding of governor.

2586. Zorrilla, Juan Fidel. El poder colonial en Nuevo Santander. México, Manuel Porrúa, 1976. 333 p.

Outlines foundation and development of Nuevo Santander, a region incorporated relatively late to colonial Mexico, and one which was colonized by families and people from various socioeconomic and ethnic groups. Role of José de Escandón as leader of this settlement and organizer of whole region is strongly delineated. Study is chronologically arranged following government of commandants in charge of this area. Although there are no startling revelations in text, narrative is smooth and work makes good general reading.

19th CENTURY, REVOLUTION AND POST-REVOLUTION

RICHARD E. GREENLEAF

Director
Center for Latin American Studies
Tulane University

DON M. COERVER

Assistant Professor of History
Texas Christian University

THE PAST BIENNIUM HAS WITNESSED the publication of several outstanding contributions along with the usual proportion of solid monographs, antiquarian books and articles, and reprints of old classics. Special attention should be directed to the papers delivered at the IV International Congress of Mexican History on the subject of contemporary Mexico edited by Wilkie, Meyer, and Wilkie (see item 2730). The following books devoted to 19th-century topics are worthy of special note: Anderson on industrial workers in the late Porfiriato (item 2587); Coatsworth on the impact of the railroads (item 2604); Knowlton on Church property and the Reforms (item 2622); and Raat on positivism during the Porfiriato (item 2652). The most significant articles on 19th-century topics are the following: Coatsworth on Porfirian agricultural production (item 2603); Hart on the Mexican anarchist movement (item 2621); Powell on priest-peasant relations in the 1840s and 1850s (item 2649); Raat on US-Mexican diplomacy of suppression (item 2651); and Weber's historiographical essay on the northern frontier (item 2673). The following monographs on 20th-century topics merit special attention: Carr on the labor movement and government in the first two decades of the Revolution (item 2701); and Meyer on the Cristero Rebellion (item 2752). Superior articles on 20th-century themes are: Aguilera Gómez on land reform during the Echeverría administration (item 2682); Burke on the relationship between UNAM and the Revolution (item 2695); and Naylor on Villa's Sonora campaign (item 2759).

Several themes emerged during the last two years. Considerable interest was directed to the labor movement and its relation to government policy. In addition to the above-mentioned books and articles by Anderson, Carr, and Hart, the following studies on the labor movement should be mentioned: Huitrón's history of the early labor movement (item 2729); Ruíz on labor during the early years of the Revolution (item 2771); Trejo Delarbe's overview of the labor movement since the Revolution (item 2782); and Leal and Woldenberg's annotated bibliography on the labor movement from 1867-1914 (item 2739).

Studies of Porfirian economics were also very popular. These include (in addition to the above-mentioned works by Coatsworth and Knowlton) the following: Coerver on the Department of Fomento (item 2606); Meyers on the Company Tlahualilo (item 2632); Theisen on the Mexicanization of the country's industry (item 2664); and Yeager on Porfirian commercial propaganda (item 2675).

Immigration history received considerable attention. Barker's article on the French colony in Mexico revealed much about the background to the "Pastry War" (item 2591). Berninger added to knowledge of Mexican opinion on 19th-century immigration to Mexico (item 2598). Cardoso (items 2698-2699); Carreras de Velasco (item 2702); Dinwoodie (item 2712); Hoffman (items 2727-2728); and Reisler (item 2763) wrote on the problems associated with immigration to the US.

The recent change in administration has provoked a flood of articles dealing with the Echeverría government or its consequences: Grindle (item 2720); Jones and LaFrance (item 2731); Martínez de la Vega (item 2747); Rodríguez Araujo (item 2766); and Shapira (item 2774). US-Mexican border problems and diplomacy are very popular subjects of study. A large number of these works, however, rely exclusively on English courses. Only a smattering of social history appeared during the last two years. Meyer dealt with the social origins of the federal and various revolutionary armies between 1910-30 (item 2753), but women's history in particular seems to be coming into vogue: Arrom on Mexican women and ecclesiastical divorce (item 2589); and Dysart on Mexican women in San Antonio (item 2609).

A trend away from political history in general and political biography in particular can be discerned. Only local political history seems to be attracting increasing attention. Some of the better studies in this category for the 19th century are: Bryan on Governor Bernardo Reyes of Nuevo León (item 2600); Coerver on Sonoran political struggles (item 2605); Falcone on Oaxacan politics (item 2610); and Macune on conflicts between the national government and the state of Mexico (item 2628). The Biblioteca del Instituto de Estudios Históricos de la Revolución Mexicana continues to publish useful monographs on local revolutionary history, but the majority have been written by amateur historians. The best works on local aspects of the Revolution are: Beezley on Carranza's governorship in Coahuila (item 2691); Deeds on Maytorena's administration in Sonora (item 2710); and Joseph on the Revolution in Yucatan (item 2732).

Finally, the Secretaría de Educación Pública must be commended for the quantity and quality of its SepSetentas publications: Arreola Cortés (item 2588); Arrom (item 2589); Bataillon and Rivière (item 2689); Berninger (item 2597); Britton (item 2694); Carr (item 2701); Coatsworth (item 2604); Luna (item 2626); Matute (item 2751); Monjarás-Ruíz (item 2757); Monroy Huitrón (item 2758); Powell (item 2648); Raat (item 2652); Reyna (item 2653); and Velasco Márquez (item 2670).

In summary, the major trends of the past biennium are toward diplomatic, economic, immigration, and labor history. Special recognition is due this biennium to Lawrence J. Rohlfes who screened the literature and helped write this section. Barbara Johnson Encinas helped with the literature in journals published in languages other than Spanish and English.

19th CENTURY

2587. Anderson, Rodney D. Outcasts in their own land: Mexican industrial workers, 1906-1911. De Kalb, Northern Illinois Univ. Press, 1976. 407 p., bibl., illus., facsims., maps, plates, tables (The origins of modern Mexico, 2)

Important well-researched study of Mexican industrial workers on eve of Revolution. Anderson argues convincingly that Spanish anarchists and PLM had little influence on Mexican workers. Instead stresses workers' concern for dignity, equality, and respect. They sought aid from Porfirian government when employers ceased to perform traditional role of *patrón*, and when government failed them its legitimacy was lost.

2588. Arreola Cortés, Raúl *ed.* Melchor Ocampo: textos políticos. México, Secretaría de Educación Pública, 1975. 190 p., plates (SepSetentas, 192)

Useful collection of Melchor Ocampo's political texts covering period 1842-61.

2589. Arrom, Silvia M. La mujer mexicana ante el divorcio eclesiástico: 1800-1857. México, Secretaría de Educación Pública, 1976. 222 p.

Study of interest not only to social historians but also to legal and church historians. Author examines social meaning of "divorce" in its 19th-century Mexican form (actually limited form of separation) and concludes that divorce was used as control device in male-dominated society.

2590. Baker, George T. Una propuesta mexicana para la ayuda militar norteamericana o sea, un recuerdo del liberalismo mexicano desconocido (UNAM/AH, 8, 1976, p. 249-260)

Article contains document identified by author in brief annotation as proposal written by Francisco Carbajal to American military officer in 1847. Document requests American military aid to implement liberal reforms in Mexico.

2591. Barker, Nancy Nichols. The French colony in Mexico, 1821-61: generator of intervention (French Historical Studies [Society for French Historical Studies, Columbus, Ohio] 9:4, Fall 1976, p. 596-618, bibl., tables)

Excellent study of French subjects in Mexico drawn primarily from archives of French Foreign Ministry and Mexican Embassy in Paris. Concludes that France's interventionist posture was strongly influenced by vulnerability of large French community in face of Mexico's chronic civil disorders.

2592. Bazant, Jan. La familia Alamán y los descendientes del conquistador: 1850-1907 (CM/HM, 26:1, julio/sept. 1976, p. 48-69, bibl.)

Another informative installment from author's continuing research into disposition of property in 19th-century Mexico. Lucas Alamán and son Juan energetically defended Mexican interests of conqueror's Italian heirs against Liberal property legislation. Juan, particularly, enjoyed great success through cultivation of personal associations with important liberals, especially Sebastián Lerdo de Tejada.

2593. ———. Landlord, labourer, and tenant in San Luis Potosí, northern Mexico, 1822-1910 (*in* Duncan, Kenneth; Ian Rutledge; and Colin Hardings eds. Land and labour in Latin America [see item 2156] p. 59-82, bibl., maps)

Synthesis, with additional information, of two of author's previous works published in Spanish (see *HLAS 38:2578*). [A. Lavrin]

2594. Benjamin, Thomas. International Harvester and the henequen marketing system in Yucatan, 1898-1915: new perspective (IAMEA, 31:3, Winter 1977, p. 3-19)

Examination of traditional interpretation that domination of henequen market by International Harvester was responsible for decline in henequen prices in early 1900s. Author argues that decline is more correctly attributed to movements in world fiber market, fluctuations in business cycle, Mexican monetary reform and decline in US agricultural production and resulting drop in demand for henequen.

2595. Bennett, E. Fay. An afternoon of terror: the Sonoran earthquake of May 3, 1887 (UA/AW, 19:2, Summer 1977, p. 107-120, plates)

Description of earthquake which struck Sonora, Ariz., and New Mexico and of scientific investigation which it prompted. While most of narrative deals with Arizona, there is some attention devoted to its impact upon Sonora. Includes photographs.

2596. Berge, Dennis E. *ed.* and *trans*. Considerations on the political and social situation of the Mexican Republic: 1847. El Paso, Univ. of Texas [and] Texas Western Press, 1975. 62 p. (Southwestern studies, 45)

English translation of *Consideraciones sobre la situación política y social de la República Mexicana, en el año 1847*, liberal political tract signed by "varios mexicanos" which denounced Spanish colonial heritage and urged acceptance of a US protectorate over Mexico.

2597. Berninger, Dieter G. Immigration and religious toleration: a Mexican dilemma, 1821-1860 (AAFH/TAM, 32:4, April 1976, p. 549-565)

Citing extensively from contemporary polemical literature, author traces dispute over religious toleration in early 19th century. In order to gain hearing, liberals tied issue to question of immigration, which most Mexicans favored. Conservatives prevailed, however, until 1860 when liberal military victory enabled Juárez to impose toleration by decree.

2598. ———. La inmigración en México: 1821-1857. Traducción de Roberto Gómez Ciriza. México, Secretaría de Educación Pública, 1974. 198 p., bibl. (SepSetentas, 144)

Examines spectrum of Mexican opinion on immigration question between 1821-57.

2599. Bonfil Batalla, Guillermo. Cholula: la ciudad sagrada en la era industrial. México, UNAM, Instituto de Investigaciones Históricas, Sección de Antropología, 1973. 296 p., bibl., fold. map, illus. (Serie antropológica, 15)

Anthropological study of persistence of traditional institutions in urbanized society. Valuable to historians with interest in society and culture of present-day Cholula.

Brack, Gene M. Mexico views Manifest Destiny, 1821-1846: an essay on the origins of the Mexican War. See *HLAS 39:8683*.

2600. Bryan, Anthony T. El papel del General Bernardo Reyes en la política nacional y regional de México (UNL/H, 13, 1972, p. 331-349)

Case study of state and local government under Porfiriato argues, among other things, that governors were not ordinarily puppets. Maintenance of local order and solution of local problems were crucial to success of Porfirian regime nationwide.

2601. ———. Political power in Porfirio Díaz' Mexico: a review and commentary (PAT/TH, 38:4, Aug. 1976, p. 648-668)

Valuable survey of current state of research on Porfiriato. Includes suggestions for future. Footnotes include extensive bibliographic matter.

2602. Cardero García, María Elena. Evolución financiera de México: Porfiriato y revolución (UNAM/RMS, 38:2, abril/junio 1976, p. 359-387, tables)

Graphic overview of financial stagnation fostered by Porfirian policy of elitist concentration of capital and dependence upon foreign economic catalysts.

2603. Coatsworth, John H. Anotaciones sobre la producción de alimentos durante el Porfiriato (CM/HM, 26:2, oct./dic. 1976, p. 167-187, tables)

Important study reveals limitations of existing statistical work on Porfirian agricultural production and questions hypothesis that production of basic foodstuffs declined during second half of Porfiriato as export and industrial crop production increased.

2604. ———. El impacto económico de los ferrocarriles en el Porfiriato: crecimiento y desarrollo. México, Secretaría de Educación Pública, 1976. 2 v. (150, 158 p.) maps, tables.

Important study utilizes econometric techniques to measure impact of railroads upon Porfirian economy. Concludes that railroads in Mexico sparked greater amount of economic activity than railroads in countries already possessing industrial establishment. Railroads contributed little to industrial growth, however, because freight consisted primarily of raw materials for export. Coatsworth also shows that railroads helped perpetuate latifundismo.

2605. Coerver, Don M. Federal-state relations during the *Porfiriato*: the case of Sonora, 1879-1884 (AAFH/TAM, 33:4, April 1977, p. 567-584)

Examines several political struggles which took place in Sonora prior to and during presidential administration of Manuel González. Emphasizes central government's inability to exercise absolute control over local and federal authorities in provinces. Well documented from Col. Gen. Porfiro Díaz.

2606. ———. The perils of progress: the Mexican Department of Fomento during the boom years, 1880-1884 (IAMEA, 31:2, Autumn 1977, p. 41-62)

Examination and analysis of Dept. of Fomento's promotion of economic development during Manuel González' administration, 1880-84. Article demonstrates that economic ambitions of González administration outstripped its financial resources.

2607. Costeloe, Michael P. Santa Anna and the Gómez Farías administration of México: 1833-1834 (AAFH/TAM, 31:1, July 1974, p. 18-50)

Interesting insights into motivations behind Santa Anna's political activities during 1833-34 period.

Díaz Ramírez, Manuel. Apuntes sobre el movimiento obrero y campesino de México: 1844-1880. See *HLAS 39:7117*

2608. Documentos inéditos de José Ives Limantour: apuntes relativos a una conversación habida con el Sr. Presidente en presencia de los Sres. Ramón Corral y Olegario Molina, Mayo 13 de 1908 (FCE/TP, 1:1, julio/sept. 1975, p. 125-138)

Limantour's notes of discussion with President Díaz concerning transfer of power. Also includes discussion with Madero's father and Francisco Vázquez Gómez over revolutionaries' terms.

2609. Dysart, Jane. Mexican women in San Antonio, 1830-1860: the assimilation process WHQ, 7:4, Oct. 1976, p. 365-375)

Good insight into social mores on frontier where Anglo and Mexican cultures came into contact and conflict. Based on ecclesiastical and civil archives.

2610. Falcone, Frank S. Benito Juárez versus the Díaz brothers: politics in Oaxaca, 1867-1871 (AAFH/TAM, 33:4, April 1977, p. 630-651, tables)

Félix Díaz, younger brother of Porfirio Díaz, was elected governor of Oaxaca in Nov. 1867. Article shows how Díaz brothers used patronage powers of governorship to build political following in native state of then president of Mexico, Benito Juárez. On eve of Plan of La Noria in 1871 Oaxaca was for all intents and purposes politically independent of federal government.

2611. Fuentes Mares, José. La Emperatriz Eugenia y su aventura mexicana. México, El Colegio de México, 1976. 243 p., bibl., illus.

Well-written diplomatic history of Mexican monarchist plots, European background to French Intervention, and selection of Maximilian as Emperor of Mexico.

2612. Gamilscheg, Felix. 8.000 [i.e. Achttausend] Österreicher mit Maximilian in Mexiko (OLI/ZLW, 11, 1976, p. 40-53)

Deals with 8,000 European volunteers of primarily Austrian origin who came to Mexico in 1865 to fight for Maximilian. Majority returned to Europe in 1867, but some remained until Emperor's death. Includes Spanish abstract of German text.

2613. García, Genaro ed. Correspondencia secreta de los principales intervencionistas mexicanos. El sitio de Puebla en 1863. Causa contra el Gral. Leonardo Márquez. 2. ed. México, Editorial Porrúa, 1972. 807 p., plate (Biblioteca Porrúa. Documentos inéditos o muy raros para la historia de México, 51)

Reprints five vols. in series "Documentos Inéditos o Muy Raros para la Historia de México:" t. 1, 4, 13, *Correspondencia* . . .; t. 23, *El sitio* . . .; t. 8, *Causa contra* . . . .

2614. Gaxiola, Francisco Javier. Gobernantes del estado de México: Múzquiz; Zavala; Olaquíbel. Ed. facsimilar de la de 1899 preparada por Mario Colín. México, Gobierno del Estado de México, 1975. 106 p., facsims. (Biblioteca enciclopédica del estado de México, 43)

Facsimile of 1899 ed. Contains biographical sketches of three governors of State of Mexico: Melchor Múzquiz, Lorenzo de Zavala and Francisco Modesto de Olaquíbel.

2615. Giron, Nicole. La idea de "Cultura Nacional" en el siglo XIX: Altamirano y Ramírez (*in* Aguilar Camín, Héctor and others. En torno a la cultura nacional [see item 2418] p. 51-84)

Both Altamirano and Ramírez exemplified elitist 19th-century liberal thought. They ignored or did not understand indigenous cultures and extolled foreign cultural values, confusing technological development with civilization. Giron sees them as necessary stages in definition of national culture. Interesting analysis. [A. Lavrin].

2616. González, Luis and others. La economía mexicana en la época de Juárez. Introducción de Carlos Torres Manzo. Prólogo de José Luis Ibáñez Cabrera. México, Secretaría de Educación Pública (SEP), Dirección General de Divulgación, 1976. 190 p., illus. (SepSetentas, 236)

Contains five essays on various aspects of Mexican economy between 1850-72:
Luis González "La Era de Juárez" p. 11-55
Enrique Florescano and María del Rosario Lanzagorta "Política Económica: Antecedentes y Consecuencias" p. 57-106
Romero Flores Caballero "Etapas del Desarrollo Industrial" p. 107-128
Inés Herrera Canales "Comercio Exterior" p. 129-154
Jan Bazant "Desamortización y Nacionalización de los Bienes de la Iglesia" p. 155-190.

2617. González Navarro, Moisés. Las guerras de castas (CM/HM, 26:1, julio/sept. 1976, 70-106)

Treats Indian rebellions of 1840s in northern and southern Mexico. Lacks clear focus and a sufficient degree of analysis.

2618. Grajales, Gloria ed. México y la Gran Bretaña durante la intervención: 1861-1862. 2. ed. México, Secretaría de Relaciones Exteriores, 1974. 241 p., bibl. (Col. del Archivo Histórico Diplomático Mexicano. Serie documental, 9)

Collection and translation into Spanish of documents relating to Great Britain's participation in Tripartite Intervention of 1860-61. For political scientist's comment, see *HLAS 39:8693*.

2619. Green, Michael Robert. El soldado mexicano: 1835-1836 (Military History of Texas and the Southwest [Military History Press, Austin] 13:1, 1975, p. 5-10)

Description of disorganized state of Mexican Army on eve of Texas Revolution. Includes discussion of organization, tactics and logistics.

2620. Hardy, R.W.H. Travels in the interior of Mexico, in 1825, 1826, 1827, & 1828. Preface by Robert B. McCoy. Introduction by David J. Weber. Glorieta, N. Mex., The Rio Grande Press, 1977. 558 p., fold. map (A Rio Grande classic)

Reprint of 1829 ed. (London, H. Colburn and R. Benley). Description of northwestern Mexico through eyes of 19th-century Englishman. Especially valuable for its commentaries on society and culture of provincial Mexico.

2621. Hart, John M. Nineteenth century urban labor precursors of the Mexican Revolution: the development of an ideology (AAFH/TAM, 30:3, Jan. 1974, p. 297-318)

Focuses on Mexican anarchist movement of 1860s and 1870s. Maintains that anarchist followers of Plotino C. Rhodakanaty made significant contributions to ideology of Revolution of 1910s Casa del Obrero Mundial.

2622. Knowlton, Robert J. Church property and the Mexican reform: 1856-1910. De Kalb, Northern Illinois Press, 1976. 265 p., bibl., facsims., illus., tables (The origins of modern Mexico, 1)

Excellent detailed study of the disamortization and nationalization of ecclesiastical property and their impact upon Mexican society in context of Church-State relations between 1856-1910.

2623. Krause, Corinne Azen. Positivist liberalism in Mexico: the career of Isidoro Epstein, 1851-1894 (UM/JIAS, 18:4, Nov. 1976, p. 475-494, bibl.)

Examines career of 1848 German exile in Mexico. Epstein was Jew, liberal, and technocrat (engineer and mathematician) and thus blended well in progressive intellectual and political circles which sought to flaunt anti-clericalism, anti-traditionalism, and commitment to "scientific" material development.

2624. Leonard, Glen M. Southwestern boundaries and the principles of statemaking (WHQ, 8:1, Jan. 1977. p. 39-53, map)

Look at legislative criteria for formation of permanent boundaries of statehood in US Southwest. Stresses importance of geography and preeminence of people. Examines historical, social and geographical factors.

2625. Long, Robert W: José Matías Moreno: jefe político de la frontera, Baja California, 1861-1862: pts. 1/3 (UP/PH, 21:1, Spring 1977, p. 55-69; 21:2, Summer 1977, p. 215-221; 21:3, Fall 1977, p. 262-267; 21:4, Winter 1977, p. 395-410, bibl.)

Anecdotal narrative of life on Mexican periphery in middle of 19th century. Manner of presentation makes study disjointed and repetitious. Topics and time period covered are considerably broader than title would suggest.

2626. Luna, Jesús. La carrera pública de Don Ramón Corral. Traducción de Antonieta S. de Hope. México, Secretaría de Educación Pública, 1975. 182 p., bibl. (SepSetentas, 187)

Documented study of Ramón Corral's public careers.

2627. MacKinnon, Richard M. The Sonoran miners: a case of historical accident in the California gold rush (CCGT/CG, 11, 1970, p. 21-28, illus., map)

North American domination of California gold rush obscures important role played by miners from many countries and in particular Mexicans from Sonora.

2628. Macune, Charles W., Jr. Conflictos entre el gobierno nacional y el estado de México: 1823-1835 (CM/HM, 26:2, oct./dic. 1976, p. 216-237)

Examines several conflicts which arose between state of Mexico and national government after establishment of federal system in 1824.

2629. Meier, Matt S. María Insurgente (CM/HM, 23:3, enero/mayo 1974, p. 466-482)

Examines political use of Virgin of Guadalupe by Miguel Hidalgo and José María Morelos during wars in independence. Author maintains that Guadalupana was very effective symbol of nationalism for insurgents.

2630. Mertens, Hans-Günther and **Hans Pohl.** Die Entwicklung der Mexikanischen Landwirtschaft während des Porfiriats (IAA, 1, 1975, p. 61-103, bibl., table)

Porfirian efforts to modernize Mexican agriculture concentrated on large-scale production of raw materials for domestic industry and cash crops for export. When combined with prevailing trend of concentration of lands into *latifundia*, process aggravated tensions ultimately leading to agrarian revolt.

2631. Mexico. Secretaría de la Presidencia. Dirección General de Estudios Administrativos. La administración pública en la época de Juárez. t. 1/3. México, 1973/1974. 3 v. (800, 710, 1466 p.) bibl., illus., tables.

Useful compilation of federal government legislative dispositions along with well-written summaries of each public administration between 1851-72. Vol. 1 begins with administration of Mariano Arista and concludes with government of Ignacio Commfort. Vol. 2 is devoted to Benito Juárez' administration during War of Reform and European intervention. Vol. 3 deals with Restored Republic until death of Juárez.

2632. Meyers, William K. Politics, vested rights, and economic growth in Porfirian Mexico: the Company Tlahualilo in the Comarca Lagunera, 1885-1911 (HAHR, 57:3, Aug. 1977, p. 425-454)

Well-researched study of important water rights controversy in context of local and national politics, Porfirian economic policy, and foreign investment vs. national development.

2633. Montaigne, Sanford H. Blood over Texas. New Rochelle, N.Y., Arlington House, 1976. 160 p., bibl., illus.

Inadequately documented defense of US role in Mexican War.

2634. Morales, María Dolores. Estructura urbana y distribución de la propiedad en la ciudad de México en 1813 (CM/HM, 25:3, enero/marzo 1976, p. 363-402, maps, tables)

Among many fine studies produced by INAH's Seminario de Historia Urbana. Represents first stage in author's project to survey changes in Mexico City's urban structure and distribution of urban property during 19th century. In 1813, the Church was largest proprietor of urban real estate. Private individuals were second with expected extreme concentration into few hands. For summary of entire project which indicates that confiscation of Church wealth in no way favored broader distribution of urban property, see item 2636.

2635. Moreno, Roberto. La introducción del Darwinismo en México (UNAM/AH, 8, 1976, p. 121-150)

Well-written article examines reception and diffusion of Darwinism in Mexico with emphasis upon its connections with positivist philosophy, religion, education, and science.

2636. Moreno Toscano, Alejandra and others. Research in progress in urban history: pt. 1, Mexico (LARR, 10:2, Summer 1975, p. 117-131, tables)

Summaries of research projects presented before Seminario de Historia Urbana of INAH's Depto. de Investigaciones Históricas. Projects deal with Mexico City in 19th century and employ machine analysis of archival data related to demography, patterns of settlement and construction, distribution of urban property, and permanence of structures. These works demonstrate promise of seminar's ambitious program of research and publications which aims ultimately at an overall synthesis.

2637. Moseley, Edward H. Los Planes de Ayutla y Monterrey (UNL/H, 13, 1972, p. 365-381)

Well-documented discussion of Plan of Monterrey (less appreciated by historians than its southern counterpart, Plan of Ayutla) and role of its adherents, including Santiago Vidaurri and Juan Zuazúa, in final overthrow of Santa Anna.

2638. Mullins, William H. The British press and the Mexican War: Justin Smith revised (UNM/NMHR, 52:3, July 1977, p. 207-227)

While supposedly concerned with revising Justin Smith's interpretation of attitude of British public toward Mexican war, author devotes most of his attention to reaction of British government and press. Smith is depicted as "strong Anglophobe" who misinterpreted response of both British government and press to conflict.

2639. Núñez Ortega, Angel. Los primeros consulados de México, 1823-1872. Tlatelolco, Mex., Secretaría de Relaciones Exteriores, 1974. 102 p., fold. map, table (Col. del Archivo Histórico Diplomático Mexicano. Serie documental, 7)

Listing of Mexican consuls and consulates in Europe and America, 1823-72. Originally compiled by Núñez Ortega, Mexican diplomat, under auspices of Secretaría de Relaciones Exteriores in 1872. For political scientist's comment, see *HLAS 39:8700*.

2640. Olliff, Donathon C. Mexico's mid-nineteenth-century drive for material development (SECOLAS/A, 8, March 1977, p. 19-29)

Maintains that liberal leaders of Reforma period gave high priority to economic questions. They believed that government should play active role in economy rather than take laissez-faire approach.

2642. Paredes, Raymond A. The Mexican image in American travel literature: 1831-1869 (UNM/NMHR, 52:1, Jan. 1977, p. 5-29)

Fascinating description of how travel literature helped promote Mexican stereotype in the American mind as well as justify American expansionism in Southwest. Contains some favorable reports by travelers and constitutes annotated bibliography of sorts for many primary accounts of period.

2643. Pasquel, Leonardo. El conflicto obrero de Río Blanco en 1907. México, Editorial Citlaltepetl, 1976. 104 p., bibl., facsims., fold. illus., illus. (Col. Suma veracruzana. Serie historiografía)

Brief treatment of Río Blanco strike drawn from published primary and secondary sources.

2644. Penor, J. L'expansion commerciale française au Mexique et les causes du conflit franco-mexicain de 1838-1839 (UB/BH, 75:1/2, janvier/juin 1973, p. 169-201)

Extensive research in French diplomatic and naval archives reveals political and economic background to so-called "Pastry War." Although based entirely upon French sources, record of abuses and violence to French merchants and residents suggests claims against Mexico not so trivial as popular name of conflict suggests. Author argues, however, that real purpose of French action was to obtain advantageous commercial treaty to protect what July Monarchy considered vital branch of French economy.

2645. Perry, Laurens Ballard. El modelo liberal y la política práctica en la

República Restaurada: 1867-1876 (CM/HM, 23:4, abril/junio 1974, p. 646-699, tables)

Contains three parts: 1) summarizes liberal principles embodied in Constitution of 1857; 2) points out contradictions between liberal program and Mexican reality; and 3) examines federal government's response to election disputes in four states. Concludes that presidents of Restored Republic bent liberal theory by taking advantage of election disputes to encourage formation of political machines in states.

2646. Peterson, Richard H. The Foreign Miner's Tax of 1850 and Mexicans in California: exploitation or expulsion (UP/PH, 20:3, Fall 1976, p. 265-272)

Brief discussion of evidence on this issue. Frontier egalitarianism did not apply to all ethnic groups.

2647. Pletcher, David M. Consul Warner P. Sutton and American-Mexican border trade during the early Díaz period (TSHA/SHQ, 79:4, April 1976, p. 373-399)

Career of "an unusually able and perceptive American consular official" (p. 373) reflects day-to-day problems of US-Mexican relations, process of North American penetration of Mexican economy, and changes that occurred in Rio Grande Valley in the critical years of Porfiriato. For political scientist's comment, see *HLAS 39:8706*.

2648. Powell, T.G. El liberalismo y el campesinado en el centro de México: 1850-1876. Traducción de Roberto Gómez Ciriza. México, Secretaría de Educación Pública, 1974. 189 p., bibl.

Examines impact of Reforma legislation on Indian communities in central area of Mexico.

2649. ———. Priests and peasants in Central Mexico: social conflict during "La Reforma" (HAHR, 57:2, May 1977, p. 296-313)

Examination of priest-peasant relations in Archbishopric of Mexico during 1840s and 1850s. Concludes that peasant indifference to Church's plight during wars of Reforma can be traced in part to corruption among rural priests and failure of Mexican hierarchy to discipline them. Based on archival research from Ramo de Bienes Nacionales of AGN.

2650. Raat, William Dirk. The antipositivist movement in pre-revolutionary Mexico: 1892-1911 (UM/JIAS, 19:1, Feb. 1977, p. 83-98, bibl.)

Author suggests that "for the intellectual history of the Porfiriato the issue of antipositivism was more important politically and socially than that of positivism" (p. 83). Mexicans of all political persuasions found explanations for national ills in "positivism" of their opponents. Overuse of the epithet in contemporary polemics rendered the term essentially meaningless.

2651. ———. The diplomacy of suppression: *Los revoltosos*, Mexico, and the United States (HAHR, 56:4, Nov. 1976, p. 529-550)

Important study, employs wealth of US and Mexican archival sources. Roosevelt and Taft administration cooperated with Díaz in operating extensive espionage network on both sides of border. Official and semi-official pursuit and harassment was effective against Flores Magón brothers and other "amateur" revolutionaries in US, less so against Madero's compact, well-financed, "professional" operation.

2652. ———. El positivismo durante el Porfiriato: 1876-1910. Traducción de Andrés Lira. México, Secretaría de Educación Pública, 1975. 175 p., bibl.

A more precise, if not revisionist, analysis of intellectual currents of Porfiriato. Author identifies need for greater precision in categorizing ideas of period, especially task of distinguishing between Comte's positivism and "scientism" that became so popular.

2653. Reyna, María del Carmen. La prensa censurada durante el siglo XIX. México, Secretaría de Educación Pública, 1976. 189 p., table (SepSetentas, 255)

Documents instances of press censorship between 1820-82 by both liberal and conservative governments.

2654. Roldán Oquendo, Ornán. Las relaciones entre México y Colombia: 1810-1862. Tlatelolco, Méx., Secretaría de Relaciones Exteriores, 1974. 263 p., bibl. (Col. Del archivo histórico diplomático mexicano. Serie de obras monográficas, 5)

Detailed examination of Mexican-Colombian diplomatic and commercial relations between 1810-62. Author consulted impressive number of archival sources in both countries. For political scientist's comment, see *HLAS 39:8709*.

2655. Ruibal Corella, Juan Antonio. ¡Y Caborca se cubrió de gloria ...!: la expedición filibustera de Henry Alexander Crabb a Sonora. Prólogo de Alejandro Sobarzo. México, Editorial Porrúa, 1976. 231 p., bibl., facsims., illus., table.

Commemorates defeat of group of filibusters under Henry Alexander Crabb's leadership at Caborca, Sonora, 6 April 1857.

2656. Ruiz Castañeda, María del Carmen. La guerra del 47 vista por Guillermo Prieto (UNAM/A, 6, 1973, p. 39-96)

Guillermo Prieto, "Fidel," tells unpleasant story of young soldier in Santa Anna's command in 1847. Author maintains such *costumbrista* sketches aid understanding of social and cultural history of early 19th-century Mexico.

2657. Saldaña, José P. Próceres de la Reforma y de la Intervención Francesa (UNL/H, 17, 1976, p. 441-461)

Biographical sketches of seven liberal neoleoneses who participated in military or political capacities in Reform wars and French Intervention.

2658. Sayles, Stephen. The Romero-Frelinghuysen Convention: a milestone in border relations (UNM/NMHR, 51:4, Oct. 1976, p. 295-311)

Description of political, economic and diplomatic events leading up to reciprocal-crossing agreement of 1882. Based primarily on US diplomatic correspondence.

2659. Schoonover, Thomas. Dollars over dominion: United States economic interests in Mexico, 1861-1867 (UC/PHR, 45:1, Feb. 1976, p. 23-45)

Description of transitional period when the US was moving from policy of territorial expansion to one favoring trade and investment. Author clearly demonstrates that limited American penetration of Mexican economy during 1860s was not only encouraged by US government but also welcomed by Mexican government. Based primarily on archival sources and diplomatic correspondence. For political scientist's comment, see *HLAS 39:8710*.

2660. Seba Patrón, Francisco. Historia y leyenda de Antonio López de Santa Anna en Turbaco, Nueva Granada (UY/R, 16:96, nov./dic. 1976, p. 37-53)

Account of Santa Anna's activities in Turbaco, Colombia, during his years of exile from Mexico.

2661. Semo, Enrique and **Gloria Pedrero. La vida en una hacienda-aserradero mexicana a principios del siglo XIX** (*in* Florescano, Enrique *ed.* Haciendas, latifundios y plantaciones en América Latina [see *HLAS 38:2190*] p. 273-306, map, tables)

Account of hacienda-sawmill on Lake Chalco at turn of 19th century. Stresses enterprising aspect of hacienda life often overlooked.

2662. Seward, John H. The Veracruz massacre of 1879 (AAFH/TAM, 32:4, 1976, p. 585-596)

Role of Porfirio Díaz in cold-blooded shooting of Veracruz merchants will probably never be established. Nevertheless, author concludes action important in encouraging respect for smuggling laws and, thereby, enabling Díaz regime to stabilize public finances.

2663. Tenenbaum, Barbara H. Straightening out some of the *lumpen* in the development (LAP, 2:2, Summer 1975, p. 3-16, bibl.)

Author uses Mexico (1821-56) to critique André Gunder Frank's assertion that Latin American "bourgeoisie" worked with foreign capitalists to increase Latin America's dependence on developed countries. Using mainly secondary sources, author concludes that in post-independence Mexico the "bourgeoisie" as a class was much less cohesive than Frank assumed, and that alliances between Mexican and foreign capitalists were not voluntary arrangements on part of former.

2664. Theisen, Gerald. La mexicanización de la industria en la época de Porfirio Díaz (CM/FI, 12:4, abril/junio 1972, p. 497-506)

Author argues that Mexico was near "take off point" on eve of Revolution. Industry (especially manufacturing) was attracting more Mexican capital than foreign; Díaz government was making efforts to promote this trend as well as to limit foreign control of Mexican economy; and group of modernizing, nationalist leaders (including José Ives Limantour) was emerging. Author questions inevitability of violence in transition from traditional to modern society, but does not then sufficiently explain why Mexican Revolution occurred or, given its occurrence, how his view of Profiriato offers "hope" to "those who deplore the violence and death revolution produces" (p. 506).

2665. Timmons, Wilbert H. *ed.* **John F. Finerty reports on Porfirian Mexico: 1879.** El Paso, Texas Western Press, 1975. 334 p., bibl.

Account by Chicago *Times* reporter of his Mexican travels in 1879. Drafted in 1904, John F. Finerty's manuscript remained unpublished until now.

2666. Torre Villar, Ernesto de la. La Reforma como proceso ideológico y cultural (CAM, 213:4, julio/agosto 1977, p. 178-189)

Despite title and introductory paragraph, work is not so much an examination of La Reforma as discussion of reform movement from its European origins to 1860s. Author raises certain issues such as long-range impact of reform and its international nature that cannot be adequately examined in such brief space.

2667. Valadés, José C. Maximiliano y Carlota en México: historia del Segundo Imperio. México, Editorial Diana, 1976. 398 p., illus.

This very readable and well-illustrated biography of Maximilian and Carlota in Mexico is solidly documented with manuscript and published sources.

2668. Vanderwood, Paul J. Mexico's Rurales: reputation versus reality (AAFH/TAM, 1, July 1977, p. 102-112)

Deflates romanticized reputation of Rurales and shows that they were often ineffectual and sometimes inept. It was their public image and not their reality which made them symbol of national pride and recipient of international praise.

2669. ———. Response to revolt: the counter-guerrilla strategy of Porfirio Díaz (HAHR, 56:4, Nov. 1976, p. 551-579)

Military history of Madero revolt in North discussed in context of guerrilla warfare theory. Díaz understood well enough strategy and tactics of counter-insurgency but corruption and personalism weakened this regular army while 30 years of accumulated grievances robbed him of advantage on equally important political front.

2670. Velasco Márquez, Jesús. La guerra del 47 y la opinión pública: 1845-1848. México, Secretaría de Educación Pública, Dirección General de Divulgación, 1975. 165 p., illus. (Sep-Setentas, 196)

Employs Mexico City newspapers in attempt to explain why Mexican public opinion insisted upon bellicose conflict with US. Author also comments upon certain long run benefits which he believes Mexico derived from war. Introduction contains good survey of major newspapers.

2671. Webb, Walter Prescott. The Texas Rangers in the Mexican war. Austin, Jenkins Garrett Press, 1975. 106 p., bibl., maps.

Discusses role of Texas Rangers in military campaigns of Zachary Taylor and Winfield Scott. Originally presented as MA thesis, Univ. of Texas, 1920.

2672. Weber, David J. Mexico's far northern frontier, 1821-1845: a critical bibliography (UA/AW, 19:3, Autumn 1977, p. 225-266, bibl.)

After brief introduction, author provides lengthy annotated bibliography organized on geographical and chronological basis. Includes literature published through 1976. Valuable reference tool for those interested in borderlands areas.

2673. ———. Mexico's far northern frontier, 1821-1854: historiography askew (WHQ, 7:3, July 1976, p. 279-293)

Beginning with thesis that historiography of northern frontier between 1821-54 has been "notably unbalanced, ethnocentric, and incomplete," author proceeds in well organized and often humorous manner to prove his point. One of better historiographical essays in recent years.

2674. Wortman, Miles. Legitimidad política y regionalismo: el Imperio Mexicano y Centroamérica (CM/HM, 26:2, oct./dic. 1976, p. 238-262)

Indicates some factors involved in Gen. Vicente Filísola's able but unsuccessful efforts to stem tide of regional separation in Central America during Agustín de Iturbide's reign.

2675. Yeager, Gene. Porfirian commercial propaganda: Mexico in the world industrial expositions (AAFH/TAM, 34:2, Oct. 1977, p. 230-243)

Examines Dept. of Fomento's efforts to stimulate trade and attract foreign investment through its extensive participation in world industrial expositions.

2676. Zavala, Lorenzo de. Obras. Ensayo crítico de las revoluciones de México desde 1808 hasta 1830. Prólogo, ordenación y notas de Manuel González Ramírez. México, Editorial Porrúa, 1969. 969 p., illus., table (Biblioteca porrúa, 31)

Reprint of 1831-32 ed.

2677. ———. Obras. Viaje a los Estados Unidos del Norte de América. Noticias sobre la vida y escritos de Zavala por Justo Sierra O'Reilly. La cuestión de Texas. Memorias. Prólogo, ordenación y notas de Manuel González Ramírez. México, Editorial Porrúa, 1976. 973 p., bibl., illus., map, tables (Biblioteca porrúa, 64)

Includes following: reprint of 1834 ed. of Zavala's *Viaje a los Estados Unidos*; Justo Sierra's preface to second (1846) ed.; convenient collection of docu-

2678. ———. **Páginas escogidas.** Introducción y selección de Fernando Curiel. México, UNAM, 1972. 176 p. (Biblioteca del estudiante universitario, 66)

Contains excerpts from Zavala's two major works: *Ensayo histórico de las revoluciones de México, desde 1808 hasta 1830* (see item 2676) and *Viaje a los Estados Unidos del Norte de América* (see item 2677). Sympathetic portrayal of Zavala's life is presented in editor's introduction.

2679. Zerecero, Anastasio. Memorias para la historia de las revoluciones en México. Estudio historiográfico de Jorge Gurría Lacroix. 2. ed. México, UNAM, Dirección General de Publicaciones, 1975. 346 p., bibl., plate (Nueva biblioteca mexicana, 38)

Reprint of 1869 ed. prefaced by lengthy historiographical study.

REVOLUTION AND POST REVOLUTION

2680. Aguilar, José Angel. La Revolución en el estado de México. t. 1. México, Biblioteca del Instituto Nacional de Estudios Históricos de la Revolución Mexicana, 1976. 197 p. (Biblioteca, 68)

Overview of Revolution in State of México from 1910-13.

2681. Aguilar Camín, Héctor. Nociones presidenciales de "cultura nacional:" de Alvaro Obregón a Gustavo Díaz Ordaz: 1920-1968 (*in* Aguilar Camín, Héctor and others. En torno a la cultura nacional [see item 2418] p. 95-134)

By examining ideological content of speeches of Mexico's presidents, author seeks to trace changing concept of role of education in country. Education is variously perceived as tool for social redemption, transformation of society, cultivation of civic nationalism or as necessary premise for future accomplishment of Revolution's tenets. Intriguing interpretative essay. [A. Lavrin]

2682. Aguilera Gómez, Manuel. El eterno problema de la tierra en México (CAM, 208:5, sept./oct. 1976, p. 36-55)

Examination of land seizures during Echeverría administration using three basic categories: roots of conflict ("urban ruralization and rural proletarization"); specific causes (a combination of inflation and unemployment); and government's response (essentially political). With solid research and good organization, this is one of best articles on Mexican economic history for last reporting period.

2683. Alamillo Flores, Luis. Memorias: luchadores ignorados al lado de los grandes jefes de la Revolución mexicana. Prólogo de Xavier Olea Muñoz. México, Editorial Extemporáneos, 1976. 617 p., plates (Col. Ediciones especiales)

Autobiography of lesser known general may be of use to students of 20th-century military history.

2684. Ames, Charles R. Along the Mexican boundary—then and now (Journal of Arizona History [Arizona Historical Society, Tucson] 18:4, Winter 1977, p. 431-446, plates)

Photographic essay on marking of boundary between Arizona and Sonora. Photos used date from 1892 to 1969.

2685. Andrews, George Reid. Toward a reevaluation of the Latin American family firm: the industry executives of Monterrey (IAMEA, 30:3, Winter 1976, p. 23-40, illus., tables)

Article analyzes biographical data of Monterrey's socially elite citizens to test traditional view of Latin American family company as closed, conservative, and unscientific type of business organization. Reveals that city's industrial firms are not reluctant to hire non-family members to fill executive positions, that intermarriage among old-families and outsiders is surprisingly frequent, that high percentage of executives received highly technical education, that social organizations offer many opportunities for contacts between industrial executives and lesser commercial figures, and that industrial elite is not openly involved in politics.

2686. Ballé, Catherine. Industrialisation et développment au Mexique: la création du complexe sidérurgique Las Truchas (PUF/AS, 25:3, 1974, p. 45-81, bibl., tables)

Sociological case study of establishment in 1971 of steel complex on Guerrero-Michoacán coast. History of project is revealing on operation of political and economic restraints on development policy. Case also provides study in microcosm on effects of industrialization in traditional, non-industrial, non-urban region. Author notes polarization among students of industrialization between those who emphasize creation of new structures and attitudes and those who emphasize destructive and dislocatory aspects. Concludes issue is very complex and such easy positions misleading.

2687. Bartra, Armando comp. Regeneración, 1900-1918: la corriente más radical de la Revolución de 1910 a través de su periódico de combate. Artículos de Ricardo Flores Magón and others. Prólogo, selección y notas de . . . México, HADISE, 1972. 541 p., bibl., plates, tables.

Useful collection of articles published in Regeneración, El Hijo del Ahuizote, Revolución and Punto Rojo between 1900-18 by Ricardo Flores Magón and other magonistas.

2688. Basurto, Jorge. El conflicto internacional en torno al petróleo de México. México, Siglo XXI Editores, 1976. 138 p., table (Historia)

Uses British Foreign Office records to retell history of Mexican oil expropriation in attempt to expose "corruption" of world-wide capitalist system. For political scientist's comment, see HLAS 39:8681.

2689. Bataillon, Claude and Hélène Rivière D'Arc. La ciudad de México. Translated by Carlos Montemayor and Josefina Anaya. México, Secretaría de Educación Pública, 1973. 183 p., bibl., illus., maps, tables (SepSetentas, 99)

After brief discussion of historical and spatial evolution of Mexico City, authors concentrate on current problems and structures. Picture that develops is essentially one of Mexico City in early 1970s. Various topics are examined including population movements, land utilization, residential patterns, and economic impact of city on surrounding countryside. While continuing rapid growth of Mexico City dates some of the information, study is valuable addition to urban history of Latin America.

2690. Beer, Gabriella de. Los cien años de Luis Cabrera: actualidad de su pensamiento revolucionario (CAM, 209:6, nov./dic. 1976, p. 80-91)

Part of homenaje on centennial of Cabrera's birth. Author discusses Cabrera's political thought beginning with his criticism of científicos in 1909 and emphasizing especially his theories on revolution in general and Mexican Revolution in particular. Abbreviated version of the article appeared in Luis Cabrera: semblanzas y opiniones, see also items 2748 and 2776.

2691. Beezley, William H. Governor Carranza and the Revolution in Coahuila (AAFH/TAM, 33:1, July 1976, p. 50-61)

Discussion and evaluation of Madero's plan to decentralize Revolution using Carranza's governorship in Coahuila from 1911-13 as case study. Basing his account on extensive archival resources, author concludes that Carranza as governor demonstrated possibilities as well as limitations of state reform programs and that this experience convinced Carranza of need to discard federalism in favor of reform program under federal auspices.

2692. Blanco, José Joaquín. El proyecto educativo de José Vasconcelos como programa político (in Aguilar Camín, Héctor and others. En torno a la cultura nacional [see item 2418] p. 86-94)

Evaluation of José Vasconcelos' role as builder of national culture. He is seen as originator of: 1) criollo idea of nationality; 2) introduction of mestizaje as vehicle of national unity; 3) concept of Iberoamerican civilization; and 4) assimilation of Nitzchean concept of value of non-European civilization as source of new artistic freedom. Author maintains that much of what was original in Vasconcelos' concepts and his methods for creation of national culture has been lost in bureaucratic development of later years. Crisp article with valuable insights. [A. Lavrin]

2693. Boils, Guillermo. Los militares y la política en México: 1915-1974. México, Ediciones El Caballito, 1975. 190 p., bibl., tables (Col. Fragua mexicana)

Study of Mexican military between 1968-74 with emphasis upon its function as socio-political control mechanism.

2694. Britton, John A. Educación y radicalismo en México. v. 1, Los Años de Bassols: 1931-1934; v. 2, Los años de Cárdenas: 1934-1940. México, Secretaría de Educación Pública, 1976. 2 v. (162, 173 p.) bibl., tables (SepSetentas, 287/288)

In-depth history of Secretaría de Educación Pública during decade of radicalism and experimentation within institution (1931-40).

2695. Burke, Michael E. The University of Mexico and the Revolution: 1910-1940 (AAFH/TAM, 34:2, Oct. 1977, p. 252-273)

Excellent description of evolution of relationship between Univ. of Mexico and revolutionary administrations. Author skillfully portrays interaction involving national politics, academic politics, student activism, and shifting educational philosophies.

2696. Camp, Roderic Ai. Autobiography and decision-making in Mexican politics (UM/JIAS, 19:2, May 1977, p. 275-283, bibl.)

Review essay of the memoirs of seven public figures who have been prominent in Mexico since 1930s: Praxedis Balboa, Alberto Bremauntz, Luis Garrido, Manuel Rivera Silva, Jesús Silva Herzog, Jaime Torres Bodet, and Eduardo Villaseñor. Author is concerned with how personnel decisions are made and with question of responsibility for decision-making.

2697. Cárdenas, Lázaro. Epistolario. v. 1. Presentación de Elena Vázquez Gómez. México, Siglo XXI Editores, 1974. 497 p., tables.

This useful collection of Lázaro Cárdenas' personal and official correspondence from 1925-70 is second part of multi-volume *Obras de Lázaro Cárdenas*. Letters are grouped into two general sections: "Asuntos Internos" and "Asuntos Externos."

2698. Cardoso, Lawrence A. Labor emigration to the Southwest, 1916 to 1920: Mexican attitudes and policy (TSHA/SHQ, 79:4, April 1976, p. 400-416)

Revolution in Mexico and war in Europe combined to encourage massive emigration of Mexican unskilled and semi-skilled workers to US. American officials actively promoted traffic. Economic and political realities of situation left Carranza government unable, even reluctant to prevent it although opposed by revolutionary nationalists. Mexican regime ultimately opted for compromise course of anti-emigration propaganda and consular protection of *braceros* in labor disputes and Selective Service cases. Based upon extensive primary documentation. For political scientist's comment, see *HLAS 39:8687*.

2699. ———. La repatriación de braceros en época de Obregón: 1920-1923 (CM/HM, 26:4, abril/junio 1977, p. 576-595, bibl.)

Examination of repatriation of Mexican workers in early 1920s caused by recession in US following World War I. Using both Mexican and US archives, author describes efforts by Obregón administration to cope with repatriation in midst of severe economic problems in Mexico. Author concludes that intensity and direction of population movement is primarily a function of US economic needs.

2700. Carman, Michael Dennis. United States customs and the Madero revolution. El Paso, The Univ. of Texas at El Paso [and] Texas Western Press, 1976. 87 p., illus., map (Southwestern studies, 48)

Brief study shows that US customs officials were unable to control flow of munitions into Mexico during Madero revolution partly because of confusion over neutrality laws. Documented from Records of Depts. of Treasury and State.

2701. Carr, Barry. El movimiento obrero y la política en México: 1910-1929. México, Secretaría de Educación Pública, 1976. 2 v. (222, 206 p.) bibl., tables.

One of number of works to appear recently on Mexican labor and certainly one of most comprehensive. While essentially a survey, work does pursue certain relationships between labor and government in in-depth manner. While revisionist in some cases such as in his evaluation of Huerta and labor, author's interpretation of relationship between labor and Obregón-Calles dynasty follows traditional line. While author demonstrates exhaustive research of secondary sources, he has also done extensive archival research.

2702. Carreras de Velasco, Mercedes. Los mexicanos que devolvió la crisis: 1929-1932. Presentación de Juan Barona Lobato. Tlatelolco, Mex., Secretaría de Relaciones Exteriores, 1974. 198 p., bibl., facsims., illus., map, tables (Col. Del Archivo histórico diplomático mexicano. Serie de obras monográficas, 2)

Studies Mexican government's perception and reaction to forced repatriation of Mexicans from US during Great Depression.

2703. Carrión, Benjamín. ¿México dado al diablo? (CAM, 206:3, mayo/junio 1976, p. 34-47)

Disjointed, impressionistic tracing of struggle of "popular" forces against repression from independence movement to 1970s. Particular attention to 1968 Tlatelolco incident.

2704. Chevalier, François. El modelo mexicano de revolución (CAM, 210:1, enero/feb. 1977, p. 172-184)

Overview of different "models" of revolution in Mexico beginning with revolutions for independence through liberal revolutions of 19th century and ending with discussion of Revolution of 1910. Author concentrates on issues of land and religion.

2705. Clements, Kendrick A. "A kindness to Carranza:" William Jennings Bryan, International Harvester, and Intervention in Yucatan (Nebraska History [Nebraska State Historical Society, Lincoln] 57:4, Winter 1976, p. 478-490)

Description of incident in which Bryan, opponent of "harvester trust," was prepared to intervene militarily in Mexico to protect interests of International Harvester. While incident was minor one in catalogue of problems between Carranza and Wilson administration, author sees it as illustrative of Bryan's "moral imperialism" and Wilsonian tendency to over-simplify diplomatic difficulties

2706. Cosío Villegas, Daniel. Un poco de historia (CM/HM, 25:4, abril/junio 1976, p. 505-529)

Selection from memoirs of Don Daniel. Topics covered include Cosío's role of bringing refugee intellectuals of Spanish Civil War to Mexico, founding of Casa de España, organization of Colegio de Mexico, financing of Fondo de Cultura Económica, and establishment of journals *Historia Mexicana* and *Foro Internacional*.

2707. Cuéllar Abaroa, Crisanto. La Revolución en el estado de Tlaxcala. t. 1/2. México, Instituto Nacional de Estudios Históricos de la Revolución Mexicana, 1975. 2 v. (213, 173 p.) bibl., illus. (Biblioteca, 65)

Survey of Mexican Revolution in Tlaxcala based on few published sources.

2708. Davis, Charles L. The mobilization of public support for an authoritarian regime: the case of the lower class in Mexico City (American Journal of Political Science [Midwest Political Science Assn., Detroit, Mich.] 20:4, Nov. 1976, p. 653-670, bibl., tables)

Examines Mexican government's use of symbolic rewards to generate public support among politically demobilized groups.

2709. Davis, Thomas B. Aspects of freemasonry in modern Mexico: an example of social cleavage. N.Y., Vantage Press, 1976. 421 p., bibl.

Interesting if at times superficial discussion of Freemasonry in 20th-century Mexico with emphasis on rivalry between Spanish-speaking grand lodge and English-speaking York rite grand lodge.

2710. Deeds, Susan M. José María Maytorena and the Mexican Revolution in Sonora: pt. 1/2 (UA/AW, 18:1, Spring 1976, p. 21-40; 18:2, Summer 1976, p. 125-148, plates)

Analysis of Maytorena's administration between 1911 and his overthrow and exile in 1915. Provides good description of Porfirian background. Author perceives Maytorena as political reformer undone by financial and military problems who "simply did not possess the leadership abilities which the times demanded." Well-researched study. Includes photographs.

2711. Dieli, Robert F. Devaluation and statism in Mexico: a review article (IAMEA, 30:4, Spring 1977, p. 85-91)

Review of Luis Pazos' *Devaluación y estatismo en México* (1976) in which Pazos attributes devaluation to mismanagement in state-owned sectors of economy and continued promotion of ejido system in agricultural sector. Reviewer thoughtfully criticizes Pazos' methods, conclusions, and proposed solutions.

2712. Dinwoodie, D.H. Deportation: the Immigration Service and the Chicano labor movement in the 1930s (UNM/NMHR, 52:3, July 1977, p. 193-206)

Beginning with description of use of deportation as weapon against labor organizers, author moves on to discussion of dichotomy between technical "liberalism" of New Deal immigration policy and repressive tactics actually implemented in the field. Based on impressive array of archival sources.

2713. Fagen, Richard R. The realities of U.S.-Mexican relations (CFR/FA, 55:4, July 1977, p. 685-700)

While acknowledging that wide variety of issues "agitate" US-Mexican relations, author maintains that economics is key feature of relationship and the most difficult about which to negotiate. Analysis of recent economic developments in Mexico, especially Echeverría's problems in 1976, leads author to conclusion that US government should support those aspects of Mexican development that promote social justice even at risk of being accused of interfering in internal affairs of Mexico. For political scientist's comment, see *HLAS 39:8690*.

2714. Falcón, Romana. El agrarismo en Veracruz: la etapa radical, 1928-1935. México, El Colegio de México, 1977. 180 p., bibl., plates, tables (Col. Centro de estudios internacionales, 18)

Monograph demonstrates that agrarian movement of Veracruz during Adalberto Tejeda's governorship was carried out in conflict with less radical agrarian program of national government.

2715. Gilderhus, Mark T. Carranza and the decision to revolt, 1913: a problem in historical interpretation (AAFH/TAM. 33:2, Oct. 1976, p. 298-310)

Effort to resolve conflicting interpretations of Carranza's political motives which run spectrum from political opportunist to defender of principles of Mexican liberalism using decision to revolt as key. Interpretation that emerges is moderate one of man committed to liberalism but "not prepared to sacrifice himself needlessly on the alter of high principle."

———. Diplomacy and revolution: U.S.-Mexican relations under Wilson and Carranza. See item 2390.

Gómez-Quiñones, Juan. Piedras contra la luna, México en Aztlán y Aztlán en México: Chicano-Mexican relations and the Mexican consulates, 1900-1920. See *HLAS 39:8692*.

2716. González, Luis. Linaje, miseria y porvenir de la historia local (UNL/H, 13, 1972, p. 301-313)

Analysis of status of local history in Mexico by one of its most distinguished practitioners. Similar to ideas presented previously (see *HLAS 34:1483* and *1492*).

2717. González Roa, Fernando. El aspecto agrario de la Revolución Mexicana. Prólogo de Fernando Paz Sánchez. México, Liga de Economistas Revolucionarios de la República Mexicana, 1975. 393 p. (Ler)

Reprint of 1919 history of agrarian problem.

2718. Grieb, Kenneth J. Sir Lionel Carden and the Anglo-American confrontation in Mexico: 1913-1914 (IAA, 1, 1975, p. 201-216, bibl.)

Sympathetic treatment of British frustration with Wilsonian idealism illustrated through efforts of British diplomat Carden to effect mediation between US and Huerta regime 1913-14. Emphasis upon US refusal to act realistically on diplomatic level.

2719. Grindle, Merilee S. Bureaucrats, politicians, and peasants in Mexico: a case study in public policy. Berkeley, Univ. of California Press, 1977. 220 p., bibl., illus., tables.

Examines Mexico's stable commodities marketing agency (CONASUPO) as case study of policy process in Mexico. Based largely upon extensive interviews with public officials.

2720. ———. Policy change in an authoritarian regime: Mexico under Echeverría (UM/JIAS, 19:4, Nov. 1977, p. 523-555, bibl.)

Description of change in economic policy from that of "developmentalism" with its emphasis on industrialization through import substitution to one favoring new rural development strategy. Includes good discussion of status of Mexican agriculture in early 1970s and different government agencies concerned with rural development. Author concludes that major policy change is basically work of very small group of individuals at top level, who may or may not be operating on "adequate or correct" information. For political scientist's comment, see *HLAS 39:7125*.

2721. ———. Power, expertise and the *técnico*: suggestions from a Mexican case study (SPSA/JP, 39:2, May 1977, p. 399-426)

Examination of relationship between *técnico* and *político* in administrative processes of Latin America, focusing on Mexican bureaucracy, particularly CONASUPO. Author concludes that it is often difficult to distinguish between two and that staffing of administrative agencies with *técnicos* does not automatically lead to more efficient and honest government.

2722. Guerrero Yoacham, Cristián. Un testigo chileno del asesinato del Presidente Madero (*in* Siete estudios: homenaje de la Facultad de Ciencias Humanas a Eugenio Pereira Salas. Santiago, Univ. de Chile, 1975, p. 81-116, plates)

Correspondence of Anselmo Hevia Riquelme, Chilean diplomat in Mexico during the *Decena trágica* of 1913. Detailed, dispassionate account preceded by biographical introduction on author.

2723. Guízar Oceguera, José. Episodios de la guerra cristera y . . .: recuerdos de un combatiente. Prólogo de Carlos Alvear Acevedo. México, B. Costa-Amic Editor, 1976. 174 p., bibl., plates.

Memories of a Cristero.

2724. Hall, Linda B. The Mexican Revolution and the crisis in Naco: 1914-1915 (JW, 16:4, Oct. 1977, p. 27-35, plates)

Well-organized and researched account of confrontation between *villista* and *carrancista* forces at Naco with its important national and international implications. Includes numerous photographs.

2725. Hanrahan, Gene Z. ed. Documents on the Mexican Revolution. v. 1, The origins of the Revolution in Texas, Arizona, New Mexico and California: 1910-1911; the beginnings of the revolutionary movement by Mexican exiles and United States governmental and popular response: pt. 1, February 1910 to April 1911; pt. 2, April 1911 to October 1911. v. 2, The Madero Revolution as reported in the confidential dispatches of U.S. Ambassador Henry Lane Wilson and the Embassy in Mexico City, June 1910 to June 1911: pt. 1, Beginnings of the Revolution to June 9, 1910; pt. 2, Madero Revolution to the overthrow of the Díaz Government, June 1911. Salisbury, N.C., Documentary Publications, 1976. 2 v. (447, 465 p.) facsims., illus., maps.

Photographic copies of selected documents from US National Archives and dispatches from Ambassador Lane Wilson and American Embassy in Mexico City. Spanish documents are translated into English and viceversa.

2726. *Historia Mexicana.* El Colegio de México. Vol. 25, No. 4, abril/junio 1976- . México.

After selection from memoirs of Daniel Cosío Villegas, remainder of issue is devoted to articles dealing with history and activities of Centro de Estudios Históricos, Colegio de México. Includes: Luis González "La Pasión del Nido;" Alejandra Moreno Toscano "El Trabajo de los Estudiantes;" Elías Trabulse "Crónica Bibliográfica;" and Josefina Zoraida Vázquez *"Historia Mexicana en el Banquillo."*

2727. Hoffman, Abraham. El cierre de la puerta trasera norteamericana: restricción de la inmigración mexicana (CM/HM, 25:3, enero/marzo 1976, p. 403-422)

Analysis of efforts made at "administrative restriction" of immigration from Mexico beginning 1929. Study shows that substantial decline in immigration occurred before Depression of 1929. Author demonstrates problem of trying to coordinate activities of State Dept., Dept. of Labor, and Immigration Service. Concludes that excessive bureaucratic red tape encouraged illegal immigration.

2728. ———. "An unusual movement:" Paul S. Taylor's *Mexican labor in the United States* monograph series (UC/PHR, 45:2, May 1976, p. 255-270)

Biographical essay on Paul S. Taylor whose 11 monographs published between 1928-34 on Mexican labor in eight areas of US are still basic sources for students and scholars.

2729. Huitrón, Jacinto. Orígenes e historia del movimiento obrero en México. México, Editores Mexicanos Unidos, 1974. 318 p., illus.

History of early labor movement by one of Mexico's leading anarchists and labor agitators. Narrative is both aided and hindered by Huitron's personal involvement in labor movement, and author has little to say on post-1920 period.

2730. International Congress of Mexican History, *IV, Santa Monica, Calif., 1973.* Contemporary Mexico: papers. Edited by James W. Wilkie; Michael C. Meyer; and Edna Monzón de Wilkie. México, El Colegio de México [and] Univ. of California, UCLA Latin American Center, Berkeley, 1976. 858 p., maps, tables (UCLA Latin American studies, 29)

Papers delivered at Santa Monica, Calif., meeting held 17-21 Oct. 1973. Interdisciplinary emphasis on 20th-century Mexico. List of contributors and papers follows (those that are annotated separately in this *HLAS* have item number in parenthesis after title):
Pt. 1: *Background of Contemporary Mexico*
Wigberto Jiménez Moreno "Legados del Pasado: prehispánico" p. 25-28
Woodrow Borah "Legacies of the Past: Colonial" p. 29-37 (see item 2453)
Jacques Lafaye "Conciencia Nacional y Conciencia Étnica en la Nueva España: un Problema Semántico" p. 38-46 (see item 2466)
Charles H. Harris "The 'Overmighty Family': the Case of the Sánchez Navarros" p. 47-61 (see item 2431)
Alejandra Moreno Toscano and Enrique Florescano "El Sector Externo y la Organización Espacial y Regional de México, 1521-1910" p. 62-96 (see item 2436)
Pt. 2: *Population, Space, and Migration*
Richard W. Wilkie "Urban Growth and the Transformation of the Settlement Landscape of Mexico, 1910-1970" p. 99-134
Eduardo Pontones Ch. "La Migración en México" p. 135-163
Pt. 3: *Elites and Masses*
Peter H. Smith "Continuity and Turnover within the Mexican Political Elite, 1900-1971" p. 167-186
Ramón Eduardo Ruiz "Madero's Administration and Mexican Labor" p. 187-203
Arnaldo Córdova "La Transformación del PNR en PRM: el Triunfo del Corporativismo en México" p. 204-227
Carmelo Mesa-Lago "Social Security Stratification and Inequality in Mexico" p. 228-255
Pt. 4: *Land Reform*
Friedrich Katz "Agrarian Changes in Northern Mexico in the Period of *Villista* Rule, 1913-1915" p. 259-273
Heather Fowler Salamini "Adalberto Tejeda and the Veracruz Peasant Movement" p. 274-292
Pt. 5: *The Church and the Military*
Alicia Olivera de Bonfil "La Iglesia en México, 1926-1970" p. 295-316
David F. Ronfeldt "The Mexican Army and Political Order since 1940" p. 317-336
Pt. 6: *Politics*
Martin C. Needler "Problems in the Evaluation of the Mexican Political System" p. 339-347
John F.H. Purcell and Susan Kaufmann Purcell "Machine Politics and Socio-Economic Change in Mexico" p. 348-366
Calman J. Cohen "Beyond the Pathological Approach to Mexican Family Research: a Study of

Authority Relations in Family and Polity" p. 367-388
Roger D. Hansen "PRI Politics in the 1970's: Crisis or Continuity?" p. 389-401
Pt. 7: *Politicoeconomic Position of Mexico in Latin America*
Manuel Gollás and Adalberto García Rocha "El Desarrollo Económico Reciente de México" p. 405-440
Olga Pellicer de Brody "El Acercamiento de México a América Latina: una Interpretación Política" p. 441-451
Clark M. Reynolds "Mexico and Brazil: Models for Leadership in Latin America?" p. 452-467
Pt. 8: *Mexico and the United States*
Lyle C. Brown "The Politics of United States-Mexican Relations: Problems of the 1970s in Historical Perspective" p. 471-493
Juan Gómez-Quiñones "Piedras contra la Luna, México en Aztlán y Aztlán en México: Chicano-Mexican Relations and the Mexican Consulates, 1900-1920" p. 494-527
Pt. 9: *The Chicano and the Mexican*
Jorge A. Bustamante "El Movimiento Chicano y su Relevancia para los Mexicanos" p. 531-541
Stanley L. Robe "Problems in Mexican-American Folk Tradition: the Southern California Scene" p. 542-555
Luis Dávila "Otherness in Chicano Literature" p. 556-563
Raúl Béjar Navarro "Estructura, Violencia, y Cambio Social del Grupo Chicano" p. 564-580
Amado M. Padilla "A Set of Categories for Combining Psychology and History in the Study of Culture" p. 581-597
Pt. 10: *Education and Cultural Life*
Rodrigo A. Medellín E. and Carlos Muñoz Izquierdo "Sistema Escolar y Sociedad en México: Aportaciones al Planteamiento de una Reforma Educativa Nacional" p. 601-617
Josefina Vázquez de Knauth "La Enseñanza de las Ciencias Sociales: un Aspecto de la Reforma Educativa" p. 618-623
Carlos Monsiváis "La Cultura Mexicana en el Siglo XX" p. 624-670
John S. Brushwood "Literary Periods in Twentieth-Century Mexico: the Transformation of Reality" p. 671-683
Pt. 11: *Periodization*
Albert L. Michaels and Marvin Bernstein "The Modernization of the Old Order: Organization and Periodization of Twentieth-Century Mexican History" p. 687-710
Jean Meyer "Periodización e Ideología" p. 711-722
Eduardo Blanquel "Esquema de una Periodización de la Historia Política del México Contemporáneo" p. 723-729
Jerry W. Knudson "Periodization of the Mexican Press" p. 747-749
Pt. 12: *Studying Mexico*
Ralph L. Beals "Anthropology in Contemporary Mexico" p. 753-768
Claude Bataillon "Estudios Regionales sobre México en Francia: Evolución desde 1966" p. 769-774
Stanley R. Ross "Twentieth-Century Mexican History: an Overview from the United States" p. 775-787
Romeo Flores Caballero "Tendencias de la Investigación Histórica en el México Contemporáneo" p. 788-799
Alvaro Matute "Perspectivas para la Historia de la Administración de Justicia" p. 800-808
François Chevalier "Nuevas Orientaciones de la Investigación Histórica sobre Méjico Contemporáneo" p. 809-811
Robert A. Potash "Mexican Historiography Revisited" p. 812-816.

2731. Jones, Errol D. and David Lafrance. Mexico's foreign affairs under President Echeverría: the special case of Chile (IAMEA, 30:1, Summer 1976, p. 45-78)

Well-researched and organized account which integrates number of different themes: Mexico's traditional foreign policy, internal problems, dependence economics, and hemisphere and Third World solidarity. While authors are essentially sympathetic to Echeverría's aspirations, their presentation highlights gap between rhetoric and reality under Echeverría's administration and accuses Echeverría of postponing "day of reckoning" on basic economic and diplomatic issues.

2732. Joseph, Gilbert M. Apuntes para una nueva historia regional: Yucatán y la Revolución Mexicana: 1915-1940 (UY/R, 19:109, enero/feb. 1977, p. 12-35)

Contends that the Revolution in Yucatán was instigated from Mexico City in 1930s. This forced revolution from outside stifled development of indigenous social revolution which failed because it did not spring from nor adapt itself to local conditions.

2733. Katz, Bernard S. Mexico's tariff policy: a study in alternatives (AJES, 35:3, July 1976, p. 235-250)

In examining period 1930-65, author explores possibility that Mexico's tariff policy might have been used to improve her terms of trade, her revenue position, or her balance of payments. Author concludes that—except for isolated instances—tariff was designed as protectionist device to promote industrial development. For economist's comment, see *HLAS* 39:2990.

2734. Katz, Friedrich. Peasants in the Mexican Revolution of 1910 (*in* Spielberg, Joseph and Scott Whiteford *eds*. Forging nations: a comparative view of rural ferment and revolt. East Lansing, Michigan State Univ. Press, 1976, p. 61-85)

Large scale distribution of lands lagged two decades behind constitutional mandate of 1917. Katz attributes failure to early cooptation of peasantry in support of political ends of non-peasants. Not until 1930s does relationship involve meaningful exchange of reward for support.

2735. Kerig, Dorothy Pierson. Luther T. Ellsworth: U.S. consul on the border during the Mexican Revolution. El Paso, The Univ. of Texas at El Paso, Texas Western Press, 1975. 80 p., illus., map (Southwestern studies, 47)

Examines activities of American Consul assigned to Ciudad Porfirio Díaz, 1907-13.

2736. Krauze, Enrique. Caudillos culturales en la Revolución Mexicana. México, Siglo XXI Editores, 1976. 329 p., illus.

Study of relationship between intellectuals and political power, focusing on entrance of student "generation of 1915" into politics and government. Author proceeds by providing in effect dual biography of two members of this group, Vicente Lombardo Toledano and Manuel Gómez Morín who ended their careers at opposite ends of political spectrum. This choice was influenced to great extent by difficulty in getting access to materials of several prominent figures; juxtaposition of Lombardo Toledano and Gómez Morín was excellent selection in any case.

Ladman, Jerry R. The development of the Mexicali regional economy: an example of export propelled growth. See *HLAS 39:2993*.

2737. Leal, Juan Felipe. El estado y el bloque en el poder en México: 1867-1914 (LAP, 2:2, Summer 1975, p. 34-47)

Leftist attempt to periodize relationship between Mexican State and development of capitalism between 1867-1914. No bibliography or footnotes.

2738. ——. The Mexican state: 1915-1973, an historical interpretation (LAP, 2:2, Summer 1975, p. 48-63, bibl., table)

Essay attempts to show that primary function of Mexican bureaucracy is to promote "the capitalistic development of the country under conditions imposed by the imperialistic system."

2739. —— and José Woldenberg comps. Orígenes y desarrollo del artesanado y del proletariado industrial en México: 1867-1914, bibliografía comentada (UNAM/RMCP, 21:80, abril/junio 1975, p. 131-159)

Useful annotated bibliography, although authors accurately state in introduction that it is neither complete nor systematic. Contains entries in following categories: "Obras Teóricas," "Fuentes Estadísticas," "Historiografía," "Publicaciones de Organizaciones Artesanas y Obreras," and "Legislación Laboral."

2740. León de Palacios, Ana María. Plutarco Elías Calles: creador de instituciones. Introducción de Andrés Caso. México, Instituto Nacional de Administración Pública (INAP), 1975. 172 p., bibl., illus. (Cuadernos INAP)

This uncritical treatment of Calles government won first prize in competition entitled "Plutarco Elías Calles, Creador de Instituciones."

2741. Lerner, Victoria. El reformismo de la década de 1930 en México (CM/HM, 26:2, oct./dic. 1976, p. 188-215, bibl.)

"Provisional essay" on Mexican government's economic policies during 1930s. Focusing on "incipient industrial bourgeoisie" and small landed proprietors, author describes economic situation prior to 1929, effects of crisis of 1929, reform responses of Abelardo Rodríguez and Cárdenas, and shift away from reformism in late 1930s. Suggestive of areas for future research.

2742. Levine, Robert M. The Mexican Revolution: a retrospective view (CUH, 66:393, May 1974, p. 195-199, 231)

Intelligent synthesis which of necessity tends to oversimplify. High potential for undergraduate classroom use as handy guide to salient issues in evaluation of Revolution.

2743. Lomnitz, Larissa. Conflict and mediation in a Latin American university (UM/JIAS, 19:3, Aug. 1977, p. 315-338, bibl.)

Description of politics (academic and otherwise) at National Autonomous Univ. of Mexico (UNAM). Author sees conflict between explicit functions of university (teaching, research, and cultural extension) and its implicit functions (channel of social criticism, new options for social mobility and, battlefield for political ideas). Author concludes university would best be served by continuing to mediate between explicit and implicit functions rather than by triumph of either set of functions.

2744. Machado, Manuel A., Jr. An industry in limbo: the Mexican cattle industry, 1920-1924 (AHS/AH, 50:4, Oct. 1976, p. 615-625)

Description of status of cattle industry following decade of dislocation and of obstacles to recovery encountered: political instability, lawlessness, drought, taxation, quotas, land reform, and disease. Period covered is generally more extensive than title would indicate.

2745. McHenry, Dean E., Jr. The Ujamaa village in Tanzania: a comparison with Chinese, Soviet and Mexican experiences in collectivization (CSSH, 18:3, July 1976, p. 347-370, tables)

Emphasis on Tanzanian case. Chief distinction of Mexican experience from this perspective is that *ejido* movement responded to popular rather than state demands, therefore, Mexican government has been in position of *permitting* rather than promoting collectivization. Only in USSR and Mexico have collective forms lost ground to other types of rural productive organization; only in Mexico to private ownership. Author concludes experiences too diverse for construction of meaningful theories of collectivization.

2746. Martínez, Oscar J. Chicanos and the border cities: an interpretive essay (UC/PHR, 46:1, Feb. 1977, p. 85-106)

Excellent analysis of impact of social and economic developments on both sides of border on Chicano community. Author deals with frequently examined problem of border cities as springboards for Mexicans entering US as well as less-explored problem of border cities as receptacles for Mexicans returning from the US. Socioeconomic picture is gloomy and focuses primarily on Ciudad Juárez-El Paso area.

2747. Martínez de la Vega, Francisco. ¿Crisis del sistema mexicano? (CAM, 208:5, sept./oct. 1976, p. 29-35)

Description of various features in Mexican political system associated with "crisis" of transfer of presidential power. Author believes that all presidents since 1923 have been "selected by unilateral decision" of preceding president and that transfer of power has been complete since 1934. Particular emphasis on Echeverría administration.

2748. ———. Luis Cabrera: cátedra en la crítica política (CAM, 209:6, nov./dic. 1976, p. 92-98)

Part of *homenaje* on centennial of Cabrera's birth. More attention to biographical data than in articles by Beer (item 2690) and Silva Herzog (item 2776).

2749. ———. Nunca estuvo México alejado de España (CAM, 212:3, mayo/junio 1977, p. 7-14)

Review of Spanish-Mexican relations— or lack of same—from fall of Spanish Republic to exchange of representatives following Franco's death. Author does excellent job of presenting Mexican attitude toward Franco's Spain but his contention that this attitude "constitutes a singular fact in the history of diplomacy" is largely undermined by his narrative which indicates that Mexico, like virtually every country, is prepared to use shifting standards in its international relations.

2750. ———. El sistema mexicano sobrevive (CAM, 210:1, enero/feb. 1977, p. 20-27)

Discussion of role of official party in Mexican political system, beginning with its establishment in 1929 and concentrating on Echeverría administration, 1970-76. Author believes peaceful transfer of power demonstrates "electoral efficacy" of PRI but also shows that party has lost its "moral authority."

2751. Matute, Alvaro *ed.* La teoría de la historia en México: 1940-1973. México, Secretaría de Educación Pública, 1974. 207 p.

Anthology of selections representing two major historiographical trends during this period: neopositivist and relativist. While relativists are well represented in works of Edmundo O'Gorman and Ramón Iglesia, some major representatives of neopositivist group such as Daniel Cosío Villegas are conspicuously absent.

2752. Meyer, Jean A. The Cristero Rebellion: the Mexican people between Church and State, 1926-1929. Translated by Richard Southern. Cambridge, U.K., Cambridge Univ. Press, 1976. 260 p., bibl., illus., maps, plates, tables (Cambridge Latin American studies, 24)

Very important one-vol. English version of author's monumental work on Cristero Rebellion (see *HLAS 38:2708*; Spanish version appeared in 1973-74, French in 1975). Massively researched study shows Cristeros to have been less than compliant tools of Church's hierarchy. Instead portrays peasant rebellion as one of Revolution's most authentically popular movements.

2753. ———. Grandes compañías, ejércitos populares y ejército estatal en la Revolución Mexicana: 1910-1930 (EEHA/AEA, 31, 1974, p. 1005-1030, table)

Perceptive treatment of federal and various revolutionary armies between 1910-30. Includes discussion on recruitment patterns, organization, size, discipline, effectiveness, corruption, strategy, and function. Also contains information on social, racial, and geographic origins of officers and enlisted men.

2754. Mols, Manfred Heinrich and Hans Werner Tobler. Mexiko: Bilanz einer Revolution; Revolution und nachrevolutionäre Entwicklung im Lichte der historischen und sozialwissenschaftlichen Forschung: pt. 1, Zur Historiographie der Mexikanischen Revolution: 1910-1940; pt. 2, Zur sozialwissenschaftlichen Analyse der

Institutionalisierten Revolution: die Jahre nach 1940 (JGSWGL, 12, 1975, p. 284-392)

Two essays on historical and social science research on Mexican Revolution. First covers period before 1940, sees trend toward more critical appraisal, greater recognition of social complexity of movement in North. Second examines approaches to institutionalization of Revolution since 1940, seeks to balance Mexican "distorted revolution" view with North American "preferred revolution."

2755. ———— and ————. Mexiko: die Institutionalisierte Revolution. Köln, FRG, Böhlau Verlag, 1976. 235 p. (Böhlau politica, 1)

Ch. 1 is devoted to historiography of Revolution (1910-40). Ch. 2 analyzes "Institutional Revolution" from sociological point of view. Ch. 3 examines issues surrounding peasant uprisings and agrarian reform. Ch. 4 deals with Luis Echeverría Alvarez presidency.

2756. **Monjarás-Ruiz, Jesús** ed. Una versión alemana de los inicios de la Revolución de 1910 (UNAM/AH, 8, 1976, p. 205-248)

Collection and translation into Spanish of materials concerning Mexican Revolution which appeared in the following German newspapers in 1910: *Kölnische Zeitung* (see item 2757), *Rheinisch-Westfälische, Düsseldofer Zeitung*, and *Allgemeine Zeitung*.

2757. ———— ed. and trans. Los primeros días de la Revolución: testimonios periodísticos alemanes. México, Secretaría de Educación Pública (SEP), Dirección General de Divulgación, 1975. 190 p. (SepSetentas, 220)

Collection and translation into Spanish of materials on Mexico published 1910-11 by Cologne newspaper *Kolnishe Zeitung*. Majority of selections deal with initial fighting phase of Mexican Revolution from centennial celebrations to exile of Porfirio Díaz.

2758. **Monroy Huitrón, Guadalupe.** Política educativa de la Revolución: 1910-1940. México, Secretaría de Educación Pública (SEP), 1975. 175 p. (SepSetentas, 203)

Collection of documents and brief laudatory summary of education policies from 1910-40.

2759. **Naylor, Thomas H.** Massacre at San Pedro de la Cueva: the significance of Pancho Villa's disastrous Sonora campaign (WHQ, 8:2, April 1977, p. 125-150)

Excellently-researched and novelesque account of Villa's unsuccessful Sonora campaign, focusing on massacre at San Pedro de la Cueva. Author attributes Villa's actions to increasing irrationality and desire for revenge against US. Essay is certainly deserving of 1976 Bolton Award in Spanish Borderlands History which it won.

2760. **O'Brien, Dennis J.** Petróleo e intervención—relaciones entre los Estados Unidos y México: 1917-1918 (CM/HM, 27:1, julio/sept. 1977, p. 103-140, bibl.)

Well-written and organized examination of American petroleum policy toward Mexico during World War I. Author shows that flow of oil to US and Allies was maintained due to combination of factors: cooperation on part of petroleum companies, effective diplomacy, acquiescence of Carranza, and "healthy dose of luck."

2761. **Peniche Vallado, Leopoldo.** El idealismo pragmático de Salvador Alvarado (CAM, 213:4, julio/agosto 1977, p. 47-66)

Analysis of Alvarado's term as Governor of Yucatan between 1915-18. Author devotes most of his attention to Alvarado's economic policies and efforts to "reconcile irreconcilable situations." There is tendency toward vagueness and unfortunate affinity for revolutionary rhetoric and economic jargon ("the monolithic, henequen-based economy controlled by an all-powerful plutocracy"). See also Silva Herzog's article on Alvarado (item 2775).

2762. **Pozas Horcasitas, Ricardo.** La evolución de la política laboral mexicana (UNAM/RMS, 38:1, enero/marzo 1976, p. 85-109)

Detailed synthetic survey based on published and secondary sources. Light on analysis.

2763. **Reisler, Mark.** Always the laborer, never the citizen: Anglo perceptions of the Mexican immigrant during the 1920s (UC/PHR, 45:2, May 1976, p. 231-254)

Analysis of how Americans viewed Mexican workers during immigration controversy of 1920s. Author demonstrates that both sides on immigration-restriction issue operated from similar stereotypes of Mexican worker as docile, indolent, and backward. Drawn primarily from Congressional hearings and government reports.

2764. **Richmond, Douglas W.** El nacionalismo de Carranza y los cambios socioeconómicos: 1915-1920 (CM/HM, 26:1, julio/sept. 1976, p. 107-131, bibl.)

Well-researched article on Venustiano Carranza's vigorous program of economic nationalism. Contends that Carranza's nationalism lay at basis of his banking reforms, agrarian policies, support of labor movement, and efforts to increase opportunities for native capitalists.

2765. ———. The Venustiano Carranza Archive (HAHR, 56:20, May 1976, p. 290-294)

Descriptions of important collection recently acquired by Centro de Estudios de Historia de Mexico cover period 1913-20 and are particularly strong on social and economic conditions. Incoming correspondence predominates.

2766. Rodríguez Araujo, Octavio. Una reforma político en México (CAM, 214:5, sept./oct. 1977, p. 7-18)

Analysis of Mexico's economic problems in 1970s and their political implications using "capitalist-vs-workers" framework and dependency theory approach. Author maintains that economic crisis has had its greatest impact in agricultural sector and that government will attempt to use political reform to lessen social effects of crisis.

2767. Roman, Richard. Hegemonía ideológica y Revolución Mexicana (UCCH/A, 3:5, 1976, p. 29-42)

Revolution of 1910 produced not only new political elite but also institutionalization of socially cohesive ideological hegemony. Author seeks to demonstrate parallel development of both phenomena from 1917 to present.

2768. ———. Political democracy and the Mexican constitutionalists: a reexamination (AAFH/TAM, 34:1, July 1977, p. 81-89)

Critique of widely-held view that Constitutionalists of 1917 were "democratizing thrust" in politics. Using four basic points: suffrage; literacy requirements for deputies to Congress; directness of electing officials; and no re-election, author concludes that Constitutionalists were not radical democrats but elitists fearful of mass participation and rise of a new dictatorship. Conclusions based on debates rather than on actual articles passed in Constitution of 1917.

2769. Ross, Stanley R. Forging a nation (PAIGH/H, 83, enero/junio 1977, p. 135-151)

Thought-provoking discussion of Revolution and its legacy in connection with Mexico's struggle for national identity.

2770. ———. La protesta de los intelectuales ante México y su Revolución (CM/HM, 26:3, enero/marzo 1977, p. 396-437, bibl.)

Beginning with observation that Mexican Revolution lacked theoreticians to give it intellectual basis, author examines relationship between intellectuals and government from anti-Díaz critics of late Porfiriato to intellectual opponents of Echeverría administration. Much attention is devoted to debate over "crisis" of Revolution beginning in 1940s and growing leftist criticism after 1958. Author clearly indicates difficulty of translating political thought into political action.

2771. Ruiz, Ramón Eduardo. Labor and the ambivalent revolutionaries: Mexico, 1911-1923. Baltimore, Md., Johns Hopkins Univ. Press, 1976. 145 p., bibl.

Study of Mexican labor movement during early years of Revolution. Drawing heavily from archival sources such as Carranza papers and Fomento records, author demonstrates continuing efforts by government—whether under Madero, Huerta, or Carranza—to control labor movement by favoring certain groups, a policy which was not always successfully implemented.

2772. Sánchez Lamego, Miguel A. Historia militar de la Revolución Mexicana en la época maderista. México, Instituto Nacional de Estudios Históricos de la Revolución Mexicana, 1976. 310 p. (Biblioteca, 67)

Information on maderista military uprisings in 1910-11. Each armed conflict is given separate treatment. Each chapter is devoted to different geographical area.

2773. Schmidt, Donald L. The indigenista novel and the Mexican Revolution (AAFH/TAM, 33:4, April 1977, p. 652-660)

Description of evolution of indigenista novel from vehicle of social protest in 1930s to "study of history and ethnology" in 1960s. Author concludes that indigenista novel dramatized socioeconomic issues raised by Revolution and also reflected changing environment in which these problems were attacked. For more on subject, see items 6616 and 6618.

2774. Shapira, Yoram. Mexico: the impact of the 1968 student protest on Echeverria's reformism (UM/JIAS, 19:4, Nov. 1977, p. 557-580, bibl.)

Operating on contention that student protest of 1968 was "distinctive" from other recent protests movements, author draws causal relationship between student protest and reformism of Echeverría's administration. Various efforts at reform are discussed: democratizing PRI, purging CTM, fiscal reform. Author refuses to get involved in debate over whether Echeverría's reformism was "stylish" or substantive but concedes that president had few allies with which to work.

2775. Silva Herzog, Jesús. Las ideas económicas, sociales y políticas de Salvador Alvarado (CAM, 213:4, julio/agosto 1977, p. 67-82)

Author devotes most of his attention to discussion of Alvarado's actions as Governor of Yucatán between 1915-18, examining number of topics such as agrarian reform, Indian policy, and treatment of women. Silva considers Alvarado's program to have been "without parallel in any other state of the Republic," especially on land question where Alvarado was first governor to have concept of "integral agrarian reform." See also Peniche Vallado's article (item 2761).

2776. ———. El licenciado Luis Cabrera, el político Blas Urrea y el literato Lucas Ribera (CAM, 209:6, nov./dic. 1976, p. 63-79)

Part of *homenaje* on centennial of Cabrera's birth. Author provides brief biography and then traces Cabrera's political thought from his criticism of *científicos* in 1909 to his denunciations of US imperialism in 1950s. Article originally appeared in modified form in *El pensamiento económico, social y político de México* (1967). See also items 2777 and 2778.

2777. ———. Narcisco Bassols, un mexicano ejemplar (CAM, 205:2, marzo/abril 1976, p. 79-100)

Somewhat eulogistic presentation of evolution of Bassols' thought on such topics as agrarian reform, education, and North American investment in Mexico. Essay first appeared in the author's *Pensamiento económico, social y político de México, 1910-1964* (p. 563-583).

2778. ———. Opiniones heterodoxas sobre la Revolución Mexicana (CAM, 206:3, mayo/junio 1976, p. 7-24)

One of most experienced observers of Mexican Revolution offers another installment in continuing debate over whether "Mexican Revolution is dead." Author provides good discussion of ideological influences on Mexican Revolution and argues that Revolution was made against rather than by bourgeoisie.

2779. Slade, James J., III. From hacienda to ejido: Puruarán, Mexico (IAMEA, 31:2, Autumn 1977, p. 71-76)

Description of hacienda in Michoacán which presents mildly-revisionist view of traditional image of hacienda as well as analysis of results of transition from hacienda to ejido. Author's conclusion that land reform in Puruarán has been successful is considerably circumscribed by picture of inefficiency and continued economic dependency presented. Subject deserves more extensive treatment.

2780. Taylor, William B. Time and community studies: four books on rural societies in contemporary Mexico (UP/PSN, 4:2, April 1975, p. 13-17)

Reflective commentary on four recent studies on Mexican rural communities in 20th century: Frank Cancian's *Change and uncertainty in a peasant economy: the Maya corn farmers of Zinacantan* (1972, see *HLAS 37:1115*); Jane F. Collier's *Law and social change in Zinacantan* (1973, see *HLAS 37:1120*); David Ronfeldt's *Atencingo: the politics of agrarian struggle in a Mexican ejido* (1973, see *HLAS 37:9744*); and Raymond Wilkie's *San Miguel: a Mexican collective ejido* (1971, see *HLAS 33:2745*).

2781. Toro, Alfonso. La Iglesia y el Estado en México: estudio sobre los conflictos entre el clero católico y los gobiernos mexicanos desde la independencia hasta nuestros días. Prólogo de Francisco Martínez de la Vega. México, Archivo General de la Nación, 1975. 501 p.

Reprint of 1927 ed. of anticlerical survey of Mexico's Church-State conflict from independence to 1926. This important work in historiography of Mexican politico-ecclesiastical relations was first published by AGN during Cristero rebellion to defend policies of Calles administration.

2782. Trejo Delarbe, Raúl. The Mexican labor movement: 1917-1975 (LAP, 3:1, Winter 1976, p. 133-153, bibl.)

Based largely on secondary sources, partisan narrative provides useful overview and thought-provoking assessment of contemporary trends. Emphasizes government cooperation of trade union leadership and worker's struggle for independence. Concludes that "the trade union system is presently the weakest point in the Mexican corporatist state" (p. 152).

2783. Vaughan, Mary Kay. Education and class struggle in the Mexican Revolution (LAP, 2:2, Summer 1975, p. 17-33, bibl.)

Cites statements made by Mexican educators in attempt to demonstrate that country's primary school policy reflected "dependent mentality" and effort on part of "bourgeois" to contain "popular forces." Author believes that such educators as Palavicini and Vasconcelos did little more than continue 19th-century policies.

Vázquez, Josefina. Nacionalismo y educación en México. See *HLAS 39:4493*.

2784. Vigness, David M. La República del Río Bravo (UNL/H, 13, 1972, p. 395-407, bibl.)

More than title suggests, short essay on origin and persistence of regional consciousness in Northeastern Mexico. No notes but extensive bibliography of primary and secondary sources.

2785. Warman, Arturo. Y venimos a contradecir: los campesinos de Morelos y el estado nacional. México, Ediciones de la Casa Chata, 1976. 351 p.

Author divides this examination of eastern Morelos peasantry into four periods: 1) Porfiriato; 2) Revolution (1910-20); 3) redistribution of land (1920-40); and 4) 1940-72 era. Concludes that peasantry has been able to maintain its economic base and lifestyle in face of pressure from large landowners, big business, and government because of endurance of household and community.

2786. Waterbury, Ronald. Non-revolutionary peasants: Oaxaca compared to Morelos in the Mexican Revolution (CSSH, 17:4, Oct. 1975, p. 410-442, bibl., tables)

Working largely from secondary sources, social anthropologist compares very different historical experiences of Morelos and Oaxaca in order "to better understand the conditions under which peasants will or will not make the revolution" (p. 411). Concludes determining factor of peasants' immediate perception of threats to personal survival rather than sympathy with or understanding of national movement.

2787. Whittaker, William G. Samuel Gompers, labor and the Mexican-American crisis of 1916: the Carrizal Incident (Labor History [Tamiment Institute, N.Y.] 17:4, 1976, p. 551-567)

Author examines response of Gompers and AFL to Punitive Expedition of 1916. While author clearly shows that US and Mexican trade unionists labored for similar goals (mainly, an end to intervention), importance he attaches to labor's role in affair seems exaggerated. Based on primary sources, including Gompers' personal papers.

2788. Wilkie, James W. El complejo militar-industrial en México durante la década de 1930: diálogo con el general Juan Andreu Almazán (UNAM/RMCP, 20:77, julio/sept. 1974, p. 59-65)

Gen. Almazán explains how revolutionary government under Calles and Cárdenas co-opted ambitious *militares* through concession of public works contracts. Claims decision to accept electoral defeat in 1940 due not to this, however, but to recognition that US favored Ávila Camacho and would not tolerate a *coup*.

CENTRAL AMERICA

MURDO J. MacLEOD

Professor of History
University of Pittsburgh

PUBLISHING ON THE SUBJECT of Central American history increased rapidly over the last two years, and, in the natural order of things, the quantity of trivial scholarship, and the unfortunately smaller amount of good work, increased too.

The work of these years was dominated by the question of the Panama Canal. Panamanian writers were at some pains, not only to defend the general Panamanian position on the issue, but also to show that Panamanian nationalism and desire for independence are much older than the canal and Theodore Roosevelt's policies. Other books and articles dealt with the epic of the building of the canal—the book by McCullough being an exceptional contribution (see item 2899)—and with the thorny question of US-Panamanian relations between then and now. The last two years have been somewhat of a bonanza for scholars working on the canal or on Panama in general. Many valuable documents have been printed for the first time, and even some of the poorer works have had worthwhile documentary appendices.

The question of the canal should not be allowed to overshadow other important work. Two notable histories of Central America appeared. Ernesto Chinchilla Aguilar published the third and final volume of his enormous, informative, narrative history (item 2794), and Ralph Lee Woodward gave us a much more concise but equally interesting survey (item 2811).

Several hardy Central American staples continued to flourish. The William Walker industry weighed in with some highly readable contributions, including books by Gerson (item 2879), Raudales (item 2909), and Rosengarten (item 2912). The interest in numismatic history reached new maturity with solid, careful works by Castillo Flores (item 2792) and Prober (item 2805). Belize, that peculiar colonial survival, was the subject of two excellent studies by Bolland and Grant (items 2790 and 2883), which, although very different in approach, complemented one another chronologically. The Biblioteca Patria of Costa Rica deserves our thanks for its inexpensive reprinting of many classic Costa Rican histories, some of them long out-of-print and hard to find. The independence years gave us the familiar litany of *próceres* and heroes, but also a fine book by Rodríguez (item 2836).

Established scholars from Central America published several noteworthy contributions. Severo Martínez Peláez broke new ground with an excellent article on the subject of colonial Indian revolts (item 2828) and the prolific Costa Rican historian Carlos Meléndez Ch. continued to give us insights to the social history of his country (item 2829).

Perhaps the greatest advances came in agrarian and economic history. The Spanish translation of Browning's work appeared in El Salvador (item 2791). Mario Rubio Sánchez published two volumes on the colonial indigo industry, the results of prolonged archival research (item 2838). The coffee industry, especially in the 19th century, at last received its due, with a group of remarkable works by Hall, McCreery, and Santana Cardoso (items 2886, 2898, and 2917). These writings show all the signs of sophistication, ability to handle statistics, and a sense of the wider implications of monocultural plantations in small societies. Together they raise Central American economic and agrarian history to a new level.

In fact the younger scholars of the isthmian region give cause for optimism. Simple minded declamatory denunciations and adulations are still with us, but they are giving way to a sophisticated economic history, often marxist in perspective, based on dispassionate yet focused analysis backed up by solid archival and field work. The splendid essays in a volume such as the one by Romero Vargas and others (item 2820) show the new levels to which this school has reached.

GENERAL

2789. Alfaro, Ricardo Joaquín. Esbozos biográficos. Prólogo de Rodrigo Miró. Panamá, Instituto Nacional de Cultura, 1974. 302 p.

Leading Panamanian journalist gathers together biographies of 27 Panamanians and 24 foreigners, which he has published during his career. Panamanian material is useful.

2790. Bolland, O. Nigel. The formation of a colonial society: Belize, from conquest to Crown Colony. Baltimore, Md., The Johns Hopkins Univ. Press, 1977. 420 p., bibl., map, tables (Johns Hopkins studies in Atlantic history and culture)

Useful history of Belize to 1870s. Dominance of European market influence of monoculture, slavery and plantation economy, and influx of people from Yucatan during Caste War, are major themes.

2791. Browning, David G. El Salvador: la tierra y el hombre. Traducción de Paloma Gastesi and Augusto Ramírez C. San Salvador, Ministerio de Educación 1975. 482 p., bibl.

Translation of major study: *El Salvador: landscape and society* (Oxford, U.K., Clarendon Press, 1971). Book can best be described as history of agriculture, economics and land tenure. Industries of colonial period, rise of coffee, land expropriations, population growth and land hunger, and various attempts at land reform, all receive attention from careful and imaginative scholar.

2792. Castillo Flores, Arturo. Historia de la moneda de Honduras. Tegucigalpa, Banco Central de Honduras, 1974. 233 p., illus., tables.

Much more than numismatics, this is well-prepared, profusely illustrated, and thoroughly researched work. Carries story from precolumbian times to present concluding with chapter on role of Bank of Honduras as manager of nation's currency.

2793. Chávez, Absalón. Historia agraria panameña (USMLA/LA, 5:6, mayo 1976, p. 29-57)

Peculiar brief history of Panamanian land and land reform which attempts to categorize influences and tendencies in rather vague manner. Much of essay studies effects of land reform on surviving Indians of Panama.

2794. Chinchilla Aguilar, Ernesto. Historia de Centroamérica. t. 1., Los jades y las sementeras; t. 2., Blasones y heredades; t. 3., La vida moderna en Centroamérica. Guatemala, Ministerio de Educación [and] Editorial José de Pineda Ibarra, 1974/1977. 3 v. (213, 551, 645 p.) bibl., plates (Seminario de integración social guatemalteca, 34/36)

Prolific Guatemalan historian offers here culmination of many years of research. This massive, narrative history covers three periods: v. 1, precolumbian; v. 2, colonial; and v. 3, modern. Traditional in approach, it shows deep knowledge of, and prolonged thought about subject. Destined to become basic manual for all research scholars interested in Central American history.

2795. Conte Porras, J. Indice general bio-bibliográfico de panameños ilustres en la *Revista Lotería*, 1941-1974. Panamá, Academia Panameña de la Historia, 1975. 62 p.

Alphabetical listing of bibliographical material from *Lotería* for above dates. More simple listing than critical index.

2796. Creedman, Theodore S. Historical dictionary of Costa Rica. Metuchen, N.J., The Scarecrow Press, 1977. 251 p., bibl. (Latin American historical dictionaries, 16)

Useful reference volume in this practical series. Book is enhanced by very full bibliography.

2797. Fernández Guardia, Ricardo. Cartilla histórica de Costa Rica. San José, Imprenta y Litografía Lehman, 1974. 171 p., illus.

Most recent of numerous editions of brief history of Costa Rica by its most famous historian.

2798. King, Arden R. Cobán and the Verapaz: history and cultural process in Northern Guatemala. New Orleans, La., Tulane Univ., Middle American Research Institute, 1974. 379 p., fold. maps, tables (Publication, 37)

History, sociology and anthropology, judiciously mixed. Demographic information is well analyzed, and three chapters on German settlers are of notable interest. Concludes with detailed and valuable tables and brief bibliography.

2799. Láscaris, Constantino and Guillermo Malavassi. La carreta costarricense. San José, Ministerio de Cultura, Juventud y Deportes, Depto. de Publicaciones, 1975. 210 p., illus., plates (Serie del folclor, 1)

History and evocation of the Costa Rican cart, until recently major means of transportation in highlands. Pleasant and nostalgic reading, but with considerable slice of economic and agrarian history.

2800. Martínez, José Francisco. Honduras histórico. Tegucigalpa, Imprenta Calderón, 1974. 499 p., bibl.

Historical biography more than history. Pts. 1 and 2 contain small biographies of some 36 notables from Honduran political history, plus some linking commentary. Pt. 3 is outline of constitutional history up to 1965, and pt. 4 is overview of economic history and economic problems.

2801. Meléndez Chaverri, Carlos *ed. and comp.* Viajeros por Guanacaste. San José, Ministerio de Cultura, Juventud y Deportes, 1974. 557 p., maps (Serie Nos Ven, 4)

Well-chosen collection of travelers' accounts, ranging all the way from Gil González Dávila and Gonzalo Fernández de Oviedo to María Fernández de Tinoco in 1935. Basic for those interested in region or Costa Rica.

2802. ——— and Quince Duncan. El negro en Costa Rica: antología. 2. ed. rev. San José, Editorial Costa Rica, 1974. 225 p., bibls., table.

New ed. contains three long introductory essays: two by Meléndez Chaverri on history of Negro in Costa Rica (see also item 6659) and one by Quincy Duncan on immigration and social life. Anthology itself, less than half of book, is composed of short pieces on diverse topics (e.g., three essays on Marcus Garvey and three others on black community of Limón port).

2803. Meyer, Harvey Kessler. Historical dictionary of Honduras. Metuchen, N.J., The Scarecrow Press, 1976. 399 p., bibl., illus., maps, tables (Latin American historical dictionaries, 13)

Perhaps best so far of this historical dictionary series. Fatter, more detailed and complete, and pleasantly illustrated.

2804. Monge Alfaro, Carlos. Historia de Costa Rica. 14. ed. corregida y aumentada. San José, Trejos Hermanos, 1976. 313 p., illus.

Yet another revised ed. of this popular basic text.

2805. Prober, Kurt. Historia numismática de Guatemala. 2. ed. Guatemala, Banco de Guatemala, 1973. 376 p., bibl., facsims., illus., tables.

Profusely illustrated history of coinage in Guatemala. Large documentary appendix contains materials of interest to social and economic historians of both colonial and national periods. Sophisticated and satisfactory treatment of minor topic.

2806. *Revista de Costa Rica.* Ministerio de Cultura, Juventud y Deportes. No. 7, agosto 1974–   . San José.

Contains articles on conquest by María M. De Lines, on history of modern tobacco industry by María Cristina A. de Castro, and selection of documents for nation's legal history chosen by Luz Alba Chacón de Umaña.

2807. ———. ———. No. 9, abril 1975–   . San José.

Most significant issue contains: José L. Vega Carballo's lengthy article on Costa Rica's agricultural history, Franco Fernández' profusely illustrated piece which evokes 19th-century Costa Rica in photographs; and archivist Luz Alba Chacón de Amaña's study of independence in Costa Rica. Also reprints various previously published documents on legal history.

2808. *Revista de la Academia Hondureña de Geografía e Historia.* Año 65, Nos. 10/12, Vol. 53, abril/junio 1970–   . Tegucigalpa.

Contains snippets on Morazán's birthplace, historical ties with Mexico, famous women in Honduran history, and annotated list of bishops of Honduras.

2809. Soley Güell, Tomás. Compendio de historia económica y hacendaria de Costa Rica. Prólogo de Carlos Monge Alfaro. 2. ed. San José, Editorial Costa Rica, 1975. 134 p. (Biblioteca patria, 12)

Another reprint of long out-of-print Costa Rican classic. Biblioteca Patria series is engaged in reprinting best-known historical works of Costa Rica in complete and inexpensive format.

2810. Watts, A. Faulkner. Perspectivas sobre el afro-panameño (LNB/L, 234, agosto 1975, p. 36-48)

Very general and superficial view of role of Negro in Panamanian life and letters. For more on subject, see item 6669.

2811. Woodward, Ralph Lee, Jr. Central America: a nation divided. N.Y., Oxford Univ. Press, 1976. 344 p., bibl., map, tables (Latin American histories)

Probably best general survey in English of history of Central America. Approach is thematic, and some may complain that Guatemala receives undue attention, but chronology remains clear. Includes extensive bibliography useful for students of area.

COLONIAL

2812. Academia de Geografía e Historia de Costa Rica, *San José.* Anales: 1967-1968, 1968-1969. San José, 1971. 263 p., bibl., plate.

Monograph consisting of two unnumbered issues of *Anales* contains essays by Carlos Meléndez on colonial Indians and black slaves in Costa Rica; by Marco Antonio Fallas B. on colonial tobacco industry, and by late Norberto Castro y Tosi on Cartago's colonial cabildo.

2813. Arellano, Jorge Eduardo. El padre-indio Dr. Tomás Ruiz: fundador de la Universidad y prócer de Nicaragua. León, Univ. Nacional Autónoma de Nicaragua, 1972. 30 p. (Col. Popular, 1)

Pamphlet extolling virtues of Indian hero of Nicaraguan independence, priest and scholar Tomás Ruiz.

2814. Arosemena, Marcia A. de. Un proyecto de Colonia Escocesa en el Darién (UNCIA/HC, 2:4, sept. 1973, p. 69-80, bibl.)

Brief essay on previously explored territory. Poor fare.

2815. Borland, Francis. La historia de Darién (UNCIA/HC, 2:4, sept. 1973, p. 101-186, facsims.)

Spanish translation of account by Francis Borland, participant of ill-fated Scots colony in Darién.

2816. Carlés, Rubén Darío. Panameños en la gesta libertaria de España, 1821-1824: Francisco Gómez Miró, José Antonio Miró, Tomás Herrera, José Domingo de Espinar; pts. 1/2 (LNB/L, 236, oct. 1975, p. 35-47; 237/238, nov./dic. 1975, p. 83-91)

More proof that Panama's independence movement started long time before canal became urgent issue.

2817. Castillero, Ernesto J. Primer intento de emancipación del Istmo de España (LNB/L, 233, julio 1975, p. 73-87)

Brief account of expedition of 1819 to isthmus of Panama led by Gen. Gregory MacGregor, which failed in its attempt to liberate region from Spanish rule.

2818. Cavallini de Arauz, Ligia. La municipalidad de Nicoya: 1820-1824 (UCR/R, 38, julio 1974, p. 73-81)

Municipalidad de Nicoya was reestablished in 1820, and played major role in attaching area to Costa Rica, rather than to Nicaragua, after independence.

2819. Chandler, Dewitt S. Jacobo de Villaurrutia and the Audiencia of Guatemala (AAFH/TAM, 32:3, Jan. 1976, p. 402-417)

By analyzing activities of one Audiencia judge, author attempts to prove that creoles were not excluded from office and other favors in late colonial Guatemala.

2820. Congreso Centroamericano de Historia Demográfica, Económica y Social, *1, Santa Bárbara, C.R., 1973.* Ensayos de historia centroamericana. Germán Romero Vargas and others. San José, Centro de Estudios Democráticos de América Latina (CEDAL), 1974. 165 p. (Col. Seminarios y documentos, 17)

Outstanding group of six essays which shows that Central American history has made some startling advances: 1) Germán Romero Vargas analyzes sources available for writing of demographic history of colonial Central America; 2) Severo Martínez Peláez presents exhaustive and deeply researched review essay of Indian riots and revolts in colonial Guatemala; 3) Omar Jaén Suárez studies real estate ownership and social structure in 1756 Panama City; 4) Oscar R. Aguilar Bulgarelli examines slavery in colonial Costa Rica; 5) José Luis Vega Carballo discusses creation of state of "bourgeois dependence" in Costa Rica; and 6) Vilma Laínes and Victor Meza study role of Caribbean banana enclave in Honduran history.

2821. Fernández, León. Historia de Costa Rica durante la dominación española: 1502-1821. 2. ed. Introito de Carlos Meléndez. San José, Editorial Costa Rica, 1975. 288 p. (Biblioteca patria, 7)

See item 2809 for comment on this fine series of reprints of Costa Rican historical classics. Introduction to this vol. by Carlos Meléndez discusses León Fernández, his life, work, and concept of history.

2822. Fernández Guardia, Ricardo. El descubrimiento y la conquista. 5. ed. Reseña histórica de Talamanca. 3. ed. Introito de Carlos Monge Alfaro. San José, Editorial Costa Rica, 1975. 228 p. (Biblioteca patria, 1)

Vol. 1 in series (see item 2809) which will include inexpensive new editions of historical classics of Costa Rica. Scheduled to appear are the works of: León Fernández, Bernardo A. Thiel, Tomás Soley Güell, and other well-known authors, especially of 19th century.

2823. Fichrer, Thomas. Hacia una definición de la esclavitud en Guatemala colonial (RCPC, 31:153, oct./dic. 1976, p. 41-55)

San Salvador is really focus of this study, which gleans known facts on Central American black slavery during colonial period, and attempts to compare these findings with other parts of Americas.

Frank, Karl Anton. Durch Guatemala ritt der Tod der Zug des Pedro de Alvarado 1524 durch Mittelamerika nach seinen eigenen und anderen spanischen Berichten sowie den Chroniken der Hochland-Maya. See item 1979.

2824. García Laguardia, Jorge Mario. Estado de la opinión sobre convocatoria a Cortes Constituyentes en 1810: la posición del Ayuntamiento de Guatemala (IAHG/AHG, 21:1/2, enero/dic. 1969, p. 77-90, plates)

Ayuntamiento and others opposed convening of Cortes unless they were allowed to participate. Article's appendix reprints appropriate documents demonstrating this.

2825. Guardia, Roberto de la. El fenómeno de la esclavitud en la civilización panameña (UNCIA/HC, 2:3, dic. 1972, p. 27-73, bibl.)

Selection of excerpts from notarial documents illustrates various aspects of slavery in Panama (e.g., slaves used as collateral for loans; sales of slaves; slaves who purchased their own freedom; exchange of slaves as presents; slaves purchasing liberty of other family members; etc.).

2826. Hüper Argüello, William. Rasgos de la esclavitud en Nicaragua (RCPC, 31:152, julio/sept. 1976, p. 76-99)

Excellent review of what is known presently about Indian slavery in colonial Nicaragua in first decades after conquest. Author explores relationship between Indian slavery and rise of powerful encomenderos.

2827. Luján Muñoz, Jorge. Indios, ladinos y aculturación en San Miguel Petapa, Guatemala, en el siglo XVIII (*in* Jornadas Americanistas, III, Valladolid, Spain, 1974. Estudios sobre política indigenista española en América [see item 2298] v. 1, p. 331-346, illus., map)

Indian population remained static, while ladino population grew through inmigration and acculturation. By 1750 both groups were of roughly equal size, with ladino group steadily increasing.

2828. Martínez Peláez, Severo. La sublevación de los zendales: pts. 1/2 (USCG/E, 11:3, julio/sept. 1973, p. 79-113; 11:4, oct./dic. 1973, p. 105-173)

Fine two-part essay: 1) "Carácter General y Causas Económicas," and 2) "Desarrollo y Represión." Discusses major Indian uprising which shook Chiapas, Tabasco and Guatemala, 1712-13. Research is based on Guatemalan archive and published writings of the time.

2829. Meléndez Chaverri, Carlos. Formas en la tenencia de la tierra en Costa Rica durante el régimen colonial (UNCR/R, 1:1, 1975, p. 104-144)

Important work on history of land tenure in colonial Costa Rica by leading historian. Finds pattern of haciendas in Guanacaste and Nicoya, small chacras around Cartago, and plantations in Matina area of Caribbean coast.

2830. ———. Nicoya y sus templos históricos (UCR/R, 38, julio 1974, p. 59-72, bibl., illus.)

Brief look at history of Nicoya's main parish church.

2831. Peccorini Letona, Francisco. La voluntad del pueblo en la emancipación de El Salvador: un estudio sobre las relaciones del pueblo con los próceres en la independencia y en la anexión a México. San Salvador, Ministerio de Educación, Dirección de Cultura, Dirección de Publicaciones, 1972. 131 p.

Author argues convincingly that independence movement's leadership in El Salvador did not have people's wholehearted support. They favored more moderate intermediate solution, such as Iturbide and Plan of Iguala.

2832. El puntero apuntado con apuntes breves. San Salvador, Ministerio de Educación, Dirección de Cultura, Dirección de Publicaciones, 1972. 1 v. (Various pagings) facsims.

Facsimile reissue with thorough explanation and annotation of curious 17th-century manual on making of indigo.

2833. Radell, David R. The Indian slave trade and population of Nicaragua during the sixteenth century (*in* Denevan, William M. *ed.* The native population of the Americas in 1492 [see item 2279] p. 67-76, map, table)

Study which favors school of high population loss following conquest. Radell argues that major factor in Nicaragua was shipping of large numbers of Indian slaves to Panama and Peru. Claims that population of more than one million in 1523 fell to less than 10,000 within about 60 years.

2834. *Revista del Archivo Nacional.* Archivo Nacional. Años 34/38, Nos. 1/12, enero 1970/dic. 1974- San José.

This journal makes up for almost five years of silence in one bound issue. Devoted entirely to printing of residencia of Costa Rican colonial Governor Lorenzo Antonio de Granda y Balbín which took place in 1713. Important document, it contains information on Indian revolts and on negotiations with zambos-mosquitos.

2835. Riismandel, John N. and **James H. Levitt.** Un estudio cuantitativo de algunos aspectos de la esclavitud en Costa Rica en tiempos de la colonia (RCPC, 31:152, julio/sept. 1976, p. 101-116, tables)

Blacks slaves were important during cacao period but fell in numbers when it declined. Freedmen and mulattoes became important part of Costa Rican population during late 18th century.

2836. Rodríguez, Mario. The Cádiz experiment in Central America: 1808-1826. Berkeley, Univ. of California, 1978. 316 p., bibl., maps.

Careful research and fine writing enhance value of this study of effects of Spanish early liberalism on Central America, just before independence. Rodríguez shows that influence of Cádiz thinking lasted well beyond independence.

2837. Rodríguez Becerra, Salvador. Encomienda y conquista: los inicios de la colonización en Guatemala. Sevilla, Univ. de Sevilla, 1977. 202 p., bibl., maps (Publicaciones del seminario de antropología americana)

Full study of encomienda in Guatemala based almost entirely on documents in Seville's AGI. Author decides that encomienda played decisive role in holding settlers in Guatemala, in stabilizing social relations, and in laying down colonial patterns.

2838. Rubio Sánchez, Manuel. Historia del añil o xiquilite en Centro América. v. 1/2. San Salvador, Ministerio de Educación, Dirección de Publicaciones, 1976. 2 v. (398, 449 p.)

Thorough economic history based on Guatemalan archives. Work is especially strong on 18th century, and on institutional role played by indigo growers in Central American colonial life. Important study for Central American historians.

2839. Samayoa Guevara, Héctor Humberto. Don Alejandro Ramírez (IAHG/AHG, 20:2, julio/dic. 1968, p. 41-60, bibl., plate)

Biography of Spanish colonial writer and official (1777-1821) who spent most of his life in Guatemala, and died as Intendente de Hacienda, La Habana.

2840. Scholes, France V. and Eric Thompson. The Francisco Pérez *Probanza* of 1654-1656 and the *Matrícula* of Tipu, Belize (*in* Jones, Grant D. *ed.* Anthropology and history in Yucatán [see *HLAS 39:1094*] p. 43-68, plate, tables)

Two renowned authors take one *probanza de méritos*, and use it to discuss workings of Spanish bureaucracy, and Indian-Spanish culture clash.

2841. Sherman, William L. La esclavitud indígena y las reformas de Cerrato (RCPC, 31:152, julio/sept. 1976, p. 62-75)

Spanish translation of 1971 article from *Hispanic American Historical Review* (see *HLAS 34:1970*).

2842. Simposium [sic] Conmemorativo de 150 Aniversario de la Independencia de Panamá de España, *Panamá, 1971.* 28 [i.e. Veintiocho] de noviembre de 1821: independencia de Panamá de España. Panamá, Instituto Nacional de Cultura y Deportes, Dirección de Patrimonio Histórico, 1973? 55 p., illus.

Series of essays designed to prove that Panamanian struggle for independence began long before US took interest in subject.

2843. Smith Fernández, Alberto. Las historias aberrantes y los autores panameños (LNB/L, 230, abril 1975, p. 40-54)

Harsh and sometimes ill-founded attack on several authors who have written about colonial Panama and its Indians.

2844. Thompson, George Alexander. Narración de una visita oficial a Guatemala viniendo de México en 1825. Traducción de Ricardo Fernández Guardia. San Salvador, Ministerio de Educación, Dirección de Publicaciones, 1971. 231 p., maps, tables.

Reissue in one vol. of Thompson's travel account and impressions of Mexico and Central America. Spanish translation by Ricardo Fernández Guardia was first published in *Anales de la Sociedad de Geografía e Historia* (3, 1926/1927).

2845. Tovar A., Romeo. El Padre Salvador M. Medrano, O.F.M., y la exclaustración de 1872 en Guatemala (PF/AIA, 35:139, julio/sept. 1975, p. 527-534)

Excerpts from diary of superior of Colegio Apostólico de Cristo Crucificado (Recolección) in year when it was confiscated by state.

2846. Valladares Rubio, Manuel. Sucesos precursores de la independencia. Introducción de Luis Beltranena Sinibaldi. Guatemala, Ministerio de la Defensa Nacional, Editorial del Ejército, 1971. 303 p., illus. (Col. Sesquicentenario)

Series of essays on period just before independence in Guatemala. Includes some useful biographies of notables of period.

2847. Veblen, Thomas T. Native Population Decline in Totonicapán, Guatemala (AAG/A, 67:4, Dec. 1977, p. 484-489)

Thorough review of printed literature on population catastrophe following conquest in one area of highland Guatemala.

2848. Wortman, Miles. Bourbon reforms in Central America: 1750-1786 (AAFH/TAM, 32:2, Oct. 1975, p. 222-238, tables)

Wortman believes that reforms had some successes in Central America. They weakened power of *comerciantes* in capital, brought local autonomy and efficiency to tax collection, and restored royal fiscal control.

NATIONAL

2849. Aguilar Bulgarelli, Oscar R. Costa Rica y sus hechos políticos de 1948: problemática de una década. 2. ed. San José, Editorial Universitaria Centroamericana (EDUCA), 1974. 564 p., bibl. (Col. Rueda del tiempo)

Pioneering historical study of events leading up to 1948 revolution and of revolution itself. Author refuses to be drawn into polemic and result is unbiased but somewhat flat account. Many interesting documents and full bibliography add to this valuable work.

2850. *Anales de la Sociedad de Geografía e Historia de Guatemala.* Revista trimestral. Sociedad de Geografía e Historia de Guatemala. Año 43, Vol. 43, Nos. 1/4, enero/dic. 1970- Guatemala.

Rather disappointing issue of usually excellent journal is taken up with members' speeches to sociedad meetings. Topics include: constituent assembly of 1872; revolution of 1871 and popular responses to it; and role of vicepresidency in Guatemalan constitutional history.

2851. Arellano, Jorge E. Historia de la Universidad de León: época moderna y contemporánea. v. 2. León, Nic., Editorial Universitaria, 1974. 208 p., bibl. (Col. Documento, 3)

For vol. 1, see *HLAS 38:2770.* Brief continuation of this university history. Half of book consists of documentary appendix and brief bibliography.

2852. Argüello Mora, Manuel. La trinchera y otras páginas históricas. Prólogo de José Marín Cañas. San José, Editorial Costa Rica, 1975. 153 p., bibl. (Col. Nuestros clásicos, 6)

Fiery, impressionistic and partisan essays on fratricidal Costa Rican political struggles of 19th century.

2853. *Avances de Investigación.* Univ. de Costa Rica, Facultad de Ciencias Sociales, Instituto de Investigaciones Sociales. Año 3, No. 24, 1977- San José.

Brief historical essay divided into three parts: 1) US intervention in Nicaragua to Antonio Somoza's rise to power; 2) from Somoza to cotton boom; and 3) from cottom boom to present (1976). Article concludes by listing growing number of organizations and groups expressing dissatisfaction with Somoza regime. Issue entitled: "Estudio sobre la Historia Contemporánea de Nicaragua."

2854. Barahona Jiménez, Luis. La Universidad de Costa Rica: 1940-1973. San José, Editorial Univ. de Costa Rica, 1976. 408 p.

Well-researched official history, but confusing in format and discussion.

2855. *Boletín Informativo del Archivo Nacional de Panamá.* Ministerio de Gobierno y Justicia. Archivo Nacional de Panamá. Vol. 7, junio 1977- Panamá.

Important issue for those interested in history of Panama Canal. Among documents published are letters exchanged between Bunau-Varilla and US and decree of 1903 approving treaty with US. Issue closes with address by Gen. Omar Torrijos.

2856. *Boletín Nicaragüense de Bibliografía y Documentación.* Biblioteca del Banco Central de Nicaragua. Nos. 6/7, julio/oct. 1975- Managua.

Issue devoted to studies of and documents about President José Santos Zelaya of Nicaragua. Includes revisionist essay by Charles Stansifer, letters from Zelaya to people as diverse as Rubén Darío and Philander Knox, and brief opinions on Zelaya by contemporaries and writers and politicians of today.

2857. Bolland, O. Nigel. The Maya and the colonization of Belize in the nineteenth century (*in* Jones, Grant D. *ed.* Anthropology and history in Yucatán [see *HLAS 39:1094*] p. 69-99, map)

Study of various transitions in Maya white relations in 19th century. Maya were first driven away, then defeated in battle, and finally incorporated as wage labor force.

2858. Cadenhead, Ivie E. The personal finances of General Jorge Ubico (UPR/CS, 13:4, Jan. 1974, p. 127-132, tables)

A look at Ubico's finances leads author to guess that dictator did not amass large personal fortune during his regime.

2859. Cambranes, J.C. Aspectos del desarrollo socio-económico y político de Guatemala, 1868-1885, en base a materiales de archivos alemanes (USCG/PS, 2:3, enero/junio 1977, p. 7-14)

Marxist interpretation of liberal revolution of 1871-85. It was incomplete but made introduction of European capitalism, especially German, easier. Attempts to bring mass bourgeois democracy to Guatemala failed again in 1944-54.

2860. Carlés, Rubén Darío. Historia del Canal de Panamá. n.p., n.p., 1973? 1 v. (Various pagings) illus., maps.

Brief history of canal by Panamanian nationalist. Pamphlet republishes many interesting documents, illustrations, maps and cartoons, and is thus of value to historian.

2861. Casey, Jeffrey J. La inmigración china (UNCR/R, 1:1, 1975, p. 145-165)

Brief selection of documents on importation of Chinese labor to Costa Rica, 1872-74.

Castillo, Rolando M. Sinopsis histórica sobre las exploraciones petroleras en Costa Rica. See *HLAS 39:3028*.

2862. Castro Díaz, Alejandro. Cartas al terruño. Selección de 110 cartas recogidas de la *Revista Tegucigalpa*. A guisa de prólogo por Jorge Fidel Durón. Tegucigalpa, Banco Nacional de Fomento, 1975. 334 p.

Cautionary and hortatory little essays in guise of letters to friend, by journalist who comments sardonically on passing scene (1917-37).

2863. Clegern, Wayne M. El tránsito de conservatismo a liberalismo en Guatemala: 1865-1871 (RCPC, 31:151, abril/junio 1976, p. 60-65)

Short article which asserts that Guatemalan revolution of 1871 was most important of 19th century in Central America after independence.

2864. Conte-Porras, Jr. Demetrio Augusto Porras: el camarada (LNB/L, 239, enero 1976, p. 1-19, plates)

Review of life and works of late Panamanian socialist, by friend.

2865. ———. Referencias históricas sobre el crédito, la banca y la moneda panameña. Panamá, Banco Nacional de Panamá, 1976. 201 p., illus., plates (Cuadernos, 9)

Official publication, designed to present bank's work to students of Panama. Pt. 3 presents brief history of banking in country.

2866. Contreras Vélez, Alvaro. En el XXX aniversario de la revolución de octubre: apuntes para la historia en remembranzas de CACTO. Guatemala, Editorial Prensa Libre, 1974. 124 p., plates.

Journalist looks back on 1944 revolution and argues that it did bring improvements to Guatemalan life. Also attacks revolutionaries of 1970s.

2867. Cospín, Miguel Angel. Ydígoras Fuentes: ante la faz de sus contemporáneos. México, Ediciones Ley, 1970. 396 p., plates.

Lengthy defense of presidency of Miguel Ydígoras Fuentes, and accompanying attack on following two executives: Col. Peralta Azurdia and Licenciado Julio César Méndez Montenegro.

2868. Costa Rica. Ministerio de Economía, Industria y Comercio. Dirección General de Estadística y Censos. Sección de Publicaciones. Censo de población: 1892. San José, 1974. 1 v. (Various pagings) facsims., illus., maps, tables.

Out of print for many years, this census is of use to 19th-century historians and demographers. Also contains wealth of information for other social scientists, e.g., number of schoolchildren enrolled, agricultural production, numbers of domesticated animals, industry, imports and exports, and port activity.

2869. Díaz Chávez, Filander. La independencia de Centro-América: dilatado proceso histórico por la liberación nacional. Tegucigalpa, Federación de Estudiantes Universitarios de Honduras (FEUH), 1973. 145 p.

Attempt to demystify heroes and events of Central American history, this essay calls for completion of task of national liberation in Honduras, begun over 150 years ago. Essay in social history by revolutionary author.

2870. Dodd, Thomas J. Los Estados Unidos en la política nicaragüense: elecciones supervisadas, 1928-1932 (RCPC, 30:148, julio/sept. 1975, p. 5-102)

Book-length article proves that US intervention from 1928-32 assured rise to power of Liberal Party which, until then, had been excluded by entrenched Conservatives.

2871. Editoriales de *La Voz del Nuevo Mundo*: Honduras-Guatemala (AHGH/R, 55:3/4, enero/junio 1972, p. 19-56)

Selection of letters, editorials and decrees published in 1883, including material from Justo Rufino Barrios, Marco A. Soto, and Manuel Gamero.

2872. El Salvador. Archivo General de la Nación. Recopilación de documentos históricos relativos a la administración del General Francisco Menéndez. Apéndice de "Repositorio." San Salvador, Archivo General de la Nación, Ministerio de Educación, Dirección de Cultura, n.d. 495 p., illus. (Col. Gobernantes salvadoreños)

Documents from presidency of Menéndez in El Salvador (1885-90). Tone of prefatory material is adulatory and documents selected cast president in favorable light, but student will find other uses for many of these valuable documents of period.

2873. Fallas Barrantes, Marco Antonio. Viva España, viva Fernando VII . . . ¡Fuego va! (UCR/R, 41, julio 1975, p. 133-157, bibl.)

Analysis of personalities and events surrounding first attempted coup d'état against Costa Rican government. Revolt started in Alajuela and was crushed (Jan. 1826).

2874. Fallas Monge, Carlos Luis. El golpe de estado de 1917 (UNCR/R, 1:1, 1975, p. 85-103)

Straightforward history of coup. Blames it on economic crisis which led government to levy new unpopular direct taxes.

2875. Fonseca, Virginia S. de. Manuel González Zeledón: Magón. San José, Ministerio de Cultura, Juventud y Deportes, Depto. de Publicaciones, 1974. 198 p. (Serie ¿quien fué y qué hizo?, 19)

Brief biography of popular Costa Rican poet and diplomat (1864-1938) who played minor role in diplomatic and cultural life of N.Y.'s and Washington's Latin communities. Latter half of book consists of anthology of his writings.

2876. García Laguardia, Jorge Mario. 1876 [i.e. Mil ochocientos setenta y séis]: la dictadura democrática, una decisión política del constitucionalismo liberal centroamericano en el siglo XIX (USCG/PS, 2:3, enero/junio 1977, p. 15-27)

Study of how late 19th-century liberals, especially in Guatemala, found themselves supporting developmentally minded dictatorship, arguing that this was necessary for intermediate period until liberal society replaced late colonial one.

2877. Gaspar Stork, Juan. Estatutos sinodales de la Diócesis de San José de Costa Rica: 1910. Edición y presentación de Julio Torres. Cuernavaca, Méx., Centro Intercultural de Documentación (CIDOC), 1971. 188 p., illus., table (Fuentes, 15. Serie segunda: sínodos diocesanos)

Unusually careful index increases value of this volume to students of Church history.

2878. Gerome, Frank. Secretary of State Philander Knox and his good will tour of Central America: 1912 (SECOLAS/A, 8, March 1977, p. 72-83)

Author doubts if Knox's tour helped him to understand region better, or did anything to allay Central American suspicions of US motives.

2879. Gerson, Noel Bertram. Sad swashbuckler: the life of William Walker. Nashville, Tenn., Thomas Nelson, 1976. 106 p., bibl.

Lively, journalistic, brief biography of William Walker.

2880. Gómez U., Carmen Lila. Los gobiernos constitucionales de Don Juan Morra Fernández: 1825-1833. San José, Univ. de Costa Rica, 1974. 294 p., map, tables (Serie historia y geografía, 16)

Brief (169 p.) life and times, backed up by massive documentation and tables. In general, book is highly favorable towards Morra Fernández.

2881. Goytía, Víctor Florencio. Capítulo séptimo: Costa Rica. San José, Talleres Gráficos de Librería, 1973. 114 p.

Unpretentious essay on Costa Rican history, and on relations with great powers. Some thoughtful and original passages.

2882. ———. El siglo XIX en Panamá: escenarios abruptos. Barcelona, Editorial Linosa, 1975. 354 p.

Contains some fine impressionistic essays about Panama's relations with Colombian government before independence, and about Colombia's relations with Central American states. No scholarly apparatus, but pleasant and informative reading.

2883. Grant, Cedric Hilburn. The making of modern Belize: politics, society and British colonialism in Central America. Cambridge, U.K., Cambridge Univ. Press, 1976. 400 p., bibl., map, plates, tables (Cambridge commonwealth series)

Thoroughly researched political and social history of Belize, which concludes that national integration and socioeconomic conflict within country, may trouble area much more than Guatemalan claim. For political scientist's comment, see *HLAS 39:7171*.

2884. Greñas Morales, Rosa. Anexión del partido de Nicoya a Costa Rica (UCR/R, 38, julio 1974, p. 7-10)

History of Nicoya, especially how it was annexed to the remainder of Costa Rica. [T.L. Martinson]

2885. Grieb, Kenneth J. The Guatemalan military and the Revolution of 1944 (AAFH/TAM, 32:4, April 1976, p. 524-543)

Split between old elite and junior officers was one of main factors behind 1944 revolution in Guatemala. Grieb believes that old guard showed great flexibility and that presidency of Ponce was an intelligent compromise attempt by old guard.

2886. Hall, Carolyn. El café y el desarrollo histórico-geográfico de Costa Rica. Traducción al español revisado por Jesús Murillo Gutiérrez. San José, Editorial Costa Rica [and] Univ. Nacional, 1976. 208 p., maps, tables.

Thorough study based on extensive research and documentation on role of coffee in Costa Rican modern history. Excellent maps and charts. Revised Spanish version of Oxford thesis prepared under David Browning's direction.

2887. Hiram, Allan K. Un poco de historia sindical tipográfica panameña. Panamá, Editora de la Nación, 1975. 67 p.

Although study is slight as title suggests, students of Panamanian labor movement may glean some facts about strike participation and about early membership in Panamanian trade union movement.

2888. Houwald, Goetz von. Científicos y viajeros alemanes en Nicaragua (Encuentro [Revista de la Univ. Centroamericana, Managua] 4, enero/feb. 1974, p. 3-11, plates)

Attempt to introduce to Nicaraguan audience large number of German scientists and scholars who have visited and studied in that nation. Popular narrative.

2889. Jaramillo Levi, Enrique *comp.* Una explosión en América: el Canal de Panamá. México, Siglo XXI Editores, 1976. 380 p., bibl.

Collection of some of best articles defending Panamanian position. Pt. 1, of most interest to historians, includes article by Ricaurte Soler on Panamanian attempts to gain independence from Colombia and another by Ernesto Castillero Pimentel on US arrival to isthmus.

2890. Jonas, Susanne and **David Tobis** *comps.* Guatemala: una historia inmediata. Traducción de Juan Jacobo Hernández and Jorge Ferreiro. México, Siglo XXI Editores, 1976. 346 p., tables.

Translation of *HLAS 38:2807*.

2891. Kantor, Harry. Bibliography of José Figueres. Tempe, Arizona State Univ., Center for Latin American Studies, 1972. 50 p.

Useful bibliography by friend of Figueres. Brief biography precedes listings.

2892. Karnes, Thomas L. The failure of union: Central America, 1824-1975. Tempe, Arizona State Univ., Center for Latin American Studies, 1976. 283 p., bibl., map, table.

Reprint of 1961 ed. Includes little new material in ch. 1, 10 and 11.

2893. LaFeber, Walter. The Panama Canal: the crisis in historical perspective. N.Y., Oxford Univ. Press, 1978. 248 p., bibl.

Basic outlines of topic and rather rapid overview. Includes sympathetic appreciation of Panamanian past and of nation's attitude towards canal question. Bibliographical essay will be of great help as teaching and research tool.

2894. Lanuza, Alberto. Nicaragua: territorio y población, 1821-1875 (RCPC, 31:151, abril/junio 1976, p. 1-22)

Careful demographic analysis of Nicaragua in 19th century, with maps of regions, and full documentation.

2895. López-Trejo, Roberto. Realidad dramática de la república: 25 años de traición a la fuerza armada y a la patria. San Salvador, Editorial Ahora, 1974. 420 p.

Rabidly anti-communist book of tracts which urges Salvadorean army to play stronger role in national affairs. Author praises US policy under Nixon, and admires him for "la eminencia, el talento, el honor y la buena fe" (p. 420). To read every word is a considerable undertaking!

2896. Lovo Castelar, Luis. La Guardia Nacional en campaña: relatos y crónicas de Honduras. San Salvador, Editorial Lea, 1971. 185 p.

Vainglorious account of Salvadorean National Guard in 1969 campaign against Honduras. Pt. 4 consists of "Anexos Documentales."

2897. Martínez B., Juan Ramón. Historia del movimiento cooperativo. Tegucigalpa, Instituto de Formación e Investigación Cooperativista, n.d. 90 p., bibl.

First 55 p. are sketch of origins of world cooperative movement. Remaining 45 p. are brief history of cooperative movement in Honduras from its origins at University to creation of a nationwide confederation in 1974.

McCann, Thomas P. An American company: the tragedy of United Fruit. See *HLAS 39:8724*.

2898. McCreery, David J. Coffee and class: the structure of development in liberal Guatemala (HAHR, 56:3, Aug. 1976, p. 438-460, tables)

Coffee boom, which created national wealth, had disastrous effect on surviving "Indian" communities of Guatemala. Also studies racist immigration policies of 19th-century liberals.

2899. McCullough, David G. The path between the seas: the creation of the Panama Canal, 1870-1914. N.Y., Simon and Schuster, 1977. 698 p., bibl., illus., maps.

Compelling account of creation of canal, with wealth of detail, judicious use of sources, and keen eye for the dramatic. Perhaps best book of 1977 on this newsworthy topic.

2900. Melgar Callejas, José María and J. Armando Dueñas C. Historia del Ministerio del Interior. San Salvador, Ministerio del Interior, 1976. 135 p., fold. table.

Official history which contains useful mini-biographies of Ministers and Under-secretaries, with few interruptions, 1841-1975. Might lend itself to studies of group biography of elite.

2901. Millet, Richard. Guardians of the dynasty: a history of the US created Guardia Nacional de Nicaragua and the Somoza family. Introduction by Miguel d'Escoto. Maryknoll, N.Y., Orbis Books, 1977. 284 p., illus.

US intervention is identified as major factor in creation of Nicaraguan Guardia and thus of Somoza dynasty. Well-researched partisan work, which avows its convictions openly.

2902. Müller, Gene A. La formación de un revolucionario del siglo XIX: El Doctor Tomás Ruiz de Centro-américa (RCPC, 32:154, enero/marzo 1977, p. 22-32)

More on Indian priest involved in "Conspiración de Belén" just before independence, this time based on documents in Guatemalan archives.

2903. Obregón Loria, Rafael. Costa Rica y la Guerra del 56: la campaña del tránsito, 1856-1857. Prólogo de Teodoro Picado Michalski. 2. ed. San José, Editorial Costa Rica, 1976. 246 p., bibl., illus., maps (Biblioteca patria, 13)

Reprint of excellent history of Costa Rican participation in war against William Walker and foreign filibusters (1856-57). Fine maps, poor bibliography and index.

2904. Pacheco, León. Dos personajes centro-americanos: el General Francisco Morazán y el Licenciado Braulio Carrillo (CAM, 212:3, mayo/junio 1977, p. 176-198)

Interesting essay contrasting Honduran warrior and Costa Rican statesman, and their influence on turbulent politics of Central America just after independence.

2905. ———. Panamá y La Frutera: análisis de una confrontación económico-fiscal. Panamá, Editorial Universitaria de Panamá, 1974? 94 p.

Strong attack on historical role played by United Brands Co. in Panama; and appeal to government to assert itself against such powerful foreign influences. Drawn up by commission of scholars at university.

2906. Parker, Franklin D. The extranjero in Nicaragua during the Vanderbilt-Walker years (RIB, 25:4. oct./dic. 1975, p. 387-407, tables)

Useful bibliographic essay on travel accounts of Nicaragua during middle years of 19th century. Parker traces carefully where each traveler went and what he saw.

2907. Peña Kampy, Alberto. El General Martínez, un patriarcal presidente dictador: vívidos relatos históricos, con comentarios de actualidad, de algunos destacados y auténticos sucesos políticos, sociales y económicos; ocurridos en una época en la República de El Salvador en Centro América. Prefacio de Rolando Velásquez. Santa Anita, Mex., Editorial Tip. Ramírez, 1973? 207 p., illus.

Essay which attempts to rehabilitate Dictator-President Maximiliano Hernández Martínez, although deplorable events are not concealed.

2908. Porras, Camilo A. Retazos de mi vida. Panamá, Litho-Impresora Panamá, 1975. 100 p., illus.

Mélange of nostalgic memories, letters and poems by distinguished Panamanian.

2909. Raudales Soto, Julio. Cinco ejércitos y un objetivo común. Ensayo. Prólogo de Oscar Falchetti. Tegucigalpa, Papelería e Imprenta Calderón, 1976. 102 p., bibl.

Account of activities of Central American armies against William Walker runs 60 p. Of more interest to historian is appendix of official documents (25 p.). Includes letters exchanged between various generals about campaigns and Walker's defense at his trial in Honduras.

2910. *Revista Lotería.* Lotería Nacional de Beneficencia. Publicación mensual. Nos. 248/249, oct./nov. 1976- Panamá.

Issue devoted to Panama Canal and relevant treaties. Documents from Bunau-Varilla, and from negotiations for treaties of 1926 and 1936 make this a valuable issue.

2911. Rodríguez Ayestas, Julio *comp*. Adolfo Zúñiga: el progreso democrático, selección de escritos. Tegucigalpa, Imprenta Soto, n.d. 225 p., plate.

Selection of writings of 19th-century journalist and constitutionalist. His most polemical work attacks Honduran generals for disorder caused by their political ambitions.

2912. Rosengarten, Frederic, Jr. Freebooters must die!: the life and death of William Walker, the most notorious filibuster of the nineteenth century. Wayne, Pa., Haverford House, 1976. 226 p., bibl., facsims., illus., maps, plate.

Somewhat sensational, but well-illustrated and competently researched life of William Walker. Early chapters deal with filibusters who preceded him in Cuba and Sonora.

2913. Ross, Delmer G. The construction of the interoceanic railroad of Guatemala (AAFH/TAM, 33:3, Jan. 1977, p. 430-456)

Although costly this railroad proved to be financial success and opened up previously undeveloped area of Guatemala. Study which emphasizes positive aspects of this undertaking.

2914. ———. Emergent Costa Rican economic nationalism: financing railway construction (SECOLAS/A, 8, March 1977, p. 84-93)

Early experiences with foreign built railroads reinforced Costa Rican nationalism contributing to government's determination to finance its own railroads, even if it meant building less of them.

2915. Salazar Valiente, Mario. El proceso político centroamericano. San Salvador, Editorial Universitaria, n.d. 124 p. (Seminario de historia contemporánea de Centro América)

Three essays: 1) Mario Salazar Valiente discusses Guatemalan politics from Arévalo through Ydígoras Fuentes; 2) David A. Luna examines Salvadorean peasant uprisings of 1932; and 3) Jorge Arias Gómez analyzes Salvadorean political events of 1944, 1948 and 1960-61.

2916. Santana Cardoso, Ciro Flamarión. The formation of the coffee estate in nineteenth-century Costa Rica (*in* Duncan, Kenneth; Ian Rutledge; and Colin Harding *eds*. Land and labour in Latin America [see item 2156] p. 165-202, maps, tables)

Following in the footsteps of Samuel Z. Stone, this well-argued essay believes that coffee industry and taxes from it raised backward Costa Rica of 1821 to leadership among Central American nations by end of 19th century. Coffee also created dependency on outside world of capital and markets. For Spanish version of this study, see *HLAS 38:2190.*

2917. ———. Historia económica del café en Centroamerica: siglo XIX, estudio comparativo (CSUCA/ESC, 4:10, enero/abril 1975, p. 9-55, illus., tables)

Important economic history of coffee in 19th century. Author compares geography, factors of production, labor, availability and nature of capital, technology, and much else in Guatemala, El Salvador, and Costa Rica, and assesses impact of coffee on national life in these nations. Major study.

2918. Schoonover, Thomas. Costa Rican trade and navigation ties with United States, Germany, and Europe: 1840 to 1885 (JGSWGL, 14, 1977, p. 269-309)

Thoroughly-researched study of beginnings of Costa Rican foreign trade in modern age. Full tables.

2919. Setzekorn, William David. Formerly British Honduras: a profile of the new nation of Belize. Newark, Calif., Dumbarton Press, 1975. 280 p., bibl., maps, tables.

Encyclopedic overview of Belize designed for the curious, with handy references companion for travelers. [F.T. Knight]

2920. Soler, Ricaurte. Panamá: nación y oligarquía, 1925-1975. Panamá, Ediciones de la *Revista Tareas*, 1976. 67 p., bibl.

Sociological analysis of last 50 years in Panama. This brief marxist essay accuses Panamanian elites of bonapartism and bourgeois nationalism.

2921. Stansifer, Charles L. La aplicación de la doctrina Tobar a Centroamérica (RCPC, 32:154, enero/marzo 1977, p. 45-57)

Rise and decline of Tobar doctrine which sought to ostracize de-facto governments. US desire for "stability," and thus recognition of governments such as that of Martínez in El Salvador, helped to undermine doctrine in Central America.

2922. Terán, Oscar. El tratado Herrán-Hay ante la opinión pública (LNB/L, 251/252, enero/feb. 1977, p. 77-167)

Summary with extensive quotations of what people wrote and said about treaty with Colombia. Years covered are 1903-05.

2923. Thompson, Nora B. Delfino Sánchez: Guatemalan statesman. n.p., The Author, 1977. 105 p.

Chatty, narrative history of 19th-century diplomat and statesman by family friend.

2924. Torres de Araúz, Reina. La leyenda de los indios blancos del Darién y su influencia en la etnografia istmeña y en la historia política (UNCIA/HC, 2:4, sept. 1973, p. 5-67, bibl., illus.)

Curious article which explains how search for mythical white Indians among Cuná (a legend perhaps based on high incidence of albinism among them) brought attention, acculturation, and world of politics to these previously isolated people.

2925. Urra Veloso, Pedro. La Guerra del Banano de la Mamita Yunai a la UPEB. B.A., Tierra Nueva, 1975. 90 p., tables (Col. Proceso, 4)

Brief history of rise of United Fruit Co. and its banana empire, and of struggle of plantation workers against it. Most of evidence is drawn from Honduras, Costa Rica, and Panama. Author's convictions are anti-imperialist and marxist.

2926. Wasserstrom, Robert. Revolution in Guatemala: peasants and politics under the Arbenz government (CSSH, 17:4, Oct. 1975, p. 443-478, tables)

Thoughtful essay which argues that Arbenz land reform was cautious one mainly because he and his advisors thought of Indian poverty as result of feudal rather than commercial agriculture.

2927. Zentner, Federico, Jr. Homenaje postumo a valores femeninos panamenos. Panamá, n.p., 1975. 31 p., plates.

Biographies of 21 important Panamanian women of late 19th and 20th centuries.

2928. Zinsser, Christian. Diplomatische Mission in Honduras (JGSWGL, 12, 1975, p. 434-455)

German diplomat's chatty account of his mission to Honduras in 1940-41. Includes observations of United Fruit Co., Tiburcio Carias Andino, German community in Tegucigalpa, and capital's small diplomatic group.

2929. Zúñiga Guardia, Carlos Iván. El desarme de la Policía Nacional de 1916. Panamá, Ediciones Cartillas Patrióticas, 1973? 31 p. (Col. Cartillas patrióticas)

Battles between Panamanian police and US soldiers led US to ask for disarmament of police (in 1915 and again in 1916). Debate in Panamanian National Assembly was acrimonious and revealing, and much of it was reported here. Panama gave in, but with deep resentment.

THE CARIBBEAN AND THE GUIANAS

FRANKLIN W. KNIGHT

Professor of History
The Johns Hopkins University

THE BIBLIOGRAPHY REVIEWED in this biennium continues to reflect the diversity and unevenness noted in *HLAS 38*. Studies on slavery and the post-slavery society dominate the field. Although the number of studies on the Cuban Revolution, especially by non-Cubans, seems to have declined, their general quality remains impressive. One also notes that there are more political biographies and works on the labor movement and less studies of peasants, crime, women, and cross-cultural characteristics.

The best general studies are Sidney W. Mintz and Richard Price's *An anthropological approach to the Afro-American past: a Caribbean perspective* (item 2946) and Franklin W. Knight's *The Caribbean: the genesis of a fragmented nationalism* (item 2941). Both works treat the region as an integrated cultural entity. The early colonial period has two outstanding additions: Demetrio Ramos Pérez's *Actitudes ante los caribes* (item 2974) and Linda Newson's *Aboriginal and Spanish colonial Trinidad* (item 2972). Four excellent new books on slavery and the slave society command the attention of anyone interested in the field: 1) Enriqueta Vila Vilar *Hispano-América y el comercio de esclavos* (item 3005) revises upwards some of the figures found in Philip Curtin's *Atlantic slave trade*, as well as provides much new data on many aspects of trade, trading, and ships during that period; 2) Barry Higman's *Slave population and economy in Jamaica, 1807-1834* (item 2983) supplies uniquely rich figures for any slave society at any time and his methodology combines the best aspects of Robert Fogel and Stanley Engerman's *Time on the cross* as well as Herbert Gutman's *The black family in slavery and freedom* (N.Y., 1976); 3) Manuel Moreno Fraginals' *The sugarmill: the socio-economic complex of sugar in Cuba, 1760-1860* (item 2985) is a competent translation of the Cuban classic first published in 1964 (see *HLAS 27:2026*) whose sensitivity for the subject remains unsurpassed; and 4) Vera Rubin and Arthur Tuden's *Comparative perspectives on slavery in New World plantation societies* (N.Y., New York Academy of Sciences, 1977) is a landmark publication with inestimable value for present scholarship and future research.

The free non-whites and the later-arriving indented Asians and East Indians are now commanding some attention. The most interesting paper on the free non-whites, Bridget Brereton's "The Development of an Identity: the Negro Middle-Class in Trinidad in the Later Nineteenth Century," is included in the published selections of the VI Conference of Caribbean Historians (see item 2931). Her conclusions contradict not only Donald Wood's and Selwyn Ryan's representations for Trinidad but Mavis Campbell's for Jamaica as well.

Contrary to what was noted in *HLAS 38*, this biennium has yielded outstanding works on the 20th-century Caribbean: Oscar Pino Santos' *La oligarquía yanqui en Cuba* (item 3061) and Carlos del Toro González' *Algunos aspectos económicos sociales y políticos del movimiento obrero cubano, 1933-1958* (item 3064) detail the background of conditions in the island which led to the Revolution. Works specifically on the rise of the labor movement, a topic on which little has been written of late, are: Angel Quintero Rivera's *Worker struggle in Puerto Rico: a documentary history* (item 3062), Frank Hill's *Bustamante and his letters* (item 3051), and *Butler versus the King*, edited by Richard Jacobs (item 3021).

In 1978, the Dominican Republic commemorated the centennial of the death of national hero Juan Pablo Duarte. As expected, the occasion elicited numerous published tributes to his life and works. Unfortunately, the voluminous outpouring was not distinguished by either scholarly or literary merit. Duarte's tributes notwithstanding, the quality of the Dominican Republic's intellectual output during the past few years has continued to rise steadily with the best scholarship to be found in studies dealing with the early national period, the socio-economic structure, and problems of slavery.

As noted in *HLAS 38*, social history continues to dominate Caribbean studies with themes such as criminality, religion, popular art, and culture attracting scholarly attention. In contrast, political history as a topic is on the wane. Two trends are discernible, 1) interest in the 19th and 20th centuries, and 2) cross-cultural studies attempting to link the Caribbean with developments in Africa, mainland Latin America, the US, Canada, and Europe. Even individual studies of separate entities are now, significantly, broader in theme in addition to being higher in quality and more sophisticated in methodology. This cross-cultural awareness reflected in the literature and stressing the need for a larger perspective and a wider scope in the study of the Caribbean augurs well for the future of scholarship in the region.

Finally, I would like to thank Dr. Arturo Santana of the Univ. of Puerto Rico, Río Piedras, for his magnanimous and spontaneous assistance not only in bringing to my attention some deserving items, but also in contributing annotations of material which otherwise might have escaped my attention. Only with help such as he provided could this section attempt the comprehensive evaluation that is necessary.

GENERAL

2930. Allen, Hubert Raymond. Buccaneer: Admiral Sir Henry Morgan. London, Arthur Barker, 1976. 193 p., bibl., maps, plates.

Sympathetic account of famous buccaneer by descendant desirous of "putting the record straight." Although containing minor corrections—probably *differences*, is a better word—of John Esquemeling, and other accounts, this is a readable, but sometimes no more credible study. Has no footnotes, and bibliography contains only ten references.

2931. Annual Conference of Caribbean Historians, VI, *Río Piedras, P.R., 1974*. Social groups and institutions in the history of the Caribbean. Mayagüez, P.R., Association of Caribbean Historians, 1975. 119 p., bibl., maps.

Papers vary in quality, with contribution by Bridget Brereton being the best. She counters portrait of dismal ambivalence of free coloreds drawn by Donald Wood and Selwyn Ryan in "The Development of an Identity: The Negro Middle Class of Trinidad in the Later Nineteenth Century" (for ethnologist's comment, see *HLAS 39:1176*).

2932. Arana-Soto, Salvador. La ceiba de la libertad y otros artículos sobre Luis Muñoz Rivera. Barcelona, Artes Gráficas Medinaceli, 1975. 79 p.

Short articles on Luiz Muñoz Rivera, some of which are in allegorical form, by prolific medical doctor and *pensador*.

2933. Estrella, Julio C. La moneda, La banca y las finanzas en la República Dominicana. t. 1, 1492-1947; t. 2, 1948-1970. Santiago, D.R., Univ. Católica Madre y Maestra, 1971. 2 v. (742, 478 p.) bibl. (Col. Estudios)

Vol. 1, colonial period, gets severely short-changed. Work is long on documentation but short on analysis. Moreover, it disappoints from both perspectives, history and economics. Vol. 2 describes in great detail how Dominican Republic completely overhauled its economic and banking structure in 1947 and problems confronted by state as well as by most agricultural exporters in decades of 1950s, 1960s and early 1970s. Unlike vol. 1, documentation had been asimilated into text.

2934. Fernández Retamar, Roberto *comp.* José Martí: nuestra América. La Habana, Casa de las Américas, 1974. 479 p. (Col. Nuestra América)

Brilliant introduction by Roberto Fernández Retamar gives context in which these varied pieces of Martí's writings are placed. Martí traveled as much as he wrote, and his poignant observations and extraordinary perceptions are well represented here as he examines the historicity of America, problems of its people, its culture and future.

2935. Figueroa, Loida. Breve historia de Puerto Rico: pt. 2. Río Piedras, P.R., Editorial Edil, 1977. 515 p.

Pt. 2 of work that purports to be general survey of Puerto Rican history (for pt. 1, see *HLAS 32:2044*). This vol. covers last decade of 19th century and thus comprises background of Spanish American War as it affected Puerto Rico, island's annexation to US and period under American military rule. [A. Santana]

2936. Géigel Polanco, Vicente. El grito de Lares: gesta de heroísmo y sacrificio. Río Piedras, P.R., Editorial Antillana, 1976. 54 p., bibl. (Col. Lares, 1)

Collection of documents pertaining to most historic occasion in Puerto Rican history during 19th century by noted poet complements study of Lidio Cruz Monclova. Extremely popular in conception and appeal.

2937. Green, William A. Caribbean historiography: 1600-1900; the recent tide (JIH, 7:3, Winter 1977, p. 509-530)

Useful review article which tries to incorporate diverse elements of Caribbean. Suggests that historiography is now at watershed.

2938. Hostos, Adolfo de. Diccionario histórico bibliográfico comentado de Puerto Rico. San Juan, P.R., Academia Puertorriqueña de la Historia, 1976. 952 p.

One vol. encyclopedia of Puerto Rican history and biography with sundry bibliographical data. [A. Santana]

2939. Ingram, Kenneth E. *comp.* Sources of Jamaican history, 1655-1838: a bibliographical survey with particular reference to manuscript sources. Zug, Switzerland, Inter Documentation Co., 1976. 2 v. (1310 p.) (Continuous pagination)

Work describes primarily manuscript sources in British, Jamaican, European and North American repositories and in private hands. Covers British colonial period until 19th century abolition of slavery. Provides useful assessments of collections/repositories in separate chapters and bibliographical tools available to researcher. Full subject, and place name indexes appear. Essential tool for Jamaican Colonial Research. [J.R. Hébert]

2940. Kirk, John M. El aprendizaje de Martí revolucionario: una aproximación psico-histórica (CAM, 210:1, enero/feb. 1977, p. 108-122)

Counters argument made by José L. Mas relating to philosophical influences on Martí's intellectual development and suggests strongest influences derived from his family and domestic circumstances.

2941. Knight, Franklin W. The Caribbean: the genesis of a fragmented nationalism. N.Y., Oxford Univ. Press, 1978. 251 p., bibl., maps, tables.

Latest in Oxford Latin American series. Covers entire Caribbean from about 1492 to 1976. First book to integrate entire area within analytical framework. Themes covered: pre-hispanic peoples; early European settlements and colonies; social structure of slavery; and societies and fragmented nations which developed during and after 19th century. Balances colonial and modern periods.

Langley, Lester D. Struggle for the American Mediterranean: United States-European rivalry in the Gulf-Caribbean, 1776-1904. See item 2190.

2942. Laurent, Gérard M. Les volontaires de St. Domingue (IFH/C, 131, nov. 1976, p. 39-57)

Relying heavily on Charles Frostin's work this article looks at volunteers from French Colony of Saint-Domingue who fought on side of American rebels against English in 1778.

2943. Le Riverend, Julio. Historia económica de Cuba. La Habana, Instituto Cubano del Libro, Editorial Pueblo y Educación, 1974. 662 p., bibl., illus., tables.

Best single volume on Cuba covers both social and economic history. Le Riverend provides enormous new data on 18th and 19th century, based on brilliant new research being done in Cuba and abroad on that period. Has up-to-date bibliography.

2944. Lluberes Navarro, Antonio. Las rutas del tabaco dominicano (EME, 21, nov./dic. 1975, p. 3-22)

In order to cover period from 1520 to 1920, article had to be tersely written, but not as superficial as this. Most interesting, if not the most important themes have been deliberately neglected.

2945. Martínez P., Marcos A. *comp.* Para la iconografía dominicana: índices de fotografías de personajes históricos en revistas dominicanas (EME, 27, nov./dic. 1976, p. 49-86)

McCullough, David. The path between the seas: the creation of the Panama Canal, 1870-1914. See item 2196.

McDowell, Robert Eugene. Bibliography of literature from Guyana. See *HLAS* 39:25.

2946. Mintz, Sidney Wilfred and **Richard Price.** An anthropological approach to the Afro-American past: a Caribbean perspective. Philadelphia, Pa., Institute for the Study of Human Issues, 1976. 64 p., bibl. (ISHI occasional papers in social change, 2)

This thoughtful essay is simply required reading for all who try to come to grips with diverse societies whether they be in the Caribbean or elsewhere. Mintz and Price have greatly succeeded in establishing basis from which all speculation must proceed concerning vitality and viability of relevance of Africa for contemporary Caribbean.

2947. **Morales Carrión, Arturo.** Albores históricos del capitalismo en Puerto Rico. 2. ed. Río Piedras? Univ. de Puerto Rico, 1974. 142 p. (Col. Uprex, 9. Serie humanidades)

Few scholars of Caribbean possess better grasp of background and problems of these fragmented societies than Morales Carrión. This little book lays out schema which applies not merely to Puerto Rico, but to the surrounding islands as well. Most valuable aspect of study is how it elucidates cross-imperial political and economic relations. Also suggests provocatively that Cuba and Puerto Rico had more in common than previously suspected while also differing in unforeseen ways. Strongly recommended.

2948. **Moya, Casimiro N. de.** Bosquejo histórico del descubrimiento y conquista de la isla de Santo Domingo y narración de los principales sucesos ocurridos en la parte espanola de ella desde la sumisión de su último cacique hasta nuestros días. t. 1. Santo Domingo, Sociedad Dominicana de Bibliófilos, 1976. 299 p. (Col. De cultura dominicana, 19)

They don't write histories like this much anymore—and they shouldn't. No need to reprint this narrative which fails to bring story down to even 19th century. Indeed, original has very little to recommend it.

2949. **Pawson, Michael and David Buisseret.** Port Royal, Jamaica. London, Oxford Univ. Press, 1975. 204 p., maps, tables.

Study of Port Royal provides greater detail in wake of newly discovered manuscript sources on trade and status of Port Royal during early period of English Settlement on island of Jamaica.

2950. **Perusse, Roland I.** Historical dictionary of Haiti. Metuchen, N.J., The Scarecrow Press, 1977. 124 p., bibl., map (Latin American historical dictionaries, 15)

Designed as supplementary reference work in long series edited by A. Curtis Wilgus, dictionary also provides historical chronology and appendix of past chiefs of state of Haiti. Information is extremely sketchy and sometimes erroneous.

2951. **Poyo, Gerald E.** Cuban revolutionaries and Monroe County reconstruction politics: 1868-1876 (FHS/FHQ, 55:4, April 1977, p. 407-422, plates)

Appraisal of strength which Cuban emigrés gave to Republican party in important Florida county, which includes city of Key West. As Democratic Party gained control of county's politics, Cubans lost their influence.

Price, Richard. The Guiana Maroons: a historical and bibliographical introduction. See *HLAS 39:1249*.

2952. **Ribera, Nicolas Joseph de.** Descripción de la isla de Cuba: con algunas consideraciones sobre su población y comercios. Estudio preliminar y notas de Hortensia Pichardo Viñals. La Habana, Instituto Cubano del Libro, Editorial de Ciencias Sociales, 1973. 179 p., facsims. (Nuestra historia)

Reprint of one of earliest guides to island of Cuba, enhanced with modern introductory essay by one of leading contemporary historians.

2953. **Seal-Coon, F.W.** An historical account of Jamaican freemasonry. Kingston, Jam., Golding Printing Service, 1976. 127 p., facsims., illus., maps, tables.

Jamaica was site of first Masonic Lodge formed under purely local initiative in English West Indies. This study covers some activities and personnel who supported masonry during past three centuries, emphasizing prominent role of local Jews in activities, as well as links with other non-English colonies.

2954. **Sheppard, Jill.** The "Redlegs" of Barbados: their origins and history. Foreword by Philip Sherlock. Millwood, N.Y., KTO Press, 1977. 147 p., bibl., illus., table (The Caribbean historical and cultural perspectives)

Although Sheppard inclines too far toward narrative, she manages to present very important description of origin and fortunes of a most peculiar type of minority group; redlegs are descendants of English and Irish immigrants some of whom were indentured serfs. For as whites in a white-controlled exploitation society, it is somewhat illogical to describe these social "drop-outs" in terms comparable to other minorities. But, in fact, that is precisely what they were. Real value of study lies in description of socio-economic conditions which create and perpetuate minority groups. "Redlegs" were yet another type formed on highly changing frontier of Caribbean societies in early days of colonialism, imperialism and slavery.

COLONIAL

Bolland, O. Nigel. The formation of a colonial society: Belize, from conquest to Crown Colony. See *HLAS 39:1185.*

2955. *Bulletin de la Société d'Histoire de la Guadeloupe.* Société d'Histoire de la Guadeloupe. Archives Départementales. No. 26, 4. trimestre 1975- . Basse-Terre.

Issue entitled "Les Colons de Saint-Domingue Passé à la Jamaique: 1792-1835." Dispersal occasioned by repercussions of French Revolution in its colony of Saint-Domingue is one of relatively underprobed themes of Caribbean history. Gabriel Debien with Philip Wright's assistance continues to pursue career of those who fled Chaos during those frightful years, and looks at Jamaica arrivals as he did those who went to Cuba. This study of who they were, what they brought, and what became of them constitutes valuable contribution to Caribbean history.

2956. Campo Lacasa, Cristina. Historia de la iglesia en Puerto Rico: 1511-1802. San Juan, Instituto de Cultura Puertorriqueña, 1977. 326 p.

Documental history of Roman Catholic Church in Puerto Rico and socio-political impact of this all encompassing institutions on island's development from early colonial days and establishment of Diocese of Puerto Rico in 1511 to early 19th century. Emphasizing institutional and cultural aspects and individual accomplishments of several bishops, it is based on extensive use of documentary material from AGI and printed primary and secondary sources. Important contribution, particularly in its documentary assemblage, in Spanish West Indian colonial historiography. [A. Santana]

Canedo, Lino Gómez. La iglesia de San Francisco en Santo Domingo. See item 261.

2957. Cárdenas, Manuel *ed.* El *Código Negro* francés para las Antillas (ICP/R, 17:64, julio/dic. 1974 [i.e. 1977] p. 26-36)

Spanish text of the *Code Noir* issued by French islands in West Indies. Original French transcription is in 1730 ed. of Pére Labat's *Voyages en Guinée et a Cayenne.* [A. Santana]

2958. Cardoso, Ciro. Propriété de la terre et techniques de production dans les colonies esclavagistes de l'Amérique et des Caraïbes au XVIIIème siècle (CDAL, 13/14, 1976, p. 127-152)

Attempt to compare and explain relative levels of development of French Guyanese, Cuban, Brazilian, French and English-Antillean sugar industries in 18th century. Model is marxist, within dependency context, but theory suffers from synchronic nature of comparison.

2959. Caro Costas, Aida R. La Real Cédula de 1789 y dos reglamentos antillanos sobre la educación, trato y ocupación de los esclavos (UPR/LT, 21:81/82, julio/dic. 1973 [i.e. 1977] p. 103-130)

Textual transcription of the *Real Cédula . . . sobre la Educación, Trato y Ocupación de los Esclavos en todos sus dominios de Indias e Islas Filipinas,* issued by Spanish monarch Charles IV on 31 May 1789. Innumerable notes contain explanatory addenda and subsequent Spanish regulations adapting Cédula to local Puerto Rican socioeconomic conditions. [A. Santana]

2960. Craton, Michael. Worthy Park, 1670-1972: cambios y continuaciones en el sistema jamaiquino de plantación azucarera (*in* Florescano, Enrique *ed.* Haciendas, latifundios y plantaciones en América Latina [see *HLAS 38:2190*] p. 537-609, map, tables)

Repeats essential points made in study of Worthy Park Estates by Craton and James Walvin.

2961. Crouch, Thomas W. A Yankee guerrillero: Frederick Funston and the Cuban insurrection. Memphis, Tenn., Memphis State Univ. Press, 1975. 165 p., bibl., illus., map.

Extremely readable and interesting account of unusual association. Less than 20 persons from US fought for Cubans against Spain, and Funston's short career in Cuba during 1896-97 tells more about times and popular notions in US than war in which he took part.

2962. Crouse, Nellis M. French pioneers in the West Indies: 1624-1664. N.Y., Octagon Books, 1977. 294 p., bibl., maps.

Crouse still provides one of few narrative accounts of early French settlements in Caribbean, and its reappearance is welcome (reprint of ed. published by Columbia Univ. Press, N.Y., 1940).

2963. Dávila, Arturo V. *ed.* La relación del Socorro de Puerto Rico en 1599 por el Jerónimo Fray Diego de Ocaña (ICP/R, 17:64, julio/dic. 1974 [i.e., 1977] p. 49-53)

Textual transcription of account by Spanish traveler of conditions and circumstances in San Juan, P.R., in 1599 after capture and relinquishment of city by English forces under Earl of Cumberland. Text, here preceded by explanatory note, is part of more extensive account of trip throughout Caribbean and South America, published in 1969 (see *HLAS 36:2481*). [A. Santana]

Dupuy, Alex. Spanish colonialism and the origin of underdevelopment in Haiti. See *HLAS 39:3071*.

2964. Fornet, Ambrosio. El ajuste de cuentas: del panfleto autonomista a la literatura de campaña (CDLA, 16:100, enero/feb. 1977, p. 49-57)

Review of resurgence of literary activity after Ten Years War, and how this renaissance contributed to sharpening of political and ideological rift with Spain.

2965. García del Pino, César. En el cincuentenario de la muerte de Carlos Baliño (BNJM/R, 18:1, enero/abril 1976, p. 85-116)

Well-researched exposition on early patriot who with words and deeds fought against Spain and warned of dangers in connection with US.

2966. *The Journal of the Barbados Museum and Historical Society.* Vol. 35, No. 1, March 1975- . Bridgetown.

Articles include: "St. Ann's Fort and the Garrison;" "The Imports of Fish into Barbados in 1698;" "Richard A. Wyvill's Visits to Barbados in 1796 and 1806-7;" "Nomenclature Changes Affecting the Flora of Barbados;" "The Evolution of Marriage Law in Barbados;" "The First Barbados Scholarships;" and book reviews.

2967. Knight, Franklin W. Patterns of colonial society and culture: Latin America and the Caribbean, 1492-1804 (South Atlantic Urban Studies [College of Charleston, Urban Studies Center and Univ. of South Carolina Press, Charleston] 2, 1978, p. 3-23)

Author suggests new paradigm for understanding diversity of American colonial societies, and constructs continuum along which settler societies and exploitation societies constitute two extreme forms. Knight thinks that patterns set by socioeconomic nature of these societies provide better clues to their later development than imperial and cultural divisions.

2968. Lamb, Ursula. Frey Nicolás de Ovando, Gobernador de las Indias. Comentarios preliminares de Miguel Muñoz de San Pedro. Santo Domingo, Sociedad Dominicana de Bibliófilos, 1977. 225 p., plates (Col. De cultura dominicana, 20)

Limited ed., luxury printing of old work originally published in Spain, on first European governor in Antilles. Many of Lamb's original conclusions still hold true, and altogether it is well worth reading again—if one can find it.

2969. Locker, Zvi. Une famille juive au Cap: membres de la Famille Depas —ou de Paz—à St-Domingue (IFH/C, 133, mars/avril 1977, p. 126-131, bibl., table)

Depas family originated in Portugal, and this brief resumé illustrates that imperial boundaries did not preclude cross-commercial and inter-imperial migrations during 18th century.

2970. Marrero, Levi. Cuba: economía y sociedad. v. 3, El siglo XVII, pt. 1. Madrid, Editorial Playor, 1975. 309 p.

Together with vols. 1/2 (see *HLAS 38:2847-2848*), this multi-volume history of Cuba offers well integrated and comprehensive account of Cuban socioeconomic process during 17th century. Closely examines wealth of data on important facets: agriculture; mining; cattle-ranching; commerce; navigation; contraband trade; fiscal policy; ecclesiastical affairs; political institutions; demography; and family life. Based on extensive manuscript material from AGI and numerous primary and secondary sources. Includes many charts and diagrams and typographical presentation is excellent. [A. Santana]

Meza Villalobos, Néstor. Historia de la política indígena del Estado Español en América: las Antillas; el Distrito de la Audiencia de Santa Fe. See item 3145.

2971. Morales Carrión, Arturo. El reflujo en Puerto Rico de la crisis dominico-haitiana: 1791-1805 (EME, 27, nov./dic. 1976, p. 19-39)

Documented analysis of military and sociopolitical impact on Puerto Rico of revolutionary flux that spread from French Saint Domingue to neighboring Spanish Santo Domingo during late 18th and early 19th century. Covers such aspects as insular repercussions of Treaty of Basel, subsequent developments in Spanish strategy and naval activities throughout West Indies, Spain's utilization of Puerto

Rico's military and naval resources in Santo Domingo and emigration from Santo Domingo to Puerto Rico. Based on printed primary and secondary sources and manuscript material from Spanish and Puerto Rican archival collections. This is chapter from forthcoming look on Puerto Rico and Dominico-Haitian Crisis (1791-1865). [A. Santana]

2972. Newson, Linda A. Aboriginal and Spanish colonial Trinidad: study in culture contact. London, Academic Press, 1976. 268 p., bibl., maps, tables.

Enlightening book on otherwise obscure period of Trinidad and Caribbean history. Despite number of "loaded" terms, Newson's research, based on substantial archival consultation in AGI, and her deductive arguments are laudable. She gives original population of between 20,000 and 30,000 ca. 1500, based on density of approximately 500 persons per 100 km^2. Very useful addition to the literature. For ethnologist's comment, see HLAS 39:1243.

2973. Oviedo y Valdés, Gonzalo Fernández de. The conquest and settlement of the island of Borinquen or Puerto Rico. Translated and edited by Daymond Turner. Illustrated with drawings by Jack and Irene Delano. Avon, Conn., Cardavon Press, 1975. 143 p., illus.

Useful for earliest history of Puerto Rico, with some illustrations which look quite out-of-place, and some words which have not been modernized in their spelling. Otherwise, a fine "luxury" ed.

2974. Ramos Pérez, Demetrio. Actitudes ante los caribes: desde su conocimiento indirecto hasta la capitulación de Valladolid de 1520 (*in* Jornadas Americanistas, III, Valladolid, Spain, 1974. Estudios sobre política indigenista española en America [see item 2298] v. 1, p. 81-110)

Suggests that Lesser Antilles were not thought of as useless by Spanish, but rather as crucial links in development of American Empire as well as valuable for entire Antillean colonial scheme.

2975. Silié, Rubén. La trata de negros en Santo Domingo: siglo XVIII (Ciencia [Univ. Autónoma de Santo Domingo] 2:3, julio/sept. 1975, p. 97-110)

Silié, an authority on Domincan sector of transatlantic slavetrade, puts it in context of broader commercial activity. Shows that poor development of regional economy led to rather sporadic commerce in slaves.

2976. Smith, Octavio. El Capitán Santiago Pita de Figueroa: las viejas milicias habaneras (BNJM/R, 18:1, enero/abril, 1976, p. 79-84)

Pita died in 1755, but this short article tells us little about man or *Milicias* which he served so well.

Tiró, Aurelio. Puerto Rico: site of the primordial University of the Americas. See *HLAS 39:4542*.

2977. Vega B., Wenceslao. La Real Audiencia de Santo Domingo: funciones y procedimientos del Primer Tribunal de Comercio (EME, 21, nov./dic.1975, p. 91-104)

Based on published material, but solid enough description of Council at very important stage of its early growth.

2978. Veitia Linaje, José de. The Spanish rule of trade to the West-Indies. N.Y., AMS Press, 1977. 367 p.

Valuable for any examination of 18th-century trade between Europe and the Americas with detailed description of size, construction and carrying capacity of vessels, and commodities which comprised Atlantic trade as well as trade courtesies of period. Extremely valuable reprint of 1702 ed. (S. Crouch, London) and reproduced from originals in collections of Brown Univ. Library and N.Y. Public Library.

PLANTATION SOCIETIES

2979. *Annals of the New York Academy of Sciences.* Vol. 292, 1977- N.Y.

Issue entitled "Comparative Perspectives on Slavery in New World Plantation Societies." With 67 principal participants from Latin America, Caribbean, North America, and Western Europe, conference on which volume is based was most solidly sustained, serious discussion of origins, nature, and consequences of slavery in the Americas. Contributions included all levels of research across wide variety of disciplines. Although not all papers are reproduced here, inclusion of main depositions and commentaries, points and counterpoints, can proudly stand as a magnificent summary of state of field research as well as eloquent pointer to work yet to be done on this important subject. Landmark effort and indispensable tool.

2980. Deschamps Chapeaux, Pedro and **Juan Pérez de la Riva.** Contribución a la historia de la gente sin historia. La Habana, Editorial de Ciencias Sociales, 1974. 282 p., illus.

Some of these articles have appeared before, but their convenient compilation here affords a wonderful opportunity to reassess contribution of non-free immigrants to development of Cuban society and economy during past centuries. Extremely valuable for studies of plantation society and economy.

2981. Frostin, Charles. Les révoltes blanches à Saint-Domingue aux XVIIe et XVIIIe siècles: Haïti avant 1789. Préface de Michel Bruguiere. Paris, Editions de l'Ecole, 1975. 407 p., bibls., illus., maps, tables (Col. Histoire et littérature haïtiennes)

Frostin places situation of Saint-Domingue within context of 18th-century Caribbean, and meticulously describes various factors which forced white minority to become restless and revolutionary class in 1789. Many of conclusions have already appeared in numerous other works of author on related topics: military defenses were weak after Seven Year's War; socioeconomic conditions of Petits Blancs were often worse than that of slaves; and vast illegal trade with US exacerbated colonial economic discontent making colony even more imperially irridentist than British North American colonies in 1789.

2982. Hall, N.A.T. Anna Heegaard: enigma (UWI/CQ, 22:2/3, June/Sept. 1976, p. 62-73)

Hall insists that Heegaard's role has been undeservedly neglected, and that she might have played a crucial role in amelioration and eventual abolition of slavery in Danish Antilles. In any case, she was a remarkable lady with a keen sense of purpose and political connections.

2983. Higman, B.W. Slave population and economy in Jamaica, 1807-1834. Cambridge, UK, Cambridge Univ. Press, 1976. 327 p., bibl., maps, tables.

Winner of 1977 Bancroft Prize, this sophisticated socioeconomic study with pronounced emphasis on demographic changes, may well be the best single study to date on any slave system anywhere. Higman's conclusions challenge those of Edward Brathwaite and Orlando Patterson, and illustrate some profound, unforeseen consequences of the abolition of the slave trade on the age, sex, occupation and location profile of Jamaica's slave population.

2984. Irwin, Graham W. Africans abroad: a documentary history of the black diaspora in Asia, Latin America, and the Caribbean during the age of slavery. N.Y., Columbia Univ. Press, 1977. 408 p., bibl.

Interesting collection which lacks a focus. Many will question pushing "Age of Slavery" back into classical antiquity." Samples cover just about every type of material from every corner of the globe. Some selections have short introduction to establish their relevance both for volume as well as their intrinsic historical significance. Suggested reading section is useful despite some surprising gaps. Not for the specialist.

2985. Moreno Fraginals, Manuel. The sugarmill: the socioeconomic complex of sugar in Cuba, 1760-1860. Translated by Cedric Belfrage. N.Y., Monthly Review Press, 1976. 182 p., illus., tables.

Excellent translation of Cuban classic, retaining highly informative footnotes and marvellous illustrations of original. There is no better analysis attempted of this crucial period in history of modern Cuba. Nor is examination done with more feeling and understanding. Despite its high price, this is a most highly recommended work, a required addition for every library. For ethnologist's comment, see *HLAS 39:1239*.

2986. Saco López, José Antonio. Memoria sobre la vagancia en la isla de Cuba. Santiago, Instituto Cubano del Libro, Sección Editorial Oriente, 1974. 80 p., illus.

Saco was among most perceptive social commentators of his time, and this pamphlet ranks among most pointed observations of his native Cuba. Covers wide variety of activities as well as economic and social conditions in general, and its reissue here is most welcome. This pamphlet is crucial for study of 19th-century Cuban conditions and author's racist thought.

2987. Silié, Rubén. Economía, esclavitud y población: ensayos de interpretación histórica del Santo Domingo español en el siglo XVIII. Presentación de Emilio Cordero Michel. Santo Domingo, Univ. Autónoma de Santo Domingo (UASD), 1976. 191 p., bibl., illus., tables (Publicaciones, 188. Col. Historia y sociedad, 20)

Most Caribbean colonies abandoned mixed agriculture for domination of sugar. In this work Rubén Silié demonstrates that Dominican Republic's experience ran in opposite direction. After first flush of success in 16th century, colony gradually passed into grazing economy. Economic retardation also derived from subordinate position of the metropolis (Spain) in economy of 18th-century Atlantic world. Colonial poverty inhibited accumulation of capital and served to perpetuate grazing economy to end of period. As result, slavery tended to be less exacting than on export-oriented plantations in neighboring colonies—a reality which did not escape field slaves of neighboring Saint-Domingue before the revolution. Author deals not only with ramifications of slave economy and society, but also with constant stream of Canary Islanders who came to colony in 17th and 18th centuries.

2988. Thomas, Mary Elizabeth. Jamaica and voluntary laborers from Africa: 1840-1865. Gainesville, The Univ.

Presses of Florida, 1974. 211 p., bibl., maps.

Essentially narrative account, which depends too much on records of Public Record Office in London, with result that it sounds very officialese. Interesting but not major study.

SLAVERY

2989. Alvarez Nazario, Manuel. Nuevos datos sobre las procedencias de los antiguos esclavos de Puerto Rico (UPR/LT, 21:81/82, julio/dic. 1973 [i.e. 1977] p. 23-37)

Miscellaneous data on various West African origins of slaves taken into Puerto Rico during 19th century in light of hitherto unpublished documentation included in collection recently published by Univ. of Puerto Rico: *El proceso abolicionista en Puerto Rico* (see *HLAS 38:2941*) [A. Santana]

2990. Arcila Farías, Eduardo. La abolición de la esclavitud en Venezuela (UPR/LT, 21:81/82, julio/dic. 1973 [i.e. 1977] p. 257-266)

Analysis of socioeconomic structures and forces contributing to abolition of slavery in late colonial and early republican Venezuela. [A. Santana]

2991. Campbell, Mavis Christine. The dynamics of change in a slave society: a sociopolitical history of the free coloreds of Jamaica, 1800-1865. Cranbury, N.J., Associated Univ. Presses, 1976. 386 p., bibl.

Although Campbell's passionate work will not lack critics, it is useful study of problems and conflicts which plagued this vital component of society only recently released from restrictions of institutions of slavery. Until recently, this sector was almost completely neglected in histories of slave and post-slave Caribbean.

2992. Davila, Arturo V. Aspectos de una pastoral de esclavitudes en Puerto Rico durante el siglo diecinueve: 1803-1873 (UPR/LT, 21:81/82, julio/dic. 1973 [i.e. 1977] p. 39-102)

Data, based mainly on unpublished manuscripts from local ecclesiastical archives, on various attitudes towards slavery and owners-slave relations, mostly moderately critical, on part of Roman Catholic hierarchy and prelates in Puerto Rico throughout 19th century. Contains a documentary appendix. [A. Santana]

2993. ———. Don Jerónimo Mariano Usera y Alarcón, Dean of Puerto Rico—1853-1863—en la crisis del sistema esclavista (UPR/LT, 21:81/82, julio/dic. 1973 [i.e. 1977] p. 131-173)

Miscellaneous data on philanthropic activities of Spanish ecclesiastic among recently arrived African slaves in San Juan in late 1850s. Based on hitherto unpublished manuscript sources from local ecclesiastical archives. [A. Santana]

2994. Díaz Soler, Luis M. La experiencia abolicionista de Puerto Rico (UPR/LR, 21:81/82, julio/dic. 1973 [i.e. 1977] p. 293-395)

Documented survey, based on printed primary and secondary sources of events, both in Spain and Puerto Rico, leading to final abolition of slavery in island in 1873. [A. Santana]

2995. ———. Participatión de Eugenio María de Hostos en el movimiento abolicionista puertorriqueño (UPR/LT, 21:81/82, julio/dic. 1973 [i.e. 1977] p. 175-202)

Documented notes on anti-slavery posture and related activities, up to abolition in 1873, of noted 19th-century Puerto Rican thinker and liberal activist, Eugenio María de Hostos (1839-1903). Based on printed primary and secondary sources. [A. Santana]

2996. Flinter, Jorge D. Examen del estado actual de los esclavos de la isla de Puerto Rico. San Juan, Instituto de Cultura Puertorriqeña, 1976. 124 p.

Facsimile ed. of opuscule originally published 1832, but now classic primary source of early 19th-century Puerto Rican history. Work of Anglo-Irish military officer in service of Spain, it impugns contemporary European reformist's efforts towards immediate abolition of slavery in West Indies and purports to show slaves under Spanish colonial system, specifically in Puerto Rico, as much better off personally than their counterparts in other European Caribbean colonies. [A. Santana]

2997. Hoetink, Harmannus. La abolición de la esclavitud en las Antillas Holandesas (UPR/LT, 21:81/82, julio/dic. 1973 [i.e. 1977] p. 283-291)

Socioeconomic and demographic aspects of historical background to slaves' emancipation in Dutch West Indies. Based on printed primary and secondary sources. [A. Santana]

2998. Klein, Herbert S. Consideraciones sobre la viabilidad de la esclavitud y las causas de la abolición en la Cuba del siglo diecinueve (UPR/LT, 21:81/82, julio/dic. 1973 [i.e. 1977] p. 307-318)

Exposition of several historiographical theories which purport to explain general acceptance of abolition of slavery in mid-19th-century Cuba as due to already obvious incompatibility of institution of slavery with contemporary colonial socioeconomic structures and realities. [A. Santana]

Lange, Frederick W. Slave mortuary practices, Barbados, West Indies. See *HLAS 39:592*.

2999. Love, Robert William, Jr. The end of the Atlantic slave trade to Cuba (UWI/CQ, 22:2/3, June/Sept. 1976, p. 51-58)

Interesting episode, but sources are skimpy, and author fails to see wider context in which events moved at that time.

3000. Manigat, Leslie F. La experiencia histórica de la abolición de la esclavitud en Haiti (UPR/LT, 21:81/82, julio/dic. 1973 [i.e. 1977] p. 203-228)

Analysis of political and socioeconomic forces leading towards destruction of slavery as institution in Haiti from French colonial days to early 19th century. Based on printed primary and secondary sources. [A. Santana]

3001. Marshall, Bernard A. Maronage in slave plantation societies: a case study of Dominica, 1785-1815 (UWI/CQ, 22:2/3, June/Sept. 1976, p. 26-32)

Bernard asserts that resistance of maroons was one factor in destruction of slave society in Antilles, and suggests their example (not their mistakes) as good case of struggle against colonialism and neo-colonialism in contemporary Caribbean.

3002. Moore, Robert J. La abolición de la esclavitud en el Caribe británico supuestos y respuestas (UPR/LT, 21:81/82, julio/dic. 1973 [i.e. 1977] p. 267-282)

Study of determining factors which contributed in 1834 to slaves' emancipation in British West Indies and most important socioeconomic consequences therefrom. [A. Santana]

3003. Morales Carrión, Arturo. El centenario de la abolición: una visión histórica (UPR/LT, 21:81/82, julio/dic. 1973 [i.e. 1977] p. 1-21)

Documented essay on various ideological, political and socioeconomic forces that, throughout first half and mid-19th-century led to final abolition of slavery in Puerto Rico in 1873. [A. Santana]

3004. Moya Pons, Frank. Notas sobre la primera abolición de la esclavitud en Santo Domingo (UPR/LT, 21:81/82, julio/dic. 1973 [i.e. 1977] p. 229-255)

Documented notes on forces and circumstances leading to abolition of slavery under aegis of invading Haitian soldiery in Spanish Santo Domingo during last decade of 18th century. Based on printed primary and secondary sources. [A. Santana]

3005. Vila Vilar, Enriqueta. Hispano-América y el comercio de esclavos. Sevilla, Escuela de Estudios Hispano-Americanos, 1977. 306 p.

Superb examination of period of transatlantic trade, between 1595-1640, when trade was handled predominantly by Portuguese. Vila Vilar looks at general conditions which created demand for Africans, licenses and licensees, economic and demographic patterns of trade, and offers suggestions on proportion of illegal trade as well as on thorny problems of quantifying transatlantic slave trade. Vila Vilar's work is indispensable for any consideration of trade in terms laid down by Philip Curtin's *Atlantic slave trade*.

HAITIAN AND CUBAN REVOLUTIONS

3006. Canto Hernández, Rosendo. Cuba: anverso y reverso. Madrid, Ediciones Sedmay, 1974. 285 p.

Thoroughly readable journalistic account of conditions which brought Castro to power in Cuba, and what keeps him there. Canto typifies softening of intelligent militant anti-Castro Cuban whose visit to Cuba changed his mind.

3007. Carré Lazcano, Elio. Girón: una estocada a fondo. Prólogo de Pedro Deschamps Chapeaux. La Habana, Partido Comunista de Cuba, Comité Central, Depto. de Orientación, 1975. 240 p., bibl., illus., maps.

Probably most detailed Cuban account of unsuccessful April 1961 invasion of island referred to as "Bay of Pigs" in US. Describes prelude to invasion, fighting, and ends with eyewitness accounts by some participants.

3008. Castro, Fidel. Obras escogidas. t. 2, 1962-1968. Madrid, Editorial Fundamentos, 1976. 231 p. (Col. Ciencia)

Speeches of Fidel, in their entirety except for his acceptance speech on being awarded Lenin Peace Prize in May 1961.

3009. Os Comités de Defesa da Revolução. Lisboa, Iniciativas Editoriais, 1975. 122 p., bibl., tables (Col. Século 20/21)

Good examination of establishment and working of major Cuban political institution (the CDR's), which reminds one how fluid and dynamic are the Revolution's institutions.

Farber, Samuel. Revolution and reaction in Cuba, 1933-1960: a political sociology from Machado to Castro. See *HLAS 39:7214*.

3010. Franqui, Carlos. Diario de la Revolución cubana. Barcelona, Ediciones R. Torres, 1976. 753 p., maps, table.

Brilliantly written and highly informative, Franqui presents curious, semi-personal history. Few have longer political and ideological connection to Revolution, hence strong partisan nature of narrative. Nevertheless, work is important because of its amazing details, account of struggle between 1952-59 for portrayal of psychology of revolution in colonial society.

Gouraige, Chislain. La Diaspora d'Haïti et l'Afrique. See item 7796.

3011. Grinevich, Emiliia Andreevna. Kuba: put' k pobede revoliutsii (Cuba: the path to the victory of the Revolution). Moscow, Izdatel'stvo "Nauka," 1975. 239 p.

Soviet history of Cuba for years 1952-59. Issued under auspices of Institute of Latin America of USSR's Academy of Sciences. Substantial bibliography with numerous references to work's by Soviet authors. [R.V. Allen]

3012. Kubánská revoluce: bibliografická, a biografická pomucka. Brno, Czechoslovakia, Knihovna J. Mahena, 1974. 56 p.

Czech compilation of monographs and periodical articles on Cuban Revolution published in Czech and Slovak languages. Includes basic data on Cuban history and biographical index of Cuban revolutionaries. [G.J. Kovtun]

3013. Lewis, Oscar; Ruth M. Lewis; and **Susan M. Rigdon.** Living the Revolution: an oral history of contemporary Cuba. v. 1, Four men. Urbana, Univ. of Illinois Press, 1977. 538 p., bibl., illus., map.

Vol. 1 of projected trilogy, based on last research project of Oscar Lewis and his research team, *Four Men* is grippingly-written book which holds one's attention from start to finish. Hard to put down, book's technique closely follows pattern familiar to readers of *Children of Sánchez* and *La Vida*. Like Bible, this work will attract strong supporters and equally strong detractors. Worthy of reading it nevertheless should not be taken for more than what it is, a photographic impression of small segment of dynamic process. *Four Men* graphically portrays transformation of both slum-dwellers and revolutionary society, but it can in no way be accepted as reliable account of general conditions in Cuba today (1978) since data was collected in 1969 and early 1970.

3014. Maidique Patricio, Hilda; Virgen Gutiérrez Mesa; and **Elena Rodríguez Pérez** *comps*. Camilo Cienfuegos: estudio bibliográfico. La Habana, Univ. de La Habana, Centro de Información Científica y Técnica, 1974? 14 p.

Cienfuegos, one of leading "barbudos" of Cuban Revolutionary cadre which overthrew Batista, perished shortly thereafter. This compilation of references by and about hero is made lest we forget. Merely a listing.

3015. Morales Carrión, Arturo. El reflujo en Puerto Rico de la crísis dóminico-haitiana, 1791-1805 (EME, 27, nov./dic. 1976, p. 19-39)

Morales Carrión looks at impact which Haitian revolution had on Puerto Rico and repeats theme that histories of Antilles have always been intertwined despite imperial boundaries. Just as in case of Cuba, disturbance on neighboring island created exile community which quickly assimilated to local economy and led to long-term connection between both regions.

3016. Nicholson, Joe, Jr. Inside Cuba. N.Y., Sheed and Ward, 1974. 234 p.

Expansion of the prize-winning article from *Harper's Magazine* (1973), which reads a little dated today, but is very well written. For political scientist's comment, see *HLAS 39:7227*.

Pérez, Louis A., Jr. *comp*. The Cuban revolutionary war, 1953-1958: a bibliography. See *HLAS 39:28*.

3017. Prendes, Alvaro. En el punto rojo de mi kolimador. La Habana, Editorial de Arte y Literatura, 1974. 328 p.

Grippingly-told narrative by one senior Cuban pilot of his role in defense of his country during ill-fated Bay of Pigs invasion of Cuba in 1961.

Vitier, Cintio. Ese sol del mundo moral para una historia de la etnicidad cubana. See item 6745.

3018. Weiss, Judith A. *Casa de las Américas*: an intellectual review of the Cuban Revolution. Chapel Hill, Univ.

of North Carolina, 1977. 171 p., bibl. (Estudios de hispánofila, 44)

Weiss' study adds most important dimension to our understanding of pervasive effects of Cuban Revolution, and nicely complements—from above— the work by Richard Fagen, *Transformation of political culture in Cuba*. She analyzes the evolution of the review as it mirrored the political course, or reality, in Cuba between 1960 and 1971. Her conclusion is that *Casa* "is a faithful mirror of Cuba's relationship with Latin America and with the intellectuals of all countries" and that *Casa* has managed to wage intellectual battle on all fronts simultaneously because it has, and has had a large, rigorously-trained and able body of supporters and editors. Highly recommended.

INDEPENDENCE

3019. Auilera, Francisco Vicente. Epistolario. La Habana, Instituto Cubano del Libro, Editorial de Ciencias Sociales, 1974. 268 p. (Pensamiento cubano)

Letters are interesting, but do not do full justice to this outstanding figure of first Cuban attempt to establish independence from Spain, Aguilera was rich planter who threw in his lot with nationalists and paid the material price.

3020. Coiscou Henríquez, Máximo. Documentos para la historia de Santo Domingo. v. 2. Madrid, Rivadenerya, 1973. 417 p.

Documents from Seville's AGI almost entirely political, e.g., normally inflated honors and decorations. Includes few which discuss security of colony and public celebrations.

3021. Jacobs, W. Richard *ed.* Butler versus the King: riots and sedition in 1937. Comments by George Weekes and Joe Young. Port of Spain, Key Caribbean Publications, 1976. 254 p., illus.

Constitutional decolonization of English Antilles gained strong momentum after series of general labor disturbances swept through Caribbean in 1937. Nowhere were riots more serious than in Trinidad, especially among oilfield workers, led by inimitable and charismatic Tubal Uriah Buzz Butler. Riots were called Butler riots and government arrested him on charge of sedition. Book is more than what title implies or collection of letters and documents surrounding Butler's trial. Enhanced by Excellent introduction, it is commendable contribution to history of rise of Caribbean labor movement in twilight of British colonialism. Contributions by George Weekes and Joe Young provide sketch which covers period after World War II and through present. Despite undisguised political rhetoric, book does provide most useful insight into workings of colonial society and conditions which gave rise to Butler, and against which he fought.

3022. Pérez Moris, José. Historia de la insurrección de Lares. Con un estudio a esta edición por Kenneth Lugo del Toro. Río Piedras, P.R., Editorial Edil, 1975. 350 p., tables (Clásicos puertorriqueños Edil)

Useful guide with some additional documents on abortive attempt to declare Puerto Rican independence in 1867.

3023. Rodríguez Objío, Manuel. Gregorio Luperón e historia de la restauración. t. 1. Santo Domingo, Editora de Santo Domingo, 1975. 364 p. (Sociedad Dominicana de Bibliófilos. Col. De cultura dominicana, 13)

Rather tedious biography of distinguished Dominican general, with excessively detailed political narrative of period 1840-66.

3024. Tena Reyes, Jorge *ed.* and *comp.* Duarte en la historiografía dominicana. Santo Domingo, Secretaría de Estado de Educación, Bellas Artes y Cultos, 1976. 810 p., bibl.

Another addition to outpouring in commemoration of Duarte's centenary. Strong in melodrama and weak in scholarship. Duarte is greatest hero in Dominican Republic and his bibliography is extensive.

NATIONAL AND 19th CENTURY

3025. Arana-Soto, Salvador. Luis Muñoz Rivera: savia y sangre de Puerto Rico. t. 3, Barbosa-Labra: la disidencia anexionista. San Juan, P.R., n.p., 1975. 323 p., bibl.

Arana-Soto's argument is that ambivalence has long history in Puerto Rico and this traces dual viewpoints of José Barbosa and Rafael María Labra on direction island should have taken during 19th century and effects that contrasting experience of Cuba had on evolution of Puerto Rican political thought.

3026. Balcácer, Juan Daniel. Pedro Santana: historia política de un déspota. Prólogo por J.I. Jiménes-Grullón. Santo Domingo, Editora Taller, 1974. 195 p., bibl. (Biblioteca taller, 50)

Political history of 19th-century Dominican leader which is also a polemic. Routine.

3027. Betances, Ramón Emeterio. Las Antillas para los antillanos. Prólogo, selección, traducciones y notas del Doctor Carlos M. Rama. San Juan,

Instituto de Cultura Puertorriqueña, 1975. 288 p., bibl.

Betances ranks foremost among Puerto Rican and Caribbean nationalists of 19th century who advocated total independence of Spanish Antilles and Haiti not only of their metropolis (Spain) but of the US. Good introduction and representative sample of this old revolutionary who spent half a century fighting imperialism.

3028. Bothwell, Reece B. and Lidio Cruz Monclova. Los documentos . . ., Qué dicen? 1869-1899. 2. ed. rev. y ampliada. San Juan, Univ. de Puerto Rico, 1974. 602 p.

Documents from Spanish and Puerto Rican newspapers giving varying opinions of period.

3029. Domínguez, Jaime. La República Dominicana en vísperas de la anexión (Ciencia [Univ. Autónoma de Santo Domingo] 3:2, abril/junio 1976, p. 77-95, illus., table)

Excellent socioeconomic analysis of structure of society and economy immediately preceding short-lived annexation with Spain. Not only does author focus on local rivalries, but also on larger competition for hegemony between Great Britain and US. Highly recommended.

3030. Fallope, J. Le problème sucrier en Guadeloupe dans la première moitié du XIXè. siècle, 1815-1860 (SHG/B, 25, 3. trimestre 1975, p. 7-34, bibl.)

Demonstrates that post-slavery problems of Guadeloupe were not uncommon to wider Caribbean of 19th century, especially those faced with limited land areas, and that scarcity of labor led to new wave of immigrants: Chinese and East Indians.

3031. Figueroa, Loida. Breve historia de Puerto Rico. v. 3, Desde el crepúsculo del dominio español hasta la antesala de la Ley Foraker, c. 1892-1900. Río Piedras, P.R., Editorial Edil, 1977. 515 p., bibl.

This is Figueroa's vol. 3 on theme which she originally offered as "short history" of Puerto Rico. This volume covers important phase in island's history and author makes very persuasive case for calculated invasion and possession of Puerto Rico by military forces of US. One strong point is way she integrates context of late Spanish colonialism in her narrative, making frequent references to Spain, Cuba and Philippines.

3032. Hoernel, Robert B. Sugar and social change in Oriente, Cuba: 1898-1946 (JLAS, 8:2, nov. 1976, p. 215-249)

Excellent articulate exposition of repercussions of US intervention both in Cuba and in sugar business in Oriente prov. Portrait is of region raped by foreigners as well as local capitalists and particularly vulnerable to economic fluctuations of international economy. Tables and figures aptly illustrate closely reasoned arguments.

3033. Kirk, John M. José Martí and the United States: a further interpretation (JLAS, 9:2, Nov. 1977, p. 275-290)

Reveals evolution of Martí's attitude toward US and radicalization of his thought as he gradually developed his perception of US role in hemispheric affairs.

3034. Langley, Lester D. Struggle for the American Mediterranean: United States-European rivalry in the Gulf-Caribbean, 1776-1904. Athens, Univ. of Georgia Press, 1976. 226 p., bibl., map.

Narrative slanted heavily from Anglo-Saxon—and especially North-American point of view. Research based on materials published primarily in English.

Lenoir, John D. Surinam national development and Maroon cultural autonomy. See *HLAS 39:1226*.

Marshall, Woodville K.; Trevor Marshall; and Bentley Gibbs. The establishment of a peasantry in Barbados: 1840-1920. See *HLAS 39:1232*.

3035. Moore, Brian L. The retention of caste notions among the Indian immigrants in British Guiana during the nineteenth century (CSSH, 19:1, Jan. 1977, p. 96-107)

Although immigration of East Indian workers to British Guiana inevitably led to severe challenge of their notion of caste as it existed in Indian subcontinent, many clung to tenets of caste. Workers' return to their native land however, had effect of immunizing them against such lapses. For ethnologist's comment, see *HLAS 39:1237*.

3036. Ortíz, Helen. Algunas consideraciones sobre el alza del azúcar en la República Dominicana: 1875-1900 (UNCR/R, 1:1, 1975, p. 1-20)

Reviews rapid development of plantation economy in Dominican Republic at end of 19th century and attributes it to expansion of world economy after 1850 and integration of Latin America's export-economies.

3037. Pérez, Louis A., Jr. Army politics in Cuba: 1898-1958. Pittsburgh, Pa.,

Univ. of Pittsburgh Press, 1976. 240 p., bibl. (Pitt Latin American series)

Interesting case study of process of change in military establishment set up to protect property rather than the state, and alienated from conventional military tradition as well as social responsibility. Study emphasizes political aspects of military activity in Cuba before 1958.

3038. Picó, Fernando. Registro general de jornaleros, Utuado, Puerto Rico: 1849-1850. Río Piedras, P.R., Ediciones Huracán, 1976. 190 p.

Textual transcription of official inventory dated 1849-50 registering agricultural day laborers of Utuado, at that time most important urban center in Puerto Rico's coffee and tobacco producing mountainous central area. Illustrative of important facet of mid-19th century social structure and of Spanish government's cumbersome regulations restricting life and working conditions of island's non-enslaved agricultural labor force. [A. Santana]

3039. Pina, Pedro Alejandrino. Vida y escritos. Santo Domingo, Editora del Caribe, 1970. 247 p. (Academia Dominicana de la Historia, 27)

Pina's claim to fame was his close friendship and collaboration with Dominican hero Duarte. A fervent nationalist, he had 19th-century flair for poetry and prose as his writings attest.

3040. Sundiata, I.K. "Cuba Africana:" Cuba and Spain in the Bight of Biafra: 1839-1869 (AAFH/TAM, 34:1, July 1977, p. 90-101)

Not well written article based on meager use of secondary sources. Skirts main issues of vital connections between Africa and New World as well as between slavery and freedom and never comes to grips with importance of island of Fernando Po.

MODERN

3041. Antuña, Vicentina. Camila Henríquez Ureña: *in memoriam* (CDLA, 14:84, mayo/junio 1974, p. 96-105)

Excellent tribute to notable Latin American feminist, literary critic and pedagogue. Member of distinguished Dominican family of intellectuals, she grew up in exile in Cuba and US. One of founders of Unión Nacional de Mujeres de Cuba, she was also organizer of one of first Women's Congresses in 1938. Author of many studies on women long before it was fashionable (e.g., women in colonial times, Romanticism, Bernard Shaw plays, etc.) she surprised many when, at advanced age and after retirement she left comforts of US to live under rigors of Revolutionary Cuba where she died much loved and respected in 1973. [Ed.]

3042. Attema, Ypie. Eustatius: a short history of the island and its monuments. Translation by Peter Daniels. Foreword by C.L. Temminck Groll. Amsterdam? De Walburg Pers Zutphen, 1976. 87 p., plates.

Good guide to forts and monuments of this curiously attractive little island about which there are few works. Historical outline confirms general impression that island and inhabitants have always been dependent on outside world given their scarce resources.

Baptiste, F.A. La captura de las autoridades holandeses de Curazao, por exilados políticos venezolanos en junio de 1929, considerada en relación con los desembarcos anglo-franceses en Aruba y Curazao en mayo de 1940. See *HLAS 39:8738*.

Bellegarde-Smith, Patrick. Haiti: perspectives of foreign policy. See *HLAS 39:8739*.

3043. Benjamin, Jules Robert. The New Deal, Cuba and the rise of a global foreign economic policy (HU/BHR, 51:1, Spring 1977, p. 57-78)

Benjamin's thesis is that relations with Cuba during New Deal foreshadowed post-World War II foreign aid programs. Author's narrow approach to study of US-Cuba connection tends to underestimate pressures from Cuban side.

3044. ———. The United States and Cuba: hegemony and dependent development, 1880-1934. Pittsburgh, Pa., Univ. of Pittsburgh Press, 1977. 266 p., bibl. (Pitt Latin American series)

Research is impressive. Nevertheless, Benjamin tends to underestimate Cuban politicians and Cuba's political system. Reviews economic relations of both countries emphasizing monetary trends and policies thus offering fresh and insightful account of problems which US faced with the new Cuba. Unfortunately, it does not offer as rich nor as insightful an account of Cuba's response to the new relation.

3045. Blouet, Brian. The post-emancipation origins of the relationship between the estates and the peasantry in Trinidad (*in* Duncan, Kenneth; Ian Rutledge; and Colin Harding eds. Land and labour in Latin America [see item 2156] p. 435-452, tables)

Concludes that present difficulties of Trinidad peasants stem directly from legacies of slavery, plantation and colonial politics of post-emancipation period.

Cassá, Roberto. Los taínos de la Española. See *HLAS 39:576*.

Clark, Truman R. Puerto Rico and the United States, 1917-1933. See *HLAS 39:3149*.

3046. Clark, Victor Selden. Puerto Rico and its problems. Preface by Harold G. Moulton. N.Y., Arno Press, 1975. 707 p., illus., tables (Arno Press Collection. The Puerto Rican experience)

This report on state of Puerto Rica ca. 1928-30 (reprint of 1930 ed.) covers urban and rural living conditions, labor movement, taxation, trade and commerce, public health, education (or better, lack thereof) agriculture, and entire public and private economic infra-structure. Excellent tables and charts support survey, carried out by team from Brookings Institution, and including late Frank Tannenbaum. Of interest mainly to historians and social anthropologists.

3047. Coll y Toste, Cayetano. La invación americana en Puerto Rico. Madrid, Artes Gráficas Corrales, 1974. 82 p.

Random undocumented notes on military aspects of American invasion of Puerto Rico during summer of 1898 by well known Puerto Rican historian (1850-1930). Unpublished until now, these are mostly personal impressions and reminiscences by author, then high-ranking officer in island's autonomous government. [A. Santana]

Descartes, Sol L. Puerto Rico: trasfondo de su economía. See *HLAS 39:3154*.

3048. Díaz Polanco, Héctor. Economía y movimientos campesinos. Santo Domingo, Editora de la Univ. Autónoma de Santo Domingo (UASD), 1976. 151 p., illus. (Publicacion, 210. Col. Historia y sociedad, 26)

Based on a Marxist concept of economic determinism this essentially theoretical study ends with an examination of case studies from Bolivia and Mexico, where author finds that peasants were not integrated into national economy, and that solidarity of peasant movement depended on outside forces. Strong influence of Arturo Warman throughout.

Dirks, Robert and Virginia Kerns. Mating patterns and adaptive change in Rum Bay, 1823-1970. See *HLAS 39:1206*.

Eaton, George. Osmond Dyce, labor leader: a life and its time; 1918-1970. See *HLAS 39:7255*.

3049. Gómez Acevedo, Labor. Sanz: promotor de la conciencia separatista en Puerto Rico. 2. ed. rev. Prólogo por Manuel Ballesteros Gaibrois. San Juan, Univ. de Puerto Rico, 1974. 320 p., bibl. (Col. Uprex. Serie humanidades)

Based on archival material from Archivo Histórico Nacional and Madrid's Biblioteca Nacional as well as Hemeroteca Municipal, this study deals with 1860s and 1870s when Puerto Rico reached a crossroad in its relation with Spain. Includes excellent bibliography and list of archival sources.

Groot, Silvia W. de. From isolation towards integration. See *HLAS 39:1214*.

3050. Hazard, Samuel. Santo Domingo, past and present: with a glance at Hayti [sic]. Santo Domingo, Editora de Santo Domingo, 1974. 511 p., bibl., illus., tables (Sociedad Dominicana de Bibliófilos. Col. Cultura dominicana, 4)

Welcome reissue of rare 1873 book. Interesting as much for its prose as for magnificent illustrations.

3051. Hill, Frank. Bustamante and his letters. Kingston, Jam., Kingston Publishers, 1976. 126 p., illus., table.

William Alexander Clark Bustamante was one of most charismatic of Caribbean leaders, and his contribution to political evolution of Jamaica is paralleled only by that of his cousin, Norman Washington Manley. In this book, Frank Hill gives short, useful review of man and politics of his times, while offering an edition of his letters which places him in league of such indefatigable Caribbean letter writers, as W.A. Domingo and Richard Moore. Letters show great wit, social concern, and no reluctance to offer opinions on any and all subjects. Although Bustamante, the politician, emerges vividly, there is very little of the private man.

Holzberg, C.S. Societal segmentation and Jewish ethnicity: ethnographic illustrations from Latin America and the Caribbean. See *HLAS 39:1218*.

3052. Hum, D.; R. Lobdell; and B. Spencer. Plantations, staple exports and the seasonality of births in Jamaica: 1880-1938 (UWI/SES, 26:1, March 1977, p. 63-85, tables)

After examining birth patterns in selected parishes of Jamaica between 1880-1938, concludes that seasonality of rural birth: "depended primarily on the nature of agricultural output rather than on the mode of production."

Kneer, Warren G. Great Britain and the Caribbean, 1901-1913: a study in Anglo-American relations. See *HLAS 39:8766*.

Kopytoff, Barbara K. The development of Jamaican Maroon ethnicity. See *HLAS 39:1222*.

———. Jamaican Maroon political organization: the effect of the treaties. See *HLAS 39:1223*.

3053. Kryzanek, Michael J. Political party decline and the failure of liberal democracy: the PRD in Dominican politics (JLAS, 9:1, May 1977, p. 115-143)

Author thinks that PRD suffered as much from its own internal weaknesses as from external damage of Balaguer and his foreign, capitalist cohorts.

3054. El libro azul. Presentación de Roberto Cassa. Edición a cargo de José del Castillo. Santo Domingo, Editora de la Univ. Autónoma de Santo Domingo (UASD), 1976. 176 p., facsims., illus. (Publicacion, 209. Col. Historia y sociedad, 25)

Reprint of elegant, 1920 bilingual ed. of Santo Domingo's Blue Book has some of best photographs of early 20th century for any Caribbean territory. Valuable historical tool which introduction describes as: "A pictorial review of the Republic of Santo Domingo (Dominican Republic) including special articles of history, geography, public instruction, transportation, mines, agriculture, commerce, industry, etc., etc., all of which are of great value to the capitalist, tourist, immigrants, etc., etc."

3055. López, José Ramón. Dos textos: Documentos: la industria azucarera dominicana a principios de siglo; La caña de azúcar en San Pedro de Macorís desde el bosque virgen hasta el mercado (Ciencia [Univ. Autónoma de Santo Domingo] 2:3, julio/sept. 1975, p. 111-141)

As title states: production figures, and general reports on development of sugar industry at beginning of 20th century.

3056. Lozano, Wilfredo. La dominación imperialista en la República Dominicana, 1900-1930: estudio de la primera ocupación norteamericana de Santo Domingo. Presentación de José del Castillo. Santo Domingo, Editora de la Univ. Autónoma de Santo Domingo (UASD), 1976. 297 p., bibl., illus., tables (Publicacion, 189. Col. Historia y sociedad, 21)

Despite relying somewhat heavily on Melvin Knight's *The Americans in Santo Domingo*, Lozano places his study squarely within theoretical context of recent dependency studies and sees Dominican role as enclave within wider imperialist sphere of US. Also looks at what occupation did for social restructuring, and creation of "pre-bourgeoisie" in Dominican Republic. Bibliography and economic charts are especially useful.

3057. Maldonado-Denis, Manuel. En las entrañas: un análisis sociohistórico de la emigración puertorriqueña. La Habana, Casa de las Américas, 1976. 212 p., bibl., tables.

In many ways a sequel to author's *Puerto Rico: a socio-economic interpretation*. Maldonado-Denis continues to regard Puerto Rican problems as stemming from its colonized, exploited, client status. It is a passionate, informed, marxist interpretation of ill-effects of dependency; poverty, internal socioeconomic dislocation, cultural debilitation and psychological insecurity. Conclusion is that local political leaders have conspired to use emigration as acceptable form of subordination. Regards recommendations of Tobin Report on island's economic status as unsatisfactory palliative.

3058. Murtil, Pierre-Albert. Indépendence pour la Guyane. Paris, La Pensée Universelle, 1977. 127 p.

Political tract outlines history of French Guiana, and appeals for independence. Includes facts and figures for 1974.

3059. Natal, Carmelo Rosario. La juventud de Luis Muñoz Marín: vida y pensamiento, 1898-1932. San Juan, P.R., n.p., 1976. 255 p., illus.

Delightfully written biography, which fills in details of early life of architect of Puerto Rico's Associated Free State Status, with examples of Muñoz Marín's and his wife Muna Lee's poetry and journalism. Author obviously admires his subject, but manages to avoid editorializing during his narration.

United States, Department of Commerce. Domestic and International Business Administration. Bureau of East-West Trade. United States commercial relations with Cuba: a survey. See *HLAS 39:3133*.

3060. Núñez Machín, Ana. Rubén Martínez Villena. Prólogo de Fabio Grobart. 2. ed. La Habana, Editorial de Ciencias Sociales, 1974. 463 p., bibls., illus. (Col. Hombre y época)

Excellent biography of young Cuban poet, lawyer, politician and nationalist who died of tuberculosis at age 35 in 1934. Martínez Villena was one of outstanding young patriots of 1920s whose political consciousness was sharpened by Gerardo Machado's dictatorship. Also contains selections of his poems and letters.

3061. Pino Santos, Oscar. La oligarquía yanqui en Cuba. Epílogo por Fidel Castro. México, Editorial Nuestro Tiempo, 1975. 207 p., bibl., tables (Col. Teoría e historia)

Clearest exposition one is liable to find of subtle and non-subtle ways in which Cuban economy became integrated in, and dependent on that of US. Pino Santos is among most learned, thoughtful, and able historians working in and on Cuba.

Quintero Rivera, Angel G. Background to the emergence of imperialist capitalism in Puerto Rico. See *HLAS 39:3213*.

3062. ———. Workers' struggle in Puerto Rico: a documentary history. Translated by Cedric Belfrage. N.Y., Monthly Review Press, 1976. 236 p., bibl.

Important study illustrates activities and growth of Puerto Rican labor movement 1904-73. Each document has introduction which places it in context and underscores its relevance.

Ramesar, Marianne D. Patterns of regional settlement and economic activity by immigrant groups in Trinidad: 1851-1900. See *HLAS 39:1251*.

Senior, Clarence. Santiago Iglesias: labor crusader. See *HLAS 39:3222*.

Sinclair, Sonja S. A fertility analysis of Jamaica: recent trends with reference to the Parish of St. Ann. See *HLAS 39:1853*.

Sio, Arnold. Race and colour in the status of the free coloured in the West Indies: Jamaica and Barbados. See *HLAS 39:1266*.

Taylor, Frank. Jamaica: the welcoming society, myths and reality. See *HLAS 39:1273*.

3063. Tellería Toca, Evelio. Congresos obreros en Cuba. La Habana, Editorial de Arte y Literatura. Instituto Cubano del Libro, 1973. 587 p., bibl., facsims., illus.

Author gives brief summary of growth of labor movement in Cuba, starting with free tobacconists, and then details organized workers' congresses beginning in 1887, and continuing erratically until 1966. Only congresses representing entire island are included, and agendas as well as delegates are described. Value of work will lie in inferences drawn from data presented.

3064. Toro Gonzáles, Carlos del. Algunos aspectos económicos, sociales y políticos del movimiento obrero cubano: 1933-1958. La Habana, Editorial Arte y Literatura, 1974. 474 p., bibl., tables.

Very impressive study dealing with labor movement, especially social ramifications of unemployment and underemployment. Includes very useful set of statistical tables on patterns of employment, education, union growth, as well as distribution of social services and income based on 1953 census. Shows how value of sugar exports increased from 74 percent of total exports in 1933 to 81 percent in 1938, while tobacco declined from 16 percent in former year, to 7 percent in latter. Employment of women increased especially in sugar industry partly because of low wages, and minimal working conditions which prevailed. Provisions of 1940 constitution were subscribed to more in breach than in observance, while local and foreign enterprises consorted with worst elements of North American organized criminals to exploit Cuba and its people.

SPANISH SOUTH AMERICA

GENERAL

MICHAEL T. HAMERLY
Pacific Northwest Bibliographic Center
Seattle, Washington

3065. Amich, José and others. Historia de las misiones del Convento de Santa Rosa de Ocopa. Edición de Julián Heras. Lima, Editorial Milla Batres, 1975. 559 p.

Republishes official chronicles of Franciscan missions of Ocopa in eastern Peru. Covers colonial period and 19th century. Editor Father Heras has added notes, documentary and other supplementary appendices

3066. Bibliografía histórica peruana: 1968-1970 (PUCP/CSH, 10, enero 1970/dic. 1972, p. 123-145)

Annotated and indexed guide to articles published on prehistory and history of Peru between 1968-70. See also *HLAS 36:2418-2419.*

3067. Bibliografía histórica peruana: 1970-1973 (PUCP/CSH, 11, enero 1973/dic. 1975, p. 97-127)

Latest installment of highly useful guide to historical output in and on Peru. To date, it has indexed 3,723 items.

3068. Campbell, Leon G. After the fall: the reformation of the Army of Peru, 1784-1816 (IAA, 3:1, 1977, p. 1-28)

Drawing on extensive original research, analyzes changing defense policies and structures in viceregal Peru. Stresses renewed reliance on army as against militia following Túpac Amaru revolt, success of Viceroy Abascal in building military strength in early part of independence period. [D. Bushnell]

3069. Carmagnani, Marcello and **Giovanna Mantelli.** Fonti quantitative italiane relative all'emigrazione italiana verso l'América Latina: 1902-1914; analisi crítica (Annali della Fondazione Luigi Einaudi [Torino, Italy] 9, 1975, p. 283-297, bibl., tables)

Análisis de las fuentes estadísticas relativas a la emigración italiana hacia América Latina. En el mismo se intenta reconstruir una serie estadística que reduzca los errores que por falta o exceso existan en las dos fuentes estudiadas. [M. Carmagnani]

3070. Congreso de Historia Argentina y Regional, *II, Comodoro Rivadavia, Arg., 1973.* Segundo Congreso de Historia Argentina y Regional. t. 1/3. Introducción por Laurio H. Destefani. B.A., Academia Nacional de la Historia, 1974. 3 v. (446, 447, 383 p.) illus., maps, tables.

Publishes papers of II Congress of Argentine and Regional History held Comodoro Rivadavia, Jan. 1973, largely devoted to history of Patagonia from discovery and conquest through early 20th century. Original contributions examine virtually every aspect of Patagonia's past. Major step forward in knowledge and understanding of largely neglected history of southern Argentina.

3071. Craig, Alan K. Franciscan exploration in the central *montaña* of Peru (*in* International Congress of Americanists, XXXIX, Lima, 1970. Actas y memorias [see *HLAS 35:5101*] v. 4, p. 127-144, bibl., illus., maps)

Calls attention to considerable ethnographical and geographical data in accounts of Franciscan missionaries active in Peruvian Oriente from 16th through 19th centuries.

Dobyns, Henry E. and **Paul L. Doughty.** Peru: a cultural history. See item 3510.

3072. La emancipación americana en Bolivia y Perú. t. 3, Siglo VIII: historia. La Paz, Editorial Casa Municipal de la Cultura Franz Tamayo, 1976. 292 p., bibl., illus., tables (Jornadas peruano-bolivianas de estudio científico del altiplano boliviano y del sur del Perú, 3. Biblioteca Paceña, nueva serie)

Miscellany of articles and papers that span Peru and Bolivia, 18th and 19th centuries, and even include something on electronic information processing ("Historia y Cibernética"). Most are quite marginal, but two topics receive fairly extensive and aerious treatment: "La Rebelión de 1780 en Arequipa," on which there is a group of entries by different authors, and the Cuzco rebellion of 1814, on which

Manuel Jesús Aparicio Vega offers some studies that in part overlap his *El clero patriota en la Revolución de 1814* (see *HLAS 38:3257*. [D. Bushnell]

3073. Fals Borda, Orlando. Capitalismo, hacienda y poblamiento: su desarrollo en la costa atlantica. Bogotá, Punta de Lanza, 1976. 70 p., facsim., maps, plates, table.

Working report on ongoing research into social and economic history of Colombia's Atlantic coast. Delineates demographic and economic, especially agricultural developments from initial exploitation of area's Indians by Spaniards in 16th century through that of its natural resources by foreign interests in late 19th and early 20th centuries.

3074. Fishman, César. Monedas del Perú de 1751 a 1975. Lima, Numismática Libertad, 1976. 143 p., illus.

Catalogue of coins minted in and for Peru between 1751 and 1975.

3075. García Chuecos, Héctor. José Vicente de Unda: vida y obra de un glorioso fundador. Introducción de Mario Briceño Perozo. Caracas, Edición Homenaje del Congreso de la República, 1975. 222 p., illus.

Reedition of *HLAS 6:3137*. Both biography of patriot clergyman (1777-1840) who eventually became Bishop of Mérida and study of Colegio de San Luis de Gonzaga de Guanare with which he was closely associated. [D. Bushnell]

3076. *Historia*. Univ. Nacional de San Agustín. Depto. Académico de Historia, Geografía y Antropología. No. 1, 1975- . Arequipa, Peru.

Inaugural issue of journal of recently reinvigorated Dept. of History, Geography and Anthropology of Univ. Nacional de San Agustín, Arequipa. Includes notices and book reviews. Although all articles and documents published in this issue which include items 3203, 3219, 3231 and 3237 are original, Editor Alejandro Málaga Medina intends to reprint out-of-print items on Arequipa and southern Peru.

3077. *Histórica*. Pontificia Univ. Católica del Perú, Depto. de Humanidades. Vol. 1, No. 1, julio 1977- Lima.

First issue of new journal (biannual) devoted primarily to history of Peru, but also willing to consider "estudios sobre historia latinoamericana, relacionados con el Perú, y sobre temas y metodología de la historia." Includes:
Jorge Basadre "Leyes Electorales Peruanas, 1890-1917: Teoría y Realidad" p. 1-36

David Cook "Estimaciones sobre la Población del Perú en el Momento de la Conquista" p. 37-60 (see item 3200)
Carlos Lazo García and Javier Tord Nicolini "El Movimiento Social en el Perú Virreinal" p. 61-92 (see item 3213)
Jeffrey L. Klaiber "Religión y Revolución en los Andes en el Siglo XIX" p. 93-111
Scarlett O'Phelan Godoy "Cuzco, 1777: el Movimiento de Maras, Urubamba" p. 113-128 (see item 3229).

3078. Huamanga: una larga historia. Lima, Consejo Nacional de la Univ. Peruana (CONUP), 1974. 429 p., plates.

Convenient anthology of sources and studies of Huamanga from refoundation as Spanish town in 1539 through present. Emphasizes colonial period and 19th century. Includes difficult to obtain items.

3079. Hurtado, Osvaldo. El poder político en el Ecuador. Quito, Pontificia Univ. Católica del Ecuador, Centro de Publicaciones, 1977. 312 p., bibl.

Probes problematic politics, past as well as present of Ecuador. Pt. 1 examines political and socioeconomic processes during colonial period; pt. 2, national period through 1949; and pt. 3 from 1950 through 1975. Although 1920s rather than 1950s strike this contributor as more critical decade of change in recent history of Ecuador, Hurtado is to be commended for his professionalism and for having given us a substantially better account than anyone else.

3080. Lovera de Sola, R.J. Contribución a la bibliografía histórica venezolana: 1969-1972 (EEHA/HBA, 17:1/2, marzo/julio 1973, p. 93-139)

Well done and highly useful thematic listing of books published between and inclusive of 1969 and 1972, abroad as well as in Venezuela on its history. Includes some studies published in anthologies and collections, but not articles.

3081. Moreno, Gabriel René. Mariano Alejo Alvarez y el silogismo altoperuano de 1808. pt. 1, Fray Antonio de la Calancha. La Paz, Consejo Nacional de Educación Superior, 1973. 107 p. (Publicación, 2)

Reproduces two of lesser works of Bolivia's classic historian: first on spokesman for American discontent at time of independence, second on author of *Coronica moralizada del Orden de S. Agustín en el Perú* (published 1638). [D. Bushnell]

3082. Ocampo, Javier. De la historiografía romántica y académica a la "nueva

History: Spanish South America, General / 203

historia" de Colombia (Gaceta [Bogotá] 1:12/13, julio/agosto 1977, p. 64-72)

Incisive review of different schools or traditions of historiography in Colombia, from early 20th century through present.

Ortiz, P. Dionisio. Las montañas del Apurimac, Mantaro y Ene. See *HLAS 39:5592*.

3083. Ponce, Fernando. Anotaciones sobre fuentes documentales de Arequipa (UNSA/H, 1, 1975, p. 95-101)

Introduction to documentary sources in and on colonial and 19th-century Arequipa.

Rama, Carlos M. Historia del movimiento obrero y social latinoamericano contemporáneo. See item 2219.

3084. Retamal Avila, Julio. Bibliografía de historia eclesiástica chilena: revistas chilenas, 1843-1973 (UCCIH/H, 11, 1972-1973, p. 163-258)

Indexes studies and documents for history of Church in Chile as published in 59 Chilean serials between 1843-1973. Major bibliographic feat.

3085. Revista del Archivo Nacional. Instituto Colombiano de Cultura, Subdirección de Patrimonio Cultural, División de Archivo Nacional. No. 1 [76], Serie 2, 1977- . Bogotá.

Reestablishes official organ of Colombia's Archivo Nacional. First series published in 75 numbers between March 1936-June 1957. This second series includes article by Director Alberto Lee López on legal and actual state of archives in Colombia; discusses history of the Archive, meetings for Archive development in Latin America, etc. Of hemisperic, not only national interest.

3086. Rodríguez Villegas, Hernán. Historia de un solar de la ciudad de Santiago: 1554-1909 (UCCIH/H, 1972/1973, p. 103-162)

Fascinating account of lot on which main office of Banco de Chile is now located in downtown Santiago, from first owner in 1554 through penultimate occupant (orphanage) and 1909 sale to Bank.

3087. Rumazo González, Alfonso. Simón Rodríguez, maestro de América: biografía. Caracas, Univ. Simón Rodríguez, 1976. 302 p., bibl. (Col. Dinámica y siembra)

Like author's other works, this is competent popular biography, taking career of Bolívar's tutor from Venezuela to Europe and back to South America, where he continued to wander, teach, and write till his death in 1854. Just a bit wordy. [D. Bushnell]

3088. La vida y obra del Mariscal Andrés Santa Cruz. t. 1/3. Prólogo de Carlos Urquizo Sossa. La Paz, Casa Municipal de la Cultura Franz Tamayo, 1976. 3 v. (353, 359, 535 p.) illus., maps, plates, tables (Biblioteca Paceña. Nueva serie)

Studies by different authors of widely varying length, covering Santa Cruz's military career in wars of independence, service as president of Bolivia and then as head of Peru-Bolivian Confederation. Entire vol. 2 is *La cultura en la época del Mariscal Santa Cruz* by José de Mesa and Teresa Gisbert. In other vols., there is some relative emphasis on military and diplomatic topics, but internal administration is not wholly neglected. In general, contents are narrative and descriptive without much critical analysis, but for sheer amount of information offered the set is nevertheless a major and welcome addition. [D. Bushnell]

3089. Villalobos R., Sergio; Fernando Silva V.; Osvaldo Silva G.; and Patricio Estellé M. Historia de Chile. Santiago, Editorial Universitaria, 1975. 4 v. (Various pagings) facsims., illus., plates (Col. Imagen de Chile. Cormorán)

Excellent introduction to history of Chile by four leading authorities. Coverage is integral and balanced. Vol. 2 covers 17th and 18th centuries, vol. 3, independence period and Republic through 1860. Vols. 1 and 4, which I have not seen, cover prehistory, conquest, and years 1860-1970 respectively. Merits translation into English for use as text.

3090. Weilbauer, Arthur. Los alemanes en el Ecuador: estudio histórico (Die Deutschen in Ekuador: Historische Studie). Versión castellana por Alicia Terán de Langpap and Augusta Cruz de Weilbauer. Quito, Colegio Alemán, 1975. 117 p., bibl., facsim., plates.

Overview of German activities in and writings on Ecuador. Useful for data and for insight into mentality of German *émigré*. Bilingual ed.

3091. Williams, John Hoyt. Paraguay's historical resources: pt. 1, Paraguay's National Archives (AAFH/TAM, 34:1, July 1977, p. 113-123)

Succinct introduction to history and holdings of Archivo Nacional of Paraguay in Asunción, by scholar intimate with that repository. Updates his 1971 description (see *HLAS 34:2342*).

COLONIAL PERIOD

MICHAEL T. HAMERLY

Pacific Northwest Bibliographic Center
Seattle, Washington

with the assistance of

JOHN HOYT WILLIAMS

Associate Professor of History
Indiana State University, Terre Haute

THE HISTORIOGRAPHY OF COLONIAL VENEZUELA AND COLOMBIA: DEVELOPMENTS OF THE LAST DECADE

RATHER THAN ATTEMPT TO EXAMINE trends, which would require more space than is now available in *HLAS* and in order to evaluate literature not reviewed from *HLAS 32* through *HLAS 40*, the remarks which follow are limited to developments in the newer approaches to the past and research related aspects thereof. Relatively few bibliographies of importance on or relating to colonial Venezuela and Colombia appeared during the decade under review (1968-77). A recent guide compiled by John V. Lombardi, Germán Carrera Damas, Roberta E. Adams and others is *Venezuelan history: a comprehensive bibliography* (see *HLAS 38:113*) which lists over 4000 items from and since discovery. The most complete coverage of historical and other letters in Venezuela, however, is Angel Raúl Villasana's *Ensayo de un repertorio bibliográfico venezolano: años 1808-1950* (5 vols. to date; Caracas, Banco Central de Venezuela, 1969-). A full scale historical bibliography for Colombia would be welcome but does not yet exist. Bibliographic landmarks of importance on the colonial period are: Agustín Millares Carlo's *Estudio bibliográfico de los archivos venezolanos y extranjeros de interés para la historia de Venezuela* (see *HLAS 36:2453*) and Torciso Higuera's very fine history of *La imprenta en Colombia* (see *HLAS 36:2814*).

There are neither one-volume accounts nor comprehensive syntheses of known sources and existing studies on colonial Venezuela but see: the new edition of vol. 1 of Federico Brito Figueroa's *Historia económica y social* (*HLAS 38:2960*); José Sucre Reyes' *La Capitanía General* (*HLAS 34:2216*); and appropriate entries in Donna Keyse Rudolph and G.A. Rudolph's *Historical dictionary of Venezuela* (*HLAS 34:2573*). And in lieu of general histories of Nueva Granada, Germán Colmenares' excellent *Historia económica y social de Colombia: 1537-1719* (*HLAS 38:3049*), and Fernando Díaz Díaz's competent if routine *Historia documental de Colombia: siglos XVI, XVII y XVIII* (*HLAS 38:3051*). More or less satisfactory in-depth coverage, incorporating recent scholarship, on the other hand, may be found in Guillermo Morón's five-volume *Historia de Venezuela* (*HLAS 34:2173*), and in the Academia Colombiana de Historia's yet to be completed *Historia extensa* (Bogotá, 1965-). On the colonial period so far only the following volumes have appeared: Manuel Lucena Salmoral's *Presidentes de capa y espada: 1628-1654* (*HLAS 36:2539*); Sergio Elías Ortiz's *Presidentes de capa y espada: 1654-1719* (see item 3147a) and *El Virreinato*, t. 2, *1753-1810* (*HLAS 36:2540*); and the first two volumes of *Historia eclesiástica* both by Father Juan Manuel Pacheco (see *HLAS 36:2541*, and in this volume, item 3148).

The historical demography of colonial Colombia has been much more cultivated on the whole as well as of late than that of colonial Venezuela, both per se and in conjunction with economic and social history. On Venezuela, the only major work in this genre to have been published during the last decade is Lombardi's demographic and geographic study and workbook on the late colonial period, *People and places in colonial Venezuela* (item 3113). Also noteworthy are Graziano Gasparini's history of the growth of *Caracas colonial* (*HLAS 36:2505*), and Bishop Martí's *visita* (*HLAS 34:2195*), a monumental source which remains to be exploited.

On colonial Colombia at least seven important books have appeared, having to do with population history in one way or another: Germán Colmenares' above mentioned *Historia económica y social* and his earlier monographs *Encomienda y población en la Provincia de Pamplona: 1549-1650* (*HLAS 34:2221*) and *La Provincia de Tunja en el Nuevo Reino de Granada: ensayo de historia social, 1539-1800* (*HLAS 36:2535*); Darío M. Fajardo's *El régimen de la encomienda en la Provincia de Vélez: población indígena y economía* (*HLAS 32:2166*); Jorge Palacios Preciado's *La trata de negros por Cartagena de Indias* (*HLAS 36:2542*); Julián Bautista Ruiz Rivera's *Fuentes para la demografía de Nueva Granada* (*HLAS 38:3067*) and his Ph.D. dissertation *Encomienda y mita en Nueva Granada en el siglo XVII* (item 3156).

Economic history, on the other hand, seems to be more in vogue in Venezuela than in Colombia, at least in terms of major monographs and publication of sources. Eduardo Arcila Farías has brought out revised and augmented editions of his basic *Economía colonial de Venezuela* (item 3100) and *El régimen de la encomienda* (*HLAS 38:3012*), and Julio de Armas is the author of a substantial history of *La ganadería* (*HLAS 38:3013*). Many of the volumes in the series entitled "Fuentes para la Historia Colonial de Venezuela" contain critical sources on one or more aspects of the economy, but undoubtedly the most important in this regard are: Antonio Arellano Moreno's compilation *Documentos para la historia económica* (*HLAS 34:2179*); Manuel Nunes Dias' *El Real Consulado de Caracas* (*HLAS 36:2500*); and Ermila Troconís de Veracoechea's *Las obras pías en la Iglesia colonial* (*HLAS 34:2179*). Also important, although published separately is Enrique Bernardo Nuñez's compilation of documents on *cacao* (*HLAS 36:2516*).

When turning to Colombia, the works of Colmenares come to mind. In addition to his *Historia económica y social*, we owe to his productivity and rigorous research the following studies: *Haciendas de los jesuitas en el Nuevo Reino de Granada* (*HLAS 38:3048*), his recent *Cali: terratenientes, mineros y comerciantes* (see item 3131), and together with Fajardo and Melo, *Fuentes coloniales para la historia del trabajo* (*HLAS 32:2163*). There are, moreover, several important articles on Colombia by other authors (which lack of space prevents us from mentioning) as well as the titles already cited in demographic history.

Venezuelan and Colombian scholars appear to have been about equally interested in social history during the course of the last decade, not that this genre is in any danger of being depleted. In addition to several of the works already cited, which could be classified just as well under social as well as demographic and/or economic history, the following merit attention: Guillermo Boza's *Estructura y cambio en Venezuela colonial* (*HLAS 38:3016*); Jesús María G. López Ruiz's *Hernández de Serpa y su "hueste" de 1569* (*HLAS 38:3028*); Ambrosio Pereira's *Historia de la organización de pueblos antiguos de Venezuela* (*HLAS 36:2519*); Troconis de Veracoechea's *Documentos para el estudio de los esclavos negros* (*HLAS 34:2218*), the introduction to which constitutes a full-scale monograph and her recent Ph.D. dissertation, *Historia de El Tocuyo colonial* (Caracas, Univ. Central de Venezuela, 1977). Also worthy of attention are Margarita González's *El resguardo en el Nuevo Reino de Granada* (item 3135a); Jaime Jaramillo Uribe's *Ensayos sobre historia social colombiana* (*HLAS 38:3054*); Néstor Meza Villalobos' monumental *Historia de la política indígena del Estado Español en América: las Antillas; el Distrito de la Audiencia de Santa Fe* (item 3145); and Inés Pinto Escobar's *La rebelión del común* (item 3151).

Surprisingly, the history of institutions seems to have been neglected of late in Colombia, to the extent that I have not seen a single major study. In Venezuela, on the other hand, the study of institutions is in renaissance. In first place are the 1972 and 1975 *Memorias* of the I and II Congresos Venezolanos de Historia held in 1971 and 1974, the important contributions to which are noticed in *HLAS 36* and in this *HLAS* (see item 3094). The first congress was given over largely to cabildos, and the second to *visitas* and *residencias*. Running close second are the 1970 and 1975 *Memorias* of the I and II Congresos Venezolanos de Historia Eclesiástica of 1969 and 1972. The participants in the first Congress of Church History examined published and archival sources, and those in the second, concentrated on the interrelated themes of missionaires and proselytization as reported upon in *HLAS 38:3022*. Another important study is José Llavador Mira's *La gobernación de Venezuela en el siglo XVII* (*HLAS 34:2204*).

Venezuelans have also been more active than Colombians in publishing sources, but then this is largely due to the fact that the Venezuelan Academia Nacional de la Historia as well as other entities are much better endowed than their Colombian counterparts. The series entitled "Fuentes para la Historia Colonial de Venezuela," for example, now totals at least 74 volumes (i.e., as of 1977). On Colombia one would be hard pressed to cite 10 major collections of documents on the colonial period in as many years; in fact, I have seen only seven: vols. 3 and 4 of the *Archivo epistolar del sabio naturalista Don José Celestino Mutís* (item 3138); Roberto Arrazola's anthology on *Palenque* (*HLAS 38:3042*); Díaz Díaz's *Historia documental* (*HLAS 38:3051*); *Documentos coloniales originados en el Santo Oficio del Tribunal de la Inquisición de Cartagena de Indias* (*HLAS 36:2536*); Juan Friede's *Fuentes documentales para la historia del Nuevo Reino de Granada desde la instalación de la Real Audiencia de Santafé* (eight vols. to date; Bogotá, Banco Popular, 1975-1976), which cover the second half of the 16th century; and Ruiz Rivera's compendium of *Fuentes para la demografía*.

Few foreign scholars appear to take an interest in colonial Venezuela, at least only a handful have published during the last decade. These include only two North Americans, Stephanie Blank (see *HLAS 36:2492* and *HLAS 38:3015*) and John V. Lombardi and Spaniards such as the Franciscans Lino Gómez Canedo and Odilo Gómez Parente. On the other hand, no less than 10 North Americans have published on colonial Colombia in recent years: Maurice P. Brungardt (see *HLAS 38:3045*); David L. Chandler (*HLAS 38:3046*); Gary W. Graff (item 3137); Allan J. Kuethe (*HLAS 34:2217-2218* and *HLAS 38:3055*) and *Military reform and society in New Granada: 1773-1808* (Gainesville, Univ. of Florida Press, 1978); Peter Marzahl (*HLAS 38:3060*); Norman A. Meiklejohn (*HLAS 38:3061*); the late John Leddy Phelan, *The people and the King: the Comunero Revolution in Colombia, 1781* (Madison, Univ. of Wisconsin Press, 1978); G. Earl Sanders (item 3158); William F. Sharp (*HLAS 38:3069* and in this volume, item 3159). And one could list just as many, if not more Spaniards, including the newcomers María del Carmen Borrego Pla (items 3129-3130), Trinidad Miranda Vásquez (item 3146); and of course also Ruiz Rivera. Why North American and Spanish historians should be more interested in colonial Colombia than in Venezuela, and why hardly any scholars of other nationalities appear to be concerned with either country are intriguing questions. Space limitations preclude answering them here.

In retrospect, we still lack a guide to the historiography of Colombia, and a handbook on its repositories. No good succinct histories of colonial Venezuela and Colombia, let alone of their entire past, exist in either Spanish or English. At least none have come to our attention. The demographic history of Venezuela continues to be ignored for the most part. That of Colombia is much better known, a synthetic account of which would be helpful, as would also manuals on the historical geography of both countries.

The economic history of Venezuela is much better known than that of Colombia and continues to receive more attention. Nonetheless, no major monographs have been published on the agricultural sector, especially on the emergence of the great estate. It is encouraging that Venezuelan and Colombian scholars as well as of course several foreigners have been researching different aspects of colonial society, but much more remains to be done than is possible to mention here.

No doubt 10 years from now much more and better work will have appeared along these and other lines, especially as the research has been or is being done, in large part by scholars who emerged during the preceding decade. Also, and this is another point that could be pursued elsewhere, most of the younger Venezuelan and Colombian scholars are professionally trained and in the process of training others. In 1968, the history of colonial Venezuela and Colombia was still largely unknown. As of 1978, much has been achieved but far more remains to be done.

GENERAL

Bronner, Fred. Peruvian encomenderos in 1630: elite circulation and consolidation. See item 3195.

3092. Céspedes, Guillermo. América Latina colonial hasta 1650. Mexico, Secretaría de Educación Pública, 1976. 206 p. (SepSetentas, 260)

Second Spanish language ed. of *HLAS 38:2264*.

3093. Coleti, Giandomenico. Diccionario histórico-geográfico de la América Meridional. Bogotá, Banco de la República, 1974-1975. 2 v. (493 p.) (Continuous pagination) facsims., map (Archivo de la economía nacional, 35)

Welcome reedition in Spanish translation of *Dizionario storico-geografico dell' America Meridionale*, originally published Venice 1771 and long unavailable. Major, still useful source upon which Antonio de Alcedo Herrera relied extensively in compiling his *Diccionario geográfico de la América Meridional*. Coleti (1727-98) was Italian Jesuit who spent 10 years in Quito prior to Order's expulsion.

3094. Congreso Venezolano de Historia, II, Caracas, 1974. Memoria. Caracas, Academia Nacional de Historia 1975. 3 v. (518, 555, 515 p.) bibl., plates, tables.

Publishes papers delivered at this congress mostly on administrative reviews (*visitas* and *residencias*), audiencias and lesser tribunals. Studies amplify and clarify our knowledge of them in colonial Venezuela and other parts of Spanish America. Individual contributions of significance are annotated separately, and entered under each author's name.

3095. Reig Satorres, José. Ordenanzas de la Real Audiencia de Quito: 1563 (Anuario Histórico Jurídico Ecuatoriano [Corporación de Estudios y Publicaciones, Quito] 4, 1976, p. 311-445)

Comparative study of 1563 ordinances and those issued upon erection of earlier audiencias. Of interest to legal and institutional historians.

3096. Szászdi, Adám. Spain and American treasure: the depreciation of silver and monetary exchange in the Viceroyalty of Lima, 1550-1610 (The Journal of European Economic History [Rome] 4:2, Fall 1975, p. 429-458, tables)

Discusses fluctuating value of gold and silver coinage in 16th-century Peru, especially in Audiencia of Quito. Does not include summary tables.

3097. Vigneras, Louis-André. The discovery of South America and the Andalusian voyages. Chicago, Ill., The Univ. of Chicago Press *for* the Newberry Library, 1976. 170 p., bibl., maps (Studies in the history of discoveries)

Rescues from neglect 11 voyages of 1499-1505/06 to Spanish Main, wrongly thought of as "minor" until now. Vigneras demonstrates their importance through fresh materials uncovered by him in Archivo de Protocolos in Seville, details financial role played by Seville's merchants. Fine example of how a diligent historian can offer further insights into a much studied topic.

3098. Zúñiga, Neptalí. Historia de la independencia de América Latina: movimientos precursores. Quito, Editorial Universitaria, 1975. 2 v. (671 p.) (Continuous pagination)

Title of work stems from author's unshakable belief that movements for independence, at least in Viceroyalty of Peru, began with Gonzalo Pizarro's rebellion. Zúñiga's beliefs notwithstanding, specialists will find some new data, mostly from the Archivo Histórico Nacional in Madrid, on conquest and civil wars of Peru, especially on Quito in this otherwise routine work.

CARACAS

3099. Arcila Farías, Eduardo. La administración de la Renta del Tabaco en Venezuela (EEHA/AEA, 31, 1974, p. 55-77, tables)

Examines establishment of Royal Tobacco Monopoly in Captaincy General of Caracas, its administration, monopoly as source of revenue, and question of profits.

3100. ———. Economía colonial de Venezuela. 2. ed. Caracas, Italgráfica, 1973. 2 v. (360, 347 p.) bibl., tables.

Revised and augmented ed. of basic work (1. ed. Mexico, 1946) on economic history of colonial period to which Arcila Farías has contributed substantially in this and other studies. Based on many years of research in Venezuela, Mexico, US and Spain.

3101. ———. Establecimiento del estanco del tabaco (IEH/A, 1, 1974, p. 7-31)

Primarily concerned with difficulties encountered by Intendant of Caracas and subordinates in establishing Royal Tobacco Monopoly in several provinces of Captaincy General. Appendix publishes royal cedula of erection 24 June 1777.

3102. Arellano Moreno, Antonio. Los planteamientos economicos del Visitador Chávez y Mendoza en 1784 (*in* Congreso Venezolano de Historia, II, Caracas, 1974. Memoria [see item 3094] v. 1, p. 89-108)

Brief review of the 1783-84 general inspection of Cumaná prov. by Luis de Chávez y Mendoza, Dean of Audiencia of Santo Domingo, and of economic reforms proposed by him.

3103. Briceño Perozo, Mario. El Juez Visitador Alonso Vásquez de Cisneros (*in* Congreso Venezolano de Historia, II, Caracas, 1974, Memoria [see item 3094] v. 1, p. 151-177)

Informative albeit simplistic appreciation of Vásquez de Cisneros' 1619-20 inspection of apparently never before visited Partido de Mérida, at least not by an oidor. See also item 3108.

3104. Canedo, Lino Gómez. Notas de historia caraqueña: algo más sobre la fundación de un colegio de la Compañía de Jesús en Caracas, 1735-1736 (UCAB/M, 5, 1976, p. 1049-1052)

Explicit in title, this brief article consists of additional notes on latent foundation of Jesuit school in Caracas, based on continuing archival research.

3105. ———. San Francisco de Caracas: su papel en la historia de Venezuela (VANH/B, 59:233, enero/marzo 1976, p. 47-62)

Lecture delivered during IV Centennial of foundation of Franciscan Convent in Caracas, in which Father Canedo ably summarizes its role in history of Venezuela, especially Caracas from 1575 through late 19th century.

3106. ——— *ed.* Un importante documento para la historia de Guayana (VANH/B, 59:236, oct./dic. 1976, p. 767-775)

Publishes informative 1812 document by Bishop elect José Ventura Cabello on state of Diocesis of Guayana.

3107. Carrocera, Buenaventura de. Aportación indigenista cultural y civilizadora del misionero y asimilación por parte del indio venezolano (*in* Jornadas Americanistas, III, Valladolid, Spain, 1974. Estudios sobre política indigenista española en América [see item 2298] v. 2, p. 87-121)

On one hand, useful summary of Augustinian, Dominican, Franciscan, Jesuit and Capuchin missionary endeavours in what is now Venezuela during colonial period. On other, defense of same against anthropologists' criticisms.

3108. Contreras D., Milagros. Aportación al estudio de las visitas de audiencias (*in* Congreso Venezolano de Historia, II, Caracas, 1974. Memoria [see item 3094] v. 1, p. 179-221)

Excellent two-part study: pt. 1, which offers new, highly suggestive classification of *visitas*; pt. 2, is detailed case study of 1619-20 and 1655-57 inspections of Mérida district and results thereof.

3109. Duviols, Jean-Paul *ed.* Pascual Martínez Marco, "Viaje y Derrotero de la Ciudad de Cumaná a Santa Fé de Bogotá, 1749:" récit inédit (UTIEH/C, 26, 1976, p. 19-33, table)

Publishes excerpts from 1749 Spanish lieutenant's manuscript diary recently discovered in Paris bookstore. Describes journey from Cumaná up Orinoco to Bogotá. Entire diary deserves to be published as it is rich in botanical, ethnographic, and geographic observations.

3110. Giménez de Arcondo, Floraligia *ed.* Casos en la Real Audiencia de Caracas: homicidios y robos (*in* Congreso Venezolano de Historia, II, Caracas,

1974. Memoria [see item 3094] v. 1, p. 433-472, table)

Publishes and summarizes tabularly 12 sentences issued by Audiencia of Caracas between its establishment in 1795 and 1808, six of which were for homicides, others for theft. Of interest to social as well as legal historians.

3111. Gómez Parente, Odilo. Los franciscanos en Venezuela durante el siglo XVI (PF/AIA, 36:142/143, abril/sept. 1976, p. 243-300)

Fifth and final part of minute study of initial activities of Franciscans in Santa Cruz Prov. and Caracas upon their arrival in late 16th century. For pts. 1/2, see *HLAS 38:3027*; pts. 3/4 have not been seen and apparently appeared in 1975.

3112. ———. Ilustrísimo padre Fray Juan Ramos de Lora: fundador de la Universidad de los Andes (UCAB/M, 3, 1974, 473-591)

Details and documents life and career of founder of Colegio de San Buenaventura de Mérida, now Univ. of the Andes, and events leading up to its 1785 foundation.

3113. Lombardi, John V. People and places in colonial Venezuela. Maps and figures by Cathryn L. Lombardi. Bloomington, Indiana Univ. Press, 1976. 484 p., illus., maps, tables.

Basic source book on population history. Pt. 1, "The Population of the Bishopric of Caracas in the Late Colonial Period," describes Venezuela as it was in 18th and early 19th centuries, discusses demographic sources, especially census returns, analyzes such variables as urban size, "race," sex, marriage patterns and family size, and offers case study of demography of San Carlos de Austria during period in question. Pt. 2, "A Workbook in the Historical Demography of Venezuela: The Bishopric of Caracas, 1771-1838" publishes parish-by-parish in six computer print out tables, figures on which pt. 1 is and future studies are to be based. Altogether most significant contribution to late colonial history of Venezuela in recent years, and important benchmark in quantification of Latin American historiography. See also exchange between Lombardi and Robert McCaa in *Latin American Research Review* (13:1, 1978, p. 195-204).

3114. López Cantos, Angel. Don Francisco de Saavedra: segundo intendente de Caracas. Prólogo de Francisco Morales Padrón. Sevilla, Escuela de Estudios Hispano-Americanos, 1973. 170 p., bibl. (Publicación, 211)

Original senior thesis on the intendancy (1783-88) of reform minded Saavedra. Mostly given over to examination of coeval economy, which Saavedra attempted to stimulate. Data are useful but analysis is weak.

3115. Pardo, Isaac J. Esta tierra de gracia: imagen de Venezuela en el siglo XVI. 3. ed. Caracas, Consejo Municipal del Distrito Federal Caracas, 1975. 178 p., bibl., illus.

Although not scholarly in usual sense, work is competently documented and exceptionally well written attempt to evoke essence of 16th-century Venezuela. In brief, a literary, almost lyrical portrait of early colony. Originally published 1955, text has not been altered but notes and bibliography have been updated.

3116. Ramos Pérez, Demetrio. El presidente de la Real Audiencia de Caracas, en su fase inicial, y su intento de concentración de todos los poderes (*in* Congreso Venezolano de Historia, II, Caracas, 1974. Memoria [see item 3094] v. 2, p. 465-498)

Administrative reforms of later Bourbons were more complex than most scholars realize. They involved appointing separate men to offices of Viceroy or Governor and Captain General, Intendant, and occasionally Regent President of Audiencia. In this enlightening case study, Ramos Pérez examines clashes between these officials and attempts by Governor Captain General to regain full power in Caracas in 1780s and 1790s. Parenthetically, this critical issue is in need of clarification for other audiencias as well, in some of which it was not unusual for one man to wear all four hats.

3117. Reixach Vilá, Pedro. La Provincia de la Nueva Cataluña en el siglo XVII (VANH/B, 59:233, enero/marzo 1976, p. 132-159, bibl.)

Documented chronology of former Province of Nueva Cataluña, whose capital was Nueva Barcelona and which had ephemeral existence (1631-54).

3118. Rengifo, Diana. La gobernación del canario Marcos de Betancourt, en la provincia de Venezuela, 1716-1720: el problema del contrabando (VANH/B, 59:235, julio/sept. 1976, p. 498-516, bibl.)

Interesting example of extent to which peninsular officials were subject and sympathetic to colonial interests. Venezuelan commerce became adversely affected by War of Spanish Succession and open to contraband anyway, Governor Betancourt opted to regulate illicit trade rather than attempt to suppress it.

Rey Fajardo, José del. Apuntes para una historia de la cartografía jesuítica en Venezuela. See *HLAS 39:5626*.

3119. ———. Filósofos y teólogos jesuitas en la Venezuela colonial (UCAB/M, 3, 1974, p. 7-51)

Well documented bibliographic notes on Jesuit philosophers and theologians assigned to or born in colonial Venezuela. Important contribution to history of higher education in Venezuela, indeed of colonial Spanish America in general.

3120. Robinson, David J. The syndicate system of the Catalán Capuchins in colonial southeast Venezuela (PAIGH/H, 79, enero/junio 1975, p. 63-76, table)

Detailed examination of Capuchin missionary activities, especially their economic aspects, among Caroni Indians in Venezuelan Guayana during second half of 18th century. Based on field and archival research.

3121. Rodríguez Leal, Edgard. Fray Antonio Caulín: ideología e historia. Caracas, Univ. Central de Venezuela, Facultad de Humanidades y Educación, Instituto de Antropología e Historia, 1975. 203 p., bibl.

Routine study of philosophy of history of Father Antonio Caulín (1719-1802) as manifest in his *Historia corográfica, natural y evangélica de la Nueva Andalucía, provincias de Cumaná, Guayana y vertientes del Río Orinoco*, finished in 1759 but not published until 1779.

3122. Solano, Francisco de. Nivel cultural, teatro y diversiones colectivas en las ciudades de la Venezuela colonial: 1747-1760 (VANH/B, 59:233, enero/Marzo 1976, p. 63-102, facsims., table)

Interesting study of theatre and popular diversions in mid-18th century Venezuela. Author has been able to identify 19 plays performed then and there, all of which were Spanish comedies from previous or "golden century." Solano also examines celebrations in honor of ascensions to throne of Ferdinand VI and Charles III, examples of which he gives in appendix. Significant contribution to social and cultural history.

3123. Tosta, Virgilio. Dos juicios de residencia en la ciudad de Barinas y su jurisdicción, provincia de Mérida (*in* Congreso Venezolano de Historia, II, Caracas, 1974. Memoria [see item 3094] v. 3, p. 235-256)

Emphasizes importance of economic and social data to be found in administrative reviews as exemplified by 1681 and 1687 *residencias* of Barinas' governors.

3124. Troconis de Veracoechea, Ermila. La "Limpieza de sangre" a través de la Real Audiencia de Caracas (*in* Congreso Venezolano de Historia, II, Caracas, 1974. Memoria [see item 3094] v. 3, p. 353-385)

Highly original and informative paper on "limpieza de sangre" one of most interesting social phenomena in colonial Spanish America, by one of Venezuelas' leading researchers. Also deals with growing problem of foundlings (*expósitos*) from whom Crown removed stigma of illegitimacy in 1790s by declaring them legally "white" regardless of caste.

3125. ———. El río y la terra en el Tocuyo colonial (IEH/A, 1, 1974, p. 33-45)

Overview of River Tocuyo's role in history of Nuestra Señora de la Concepción del Tocuyo and its district. Appetizer as it were to author's recent Ph.D. dissertation, *Historia del Tocuyo colonial* (Caracas, Univ. Central de Venezuela, 1977), which promises to be one of most detailed and soundly documented contributions to local history ever produced in Venezuela.

3126. ———. Tres cofradías de negros en la Iglesia de San Mauricio en Caracas (UCAB/M, 5, 1976, p. 339-376, bibl.)

Fascinating social and economic study of three black religious brotherhoods; San Juan Bautista (founded 1611), Nuestra Señora de Guía (1701) and Santísimo Sacramento (1751), sponsored by Caracas' San Mauricio parish (today Santa Capilla). See also author's "Las Cofradías del Montón, en Caracas" in *Boletín de la Academia Nacional de la Historia* (Caracas, 55:220, oct./dic. 1972).

3127. Venezuela. Academia Nacional de la Historia. Departamento de Investigaciones. Investigación sobre los juicios de residencia en Venezuela (*in* Congreso Venezolano de Historia, II Caracas, 1974. Memoria [see item 3094] v. 1, p. 223-286, bibl.)

Reports on ongoing research into administrative reviews in colonial Venezuela. Lists archival materials and published studies and sources being consulted, which other researchers will also find useful.

3128. Vila, Pablo. Gestas de Juan Orpin en su fundación de Barcelona y defensa de Oriente. Prólogo de Carlos Augusto León. Caracas, Univ. Central de Venezuela, Dirección de Cultura, 1975. 501 p., maps, plates.

Very readable, semischolarly account of foundation of Nueva Barcelona on Caribbean coast of Venezuela in 1638 by Catalan Juan Orpin.

NUEVA GRANADA

Alvarez Díaz, Enrique. Herencia colonial en la vida rural colombiana. See item 269.

3129. Borrego Pla, María del Carmen. El indio de encomienda en Cartagena de Indias: siglo XVI (*in* Jornadas Americanistas, III, Valladolid, Spain, 1974. Estudios sobre política indigenista española en América [see item 2298] v. 2, p. 419-425, table)

Pithy examination of difficult to document subject: exploitation of encomienda Indians during 16th century in Cartagena de Indias district, when and where they appear to have been utilized mostly as *bogas*.

3130. ———. Palenques de negros en Cartagena de Indias a fines del siglo XVII. Prólogo de Luis Navarro García. Sevilla, Escuela de Estudios Hispano-Americanos, 1973. 140 p., maps (Publicación, 216)

Well documented senior thesis on runaway slave problem in late 17th-century Colombia. Details excursions made against rebel slave communities (*palenques*) and examines polemic provoked by Royal Cedula of 23 Aug. 1691 which ordered pacific reduction and manumission of these rebel slaves.

3131. Colmenares, Germán. Cali: terratenientes, mineros y comerciantes, siglo XVIII. Cali, Colombia, Univ. de Valle, División de Humanidades, 1975. 263 p., maps, tables.

First scholarly attempt to reconstruct economy and society of Santiago de Cali and district during colonial period, especially 18th century. Drawing on considerable research in Spain, Bogotá and local notarial registers—critical data in which are abstracted in appendix (p. 205-263)—and employing newer approaches to past (prosopographic as well as quantitative analysis), Colmenares first traces evolution and development of landed estates in Valley from early 17th century through mid-19th, paying special attention to slaves and problem of credit or financing. He then takes up mining and commerce, and finally city, its social and political structures. One of most important contributions ever penned on Colombia's socioeconomic as well as regional history by one of country's leading practitioners of both genres.

Colombia. Instituto Geográfico Agustín Codazzi. República de Colombia: mapa histórico-político, descubrimiento, conquista e independencia. See *HLAS 39:5890*.

Duviols, Jean-Paul *ed.* Pascual Martínez Marco, "Viaje y Derrotero de la Ciudad de Cumaná a Santa Fe de Bogotá, 1749." See item 3109.

3132. Eugenio Martínez, María Angeles. El puerto y camino de Carare en Nueva Granada (EEHA/AEA, 30, 1973, p. 263-294, map)

Detailed examination of Canare's role as way station or riverine port between Bogotá and Barranquilla in 16th century. Aslo sheds considerable light on problems of communication and transportation in general between interior and Caribbean during those early years.

3133. ———. Tributación indígena en el Nuevo Reino de Granada: siglo XVI (*in* Jornadas Americanistas, III, Valladolid, Spain, 1974. Estudios sobre política indigenista española en América [see item 2298] v. 2, p. 401-417, bibl.)

Systematic exposition of tribute schedules and abuses in their collection in Nueva Granada from inauguration of Santa Fé Audiencia 1550 through end of century.

3134. Fernández, Matilde and **Norma Rubio.** Catálogo cronológico de documentos sobre los Panches, existentes en el Archivo Histórico Nacional: materiales para una etnohistoria Panche (PUJ/UH, 3, julio 1972, p. 229-233)

Useful chronological list, spanning years 1568-1807, of 30 documents in Bogotá's Archivo Historico Nacional on Panches, highland Indians whose history remains to be written.

3135. Fernández de Piedrahita, Lucas. Noticia historial de las conquistas del Nuevo Reino de Granada. Prólogo de Sergio Elías Ortíz. Bogotá, Ministerio de Educación Nacional, Instituto Colombiano de Cultura Hispánica, 1973. 2 v. (830 p.) (Continuous pagination) facsim., plate (Ediciones de la *Revista Ximénez de Quesada*, 31/32)

Welcome reedition of basic but heretofore scarce chronicle on New Granada's conquest by native son, Bishop Fernández de Piedrahita (1624-88) who did considerable original research. *Noticia historial* not only contains data on conquest not available elsewhere—among other accounts he had access to lost original of Jiménez de Quesada—but also on early ethnography of Colombia.

3135a. González, Margarita. El resguardo en el Nuevo Reino de Granada.

Bogotá, Univ. Nacional de Colombia, Dirección de Divulgación Cultural, 1970. 196 p.

Two-part study on Indian held lands, especially those guaranteed by Crown (i.e., those to which titles were issued and/or recognized). Pt. 1 is case study of *resguardos* in colonial provinces of Santa Fé and Tunja, where they were more important and numerous than elsewhere. Pt. 2 (p. 81-196) publishes basic documentation on which pt. 1 is based.

3136. **González Luna, María Dolores.** La política reformista en los resguardos en el siglo XVIII (*in* Jornadas Americanistas, III, Valladolid, Spain, 1974. Estudios sobre política indigenista española en América [see item 2298] v. 3, p. 201-219, bibl.)

General review of adverse effects of Bourbon instigated land reforms on *resguardos* or lands reserved for Indians since 1591, measures which resulted in their virtual suppression in highlands. Also includes notes on resguardos in Caribbean lowlands where their history was not surprisingly different. See also items 3144 and 3152.

3137. **Graff, Gary W.** Spanish parishes in colonial New Granada: their role in town building on the Spanish-American frontier (AAFH/TAM, 33:2, Oct. 1976, p. 336-351)

Important contribution to little known history of lesser communities in late 17th and 18th-century Colombia. Graff examines role of rural parishes in emergence of new towns. Also informs us about brotherhoods or sodalities (*cofradías*), on which Graff wrote his dissertation and which merits publication.

3138. **Hernández de Alba, Guillermo** *ed.* and *comp.* Archivo epistolar del sabio naturalista Don José Celestino Mutís. Bogotá, Instituto Colombiano de Cultura Hispánica [and] Editorial Kelley, 1975. 2 v. (431, 334 p.) (Col. José Celestino Mutís, 5/6)

Publishes bulk of correspondence addressed to Mutís, head of late 18th-century botanical expedition to New Granada. Includes letters sent 1760-1808 from France, Sweden, Spain, Mexico, Quito, and New Granada itself by many well and lesser known individuals. Mutís' own letters appear in vols. 1/2 (published 1968, see *HLAS 32:2184*). Altogether highly informative compendium of sources on late colonial viceroyalty, Royal Botanical Expedition, and Mutís himself.

3139. **Lucena Salmoral, Manuel.** Los diarios anónimos sobre el ataque de Vernon a Cartagena existentes en Colombia: su correlación y posibles autores (EEHA/AEA, 30, 1973, p. 337-469)

Fascinating critical analysis of eight diaries published between 1884-1968 on Cartagena's 1741 defense. Author demonstrated there are only three known diaries, others being different versions, delineates flaws in transcriptions and publishes new literal version of "Diario de lo Acaezido en la ymbación Echa por los Yngleses á la Plaza de Cartagena de Yndias desde 13 de Marzo de 1741, hasta 20 de Mayo del Mismo Año (p. 387-469). Its importance as source aside, one notes lesson drawn from this, that published sources are not always faithful to originals.

3140. ———. El indofeudalismo Chibcha, como explicación de la fácil conquista quesadista (*in* Jornadas Americanistas, III, Valladolid, Spain, 1974. Estudios sobre política indigenista española en América [see item 2298] v. 1, p. 111-160)

Cogent reexamination of nature of conquest of New Granada. Author argues that organization of Mwiska or highland Chibcha into two major confederations (those of the Zipa and Zaque) facilitated conquest. Also demonstrates that Jiménez de Quesada attempted to take lasting advantage of situation by founding two Spanish cities (Santafé de Bogotá and Tunja) as centers for exploitation of Zipa and Zaque, jurisdictions which were to be respected.

3141. **Mateos, Francisco** *ed.* Constituciones sinodales de Sante Fé de Bogotá: 1576 (ISTM/MH, 31:93, sept./dic. 1974, p. 289-368)

Publishes literal transcriptions of 1576 "Cathecismo" of Archbishop Zapata de Cárdenas, one of earliest such ordinances issued on proselytization of Indians. Critical source on early missionary activities in Colombia and last in series of texts of early Councils and Synods (barring discovery of others) which Father Mateos intends to publish.

3142. **Matta Rodríguez-Caso, Enrique de la.** La "rebelión" de Diego de los Ríos: una página inédita en la historia de Cartagena de Indias (EEHA/AEA, 31, 1974, p. 955-971)

Narrative account of little known episode in Cartagena's history or Governor Diego de los Ríos' attempt to elude trial for having failed to ward off French attack and port's capture in 1697.

3143. **Mesa, Carlos E.** Concilios y sínodos en el Nuevo Reino de Granada, hoy Colombia (ISTM/MH, 31:92, mayo/agosto 1974, p. 129-171)

Meaty account of seven diocesan Synods realized in New Granada, first of which was held in Popayán in

1555 and last Cartagena 1789. One of more important points made by Father Mesa is that Church legislators in Colombia were influenced not only by Trent but also by first Mexican and Limeño Councils, decrees of which were "más adaptados a la realidad americana."

3144. Meza Lopehandia, Juan N. Racionalización de la situación del indio en Nueva Granada hacia 1780 (*in* Jornadas Americanistas, III, Valladolid, Spain, 1974. Estudios sobre política indigenista española en América [see item 2298] v. 2, p. 203-224, table)

Careful examination of indigenist aspects of general inspection of Visitador General Francisco Gutierrez de Piñeres, who brought to halt albeit too late for most part, Moreno y Escandón's consolidation of Indian pueblos (i.e., suppression of *resguardos*). See also items 3136 and 3152.

3145. Meza Villalobos, Néstor. Historia de la política indígena del Estado Español en América: las Antillas; el Distrito de la Audiencia de Santa Fé. Santiago, Univ. de Chile, 1975. 1059 p., maps.

Minute and massive reexamination of efforts actual and legislative taken by Crown and its agents to preserve and protect Indians in Antilles and Audiencia of Santa Fé de Bogotá during first half of colonial period. Also details Indian demography, economy and society of 16th and 17th centuries, and hence serves as primer for ethnohistorians as well as colonialists.

3146. Miranda Vásquez, Trinidad. La Gobernación de Santa Marta: 1570-1670. Prólogo de Luis Navarro García. Sevilla, Escuela de Estudios Hispano-Americanos, 1976. 188 p. facsims., map, tables (Publicación, 232)

Original senior thesis on first century and half of largely neglected region, Governorship of Santa Marta on northeast coast of Colombia. Contributes much new data on native populations, demography, trade, mining and encomiendas as well as administration and defense.

3147. Ordenanças del señor doctor Antonio González y del señor Miguel de Ybarra (PUJ/UH, 3, julio 1972, p. 243-260)

Literal transcription of 1593 ordinances issued to *corregidores de indios* on administration of Indian pueblos and treatment of inhabitants.

3147a. Ortíz, Sergio Elías. Nuevo Reino de Granada: Real Audiencia y presi- dentes. t. 3, Presidentes de capa y espada: 1654-1719. Bogotá, Academia Colombiana de Historia [and] Ediciones Lerner, 1966. 423 p., bibl., facsims., maps, plate (Historia extensa de Colombia, 3)

Balanced account of Colombia's history from mid-17th century through erection of first Viceroyalty of New Granada. Although organized chronologically by presidencies, there is substantial coverage of wide variety of events other than administrative, as for example alcoholism and natural disasters. Based on considerable archival research is Spain and Colombia as well as appropriate literature. For vol. 3, t. 2 of *Historia extensa de Colombia*, see *HLAS 36:2539* (first tome not yet available).

3148. Pacheco, Juan Manuel. Historia eclesiástica. t. 2, La consolidación de la iglesia: siglo XVII. Bogotá, Academia Colombiana de Historia [and] Ediciones Lerner, 1975. 740 p., bibl. (Historia extensa de Colombia, 13)

Vol. 2 of projected five or six vol. history of Church in Colombia (for review of vol. 1, see *HLAS 36:2541*). Covers 17th century and observes much the same plan. Details ecclesiastical developments within Archdiocesis of Santafé de Bogotá and Dioceses of Cartagena, Santa Marta, and Popayan, takes up activities of secular and religious clergy, and relates missionary endeavours of latter among Negro slaves and frontier Indians. Exceptionally well researched.

3149. ———. La ilustración en el Nuevo Reino (UCAB/M, 4, 1975, p. 9-188, bibl.)

Original monograph on arrival to, diffusion in, and impact of Enlightenment in Colombia, to which movement several native *pensadores* and naturalists contributed considerably. Well balanced, informative contribution to history of ideas, limited by no means to Mutís, Nariño and Caldas.

3150. Pérez de Tudela y Bueso, Juan. Sobre la resistencia contra la visita: el caso del licenciado Monzón en el Nuevo Reino de Granada (*in* Congreso Venezolano de Historia, II, Caracas, 1974. Memoria [see item 3094] v. 2, p. 325-416)

Careful case study of failure of general inspection by Monzón of Nueva Granada in early 1570s, largely because of resistance of Audiencia of Santa Fé.

3151. Pinto Escobar, Inés. La rebelión del común. Tunja, Colombia, Univ. Pedagógica y Tecnológica de Colombia, Secretaría de Investigaciones y Extensión Universitaria, Fondo Especial de Publicaciones, 1976. 242 p., bibl., plates (Ediciones La Rana y el Aguila)

Revisionist study of *comuneros'* 1781 rebellion. Drawing on AGI as well as published studies and sources, Pinto Escobar details and analyzes social and especially economic aspects of rebellion. Ch. 3 and 12 on Cajas Reales, are noteworthy.

3152. Restrepo Ricaurte, Inés. La supresión del resguardo de Tasco y su traslado a Socha (*in* Jornadas Americanistas, III, Valladolid, Spain, 1974. Estudios sobre política indigenista española en América [see item 2298] v. 3, p. 221-260, maps, plates, tables)

Well documented case study of deliberately misinterpreted cedula of 3 Aug. 1774, according to which Indian districts losing population were regrouped to facilitate administration. Fiscal and Protector de Indios Francisco Moreno y Escandón used this cedula at connivance of all others involved save Indians, to suppress many resguardos such as Tasco, which in turn were opened up to Creole and mestizo occupation. Includes documentary appendix with demographic data.

3153. Restrepo Tirado, Ernesto. Historia de la Provincia de Santa Marta. Bogotá, Instituto Colombiano de Cultura, Subdirección de Comunicaciones Culturales, División de Publicaciones, 1975. 561 p., plates (Publicaciones especiales)

Reprint of well known and still useful chronicle of Santa Marta Prov. from discovery and conquest through 1821. Based on considerable research in AGI. Originally published Spain 1921, two volumes.

3154. Rey Fajardo, José del *ed.* La biblioteca del Seminario de San Bartolomé en 1767 (VANH/B, 58:230, abril/junio 1975, p. 316-327)

Publishes inventory (5 Aug. 1777) of library of San Bartolome's Jesuit Seminary, Bogotá.

3155. Rodríguez Plata, Horacio. Don Miguel de Santiestevan, Juez de residencia del Virrey del Nuevo Reino de Granada don José de Solís y Folgh de Cardona (*in* Congreso Venezolano de Historia, II, Caracas, 1974. Memoria [see item 3094] v. 3, p. 11-38)

Notes on life and multifaceted career of Spanish born Miguel de Santiestevan (1685-1776), bureaucrat and naturalist, who spent his last years in Bogotá as Mint's superintendant. Interesting personage about whom we would like to know more as he also served in what are now Peru and Ecuador, and was instrumental in the discovery of quinine bark.

3156. Ruiz Rivera, Julián Bautista. Encomienda y mita en Nueva Granada en el siglo XVII. Prólogo de Luis Navarro García. Sevilla, Escuela de Estudios Hispano-Americanos, 1975. 454 p., maps, tables (Publicación, 228)

Solid and substantial demographic as well as economic study of Indian tributaries and labor systems in 17th-century Colombia. Strong on sources, several of more important of which Ruiz Rivera edited earlier (see *HLAS 38:3067*).

3157. ———. Las visitas a la tierra en el siglo XVII como fuente de historia social (*in* Jornadas Americanistas, III, Valladolid, Spain, 1974. Estudios sobre política indigenista española en América [see item 2298] v. 1, p. 197-214)

Demonstrates that land surveys (*visitas a la tierra*) are major source for study of social history, especially as they are rich in data on Indian pueblos. Ruiz Rivera has located 18 such surveys from 17th century and notes their nature and characteristics.

3158. Sanders, G. Earl. Counter-contraband in Spanish America handicaps of the governors in the Indies (AAFH/TAM, 34:1, July 1977, p. 59-80)

Enlightening case study of considerable problems faced by local authorities in their attempts to combat contraband. Place and time, Cartagena de Indias and district during first half of 18th century.

3159. Sharp, William Frederick. Slavery on the Spanish frontier: the Colombian Chocó, 1680-1810. Norman, Univ. of Oklahoma Press, 1976. 253 p., bibl., illus., maps, plates, tables.

Piecing together manuscript sources from Andagoya, Bogotá, Popayán, Quibdó, Seville and elsewhere and employing quantitative analysis, Sharp has produced work broader in scope than title implies, history of gold production and slavery in Chocó about whose past little was known. He is to be commended for readability, originality and choice of tropical area where research difficulties are formidable.

3160. Vaughan Ricaurte, Mary Jane and **Guillermo Ramón García-Herreros.** Catálogo de documentos existentes en el Archivo Histórico Nacional para el período 1564-1580: período de los presidentes togados Venero de Leiva,

Francisco Briceño, Cortés de Mesa y Lopez Díaz Aux de Armendariz (PUJ/UH, 3, julio 1972, p. 151-228)

Lists sources in Archivo Histórico Nacional in Bogotá for years 1564 through 1580, by presidential period, series (*fondo*), year, volume and folio as indexed. Although useful enough guide to materials on years in question it does not correct errors of existing indexes.

3161. Villamarín, Juan A. Haciendas en la Sabana de Bogotá, Colombia, en la época colonial: 1539-1810 (*in* Florescano, Enrique, *ed*. Haciendas, latifundios y plantaciones en América Latina [see *HLAS 38:2190*] p. 327-345, bibl.)

Sketches history of haciendas in Bogotá's Sabana from earliest beginnings through end of colonial period. Preliminary report on ongoing research. Not surprisingly, Villamarín finds that estates in question were capitalistic and market oriented.

3162. Wilhite, John F. Foreign ideas in New Granada, 1760-1830 (SECOLAS/A, 8, March 1977, p. 5-18)

Résumé of intellectual developments in late colonial New Granada in which Wilhite reveals new data but little depth. Treats liberalism and enlightened thinking as synonymous. Attributes appearance of both to Mutis implying Colombia lived in cultural darkness prior to famed botanist's arrival.

QUITO

3163. Alcina Franch, José. El problema de las poblaciones negroides de Esmeraldas, Ecuador (EEHA/AEA, 31, 1974, p.33-36, plate, tables)

Working paper on ongoing research into ethnohistory of Ecuador's northwest coast. Examines problems of survival faced by those 23 African slaves (17 men and six women) who ship-wrecked off Esmeraldas' coast in 1553, fled inland and literally gave birth to province's mulatto and zambo population.

3164. Anda Aguirre, Alfonso. El Corregidor de Loja Don Melchor de Peñalosa. Loja, Ecua., Ediciones Casa de la Cultura Ecuatoriana, Núcleo Provincial de Loja, 1976. 110 p.

Well documented but amateurish biography of early 17th-century corregidor of Loja.

3165. Barnadas, Josep M. La Biblioteca Jesuita de Quito en el siglo XVII: breve panorama analítico (UCP/IAP, 8, 1974, p. 151-161, table)

Content analysis of Colegio Máximo's Jesuit Library in Quito, based on 1682 inventory and 1703 updating. Concludes that library was reasonably well stocked and up to date for times.

3166. *Boletín del Archivo Nacional de Historia.* Casa de la Cultura Ecuatoriana. Año 14, No. 20, sept. 1976-   . Quito.

Re-issue of former *Boletín* (entitled *Arnahis* between 1968-73) is devoted to publication of 17 *relaciones geográficas* (1766-1815) of pueblos and provinces of highlands and Oriente. Useful group of sources on demography, economy and society of late colonial period at local level.

3167. Conniff, Michael. Guayaquil through independence: urban development in a colonial system (AAFH/TAM, 33:3, Jan. 1977, p. 385-410, tables)

Drawing mostly on secondary studies and published sources, Conniff reviews selected aspects of economic, social and political history of Guayaquil in attempt to explain why coast's society, especially port city's was more open, free and enterprising than elsewhere in colonial Spanish America. Comparison may hold vis-à-vis highlands of Ecuador but hardly with other colonies.

3168. Deler, J.P. L'evolution du systeme urbain et la formation de l'espace en Equateur (IFEA/B, 5:3/4, 1976, p. 13-47, bibl., illus., maps, tables)

Interesting if error marred attempt to determine origins of cities in Ecuador and to establish patterns of urban hierarchy, from pre-Inca times through end of colonial period. Regrettably author is insufficiently familiar with history of Ecuador to have made discerning use of relatively few secondary studies and published sources on which he relied.

3169. Ecuador. Fuerzas Armadas [and] **Dirección de Historia y Geografía Militar del Estado Mayor.** Documentos para la historia militar. Quito, Editorial Casa de la Cultura Ecuatoriana, 1974/1975. 2 v. (356, 486 p.)

Potpourri of documents on "military" aspects of colonial and independence periods. Vol. 1 publishes 1586 *probanza de méritos* of Gerónimo Puento, cacique of Cayambe, important ethnohistorical source, and republishes number of well known documents on Quito rebellions of 1809 and 1810-12 and Quito's liberation 12 years later as spearheaded by Guayaquil. Vol. 2, more interesting and wholly original, consists of documents on conquest, colonial disturbances, pirate attacks, and new sources on Quito's independence movements.

3170. Grohs, Waltraud. Los indios del Alto Amazonas del siglo XVI al XVIII: poblaciones y migraciones en la antigua Provincia de Maynas. Versión castellana de Juan R. Castro y Velázquez. Bonn, n.p., 1974. 133 p., bibl., maps, tables (Bonner Amerikanistische Studien, 2)

M.A. thesis on Upper Amazon demography (former Mainas prov.) from initial contact through Jesuits' expulsion. Competent résumé and analysis of existing state of knowledge.

3171. Guerra B., Samuel M. Apuntes para una crítica a los estudios sobre Eugenio Espejo (Quitumbe [Pontificia Univ. Católica del Ecuador, Facultad de Pedagogía, Depto. de Historia, Quito] 4, 1976, p. 59-83)

Critical analysis of existing state of knowledge and literature on late 18th-century *precursor* and *pensador* Eugenio Espejo (1747-95). Exceptionally well done.

3172. Hamerly, Michael T. El comercio del cacao de Guayaquil durante el período colonial: un estudio cuantitativo. Quito, Comandancia General de Marina, 1976. 75 p. (Historia marítima del Ecuador. Documentación y estudio del Depto. de Historia de la Marina del Ecuador, 4)

With abundance of numerical data (both commercial and fiscal), surveys rise of Guayaquil cacao trade from 17th century origins through boom of later colonial period. In passing, has something to say also on general economic development of coastal Ecuador. Almost all based on new archival research; documentary appendix. [D. Bushnell]

Hurtado, Osvaldo. El poder político en el Ecuador. See item 3079.

3173. Landazuri Camacho, Carlos. El Dr. Antonio de Morga, octavo Presidente de la Real Audiencia de Quito: 1615-1636 (Quitumbe [Pontificia Univ. Católica del Ecuador, Facultad de Pedagogía, Depto. de Historia, Quito] 3, 1973, p. 1-112, bibl.)

Original senior thesis which contributes new data not just on administration of Morga, but also on state of and events in Audiencia of Quito during early 17th century.

3174. Larrain B., Horacio and **Cruz Pardo D.** Apuntes para un estudio de la población del Corregimiento de Otavalo a fines del siglo XVI (Sarance [Instituto Otavaleño de Antropología, Otavalo, Ecua.] 4, julio 1977, p. 63-95, maps, tables)

Analyzes 16th-century demographic data on Otavalo and its district as found in *Relaciones geográficas de Indias-Perú*. Maps and tables are well done and informative.

3175. Larrea, Carlos Manuel. Cartografía ecuatoriana de los siglos XVI, XVII, y XVIII. Quito, Corporación de Estudios y Publicaciones, 1977. 177 p., plates.

Useful introduction to charts, maps and plans of Audiencia of Quito, districts and towns. Quality of reproductions is poor but somewhat better than that of ed. by Casa de la Cultural Ecuatoriana, 1976.

3176. León Borja, Dora. Los indios balseros como factor en el desarrollo del puerto de Guayaquil (*in* Jornadas Americanistas, III, Valladolid, Spain, 1974. Estudios sobre política indigenista española en América [see item 2298] v. 2, p. 281-311, tables)

Pioneering study of economic, especially but not exclusively, maritime infrastructure and activities of 16th-century littoral Indian pueblos. Several *parcialidades*, if not entire pueblos drew their livelihood from sea, not just as fishermen but also as traders and freighters. Significant addition to ethnohistory of Guayaquil and its district. See also item 3185.

3177. Libro segundo de Cabildos de Cuenca: 1563-1569. Versión de Juan Chacón Zhapan. Prólogo de Julio Estrada Ycaza. Guayaquil, Ecua., Publicaciones del Archivo Histórico del Guayas, 1977. 240 p., facsims. (Col. Monográfica, 9)

Important source on early history of Cuenca, third most important city in Ecuador, indeed for the then colony as a whole.

Miño Grijalva, Manuel. Los cañaris en el Perú: una aproximación etnohistórica. See item 3223.

3178. Moreno Yañez, Segundo. Sublevaciones indígenas en la Audiencia de Quito desde comienzos del siglo XVIII hasta finales de la colonia. Bonn, n.p., 1976. 453 p., bibl., map (Bonner Amerikanistische Studien, 5)

Detailed, documented account of 10 Indian rebellions in Ecuador's highlands, beginning with Pomallacta's in 1730 and concluding with Guamote's and Columbe's in 1803. Also includes solid analysis of these movements. Substantial contribution to all but unknown social history of Quito's Audiencia. Moreno is first Ecuadorian to be trained in ethnohistory having earned his doctorate (this is his dissertation) at Bonn under Udo Oberem.

3179. Oberem, Udo. Los cañaris y la conquista española de la sierra ecuatoriana: otro capítulo de las relaciones interétnicas en el siglo XVI (SA/J, 58, 1974/1976, p. 263-274, bibl.)

Details Cañaris' role as Spaniards' allies in Quito's conquest and in suppression of rebellions later in century, especially in Oriente. See also items 3183 and 3223.

3180. ·Ordenanças Reales de la Real Audiencia de Quito. Transcripción e introducción de Jaime E. Rodríguez O. Revisión de Juan Freile-Granizo (Anuario Histórico Jurídico Ecuatoriana [Corporación de Estudios y Publicaciones, Quito] 4, 1976, p. 259-310)

Publishes 1563 Ordinances of Quito's Royal Audiencia which served as model for audiencias that followed.

3181. Probanza de Diego de Sandoval, 19.XI.1539. Transcripción de Juan Freile Granizo (AHG/R, 4:7, junio 1975, p. 73-104)

Important source on conquest of what is now Ecuador. Sandoval came with Alvarado from Guatemala and joined Benálcazar in settlement and pacification of Quito, La Culata (i.e., Guayaquil), Puná and other towns and/or areas. See also in this same journal, "Información de Diego de Sandoval, 7.III.1542" as transcribed by Freile (p. 105-114).

3182. Probanza de méritos de Martín Ramírez de Guzmán, Quito, 12.XI.1574. Transcripción de Juan Chacón Zhapan (AHG/R, 5:10, dic. 1976, p. 27-146, facsims.)

Major source on early history of Ecuador's coast Ramírez de Guzmán was son of one of Quito's conquerors and important *vecino* of Guayaquil. In fact, this *probanza* has mostly to do with Rodrigo de Vargas' *hazañas*.

Reig Satorres, José. Ordenanzas de la Real Audiencia de Quito: 1563. See item 3905.

3183. Segarra Iñiguez, Guillermo *ed.* Probanza de don Juan Bistancela cacique de Toctesí de su noble y limpia sangre y de los servicios que prestó su padre al Rey: 1594. Quito, Comintur, 1976. 37 p., facsims. (Cuadernos Guapnondelig, 1)

Illuminates Cañari's role in conquest of Tahuantinsuyu. Like Huanca's Cañaris allied with Spaniards, latter not staying grateful for very long (see item 3179).

3184. Segundo tomo de recopilación de cédulas despachadas en diferentes tiempos por su Majestad y Señores de su real Consejo de Indias para la Audiencia y Cancillería Real de la ciudad de San Francisco del Quito del Perú. Transcripción e introducción de Juan Freile-Granizo (Anuario Histórico Jurídico Ecuatoriana [Quito] 4, 1976, p. 1-255)

Basic source on administration of Antonio de Morga, President of Quito (1615-36), and early colonial institutions in general. Preceded by solid introduction on "Cédulas y cédularios" (p. xiii-xxii) by Freile, who has also added indexes (p. xxiii-xxxii and 252-255).

3185. Szászdi, Adám. D. Diego Tomalá, cacique de la isla de la Puná (*in* Jornadas Americanistas, III, Valladolid, Spain, 1974. Estudios sobre política indigenista española en América [see item 2298] v. 3, p. 157-182, illus.)

Excellent essay on Diego and his son Francisco Tomalá, caciques and governors of Puná and dependent Machala in the 16th century. Illuminates ways in which some Indian notables benefited by their cooperation with Spaniards. Important contribution to little known early history of Ecuador's coast.

3186. —— and **Dora León Borja.** Localización del pueblo aborigen de Guayaquil (Cuadernos Prehispánicos [Univ. de Valladolid, Seminario Americanista, Valladolid, Spain] 3, 1975, p. 5-18, map)

Argues that Indian pueblos of Yaguache and Guayaquil were located on R. Bulubulu-Boliche, former approximately 18 and 1/2 leagues to Guayas' east and latter somewhat further downstream. Sources I have seen, including coeval maps of Yaguache suggest another location in as much as San Antonio de Yaguache appears to have been near what is now Yaguachi Viejo or Cone that is to say on the river of the same name (then the Guayaquil). Nonetheless, the Szaszdis offer new, important data on Indian Guayaquil.

3187. —— and ——. Santiago de Quito—Santiago de Guayaquil, 1534-1536 (IGFO/RI, 139/142, enero/dic. 1976, p. 17-81, map)

Argues that Santiago de Quito as founded by Diego de Almagro on 15 Aug. 1534 at the Indian Riobamba was one and same city as Santiago de la Nueva Castilla (i.e. de Guayaquil) as refounded by Francisco de Orellana towards end of 1537, an unconvincing thesis. Nevertheless, the Szászdis offer some new data on and insight into conquest and colonization of what is now Ecuador.

3188. Vargas, José María. Historia del Ecuador: siglo XVI. Quito, Pontificia Univ. Católica del Ecuador, Centro de Publicaciones, 1977. 344 p.

Not history of Ecuador but chronicle of Quito during 16th century. Neither synthesis nor original research, work is routine compendium of data organized chronologically and somewhat thematically, drawn from Publications of Quito's Archivo Municipal, especially *Actas del Cabildo*, Vacas Galindo Collection (which consists of suspect transcripts from AGI) and *Relaciones geográficas de Indias-Perú*.

3189. Vasco de Escudero, Grecia. Los archivos quiteños. Quito, Instituto Panamericano de Geografía e Historia, Sección Ecuatoriana, 1977. 178 p., plates (Biblioteca Ecuador)

Introduction to Quito's archives.

PERU

3190. Alvarez Salas, Juan. Indice del protocolo de Gaspar Hernández: Arequipa 1550 (PEAGN/R, 4/5, 1975/1976, p. 81-114)

Index 1550 register of Notary Gaspar Hernández by date, entry title, folio, and persons. Useful research aid.

3191. Birckel, Maurice. El Padre Miguel de Fuentes, S.J. y la Inquisición en Lima (PMNH/HC, 6, 1973, p. 5-92)

Spanish version of French study (see *HLAS 32:2221*).

3192. Bradley, Peter T. The defence of Peru: 1600-1648 (IAA, 2:2, 1976, p. 79-112, bibl., illus.)

Careful study of measures taken by Viceroys of Peru during first half of 17th century to defend Lima and Callao from Dutch attack. Based on extensive research in England, Spain and Peru.

3193. ———. Some considerations on defence at sea in the Viceroyalty of Peru during the seventeenth century (PAIGH/H, 79, enero/junio 1975, p. 77-97)

Bradley examines defenses at sea, especially chequered history of Armada del Mar del Sur, focusing on 1624 proposal to dispatch supplementary fleet from Spain and late 17th-century venture by private individuals, mostly merchants, to organize squadron of their own, the sometime successful Company of Nuestra Señora de Guía. Together with item 3192, this is best study in English on defense of viceroyalty in 17th century.

3194. Bravo Guerreria, María Concepción. La muerte de Atahualpa: un análisis de las circumstancias que concurrieron en ella (EEHA/AEA, 31, 1974, p. 91-103)

Reexamines "circumstances" leading up to and culminating in Atahualpa's execution. Bravo argues that one of, if not decisive factor was pressure brought to bear on Pizarro and Almagro by numerous Indian groups discontent with Inca rule and/or Atahualpa himself, who apparently was somewhat a tyrant.

3195. Bronner, Fred. Peruvian encomenderos in 1630: elite circulation and consolidation (HAHR, 57:4, Nov. 1977, p. 633-659, tables)

Carefully researched examination of makeup of encomenderos in greater Peru (i.e., Quito. Lima and Charcas) as of 1630. Focusing primarily on interrelated issue of elite status, this article illuminates social structure and change in established colony.

3196. Burga, Manuel and Alberto Flores Galindo. La producción agrícola y las sublevaciones durante el siglo XVII: apuntes metodológicos (UNCP/AC, 4, 1975, p. 167-184, tables)

Many scholars have argued that Peru's economy was in crisis during late colonial period, and that this crisis underlay not only independence movements but Indian and Negro slave uprisings as well. For most part, however, these interpretations are based on impressionistic data. One way to determine what in fact was happening, particularly in little studied agricultural sector, is to use tithe (*diezmo*) figures as barometers, research on which Burga and Flores Galindo regrettably have yet to publish.

3197. Campbell, Leon G. The Army of Peru and the Túpac Amaru revolt: 1780-1783 (HAHR, 56:1, Feb. 1976, p. 31-57, tables)

Examines Army's performance in putting down Túpac Amaru's revolt, and subsequent reorganization, especially demobilization of creole militia in 1784. See also Campbell's companion, prize-winning article in *The Americas* (*HLAS 38:3112*), and "After the Fall: the Reformation of the Army of Peru, 1789-1816" in *Ibero-Amerikanischer Archiv* (4:16, Nov. 1976).

3198. Cárdenas Ayaipoma, Mario. El Colegio de Caciques y el sometimiento ideológico de los residuos de la nobleza aborigen (PEAGN/R, 4/5, 1975/1976, p. 1-24, table)

Brief but well documented account of Colegio de Caciques of Lima, founded 1589. Among other things, demonstrates that this School served as center of higher education for sons of Indian nobles only during 17th century, but that in 18th, especially after expulsion of Jesuits who ran it, relatively few *principales* attended. Includes prosopographic table on post-1776 students.

3199. Clayton, Lawrence A. Sources in Lima for the study of the colonial Consulado of Peru (AAFH/TAM, 33:3, Jan. 1977, p. 457-469, facsim.)

Majority of extant papers of Tribunal del Consulado de Comercio de Lima (1613-1887) are in ex-Archivo Histórico del Ministerio de Hacienda y Comercio, now a *fondo* of the Archivo General de la Nación (formerly Archivo Nacional), separately within this Archivo itself and in Ministerio de Relaciones Exteriores. In this article, Clayton samples and comments on utility of manuscripts from colonial period, stressing among other aspects, their importance for research into economic history not just of Peru but of Viceroyalty as a whole, and fact that we still lack complete history of Consulado itself.

3200. Cook, Noble David. Estimaciones sobre la población del Perú en el momento de la conquista (PUCP/H, 1:1, julio 1977, p. 37-60, bibl., map, tables)

Methodologically sophisticated attempt to estimate magnitude of population of Peru proper as of 1530. Utilizing recently recovered data such as results of Toledo visita (see *HLAS 38:2103*) and professionally acceptable demographic techniques, Cook demonstrates minimum and maximum contact populations of highlands and coast considered together would have been 3,000,000 and 12,000,000. He himself, however, continues to opt for 6,000,000.

3201. ———. La población indígena de Végueta, 1623-1683: un estudio del cambio en la población de la costa central del Perú en el siglo XVII (PMNH/HC, 8, 1974, p. 81-89, tables)

Analysis of 1623 and 1683 censuses of Indian population of Végueta, just north of Huara River on coast. Significant contribution to little known demography of 17th century Peru.

Craig, Alan K. Franciscan exploration in the central *montaña* of Peru. See item 3071.

3202. Crespo, Juan Carlos *ed.* La relación de Chincha: 1558 (PMNH/HC, 8, 1974, p. 91-104)

New critical ed. of 1558 account of southern coastal Valley of Chincha. Important demographic and ethnohistorical source.

3203. Davies, Keith. La tenencia de la tierra en Arequipa colonial: 1540-1650 (UNSA/H, 1, 1975, p. 29-46, tables)

Examines origins and organization of rural estates, especially those given over to viniculture, in and around Arequipa from city's foundation through 1650. Includes data on prices of slaves and wine. Well documented.

Dobyns, Henry E. and **Paul L. Doughty.** Peru: a cultural history. See item 3510.

Espinoza Soriano, Waldemar. Los mitmas de Nasca en Ocoña, Citor y Camaná, siglos XV y XVI: una tasa inédita de 1580 para la etnohistoria andina. See item 2049.

3204. Fisher, John R. Miners, silver merchants and capitalists in late colonial Peru (IAA, 2:3, 1976, p. 257-268, bibl., tables)

Critical study of role of capitalists and silver merchants (*aviadores*) in expansion of silver mining and output in Peru between 1771-1824. Argues that unlike in Mexico, capitalists were unwilling to invest heavily as well as directly in silver mining, which retarded both its growth and modernization.

3205. ———. Silver mines and silver miners in colonial Peru: 1776-1824. Liverpool, UK, Univ. of Liverpool, Center for Latin American Studies, 1977. 150 p., bibl., maps, tables (Monograph series, 7)

Detailed reexamination of mining sector of economy of Peru from the loss of Upper Peru to the Viceroyalty of Rio de la Plata through battle of Ayacucho. Fisher reviews history of mining in Peru before 1776, its initial reorganization under later Bourbon viceroys, Mining Guild and Tribunal, Nordenflicht mission, problems of mercury supply, labor and capital, and question of output, contributing much new data and insight. Perhaps his most important finding is that silver mining did not decline but expanded after 1776 and "remained relatively healthy until" wars of independence. In brief, this is the monograph on the subject. See also item 3204 and *HLAS 38:3119*.

3206. Fuentes Rueda, Helard L. Cuadros estadísticos de escribanos de Arequipa del siglo XVI (PRAGN/R, 4/5, 1975/ 1976, p. 201-212, tables)

Useful schematic guide to Archivo Departamental de Arequipa's holdings of 16th century notary registers (*protocolos de escribanos*).

Galdós Rodríguez, Guillermo. Visita a Atico y Caravelí: 1549. See item 2053.

3207. Gentile Lafaille, M.E. Distintos aspectos del tributo entre los yauyos de Chaclla: siglo XV-XVIII (IFEA/B, 5:3/4, 1976, 77-89, bibl., table)

Brief case study of consequences of commutation of tribute from labor to cash among Yauyos of Chaclla, highland Indian group just east of Lima.

3208. Hanke, Lewis and **Celso Rodríguez.** El Visitador Licenciado Alonso Fernández de Bonilla y el Virrey del Perú, el Conde del Villar: 1590-1593 (*in* Congreso Venezolano de Historia, II, Caracas, 1974. Memoria [see item 3094] v. 2, p. 11-127, facsim.)

Brief appreciation of general inspection of 1590/1603, certainly one of, if not longest visita on record. It is however, not as important as mass of documentation Bonilla compiled on virtually every aspect of administration of and life in the viceroyalty's, sources which remain as virgin as the day they were dispatched to Spain, and which are exemplified in extensive documentary appendix (p. 29-128).

3209. Harth-Terré, Emilio. Indios del común propietarios de esclavos: un testamento de la sociedad virreinal no historiado (*in* Jornadas Americanistas, III, Valladolid, 1974. Estudios sobre política indigenista española en América [see item 2298] v. 3, p. 183-200)

Notes on Indians, especially artisans in Lima, as owners of black slaves. History of Indian parishes and/or groups in Spanish cities and towns such as viceregal capital needs to be refined and researched in depth.

3210. Holguín Callo, Oswaldo. El Visitador Areche y el Consulado del Comercio de Lima: el problema de la alcabala de reventas (IRA/B, 9, 1972/ 1974, p. 83-109)

Details quarrel between Areche and Consulado de Comercio of Lima over payment of tax on resales, reappraised in 1773, but several years in arrears. Constitutes new chapter as it were on Areche, his *visita*, Consulado, and economic conditions in late 18th century Lima.

3211. Kapsoli E., Wilfredo. Sublevaciones de esclavos en el Perú: siglo XVIII. Lima, Univ. Ricardo Palma, Dirección Universitaria de Investigación, 1975. 153 p., tables.

Brief but meaty examination of slave rebellions of 1768, 1779, and 1786 on sugar plantations in coastal Valley of Nepeña. Supplemented by extensive documentary appendices (p. 79-153).

3212. Keith, Robert G. Conquest and agrarian change: the emergence of the hacienda system on the Peruvian coast. Cambridge, Mass., Harvard Univ. Press, 1976. 176 p., bibl., maps, tables (Harvard historical studies, 93)

Original monograph which outlines all but unknown early agrarian history of Peru's coast, both before and after Spaniards' arrival. Also important because it demonstrates that much more documentation on 16th century has survived in Peru than some scholars realize. Unfortunately, editors eliminated many details found in his Ph.D. dissertation, of which this is more abridgement than revision.

3213. Lazo García, Carlos and **Javier Tord Nicolini.** El movimiento social en el Perú virreinal (PUCP/H, 1:1, julio 1977, p. 61-92, bibl.)

Interesting attempt to define, interrelate and explain social tensions and conflicts in colonial Peru, especially those between special interest groups, classes and "races."

3214. Lehnertz, Jay. Juan Santos: primitive rebel on the Campa frontier: 1742-1752 (*in* International Congress of Americanists, XXXIX, Lima, 1970. Actas y memorias [see *HLAS 35:510*] v. 4, p. 111-125, bibl.)

Although Lehnertz has uncovered little that is new about this mid-18th-century rebel, he does offer new interpretation, namely that Juan Santos was not so much leader of local or Campa revolt but would-be spokesman of frustrated pan-Andean attempt to expel Spaniards altogether. Only further research will tell. See also *HLAS 38:3136*.

3215. Lohmann Villena, Guillermo. Los ministros de la Audiencia de Lima en el reinado de los Borbones, 1700-1821: esquema de un estudio sobre un núcleo dirigente. Sevilla, Escuela de Estudios Hispano-Americanos, 1974. 198 p., plates, tables (Publicación, 222)

Tripartite study of members of Audiencia of Lima under Bourbons. Pt. 1 (p. v-cxxiv) is prosopographic analysis of 158 men who served or were appointed between 1700-1821: pt. 2 (p. 1-147) summarizes career of each minister and lists biographical sources on him; and pt. 3 (p. 149-195) provides comparable data on 51 Creoles and peninsulars married to Creoles who served in Lima under Habsburgs. Not as methodologically sophisticated as Burkholder and Chandler's *From impotence to authority* (see item 2265), but richer in detail.

3216. ———. Victorino Montero del Aguila y su *Estado político del Reyno del Perú*, 1742 (EEHA/AEA, 31, 1974, p. 751-807)

Biobibliographical study of limeño Montero del Aguila (1696-1755), one time Corregidor of Piura, merchant, newspaperman, and social critic, whose polemical *Political state of the Kingdom of Peru* (1742) presaged need for major reforms.

3217. López Soria, José Ignacio. Ideología económica del *Mercurio Peruano*. Lima, Publicaciones de la Comisión Nacional del Sesquicentenario de la Independencia del Perú, 1972. 164 p., bibl.

Employs content analyses to establish political economic thinking of contributors to *Mercurio Peruano* (1791-94), organ of Society of Friends of Lima. Concludes that as group they reflected mentality of coeval reform minded bourgeois elsewhere, especially in Europe.

3218. Macera Dall'Orso, Pablo *comp*. Historia económica peruana: documentos. Lima, The Author, 1975. 320 p. (Biblioteca andina)

Publishes 48 documents, mostly from Archivo General de la Nación (formerly Archivo Nacional) and Biblioteca Nacional in Lima, from 1571 through 1914, but largely from 18th century on haciendas, *obrajes* (textile sweat shops), slavery, irrigation of the coastal valleys, and mining. Highly personal selection, but nonetheless useful compilation.

3219. Málaga Medina, Alejandro. Los corregimientos de Arequipa: siglo XVI (UNSA/H, 1, 1975, p. 47-85)

Details division of Arequipa prov. into seven corregimientos, following Toledo's reforms, correlates their limits with prehispanic units, and depicts their organization in terms of *cacicazgos* and *repartimientos*. Includes demographic and economic data. Basic contribution to historical geography as well as adminitrative history of southern Peru.

3220. ———. Indice de los manuscritos arequipeños existentes en el Archivo General de la Nación. Arequipa, Peru, Editorial El Sol, 1975? 78 p.

Lists documents on Arequipa in those fondos of Archivo General de la Nación in Lima (formerly Archivo Nacional) which have been catalogued.

3221. ———. Las reducciones en el Perú: 1532-1600 (PMNH/HC, 8, 1974, p. 141-172, bibl., table)

This item is fourth version of a single study by Málaga Medina in which he reexamines attempts to regroup declining Indian populations into larger settlements before, during, and after the Toledan reforms. Other three versions were published in: 1) *Revista de Historia de América* (80, julio/dic. 1975, p. 9-52); 2) *Kollasuyo* (see *HLAS 38:3230*); 3) *Anuario de Estudios Americanos* (31, 1974, p. 819-842). Although all four articles contain new data, we need detailed case studies such as the one on Arequipa by Málaga Medina himself (see *HLAS 38:2128*) and this one on Santiago del Cercado.

3222. Martín, Luis and **Jo Ann Geurin Pettus** *comps*. Scholars and schools in colonial Peru. Dallas, Tex., Southern Methodist Univ., School of Continuing Education, 1973. 206 p., bibl.

Competently edited and translated anthology of excerpts from writings of 16th, 17th and 18th-century Peruvian intellectuals, and of coeval documentation on state of education, especially in Lima and Cuzco. May be used with profit in advanced courses on Andean countries as guide to colonial mentalities as well as intellectual developments.

3223. Miño Grijalva, Manuel. Los cañaris en el Perú: una aproximación etnohistórica. Quito, Pontificia Univ. Católica del Ecuador, 1977. 109 p., bibl., illus., map.

Preliminary attempt to establish role played by Cañari in Tahuantinsuyu's downfall, first as allies of Huascar against Atahualpa and then of Spaniards, especially Benalcázar against Atahualpa. Also includes notes on massive removal of Cañari by Huayna Capac to Peru in late 15th century, and their subsequent utilization as *mitmaq* and *yanaconas* through 1575, and what became of them after Toledo reorganization of Viceroyalty. Based on archival and field research. See also items 3179 and 3183.

3224. Mörner, Magnus. En torno a las haciendas de la región del Cuzco desde el siglo XVIII (*in* Florescano, Enrique *ed*. Haciendas, latifundios y plantaciones en América Latina [see *HLAS 38:2190*], p. 346-392, bibl., tables)

This item and item 3225 are preliminary reports on ongoing research. Here Mörner outlines demographic, economic and social structures of Intendancy/Dept. of Cuzco from late colonial period through present. Section on archival sources and bibliography are very useful.

3225. ———. Some characteristics of agrarian structure in the Cuzco region towards the end of the colonial period (CEDLA/B, 18, junio 1975, p. 15-29, map, tables)

More detailed examination of demography and economy of rural Cuzco as of late 18th century.

3226. Moreno Cebrián, Alfredo. Dictámenes contrapuestos de dos ex-corregidores sobre los repartos de mercancías a los indios del Perú: 1778 (*in* Jornadas Americanistas, III, Valladolid, Spain, 1974. Estudios sobre política indigenista española en América [see item 2298] v. 3, p. 107-145)

Detailed analysis of divergence of opinion of two former corregidores, Demetrio Egan, peninsular and military, and Miguel Feijó de Sosa, Creole and litterato, on forced distribution of merchandise among Indians. Egan and Feijó's opinions were solicited by Viceroy Guirior at Council of Indies' insistence and in order to minimize, if not eliminate this abuse altogether, legally that is.

3227. Mugaburu, Josephe de. Chronicle of colonial Lima: the diary of Josephe and Francisco Mugaburu, 1640-1697. Translated and edited by Robert Ryal Miller. Norman, Univ. of Oklahoma Press, 1975. 342 p., illus.

Not entirely satisfactory translation and ed. of one of few known colonial diaries, that of Spaniard Josephe de Mugaburu y Honton (1607-86). Mugaburu was sergeant in viceregal palace guard, and his diary is useful chronicle of daily as well as official life in Lima from 1630 through his death. Entries added by his son Francisco (b. 1647) for years 1687-97 are few and far less informative.

3228. Mujica Barreda, Elías. Changuco y Xacon: su probable ubicación (IFEA/B, 5:1/2, 1976, p. 113-120)

Uses archaeological evidence and historical source (see item 3232) to establish location of Indian pueblos of Changuco and Xacon in Moche Valley.

3229. O'Phelan Godoy, Scarlett. Cuzco 1777: el movimiento de Maras, Urubamba (PUCP/H, 1:1, Julio 1977, p. 113-128, bibl.)

Examines 1777 anti-tax uprising by Indians of Maras, ayllu in Urubamba prov. Author argues correctly that this and other minor protest movements of 1770s in altiplano, most of which remain to be studied, were symptomatic of general unrest which culminated in rebellion of Tupac Amaru several years later.

3230. Pereña Vicente, Luciano. La pretensión a la perpetuidad de las encomiendas del Perú (*in* Jornadas Americanistas, III, Valladolid, Spain, 1974. Estudios sobre política indigenista española en América [see item 2298] v. 2, p. 427-469)

Exceptionally well-researched essay on debate at court over proposed concession in perpetuity of encomiendas, which polemic culminated in intervention of Las Casas, his last, and preparation of his lesser known but no less important *De Thesauris del Perú*.

Ponce, Fernando. Anotaciones sobre fuentes documentales de Arequipa. See item 3083.

3231. Quiroz Paz-Soldán, Eusebio. Producción y consumo de trigo en Arequipa: 1780 (UNSA/H, 1, 1975, p. 103-113, tables)

Quantitative study of production and consumption of bread in Arequipa in 1780.

3232. *Relación sacada de la probanza fecha por parte de Pedro Lozano en el plieto que trata con Melchor Verdugo sobre el Prencipal Guaman e sus sujetos*: transcripción de Guillermo Cock (IFEA/B, 5:1/2, 1976, p. 121-147)

Undated mid-16th-century lawsuit which constitutes important ethnohistorical source on northern coast of Peru, especially *curacazgo* of Changuco (see also items 2111 and 3228).

3233. Rostworowski de Diez Canseco, María. Los ayarmacas (Cuadernos Prehispánicos [Univ. de Valladolid, Seminario Americanista, Valladolid, Spain] 3, 1975, p. 53-97, bibl., map, tables)

Ayarmacura were important *curacazgo* in and around Acamana before latter became Cuzco and Incas emerged as dominant group in southern altiplano. In this study ethnohistorian Rostworowski pieces together archaeological evidence and historical sources to outline their history from pre-Inca times through present. Notable contribution to rapidly emerging ethnohistory of Peru.

———. El señorío de Changuco. See item 2111.

3234. ———. El tributo indígena en la primera mitad del siglo XVI en el Perú (*in* Jornadas Americanistas, III, Valladolid, Spain, 1974. Estudios sobre política indigenista española en América [see item 2298] v. 2, p. 393-399)

Reaffirms what is increasingly patent, tribute under the Incas was and is not comparable to that demanded by the Spaniards. Includes tribute data from the general visita of Viceroy La Gasca (1549), part of which Rostworowski was able to locate in the Archivo General de Indias.

Saeger, James S. Clerical politics en eighteenth-century Peru: the trial of José de Antequera. See item 3300.

Shea, Daniel E. A defense of small population estimates for the Central Andes in 1520. See item 2116.

3235. Tord Nicolini, Javier. El corregidor de indios del Perú: comercio y tributos (PMNH/HC, 8, 1974, p. 173-214, bibl., tables)

General study of interrelations between amount of Indian tribute collectable and volume of trade imposed on them by corregidores. Primarily useful for lists of 18th-century archival sources needed for neglected study of *corregidores de indios* in first half.

3236. Valcárcel, Carlos Daniel comp. Relaciones de méritos y servicios (Revista del Instituto Peruano de Investigaciones Genealógicas [Lima] 16, junio 1975, p. 127-294, facsims.)

Publishes 74 18th-century "relaciones de meritos y servicios" of civil servants, priests, lawyers and military men, 47 of whom were criollos, 20 peninsulares, six of unspecified origin but probably criollos, and one German, Antonio de Malnerschitsch. Important biographical source.

3237. Visita de Camaná: 1789. Transcripción de Alejandro Málaga Medina (UNSA/H, 1, 1975, p. 117-225)

Publishes for first time 1789 *visita* of Camaná, one of seven partidos (formerly corregimientos) of Intendency of Arequipa. Primarily demographic source, in fact exceptionally rich one as it lists population, family by family, and includes parish register data.

ALTO PERU

Huber, Siegfried. Im Reich der Inka: die Alteperuanischen Königreiche. See *HLAS 39:934*.

3238. Martire, Eduardo. El Código Carolino de Ordenanzas Reales de las Minas de Potosí y Demás Provincias del Río de la Plata (1794) de Pedro Vicente Cañete. B.A., Univ. de Buenos Aires, 1973/1974. 2 v. (353, 436 p.)

Vol. 2 published 1794 mining code for Potosí as drafted by Paraguayan Cañete, legal advisor (*asesor*) to Intendant of Potosí and first appointee to that office in 1785. Vol. 1 is legal study of these ordinances.

3239. ———. Tolerancias, prevenciones y regulación participadora de los indios "capchas" de Potosí, en la explotación del cerro (*in* Jornadas Americanistas, III, Valladolid, Spain, 1974. Estudios sobre política indigenista española en América [see item 2298] v. 3, p. 291-303)

Fascinating notes on highly organized illegal miners of Potosí, infamous *capchas*—not all of whom were Indians by any means—especially as found in 18th-century materials.

3240. Meza Villalobos, Néstor. Felipe V y el problema ético-político de la provisión de mano de obra a la minería del Perú y Nuevo Reino de Granada (*in* Jornadas Americanistas, III, Valladolid, Spain, 1974. Estudios sobre política indigenista española en América [see item 2298] v. 2, p. 313-343)

Details all but forgotten debate of late 17th and early 18th centuries over continuing provision of forced Indian labor to mines, issue resuscitated by Viceroy Count of Monclova and brought to attention of first Bourbon, Philip V, who suppressed mining mita in Cundinamarca but ordered it continued in Potosí to relief of all other parties concerned.

Ponce Sanginés, Carlos. Apuntes para el estudio de la demografía histórica de Tiwanaku durante el período colonial. See item 2101.

3241. Rípoda Ardanaz, Daisy. Bibliotecas privadas de funcionarios de la Real Audiencia de Charcas (*in* Congreso Venezolano de Historia, II, Caracas, 1974. Memoria [see item 3094] v. 2, p. 499-555)

Informative study of libraries of 22 members, including presidents as well as regents, oidores and prosecutors, of Audiencia of Charcas between 1681-1825. Titles these men collected and presumably consulted are indicative of their professional formation and intellectual interests.

3242. Santamaría, Daniel J. Potosí entre la plata y el estaño (PAIGH/G, 79, dic. 1973, p. 71-115, maps, tables)

Solid introduction to history of city of Potosí, from beginnings as silver mining camp through tin mining present. Especially strong on demographic and economic aspects, to which author adds new details from his own, original research.

3243. Tormo Sanz, Leandro. Algunos datos demográficos de Moxos (*in* Jornadas Americanistas, III, Valladolid, Spain, 1974. Estudios sobre política indigenista española en América [see item 2298] v. 2, p. 191-202, tables)

Brief study of demography of Mojos from contact in late 17th century through census of 1950.

3244. Vázquez Machicado, José *comp.* Catálogo descriptivo del material del Archivo General de Indias referente a la historia de Bolivia. v. 1, pts. 1/2, Audiencia de Charcas; v. 2, pts. 1/2, Audiencia de Buenos Aires; v. 3, Audiencia de Lima. La Paz, Univ. Mayor de San Andrés, Centro de Planificación y Coordinación de la Investigación Científica y Tecnológica, Instituto de Investigaciones Históricas, Archivo de La Paz, 1976. 3 v. (379, 244, 129 p.)

Welcome publication of major guide to holdings of AGI on colonial Bolivia. Originally compiled 1933 and until now available only in typescript to fortunate few. Vol. 1 lists 3,334 documents in Patronato and Audiencia *fondos*; v. 2 lists 1,118 documents as found in Audiencia de Buenos Aires *fondo*; and vol. 3 lists 578 items in Audiencia of Lima *fondo*.

CHILE

3245. Bermúdez, Oscar. Pica en el siglo XVIII: estructura económica y social (SCHG/R, 141, 1975, p. 7-56)

Delineates economy, particularly agrarian and mining sectors, and society of Pica, northern Chile, during 18th century, especially latter half during Pica's prime. Significant contribution to local history.

3246. Casassas Canto, José María. Algunas noticias sobre los Partidos de Arica y Tarapacá hacia fines del siglo XVIII y principios del XIX (UCC/NG, 1:2, dic. 1974, p. 217-226)

Tabulates total intake and outflow of Cajas Reales of Arica, Tarapacá and Pica during late 18th and early 19th centuries. Tabulation by individual surcharge and tax (e.g. tithe, sales tax, customs duties and the like) would have been more revealing.

3247. Contreras A., Juan and others. La población y la economía de Chiloé durante la colonia: 1567-1826. Concepción, Chile, Univ. de Concepción, Instituto Central de Historia, 1971. 48 p., bibl.

Despite title, this monograph advances only to 1700, being pt. 1, two-part study. Moreover, it is working paper on ongoing group research into demography and economy of colonial Chiloé. Contains much revealing detail and interesting comments in notes on problems of methodology and interpretation.

3248. Cunill Grau, Pedro. La temprana sementera urbana chilena y los comienzos del deterioro ambiental (*in* Siete estudios: homenaje de la Facultad de Ciencias Humanas a Eugenio Pereira Salas. Santiago, Univ. de Chile, 1975, p. 59-80, maps)

Chronicles deforestation in Chile between Salado and Bío-bío Rivers from 1542 through 1850 as brought about by mining activities and urban growth. More of interest to geographers than historians as author spells out significance in terms of land rather than man.

3249. Fichandler, Joseph B. and **Thomas F. O'Brien, Jr.** Santiago, Chile, 1541-1581: a case study of urban stagnation (AAFH/TAM, 33:2, Oct. 1976, p. 205-225)

Authors demonstrate that encomenderos as group dominated Cabildo of Santiago de Chile during that city's first 40 years and argues that encomenderos used their concomitant power almost exclusively to their own behalf, thwarting interests of all other groups, including merchants, artisans and "the lower classes" in general. No doubt Fichandler and O'Brien are right to some extent, but it is equally doubtful that well being of Santiago de Chile as colony and preindustrial society was all that dependent upon actions of its immediate rulers.

3250. Hanisch, Walter. El historiador Alonso de Ovalle (UCAB/M, 5, 1976, p. 585-874)

Exhaustive, exceptionally well researched essay on life of Chilean Jesuit Alonso de Ovalle (1603-51), importance of his truly great *Histórica relación del Reino de Chile* (Rome, 1646, for best available ed., see *HLAS 34:2305*) and his impact on contemporary and later letters. It is fascinating, for example, to learn that Ovalle was cited 1,004 times, 316 of which as sole authority, in first official *Diccionario de la lengua castellana* to be issued by Real Academia Española de la Lengua (6 vols.; 1726-39).

3251. ———. Juan Ignacio Molina: sabio de su tiempo (UCAB/M, 3, 1974, p. 205-308)

On the one hand, a study of ideas of 18th-century Chilean Jesuit Molina (1740-1829) as present in his several histories (e.g., *Compendio della storia geo-*

grafica, naturale el civile del Regno del Chile, Bologna, 1776). And on the other, catalogue of coeval and later authors who drew on Molina. Carefully done.

3252. Lira Montt, Luis. Estudiantes chilenos en la Real Universidad de Córdoba del Tucumán: 1670-1815 (JEHM/R, 2:8, 1975, p. 649-671)

Biobibliographical notes on 88 Chileans who studied at Univ. of Córdoba in what is now Argentina, between 1670 and 1815.

3253. Mellafe Rojas, Rolando. Las primeras crisis coloniales, formas de asentamiento y el origen de la sociedad chilena: siglos XVI y XVII (*in* Siete estudios: homenaje de la Facultad de Ciencias Humanas a Eugenio Pereira Salas. Santiago, Univ. de Chile, 1975, p. 117-135)

Seminal essay on "neglected," particularly economic aspects of 16th and 17th centuries by leading Chilean historian. Mellafe outlines what he considers to be their salient features as, for example, open frontier, encomienda and seignioralism in 16th century, and metamorphosing impact of crises such as Indian rebellions of 1598 and 1655, and 1647 earthquake. Basic reading.

3253a. Orrego Vicuna, Claudio. Libertad e igualdad en la historia de Chile. pt. 1, La conquista, La Guerra de Arauco y la colonia. Santiago, Instituto Latinoamericano de Estudios Sociales (ILADES) [and] Instituto Chileno de Estudios Humanísticos (ICHEH), 1976? 131 p.

Useful, interpretative study with colonial focus which attempts (with some success) to account for Chilean national character in terms of what shaped its basic culture: fact that between 1541 and 1883, Chilean people never enjoyed "total peace" due to Araucanian wars. Well-documented work finds that dangerous frontier led to sense of mutual dependence among Chileans, commitment to "justice," and avoidance of extremes, all brought about because of long-term need for *"un esfuerzo colectivo."*

3254. Ramón, Armando de. Santiago de Chile: 1650-1700 (UCCIH/H, 12, 1974/1975, p. 93-373, fold. map, tables)

Block by block, property by property account of holdings in parishes of Sagrario or Iglesia Matriz, and Santa Ana but only as far as present day San Martín Street, during second half of 17th century. Each entry details history, limits, extent, value, liens if any, and sources on corresponding property. To be continued. Offshoot of larger study on origins of class structure of which assets are indicators as well as determinants.

Retamal Avila, Julio. Bibliografía de historia eclesiástica chilena: revistas chilenas, 1843-1973. See item 3084.

Rodríguez Villegas, Hernán. Historia de un solar de la Ciudad de Santiago: 1554-1909. See item 3086.

3255. Salinas Meza, René. Raciones alimenticias en Chile colonial (UCCIH/H, 12, 1974/1975, p. 57-76, tables)

Careful analysis of sailors' rations as of 1768. First systematic attempt to determine daily diet of any group in colonial Chile.

3256. Salzedo y Pineda, Manuel de and **Antonio Narssiso de Santa María Escobedo.** Informe sobre las Plazas Fuertes del Reino de Chile (SCHG/R, 140, 1972, p. 72-110)

Report (1763) on state of Southern or Araucanian frontier by two army officers. Based on personal inspection.

Villalobos R., Sergio; Fernando Silva V.; Osvaldo Silva G.; and Patricio Estellé. Historia de Chile. See item 3089.

3257. Weischet, W. and **E. Schallhorn.** Altsicdelkerne und fränkolonialer Ausbau in der Bewässerungskulturlandschaft Zentralchiles (UBGI/E, 4:28, dez. 1974, p. 295-303, bibl., maps, plates)

Utilizes aerial photography to pin-point early agricultural settlements, especially those which were nuclei of later irrigated field systems.

RIO DE LA PLATA

3258. Abadie-Aicardi, Aníbal. La *Relación exacta* versificada de la expedición de Cevallos a Santa Catalina y el Plata, 1776-1777 (EEHA/HBA, 18:2/3, 1974, p. 153-194)

Relación exacta is long poem written by sergeant who served with Viceroy Cevallos against Portuguese, which Abadie-Aicardi has rendered into modern Spanish, added explanatory footnotes and comprehensive introduction dealing with campaign, region and Cevallos himself. Original ms. in Biblioteca Nacional, Madrid.

3259. ———. El Uruguay en los albores del siglo XIX: su *Breve descripción* por el Dr. Miguel de Lastarria (CEHA/NH, 7:13, dic. 1974, p. 5-15)

Well-edited 1803 account of Montevideo, fascinating survey of people and customs. Original ms. is in Archivo Histórico Nacional, Madrid. Explanatory footnotes and good, brief introduction place Lastarria in perspective.

3260. Alvarez Romero, José María. La confirmación póstuma de Olañeta como Virrey del Río de la Plata (EEHA/AEA, 31, 1974, p. 47-54)

Consists of several documents with scanty, related narrative, having to do with Council of Indies appointment of Gen. Olañeta as (last) Viceroy of Río de la Plata, 1825. Olañeta, who had been accused by viceroy of Peru of treason, died of wounds acquired at battle of Tumusla before news of his elevation reached area.

3261. Archivo Histórico de Tucumán, Arg. Indices documentales: sección Actas Capitulares; copia de Samuel Díaz. v. 11/14, 1784/1824. Tucumán, Arg., 1975. 122 p. (Publicación, 29. Serie 5, 7)

Mimeo copy of index, with short descriptions of documents, their folio numbers and specific dates. Chronologically organized.

3262. Argentina. Academia Nacional de la Historia. Actas capitulares de Mendoza. t. 3, Años 1652-1675. Advertencia de Victor Tau Anzoátegui. Introducción de Edberto Oscar Acevedo. B.A., 1974. 667 p.

Vol. is continuation of what will be very long series of useful publications (vol. 1 appeared 1945, vol. 2 1961). Covering third quarter of 17th century, work (which contains actas in their entirety) is complemented by excellent introduction, which includes (among other things) lists of all *cabildantes*, with their years of service and short description of notable events mentioned in documents. Long and detailed alphabetic index of contents facilitates volume's use.

3263. Armani, Alberto. Città di Dio e Città del Sole: lo stato gesuita dei guarani, 1609-1768. Roma, Edizioni Studium, 1977. 251 p., bibl.

Excelente síntesis basada en bibliografía existente. El autor describe la evolución del "estado" jesuita guaraní en base a la acción colonial del estado español y del desarrollo de factores internos del Paraguay. Por lo tanto, logra retornar la realidad histórica de utopías basadas en un mito. [M. Carmagnani]

3264. Assef, Alberto E. La creación del Virreinato del Río de la Plata y la disgregación nacional (IAEERI/E, 42, sept./oct. 1976, p. 104-118, map, tables)

Provocative examination of B.A.'s role in opting for *patria chica*, which it could control (and dominate) rather than larger Río de la Plata, in which it would have lesser role. Assef sees Artigas and other figures of *"norte"* as proponents of "true" nationalism, while porteños pursued only their own interests.

Cañete y Domínguez, Pedro Vicente. Syntagma de las resoluciones prácticas cotidianas del derecho del Real Patronazgo de las Indias. See item 2266.

3265. Caravaglia, Juan Carlos. Los actividades agropecuarias en el marco de la vida económica del pueblo de indios de Nuestra Señora de los Santos Reyes Magos de Yapeyú: 1768-1806 (*in* Florescano, Enrique *ed*. Haciendas, latifundios y plantaciones en América Latina [see *HLAS 38:2190*] p. 464-485, map)

Carefully researched study of the Indian pueblo of Yapeyú and its more than 20 estancias in years after expulsion of Jesuits, showing precipitous decline in livestock common to all former missions, but stressing survival of community and commercial importance of locally woven textiles.

3266. Chaves, Osvaldo. La formación del pueblo paraguayo. B.A., Ediciones Amerindia, 1976. 178 p., bibls.

Short, semi-Marxist survey of Paraguay's colonial past by one of its many political exiles. Text lacks notes, but does provide short bibliography at end of each chapter. Focus is predictably upon economic growth and social issues, especially "el vigor del mestizaje." There is little new here for serious scholar despite synthesis' readability.

3267. Comadrán Ruiz, Jorge. Notas para una historia institucional del Corregimiento de Cuyo: en torno al beneficio por la corona del oficio de Corregidor, 1689-1773 (EEHA/AEA, 31, 1974, p. 189-227)

Examines negative impact on Cuyo of sale by Crown of office of Corregidor, which practice began in 1689 and lasted until 1773. This office, which before had more often than not gone to native sons or at least to creoles, during period in question was usually purchased by peninsulars, who were more interested in recouping their investment than in dispensing justice.

Congreso de Historia Argentina y Regional, *II, Comodoro Rivadavia, Arg., 1973*. Segundo Congreso de Historia Argentina y Regional. See item 3070.

3268. **Destéfani, Laurio Hedelvio.** Los marinos en las invasiones inglesas. B.A., Dirección de Abastecimientos Navales, 1975. 459 p., bibl., illus., maps (Historia naval argentina. Serie B, 15)

Impressive, very detailed study of naval aspects of the British invasions of 1806 and 1807. Well-illustrated and equally well-documented from Spanish and Argentinian archives. More such studies on other aspects of invasions are needed.

3269. **Disandro, Carlos A.** and **Jorge L. Street.** La compañía de Jesús contra la Iglesia y el estado: documentos americanos, siglo XVII. La Plata, Arg., Instituto Cardenal Cisneros, 1970. 370 p. (Col. Homo conditor, 1, Serie Americana y Argentina)

Long, fascinating introduction (164 p.) sets legalistic framework for 10 lengthy documents from 1640s and 1650s, which deal with clash of wills and purposes between Jesuits on one hand, and Royalist secular clergy and Crown on other. Supplemented by three appendices. Vol. of projected series, this work is limited to Río de la Plata.

3270. **Duviols, Jean-Paul** ed. *Montevideo et sa Région en 1767*: extraits inédits du journal de Ch[arles] F.P. Fesche (UTIEH/C, 24, 1975, p. 7-17)

Aboard Bougainville's famed voyage of circumnavigation, Fesche wrote detailed treatise on trip (now reposing in Library of Museum of Natural History, Paris). Duviols presents us with six and a half p. of extracts from original, treating Indians, wildlife, cattle, agriculture and Montevideo. Worthwhile article.

3271. *Estudios Paraguayos.* Univ. Católica Nuestra Señora de la Asunción. Vol. 1, No. 1, nov. 1973-   Asunción.

Journal which began publication Nov. 1973 contains many historical articles of high caliber, written by foreign scholars as well as Paraguayans. Somewhat irregular in appearance. Vol. 1 consisted of only one issue, vol. 2 came in two parts, published June and Dec. 1974. Vol. 3 is reportedly in press and will soon appear.

3272. **Fajardo Terán, Florencia.** El proceso colonizador en el Río de la Plata: Pérez del Puerto y los orígenes de Rocha (EEHA/AEA, 31, 1974, p. 269-322, facsim., plates)

Detailed, documented chronicle of events leading to foundation of Villa de Nuestra Señora de los Remedios de Rocha in 1793 by Rafael Pérez del Puerto, which constituted Spain's latent recognition of strategic importance of what is now southeastern Uruguay. But Rocha was founded not only as military outpost but also as settlement of peninsular colonists, about whom Fajardo does not tell us enough.

3273. **Fidente, Enrico.** La difesa di Buenos Aires nel sec. XVII. Roma, Minerva Historica, 1972. 115 p., bibl.

Dealing basically with Portuguese/Spanish boundary conflict of 1670s, this slim volume focuses on origins of Colonia de Sacramento in Banda Oriental, and local Spanish reaction to Portuguese advance. Based largely on documents from AGI in Seville, this study is most valuable in its treatment of raising of Indian army from region's Jesuit misssions—only defensive force available to governor.

3274. **Gammalsson, Hialmar Edmundo.** El Virrey Cevallos. B.A., Editorial Plus Ultra, 1976. 214 p.

Valuable biography of major military and administrative figure who seems to have been involved in one capacity or another in most important crises which wracked Río de la Plata region in second half of 18th century. Soundly documented.

3275. **Garay, Blas.** El comunismo de las misiones: la revolución de la independencia del Paraguay. Asunción, Instituto Colorado de Cultura, 1975. 252 p. (Biblioteca clásicos colorados, 2)

New ed. of two minor "classics" a half century out of print. First work, on Jesuits, is thoughtful and thought-provoking, slim treatment of independence movement is not. Garay, who died tragically young, is rightfully considered a founder of Paraguayan historiography.

3276. **González, Juan Natalicio.** Proceso y formación de la cultura paraguaya. 2. ed. Asunción, Instituto Colorado de Cultura, 1976. 416 p. (Biblioteca clásicos colorados, 6)

This, vol. 6 in series "Biblioteca Clásicos Colorados" is good, general work by one of Paraguay's finest historian-philosopher-*pensadores*. Running entire gamut from Guaraní culture before conquest (heavy with both mythology and linguistics) to and through selective cultural aspects of colonial era, book is filled with thought and thought-provoking vignettes. It is unfortunate that this valuable search for national *raíces* is seriously hampered by an appalling lack of organization and lack of either notes or bibliography. One can still consider it, however, a standard work.

3277. **Halperin-Donghi, Tulio.** Una estancia en la campaña de Buenos Aires, Fontezuela, 1753-1809 (*in* Florescano, Enrique *ed.* Haciendas, latifundios y plantaciones en América Latina [see HLAS 38:2190] p. 447-463, tables)

Excellent quantitative study of operation of very successful estancia owned and managed by the Bethlamite Order in Buenos Aires prov. Based on account records, includes wealth of data on work force, value of slaves, wages paid to peons, cereal production and price of commodities purchased for estancia.

3278. **Hernández, Angel Santos.** Forma de vida y régimen económico de los indios en las reducciones jesuíticas del Paraguay (*in* Jornadas Americanistas, III, Valladolid, Spain, 1974. Estudios sobre política indigenista española en América [see item 2298] v. 2, p. 123-166)

Title notwithstanding, this is one-sided and short-sighted defense of Jesuits and Franciscans and their missions in what are now Paraguay and Uruguay, based entirely on secondary studies as written by members of those orders. Author, Spanish Jesuit, resorts to shibboleth that Guarani were children by nature and hence had to be protected from themselves as well as outsiders. Interesting example of extent to which White Legend pervades.

3279. **Isola, Ema.** La esclavitud en el Uruguay desde sus comienzos hasta su extinción: 1843-1852. Montevideo, Comisión Nacional de Homenaje del Sesquicentenario de los Hechos Históricos de 1825, 1975. 334 p., bibl., tables.

Prosaic history of slavery in Uruguay, largely culled from secondary studies.

3280. **Johnson, Lyman L.** The silversmiths of Buenos Aires: a case study in the failure of corporate social organization (JLAS, 8:2, Nov. 1976, p. 181-213, tables)

Excellent study of failure of B.A.'s silversmiths to organize themselves into guild and corresponding religious brotherhood (*cofradía*) in 1790s—a failure which author correctly notes, led to social organization far different from that of Lima or Mexico City, whose experiences should not be so readily generalized.

3281. **Lockhart, Washington.** Soriano: antecedentes, fundación, consecuencias. Montevideo, Fundación de Cultura Universitaria, 1975. 132 p., illus., maps.

Well-documented account of events leading to foundation of Soriano in 1622 and subsequent history through end of colonial period. Soriano was originally *reducción* of remnants of Chanáes and Charrúas ethnic groups.

3282. **López, Adalberto.** The revolt of the comuneros, 1721-1735: a study in the colonial history of Paraguay. Cambridge, Mass., Schenkman, 1976. 214 p., bibl., maps.

Scholarly study of political disturbances which wracked Asunción in early 18th century. López interprets comuneros' rebellion as attempt to rid Paraguay of Jesuits and to maintain autonomy. Summarizes and analyzes both traditions of autonomy and Jesuit establishment in pts. 1/2, before taking up revolt in pt. 3. Well written, moreover, one of few acceptable books on Paraguay history in English. (Both title page and dust jacket unfortunately marred by misprint: *comuñero*).

3283. **Luque Colombres, Carlos.** Para la historia de Córdoba. t. 2, Monografías, artículos y otros escritos. Córdoba, Arg., Biffignandi Ediciones, 1973. 457 p., illus. (Col. Alma de Córdoba, 8)

Extended vignettes of lives of six men who had significant impacts on Córdoba. Three of these (Capt. Gaspar de Medina, Diego de Villarroel and Juan Alonso de Vera y Zarate) were 16th-century founders, while one (Capt. Diego Navarro de Velasco) was a 17th-century figure, and two (Dean Gregorio Funes and Dr. Victorino Rodríguez) pertain to late 18th and early 19th centuries. While there is no bibliography per se, volume is well-documented and can be very useful to scholar of Argentina.

3284. **Maeder, Ernesto J.A.** and **A.S. Bolsi.** La población de las misiones guaraníes entre 1702 y 1767 (UCNSA/EP, 2:1, junio 1974, p. 111-138)

Superior study which can be regarded as only valid one on subject. Based solidly upon extensive research, this article should be read by all who are interested in historical demography.

3285. **Mariluz Urquijo, José María.** La Real Audiencia de Buenos Aires y el Juzgado de Provincia (*in* Congreso Venezolano de Historia, II, Caracas, 1974. Memoria [see item 3094] v. 2, p. 129-166)

Sound institutional and case study of B.A.'s Provincial Court, which was manned by oidor of audiencia on rotating basis and concerned with civil and criminal jurisdiction in first instance within city and immediate district (i.e., *alfoz*). Juzgado de Provincia functioned between installation of B.A.'s second Audiencia in 1785 and suppression of Provincial Courts in 1812 by Cortes of Cádiz.

3286. Martinič B., Mateo. Los españoles en Magallanes. Punta Arenas, Chile, Hersaprint, 1976. 28 p., bibl.

Interesting if overly brief history covering 1520-1920s era, which assiduously avoids Chilean-Argentinian crisis of conflicting claims to area. Bibliography is very scanty, but description of European discovery of and impact upon desolate Magallanes territory is well told.

3287. Mendoza, Diego de. Crónica de la Provincia de S. Antonio de los Charcas del orden de ño seráphico P.S. Francisco en las Indías Occidentales, Rayno del Peru. 2. ed. La Paz, Editorial Casa Municipal de la Cultura Franz Tamayo, 1976. 601 p., facsims.

Fascinating facsimile reproduction of Franciscan crónica written by order of Crown in 1653 at Cuzco by very well-informed cleric familiar with subject. Volume is very eclectic compendium of ethnic description, customs of white, red and black, and mineralogical surveys. While focus is naturally upon good deeds and trials and tribulations of Franciscan *railes*, it is much more than that. Quality of reproduction is quite good, but work would have been much improved by addition of decent introduction, biographical data concerning author, and few explanatory notes.

3288. Mora Mérida, José Luis. Cedulario para la Governación de Paraguay: 1700-1716 (EEHA/AEA, 31, 1974, p. 1031-1047)

Abstracts royal cedulas concerning Paraguay issued between 1700-16. Useful research notes.

3289. ———. Historia social del Paraguay: 1600-1650. Prólogo de Luis Navarro García. Sevilla, Escuela de Estudios Hispano-Americanos, 1973. 366 p., maps, plate, tables (Publicación, 214)

Quantitative monograph on demography, economy and society of Paraguay during first half of 17th century. Includes chapters on Spanish origins of Paraguay, its civil and ecclesiastical administration and administrators during the period, and documentary appendix on state of encomiendas as of 1674. Well-written, organized and documented, this work adds appreciably to our knowledge of early history of Paraguay. See also author's *Iglesia y sociedad en Paraguay en el siglo XVIII* (Sevilla, Escuela de Estudios Hispano-Americanos, 1978?) not available at press time for review in this *HLAS*.

3290. ———. Notas sobre el episcopologio paraguayo (EEHA/AEA, 30, 1973, p. 317-336)

Professionally-documented survey of bishops who actually served Diocese of Asunción (from 1555 through 1838) with appendices of bishops named (many) and bishops who reached Asunción (few). Author correctly states that this is area of Paraguayan history almost unknown, and his new data reveal that of 19 bishops who took up their posts, a surprising 15 were *regulares*.

3291. ———. La población indígena paraguaya no reducida (*in* Jornadas Americanistas, III, Valladolid, Spain, 1974. Estudios sobre política indigenista española en América [see item 2298] v. 1, p. 347-362, map, tables)

Mora, a fine historian, has chosen to trace a very slim thread in this piece which deals with settled Indians *not* under control of lay or ecclesiastical administrators. Describes ups and downs (numerically) of that segment of population and resultant survival of some Guaraní cultural traits.

3292. Musso Ambrosi, Luis Alberto. El Río de la Plata en el Archivo General de Indias de Sevilla: guía para investigadores. Prólogo de Josefa Emilia Sabor. 2. ed. Montevideo, n.p., 1976. 224 p., bibl.

Exceedingly valuable research tool for Río de la Plata scholars which describes sources available in each of AGI's nine sections. Musso even provides archival call numbers of various documents and general description of each section, as well as number of detailed indices for relevant documents in each. Highly recommended.

3293. Notas sobre el Virreinato del Río de la Plata (UBN/R, 14, marzo 1976, p. 95-123)

Selection from much longer work written London 1808 by anonymous English officer who participated in 1807 conquest of Montevideo. Pintos provides short, succinct introduction to officer's very accute recording of commercial, cultural and social life under British rule in Montevideo.

3295. Paula, Alberto S.J. de; Ramón Gutiérrez; and Graciela María Viñuales. Del pago del Riachuelo al partido de Lanús: 1536-1944. La Plata, Arg., Archivo Histórico de La Provincia de Buenos Aires Ricardo Levene, 1974. 206 p., maps, plates.

Excellent, detailed study of *partido* and *municipio* of Lanś, now part of B.A. Drawing on documents from six archives, authors emphasize 18th and 19th-century integration of rural Lanús into growing port city (in large part completed with opening of railroads in late 19th century). Detailed documental appendices concern changing land ownership in partido, 1580-1859.

3296. Piossek Prebisch, Teresa. La rebelión de Pedro Bohorquez, el Inca de Tucumán: 1656-1659; relato histórico-documental. B.A., Juárez Editor, 1976. 258 p., bibl., maps.

Detailed, well-researched monograph on fake Inca of Tucumán and Calchaquí rebellion which he spearheaded. See also *HLAS 38:3008*.

3297. Pistoia, Benito Honorato. Los franciscanos en el Tucumán: 1566-1810. Salta, Arg., Cuadernos Franciscanos, 1973. 88 p., bibl.

Detailed, documented if partial history of Franciscans in Tucumán, especially Córdoba, during colonial period.

3298. Plá, Josefina. Los talleres misioneros, 1609-1797: su organización y funcionamiento (PAIGH/H, 75/76, enero/dic. 1973, p. 9-56, bibl.)

Excellent, securely-grounded article on neglected subject of great importance: local manufacturing. Emphasizing "oficios mayores" such as goldworking, saint-making, silverware and furniture production, Pla delves into methods of apprenticeship, materials, and many other facets of manufacturing in (mostly jesuit) *reducciones* of northern Río de la Plata.

3299. Robinson, David J. and Teresa Thomas. New towns in eighteenth century northwest Argentina (JLAS, 6:1, May 1974, p. 1-33, maps, tables)

Well-balanced article dealing with process of founding new towns in Salta, Jujuy and Córdoba provs., and social, economic and defensive functions of new entities. Notes 17 such towns and includes fairly detailed analysis of creation of one (Nueva Oran) illustrating changes in status from rural village to incorporated town, and growing centralization of authority. We need more such thoughtful studies.

3300. Saeger, James S. Clerical politics in eighteenth-century Peru: the trial of José de Antequera (BU/JCS, 17:1, Winter 1975, p. 81-96)

Excellent article which uses trial of comunero leader of Paraguay to illustrate complexities and confusions of Church/State and Church/Church relations and rivalries. Tensions between Franciscans and Jesuits, fearful vacilation of viceroy and potential for social upheaval in Lima (where trial was eventually held) made circus of Antequera affair (he was arrested in 1726 but not executed until 1731, after new rebellion had begun in Paraguay).

3301. Segreti, Carlos S.A. *ed.* Córdoba: ciudad y provincia, siglos XVI-XX, según relatos de viajeros y otros testimonios. Córdoba, Arg., Junta Provincial de Historia de Córdoba, 1973. 555 p.

Well-organized and presented anthology of Córdoba (often neglected subject among Río de la Plata scholars) which includes extracts from letters and travelers' accounts (beginning with *Relación of Jerónimo de Cabrera*, city's 1573 founder and ending in early 20th century. Extracts are well-chosen and informative, especially those which deal with 18th and 19th centuries.

3302. Sola, José Vicente. Diccionario de regionalismos de Salta. Prólogo de Carlos Ibaguren. B.A., Editorial Plus Ultra, 1975. 365 p., bibl.

Sola makes valiant attempt to save parts of old, regional expressions of his province in face of what he calls "rapidly changing Argentina." Includes very substantial bibliography and for archive-crawling Argentinist, this dictionary can be of considerable value.

3303. Storni, Hugo. Documentación y bibliografía sobre los beatos mártires ríoplatenses (AHSI, 45:90, luglio/dic. 1976, p. 318-348)

Work is very detailed bibliography of some 372 documents and printed works concerning martyrs and martyrdom of Roque González de Santa Cruz (b. Asunción 1576; killed Paraguay 1628) and two who died with him: Alonso Rodríguez and Juan del Castillo. Bibliography is carefully annotated and useful to scholar concerned with Jesuits in Paraguay, and/or Indians and their culture. Includes two-page author index. Good reference work.

3304. Tanzi, Héctor José. El Río de la Plata en el época de los Virreyes Loreto y Arredondo (PAIGH/H, 83, emero/junio 1977, p. 153-192)

Excellent article composed of long introduction concerning population and economic activities of various parts of viceroyalty and shorter history of rule of two viceroys (1784-94). Tanzi shows region undergoing unusually fast change and growth, and focuses in part on increasing conflict between B.A.'s Cabildo and imperial bureaucracy, which seemed to increase in size each year.

3305. Velázquez, Rafael Eladio. Cabildos en el Paraguay (*in* Congreso Venezolano de Historia, II, Caracas, 1974. Memoria [see item 3094] v. 3, p. 333-352)

Solid introduction to history of Spanish and Indian cabildos in colonial Paraguay, which at same time notes sources which have survived from and on them.

3306. ———. Navegación paraguaya de los siglos XVII y XVIII (UCNSA/EP, 1:1, nov. 1973, p. 45-84)

Carefully researched study by one of Paraguay's foremost younger historians. Working essentially from documents, Velázquez demonstrates that trade and navigation along both Paraná and Paraguay rivers was substantial, despite high taxation, dangerous fluvial Indians and Crown restrictions. Excellent illumination of shadowy *corners* of Paraguay's colonial past.

3307. ———. La población del Paraguay en 1682 (CPES/RPS, 9:24, mayo/agosto 1972, p. 128-148, map)

Pioneering study which not only analyzes Paraguayan population but which shows that in decade of 1670s, populated area of Paraguay actually decreased notably in size due to Indian raids and resurgent Luso-Brazilian threat. Paraguay was under seige. Raw data used is Fray Faustino de Casas' census of 1682, but Velázquez has put that census into perspective with his detailed discussion of preceding decade. Excellent work.

Williams, John Hoyt. Paraguay's historical resources: pt. 1, Paraguay's National Archives. See item 3091.

3308. Williman, José Claudio and **Carlos Panizza Pons.** Historia uruguaya. t. 1, 1503-1810: la Banda Oriental en la lucha de los imperios. Montevideo, Ediciones de la Banda Oriental, 1975. 259 p.

First 80 p. deal with most general of subjects ("The Spain of the Conquest") but p. 109-259 are very good examination of imperial rivalries in what would become Uruguay. Unfortunately, despite quality of text, there is no bibliography and only handful of notes. This study deserves better treatment than that.

3309. Ygobone, Aquiles D. Viajeros científicos en la Patagonia durante los siglos XVIII y XIX. B.A., Editorial Galerna, 1977. 193, p., bibl., illus., maps.

Excellent treatment of major "travelers," introduced with 16th through early 18th-century background, volume then deals at length with three Englishmen (Missionary Thomas Falkner, scientist Charles Darwin, and *sabio* George Chatsworth Musters) and Argentinian Francisco Pascasio Moreno. All four spend considerable time in Patagonia and left impressive literature about region (written between 1730s and 1880s). Ygobone presents excellent bio-bibliographical data on all four, although he emphasizes Falkner (author of *Descripción de Patagonia*) first of his subjects in time. Includes excellent bibliography.

INDEPENDENCE PERIOD

DAVID BUSHNELL

Professor of History
University of Florida

THE MOST OBVIOUS TRENDS THAT EMERGE from the items annotated below concern the geographic origin of publications. Seemingly exhausted by their special sesquicentennial observances which extended well beyond 1971, Peruvian historians have cut back their independence output to more or less what used to be the normal level. The Argentine contribution is also down, for no obvious reason. Bolivians, on the other hand, have been busier than usual—perhaps because the sesquicentennial of their definitive independence came in 1975, although the earlier phases of the struggle in Bolivia continue to attract somewhat greater attention. And Venezuelans continue to spend a significant percentage of petroleum income printing things about Bolívar and his epoch. Unfortunately, they have not quite matched in over-all quality what they achieve in quantity. The two best items of Venezuelan authorship included here are both by the same historian, Germán Carrera Damas, and both are reeditions of earlier works (items 3347-3348) as he has not lately been working on the independence period. But a Venezuelan university press did give us a biography of Sucre by the North American author John P. Hoover (item 3322) that easily eclipses those previously available.

The Panama Congress sesquicentennial produced rather little of permanent value (items 2207, 2249 and 2345-2346). The American Revolution bicentennial produced somewhat more: there are items on the relationship of Anglo-American ideas and antecedents to Latin American independence both listed in this *HLAS*, the section entitled HISTORY: GENERAL (see items 2223-2224, 2371 and 2374) and, with specific application to the Gran Colombian area, see below, items 3338-3339 and 3343. Apart from these special commemorations, the mix of topics treated was much the same as always. Military activities were studied in a substantial number of works, among which Vergara's book on partisan irregulars in Peru (item 3379) particularly stands out. Of course, the biography of Sucre already alluded to is also mainly military in emphasis. In conventional political history there is nothing quite as noteworthy, although Reyes Abadie's general view of the Platine revolution (item 3410) and Salvat Monguillot's excellent case study of the treatment of suspected disloyalty in Chile (item 3397) are just two examples of the continuing serious work done in this field. On political ideas, Héctor José Tanzi has contributed a study of ideological antecedents (item 2378) which is very well done though scarcely trailblazing, and Walter Hanisch Espíndola an examination of the Chilean climate of opinion (item 3393) that is narrower in focus but excellent (and regrettably late in reaching the *Handbook*). In a closely related field, Febres Cordero's study of printing and journalism in Venezuela (item 3351) deserves mention. And in socioeconomic history, alongside the interesting study of "daily life" by a group of Bolivian authors (item 3385), there are a number of significant articles on such specialized topics as Chilean trade by Rector (item 3395), slavery in Venezuela by Veracoechea (item 3358), and the economic and demographic impact of the struggle itself, also in Venezuela, by the Chilean Cunill Grau (item 3350). Naturally, too, the publication of source materials never ceases. Just from Colombia, for example, we have two previously hard-to-find contemporary descriptions of the Gran Colombian period (items 3336-3337), not to mention a welcome compilation of key documents on foreign relations (item 3341). The usual volumes of *próceres'* correspondence have been appearing (see item 3333), and allegedly some more volumes of the monumental series entitled "Colección Documental de la Independencia del Perú" have become available since those noted in *HLAS 38:3259*, although neither the Library of Congress nor the Univ. of Florida library seems able to maintain control of the series in question. Maybe next time.

GENERAL

3310. Avila Martel, Alamiro de. Presencia de Bolívar en Chile en 1819 (ACH/B, 38:85, 1971, p. 39-77)

Following extended tribute to Chilean historian Raúl Silva Castro whose seat Avila Martel was taking in Academia Chilena de Historia (this being his *discurso de incorporación*), discusses image of Bolívar in Chilean press 1812-19 and concludes with mention of an *Elogio* of Bolívar by student of Juan Egaña. Appendix details 133 press references. Principal part of this work was also published separately under different title.

3311. Burke, William. Additional reasons for our immediately emancipating Spanish America. N.Y., AMS Press, 1976. 91 p.

Plea for British aid to schemes of Miranda. Reprint of 1808 ed. London, J. Ridgway.

3312. Carrera Damas, Germán. Bolívar. Montevideo, n.p., 1974. 241 p. (Biblioteca de marcha. Col. Los nuestros, 10)

Another Bolívar anthology, whose introductory essay "Vigencia de Bolívar" serves as author's own condensation of his brilliant *El culto a Bolívar* (see *HLAS 32:2418*). It is followed by lucid short biographical sketch, then selections themselves, which are all Bolívar's words and well chosen but unfortunately not annotated.

3313. Costa de la Torre, Arturo. Ildefonso de las Muñecas y los mártires de la Republiqueta de Larecaja. La Paz, Editorial Casa Municipal de la Cultural Franz Tamayo, 1976. 225 p. (Jornadas peruano-bolivianas de estudio científico del altiplano boliviano y del sur del Perú, 4)

Having participated in abortive Cuzco revolution of 1814, Ildefonso de las Muñecas continued guerrilla-type resistance to Spanish rule in area north of La Paz. This account is strictly amateur history, with documentary sources both in appendix and incorporated in text.

3314. Durand Flórez, Guillermo. Correspondencia de misiones diplomáticas en Chile: 1823-1824 (PEAGN/R, 2, 1974, p. 5-32)

With brief introduction, select documents pertaining to Peruvian-Chilean relations.

3315. Estévez, Alfredo and **Oscar Horacio Elía.** Aspectos económico-financieros de la campaña sanmartiniana. Prólogo de Eugenio J. Folcini. 2. ed. aumentada con un apéndice. B.A., Editorial El Coloquio, 1976. 332 p., bibls.

Reedition of work first published 1961 (see HLAS 28:953) which is mainly description of measures adopted in economic and fiscal areas but is important because of relative scarcity of more comprehensive and analytical treatments. "Appendix" is group of additional short studies chiefly concerned with economic conditions of Cuyo provinces and their contribution to San Martín's expedition to Chile.

3316. Estrada Ycaza, Julio. La invasión de Brown (Historia Marítima del Ecuador, Documentación y Estudios [Marina del Ecuador, Depto. de Historia, Quito] 2, dic. 1975, p. 9-36)

Solidly documented article on Platine corsair activities 1816-18 off Ecuadorian coast. Certain related documents follow (p. 37-47).

3317. Fitte, Ernesto J. El fusilamiento de los Carrera y las publicaciones de la época (ANH/IE, 20, enero/junio 1976, p. 177-203, bibl.)

Looks at polemics unleashed by execution, in Argentina, of the three Chilean brothers Carrera in 1818 and 1821. "Epoch" in title extends to mid-century, to include, e.g., charges made by Benjamín Vicuña Mackenna. Fitte vigorously defends San Martín against attacks by Carreras and their partisans; but a useful historical (and historiographical) contribution.

3318. Freile Granizo, Juan *comp*. Más sobre el insurgente Brown. Quito, Comandancia General de Marina, Depto. de Historia, 1977. 70 p. (Historia marítima del Ecuador. Documentación y estudios, 5)

Documents from Ecuadorian archives, 1816-17, on activities of Platine corsair Guillermo Brown in Pacific waters.

3319. González Echenique, Javier. Notas sobre la regulación jurídica de la expedición libertadora de 1820: noviembre de 1818 a agosto de 1820 (ACH/B, 38:85, 1971, p. 105-119)

Reviews legal provisions (both pre-existing in Spanish legislation and adopted for occasion) that governed preparation of expedition of San Martín from Chile to Peru: command, recruitment, supply, etc. Solidly researched work, which also appeared in *HLAS 38:3260* (vol. 4, p. 223-237).

3320. Grases, Pedro *comp*. Contribución a la bibliografía de Antonio José de Sucre, Gran Mariscal de Ayacucho: 1795-1830. Caracas, Ministerio de la Defensa, 1974. 165 p.

Though prepared by expert bibliographer and of obvious importance, this work was completed in 1945 and is only now published, without updating. Lists many newspaper articles and other ephemeral items of more interest for study of cult than actual life and times of Sucre.

3321. Guarda Geywitz, Gabriel. Repercusión en Chile de la independencia del Perú (ACH/B, 38:85, 1971, p. 121-140)

Examines reactions among both patriots and royalists in Chile to news of Peru, from liberation of Lima to intervention of Bolívar. This was another paper presented by Chilean delegates to V Congreso Internacional de Historia de América held Lima 1971 and which like item 3319, also appeared in congress proceedings (see *HLAS 38:3260*, vol. 4, p. 238-257).

3322. Hoover, John P. Sucre, soldado y revolucionario. Cumaná, Ven., Univ. de Oriente, 1975. 372 p., bibl.

Best biography yet published on Sucre. Though conventional in approach and showing familiarity with not quite all of recent work pertinent to topic, it does reflect thorough examination of traditional sources, including material in Venezuelan archives. Balanced in coverage and competently executed.

3323. Kossok, Manfred. Die Unabhängigkeitsrevolution Lateinamerikas als Gegenstand der historisch-vergleichenden Methode (WZHUB, 24:1, 1975, p. 13-28)

Analysis of mainly Eastern European historiography on Latin American independence movements. Compares various perspectives in historical approaches to independence period, including newest trends. [G.M. Dorn]

3324. Lechín Suárez, Juan. Estrategia del altiplano boliviano: en una recapitulación histórica. La Paz, Editorial Los Amigos del Libro, 1975. 69 p.

Critique of San Martín's decision to strike via Chile at Lima, instead of continuing Upper Peruvian strategy of previous Argentine leaders, which author thinks would have brought faster results. Nothing literally new but suggestive treatment by Bolivian general. Previously published as article (see *HLAS 36:2950*).

3325. Lotería. Lotería Nacional de Beneficencia. Nos. 243/244, mayo/junio 1976- . Panamá.

Special issue in homage to Bolívar and commemoration of Panama Congress. Contains numerous short pieces, mostly of slight importance, but several rather useful ones referring to Panama in independence period.

3326. Mendoza, Cristóbal L. Páginas de devoción bolivariana. Prólogo de Carlos Felice Cardot. Caracas, Academia Nacional de la Historia, 1973. 350 p.

Volume put together from writings of leading traditionalist exponent of Bolívar cult. Some worth reading for substantive content, others as manifestations of cult itself.

3327. Mieres, Antonio. Bolívar y el periodismo (IEH/A, 1, 1974, p. 65-82, bibl.)

For what it may be worth, reference or otherwise, largely inventory of quotations from Bolívar on different aspects of role of press.

3328. Miller, William. Memorias del general Guillermo Miller. Lima, Editorial Arica, 1975. 2 v. (334, 376 p.)

New edition of 1829 Spanish translation of one of standard sources, by English officer who came to Peru with San Martín and stayed to fight under Bolívar. As English original was recently reprinted (see *HLAS 36:2725*), this is noted only because of very useful "Estudio Preliminar" by Percy Cayo Córdova (p. xxvi-lxvii) which discusses Miller, his work, and its place among sources on independence.

3329. Ornstein, Leopoldo R. Lo que nunca se dijo de la batalla de Chacabuco (JEHM/R, 1:8, 1975, p. 47-64)

Ornstein himself had said before that San Martín's cool-headed valor saved what O'Higgins' impetuosity almost lost, but here his version of Chacabuco is set forth in form of a quite readable address and incorporating some little known, scathing marginal comments by the Argentine Liberator.

3330. Rojas, Armando. Bolívar y Santa Cruz: epistolario. Caracas, Oficina Central de Información (OCI), 1975. 177 p., bibl., illus.

Most of this correspondence between Bolívar or his secretariat and Andrés Santa Cruz had been published before, but the collection does contain some new pieces, and it conveniently brings together source material pertinent for history of Peru and Bolivia 1822-31. There is a fairly extensive though pedestrian "Estudio preliminar."

3331. Salcedo-Bastardo, J.L. El primer deber: con el acervo documental de Bolívar sobre la educación y la cultura. Caracas, Equinoccio, 1973. 643 p., plates.

In somewhat the same fashion as in his earlier works on Bolivarian themes, Salcedo-Bastardo here analyzes the Liberator's thought and action in education and related fields. Largest part is then devoted to chronological compilation of pertinent items from Bolívar's writing. Useful, elegantly presented.

3332. Sañudo, José Rafael. Estudios sobre la vida de Bolívar. Medellín, Colombia, Editorial Bedout, 1975. 511 p.

Reedition of classic anti-Bolivarian biography, by *pastuso* historian; first version appeared 1925.

3333. Sucre, Antonio José de. Archivo de Sucre. t. 1, 1812-1821; t. 2, 1822; t. 3, 1823. Caracas, Fundación Vicente Lecuna, Banco de Venezuela, 1974. 3 v. (606, 614, 639 p.) illus.

Documents by, to, and relating to Sucre, many of which had been published before but many not. Pedro Grases' "El Archivo de Sucre: Notas para su Historia" (t. 1, p. xxi-xxxix) explains location of Sucre papers, which do not constitute single archival collection in themselves but are dispersed through a great many collections.

3334. Vargas, Francisco Alejandro. Un fiel edecán del Libertador: General en Jefe Juan Nepomuceno Santana (FJB/BH, 42, sept. 1976, p. 420-459)

Factual, documented, pedestrian; main emphasis on Santana's service with Bolívar in Peru. Briefer mention of early career, later association with Urdaneta dictatorship in New Granada, and retirement in native Venezuela.

GRAN COLOMBIA

3336. Banco de la República, *Bogotá*. Cartas escritas desde Colombia durante un viaje de Caracas a Bogotá y desde allí a Santa Marta en 1823. Bogotá, 1975. 140 p. (Archivo de la economía nacional, 36)

Translation of one of more interesting foreign travelers' accounts, originally published in English (London, 1824) but hard to find; of uncertain authorship. Good short prologue by Malcolm Deas.

3337. ———, ———. Relación geográfica, topográfica, agrícola, comercial y política de este país. Bogotá, 1974. 2 v. (435, 453 p.) fold. map, plates (Archivo de la economía nacional, 34)

Another valuable reedition: compendium originally published London 1822, in both English and Spanish. Vol. 1 contains historical-bibliographical "Presentación" by Sergio Elías Ortiz.

3338. Bowman, Charles H., Jr. *comp.* Correspondence of William Duane in two archives in Bogotá (PAIGH/H, 82, julio/dic. 1976, p. 111-125)

Letters of 1819-23 from Philadelphia publicist and strong supporter of Spanish American independence to various Gran Colombian figures. In same issue, compiler presents "Calendar of Correspondence of Colombian Agents in the United States, 1816-1824," (p. 139-157) inventory of materials existing in Bogotá archives; most of items listed are directed to or from Manuel Torres, who shortly before his death in 1822 was received as first Gran Colombian minister to US.

3339. Bushnell, David. El ejemplo norteamericano y la generación colombiana de la independencia (ACH/BHA, 63:714, julio/sept. 1976, p. 359-369)

This article and "Los Usos del Modelo: la Generación de la Independencia y la Imagen de Norteamérica" in *Revista de Historia de América* (Instituto Panamericano de Geografía e Historia, México, 82, julio/dic. 1976, p. 7-27) are two offshoots of same research project, concerning impact of US "model" in Nueva Granada and Gran Colombia. First is general overview; second more detailed look at some lesser-known applications. No clear conclusions as to significance of it all.

3340. Castellanos, Rafael Ramón. Gual, periodista: una tesis de revisionismo histórico (ACH/BHA, 64:716, enero/marzo 1977, p. 109-154, bibl.)

Consists largely of lengthy excerpts from Venezuelan patriot Pedro Gual's articles in important but rare *El Observador Colombiano* of Cartagena (1813), in which he made a reasoned attack on federalism and called for close unity of Venezuela and New Granada. Detailed notes.

3341. Cavelier, Germán. Documentos para la historia diplomática de Colombia. t. 1, 1820-1830. Bogotá, Editorial Kelly, 1976. 243 p.

Very useful collection of documents on foreign affairs of Gran Colombia; covers armistice negotiations with Spain, recognition, Spanish American relations, Panama Congress and other matters.

Colombia. Instituto Geográfico Agustín Codazzi. República de Colombia: mapa histórico-político, descubrimiento, conquista e independencia. See *HLAS 39: 5890.*

·3342. Dziubiński, Andrzej. Intentos de establecer relaciones diplomáticas entre Colombia y Marruecos en los años 1825-1827 (PAN/ES, 3, 1976, p. 51-67)

Intriguing marginal note, based on esoterically original research by Polish historian. Efforts referred to were in effect a by-product of Colombian corsair operations in Spanish vicinity, which went back to about 1820.

3343. Ocampo López, Javier. Las ideas sobre la integración de la Gran Colombia en el Congreso de Cúcuta (FJB/BH, 40, enero 1976, p. 7-47)

Analyzes both antecedents (including thought of Miranda and Bolívar) and debates of 1821 constituent congress, concerning formation of larger union of Venezuela and Nueva Granada and its internal organization.

3344. Peña, Miguel and Leonardo Infante. Dos procesos célebres. Prólogo de José Antonio de Armas Chitty. Recopilación de Nicolás Vegas Rolando. Caracas, Ediciones Vegas Rolando, 1975. 349 p. (Serie Fermín Toro)

Useful compilation of primary and secondary sources (none recent) on two related *causes célebres*, involving Venezuelans Leonardo Infante and Miguel Peña, which reflected and contributed to both military-civilian and New Granada-Venezuela tensions.

3345. Santander, Francisco de Paula. Memorias del General Santander. Bogotá, Banco Popular, 1973. 418 p., facsims., plates (Biblioteca Banco Popular, 50)

Contains his *Apuntamientos* which cover basically his entire career, plus certain other historical writings and select correspondence referring exclusively to independence struggle and Gran Colombian period. Obviously important source material, hitherto mostly available in inconvenient collections on crumbling paper.

3345a. Venezuela. Academia Nacional de la Historia. Sociedad Venezolana de Historia de la Medicina. Enfermedad y muerte del Libertador. Caracas, 1976. 297 p., bibl., illus.

Reedition of proceedings of 1962-63 symposium previously published but not noted in *HLAS*. Both medical and general historians contribute. Of primarily biographical interest, but not without some bearing on broader history of period, particularly in closing days of Gran Colombia.

VENEZUELA

3346. Beaujón, Oscar. El Libertador en Coro (VANH/B, 60:237, enero/marzo 1977, p. 1-24, bibl.)

Local case study of Bolivarian cult: details when the Liberator was in Coro, later tributes and monuments to him, etc.

3347. Carrera Damas, Germán. Boves: aspectos socioeconómicos de la guerra de independencia. 3. ed. Caracas, Univ. Central de Venezuela, Ediciones de la Biblioteca, 1972. 263 p., bibl., plate (Col. Temas, 48)

Exact reproduction of 2. ed. (1968), including its new prologue that commented on criticisms and other observations aroused by first (see *HLAS 28:978*).

3348. ———. La crisis de la sociedad colonial venezolana. Caracas, Dirección de Cultura de la Gobernación del Distrito Federal, 1976. 101 p. (Cuadernos de difusión, 5)

Conceptually penetrating overview of origins, progress, and general significance of Venezuelan independence movement, already noted when it first appeared as introductory essay (see *HLAS 34:2196* and *HLAS 36:2683*).

3349. Castillo Lara, Lucas G. José Laurencio Silva: viaje alrededor de una lealtad. Caracas, Archivo General de la Nación, 1973. 431 p., bibl., illus. (Biblioteca venezolana de historia, 18)

Traditional political-military biography, laudatory but at least documented, concerning Venezuelan military figure of independence who fought his way down to Peru and lived on to participate in Venezuelan affairs through the Federal War.

3350. Cunill Grau, Pedro. Cambios en el paisaje geográfico venezolano en la época de la emancipación (VANH/B, 60:237, enero/marzo 1977, p. 25-60, bibl.)

Highly informative and balanced overview, quite fully documented, of impact of independence struggle on Venezuelan human and economic geography. Treats decline and displacement of population and animal stocks, disruption of agriculture and other related matters. This article was previously published in *Boletín de la Acadmia Chilena de Historia* (86, 1972, p. 49-95).

3351. Febres Cordero, Julio. Historia de la imprenta y del periodismo en Venezuela: 1800-1830. Caracas, Banco Central de Venezuela, 1974. 262 p., facsims. (Col. Cuatricentenario de Caracas)

Not single integrated account of development of printing and journalism so much as collection of separate monographic chapters. Much miscellaneous information, but authoritative and, taken together, comprehensive.

3352. Lambert, Eric T.D. Carabobo 24 June 1821: some accounts written in English. Caracas, Fundación John Boulton, 1974. 103 p.

Mainly contemporary descriptions, naturally emphasizing role of British legion, usefully annotated by Lambert. Bilingual ed.

3353. Lucena Salmoral, Manuel. Don Simón Bolívar: consiliario electo para el Consulado caraqueño de 1809, impedido de posesionarse por parentesco con don Pedro de Vega (VANH/B, 59:235, julio/sept. 1976, p. 489-497)

Very interesting brief note that reveals mechanism of Consulado elections, extent to which that mechanism was dominated by few interlocking aristocratic families, and incidentally disqualification of Bolívar as *hacendado* representative.

3354. Motín en La Soledad (FJB/BH, 41, mayo 1976, p. 281-324)

Transcribes *proceso* drawn up following mutiny of British legionnaires near Angostura, Sept. 1820; it had been triggered by incident among British themselves.

3355. Pinto, Manuel *ed.* and *comp.* Documentos para la historia de la vida de José Antonio Páez. t. 1. Prólogo de Nicolás Perazzo. Caracas, Academia Nacional de la Historia, 1976. 419 p. (Biblioteca de la Academia Nacional de Historia, 21. Fuentes para la historia republicana de Venezuela)

Documents from various archives, some previously published and others not, spanning Páez' entire career; about equally divided pre- and post-1830. No precise explanation of criteria for selection. Prologue on his "origen y formación."

3356. Princep, John. Diario de un viaje de Santo Tomé de Angostura en la

Guayana Española, a las misiones capuchinas del Caroní. Prólogo de Efraín Schacht Aristeguieta. Introducción y notas de Jaime Tello. Caracas, Ediciones de la Presidencia de la República, 1975. 94 p., illus. (Col. Viajeros y legionarios, 3)

Account of 1818 by British trader taking supplies to Guayana. Appendix contains data on trade and shipping of Guayana 1817-20.

3357. Rosas Marcano, Jesús. Languideció sin extinguirse la escuela primaria, durante la Independencia (FJB/BH, 42, sept. 1976, p. 483-490)

Few brief notes rather than over-all analysis or description, but worth noting in lack of much else on subject.

3358. Veracoechea, Ermila de. Notas sobre los esclavos y la guerra de independencia de Venezuela (UCV/CA, 1:1, 1975, p. 159-170)

Considers two examples (from Venezuelan archives) of operation of opportunities for freedom provided by independence movement. In both, self-styled owners sought after 1830 to reduce ex-slaves to renewed slavery—and failed.

NUEVA GRANADA

3359. Actuaciones del cabildo de Tunja después de la Batalla de Boyacá (Repertorio Boyacense [Tunja, Colombia] 61:292/293, julio/dic. 1977, p. 4391-4400)

Miscellaneous documentation on activities of local government, including elections and asessment of forced loans; largely 1819-20.

3360. Bastidas Urresty, Edgar. La vendée americana: pt. 2, Las guerras de Pasto (UV/L, 6, junio 1973, p. 51-100, bibl.)

Continuation of HLAS 38:3248, which completes discussion of Pasto in independence period and briefly traces regional history to 1863.

3361. Caballero, José María. Diario de la independencia. Bogotá, Banco Popular, 1974. 253 p. (Biblioteca, 71)

New ed. of classic contemporary account.

3362. Hammett, Brian R. The counter revolution of Morillo and the insurgent clerics of New Granada: 1815-1820 (AAFH/TAM, 32:4, 1976, p. 597-617)

Though including appendix list of suspect clergymen, mainly discusses alienation from Spanish regime of certain key figures as result of perceived threats to their personal and corporate interests, and Spain's inability to win them back despite their similar troubles with patriots. Weak on general background but good original research.

3363. Molina Lemus, Leonardo. El proceso contra Bartolomé Lizón (ACH/BHA, 63:712, enero/marzo 1976, p. 39-55, bibl.)

Royalist execution of prisoners and related outrages against people of Cúcuta, following battle of Llano del Carrillo in Oct. 1813; as revealed in unpublished royalist trial proceedings.

3364. Ocampo López, Javier. La agitación revolucionaria en el Nuevo Reino de Granada y el ejemplo de la independencia de Estados Unidos (PAIGH/H, 82, julio/dic. 1976, p. 29-52)

Considers pre-1810 reverberations of US independence in Nueva Granada, then efforts to apply Anglo-American political model during independence period itself, with special reference to federalism in first stage of revolution.

3365. Rodríguez Avellaneda, Antonio José. Biografía del Coronel Juan José Buenaventura de Ahumada y Gutiérrez. Bogotá, Imprenta y Litografía de las Fuerzas Armadas, 1974. 409 p., bibl., facsims., plates (Col. De oro del militar colombiano, 7)

Despite its appearance in military publication series, this work of well-informed amateur of historical writing contains little of conventional military history. Ahumada (1786-1838) did serve in war of independence but is chiefly remembered as an energetic alcalde and jefe político of Bogotá in Gran Colombian period. Alongside biographical details (with special emphasis on his studies at Colegio del Rosario), one finds a great amount of interesting though not necessarily new costumbrista and other information on Bogotá.

3366. Tisnés Jiménez, Roberto María. La independencia en la costa atlántica. Bogotá, Academia Colombiana de Historia [and] Editorial Kelly, 1976. 444 p., bibl. (Biblioteca de historia nacional, 134)

Hodgepodge, useful essentially in absence of any systematic study to date of independence movement on Caribbean coast of Nueva Granada. With it comes facsimile reproduction of Catecismo o instrucción popular (Cartagena, 1814), by patriot priest Juan Fernández de Sotomayor.

QUITO

3367. Ferro, Carlos A. San Martín y la revolución ecuatoriana. B.A., Editorial Cuarto Poder, 1976. 183 p. (Col. Historia de Latinoamérica)

Synthetic treatment—originally presented in form of lectures—of contribution made by Argentina and particularly San Martín to Ecuadorian independence, with brief final glance at Guayaquil interview. Appendix offers some pertinent documents. Nothing new, but rather good overview.

3368. Fuentes-Figueroa Rodríguez, Julián. La emancipación del Ecuador: el Libertador y Sucre en el sur. t. 1/3. Caracas, Gráficas Herpa, 1974. 3 v. (323, 321, 396 p.) illus. (Historia general de Venezuela)

Hardly work of original research, but does bring a lot of things together. Vol. 1 takes story from "Precursor" Eugenio Espejo to Nov. 1821, with numerous long quotations from primary and secondary sources. Rest of work continues to departure of Bolívar for Peru, with most of its "chapters" wholly consisting of reprinted decrees or correspondence.

3369. Larrea Alba, Luis. Sucre, alto conductor político y militar: la Campaña Libertadora de 1821-1822. Prólogo de José Luis Salcedo Bastardo. Quito, Editorial Casa de la Cultura Ecuatoriana, 1975. 226 p., bibl., fold. maps.

This is strictly military history, of events culminating in battle of Pichincha. Based on standard sources but very clearly organized and, despite title, not afraid to criticize Sucre's leadership.

3370. Loor Moreira, Wilfrido. La Provincia de Guayaquil en lucha por su independencia. Guayaquil, Ecua., Editorial Gregorio de Portoviejo, 1974. 90 p.

History of independent Guayaquil, to its definitive incorporation into Gran Colombia. Pedestrian, and somewhat uneven in coverage and organization, but by conscientious local historian who knows his material.

PERU

3371. Grisanti, Angel. La batalla, la capitulación y las actas de Ayacucho. Caracas, Ministerio de la Defensa, 1974. 193 p., facsims.

Series of newspaper articles, with good bit of argumentation on points of specialized interest. They mainly concern not the battle but capitulation and copies thereof.

3372. La independencia nacional: conferencias dictadas por encargo de la Comisión Nacional del Sesquicentenario de la Independencia del Perú; tercer ciclo. Lima, Comisión Nacional del Sesquicentenario de la Independencia del Perú, 1974. 143 p.

Concluding "cycle" of lectures aimed at Peruvian history teachers mostly by recognized scholars. These deal with Bolivarian phase. The most substantial, by Lt. Col. Abel Carrera Naranjo "Bolívar: Campaña de 1824" (p. 73-139) unhesitatingly accepts him as "Liberator of Peru."

3373. *Nuevo Día del Perú.* Semanario. No. 1, 1 julio 1824 [through] No. 12, 25 sept. 1824- . Trujillo, Peru.

Short-lived (July-Sept. 1824) weekly periodical which served chiefly as journal of comment and opinion. Directed by Hipólito Unanue, it was published in Trujillo. This facsim. ed. includes historical introduction by Eugenio Alarco and was printed Lima 1974.

3374. Pease G.Y., Franklin. Un movimiento mesiánico en Lircay, Huancavélica: 1811 (PEMN/R, 40, 1974, p. 220-252, bibl.)

Useful reminder that religious cults did not cease because there was an independence movement underway. Presents document concerning one such, with good introduction.

3375. Perazzo, Nicolás. Sánchez Carrión y Unanue: ministros del Libertador. Caracas, Oficina Central de Información (OCI), 1975. 251 p., bibl.

Brief biographies of José Sánchez Carrión and Hipólito Unanue, emphasizing their collaboration with Bolívar, followed by substantial group of pertinent documents.

3376. Pereyra Plasencia, Hugo. La campaña libertadora de Junín y Ayacucho. Lima, Comisión Nacional del Sesquicentenario de la Independencia del Perú, 1975. 114 p., bibl.

Another narrative of the decisive 1824 campaign. Factual, orderly presentation, based on standard sources.

3377. Selección documental del período bolivariano (PEAGN/R, 3, 1974, p. 9-255)

Special issue, whose contents are mostly inedited and largely military or political. Includes:
"Documentación Patriota" p. 9-76
"Documentación Realista" p. 77-115
"Documentación 1825-1828: Período Inicial de la

República" p. 117-187 "Indices y Copiadores de Oficios: 1823-1826" p. 189-255.

3378. Temple, Ella Dunbar. Comisión Nacional del Sesquicentenario de la Independencia del Perú (PAIGH/H, 79, enero/junio 1975, p. 148-154)

Succinct summary of official sesquicentennial observances, including major publication ventures.

3379. Vergara Arias, Gustavo. Montoneras y guerrillas en el etapa de la emancipación del Perú: 1820-1825. Lima, Imprenta y Litografía Salesiana, 1974. 262 p., bibl., facsims., map, tables.

Tightly organized, fact-crammed volume in which preliminary chapters on sources and on general characteristics of both *montoneras* and guerrillas are followed by detailed account of their activities. Author frankly acknowledges his aim of demonstrating importance of "popular" contribution to Peruvian independence; he has worked extensively in both archival and other sources in order to do so.

3380. Villanueva Urteaga, Horacio. Cajamarca: apuntes para su historia. Cuzco, Perú, Editorial Garcilaso, 1975. 269 p., bibl., illus., plates.

Brief but documented examination of activities of Bolívar in Cajamarca, men and money he extracted from the region.

3381. ———. Simón Bolívar en el Cuzco. Caracas, Biblioteca Venezolana de Historia, 1971. 103 p. (Biblioteca venezolana de historia, 14)

Study of what Bolívar did in or relating to Cuzco, over half devoted to pertinent documents. Sticks closely to a limited topic, covers it admirably.

ALTO PERU

3382. Abecia Baldivieso, Valentín. Historiografía de la Independencia de Bolivia (PAIGH/H, 83, enero/junio 1977, p. 193-208)

Refers to sources written during period of independence itself, defined as 1780-1825. Coverage uneven, and too much time spent complaining about writers' ignorance of modern historiographical standards; but still worth consulting.

3383. Bedoya Ballivián, Mario. Manuel Victorio García Lanza: protomártir de la independencia. La Paz, Editorial Los Amigos del Libro, 1975. 203 p., facsims., plates.

Slightly novelized but documented story of one of martyrs of 1809 La Paz revolution. Short documentary appendix, portraits of descendants.

3384. Costa de la Torre, Arturo. Bibliografía de la revolución del 16 de julio de 1809. La Paz, Editora Universo, 1974. 127 p.

Exhaustive listing of sources, from unpublished manuscripts to recent newspaper articles.

3385. Crespo R., Alberto; René Arze Aguirre; Florencia B. de Romero; and Mary Money. La vida cotidiana en La Paz durante la guerra de la independencia: 1800-1825. La Paz, Univ. Mayor de San Andrés, 1975. 278 p., bibl., plates.

Collection of often fascinating details, held together by analysis of varying depth, on population, taxation, housing, letters, Church and independence, and much more. Coverage sometimes uneven, but solidly grounded in research; a highly welcome contribution.

3386. Fernández, Emilio. La revolución del 25 de mayo de 1809: recomposición. Prólogo de Joaquín Gantier V. La Paz, Biblioteca del Sesquicentenario de la República, 1975. 404 p., bibl. (Biblioteca, 11)

Chronicle of abortive preliminary uprising in Chuquisaca, in which Audiencia deposed President of Charcas accused of carlotist sympathies. Devoid of professional sense and too eager to read far-reaching significance into events, but contains much detailed information, chiefly by incorporation of documents (or excerpts from same) into text.

3387. Urquizo Sossa, Carlos ed. and comp. Proclama de la Junta Tuitiva de 1809: esclarecimiento para la historia. La Paz, Casa Municipal de la Cultura Franz Tamayo, 1976. 145 p., facsims.

Historiographical references, handwriting analysis, and other proofs are brought together here to demonstrate authenticity of commonly accepted version of radical 27 July 1809 proclamation of La Paz revolutionary junta.

3388. Vázquez Machicao, Humberto. Orígenes históricos de la nacionalidad boliviana. La Paz, Univ. Mayor de San Andrés, 1975. 191 p.

Collection of essays by one of Bolivia's principal modern historians, mostly dealing with independence period, some published before and others not. Most important among the latter are "La Creación de la República de Bolivia," which chiefly reviews events of 1825, and the one that gives its name to volume as a whole, stressing colonial roots and nature of settlement of Bolivian *Oriente*.

3389. Villarroel Triveño, Augusto *ed.* and *comp.* La fundación de Bolivia: documentos para su historia. Cochabamba, Bol., Centro de Investigaciones Históricas de la Normal Superior Integrada Católica, 1975. 224 p., bibl., facsims.

Contains correspondence and other documents on conclusion of military struggle and convocation and proceedings of Assembly of 1825 that created independent Bolivia, e.g. minutes of Assembly's sessions. Compiler's preliminary discussion is not especially noteworthy; but a good documentary collection.

CHILE

3390. Avila Martel, Alamiro de. Impresos relativos a la Declaración de la Independencia de Chile. Santiago, Editorial Jurídica de Chile, 1969. 135 p., facsims., plates.

Good preliminary study; facsimiles of *Gazeta* issues, manifestos, etc.; portraits of some key figures involved.

3391. Carrera, José Miguel. Diario de José Miguel Carrera. Santiago, Editora Nacional Quimantu, 1973. 252 p. (Serie nuestra historia. Col. Camino abierto)

New ed. of major source which apparently had not been reprinted in full for surprisingly long time.

3392. Estellé, Patricio. Gestiones carlotinas en el Reino de Chile: 1808-1809 (EEHA/HBA, 18:2/3, 1974, p. 195-212)

Based in considerable part on British records (some of them reproduced in documentary appendix), examines intrigues of Princess Carlota in Chile, for which a British merchant who worked between B.A. and Rio served as intermediary. They generated rumors and suspicions but not, of course, positive results.

3393. Hanisch Espíndola, Walter. El catecismo político-cristiano: las ideas y la época, 1810. Santiago, Editorial Andrés Bello, 1970. 147 p.

Systematic contribution to intellectual history of independence, which first analyzes content of anonymous *Catecismo* as key document of Chilean revolution, reviews possible sources of ideas expressed, then discusses incidence of same or related ideas at beginning of independence movement. Situates *Catecismo* itself squarely in "populist scholastic" tradition.

3394. Heise González, Julio. O'Higgins, forjador de una tradición democrática. Santiago, Talleres de Artesanía Gráfica R. Neupert. 1975. 187 p., bibl., plate.

Brief but heavily documented, interpretative study (highly favorable to O'Higgins) but with no lack of concrete supporting data. Focuses on revolution's political course and O'Higgins' government.

3395. Rector, John. Transformaciones comerciales producidas por la independencia de Chile (SCHG/R, 143, 1975, p. 106-126)

Important though brief article, sketchy on some points but based on original research. Treats impact of military events and new regulations on quantity and composition of commerce, decline of prerevolutionary leading merchants, emergence of new ones (especially foreign).

3396. Rodríguez S., Juan Agustín. La vida militar de O'Higgins: síntesis de la historia de la independencia. Santiago, Editora Nacional Gabriela Mistral, 1975. 258 p.

Based on traditional historical literature and undocumented, but a convenient reference as it gives concentrated attention to military aspects of O'Higgins' career. Also strongly defends him against criticism of. e.g. Francisco Encina

3397. Salvat Monguillot, Manuel. El delito de infidelidad a la patria: un caso chileno (ANH/B, 40:87, 1973, p. 17-39)

After brief review of treatment of disaffected by both patriots and royalists, examines in more detail the case of *oidor* José de Santiago Concha, whose difficulties under insurgents were not severe enough to clear him of suspicion during Spanish Reconquest. Instructive and documented case study.

RIO DE LA PLATA

3398. Alen Lascano, Luis C. Dependencia y liberación en los orígenes argentinos. B.A., Editorial El Coloquio, 1974. 193 p. (Col. Ensayos, 3)

Another treatise on disastrous economic effects of "free trade" as unleashed at time of independence by English and their native collaborators. Though facts and interpretation are all familiar, they are coherently presented; good short introduction to topic.

3399. Cabral, Salvador. Artigas como caudillo argentino. Prólogo de J.E. Spilimbergo. B.A., Ediciones Octubre, 1975. 218 p.

Popular synthesis, frankly following left-nationalist line of Jorge Abelardo Ramos. Emphasizes importance of Artigas as popular caudillo with social program (as noted by Uruguayan leftist admirers) and also as dedicated foe of "Balkanization" of Latin America at hands of British imperialism and its lackeys.

3400. Carámbula de Barreiro, Margarita. La revolución rioplatense en las notas del periódico *Barbados Mercury and Bridge-Town Gazette*: 1815-1819 (UMHN/RH, 46:136/138, feb. 1975, p. 225-244, facsim.)

Brief introduction followed by selection of articles (in translation) dealing with revolution in general and, more specifically, activities of Platine corsairs.

3401. Destefani, Laurio H. Los Marinos en las invasiones inglesas. B.A., Comando General de la Armada, Depto. de Estudios Históricos Militares, 1975. 459 p., bibl., maps, plates (Serie B. Historia naval argentina, 15)

Highly detailed treatment of participation of naval forces in 1806-07 defense of Río de la Plata against British; authoritative though somewhat pedestrian in tone. Has epilogue on later careers of principal figures. Of importance to independence studies because of light shed on formative antecedents of military establishment.

3402. Doucet, Gastón Gabriel. "El Curioso Católico" y una crónica eclesiástica de Salta en tiempos de la revolución (ANH/IE, 20, enero/junio 1976, p. 323-339)

Good description and analysis of manuscript by anonymous disgruntled clergyman concerning revolution of independence and its consequences. Reproduces, with notes, a segment dealing with history of Church in Salta 1808-29.

3403. Gandía, Enrique de. Prolegómenos de la desorganización nacional en la Argentina (JEHM/R, 1:8, 1975, p. 147-179)

Events (political, military, diplomatic) of 1819, last year before national unity dissolved; from B.A. perspective, and in purely chronological order. Very lack of thematic structure does give an idea of how miscellaneous developments must have appeared to contemporaries, and for some reference purposes may be an advantage.

3404. Grenón, Pedro. Episodios de la resistencia española íntima a la Revolución de Mayo (ANH/IE, 19, julio/dic. 1975, p. 367-422)

With extensive quotations from Córdoba archives, presents series of episodes involving real or alleged antipatriot activities and/or minor disputes of police or administrative nature.

3405. Heredia, Edmundo A. Manuel Moreno al servicio de la Corona española en 1817 (CEHA/NH, 3:8, mayo 1970, p. 67-79)

Interesting brief note with documents. Mariano's brother, exiled from Argentina, contacts Spanish minister to US to discuss restoration of Spanish rule—only to have the minister show scant interest as he is proposing cession of Platine area to Portugal.

3406. Martín, María Haydée. El censo del año 1813 en la provincia de Buenos Aires (América [Revista cuatrimestral de asuntos históricos, B.A.] 1:1, abril 1976, p. 13-20, map, table)

Background discussion and brief description of incomplete (or at least incompletely preserved) provincial census.

3407. Martín de Codoni, Elvira Luisa. El intento de gobierno de juntas de 1811 en el Río de La Plata (EEHA/AEA, 31, 1974, p. 843-953)

Well-researched article that despite its somewhat narrow focus sheds considerable light on political process of independence period. It examines terms and implementation of Feb. 1811 *reglamento* for establishment of juntas to head government in interior cities, noting impact on local ambitions and rivalries; then covers specific case of Mendoza in more detail, to abolition of its junta in early 1812.

3408. Molina-Muñoz, Stella-Maris. La expedición pacificadora al Río de la Plata de 1819 (SHM/RHM, 21:42, 1977, p. 51-75, facsim.)

Mostly familiar, but some new research concerning organization, delays, and other problems facing expedition whose departure was ultimately thwarted by Riego revolt of Jan. 1820.

3409. Préstamos y donaciones de patriotas, españoles y portugueses vecinos de Mendoza en los años 1813 a 1817 (JEHM/R, 2:8, 1975, p. 911-926)

Listing of individuals and their respective "donations" for patriot cause, of obvious interest for regional social history as well as providing further illustration of wartime financing.

3410. Reyes Abadie, Washington. Artigas y el federalismo en el Río de La Plata. t. 2, 1810-1820. Montevideo, Ediciones de la Banda Oriental, 1974. 328 p. (Historia uruguaya, 2)

In reality a general synthesis, largely political and military, of Platine revolution; with particular emphasis on Artigas and federalism as stated in title. Quite systematic. Naturally critical of *unitarismo porteño*, but not mere polemicizing.

Tanzi, Héctor José. El poder político y la independencia argentina. See item 2378.

3411. Villegas, Alfredo G. San Martín y su época. t. 1. B.A., Ediciones Depalma, 1976. 327 p., bibl., facsims.

This t. 1 (of which about half is documentary appendix) takes San Martín from family origins to participation in Oct. 1812 coup against First Triumvirate. Based on extensive research, clearly organized (with numbered paragraphs), traditional in tone despite certain revisionist pretensions, but not mere eulogy.

PARAGUAY

3412. Autos de la Revolución del Paraguay del 15 de mayo de 1811. Asunción, Academia Paraguaya de la Historia, 1976. 1 v. (Unpaged) facsims.

Mostly unpublished documentation relating to coup that launched Paraguay on independent career, including its repercussions mainly within Paraguay itself though also on relations with B.A. Items appear in facsimile only, but most are quite legible.

URUGUAY

3413. Abadie-Aicardi, Aníbal and C. Alberto Roca. Montevideo y la Corona española: 1806-1812 (CEHA/NH, 8:16, dic. 1975, p. 195-210)

Montevideo as bastion of loyalty seeks assorted honors and other favors from Spain, receives mostly honors. Original though somewhat narrow research note.

3414. Gadea, Juan Alberto. Informe a la Comisión Nacional Archivo Artigas (EMGE/BH, 141/144, 1974, p. 73-139)

Report actually written 1945, concerning certain local archives of Montevideo and their holdings, with special reference to matters of *artiguista* interest. Some *expedientes* of latter sort are discussed more fully.

3415. García, Flavio A. Las instrucciones de Maldonado, 1813: contribución al estudio de la Asamblea General Constituyente (ANH/IE, 19, julio/dic. 1975, p. 347-365)

Another discussion of Uruguayan objectives and demands for representation at time of 1813 Platine constitutional assembly. Says nothing new on underlying issues and tensions but further rounds out picture of events.

3416. Melogno, Tabaré. Artigas, la causa de los pueblos. Montevideo, Ediciones de la Banda Oriental, 1976. 111 p., illus (Historia uruguaya. Serie, 2. Los hombres, 1)

Good, short, attractively presented biography.

19th AND 20th CENTURIES

COLOMBIA AND VENEZUELA

WINTHROP R. WRIGHT

Associate Professor of History
University of Maryland, College Park

VENEZUELAN HISTORIOGRAPHY HAS REACHED a transition point. Although old-school historians, doctors, and lawyers still publish the bulk of the works on modern Venezuelan history, a new generation of young North American and Venezuelan historians has begun to make important contributions. The Venezuelan public has discovered the richness of contemporary history. Students crowd into history classrooms throughout the nation and demonstrate considerable interest in the post-1850 period, with special emphasis upon the Castro/Gómez era. Thanks to the efforts of Professor Oscar Abdala, both the Univ. Católica Andrés Bello and the Univ. Central de Venezuela have expanded their offerings in history and now teach courses in US, European, African, and Asian history.

Most Venezuelan historians continue to write along traditional lines, as best demonstrated by two recent books by the leading historiographer Germán Carrera Damas (see items 3444-3445). A study of Venezuela during 1902 by Manuel Rodríguez Campos (item 3458), prepared under the direction of Eduardo Arcila Farías for the Univ. Central de Venezuela's Castro/Gómez project, sticks to the usual political descriptions. Further traditional history appears in the latest volumes of a political history written by the former activist Juan Bautista Fuenmayor (item 3449), who reflects the influence of his mentor Federico Brito Figueroa in his approach to modern politics. A predilection for documentary collection absorbs the energy of many Venezuelan historians. Tómas Enrique Carrillo Batalla has presented a useful study of public finance during the 1860s as part of a documentary series edited by Pedro Grases (item 3443). A new document series published by the Univ. Católica Andrés Bello begins with a two-volume set edited by Naudy Suárez Figueroa on political movements and parties between 1899 and 1948 (item 3460). Clara Posani has put together a vivid image of the Gómez era in her compilation of photographs taken from the collection of Luis F. Toro, official photographer of Gómez. As in the past, the *Boletín del Archivo Histórico de Miraflores* makes available rich information on the Castro and Gómez administrations (see items 3440-3442).

A growing interest in Venezuelan history in the US has resulted in a number of dissertations in recent years. Several chapters and distilled articles have been published. A book of essays on Venezuelan political development and economic growth, published by the Fundación John Boulton (item 3453), includes excellent chapters by Robert P. Matthews on the Monagas decade, Benjamin A. Frankel on the Guerra Federal, and Mary B. Floyd on the Guzmán-Blanco period. The book also has a chapter by a young Venezuelan, Nikita Harwich Vallenilla, grandson of Laureano Vallenilla Lanz. Judith Ewell has condensed her dissertation on the extradition of Marcos Pérez Jiménez into an excellent article (item 3448). Two other dissertations recently published in full-length translation were not available for review: Robert P. Matthews' study of the origins of the Guerra Federal, and Harrison Howard's treatment of Rómulo Gallegos' political career. They will appear in *HLAS 42*.

With few notable exceptions, the topics of Church and State continue to monopolize the literature on Colombia. Its historians do not seem to use any new methodological techniques and, in contrast to the growing interest of foreigners in the country's colonial history noted in this volume by Hamerly (see p. 206), few foreigners have published works on modern Colombia. Richard L. Sharpless has written a solid political biography of Jorge Eliécer Gaitán, well worth reading (item 3436). Two excellent chapters on land and labor, written by Malcolm Deas and Michael Taussig (items 3426 and 3437) comprise part of Duncan, Rutledge, and Harding's *Land and labour in Latin America* (see item 2156). Charles W. Bergquist's study of the presidential election of 1897 is well written (item 3419). Other than the above mentioned works, very little of note has been written on modern Colombia. Readers might like to compare the Sharpless work with a partisan account of the organization of agrarian labor between 1925 and the 1930s, written by Gloria Gaitán (item 3427).

COLOMBIA

3417. Agudelo Villa, Hernando. Antioquia liberal: de la resistencia a la libertad democrática. Bogotá, Ediciones Tercer Mundo, 1974. 157 p.

Polemical treatment of new leftism in recent Colombian political development. Emphasizes importance of Antioquia in movement.

Alvarez Díaz, Enrique. Herencia colonial en la vida rural colombiana. See item 269.

Bastidas Urresty, Edgar. La vendée americana: pt. 2, Las guerras de Pasto. See item 3360.

3418. Bateman, Alfredo D. Páginas para la historia de la ingeniería colombiana: galería de ingenieros colombianos. Bogotá, Editorial Kelly, 1972. 634 p. (Biblioteca de historia nacional, 114)

Deals with history of engineering in Colombia from colonial times to present. Emphasizes role of various institutions, including Observatorio Astronómico

Nacional, Faculty of Engineering, Sociedad Colombiana de Ingenieros, and works of Ministerio de Obras Públicas, as well as brief biographical sketches of over 90 Colombian and foreign engineers who made outstanding contributions.

3419. Bergquist, Charles W. The political economy of the Colombian presidential election of 1897 (HAHR, 56:1, Feb. 1976, p. 1-30, table)

Argues that Colombian parties in 1897 divided along lines of elite ties to evolving capitalist system of North Atlantic. Parties represented divergent economic interests.

3420. Caicedo Castilla, José Joaquín. Historia diplomática. t. 1/2. Bogotá, Academia Colombiana de Historia [and] Ediciones Lerner, 1974. 2 v. (441, 486 p.) bibl., map, plates.

Generally non-interpretive compilation of data related to Colombia's foreign relations 1810 to 1970s. Vol. 1 ends with material related to question of political asylum for Víctor Raúl Haya de la Torre at Colombian Embassy in Lima. Mostly excerpts from treaties. Based on secondary works.

3421. Colombia. Departamento Administrativo Nacional de Estadística. Estadísticas históricas. Bogotá, 1975. 200 p., tables.

Useful data on 19th century. Includes census data from 1780 to 1905, as well as information on education, health, justice, fiscal affairs, and foreign trade.

3422. Davis, Robert H. Education in New Granada: Lorenzo María Lleras and the Colegio del Espíritu Santo, 1846-1853 (AAFH/TAM, 33:3, Jan. 1977, p. 490-503)

Educational progress aborted by politics, bureaucratic restrictions, lack of finances, and personal problems. Private school failed in mid-19th century, but did introduce new concepts to Colombian education.

3423. ———. Historical dictionary of Colombia. Metuchen, N.J., The Scarecrow Press, 1977. 280 p., bibl.

Useful for basic information. Short definitions and descriptions limit usefulness to general readers.

3424. Deas, Malcolm. A Colombian coffee estate: Santa Bárbara, Cundinamarca, 1870-1912 (*in* Duncan, Kenneth; Ian Rutledge; and Colin Hardings *eds.* Land and labour in Latin America [see item 2156] p. 269-298, maps, tables)

Excellent description of relations among coffee plantation owners, their mayordomos, and peasants during late 19th century. Based on rich correspondence between liberal plantation owner, Roberto Herrera Restrepo, who resided in Bogotá, and his administrator, Cornelio Rubio. Article shows well human side of land and labor relations in Colombia and aptly describes conditions that prevailed. Deas' political discussions are clear, and reveal dilemma of pacifist Herrera, who tried to protect his sharecroppers and peasants from ravages of civil wars. Herrera, a liberal, suffered from fact that town closest to his estate was controlled by conservatives. Good description of sharecropping, with explanations of tensions *hacienda/arrendatario* system created.

3425. Duque Botero, Guillermo. Historia de Salamina: vida municipal, siglos XIX y XX. Manizales, Colombia, Biblioteca de Autores Caldenses, 1974. 292 p., facsims., maps, plates, tables.

Pedestrian, Church related local history. Perhaps useful to someone interested in details of local or regional social history. [D. Bushnell]

3426. Echeverri M., Aquiles. Sangre irlandesa en Antioquia: biografía del Doctor Hugo Blair Brown, miembro de la Legión Británica y médico-coronel de los ejércitos patriotas. Prólogo de Jaime Serna Gómez. Medellín, Colombia, Academia Antioqueña de Historia, 1972. 141 p., bibl. (Col. Academia antioqueña de historia, 17)

Discursive and anecdotal sketch of military surgeon with Bolívar's armies who settled in Antioquia, there founding a family whose various branches are traced. Modest contribution, of interest mainly for regional social history. [D. Bushnell]

Fals Borda, Orlando. Capitalismo, hacienda y poblamiento: su desarrollo en la costa atlántica. See item 3073.

3427. Gaitán, Gloria. Colombia: la lucha por la tierra en la década del treinta: génesis de la organización sindical campesina. Bogotá, Ediciones Tercer Mundo, 1976. 102 p., tables.

Partisan account of organization of agrarian labor between 1925 and late 1930s. Written by daughter of Jorge Eliécer Gaitán.

Gallo, Carmenza. Hipótesis de la acumulación originaria de capital en Colombia. See *HLAS 39:3253*.

3428. Galvis Galvis, Alejandro. Memorias de un político centenarista. t. 1. Bucaramanga, Colombia, n.p., 1975. 545 p., illus.

Memoirs of 20th-century politician, member of Liberal party.

3429. Gómez Picón, Alirio. Semblanza de Antonio José Restrepo. v. 4. Bogotá, Editorial Kelly, 1974. 361 p., illus.

Traditional treatment of political career of illustrious Colombian from Antioquia.

González G., Fernán E. Iglesia católica y partidos políticos en Colombia. See *HLAS 39:7294*.

Guzman G., Manuel José. Los andokes: historia, conciencia étnica, y explotación del caucho. See *HLAS 39:1333*.

3430. Helguera, J. León. Indigenismo in Colombia: a facet of the national identity search, 1821-1973. Buffalo, N.Y., SUNY at Buffalo, Council on International Studies, 1976. 21 p. (mimeo) (Special studies series)

Brief summary of conquest and assimilation of Colombian Indians and their role in country's history. Seen as rural and weak minority since conquest, with few exceptions. Brief discussion of New Indigenistas movement of 1930s-40s. Mentions impact of Manuel Quintan Lame, Juan Friede, and Victor Daniel Bonilla on *indigenismo*.

Hobsbawm, Eric J. Ideology and social change in Colombia. See *HLAS 39:7297*.

3431. Lleras Camargo, Alberto. Mi gente. v. 1. Bogotá, Ediciones del Banco de la República, 1975. 153 p.

Pt. 1 of memoirs of 20th-century politician. Much emphasis upon recounting family history, especially 19th-century politicos. Mostly anecdotal, though detailed, treatment of grandfather, uncles and other important figures. Interesting insights into family through account of early childhood.

3432. Lleras Restrepo, Carlos. Borradores para una historia de la república liberal. t. 1. Bogotá, Canal Ramírez Antares, 1975. 460 p., plates.

First of series of historical sketches written about liberal experiences since 1930. Vol. 1 deals with period 1929-35. Polemical, but informative as view of participant and party insider.

3433. Noguera, María Luz de. Vestido, modas y confecciones. Bogotá, Canal Ramírez-Antares, 1974. 294 p., plates (Enciclopedia del desarrollo colombiano. Col. Los fundadores, 4)

Encyclopedia of fashion in Colombia from conquest to 1974. Gives brief descriptions of modes of dress in each epoch, for men and women, and for all classes. Brief summary in English. Lists leading producers, models, textile companies, and the like. Useful if not inspired, especially for seeing foreign and indigenous influence upon dress.

Ocampo, Javier. De la historiografía romántica y académica a la "nueva historia" de Colombia. See item 3082.

3434. *Papel Periódico Ilustrado.* Año 2, No. 25, 1882 [through] Año 3, No. 48, 1883- . Bogotá.

Facsim. ed. (printed Cali, Colombia, Carvajal & Co., 1976) of several issues semi-monthly periodical published in Bogotá (Aug. 1881-May 1888) and edited by Alberto Urdaneta.

3435. Restrepo Canal, Carlos. La Nueva Granada. t. 1, 1840-1849. Bogotá, Academia Colombiana de Historia [and] Ediciones Lerner, 1975. 508 p., map, plate (Historia extensa de Colombia, 8)

Continuation of essentially detailed narrative chronology of war and factionalism in Colombia during formative years of Republic. Based mostly on secondary sources, though more primary material was used than in vol. 1 of series. Also, women are recognized, though minimally, for at least their physical participation in wars of period. Useful for detailed political facts.

Revista del Archivo Nacional. See item 3085.

Roldán Oquendo, Ornán. Las relaciones entre México y Colombia: 1810-1862. See *HLAS 39:8709*.

3436. Sharpless, Richard E. Gaitán of Colombia: a political biography. Pittsburgh, Pa., Univ. of Pittsburgh Press, 1978. 229 p., tables.

Clearly written, well-documented study of Gaitán's political life. Argues that Gaitán was most innovative and popular politician in Colombia at time of his 1948 assassination. Perceives Gaitán as populist, socialist who believed that gaining control of traditional Liberal Party was only way to bring about social change in Colombia.

3437. Taussig, Michael. The evolution of rural wage labour in the Cauca Valley of Colombia: 1700-1970 (*in* Duncan,

Kenneth; Ian Rutledge; and Colin Hardings eds. Land and labour in Latin America [see item 2156] p. 397-434, map)

Well-written article which traces metamorphosis of predominantly black labor force of Cauca Valley from slavery, through subsistence farming, to migrant labor as alienated peasants. Free peasants lost their status as squatters when new class of rural capitalists took over large estates. Rural capitalists finally won out over labor, and forced peasants into accepting role as wage-earning proletarians. Change largely explained by four factors: 1) political unification of upper class and consolidation of nation-state; 2) massive increase in US investment; 3) opening of valley to sea by rail; and 4) sharp increase in local rural population (p. 422). Labor surplus sealed fate of valley wage-workers. Their poverty continues as result of combination of their religious beliefs, spending habits, and contractual relations with rural capitalists.

3438. Tirado Mejía, Alvaro. Aspectos sociales de las guerras civiles en Colombia. Bogotá, Editorial Andes, 1976. 493 p., bibl., illus., tables.

Collection of secondary readings related to causes and consequences of civil wars in Colombia during 19th century. First 66 p. present author's views on subject in interpretive essay. Shows some social aspects of civil wars.

3439. ———. Colombia en la repartición imperialista: 1870-1914. Medellín, Colombia, Ediciones Hombre Nuevo, 1976. 231 p.

Attempt to write Colombian history at "popular level" from foreign point of view. Polemical, but based on French archival material related to diplomatic questions concerning US hegemony over Panama Canal and United Fruit lands, and other late 19th-century "interventions" such as British at Timbiqui mines and Germans at Bucaramanga. Also touches upon 19th-century reclamation claims cases.

Torres León, Fernán. Trayectoria histórica de la universidad colombiana. See *HLAS 39:4456*.

Uribe Garras, Carlos. Panorama de la economía colombiana. See *HLAS 39:3286*.

VENEZUELA

Ascanio Jiménez, Augustín. El Golfo de Venezuela es territorio venezolano. See *HLAS 39:8790*.

3440. *Boletín del Archivo Histórico de Miraflores.* Presidencia de la República. Secretaría General. Año 17, No. 87, sept./oct. 1975- . Caracas.

Deals mostly with events in 1900, including relations between Castro and Gómez following Caracas earthquake of 29 Oct. 1900. Strained relations between Castro Tachirense faction and Gómez. Also has documents on affairs in Oriente and Central region of Venezuela during Oct. and Nov. 1900, as Castro tried to consolidate his power. One segment deals with Juan Francisco Castillo's death, another with Monseñor Jáurequi Moreno's role. Final section comprises telegrams from Feb. 1905 that shed light on machinery of Castro's political system.

3441. ———. ———. ———. Año 17, No. 88, nov./dic. 1975- . Caracas.

Begins with speech by Nicolás Hernández (leading anti-gomecista living in exile) to Masonic Lodge in Puerto Rico in 1921, in which he attacked Venezuelan Masons associated with Gómez. Other sections treat Castro's trip to Guárico, Apure, Bolívar, Sucre, Anzoátegui, and Margarita in 1905, and events from Dec. 1900, including relations Castro and Gómez had with Colombian Liberals.

3442. ———. ———. ———. Año 17, No. 90, marzo/abril 1976- Caracas.

Contains documents concerning mixed bag of issues during Gómez regime, including territorial limits with Colombia (1918), biography of Castro published in France (1913), internal conflicts within Gómez family, problems related to Zulia and Sucre in mid-1920s, as well as section on *Falke* incident (1929).

3443. Carrillo Batalla, Tomás Enrique. Historia de las finanzas públicas en Venezuela. v. 15, 1863-1865. Caracas, Editorial Arte, 1976. 348 p., tables.

Very useful and well edited collection of documents related to fiscal practices and policies, especially international loans, at end of Federal Wars. Introductory essay deals with means by which Venezuela's great international debt burden served everyone but public. Vol. 15 in series edited by Pedro Grases.

3444. Carrera Damas, Germán. Historia contemporánea de Venezuela: bases metodológicas. Caracas. Univ. Central de Venezuela, 1977. 258 p., table.

Good book for understanding modern Venezuelan historiography. Chapters on methodology and periodization are most revealing. Author believes that World War II was turning point in evolution of Venezuela, with new oruer emerging after 1945. Carrera concludes by stating that historians should take part in planning new society at all levels.

3445. ———. Validacón del pasado: discursos, conferencias y ponencias.

Caracas, Univ. Central de Venezuela, 1975. 230 p. (Ediciones de la biblioteca)

Collection of provocative lectures by Venezuela's leading historiographer. Includes text of Bolívar's speech of 15 Feb. 1818 to Angostura Congress.

3446. Dávila, Mauro. Arqueo hemerográfico de la ciudad de Mérida: siglo XIX. Mérida, Ven., n.p., 1972. 214 p.

List of newspapers, publishers, and dates of publications for Mérida (1840-98) found in Venezuelan archives and collections.

3447. Escovar Salom, Ramón. Evolución política de Venezuela. Caracas, Monte Avila Editores, 1975. 168 p., bibl.

Essentially a wide-ranging constitutional study, which shows continuity in many Venezuelan Constitutions promulgated between 1811-1961. Also treats origins of Venezuelan laws, with brief comments on colonial heritage. Essay in which author synthesizes existing interpretations and data, rather than introduces new material.

3448. Ewell, Judith. The extradition of Marcos Pérez Jiménez, 1959-63: practical precedent for enforcement of administrative honesty? (JLAS, 9, pt. 2, Nov. 1977, p. 291-313)

Well-written and objective account of events that led up to extradition of Venezuelan dictator Marcos Pérez Jiménez. Based on Venezuelan and US court documents, interviews, and secondary material. Reveals expense of extradition process. Also treats diplomatic aspects of case and their bearing on legal proceedings. Very good article.

3449. Fuenmayor, Juan Bautista. Historia de la Venezuela política contemporánea: 1899-1969. t. 2; t. 3, pt. 1/2. Caracas, Miguel Angel García, 1976. 2 v. (461, 749 p.) (Continuous pagination) tables.

Continuation of multi-volume and polemical, essentially political, history of Venezuela by founding member of Venezuelan Communist Party (for vol. 1, see *HLAS 38:3384*). Vol. 2 treats era of petroleum (1923-37), stressing US influence on Venezuela and its dependence on US. Author is critical of US and offers insightful analysis of failure of Communist Party. Vol. 3 (in two separate volumes, pts. 1/2) carries struggle of left through 1942. This last volume is especially good in polemics between clandestine parties, taken from private archives of previously unpublished materials. Author has presented much useful information, although his own interpretations often fall short.

3450. Gallegos Ortiz, Rafael. El Cachorro Juan Vicente Gómez. Caracas, Editorial Fuentes, 1976. 206 p.

Uninspired and nothing new, yet in light of recent works that have made Gómez into a simpático organizer of nation, Gallegos Ortiz puts dictator's crimes in focus and sees Gómez as loyal servant of imperialists. Venezuela would have been a rich country with or without Gómez. With Gómez it remained underdeveloped, with illiterate and tubercular population. Good reading to offset recent gómezmania fomented by Tachirense authors.

3451. Grases, Pedro. La obra de . . . Caracas, Editorial Arte, 1976. 300 p.

Collection of tributes paid to the Spanish-born bibliophile and historian, Pedro Grases. Includes list of publications and edited works prepared by Grases.

3452. Hood, Miriam. Gunboat diplomacy, 1895-1905: great power pressure in Venezuela. London, George Allen and Unwing, 1975. 202 p., illus., bibl.

Examines Venezuela's credit relations with Great Britain in late 19th century. Sums up Guzmán Blanco's dealings and subsequent efforts relating to foreign debt. Emphasizes Venezuela's domestic weaknesses and international vulnerability.

3453. Izard, Miguel and others. Política y economía en Venezuela: 1810-1976. Caracas, Fundación John Boulton, 1976. 292 p., tables.

Series of articles that present panorama of interaction of politics and economic development in Venezuela from struggle for independence to 1976. Published by Fundación John Boulton to commemorate 150th year of Boulton's activities in La Guaira. Includes essays by Miguel Izard (1810-30); Manuel Pérez Vila (1830-48); Robert P. Matthews (1847-58); Benjamin A. Frankel (1859-69); Mary B. Floyd (1870-88); Nikita Harwich Vallenilla (1888-1908); William M. Sullivan (1908-35); and José Antonio Mayobre (1936-76).

Lovera de Sola, R.J. Contribución a la bibliografía histórica venezolana: 1969-1972. See item 3080.

Malavé Mata, Héctor. Formación histórica del antidesarrollo de Venezuela. See *HLAS 39:3316*.

Oficina de Estudios Socioeconómicos, *Caracas*. Evolución histórica del sector agropecuario y su crisis actual. See *HLAS 39:3326*.

3454. Petras, James F.; Morris Morley; and Steven Smith. The nationalization of Venezuelan oil. N.Y., Praeger, 1977. 173 p., tables.

Authors, all sociologists, have written useful and provocative study of process of change that led to nationalization of Venezuelan oil. Though hastily researched, work is well documented and demonstrates leverage of US-based corporations in dealing with Venezuelan governments. Nationalization of oil seen as result of association between Venezuelan capitalist class and diversified US industrial and service sectors. Nationalization was not a revolutionary act, but one that led to better alliance between national capitalists and US corporate structure. Attempt it made to show why Pérez government was not overthrown as result of nationalization of oil. Filled with minor historical and factual errors, but worth reading for better understanding of crucial Venezuelan issue.

Pimentel y Roth, Francisco. Historia del crédito público en Venezuela. See *HLAS 39:3332*.

3455. Pinedo Nava, Angel Genaro. Memorias de un viajero. Caracas, Gráficas Armitano, 1976. 185 p., plates.

Well illustrated anecdotal tales of travels in Venezuela from 1903 onward by former medicine/drug company representative and automobile salesman. Fascinating glimpses of Venezuela before atuomobile and equally entertaining stories of early stages of automobile travel.

3456. Posani, Clara *ed.* and *comp.* Apenas ayer: 20 años de fotografía de Luis F. Toro. Caracas, Fundación Neumann, 1972. 77 p., plates.

Consists of 75 photographs of Caracas and environs from first decades of 20th century, taken by Luis F. Toro, official photographer for Juan Vicente Gómez. Excellent visual presentation of Venezuela during Gómez era. Introduction includes interviews with friends and relations of Toro, one with his daughter and another with Gonzalo Gómez.

3457. Quintero, José Humberto. Para la historia. Caracas, Editorial Arte, 1974. 261 p., facsim., plates.

Two historical essay/documentaries on Church, written by Archbishop of Caracas. First deals with expulsion from Venezuela of Bishop of Valencia, Monseñor Montes de Oca because of his intransigent position on marriage. He did not accept civil marriage in 1929. Gómez finally let bishop return in 1931. Second essay deals with ecclesiastical matters after earthquake of 1900, during which time Archbishop of Caracas suffered from incurable disease that had incapacitated him.

3458. Rodríguez Campos, Manuel. Venezuela 1902, la crisis fiscal y el bloqueo: perfil de una soberanía vulnerada. Caracas, Univ. Central de Venezuela, 1977. 453 p., bibl., facsims., tables.

Part of ongoing project on Castro/Gómez, directed by Eduardo Arcila Farías. Reviews economic and political background to intervention, both from internal and international perspectives. Very little new evidence, but well-written, clear and detailed. Stresses economic factors. Shows Venezuela's dependence role. Deals with Revolución Libertadora led by Matos and supported by foreign interests, and shows use of nationalism to end that revolution. Concludes that intervention was aimed at blocking US expansion.

3459. Stan, E. Jeffrey. Transportation and urbanization in Caracas, 1891-1936 (UM/JIAS, 17:1, Feb. 1975, p. 82-100, maps)

Compares transportation and urban growth patterns to C.S. Sargent's model for B.A. Brief and sketchy.

3460. Suárez Figueroa, Naudy *ed.* Programas políticos venezolanos de la primera mitad del siglo XX. t. 1, De Cipriano Castro a Eleazar López Contreras: 1899-1941; t. 2, De Isaías Medina Angarita a Rómulo Gallegos: 1941-1948. Caracas, Univ. Católica Andrés Bello, 1977. 2 v. (295, 235 p.) tables.

Well-selected documents related to leading political movements and parties between 1899 and 1948. Short introductory essay (p. 11-28) sets scheme of collection. Useful, though several documents have been included in other published works.

Sullivan, William J. Bibliografía comentada de la era de Cipriano Castro: 1899-1908. See item 37.

Tugwell, Franklin. The politics of oil in Venezuela. See *HLAS 39:7537*.

Veracoechea, Ermila de. Notas sobre los esclavos y la guerra de la independencia de Venezuela. See item 3358.

Yépez Tamayo, Gerardo. Ensayo sobre la historia de las ciencias en Venezuela. See *HLAS 39:4525*.

ECUADOR AND PERU

VINCENT C. PELOSO

Associate Professor of History
Howard University

THE VOLUME AND QUALITY OF STUDIES on Ecuador and Peru grows at a rapid rate. The quality of work on Peru remains high and on the rise, while the evidence on Ecuador suggests that whimsical and idiosyncratic narratives are making way on the proverbial shelf for works with broader meaning. On the whole, studies reviewed for this installment deal with historical problems far more than they describe institutions or narrate events. Those problems which have drawn the greatest attention include the state, the intelligentsia, the ruling class, and agriculture. In a notable departure from past practices, the study of agricultural history in turn has benefitted from the adoption of a regional perspective, a practice which is certain to stimulate further debate among social scientists.

Studies of the state focus most often on government policy in response to internal processes and external pressures. Largely 20th-century studies, many of them breach the wall between domestic politics and foreign policy, and though diplomacy continues to arouse interest, especially in the period since World War II, the meticulous work of E.V.K. Fitzgerald (item 3514) exemplifies recent efforts. Fitzgerald examines the relation between state and domestic capital on the one hand and foreign capital on the other, and suggests that by replacing domestic capital in the political economy of Peru since 1968 the state has formed a new relation with foreign investors. By comparing corporate and household economies since the late 1950s, he concludes that class polarization has increased rather than diminished, and in the end he suggests that the "intermediate" military regime's ownership of major industries is a positive step toward fuller restructuring of society.

Fitzgerald's historical analysis complements works which concentrate on past movements to reform the state or to destroy it. APRA studies far out number others of this type. A new general history of the movement by Murillo Garaycochea (item 3551) exemplifies the genre and must be considered the standard work on the subject thus far. The role of intellectuals in this process, meanwhile, has remained the most ignored of subjects in Peruvian history, a point which contributes significantly to the problem. In the past students of Peruvian intellectual history wavered between the discomforting thought that no ideas ever have originated in Latin America and the suspicion that somehow derived ideas are tawdry, rather than consider that derivation and adaptation are themselves inventive processes. Recent essays that sweep this ambivalence aside are the examination of Haya de la Torre's political philosophy by Portocarrero (item 3557) and Rama's essay on Flora Tristán (item 3558) which illustrates the impact of derivation on 19th-century socialism.

Closely tied to the state and the intelligentsia is the historic power of the ruling class. Studies of this class evoke stimulating interpretations of the bourgeoisie in the 19th and 20th centuries. They continue to be seen as wholly dependent by Bonilla (items 3494-3496), who presents a formidable collection of London documents for general study of the problem, and a parallel outlook emerges in the internal dissection of guano production by Mathew (item 3544). On the other hand, some scholars feel it necessary to clarify the internal behavior of this class, and their methods are exemplified by Chueca Posadas and Alfaro Vallejos (item 3506), whose sophisticated research and organizing talent draws a picture of the business activities of an Italian-immigrant Peruvian who pioneered in oil exploration and the family network which followed in his footsteps to create one of the largest "unreformed" business empires in the country. Outstanding efforts to characterize the nature of the ruling class are those by Caravedo Molinari (item 3500-3501) which examine the debate over unity and division within the ruling class from 1919 to 1945. His delineation of an industrial sector in bourgeois politics as early as the 1920s provocatively challenges dependency theory at its "core," calling into question its primacy for elucidating the social history of Peru.

Most stimulating, however, is the tendency for regional studies to dominate the literature: valleys, provinces, and departments have become the framework for writers who, wrapping the country in its geography, deplore the equation of the government with the nation, or the aristocracy with the people. Their choice of a regional setting is equally a product of sociological findings since the mid-1960s which encourage the use of archives that lie outside the cross formed by Avenida Arequipa and "La Colmena." At this point, two regions attract intensive research, the southern highlands and the coast.

Studies of the Pacific littoral, divided by Lima, focus either on the north (Norte Chico) or the southern desert (Sur Chico). On the least-studied south coast an outstanding recent work is that of Bill Albert (item 3482), based on several years of research in the CDA and other collections and extensive conversations with a fascinating Anglo-Peruvian whose lifetime of agricultural experience is clear. Albert's work challenges earlier studies of coastal agriculture, chiefly that of Klarén (see *HLAS 34:2617*), when he finds that during World War I, an era of great stress, social relations of production were far more central to understanding the character of class formation than any other variable. Studies of north coast regions, meanwhile, challenge the direct, linear equation of foreign monopolization of land with mass political consciousness. Skepticism arises in the study of the Chancay valley, for example, through the pioneer work on sharecropping by Matos Mar (item 3545) and the briefer essay by Mejía and Díaz Suárez (item 3547) which asserts that since 1940 neither APRA nor the Communist Party seems capable of giving direction to the agrarian labor movement. Without question the best work reviewed in this biennium is that of Burga (item 3498) on the north coast Jequetepeque valley from the 16th to the 20th century, a work whose reflections on the struggle over agricultural values contested by landowners and tillers highlights a number of important ideas. Among them, Burga documents the varied forms class struggle takes on different plantations but he reveals that central to each of them is the subjugation and mobilization of the masses of tillers. This profoundly anthropological conclusion relegates centralization of ownership and market demand to essential but secondary importance.

Studies of the labor movement in the central highlands and even in the *montaña*, the region that slopes down to the Amazonian thickets, such as those of Kapsoli (item 3528) on the pastoral and mining workers of Cerro de Pasco, and by Flores Marín (item 3516) and Bonilla (item 3494) on rubber exploitation, hint that the mobility of labor from 1880 forward raises questions about the distinctions often made between the three principal regions of Peru, especially within the framework of the "dual society" explanation of underdevelopment. Bonfiglio's preliminary effort to study the steel workers (item 3493) and that of Colque Valladares (item 3507) to note the character of labor in highland Arequipa over this century also help to sketch some of the outstanding commonalities in the labor movement. Dore and Weeks (item 3511) give continuity to the quest in their concern with the attack upon labor by the present military regime, as does Santisteban (item 3563), who delineates the compromising nature of the *comunidad industrial*. Most useful to historians, however, is the appearance of the work of Sulmont (item 3564), an interpretive view of the 20th-century labor movement which sets the parameters for further research from a class perspective. Finally, an affirmation of institutional support for historical research is made clear in the establishment of a new journal, *Histórica* (item 3527), while an impressive sign that interdisciplinary history that employs various methodologies is avidly sought after in Peru.

Similar signs of new vigor have appeared in Ecuadorian academic circles. Especially notable is an interpretive historical volume by economists who encourage historians to stress class conflict in 19th and 20th-century studies (item 3472), while a history of 19th-century banks by Estrada Ycaza (item 3465) sets a standard for further studies of its kind. Intellectual history also received guidelines from the generational interpretation by Valdano Morejón (item 3478), and the memoirs of Robalino Dávila (item 3476a). Work on political leadership, meanwhile, is strengthened by the appearance of a volume on Rocafuerte by Rodríguez O. (item 3477) and an interpretation of Velasco Ibarra by Cuvi (item 3463). These plus the work of Hamerly and Estrada Ycaza (item 3466) on medical history leave the impression that the social history of Ecuador is following that of Peru in emerging as the leading theme of new work. It is also a sure sign that controversy soon will stimulate improvements in Ecuadorian historical debate as it has in Peru.

ECUADOR

3461. *Anales de la Universidad de Cuenca.* Univ. de Cuenca. Depto. de Difusión Cultural. Vol. 32, abril 1977- . Cuenca, Ecua.

Work that commands attention in this issue is essay by César Hermida Piedra, "Resumen de la Historia de la Medicina en el Ecuador" (p. 9-106) which surveys establishment of medical profession from colonial period on with emphasis on 18th and 19th centuries. No sources cited but bibliography appended.

3462. **Bossano, Guillermo.** *Vicisitudes de la nacionalidad ecuatoriana: mirajes histórico-sociológicos de la conquista a través del proceso vital patrio.* 3. ed. Quito, Editorial Casa de la Cultura Ecuatoriana, 1975. 256 p.

Although it begins with promise of broad approach to problem, perhaps even an anthropo-historical one, it ends with tunnel vision. At end of the tunnel: Ecuadorian nationality is reducible to correct delineation of border with Peru.

3463. **Cuvi, Pablo.** *Velasco Ibarra: el último caudillo de la oligarquía.* Quito, Univ. Central del Ecuador, Instituto de Investigaciones Económicas, 1977. 263 p., tables.

Interpretive essays that set Velasco phenomenon in context of 20th-century history of liberalism, dictatorship and activities of Ecuadorian oligarchy. Interspersed with interviews conducted by author with Velasco in B.A., Aug. 1975, while caudillo was once more in exile. Evocative questions and revealing answers. Valuable and imaginative study.

3464. **Ecuador. Fuerzas Armadas. Estado Mayor Conjunto. Dirección de Historia y Militar.** *Documentos para la historia militar.* t. 1/2. Quito, Editorial Casa de la Cultura Ecuatoriana, 1974/1975. 2 v. (356, 486 p.) (Boletín del departamento de historia)

Vol. 1 consists largely of materials from Ecuadorian archives on rebellions and conspiracies in years 1809-22. Vol. 2 offers strange mixture of documents chosen apparently at random concerning Audiencia de Quito and other subjects stretching back to 16th century, but also including more documents from 1809-22. No explanations offered. Colonial material from AGI. Of limited value on whole.

3465. **Estrada Ycaza, Julio.** *Los bancos del siglo XIX.* Guayaquil, Ecua., Archivo Histórico del Guayas, Casa de la Cultura Ecuatoriana, Núcleo del Guayas, 1976. 323 p., bibl., facsims., plates, tables (Col. Monográfica, 8)

Surveys establishment of credit agencies and lending establishments linked to coastal commerce in Ecuador from colonial period forward with emphasis on period 1810-1910. Indicates origins, successes, failures in terms of capitalization or lack of it of various banking ventures, and establishes links among different types of banks—savings, mortgages, etc.—that demonstrate centralization process although author is reluctant to draw this or any conclusion. Nevertheless, fundamental study that will be part of promised more general economic history of Ecuador. Based on relevant, systematic archival research.

3466. ——— **and Michael T. Hamerly.** *Los Bernales del hospital* (AHG/R, 4:8, dic. 1975, p. 7-25)

Contribution to history of medicine in Ecuador and administration of public medicine in 19th-century Guayaquil. This essay explores identity of early administrators of Hospital of Guayaquil, making careful use of records of sessions of city's cabildo.

3467. **Galarza Zavala, Jaime.** *El yugo feudal: visión del campo ecuatoriano.* 3. ed. ampliada. Quito, Ediciones Solitierra. 200 p., illus., tables.

Within framework that expresses outrage at contradictions between promise and performance, this essayist attacks gross failures of Ecuadorian agrarian reforms and insists that feudalism has reigned as dominant system since conquest in that country. Polemical essays based on research in archives, unfortunately defective copy under review is missing end pages.

3468. García Moreno, Gabriel. *Epistolario diplomático del Presidente . . .: 1859-1869.* Edición preparada y prologada por Jorge Villalba. Quito, Ediciones Univ. Católica (EDUC), 1976. 1 v. (Various pagings) bibl., plates (Publicaciones del Archivo Juan José Flores)

Documents on diplomatic history of Ecuador from Juan José Flores' archives. Part of personal materials of García Moreno. Includes relations with Colombia and Vatican in 1860s.

3469. Hamerly, Michael T. El antiguo *Rejistro Municipal,* 1835?-1861, de Guayaquil (AHG/R, 4:7, junio 1975, p. 64-70a, fold. tables, tables)

Brief essay indicating importance of this source for study of Ecuadorian local history in early 19th century. Value illustrated by appending of 1840 census of Cantón de Guayaquil done by municipio. Part of valuable continuing effort to unearth archival sources for study of Ecuador.

Hurtado, Osvaldo. El poder político en el Ecuador. See item 3079.

3470. Judde, Gabriel. *Viaje a la República del Ecuador en 1852* por Henri Comynet (EEHA/AEA, 31, 1974, p. 597-680, maps, tables)

Commentary on and analysis of report by French geologist Henri Comynet on his trip from Ecuador into Amazon region. These introductory remarks, with maps and notes, preface this edition of original manuscript report in French. Manuscript records valuable insights into Quito society, especially on color, class, markets, the state, etc. Includes comments on Río Napo region, local population figures from unstated sources, Church-State relations, commercial prices, and other remarks. Valuable travel source for mid-19th century Ecuador.

3471. Larrea, Carlos Manuel. Antonio Flores Jijón: su vida y sus obras. Quito, Corporación de Estudios y Publicaciones, 1974. 281 p., illus.

Overly laudatory biography of son of Juan José Flores, general, diplomat and president (1888-92) in his own right. Earlier had been Ecuador representative to Vatican under García Moreno, charged with adjusting terms of Concordat; during presidency treated with Peru on mutual border, fostered agricultural improvement, among other things, opposed by Eloy Alfaro. This work flits lightly over subject.

3472. Mejía, Leonardo and others. Ecuador: pasado y presente. Quito, Univ. Central del Ecuador, Facultad de Ciencias Económicas, 1975. 273 p.

Group of interpretive essays set within framework of historical materialism which attempts to formulate fresh view of Ecuadorian historical process. Authored by social scientists, essays sweep through epochs from "primitive" society, through Audiencia de Quito, to independence and heights of export, capitalism and class struggle in 19th century and on into crises of 1960s. Not product of original research but sure to become basis for further studies by these authors. Among them: Leonardo Mejía, Fernando Velasco, José Moncada, Alejandro Moreano, Agustín Cueva and René Báez.

3473. Mörner, Magnus. La fragata sueca *"Eugènia"* y la expedición de Flores contra Guayaquil en 1852 (CCE/CHA, 24:41, 1974, p. 155-171)

Swedish ship's captain found himself caught between rivals for power in Ecuador in case which nearly mushroomed into international politics in mid-19th century. Episode also reflects era's liberal-conservative ideological battles. Unfortunately, defective copy reviewed was missing p. 161, 162, 167.

3474. Ochoa O., Octavio. Tragedia ecuatoriana, 1941. Quito, Gráfica Chimborazo, 1976. 340 p., tables.

Another recapitulation of Ecuadorian military perspective on what happened in Peru-Ecuador confrontation of that year. Appends lists of Ecuadorian soldiers and officers, by battle and unit, who fought those campaigns.

3475. Peralta, José. Eloy Alfaro y sus victimarios: apuntes para la historia ecuatoriana. 2. ed. Cuenca, Ecua., n.p., 1977. 495 p., illus. (Obras completas de José Peralta)

Last government of Eloy Alfaro (1906-11) ended in general's assassination and his subsequent elevation to status of hero of Ecuadorian liberalism. Author of this account, originally published 1918, was member of Alfaro's party and his governments as officer, party leader and diplomat. This reprint will be helpful to students of period.

3476. *Revista del Instituto Ecuatoriano de Historia Eclesiástica.* Pontificia Univ. Católica del Ecuador. No. 1, 1974- . Quito.

Jorge Villalba F., S.J., does three short studies on Federico González Suárez, one on his youth, another on his decade with Jesuits and another on his first writings. Why he left Jesuit order in 1872 is not revealed, and remainder is biographical minutiae. Might be of interest to biographer although largely drawn from his own memoirs.

History: Spanish South America, 19th and 20th Centuries, Peru / 253

3476a. Robalino Dávila, Luis. Memorias de un nonagenario. Quito, Editorial Ecuatoriana, 1974. 407 p., plates.

Edited by famed historian and diplomat's daughter, volume contains essays, letters, speeches and other memorabilia culled from his files. Nothing long enough nor pungent enough to attract serious attention.

3477. Rodríguez O., Jaime E. Estudios sobre Vicente Rocafuerte. Prólogo de Julio Estrada Ycaza. Guayaquil, Ecua., Archivo Histórico del Guayas, 1975. 390 p., bibl. (Col. Monográfica, 7)

Series of well-documented essays on subject's political life, followed by collection of new materials demonstrating his political activities, 1810-43, as second president of Ecuador, as Mexican diplomat, and in politics of Gran Colombia, independence of Ecuador and liberalism in early 19th century. Materials drawn from Mexican Foreign Relations archive, Rocafuerte's correspondence, journals. Useful for studies of independence problems and early 19th-century liberalism.

3478. Valdano Morejón, Juan. La pluma y el cetro: intelectuales, cultura y generaciones en el Ecuador (UC/A, 31:3/4, julio/dic. 1975, p. 13-71, tables)

Attempt to explore meaning of being an intellectual in Ecuador, this essay probes for definition of word, then suggests that in underdeveloped societies intellectual provides a "cosmovision" of future in context of tensions between powerful oligarchies and powerless masses, and in Latin America he must be *engagé*. In the mode of Juan José Arrom, applies generational scheme to try to determine how well intellectuals of Ecuador have expressed country's cultural evolution. Asserts that intellectual generations of that country had their origins in early 18th century with Pedro Vicente Maldonado and Juan de Velasco, and rather than apply chronological criteria argues that each 30-year generation is marked by "vital sensibilities" that bracket it. Last generation whose members are listed is that of 1944. Provocative essay which promises to continue.

3479. Velasco Ibarra, José María. Obras completas. v. 1/15. Edited by Juan F. Velasco Espinosa. 2. ed. Quito, Imprenta y Ediciones Lexigrama, 1973/1975. 15 v. (230, 227, 259, 143, 201, 111, 88, 212, 234, 198, 223, 496, 601, 320, 103 p.) plates.

Speeches, essays, polemics which have appeared in the twists and turns of this enigmatic figure's political career spanning much of 20th-century Ecuador. Subjects range over usual experiences of durable, practical politician, heavy on philosophy of constitutional and international law, Christianity and Marxism, religiosity and others. Historians will find presidential messages in vol. 12 particularly useful. They are selections from each of his terms of offiice, 1934-35, 1944-47, 1952-56, 1960-61, 1968-72. These volumes are the public Velasco Ibarra.

3480. Villacres Moscoso, Jorge W. Historia diplomática de la República del Ecuador. t. 4, La política exterior de la República del Ecuador desde 1932 a 1944. Guayaquil, Ecua., Univ. de Guayaquil, 1976. 537 p., bibl.

Continuation of narrative, strictly diplomatic approach to subject, this volume covers events leading up to conflict with Peru in 1941 and diplomacy of settlement that followed conflict. Important for its presentation of Ecuadorian point of view on border issue, though not full exposition of that position. Still useful as standard diplomatic history of Ecuador.

Weilbauer, Arthur. Los alemanes en el Ecuador: estudio histórico. See item 3090.

PERU

3481. Alba, Víctor. Peru. Boulder, Colo., Westview Pres,s 1977. 245 p., bibl.

Topically structured in 10 chapters, last dealing with events since 1968, ends with note on "world opinion." Appears aimed at the well-educated businessman/traveler. Although trenchantly written, volume is occasionally marred by over-use of clichés.

3482. Albert, Bill. An essay on the Peruvian sugar industry, 1880-1920, and the letters of Ronald Gordon, administrator of the British Sugar Company in the Cañete, 1914-1920. Norwich, U.K., Univ. of East Anglia, School of Social Studies, 1976. 1 v. (Various pagings) maps, tables.

Consists of over 545 p. quarto-sized, in mimeograph form, of wealth of material on agricultural history of 20th-century Peru. Of two major sections, one is unedited but copiously annotated letterbook of R.M.J. Gordon, administrator of south coast plantation during World War I. Other section is essay on formation of sugar plantation industry in Peru from 1880 to 1920s along with historical essay on British Sugar Company in particular. Appendix places system of sharecropping within framework that gives it meaning in changes that overcame coastal agriculture early in this century. Gordon letters, all in English, contain wealth of detailed information on every aspect of plantation management, revealing great concern Gordon felt for efficient productivity at same time that they show his grasp of farming detail. Presents production figures, estimates of yields in cotton and sugar and other data. Also gives technical information on sugar milling and refining. Section concerned with history of sugar in Peru rests upon accounts and correspondence of Hacienda Cayaltí, north-coast Zaña valley property. Albert questions assertion that centralization of landholding that occurred earlier this century necessarily resulted in foreign control of land, and suggests that in Zaña valley at any rate it meant fierce competition among Peruvian families, a conclusion that challenges finding of P. Klarén (see *HLAS 34:2617* and *HLAS 36:2912*) that Chicama valley was typical of coast. Finds that in other coastal valleys of period most significant change was entry of new, capitalist planter group into business who joined process of land amalgamation and technological improvement. Other sections of this work dip into labor recruitment and beginnings of agricultural labor movement, changes brought about by World War I, growth in cotton farming, food prices, wages, post-war labor on plantations. Index is followed by essay on coastal *yanaconaje*. Altogether, a mine of information, a challenging study which makes strong inroad into questions raised by earlier studies of nature of underdevelopment in Peru as it is reflected in process of agricultural growth since about 1860. Indispensable work for specialist in Latin American economic history.

3483. Alvarez Ganoza, Pedro L. Origen y trayectoria de la aplicación de la pena de muerte en la historia del derecho peruano, época republicana, 1821-1937, y algunos antecedentes coloniales. Lima, Editorial Dorhca, 1974. 207 p., bibl.

Brief recapitulation of history of application of death penalty with little analysis of subject. Based on doctoral thesis at Univ. Católica.

Amich, José and others. Historia de las misiones del Convento de Santa Rosa de Ocopa. See item 3065.

3484. Aquésolo Castro, Manuel comp. La polémica del indigenismo. Lima, Mosca Azul Editores, 1976. 172 p.

Evidence of witty and penetrating invective traded in Peruvian literary and political magazines of 1926-30 among people like Mariátegui Sánchez, López Albújar, L. Valcárcel, and others, some of whom formed initial staff of *Amauta*. Compiled from pages of *Amauta, Mundial, La Prensa*, and others, but not systematic treatment of topic.

3485. Barrios, D. Walter and **José Antezana.** Diccionario histórico geográfico de Tacna. Tacna, Perú, Jorge Hugo Girón Flores, 1973. 147 p., bibl., plates.

Thinking behind this slim volume becomes evident when Luis Banchero Rossi gets two columns and Jorge Basadre merits less than one, while Guillermo Billinghurst, president of Perú, 1914-15, is summed up in 10 lines. Nevertheless, could prove useful to local studies. Not well researched and very poorly bound.

3486. Basadre, Jorge. Los conflictos de pasiones y de intereses en Tacna y Arica: 1922-1929 (PMNH/HC, 8, 1974, p. 5-68, table)

Chapter from author's memoirs (see item 3488), this study provides details on public reponse to final Tacna-Arica dispute negotiations. Author was involved through his earliest posts in Ministry of Foreign Affairs and as Tacneño. Describes in detail official events leading to plebiscite from Peruvian side and comments on US contingent under General J.J. Pershing, there to keep order. This essay roams around comfortably in recollection of episodes of nationalist enthusiasm, says many Chilean voters in Arica were fictitious names. Much useful detail gleaned from US and Peruvian foreign affairs documents. Engaging diplomatic history.

3487. ———. Reconsideraciones sobre el problema histórico de la Confederación Perú-Boliviana (PAIGH/H, 83, enero/junio 1977, p. 93-119, tables)

Decision-making framework is used to study diplomatic strategy and tactics in historical context of Peru-Bolivia Confederation (1835-39). Considers geo-economic ties that bound countries, military and diplomatic factors that sustained confederation, weight of public sympathy in south of Peru and of antipathy in north and center, along with strained personal relationships among political leaders. Concludes that confederation was not solid construction and that Andrés Santa Cruz, its president, could not swim against current of his time. Though revival dream remained alive for a while, it ended when Chile occupied port of Arica after 1879. Survey of problem.

3488. ———. La vida y la historia: ensayos sobre personas, lugares y problemas. Presentación de Alonso Polar Campos. Lima, Fondo del Libro del Banco Industrial del Perú, 1975. 612 p., facsims., plates.

As author points out, this is not traditional memoir. Documentation from his wide reading amplifies and supports set of essays that display historian as participant. All of them are historically important aspects of his engagement in events over a productive lifetime of passionate political involvement and historical writing. None of them deals with a past long dead but rather with a past that intrudes into present: essay on "Infancia en Tacna" includes section on youth of today; while in section on higher education he talks about "the mirage of progress in the world" and about "the deceitful proofs of examinations." Follows with two sections on university reform in Peru and especially at San Marcos (1920-29) including comments on specific reform laws, detour into settlement of Chile boundary dispute as aspect of regional and national passions, long and important essay on his years as Director of Biblioteca Nacional, life and history in Germany and Spain, and with his personal views on presidential politics in Peru since Bustamante (1945-68), including final remarks on beginnings of "rupturing" process of 1968. Indispensable source of 20th-century Peruvian intellectual history.

3489. Bertram, Geoff. Modernización y cambio en la industria lanera en el sur del Perú, 1919-1930: un caso frustrado de desarrollo (UP/A, 2:6, 1977, p. 3-22, tables)

Studies Puno wool region in period. Points out that though big landowners wanted to expand production with help of foreign companies, local peasant shepherds and Arequipa merchants were strongly opposed. Ensuing struggle, plus fall in world wool prices in 1920s, left industry backward and relations of production pre-capitalist, and also left Arequipa merchant houses strengthened. Process of collision among these elements was set in motion by efforts at technological improvements in cattle-raising and enclosure. Wave of peasant uprisings, plus falling prices of 1920s, blocked effort to expand landed holdings as part of process of capitalization. Effective use made here of plantation records, public sources and newspapers.

Bibliografía histórica peruana: 1968-1970 [and] 1970-1973. See items 3066-3067.

3490. Blanchard, Peter. A populist precursor: Guillermo Billinghurst (JLAS, 9:2, Nov. 1977, p. 251-273)

Careful research in Lima dailies and effective use of CDA materials help this probe of meaning of populism. Suggests that emergence of this type of politics predated 1930 if career of Billinghurst is good example. Links his labor sympathies to his Pierolista background and impact on him of 1907 Iquique massacre in Chile, all of which led to welfare reforms when he was mayor of Lima and demonstrations by workers on his behalf. As president, however, he failed to capitalize on worker support to build political party, nor solidified support in Congress. Congressional-military conspiracy against him, plus continued strikes resulted in his overthrow in Feb. 1914. Shows rising influence of urban labor in politics in era before Leguía. But too much to say Billinghurst began "new era" in Peru politics.

3491. Blanco, José María. Diario del viaje del Presidente Orbegoso al sur del Perú. Edición, prólogo y notas de Félix Denegri Luna. t. 1/2. Lima, Pontificia Univ. Católica del Perú, Instituto Riva-Agüero, 1974. 2 v. (317, 201 p.) (Archivo del Gran Mariscal Orbegoso, 1/2)

Originally published in 1929, forms part of collection of materials from life of Orbegoso, 19th-century general who peaked during Peru-Bolivia Confederation and whose exile was result of Arequipa regional politics. These volumes were gathered by author/priest chiefly interested in descriptive and historical ruminations on customs and traditions of southern region. Present edition comes with explanatory introduction and vol. 2 constitutes set of detailed, descriptive notes that significantly amplify text. Of interest mainly to 17th- and 18th-century scholars, major attention given to local language, customs and politics, 1650-1840, in notes.

3492. Bolo Hidalgo, Salomón. Micaela Bastidas Puiucagua: la mujer más grande de América. Lima, n.p., 1977. 670 p.

Long, self-described polemic that cites Bible, Dante, occasional articles from popular magazines, few documents from Seville's AGI, and standard accounts by Peruvian historians on Tupac Amaru in order to sing praises of woman whose story should be told. Micaela Bastida awaits her biographer.

3493. Bonfiglio, Giovanni. Antecedentes históricos del movimiento sindical metalúrgico en el Perú. Lima, Pontificia Univ. Católica, Programa Académico de Ciencias Sociales, Taller de Estudios Urbano-Industriales, 1976. 48 l. (Serie estudios sindicales, 3)

Focuses on steelworkers' movement from 1940s to major strikes of 1964 which were accompanied by takeovers of factories by workers, repression of their movement and fall and recovery of FETIMP, steelworkers federation. Thinly supported but uses some materials from archives of Ministry of Labor.

3494. Bonilla, Heraclio. El caucho y la economía del Oriente peruano (PMNH/HC, 8, 1974, p. 69-80, tables)

Uses annual consular reports on Iquitos trade to graph direction and value of Peruvian rubber exports and points out two intensive phases of production, 1892-1910 and 1910-14. Crisis in industry in 1910 was precipitated by depression in market and Peru-Ecuador border war. Nevertheless, exploitation of local labor and enclaved character of exports did not contribute to Peruvian economy. Calls for rigorous study of local mode of production in any industry rather than concentrating on its contacts with external world economy. Part of author's five-volume documentary publication with essay on British consular reports.

3495. ———. La emergencia del control norteamericano sobre la economía peruana: 1850-1930 (CSUCA/ESC, 5:13, enero/abril 1976, p. 97-122, tables)

Seeks to establish chronology that demonstrates character of US-Peru relations and to show mechanisms of emergence of US control in that relationship. Based on US public sources and consular reports, locates its beginnings in demand for guano in 1840s, and though control down to 1900 rested with Great Britain, after 1900 US hegemony mounted with spectacular increases in trade, entrance of US banks into Peru and after World War I demand for Peruvian primary materials. After 1913, US displaced England as major importer of Peruvian goods. US firms entered country more fully in 1920s and 1930s under Leguía dictatorship. Accompanied by ample statistical support, but assertion that "control" was result of such expansion has broad implications that require further research. For political scientist's comment, see *HLAS 39:8798*.

3496. ——— *ed.* and *comp.* Gran Bretaña y el Perú: informes de los cónsules. v. 3, Callao, Iquitos y Lambayeque: 1867-1913; v. 4, Islay, Mollendo, Arica e Iquique: 1855-1913; v. 5, Los mecanismos de un control económico. Lima, Instituto de Estudios Peruanos [and] Banco Industrial del Perú, Fondo del Libro, 1976-1977. 3 v. (392, 302, 222 p.) bibl., tables (Serie estudios históricos, 2)

Vol. 3/4 continue compilation on consular reports previously noted in *HLAS 38:3457*. Vol. 5 is particularly useful because it places first four volumes in their political and economic nexus, particularly efforts to subordinate Peruvian economy to international market. Emphasis on historical formation of foreign debt and its links to guano, already studied elsewhere, Peruvian Corporation's activities, economy between War of Pacific (1879-83) and World War I, industrial development, etc. Bases of commercial expansion in 19th century are viewed through wool and rubber industries. Extensive tables and charts on patterns of commercial growth and decay. Invaluable resources for economic history of 19th-century Peru, these documents are said to be all the commercial and financial reports from Foreign Office that were published in British Parliamentary Papers, along with few early ones from Foreign Office records that did not appear in British Parliamentary Papers.

3497. Burga, Manuel. De la encomienda a la hacienda capitalista: el valle del Jequetepeque del siglo XVI al XX. Presentación de Ruggiero Romano. Lima, Instituto de Estudios Peruanos, 1976. 319 p., bibl., fold. map, tables (Serie estudios de la sociedad rural, 4)

Study of north coast valley from colonial period to present era, begins in Braudelian fashion with interrelation of human and natural resource use that resulted in encomienda. Next focuses on processes that formed rural properties in 16th-19th centuries, from cattlemen and churchmen to secular families in rice, cotton and sugar, surrounded by minifundios. Third part deals with intensive capitalization of valley's lands by export commercial agriculture under Peruvian Sugar Company leadership, response of different plantations to these efforts, impact on land values of numerous ownership changes, uprooting of labor and creation of rural proletariat, economic crises of 20th century, increased technology of production, etc. Concluding chapter assesses relationships between these phenomena over entire period. Little attention to related political developments; nevertheless its reliance upon archival materials in Lima, property registers in Trujillo, and wide reading in published materials makes this an exemplary study.

3498. ———. El surgimiento de la hacienda capitalista en la costa norte: el caso de dos haciendas en el Valle del Jequetepeque (PENM/R, 41, 1975, p. 395-422, tables)

Amplification of chapter in author's recent study (see item 3497) of Jequetepeque valley, 16th to 20th centuries. In this key essay two plantations are compared, one expansive, other involutionary, despite their location in same valley, point which illustrates dangers of easy generalizations made on basis of crops, exports, size of land and other variables.

3499. Campo, José Rodolfo del. Campaña naval, 1879. Introducción biográfica y glosario de términos náuticos por H. Buse. Lima, Instituto de Estudios Histórico-Marítimos del Perú, 1976. 268 p., fold. plate, plates (Serie crónicas y testimonios)

Essays by correspondent on Peruvian warships, describing conditions of battle. Most of these reports are brief, taken from *El Comercio* of that year. Of purely naval history value.

3500. Caravedo Molinari, Baltazar. Burguesía e industria en el Perú: 1933-1945. Presentación de Heraclio Bonilla. Lima, Instituto de Estudios Peruanos, 1976. 187 p., bibl., tables (Serie estudios históricos, 3)

Analyzes Peruvian bourgeoisie of mid-20th century to determine its unity of purpose and its divisions as they appeared in response to world market conditions. Notes that division occurred in wake of damages wrought by World War I and Depression, such that local capital accumulated after World War II was invested increasingly in industrialization rather than agricultural exports. Rising tensions that followed spilled into election of 1936 with formation of National Front and cancelation of results because of APRA participation. Benavides regime encouraged industrial investment and Prado government (1939-45) paved way for APRA strength in election of 1945. Based on commercial, industrial, banking publications and government materials. Provocatively suggests a more divided **bourgeoisie** in 1930s than has been assumed.

3501. ——. Clases, lucha política, y gobierno en el Perú, 1919-1933: el oncenio ante la historia ¿se puede hablar de un período revolucionario? agroexportadores versus industriales, el capital imperialista en el Perú. Lima, Retama Editorial, 1977. 124 p., bibl., tables (Historia política, 1)

Illustrates emergence of class struggle (1900-19) in three regions of Peru, linking them generally to perspectives of political parties on eve of Oncenio (1919-30). Distinguishes "honeymoon" period of Leguía's rule from turn of reliance on US investors and emergent industrial bourgeoisie. Growth of both proletariat and petit-bourgeoisie in same era suggests that Peru was on verge of far wider revolution in 1930-33 than Trujillo uprising alone suggests. Suggests that growth of industrial bourgeoisie has been ignored by dependency theory and that Leguía's death left field wide open for popular support of APRA. Provocative interpretation of key era.

3502. Carbone Mora, Pablo V. El problema agrario en el Departamento de La Libertad, 1932. Lima, Univ. Nacional Mayor de San Marcos, Seminario de Historia Rural Andina, 1976. 26 l., bibl.

Reprint of 1932 thesis interesting because it focuses on agricultural economy of La Libertad dept. on eve of Trujillo uprising. Author's historical scheme coincides with that offered in recent years by work of Klarén and he proposes policies to correct negative effects of centralization of land ownership process that he had deplored. A real find.

3503. Carlin Arce, Jorge. Antología documental del Departamento de Tumbes. Lima, Ministerio de Guerra, 1977. 339 p., illus., maps, tables.

Supplements author's history of province (see item 3504). Collection of essays on historical topics largely in 19th and 20th centuries, including some on land tenancy in department. Section on geographic aspects concentrates on oil, irrigation and property. Last section on local traditions.

3504. ——. Reseña histórica del Departamento de Tumbes. Lima, Ministerio de Guerra, 1976. 506 p., bibl., illus., tables.

Survey of this northernmost dept. from pre-colonial times to present. Traditional approach with much detail on local political events useful if often disorganized. Interesting tables on property ownership in 19th century, census data, etc.

3505. Cerda Catalán, Alfonso. La misión de Jacinto Albístur al Perú en 1865 (UMHN/RH, 47:139/141, nov. 1975, p. 1-46)

Spanish career diplomat's last mission, a futile unfortunate one in Peru for five months, after which he retired in Uruguay. His efforts to settle the peace and reclamations in aftermath of Spanish war with Chile and Peru (1864-66), refers especially to attacks on Basque immigrants in Peru. Negotiations halted by uprising in Peru and Albístur was later charged with neglect and held responsible for Spanish failures at end of war. Sidelight of Peruvian diplomatic history.

3506. Chueca Posadas, Susana and Florinda Julia Alfaro Vallejos. El proceso de hacer la América: una familia italiana en el Perú. Lima, Pontificia Univ. Católica del Perú, Escuela de Graduados de Ciencias Sociales, 1975. 1 v. (Various pagings) bibl., tables.

Relies on interviews, material from Archivo del Museo Naval, and newspaper collection of Univ. Católica and Biblioteca Nacional. First part studies problem of European immigrant in America, especially to Peru, and place of Italian families in that framework. Second part specifically analyzes case of Piaggio family, their marriage network and their fortunes. Two final chapters speculate on power derived from family network of this type and tries to elaborate model for further study. Piaggio family pioneered oil exploration in 1879, and from this point on family went into shipping, fishing, commerce, cattle, mines, industry, finance and other areas of enterprise, but core of empire is Compania Nacional de Cerveza, makers of *Cristal*, a property acquired in 1904. Contains genealogical tables and company directorships. Excellent case study.

3507. Colque Valladares, Víctor. Dinámica del movimiento sindical en Arequipa: 1900-1968. Lima, Pontificia Univ. Católica, Programa Académico de Ciencias Sociales, Taller de Estudios Urbano Industriales, 1976. 128 p., bibl., tables (Serie estudios sindicales, 4)

Based on newspapers, interviews and Arturo Sabroso Archive at Univ. Católica, explores differences between anarcho-syndicalist workers movement in Arequipa, led by railway workers and artisans, and popular labor movements in 1930s Lima, noting that Arequipa movement was linked to cattle industry and its derivatives. APRA and CP penetrated local structure in mid-1940s, and after repressions of Odría years (1948-56), local popular movements helped to favor CP labor leadership. Increased export-oriented industrialization of Arequipa in 1960s hit labor hard and migrants to region meant heightened class struggle down to 1968. Valuable for overall view of regional labor in this century.

3508. Comisión para Escribir la Historia Marítima del Perú, *Lima*. Historia marítima del Perú. t. 6, v. 1, La República: 1826-1851; t. 7, La intervención de las potencias europeas en Latinoamérica: 1864-1868. Lima, Editorial Ansonia, 1975? 2 v. (501, 612 p.) bibl., illus., maps, plates, tables (Col. Historia marítima del Perú)

Vol. 6 follows same format as others and emphasizes military aspects of politics and commerce. Formation of a navy, conflicts with Colombia, Peruvian occupation of Guayaquil in 1829, fortunes of navy under several early governments, role in Peru-Bolivia Confederation, war with Chile, and demise. Notes accompany each chapter, showing ample and effective use of contemporary official and published contemporary sources. Vol. 7 consists of diplomatic narrative of international politics that bore on War with Spain (1864-66). Emphasizes Peru's participation; surveys Chincha Island claims of several countries, Congress of Lima and the Vivanco-Pareja Treaty the Peruvian case rested on; breakdown of diplomacy after 1865; war and the mediation which brought it to an end. Impressive bibliography cites materials from foreign relations archives of Europe, US, Chile and Peru, plus manuscripts and contemporary publications.

3509. Cuche, Denys. Pouvoir et participation dans les coopératives agraires de production au Pérou: le cas des coopératives cotonnières de la Côte Sud (AISCD, 40, juillet/dec. 1976, p. 125-146)

Examines results obtained by 1969 agrarian reform in context of debate in Peru between "extreme left" and government over successes and failures. Government claims reform altered social cleavages while opponents claim reform only aided and strengthened bourgeoisie. Debate issues taken to Chincha valley cotton cooperatives visited in 1974-75, where credit and sales of cotton remain dependent on Lima, rural unemployment still high, authoritarianism prevails in cooperatives and salary inequalities continue. Documents mini-rebellions in cooperatives Sinchi Roca and Manco Capac in valley during his stay and concludes that self-management is made authoritarian when participation by workers is severely restricted by government-controlled, technician-oriented committees, thus perpetuating social cleavages of pre-reform period. Based on interviews and newspapers.

DeWind, Adrian. De campesinos a mineros: el origen de las huelgas en las minas peruanas. See *HLAS 39:1453*.

3510. Dobyns, Henry F. and **Paul L. Doughty.** Peru: a cultural history. N.Y., Oxford Univ. Press, 1976. 336 p., bibl., maps, tables (Latin American histories)

Survey of processes by which culture of Peru has matured and continues to distinguish itself from others, looked at from both powerful and powerless institutions and people. Five of 11 chapters devoted to pre-conquest, conquest and colonial periods. Ch. 5 and 6 survey 18th-century reforms and rebellions as well as political struggles of independence period. Ch. 7 deals with era of Ramón Castilla and ch. 8 emphasizes politics of modernization. Last three chapters concentrate on 20th century: role of "governing elite" in modernization process, clash between political parties—especially Partido Aprista Peruano—and army, and "revolutionary" military regime of 1970s. Followed by chronology of Peruvian ethnohistory and history, bibliographical essay and tables. On whole, attractive mix of traditional narrative and an interdisciplinary perspective yet little effort to relate economic problems to cultural developments, modernization seems to mean recitation of growth statistics, surprisingly little on Leguía regime (1919-30). Nevertheless will be valuable text for advanced undergraduates and graduate students interested in historical problems of Peru. Worthwhile addition to series. For anthropologist's comment, see *HLAS 39:1455*.

3511. Dore, Elizabeth and **John Weeks.** The intensification of the assault against the working class in "revolutionary" Peru (LAP, 3:2, Spring 1976, p. 55-83, tables)

Demonstrates the intensification since 1975 of a process set in motion by the 1968 military coup. Argues that the assault on the Peruvian working class has been generated by the reemergence of a crisis for the state in the form of a balance of trade and payments deficit engendered in turn by demands coming from international lending agencies and banks. The Aprista-Civil Guard uprising of February 1975 and the expulsion of Velasco from the presidency in August afterward represented internal manifestations of the crisis. Taken together these developments mean an end to the alliance of the national and petit-bourgeoisies and signalled the increased repression of labor. Theoretically challenging. For political scientist's comment, see *HLAS 39:7355*.

3512. Estado y política agraria: cuatro ensayos. Lima, Centro de Estudios y Promoción del Desarrollo (DESCO), 1977. 351 p., tables.

Interpretive essays based on secondary sources that try to analyze essential characteristics of social-agrarian process in Peru since 1950, especially as it relates to state's role. Essays concentrate on setting out background of 1969 agrarian reform and political response to it made by peasant organizations, agricultural bourgeoisie, small owners, National Agrarian Society and others. Major analysis of agrarian reform activities of state, their expansion under reform and impact on bourgeoisie.

Faron, Louis C. Peruvian social stratification and the history of agrarian reform. See *HLAS 39:1468*.

3513. Fernández Montagne, Ernesto and **Germán Granda Alva.** Apuntes socio económicos de la inmigración China en el Perú, 1848-1874. Lima, Univ. del Pacífico, Centro de Investigación (CIUP), 1977. 134 l., bibl., facsims., map (Serie tesis, 1)

Based on 1968 thesis presented for bachelor's degree, essay is remarkable largely because authors conducted their research in Archive of the Ministry of Foreign Relations, Archive of Museo Naval and Biblioteca Nacional. While coming up with nothing new, authors demonstrate importance of these archives for subject and devote more attention to impact of indenture system of plantation Chinese and guano islands than did Watt Stewart in his original study. Also demonstrates importance of theses for further studies.

Fishman, César. Monedas del Perú de 1751 a 1975. See item 3074.

3514. Fitzgerald, E.V.K. State capitalism in Peru (CEDLA/B, 20, junio 1976, p. 17-33, tables)

Examines relation between state and domestic capital on one hand and foreign capital on other, and suggests that since 1968 state replaced domestic capital in political economy and thus formed a new relationship with foreign capital, wherein dependent export economy has since 1950s altered ruling sector while it has left urban poor and peasants virtually untouched. Since 1968 state activity in exports has expanded at same time that domestic capital has concentrated in safe, lucrative manufacturing and construction. Despite increased state control of exports, banking and heavy industry lately, foreign interest in oil and copper has remained high, resulting in worsening of balance of payments. Since 1973 external debt has risen sharply, necessitating further dependence on major multinationals. Speculates whether this can be called "state capitalism" and elects to call this regime "intermediate" one, à-la-M. Kalecki. Maintains that to develop economy, this regime must integrate industry with remaining sectors by extending state control over most influential private firms. Without radical restructuring of production, transition to socialism cannot be made. Tables demonstrate relative size of production, employment, finance sectors and debt. This is extract from larger, important book reviewed by economist, see *HLAS 39:3436*.

3515. Flores-Galindo, Alberto. Arequipa y el sur andino: ensayo de historia regional, siglos XVIII-XX. Lima, Editorial Horizonte, 1977. 194 p., bibl., fold. map, maps, tables.

Uses regional focus to emphasize problems of country whose history is characterized by lack of effective internal market and absence of "nation." Conscious effort to counter-balance perspective from capital. Region includes Arequipa, Cuzco, Puno and corresponding coastline. Explores social tensions within this framework and commerce they spawned, resulting in hegemony of Arequipa merchants. Speculates on why internal market has not emerged in 20th century, a point which maintains regional dependency on wool exports. Employs previous work on Arequipa and wool, though more frequently relies upon archival materials. Sources include departmental archives, especially those containing notarial records, plantation records, Archbishopric Archive of Cuzco and municipal libraries. Methodologically challenging and indicative of trends among Peruvian historians.

3516. Flores Marín, José A. La explotación del caucho en el Perú. Presentación de Honorio Pinto H. Lima, Univ. Nacional Mayor de San Marcos, Seminario de Historia Rural Andina, 1977. 1 v. (Various pagings) bibl., tables.

Basic study of Tambopata Rubber Syndicate Ltd., English company that exploited Amazon rubber in Peru, 1900-10, and whose brutalization of local people as laborers provoked international scandal. Makes use of company records, housed in Centro de Documentación Agraria, Lima, to link Peruvian rubber to world market, define its social relations of production and especially to analyze system of *enganche* in jungle region of Peru. Company data span period 1907-13 but other public records contribute to examination of era 1880-1910. Concludes that Peruvian rubber was an extractive capitalist dependency, distinguishes between destructiveness of rubber cutting and rubber plant farmers, shows that labor exploitation produced violent confrontations and that local government agencies were employed by rubber companies to facilitate their objectives. End of rubber boom meant stagnation of jungle economy and depopulation of region, leaving only city of Iquitos as reminder of era.

3517. Freyre J., Iris. Exportaciones e industria en el Perú: el caso de Grace y Paramonga. Lima, Pontificia Univ. Católica del Perú, Depto. de Ciencias Sociales, Area de Sociología, 1976. 60 p., tables (Serie publicaciones previas, 15)

Attacks dual society perspective through which past studies have viewed Peru by examining the circulation of capital as a productive activity, using sugar production at Hacienda Paramonga, owned formerly by W.R. Grace, as case. Lacks Grace Co. records but effectively employs property and mercantile registers along with public documentation in this admittedly tentative effort. Concludes that Grace activities must be studied through its mode of accumulation rather than by market pressures and that this leads one to ask how export-oriented plantations proletarianized Peruvian workers.

3518. García-Sayán, Diego. El caso Marcona: análisis histórico-jurídico de los contratos. Lima, Centro de Estudios y Promoción del Desarrollo (DESCO), 1975. 196 p., bibl., tables.

Examines legal history of penetration and control of mining in Peru in 20th century by North American companies, using Marcona Mining Co. as illustration of general tendency to manipulate laws in favor of foreign interests. Cautions that character of state in this period might not be same as that studied in another epoch and that search for consensus rules relations between hegemonic interests of capital and underdeveloped states. Concludes that principal social effect of legal relationship studied here is maintenance and reproduction of imperialist dependency in Peru. Closely reasoned examination of mining laws in historical perspective.

3519. Gargurevich, Juan. Introducción a la historia de los medios de comunicación en el Perú. Lima, Editorial Horizonte, 1977. 217 p., bibl., tables.

Preliminary scholarly survey of history of communications media—newspaper, radio, television—in Peru since their founding. Emphasis on relations between the law, the state and owners of media, with considerable citation of data on character of ownership, lists of stockholders, dates of founding, distribution figures for both provinces and Lima, of newspapers, radio and television, with chronologies of important dates in history of separate media. Expropriation process studied for its impact on changes. Journalist author finds that although media gives greater attention to popular culture since 1970, this does not necessarily contribute to socialization of Peru. Expropriations created a "revolution of hope" but implies this not yet accomplished. Good beginning for further study of Peru media with basic bibliography.

3520. Gómez Rodríguez, Juan de la Cruz. Reforma agraria y campesinado de Caylloma. Arequipa, Perú, Editorial Universitaria, 1976. 111 p., bibl., tables.

Interpretive analysis of impact of 1969 agrarian reform on major province of Arequipa Dept. Caylloma is cattle hacienda region whose affected properties were shaped into a SAIS. Based largely on published not primary materials. Concludes that implementation of SAIS after 1969 consolidated precapitalist relations of production that came into being after World War I.

3521. González Vigil, Francisco de Paula. Educación y sociedad: importancia y utilidad de las asociaciones; importancia y necesidad de la educación popular. v. 1. Compilación y estudio preliminar de Alberto Tauro. Lima, Instituto Nacional de Cultura, 1973? 88 p.

Series of essays by well-known mid-19th century ecclesiastic from Tacna. Reprinted from difficult-to-find sources. Useful introductory biographical remarks.

3522. ———. Importancia de la educación del bello sexo. Prólogo de Helen Orvig de Salazar. Lima, Instituto Nacional de Cultura, 1976. 178 p.

Reprint of thoughts on education of women by well-known 19th-century cleric was encouraged by declaration of 1975 as "Año de la Mujer Peruana." Consists of essays that originally appeared in 1858 and 1872.

3523. Guerra M., Margarita. Documentos sobre tema peruano existentes en el Archivo Nacional de París: 1831-1841 (PUCP/CSH, 8:10, enero 1970/dic. 1972, p. 31-70)

Inventory of materials from Archives Nationales de Paris, Section Maritime, dealing with the Peru-Bolivia Confederation. Presented by legajo, they often form part of records dealing with other countries. Unannotated.

3524. Gutiérrez, Laura and others. Bibliografía histórica peruana: 1968-1970 (PUCP/CSH, 8:10, enero 1970/dic. 1972. p. 123-145)

Includes items from selected Peruvian, French, US and Spanish journals, classified by category (bibliography, etc.) and period. Divided into "History of America" and "History of Peru" and annotated. Of limited use.

3525. Herrick, Paul B., Jr. and Robert S. Robins. Varieties of Latin American revolutions and rebellions (JDA, 10:3, April 1976, p. 317-336)

Attempt to formulate typology of revolution to make concept more instrumental, quantifiable and analytic. Authors prefer four-fold typology, distinguishing revolutions on continuum of degree of disruption that extra-legal movements pose for a state. Items are: total revolution, political revolution, policy rebellion and a palace rebellion, all of which are examined for the "discontinuities" they produce. This framework imposed tentatively on four Latin American revolutions to test its validity: Mexico, 1910-40; Brazil, 1964; Venezuela, 1948; and Bolivia, 1920. Revolutions chosen questionable, categories unconvincing.

3526. Heysen, Luis E. El apóstol del APRA en Buenos Aires. Lima, Enrique Bracamonte Vera, 1973. 32 p., illus.

In homage to recently deceased Enrique Cornejo Koster, this essay of recollections of founding episodes of APRA in Peru was set out by Luis E.

Heysen, one of early leaders along with Haya and Cornejo. Printed with essays by Cornejo that appeared in various journals between 1923-55, this becomes a brief memoir.

Historia. See items 3076-3077.

3527. *Histórica.* Pontificia Univ. Católica del Perú, Depto. de Humanidades. Vol. 1, No. 1, julio 1977- . Lima.

Edited by Franklin Pease G.Y. of the Univ. Católica, Social Science faculty, along with team of his colleagues, this new journal devotes one section to articles on Peruvian history, another to extended reviews of major works in all languages and at end gives professional notices. In-line footnotes, in social-science journal style, plus listing of sources at end of essay, is preferred style. Attractive format and important articles make this a journal of high quality. First issue contains: J. Basadre "Leyes Electorales Peruanas, 1890-1917: Teoría y Realidad;" N.D. Cook "Estimaciones sobre la Población del Perú en el Momento de la Conquista;" C. Lazo García and J. Tord Nicolini "El Movimiento Social en el Perú Virreinal;" J. Kaliber "Religión y Revolución en los Andes en el Siglo XIX;" and S. O'Phelan Godoy "Cuzco 1777; El Movimiento de Maras, Urubamba."

Huamanga: una larga historia. See item 3078.

3528. Kapsoli E., Wilfredo. Los movimientos campesinos en Cerro de Pasco: 1880-1963. Lima, P.L. Villanueva, 1976. 161 p., maps, tables.

Brief excursion into the subject, but makes the important distinction between plantation-based uprisings and those undertaken in communities of freeholders. The two types examined in the department where Cerro Corporation played large role in mining and where major cattle ranches located. Fernandini family papers, in Centro de Documentación Agraria, not consulted, but good sources from archive of Ministerio de Trabajo y Comunidades, mostly from 1940s. Concludes that comunidad activities vs. haciendas made Cerro de Pasco region a high priority area for agrarian reform of 1969. Appeared previously as article in *Anales Científicos* (Lima, 4, 1975, p. 185-334).

3529. Klaiber, Jeffrey L. Religion and revolution in Peru: 1824-1976. Notre Dame, Ind., Univ. of Notre Dame, 1977. 259 p., bibl.

Study of interaction of reformist politics and popular religiosity in Peru mainly since 1885. To do so reviews anti-clericalism in 19th century, influence of Manuel González Prada on reformist outlook and sierra uprisings, 1860s and 1890s, emphasizing one led by P.P. Atusparia in Callejón de Huaylas, 1885. Examines indigenista movement of 1889-1930 as viewed by novelists and essayists around whom movement formed: Mariátegui's early experiences said to have made him a "spiritual" Marxist, and suggests that APRA's moral stance gave it widespread appeal, labeled "political messianism," despite early anti-clericalism of its leaders. APRA's effort to coopt Catholic sentiment allowed it to develop strong following among masses and paved way for emergence of social Christianity. Discusses post World War II challenge to APRA laid down by Christian Democrats through Popular Action party and by socially conscious military, a point which leads to consideration of influence of Church on policies of military government since 1968. Little consideration for left-wing political anti-clericalism, and no treatment of economic bases of APRA or Church programs. Nevertheless ends by nothing that tradition which includes *indigenismo*, Mariátegui, APRA, military and Church has created psychological and intellectual climate in which religion and revolution could be viewed as harmonious and complementary realities in Peru.

3530. Klarén, Peter F. Formación de las haciendas azucareras y orígenes del APRA. 2. ed. Lima, Instituto de Estudios Peruanos, 1976. 298 p. (Perú problema, 5)

Introduction to this ed. by Heraclio Bonilla points out that later studies have modified two points originally made here: 1) that similar enclaves elsewhere in Peru experienced same results as did Trujillo; and 2) that although rural proletariat developed in Piura APRA was not strong there. Suggests that this work cannot account fully for militancy displayed by rural workers, and calls for further study of impact of APRA on structure, thought and ideology of urban and rural proletariat of Peru. This ed. essentially unchanged from original (see *HLAS 34:2617*).

3531. ———. The social and economic consequences of modernization in the Peruvian sugar industry: 1870-1930 (*in* Duncan, Kenneth; Ian Rutledge; and Colin Hardings eds. Land and labour in Latin America [see item 2156] p. 229-252, map, tables)

Focuses on same period as book (see item 3530) and studies relationship between centralization of land, mechanization of sugar production, dispossession of small owners and provision of agro-industrial labor, all of which led to labor unrest, in essentially unchanged synopsis of item 3530. Good tables on wages and cites CDA documentation on wages at Hacienda Cayaltí in 1920s and labor specialization in 1940s.

3532. *Latin American Perspectives.* Univ. of California. Vol. 4, No. 3, Summer 1977- . Riverside.

Entire issue devoted to coherent class analysis of Peru's military regime in power since 1968. Introductory essay by E. Dore and J. Weeks "Class Alliances and Class Struggles in Peru" dissects character of class struggle on eve of coup of Oct. 1968, and by way of strong theoretical analysis, dismisses utility of dependency theory for explaining recent events in Peru. Essay by W.Bollinger "The Bourgeois Revolution in Peru: a Conception of Peruvian History" clarifies role of national bourgeoisie in country's 20th-century history. In "Petty-Bourgeois Ideology of the Peruvian Aprista Party" V. Villanueva shows how social composition of PAP led it to betray its leadership of working class, after which E. Dore's "Crisis and Accumulation in the Peruvian Mining Industry, 1968-1974" examines restructuring of capital that took place in period as consequence of nationalizations, especially as it reflected in cost of labor. Statistics were drawn from Ministry of Development and Public Works in 1950s and 1960s. B. Caravedo Molinari "The State and the Bourgeoisie in the Peruvian Fishmeal Industry" examines struggle to expand fishing, 1948-68, and crisis that came about in industry under military regime. J. Weeks "Backwardness, Foreign Capital, and Accumulation in the Manufacturing Sector of Peru, 1954-1975" explores role of foreign capital in process of accumulation, combining Marxist-Leninist analysis with public statistics to conclude that foreign capital-led accumulation, 1956-67, accelerated onset of crisis in Peruvian capital, and that without revolutionized agriculture class struggle is thereby intensified. Final essay "Sobre el Carácter de la Reforma Agraria Peruana" by J.M. Caballero, shows that agrarian reform which ended officially in 1976 thus far has benefitted military state above all and has not strongly affected structure of productivity of capital. This has created conflict in agriculture between workers and state which in turn eliminates possibility that a class of small capitalist farmers might emerge. Series of penetrating essays indispensable for any further study of Peruvian political economy of past decade.

3533. Macera, Pablo. Agricultura en el Perú: siglo XX. v. 1/2. Documentos. Presentación de Honorio Pinto H. Lima, Univ. Nacional Mayor de San Marcos, Seminario de Historia Rural Andina, 1977. 2 v. (307 p.) (Continuous pagination) tables.

Reprints reports made by administrators or technicians to owners of plantations or to government officials (1907-18) from various regions, containing data on labor, prices of cattle and produce, costs of production and transportation, enganche, capital, irrigation and other matters of technical importance for agricultural production. Valuable reports.

3534. ———. Cayaltí 1875-1920: organización del trabajo en una plantación azucarera del Perú. Lima, Univ. Nacional Mayor de San Marcos, Seminario de Historia Rural Andina, 1973. 311 p.

Reprints typed, documents from Accounts and Correspondence of Hacienda Cayaltí, materials located in Centro de Documentación Agraria, Lima. Materials presented here are random sampling of 127 documents out of more than 120 vols. of correspondence and other materials available for study of major coastal sugar plantation. Documents in this volume cover years 1875-1951 and touch on all manner of plantation activities. Useful sampling of whole collection though marred by hurried issue. Categories of subject are merely labeled "administration," "labor," and "various."

3535. ———. Palto: hacendados y yanaconas del algodonal peruano; documentos, 1877-1943. Presentación de Honorio Pinto H. Lima, Univ. Nacional Mayor de San Marcos, Seminario de Historia Rural Andina, 1976. 150 p., fold. maps, fold. tables, tables.

Transcription and printing of selections from massive collection of accounts and correspondence of Hacienda Palto, cotton plantation located in Pisco valley of coastal Peru. Selections emphasize problems of administration. Documents will encourage further studies of plantations in historical perspective.

3536. ———. Tierra y población en el Perú: siglos XVIII-XIX. v. 1/4. Lima, Univ. Nacional Mayor de San Marcos, Seminario de Historia Rural Andina, 1972. 4 v. (942 p.) (Continuous pagination) fold. tables, tables.

Bulk of documents brought together here come from Archivo General de la Nación and Archivo Histórico del Ministerio de Hacienda, and Biblioteca Nacional in Lima as well as from occasional publications of 18th and 19th centuries. Materials from part of records that were required for accurate accounts of tribute payments. Most of them from AGN where they are located under diverse headings, and most of which were collected in 1965-67. The 285 tables reproduced with written sources cover period 1723-1853, while documents cover 1769-1889. These materials will aid in further Andean demographic, land tenure, kinship and social conflict studies. Macera promised an essay on colonial tributes to accompany this publication.

Macera Dall'Orso, Pablo *comp.* Historia económica peruana: documentos. See item 3218.

3537. Malpica Silva Santisteban, Carlos. El desarrollismo en el Perú: década de esperanzas y fracasos, 1961-71. Lima, Editorial Horizonte, 1975. 159 p., tables (Serie realidad peruana)

Brief, critical cataloguing of failures of goals of 1961 Charter of Punta del Este which outlines Alliance for Progress, as manifested in Peru. Military regime in power since 1968 also comes in for share of criticism. Rather than examine why failures occurred, however, prefers only to show that they happened. Uses UN sources and concludes that things have gotten worse, not better in Peru, relative to other Latin American countries over the decade in question. Uses UN statistics but occasionally commits errors. Table (p. 105) which compares Peru's life expectancy to neighboring countries left out Peru's statistics.

3538. El Mariscal Benavides: su vida y su obra. v. 1, Lima, Editorial Atlántida, 1976. 336 p., fold. plates.

First of projected two-volume study of general whose best recollected career was as ruler in Peru during 1930s after assassination of Luis Sánchez Cerro. This vol. 1 apparently written by his children (though they do not claim authorship), records details of his life up to 1921. Published on 30th anniversary of his death. Major figure in Peruvian politics from 1915 to his death, Gen. Oscar R. Benavides Larrea (1876-1945) confronted American oil companies at La Brea and Pariñas oil fields and created national oil enterprise. He was exiled by Augusto Leguía, returned in early 1930s and ruled 1932-39, then led campaign against Ecuador in 1941. This hagiographic vol. predictably over-emphasizes narrow military history but it also suggests connections between Peruvian and French military systems made between 1870 and 1914. Details general's early jungle expeditions before 1915. Apparently based on family records but this is not indicated.

3539. Martín, José Carlos. Infancia de José Pardo y Barreda (IRA/B, 9, 1972/1974, p. 123-137)

Minutely documented genealogical study of kin of Manuel Pardo y Barreda, first civilian president of Peru (1872-79), and descendant of Felipe Pardo y Aliaga. Hews closely to genealogical concerns and provides interesting links among landowning families that could be useful to social historians. Based on parish records.

3540. Martinet, Jean Baptiste H. La agricultura en el Perú. Presentación de Honorio Pinto. Lima, Centro Peruano de Historia Económica, 1977. 165 p., fold. table.

Reprint of 100-year old classic originally published as report by French agronomist with keen insight into country. unique study of Peru's 19th-century agriculture is complemented by other publications in this series. Martinet saw agriculture being abandoned and was convinced that teaching of agricultural methods had to be intensified, especially in order to bring out its scientific nature. His views are policy-oriented. One warning: typing of manuscript resulted in pagination error: number of pages cited above is less than true size of this mimeograph ed. by some 35 p. Nevertheless, valuable resource for study of 19th-century agriculture.

3541. ———. Carestía de víveres en Lima, 1875. Presentación de Honorio Pinto. Lima, Centro Peruano de Historia Económica, 1977. 41 p.

Reprint of essay originally published in *Revista de Agricultura* (Lima, 1875-76). Its relevance to current and past (1870s) problems of Peru is vividly clear. Discusses relationship between agricultural production, rising capital costs, increase in population and scarcity of capital.

3542. Martínez-Alier, Juan. Haciendas, plantations and collective farms: agrarian class societies—Cuba and Peru. London, Frank Cass, 1977. 185 p., bibl.

Some of these interpretive essays have appeared before in journals, collections of essays or as separate works. Nevertheless, collection heightens usefulness to agrarian historians. Long introductory statement argues with A.V. Chayanov and his epigones on agrarian classes, the state and capital accumulation. Succeeding chapters compare cases from 1934 to 1960, in illustration of disagreement with Chayanov, and ends with discussion of problems of management of agriculture in socialist economy. Insightful shifting from empirical to theoretical considerations throughout. Important set of essays for 20th-century agrarian themes.

3543. Masterson, Daniel M. Soldiers, sailors, and *Apristas*: conspiracy and power politics in Peru, 1932-1948 (*in* Bratzel, John F. and Daniel M. Masterson eds. The underside of Latin American history. East Lansing, Michigan State Univ., The Latin American Studies Center, 1977, p. 24-42 [Monograph series, 16])

Detailed study of impact of APRA conspiracies (1932-48) upon relations between Apristas and progressive military who were convinced of movement's political effectiveness. By 1948, when most serious uprisings since 1932 failed, indecision and inaction of APRA leaders at key moments seriously damaged their image. Disillusionment with their revolutionary tactics grew thereafter but legacy of their plotting and intrigue remained. Makes use of US National Archives material, interviews with Haya and Víctor Villanueva, plus Villanueva's works. Convincing explanation of 1948 events.

3544. Mathew, W.M. A primitive export sector: guano production in mid-nineteenth century Peru (JLAS, 9:1, May 1977, p. 35-57)

Peers into internal operation of guano business to determine mechanics of production, costs, efficiency and or export, in order to judge its impact on overall economy of Peru. Decides that Peruvian state—uniquely among backward economies of 19th century—was able to retain considerable part of net returns from extraction. Examines activities of contractors, character of labor force, and complications of shiploading guano. Speculates that exploitation of contract labor was more advantageous than free labor despite inefficiencies, and that Chinese workers had little impact on mainland domestic production. Peruvian government used its earnings to secure loans from guano merchants which, with poor investment, led to extraordinary debts of 1870s. This work suggests consequences of failure of a national bourgeoisie to emerge in mid-19th century.

3545. Matos Mar, José. Yanaconaje y reforma agraria en el Perú: el caso del valle de Chancay. Lima, Instituto de Estudios Peruanos, 1976. 278 p., bibl., tables.

General introduction to historical problem of yanaconaje in Peru sets tone for study based on extensive interviews, newspapers, government publications and previous works. Divided into three sections: 1) outlines changes in Chancay valley from "traditional" to "modern" agricultural relations, including 20th-century advent of share-cropping aided by importation of Chinese and Japanese labor and culminating in sharecropping law of 1947; 2) examines sharecropping in its "final" stage (1949-61); and 3) assesses gradual abolition of share-cropping as system of surplus extraction from 1964 to 1975. Handy overview of subject in 20th century especially because of its discussion of structure of this system. Limited to one valley and does not examine closely mechanics of yanaconaje.

3546. ——— ed. Hacienda, comunidad y campesinado en el Perú. 2. ed. rev. Lima, Instituto de Estudios Peruanos, 1976. 390 p., bibl., tables (Perú problema, 3)

Edition amplified and revised from 1970 original. Originally a set of essays in historical sociology, it was a suggestive examination by a number of highly regarded historians and other social scientists of the rural social process in Peru from three angles: 1) plantations (from origins to 20th century changes): 2) community (organization and activity); and 3) peasant (political organization and activity). Continued scholarly debate on aspects of rural society and history justify re-edition.

3547. Mejía, José Manuel and Rosa Díaz Suárez. Sindicalismo y reforma agraria en el Valle de Chancay. Lima, Instituto de Estudios Peruanos, 1975. 151 p., bibl., tables (Proyecto de estudios etnológicos del valle de Chancay, 5)

Sources such as volumes of study entitled *Las huelgas en el Perú* and *Asociaciones sindicales* issued by Ministerio de Trabajo y Comunidades (1966-71), and annual reports of Sociedad Nacional Agraria (1946-47, 1959-60) plus secondary materials, allow authors to draw conclusion that movement of agrarian labor unionism has moved beyond capabilities of either APRA or Community Party to keep up with them. Develops this view by examination of organization efforts among sharecroppers and wage laborers of Chancay (1930s-40s) and role of APRA and CP in 1950s and 1960s. Ends with response to agrarian reform of 1969 in valley and peasant convention of 1972. Good agrarian reform charts.

3548. Mendiburu, Manuel de. Diccionario histórico-biográfico del Perú. t. 1, ABAD-AMAT. 3. ed. con adiciones y notas bibliográficas por Evaristo San Cristóval. Estudio biográfico del General Mendiburu por D. José de la Riva-Agüero y Osma. Lima, Editorial Arica, 1976. 380 p., illus. (Col. Perú historia)

Reprint of standard source in field. Volume contains appended subject index. Originally published 1874-80 in four volumes.

3549. Miller, Rory. The making of the Grace Contract: British bondholders and the Peruvian government, 1885-1890 (JLAS, 8:1, May 1976, p. 73-100, tables)

Explores relations between post-Chilean war economic recovery of Peru and Grace agreement in context of interests of bondholders, businessmen and Peruvian government. Examines reasons why contract was made, dictates of politics pursued by both bondholders and government and consequences of contract. Concludes that bondholders were unable to control negotiations that led to contract, nor were they able to get the strong support from Foreign Office that they wanted, while Cáceres government was weak throughout affair. Also, real impact of bonds issued once contract was made appeared not in modernization of sierra agriculture but in copper mining. More than anyone else, beneficiary was Michael Grace. Fine study based on Foreign Office records, private collections in England, including Peruvian Corporation Archive in Univ. of London, and newspapers.

3550. ———; Clifford T. Smith; and John Fisher *eds.* Social and economic change in modern Peru. Liverpool, U.K., Univ. of Liverpool, Centre for Latin-American Studies, 1976. 198 p., bibl., maps, tables (Monograph series, 6)

Studies originally presented at Univ. of Liverpool 1974 conference whose unifying theme is regional analysis of Peruvian development. Special attention is given to use of dependency analysis and to problems of relation of export economy to development. Second theme that interests these scholars is state's role in transition from pre-capitalist to capitalist economy in 20th-century Peru. Mostly new material largely based on archival research in Peru. They include: John Fisher "Silver Mining and Silver Miners in the Viceroyalty of Peru, 1776-1824: A Prolegomenon;" R. Miller "Railways and Economic Development in Central Peru, 1890-1930;" R. Thorp and G. Bertram "Industrialization in an Open Economy: A Case Study of Peru, 1890-1940;" C.T. Smith "Agrarian Reform and Regional Development in Peru," which examines conduct of 1969 agrarian reform; C. Harding "Agrarian Reform and Agrarian Struggles in Peru," which has appeared elsewhere; and B. Roberts "The Social History of a Provincial Town: Huancayo, 1890-1972." Effective presentation of set of disparate but useful studies.

Mörner, Magnus. En torno a las haciendas de la región del Cuzco desde el siglo XVIII. See item 3224.

3551. Murillo Garaycochea, Percy. Historia del APRA, 1919-1945. Prólogo de Andrés Townsend Ezcurra. Edición de Delgado Valenzuela. Lima, Imprenta Editora Atlántida, 1976. 498 p., bibl., facsims., illus.

Dedicated to martyrs to: "ideals of liberty and social justice that Aprismo incarnates." Volume relies for most part on standard works, Haya's essays and *La Tribuna*, APRA's newspaper, to examine in detail founding of movement, split with Mariátegui, founding of PAP, 1931 electoral politics, 1932 Trujillo uprising and relations with Sánchez Cerro afterward, and ends with commentary on clandestine operations of 1930s and APRA in World War II. Fascinating photo reproductions are best part of this work which nevertheless must be considered standard history of movement and party at this point. Far from definitive.

Peru. Ministerio de Relaciones Exteriores. Confederación Perú-Bolivia: 1835-1839. See *HLAS 39:8874*.

3552. Philip, George. The limitations of bargaining theory: a case study of the International Petroleum Company in Peru (WD, 4:3, March 1976, p. 231-239)

Uses IPC conflict with Peruvian government in decade preceding nationalization decree to illustrate point that bargaining theory too often presumes existence of strong state whose policies on nationalization will benefit development. Suggests this may not be the case. Though political science, worthy of consideration by historians of recent period. For political scientist's comment, see *HLAS 39:7376*.

3553. ———. The soldier as radical: the Peruvian military government, 1968-1975 (JLAS, 8:1, May 1976, p. 29-51)

Relates accepted theoretical assumptions about military government to Peruvian case (1968-75) to determine fairness of accusations made against generals. Focuses on degree of internal unity within military and its relations with civilian ruling class. Finds this unity spurred by training system and by military contempt for civilian ineptitude, nursed by anti-APRA outlook and strained relations with US. Argues that obstacles to effective military radicalism have not appeared. However, problem of popular participation in government a major weakness, indicated by effort to create state political organizations (SINAMOS, etc.), but army continues to assert central position of state in development policy without strong social base. For political scientist's comment, see *HLAS 39:7377*.

3554. Pike, Fredrick B. The United States and the Andean republics: Peru, Bolivia, Ecuador. Cambridge, Mass., Harvard Univ. Press, 1977. 493 p., maps (The American foreign policy library)

Synthesis of history of "national culture" of these countries. Early chapters devoted to creating framework of common experiences in region. Does so by contrasting patron-client and corporativist model for Andean historical behavior with individualistic model commonly accepted for US. This leads to advocacy of paternalistic and fatalistic policies by US with reference to Andean countries. Patron-client, corporatist model allows in succeeding chapters for explanation of cleavage between highland and coastal cultures in pre-conquest, conquest and colonial periods and lays groundwork for explanation of dominance of commercial capitalism on coast over traditionalism of highlands after 1825. Comparisons with US culture made throughout. Quest for stability and progress in 19th century fails to give much attention to guano's role in political economy of Peru though much to arguments of liberal and conservative intellectuals, while almost one chapter devoted to military and diplomatic aspects of War of Pacific (1879-83). Ch. 6 discusses liberalism and rise of US penetration of Peruvian economy, as does ch. 7. Ch. 8/9 devoted to comment on challenges to ruling establishment, reformism, impact of world depression and World War II. Bolivian revolution of 1952 allows for fuller discussion of US diplomacy in Andean region and this followed in ch. 11 by full treatment of US impact vis-à-vis Alliance for Progress, plus discussion of dependency theory, patron-client relations, nation-building through corporatism, etc. Discussion of military regimes leads nevertheless to pessimistic conclusions. Epilogue is couched in framework of "sociobiology" in order to compare US and Andean America. Ends by noting that corporatism cannot be a panacea for Andean region because it does not destroy alienation born of "class and division-of-labor conflicts." Notes will be useful to beginning students of region.

3555. Pinto, Honorio and Alvaro Goicochea. Ocupaciones en el Perú: 1876. Lima, Univ. Nacional Mayor de San Marcos, Seminario de Historia Rural Andina, 1977. 46 l., tables.

Attempts to make census of 1876 more useful to researchers by distilling from it information on occupations. Problems arise in construction of categories, alluded to in preliminary remarks by Pablo Macera, who notes that some stated occupations of that era are now unintelligible. Nevertheless, important effort at refinement.

Ponce, Fernando. Anotaciones sobre fuentes documentales de Arequipa. See item 3083.

3556. ———. La ciudad en el Perú. Lima, Retablo de Papel, 1975. 186 p., bibl., illus., maps, tables (Retablo de papel ediciones, 21)

Marshals demographic data from censuses, other ministries, and wide reading of dependency theory and related studies, to draw conclusions about urban process in Peru since about 1920. Finds that enclavement and migration have significantly distorted demographic structure of rural areas, that services tend to be available only in cities, and that since 1969-70 Lima-Callao may not have primacy they once did. Brief and somewhat schematic but gathers important data on urbanization and relates it to policy.

3557. Portocarrero M., Felipe. El pensamiento político de Haya de la Torre (ANA, 1, enero/marzo 1977, p. 37-48, bibl.)

Precise, careful analysis of APRA's political philosophy as set forth in Haya's writings, especially in *El antimperialismo y el APRA*. Notes petit-bourgeois jacobinism of his ideas, their conception of neutral anti-imperialist state, and inherent consequences for relations between middle class and workers and peasants. Concludes that such conceptions could never lead to socialism. Excellent sociological analysis that will be of great value to historians of APRA and of intellectual history of Peru.

3558. Rama, Carlos M. Flora Tristán en América del Sur (CAM, 36[214]:5, sept./oct. 1977. p. 159-168)

Surveys some of literature on utopian socialism in 19th-century Europe and places Flora Tristán in that tradition. Less convincing is view that she had precursorial impact upon Peruvian socialist tradition similar to that of González Prada and Mariátegui. Useful survey of her thinking on socialism, reviews writings by her and about her.

Ramírez Gastón, José M. 150 [i.e. Ciento cincuenta] años: economía y finanzas en el Perú; 1821-1971 y en el Virreynato: 1544-1824. See *HLAS 39:3457*.

3559. Riva-Agüero, José de la. Obras completas. t. 11, Escritos políticos. Prólogo de Carlos Rodríguez Pastor. Lima, Pontificia Univ. Católica del Perú, 1975. 343 p. (Publicaciones del Instituto Riva-Agüero, 91)

Short speeches and letters, chosen at random, covering years 1904-44, of best-known academic spokesman of fascism in Peru, especially in 1930s. Those statements concerning his views on political process, though only part of this volume, are the most interesting. His academic career, evolution of his thinking, events in his life, are subject of prologue by Carlos Rodríguez Pastor.

3560. Rowe, Leo Stanton. El Perú y la guerra de 1914. Prefacio de David Kinley. Lima, Biblioteca Andina, 1975. 41 l., tables.

Originally wirtten immediately after war, this essay was preliminary presentation of views that were more fully developed in Rowe's much larger work, itself part of series issued by Carnegie Foundation. Tables and conclusions are limited to early years, 1911-14, nevertheless critical examination based on US Commerce Dept. and public statistics of Peru. Exports and imports broken down by product and values given.

3561. Saint John, Ronald Bruce. The end of innocence: Peruvian foreign policy and the United States, 1919-1942 (JLAS, 8:2, Nov. 1976, p. 325-344)

Peruvian diplomatic relations with US examined through resolution of border conflicts with Chile, Colombia and Ecuador. US diplomatic attention increased by Tacna-Arica plebiscite of 1925, Salomón-Lozano Treaty of 1922 which gave Colombia part of Leticia Trapezoid, and Marañón dispute with Ecuador. Leguía's overthrow said to partially reflect these losses. Sánchez Cerro refused US entreaties and Benavides reaffirmed 1922 treaty with Colombia. Ecuador question became mark of Peruvian national self-confidence and continued mistrust of US, thereafter central to Peruvian foreign policy.

3562. Sánchez, Luis Alberto. Mito y realidad de González Prada. Lima, P.L. Villanueva, 1976? 90 p., facsims., illus.

Essay which argues that subject has been more influential in political debates of 20th-century Peru than any other figure, and raises question with reference to labor, educational debates and others. Appendix is chronology of activities of González Prada family in Peru since early colonial period.

3563. Santisteban, Jorge. Aproximación histórica a la comunidad industrial (UCCH/A, 3:5, 1976, p. 3-28)

Evidence culled from congressional debates down to 1964 and other sources seeks to set worker participation in industrial management in historical perspective. Points out that participation by labor in gains from private enterprise was legislated in 1949 but never implemented, and that debate on this issue continued down to 1970 when industrial communities were created in Peru, giving workers participation in profits and access to property. This was new in that it sought to harmonize goals of capital and labor. Reveals that military government tried to convince industrial capitalists of seriousness of their program while owners opposed it by every possible means. Though labor unions favored legislation, rank-and-file members were apathetic. By March 1973 National Confederation of Industrial Communities (CONACI) was formed and afterward workers pressed toward 50 percent participation in industrial returns the law set as goal. Author's language suggests that worker participation up to now has fallen far short of government claims and that 50 percent participation in returns is unrealizable under present conditions.

3564. Sulmont, Denis. El movimiento obrero en el Perú: 1900-1956. Lima, Pontificia Univ. Católica del Perú, Fondo Editorial, 1976. 356 p., bibl., facsims., tables.

Rather than history based on movement documents, this is initial interpretive synthesis of trajectory of labor's struggle. Set within dependency framework, it draws on wide variety of published materials. Newspapers and interviews with labor leaders dissect formation of different sectors of working class. Argues significantly that APRA's popular radicalism was outgrowth of extremely weak bourgeoisie which also explains why workers saw APRA as their party. Also describes rise of labor federations and their competition in context of APRA politics and offers explanation of splits in left during Odría period as result of complete cooptation of APRA. Points way to further research.

3565. Valderrama, Mariano. 7 [i.e. Siete] años de reforma agraria peruana: 1969-1976. Lima, Pontificia Univ. Católica del Perú, 1976. 632 p., tables.

Critical, helpful description of major events in process of agrarian reform of period. Pt. 1 develops dynamics of reform; pt. 2 presents strict chronology of it; and pt. 3 consists of documents from reform which indicate positions taken on issues by the state, peasant organizations, and dispossessed landlords. Tables show extent of expropriation by area and their disposition. Author coordinated rural study workshop at Univ. Católica and based this work on newspapers and government sources.

3566. Van Cleve, John V. The Latin American policy of President Kennedy: a reexamination case, Peru (IAMEA, 30:4, Spring 1977, p. 29-44)

Takes to task Lieuwen-Schlesinger, Jr. *et al.* view that social idealism was at root of Kennedy's Latin American policy. Refers to US response to Peru events in summer of 1962 to argue that Kennedy's commitment to Cold War and material interests of US were stronger motivations. Thus, US failed to recognize military government that toppled Prado in 1962 even though generals respected civil rights and began reforms. Kennedy's policy rested on fear that coup would open door for gains by Communist labor unions. Also, Kennedy saw military as obstacle to his favorites, Haya and APRA. Interesting thesis even if depiction of generals is a bit much.

Van den Berghe, Pierre L. and George P. Primov. Inequality in the Peruvian Andes: class and ethnicity in Cuzco. See *HLAS 39:1568.*

3567. Vásques, Emilio. La rebelión de Juan Bustamante. Lima, Editorial Juan Mejía Baca, 1976. 408 p., plates.

An 1866 uprising in Lake Titicaca area of Puno dept. in which peasants attempted to have wrongs of landlords corrected, found Bustamante at its head. Son of landlord family, portrayed here as "precursor of the Peruvian desire for authentic social reform," a world traveler, congressman and prefect of Cuzco at different times, author and contemporary of Manuel A. Fuentes. Also said to be friend of Ramón Castilla and after 1846 constant agitator for fairness to peasants. Assisted in founding in 1867 of Sociedad Amiga de los Indios which became vehicle for general peasant rebellion. Movement ended one year later with capture and beheading of leaders and suffocation of 70 followers. Story told with too little analysis, bit of hagiography and lots of quotes from contemporary sources. Follow-up investigation dragged on without conclusive results. This work hardly closed the subject.

3568. Vera, Gustavo Adolfo. Cuzco: reforma agraria y cambios en la propiedad de la tierra, 1969-1974. Lima, Univ. Nacional Mayor de San Marcos, Seminario de Historia Rural Andina, 1976. 136 p., bibl., fold. table, tables.

Based on field work in region, this thesis carefully examines application of agrarian reform laws in 1960s and 1970s with eye toward their impact on agrarian social relations. Employs agropecuario census data, agrarian reform laws, other government data to study land seizures, land concentration, and productivity. Decides that 1969 reform set in motion collapse of pre-capitalist agriculture in Cuzco and amplified regional market structure. Nevertheless says that dependent capitalist agriculture remains and calls for collectivization of agriculture in Peru.

3569. Villanueva, Víctor. El APRA y el ejército: 1940-1950. Lima, Editorial Horizonte, 1977. 174 p., bibl.

Takes up where *El APRA en busca del poder* left off (see *HLAS 38:3520*), explaining development of Haya's collaborationist views and his growing relationship with sector of military. Relies on correspondence between Aprista executives exiled in Chile and Haya, US State Dept. materials, 1976 Michigan State dissertation on Peruvian military, newspapers and author's own archives. Considers APRA conspiracy of 1948 and start of relations between Odría and Haya. Altogether spellbinding interpretation by insightful, unorthodox retired officer.

3570. ——. Así cayó Leguía. Lima, Retama Editorial, 1977. 155 p. (Historia política, 2)

Testimonial of what author, young idealist officer at time, saw and heard in Aug. 1930, concerning Leguía's resignation, US' role in process, and accompanying rise of Luis Sánchez Cerro. Interesting that he relates those events to specific situations in uprising of Feb. 1975, drawing parallels about crown behavior, infighting among officers, etc. Engaging, insightful essay that serves as both memoir and history.

3571. Zevallos Paz-Soldán, Carlos Ortiz de *ed.* Perú y Bolivia: 1840-1843. Lima, Ministerio de Relaciones Exteriores del Perú, 1976. 281 p. (Archivo diplomático peruano, 10)

Contains carefully selected documents, arranged in chronological order, on Confederation of Peru and Bolivia, especially on activities of Generals Orbegoso, Salaverry and Santa Cruz. These years characterized as "chaotic" by editor, and indeed, arrangement of materials is by year.

3572. Zimmermann Zavala, Augusto. El Plan Inca: objetivo, revolución peruana. Barcelona, Ediciones Grijalbo, 1975. 242 p. (Col. Nuevo norte, 16)

From pen of Press Secretary to former President, appointed when military government took power in 1968. This must be considered memoir that gives unofficial version of military view of why coup took place. Sets events in context of "secret history" of Peruvian oil, bungling politics of Acción Popular and military nationalization of IPC.

BOLIVIA AND CHILE

THOMAS C. WRIGHT

Associate Professor of History
University of Nevada, Las Vegas

ALTHOUGH SERIOUS HISTORICAL SCHOLARSHIP on Bolivia is still in the embryonic stage, the pace of research and publication within the country has quickened somewhat under the stimulus of the sesquicentennial of Bolivian independence (1975). The government-sponsored Biblioteca del Sesquicentenario de la República published several worthwhile books, most notably the four-volume *Monografía de Bolivia* (see item 3580) and Editorial Los Amigos del Libro has continued to promote historical publications. Unfortunately, despite some qualitative advances, most Bolivian historians still refuse to adopt the standard practice of citing sources, thus reducing the utility of their products. Another negative note: the historical journal *Kollasuyo* (see *HLAS 38:3539*) has apparently suspended publication, eliminating a good source of article literature.

Individual political figures, the Chaco War, and the background and results of the 1952 Revolution have been the favorite themes of recent scholarship. Gómez's study of Bautista Saavedra is the best of several political biographies (item 3590). The revised edition of Querejazu Calvo's book (item 3596) and Céspedes' work (item 3581) are useful additions to the literature on the Chaco War. Among the contributions on the National Revolution, the books by Andrade (item 3573), Quiroga Ochoa (item 3597), and the new edition of Céspedes' study (item 3582) are worthy of note, as are the articles by Dandler (item 3584) and Gudmundson (item 3591) on specialized related themes.

Four other books deserve mention. Debray's work is important for its insights into Che Guevara's failure in Bolivia (item 3585). Fellman Velarde's cultural history, despite some shortcomings, is useful (item 3586) and Querejazu Calvo's history of tin mining is an excellent synthesis (item 3595). The general history by Finot and Baptista Gumucio provides a solid single volume history of Bolivia to the 1970s (item 3587).

Research and publication in Chile continue to be hampered by the political climate, and Arnold J. Bauer's remarks in *HLAS 38* (p. 295-296) on the ramifications of the military coup for historical scholarship are still essentially valid. Nonetheless the early post-coup dedication to works of hero worship may have peaked, and several important books and articles on the national period have appeared in Chile as well as abroad.

The torrent of writings on contemporary history since 1970 continues unabated (for more extensive coverage of the UP, the coup, and military government, see *HLAS 37*, p. 483-491 and *HLAS 39*, p. 560-571). Recently, several Chileans have turned to history for clues to the election of Allende, the collapse of democracy, and the new role of the military. Among the noteworthy writings in this vein are articles by Borón (item 3615), de Riz (item 3660), Tapia-Videla (item 3665) and Donoso Letelier (item 3627). Nunn's book provides a thoughtful analysis of civil-military relations that places the 1973 coup and the military government in historical perspective (item 3654).

Rural history has continued to receive the attention of excellent scholars. Loveman's analysis of the struggle for rural unionization and agrarian reform is an important contribution (item 3645). The articles by Kay (item 3640) and Bauer and Johnson (item 3612) perceptively examine changes in agrarian systems and rural society.

A few other publications deserve mention. The memoirs of González Videla will be a valuable source for students of politics since the 1930s (item 3634). Varona's book brings to light new information on Francisco Bilbao (item 3667). Rossignol's study of popular warfare (item 3661) and Blancpain's article on immigration (item 3614) are incisive, and Remmer's reassessment of the Parliamentary Period is useful (item 3659). Nineteenth-century historians and their works have received the careful attention of Woll (item 3673); also, Collier's study of the historiography of the 1830-91 period is an excellent synthesis (item 3624).

BOLIVIA

3573. Andrade, Víctor. My missions for revolutionary Bolivia: 1944-1962. Edited and with an introduction by Cole Blasier. Pittsburgh, Pa., Univ. of Pittsburgh Press, 1976. 200 p., plate (Pitt Latin American series [PLAS])

These memoirs of important figure of MNR and long-time Ambassador to US (1944-46 and 1952-62) provide valuable insights into international aspects of MNR's bid to gain and consolidate power. Andrade was key element in crucial struggle between tin barons and MNR for Washington's vital support, both before and after National Revolution. Important work. For political scientist's comment, see *HLAS 39:8789*.

3574. Araujo Subieta, Mario. Luis Subieta Sagárnaga: estudio biográfico — estimativo. Ilustración de Lalo Flores. La Paz, Ediciones ISLA, 1975. 208 p., illus., plates (Col. Destinos, 18)

Biography of the 20th-century historian of Potosí and Bolivia and analysis of his major works, by subject's grandson. Although Subieta's importance within Bolivian historiography is exaggerated, this study of the man and his scholarship is useful.

3575. Ayala Z., Alfredo. Historia de Bolivia en cuadros sinópticos. La Paz, Editorial Don Bosco, 1976. 424 p.

Curious factual outline history of Bolivia comparable to "College Outline Series" familiar to US students. Potentially useful as reference work or aid to memorization.

3576. Baptista Gumucio, Mariano. Ensayos sobre la realidad boliviana. La Paz, Comité Nacional del Sesquicentenario de la República, 1975. 271 p. (Biblioteca del sesquicentenario, 10)

Worthwhile collection of previously published essays by well-known historian, essayist and journalist. Includes historical vignettes, anecdotes, critical commentary, biographical sketches, and thoughtful section on Bolivia's international position.

3577. ———. Historia gráfica de la Guerra del Chaco. 2. ed. Pinturas de Gil Coimbra. Fotografías de Luis Bazoberry. La Paz, Editorial Ultima Hora, 1976. 254 p., facsims., illus., maps (Biblioteca popular boliviana de ultima hora. Col. Historia)

Enlarged ed. of interesting and useful photographic history of Chaco War. Contains diverse information on geography, weaponry and war personalities.

3578. ———. **Páginas escogidas.** La Paz, Editorial Los Amigos del Libro, 1975. 388 p., plates

Collection of writings and speeches by Mariano Baptista Caserta, 19th-century political figure and President of Bolivia (1892-96). Consists of four parts: 1) selected speeches; 2) biographical sketches of contemporary national public figures; 3) articles on political topics; and 4) personal and public letters.

3579. Benavides M., Julio. José Gutiérrez Guerra en nuestra historia económica. La Paz, n.p., 1975. 101 p., tables.

Attempts to resurrect figure of Gutiérrez Guerra (President, 1917-20) from obscurity to which Bolivian historiography has relegated him. Based on secondary works and passion, study traces career of accountant, financier and last President of the liberal oligarchy, and concludes that his administration has been undeservedly maligned.

3580. Bolivia. Comité Nacional del Sesquicentenario de la República. Monografía de Bolivia. t. 1, Chuquisaca-Potosí; t. 2, La Paz-Cochabama; t. 3, Oruro-Santa Cruz. La Paz, 1975. 4 v. (401, 442, 439 p., unavailable) bibl., facsims., illus., maps, plates, tables.

This ambitious work, culminating effort of Comité Nacional del Sesquicentenario de la República, offers solid and comprehensive reference manual on Bolivian geography, archaeology, sociology, popular culture, economy, and particularly history. Covering Bolivia's nine depts. in four volumes (t. 4, Beni-Pando-Tarija, not available at press time) this well-illustrated compendium contains essays of varying but generally high quality by several national historians and other academics, and provides useful bibliographies in some sections. This attractive and sophisticated publication will be of considerable value to specialist as well as casual student of Bolivia.

3581. Céspedes, Augusto. Crónicas heroicas de una guerra estúpida. La Paz, Librería Editorial Juventud, 1975. 139 p.

Collection of reprinted newspaper reports from Chaco front in 1933, accompanied by author's previously unpublished diary giving soldier's view of war in 1934. Valuable and interesting anthology which confirms horrors of Chaco War for Bolivian participant.

3582. ———. El presidente colgado. 2. ed. B.A., EUDEBA, 1975. 285 p.

Second ed. (for first, 1966, see *HLAS 30:2307*) of Céspedes' lively political history of 1939-46 period, written from extremely partisan MNR viewpoint. Valuable insider's perspective on US involvement and other events leading to assassination of President Villarroel.

3583. Crespo Gutiérrez, Alberto. Los tratados suscritos con Chile en 1895. La Paz, Editorial Los Amigos del Libro, 1975. 80 p. (Mini Col. Un siglo y medio)

Serious and intelligent analysis of stillborn 1895 peace treaties between Bolivia and Chile, containing lengthy documentary quotations. Author blames naiveté of opposition Liberals in Congress for modifying treaties—which would have guaranteed a sovereign Bolivian corridor to sea—in ways unacceptable to Chile, and thus for losing Bolivia's best opportunity for a favorable treaty.

Dandler, Jorge. Campesinado y reforma agraria en Cochabamba: dinámica de un movimiento campesino en Bolivia. See *HLAS 39:1450*.

3584. ———. "Low classness" or wavering populism?: a peasant movement in Bolivia, 1952-1953 (*in* Nash, June and Juan Corradi eds. Ideology and social change in Latin America [see *HLAS 38:2394*] v. 2, p. 33-64, bibl.)

Elaboration of Dandler's earlier pioneering work, this valuable article analyzes experience of Cochabamba as case study of peasant participation in revolution and points up inadequacy of existing theory of peasant movements for explaining Bolivian phenomenon.

3585. Debray, Régis. Che's guerrilla war. Translated by Rosemary Sheed. Harmondsworth, U.K., 1975. 156 p., maps (Pelican books)

Analysis of failure of Che Guevara's Bolivian *foco* strategy by participant and theoretician of this concept of revolution. Debray argues that choice of Bolivia for launching continental revolution was essentially correct, but failure to coordinate with urban groups and choice of terrain were fatal to Che's enterprise. This work is indispensable to students of contemporary Latin American politics. French original: *La Guérilla du Che* (Paris, Editions du Seuil, 1974). For political scientist's comment, see *HLAS 39:7394*.

3586. Fellman Velarde, José. Historia de la cultura boliviana: fundamentos socio-políticos. La Paz, Editorial Los Amigos del Libro, 1976. 501 p., bibl.

Competent, serious survey of thought, science, letters, arts, education and popular culture from beginnings of civilization to 1971, set within synthesis of Bolivian history. Essentially a compendium of names and works with little critical analysis but still valuable as introduction to Bolivian cultural history.

3587. Finot, Enrique and **Mariano Baptista Gumucio.** Nueva historia de Bolivia: ensayo de interpretación sociológica. pt. 1, Nueva historia de Bolivia: ensayo de interpretación sociológica de Tiwanaku a 1930; pt. 2, Historia contemporánea de Bolivia, 1930-1976. 5. ed. La Paz, Librería y Editorial Gisbert, 1976. 763 p.

Pt. 1 consists of fifth ed. of Finot's dated but sound and still standard history of Bolivia to Chaco War. Pt. 2 is Baptista Gumucio's new contemporary history of Bolivia since 1930. Primarily political history, written with obvious sympathy for men and accomplishments of 1952 Revolution, Baptista's study also follows social and economic developments and covers cultural life in cursory fashion. Important and ambitious publication which offers solid, readable history of Bolivia in one volume.

3588. Francovich, Guillermo. Alberto Ostria Gutiérrez. Ilustración de Lalo Flores. La Paz, Ediciones ISLA, 1974. 110 p., illus., plates (Col. Destinos, 17)

Less than full-scale biography, this short book presents author's personal memories and invariably favorable impressions of well-known writer, diplomat and critic of MNR and its revolution.

3589. Friedl Zapata, José *comp.* Del coloniaje al siglo XX: alemanes interpretan a Bolivia. La Paz, Editorial Los Amigos del Libro [and] Horst Erdmann Verlag, Tübingen, FRG, 1976. 197 p., bibl.

Diverse collection of previously published essays and excerpts from books on Bolivia by authors of German nationality or descent. Topics include: Bolivian anthropology, archaeology, geography and literature. Authors range chronologically from Tadeo Haenke in late colonial period to several contemporary writers.

3590. Gómez, Eugenio. Bautista Saavedra. El ayllu: estudios sociológicos [de] Bautista Saavedra. La Paz, Comité Nacional del Sesquicentenario de la República, 1975. 558 p. (Biblioteca del sesquicentenario, 12)

Laudatory but thoughtful and documented biography of founder of Republican Party, President of Bolivia (1921-25), and scholar. Based on variety of primary and secondary sources, this should supersede previous biographies. Contains Saavedra's famous study of prehispanic *ayllu*.

3591. Gudmundson K., Lowell. El populismo y la integración de las clases obreras en Bolivia: 1952-1957 (UNCR/R, 1:2, 2. semestre 1976, p. 17-81, bibl., tables)

Important and informative article which examines organized labor in postrevolutionary Bolivia within analytical framework of populism. Argues through decisional tests and structural analysis that real power of labor in early revolutionary period was far less than generally assumed, and that it suffered irreparable decline after 1957 stabilization program.

3592. Montenegro, Armando. Cuadros de Cochabamba: imágenes de ayer y de hoy. Cochabamba, Bol., Editorial Canelas, 1975. 233 p., illus.

Anthology of anecdotes and legends from Cochabamba, primarily set in early 20th century. Potentially useful to folklorist and social historian.

3593. Peru. Ministerio de Relaciones Exteriores. Confederación Perú-Bolivia. v. 1, Estado nor-peruano, estado sur-peruano: 1835-1839; v. 2, Perú y Bolivia: 1840-1843. Lima, 1972-1976. 2 v. (601, 281 p.) (Archivo diplomático peruano, 9/10)

Collection of previously unpublished diplomatic correspondence and documentation from archives of Peruvian Ministry of Foreign Relations. These volumes are part of series on relations between both republics since independence. V. 1 contains correspondence pertaining to establishment of Peru-Bolivia Confederation; v. 2 covers turbulent period following its liquidation. For political scientist's comment, see *HLAS 39:8874*.

Pike, Fredrick B. The United States and the Andean Republics: Peru, Bolivia, Ecuador. See item 3554.

3594. Ponce Sanginés, Carlos *ed.* and *comp.* La República Federal de los Inkas: los Protocolos de 1880, material para su estudio. La Paz, Casa Municipal de la Cultura Franz Tamayo, 1975. 117 p., tables (Biblioteca paceña. Nueva serie)

Facsimile reproduction of three important documents, originally published c. 1880, related to projected federal union of Bolivia and Peru after their defeat in War of Pacific. Potentially useful for diplomatic and political historian of Bolivia or Peru.

3595. Querejazu Calvo, Roberto. Llallagua: historia de una montaña. La Paz, Editorial Los Amigos del Libro, 1977. 379 p. bibl., plates.

Solid, comprehensive economic, social and political history of Bolivian tin from War of Pacific to 1952, based on previously unused Patiño Co. archives and other primary sources. Traces rise of tin-mining and tin barons, working conditions and growth of unions, and attempts to extend state control over tin industry, culminating in 1952 nationalization. Despite unfortunate lack of documentation, this is an important and useful work.

3596. ———. Masamaclay: historia política diplomática y militar de la Guerra del Chaco. 2. ed. La Paz, Editorial Los Amigos del Libro, 1975. 540 p., bibl., maps.

Authoritative, comprehensive work on Chaco War. Sections on diplomacy are enlarged after further archival research (for first ed., 1965, see *HLAS 30:2316a*).

3597. Quiroga Ochoa, Ovidio. En la paz y en la guerra al servicio de la patria: 1916-1971. La Paz, Librería y Editorial Gisbert, 1974. 358 p.

Memoirs of former Commander-in-Chief of Bolivian armed forces, from beginnings of his career to 1952 Revolution with brief comment on his subsequent activities. Written with consistently anti-MNR bias, this work provides valuable insights into political machinations of armed forces, particularly after Chaco War.

3598. René-Moreno, Gabriel. Casimiro Olañeta: esbozo de biografía, papeles inéditos. Recopilación y ensayo de Humberto Vázquez Machicado. La Paz, Academia Bolivia de la Historia [and] Banco Central de Bolivia, 1975. 150 p. (Serie historia, 1)

Biographical notes on important and controversial figure of Bolivian independence and early Republic, compiled by late Humberto Vázquez-Machicado from papers of 19th-century historian and man of letters Gabriel René-Moreno. Confirms common view of Olañeta as opportunist and political chameleon. Includes Vázquez-Machicado's brief essay on René-Moreno's unpublished papers.

3599. ———. Matanzas de Yáñez. La Paz, Librería Editorial Juventud, 1976. 346 p., bibl.

New ed. of detailed investigative account of slaughter of 70 political prisoners in La Paz in 1861, by outstanding 19th-century historian and bibliographer.

Roca, Omar. El sesquicentenario de la independencia de Bolivia. See *HLAS 39:7398*.

3600. Saint John, Ronald Bruce. Hacia el mar: Bolivia's quest for a Pacific port (IAMEA, 31:3, Winter 1977, p. 41-73)

Useful survey of Bolivia's attempts to gain suitable sovereign port on Pacific from independence, through War of Pacific, to present. Concludes that prospects for satisfactory solution may have diminished with passage of time.

3601. Salamanca, Daniel. Mensajes y memorias póstumas. Cochabamba, Bol., Editorial Canelas, 1976. 194 p.

Collection of memoirs and official messages relating President Salamanca's version of his conduct of the Chaco War, published by anonymous descendants to exonerate him. Much of same material appeared in four volume collection edited by Eduardo Arze Quiroga (see *HLAS 38:3526*).

3602. Salinas Mariaca, Ramón. Viva Belzú: compendio de la vida y obra de éste gran caudillo. La Paz, Ediciones Abaroa, n.d. 195 p.

Popular, hagiographic biography of controversial 19th-century caudillo.

3603. Sanders, G. Earl. The quiet experiment in American diplomacy: an interpretive essay on U.S. aid to the Bolivian Revolution (AAFH/TAM, 33:1, July 1976, p. 25-49)

Examines reasons for reversal of US attitude toward the MNR after 1952 which resulted in large-scale aid to revolutionary government. Concludes that despite its success in helping to consolidate moderates' power in Bolivia, in broader terms "quiet experiment" failed to educate US diplomacy to deal effectively with other nationalist revolutionary movements. See also item 3573.

3604. Sanjinés Goitia, Julio. El militar ingeniero. Prólogo de Héctor Ormachea Peñaranda. La Paz, Editorial Los Amigos del Libro, 1975. 424 p., bibl., fold. tables, illus., maps, tables.

Over half of book is history of military engineering in America and the world. Latter third provides detailed information on origins, development and functions of engineering branch of Bolivian armed forces. Of interest primarily to specialist in military history.

Santamaría, Daniel J. Potosí entre la plata y el estaño. See item 3242.

3605. Sashin, G.Z. Boliviia: ocherk

noveishei istorri (Bolivia: an outline of recent history). Moscow, Izdatel'stvo Mysl", 1976. 278 p.

Soviet history of Bolivia, with special attention given to years since 1952. Although footnotes are somewhat sparse, there is a substantial bibliography. [R. V. Allen]

Siles Salinas, Jorge. Historia de Bolivia en los textos escolares. See *HLAS 39:4402*.

3606. Vidaurre Retamoso, Enrique. El Presidente Daza. La Paz, Comité Nacional del Sesquicentenario de la República, 1975. 343 p. (Biblioteca del sesquicentenario de la República, 3)

Polemical defense of Gen. Hilarión Daza (President, 1876-79) against common charges of mismanagement and treason during War of Pacific. Author exonerates Daza in text heavily laden with lengthy eulogistic quotations and documents lacking citations.

Zeerten, Federico. Colonización en Bolivia. See *HLAS 39:9246*.

CHILE

3607. Alamos V., María Ignacia and others. Perspectiva de Alberto Edwards V. Introducción de Eduardo Palma Carvajal. Santiago, Ediciones Aconcagua, 1976? 117 p., bibl. (Col. Lautaro)

Consists of three essays: man and his time; influence of Spengler; and Edwards' interpretation of Chilean history. Good introduction to historian and his perennially popular *La fronda aristocrática*.

3608. Aldunate Phillips, Arturo. Chile mira hacia las estrellas: pequeña historia astronómica. Santiago, Editora Nacional Gabriela Mistral, 1975. 265 p., facsims., illus., maps, tables.

After lengthy, impressionistic introduction to Chilean history, Aldunate offers competent survey of astronomical science in Chile from US Naval (Gillis) Expedition of 1849-52 to present, emphasizing foreign and international observatories established during and since 1950s.

3609. Altamirano, Carlos. Dialéctica de una derrota. México, Siglo XXI Editores, 1977. 300 p. (Historia inmediata)

Critical examination of UP government's failure by Secretary of Socialist Party during this period. Recognizes government's errors—particularly, failure to develop military policy and to hold plebiscite in 1971—but argues that crucial factors were strength and determination of the domestic and foreign opposition. Valuable insider's view.

3610. Barrera V., Humberto. Los antiguos caminos entre Santiago de Chile y Mendoza (JEHM/R, 1:8, 1975, p. 189-210, plates, map)

Informative but disjointed study of five trans-Andean roads linking Mendoza with Santiago prov. from 18th century forward. Presents primarily physical descriptions of routes based on historical documents and author's and other contemporaries' explorations. Of special interest to *andinistas* and geographers.

3611. Barros Jarpa, Ernesto. Reminiscencias anecdóticas: épocas de Arturo Alessandri Palma y Gustavo Ross Santa María. Santiago, Impresora Camilo Henríquez, 1974. 59 p.

Brief memoirs of Barros Jarpa's role in selected episodes of Chilean public life in 1920s and 1930s, with revealing commentary on Arturo Alessandri, Gustavo Ross, Eliodoro Yáñez, and other political figures of the day.

3612. Bauer, Arnold and **Ann Hagerman Johnson.** Land and labour in rural Chile: 1850-1925 (*in* Duncan, Kenneth; Ian Rutledge; and Colin Harding eds. Land and labour in Latin America [see item 2156] p. 83-102, map, tables)

Lucid analysis of changes in land tenure and labor usage under impact of expanding markets, based on close analysis of tax rolls and other data. Authors argue persuasively against common notion that Chile was dominated by few huge feudal estates, and assert that persistence of traditional forms of labor organization rather than presumed maldistribution of land should be blamed for continuing backwardness of Chilean agriculture.

3613. Blanc Renard, Neville ed. Homenaje al Profesor Guillermo Feliú Cruz. Santiago, Editorial Andrés Bello, 1973? 1200 p., illus., plates (Biblioteca del Congreso Nacional)

Fine collection of essays honoring late Guillermo Feliú Cruz contains pieces on varied topics by 43 Chilean and foreign scholars. Essays are of generally high quality and deal primarily with themes from Chilean history.

3614. Blancpain, Jean-Pierre. Economie et société immobiles: les campagnes chiliennes au XIX$_e$ siècle (CDAL, 15, 1. semestre 1977, p. 47-86)

Drawing on his previous excellent work, Blancpain examines 19th-century immigration to Chile with special attention to its potential impact on institutions and attitudes of traditional agrarian society. Argues that vision of transforming Chile through introduction of Europeans failed. owing in large part to limited objectives of early immigration policy (to 1880s) and later to growth of xenophobia in reaction to limited amount of immigration that did take place.

3615. Borón, Atilio Alberto. Notas sobre las raíces histórico-estructurales de la movilización política en Chile (CM/FI, 16:1, julio/sept. 1975, p. 64-121, tables)

Thoughtful interpretive essay that examines historical roots of popular mobilization and argues that hegemonic crisis of dominant classes prevented their stopping Allende's election. Concludes that political conjuncture of 1970 was not fortuitous but logical outgrowth of Chile's prior pattern of development.

3616. Bowers, Claude G. Chile through embassy windows: 1939-1953. Westport, Conn., Greenwood Press, 1977. 375 p.

Reprint of memoirs of US ambassador to Chile, 1939-53 (for 1958 ed., see *HLAS 21:3412*). Useful for observations of political and social scene.

3617. Braun Menéndez, Armando. Pequeña historia Antártica. Santiago, Editorial Francisco de Aguirre, 1974. 180 p., bibl., plates.

Fifth and final book in the popular "Pequeña Historia" series by prolific historian of America's extreme south. Useful survey of Antartica from discovery to 1960s, with special attention to roles of Chile and Argentina.

3618. Bulnes, Gonzalo. Resumen de la Guerra del Pacífico. Redacción de Oscar Pinochet de La Barra. Santiago, Editorial del Pacífico, 1976. 269 p., fold. maps, maps, plates.

Well-illustrated, readable synopsis of Bulnes' classic and ever popular history of war with Peru and Bolivia, originally published 1912-19 in three volumes.

3619. Bunster, Enrique. Distinguidas historias. Santiago, Editora Nacional Gabriela Mistral, 1976. 230 p.

Collection of colorful sketches and vignettes without discernible unifying theme, ranging from colonial "cal y canto" bridge to biographical sketch of Eduardo Cruz Coke. Amusing and potentially useful to historian.

3620. Carrière, Jean. Conflict and cooperation among Chilean sectoral elites (CEDLA/B, 19, dic. 1975, p. 16-27, tables)

This article proposes and executes empirical test of degree of consensus and conflict among Chilean sectoral elites between 1932-64. Several hundred "conflict situations" involving organized landowners are identified and categorized, but implications for Chilean elite studies are not fully explored. For sociologist's comment, see *HLAS 39:9248*.

3621. Cassassas Cantó, José María *comp.* Inventario de los Archivos del Arzobispado de Antofagasta, de la Prelatura de Calama y de sus respectivas parroquias (UN/A, 8, 1970, p. 141-303, bibl.)

Inventory and catalogue of all existing archives of secular church in Antofagasta prov. Includes material from 17th century to present, with preponderance dating from Chilean annexation in 1879. This guide should be of great value to social, demographic and religious historians of Norte Grande.

3622. Cavarozzi, Marcelo. La etapa oligárquica de dominación burguesa en Chile. B.A., Centro de Estudios de Estado y Sociedad (CEDES), 1977. 46 l., bibl. (Documento CEDES/CLASCO, 7)

Sound, suggestive study of Chilean elites employing dependency theory and close political analysis. Examines nature of 19th-century oligarchy and loss of its power monopoly between 1918-38.

3623. Cea Egaña, José Luis. La representación funcional en la historia constitucional de Chile. Santiago, Univ. Católica de Chile, Instituto de Ciencias Políticas, 1976. 74 l., tables (Cuadernos, 9)

Competent overview of corporatist thought and tendencies in Chile from independence to present, as background to current debate on country's future political institutional structure. Not surprisingly, it argues that previous political institutions were based on foreign concepts and that Chilean reality should support a system of functional representation.

3624. Collier, Simon. The historiography of the "Portalian" period, 1830-1891, in Chile (HAHR, 57:4, Nov. 1977, p. 660-690)

In this valuable synthesis, Collier traces historiography of Portalian period from "Whig" interpretations of contemporaries through revisionism of Alberto Edwards and Encina, later social and economic approaches of Jobet, Segall and Ramírez Necochea, to varied interests and methods of current scholarship. Author's own detailed knowledge of period provides setting for his analysis of historical schools and individual scholars' works. Concludes by pointing out areas in need of more research.

3625. Couyoumdjian, Ricardo. El mercado del salitre durante la primera guerra mundial y la post-guerra, 1914-1921: notas para su estudio (UCCIH/H, 12, 1974/1975, p. 13-55, illus., tables)

Close analysis of impact of war on nitrate prices and sales and on organization of nitrate production and marketing. Based on wide range of primary sources, this article examines interplay of foreign governments, private companies, and Chilean state, demonstrating extreme vulnerability of nitrate economy.

Cunhill Grau, Pedro. La temprana sementera urbana chilena y los comienzos del deterioro ambiental. See item 3248.

3626. Donoso, Ricardo. Las ideas políticas en Chile. 3. ed. B.A., EUDEBA, 1975. 439 p., bibl. (Iberoamérica en la historia)

Donoso's seminal and still indispensable work on role of ideas in Chile's 19th-century political evolution (for first ed., 1946, see *HLAS 12:2117*).

3627. Donoso Letelier, Crescente. Notas sobre el origen, acatamiento y desgaste del régimen presidencial: 1925-1973 (UCCIH/H, 13, 1976, p. 271-352)

Intelligent analysis of origins and evolution of system of presidential supremacy enacted in 1925, emphasizing central roles of military and Carlos Ibáñez, in establishing new constitution. Argues that important elements of parliamentary system—notably, attitudes of political parties—survived informally under new regime, contributing to its eventual demise.

3628. Edwards, Agustín. Apuntes biográficos de Don Federico Santa María y breve noticia de la fundación que lleva su nombre. Ilustraciones de A. Gómez Palacios. Valparaíso, Chile, Editorial de la Univ. Técnica Federico Santa María, 1975. 161 p., fold. illus., illus.

Reprint of Edwards' 1931 biography of Federico Santa María (1845-1925), expatriate Chilean business magnate who left substantial fortune to further technical education at all levels in Chile.

3629. Escala Escobar, Manuel. Geografía policial y otros estudios. Santiago, Talleres de *Revista Aquí Está*, 1976. 152 p.

Diverse collection of documents with extensive commentary, related directly or indirectly to history of uniformed police in Chile, ranging chronologically from 18th century to 1970s.

3630. Estellé Méndez, Patricio. Presiones extranjeras en la anexión y primeros años de Chiloé independiente (UC/AT, 432, 1975, p. 71-98, tables)

Details role of foreign powers in incorporation of Chiloé into Chilean Republic (1826) and subsequent Franco-British rivalry over island's status, through 1830. Reproduces two contemporary letters on subject.

3631. Feliú Cruz, Guillermo comp. Bío-bibliografía de Eugenio Pereira Salas (*in* Siete estudios: homenaje de la Facultad de Ciencias Humanas a Eugenio Pereira Salas. Santiago, Univ. de Chile, 1975, p. 27-57)

Exhaustive unannotated bibliography of works of Eugenio Pereira Salas. Begun by late Feliú Cruz, project was completed by his students.

3632. Ffrench-Davis, Ricardo. La importancia del cobre en la economía chilena: antecedentes históricos. Santiago, Centro de Estudios de Planificación Nacional (CEPLAN) [and] Univ. Católica de Chile, 1973. 44 l., tables (Estudios de planificación, 34)

Reviews copper production, exports and prices to determine role of "gran minería del cobre" in Chilean gross national product, balance of payments and national budget between 1952 and nationalization in 1971.

3633. Francis, Michael J. The United States and Chile during the Second World War: the diplomacy of misunderstanding (JLAS, 9:1, May 1977, p. 91-113)

Detailed survey of US-Chilean relations from Río meeting of American foreign ministers (Jan. 1942) which called for breaking diplomatic relations with Axis powers, to Chilean government's break in Jan. 1943, with brief follow-up through 1945. Sound exposition, but use of Chilean sources is minimal and Chilean context inadequately developed.

3634. González Videla, Gabriel. Memorias. Santiago, Editora Nacional Gabriela Mistral, 1975. 2 v. (1564 p.) (Continuous pagination) plates.

Massive political autobiography covers: 1) González Videla's youth (101 p.); 2) pre-presidential political and diplomatic career (349 p.); 3) presidential administration of 1946-52 (774 p.); and 4) return to political life as opponent of UP government and subsequently apologist for military regime (306 p.). Memoirs emphasize consistent anti-communism that inspired his administration's outlawing of Communist Party in 1949 and his active opposition to Allende government. This will be an invaluable source to historians of period of Radical ascendancy (1938-52), particularly since both other Radical presidents, Aguirre Cerda and Ríos, died in office without leaving memoirs.

3635. Heise González, Julio. O'Higgins: forjador de una tradición democrática. Prólogo de Roberto Larraín Gundián. Santiago, Artesanía Gráfica R. Neupert, 1975. 187 p., bibl.

Worthwhile addition to literature on O'Higgins, this partisan but well documented study refutes common charge that O'Higgins ruled dictatorially. Rather, author argues that O'Higgins used extensive powers granted him with circumspection and respect for legality, establishing precedents for Chile's future political development.

3636. Horowitz, Irving Louis ed. The rise and fall of Project Camelot: studies in the relationship between social science and practical politics. 2. ed. rev. Cambridge, Mass., The MIT Press, 1974. 409 p., tables.

Revised ed. of important study of Project Camelot, controversial US Dept. of Defense-sponsored project that embittered US-Chilean relations when its existence was revealed in 1965 (first ed. 1967).

3637. Infante Barros, Marta. Testigos del treinta y ocho. Santiago, Editorial Andrés Bello, 1972. 194 p.

Sound analysis of personalities, issues and events of 1938 presidential campaign and early months of Popular Front government, based on selections from all segments of Santiago press. Illustrates role of formerly free press and suggests constancy of issues and invective in divisive campaigns such as those of 1920, 1938, 1964 and 1970.

3638. Izquierdo Fernández, Gonzalo. Octubre de 1905: un episodio en la historia social chilena (UCCIH/H, 13, 1976, p. 55-96, map, plates, tables)

Detailed examination of 1905 "Red Week" in Santiago, in which orderly protests against high meat prices gave way to serious rioting and repression. Concludes that this explosion was symptomatic of period's social conditions.

3639. Kay, Cristóbal. Chile: the making of a coup d'état (SS, 39:1, Spring 1975, p. 3-25)

Argues that growth of working class strength and militance during UP years eventually isolated that sector, contrary to Allende's strategy, allowing opposition to turn resulting middle-class fears into pro-golpista sentiment. Useful contribution to literature on Allende years.

3640. ———. The development of the Chilean *hacienda* system: 1850-1973 (*in* Duncan, Kenneth; Ian Rutledge; and Colin Harding eds. Land and labour in Latin America [see item 2156] p. 103-139, tables)

Provocative survey of evolution of Chilean hacienda system over past century and quarter, as it responded to changes in market, growth of urban population, and political radicalization. Employing "multi-enterprise approach" introduced by Rafael Baraona, Kay analyzes hacienda system as ongoing conflict between landlord and peasant economies, and asserts that peasant became increasingly proletarianized after 1880s until agrarian reform reversed process.

3641. Krebs Wilckens, Ricardo. Eugenio Pereira Salas: historiador (*in* Siete estudios: homenaje de la Facultad de Ciencias Humanas a Eugenio Pereira Salas. Santiago, Univ. de Chile, 1975, p. 15-25)

Useful analysis of works of one of Chile's most prolific and respected historians. Attributes Prof. Pereira Salas' eminence to meticulous research and documentation combined with literary skill and interpretive ability.

3642. Lambert, Charles James. Sweet Waters: a Chilean farm. Westport, Conn., Greenwood Press, 1975. 212 p., maps, plates.

Reprint of Anglo-Chilean's reminiscences of the good life on large estate in Central Chile in 1920s. This is valuable source for rural customs, agricultural practices, and social attitudes and relations, and can be used profitably by students of rural history (for 1952 first ed., see *HLAS 18:2101*).

3643. Larraín Errázuriz, Manuel. La voz profética: recopilación de discursos y escritos, textos íntegros. Presentación de Carlos Camus Larenas. Santiago, Ediciones Mundo, 1976? 88 p.

Collection of speeches and writings of Manuel Larraín Errázuriz (1900-66), long-time Bishop of Talca and spokesman for social progressivism in Chilean church. Includes messages of spiritual and social content.

3644. López Urrutia, Carlos. Episodios chilenos en California: 1849-1860. Valparaíso, Chile, Univ. Católica de Valparaíso, 1975. 202 p., bibl., illus., maps, plates, tables (Col. El rescate)

Valuable monograph on Chileans in California during Gold Rush period which author divides into three categories: a) "gringos achilenados" such as Atheront and Ellis; b) miners proper who introduced many new techniques into California; and c) most famous group of all: adventurers which included aristocrats such as Vicente Pérez Rosales (see *HLAS 38:2610*), newspaperman Ramón Gil Navarro (later Urquiza's secretary) as well as bandits such as Narrato Ponce. Includes good reproductions of period paintings and photos, and extensive bibliography with careful listing of primary sources. [Ed.]

3645. Loveman, Brian. Struggle in the countryside: politics and rural labor in Chile, 1919-1973. Bloomington, Indiana Univ. Press, 1976. 439 p., bibl., maps, tables.

Thorough, heavily documented examination of changing social and property relations in rural Chile, utilizing interviews and rich sources of Labor Dept. archives. Loveman skillfully sets rural question within context of national politics, reviewing both long-standing attempts of urban parties to penetrate countryside and impact of political transactions on outcome of struggle at various junctures. Develops picture of peasant militancy since 1919 that is not entirely borne out by evidence, but does put to rest myth of peasant passivity prior to 1960s. Important contribution on crucial topic. For political scientist's comment, see *HLAS 39:7463*.

3646. Manns, Patricio. La revolución de la escuadra. Presentación de Javier Martínez. Valparaíso, Chile, Ediciones Universitarias de Valparaíso, 1972. 160 p., bibl., illus. (Col. El rescate, 4)

Lively, illustrated revisionist history of 1931 naval rebellion whose importance, author argues, has been ignored due to government cover-ups and "conspiracy of silence" by unsympathetic historians. Manns depicts mutiny of petty officers and enlisted men as not merely protest over salary cuts and bad treatment, but as real proto-revolution à-la-*Potemkin*.

3647. Martinič Beros, Mateo. Las actividades económicas iniciales de José Menéndez: 1875-1885. Punta Arenas, Chile, Instituto de la Patagonia, 1975. 21 p., bibl. (Serie monografías, 8)

Deals with José Menéndez's early entrepreneurial activities in Punta Arenas which laid basis for his economic pre-eminence in Magallanes.

3648. ———. Recorriendo Magallanes antiguo con Theodor Ohlsen. Diseño gráfico de Rosa da Venezia. Santiago, Editorial Andrés Bello, 1975. 90 p., illus., plates.

Consists of 35 sketches of Magallanes between 1883-93 by German Theodor Ohlsen, reproduced from artist's 1894 book and accompanied by Martinič's descriptive commentary. Many plates depict Ona and other Indians.

3649. Michaels, Albert L. The Alliance for Progress and Chile's "revolution in liberty:" 1964-1970 (UM/JIAS, 18:1, Feb. 1976, p. 74-99)

This well-reasoned article analyzes strategies and programs of Alliance for Progress in Chile under Christian Democrats. Contends that basic endeavor for Alliance was to shore up US economic interests, and that contradictions between social and developmental goals and needs of US economy led to its failure in country that offered greatest hope for success. For political scientist's comment, see *HLAS 39:8853*.

3650. Molina Silva, Sergio. El proceso de cambio en Chile: la experiencia, 1965-1970. Prólogo de Raúl Prebisch. Santiago, Editorial Universitaria, 1972. 220 p., tables (Textos del Instituto Latinoamericano de Planificación Económica y Social)

Analysis of Christian Democratic administration by Frei's Minister of Finance. Not mere apologia, this personal account provides valuable insider's perspective on economic accomplishments and failures of Frei government. Includes section on planning.

3651. Musalem, José. Crónica de un fracaso: frustración de un pueblo. Presentación de Jaime Castillo V. Santiago, Editorial del Pacífico [and] Instituto de Estudios Políticos (IDEP), 1973. 399 p., tables.

Anthology of speeches, interviews and articles (1970-72) by former Christian Democratic Senator José Musalem, criticizing UP government and its policies. Useful addition to polemical literature on Allende years.

3652. Neghme, Amador. El profesor doctor Juan Noé, maestro de la parasitología iberoamericana (CSIC/A, 25, 1973, p. 253-267, bibl.)

Biographical sketch of Italian-born Chilean parasitologist and professor of medical zoology at Univ. of Chile, who directed sweeping public health measures in 1930s and 1940s, including eradication of malaria.

3653. Niemeyer, E.V., Jr. Three North Americans in Chile (UC/AT, 433, 1976, p. 61-68)

Biographic and bibliographic sketches of three North American students of Chile: Col. Charles W. Furlong, explorer of Tierra del Fuego; Isaiah Bowman, geographer of the Atacama Desert; and George McBride, geographer and author of classic *Chile: land and society*.

3654. Nunn, Frederick M. The military in

Chilean history: essays on civil-military relations, 1810-1973. Albuquerque, Univ. of New Mexico Press, 1976. 343 p., bibl.

Most ambitious study to date of the military in Chilean history. In series of chronologically defined essays, Nunn provides wealth of information on military activities, attitudes and involvement in political system. This will not be final word, but clearly is major contribution to understanding Chile's peculiar historical pattern of civil-military relations and military's new role since 1973.

3655. Orrego Vicuña, Claudio ed. Horacio Walker y su tiempo. Santiago, Ediciones Aconcagua, 1976. 223 p., bibl. (Col. Lautaro)

Consists of four essays by Sofía Correa, Nicolás Cruz, Virginia Krzeminski and Sol Serrano which analyze, in chronological order, thought and influence of leading proponent of social Christian principles, active in Conservative Party from 1920s to 1950s. Much more than political biography, this important contribution explores Conservative Party's failure to adapt to mass competitive politics and thus explains party's eclipse after 1950s.

———. Libertad e igualdad en la historia de Chile. See item 3294.

Palma Zuñiga, Luis. Reseña histórica: la Facultad de Ciencias Económicas, 1934-1972. See *HLAS 39:3403*.

3656. Paul, Irven. A Yankee reformer in Chile: the life and works of David Trumbull. Foreword by Charles W. Forman. South Pasadena, Calif., William Carey Library, 1973. 155 p., bibl., plates.

Biography of influential missionary in Chile (1845-89), this work sheds light on early Protestant effort and on Church-State question in Chile.

3657. Pereira Salas, Eugenio. Las tendencias actuales en la historiografía chilena (RIB, 25:2, abril/junio 1975, p. 122-133)

Rather than a survey of contemporary trends as suggested by title, this is overview of major currents of scholarship by 20th-century Chilean historians. Useful but selective listing of individual historians, with little analysis of their works.

3658. Ramírez Necochea, Hernán. Esquema de la evolución social y política de la República de Chile: 1810-1970 (UCP/IAP, 7, 1973, p. 101-142)

Marxist interpretation of Chilean social and political evolution that seeks to explain why Unidad Popular government was elected and seated. Identifies three periods in national history to 1970: conservative republic (1830-59); bourgeois republic (1859-1920); and bourgeois democratic republic (1920-70).

Remmer, Karen L. Economic dependency and political conflict: Chile and Argentina, 1900-1925. See *HLAS 39:7684*.

3659. ———. The timing, pace and sequence of political change in Chile: 1891-1925 (HAHR, 57:2, May 1977, p. 205-230, tables)

Sound study argues that beneath surface appearance of inertia and sterility, Parliamentary Period (1891-1925) was important to Chile's future political development. In particular, creation of well-defined party structure during this period of limited participation was key to competitive but relatively stable political system that characterized Chile until 1973.

Retamal Avila, Julio. Bibliografía de historia eclesiástica chilena: revistas chilenas, 1843-1973. See item 3084.

3660. Riz, Liliana de. La lucha de clases en la sociedad chilena: hipótesis para su interpretación (UNAM/RMS, 38:1, enero/marzo 1976, p. 127-147)

Historical analysis of forms of political domination in Chile as background to understanding failure of Unidad Popular government. Suggests that peculiarities of Chile's development within context of dependent societies resulted from establishment of strong national state prior to foreign economic enclave. For political scientist's comment, see *HLAS 39:7493*.

Rodríguez Villegas, Hernán. Historia de un solar de la Ciudad de Santiago: 1554-1909. See item 3086.

3661. Rossignol, Jacques. Guerra populaire et société dans les mouvements révolutionnaires chiliens au XIXe siècle (CDAL, 15, 1. semestre 1977, p. 1-45)

Provocative article examines results of popular mobilization during Chilean independence wars and subsequent internal struggles to 1830. Contends that, particularly in frontier area, political struggles gave rise to popular warfare and social banditry organized along guerrilla or montonera lines, which government overcame with some difficulty. Considers revolutions of 1851 and 1859 as last manifestations of these archaic forms of popular violence.

3662. Sater, William F. Economic nationalism and tax reform in late nineteenth-century Chile (AAFH/TAM, 33:2, Oct. 1976, p. 311-335)

Sater refutes standard argument that free trade set back Chile's economic development in 19th century. Based on close examination of tariff laws and accompanying congressional debates, this important article demonstrates that free trade principles prevailed only briefly in 1860s, and that moderate protectionism in various forms was restored in 1870s and 1880s. For economist's comment, see *HLAS 39:3405*.

Steenland, Kyle. Notes on feudalism and capitalism in Chile and Latin America. See *HLAS 39:7502*.

3663. Stuardo Ortiz, Carlos. Vida de Claudio Gay, 1800-1873, seguida de los escritos del naturalista e historiador, de otros concernientes a su labor y de diversos documentos relativos a su persona: obra póstuma; escritos y documentos. Estudio sobre Gay a través de su correspondencia de Guillermo Feliú Cruz. t. 1/2. Santiago, Fondo Histórico y Bibliográfico José Toribio Medina [and] Editorial Nascimento, 1973. 2 v. (677, 404 p.) tables.

Important contribution to literature on Claudio Gay, French naturalist and historian of Chile, published to commemorate centennial of his death (see also *HLAS 38:3588* and *3630*). Vol. 1 contains two essays by the late Feliú Cruz: one on Gay the historian, the other on late historian Stuardo Ortiz, whose lengthy biography of Gay follows. Vol. 2 consists of another essay by Feliú Cruz on Gay as seen through his correspondence and of extensive appendices of materials by and about Gay.

3664. Sutulov, Alexander. Minería chilena: 1545-1975. Santiago, Centro de Investigación Minera y Metalúrgica (CIMM), 1976. 260 p., bibl., fold. tables, illus., tables.

Profusely illustrated attempt by mining engineer at comprehensive history of Chilean mining from its inception to 1975. Useful summary of secondary literature, but lack of documentation and failure to elucidate methodology vitiate presentation of extensive quantitative data.

3665. Tapia-Videla, Jorge. The Chilean Presidency in a developmental perspective (UM/JIAS, 19:4, Nov. 1977, p. 451-481)

Examines evolution of constitutional and functional relationship between executive and legislative branches of government from 1833 constitution to 1973. Demonstrates that several constraints on presidential authority frustrated objectives of 1925 constitution, resulting in "social deadlock and political immobilism," and analyzes collapse of Chilean democracy in light of institutional conflict between Presidency and Congress.

3666. Vargas Cariola, Juan Eduardo. La Sociedad de Fomento Fabril: 1883-1928 (UCCIH/H, 13, 1976, p. 5-52, tables)

Useful analysis of membership, purposes and activities of voluntary association of industrialists from its founding to 1928. Concludes that by 1928 organization had acquired essential characteristics that it retains today.

3667. Varona, Alberto J. Francisco Bilbao, revolucionario de América: vida y pensamiento; estudio de sus ensayos y trabajos periodísticos. Panamá, Ediciones Excelsior, 1973. 457 p., bibl.

This important addition to literature on 19th-century Chilean pensador and revolutionary is thoroughly researched and well-documented. Includes particularly valuable sections on little-known Bilbao essays published in Peru, Ecuador and France, and on Bilbao's three years as journalist in Argentina. Contains extensive bibliography.

3668. Véliz, Claudio. Egaña, Lambert, and the Chilean mining associations of 1825 (HAHR, 55:4, Nov. 1975, p. 637-663, tables)

Detailed account of activities of four London based mining companies and of French metallurgist Charles Lambert in Chile. Argues that although brief and financially disastrous, companies' experience was important to Chile for two reasons: 1) companies introduced new mining technology; and 2) their failure strengthened position of conservatives and protectionists such as Mariano Egaña (envoy to Great Britain at the time) over liberal free trade interests.

3669. Verniory, Gustave. Diez años en Araucanía: 1889-1899. Nota preliminar por Guy Santibáñez. Traducción de Eduardo Humeres. Santiago, Ediciones de la Univ. de Chile, 1975. 499 p., illus.

Diary of Belgian engineer involved in railroad construction in south is especially valuable for its incisive and entertaining commentary about Mapuches, frontier's social conditions, wages and working conditions in railroad and general construction, and for observations on 1891 civil war.

3670. Vicuña Mackenna, Benjamín. Vida del Capitán General Don Bernardo

O'Higgins. Introducción por Claudio Orrego Vicuña. Santiago, Editorial del Pacífico, Instituto de Estudios Políticos, 1976. 675 p.

Fourth ed. of classic originally published 1861 contains only minor changes from previous 1936 ed.

3671. Villalobos R., Sergio. La aventura chilena de Darwin. Santiago, Editorial Andrés Bello, 1974. 103 p., illus., map, plates.

Lavishly illustrated, popular biography of Charles Darwin emphasizes his impressions of Chile during his extended visit there between 1833-35. Good introduction to Darwin in Chile.

———; **Fernando Silva V.; Osvaldo Silva G.; and Patricio Estellé M.** Historia de Chile. See item 3089.

Vylder, Stefan de. From colonialism to dependence: an introduction to Chile's economic history. See *HLAS 39:3412*.

3672. Wegmann H., Osvaldo. Magallanes histórico. Punta Arenas, Chile, Impresos Coiron, 1974? 111 p., illus. (Col. Magallanes, 1)

Popular, profusely illustrated narrative history of Magallanes, useful to general reader.

Williams, Lee H., Jr. *comp.* The Allende years: a union list of Chilean imprints, 1970-1973, in selected North American libraries, with a supplemental holdings list of books elsewhere for the same period by Chileans or about Chile or Chileans. See *HLAS 39:12*.

3673. Woll, Allen. The Catholic historian in nineteenth century Chile (AAFH/TAM, 33:3, Jan. 1977, p. 470-489)

Examines evolution of Catholic interpretations of Chilean history through 19th century, against the backdrop of rising anti-clericalism in politics and historiography. Considers works of Crescente Errázuriz, Archbishop Valdivieso and other Catholics essentially as ideological weapons in struggle against secularization of Chilean society.

ARGENTINA, PARAGUAY AND URUGUAY

HOBART A. SPALDING, JR.

Associate Professor of History
Brooklyn College of CUNY

ONLY A SMALL NUMBER OF SIGNIFICANT contributions appear in this biennium. In all, publication continues unabated, but overall quality fails to match quantity. In English, Ronald Newton's book on the German community in B.A. stands out among several excellent works on immigration themes (item 3821). In Spanish, José Campobassi's lengthy biography of Domingo F. Sarmiento is the best book in years on that important figure of the Platine past (item 3712). José Pedro Barrán and Benjamín Nahum's two volumes on rural Uruguay in the early 20th century reaffirm their place among the foremost contemporary Uruguayan historians (item 3927). Moreover, a number of worthy articles have appeared, many by a generation which is now beginning to publish. The solid and detailed work in English of Donna Guy, Ian Rutledge, Eugene Sofer, and Mark Szuchman is representative of this trend (items 3778-3779, 3852, 3865-3866 and 3872). In Spanish, Hugo Raúl Galmarini's and Javier Lindeboim's articles on the 1820s and 1930s respectively (items 3757 and 3798) deserve attention for applying interest-group analysis. Works by Andrés Carretero (items 3719-3720), Susana Rato de Sambuccetti (item 3844), Arthur P. Whitaker (item 3882), and Peter Winn (items 3955-3956) also merit notice.

ARGENTINA. Turning to Argentina, a number of old and some newer trends continue to prevail. Works designed for popular consumption still dominate much of the historical output. Within this genre, the "Memorial de la Patria" series edited by Félix Luna maintains a high standard, although most volumes highlight political events. Almost all 30 titles projected in this series have now been published. The short monographs of "Cuadernos de Crisis" continue to appear, many of them by historians of national repute. Some of the slim volumes represent a fine synthesis. Lastly, *Todo es Historia* (item 3875) a monthly magazine, delves into varied aspects and episodes of the past. Many of its articles form the basis for subsequent monographs.

There continues to be considerable interest in the 19th-century frontier, Patagonia, struggles against the Indians, and the southern lands in general. On these subjects, re-editions of writings by old campaigners predominate over more recent studies. On the frontier, Pedro Daniel Weinberg's essay (item 3695) makes a nice introduction to the topic. Local history, often arising from anniversary celebrations, is attracting writers and although most of it is of local interest, certain works deserve mention. The II Congreso de Historia de los Pueblos de la Provincia de Buenos Aires published its proceedings (item 3732). We may hope that future gatherings will build on the research already done and provide a solid core of data to support monographic efforts as well as synthesis. The research team headed by César A. García Belsunce (item 3760) completed the first of four volumes about B.A. from 1800-30. Their findings include a wealth of information about the population living in the city and surrounding areas. Marta B. Goldberg's article on blacks and mulattos in B.A. in 1810-40 (item 3767) begins to unravel the puzzle concerning the fate of the black population after independence.

On the decades immediately after 1810, three documentary collections should ease the task of investigators by making available materials on government, civil wars, and Church-State relations (items 3699, 3707, and 3768). Ernesto J. Fitte's nationalistic account of the French naval attack of 1929 also contains a lengthy documentary section (item 3752). Much continues to be published on Rosas and the Rosas period, although the volume has decreased since *HLAS 36* and *HLAS 38*. In all, little new has surfaced in the pro- and anti-Rosas controversy. Historians studying the period rather than the man himself produced the most solid work. Andrés M. Carretero advanced his studies on land tenure to 1852 and shows patterns of continuity between elites and large holdings (item 3719). Juan Carlos Nicolau looks at the 1835 and 1854 customs laws, arguing that the former stifled national industrial development (item 3822). Carlos A. Segreti adds to banking and monetary history (item 3864) and Jonathan C. Brown examines the commercial boom to 1862 finding that creoles and foreigners without external connections played a leading role (item 3706).

A number of monographs and articles examine the post-Rosas period through World War I. Eduardo A. Zalduendo's study on railroads marks a major step in comparative economic history (item 3886). Francisco L. Romay completed another volume on the Federal Police, this one covering 1880-1916 (item 3848). Susana Rato de Sambuccetti argues that President Avellaneda should be viewed as a stronger executive than previously thought (item 3844). Alfredo Terzaga's unfinished biography of Julio A. Roca ends in 1880, but it makes interesting reading (item 3874). More important, José Campobassi published a major biography on Domingo Faustino Sarmiento, evaluating his life and times sympathetically (item 3712). Studies on Alberdi prove less rewarding, most tending towards partisan interpretations (items 3813, 3824 and 3887). The publication of another volume from the Elizalde archives adds to available primary sources for the 1860s (item 3745). Germán O. Tjark's lengthy article on the ideological setting behind the formation of the Triple Alliance attests to the value of the Elizalde Papers (item 3919). Francisco J. Delich contributes a study on land-holdings in Córdoba highlighting the role of speculative buying as a deterrent to investment (item 3740).

The peronist experiences and recent events received considerable attention. The historiography of peronism is manifesting certain similarities to that of the Rosas period as noted in *HLAS 38*. Although the number of works on peronism declined, no doubt due to voluntary or enforced censorship, their polemical tones have not. In addition to documents (item 3833), supporters and activists churned out their particular versions of the phenomenon from a variety of points of view (items 3683, 3708, 3721, 3744, 3790, 3861-3862, 3880 and 3885). Detractors fired volleys from both right (items 3676 and 3814) and left (item 3846). Fortunately, some works will prove useful in unravelling the complicated strands entwining contemporary Argentine history. A chronology and documentary (item 3689), Donald C. Hodges' monograph (item 3782), and François Géze and Alain Labrousse's interesting survey (item 3762) are partisan works which nevertheless present coherent positions and arguments in explaining peronism's 35-year external and internal struggles to regain or remain in power. Current information in *Argentina Outreach* especially on human rights, supplements the above studies (item 3688).

Also, some valuable general works have appeared. Horacio Juan Cuccorese's evaluation of socio-economic literature through the 1950s provides a nice summary (item 3738). Enrique Zuleta Alvarez completed a thoughtful two-volume set on nationalist ideas and schools of thought (item 3888). Other historiographical offerings proved less detailed (item 3862). Three other studies also deserve mention: Laurio H. Destefani's exploration of naval history (item 3741); Ambrosio Romero Carranza, Alberto Rodríguez Varela, and Eduardo Ventura Flores Pirán's political history (item 3850); and the expansion of revisionist Fermín Chávez's interpretive essay (item 3725). Finally, leftist authors also offer their versions of the past (items 3817, 3834 and 3855).

Some of the most exciting work in the last two years is found in immigration studies. Ronald C. Newton's monograph on the German community of B.A. (1900-33) broke new ground by challenging old myths, showing in particular how class factors influenced the trajectory of the group (item 3821). The collective and individual work of Eugene P. Sofer and Mark Szuchman also attacked the "melting pot" thesis (items 3865, 3866 and 3872). Moreover, these works shed light on immigrants groups—Jews and French in particular—in B.A. and Córdoba. Glynn Williams dealt sympathetically but thoroughly with the Welsh settlements in Patagonia (item 3884).

Labor and working-class history, once a promising arena for new scholarship, received only limited attention. Nevertheless, some provocative and high quality research has emerged. Elizabeth Jelin revives the notion of spontaneity as a factor in current worker-struggles in Argentina and elsewhere in Latin America. She pinpoints the hierarchical nature of union bureaucracy as one cause for this (item 3793). In another article she examines the contemporary labor scene, showing the contradiction between economic demands and radical action in declining resource base situations (item 3792). Iaacov Oved's thorough article on the Law of Residence argued that the Law probably strengthened the anarchist cause rather than damaging it as intended (item 3826). Donna Guy (item 3779) and Ian Rutledge (item 3852) concentrate on the rural Northwest. Guy, supplementing her studies on the Tucumán sugar industry within the national context, forcefully puts the case for rural-labor studies and specifically shows the possibilities of such a topic (items 3778-3779). Rutledge's piece on the sugar economy demonstrates the feasibility of provincial labor histories and clearly underscores the need to support theory with empirical research. CEIL's research plan for a major study on the labor movement may indicate that the eclipse of labor studies is ending (item 3852).

Several publications featuring socialists or anarchists have appeared. Richard Walter's monograph on the political activities of the Socialist Party opens new ground (item 3881). Juan Antonio Solari contributes several items on socialists (items 3867-3870) and Jan Klima's short efforts are unusual in their use of materials from Czechoslovakian archives (items 3795-3796). Osvaldo Bayer's essays on Simón Radowitzky and anarchists of the 1920s as well as other historical themes serve to maintain his position as a leading investigator (item 3696).

In diplomatic history, Arthur P. Whitaker's substantial book provides a useful summary and interpretation of both Argentina and Uruguay as well as their relations with the US (item 3882). Roger Gravil extends his explorations into 20th-century diplomacy with a provocative argument that World War I tightened economic ties between Argentina and the metropolitan nations (item 3772). He also sheds more light on the specifics of Anglo-US rivalry for Argentine trade, a theme Mario Rapoport develops for the 1930s and early 1940s (item 3842). Rapoport also traces the influence of this rivalry on changing diplomatic relations with Argentina. Another work explores the interconnections between foreign oil companies and Argentine nationalization plans (item 3808).

Studies of two interest groups deepen our knowledge of the past. Hugo Raúl Galmarini delineates the "Costa Group" in the 1820s (item 3757) and Javier Lindeboim contributes a pioneering study of industrialists' organizations from 1930-46 (item 3798), a topic which merits further investigation as one key to understanding events of the 1940s and the transitional period of the 1930s. Three studies on women by Ana María Marini (item 3804), Marysa Navarro (item 3820), and Nancy Caro Hollander (item 3783) add to the meager bibliography on the subject. In particular, Navarro's measured interpretation of Evita Perón and Hollander's synthesis of women in the labor force deserve recognition.

A number of intellectuals and activists compiled their memoirs or collected works which tend to shed more light on the writer than on the historical process (items 3675, 3763, 3786 and 3810). In addition, publishing houses re-issued several classics or near-classics (items 3731, 3791, 3809 and 3854).

PARAGUAY. The Chaco War and the War of the Triple Alliance continue to account for the majority of works about the Paraguayan past. With the exception of François Chartrain's competent article on the conflict's origins (item 3896), writings on the Chaco War consist primarily of military histories written by veterans. Among these Carlos José Fernández's final volume of a lengthy set stands out (item 3899). On the 1864-70 events, Pierre Mondain surveys its causes and conduct (item 3906) and Germán O. Tjarks raises interesting questions for further research on the Triple Alliance's formation (item 3919). Two excellent items cover longer time spans. Josefina Plá's careful monograph on the British in Paraguay from 1850-70 (item 3909) and John Hoyt Williams' article on foreign *técnicos* from 1840-70 (item 3923) portray the substantial contributions by foreigners. Williams, the only US historian consistently publishing on Paraguay, continues his meticulous investigations into the 19th century with a suggestive analysis of the 1846 census indicating a lower population figure for Paraguay than previously accepted (item 3924). On other topics, Antonio R. Ramos studies Brazil's role in Paraguayan independence (item 3911). The *Revista Paraguay de Sociología* maintains its high quality in articles such as Chartrain's on social history from 1870-1936 (item 3897) and Irene S. de Arad's on the livestock sector after 1870 (item 3891).

URUGUAY. The appearance of two more volumes in Juan Pedro Barrán and Benjamín Nahum's excellent series on the formation of rural society, highlight an otherwise sparse two years (item 3927). These works cover 1905-14, a key period on the country's modern formation. Both show how foreign influences—capital, technology, and markets—shaped the rural sectors and connected industries. These volumes also describe how those sectors successfully resisted many of the reforms instituted during the Batllista period, while adapting to changes within the economy. Noteworthy too are Peter Winn's persuasive contributions supporting the theory of Great Britain's informal empire in Uruguay (items 3955-3956).

Several publications resulted from the Commission for the 150th Anniversary of 1825 including documents and primary source collections (items 3936 and 3946) as well as re-editions of earlier works (items 3949 and 3954) and collected works (item 3951). The *Revista Histórica* published more articles on the 19th century (item 3947) and books appeared on the British in Uruguay (item 3939) as well as a history of the Air Force (item 3944). Finally, Ediciones de la Banda Oriental issued several slim volumes intended for popular consumption but of a high standard (items 3926, 3928,

3931, 3941-3943, 3948 and 3953). Unfortunately, the fine monographic tradition established at the National Univ. and noted in *HLAS 38* did not continue, surely a result of the continuing national crisis which also affects academic circles.

ARGENTINA

3674. Abeijón, Asencio. Recuerdos de mi primer arreo: memorias de un carrero patagónico. B.A., Editorial Galerna, 1975. 182 p.

Companion piece to *HLAS 38:3641* contains more stories and memoirs about turn-of-century Patagonia.

3675. Agosti, Héctor Pablo. Prosa política. B.A., Editorial Cartago, 1975. 275 p.

Articles, speeches, and conferences dating 1937-70s by leading Communist Party intellectual on various national political, historical, and philosophical problems.

3676. Aizcorbe, Roberto. El mito peronista: un ensayo sobre la reversión cultural ocurrida en la Argentina en los últimos 30 años. B.A., Ediciones 1853, 1976. 609 p.

Passionate and highly unfavorable view of peronism concentrating on 1970s. Throughout equates peronism with totalitarianism. English translation (N.Y., Exposition Press, 1975) not available at press time.

3677. Alén Lascano, Luis C. La Argentina ilusionada: 1922-1930. B.A., Editorial Astrea, 1975. 391 p. (Ediciones La Bastilla)

Historical overview concentrating more on political and cultural aspects of these Radical years. Includes fairly lengthy chronology of events.

3678. ———. Desarrollo histórico socio-económico de la Provincia de Santiago del Estero. San Carlos de Bariloche, Arg., Fundación Bariloche, Depto. de Sociología, 1974. 129 l., tables.

Highly informative study of socioeconomic development of Santiago del Estero for purpose of isolating those factors causing unemployment and migration of human resources from province. Most valuable for data which stops in 1970. Lacks any real conclusions or adequate summation.

3679. ———. Ibarra: un caudillo norteño. B.A., Editorial Crisis, 1976. 80 p., bibl., facsims., illus. (Cuadernos de crisis, 25)

Short, popular biography by foremost provincial historian.

3680. ———. Rosas. B.A., Editorial Crisis, 1975. 79 p., bibl., facsims., plates (Cuadernos de crisis, 21)

Favorable review of man and his career.

3681. Ales, Oreste Carlos. D. Manuel de Sarratea: ensayo histórico. B.A., Editorial Lito, 1975. 98 p., facsims.

Brief biography of first Governor of Buenos Aires prov. Focuses on his role in Treaty of Pilar which author sees important antecedent to 1853 Constitution. Includes appendix of 16 documents from year 1820 reproduced photographically.

3682. Alonso Piñeiro, Armando. La historia Argentina que muchos argentinos no conocen. B.A., Ediciones Depalma, 1976. 492 p.

Divided into three parts: 1) 41 short anecdotes about Argentina from the colonial period to 1930s; 2) similar short pieces on Latin America; and 3) contemporary anecdotes of "An Argentine historian in the United States."

3683. Antonio, Jorge. Ahora o nunca: 1945-1975; recapitulación del pasado, crónicas del presente y aportes para el futuro argentino. B.A., The Author, 1975. 139 p., facsim.

Peronist politican's vision of his country since and during Perón's presidencies.

3684. Aráoz de la Madrid, Gregorio and others. Las guerras civiles, el rosismo. Rosario, Arg., Editorial Biblioteca, 1974. 424 p., illus. (Col. Conocimiento de la Argentina, B. Escritos testimoniales, 2)

Short prologue by Adolfo Prieto leads into selections from Memoirs of Aráoz, Pedro Ferré, José María Paz, Tomás de Iriarte, Juan Estanislao de Elías, and Miguel Otero, all principal figures of Rosas epoch. Selections are well-chosen and well-edited: useful compendium for Argentinist.

3685. Arce, Facundo A. and **Francisco Maximiliano Ibañez.** Las lechiguanas: el conflicto jurisdiccional y la soberanía de Entre Ríos. Paraná, Arg., Editorial de la Mesopotamia, 1974. 74 p.

Documents and legal history of conflict between Buenos Aires prov. and Entre Ríos prov. around ownership of islands in Paraná delta. Resolved 1968.

3686. Arcocha, Carlos Enrique. Hidrocarburos gaseosos: historia, régimen legal (UNL/U, 83, sept./dic. 1975, p. 37-101, bibl., tables)

Brief historical section covers legislation, contracts, companies, and concessions up through establishment of Gas del Estado.

3687. Argentina. Consejo Nacional de Investigaciones Científicas y Técnicas. Centro de Estudios e Investigaciones Laborales (CEIL). Breve reseña histórica del desarrollo del sindicalismo en Argentina (UNLP/CA, 45, sept./dic. 1974, p. 5-36)

Short historical sketch of labor movement from origins to 1973 which will serve as departure point for CEIL's longer study on Argentine labor movement. Article by itself, however, makes nice summary.

3688. *Argentina Outreach.* Argentine Information Service Center. Vol. 1, No. 1, April 1976 [through] Vol. 2, No. 10, Oct. 1977- . Berkeley, Calif.

Excellent source for information on human rights debate concerning Argentina and for current political news and views both from inside and outside Argentina. Presents variety of anti-military government positions.

3689. Argentine: chronologie de la Présidence de Perón; la prise du pouvoir par la Junte Militaire chronique du coup d'état, 24-31 mars 1976 (FDD/NED [Problèmes d'Amérique Latine, 40] 4292/4293, 20 mai 1976, p. 23-80)

Useful chronology of events from Jan. 1974 through March 1976 coup. Biographical sketches of Junta's members and texts of Junta's economic and political programs.

3690. Arnaudo, Lidia. Del Buenos Aires de ayer: de cómo se vivía en el barrio de Palermo a fines del siglo pasado y principios de 1900. B.A., Ediciones Acanto, 1976. 95 p.

Sketches of turn-of-century B.A., personal memoirs of mostly upper-class life.

3691. Avellá Cháfer, Francisco. La Santa Sede y el Río de la Plata: 1823-1825 (CEHA/NH, 8:16, dic. 1975, p. 211-217)

Brief description of Apostolic Delegates and their work in this period as well as mission of new Apostolic Vicar of 1823.

3692. Baigorria, Manuel. Memorias. Prólogo de Félix Luna. Cronología comentada de J.A. de Diego. B.A., Solar/Hachette, 1975. 169 p. (Col. Dimensión argentina)

Memoirs of military man, who after defeat of unitarios lived with Ranquel Indians before rejoining army in 1852.

3693. Baldrich, J. Amadeo. Historia de la Guerra del Brasil: contribución al estudio razonado de la historia militar argentina. 2. ed. B.A., EUDEBA, 1974. 472 p., bibl., fold. map (Cuestiones de geopolítica)

Re-edition of 1905 work focusing on military aspects of war, but not neglecting social and economic ones. Includes documentary appendix (130 p.). Generally falls into mitrista tradition.

Barrera, Mario. Information and ideology: a case study of Arturo Frondizi. See *HLAS 39:7641*.

3694. Barrientos, José P. Historia del periodismo de Tandil. Introducción, notas e investigaciones ampliatorias, actualización: 1956-1974 y apéndice de Daniel E. Pérez. B.A., Grafitán, 1975. 261 p., bibl., facsims., illus., map, plates.

Brief historical notes on press and section on Barrientos. Covers 1854 to 1974 giving brief notes on most newspapers with facsimiles of each.

3695. Barros, Alvaro. Indios, fronteras y seguridad interior. Estudio preliminar de Pedro Daniel Weinberg. B.A., Solar/Hachette, 1975. 366 p. (Col. Dimensión argentina)

Re-edition of three works originally published in 1870s: *La guerra contra los indios, Actualidad financiera de la República Argentina,* and *La memoria especial de Ministro de la Guerra* by man who fought on frontier and who later became Governor of B.A. and national and local legislator. Mostly concerns problem of defense and development of frontier but also examines and criticizes country's economic policies. Initial essay by Daniel Pedro Weinberg forms solid introduction to work and to problem of frontier in Argentine history.

3696. Bayer, Osvaldo. Los anarquistas expropiadores, Simón Radowitzky y otros ensayos. B.A., Editorial Galerna, 1975. 271 p.

Six essays in usual flowing style of Argentina's leading historian of anarchists. First three treat various themes about Argentine and international anarchism, last three discuss 1940 scandal that shook government, wreck of vessel *Rosales* in 1892, and *Graf Spee* incident. All previously published in journal *Todo es Historia*.

3697. Bazán, Raúl; Gaspar H. Guzmán; Gerardo Pérez Fuentes; and **Ramón R. Olmos.** Felipe Varela: su historia. B.A., Plus Ultra, 1975. 175 p., facsims., plates (Col. Los argentinos, 5)

Essentially revisionist work on life and times of Catamarca caudillo. Concluding chapter presents neat summary of Varela's ideology and importance.

3698. Belza, Juan E. En la Isla del Fuego. v. 2, Colonización. B.A., Instituto de Investigaciones Históricas Tierra del Fuego, 1975. 366 p., maps, plates, tables.

Vol. 2 of series (see *HLAS 38:3655*) covering 1893-1905. Contains chapters on leading settlers, territorial governors, land settlement, and missionary efforts. Many photographs and maps.

3699. Benencia, Julio Arturo *ed.* Partes de batalla de las guerras civiles: 1822-1840. Prólogo de Enrique M. Barba. v. 2. B.A., Academia Nacional de la Historia, 1976. 681 p. (Biblioteca de publicaciones documentales, 11)

Includes 251 documents from archival and published sources covering period Jan. 1822-Nov. 1840. Preserves original orthography. Excellent source for military, social and political history.

3700. Bennassar, Bartolomé. La inmigración francesa a la Argentina a finales del siglo XIX: el caso de la Colonia Pigüe y el problema de las fuentes (JGSWGL, 13, 1976, p. 174-180)

Short historical notes on 1884 French settlers in Pigüe and why they came to Argentina.

3701. Biedma, José Juan. Crónicas militares: antecedentes históricos sobre la campaña contra los indios. B.A., EUDEBA, 1975. 303 p., tables (Lucha de fronteras con el indio)

Re-edition of two volumes published 1924-31. Covers struggles against the Indians from legal and military aspects in colonial period through 1820.

3702. Birabent, Mauricio. Chivilcoy: después de un siglo. B.A., Instituto Social Agrario, 1973. 89 p.

Collection of articles and conferences on local history.

3703. Bischoff, Efraín U. El cura Brochero: un obrero de Dios. 2. ed. rev. B.A., Editorial Plus Ultra, 1977. 430 p. (Col. Los argentinos, 6)

Expanded and corrected ed. of 1953 biography of priest who worked in western Córdoba from 1860s through early 20th century. Uses local sources, Church records, and folklore.

3704. ———. Por qué Córdoba fué invadida en 1829. B.A., Plus Ultra, 1975. 238 p. (Col. Esquemas históricos, 27)

Veteran historian of Córdoba looks at clash between Generals Paz and Bustos and its impact and future consequences for that province.

Bowen, Nicholas. The end of British economic hegemony in Argentina: Messersmith and the Eady-Miranda Agreement. See *HLAS 39:8800*.

3705. Brañas, Balbino. Ayer: mi tierra en el recuerdo. Posadas. Arg., Talleres de Skanata Offset, 1975. 120 p., plates.

Memoirs about Posadas in first decades of 20th century.

3706. Brown, Jonathan C. Dynamics and autonomy of a traditional marketing system: Buenos Aires, 1810-1860 (HAHR, 56:4, Nov. 1976, p. 605-629, tables)

Describes B.A.'s commercial boom and convincingly argues that creole businessmen and foreign-born entrepreneurs without outside commercial interests played substantial role in developing regional economic infrastructure.

3707. Buenos Aires (prov.), *Arg.* **Gobernación. Ministerio de Educación. Subsecretaría de Cultura.** Mensajes de los Gobernadores de la Provincia de Buenos Aires: 1822-1849. v. 1/2. La Plata, Arg., Archivo Histórico de la Provincia de Buenos Aires Ricardo Levene, 1976. 2 v. (301, 286 p.) plates, table (Col. Mensajes de los gobernadores de la provincia de Buenos Aires. Serie, 6)

Covers messages of Rivadavia and Rosas (1 May 1822 through 27 Dec. 1849). Useful collection but lack of index hampers use.

3708. Cairo, Angel. Peronismo claves. B.A., Ediciones Centro de Estudios Aporte, 1975. 188 p.

Augmented version of author's essay "El Peronismo: sus Luchas y sus Crisis, 1955-68" (see *HLAS*

38:3678). Also contains articles written between 1959-73, conferences, and two unpublished essays which treat peronism in general, particular world events, and Argentine politics. Focus is nationalist-Catholic-peronist.

3709. Calabrese, Humberto. Juan Manuel de Rosas: cien respuestas acerca de su dictadura. La Plata, Arg., Instituto Cardenal Cisneros, 1975. 211 p., facsims., plate.

Generally sympathetic treatment.

3710. Calgaro, Orlando Florencio. FORJA: cuarenta años después. Rosario, Arg., Ediciones La Ventana, 1976. 90 p. (Col. Ensayos para la liberación)

Short essay on FORJA (Fuerza de Orientación de la Joven Argentina, group of nationalist intellectuals, active late 1930s). Includes documentary appendix of important documents pertaining to organization and some newspaper articles about it.

3711. Campana antiguo. Autores varios. B.A., Ediciones Crisol, 1975. 188 p., tables.

Short articles on various aspects of 19th and 20th-century local history. Documentary appendices. Topics include: railroads, education, *tiro federal*, institutions, etc.

3712. Campobassi, José Salvador. Sarmiento y su época. v. 1, Desde 1811 a 1863; v. 2, Desde 1863 a 1888. B.A., Editorial Losada, 1975. 2 v. (553, 554 p.)

Serious life-and-times biography based on secondary and archival works. As such it is a contribution to Argentine historiography, although it belongs to school of those who admire and support Sarmiento. Concluding chapter provides nice summary of Sarmiento's place inside Argentine historical studies and polemics.

3713. Camusso, Guillermina G. de and **Nelly Schnaith.** Proceso a Rosas. B.A., Ediciones Caldén, 1975. 225 p. (Col. Procesos)

Extensive documentary section covers Rosas as representative of order, the Confederation, national sovereignty, and B.A. Short introduction locates Rosas within natural historical progression whose moving force ultimately lies with developing world capitalist system.

Candido, Salvatore. La emigración política italiana a la América Latina: 1820-1870. See item 2349.

3714. Cárdenas, Eduardo J. and **Carlos M. Payá.** En camino a la democracia política: 1904-1910. B.A., Ediciones La Bastilla, 1975. 417 p., bibl. (Col. Memorial de la patria)

Broader than some books in this series in that it integrates social phenomena. Includes chapters on international situation, politics, provinces, economy, society, and intellectuals. Sympathetic to Radicals.

3715. Cárdenas, Felipe. El Chacho: vida, muerte y resurrección. B.A., Editorial El Alba, 1974. 65 p., plates (Col. Liberación, 2)

Short popular biography.

3716. Cárdenas, Felipe, h. El testamento de Rosas. B.A., Editorial Marlona, 1973. 97 p., facsims., plates.

Popular synthesis including biographical data, and short expositions on Rosas and economic independence, national sovereignty, confronting European aggression, and his last will and testament.

3717. Carlino, Carlos. Gauchos y gringos en la tierra ajena. B.A., Editorial Plus Ultra, 1976. 332 p. (Temas contemporáneos, 2)

Series of short sketches mostly referring to 19th-century life, customs, and events on pampas.

3718. Carreño, Virginia. La "Santa Maria" de Oldendorff, en 1869 (SRA/A, 110:1/3, enero/marzo 1976, p. 34-39, illus.)

About model estancia of early pioneer of agricultural science in Argentina.

3719. Carretero, Andrés M. La propiedad de la tierra en la época de Rosas. B.A., Editorial El Coloquio, 1972. 160 p. (Col. De temas de historia argentina)

Sequel to authors previous work (see *HLAS 34:2684c*) which examined structure of landholdings up to 1830. This book examines period 1830-52. Introductory essay notes continued concentration of lands in relatively few hands, stability of landholding from previous period, and marked connection between officialdom and landholdings. It also examines prices and condition of those who worked land. Excellent study based on archival research.

3720. ———. La Santa Federación: 1840-1850. B.A., Ediciones La Bastilla, 1975. 251 p., bibl. (Memorial de la patria)

Synthesis by leading historian of period. Includes material on daily life, culture, people, and customs in both B.A. and provinces.

3721. Casco, Marcos. Peronismo dentro del peronismo. Santa Fe., Arg., Gobierno de la Provincia de Santa Fe, Ministerio de Educación y Cultura, Subsecretaría de Cultura, 1974. 143 p., illus., plates (Col. Biblioteca de la doctrina nacional, 3)

Brief historical survey of Argentina from 1810 to 1973. Laudatory of Perón, his role within movement, and his place in Argentine history.

3722. Los caudillos de este siglo. B.A., Todo es Historia, 1976. 143 p., illus., table (Todo es historia, 4)

Articles originally published in magazine *Todo es Historia:*
Dardo Olguín "Los Lencinas: los Gauchos de Mendoza" p. 7-62
Ernesto Córdova Alsina "Juan Ramón Vidal: el 'Rubichá' de Corrientes" p. 63-91
Celso Rodríguez "Los Cantoni: Clan Populista Sanjuanino" p. 93-143.

3723. Chatwin, Bruce. In Patagonia. N.Y., Summit Books, 1977. 205 p., bibl., map.

Remarkable account of Patagonia by British journalist destined to become travel classic in the tradition of Montaigne's *Journal of voyage* or Burton's *Pilgrimage to Mecca.* Delightful blend of region's human and natural history by writer of subtle wit and unusual power. Of particular interest to social historians and naturalists. Book lacks notes but includes well-selected bibliography of primary and secondary sources (p. 200-205). [Ed.]

3724. Chávez, Fermín. General Angel Vicente Peñaloza: El Chacho. B.A., Crisis, 1975. 78 p., plates (Cuadernos de crisis, 16)

Concise summary by one of leading students of this famed caudillo of the interior.

3725. ——. Historia del país de los argentinos. 2. ed. corregida y notablemente aumentada. B.A., Ediciones Theoría, 1977. 345 p. (Biblioteca Argentina de letras)

Revisionist history from discovery through 1930. This interpretative essay is strongest for 19th century.

3726. —— *ed.* and *comp.* La Confederación: un proyecto nacional olvidado. B.A., Crisis, 1976. 64 p. (Cuadernos de crisis, 29)

Collection of 23 writings about Confederation dating from 1850s to early 20th century. Introduction by editor, leading revisionist historian, places texts in perspective. Mostly favorable to Confederation.

3727. —— *ed.* and *comp.* Testamentos de San Martín y Rosas y la Protesta de Rosas. B.U., Ediciones Theoría, 1975. 47 p. (Col. De textos rosistas, 1)

Briefly annotated versions of wills of San Martín and Rosas along with latter's protest against law that declared him criminal in B.A. Short introduction by noted revisionist historian.

3728. Chianelli, Trinidad Delia. El gobierno del puerto: 1862-1868. B.A., Ediciones La Bastilla, 1975. 311 p., bibl. (Col. Memorial de la patria)

Reasonably well-balanced interpretation. Does present, however, a pro-Argentine position on the Paraguayan war.

3729. Chumbita, Hugo. Bairoletto: prontuario y leyenda. n.p., n.p., 1974? 96 p.

Expanded version of 1968 article from *Todo es Historia* about 20-year career and legend of classic social bandit of pampa regions in southern B.A. prov.

3730. Cichero Pitré, Aníbal. De mi anotador porteño. B.A., Librería Platero, 1975. 247 p., plates.

Collection of essays, speeches, and articles about diverse themes, e.g., B.A.'s and Argentine forest-products industry.

3731. Ciria, Alberto. Partidos y poder en la Argentina moderna: 1930-1946. 3. ed. B.A., Ediciones de la Flor, 1975. 414 p., bibl.

Re-edition of 1969 work (see *HLAS 32:2519*).

Congreso de Historia Argentina y Regional, *II, Comodoro Rivadavia, Arg., 1973.* Segundo Congreso de Historia Argentina y Regional. See item 3070.

3732. Congreso de Historia de los Pueblos de la Provincia de Buenos Aires, *II, Tandil, Arg., 1972.* Segundo Congreso de Historia de los Pueblos de la Provincia de Buenos Aires. v. 1. Advertencia preliminar por Tomás Diego Bernard. La Plata, Arg., Archivo Histórico de la Provincia de Buenos Aires Ricardo Levene, 1974. 302 p., fold. maps, map, tables (Publicaciones, 4)

History: Spanish South America, 19th and 20th Centuries, Argentina / 289

Includes works by established and younger historians on variety of themes as well as specific towns in province.

3733. Converso, Félix and others. Estudios de historia argentina. t. 1/2. Córdoba, Arg., Univ. Nacional de Córdoba, Facultad de Filosofía y Humanidades, 1974. 2 v. (188, 174 p.) tables (Cuadernos de la cátedra de historia argentina, 1:11) (mimeo)

Good group of monographic articles based on original research which deserves better than mimeographic format of this publication. Authors and topics: Segreti on Belgrano; Converso, Grossi Belaúnde and Solveira on 19th-century commerce between Córdoba and Catamarca; Vera de Flachs on Roca era in Córdoba; González de Martínez on Argentine-Belgian meat trade in 1920s; Solveira on Córdoba's encomiendas, 1500s-1700s; Segreti on San Martín and Bustos; Giordano on Bustos' government in Córdoba; Pavoni on Gen. Paz' ideology; Converso on relations of Córdoba and Confederation with frontier Indians 1850s; and Vera de Flachs on 1905 Radical revolution in Córdoba. [D. Bushnell]

3734. Corbière, Emilio J. Juan B. Justo: socialismo e imperialismo. n.p., n.p., n.d. 95 p., plates.

Series of interpretative essays on various aspects of Justo's life and writings. On balance sees Justo as positive force within development of Argentine socialism.

3735. Córdoba, Tomás. La Argentina, Perón y después. Caracas, Ediciones CIDAL, 1975. 221 p. (Col. Análisis)

Interpretive essay concentrating on post-World War II period. Tries to show inadequacy of various national plans undertaken in period and ends on optimistic note that since things cannot get worse, they can only get better. Events since 1975 cast doubt on author's thesis.

3736. Correas, Edmundo. Historia y crisis del federalismo argentino. Mendoza, Arg., Junta de Estudios Históricos, 1973. 29 p.

Text of 1973 conference by mendocino historian on historical deterioration of Argentine federalism and need for its revival.

3737. Cosmelli Ibáñez, José Luis. Historia cultural de los argentinos. t. 1, Del período prehispánico a la época de Rosas; t. 2, Desde 1852 a la actualidad. B.A., Editorial Troquel, 1975. 2 v. (643, 706 p.) bibl., facsims., illus., maps.

Reference work. Specific sections include: arts, sciences, cultural institutions, education, etc. Indexed by name and includes chronology.

3738. Cuccorese, Horacio Juan. Historia crítica de la historiografía socioeconómica argentina del siglo XX. La Plata, Arg., Univ. Nacional de La Plata, Facultad de Humanidades y Ciencias de la Educación, Depto. de Historia, 1975. 443 p., plates (Monografías y tesis, 9)

Important book which delivers less than title promises. Pt. 1 on birth and development of Argentine socioeconomic historiography examines works of Juan Agustín García, Juan Alvarez, Juan B. Justo, and José Ingenieros; pt. 2, new history, includes Carbia, Korn, and Ravignani, then Levene and Emilio Coni; pt. 3, nationalist variant, looks at work of Raúl Salabrini Ortiz and Ricardo Ortiz. Each section examines leading work of particular individuals and includes summaries of contemporary and more recent critiques. By cutting-off at Ortiz, author unfortunately excludes important work done in 1960s by figures such as José Luis Romero, or more currently Halperin Donghi or those connected with Instituto Di Tella. Nevertheless, if author's vision is partial, his contribution to Argentine historiography is solid.

3739. Daza, José S. Episodios militares. B.A., EUDEBA, 1975. 135 p. (Col. Lucha de fronteras con el indio)

Memoirs of Indian fighter of 1870s and 1880s. Includes articles published in 1889, 1900, and 1901 on diverse military themes.

3740. Delich, Francisco J. Empresas agrícolas en gran escala (CPES/RPS, 10:27, mayo/agosto 1973, p. 119-176, bibl., tables)

Studies process of colonization in Córdoba prov. to 1914 based on data from Unión and Juárez Celman depts. Concludes that large land-owning enterprises speculated with colonization depriving most arrivals of possibility of owning land and driving up its prices. In return, system of renting for short periods both isolated immigrant population and resulted in little capital investment in land.

3741. Destefani, Laurio H. Manual de historia naval argentina. 2. ed. aumentada y corregida. B.A., Armada Argentina, Dirección de Abastecimientos Navales, 1975. 212 p., bibl., illus., tables (Historia naval argentina. Serie B, 18)

Brief history from independence to present, but concentrates on 19th and early 20th centuries.

3742. Díaz, Benito. Inmigración y agricultura en la época de Rosas. B.A., Editorial El Coloquio, 1975. 77 p. (Comunicaciones, 1)

3743. Doll, Ramón. Acerca de una política nacional. Del Servicio Secreto Inglés al judío Dickmann. Itinerario de la Revolución Rusa de 1917. Hacia la liberación. Reconocimientos. B.A., Ediciones Dictio, 1975. 470 p. (Biblioteca del pensamiento nacionalista argentino, 5)

Varied writings and studies from 1930s by right-wing nationalist. Markedly anti-leftist, anti-liberal, and anti-Semitic.

3744. Duarte, Erminda. Mi hermana Evita. B.A., Ediciones Centro de Estudios Eva Perón, 1972. 188 p.

Personalistic memoirs by Evita's sister. Primarily anecdotal.

3745. Elizalde, Rufino de. El Doctor Rufino de Elizalde y su época visita a través de su archivo. v. 4. B.A., EUDEBA, Facultad de Filosofía y Letras, Instituto de Historia Argentina Doctor Diego Luis Molinari, 1974. 467 p. (Documento para la historia argentina, 45)

Consists of 923 entries covering 1863-64. Index by name makes it easier to use. For vols. 1/2, see *HLAS 36:3112* and for vol. 3, see *HLAS 38:3699*.

3746. Etchepareborda, Roberto. La estructura socio-política argentina y la generación del ochenta (LARR, 8:1, 1978, p. 127-134)

Short evaluation of past research and outline of themes and problems for future investigation.

3747. ———. Problemas internacionales sudamericanos: Las Guayanas, vocación continental de algunos argentinos — Vicente G. Quesada, Paul Groussac y Martín García Merou (ANH/B, 47, 1974, p. 219-225)

Based on writings of three personages of period, author argues that public opinion at the turn of the century favored a continentalist perspective.

3748. Los excéntricos. B.A., Todo es Historia, 1977. 140 p., illus. (Todo es historia, 9)

Articles originally published in magazine *Todo es Historia*:
Ernesto Goldar "Asuero: Trigémino y Política" p. 7-52
Ernesto Goldar "El Hombre de la Vaca" p. 53-78

Héctor J. Iñigo Carrera "El Diputado Bromosódico" p. 79-122
Hernán Ceres "Baigorri: el Mago de la Lluvia" p. 123-140.

3749. Falgalde, Lauro. El interior al poder: de Caseros a Roca. B.A., Editorial Los Andes, 1975. 126 p.

Short synthesis concentrating primarily upon political events from pro-interior Liberal viewpoint.

3750. Fernández Balzano, Oscar Alberto. Estudios sobre la realidad social, cultural, política y económica argentina. B.A., Centro Argentino de Estudios e Investigaciones Sociopolíticas, 1975. 62 p.

Short interpretive essay on contemporary Argentina.

3751. Ferrero, Roberto A. Del fraude a la soberanía popular: 1938-1946. B.A., Ediciones La Bastilla, 1976. 418 p., bibl. (Col. Memorial de la patria)

Adequate volume about most difficult period. In places tends to accept portions of peronist myth and show undue partisan judgements about opposition groups.

3752. Fitte, Ernesto J. La agresión francesa a la escuadra argentina en 1829. B.A., Editorial Plus Ultra, 1976. 369 p., fold. facsims.

Brief text accompanied by 151 documents. Implicates Rosas for playing an overly pacific role before foreign aggression.

3753. Furlong, Guillermo. Como juzgó Carlos Darwin a nuestros gauchos (ANH/B, 47, 1974, p. 205-209)

Reflections on defenders and attackers of gauchos by leading historian. Cites Darwin's opinions about "superiority" of gauchos to townspeople.

3754. Galasso, Norberto. Scalabrini Ortiz. B.A., Crisis, 1975. 80 p., facsims., illus., plates (Col. Cuadernos de crisis. Serie, 22)

Good short biography. Concentrates mostly on politics and impact of Scalabrini's ideas.

3755. Gallardo, Guillermo. Un revolucionario de 1874: Florencio Cantilo (ANH/B, 47, 1974, p. 243-250)

Brief biographical introduction and text of letter written by Mitre's secretary about Revolution of 1874.

3756. Gallo, Ezequiel. The cereal boom and changes in the social and political structure of Santa Fe, Argentina: 1870-95 (*in* Duncan, Kenneth; Ian Rutledge; and Colin Harding *eds*. Land and labour in Latin America [see item 2156] p. 323-342, map, tables)

See *HLAS 38:3716* for Spanish version.

3757. Galmarini, Hugo Raúl. Negocios y política en la época de Rivadavia: Braulio Costa y la burguesía comercial porteña, 1820-1830. B.A., Librería y Editorial Platero, 1974. 213 p., bibl. (Col. Ensayos e investigaciones históricas)

Well-presented and argued monograph about "Costa Group" including its financial activities around Baring Loan and National Banks as well as its mining speculations. Details its links to London money markets, and to provincial and porteño elites. Shows how political connections and frequent changes of position served to further particular interests of these groups. Includes copious footnotes and documentary appendix. Solid contribution to our knowledge of early Argentina financial and political elites.

3758. Gálvez, Manuel. Vida de Ceferino Namuncurá: el santito de la toldería. B.A., Club de Lectores, 1976. 235 p., bibl., illus. (Col. Retorno a los testimonios)

Re-edition of 1947 work depicting life of Indian chief who dedicated his life to the Church and his people.

3759. Gandulfo Arce de Ballor, Josefina. Auténticos paladines de la Patagonia en Valcheta: Lino Oris de Roa y el Fortín de Valcheta, Francisco R. Moreno, Ramón Lista, Arturo Casas, Domingo Pronsato, 1833-1976. Valcheta?, Arg., n.p., 1977? 1 v. (Unpaged)

Short biographies of Patagonian explorers and settlers.

3760. García Belsunce, César A. Buenos Aires su gente: 1800-1830. t. 1. Nota preliminar de Julio E. Álvarez. B.A., Emecé, 1976. 256 p., fold. map, illus., maps, tables.

Vol. 1 of projected four-volume set on B.A. 1800-30 done by research team of five persons under author's direction. Studies urban and rural areas based on available primary and secondary materials. Concludes, among other things, that city and country grew at relatively even pace, that two areas mutually complemented each other in terms of skills and services, that relatively youthful population existed, that foreigners mostly lived in city, that rapid whitening of population took place, that most slaves lived in urban area, and that traditional family structure existed with low-fertility indices. Interesting initial volume containing valuable data.

3761. Garretón, Juan Antonio. Partes detallados de la expedición al desierto de Juan Manuel de Rosas en 1833. Introducción de Adolfo Garretón. B.A., EUDEBA, 1975. 197 p., tables (Lucha de fronteras con el indio)

Diary of officer with Rosas' expedition to desert covering April-Nov. 1833. Introduction includes biographical notes and 1819 letter on independence movement and Spain.

3762. Gèze, François and **Alain Labrousse.** Argentine: révolution et contre-révolutions. Paris, Editions du Seuil, 1975. 287 p., bibl., maps.

Marxist analysis of contemporary Argentina from Perón through 1975. Particularly useful for its analysis of leftist groups and parties as well as its provocative global vision of Argentina within world framework.

3763. Ghioldi, Rodolfo. Escritos. t. 1/2. Nota biográfica de Salvador Marini. B.A., Editorial Anteo, 1975/1976. 2 v. (254, 319 p.)

Two volumes include writings and speeches on variety of national and international topics by one of founders of Argentine Communist Party who has occupied key party posts since then. Valuable for students of party as well as for insights into Argentina or international situation.

3764. Gianello, Leoncio. El sesquicentenario de Juan Crisóstomo Lafinur (ANH/B, 47, 1974, p. 251-260)

Biographical notes about Argentine intellectual of early 19th century (1797-1824) whom author cites as one of first to introduce ideology into Argentine thought.

3765. Giménes Vega, Elías S. Alerta en el sur. B.A., Luis Lasserre, 1974. 233 p.

Rambling series of nationalistic revisionist essays bemoaning Argentina's failure to become continental power in 1810 or later.

3766. Giménez Zapiola, Marcos *ed.* and *comp*. El régimen oligárquico: materiales para el estudio de la realidad argentina hasta 1930. v. 1. B.A., Amorrotu Editores, 1975. 361 p., tables.

First of projected three-volumes (vol. 2 will cover 1930-55; vol. 3, 1955-73) contains previously published articles. Zapiola's introduction pulls several threads together around theme of growth and changes in historical dynamics between nation (Argentina) and imperialism (Great Britain).

3767. Goldberg, Marta B. La población negra y mulata de la ciudad Buenos Aires: 1810-1840 (IDES/DE, 16:61, abril/junio 1976, p. 75-99, tables)

Based on available demographic data, this article suggests basic causes for disappearance of B.A.'s black and mulatto population. Throughout period, they suffered from lower birth rates, higher infant mortality and death rates than white population. Further, proportion of males to females remained low. Also suggests that slaves' quality of life deteriorated after emancipation. Solid and precise article. Includes a discussion on methodology.

3768. Gómez Ferreyra, Avelino Ignacio ed. and *comp.* Viajeros pontificios al Río de la Plata y Chile, 1823-1825: la primera Misión Pontificia a Hispano-América relatada por sus protagonistas. Córdoba, Arg., Gobierno de la Provincia de Córdoba, 1970. 747 p., bibl.

Contains three accounts of mission by Abbott Giuseppe Sallusti including his secret memorandum to Pope Leon XII, by Canon Juan María Mastai Ferretti, and by Monsignor Juan Muzi. Also includes supplementary correspondence and documentation in addition to annotations. Valuable for early Church-State relations.

3769. González Arzac, Alberto Ricardo. El papelón de Manuel Quintana. B.A., Editorial Korrigan, 1974. 96 p., plates (Col. Procesos, 1)

Short monograph on conflict between Banco de Londres and Santa Fe prov. Originally article in *Todo es Historia*, this augmented version includes 12 documents. Author's sympathy with "nationalists" against British imperialism does not detract from case study.

3769a. González Climent, Anselmo. Historias del puerto de Buenos Aires. B.A., Emecé Editores, 1975. 1 v. (Unpaged) illus., plates.

Fine collection of old plates of B.A.'s port.

3770. Goodwin, Paul B., Jr. The Central Argentine Railway and the economic development of Argentina: 1854-1881 (HAHR, 57:4, Nov. 1977, p. 613-632, map, tables)

Contends that "railroads not only contributed to Argentine economic growth but also were built in response to clearly discerned market patterns and economic opportunity" and that "transportation innovation was intimately linked to economic demand."

3771. Los grandes negociados. B.A., Todo es Historia, 1976. 120 p., facsims., illus. (Todo es historia, 2)

Articles originally published in magazine *Todo es Historia*:
Miguel Scenna "El Escándalo del Siglo" p. 9-60
Osvaldo Bayer "Palomar: el Negociado que Conmovió a un Régimen" p. 67-93
Hernán Ceres "Los Niños Cantores" p. 101-120.

3772. Gravil, Roger. Argentina and the First World War (USP/RH, 54:108, out./dez. 1976, p. 385-417, tables)

Excellent, provocative article which argues that during World War I economic ties between Argentina and metropolitan countries tightened. Examines, in particular, grain and meat trades in view of Britain's policies and rivalries among Germany, Britain, and US, and where applicable Argentine interests. See also Gravil's article "The Anglo-Argentine Connection and the War of 1914-1918" in *Journal of Latin American Studies* (Cambridge, U.K., 9:1, May 1977, p. 59-89).

3773. Grela, Plácido. Alcorta: origen y desarrollo del pueblo y de la rebelión agraria de 1912. Rosario, Arg., Litoral Ediciones, 1975. 219 p., bibl., map, plates.

Historian of 1912 movement in Alcorta writes about this community, its founding and development, the strike, Federación Agraria Argentina, and more recent need for land reform. Includes proposal for land-reform law. Less valuable as historical study than author's other works.

3774. ———. El espinillo: reseña histórica del otrora pueblo Paganino hoy ciudad Granadero Baigorria. Grandero Baigorria, Arg., Editorial El Remanso, 1975. 32 p., plates.

Local history.

3775. Guerrero, César H. Sarmiento: fundador de la Sociedad Argentina Protectora de los Animales. San Juan, P.R., Asociación Amigos de la Casa Natal de Sarmiento, 1975. 44 p., illus.

Short exposition on Sarmiento's role in this society.

3776. Guido, Horacio J.M. Secuelas del Unicato: 1890-1896. B.A., Ediciones La Bastilla, 1977. 367 p., bibl. (Memorial de la patria)

Volume covers background to Revolution of 1890-96. Dwells almost exclusively on political history which detracts from its value as general statement about this period.

3777. **Gutiérrez, Guillermo.** La clase trabajadora nacional: su confirmación histórica. B.A., Editorial Crisis, 1975. 80 p., facsims., plates, table (Cuadernos de crisis, 18)

Brief historical overview of formation of Argentine working class from left-peronist perspective.

3778. **Guy, Donna J.** The rural working class in nineteenth century Argentina: forced plantation labor in Tucumán (LARR, 13:1, 1978, p. 135-145, tables)

Suggestive article showing possibilities for studies of rural workers and arguing persuasively that topic must be focused within bounds of local histories.

3779. ———. Tucumán sugar politics and the Generation of Eighty (AAFH/TAM, 32:4, April 1976, p. 566-584, table)

Solid article showing how internal political alignments defeated attempts at regional development in the case of Tucumán's sugar industry. Contains many insights into personal political relationships between provinces and B.A. and their impact at national and local levels.

3780. **Halperin Donghi, Tulio.** ¿Para qué la inmigración? ideología y política inmigratoria y aceleración del proceso modernizador: el caso argentino, 1810-1914 (JGSWGL, 13, 1976, p. 437-489)

Interpretive essay on ideologies of and attitudes toward immigration written in characteristic brilliant but rambling style of one of Argentina's foremost historians. Deals with, among others, ideas of J.B. Alberdi, D.F. Sarmiento, Fray Mocho, J.B. Justo, and Manuel Gálvez. Nicely brings out love-hate relationships on both sides.

3781. Historia de la evolución de Campana: centenario de la ciudad municipalidad de Campana, 1875-1975. t. 3. B.A., Ediciones Crisol, 1975. 186 p., plates.

Covers mostly late 19th to early 20th century. Includes isolated episodes about railroad, local clubs, *frigorífico*, institutions.

3782. **Hodges, Donald C.** Argentina: 1943-1976, the national revolution and resistance. Albuquerque, Univ. of New Mexico Press, 1976. 207 p., bibl.

Detailed analysis of varied peronist strategies and tactics developed since 1955. Written from sympathetic point of view, its coverage of internal debates inside peronism is excellent. Author's attempt to extrapolate peronist experience onto a continental plane, however, is less solidly rooted in historical research.

3783. **Hollander, Nancy Caro.** Women workers and the class struggle: the case of Argentina (LAP, 1/2, Winter/Spring 1977, p. 180-193)

Penetrating article on women in the labor force in 19th and 20th-century Argentina. Outlines peronism's appeal to women and contradictory nature of its policies. Good introduction to women under capitalism and in Argentina.

3784. **Instituto Bibliográfico Antonio Zinny,** *Buenos Aires*. Indice historiográfico argentino: 1970. B.A., Biblioteca F.V., 1973. 338 p.

Valuable index for specialist. Includes 2021 items from 107 sources divided into 59 categories and includes author and subject indexes. Each item is briefly annotated mostly for content alone. Coverage includes newspapers, magazines, journals, both provincial and national plus smattering of foreign publications.

3785. **Instituto de Estudios Sociales,** *Buenos Aires*. Pueblo y antipueblo: 1880-1930. v. 1, El granero del mundo. B.A., Editorial Ciencia Nueva, 1974? 240 p., maps, tables (Col. América nueva)

Encompasses first two parts of five-part study of period. Covers outline of main events as well as brief economic history. Intended as political education manual for left peronists.

3786. **Irazusta, Julio.** Memorias: historia de un historiador a la fuerza. B.A., Ediciones Culturales Argentinas [and] Ministerio de Educación y Justicia, Secretaría de Estado de Cultura, 1975. 238 p., facsim., plates (Col. Autobiografías, memorias y recuerdos)

Autobiography of leading spokesperson of the nationalist school in the 1930s. Somewhat disappointing in that it dwells more on personal material than on politics. Covers up through early 1930s only.

3787. ———. El tránsito del siglo XIX al XX: 1896-1904. B.A., Editorial Astrea, 1975. 248 p., bibl.

Focuses mostly on politics, diplomacy, and culture with some reference to internal economic problems. Almost total neglect of social problems or emerging labor movement weakens this popular history.

3788. ———. Urquiza y su pronunciamiento contra Rosas. 2. ed. B.A., Biblioteca F.V., 1975. 93 p.

Essay severely criticizing Urquiza's uprising against Rosas. Argues that change of government disturbed Argentine development and sold out country to representatives of "cosmopolitan mercantilism" in favor of European powers and Brazil in America.

Isaacson, José *ed.* El populismo en la Argentina. See *HLAS 39:9273*.

3789. James, Daniel. The peronist left: 1955-1975 (JLAS, 8:2, Nov. 1976, p. 273-296)

Descriptive presentation of topic. Its admittedly negative cast gives article unreal quality. Should be read in conjunction with Hodges' work (see item 3782) who presents progressive view of some phenomena. Description of ideological positions in vacuum without reference to economic data may leave reader disoriented as to the why and how of appearance and disappearance of many currents that swirled in and around peronism in this period.

3790. Jassén, Raúl. ¡Romper al peronism!: la doctrina justicialista, espíritu histórico de Perón. Córdoba, Arg., Editora de la Reconquista Criolla, 1976. 267 p., illus. (Col. Rosa de los vientos)

Conferences and articles on contemporary themes by veteran justicialist newspaper person. Stresses both internal crisis within movement and need to strengthen its ranks. Expounds viewpoint that Justicialism's principal enemy is Marxism.

3791. Jauretche, Arturo. Ejército y política. B.A., A. Peña Lillo Editor, 1976. 216 p., bibl., (Biblioteca de estudios americanos, 13)

Originally published 1958 and written from exile in Montevideo, this interpretive essay from one of Argentina's leading nationalist writers places country's history in terms of Patria Chica and Patria Grande. In this framework, postulates that only latter point of view can develop national political strategy and military that functions as army not police force.

3792. Jelin, Elizabeth. Conflictos laborales in la Argentina: 1973-1976. B.A., Centro de Estudios de Estado y Sociedad, 1977. 52 p. (Estudios sociales, 9)

Excellent summary and exposition of current labor strife in Argentina. Argues that redistributive policies in declining resource-base economies tend to fragment labor movement, but that it is also at such times that new directions are adopted by labor ranks.

3793. ———. Spontanéité et organisation dans le mouvement ouvrier: le cas de l'Argentine, du Brésil, et du Mexique (ADST/SDT, 18:2, avril/juin 1976, p. 139-168)

Sociological study of 1958 railroad strikes in Mexico, Contagem strike in Brazil of 1968, and Argentine Cordobazo and aftermath. Postulates appearance of new type of spontaneity among Latin American workers based on struggle against both trade union structures and prevailing distribution of material and political power.

3794. Jouve, Marta Luisa. Sabattini: una reforma agraria profunda desde la democracia. Prólogo de Medardo Avila Vázquez. Córdoba. Arg., n.p., 1976. 137 p., bibl., tables.

Life-and-times study of Radical Governor of Córdoba stressing his agrarian reforms. Concludes that political configurations at the national level frustrated his plans although he did achieve limited results.

3795. Klíma, Jan. La asociación bonaerense *Vorwärts* en los años del siglo pasado (UCP/IAP, 8, 1974, p. 111-134, plates)

Interesting article based on Neugebauer collection in Litomysl (see item 3796) examines pamphlet and periodical literature in collection and especially *Vorwärts*. Rich in details for specialists.

3796. ——— and **Vysoké Mýto-Bohemia.** Antonio Neugebauer y los orígenes del socialismo en la región de La Plata (UCP/IAP, 7, 1973, p. 171-173, plate)

Interesting historical note about Czech socialist who lived in B.A. during 1880s and participated in various activities there.

Korolev, Nicolai. Emigración de Rusia a América Latina a fines del siglo XIX, comienzos del siglo XX. See item 2188.

3797. Lacroix, Federico. Por nuestra América: historia de la Patagonia, Tierra del Fuego, e Islas Malvinas (UCLV/I, 50, enero/abril 1975, p. 168-212, maps, plates)

Selection from 1841 work with brief historiographical introduction. Mostly description of voyages, local customs, etc.

3798. Lindenboim, Javier. El empresariado industrial argentino y sus organizaciones gremiales entre 1930 y 1946 (IDES/DE, 16:62, julio/sept. 1976, p. 163-201, tables)

Groundbreaking study on Industrial Associations. Argues, among other points, that industrial bourgeoisie did not exist, but rather sectors of it with interests in industry. Also shows existence of small industrialists who presented alternative economic plans to dominant ideas of period. Finally, suggestions that both process of concentration and foreignization (in sector) had advanced significantly by this time. Includes methodological appendix.

3799. Lironi, Julio Víctor. Génesis de la aviación argentina, 1910-1915: su historia y sus hombres. Prólogo de Edmundo Civati Gernasconi. B.A., Artes Gráficas Congreso, 1971 [i.e. 1973]. 454 p., plates, table.

Detailed year-by-year study of aviation including long biographical sketches of early aviators. Based on Aero-Club Argentino archives, newspapers, and magazines. Includes military and civilian aviation. Excellent photographs.

3800. Locria, Carlos Ignacio. Un diplomático entre los caudillos: ensayo documental sobre Domingo de Oro (Boletín de la Biblioteca del Congreso de la Nación [B.A.] 103/104, enero/junio 1976, p. 11-92)

Article about relatively unknown figure who, nevertheless, hob-nobbed with greats of the time, e.g., Rosas, Mansilla, Mitre, Quiroga. Based on archival materials, documentary appendix includes Oro's 1840 work about Rosas written from exile in Chile and essay on early days of independence in South America.

3801. López Rosas, José Rafael. Entre la monarquía y la república: 1815-1820. B.A., Ediciones La Bastilla, 1976. 388 p., bibl. (Col. Memorial de la patria)

Deals mostly with political events on national and international levels.

3802. Madsen, Andreas. La Patagonia vieja. B.A., Editorial Galerna, 1975. 220 p.

Short anecdotal sketches of life in Patagonia during late 19th and early 20th centuries.

3803. Marianetti, Benito. Manuel Ugarte: un precursor en la lucha emancipadora de América Latina. B.A., Ediciones Sílaba, 1976. 160 p.

Brief biography by leftist covering Ugarte's early years, his overseas trips, his literary relationships, and his ambivalent participation in Socialist Party. Stresses Ugarte's anti-imperialism and rejects those who see him as nationalist or merely Americanist.

3804. Marini, Ana María. Women in contemporary Argentina (LAP, 4:4, Fall 1977, p. 114-120)

Personalistic account of contemporary Argentina. Includes material on current status of women's movement and military governments anti-birth-control policies.

3805. Martínez, Pedro Santos. La nueva Argentina: 1946-1955. B.A., Ediciones La Bastilla, 1976. 2 v. (360, 369) bibl., tables (Col. Memorial de la patria)

These two volumes deal with vast complexities that made up first two Perón administrations. On whole, they present adequate descriptive history of that period although almost everyone will find something to disagree with in so controversial a topic. Those looking for new interpretations or a synthesis, however, should look elsewhere.

3806. Martínez Ruiz, Bernabé. Patagonia histórica. B.A., Editorial Galerna, 1976. 190 p., bibl.

Sweeping history from discovery to early 20th century.

3807. Matijevic, Nicolás *comp.* Bibliografía patagónica y de las tierras australes (*in* Congreso de Historia Argentina y Regional, II, Comodoro Rivadavia, Arg., 1973. Segundo Congreso de Historia Argentina y Regional. B.A., Academia Nacional de la Historia, 1975. v. 3, p. 53-58)

Brief selective essay and compilation.

3808. Mayo, Carlos A.; Osvaldo R. Andino; and **Fernando García Molina.** Diplomacia, política y petróleo en la Argentina: 1927-1930. B.A., Ediciones Rincón, 1976. 200 p., bibl., tables.

Good monograph on foreign oil companies, plans for nationalization, and events through 1930 coup. Argues that US proceeded softly on matters concerning nationalization (unlike Mexican case) for fear of arousing anti-US sentiment and because it knew that nationalization measures would not pass at that time. Also discounts any direct participation by oil companies in 1930 coup, although that issue certainly played part in political maneuverings around Yrigoyen's overthrow. Stronger on the Argentine side of the problem.

3809. Mazo, Gabriel del. El radicalismo: ensayo sobre su historia y doctrina. t. 1/5. B.A., Ediciones Cardon, 1975. 5 v. (189, 187, 197, 147, 196 p.) plates.

Reedition of 1952 work (see *HLAS 20:2222*). No footnotes or bibliography, but documents and names abound throughout. Still valuable source.

3810. ———. Vida de un político argentino: convocatoria de recuerdos. B.A., Plus Ultra, 1976. 253 p., plate.

Collection of essays containing personal memoirs from childhood through Yrigoyen period. Also, includes section on leading figures whom author dealt with over his career. Disappointing in that contents are more personal statement than presentation of important events in which author participated.

3811. Melli, Oscar Ricardo. Historia de Carmen de Areco: 1771-1970. La Plata, Arg., Archivo Histórico de la Provincia de Buenos Aires Ricardo Levene, 1974. 295 p., facsims., maps, plates (Col. Contribución a la historia de los pueblos de la provincia de Buenos Aires, 41:2)

Detailed local history including material on demography, education, etc.

3812. Melo, Carlos R. La acefalía del Poder Ejecutivo Nacional y el Congreso de 1862 (Boletín de la Facultad de Derecho y Ciencias Sociales [Univ. Nacional de Córdoba, Arg.] 39:1/3, enero/junio 1975, p. 343-363)

Conference given at Instituto Popular de Conferencias in B.A. Reproduces much congressional debate about presidential succession during Mitre's provisional presidency. Emphasizes theme of constitutional legality.

3813. Méndez Acebal, Ramón. Alberdi, el predestinado. Prólogo de Francisco Romeo Grassç. B.A., Editorial Plus Ultra, 1977. 153 p., bibl., illus.

Biographical sketch and sociological analysis of Alberdi and his principal ideas.

3814. Mercier Vega, Luis. Autopsie de Perón: le bilan de péronisme. Paris, Duculot, 1974. 205 p. (Sociologie nouvelle. Situations, 8)

Rather subjective essay (no footnotes or bibliography) which leans towards interpreting peronism as personalistic phenomenon.

3815. Minutolo, Cristina V. Fracasada invasión militar a Entre Ríos, 1852: un doble plan obstruccionista contra la Organización Nacional. Prólogo de Richard R. Caillet-Bois. B.A., Leonardo Impresora, 1977. 318 p., bibl., illus., maps.

Detailed monograph on land-and-sea expedition to Entre Ríos sent by B.A. and its failure. Solid contribution to complicated history of post-Caseros period and endless maneuverings by factions in provinces and B.A. Lengthy documentary appendix includes diary of admiral in charge of naval operations.

3816. Molina, Carlos A. and **Emilio A. García Méndez.** El imperialismo y los "enemigos buenos:" Alvear, Lonardi, Frondizi. B.A., El Cid Editor, 1974. 63 p. (Col. Liberación o dependencia, 7)

Short essay about recent Argentine history from nationalist perspective. Examines in particular regimes of Alvear, Lonardi, and Frondizi to show vascillating role of middle groups when confronting oligarchy and imperialism.

3817. Moreno, Nahuel and **Hugo Kasevich.** Método de interpretación de la historia argentina. B.A., Ediciones Pluma, 1975. 210 p. (Col. Teoría y crítica)

Amplified versions of political education pamphlets by leading Argentine Trotskyist theoreticians. Argues for a position against "mystification and falsehoods of liberal and revisionist historiography."

3818. Nario, Hugo. Tata Dios: el Mesías de la última montonera. B.A., Editorial Plus Ultra, 1976. 222 p., bibl., illus., map.

Study of 1872 incident in Tandil where group of gauchos under influence of traveling religious person killed 40 foreigners in order to "protect the country and the true religion against foreigners and Masons." Based on local police reports and other documents.

3819. Nava, Juan Carlos. Los ingleses no devolverán las Malvinas. B.A., Editores Atamisqui, 1974? 93 p., plates (Col. Los casos)

Nationalistic plea by journalist urging Argentina to occupy the Malvinas which are rightfully hers and to assert her rights in Antarctic.

3820. Navarro, Marysa. The case of Eva Perón (Signs [Chicago, Ill.] 3:1, Autumn 1977, p. 229-240)

Short synopsis of Eva Peron's role between 1943-52. Clearly shows contradictory nature of her actions and position within Argentine society. Suggests that most standard interpretations of Evita need reevaluation, something author's forthcoming biography should accomplish. Part of special issue of journal *Signs* devoted to women and national development.

3821. Newton, Ronald C. German Buenos Aires, 1900-1933: social change and cultural crisis. Austin, Univ. of

Texas Press, 1977. 225 p., bibl., tables (Texas Pan American series)

Excellent study of German community from World War I to 1933 based on archival and secondary sources. Shows clearly factors of class and culture as they affected community over time; challenges thesis of upward immigrant mobility; and documents manipulations of German economic elite for its own gain and profit. Valuable work for students of immigration in general.

3822. Nicolau, Juan Carlos. Industria argentina y aduana: 1835-1854. B.A., Editorial Devenir, 1975. 175 p., bibl. (Col. Reconstrucción histórica)

Examines 1835 customs law and then its overall impact on industry in B.A. and interior. Also analyzes debates around subsequent customs law of 1854. Argues that first law, in conjunction with government policy, worked against national industrial development.

3823. Núñez, M. Bustos: el caudillo olvidado. Supervisión de Jorge B. Rivera. B.A., Crisis, 1975. 80 p., facsims., illus., plates (Cuadernos de crisis, 15)

Short life-and-times biography of Córdoba's Federalist chieftain who ruled 1820-29.

3824. Oliver, Juan Pablo. El verdadero Alberdi: génesis del liberalismo económico argentino. B.A., Ediciones Dictio, 1977. 741 p. (Biblioteca dictio, 3. Sección historia)

Lengthy biography by economic historian based extensively on Alberdi's own writings. Labels Alberdi "lawyer-writer" and singles out his lack of faith in Argentina as predominant legacy. Also includes stinging review of Alberdi literature. Author however, does recognize his subject's considerable talents.

3825. Ortega, Ezequiel César. Cómo fué la Argentina: 1516-1972. t. 1/2. Prólogo de Armando Alonso Piñeiro. B.A., Editorial Plus Ultra, 1973. 2 v. (330, 331 p.) (Col. Esquemas históricos, 11/12)

Summary of political history divided into four stages: vol. 1, "Argentina Inicial, 1516-1810" and "Argentina Media, 1810-1880;" vol. 2, "Argentina Moderna, 1880-1930" and "Argentina Reciente, 1930-1973." For the general reader.

3826. Oved, Iaacov. El trasfondo histórico de la Ley 4144 de Residencia (IDES/DE, 16:61, abril/junio 1976, p. 123-150)

Interesting article based on primary sources. Argues that 1902 Law of Residence was passed in direct response to growing spread of anarchist tendencies within working-class movement and especially unions. It constituted attempts to isolate people of that persuasion by singling them out for special sanctions. Effect, however, was to strengthen their influence.

3827. Páez de la Torre, Carlos. El derrumbe de la Confederación: 1855-1862. B.A., Ediciones La Bastilla, 1977. 312 p., bibl. (Memorial de la patria)

Nice summary showing cross-currents that swirled inside political and economics events of period, both in porteño and provincial camps.

3828. Partido Revolucionario de los Trabajadores, Buenos Aires. Documentos del Comité Ejecutivo Comandante Mario R. Santucho, abril de 1977. Madrid, Gráficas Halas, 1977. 94 p.

Resolutions of PRT's Executive Committee covering national and international situations.

3829. Patton, Elda Clayton. Sarmiento in the United States. Evansville, Ind., The Univ. of Evansville Press, 1976. 192 p., bibl., plates.

Pt. 1 briefly describes Sarmiento's Argentina, his life and works, and his travels in Europe and Africa. Pt. 2 specifically treats his visit of 1847 and stay of 1865-68 as Ambassador. Mostly presents Sarmiento's views and ideas on specific aspects of US and calls attention to deep impression this country made on him.

Paula, Alberto S.J. de; Ramón Gutiérrez; and Graciela María Viñuales. Del pago del Riachuelo al Partido de Lanús: 1536-1944. See item 3295.

3830. Peers de Perkins, Carmen. Crónicas del joven siglo: cartas de Roca y Wilde. B.A., Editorial Plus Ultra, 1976. 113 p., plates.

Letters dating 1900-10 filled mostly with social and some cultural observations.

3831. Pellegrini, Enrique. Paso de los Libres: crónicas y ensayos. B.A., López Libreros Editores, 1974. 275 p., facsims., maps, plates.

Mostly collection of newspaper stories on various aspects of local history up to 1910 with some recent data. Covers people, places, incidents, institutions, etc.

3832. Pereyra, Mario Luis. Nicasio Oroño, el soslayado: ensayo. Santa Fe, Arg., Librería y Editorial Colmegna, 1976. 165 p., bibl.

Biography of 19th-century politican and parliamentarian divided by topics.

3833. Perón, Juan Domingo. Organización peronista. B.A., Editorial de la Reconstrucción, 1976. 410 p. (Col. La comunidad organizada)

Short selections from Perón's speeches and radio broadcasts during his first presidencies. Divided by general themes including: organizational principles, Argentine economic structure, how society should be organized, etc.

3834. El peronismo. v. 1. B.A., Todo es Historia, 1976. 151 p., bibl., illus. (Todo es historia, 5)

Articles originally published in magazine *Todo es Historia*:
Miguel A. Scenna "Braden y Perón" p. 2-53
César A. Ross "El Comienzo del Exilio" p. 57-79
Carlos A. Floria "El Peronismo" p. 83-131
Miguel A. Scenna "Perfiles Peronis:as" p. 133-151.

Peterson, Harold F. Diplomat of the Americas: a biography of William I. Buchanan, 1852-1909. See *HLAS 39:8620*.

3835. Piccirilli, Ricardo. Quiénes recogieron al Capitán Sarmiento en el campo de batalla (ANH/B, 47, 1974, p. 239-242)

Brief note on Sarmiento's adopted son Dominguito, and recovery of his body from battlefield in Paraguay.

3836. Pino, Amalia del. Alberto M. de Agostini. B.A., Asociación Dante Alighieri, 1976. 57 p., plate (Grandes italo-argentinos, 1)

Biographical essay on Salesian priest who was frequen traveler and explorer in Patagonia. Includes chronology and list of his publications.

Pintos Carbajal, Mireya. La presencia de la Cruzada Lavallejista en la prensa porteña de 1825. See item 3945.

3837. Poggi, Rinaldo Alberto. Necesarias precisiones acerca de la Batalla de San Carlos, 1872 (CEHA/NH, 8:15, agosto 1975, p. 139-159)

Study of background of problems concerning frontier's defense in year before the battle. Indicates state of unpreparedness on part of national authorities.

Polišenský, Josef. La emigración checoslovaca a América Latina, 1649-1945: problemas y fuentes. See item 2217.

3838. Prado, Manuel. La guerra al malón. B.A., Editorial Xanadú, 1976. 156 p., illus., plates (Serie América, 4)

Re-edition of 1907 publication containing memoirs of 1870s Indian fighter.

3839. Presas, Juan Antonio. Nuestra Señora del Buen Viaje: Morón. B.A., Tallares del Instituto Salesiano de Artes Gráficas, 1972. 396 p., fold. maps, illus.

Divided into three parts: 1) history of municipality; 2) documents from 16th through 19th centuries; and 3) maps. Author says: "nuestro prisma de vista al contar la historia de Morón es eminentemente religioso y mariano."

3840. Los radicales. v. 1. B.A., Todo es Historia, 1976. 126 p., illus. (Todo es historia, 1)

Articles originally published in magazine *Todo es Historia*:
Félix Luna "A Modo de Presentación" p. 7-10
Eduardo H. Passalacqua "El Yrigoyenismo" p. 15-83
Felipe Cárdenas h. "Ese Enigmático Conductor" p. 87-99
Alberto González Arzac "Hipólito Yrigoyen, Doctor" p. 105-126.

3841. Ramayón, Eduardo E. Las caballadas en la Guerra del Indio. 2. ed. B.A., EUDEBA, 1974 [i.e. 1975]. 132 p. (Col. Lucha de fronteras con el indio)

Reprint of 1920 ed. by Indian fighter of 1870s and 1880s. Includes material on mules, horses, and dogs used in campaign plus some historical material.

Ramos, R. Antonio. La independencia del Paraguay y el imperio del Brasil. See item 3911.

3842. Rapoport, Mario. La política británica en la Argentina a comienzos de la década de 1940 (IDES/DE, 16:62, julio/sept. 1976, p. 203-228, tables)

Excellent article showing how Anglo-US rivalries influenced conduct of foreign policy during early 1940s. Argues that each country jockeyed for positions in post-war world. Particularly useful in explaining attitudes of each toward Argentine governments of period. Based on primary research, mostly British sources.

3843. Rasgos de la vida pública de Juan Manuel de Rosas. B.A., Editorial Freeland, 1975. 222 p. (Col. Estudios de nuestra patria)

Consists of 92 documents covering various aspects of Rosas' public career to 1841.

3844. Rato de Sambuccetti, Susana. Avellaneda y la Nación versus la Provincia de Buenos Aires: crisis económica y política, 1873-1880. B.A., Editorial La Pleyade, 1975. 141 p., tables.

Fine study based on primary sources, argues that Avellaneda was stronger President and leader than generally recognized. Also discusses in detail financial maneuverings and intrigues between National Bank and B.A.'s Provincial Bank.

Remmer, Karen L. Economic dependency and political conflict: Chile and Argentina, 1900-1925. See *HLAS 39:7684*.

3845. *Revista de la Junta de Estudios Históricos de Mendoza.* Junta de Estudios Históricos de Mendoza. Vol. 1/2, No. 8, 2. época, 1975- . Mendoza, Arg.

Vol. 1 contains conferences and historical notes of interest to historians of Argentina and particularly to those who study Andean regions. Also includes section of travelers' accounts and "homenajes y recuerdos" as well as listing of provincial governors and legislators at national level from 19th century to present. Vol. 2 contains reprints of short articles of local and historical interest plus section on historical monuments and several documents covering miscellaneous 19th and 20th-century topics.

3846. Rivera Echenique, Silvia. Militarismo en la Argentina: golpe de estado de junio de 1966. México, UNAM, Facultad de Ciencias Políticas y Sociales, 1976. 123 p., bibl. (Serie estudios, 50)

Leftist interpretation of Argentina from Onganía to 1973 elections. Claims that lack of true workers' party permitted economic deterioration and led to manipulation by dominant classes of 1973 election results.

3847. Rodríguez, Augusto G. Roca y Sarmiento: identificación espiritual de dos soldados argentinos (ANH/B, 47, 1974, p. 281-286).

Brief discussion of relations between both men and similarities of their actions.

3848. Romay, Francisco L. Historia de la Policía Federal Argentina. v. 6, 1880-1916. B.A., Editorial Policial, 1975. 573 p., bibl., facsims., illus., map, tables.

Vol. 6 of set (for vols. 1/5, see *HLAS 28:1134*) which consists of detailed history of Federal Police as institution. Rich source of information which deals with social and political themes. Nevertheless, one regrets that access to police archives did not lead author to write a more comprehensive account relating police actions to broader trends.

3849. Romero, Luis Alberto. La feliz experiencia: 1820-1824. B.A., Ediciones La Bastilla, 1976. 288 p., bibl. (Memorial de la patria)

One of most balanced books in this series, it studies crucial period in formation of 19th-century Platine configurations and sees in them both seeds of future problems as well as buds of future solutions.

3850. Romero Carranza, Ambrosio; Alberto Rodríguez Varela; and **Eduardo Ventura Flores Pirán.** Historia política de la Argentina. v. 3, Desde 1862 hasta 1928. B.A., Ediciones Pannedille, 1975. 628 p., bibl.

Final volume of series (for others, see *HLAS 34:2790a*) encompassing pt. 6: "Crecimiento del Estado Argentino." Chronological narrative written from pro-Catholic position outlines major political developments at national and provincial levels.

3851. Rosa, José María. Defensa y pérdida de nuestra independencia económica. B.A., A. Peña Lillo Editor, 1975.

Revisionist historian looks at period 1810-60s to show how Argentina lost, won, and then lost again its economic independence. Anti-Liberal, anti-British, and pro-Rosas.

3852. Rutledge, Ian. The integration of the highland peasantry into the sugar cane economy of northern Argentina, 1930-43 (*in* Duncan, Kenneth; Ian Rutledge; and Colin Hardings *eds.* Land and labour in Latin America [see item 2156] p. 205-228, maps, tables)

Extension of author's previous work (see *HLAS 38:3838*) showing process of labor recruitment for sugar-mills through semi-proletarianization of Indian peasantry. Concludes that means adopted formed most rational capitalist response to labor problem. Of interest for its implications about local history and plantation societies in general.

3853. Sáenz, Jimena. Mar del Plata: siglo I, 1874-1974. B.A., Editorial El Alba, 1974. 96 p., plates (Col. Liberación, 3)

Personalistic descriptive history mostly on the "belle époque" of Mar del Plata.

3854. Saldías, Adolfo. Historia de la Confederación Argentina: Rozas y su época. 3 v. Prólogo de José María Rosa. B.A., Ediciones Clio, 1975. 3 v. (559, 620, 653 p.) illus., plates.

Reprints three additional volumes of classic (for previous ones, see *HLAS 36:3295-3296* and *HLAS 38:3840-3842*).

3855. San Esteban, Ricardo. El agro argentino: proceso histórico. B.A., Editorial Cartago, 1975. 188 p.

Sweeping historical panorama divided into: slave mode of production, feudal mode of production, and capitalist period up through first peronist experience.

3856. Sanguinetti, Horacio. La democracía ficta: 1930-1938. B.A., Editorial Astrea, 1975. 166 p., bibl. (Ediciones La Bastilla)

Interpretive essay covering terms of Uriburu and Justo. Discusses economics, politics, society and culture. Also includes brief chronology.

3857. Sanz, Pablo R. El espacio argentino. B.A., Editorial Pleamar, 1976. 380 p., bibl., maps (Col. Estrategia y política)

Geo-political interpretation of Argentine history and country's relations with border nations in particular. Some material on Argentine-Brazilian rivalry.

3858. Saraví, Mario Guillermo. Rosas y Cullen en 1833: algunos entretelones de una enemistad duradera (CEHA/NH, 8:15, agosto 1975, p. 131-138)

Brief article, based mostly on primary sources, about intrigues against Rosas centering on figure of Domingo Alejandro Lorenzo Cullen.

3859. ———. La suma del poder: 1835-1840. B.A., Ediciones La Bastilla, 1976. 241 p. (Col. Memorial de la patria)

Concentrates mostly on politics and B.A.-provinces conflicts, but also includes chapters on economy, culture, and daily life.

3860. Sarmiento, Domingo Fidel. Correspondencia de Dominguito en la Guerra de Paraguay. Estudio preliminar, selección y notas de Andrés M. Carretero. B.A., Ediciones Librería El Lorraine, 1975. 107 p.

Letters sent from Paraguayan front by Sarmiento's adopted son, dated 1865-66 and in Archivo General de la Nación.

3861. Scenna, Miguel Angel. Braden y Perón. B.A., Editorial Kirrigan, 1974. 95 p., plates (Col. Libertad, 1)

Popularized account of famous 1945-46 confrontation.

3862. ———. Los que escribieron nuestra historia. B.A., Ediciones La Bastilla, 1976. 430 p., bibl. (Col. Memorial de la patria)

Sweeping chronological treatment covering early colonial period to present generation. Mostly short passages about individual historians or institutions such as Academia. Lists main works and points of view of each group.

3863. Schindler, Helmut. Die Friedensverhandlungen Juan Manuel Rosas' mit den Indianern der Pampa (JGSWGL, 10, 1973, p. 331-348)

Rosas was in charge of peace negotiations with various Indian tribes roaming pampas and Patagonia, 1825-28. Main source of negotiations was a *Memoria* by Rosas to B.A. government. Schindler shrewdly analyzes Rosas' documents first published by Quesada 1864. [G.M. Dorn]

3864. Segreti, Carlos S.A. Moneda y política en la primera mitad del siglo XIX: contribución al estudio de la historia de la moneda argentina. Tucumán, Arg., Fundación Banco Comercial del Norte, 1975. 268 p. (Ediciones, 4)

Careful examination of money and banking, 1810-48. Examines subject of both national and provincial levels. Includes documents relevant to emissions, banks, and bonds.

——— ed. Córdoba: ciudad y provincia, siglos XVI-XX, según relatos de viajeros y otros testimonios. See item 3301.

3865. Sofer, Eugene F. Invisible walls: Jewish residential patterns in Gran Buenos Aires: 1890-1947. N.Y., New York Univ., Center for Latin American and Caribbean Studies, 1977. 36 p., maps, tables (Occasional papers 26)

Argues cogently, based on primary and secondary sources, that Jewish Ghetto existed in B.A. and that it changed in conformity to patterns found elsewhere. Provocative article.

3866. —— **and Mark D. Szuchman.** Educating immigrants: voluntary associations in the acculturation process (*in* La Belle, Thomas J. *ed.* Educational alternatives in Latin America. Los Angeles, Univ. of California, Latin American Center Publications, 1975, p. 334-359)

Fine comparative study of two associations, one of French immigrants in Córdoba and Jewish one in B.A. Shows how differing goals of leaders, social constituencies, and relations with state shaped each association and, therefore, acculturation process of immigrant groups.

3867. Solari, Juan Antonio. Francisco Cúneo: un obrero socialista en el Parlamento Argentino. B.A., Editorial Afirmación, 1975. 109 p., plates.

Sympathetic account by fellow Socialist who lived many of the events in question.

3868. ——. José Ingenieros en las jornadas fundadoras del Partido Socialista. B.A., Editora La Vanguardia, 1976. 34 p., plate.

Short pamphlet based on newspaper articles about Ingenieros' early days in Socialist Party.

3869. ——. Recuerdos y anécdotas socialistas. B.A., Editorial La Vanguardia, 1976. 276 p.

Short sketches by long-time Socialist Party militant of his life and times. Includes sections on Juan B. Justo, Nicolás Repetto, Enrique del Valle Ibarlucea, Alfredo L. Palacios, Mario Bravo, Enrique Dickmann, José Ingenieros, Carlos Sánchez Viamonte. Covers from Party's founding through last decades.

3870. ——. La Vanguardia: su trayectoria histórica: hombres y luchas. B.A., Editorial Afirmación, 1974. 44 p.

Reminiscences about Socialist newspaper by long-time party leader told through brief sketches about people close to the publication.

3871. Stahringer de Caramuti, Ofelia I. La política migratoria Argentina. B.A., Ediciones Depalma, 1975. 139 p., bibl., maps, tables.

Brief resumé of Argentine immigration from colonial times to present. Touches colonization, immigration and urbanization, legal aspects, etc. Mostly summary.

3872. Szuchman, Mark D. The limits of the melting pot in urban Argentina: marriage and integration in Córdoba, 1869-1909 (HAHR, 57:1, Feb. 1977, p. 24-50, tables)

Persuasively attacks "melting pot" thesis for Córdoba and suggests that similar patterns prevailed in other cities during period. Shows that non-Argentines predominantly married non-Argentines through first generation and also indicates that upward mobility through marriage was restricted phenomenon limited to upper-status persons.

3873. Tejerina Carreras, Ignacio G. Los Peñaloza y sus ramas cordobesas. Presentación de Alejandro Moyano Aliaga. Córdoba, Arg., Centro de Estudios Genealógicos de Córdoba, 1974. 35 p.

Covers branches of family in 18th and 19th centuries. Based on archival data.

3874. Terzaga, Alfredo. Historia de Roca. De soldado federal a Presidente de la República. t. 1/2. B.A., A. Peña Lillo Editor, 1976. 2 v. (346, 264 p.) bibls. (Col. Biblioteca de estudios americanos. Serie, 11)

First two installments of unfortunately never completed life-and-times study due to author's death in 1974. Leans towards revisionist interpretation and covers period up to Roca's presidential inauguration in 1880.

3875. *Todo Es Historia.* Años 9/10, Nos. 104/109, enero/junio 1976- B.A.

Continuation of popular series under editorship of Félix Luna. Major articles of most interest to historians are listed below. Also includes material on letters and culture. Issue No. 104, Jan. 1976: Ricardo Mercado Luna "Rioja 1913: la Revolución de Don Pelagio [B. Luna]" and Roberto I. Bader "Banco de la Provincia de Buenos: Mucho Más que un Banco." Issue No. 105, Feb. 1976: Carlos Páez de la Torre "Octaviano Vera: el Tucumano Radical," Carlos Marichal "Los Ferrocarriles Franceses en la Argentina," and Juan Carlos Torre "La CGT y el 17 de Octubre de 1945" (see *HLAS 38:3869*). Issue No. 107, April 1976: Juan Carlos Vedoya "Los Usurpadores de las Malvinas," Diana Hernando Ling "Linajes y Política" (interesting study of leading families and their common characteristics) and Antonio Emilio Castello "Caa-Guazú: la Gloria Efímera." Issue No. 108, May 1976 consists of three articles on 1930s: Horacio Sanguinetti "Política y Estado," Leandro de Sagastizábal "Economía y Sociedad," and Rodolfo H. Gerrano "Ideología y Cultura." Issue No. 109, June 1976: Miguel Bravo Tedín "Tribulaciones de un Comerciante en las Guerras Civiles."

3876. Troncoso, Rosa Coralia. Santa Fé y la guerra contra el imperio brasileño. Paraná, Arg., n.p., 1973. 34 p.

Argues that in 1822-28 and despite enormous social, political and economic difficulties, Santa Fé defended Argentine national interests against Brazilian designs. Includes documentary appendix.

3877. Van Steenberghe de Dourmont, Roberto. Ensayo sobre la encuadernación en Córdoba. Córdoba, Arg., Ministerio de Educación y Cultura [and] Junta Provincial de Historia de Córdoba, 1973. 109 p., bibl., plates.

History of book trade in Córdoba through centuries.

3878. Vedoya, Juan Carlos. Argentina rica, con veda y sin plata: Pacto Roca-Runciman. B.A., Editorial Marlona, 1974. 96 p., bibl., plates, tables (Col. Figuras, 3)

Series of essays on Roca-Runciman Pact, Central Bank, and monetary policy in 1920s and 1930s. In general, attacks foreign capitalist influences and defends Yrigoyen in particular along with those who opposed foreign interests in 1930s.

3879. ———. Mosconi: el petróleo y los trusts. B.A., Editorial Lañon, 1974. 94 p., maps, plates, tables (Col. Libertad, 1)

Brief background history of exploitation and laws covering Argentine petroleum industry, followed by examination of Mosconi's efforts between 1922-30 to formulate a nationalist petroleum policy. Lack of documentation weakens presentation.

3880. Waidatt Herrera, Domingo. El perfil auténtico e histórico de una mujer predestinada: documental histórico. B.A., Talleres Gráficos Lucania, 1974. 61 p., plates.

Tribute to María Estela Martínez de Perón.

3881. Walter, Richard J. The Socialist Party of Argentina: 1890-1930. Austin, Univ. of Texas, Institute of Latin American Studies, 1977. 284 p., bibl., tables (Latin American monographs, 42)

Documents party's development during its most prolific period. Centers on political activities of key figures, e.g., Justo, Bravo, Dickmann, Palacios and Repetto, and their continuity within party. Attempts to explain party's inability to capture consistent labor support and to offset Radical successes. Appendix provides data on registered voters in 1918 in federal capital, by electoral district and by profession. Walter's conclusions include update of party activities after 1930. Useful chronological study. [J.R. Hébert]

3882. Whitaker, Arthur P. The United States and the southern cone: Argentina, Chile, and Uruguay. Cambridge, Mass., Harvard Univ. Press, 1976. 464 p., bibl., maps (The American foreign policy library)

Well-known historian of Latin America and Argentina presents national histories, draws comparisons between nations of Southern Cone, and examines relationships between each country and US. Cast in essentially conservative mold, material does provide useful summary.

3883. Williams, Glyn. The desert and the dream: a study of Welsh colonization in Chubut, 1865-1915. Cardiff, U.K., Univ. of Wales Press, 1975. 230 p., bibl., maps, plates, tables.

Probably the definitive history of Welsh colonization in Chubut written from Welsh perspective. Explores conditions in Wales during 19th century, discusses history of Patagonia prior to arrival of Welsh and then details colony's history in multiple aspects. Concludes that desire to promote and retain cultural unity and identity led most Welsh to Argentina, but that gradually economic forces induced slow process of assimilation. Also notes substantial contributions of Welsh to area in particular and Argentina in general.

3884. ———. La emigración galesa a la Patagonia: 1865-1915 (JGSWGL, 13, 1976, p. 239-292, illus., maps)

Detailed study of Welsh in Patagonia showing interaction between conditions in Wales which led to emigration and those in Argentina which influenced its flow. Conclusion that Welsh case is special one based on convincing evidence. For author's definitive study of subject, see item 3883.

3885. Wilner, Norberto. La recuperación de la historia: la visión justicialista. B.A., Cimarrón Librería Editorial, 1975. 94 p.

Brief exposition of peronist ideology from its roots in Locke, Artigas, Hegel, and Marx to present day. Will not satisfy those wishing a clearer exposition of Justicialismo. Also discusses Third Worldism, national revolution, and social revolution.

Ygobone, Aquiles D. Viajeros científicos a la Patagonia durante los siglos XVIII y XIX. See item 3309.

3886. Zalduendo, Eduardo A. Libras y rieles: las inversiones británicas para el

History: Spanish South America, 19th and 20th Centuries, Paraguay / 303

desarrollo de los ferrocarriles en Argentina, Brasil, Canadá e India durante el siglo XIX. B.A., Editorial El Coloquio, 1975. 595 p., maps, tables.

Major study in comparative economic history on role of British capital and technology in developing railroads in Argentina, Brazil, Canada, and India from 1850-1900. Set within traditional economic terms, study argues pragmatically that railroad development benefitted countries involved and that, given historical moment, no alternatives existed that would have produced similar results. Argentine section appears somewhat more detailed than others, no doubt due to author's familiarity with this country. Text is studded with charts, diagrams, maps, and figures which present wealth of material.

3887. Zarza, Idalia Flores G. de. Juan Bautista Alberdi y la defensa del Paraguay en la Guerra contra la Triple Alianza. Prólogo por Enrique de Gandía. B.A., n.p., 1976. 420 p., bibls., fold plates, plate.

Based on thesis from National Univ. of B.A., concentrates upon Alberdi's defense of Paraguay during 1864-70 war. Primary and secondary sources include lengthy documentary section containing letters and articles of Alberdi on Paraguay. Concludes that Alberdi's position on Paraguay derived from authentically pro-Argentine motives.

3888. Zuleta Alvarez, Enrique. El nacionalismo argentino. t. 1/2. B.A., Ediciones La Bastilla, 1975. 881 p. (Continuous pagination) (Serie Jaque al rey)

Monumental attempt to present development of nationalist ideas in Argentina from 19th century to present. Concentrates on 1930 onwards. Includes at least brief coverage of every major nationalist school as well as individuals who have written on subject. Valuable historiographical work and interesting interpretation of Argentina's past, present and future.

PARAGUAY

3889. Al'perovich, Moisei Samuilovich. Revoliutsiia i diktatura v Paragvae: 1810-1840 (Revolution and dictatorship in Paraguay: 1810-1840). Moscow, Izdatel'stvo Nauka, 1975. 390 p.

Detailed Soviet study of Paraguay under Dr. Francia, based on wide use of both primary and secondary materials. Emphasis is placed on his positive accomplishments. Author is one of deans of Soviet Latin Americanists. [R.V. Allen]

3890. Alvarez, Raúl and others. El P. Antonio Ruiz de Montoya: su vida y su obra. Posadas, Arg., Instituto Superior del Profesorado Antonio Ruiz de Montoya, Depto. de Historia, 1974. 103 p.

Six essays by students from Dept. of History Seminar of Instituto Superior del Profesorado A.R. de Montoya on work of Padre Montoya in reducciones of Paraguay.

3891. Arad, Irene S. de. La ganadería en el Paraguay: período 1870-1900 (CPES/RPS, 10:28, sept./dic. 1973, p. 183-223, tables)

Solid summary article on recovery of livestock after 1870. Covers exports, internal consumption, and growth of large land-holdings by state.

3892. Ayala Queirolo, Víctor. Paz del Chaco: período 15 julio 1935- 21-1-1936: gestión Dr. Gerónimo Zubizarreta. v. 1, Gerónimo Zubizarreta: su actuación en la Conferencia de Paz. Asunción, Editorial Casa-Libro, 1976. 342 p., fold. map, table.

Concentrates on Chaco War peace proceedings and especially on exchange of prisoners. States that Paraguayan proposal on exchange failed due to cost of continued mobilization and due to external pressures. Exchange on Bolivian time-table, however, worked out fairly to both sides.

3893. Balbuena Rojas, Dionisio. Sucesos inéditos de la Batalla de El Carmen. Asunción, Dirección de Publicaciones de las Fuerzas Armadas de la Nación, 1976. 270 p., bibl., plates.

Veteran of Chaco War writes about battle he took part in and sees it as major turning point of war. Uses some Bolivian sources. Mostly military history.

Bejarano, Ramón César. Estudio de un Pacto de No Agresión entre Bolivia y Paraguay: Pitiantuta, cronología. See *HLAS 39:8794*.

3894. Bordón, F. Arturo. Historia política del Paraguay: era constitucional. t. 1. Asunción, Orbis, 1976. 302 p.

Somewhat schematic but detailed history. Contains lengthy documentary section.

3895. Cardozo, Efraim. Hace cien años: crónica de la Guerra de 1864-1870, publicadas en *La Tribuna* de Asunción en el centenario de la epopeya nacional. v. 8, 1 de enero de 1868 a 31 de mayo de 1868. Asunción, Ediciones EMASA, 1976. 428 p.

Continuation of series reviewed in *HLAS 30:2347a*, *HLAS 34:2871a*, and *HLAS 36:3359*. This portion covers 1 Jan. 1868 to 31 May 1868 and consists, like others of articles published in *La Tribuna* of Asunción, as part of journalistic recreation of Paraguayan War.

3896. Chartrain, François. Causes de la Guerre du Chaco: elements de jugement (UTIEH/C, 14, 1970, p. 97-123, bibl.)

Study of origins of Chaco War that concentrates on issue of Standard Oil's involvement. After examining other relevant factors, concludes that war would have broken out with or without that issue, but notes that US did little to stop conflict.

3897. ———. El mundo del trabajo en Paraguay entre 1870 y 1936: reflexiones sobre el estudio histórico (CPES/RPS, 10:27, mayo/agosto 1973, p. 93-100)

Short exposition on possibilities for writing more complete history of Paraguay in this period, one that would include majority (urban and rural workers) not just minority (ruling elites).

3898. Encina, Eulogio. Por la senda del honor y del coraje. Asunción, Dirección de Publicaciones de las Fuerzas Armadas de la Nación, 1975. 153 p., plates.

Memoirs of participant in Chaco War.

3899. Fernández, Carlos José. La guerra del Chaco. v. 6, El final de la lucha: Ybybobo, Villa Montes, Charagua, Ingavi, Armisticio, del 28 noviembre de 1934 al 14 de junio de 1935. Asunción, Imprenta Militar de Dirección de Publicaciones de las Fuerzas Armadas de la Nación, 1976. 279 p., maps, tables.

Final volume of lengthy war history by ex-Commander of Paraguayan Army's I Corps. Based on war diaries, but mostly summary and chronology (for previous vols. see *HLAS 26:1165*, *HLAS 32:2701a*, and *HLAS 36:3364*).

3900. Ferreira, Arnaldo Amado. Um fato histórico esclarecido: Marechal Francisco Solano López (IHGSP/R, 70, 1973, p. 365-376)

Examines in detail question of how López died.

3901. Franco, Victor I. La sanidad en la Guerra contra la Triple Alianza. Asunción, Círculo Paraguayo de Médicos, 1976. 96 p., bibl., plates.

Conference held in 1975 contains names of doctors, hospitals, and information on medical problems encountered during Paraguayan War.

3902. González, Antonio E. Tríptico del Chaco: la guerra, el hombre, la paz. Prólogo de Francisco Pérez-Maricevich. Asunción, Ediciones Comuneros, 1977. 306 p., bibl., maps.

Socio-historical essay on war stressing sociological factors inherent in formation of Paraguayan people that helped conduct this war. Also includes similar analysis for Bolivia.

3903. Guanes, Alejo H. Verde olivo!!: reflexiones de un lisiado de guerra. Asunción, The Author, 1975. 62 p.

Somewhat wandering narrative about years leading up to Chaco War, author's experiences in that war and aftermath.

3904. Kahle, Günther. Österreich-Ungarn und Paraguay: 1847-1918 (OLI/ZLW, 11, 1976, p. 5-19)

Historical sketch of diplomatic relations between Austro-Hungarian Empire and Paraguay from 1847 to 1918. Empire recognized Paraguay in order to support monarchy in Brazil and strengthen resistance to spread of democratic ideas in South America.

3905. Méndez Fleytas, Epifanio. Lo histórico y lo antihistórico en el Paraguay: carta a los colorados. B.A., Artes Gráficas Negri, 1976. 367 p., facsims., illus.

Rambling partisan account of recent Paraguayan history by leader-in-exile of anti-Stroessner wing of Colorado Party. Discusses origins of movement, its development, and also discusses links to peronism, CIA, etc.

3906. Mondain, Pierre. Un conflit oublié: la Guerre du Paraguay contre la Triple Alliance: 1864-1870 (PUF/RH, 520, oct./dec. 1976. p. 385-418)

General survey of causes and conduct of war.

3907. O'Leary, Juan Emiliano. El Paraguay en la unificación argentina. La Guerra de la Triple Alianza. Asunción, Instituto Colorado de la Cultura, 1976. 521 p. (Biblioteca clásicos colorados, 4)

Re-edition of two works published in 1924 and 1911 by Paraguayan "revisionist" historian and writer. They represent some of first attempts to de-vilify Francisco Solano López.

3908. Parola, Luis. Historia contemporánea de la Compañía de Jesús en el Paraguay: 1927-1969. Asunción, Ediciones Loyola, 1973. 608 p., plates. table.

Detailed place-by-place summary of Jesuits' work in Paraguay. Includes documentary section and brief historical introduction. Documents date from 19th century onwards.

3909. Plá, Josefina. The British in Paraguay: 1850-1870. Translated from the Spanish by Brian Charles MacDermot. Oxford, U.K., Oxford Univ., St. Anthony's College. 1976. 277 p., bibl., fold. map, tables.

This monograph details activities of British, most of them contract personnel. Discusses their roles in: metallurgy, shipyards, arsenals, military, medical services, public works, railways, and building. Generally shows that foreigners, and in particular, English provided much of technical expertise in Francia's and López' modernization and war programs. Based on archival research and includes documentary material.

3910. Ramos, R. Antonio. Falsedades en la historia del Dr. José Gaspar Rodríguez de Francia. Asunción, n.p., 1975. 31 p.

Text of conference given at Academia Paraguaya de la Historia roundly defending Francia from his detractors. Deals specifically with foreign relations and founding of modern-day Paraguay.

3911. ———. La independencia del Paraguay y el imperio del Brasil. Prólogo de José Antonio Soares de Souza. Rio, Conselho Federal de Cultura [and] Instituto Histórico e Geográfico Brasileiro, 1976. 586 p.

Copiously documented study on establishment of Paraguayan independence and gradual recognition of that country by other nations ending in 1850s. Documents Brazil's role in this process as friendly neighbor and anti-Rosas force.

3912. Recalde A., Sergio. Crónica de un estirpe prócer. Asunción, Orbis, 1976. 298 p., tables.

Genealogical and historical study of Recalde family from colonial times through 1920s, but concentrating on 20th century and family's role in national politics and especially Revolution of 1904.

3913. Riquelme García, Benigno. El Ejército de la Epopeya. t. 1/2. Prólogo de Leandro Prieto Yegros. Asunción, Ediciones Cuadernos Republicanos, 1976-1977. 2 v. (401 p.) (Continuous pagination) illus.

Military history. Consists of short biographies of officers who served in Paraguayan War; several chapters on diverse aspects of army and war such as clergy who participated, decorations, names of sergeants, etc.; more short biographies; some studies of institutions like telegraph and railroad and foundry; women at home; and war diary.

3914. Rolón, Raimundo. Guerra del Chaco: 1932-1935, el bautismo de fuego de la artillería paraguaya en Boquerón, Boquerón 40 años después. Asunción, Dirección de Publicaciones de las Fuerzas Armadas, Talleres de la Imprenta Militar, 1975. 95 p., maps.

Paraguayan artillery officers' personal account of Battle of Boquerón. Includes some documents.

3915. Saldívar, Julio P.M. Guerra del Chaco: 1932-1935; Yrendague y otros episodios de la Guerra del Chaco. Asunción, Dirección de Publicaciones de las Fuerzas Armadas, Talleres de la Imprenta Militar, 1975. 128 p., plates.

Participant recalls deeds of Regimiento Batallón 40, in 1934-35.

3916. Salum-Flecha, Antonio. Historia diplomática del Paraguay de 1869 a 1938. Asunción, Editorial EMASA, 1972. 215 p., bibl., maps.

Brief descriptive history of Paraguay's foreign relations almost exclusively dedicated to border questions and commercial treaties.

3917. Samaniego, Marcial. El Chaco paraguayo: conferencia pronunciada a los Alumnos del Colegio Nacional de Guerra. Asunción, Imprenta Militar, 1976. 95 p., maps, tables.

Describes area and its development since Chaco War.

3918. Sánchez Domínguez, Enrique. La rendición del Tcnel. Marzana en Boquerón. Asunción, Imprenta Militar, 1976. 38 p., facsims., fold. map, maps.

Short exposition and chronology of military campaign leading to fall of Boquerón.

3919. Tjarks, Germán O.E. Nueva luz sobre el origen de la Guerra de la Triple Alianza (UNCR/R, 1:1, 1975, p. 21-85, bibl.)

Lengthy and copiously documented article, largely based on materials from Elizalde Archives. Argues that Paraguayan War of 1865 must be seen within context of Liberal ideology of times which cemented bonds between partners of Triple Alliance.

3920. Trías, Vivian. El Paraguay: de Francia, El Supremo, a la Guerra de la Triple Alianza. B.A., Crisis, 1975. 79 p., plates (Cuadernos de crisis, 19)

Argues that the two López' demonstrated that a successful independent development model could work and that only war crushed it. Concludes that then, as now, continental unity is a necessary concomitant to liberation.

3921. Vázquez, José Antonio. El Doctor Francia visto y oído por sus contemporáneos. Prólogo de Jorge Abelardo Ramos. B.A., EUDEBA, 1975. 420 p., plates (Iberoamérica en la historia)

Collection of 465 short pieces preceded by introductory essay consisting of observations about Dr. Francia.

3922. Vittone, Luis. Dos siglos de política nacional: siglos XIX-XX, aspectos y episodios sobresalientes. Asunción, Imprenta Militar de la Dirección de Publicaciones de las Fuerzas Armadas de la Nación, 1975. 621 p., bibl., plates.

Colorado Party and armed forces member presents his vision of Paraguay from founding of Asunción to mid-1970s. Primarily political history with some social and cultural commentary.

3923. Williams, John Hoyt. Foreign técnicos and the modernization of Paraguay: 1840-1870 (UM/JIAS, 19:2, May 1977, p. 233-257, bibl.)

Solid article, based on primary sources, about foreign contributions to Paraguayan development in period. Most of these efforts, however lay in areas related to military strength, not in agriculture or general industry. Also, notes growing presence of foreigners in small middle sectors. Finally shows how almost everything that foreigners built was destroyed by war.

3924. ———. Observations on the Paraguayan census of 1846 (HAHR, 56:3, Aug. 1976, p. 424-437, tables)

Includes several interesting observations: that black population probably was lower than previously supposed, and that, if this census is nearly accurate, population of Paraguay at outbreak of 1864 War was far less than has been assumed.

———. Paraguay's historical resources: pt. 1, Paraguay's National Archives. See item 3091.

Zarza, Idalia Flores G. de. Juan Bautista Alberdi y la defensa del Paraguay en la Guerra contra la Triple Alianza. See item 3887.

URUGUAY

Anastasia, Luis V. Pedro Figari, americano integral. See item 9493.

3925. Arismendi, Rodney. Obras escogidas. t. 1. B.A., Perspectiva, 1975. 511 p.

Writings by Uruguay's leading Communist Party intellectual. Includes essays on contemporary Latin America and Uruguay. Also selections on Lenin, Marxism-Leninism, and theory of guerrilla warfare.

3926. Barrán, José Pedro. Apogeo y crisis del Uruguay pastoril y caudillesco: 1838-1875. Montevideo, Ediciones de la Banda Oriental, 1974. 144 p., bibl. (Historia uruguaya, 4) See item 3931.

3927. ——— and Benjamín Nahum. Historia rural del Uruguay moderno. v. 5, La prosperidad frágil, 1905-1914; v. 6, La civilización ganadera bajo Batlle, 1905-1914. Montevideo, Ediciones de la Banda Oriental, 1977. 2 v. (183, 487 p.) tables.

Continuation of major study which maintains high standards set by previous volumes (see *HLAS 32:2718a, HLAS 34:2885* and *HLAS 36:3387b*). Vol. 5 looks at modernization of export sectors and ties of dependency that bound Uruguay. Vol. 6 examines "triumph of the frigorífico" and foreign penetration of that sector. Concludes that traditional society, despite Batlle's reforms, maintained its positions preventing any profound structural changes.

3928. Barrios Pintos, Aníbal. Lavalleja: la patria independiente. Montevideo, Ediciones de la Banda Oriental, 1976. 133 p., bibl., facsims., illus., maps, tables (Historia uruguaya, 2. Serie Los hombres, 2)

Series of biographies designed for popular consumption. Most are useful summaries, particularly for those unfamiliar with 19th-century Uruguayan history. In general, they avoid extreme interpretations. Documentary sections and chronologies are included. For other works in this series see items 3929, 3941-3942, 3948, and 3953.

History: Spanish South America, 19th and 20th Centuries, Uruguay / 307

3929. Canessa de Sanguinetti, Marta. Rivera: un oriental liso y llano. Montevideo, Ediciones de la Banda Oriental, 1976. 124 p., bibl., facsims., illus. (Historia uruguaya, 2. Serie Los hombres, 3)

See item 3928.

3930. Castellanos, Alfredo R. Aparicio Saravia: el caudillo y su tiempo. Montevideo, Arca Editorial, 1975. 145 p. (Bolsilibro Arca, 100)

Short historical sketch concentrating on years 1893 to 1904. Mostly sympathetic.

3931. ———. La Cisplatina, la independencia y la República Caudillesca: 1820-1838. Montevideo, Ediciones de la Banda Oriental, 1974. 124 p., bibl. (Historia uruguaya, 3)

Series entitled *Historia uruguaya* is designed for popular consumption or beginning history students and concisely summarizes basic political and economic developments of Uruguayan society. Vol. 4 (see item 3926) and vol. 5 (see item 3943), however, pay more attention to social and cultural events. Some topics are neglected as, for example, in vol. 5 (item 3943) which dismisses growing labor movement in less than one page. Nevertheless, most of them contain useful summary data and tables.

3932. ———. *ed.* La Cruzada de los 33: textos originales. Montevideo, Editorial Salamandra, 1975. 36 p.

Consists of 13 documents by or about the 33 individuals who began movement for Uruguayan independence from Brazil in 1825.

3933. Cigliuti, Carlos Walter. Vida de Don Tomás Berreta: las opciones de la democracia. Montevideo, Imprenta Rosgal, 1975. 217 p.

Biography of citizen and politician from Canelones who as follower of Batlle, held numerous local and national offices including Deputy, Senator, and until his death in 1947, President of the Republic. Favorable account which unfortunately lacks footnotes or other scholarly apparatus.

3934. Faraone, Roque. Introducción a la historia económica del Uruguay: 1825-1973. Montevideo, Arca Editorial, 1974. 178 p. (Bolsilibro Arca, 97)

Overview for non-expert. Strongest on period before 1938. Includes glossary of economic terms.

3935. Fernández Cabrelli, Alfonso. Coronel Latorre: su gobierno, su obra, su final. n.p., Ediciones Grito de Asencio, 1975. 139 p. (Serie raíces, 10)

Somewhat disconnected series of writings which generally defend Latorre's actions concerning problem of strong government in 1870s. Contains various historiographical references to those who have written about Latorre.

3936. García, Flavio A. *ed.* and *comp.* Los acontecimientos de 1825 en la Provincia Oriental a través de la prensa rioplatense: presentación, selección periodística. t. 1/2. Montevideo, Comisión Nacional de Homenaje del Sesquicentenario de los Hechos Históricos de 1825, 1976. 2 v. (596 p.) (Continuous pagination) facsims., map, table.

Vol. 1 includes brief historical account of period 1821-25, short section on major newspapers of time, chronology of events and selection of articles from newspapers through July 1925. Vol. 2 continues newspaper selections through Feb. 1826.

3938. Herrera, Luis Alberto. La misión Ponsomby (sic). v. 1/2. Introducción de Jorge Abelardo Ramos. B.A., EUDEBA, 1974. 2 v. (429, 296 p.) (Col. Iberoamérica en la historia)

Re-edition of work originally published 1930 by leading Blanco politician. Interpretation is favorable to Ponsonby and British diplomacy in creation of Uruguay as sovereign state. Vol. 2, contains translations of correspondence between main diplomatic protagonists. Introductory note sets volumes in revisionist perspective.

3939. Hirst, Lloyd. Britons at Maldonado. Montevideo, Ediciones Géminis, 1975. 149 p., map, tables (Col. Novus orbis)

Retired British naval officer writes about British activities in River Plate from Drake to "Battle of the River Plate" in which he took part. Also discusses, in general, role of British in area.

Isola, Ema. La esclavitud en el Uruguay desde sus comienzos hasta su extinción: 1843-1852. See item 3279.

3940. Jacob, Raúl. El Uruguay en la crisis de 1929: algunos indicadores económicos. Montevideo, Fundación de Cultura Universitaria (FCU), 1977. 92 p., tables.

Brief commentary with statistical indicators on: foreign commerce, agriculture, banks, industry, finance, foreign debt, real property, production, etc.

3941. Lockhart, Washington. Leandro Gómez: la defensa de la soberanía. Montevideo, Ediciones de la Banda Oriental, 1977. 116 p., bibl., illus. (Historia uruguaya, 2. Serie Los hombres, 6)

See item 3928.

3942. ———. Venancio Flores: un caudillo trágico. Montevideo, Ediciones de la Banda Oriental, 1976. 110 p., bibl., illus. (Historia uruguaya, 2. Serie Los hombres, 5)

See item 3928.

3943. Méndez Vives, Enrique. El Uruguay de la modernización: 1876-1904. Montevideo, Ediciones de la Banda Oriental, 1975. 129 p., bibl., tables (Historia uruguaya, 5)

See item 3931.

3944. Meregalli, Jaime and **Carlos Leonel Bernasconi.** Aportes para la historia de la Fuerza Aérea Uruguaya. Montevideo, Imprenta Nacional, 1974. 727 p., plates, tables.

Chronology, documents, and biographies of nationals and foreigners who helped develop Uruguayan aviation from its early pioneers to recent US military missions. Index by names.

3945. Pintos Carbajal, Mireya. La presencia de la Cruzada Lavallejista en la prensa porteña de 1825 (UBN/R, 10, sept. 1975, p. 51-143, plates)

Brief historical introduction followed by reproduction of articles from *El Argos, El Piloto, El Argentino, El Nacional* and *El Mensajero Argentino* which allows for detailed study of events in Banda Oriental between May and Dec. 1825.

3946. ——— comp. Bibliografía y fuentes relativas al año 1825. Montevideo, Ediciones del Sesquicentenario de los Hechos Históricos de 1825, Biblioteca Nacional, Depto. de Investigaciones, Sección de Historia Uruguaya, 1975. 76 p.

Includes listing of foreign and national books and periodicals.

3947. *Revista Histórica*. Museo Histórico Nacional. Año 69, t. 47, nos. 139/141, nov. 1975- . Montevideo.

Consists of three issues bound in one volume (929 p.). Includes articles by Alfonso Cerda Catalán "La Misión de Jacinto Albístur al Perú en 1865" and Ladislao Szabó "El General José de San Martín y la Presencia de Francia en la Polinesia." Also documents on Alfredo Vázquez Acevedo and "Informes Diplomáticos de los Representantes de España en el Uruguay: 1849."

3948. Reyes Abadie, Washington. Latorre: la forja del estado. Montevideo, Ediciones de la Banda Oriental, 1977. 132 p., bibl., illus. (Historia uruguaya, 2. Serie Los hombres, 9)

See item 3928.

3949. Salterain y Herrera, Eduardo de. Lavalleja: la redención patria. v. 1/2. 2. ed. Montevideo, Comisión Nacional de Homenaje del Sesquicentenario de los Hechos Históricos de 1825, 1975. 2 v. (285, 344 p.)

Re-edition of biography published in 1950s (not annotated in *HLAS*).

3950. Schinca, Milton A. Boulevar Sarandí: 250 años de Montevideo: anécdotas, gentes, sucesos. Montevideo, Ediciones de la Banda Oriental, 1976. 157 p., bibl. (Boulevar Sarandí, 56)

Short sketches and stories dating from end of 19th and early 20th century about this thoroughfare in Montevideo.

3951. Seluja Cecín, Antonio *ed.* and *comp.* Juan Zorrilla de San Martín en la prensa: escritos y discursos. Montevideo, Comisión Nacional de Homenaje del Sesquicentenario de los Hechos Históricos de 1825, 1975. 300 p. (Ediciones del sesquicentenario)

Collection of writings and speeches (1871-1919) of leading personage of period. Divided thematically.

3952. Suárez, Hebert. 25 [i.e. Veinticinco] de agosto: interpretación y compromiso. Montevideo, Talleres Gráficos, 1975. 102 p.

Brief history of the day and laws about it.

3953. Torres Wilson, José A. de. Oribe: el drama del estado oriental. Montevideo, Ediciones de la Banda Oriental, 1976. 118 p., bibl., facsims., illus., map (Historia uruguaya, 2. Serie Los hombres, 4)

See item 3928.

3954. Vico, Horacio J. La Batalla de Sarandí. Montevideo, Comisión Nacional de Homenaje del Sesquicentenario de los Hechos Históricos de 1825, 1975. 152 p., fold., map.

Re-edition of 1937 work. Concentrates primarily upon military aspects and includes short documentary section.

Whitaker, Arthur P. The United States and the southern cone: Argentina, Chile, and Uruguay. See item 3832.

3955. Winn, Peter. British informal empire in Uruguay in the nineteenth century (PP, 73, Nov. 1976, p. 100-126)

Cogently argued piece based on primary materials. Contends that informal empire was both British policy and Latin American reality and that continuity of foreign control was underlying condition of economic and political life in Latin America during 19th century. For author's book on this subject, see item 3956.

3956. ———. El imperio informal británico en el Uruguay en el siglo XIX. Traducción de José de Torres Wilson. Montevideo, Ediciones de la Banda Oriental, 1975. 84 p.

Condensed and revised version of author's dissertation which applies theory of "informal empire" as developed by Ronald Robinson and John Gallagher to 19th-century Uruguayan history. Argues persuasively that such an informal empire did exist.

BRAZIL

COLIN M. MACLACHLAN

Associate Professor of History
Newcomb College, Tulane University

JEAN A. BARMAN

University of British Columbia
Vancouver, Canada

RODERICK J. BARMAN

Associate Professor of History
University of British Columbia
Vancouver, Canada

THE PAST TWO YEARS HAVE BEEN NOTABLE for the volume of material published. The decline of interest in the colonial period has been more than compensated for by the flood of studies on the national period. In part, this growth is due to the professional level attained by history in Brazil. São Paulo remains the center of research, as the innovative and incisive studies on the early Empire by Schorer Petrone (item 4149) and Berrance de Castro (item 4801) attest; but the more modest graduate program at Curitiba, which has concentrated on the socio-demographic history of the state, is also bearing fruit (item 4184). Interest continues not only in historiography as such (item 3999) but in the special relationship in Brazil of the past to the present (items 3989, 4013 and 4121). This concern with relevance is reflected in the strong interest in the Old Republic and Vargas era, and more specifically in the concentration on the themes of crisis, confrontation and disequilibrium (items 4059, 4085, 4088, 4104, 4123 and 4151). Douglas Teixeira Monteiro's study of the Contestado is perhaps the most outstanding (item 4136). Also of interest, particularly for the future of history in Brazil has been the appearance of texts especially designed for student use (items 3981, 4036 and 4151).

The increase in historical materials must, however, be in part attributed to the growing involvement of the state at all levels, national to municipal, in the process of publication. What was first evident as a plethora of works sponsored for the *sesquicentenario* of 1972 now amounts to a considerable if uncoordinated program to subsidize the publication of materials that enhance, or seem to enhance, the national heritage. The most obvious example in the last two years has been the prizes offered for the best works commemorating the centennials of Italian and German immigration into Rio Grande do Sul. If the results have been of predictably uneven quality, they are fascinating in their very diversity, ranging from graphic personal memoirs written in old age (items 4087, 4105 and 5127) to highly synthetic analyses interpreting the place of immigration in the evolution of Brazilian culture (items 4057, 4062 and 4170).

Another result of government encouragement has been the republication of many of the classic studies on Brazil—travel accounts, national and local histories, collected writings, and other works with a seminal impact on Brazilian thought and self-perception. If space does not permit their separate inclusion, certain series should be mentioned. The Univ. of São Paulo in its series entitled "Coleção Reconquista do Brasil" has already reedited some 40 travel accounts; Rio's Instituto de Planejamento Econômico e Social is reprinting classics of economic thought; and Editora Vozes of Petrópolis, under contract with the Ministry of Education and Culture, is republishing seminal essays and histories in the series entitled "Coleção Dimensões do Brasil." In addition, many key 19th-century provincial histories are being reprinted by local academic and cultural institutions.

It is by contrast sad to suggest that scholarship outside Brazil has not kept pace with that in the country, although this probably reflects the general academic crisis in the Anglophone world with Brazil far too often being the dispensable segment of Latin American history. Such an unfortunate development makes it even more important for the *Handbook* to call attention to the significant Brazilian works, while awaiting a revival of energy in the English-speaking world. Certainly, some fine works have appeared, above all John Wirth's outstanding study of Minas Gerais, 1889-1937 (item 4187) and Warren Dean's excellent analysis of a São Paulo coffee area (item 4089). Also, new fields are being probed, as evidenced by two stimulating essays on women's role in turn-of-the-century Brazil (item 4156). Yet it is difficult not to conclude that the cutting edge of scholarship has moved to Brazil.

This development will, however, be incomplete as long as little or nothing is done to remedy the appalling book distribution system which continues to exist in Brazil. To obtain works published in such major centers as São Paulo and Rio demands considerable persistence, while to get sight of publications from the other states is almost impossible. Historians in North America are fortunate indeed that the Library of Congress Office in Brazil collects such a wide range of materials from all parts of the country, that the *Handbook* annotates the most significant of these, and that the Inter-Library Loan System makes them available.

In sum, then, the publications of the past two years suggest that Brazil is finally taking charge of its own history, a development which can only be applauded as signifying the growth of an independent, professional Brazilian scholarship, but one which must be watched, particularly by Brazilians themselves, to the extent that the growth is increasingly subsidized and possibly directed by the judicious application of state funds.

GENERAL

Affonso, João. Três séculos de modas: a propósito do tricentenário da fundação da cidade de Santa Maria de Belém, capital do estado do Grão-Pará. See item 526.

3957. Andrade, Manoel Correira de. Jundiá, um engenho de açucar no Vale do Sirijí (USP/RH, 50 [2]:100, 1974, p. 609-626)

Study of Pernambucan plantation belonging to author's family presents in microcosm history of *zona da mata* since 1809 and reveals complexities within development of a monoculture.

3958. Araújo, Antonio Gomes de. Povoamento do Cariri. Crato, Brazil, Univ. Federal do Ceará, Faculdade de Filosofia do Crato, 1973. 141 p. (Obras do Padre Antonio Gomes de Araújo, 2. Col. Estudos e pesquisas, 6)

Genealogical study by cleric filled with information taken from marriage registers with some brief commentary. Dedicated social historians or demographers interested in Ceará might find it useful. Surprisingly well documented.

3959. Bahia (state), *Brazil.* Conselho Estadual de Cultura. Secretaria de Educação e Cultura. Almanach para a

Cidade da Bahia, anno 1812. Salvador, Brazil, 1973. 264 p.

Facsimile reproduction of almanac or city directory listing information on administrative system, holidays, names of public functionaries, Church and military officials, members of important organizations, lists of local merchants and much more. Actually compiled and published in 1811. Specialist will find it extremely useful.

3960. Bandecchi, Brasil and others. Dicionário de história do Brasil: moral e civismo. 4. ed. São Paulo, Edições Melhoramentos, 1976. 618 p., bibl.

Dictionary listing major historical figures and events. Includes recommended bibliography as well as information on agencies, and their powers under Constitution of 1969. Of use to students, general reader.

3961. Barata, Mário. Poder e independência no Grão-Pará, 1820-1823: gênese, estrutura e fatos de um conflito político. Apresentação de Maria Annunciada Chaves. Belém, Brazil, Conselho Estadual de Cultura, 1975? 246 p. (Col. História do Pará. Série Arthur Vianna)

Thorough narration of political events in Pará during Independence, incorporating frequent excerpts from contemporary primary sources.

Barreto, Abellard *comp*. Bibliografia sul-riograndense: a contribuição portuguesa e estrangeira para o conhecimento e a integração do Rio Grande do Sul. See item 1.

3962. Bartley, Russell H. The inception of Russo-Brazilian relations: 1808-1828 (HAHR, 56:20, May 1976, p. 217-240, table)

Study, makes best use of limited evidence, of the not very significant relations between two countries, both of strategic importance in global terms but both economic dependencies of Europe.

3963. Blaas, Richard. Österreichs Beitrag zur Erforschung Brasiliens: 1814-1848 (OLI/ZLW, 11, 1976, p. 20-39)

Interesting account of Austrian scientific expedition sent to Brazil, 1817-35, consequent on Leopoldina's marriage to Pedro I. Relates separate travel accounts later published by such participants as Spix, Martius, Pohl and Ender to import of whole. Soundly based on Austrian archival sources. Includes Spanish abstract.

3964. Brandão, Wilson de Andrade. História da independência no Piauí. Teresina, Brazil, Companhia Editora do Piauí (COMEPI), 1975? 319 p., bibl.

Readable, well-done general study that places Independence movement in context of general ideas and colonial developments. Of interest to student, general reader.

3965. Buescu, Mircea. Notas sobre o custo da mão-de-obra escrava (UC/V, 31:3, set. 1975, p. 33-44, tables)

Calculations to show that ample supply of slaves made slave labor cheaper than free labor in Brazil. When slave labor became scarce, cost of slave "wages" was driven up to free labor levels.

3966. Camello, Maurílio José de Oliveira. Caraça: centro mineiro de educação e missão, 1820-1830. Belo Horizonte, Brazil, Imprensa Oficial, 1973. 208 p.

Although drawing on school's archives, this study of establishment of Lazarist College in Minas Gerais is too unimaginative and laudatory to be satisfactory. Lengthy appendix of documents.

3967. Congresso de História da Independência do Brasil, *Río, 1972*. Anais. Rio, Instituto Histórico e Geográfico Brasileiro, 1975. 7 v. (336, 349, 352, 361, 362, 340, 205 p.) facsims.

Contains some 60 papers, with supporting documents and historiographical material, presented to congress on 150th anniversary of independence organized by Instituto Histórico e Geográfico Brasileiro. Areas of concentration are: 1) independence in provinces: 2) role of royal family members; 3) contribution of navy and role of military school; 4) attitudes of US and its diplomats; and 5) biographies of individuals of varying importance. Many documents have been previously published and papers are of uneven quality, but volumes are nonetheless useful source of reference on independence period.

3968. Costa, Francisco Augusto Pereira da. Cronologia historica do Estado do Piauí. Rio, Editora Artenova, 1974. 2 v. (212, 597 p.)

New edition of work first published 1909 that presents random information year-by-year (1535-1889). Totally useless index. Work may have some value to dedicated researcher.

3969. ———. A Ordem Carmelitana em Pernambuco. Prefácio de Mauro Mota. Recife, Brazil, Secretaria da Justiça, Arquivo Público Estadual, 1976. 200 p., facsim.

Useful introductory study of order, its Portuguese roots, activity in Brazil, politics, major convents and organizational difficulties. Includes information on third order and its activities. Unfortunately with little indication of sources and no index.

3970. Costa, Joaquim Ribeiro. Conceição do Mato Dentro: fonte da saudade. Belo Horizonte, Brazil, Editora Itatiaia *em convênio com o* Instituto Nacional do Livro (INL), Brasília, 1975. 245 p. (Biblioteca de estudos brasileiros, 10)

Enjoyable if not profound account of religion and folk culture in mining town of northwest Minas Gerais that has not been important since late 18th century.

3971. O debate político no processo da independencia. Introdução de Raymundo Faoro. Rio, Conselho Federal de Cultura, 1973. 106 p., facsims.

Facsimile re-edition of six contemporary pamphlets on issue of independence for Brazil but none of the calibre of Thomas Paine's *Commonsense*. Independence is supported on largely economic grounds and opposed on basis of tradition and morality.

3972. Diégues Júnior, Manuel. O processo da independência em seus aspectos heróicos e suas implicações sociais (UC/V, 31:2, 1975. p. 3-15)

Succinct, sophisticated survey, fairly orthodox in approach, of dynamics of independence in Brazil and effects of nationhood on dominant social elements.

3973. Dietmann, Alfonso. Los brasileiros en la trata de esclavos negro-africanos (UCV/CA, 1:1, 1975, p. 31-47)

Briefly examines historical evolution of African slave trade, notes some socio-cultural consequences and modern day survivals. Of interest to general reader, student; specialist will not encounter anything new.

3974. Duarte, Abelardo. As Alagoas na Guerra da Independência. Maceió, Brazil, Conselho Federal de Cultura [and] Arquivo Público de Alagoas, 1974. 241 p.

Conventional, rather dull study of events in Alagoas, 1817-23. Useful as comprehensive account written from local viewpoint and fairly well-documented.

3975. Ehlke, Cyro. A conquista do Planalto Catarinense: primeira fase; bandeirantes e tropeiros do Sertão de Curitiba. Rio, Editora Laudes, 1973. 193 p., bibl.

Exploration and early development of region of Paraná and Santa Catarina based mostly on secondary sources with occasional refreshing forays into primary archival material. Useful gathering of information of interest to general reader, student.

3976. Ferreira, Arthur. História geral do Rio Grande do Sul: 1503-1974. 4. ed. Porto Alegre, Brazil, Editora Globo, 1974. 285 p., bibl., illus.

Excellent general history that refreshingly notes, without malice, the bad as well as the good, and attempts to present state's past as historical process. Specialists and students will find it enlightening and enjoyable.

3977. Ferrez, Gilberto. Colonização de Teresópolis à sombra do dedo de Deus: 1700-1900, da Fazenda March a Teresópolis. Rio, Minstério da Educação e Cultura, Depto. de Assuntos Culturais, 1970. 146 p. (Publicações do Patrimônio Histórico e Artístico Nacional, 24)

Uneven, but interesting study of city and region drawn from accounts by foreign travelers supplemented with some archival material. Includes useful map, illustrations and excellent photographs.

3978. Freitas, Décio. Insurreições escravas. Revisão de Myrna Bier Appel. Porto Alegre, Brazil, Editora Movimento, 1976. 102 p. (Col. Documentos brasileiros, 11)

Short introductory study, quite intelligently done, of slave uprisings in Bahia, 1807-35.

3979. Frota, José Tupinambá da. História de Sobral. 2. ed. Fortaleza, Brazil, Editora Henriqueta Galeno, 1974. 629 p., illus.

Better-than-average municipal history by Bishop of Sobral. Contains bits and pieces of information to delight heart of dedicated social historian. Inadequate index is of little use and sources are difficult to trace. General reader, specialist.

3980. Gaioso, Raimundo José de Sousa. Compêndio histórico-político dos princípios da Lavoura do Maranhão. Rio, Editora Livros de Mundo Inteiro *sob o patrocínio da* Superintendência do Desenvolvimento do Maranhão (SUDEMA), 1970. 337 p., facsims., tables.

History of discovery and establishment of Maranhão, and of most value, description of region, population including classes, administrative bodies, and economic prospects in late 18th, early 19th century. Formerly difficult to locate, this facsim. ed. of original (Paris, L'Hirondelle, 1818) will delight specialists.

3981. Gasman, Lydinéa *comp*. Documentos históricos brasileiros. Rio, Ministério da Educação e Cultura, Fundação Nacional de Material Escolar, 1976. 302 p., bibl., illus.

Product of experimentation at secondary level presents country's history in selected documents preceded by short introductory statement. Includes useful bibliographical details. Excellent secondary teaching text, well illustrated.

3982. Gomes, Manoel. A Maçonaria na história do Brasil. Rio, Gráfica Editora Aurora, 1976? 138 p., bibl., illus.

Contribution of masonic order to Brazilian history from Tiradentes to religious question to Republic's establishment. Includes list of famous masons. May be of some use to specialists.

3983. Gouvêa, Fernando da Cruz. Oliveira Lima: uma biografia. v. 1/3. Prefácio de Barbosa Lima Sobrinho. Recife, Brazil, Instituto Arqueológico, Histórico e Geográfico Pernambucano *em convênio com o* Ministério da Educação e Cultura, Depto. de Assuntos Culturais, 1976. 3 v. (1787 p.) (Continuous pagination) facsims., plates.

Major and thorough study, based on ample documentation, of leading writer, historian and diplomat of Old Republic.

3984. Humphreys, R.A. Robert Southey and his history of Brazil. London, Hispanic and Luso-Brazilian Council, 1978. 19 p. (Diamante series, 28)

Succinct introduction to Southey and his important, if little read, history of colonial Brazil. Useful for students.

3985. Karasch, Mary C. The African heritage of Rio de Janeiro (*in* Pescatello, Ann M. *ed.* Old roots in new lands: historical and anthropological perspectives on black experiences in the Americas. Westport, Conn., Greenwood Press, 1977. p. 36-76, tables [Contributions in Afro-American and African studies, 31])

Based on travelers' accounts and contemporary records, this close and graphic study of Rio slave society in first half of 19th century makes substantive contribution to literature. Recommended reading for both specialist and student.

3986. Keith, Henry H. and **Robert A. Hayes** *eds.* Perspectives on armed politics in Brazil. Tempe, Arizona State Univ., Center for Latin American Studies, 1976. 258 p., illus., maps, plates, tables.

Series of short, introductory essays on history of military in Brazil. Useful for beginning student in conjunction with other materials. For political scientist's comment, see *HLAS 39:7576*.

3987. Komissarov, Boris N. Pervaia Russkaia ekspeditsiia v Braziliiu (First Russian expedition to Brazil). Leningrad, USSR, Akademiia Nauk SSSR, 1977. 136 p., map, illus. (Seriia "Istoriia nauki i tekhniki")

Definitive study of Russian scientific expedition through Brazil (1821-29) published by Soviet Academy of Sciences of USSR. Particularly interesting for its use of previously undeciphered diary of expedition's leader, G.I. Langsdorff (for more on him see *HLAS 38:3969-3971* and *HLAS 36:3553*).

3988. ———. Russkiie istochniki po istorii Brazilii pervoi treti XIX veka (Russian sources for Brazilian history on first third of 19th century). Leningrad, USSR, Leningradskii Univ., 1977. 168 p.

Definitive survey of Russian archival and published sources on Brazil, 1800-33 (in particular materials from round-the-world voyages, diplomatic and consular missions, and Langsdorff expedition see item 3987). Study so thoroughly analyzes content of data that it provides useful overview of events themselves.

3989. Lapa, José Roberto do Amaral. A história em questão: historiografia brasileira contemporânea. Petrópolis, Brazil, Editora Vozes, 1976. 204 p., bibl., illus.

Proceeding from premise that "the history of Brazil is in a crisis" both of content and of ideological interpretation, author—established historian of São Paulo—examines contemporary Brazilian historiography and analyzes central issues of Brazilian history. Argues for greater self-examination and for a new, fresh approach which discards traditional myths and utilizes conceptual insights of social sciences.

3990. ———. Para uma história da historiografia brasileira (SBPC/CC, 28:6, junho 1976, p. 645-653, bibl.)

Presents basic critical bibliography of Brazil historiography. Useful to specialists and students.

3991. Leonardos, Othon Henry. Geociências no Brasil: contribuição germânica. Prefácio de Aristides Azevedo Pacheco Leão. Rio, Forum Editora, 1973. 345 p., bibl.

Detailed factual account, with much biographical data, of geological and related investigations undertaken by Germans in Brazil from 16th century to present. Excellent bibliography of German and Brazilian sources. Index of names.

3992. Lima, Heitor Ferreira. História do pensamento econômico no Brasil. São Paulo, Companhia Editora Nacional *com a colaboração do* Instituto Roberto Simonsen, 1976. 198 p., tables (Brasiliana, 360)

Short, introductory study of principal trends of Brazilian economic development, identifying main schools of economic thought and their exponents in Brazil.

3993. Loureiro, María Amélia Salgado *comp*. História das universidades. São Paulo, Estrela Alfa Editora, 1975? 510 p., plates.

Contains brief information on leading universities in Europe, North America, Asia, Africa, Oceania and Latin America. Includes essay on modern university, historical survey of higher education in Brazil and information on selected Brazilian universities. Reflects current attitude towards university development.

3994. Martinho, Lenira Menezes. Organização do trabalho e relações sociais nas firmas comerciais do Rio de Janeiro: primeira metade do século XIX (USP/RIEB, 18, 1976, p. 41-62, bibl.)

Despite pedestrian handling of subject, this study contains fascinating data on life of clerks in commercial houses of Rio city, many being Portuguese who came to Brazil aged 10 to 14!

3995. Martins, Antônio Egídio. São Paulo antigo: 1554 a 1910. Edição organizada por Fernando Góes. Prefácio e notas de Byron Gaspar. São Paulo, Secretaria de Cultura, Esportes e Turismo, Conselho Estadual de Cultura, 1973? 423 p. (Col. Historia, 18)

New edition of classic early study of city this time with extensive index. Provides information on important and minor events, structures, institutions, individuals, streets, churches, etc. Of great interest to social and urban historians.

3996. Martins, Wilson. História da inteligência brasileira. v. 1, 1550-1794. São Paulo, Editora Cultrix *com a colaboração da* Editora da Univ. de São Paulo [and] Secretaria de Cultura, Ciência e Tecnologia, 1976. 585 p., facsims., maps, plates.

Vol. 1 of a seven volume set which makes massive contribution to history of Brazilian culture. Perhaps most useful as series of linked essays on all aspects of culture—thought, literature, art, music, etc. Excellent work of reference for further study of topics covered, due to generous incorporation of original sources into text. See also item 7692.

3997. Matos, Odilon Nogueira de. Afonso de Taunay, historiador de São Paulo e do Brasil: perfil biográfico e ensaio bibliográfico. São Paulo, Univ. de São Paulo [and] Fondo de Pesquisas do Museu Paulista, 1977. 267 p., plate (Col. Museu Paulista. Série ensaios, 1)

Useful aid for guiding researchers through the massive output of one of most important if most prolific of traditional Brazilian historians.

3997a. Mattoso, Katia M. Queiróz. Um estudo quantitativo de cultura social: a cidade de Salvador, Bahia de Todos os Santos no século XIX: primeiras abordagens, primeiros resultados (FFCLM/EH, 15, 1976, p. 7-28)

Preliminary attempt to determine, from 100 estate inventories, socioeconomic structure of Salvador, Bahia, in early 19th century. Findings more suggestive than conclusive.

3998. Mauro, Frédéric. Les grands problèmes de l'histoire économique du Brésil (USP/RH, 50[2]:100, 1974, p. 529-542)

Discussion of principal issues of Brazilian economic history. Neither thorough nor original. Disappointing from historian of Mauro's calibre.

3999. Mota, Carlos Guilherme. A historiografia brasileira nos últimos quarenta anos: tentativa de avaliação crítica (SBPC/CC, 27:5, maio 1975, p. 472-486)

Incisive discussion of development of national historiography in Brazil since 1930, written by leading exponent of predominant *marxisant* school. Interesting for conception of history presented as for its information on sources.

4000. Mott, Luiz R.B. Pardos e pretos em Sergipe: 1774-1851 (USP/RIEB, 18, 1976, p. 7-37, tables)

Using wealth of demographic data examines social standing and attitudes towards person of color and blacks. Presents number of interesting tables including one that lists revolts indicating location, author, against what element, and method of suppression. Of interest to specialist.

4001. Museu do Açúcar, *Recife, Brazil.* História social da agro-indústria canavieira. Conferencistas: Manuel Correia de Andrade, Amaro Quintas, Tadeu Rocha, Nilo Pereira, Nelson Saldanha, Costa Porto, Gilberto Freyre, Vamireh Chacon. Recife, Brazil, Instituto do Açúcar e do Alcool, 1974. 127 p.

Series of interpretive essays by well-known authorities that examine socio-cultural impact of sugar from 16th century to modern times. Deals with, among other elements, free and slave labor, patriarchal politics, and attitudes. General reader.

4002. Neves, Abdias. A guerra do Fidié. 2. ed. Rio, Editora Artenova, 1974. 274 p.

Re-edition of well-written narrative, published 1907, of confused political and military events of independence struggle in Piauí, Ceará and Maranhão, 1822-23.

4003. Palacin, Luis and **Maia Augusta de Sant'anna Moraes.** História de Goiás: 1722-1972. Goiânia, Brazil, Univ. Federal de Goiás, 1975. 125 p., plates.

General study, including socioeconomic data, intended for students. Provides useful introduction to region's history for general reader.

4004. Pauli, Evaldo. A fundação de Florianópolis. Florianópolis, Brazil, Indústria Editorial e Gráfica (EDEME), 1973. 162 p., illus.

Well written, in spite of curious use of numbered paragraphs, general survey of founding of municipal center and development of Santa Catarina. Provides basic demographical information, but with little documentation and no index.

4005. Peláez, Carlos Manuel. The establishment of banking institutions in a backward economy: Brazil, 1800-1851 (HU/BHR, 49:4, Winter 1975, p. 446-472, tables)

Based on rather narrow published sources, argues that "free banking" periods were most beneficial to economic growth of Brazil. Omits any consideration of metallic currency and banking partnerships.

4006. Pinto, Luis. Fundamentos da história e do desenvolvimento da Paraíba: 1574-1970. Rio, Editora Leitura, 1973? 281 p.

Gold mine of random information, statistics, biographical data from 1574-1970. Lacks index, thus only for the brave and dedicated.

4007. Porto, Carlos Eugênio. Roteiro do Piauí. Rio, Editora Artenova, 1974. 192 p., illus., maps, tables.

Historical and physical introduction by medical doctor involved in disease control. Best sections deal with matters of public health. First published 1955 now with new material added. Specialist, general reader.

4009. Rebello, Edgardo de Castro. Mauá & outros estudos. Introdução de Francisco de Assis Barbosa. Rio, Livraria São Paulo, 1975. 349 p.

Re-edition of complete works of Castro Rebello. Valuable not because of scholarly depth but for display of skeptical, probing attitude towards orthodoxies of Brazilian history, best demonstrated in debunking of Alberto de Faria's *Mauá* (Rio, 1926).

4010. Rego Neto, Hugo Napoleão do. Fatos da história do Piauí. Rio, APEC Editora, 1974. 181 p.

Yet another regional history devoted to principal events from discovery to present. Includes useful bibliography and index of some interest to general reader.

4011. Reis, Arthur Cesar Ferreira. Economic history of the Brazilian Amazon (*in* Wagley, Charles *ed.* Man in the Amazon [see *HLAS 37:523*] p. 33-44, bibl., tables)

Concise if not profound overview, from traditionalist viewpoint, of Amazon area by region's most eminent historian.

4012. Renault, Delso. Indústria, escravidão, sociedade: uma pesquisa historiográfica do Rio de Janeiro no século XIX. Apresentação de Arthur Cesar Ferreira Reis. Rio, Civilização Brasileira *em convênio com o* Ministério da Educação e Cultura (MEC), Instituto Nacional do Livro (INL), Brasília, 1976. 186 p., bibl., facsim., illus. (Col. Retratos do Brasil, 103)

Separate studies, using newspaper ads, on early industrialization, on extremes of slavery and social customs in Imperial Rio.

4013. Rodrigues, José Honório. Os estudos brasileiros e os "Brazilianists" (USP/RH, 54:107, julho/set. 1976, p. 189-219)

Survey of apparatus of Brazilian studies existing in North America and elsewhere. Emphasizes fear that Brazilians are losing control of their history and national heritage to foreigners.

4014. Santos, Paulo Rodrigues dos. Tupaiulândia: Santarém. v. 1/2. Belém, Brazil, Imprensa Oficial do Estado, 1971? 2 v. (251, 172 p.)

Useful study of important upriver urban center from its humble beginnings to early part of present century. Compiles much random information, such as listing its newspaper and known dates of publication, that will please dedicated social or urban historian. Unfortunately lacks index.

4015. Santos, Silvio Coelho dos. Nova história de Santa Catarina. Florianópolis, Brazil, The Author, 1974. 124 p., bibl., maps, plates.

Short elementary account of Santa Catarina and its development, with good maps, and photos. Intended to arouse popular pride in state and its heritage.

4016. Santos Filho, Lycurgo de Castro. História geral da medicina brasileira. v. 1. São Paulo, Editora de Humanismo, Ciência e Tecnologia (HUCITEC), *com a colaboração da Editora da Univ. de São Paulo,* 1977. 436 p., facsims., plates.

Study of development of all types, and not simply European, medicine in Brazil. Although based largely on printed materials, probably best work available on subject.

4017. Stepan, Nancy. Beginnings of brazilian science: Oswaldo Cruz, medical research and policy, 1890-1920. N.Y., Science History Publications, 1976. 225 p., bibl., plates, table.

Clear, succinct introduction to science and medicine in Brazil centering on Oswaldo Cruz Institute and its work against disease. Enjoyable and useful reading for both student and specialist.

4018. Tavares, Luis Henrique Dias. História da Bahia. Salvador, Brazil, Univ. Federal de Bahia, 1974. 257 p., bibl., maps.

Short history of Bahia from discovery through Revolution of 1964. Presents much interesting, but relatively unconnected information. Sources are clearly indicated, and useful bibliography is included. Lack of index is partly compensated for by descriptive table of contents. General reader, student.

4019. Tavares-Neto, José and Eliane S. Azevêdo. Racial origin and historical aspects of family names in Bahia, Brazil (WSU/HB, 49:3, Sept. 1977, p. 287-299, bibl., tables)

Survey of 6000 individuals indicates correlation between devotional surnames and Negro admixture, which supports related finding that freed slaves preferred devotional surnames different from master's family name. Stimulating study breaking new ground.

4020. Uchôa, Célia Ribeiro. Cantagalo, cantagalenses e a independência do Brasil. Niterói, Brazil, Lumak, 1973? 124 p., facsims.

Local history filled with poems and biographical information on region's illustrious sons and daughters. Only for most dedicated social historians.

4021. Vianna, Hildegardes. A Bahia: já foi assim, crónicas de costumes. Salvador, Brazil, Editora Itapuã, 1973. 227 p.

Series of vignettes by a well known folklorist that captures flavor of times, popular and traditional customs, old sayings and terms, superstitions, etc. Social historians will find it useful in reconstructing era.

4022. Willeke, Venâncio. Franciscanos no Brasil (VOZES, 69:5, junio/julho 1975, p. 29-38)

Brief, well written history of Rio's Franciscan prov. from 16th century to modern times by well-known specialist in order's history. General reader, student.

4023. ———. Missões franciscanas no Brasil: 1500-1975. Petrópolis, Brazil, Editora Vozes, 1974. 201 p., bibl., maps (Publicações do Centro de Investigação e Divulgação História, 3)

Well documented and indexed study of order's mission system through present. Includes text of many important documents. Provides information on individual missions, general activities, successes and failures. Of use to specialists.

COLONIAL

4024. Alden, Dauril. The significance of cacao production in the Amazon region during the late colonial period: an essay in comparative economic history (APS/P, 120:2, 15 April 1976, p. 103-125, tables)

Translation of *HLAS 38:3935*.

4025. Benites Vinueza, Leopoldo. Los descubridores del Amazonas: la expedición de Orellana. Madrid, Ediciones Cultura Hispánica, 1976. 209 p.

Based on published primary and selected secondary material, study presents vivid picture of Orellana's Amazonian adventure. Of interest to general reader.

4026. Costa, Iraci del Nero da. Análise da morbidade nas Gerais: Villa-Rica, 1799-1801 (USP/RH, 54:107, julho/set. 1976, p. 241-262, tables)

Using existing parish records author demonstrates death rate by race, slave or free, general African origin and cause of death with separate data on infant mortality. Of great interest to specialists.

4027. D'Abbeville, Claude. História da Missão dos Padres Capuchinhos na llha do Maranhão e terras circunvizinhas. Apresentação de Mário Guimarães Ferri. Belo Horizonte, Brazil, Livraria Itatiaia Editora, 1975. 297 p., illus. (Col. Reconquista do Brasil, 19)

Well done new ed. of 1614 study by French friar who accompanied La Ravardiere's 1612 expedition. Serves as primary source for that period. Of interest to specialists.

4028. Dias, Cicero *comp.* Catálogo de documentos referentes ao Brasil. Nota preliminar por José Antônio Soares de Souza. Brasília, Ministério das Relações Exteriores, Comissão de Estudo dos Textos da História do Brasil, 1975. 335 p.

Excellent calendar of some 1600 diplomatic documents concerning Brazil, mostly correspondence, sent by French mission in Lisbon (1665-1774) held in Archives Nationales de France. Thorough, pithy introduction sets events mentioned in documents into larger context of Franco-Luso-Brazilian relations. Work's title does not adequately convey its significance.

4029. Galloway, J.H. Nordeste do Brasil: 1700-1750; reexame de uma crise (IBGE/R, 36:2, abril/junho 1974, p. 85-102, tables)

Decline of old sugar coast is often blamed on discovery of gold that shifted economic center to south-center. Author attempts to assess all the reasons, concludes price of sugar was most important variable. Based on archival sources, presents some data on slave imports in Pernambuco, Paraiba, and Bahia. Of interest to specialists.

4030. Hoornaert, Eduardo. Formação do catolicismo brasileiro: 1550-1800. Petrópolis, Brazil, Editora Vozes, 1974. 140 p. (Publicações Centro de Investigação e Divulgação. História da igreja, 1)

Interesting interpretive study of activities of colonial Church and its adaptation to Brazilian environment, economy and population including slaves and Indians. Concludes work of most value was among Indians. Of interest to general reader, specialist.

4031. Lavradio, Luis de Almeida Soares Portugal Alarcão Eça de Melo, *marquês de.* Cartas do Rio de Janeiro: 1769-1776. v. 1. Rio, Ministério da Justiça, Arquivo Nacional, 1975. 191 p.

Personal letters of viceroy filled with interesting data much of it very minor yet useful to reconstruct times. Unfortunately, index is not analytical. Of interest to specialists.

4032. Lisboa, João Francisco. Crônica do Brasil colonial: apontamentos para a história do Maranhão. Introduções de Peregrino Júnior e Graça Aranha. Petrópolis, Brazil, Editora Vozes *em convênio com o* Ministério da Educação e Cultura, Instituto Nacional do Livro, Brasília, 1976. 631 p., bibl. (Dimensões do Brasil, 2)

Excellent ed. of 19th-century work by journalist and historian written to explain as well as establish Maranhão's own distinct culture through its history. Based on Portuguese archival material including some documents published in part and full. Unfortunately, poor citations will hinder tracing of sources. Two biographical and bibliographical essays place author in context of his time and personality. Of most interest to historian of ideas.

4033. Maranhão, Marcos. O forte dos Reis Magos e a história colonial. n.p., Fundação José Augusto, n.d. 74 p., bibl., illus.

Sketchy history of Rio Grande do Norte as seen from ramparts of fort constructed in 1598 under guidance of then Jesuit, former military architect. Curiously interesting, but of uncertain value. General reader.

4034. Mattos, Florisvaldo. A comunicação social na Revolução dos Alfaiates. Salvador, Brazil, Univ. Federal da Bahia, Núcleo de Publicações do Centro Editorial e Didático, 1974. 111 p., bibl. (Col. Estudos baianos, 9)

Study of "Revolt of the Tailors" as communication problem in society dependent on spoken, rather than written word. Of value to those interested in spread of knowledge and revolt in such societies.

4035. Mello, José Barboza. História das lutas do povo brasileiro: marcha de 4 séculos pela emancipação do país. Rio, Editora Leitura, 1973. 421 p., bibl.

Attempt to place history of Portuguese America within framework of continuous struggle for political, economic and social emancipation of Indians, slave resistance, civil uprisings and rebellions ending with Tiradentes.

4036. Mendes Júnior, Antonio; Luiz Roncari; and Ricardo Maranhão. Brasil história: texto e consulta. v. 1, Colônia. São Paulo, Editora Brasiliense, 1976. 300 p., tables.

First of four-volume series treating different periods of history. Consists of short essays divided into units with extensive bibliography for each section. Well done attempt to structure colonial history for secondary teaching purposes.

4037. Mont'Alegre, Omen. Açúcar e capital. Brasilía, Ministério do Industria e Comércio (MIC), Instituto do Açúcar e do Alcool, Divisão Administrativa, Serviço de Documentação, 1974. 275 p., tables (Col. Canavieira, 14)

Useful general study of colonial sugar industry drawn mainly from secondary sources. Includes number of interesting tables. Serves more as introduction suggesting more work needed in certain areas. General reader.

4038. Morão, Simão Pinheiro. Queixas repetidas em ecos dos Arrecifes de Pernambuco contra os abusos médicos que nas suas capitanias se observam tanto em dano das vidas de seus habitadores. Leitura, explicação e nótulas do Jaime Walter. Lisboa, Junta dos Investigadores do Ultramar, 1965. 180 p.

Although published 13 years ago, this is fascinating study of state of medicine in general and in Pernambuco in particular written in 1677 by medical man who retreated to Brazil under pressure from inquisition. Social and medical historian will find it useful.

4039. Nicodemos, José Pedro. A contribuição historiográfica de Frei Vicente do Salvador. Prefácio de Juarez Batista. João Pessoa, Brazil, Univ. Federal da Paraíba, 1971. 137 p.

Critical study of the author of Brazil's first history (1627) and his work that attempts to judge amount of myth vs. reality as well as assess his contribution. Of some interest to intellectual historian, specialist.

4040. Pernambuco (state), *Brazil.* **Conselho Estadual de Cultura.** Pernambuco no movimento da independência. Recife, Brazil, 1973. 184 p.

Official correspondence of last colonial administration between Aug./Oct. 1821 on eve of independence gathered from State Library and National Archive. Collectively demonstrates weakening of authority and power. Unfortunately without an index. Of interest to specialist.

4041. Pinto, G. Hércules. Calabar o patriota. Rio, Conquista, 1976. 183 p., bibl., illus. (Col. Terra dos papagaios)

Interesting attempt to place Calabar, who defected from Portugueses to help Dutch during struggle over Pernambuco, in context of fighter for Indian respect and civil rights worthy of esteem by modern Brazilians. Without much scholarly backup, of interest to general reader and student.

4042. Ramos, Donald. Social revolution frustrated: the conspiracy of the tailors in Bahia, 1798 (UW/LBR, 13:1, Summer 1976, p. 74-90)

Succinct and perceptive analysis of the causes and significance of little-known protest of late colonial Brazil. Well worth reading.

4043. Ramos Gómez, Luis J. El Brasil holandés, en la pugna entre Felipe IV y las provincias unidas (PAIGH/H, 80, julio/dic. 1975. p. 43-86)

Informative article drawing heavily on archival sources that places Dutch Brazil in context of Spain's struggle with Netherlands revolt. Of interest to specialist, general reader.

4044. Rodrígues, José Honório. A Revolução Americana e a Revolução Brasileira da Independência: 1776-1822 (PAIGH/H, 83, enero/junio 1977, p. 69-91)

Concludes American Revolution broke economic dependency opening country to full impact of capitalism, while in Brazil counter-revolutionary interest succeeded in preserving old system in spite of independence.

4045. Russell-Wood, A.J.R. Women and society in colonial Brazil (JLAS, 9:1, May 1977, p. 134)

Traces importance of women of European origin in Portuguese America. Notes and analyzes differences between Spanish and English colonial women. Concludes that although cultural transmission differed, women proved very adaptable. Of interest to specialists and general reader.

4046. Salvador (city), *Brazil.* **Diretoria do Arquivo, Divulgação e Estatística.** Cartas do Senado, 1710-1730. v. 6. Apresentação de Elyette G. de Magalhães. Salvador, Brazil, Secretaria de Educação e Cultura do Município, Depto. de Cultura, Divisão de Cultura e Arquivo, Prefeitura da Cidade do Salvador, 1973. 146 p. (Documentos históricos do Arquivo Municipal)

Letters of Municipal Council directed to King at time of political and economic decline preceding transfer of colonial capital to Rio. Letters are filled with socioeconomic data. Subject, name, and place name index make this collection doubly useful to specialist.

4047. Santos, Corcino Medeiros dos. Algumas notas para o estudo da economia de São Paulo no final do século XVIII (FFCLM/EH, 13/14, 1975, p. 85-112, tables)

First rate, well-documented study concerning revival of trade between Santos and Lisbon in last one-third of century. Notes efforts of various governors and factors that made it possible in spite of difficulties. Of interest to specialists.

4048. Schubert, Guilherme. A data da criação da Diocese do Rio de Janeiro (IHGB/R, 311, abril/junho 1976, p. 5-12, facsims.)

Attempts to establish, using Vatican sources, exact day in Nov. 1676 when Pope created Diocese of Rio. Useful bibliographical model of what sources to use in order to dig up such information. Of passing interest to specialists.

4049. Schwartz, Stuart B. Resistance and accommodation in eighteen-century Brazil: the slaves' view of slavery (HAHR, 57:1, Feb. 1977, p. 69-81)

Based on magistrate's letter concerning group of runaways and peace treaty they proposed to their former master, author presents slaves' view of their situation. Indicates their demands concerning conditions of labor and certain cultural traditions they wanted to protect. Both documents are appended. Of interest to specialists.

4050. Semana de Estudos Históricos, *I, Ponte Nova, Brazil, 1972*. O Brasil século XVIII: o século mineiro. Ponte Nova, Brazil, Univ. Católica de Minas Gerais, Faculdade de Ciências Humanas de Ponte Nova, 1972. 152 p.

Collection of seven papers of mixed interest presented at regional conference organized by Catholic Univ. of Minas Gerais in 1972 (e.g., Almir de Oliverrás essay on society in 18th century and Francisco Iglésias' on economic and political development centered on Minas are of interest).

4051. Silva, Maria Beatriz Nizza da. Educação feminina e educação masculina no Brasil colonial (USP/RH, 55:109, 1977, p. 149-164)

Interesting comparison of Azeredo Coutinho's rules for female education with Fénelon's *Traité sur l'éducation des filles*—in places a direct, literal translation from French. Author also notes some problems encountered in attempting a reconstruction of colonial education. Of interest to specialist.

Sousa, Gabriel Soares de. Notícia do Brasil. See *HLAS 39:5768*.

4052. Spix, Johann Baptist von and Karl Friedrich Philipp von Martius. Viagem pelo Brasil: a grande aventura de Spix e Martius; condensação. Translated by Mario Garcia de Paiva. Brasília, Ministério da Educação e Cultura, Instituto Nacional do Livro, 1972. 212 p., fold. map, plates (Col. Documentos, 5)

Condensation of three-volume, 1000 p. *Viagem pelo Brasil* (1817-20) by both German scientists. Excludes any discussion of preparation, ship travel, stay in Rio and trip to São Paulo as well as extensive scientific observation, but includes travels in interior as well as selection of illustration and maps. Serious researchers will want to consult larger work; however, general reader will be grateful for this considerably shorter one.

4053. Tavares, Luís Henrique Dias. História da sedição intentada na Bahia em 1798: "A Conspiração dos Alfaites." São Paulo, Livraria Pioneira Editora, *em convênio com o* Ministério da Educação e Cultura, Instituto Nacional do Livro, 1975. 144 p., tables (Biblioteca pioneira de estudos brasileiros)

Good study of "Revolt of the Tailors" that moves step by step through documentation. With aid of number of useful chronological list of arrests and investigations, does much to clear up confusion. Of interest to specialists.

4054. Trias, Rolando A. Laguarda. Rio de Janeiro: historia de sus denominaciones. Lisboa, Junta de Investigações do Ultramar, Agrupamento de Estudos de Cartografia Antiga, 1972. 31 p. (Secção de Lisboa, 66)

Traces various names applied to geographical features of Rio and vicinity by explorers and mapmakers and attempts to date their use. Of interest to specialists.

Valente, José Augusto Vaz. A carta de Pero Vaz de Caminha. See *HLAS 39:5782*.

4055. Vicente do Salvador, brother. História do Brasil: 1500-1627. 6. ed. São

Paulo, Edições Melhoramentos *em convênio com o* Ministério da Educação e Cultura, Instituto Nacional do Livro, Brasília, 1975. 437 p., bibl., illus., maps, plates.

Delightful ed. of first history of Brazil (1627) as edited and corrected by series of notable historians, Venancio Willeke, OFM, most recent. Filled with well done maps, illustrations, and serviceable index. General reader, specialist.

NATIONAL

4056. Aguiar, Manoel Pinto de. Os precursores brasileiros da aeronáutica. Rio, Civilização Brasileira [and] Instituto Nacional do Livro (INL), Brasília, 1975. 212 p., bibl., illus. (Col. Retratos do Brasil, 92)

Biographical sketches, with emphasis on their technical achievements of five Brazilian pioneers in aviation: Bartolomeu Lourenço de Gusmão, Júlio Cesar Ribeiro de Souza, José do Patrocínio, Augusto Severo Albuquerque Maranhão, and—at Length—Alberto Santos Dumont. No original research but good coverage of contemporary reactions.

4057. Amado, Janaina. Contribuição ao estudo da imigração alemã Rio Grande do Sul: São Leopoldo, 1824-1874 (SBPC/CC, 29:7, julho 1977, p. 735-770, table)

Heavy (being thesis chapter) but rewarding study, using anthropological approach, of German colony of São Leopoldo and its development from "egalitarian" society (1824-46) to "unequal one" (1846-74). Includes good descriptions of changing ways of life.

4058. Amaral, Francisco Pacífico do. Escavações: fatos da história de Pernambuco. Prefácio de Mauro Mota. Recife, Brazil, Edição do Arquivo Público Estadual, 1974. 294 p.

First published 1884, presents view of everyday life, customs, politics, biographical data by intellectual-para-journalist. Of interest to historian of social and intellectual history.

4059. Amaral, Pedro Ferraz do. Celso Garcia. São Paulo, Livraria Martins Editora, 1972? 361 p., bibl., illus.

Closely written, well researched biography of Afonso Celso Garcia (1869-1908), São Paulo journalist and politician who achieved considerable popular standing as social reformer in first two decades of Old Republic. Does not, alas!, list any sources.

4060. Araujo, Antonio Amaury Corrêa de. Assim morreu Lampião. São Paulo, Brusco, 1975. 135 p., plates.

Rambling compilation of personal memoirs, newspaper accounts, songs and miscellaneous information on events surrounding Lampião's death.

4061. Assis, José Eugênio de Paula. Prudente de Morais: sua vida e sua obra. São Paulo, Gráfica Sangirard, 1976. 260 p.

Superficial and derivative biography of first civilian president of Old Republic (1894-98). Some documents transcribed in text.

4062. Azevedo, Thales de. Italianos e gaúchos: os anos pioneiros da colonização italiana no Rio Grande do Sul. Prefácio de Guilhermino Cesar. Port Alegre, Brazil, Instituto Estadual do Livro, 1975. 310 p., bibl., maps.

Well-organized and perceptive analysis, by leading Brazilian anthropologist and scholar, of early Italian immigration and settlement in Rio Grande do Sul, concentrating on colony of Caxias do Sul and problems of acculturation. Based on thorough research and can serve as guide when using other works on subject.

Baldrich, J. Amadeo. Historia de la Guerra del Brasil: contribución al estudio razonado de la historia militar argentina. See item 3693.

4063. Barman, Roderick J. The Brazilian peasantry reexamined: the implications of the Quebra-Quilo Revolt, 1874-1875 (HAHR, 57:3, August 1977, p. 401-424, map)

Argues that this revolt, often seen as senseless and fanatic uprising, was a successful and sophisticated move by Northeast peasants to protect their socioeconomic position.

4064. ———. Politics on the stage: the late Brazilian Empire as dramatized by França Júnior (UW/LBR, 13:2, Winter 1976, p. 244-260)

Impressionistic study of writer and his works as source of sociopolitical information.

4065. ——— and **Jean Barman.** The role of the law graduate in the political elite of imperial Brazil (UM/JIAS, 18:4, Nov. 1976, p. 423-450, bibl., illus., tables)

Award-winning essay that traces elite of imperial Brazil through role of law graduate. Concludes that in early period degree gave one automatic access. By 1850, supply exceeded demand, and by end of empire elite recruitment depended on other factors causing some disillusionment with Empire. Of interest to specialist and general reader.

Basbaum, Leôncio. Uma vida em seis tempos: memórias. See *HLAS 39:7543*.

4066. Bastos, Wilson de Lima. O Engenheiro Henrique Guilherme Fernando Halfeld: sua vida, sua obra, sua descendência. Juiz de Fora, Brazil, Edições Paraibuna, 1975. 171 p., facsims., plates.

Poorly organized compilation of documents, genealogies and miscellaneous information on German engineer who immigrated to Juiz da Fora, Minas Gerais, in 1825 and founded dynasty that became part of local commercial-agricultural elite.

4067. Beiguelman, Paula. Os companheiros de São Paulo. Nota de Edimilson Antonio Bizelli. São Paulo, Edições Símbolo, 1977. 111 p. (Col. Ensaio e memória, 2)

Detailed chronological description, based on newspaper reports and comments, of labor disputes in São Paulo state, 1889-1920. Good guide to subject.

4068. Beni, Mário. Adhemar. São Paulo, Sociedade Editora e Impressora, 1973? 343 p., bibl.

Author, long-time associate and political follower of Adhemar de Barros, observes that "this is not a proper biography." Gives insider's view of Adhemar and is revealing of attitudes and outlook of those who supported São Paulo governor in his state and national career (1945-65).

4069. Besouchet, Lídia. Exílio e morte do Imperador. Rio, Editora Nova Fronteira, 1975. 465 p., bibl., facsims. (Col. Grandes vidas)

Despite title, this long and rambling account covers Pedro II's entire life. In view of new evidence unearthed by author, he should have concentrated on Pedro's psychology and his relationships with his lady friends. Includes facsimiles of many of his private letters, but often without provenance.

Boruszenko, Oksana; Rachel Costa da Rocha Loures; and **Mitiko Okazaki.** Arquivo da Paróquia São Josafat em Prudentópolis. See *HLAS 39:44*.

4070. Bratzel, John F. and **Daniel M. Masterson.** *O Exemplo*: Afro-Brazilian protest in Porto Alegre (AAFH/TAM, 33:4, April 1977, p. 585-592)

Short description of black newspaper published in far South (1892-95) whose increasing radicalism may have reflected strong localized racism.

4071. Brazil. Assembléia Constituinte e Legislativa. Diario da Assembléia Geral Constituinte e Legislativa do Imperio do Brasil: 1823. Introdução de Pedro Calmon. Brasília, Senado Federal, 1973. 2 v. in 4 (29, 381, 408, 774 p.) facsims.

Very welcome facsimile reedition, produced in honor of 1972 celebrations of independence, of proceedings of Constituent Assembly of 1823. Excellent source for study of political and philosophical beliefs then predominating.

4072. ———. Congresso. Câmara dos Deputados. Centro de Documentação e Informação. Coordenação de Publicações. Deputados brasileiros: 1826-1976. Brasília, 1976. 236 p., plates, tables.

Useful (if alphabetized by first name) list of all national deputies since independence, including political affiliation, term of office and state represented.

4073. Browne, George P. Secularization and modernization in Imperial Brazil, the question of non-Catholic marriage (PAIGH/H, 83, enero/junio 1977, p. 121-133)

Short study of background to law of 1861 which legalized non-Catholic marriages.

4074. Buescu, Mircea. Evolução dos vencimentos públicos federais no início da república: 1889-1902 (UC/V, 32:2, julho 1976, p. 87-105, tables)

In view of importance of *empreguismo* in Brazilian history, this pioneering study is especially important for its handling of problems of data and methodology involved in measuring real income of public funcionaries. Specifically concludes that from 1890 to 1900 their earning power sank due to lack of coherent, effective wage policy.

4075. Calmon, Pedro. História de D. Pedro II. t. 1, Infância e mocidade, 1825-1853; t. 2, Cultura e política: paz e guerra, 1853-1870; t. 3, No país e no estrangeiro, 1870-1887; t. 4, A abolição e a República, 1887-1889; t. 5, Memórias do exílio, 1889-1891. Rio, Livraria José Olympio Editora *em convênio com o* Ministério da Educação e Cultura (MEC), Instituto Nacional do Livro (INL), 1975. 5 v. (2008 p.) (Continuous pagination) bibl., facsims., illus., plates (Col. Documentos brasileiros, 165)

This study replaces all existing works on Pedro II by incorporating lifetime's research and because of its range and materials. Still, somewhat limited theoretically by concern for detail and failure to probe Emperor's weaknesses.

4076. Câmara, Jaime. Nos tempos de Frei Germano. Goiânia, Brazil, Livraria e Editora Cultura Goiana, 1974. 284 p., illus.

Impressionistic, semi-factual evocation of life in urban Goiás during 1920s and 1930s.

Candido, Salvatore. La emigración política italiana a la América Latina: 1820-1870. See item 2349.

4077. Carone, Edgard. O Estado Novo: 1937-1945. Rio, Difusão Européia do Livro (DIFEL), 1976. 387 p., bibl., tables (Col. Corpo e alma do Brasil, 47)

Continues in same style as item 4078 up to 1945. With this volume, author completes series on formation of Republican Brazil (1889-1945, see *HLAS 36:3570*).

4078. ———. A República Nova: 1930-1937. São Paulo, Difusão Européia do Livro (DIFEL), 1974. 414 p., bibl. (Corpo e alma do Brasil, 40)

Detailed, but rather heavy and unimaginative, account of period 1930-37 which attempts to put political developments in their socioeconomic setting. See also item 4077.

4079. ———. O tenentismo: acontecimentos, personagens, programas. São Paulo, Difusão Européia do Livro (DIFEL), 1975. 518 p., bibl. (Corpo e alma do Brasil, 43)

Wide-ranging collection of source materials on impact of *tenentismo* on Brazil (1922-35). Primarily decrees, letters, newspaper reports, memoirs, and extracts from secondary accounts. Very useful guide to subject.

———. A Terceira República: 1937-1945. See *HLAS 39:7552*.

Carrion, Francisco Machado. O modelo brasileiro: impasses e alternativas. See *HLAS 39:3594*.

4080. Cascudo, Luís da Câmara. Uma história da Assembléia Legislativa do Rio Grande do Norte: conclusões, pesquisas e documentário. Natal, Brazil, Fundação José Augusto, 1972. 488 p.

Poorly organized and repetitive but plum full of facts about Legislative Assembly of Rio Grande do Norte, 1823-1970, and its members. Prime raw material for historian gathered by state's most prolific historian.

4081. Castro, Jeanne Berrance de. A milícia cidadã: a Guarda Nacional de 1831 a 1850. Prefácio de Sérgio Buarque de Hollanda. São Paulo, Companhia Editora Nacional, *em convênio com o* Instituto Nacional do Livro (INL), 1977. 260 p., bibl., tables (Brasiliana, 359)

Pioneering and indispensable study of the National Guard, a key institution for social stability and social control in the Regency and the early Second Reign (1831-50). Highly recommended.

4082. Cleveland, Donald, Jr. Slave resistance and abolitionism in Brazil: the Campista Case, 1879-1888 (UW/LBR, 13:2, Winter 1976, p. 182-193)

Good case study (suppression of Quilombo do Travessos) of difficulties of slave control in Imperial Brazil and of ties of fugitive slave communities with ordinary population.

4083. Coelho, Salvador José Correia. Passeio a minha terra. Introdução de Newton Carneiro. Rio, Livraria Kosmos Editora, 1970? 86 p., facsims.

Shortage of autobiographical, introspective materials from 19th-century Brazil makes this nostalgic account by São Paulo law student of his trip home to Paraná in 1844 of considerable interest. Includes acute geographical and sociological comments. Reprint of 1860 ed.

4085. Corrêa Filho, José. O turbilhão dos punhais: ecos da intervenção setembrino de Carvalho; subsídios inéditos para a história do Ceará. Rio, Edição da Gráfica Barbero, 1975. 125 p., plates.

Very minor participant in events recalls, analyzes and denounces, for its excesses, 1914 federal intervention in Fortaleza, Ceará, in favor of Padre Cicero.

4086. Costa, Rovílio; Irineu Costella; Pedro A. Salame; and **Paulo J. Salame.** Imigração italiana no Rio Grande do

Sul: vida, costumes e tradições. Porto Alegre, Brazil, Livraria Sulina, 1974. 142 p., bibl., plates.

Anthropologically-oriented study reconstructing culture of early Italian immigrants in Rio Grande do Sul. Based on extensive use of interviews with founders and their children of Alfredo Chaves colony (now Veranópolis), begun in 1885 and remaining in relative isolation until 1950s.

4087. Cupello, Francisco. Memórias de um imigrante. Rio, Casa Editora Vecchi, 1973. 116 p., tables.

Very readable memoir of 1927 Italian immigrant to Rio state who worked himself up from cobbler to successful businessman through development of national cinema chain. Excellent material for historian.

4088. Dantas, José Ibarê. O tenentismo em Sergipe: da revolta de 1924 à revolução de 1930. Petrópolis, Brazil, Editora Vozes, 1974. 252 p., bibl., facsims., plates.

Well-written, analytical account of socio-political structure of Sergipe and causes of *tenentes'* revolts of 1924 and 1926, emphasizing lack of social content to revolt. Good use of interviews and printed materials.

4089. Dean, Warren. Rio Claro: a Brazilian plantation system, 1820-1920. Stanford, Calif., Stanford Univ. Press, 1976. 234 p., maps, tables.

Close study of social and economic structure of coffee frontier in western São Paulo based on state archives and printed sources. Particularly good on attempt in 1850s to bring in immigrant sharecropper labor. Useful reinforcement of existing work on plantation society.

4090. Debes, Célio. O Partido Republicano de São Paulo na propaganda: 1872-1889. São Paulo, n.p., 1975. 150 p., bibl.

Perceptive and interesting analysis of Republican Party development in São Paulo province in late Empire. Well documented from contemporary printed materials.

4091. Delgado, Luiz. Carlos de Lima Cavalcanti: um grande de Pernambuco. Recife, Brazil, Companhia Editora de Pernambuco, 1975. 170 p.

Personal recollections about leader of 1930 Revolution in Pernambuco who served as state governor until 1937 coup written by his Secretary of Education. Rather narrow in scope but gives a good impression of what it was to be a state bureaucrat during Vargas period.

History: Brazil, National / 323

Delhaes-Guenther, Dietrich von. Industrialisierung in Südbrasilien: die Deutsche Einwanderung und die Anfänge der Industrialisierung in Rio Grande do Sul. See *HLAS 39:3606*.

4092. Della Cava, Ralph. Catholicism and society in twentieth-century Brazil (LARR, 11:2, 1976, p. 7-50, illus.)

Fine and thorough analysis of development, strength and weakness of Catholic Church since 1916. Author's sympathies, while clear, do not interfere. Highly recommended as introduction to subject. For political scientist's annotation, see *HLAS 39:7556*.

4093. Derenzi, Luiz Serafim. Os italianos no Estado do Espírito Santo. Rio, Editora Artenova, 1974. 177 p., plates, tables.

Readable, intelligent account of some aspects of Italian colonization in Espírito Santo, primarily during years 1870-1900. Lacks insight into immigration as social process but very useful for its recording of local traditions and for its excellent photos.

4094. Dourado, Angelo. Voluntário do martírio: narrativa da revolução de 1893. Reprodução fac-similar da edição de 1896. Coordenação editorial e notas de Rodrigues Till. Porto Alegre, Brazil, Martins Livreiro Editor, 1977. 432 p.

Facsimile reprint of emotional account by participant of Federalist uprising of 1893. Useful as contemporary source.

4095. Duarte, Paulo. Júlio Mesquita. São Paulo, Editora de Humanismo, Ciência e Tecnologia (HUCITEC) *em coedição a* Secretaria da Cultura, Ciência e Tecnologia, 1977. 354 p. (Obras de Paulo Duarte)

Fulsome, almost sycophantic, set of essays on leading journalist-publisher in São Paulo (1862-1927), using only his writings in newspaper *Estado de São Paulo*.

4096. Dudley, William S. Professionalization and politicization as motivational factors in the Brazilian Army coup of 15 November 1889 (JLAS, 8:1, May 1976, p. 101-125)

Attempt to place dreams and discontents of Brazilian military (1870-1889) within larger context of military-civil relations. Best on question of professionalization.

4097. Eisenberg, Peter L. The consequences of modernization for Brazil's sugar plantations in the nineteenth century (*in* Duncan, Kenneth; Ian Rutledge; and Colin Harding eds. Land and labour in Latin America [see item 2156] p. 345-367, map, tables)

Argues that while sugar economy could have recovered in the late 19th century only by "integration into a northern hemisphere market via recolonization" or through radical structural reform centered on land redistribution, landowners were yet able to retain their socio-political position after abolition (perceived as economically motivated) by passing on their losses to free workers through low wages and poor working conditions.

4098. Erickson, Kenneth Paul. The Brazilian corporative state and working-class politics. Berkeley, Univ. of California Press, 1977. 225 p., bibl., map, tables.

Despite title, basically study of trade-unions, 1930-76 (being strongest on the Goulart period), emphasizing their total dependence on the government. Good introduction to subject.

4099. Evans, Peter B. Continuities and contradictions in the evolution of Brazilian dependence (LAP, 3:2, Spring 1976, p. 30-54, tables)

Straightforward, not very original but readable, account of Brazil's development as economic dependency since 1889. Useable as introductory text.

Ferreira, Arnaldo Amado. Um fato histórico esclarecido: Marechal Francisco Solano López. See item 3900.

4100. Ferreira Filho, Arthur. Revolução de 1923. Porto Alegre, Brazil, Imprensa Oficial do Estado, 1973. 140 p., bibl., plates.

Recounting, not particularly original, of 1923 uprising against Borges de Medeiros' re-election as governor of Rio Grande do Sul. Concentrates on military aspects. Few documents.

4101. Ferri, Gino. Os monges de Pinheirinho. 2. ed. n.p., Gráfica Encantado, 1975. 163 p., plates.

Unsophisticated but valuable study of messianic group, known as "Monks of Pinheirinho," who in 1902 settled near Encantada, Rio Grande do Sul. After clash with local inhabitants, group was suppressed by state police. Topic worth further investigation. Some contemporary photos.

4102. Flory, Thomas. Race and social control in Independent Brazil (JLAS, 9:2, Nov. 1977, p. 199-224, table)

From a stimulating and original analysis of Rio's mulatto press and of open use of race in politics in early 1830s, generalizes, perhaps too broadly vis-à-vis cause and effect, about subsequent racial conditions in Brazil.

4103. Fonseca, Nair de Teffé Hermes. A verdade sobre a revolução de 22. Rio, Gráfica Portinho Cavalcanti, 1974. 189 p., illus.

Although intended to describe and justify Hermes da Fonseca's (non) participation in revolt of 1922, this autobiographical account really gives vivid view of high social life in Rio of 1900-14, of author's career as talented caricaturist ("Rian"), and of her courtship by and marriage to then Brazilian president, Hermes da Fonseca, 40 years her senior. Useful reproduction of author's caricatures of Old Republic personalities.

4104. Fraga, Clementino. Vida e obra de Osvaldo Cruz. Prefácio de Raimundo Moniz de Aragão. Rio, Livraria José Olympio Editora *em convênio com o Instituto Nacional do Livro (INL)*, Brasília, 1972. 186 p., illus., plates (Col. Documentos brasileiros, 153)

Well-written, succinct biography of Brazil's leading public health doctor, first to deal effectively with yellow fever. Work, while not original, profits from author's expertise in same field.

4105. Galeazzi, Pio Vitório. Galeazza: um emigrante italiano contra sua história. 2. ed. Porto Alegre, Brazil, Livraria Sulina, 1975. 111 p., plates, tables.

Fascinating account, written by author in old age, of reasons why fairly well-off family emigrated from Italy to Brazil in 1888-89. Some information on Brazilianization of author and his descendants.

4106. Galvão, Walnice Nogueira. No calor da hora: a Guerra de Canudos nos Jornais, 4. expedição. São Paulo, Atica, 1974. 510 p., bibl. (Col. Ensaios)

Unedited reprint of contemporary newspaper reports written mainly by correspondents who accompanied expedition of fourth and final campaign against Canudos in 1897. Lengthy introduction analyzes nature and approach of reports.

4107. Giacomel, Fortunato; Hermenegildo Polesso; and **Humberto Cherubini.** Pioneiros às margens do Uruguai: a vida nos primórdios das novas colônias italianas do Alto Uruguai. Tradução, notas e introdução de Luís Alberto de Boni. Porto Alegre, Brazil, Livraria Sulina, 1975. 99 p., facsims., plates.

Three separate memoirs by children of Italian immigrants, who are now all Capuchins, on Italian immigrant community of northeast of Rio Grande do Sul in 20th century. Focuses on problems of acculturation and role of religion. Photos.

4108. Giron, Loraine Slomp. Caxias do Sul: evolução histórica. Apresentação de Luis A. De Boni. Capa de Valdir dos Santos. Arte de Vera Gonzatto e Diva Guizzo. Caxias do Sul, Brazil, Prefeitura Municipal [and] Univ. de Caxias do Sul, Escola Superior de Teologia São Lourenço de Brindes, Porto Alegre, 1977. 99 p., facsims., plates, tables (Col. Centenário da imigração italiana, 17)

Slim but useful study of socioeconomic evolution of first Italian immigrants in Brazil. Includes much statistical data on early immigrants and photos.

4109. Graham, Richard. Government expenditures and political change in Brazil, 1880-1899: who got what (UM/JIAS, 19:3, Aug. 1977, p. 339-368, bibl., tables)

Preliminary examination of thesis which holds that shifts in four main political sectors of Empire's last and Republic's first decade can be measured through changing allocations of national expenditure. Concludes that no significant changes occurred, perhaps in part because socio-political reality was more complex than postulated in thesis. Key subject which needs development.

4110. Guerra, Flávio. O Conde da Boa Vista e o Recife. Recife, Brazil, Fundação Guararapes, 1973. 158 p., illus.

Detailed study of modernization of capital of Pernambuco prov. during presidency of Francisco do Rego Barros (1837-41), providing prime example of influence of French culture on both elite and urban life during Empire.

4111. Hahner, June E. Jacobinos versus Galegos: urban radicals versus Portuguese immigrants in Rio de Janeiro in the 1890s (UM/JIAS, 18:2, May 1976, p. 125-154, bibl.)

Very useful, introductory investigation of topic—hostility to Portuguese immigrant—which is recurring theme in Brazilian history but which has been rarely studied by historians.

4112. Hall, Michael M. Immigration and the early São Paulo working class (JGSWGL, 12, 1975, p. 393-407)

Contests accepted view which contrasts apolitical native worker with radical immigrant workers: few workers were native-born and, despite radical minority, most immigrants were not and, for various reasons, could not be radical.

4113. Hilton, Stanley E. Vargas and Brazilian economic development, 1930-1945: a reappraisal of his attitude toward industrialization and planning (EHA/J, 35:4, Dec. 1975, p. 754-778)

Argues skillfully that Vargas' attitude to industrialization prior to 1937 was far more positive than often assumed, but lacks documentation necessary to prove point. For economist's comment, see *HLAS 39:3632*.

4114. Holloway, Thomas H. The coffee *colono* of São Paulo, Brazil: migration and mobility, 1880-1930 (*in* Duncan, Kenneth; Ian Rutledge; and Colin Harding eds. Land and labour in Latin America [see item 2156] p. 301-321, map, tables)

Useful examination of agricultural labor in São Paulo coffee area during its "Golden Age" showing that while *colonos*, predominantly first-generation European immigrants, were economically tied to plantation owners by very precise contractual terms they yet retained sufficient independence and mobility for "small proportion" to become independent farmers.

Ilg, Karl. Die österreichische Emigration nach Südamerika. See item 2180.

4115. Joffily, Geraldo Ireneo. O Quebra-Quiló: a revolta dos matutos contra os doutores, 1874 (USP/RH, 54:107, julho/set. 1976, p. 69-145, bibl.)

Useful detailed resumé of published material on this Northeast uprising. Should be supplemented by item 4063.

4116. Johnson, Phil Brian. Rui Barbosa e a reforma de ensino de 1882: recordações e repercussões: pt. 1, 1882-1930 (IHGB/R, 312, julho/set. 1976. p. 241-262)

First of two-part article dealing with Rui's still-born educational reforms presented in 1882. Rejection may have been one of factors in his break with monarchy and participation in establishment of republic. Of interest to specialist.

4117. ———. Rui Barbosa e a reforma educacional: "As Lições de Coisas." Rio, Fundação Casa de Rui Barbosa, 1977. 45 p.

Interesting account of struggle to publish Brazilian edition of Norman Calkin's *Primary object lession* that reflected Rui's belief that social change could best be brought about through education. With characteristic wit author notes less idealistic motivations of rising young politician. General reader, specialists.

4118. José Aleixo, *brother.* Nuporanga, minha terra: 1861-1930. n.p., Editora Cupolo, 1975. 293 p., facsims., plates.

Poorly written but quite informative account of socioeconomic and political history of Nuporanga, typical coffee town in northern São Paulo, which was founded and flourished during Old Republic.

Keith, Henry H. and **Robert A. Hayes** *eds.* Perspectives on armed politics in Brazil. See *HLAS 39:7576.*

Korolev, Nicolai. Emigración de Rusia a América Latina a fines del siglo XIX, comienzos del siglo XX. See item 2188.

4119. Kubitschek, Juscelino. Meu caminho para Brasília. v. 1, A experiência da humildade; v. 2, A escalada política. Rio, Bloch Editores, 1974-76. 2 v. (355, 502 p.) plates.

Vol. 1, while discrete on political side, gives masterly account of the formation and rise of the ambitious son of a poor but cultured family; vol. 2, dominated by politics, is characterized by tone of personal idealism and strong dislike for UDN, which opposed author. Both volumes attest to strong charisma of most successful president in Democratic Republic period (1945-64) and make highly enjoyable reading.

4120. Lacombe, Lourenço Luiz. Os Chefes do Executivo Fluminense. Petrópolis, Brazil, Ministério da Educação e Cultura, Depto. de Assuntos Culturais, Museu Imperial, 1973. 117 p., bibl. (Série monografias, 1)

Brief biographies of Rio's presidents and governors, 1834-1971. Useful reference aid.

4121. Lamounier, Bolivar. Brasil: la formación de un pensamiento político autoritario en la primera república; una interpretación (IDES/DE, 16:62, julio/sept. 1976, p. 253-280)

More a consideration of validity of conceptual frameworks which have been employed to analyze political thought under Old Republic than actual discussion of that thought.

4122. Lavenére-Wanderley, Nelson Freire. História da Força Aérea Brasileira. 2. ed. n.p., n.p., 1975. 384 p., bibl., maps, plates, tables.

Poorly organized institutional history with little analysis. Always laudatory, being recommended reading for young air-force officers, but contains much information and good illustrations.

4123. Leal, Hamilton. A grande legenda: 5 de julho. Prefácio de José Eduardo do Prado Kelly. Rio, Livraria Agir Editora, 1976. 366 p., bibl.

Ostensibly analysis of civil-military relations from Copacabana uprising to Vargas' fall (1922-45). In reality justification of ideals and conduct of Eduardo Gomes, with whom author was closely associated during founding of UDN Party.

4124. Leitman, Spencer L. The black ragamuffins: racial hypocrisy in nineteenth century southern Brazil (AAFH/TAM, 33:3, Jan. 1977, p. 504-518)

Discussion of role of slave soldiers in Rio Grande do Sul rebel forces (1836-44) which argues that, notwithstanding their grant of freedom written into peace treaty, they were badly treated by both sides.

4125. Lima, Alexandre José Barbosa. A verdade sobre a revolução de Outubro: 1930. São Paulo, Editora Alfa-Omega, 1975. 199 p., bibl. (Biblioteca Alfa-Omega de ciencias sociais. Série historia, 1:4)

Unchanged re-edition of classic study on 1930 Revolution and its causes, first published 1933.

4126. Lopes, José Antonio Dias. A Cidade de Dom Pedrito. Porto Alegre, Brazil, Livraria do Globo, 1972. 119 p.

Short survey of development of cattle town on Uruguayan border from its founding in 1854 to 1900. Slight but exact and vivid. Uses some local documents of value. Excellent illustrations.

4127. Lorenzoni, Júlio. Memórias de um imigrante italiano. Tradução de Armida Lorenzoni Parreira. Prefácio de Itálico Marcon. Porto Alegre, Brazil, Livraria Sulina Editora, 1975. 264 p. (Estante do centenário da imigração italiana, 1)

Memoir written in old age by Italian who emigrated in 1877 to Rio Grande do Sul. Covers period to 1920. Very intelligent recording of events, particularly founding of Silveira Martins colony. Originally written in Italian, memoir shows little acculturation. Photos.

4128. Lustosa, Eduardo Magalhães. Um jesuíta brasileiro: o Padre José Manuel de Madureira (UC/V, 31/1, jan./março 1975, p. 3-126)

Reprint of 1930 eulogy of José Manuel de Madureira (1865-1930), leading Jesuit educator and writer. Interesting details on influence of Jesuits and of Italian Catholicism on Old Republic.

Luz, Nícia Vilela. A luta pela industrialização do Brasil. See *HLAS 39:3641*.

4128a. Magalhães, José Vieira Conto de. Diário do General Couto de Magalhães: 1887-1890. Com prefácio de Brasil Bandecchi. São Paulo, n.p., 1974. 32 p., facsims., illus. (Col. da *Revista de História*, 58)

Rarity of autobiographical materials from 19th century makes especially significant this diary kept by wealthy Paulista intellectual who was president of his province in 1889. Published in well-prefaced facsimile ed. (with fairly legible hand-writing), diary is notable for its introspection, details on personal finances, and insights on patronage and administration in late Empire.

4129. Maia, Jerônimo Vingt-Un Rosado and **América Rosado.** Alguns subsídios à saga quase centenária da abolição mossoroense: homenagem ao ano X da Escola Superior de Agricultura de Mossoró. Mossoró, Brazil, Gráfica ASTECAM, 1977. 226 p., bibl., (Col. Mossoroense, 53)

Wide miscellany of source materials from vocal northeast centre of abolitionist movement. Also includes lists of baptized slaves (1843-74) and birth records from 1871.

4130. Maram, Sheldon L. Labor and the Left in Brazil, 1890-1921: a movement aborted (HAHR, 57:2, May 1977, p. 254-272)

Good introductory study, but not substantially different in content and approach from other published works by author.

4131. Mattoon, Robert H., Jr. Railroads, coffee, and the growth of big business in São Paulo, Brazil (HAHR, 57:2, May 1977, p. 273-295, table)

Analysis of how railroads came to be built in São Paulo emphasizing relationship between foreign finance and local initiative.

4132. Mauá, Irineu Evangelista de Sousa. Correspondência política de Mauá no Rio da Prata: 1850-1885. Prefácio e notas de Lídia Besouchet. 2. ed. São Paulo, Companhia Editora Nacional *em convênio com o* Ministério da Educação e Cultura (MEC), Instituto Nacional do Livro (INL), Brasília, 1977. 193 p. (Col. Brasiliana, 227)

Source material that indicates why Mauá got into such a dreadful mess in his business affairs in Río de la Plata.

4133. Mello, José Antonio Gonsalves de comp. O Diario de Pernambuco e a história social do Nordeste: 1840-1889. v. 1/2. Recife, Brazil, Diario de Pernambuco, 1975. 2 v. (975 p.) (Continuous pagination) fold. tables, tables.

Selected articles from *Diario de Pernambuco* (1845-87) divided into sections on economy, society, culture, Pernambucan history and biography. Excellent new primary source for students and specialists.

4134. Menezes, Jayme de Sá. Vultos que ficaram os Irmãos Mangabeira: Francisco, João e Otávio. Com 70 ilustrações fora do texto. Prefácio de Sylvio Abreu Fialho. Salvador, Brazil, MF Editora, 1977. 340 p., facsims., illus., plates.

Rather frothy account of the three Mangabeira brothers, first was poet who died young, other two were leading politicians whose careers spanned Old Republic, Estado Novo and Democratic Republic. Interesting study of non-elite family.

4135. Menezes, Raimundo de. Vida e obra de Campos Salles. São Paulo, Prefeitura Municipal de Campinas, Secretaria de Educação, Cultura, Esportes e Turismo *coedição com a* Livraria Martins Editora, 1974. 259 p., plate.

Well-written introductory biography of second President of Republic (1898-1902) that draws on existing printed sources and does not pretend to break new ground.

4136. Monteiro, Duglas Teixeira. Os errantes do novo século: um estudo sobre o surto Milenarista do contestado. São Paulo, Duas Cidades, 1974. 281 p., map. (Série universidade, 2)

Exciting, innovative study of millenarian uprisings in 1912-15 in Contestado area between Paraná and Santa Catarina. Skillful and perceptive analysis of social and psychological conditions in frontier society affected by modernization. Highly recommended as model work on history of modern Brazil.

4137. Monteiro, Norma de Góes. Imigração e colonização em Minas: 1889-1930. Belo Horizonte, Brazil, Imprensa Oficial, 1974. 213 p., bibl., tables.

Well-researched but rather unimaginative study of immigration into Minas Gerais from mid-19th century. Concentrates on legal and institutional aspects and is written from "official" viewpoint. Little consideration of social and economic effects of immigration or of acculturation.

Moraes, Eduardo R. Affonso de. História da Universidade Federal de Minas Gerais. See *HLAS 39:4636*.

4138. Moura, Ismar de. A admirável mulher do Capitão Zeferino. v. 1, no title; v. 2, Viuvez e exílio. Recife, Brazil, Edição Dialgraf, 1973. 2 v. (159, 174 p.) facsims. (Edição da Biblioteca Ana Eufrásia)

Retelling, in full detail and with facsimile documents, of woman school-teacher's life in Pernambucan *sertão* (1873-1960). Hard to read but important, since historical materials are rare on *professoras*, a significant but neglected group in Brazil since independence.

4139. Nabuco, Joaquim. Abolitionism: the Brazilian antislavery struggle. Translated and edited by Robert Conrad. Urbana, Univ. of Illinois Press, 1977. 186 p., bibl., plates (Blacks in the New World)

Welcome translation of classic argument against slavery published in 1883 by scion of national elite. Extremely revealing in its general conceptions of politics and society. Recommended for students.

4140. Nachman, Robert G. Positivism, modernization and the middle class in Brazil (HAHR, 57:1, Feb. 1977, p. 1-23)

Very useful study of forms and extent of Positivist influence on politics and ideas in Old Republic. Demonstrates that positivism in Brazil should not be equated with Positivist Church as did previous study (see *HLAS 30:5133*).

4141. ———. Positivism and revolution in Brazil's First Republic: the 1904 revolt (AAFH/TAM, 34:1, July 1977, p. 20-39)

Argues that unsuccessful 1904 Rio revolt, superficially a protest against compulsory vaccination, was in reality attempt by Positivists to overthrow government with which they had become disillusioned.

4142. Naziazene, Ademar. Policia militar da Paraíba: sua história de 1831 a 1957. João Pessoa, Brazil, Senado Federal, Centro Gráfico, 1972. 252 p., bibl., plates, tables.

Historical chronology of military police of Paraíba written by one of its officers. Basically recapitulation of documents at hand. Best on 1930s.

Neme, Mario. Apossamento do solo e evolução da propriedade rural na zona de Piracicaba. See *HLAS 39:5735*.

4143. Nogueira, Arlinda Rocha and Lucy Maffei Hutter. A colonização em São Pedro do Rio Grande do Sul durante o Império: 1824-1889. Prefácio de Egon Schaden. Porto Alegre, Brazil, Editora Garatuja *em co-edição com o* Secretaria de Educação e Cultura do Rio Grande do Sul, Depto. de Assuntos Culturais, Instituto Estadual do Livro, 1975. 162 p., bibl., fold. map, tables (Série biênio da colonização e imigração, 4)

Interesting discussion of general socioeconomic aspects of colonization drawing on experiences of individual colonies in Rio Grande do Sul.

4144. Oberacker, Carlos H., Jr. Jorge Antônio von Schaeffer: criador da primeira corrente emigratória alemã para o Brasil. Prefácio de Carlos H. Hunsche. Porto Alegre, Brazil, Editora Metrópole *em convênio com o* Secretaria de Educação e Cultura do Rio Grande do Sul, Depto. de Assuntos Culturais, Instituto Estadual do Livro, 1975. 125 p., bibl., plate, tables (Série biênio da colonização e imigração, 6)

Sophisticated study of Schaeffer's role as initiator of German colonization in southern Brazil. Well researched in German and Brazilian sources.

4145. O'Donnell, Francisco Talaia. Oswaldo Aranha. Prefácio de Justino

Vasconcelos. Porto Alegre, Brazil, Editora Garatuja em co-edição com o Secretaria de Educação e Cultura, Depto. de Assuntos Culturais, Instituto Estadual do Livro, 1976. 267 p., plates.

Laudatory study of early life (up to 1930) of Vargas' ablest and most dedicated follower. Valuable for its quotes from Aranha archive.

Passos, Juliana Maria do Nascimento. Monlevade: vida e obra. See *HLAS 39:5737*.

4146. Pauli, Evaldo. Hercílio Luz: governador inconfundível. Florianópolis, Brazil, Governo do Estado de Santa Catarina, Secretaria do Governo, 1976. 365 p., bibl. (Col. Cultura catarinense. Série história)

Based on newspapers and other sources, this study of technocrat who through his role in civil war of 1893, became three times governor of Santa Catarina is a most interesting political history of state from 1889 to 1924.

4147. Pescatello, Ann M. *Prêto* power, Brazilian style: modes of re-actions to slavery in the nineteenth century (*in* Pescatello, Ann M. *ed.* Old roots in new lands: historical and anthropological perspectives on black experiences in the Americas. Westport, Conn., Greenwood Press, 1977, p. 77-106, tables [Contributions in Afro-American and African studies, 31])

Reworks, without breaking new ground, basic published materials on Northeast slave protests in early 19th century and on abolitionist movement from perspective of non-white involvement.

4148. Pestana, Francisco Rangel. O *Memorial político* Rangel Pestana: 1889. Edited by Célio Debes. São Paulo, n.p., 1977. 23 p., facsim. (Col. da *Revista de História*. Serie textos e documentos, 2)

Welcome reprint of important source on *evolução-revolução* (direct vs. constitutional action) argument that divided Republican Party at end of Empire. Original entitled *Memorial político ao Congresso Republicano Paulista: documento reservado* (São Paulo, Tipografia de Provincia de São Paulo, 1889).

4149. Petrone, Maria Theresa Schorer. As crises da Monarquia e o Movimento Republicano (USP/RIEB, 16, 1975, p. 31-41)

Short but incisive analysis which equates downfall of Empire with crisis in growth that occurred in most fields in Brazil after 1850.

4150. Piccolo, Helga Iracema Landeraf. A política rio-grandense no Segundo Império: 1868-1882. Apresentação de Luís Carlos de Mesquita Rothman. Nota de Dante de Laytano. Porto Alegre, Brazil, Univ. Federal do Rio Grande do Sul, Instituto de Filosofia e Ciências Humanas, Gabinete de Pesquisa de História do Rio Grande do Sul, 1974. 155 p., bibl.

Based on published provincial legislative documents traces development of party politics in Rio Grande do Sul up to establishment of Republican Party. Useful political study. General reader, specialist.

4151. Pinheiro, Paulo Sérgio de M.S. Política e trabalho no Brasil: dos anos vinte a 1930. Rio, Paz e Terra, 1975. 191 p., bibl. (Estudos brasileiros, 5)

Distinctly thin study of Old Republic's fall, based on single and undeveloped insight: "that the study of the working classes is the key to understanding the historical development of 20th-century Brazil." Originally doctoral thesis at Univ. of Paris.

4152. Pinheiro Filho, Celso and **Lina Celso Pinheiro.** Soldados de Tiradentes: história da polícia militar do Piauí. Rio, Editora Artenova, 1975. 145 p., plates, tables.

Officially sponsored history of military police of Piauí. First two-thirds of book presents quite perceptive, reasonably documented history and overview of understudied Brazilian institution while last third, written by author's daughter after his death, is no more than ill-organized eulogy to force's current commander.

4153. Pinkuss, Fritz. Um ensaio acerca da imigração judaica no Brasil após o cataclismo de 1933 e da Segunda Guerra Mundial (USP/RH, 50[2]:100, 1974, p. 599-608)

This evocative account, written by participant, is good introduction to characteristics of Jewish migration to Brazil after 1933.

Pondé, Francisco de Paula e Azevado. Os transportes no Segundo Reinado. See *HLAS 39:5743*.

4154. Porto, José da Costa. O Marquês de Olinda e o seu tempo. Recife, Brazil, Governo de Pernambuco, Conselho Estadual de Cultura, 1974. 304 p.

Political biography of important imperial political figure. Educated in Portugal, judge, deputy to Lisbon Cortes in 1821, Minister under both Pedros as well as regent. General reader, specialist.

4155. Prantner, Johanna. Kaiserin Leopoldine von Brasilien: Der Beitrag des Hauses Habsburg-Lothringen und österreichischen Geistesgutes zur Entwicklung Brasiliens während der Monarchie im 19. Jahrhundert. Wien, Verlag Herold, 1974. 224 p., plate.

While centering on Empress Leopoldina, work also covers lives of Pedro I and Pedro II and Austrian contacts with Brazil. Fairly simple but useful survey of topic and of relevant literature in German.

4156. Rachum, Ilan. Feminism, woman suffrage, and national politics in Brazil: 1922-1937 (UW/LBR, 14:1, Summer 1977, p. 118-134)

Basically study of Berta Luz (b. 1894) and Federação Brasileira pelo Progresso Feminino which she founded. If not profound, well-written and stimulating work on neglected topic.

Ramos, R. Antonio. La independencia del Paraguay y el imperio del Brasil. See item 3911.

4157. Rau, Wolfgang Ludwig. Anita Garibaldi: o perfil de uma heroína brasileira. Prefácio de Oswaldo Rodrigues Cabral. Florianópolis, Brazil, Editora Lunardelli, 1975. 524 p., facsims., illus., plates.

Every last detail on *vida passionante* of Anita, the Brazilian girl who ditched her husband to follow Giuseppe Garibaldi, hero of Italy's Risorgiamento. Well documented with lots of illustrations including Miss Santa Catarina 1964 in Anita's typical costume.

4158. Reis, Jaime. From *banguê* to *usina*: social aspects of growth and modernization in the sugar industry of Pernambuco, Brazil, 1850-1920 (*in* Duncan, Kenneth; Ian Rutledge; and Colin Harding eds. Land and labour in Latin America [see item 2156] p. 369-396, tables)

Argues skillfully that modernization of sugar industry, while not significantly changing social position of rural workers, did produce decline in their material condition.

4159. Reis Júnior, Pereira. Os Presidentes do Brasil: sínteses biográficas. Rio, Divulbrás Editora Livros, 1975. 258 p., bibl., plates.

Semi-official, carefully orthodox biographies of Brazil's presidents. Useful source of basic information.

4160. Renault, Delsa. Proteção ao menor: Leon Renault; um pioneiro. Belo Horizonte, Brazil, Imprensa Oficial, 1974. 236 p.

Competent account by his daughter of the contributions of Minas educator (1877-1961), active primarily in an innovative technical school in Belo Horizonte for abandoned children—Instituto João Pinheiro.

4161. Resor, Randolph R. Rubber in Brazil: dominance and collapse, 1876-1945 (HU/BHR, 51:3, Autumn 1977, p. 341-366)

Factual account of Amazonian rubber-boom demonstrating that excessive costs of production both permitted its easy displacement by Asian cultivated rubber and have prevented any subsequent recovery.

4162. Ridings, Eugene W. Interest groups and development: the case of Brazil in the nineteenth century (JLAS, 9, pt. 2, Nov. 1977, p. 225-250)

Describes commercial associations merely as functioning interest groups of the Empire.

Rocha, Carlos Eduardo da. Museu do Recôncavo Wanderley Pinho: o engenho freguesia. See item 500.

4163. Roche, Jean. A colonização alemã no Espírito Santo. Tradução de Joel Rufino dos Santos. São Paulo, Editora da Univ. de São Paulo, 1968. 367 p., illus., map (Col. Corpo e alma do Brasil, 18)

Stolid, meticulous examination of economy and cultural geography of areas in Espírito Santo originally settled by German colonists. Based primarily on modern census data combined with author's personal observations from 1950s. Although more than 10 years old, it was not annotated in previous *HLAS*.

4164. Rocque, Carlos. Antônio Lemos e sua época: história política do Pará. Prefácio de Nélio Lobato. Belém, Brazil, Amazônia Edições Culturais, 1973? 477 p., plates.

Detailed, broadly based study of Pará journalist and politician, Antônio Lemos (1843-1913), who served in Old Republic as intendente of Belém and national senator. Revealing portrait of Pará politics, especially development of party machinery in post-Imperial period.

4165. Rosa, Joaquim. Por esse Goiás afora. Goiânia, Brazil, Livraria e Editora Cultura Goiana, 1974. 258 p., facsims., plates.

Highly enjoyable, perceptive autobiographical recollections of Goiás interior in first half of this century. Vivid descriptions of socioeconomic conditions and local politics. Special attention given to events surrounding Revolution of 1930, during which author was leading journalist in town of Ipamerí.

4166. Saes, Décio Azevedo, *marques de.* Classe média e política na Primeira República Brasileira: 1889-1930. Petrópolis, Brazil, Editora Vozes, 1975. 111 p., bibl. (Col. Sociologia brasileira, 3)

Attempt to explain, within Marxist framework, minimal strength and role of "middle urban groups" and their relationship with military during Old Republic (1889-1930).

4167. Salles, José Bento Teixeira de. Milton Campos: uma vocação liberal. Belo Horizonte, Brazil, Editora Vega, 1975. 225 p., facsims., plates.

Long-time associate's personal recollections of Milton Campos, Governor of Minas Gerais (1947-51) and supporter of 1964 Revolution. Laudatory in tone but informative portrayal, with facsimile documents, of typical, highminded yet elitist politician of Democratic Republic (1945-64).

4168. Schmeling, Gila do Amaral von. A família Souza Queiroz e a Associação Barão de Souza Queiroz de Proteção à Infância. São Paulo, The Author, 1974. 161 p., plates, tables.

Detailed genealogical study of descendants of Barão de Souza Queiroz. Although intended for family distribution, provides useful information on life-style of wealthy São Paulo coffee clan, especially in late 19th century.

Schwartzman, Simon. São Paulo e o estado nacional. See *HLAS 39:7610.*

──── . Veinte años de democracia representativa en Brasil: 1945-1962. See *HLAS 39:7611.*

4169. Serrão, Joel. A emigração portuguesa para o Brasil, na segunda metade do século XIX: esboço de problematezação (JGSWGL, 13, 1976, p. 84-106, bibl., tables)

Using Portuguese statistics from 1870s, finds that despite wider opportunities in Brazil emigrants still concentrated on Rio commercial world and that significant minority later returned to Portugal, neither very wealthy nor indigent.

4170. Seyferth, Giralda. A colonização alemã no Vale do Itajaí-Mirim: um estudo de desenvolvimento econômico. Porto Alegre, Brazil, Editora Movimento, 1974. 159 p., bibl., tables.

Outstanding short analysis, within strong theoretical framework, of migration of German peasants to Santa Catarina in 1860s, creation of peasant economy adapted to local economy, and subsequent transition to industrialism. Excellent use of evidence. Highly recommended.

4171. Siegel, Bernard J. The Contestado Rebellion, 1912-16: a case study in Brazilian messianism and regional dynamics (UNM/JAR, 33:3, Summer 1977, p. 202-213, bibl., map)

Emphasizes importance of economic development and consequent social dislocation as causes of uprising. Clear analysis, good for students, but experts will prefer item 4136.

4172. Silva, Hélio. O ciclo de Vargas. v. 15, 1945 [i.e. Mil novecentos quarenta e cinco]: por que depuseram Vargas. Com a colaboração de Maria Cecília Ribas Carneiro. Rio, Civilização Brasileira, 1976. 562 p., plates, tables (Col. Documentos da historia contemporânea, 69)

Account of principal events in Vargas' overthrow through reproduction of contemporary documentation and transcription of interviews with leading participants. Some commentary and analysis, highlighting military's role. For earlier volume, see *HLAS 38:4125.*

──── and **Maria Cecília Ribas Carneiro.** 1964 [i.e. Mil novecentos sessenta e quatro]: golpe ou contragolpe? See *HLAS 39:7614.*

4173. Singer, Paul. O Brasil no contexto do capitalismo internacional: 1889-1930 (UNAM/RMS, 36:3, julio/sept. 1974, p. 547-593, bibl.)

Largely account of Brazil's export monoculture, of its dependence on foreign capital, and of Percival Farquhar's attempt to monopolize transport-energy systems of Brazil.

4174. Smith, Peter Seaborn. The Góes Monteiro papers (USP/RH, 55:109, 1977, p. 205-225)

Well-annotated check list of papers of key member of Brazilian government in Vargas era.

4175. Souza, Luiz de Castro. O poeta Maciel Monteiro: de médico a embaixador, 1804-1868. Prefácio de Leduar de Assis Rocha. Recife, Brazil, Prefeitura Municipal do Recife *with the collaboration of* Secretaria de Educação e Cultura [and] Conselho Municipal de Cultura, 1975. 148 p., facsims., illus., plates.

Although this is superficial, only study available of physician-politician-poet, colorful yet typical member of original national elite of Empire.

4176. Stawinski, Alberto Victor. Primórdios da imigração polonesa no Rio Grande do Sul: 1875-1975. Apresentação de Rovílio Costa. Caxias do Sul, Brazil, Univ. de Caxias do Sul [and] Escola Superior de Teologia São Lourenço de Brindes, Porto Alegre, Brazil, 1976. 255 p., map, plates (Col. Imigração polonesa, 1)

Reasonably well-integrated insider study combining general analysis of immigration and assimilation with individual letters and biographical data.

4177. Stols, Eddy. O Brasil se defende da Europa: suas relações com a Belgica: 1830-1914 (CEDLA/B, 18, junio 1975, p. 57-73)

Portmanteau article that covers most aspects, from press propaganda (hence title) through banking to penal colonies, of contacts between Brazil and Belgium.

———. Penetração econômica, assistência técnica e "brain drain:" aspectos da emigração Belga para a América Latina por volta de 1900. See item 2409.

4178. Théberge, Pedro. Esboço histórico sobre a Província do Ceará. v. 1. 2. ed. Fortaleza, Brazil, Secretaría de Cultura, Desporto e Promoção Social [and] Editora Henriqueta Galeno, 1973. 218 p.

First published in 1869 work belongs to early historiography of Ceará. Some of the information has since been interpreted differently, fortunately well annotated by editor. Still useful and well done study.

4179. Titara, Ladislau dos Santos. Paraguassú: epopéia da Guerra da Independência na Bahia. São Paulo, Instituto Histórico Brasileiro *com a cooperação do* Conselho Federal de Cultura, 1973. 570 p., facsims. (Brasiliensia documenta, 8)

Facsimile ed. of great epic poem first published 1835 commemorating struggle for independence in Bahia. Includes useful biographical essay by Pedro Calmon. Of interest to specialist.

Tito Filho, A. Governos do Piauí: capitania, provinicia, estado. See *HLAS 39:7616.*

Tobias, José Antonio. História da educação brasileira. See *HLAS 39:4698.*

4180. Uricoechea, Fernando. A formação do estado brasileiro no século XIX (IUP/D, 14, 1977, p. 85-109, tables)

First half of innovative two-part study of 19th-century politico-administrative change which, in this part, utilizes public expenditure patterns at national and provincial levels, to analyze gradual shift from "patrimonialization" to "bureaucratization."

4181. Vargas, Túlio. A última viagem do Barão do Serro Azul. Curitiba, Brazil, Instituto Assistencial de Autores do Paraná, 1972? 168 p., bibl., plates (O formigueiro, 28)

Highly-dramatized but sound account of career of leading Paraná businessman, Ildefonso Pereira Correia, and his role in civil war of 1893-94. Quotes extensively from contemporary sources to support pro-Federalist stance.

4182. Villaça, Antonio Carlos. História da questão religiosa. Rio, Livraria Francisco Alves Editora, 1974. 177 p., bibl.

This chronology of Religious Question (1872-75), while based on excellent bibliography, fails to transcend orthodox Catholic view, well presented by Sister Mary C. Thornton (see *HLAS 14:2338*), praising two bishops and condemning Masons.

4183. Wachowicz, Romão. A saga de Araucária. Tradução de Mariano Kawka. Curitiba, Brazil, Gráfica Vicentina, 1975. 166 p., facsims., plates, tables.

Local history of century-old Polish community in Paraná, most useful for its insider information. Polish original entitled: *Araukaria spod Pluga.*

4184. Wachowicz, Ruy Christovam. Abranches: um estudo de história demográfica. Curitiba, Brazil, Editora Gráfica Vicentina, 1976. 84 p., bibl., tables.

Sophisticated statistical analysis of parish of Abranches, Paraná, especially of its Polish immigrant population which arrived in 1870s. Part of larger project of Federal Univ. of Paraná on state's historical demography.

4185. ——. Orleans: um século de subsistência. Curitiba, Brazil, Edições Piaol, 1976. 92 p., fold. map, plates, tables.

Succinct and interesting analysis of formative years of Polish agricultural colony established 1876 near Curitiba. Successfully incorporates contemporary statistics, comments, and photos.

4186. Williams, Margaret Todaro. Church and State in Vargas' Brazil: the politics of cooperation (BU/JCS, 18:3, Autumn 1976, p. 443-462)

Perceptive study of how in 1930s Catholic Church regained semi-official status, mainly through pressure group tactics and Cardinal Leme's personal diplomacy. Useful for students.

4187. Wirth, John D. Minas Gerais in the Brazilian Federation: 1889-1937. Stanford, Calif., Stanford, Univ. Press, 1977. 322 p., bibl., maps, plates, tables.

Sophisticated, well-written and innovative analysis combining traditional and quantitative methods to explain development of key area of Brazil between Empire and Estado Novo. Indispensible reading for both content and methodology.

4188. Wolff, Egon and Frieda Wolff. Judeus no Brasil Imperial: uma pesquisa nos documentos e no noticiário carioca da época. São Paulo, Univ. de São Paulo, Faculdade de Filosofia, Letras e Ciências Humanas, Centro de Estudos Judaicos, 1975. 548 p. (Publicação, 1)

Pioneer work containing immense amount of data, primarily from newspapers, about persons of Jewish descent (not necessarily practicing) in Brazil (1808-89). Little or no synthesis, but impressive beginning. Indexed by surname.

4189. Xavier, Livio. Infancia na Granja. São Paulo, The Author, 1974. 113 p., illus., plates.

Transcript of oral interviews probing for recollections of growing up in early 20th-century Granja and Fortaleza, Ceará, as son of wealthy merchant. Interesting facts and observations on family relations, education and cultural life, commerce and its demands, and local politics. Successful if rather self-conscious use of new historical technique. Photos.

4190. Zagonel, Carlos Albino. Igreja e imigração italiana: Capuchinhos de Sabóia; um contributo para a Igreja no Rio Grande do Sul, 1895-1915. Porto Alegre, Brazil, Escola Superior de Teología São Lourenço de Brindes [and] Livraria Sulina, 1975. 287 p., bibl., plates (Col. Centenário da imigração italiana, 5)

Close study glorifying mission of French Capuchins, active from 1895 among Italian immigrant colonies in Rio Grande do Sul. Sees missions as principal means of acculturation. Intensive use of Brazilian and European religious archives.

Zalduendo, Eduardo A. Libras y rieles: las inversiones británicas para el desarrollo de los ferrocarriles en Argentina, Brasil, Canadá e India durante el siglo XIX. See item 3886.

JOURNAL ABBREVIATIONS

AAAS/S	Science. American Association for the Advancement of Science. Washington.
AAFH/TAM	The Americas. A quarterly publication of inter-American cultural history. Academy of American Franciscan History. Washington.
AAG/A	Annals of the Association of American Geographers. Lawrence, Kan.
ACH/B	Boletín de la Academia Chilena de la Historia. Santiago.
ACH/BHA	Boletín de Historia y Antigüedades. Academia Colombiana de la Historia. Bogotá.
ADST/SDT	Sociologie du Travail. Association pour le Développement de la Sociologie due Travail. Paris.
AHA/R	American Historical Review. American Historical Association. Washington.
AHGH/R	Revista de la Academia Hondureña de Geografia e Historia. Tegucigalpa.
AHS/AH	Agricultural History. The quarterly journal for the Agricultural History Society by the Univ. of California Press. Berkeley.
AHSI	Archivum Historicum Societatis Iesu. Roma.

AI/A	Anthropos. Anthropos-Institut. Psoieux, Switzerland.
AISCD	Archives Internationales de Sociologie de la Coopération et du Développement. Paris.
AJES	The American Journal of Economics and Sociology. Francis Neilson Fund [and] Robert Schalkenbach Foundation. N.Y.
ANA	Análisis. Cuadernos de investigación. Lima.
ANH/B	Boletín de la Academia Nacional de Historia. B.A.
ANH/IE	Investigaciones y Ensayos. Academia Nacional de la Historia. B.A.
APS/P	Proceedings of the American Philosophical Society. Philadelphia, Pa.
ARBOR	Arbor. Madrid.
ASAWI/B	Bulletin. African Studies Assn. of the West Indies. Kingston.
AT/A	Antiquity. A quarterly review of archaeology. The Antiquity Trust. Cambridge, U.K.
BBAA	Boletín Bibliográfico de Antropología Americana. Instituto Panamericano de Geografia e Historia, Comisión de Historia. México.
BNJM/R	Revista de la Biblioteca Nacional José Martí. La Habana.
BU/JCS	A Journal of Church and State. Baylor Univ., J.M. Dawson Studies in Church and State. Waco, Tex.
CAM	Cuadernos Americanos. México.
CCE/CHA	Cuadernos de Historia y Arqueología. Casa de la Cultura Ecuatoriana, Núcleo del Guayas. Guayaquil, Ecua.
CCGT/CG	The California Geographer. Annual publication of the California Council of Geography Teachers. Long Beach, Calif.
CDAL	Cahiers des Amériques Latines. Paris.
CDLA	Casa de las Américas. Instituto Cubano del Libro. La Habana.
CEDLA/B	Boletín de Estudios Latinoamericanos. Centro de Estudios y Documentación Latinoamericanos. Amsterdam.
CEHA/NH	Nuestra Historia. Centro de Estudios de Historia Argentina. B.A.
CELRG/A	Araisa. Anuario del Centro de Estudios Latinoamericanos Rómulo Gallegos. Caracas.
CFR/FA	Foreign Affairs. Council on Foreign Relations. N.Y.
CH	Cuadernos Hispanoamericanos. Instituto de Cultura Hispánica. Madrid.
CM/FI	Foro Internacional. El Colegio de México.
CM/HM	Historia Mexicana. El Colegio de México.
CONAC/RNC	Revista Nacional de Cultura. Consejo Nacional de Cultura. Caracas.
CPES/RPS	Revista Paraguaya de Sociología. Centro Paraguayo de Estudios Sociológicos. Asunción.
CSIC/A	Asclepio. Consejo Superior de Investigaciones Científicas, Instituto Arnau de Vilanova de Historia de la Medicina, Archivo Iberoamericano de Historia de la Medicina y Antropología Médica. Madrid.
CSSH	Comparative Studies in Society and History. An international quarterly. Society for the Comparative Study of Society and History. The Hague.
CSUCA/ESC	Estudios Sociales Centroamericanos. Consejo Superior de Universidades Centroamericanas, Confederación Universitaria Centroamericana, Programa Centroamericano de Ciencias Sociales. San José.
CU/JIA	Journal of International Affairs. Columbia Univ., School of International Affairs. N.Y.
CUH	Current History. A monthly magazine of world affairs. Philadelphia, Pa.
DGV/ZE	Zeitschrift für Ethnologie. Deutschen Gesellschaft für Völkerkunde. Braunschweig, FRG.
ECO	Eco. Bogotá.
EEHA/AEA	Anuario de Estudios Americanos. Consejo Superior de Investigaciones Científicas [and] Univ. de Sevilla, Escuela de Estudios Hispano-Americanos. Sevilla.
EEHA/HBA	Historiografía y Bibliografía Americanista. Escuela de Estudios Hispano-Americanos de Sevilla. Sevilla.
EHA/J	Journal of Economic History. New York Univ., Graduate School of Business Administration *for* The Economic History Association. Rensselaer, N.Y.

EME	Revista Eme-Eme. Estudios dominicanos. Univ. Católica Madre y Maestra. Santiago de los Caballeros, R.D.
EMGE/BH	Boletín Histórico del Estado Mayor General del Ejército. Sección Historia y Archivo. Montevideo.
FAIC/CCPT	Comunicaciones Proyecto Puebla-Tlaxcala. Fundación Alemana para la Investigación Científica. Puebla, Mex.
FCE/TP	Trimestre Político. Publicación trimestral del Fondo de Cultura Económica. México.
FDD/NED	Notes et Études Documentaires. Direction de la Documentation. Paris.
FFCLM/EH	Estudos Históricos. Faculdade de Filosofia, Ciências e Letras, Depto. de História. Marília, Bra.
FHS/FHQ	The Florida Historical Quarterly. The Florida Historical Society. Jacksonville.
FJB/BH	Boletín Histórico. Fundación John Boulton. Caracas.
FPRI/O	Orbis. A journal of world affairs. Foreign Policy Research Institute, Philadelphia, Pa. *in association with* Tufts Univ., Fletcher School of Law and Diplomacy, Medford, Mass.
HAHR	Hispanic American Historical Review. Duke Univ. Press *for the* Conference on Latin American History of the American Historical Association. Durham, N.C.
HU/BHR	Business History Review. Harvard Univ., Graduate School of Business Administration. Boston, Mass.
IAA	Ibero-Amerikanisches Archiv. Ibero-Amerikanisches Institut. Berlin, FRG.
IAEERI/E	Estrategia. Instituto Argentino de Estudios Estratégicos y de las Relaciones Internacionales. B.A.
IAHG/AHG	Antropología e Historia de Guatemala. Instituto de Antropología e Historia de Guatemala. Guatemala.
IAHR/N	Numen. International review for the history of religions. International Association for the History of Religions. Leiden, The Netherlands.
IAMEA	Inter-American Economic Affairs. Washington.
IBGE/R	Revista Brasileira de Geografia. Conselho Nacional de Geografia, Instituto Brasileiro de Geografia e Estatística. Rio.
ICP/R	Revista del Instituto de Cultura Puertorriqueña. San Juan.
IDES/DE	Desarrollo Económico. Instituto de Desarrollo Económico y Social. B.A.
IEH/A	Anuario. Univ. Central de Venezuela, Instituto de Estudios Hispanoamericanos. Caracas.
IFEA/B	Bulletin de l'Institut Français d'Etudes Andines. Lima.
IFH/C	Conjonction. Institut Français d'Haïti. Port-au-Prince.
IGFO/RI	Revista de Indias. Instituto Gonzalo Fernández de Oviedo [and] Consejo Superior de Investigaciones Científicas. Madrid.
IGM/U	L'Universo. Rivista bimestrale dell'Instituto Geografico Militare. Firenze, Italy.
IHGB/R	Revista do Instituto Histórico e Geográfico Brasileiro. Rio.
IHGSP/R	Revista do Instituto Histórico e Geográfico de São Paulo. São Paulo.
III/AI	América Indígena. Instituto Indigenista Interamericano. México.
IRA/B	Boletín del Instituto Riva-Agüero. Pontificia Univ. Católica del Perú. Lima.
ISTM/MH	Missionalia Hispanica. Instituto Santo Toribio de Mogrovejo [and] Consejor Superior de Investigaciones Científicas. Madrid.
IUP/D	Dados. Publicação semestral do Instituto Universitário de Pesquisas do Rio de Janeiro. Rio.
JBA	Journal of Belizean Affairs. Belize City.
JDA	The Journal of Developing Areas. Western Illinois Univ. Press. Macomb, Ill.
JEHM/R	Revista de la Junta de Estudios Históricos de Mendoza. Mendoza, Arg.
JGSWGL	Jahrbuch für Geschichte von Staat, Wirtschaft und Gesellschaft Lateinamerikas. Köln, FRG.
JIH	The Journal of Interdisciplinary History. The MIT Press. Cambridge, Mass.

JLAS	Journal of Latin American Studies. Centers or institutes of Latin American studies at the universities of Cambridge, Glasgow, Liverpool, London and Oxford. Cambridge Univ. Press. London.
JW	Journal of the West. Los Angeles, Calif.
LAP	Latin American Perspectives. Univ. of California. Riverside, Calif.
LARR	Latin American Research Review. Univ. of North Carolina Press *for the Latin American Studies Association*. Chapel Hill.
LI/IA	Ibero-Americana. Research news and principal acquisitions of documentation on Latin America in Denmark, Finland, Norway and Sweden. Latinamerika Institutet. Stockholm.
LNB/L	Lotería. Lotería Nacional de Beneficencia. Panamá.
MAGN/B	Boletín del Archivo General de la Nación. Secretaría de Gobernación. México.
MH	Mundo Hispánico. Madrid.
MR	Monthly Review. An independent socialist magazine. N.Y.
OAS/AM	Américas. Organization of American States. Washington.
OLI/ZLW	Zeitschrift für Lateinamerika Wien. Osterreichisches Lateinamerika-Institut. Wien.
PAIGH/G	Revista Geográfica. Instituto Panamericano de Geografia e História, Comissão de Geografia. Rio.
PAIGH/H	Revista de Historia de América. Instituto Panamericano de Geografía e História, Comisión de Historia. México.
PAN/ES	Estudios Latinoamericanos. Polska Akademia Nauk (Academia de Ciencias de Polonia), Instytut Historii (Instituto de Historia). Warszawa.
PAT/TH	The Historian. A journal of history. Phi Alpha Theta, National Honor Society in History. Univ. of Pennsylvania. University Park, Pa.
PCCLAS/P	Proceedings of the Pacific Coast Council on Latin American Studies. Univ. of California. Los Angeles.
PEAGN/R	Revista del Archivo General de la Nación. Instituto Nacional de Cultura. Lima.
PEMN/R	Revista del Museo Nacional. Casa de la Cultura del Perú, Museo Nacional de la Cultura Peruana. Lima.
PF/AIA	Archivo Ibero-Americano. Los Padres Franciscanos. Madrid.
PMNH/HC	Historia y Cultura. Museo Nacional de Historia. Lima.
PP	Past and Present. London.
PPO	Pensamiento Político. Cultura y ciencia política. México.
PUCP/CSH	Cuadernos del Seminario de Historia. Pontificia Univ. Católica del Perú, Instituto Riva-Agüero. Lima.
PUCP/H	Histórica. Pontificia Univ. Católica del Perú. Depto. de Humanidades. Lima.
PUF/AS	L'Année Sociologique. Presses Universitaires de France. Paris.
PUF/RH	Revue Historique. Presses Universitaires de France. Paris.
PUJ/UH	Universitas Humanistica. Pontificia Univ. Javeriana, Facultad de Filosofía y Letras. Bogotá.
RCPC	Revista del Pensamiento Centroamericano. Centro de Investigaciones y Actividades Culturales. Managua.
RIB	Revista Interamericana de Bibliografía [Inter-American Review of Bibliography]. Organization of American States. Washington.
SA/J	Journal de la Société des Américanistes. Paris.
SAR/P	El Palacio. School of American Research; the Museum of New Mexico; and the Archaeological Society of New Mexico. Santa Fe, N. Mex.
SBPC/CC	Ciência e Cultura. Sociedade Brasileira para o Progresso da Ciência. São Paulo.
SCHG/R	Revista Chilena de Historia y Geografía. Sociedad Chilena de Historia y Geografía. Santiago.
SDHS/J	The Journal of San Diego History. The San Diego Historical Society. San Diego, Calif.
SECOLAS/A	Annals of the Southeastern Conference on Latin American Studies. West Georgia College. Carrollton, Ga.

SHG/B	Bulletin de la Société d'Histoire de la Guadeloupe. Archives Départamentales *avec le concours du* Conseil Général de la Guadeloupe. Basse-Terre, W.I.
SHM/RHM	Revista de Historia Militar. Servicio Histórico Militar. Madrid.
SPSA/JP	The Journal of Politics. The Southern Political Science Association *in cooperation with the* Univ. of Florida. Gainesville, Fla.
SRA/A	Anales de la Sociedad Rural Argentina. Revista Pastoril y agrícola. B.A.
SS	Science and Society. N.Y.
TSHA/SHQ	Southwestern Historical Quarterly. Texas State Historical Association. Austin.
UA/AW	Arizona and the West. Univ. of Arizona. Tucson.
UAEM/H	Histórica. Univ. Autónoma del Estado de México, Instituto de Investigaciones Históricas. México.
UASD/R	Revista Dominicana de Antropología e Historia. Univ. Autónoma de Santo Domingo, Facultad de Humanidades, Depto. de Historia y Antropología, Instituto de Investigaciones Antropológicas. Santo Domingo.
UB/BH	Bulletin Hispanique. Univ. de Bordeaux *avec le concours du* Centre National de la Recherche Scientifique. Bordeaux, France.
UBGI/E	Erdkunde. Archiv für Wissenschaftliche Geographie. Univ. Bonn, Geographisches Institut. Bonn.
UBN/R	Revista de la Biblioteca Nacional. Ministerio de Instrucción Pública y Previsión Social. Montevideo.
UC/A	Anales de la Universidad de Cuenca. Cuenca, Ecua.
UC/AT	Atenea. Revista de ciencias, letras y artes. Univ. de Concepción. Concepción, Chile.
UC/CA	Current Anthropology. Univ. of Chicago. Chicago, Ill.
UC/HR	History of Religions. International journal for comparative historical studies. Univ. of Chicago. Chicago, Ill.
UC/PHR	The Pacific Historical Review. Univ. of California Press. Los Angeles.
UC/V	Verbum. Univ. Católica. Rio.
UCAB/M	Montalbán. Univ. Católica Andrés Bello, Facultad de Humanidades y Educación, Institutos Humanísticos de Investigación. Caracas.
UCC/NG	Norte Grande. Revista de estudios integrados referentes a comunidades humanas del Norte Grande de Chile, en una perspectiva geográfica e histórico-cultural. Univ. Católica de Chile, Instituto de Geografía, Depto. de Geografía de Chile, Taller Norte Grande. Santiago.
UCCH/A	Apuntes. Revista de teatro. Univ. Católica de Chile. Santiago.
UCCIH/H	Historia. Univ. Católica de Chile, Instituto de Historia. Santiago.
UCLA/JLAL	Journal of Latin American Lore. Univ. of California, Latin American Center. Los Angeles, Calif.
UCLV/I	Islas. Univ. Central de las Villas. Santa Clara, Cuba.
UCNSA/EP	Estudios Paraguayos. Univ. Católica Nuestra Señora de la Asunción. Asunción.
UCP/IAP	Ibero-Americana Pragensia. Univ. Carolina de Praga, Centro de Estudios Ibero-Americanos. Prague.
UCR/R	Revista de la Universidad de Costa Rica. San José.
UCV/CA	Cuadernos Afro-Americanos. Univ. Central de Venezuela, Consejo de Desarrollo Científico y Humanístico, Facultad de Humanidades y Educación, Instituto de Antropología e Historia. Caracas.
UFB/AA	Afro-Asia. Univ. Federal da Bahia, Centro de Estudos Afro-Orientais. Bahia, Bra.
UHB/EHA	Etudes Hispano-Américaines. Univ. de Haute Bretagne, Centre d'Etudes Hispaniques, Hispano-Américaines et Luso-Brésiliennes. Rennes, France.
UIA/C	Comunidad. Revista de la U.I.A. Cuadernos de difusión cultural. Univ. Iberoamericana. México.
UM/JIAS	Journal of Inter-American Studies and World Affairs. Univ. of Miami Press *for the* Center for Advanced International Studies. Coral Gables, Fla.

UM/R	Revista Universidad de Medellín. Univ. de Medellín, Centro de Estudios de Posgrado. Medellín, Colombia.
UMHN/RH	Revista Histórica. Museo Histórico Nacional. Montevideo.
UN/A	Anales de la Univ. del Norte. Antofagasta, Chile.
UNAM/A	Anglia. Anuario de estudios angloamericanos. Univ. Autónoma de México. Facultad de de Filosofía y Letras. México.
UNAM/AA	Anales de Antropología. Univ. Nacional Autónoma de México. Instituto de Investigaciones Históricas. México.
UNAM/AH	Anuario de Historia. Univ. Nacional Autónoma de México. México.
UNAM/RMCP	See UNAM/RMCPS.
UNAM/RMCPS	Revista Mexicana de Ciencias Políticas y Sociales. Univ. Nacional Autónoma de México. Facultad de Ciencias Políticas y Sociales. México.
UNAM/RMS	Revista Mexicana de Sociología. Univ. Nacional Autónoma de México, Instituto de Investigaciones Sociales. México.
UNCIA/HC	Hombre y Cultura. Revista del Centro de Investigaciones Antropológicas de la Univ. Nacional. Panamá.
UNCP/AC	Anales Científicos de la Univ. del Centro del Perú. Huancayo, Peru.
UNCR/R	Revista de Historia. Univ. Nacional de Costa Rica, Escuela de Historia. Heredia, C.R.
UNL/H	Humanitas. Univ. de Nuevo León, Centro de Estudios Humanísticos. Monterrey, Mex.
UNL/U	Universidad. Univ. Nacional del Litoral. Santa Fe, Arg.
UNLP/CA	Ciencias Administrativas. Univ. Nacional de La Plata, Facultad de Ciencias Económicas, Instituto de Investigaciones de Ciencias Administrativas. La Plata, Arg.
UNM/JAR	Journal of Anthropological Research. Univ. of New Mexico, Depto. of Anthropology. Albuquerque, N. Mex.
UNM/NMHR	New Mexico Historical Review. Published jointly by the Historical Society of New Mexico [and] the Univ. of New Mexico. Albuquerque.
UNSA/H	Historia. Univ. Nacional de San Agustín, Depto. Académico de Historia, Geografía y Antropología. Arequipa, Peru.
UP/A	Apuntes. Univ. del Pacífico, Centro de Investigación. Lima.
UP/E	Ethnology. Univ. of Pittsburgh. Pittsburgh, Pa.
UP/EA	Estudios Andinos. Univ. of Pittsburgh, Latin American Studies Center. Pittsburgh, Pa.
UP/PH	Pacific Historian. Univ. of the Pacific. Stockton, Calif.
UP/PSN	Peasant Studies Newsletter. Univ. of Pittsburgh, Center for International Studies [and] Dept. of History, Pittsburgh, Pa.
UPR/CS	Caribbean Studies. Univ. of Puerto Rico, Institute of Caribbean Studies. Río Piedras.
UPR/LT	La Torre. Univ. de Puerto Rico. Río Piedras.
URSS/AL	América Latina. Academia de Ciencias de la URSS [Unión de Repúblicas Soviéticas Socialistas]. Moscú.
USCG/E	Economía. Revista del Instituto de Investigaciones Económicas y Sociales. Univ. de San Carlos de Guatemala, Facultad de Ciencias Económicas. Guatemala.
USCG/PS	Política y Sociedad. Univ. de San Carlos de Guatemala, Facultad de Ciencias Jurídicas y Sociales, Escuela de Ciencia Política, Instituto de Investigaciones Políticas y Sociales. Guatemala.
USMLA/LA	La Antigua. Univ. de Santa María La Antigua, Oficina de Humanidades. Panamá.
USP/RH	Revista de História. Univ. de São Paulo, Faculdade de Filosofia, Ciências e Letras, Depto. de História [and] Sociedade de Estudos Históricos. São Paulo.
USP/RIEB	Revista do Instituto de Estudos Brasileiros. Univ. de São Paulo. São Paulo.
USSR/SS	Scoial Sciences. USSR Academy of Sciences, Section of the Social Sciences. Moscow.

UTIEH/C	Caravelle. Cahiers du monde hispanique et luso-brésilien. Univ. de Toulouse, Institute d'Études Hispaniques, Hispano-Americaines et Luso-Brésiliennes. Toulouse, France.
UV/L	Logos. Univ. del Valle, Depto. de Humanidades. Cali, Colombia.
UW/LBR	Luso-Brazilian Review. Univ. of Wisconsin Press. Madison, Wis.
UWI/CQ	Caribbean Quarterly. Univ. of the West Indies. Mona, Jam.
UWI/SES	Social and Economic Studies. Univ. of the West Indies, Institute of Social and Economic Research. Mona, Jam.
UY/R	Revista de la Universidad de Yucatán. Mérida, Mex.
VANH/B	Boletín de la Academia Nacional de la Historia. Caracas.
VME/R	*See* CONAC/RNC.
VOZES	Vozes. Revista de cultura. Editora Vozes. Petrópolis, Brazil.
WD	World Development. Pergamon Press. Oxford, U.K.
WHQ	The Western Historical Quarterly. Western History Assn., Utah State Univ. Logan, Utah.
WSU/HB	Human Biology. Official publication of the Human Biology Council. Wayne State Univ., School of Medicine. Detroit, Mich.
WZHUB	Wissenschaftliche Zeitschrift der Humboldt- Univ. Gesellschafts- und Sprachwissenschaftliche Reihe. Berlin.
ZMR	Zeitschrift für Missionswissenschaft and Religionswissenschaft. Lucerne, Switzerland.

LANGUAGE

D. LINCOLN CANFIELD

Professor Emeritus of Spanish
Southern Illinois University

BOOKS AND ARTICLES THAT HAVE BEEN REVIEWED for this volume again include many special vocabularies, some in Spanish and some in Portuguese: Portuguese baby-talk, onomatopoeic noises in English and Spanish, words associated with the culture of corn in Colombia, marketing vocabulary of Brazil (nearly half English), architectural terminology in Mexico, the soccer vocabulary of sports writers in Brazil, tourism lexicon for Brazil, social science terminology used in Latin America.

Dialect studies have been numerous and show a slight shift in interest toward sociolinguistics and languages in contact. Two articles, one in Spanish and one in Portuguese deal with allophonic alternatives in Caribbean Spanish and Brazilian Portuguese respectively (see item 6093 and item 6063).

The problems brought about by the fact that Creole speakers in many areas have to use an "official" language in school and in certain business and judicial situations have concerned several writers, especially in the English-speaking parts of the Caribbean.

Perhaps the most significant studies to report are again in the realm of bibliography: *Spanish and English of the United States Hispanos: a critical annotated linguistic bibliography* by Richard Teschner, general editor, and Garland D. Bills and Jerry R. Craddock, associate editors (item 6013); and *A bibliography of Pidgin and Creole languages* by John E. Reinecke, David DeCamp, Ian F. Hancock, Stanley M. Tzuzaki and Richard E. Wood (item 6131).

Honorable mention should be made of Donald E. Kloe's description of onomatopoeic sounds in English and Spanish, already mentioned (item 6077) and the short but critical bibliography of *Fourteen Chicano bibliographies* by Hensley Woodbridge and Karen H. Evavik's re-examination of pedagogical materials on Spanish intonation (item 6014).

RECENT DOCTORAL DISSERTATIONS
Spanish and Portuguese Languages and Linguistics
(1975-77)

Barkin, Florence R. The influence of English on the Spanish of bilingual Mexican-American migrants in Florida. SUNY-Buffalo (Peter Boyd-Bowman).

Bjarkman, Peter C. Natural phonology and loanword phonology: with selected examples from Miami-Cuban Spanish. Univ. of Florida (B. Saciuk).

Brown, Margaret C. A transformational analysis of the Spanish neuter and related structures. Univ. of Wisconsin (Norman Sacks).
Brown, Robert A., Jr. A sociolinguistic description of the Spanish of Panama City. Georgetown Univ. (William Cressey).
Floyd, Mary Elizabeth. Tense, aspect and mood in Colorado Spanish syntax. Univ. of Colorado (Anthony G. Lozano).
Grace, Lee Ann. The effect of bilingualism on sixteenth-century Mexican Spanish. SUNY-Buffalo (Peter Boyd-Bowman).
Hammond, Robert M. Some theoretical implications from rapid speech phenomena in Miami-Cuban Spanish. Georgetown Univ. (Bohdan Saciuk).
Kirschner, Carl. Generative semantics in Spanish. Univ. of Massachusetts (John J. Staczek).
Klemme, William H. A thematic relations analysis of the syntactic and semantic domain of selected Spanish verbs. Pennsylvania State Univ. (John B. Dalbor).
La Verghetta, Raymond C. The surface structure realization of semantic categories: a study of truth and reference in Spanish. Georgetown Univ. (Gino Parisi).
Longmire, Beverly J. The relationship of variables in Venezuela Spanish to historical sound changes in Latin and the Romance Languages. Goergetown Univ. (William Cressey).
Milán, William G. Patterns of sociolinguistic behavior in Puerto Rico Spanish. Temple University (W.J. Calvano).
Pontillo, James L. Nautical terms in sixteenth-century Spanish. SUNY-Buffalo (Peter Boyd-Bowman).
Redenbarger, Wayne J. Portuguese vowel height and phonological theory: a generative re-analysis based on tongue-root features. Harvard Univ. (Francis Rogers).
Reyes, Rogelio. Studies in Chicano Spanish. Harvard Univ. (Karl V. Teeter).
Rissel, Dorothy A. An investigation of world view as manifested in a portion of the lexicon of a bilingual-bicultural situation: Spanish-English. SUNY-Buffalo (Peter Boyd-Bowman).
Santizo, Mario José. Un estudio lingüístico de *Hombres de maíz*. St. Louis Univ. (A. Taub).
Smith, Rosslyn Mynatt. Spanish clitic pronouns: a transformational description. Univ. of New Mexico (G.D. Bills).
Strozer, Judith Reina. Clitics in Spanish. Univ. of California, Los Angeles (C.L. Hulet).
Webb, John T. A lexical study of *caló* and non-standard Spanish in the Southwest. Univ. of California, Berkeley (J.R. Craddock).
Weissenrieder, Maureen M. The Spanish adverbial: form, function, and distribution. Pennsylvania State Univ. (John B. Dalbor).
Wherritt, Irene M. The subjunctive in Brazilian Portuguese. Univ. of New Mexico (John Bergen).

SPANISH

GENERAL AND BIBLIOGRAPHICAL

6001. Barbón Rodríguez, José A. La independencia lingüística (JGSWGL, 12, 1975, p. 211-229)

Polemics and serious studies on the Spanish of America since Independence, and statements by Bello and Sarmiento on whether Spanish contributions to the culture of Spanish America should be recognized.

6002. Caro, Miguel Antonio. Del uso en sus relaciones con el lenguaje. Bogotá, Instituto Caro y Cuervo, 1976. 107 p.

Speech delivered by Caro before the Academia Colombiana in 1881. Interesting now in that it reveals the old normative view of language and dialect and the role of literature in regulating.

6003. Cassano, Paul V. Theories of language borrowing tested by American Spanish phonology (UCP/RP, 30:2, Nov. 1976, p. 331-342)

Refers to statements of previous investigators who have assumed mutual influences of languages in contact. Shows that features that may be characteristic of second language are often developed internally: Náhuatl [ts] and Mexican-Spanish [ts] from *-tes* (*partes*). Points out that any phone can be borrowed at the outer-ring core, and refers to Jakobson's statement that it is impossible to borrow a feature that does not fit the pattern of the borrowing language. Value of article rests on suggestion of inner development that may resemble feature of a "loaning" language.

6004. Flórez, Luis. Apuntes de español: pronunciación - ortografía - gramática - léxico - extranjerismos - el habla en la radio y la televisión - enseñanza del idioma y de la gramática en Colombia. Bogotá, Instituto Caro y Cuervo, 1977. 229 p. (Publicaciones. Series Minor, 21)

Typically, Flórez writes against *pura pedantería* in this series of articles published in Bogotá newspaper between 1967-76, now revised and brought up to date. He had similar series between 1954-66. Cites pronunciation, especially by radio announcers, of "*veinte*" with labiodental as *el colmo de la afectación*.

6005. Hoyos Andrade, Rafael M. Dialectología hispanoamericana y enseñanza del español (USP/LL, 3, 1974, p. 171-181)

Problems of dialectology must be solved, or at least faced, by teacher of second language. Many popular misconceptions prevail with regard to language vs dialect, and in matter of unity of the language (especially true in Latin America), which some think should be furthered by school systems. Writer believes that teachers of second language should be familiar with dialectal manifestations of that language and should be objective in presenting them. Article shows Portuguese influence in spelling (*castelhano*) and accentuation (*princípios*).

6006. Leselbaum, Charles *ed.* and *comp*. Epistolario de Rufino José Cuervo y Raymond Foulché-Delbosc. Bogotá, Instituto Caro y Cuervo, 1977. 368 p., bibl., facsims., illus., plates, tables (Archivo epistolar colombiano, 11)

Letters written between 1892-1911 and now part of Institute's *Archivo epistolar*. Only one seems to have any philological significance, and much more important things are said in Cuervo's *Obras Inéditas* (1944).

6007. Milani, Virgil I. The written language of Christopher Columbus. Buffalo, State Univ. of New York, Dept. of Spanish, Italian and Portuguese, 1973. 150 p., bibl., tables. (Supplement *Forum Italicum*, June 1973)

Writer attempts to show Genovese influence in letters of Columbus, written in Spanish. It would seem that many of the peculiarities he cites as from Genoa were quite common in Spanish of period, *x* for *s*, for instance (*yglexia*), and the lexical items that he considers Genovese were common to Spanish then.

6008. Miró Quesada, Francisco and Ernesto Zierer. Siete temas de lingüística teórica y aplicada. Presentación de Walter Reinoso Sánchez-Moreno. Trujillo, Perú, Univ. Nacional de Trujillo, Depto. de Idiomas y Lingüística, 1976. 106 p.

Several essays on linguistic topics with emphasis on sociolinguistic themes. Good article on second language acquisition stresses importance of *vivenciabilidad*, a word that the writer apparently derives from *vivencia*, and which is certainly true in second language learning.

Programa Interamericano de Lingüística y Enseñanza de Idiomas (PILEI), *VI, San Juan, P.R., 1971.* Actas. See *HLAS 39:1730.*

6009. Romero, Mario Germán *ed.* and *comp*. Epistolario de Ezequiel Uricoechea con Rufino José Cuervo y Miguel Antonio Caro. Bogotá, Instituto Caro y Cuervo, 1976. 340 p., facsims., illus., tables (Archivo espitolar colombiano, 10)

Consist of 59 letters from Urichochea to Rufino José Cuervo and 12 to Miguel Antonio Caro taken directly from the Institute's Archivo Epistolar Colombiano. Interesting in stylistic aspects, proverbs, Bogotá expressions and period's idioms.

6010. Rosenblat, Angel. Los conquistadores y su lengua. Caracas, Univ. Central de Venezuela, Ediciones de la Biblioteca, 1977. 160 p. (Col. Arte y literatura, 5)

Combination of two papers delivered at meetings in Santiago and Madrid and 1940 article published in *La Nación* (B.A.). Concludes that 16th-century Spanish-American society had high percentage of *hidalgos*, clergy, *licenciados*, university people, and relatively few peasants, therefore, their language was not from the *hampa*!

6011. ———. Nuestra lengua en ambos mundos. Barcelona, Salvat/Alianza, 1971. 202 p. (Biblioteca general Salvat, 17)

6012. Subero, Efraín. El problema de definir lo hispanoamericano: estudio y bibliografía. Caracas, Univ. Católica Andrés Bello, Instituto Humanístico de Investigación, Centro de Investigaciones Literarias (CIL), 1974. 122 p., bibl.

Attempt to delve into the identity problem felt by many Spanish-speaking Americans vis-à-vis Hispanic culture, relations with Spain and subsequent isolation. Religion, language, and moral values are all factors.

6013. Teschner, Richard V.; Garland D. Bills; and **Jerry R. Craddock** *eds.* Spanish and English of the United States Hispanos: a critical, annotated, linguistic bibliography. Arlington, Va., Center for Applied Linguistics, 1975. xxii, 352 p.

Excellent, very useful compilation of 675 items which is very worthy successor to masterful study by Hensley C. Woodbridge "Spanish in the American South and Southwest: a Bibliographical Survey for the Years 1940-53" (1954). Lengthy introduction reviews geopolitical situation of 10,000,000 Spanish-speaking people of US and sketchily reports on research since Aurelio Espinosa's pioneer work on New Mexican Spanish some 70 years ago. Major categories of bibliography are: US in general; Chicanos (Mexican-Americans); Puerto Ricans; Cubans; Isleños; Peninsulares; Sephardic Jews. Each one has sub-categories, including Bibliography, General Studies, Phonology, Lexicon, Onomastics, English Influence on Spanish and Spanish on English, Code Switching. Title precisely indicates work is critical and annotated. Rather lengthy comments on many entries reveal authors' first-hand investigation and what is more important, all are well qualified to review linguistic material, especially in realm of dialectology, and all have "been around" as far as manifestations of both Spanish and English are concerned.

6014. Woodbridge, Hensley C. Fourteen Chicano bibliographies: 1971-1975 (MLTA/MLJ, 61:1/2, 1977, p. 20-25).

Characteristically thorough and critical analysis of recent bibliographies on Mexican-Americans. Some refer to works that deal with subject of Chicano as a whole, others with specific topics, such as history including references to dialect studies or glossaries. Woodbridge writes that of those examined, Arnulfo D. Trejo's *Bibliografía Chicana: a guide to information sources* (Detroit, Gale Research Co., 1975) is best one attempting overall view. Criticizes severely Frank Pino's *Mexican-Americans: a research bibliography* (East Lansing, Michigan State Univ., 1974, 2 v.) which although the most comprehensive is full of inaccuracies in entries and typos. Woodbridge believes that many of these books try to take in too much and that *Chicano* and *Mexican-American* should be better defined.

6014a. Zubatsky, Davis S. Hispanic linguistic studies in Festschriften: an annotated bibliography, 1957-75 (AATSP/H, 60, 1977, p. 656-715).

Author reviews articles on linguistic topics in some 200 *homenajes* that were published in nearly 20-year period. First considers Basque and Catalan, then Peninsular Spanish, followed by American Spanish, making categories of elements of phonology, morphology, dialectology, onomastics, etc., for Spain, while dealing with Spanish America by countries. Annotations are usually quotations from the articles. One serious omission is the *Homenaje a Federico de Onís* in *Revista Hispánica Moderna* (34:1/2; 3/4, 2 vols.) although the book contained only two articles on linguistic themes.

PHONOLOGY AND GRAMMAR

6015. Bolinger, Dwight. Again: one or two subjunctives? (AATSP/H, 59, 1976, p. 41-49).

Part of an on-going *polémica* between Bolinger and Anthony Lozano (Univ. of Colorado). Essence of Bolinger's argument is that there is one bipolar contrast between indicative and subjunctive. There are a number of classes of verbs, according to semantic features that they contain. Certain features are compatible with indicative, others with subjunctive, but none of this determines indicative or subjunctive. Determining factor is speaker's meaning, and subjunctive is so autonomous that various shades escape all regulation by set rules.

6016. Caro, Miguel Antonio. Tratado del participio. Bogotá, Instituto Caro y Cuervo, 1976. 186 p.

Study of differences in function of Latin and Castilian participle, inspired by translations of Latin works by author.

6017. Gainza, Gastón. ¿Sujeto preposicional? un problema de límites (UH/RJ, 25, 1974, p. 263-277).

Writes on change in status of *hasta* and *entre* when they occur initially. Refers to them as "nuclear modifiers" when they are part of subject.

6018. Hammarström, Göran. Dos estudios dialectológicos. Presentación de Juan M. Lope Blanch. México, Centro de Lingüística Hispánica, Instituto de Investigaciones Filológicas, 1975. 42

p., illus. (Asociación de Lingüística y filología de la América Latina. Cuadernos de lingüística, 1)

Study suggested by Juan Lope Blanch and dedicated to José Pedro Rona's memory. While dealing in *gloto-unidades* and *dia-unidades* and *socio-unidades*, writer does make significant comments about function in language of societal urge to "hablar más fino."

6019. Kvavik, Karen H. Research and pedagogical materials on Spanish intonation: a re-examination (AATSP/H, 59:3, Sept. 1976, p. 406-417, illus., tables)

Excellent examination of research that has been done on a little-understood aspect of Spanish phonology—intonation. Considers major studies of Spanish intonation that are now sources for pedagogical application, beginning with Tomás Navarro's *Manual de entonación*, which is based on "literary" or reading style of Castilian speakers, then efforts of Stockwell and Bowen, Cárdenas, Dalbor, Hadlich, Holton and Montes, Delattre, Matluck. Kvavik regrets that some of these studies show pitch curves but no frequency information, and she compiles new data from recordings of four male Spaniards and four male Mexicans. Although there isn't too much difference between two groups in conversation style, in reading the Spaniard has a much lower final tone, and Mexican's terminal styles are complex.

6020. Navarro Tomás, Tomás. La voz y la entonación en los personajes literarios. México, Colección Málaga, 1976. 191 p. (Nobles temas y bellas letras)

Stating that before the word there was the voice, Navarro examines literary masterpieces for descriptions of voice quality and intonation of characters depicted. Includes several works from Spanish America: Larreta's *Zogoibi*; Gallegos' *Doña Bárbara*; Barrios' *Gran Señor y Rajadiablos*; Asturias' *El Señor Presidente*; Yáñez' *Al filo del agua*; and García Márquez' *Cien años de soledad*. Clever interpretation of intonational descriptions.

6021. Nebrija, Antonio de. Reglas de *orthographia* en la lengua castellana. Estudio y edición de Antonio Quilis. Bogotá, Instituto Caro y Cuervo, 1977. 195 p., bibl., facsim. (Publicaciones, 40)

Using last ed. of Nebrija's *Orthographia* (González Llubera, 1926), Quilis converts original 1517 work to modern linguistic terminology. Significantly, Nebrija was reformer, and his efforts to reduce rules of his language to correspondence of grapheme to phoneme produced first grammar of a modern language.

6022. Polo Figueroa, Nicolás. Aspectos de semántica y sintaxis española. Tunja, Univ. Pedagógica y Tecnológica de Colombia, Secretaría de Investigaciones e Extensión Univ., Fondo Especial de Publicaciones, 1976. 116 p., bibl., tables (Ediciones la rana y el aguila)

Dwells on lively, continuing interest in problem of meaning. Writer uses transformational approach to reach conclusion that semantics is sub-mechanism and generator of structures from which sentences are formed. Examines process necessary to convert structure of relation to a structure of functions, that is, semantic structure into syntactic structure. Good bibliography.

6023. Stiehm, Bruce G. The information value of Spanish phonotactic occurrence (SIL, 25, April 1975, p. 49-54)

To describe syllable constraints in Spanish writer says that capacity for communicating a greater or lesser degree of conceptual distinctions is determined by number of uniquely distinguished symbolic forms that can appear in any given environment. In the Spanish word phonotactics provides support for greater number of conceptual distinctions at center of word, and lesser number of conceptual distinctions at beginning and end. Shows phonemes that can occur at various positions in Spanish word and constraints on consonants in syllable formation. Simplified presentation of all this was made by Sol Saporta and Heles Contreras in *A phonological grammar of Spanish* (1962).

6024. Suñer, Margarita. Demythologizing the impersonal "se" in Spanish (AATSP/H, 59:2, May 1976, p. 268-275)

Writer uses procedures devised from Chomsky's *Aspects of the theory of syntax* to dispell widespread myths about impersonal *se* sentences in Spanish. Myths seem to have been: 1) that *se* is a subject; 2) that there are *se* passive sentences; 3) that agreement is obligatory. She concludes that impersonal sentences are syntactically subjectless sentences, that so-called passive *se* sentences are non-existent, that agreement between verb and what follows is optional.

6025. ———. Looking down the tree in Spanish (LINGUA, 39:3, July 1976, p. 201-225, bibl., tables)

Three syntactic processes of Spanish: complementizers; subjunctive vs. indicative, and impersonal *se* construction are tested against Chomskian hypothesis which maintains existence of a certain condition on transformations. This presentation explored permissibility of transformations to reach down into lower sentences, since transformations are meaning preserving. She claims that processes support hypothesis, and demonstrate that morphological insertion and meaning preservation are complementary.

6026. Uribe-Villegas, Oscar. Las disciplinas sociolingüísticas y el énfasis sociológico en sociolingüística: un ensayo. México, Instituto de Investigaciones Sociales, 1976. 105 p., bibl.

Writer traces interest in sociolinguistics and focus of several disciplines on language. Draws heavily on Hymes and Fishman.

DIALECTOLOGY & SOCIOLINGUISTICS

6027. Albor, Hugo R. Apuntes lexicográficos del español hablado en Nariño (ICC/T, 27:2, mayo/agosto 1972, p. 333-345)

Spanish of Nariño (Colombia) divided dialectally between the highlands and the coast, shows many *quechuismos* in the highland lexicon of everyday speech. Albor uses two novels, *Chambú* and *La venganza de un cura* to illustrate how many indigenous terms occur. He then compares many of these to the vocabulary of his native Atlántico.

6028. Bareiro Saguier, Rubén. Colonialismo mental en el bilingüismo paraguayo de nuestros días (UTIEH/C. 27, 1976, p. 43-51) p. 43-51)

Writer believes that language situation in Paraguay is still reflection of existence of dominant group and dominated one. Those of elevated standing use Spanish in preference to Guaraní, but often use Guaraní in intimate situations. People of countryside and towns prefer Guaraní and use Spanish only in talking to people of some standing and, as soon as cordiality is shown, shift to Guaraní. Furthermore, bilingualism is national trait, and most are proud of it. Lima and Mexico City each have a population only 10 percent of which is bilingual. Asunción is 48.55 percent bilingual. Alphabetization in Spanish is a problem for many who speak much better Guaraní.

6029. Carvalho-Neto, Paulo de. El lenguaje de *Mi tío Atahualpa*: contribución al estudio de la fraseología popular de la costa ecuatoriana (UCAB/M, 3, 1974, p. 681-702)

Vocabulary study of work *Mi tío Atahualpa* as typical representative of speech of the Ecuadorian coast. As is the case in many of these studies, much of vocabulary is not limited to Ecuador's coast.

6029a. Cassano, Paul V. The alveolarization of the /n/, /t/, /d/ and /rt/ in the Spanish of Paraguay (LING, 93, 1 Dec. 1972, p. 22-26)

Takes Bertil Malmberg (*L'espagnol dans le Nouveau Monde*) to task for attributing alveolar articulation in the Spanish of Paraguay to Guaraní influence, and makes a good case for internal Spanish development.

6030. ———. Mexican Spanish final /-s/ in relation to Aztec influence (SIL, 25, April 1975, p. 55-61)

Discussion of various theories on reasons for "strength" of Mexican Spanish final /s/. Points out that such an /s/ exists elsewhere, so that if Aztec has had any effect on this feature of Mexican Spanish, it was perhaps reinforcement rather than influence. Refers to article by Juan Lope Blanch "La Influencia del Sustrato en la Fonética del Español de México," in *Revista de Filología Española* (1967, p. 145-161).

6031. ———. Retention of certain hiatuses in Paraguayan Spanish (LING, 109, 1 Aug. 1973, p. 12-16)

Author criticizes Amado Alonso's theory of contamination of Paraguayan Spanish by Guaraní in matter of contiguous strong vowels and corrects his transcription of certain Guaraní words, (sebo?í, not sebo'í). Glottal stop was not considered. Concludes that Spanish of Paraguay is simply conservative in retention of two-syllable renditions of such words as *país, baúl, traer, leído*.

6032. ———. The substrat theory in relation to the bilingualism of Paraguay: problems and findings (IU/AL, 15:9, Dec. 1973, p. 406-426)

Takes several writers to task on matter of assuming that substratum indigenous influence causes most phonological perculiarities of American Spanish. Examines earlier reaction of Amado Alonso to some of these theories. Questions Malmberg's statements (*L'espagnol dans le nouveau monde*) on the alveolarization of /t/, /d/, /n/ in Paraguayan Spanish.

6033. Cavazos Garza, Israel. El habla del noreste de México: comentarios (UNL/H, 1976, p. 419-426)

Mostly sketchy comments about Nuevo León's phonology: *ella* becomes [ea], *capilla* [kapía]. 50 miles away in Saltillo this is not the case. Tells of archaisms *truje, endenantes, ansina, dende*, etc. One feature of Monterrey Spanish was not mentioned: dissimilation in such combinations as *en medio* [en médjo] rather than [emmédjo].

6034. Dis, Emilio. Código lunfardo. B.A., Editorial Caburé, 1975. 258 p. (Col. Pintusa)

Vicente Emilio Disandro, of Argentina's Federal Police, tells how he learned criminal code teaching at Escuela Superior de Policía and during many years of intense and varied police work in B.A.'s "nunca acabado bullicio." Writes of ways of creating words by transposition (*zabeca* for cabeza) and describes *arrabal's* social climate.

6035. Donni de Mirande, Nélida Esther. Grupos consonánticos en Rosario (ICC/T, 29:3, sept./dic. 1974, p. 526-538)

Another good sociolinguistic study by one of Argentina's women linguists, this one of city of Rosario (pop. 700,000), using about 180 recordings of individuals, 80 between ages of 35-55, 50 24-34, and 50 over 55. Two styles of speech were recorded: formal and colloquial, and distinctions were made on basis of cultural background, urban center or barrio. Results show progressive elimination of first element of *combinación culta* from urban formal to barrio's spontaneous speech.

6036. Dubsky, Josef. Estructuración semántica de modismos (UCP/IAP, 8, 1974, p. 51-58)

Research in lexicon done in Santiago de Cuba (1971 72) in conversational idiom of the *nivel medio*, in which Czech writer tried to find semantic basis for choice of terms in idioms of the day. Some 500 are examined in categories such as *La vida del hombre* (45 percent of total), calzado, vestido, muebles, comidas y bebidas, partes de la casa, la naturaleza, vida social. Interesting examples are expressions for "having things easy:" *tener una beca, estar en el floting*.

6037. Elizaincìn, Adolfo. Algunos aspectos de la sociolingüística del dialecto fronterizo. Montevideo, Univ. de la República, Facultad de Humanidades y Ciencias, Depto. de Lingüística, 1973. 15 p. (Col. Temas de lingüística, 3)

This is a follow-up to José Pedro Rona's "La Frontera Lingüística entre el Portugués y el Español en el Norte del Uruguay" in *Veritas* (8:2, junio 1963, p. 201-219). Delivered as a paper at Congreso de Lingüística y Literatura Hispanoamericana, Salta, Arg., Jan. 1973, and describes in some detail border situation (Uruguay-Brazil) in which there is a band near border in Uruguay where only Portuguese is spoken, another farther inland in which a Portuguese with Spanish influence is spoken, and yet another in which the language is Portuguese-influenced Spanish, and finally Spanish only. Spanish does not penetrate into Brazil. For author's follow-up article on subject, see item 6038.

6038. ———. The emergence of bilingual dialects on the Brazilian-Uruguayan border (LING, 177, Aug. 1976, p. 123-134, bibl.)

Like author's earlier book (see item 6037), this is also a follow-up to José Pedro Rona's "La Frontera Lingüística entre el Portugués y el Español en el Norte del Uruguay" *Veritas* (8:2, junio 1963, p. 201-219). It is estimated that one third of the population of Uruguay speaks Portuguese rather than Spanish. Writer interviewed people of border area, who seemed aware that *dialecto fronterizo* is spoken throughout area. Some think it is same all along border, some are aware of differences, all think it will not disappear. Writer believes that review of the situation does not warrant any conclusion or recommendation for socio-educational policies, as some specialists of UNESCO suggested in 1970.

6039. Escobar, Alberto. Bilingualism and dialectology in Peru (LING, 177, 10 Aug. 1976, p. 85-96)

Attempts to account for language problem: Spanish-Quechua contact as part of Peruvian Spanish. Major part of article deals with vowel system of Quechua (/I/, /a/, /U/) and effects of this on bilinguals' Spanish. Also cites [ḷ], [f̃] ([f] final) as typical of highland Peruvian Spanish.

6040. Florez, Luis. Del español hablado en Colombia: seis muestras de léxico. Bogotá, Instituto Caro y Cuervo, 1975. 198 p. (Series Minor, 20)

Manual of samples of oral usage on two levels, learned and popular (vulgar), with two attitudes in each case (familiar and affected), and each in two environments, national and regional. Work is not normative in approach and does not condemn. Muestras: general Colombian usage, regionalisms, archaisms, sexualization and de-sexualization, indigenisms, "expressivity" (attitudes and sentiments) and the linguistic devices used, such as vowel lengthening.

6041. Fontanella de Weinberg, Marìa Beatriz. Analogía y confluencia paradigmática en formas verbales de voseo (ICC/T, 31:2, mayo/agosto 1976, p. 249-272, bibl.)

Perhaps best study yet of paradigms of verbal forms of *voseo*. Characteristically through examination of morphological details that have been rather vague. Writer's interest in this is both diachronic and synchronic (see *HLAS* 38:6079). Her emphasis is on problem presented by multiple variation observed in America in descendants of Old Spanish *-edes*. She concludes that various forms were extant in Peninsula at time of settlements in America, resulting in *és* (Central America) *éis* (Chile), and *is* (Argentina).

6042. Gagini, Carlos. Diccionario de costarriqueñismos. 3. ed. Breve nota para la tercera edición de Victor Manuel Arroyo Soto. San José, Editorial Costa Rica (ECR), 1975. 243 p. (Biblioteca patria, 20)

Old standby, first printed 1892, with second ed. in 1919, both under title *Diccionario de barbarismos y provincialismos de Costa Rica*. Long prologue by R.J. Cuervo written in 1904, and bibliography is quite good. Like many such works, idioms and vocabulary that are listed as typical of country indicated, are also to be found in several others.

6042a. García González, José. Remanentes lingüísticos munsudis: un estudio descriptivo (UCLV/I, 44, enero/abril 1973, p. 193-246, bibl., table)

Vestiges of African Congo influence in the vocabulary of sections of the population of Cuba. Much of the material (probably from the Kikongo language) had been gleaned from Leoncia Marín of Sancti-Spiritus.

6043. Geoffroy Rivas, Pedro. El español que hablamos en El Salvador. 3. ed. San Salvador, Ministerio de Educación. Dirección de Publicaciones, 1976. 177 p.

Purely lexical. For most part, list of nouns, nearly all of which are of indigenous origin (Pipil, dialect of Náhuatl). Terms listed, with etymological notes, are heard in daily conversation in El Salvador and are typical of language of area. Significant omissions: *chibola* (soda pop), *peche* (slim), *pacha* (bottle).

6044. Gnerre, Maurizio. American Spanish *palta* 'avocado': the diffusion of a Quechua word, viewed in relation to its etymology (UCP/RP, 29:3, Feb. 1976, p. 297-310, bibl.)

The term *ahuacate* (*persea gratissima* or avocado) was diffused by the Spaniards from Mexico southward, but at a certain point in southern Ecuador the fruit becomes *palta*, which turns out to be name of a tribe of Indians, a self-determination word (*my people*) with an original meaning of "flat head."

6045. Gobello, José. Diccionario lunfardo y de otros términos antiguos y modernos usuales en Buenos Aires. B.A., A. Peña Lillo Editor, 1975. 234 p.

Well known Lunfardo writer quotes from many authors, and one senses that argot is of rural and urban origins.

6046. Granda, Germán de. Elementos lingüísticos afroamericanos en el área hispánica: nuevos materiales para su estudio sociohistórico (ICC/T, 31:3, sept./dic. 1976, p. 481-501)

This member of team of investigators of *Atlas lingüístico etnográfico de Colombia* (ALEC) has long been concerned with populations of African origin in Spanish America and has certainly delved deeply into supporting literature. Article designed to give good bibliography background to those who might be interested in pursuing Afro-Hispanic American studies. Notes on sources of information take up more space than article itself.

6047. ———. Estudios sobre un área dialectal hispanoamericana de población negra: las tierras bajas occidentales de Colombia. Bogotá, Instituto Caro y Cuervo, 1977. 364 p., bibl., maps, plates (Publicaciones, 41)

Book represents recapitulation of author's notes during direct field work (1973, 1974, 1975) in Pacific Coast area of depts. of Chocó, Valle, Cauca, Antioquia and Nariño as member of team of investigators of Instituto Caro y Cuervo who have been gathering material for *Atlas lingüístico etnográfico de Colombia*, under Luis Flórez' direction. Lexically area is divided by Granda into three subzones, and he describes not only Spanish of this black population but customs and folklore. Dialectally, the discovery is an intervocalic /d/ that becomes [r], much as is the case in American English *muddy*.

Honsa, Vladimir. Clasificación de los dialectos españoles de América y la estructura de los dialectos de Colombia. See *HLAS 39:1666*.

6048. Lope Blanch, Juan M. Un caso de posible influencia maya en el español mexicano (CN/NRFH, 24:1, 1975, p. 89-100, map, tables)

In *encuestas* made by a Lope-Blanch team in Yucatán several indications of retroflex /r/ were found in Spanish of Champotón, Campeche, Mérida, Valladolid, but not in towns in south of peninsula, nor in Villahermosa. Author raises question of whether these articulations are due to Maya influence, or, since Maya does not have /r/, to *polimorfismo* inspired by Maya.

6049. ———. El estudio del español urbano culto (*in* Programa Interamericano de Lingüística y Enseñanza de Idiomas (PILEI), VI, San Juan, P.R., 1971. Comisión de Lingüística y Dialectología Iberoamericanas. Actas, informes y comunicaciones [see *HLAS 39:1730*] p. 157-168)

Progress report on project of recording on magnetic tape speech of inhabitants of major cities of Latin America and studying them in linguistic laboratories. [A.C. Wares]

6049a. Montes Giraldo, José Joaquín. El habla del Chocó: notas breves (ICC/T, 29:3, sept./dic. 1974, p. 409-428)

This article supplements the work of Luis Flórez' "El Habla del Chocó" in *Boletín del Instituto Caro y Cuervo* (6, 1950, p. 110-116), and goes into the pronunciation in much more detail, using data gathered in Nóvita, Cértegui and Tutumendo. Especially noteworthy is the intervocalic /d/ which sporadically becomes r.

6050. ———. La neutralización del consonatismo implosivo en un habla colombiana, Mechengue, Cauca (ICC/T, 30:3, sept./dic. 1975, p. 561-585)

Another spin-off of field work that has been done for the *Atlas lingüístico etnográfico de Colombia*. The town of Mechengue, Cauca, on the Pacific coast of the country seems to have considerable leveling of final consonants, to the extent that the writer claims that there are only two phonemes in an implosive position: a nasal that can be heard as [n], [ŋ], [m] or as nasalization of the preceding vowel; and an oral that can be represented by *l, r, s* or their variants. This leveling of the implosives distinguishes Pacific coast Spanish from Atlantic coast in Colombia.

6051. ——— and María Luisa Rodríguez de Montes. El maíz en el habla y la cultural popular de Colombia con notas sobre su origen y nombres en lenguas indígenas americanas. Bogotá, Instituto Caro y Cuervo, 1975. 187 p., bibl., maps, plates (Publicaciones, 33)

Another spin-off from immense corpus largely gathered by this author (1958-74) for *Atlas lingüístico etnográfico de Colombia*. Book has several maps and photographs and goes into origins of corn and various indigenous names for it. Local names for various aspects of growing corn and various parts of plant are described as they were heard by investigators in hundreds of Colombian villages.

6052. Morales P., Félix. El *voseo* en Chile (UC/BF, 23/24, 1972/73, p. 261-273, tables)

Maintains that *voseo* is rapidly spreading among youth of Chile in preference to *tuteo*, and not only in lower classes. Former idea of vulgarity that may have been associated with it is passing and it has become index of confidence and solidarity, much as in Argentina. Prevalent forms are discussed (*andai, tenís* or *teníh*). *Tuteo* has been generally form of address among intimates, but apparently many now think *voseo* more egalitarian.

6053. Moreno de Alba, José G. El español de América y el español de México (UY/R, 17:102, nov./dic. 1975, p. 12-33)

Dwells on popular misconceptions regarding differences that exist among various dialects of Spanish, but he goes back to sources of some 40 years ago for statements on dialect zones of American Spanish. Descriptions of pronunciation differences are vague or inaccurate at times.

6054. Paz Soldán y Unánue, Pedro [*pseud. for* **Juan de Arona**]. Diccionario de peruanismos. t. 1/2. Presentación, notas y suplemento de Estuardo Núñez. Nota preliminar de Ventura García Calderón. Lima, Ediciones PEISA, 1975. 2 v. (399 p.) (Continuous pagination) bibl., table (Biblioteca peruana, 48/49)

Another example of "-ismos" that are to be found in several places besides the region indicated. Work done principally in 19th century.

6055. Plá, Josefina. Español y guaraní en la intimidad de la cultura paraguaya (AAL/B, 40:157/158, julio/dic. 1975, p. 325-348)

Indicates that there were two areas of settlement in Paraguay during early colonial period, a hispanic one and *Misiones*. In first there were no white women, hence a racial mixture and bilingualism. In second, Guaraní, kept its dominance longer and is still preferred language of vast conservative majority, supported by slow transformation of cultural strata and definite predominance of rural life.

6056. Resnick, Melvyn C. Algunos aspectos histórico-geográficos de la dialectología hispanoamericana (CIDG/O, 25:2, 1976, p. 264-276)

Resnick doubts the efficacy of linguistic atlas and regrets that there has been so little systematizing of data. Lists several binary traits that divide Spanish America dialectally: /s/ syllable final; /x/; /r̄/. Supports Canfield's argument on the diachronic dimension of synchronic Hispanic dialectology and factor of accessibility to trends of Peninsula. Believes that occlusive /b, d, g/ are much more common than indicated by Canfield in 1962, especially in Puerto Rico, Yucatán, and that /č/ as [š] is more common than believed.

6057. Revilla, Angel. Los panameñismos: ¿una nueva lengua en formación? (USMLA/LA, 5:7, nov. 1976, p. 121-130)

Prologue to future book. Writer believes that there were three language zones established during conquest and settlement of Panama: 1) one of *castellanización plena,* 2) one of *ladinización* of Indians that would finally become Castilianized, and 3) an Amerindian zone that is still somewhat Indian. Thinks that study should be made on this basis, and that this would show origins of sociolinguistic differences that are so apparent today.

6058. Rey, José Antonio León. Criterios seguidos en el breve diccionario de colombianismos (ACO/B, 26:112, 1976, p. 94-109)

Report by Commission on Lexicography of Academia Colombiana de la Lengua. Object of Commission was to study Spanish usage of today, using Royal Academy Dictionary as basis of comparison, and also making comparisons with usage in other American countries of Spanish speech. Questions raised: What is an *americanismo*? What is a *colombianismo*? Gives numerous examples and states criteria for inclusion. Reports on speech by famous German consultant.

6059. Rojas, Elena M. Diminutivos y aumentativos en Tucumán (UNT/H, 18:24, 1977, p. 123-134, bibl.)

Using sociolinguistic approach, writer examines use of diminutives and augmentatives in Tucumán, Arg. Looks at suffix usage on morphological level, on semantic basis, and according to functions of language. Finds that lower economic class uses diminutives more than upper classes and with less conservative terminations where there is a choice (*llavita* instead of *llavecita*). In overall picture, Tucumán uses both diminutives and augmentatives a great deal.

6060. Rosario, Rubén del. El español antillano: resumen (*in* Programa Interamericano de Lingüística y Enseñanza de Idiomas (PILEI), VI, San Juan, P.R., 1971. Comisión de Lingüística y Dialectología Iberoamericanas. Actas, informes y comunicaciones [see *HLAS 39:1730*] p. 27-33)

Discusses phonology, morphosyntax, and vocabulary of Spanish spoken in Cuba, Santo Domingo, and Puerto Rico. [A.C. Wares]

6061. Rosenblat, Angel. El mantuano y el mantuanismo en la historia social de Venezuela (CM/NRFH, 24:1, 1975, p. 64-88)

Research into implications of popular Venezuelan term during 18th and 19th centuries that apparently first came to light in Caracas between 1700-50, to last for about 100 years. *Mantuano* originally referred to *nobles criollos* of Caracas who supported a certain caudillo, but finally came to mean anybody who belonged to an élite group of some sort.

6062. Tello, Jaime. Algunas peculiaridades del castellano en Venezuela (ICC/T, 27:1, enero/abril 1972, p. 128-131)

Reviews some contemporary usage of speakers of Venezuelan Spanish: *se los dije* (I told them); *habián tres* (there were three); *Estado Táchira* (state of Táchira); *me han informado de que* (they have informed me that); *latente* (evident); *dizque* (they say) and writes of the *leísmo* that is considered elegant usage. Most of these and other deviations from Academy usage are to be heard in many places in Spanish America.

6063. Terrell, Tracy D. La nasal implosiva y final en el español de Cuba (UNAM/AL, 13, 1975, p. 257-271)

Article forms part of "Proyecto de Estudio Coordinado de la Norma Lingüística Culta de las Principales Ciudades de Hispano-américa y de la Península Ibérica," under general direction of Juan Lope Blanch. Implosive (syllable final) nasal is subject to processes of weakening in Spanish. Writer examines 4,309 occurrences in three varieties: 1) alveolar non-assimilated, 2) assimilated varieties, 3) velar, excluding cases before a velar consonant, 4) complete loss with nasalization of the preceding vowel. Internally, the assimilated varieties were the most common, especially before voiceless fricatives. Finally, complete loss was most common, and among *panameños, cubanos,* and *puertorriqueños, panameños* nasalized the vowel most often. Article is a fine contribution to a rising interest in polymorphism.

6064. Usher de Herreros, Beatriz. Castellano-paraguayo: notas para una gramática contrastiva castellano-guaraní. Asunción, Univ. Católica Nuestra Señora de la Asunción, Centro de Estudios Antropológicos, 1976. 123 p., bibl. (Suplemento antropológico, 11:1/2)

Concerned over "incomunicación" of many Paraguayan students, writer produces this manual to meet special needs of a Guaraní-Castilian bilingual community. Much attention is given to lack of agreement (*te traigo agua frío*). It would seem from some of examples that some grammatical mistakes in Spanish by those who speak Guaraní at home are due to regional pronunciation of Spanish or are simply archaisms (*lo niños*), but significantly, writer does show lots of inter-penetration of languages in contact.

6065. Vargas, Carlos Alonso. El uso de los pronombres "vos" y "usted" en Costa Rica (UCR/RCS, 8, abril 1974, p. 7-30, bibl., tables)

In an area where *vos* is familiar form of address, there are difficulties in educational process, because many texts may come from countries where tú is familiar form. Writer also points out that the use of *vos* over *usted* is gaining ground but that there are still certain *barreras de respeto* associated with *usted*. Includes interesting chart based on interviews that depicts family usage vis-à-vis *vos* and *usted*. Father seems to rate the most respect!

6066. Vivanco, Alejandro. Introducción a un vocabulario folklórico del Perú (CIF/FA, 19, junio 1975, p. 67-80)

Encuestas made by students of several organizations; "Folkuni" UNI; Escuela Superior de Turismo; Instituto Superior de Quechua; Curso de Capacitación Turística de la Guardia Civil, mostly in the *barrios* of Lima where hundreds of people come in from out-lying provinces: Ancash, Ayacucho, Junín, etc. Lexicon arranged under folkloric categories: fiestas, music, dances, popular medicine and many others. Chief value in the archaic terms that come to light, both Spanish and Quechua.

6066a. Zapata Arellano, Rodrigo. Nota sobre la articulación del fonema /f/ en el español de Chile (UCV/S, 8[11]:1/2, 1975, p. 131-133, tables)

Referring to Oroz (*La lengua castellana en Chile*), Zapata interviews 20 informants in the area of Valparaiso, 10 of considerable education and 10 without much. He found that even at the *culto* level, 55.8 percent pronounced /f/ as [Φ], and at the lower level, 85.6 percent used the bilabial. In all cases, the tendency toward the bilabial was strongest before the back vowel.

LEXICON AND SEMANTICS

6067. Abad de Santillán, Diego. Diccionario de argentinismos de ayer y de hoy. B.A., Tipográfica Editora Argentina (TEA), 1976. 1000 p.

Very carefully organized work, in which author has drawn on many sources for his vocabulary, such as the famous *Vocabulario y refranero criollo* by Tito Saubidet (1943). Most entries have quotations to illustrate meanings and sources are listed. One of best Argentine vocabularies yet.

6068. Aschiero, Hipólito R. Diccionario de homófonos castellanos: repertorio alfabético de adjetivos, verbos y su correcta ortografía; homófonos, homógrafos, parónimos. Prólogo de Mariano P. Brotto. B.A., Editorial Victor Lerú, 1975. 120 p.

Writer bases comparisons on his own dialect of Spanish, and considers *s, c, z* (which he labels *fonemas*) as homophonous, while *ll* and *y* are not. Book also contains a repertory of adjectives, verbs and "correct" orthography.

6069. Asiaín Marquez, Carlos. El singular e inédito diccionario de Doroteo Marquez Valdéz (UBN/R, 15, abril 1976, p. 71-94)

These are comments made over years by Doroteo Marquez Valdéz (sic) on interesting "marginal vocabulary" in various editions of *Vocabulario rioplatense razonado* of D. Daniel Granada. Additions and explanations of Marquez were considered by many to have improved dictionary great deal.

6070. Boyd-Bowman, Peter. Léxico hispanoamericano del siglo XVI, reseñado por Leopoleo Sáez-Godoy (IAA, 2:2, 1976, p. 165-169)

Good thorough review of important contribution of Peter Boyd-Bowman to materials on colonial history of Latin America and to lexicology. Sáez-Godoy criticizes some listing of homonyms.

6071. Coltharp, Lurline H. Pachuco, Tirilón, and Chicano (American Speech [Columbia Univ. Press, N.Y.] 50:1/2, Spring/Summer 1975 [i.e. 1977] p. 25-29)

Author of *The tongue of the Tirilones* (Univ. of Alabama Press, 1964) recently conducted follow-up survey of attitudes toward certain terms in Second Ward of El Paso, Texas, suing 46 informants in two age groups, 19 between ages 19-31 who were university students, and 27 between the ages 16-19, high school students. She asked each what following terms meant to them: *Pachuco, Tirilones, Chicano*. Older group knew all three words but said that *Pachuco* was out of style. *Tirilones* was to them a similar designation. Half of younger group did not even recognize term *Pachuco*. To them a *Tirilón* "walks crazy." Chicano was recognized by all as a Mexican-American. "That's what I am," they said.

6072. Fernández Naranjo, Nicolás *ed.* Diccionario de bolivianismos. 3. ed. La Paz, Editorial Los Amigos del Libro, 1975. 249 p.

Interesting collection of *giros populares*. One section shows how common such forms as *yo cabo, duermimos, traye* are, and treatment of *apodos* (nicknames, usually pejorative) is especially good. Many of these are Quechua in origin.

Gamboa, Héctor. Vocabulario arqueológico costarricense. See *HLAS 39:644*.
39:644.

6073. Granda, Germán de. Un zoónimo de origen bantú en el lexico de Tumaco, Colombia: chula 'rana' (ICC/T, 29:3, sept./dic. 1974, p. 429-434)

Author's notes collected during survey for Colombian Linguistic Atlas (ALEC) in Nariño depto.

where he found word *chula* used for frog. After reviewing many meanings of word, from *moza deshonesta* to buzzard, he decided that it is derived from Bantú family of African languages—*kyula*.

6074. Grupo de Trabajo de Desarrollo Cultural. Términos latinoamericanos para el diccionario de ciencias sociales. Introducción de Juan F. Marsal. B.A., Consejo Latinoamericano de Ciencias Sociales (CLACSO) [and] Instituto Latinoamericano de Investigaciones Sociales (ILDIS), 1976. 255 p.

CLASCO began in 1972, and this publication is a group effort to fill the gaps in the *UNESCO dictionary of the social sciences* (Spanish ed. Madrid, 1975) which goes back to resolution articles on such items as *Activismo*, Communism in Latin America, *Castrismo, Bogotazo, Cristero*.

6075. Gushina, N. El *Diccionario de autoridades*, 1726-1739, y su importancia para la lexicografía hispánica (UCP/IAP, 7, 1974, p. 59-67)

Author in Czech journal points out that original *Diccionario de autoridades* and classical usage of that time has been basis for historical inventory and subsequent lexicography in Spanish America.

6076. Halil, Kiamran. Mules and mulattoes (AAC/AJ, 14:3, 1976, p. 10-13, bibl.)

Lesson on mules and hinneys and term *mulatto*, which author thinks is misnomer, because in most cases hybridinous offspring is not half and half—and mules have no offspring. Suggests that another word would be preferable, but he does not come up with anything but hybrid.

6077. Kloe, Donald R. *ed.* A dictionary of onomatopoeic sounds, tones and noises in English and Spanish, including those of animals, man, nature, machinery and musical instruments, together with some that are not imitative or echoic. (Un diccionario de las voces, sonidos, y tonos onomatopéyicos en inglés y español, incluye las de animales, hombre, naturaleza, maquinaria e instrumentos musicales, junto con algunas que no son verdaderamente ni imitativas ni ecoicas.) Introduction by Roger J. Steiner. Detroit, Mich., Blaine Ethridge-Books, 1977. 153 p., bibl.

Excellent study in onomatopoeia. Divided into four main parts plus list of pertinent verbs and a glossary: 1) sounds made by animals are described in typical Spanish way and English manner, revealing great differences in perception and modes of imitation; 2) sounds created by man are dealt with in like manner, then melodious and violent sounds of nature, such as thunder; and finally 3) sounds of machinery and instruments. Good study in popular culture and in perception.

6078. México. Secretaría del Patrimonio Nacional. Vocabulario arquitectónico ilustrado. Introducción de Pedro Moctezuma Días Infante. Prólogo de Vicente Medel Martínez. México, 1975. 539 p., bibl., illus., tables.

Very good dictionary of architectural terms, profusely illustrated, with translations into French, English, German, Italian. It is interesting to note profusion of Arabic words in Spanish column, especially in the A's. Bibliography is certainly up-to-date, and illustrations are nearly all from Mexico.

6079. Miri, Héctor F. *ed.* Diccionario de la lengua castellana con la incorporación del más moderno vocabulario adoptado por la Academia Española. B.A., Editorial Caymi, 1974. 188 p., illus.

In spite of reference to incorporation of most modern lexical items, vocabulary is quite out of date.

6080. Moreno, Alvaro J. *comp.* Voces homófonas, homógrafas y homónimas castellanas. México, The Author, 1975. 313 p., bibl.

About 5,000 terms; similarities judged from Mexican point of view. It would seem that accents are disregarded, and we have such combinations as *rey, rei; callo, calló; tope, topé*

6081. Paredes-Candia, Antonio. Refranes, frases y expresiones populares de Bolivia (1.495 paremias). Ilustraciones de Lalo Flores. La Paz, Ediciones Isla, 1976. 252 p., bibl., illus.

Unlike many works of the type, entries of this *refranero* are made on basis of initial word of phrase rather than on key item. As a result, there are many entries under *El, La, Un*, etc. Traditional Spanish proverbs are sprinkled with terms from Aymará and Quechua. Book has humorous illustrations.

6082. Peronard Th., Marianne. La partícula "así" en el habla de alumnos de ciclo básico (UCV/S, 8[11]: 1/2, 1975, p. 109-117, tables)

Good study in frequency of occurrence of certain phenomena in childhood language learning, order of acquisition, and trend toward specificity with more experience. *Así* turns out to be a space-filler early in life and almost disappears as child grows older. Early use of word: *Un doctor así particular; Es más o menos viejito así*.

6083. Savaiano, Eugene and **Lynn W. Winget.** 2001 [i.e. Two thousand and one] Spanish and English idioms (2001 [Dos mil uno] modismos españoles e ingleses). Woodbury, N.Y., Baron's Educational Series, 1976. 677 p., illus.

Spanish-English, English-Spanish compilation alphabetized under the key word of each idiom. Very practical and basic. Does not go into dialectal variants to any extent.

6084. Soler Cañas, Luis *ed*. Antología del Lunfardo. B.A., Crisis, 1976. 63 p., illus. (Cuadernos de crisis, 28)

In account designated by author as *cabalgata del lunfardo*, attempt is made to present fairly complete picture of levels, themes and directions of *lunfardo* literature, beginning during last third of 19th century.

6085. Terminología en percepción remota: documento de trabajo. v. 1/2. México, Comisión Nacional del Espacio Exterior, Instituto Panamericano de Geografía e Historia, Comité Ad-Hoc de Sensores Remotos, 1973. 2 v. (265 p.) (Continuous pagination)

Carefully prepared list of spacial terms in English, with suggested translations for Spanish of Latin America. Two evident sources are the US and USSR.

6086. Valdés Acosta, Gema. Descripción de remanentes de lenguas bantúes en Santa Isabel de Las Lajas (UCLV/I, 48, 1975, p. 67-85)

Writes of introduction of black slaves into Cuba between 1517-1880 (total of 1,200,000). In 1861 they constituted 26.5 percent of population and most came from western and Central Africa and spoke Bantu languages. Presents brief study of vestiges of language and shows how certain forms have undergone simplification: *ngulo* (pig) has become *gulo*. Advocates more study of field of investigation that has hardly been touched.

PORTUGUESE

GENERAL AND GRAMMATICAL

6087. Amaral, Amadeu. O dialeto caipira: gramática - vocabulário. Prefácio de Paulo Duarte. 3. ed. São Paulo, Editora de Humanismo Ciência Tecnologia (HUCITEC) [and] Secretaria da Cultura, Ciência e Tecnologia do Estado de São Paulo, 1976. 195 p.

Third ed. of vocabulary first published 1920. Author (d. 1929) was especially clever in his analysis of rural dialect of São Paulo area: phonetics, morphology, syntax, lexicon. Like similar studies of the *jíbaro* of Puerto Rico, *guajiro* of Cuba or *gaucho* of Argentina, many vestiges of the 16th century are brought to light.

6088. Azevedo, Milton Mariano. On passive sentences in English and Portuguese. Ithaca. N.Y., Cornell Univ., 1973. 190 p., bibl., tables (Latin American Studies Program. Dissertation series, 54)

Ph.D. dissertation on the passive that has a twofold goal: 1) to describe Portuguese and English passive sentences, considered under three formally separable but functionally related parameters; 2) present it as a contribution to the contrastive analysis of passives in Portuguese and English and the application of this to the teaching of Portuguese. The process by which passives are generated is described and problems of distribution are discussed. Advice on the forms to teach first is given.

6089. ———. O subjuntivo em português: um estudo transformacional. Petrópolis, Brazil, Editora Vozes, 1976. 56 p., bibl., tables (Col. Perspectivas lingüísticas, 14)

Transformational analysis stresses importance of social and attitudinal factors in mood of speech that is essentially subordinate.

6090. Azevedo Filho, Leodegário A. de. Os estudos filológicos e lingüísticos no Brasil (RIB, 25:4, oct./dic. 1975, p. 365-386)

Tells of imposition of Portuguese "superstratum" in 16th century, of period of imitation of Portuguese grammar in 17th and 18th centuries, of 19th-century "purista" period, and interest in vernacular during latter part of that century and of interest in philology and linguistics in 20th. Gives very good review of linguistic scholarship of last period and speaks of possibility of eventual atlas.

6091. Barbara, Leila. Síntaxe transformacional do modo verbal. São Paulo, Editora Atica, 1975. 184 p., bibl. (Ensaios, 11)

Following Katz and Postal's *An integrated theory of linguistic descriptions*, and Chomsky's *Aspects of the theory of syntax*, writer theorizes that assertive utterances always contain element of time and non-assertive never have the element. Occurrence of time in deep structure is mark of assertion and its absence makes non-assertive meaning, and distinction between declarations and orders is due to occurrence or not of element of time.

6092. Bordenave, Maria Candida Rocha de Diaz. Contribuições da lingüística para o ensino da tradução. Rio, Pontifícia Univ. Católica do Rio de Janeiro (PUC), Depto. de Letras e Artes, 1976. 130 p., tables.

Writer is concerned about application of linguistics and linguistic theory to art (or science) of translating, and about possibility of development of methodological tools for teaching this. Believes that generative grammar can help, and 50 mistakes in translation from English to Portuguese are analyzed to show that many of them are due to lack of knowledge of rules of English syntax.

6093. Brakel, C. Arthur, Jr. Portuguese //r $\stackrel{=}{}$ ř//: Lusitanean and Brazilian allophones (SIL, 24, 1974, p. 1-16, bibl.)

Perhaps best analysis to date of Portuguese sounds represented by grapheme *r*, phonemizations of these sounds, and standard descriptions of their patterning. Author contrasts standard descriptions with corpora elicited from five native speakers and concludes that biphemic interpretation of two sets of sounds is most appropriate. Informants were from Oporto, Lisbon, Paraíba, Río, Minas Gerais. He finds that today only really consistent manifestation is intervocalic /r/ as [r]. For /ř/ there are several realizations, but uvular or glottal has become most common, uvular voiced for Portugal, and uvular or glottal voiceless for Brazil.

6094. Castro, Yeda Pessoa de. Antropologia e lingüística nos estudos afro-brasileiros (UFB/AA, 12, junho 1976, p. 211-227)

Advocates interdisciplinary investigations of places in Brazil where there are vestiges of African customs and language, especially people from fields of Anthropology and Linguistics. Describes some of cults and language groups and compares situation to that of Cuba and Haiti.

6095. Elia, Silvio. Ensaios de filologia e lingüística. 2. ed. refundida e aumentada. Rio, Grifo *em convênio com o* Ministério da Educação e Cultura (MEC), Instituto Nacional do Livro (INL), Brasília, 1975. 334 p., bibl. (Col. Littera, 7)

First ed. appeared 1963. Essays draw heavily on other authors and depict Romantic origins of Modern Philology, modern tendencies, phonology of Portuguese of Brazil and dialect areas as well as difficulties through years in establishing solid orthographic system.

6095a. Gärtner, Eberhard. Zur Entwicklung der portugiesischen Sprache in Brasilien (BRP, 14:2, 1975, p. 319-351)

The political and economic development of Brazil over the centuries may have had some effect on the evolution of its speech patterns and the creation of gaps between literary usage and the dialects of the Northeast, for instance.

6096. Köpke, Carlos Burlamáqui. Ensaios de lingüística geral. São Paulo, Edições Quíron, 1975. 128 p., bibl. (Col. Logos, 4)

Introduction to historical and comparative linguistics and stylistics, with review of developments in linguistics through Chomsky.

6097. Lopes, Edward. Fundamentos da lingüística contemporânea. Prefácio de Eduardo Peñuela Cañizal. São Paulo, Editora Cultrix, 1976. 346 p., bibl., illus., tables.

Good text on origins and fundamentals of linguistics. Writer has done great deal of research, especially on semantics and grammatical notation.

6098. Martin, John. Sobre a noção do modo verbal em português: luções (UFP/RL, 24, dez. 1975, p. 191-202, bibl.)

Work attempts to demonstrate that indicative mood consists of verb forms that contain one of two morphological elements: "past" and "non-past," and that they can be related besides to secondary temporal values ("anteriority" and "subsequence"). Subjunctive mood, on the other hand, consists of verbal forms that do not contain either of two morphological elements that characterize indicative. Its manifestations *(fale, falasse)* are determined by tense value of main verb of sentence. Inflected infinitive is not an infinitive, but variant of subjunctive mood.

6099. Martins, Dileta Silveira and **Lúbia Scliar Zilberknop.** Português instrumental. Revisão: Antonio José S. Melo. Porto Alegre, Brazil, PRODIL, 1977? 335 p., bibl., fold. table, illus., map, tables.

Book on written communication: style, composition, editing, technical writing, grammar, orthography.

6100. Matos, Francisco Gomes de. Dez anos de lingüística aplicada no Brasil: 1965/1975 (VOZES, 70:1, 1976, p. 49-57)

Good review of growth of linguistic studies in Brazil since 1962, when Linguistics or Science of Language was included in curriculum of Letters by decree of Federal Council of Education. Writer lists institutions, public and private that have instituted linguistics courses since 1965 and circumstances of their establishment. It is to be noted that emphasis has shifted since 1968 to Applied Linguistics, which writer thinks will give educational system more strength ultimately.

6101. Said Ali, Manuel. Investigações filológicas. Com um estudo de Evanildo Bechara. Rio, Grifo em convênio com o Ministério de Educação e Cultura (MEC), Instituto Nacional do Livro (INL), Brasília, 1975. 317 p., plate (Col. Littera, 8)

Author lived between 1861 and 1953. His main interests seem to have been use of the gerund, Arabic phonology compared to Portuguese, names of the colors, names of marine animals.

6102. Schwab, Artur. Locuções adverbiais. Curitiba, Brazil, Gráfica Editora Ribeirão Preto, 1976. 206 p.

Good list of Portuguese adverbial phrases.

6103. Stoel-Gammon, Caroline. Baby talk in Brazilian Portuguese (SBPL/RBL, 3:1, 1976, p. 22-26, tables)

Writer finds that baby talk by adults is not only simpler but redundant, resorts to diminutives and hypochoristic effects. Study was made in Campinas, São Paulo, among middle class parents, mostly mothers, by actual observation of child-parent interaction in the home. Lexical items listed under categories: kin, body parts, qualities, animals, games, other situations. Analysis of phonological trends as well as syntax. Believes trends are similar to those of other languages.

6104. Votre, Sebastião Josué. Introdução as estruturas do português: abordagem transformacional. Prefácio [de] Celso Pedro Luft. Santo Ángelo, Brazil, FUNDAMES, 1975. 86 p., bibl., tables.

Really new contribution to study of Protuguese through transformational approach to basic rules of its grammatical structure.

LEXICON AND SEMANTICS

6105. Almeida, João de. A significação lingüística e a sua análise (FFCLM/A, 18/19, 1972/1973, p. 289-312, tables)

By clever use of a dialogue between cook and vendor, writer illustrates importance of sociolinguistic considerations in linguistic meaning, meaning that is both lexical and grammatical.

6106. Amaral, Hílton. Semántica da língua portuguesa. São Paulo, Editora Resenha Univ. [and] Univ. para o Desenvolvimento do Estado de Santa Catarina (UDESC), Florianópolis, Brazil, 1976. 88 p., tables.

While writer's main concern is Communications Theory, he shows role of semantics in Sociology, Psychology, Philosophy as well as Linguistics, and importance of *ambente* in any semantic study.

6107. Araújo, Avelino [de Pina]. Dicionário técnico de Pina (De Pina's technical dictionary). v. 2, Português-inglês (Portuguese-English). São Paulo, Editora McGraw-Hill do Brasil, 1975. 495 p.

Good technical dictionary for period of some 25 years ago. In matters of rocketry, atomic energy, computer science, it is not up-to-date.

6108. Becker, Idel. Dicionário espanhol-português e português-espanhol. 5. ed. corrigida e atualizada. São Paulo. Livraria Nobel, 1976. 371 p.

Although this ed. of 20-year old dictionary has been brought up to date in accentuation, and although it has many new terms, it is still behind times in technical vocabulary. rocketry, aviation, computer science, etc. Portuguese-Spanish section is very short compared to Spanish-Portuguese.

Campos, Cônego Apio. Algumas considerações sôbre a divisão interna dos falares brasileiros. See *HLAS 39:1610*.

6109. Dicionário inglês-português ilustrado. v. 1, Inglês-portugués. v. 2, Português-inglês. v. 3, Termos técnicos, verbos, expressões idiomáticas. São Paulo?, LISA-Livros Irradiantes, 1975? 3 v. (Various pagings, 374, 378 p.) illus., plates.

It is a shame that this elegantly-printed dictionary, with copious illustrations in color has such antiquated and generally poor definitions in English. Vol. 1 is English-Portuguese, and among terms illustrated in color are following: biddable (*obediente*); athleticism (*atletismo*); binocle (*binóculo*); impulse (*impulso*—a boy diving); girding (*faixa*); encloser (*muro*); defile (*desfile*); froth (*espuma*—of the sea); dispenser (*farmacêutico*). In Portuguese-to-English vol. we find *passarada* (crowd of birds); *inclinado*—noun (inclined); *desembarque* (landing); *cava* (hole). Phonetic transcription of English shows

British influence, but seems to avoid schwa: abolition—ébolishânn; concoction—konkokshânn. One wonders about sources and methods.

6110. Fernandes, Francisco. Dicionário brasileiro contemporâneo. 4. ed. Com a colaboração de F. Marques Guimarães e Celso Pedro Luft. Porto Alegre, Brazil, Editora Globo, 1975. 1392 p.

Search for certain scientific terms of fairly recent origin indicates that this and many other *dicionários* published in Brazil are simply not up-to-date.

6111. Fernandes, Maria do Carmo Leite de Oliveira. Futebol-fenômeno lingüístico: análise lingüística da imprensa esportiva. Prefácio de Mónica Rector. Rio, Pontifícia Univ. Católica [and] Editora Documentário, 1974. 143 p. (Col. Documenta/Brasil, 3)

Using accounts of football (soccer) in Rio newspapers and sports magazines, author makes linguistic analysis in two main parts: 1) Message; 2) Codification of message. In spite of nicknames, euphemisms, and hyperboles, like baseball in the US, language has become picturesque, humorous lingo.

6112. Ferreira, Fernando Luiz Vieira. Dicionário brasileiro de turismo. Prefácio de Olavo Lyra Maia. Rio, Colorama, 1975. 90 p.

With increase in tourism in Brazil, this little book would seem to fill need among planners, agents, consultants, as well as among tourists themselves. Includes in single alphabetical order many abbreviations, such as AIT (Alliance Internationale de Tourisme) or MAP (Modern American Plan). Even YMCA has a place. Valuable appendix indexes terms in Portuguese, English, German, Spanish.

6113. Filipak, Francisco. Glossário do Vale do Iguaçu. Curitiba?, Brazil, União da Vitória, 1977. 31 p., bibl. (Col. Vale do Iguaçu, 27)

Interesting vocabulary from southern part of Paraná state, the valley that leads to famous Iguazu falls. Much of lexicon is picturesque Portuguese, such as *destripar o mico* (to vomit), but included are several terms from Guaraní.

6114. Haseloff, Bernd Kurt. Dicionário técnico de agricultura. São Paulo, Editora Griasol, 1975. 626 p., bibl., illus., tables.

From *abacate* to *videira*, this vocabulary of agricultural terms and scientific names of all plants, includes good manual of herbicides and insecticides and fungicides, lots of illustrations and hints on planting and fertilizing.

6115. Jota, Zélio dos Santos. Dicionário de lingüística. Rio, Presença Edições, 1976. 353 p. (Col. Linguagem, 2)

General vocabulary of linguistic terminology, without bibliography.

6116. Michaele, Faris Antonio S. Gauchismos do Prata e gauchismos do Brasil. Ponta Grossa, Brazil, Gráfica Planeta, 1976. 40 p., bibl.

Comparative study that draws on literary sources (stories and poetry) to depict the *gauchismos* of Rio Grande do Sul and the Rio de la Plata region of Argentina and Uruguay.

6117. Paiva, Jorge O'Grady de. Dicionário de astronomia e astronáutica. 2. ed. correta, acrescida, atualizada. Com prefácio de Othon Costa. Rio, Fundação Romão de Mattos Duarte, 1975. 444 p.

Revision of 1968 ed. to include moon landings, for instance. Quite up-to-date on propulsion and rocketry. Quotations from Neil Armstrong.

6118. Rodrigues, Ermínio. Contribução para uma onomasiologia do português do Brasil (FFCLM/A, 18/19, 1972/1973, p. 233-242, map)

Interesting study of vocabulary related to objects, activities and concepts of daily existence of inhabitants of Brazilian countryside unfamiliar to urban populations. 600 interviews were conducted in all states and at several levels of rural society. Idea of "without tail" or "clipped tail" brought several pages of responses, among them *bicó, coleira, coto, cotoco, raboto, rabuco, rabicho*.

6119. Silva, Euclides Carneiro da. Dicionário de locuções da língua portuguesa. Rio, Edições Bloch, 1975. 419 p.

Well-ordered list of about 8,000 items, gleaned from authors of both Portugal and Brazil, with quotations to illustrate, sources, and explanations in down-to-earth terms.

6120. Silva, Zander Campos da. Dicionário de marketing e propaganda. Rio, Pallas, 1976. 200 p., bibl.

This seems to be a dialect with a semantic code of its own. Author has been assembling terms since 1962, drawing on many countries besides Brazil. Excellent picture of marketing practices that is acknowledged by Associação Brasileira de Agencias de Propaganda. Interesting is fact that almost half of vocabulary is English.

CREOLE

Abraham-van der Mark, Eva E. Confusion in the Caribbean: some notes on differences between verbal expression and actual behavior. See *HLAS 39:1169.*

6121. Alleyne, Mervyn C. Panorama de la lingüística y enseñanza de idiomas en el Caribe (*in* Programa Interamericano de Lingüística y Enseñanza de Idiomas (PILEI), VI, San Juan, P.R., 1971. Comisión de Lingüística y Dialectología Iberamericanas. Actas, informes y comunicaciones [see *HLAS 39:1730*] p. 16-28)

French, Spanish, English, Chinese, Hindi and Urdu are among languages spoken in Caribbean area, as well as Creole languages and commercial jargons. Discusses several works on Caribbean linguistics and mentions need for further sociolinguistic investigation in that area. [A.C. Wares]

6122. Baum, Paul. The question of decreolization in Papiamento phonology (LING, 173, May 1976, p. 83-93, bibl., tables)

Refers to Richard E. Wood's 1972 article "The Hispanization of creole language" (see *HLAS 36:3897*). Dutch remains official language in education, but Spanish is more popular. People like to sing in Spanish and English. Penetration of Spanish and Dutch phonology into Papiamento may be stimulated by attempts to identify with higher social levels and sophisticated ways. In time Papiamento may become official language, because there is a great deal of pride in it.

6123. Berry, Paul. Literacy and the question of creole (*in* Rubin, Vera and Richard P. Schaedel *eds*. The Haitian potential [see *HLAS 37:1288a*] p. 83-113, bibl., tables)

Question of literacy in Haiti is linked to social status of creole. Advocates use of creole in system of education and even in scientific papers. Now French is the only official language in law, communication, schools, and all written documents. Considers French great divider, because everybody speaks creole but only a few speak French, and in 1950 literacy was 10 percent.

6124. Brathwaite, Edward Kamau. La criollización en las Antillas de lengua inglesa (CDLA, 16:96, mayo/junio 1976, p. 19-32)

One of several writers who have recently defended idea of language plurality in Caribbean areas where English is official language and yet much of population—and they are not all blacks—speak English creole, and two languages are mutually unintelligible. His explanation of process of creolization goes back to slave days and patterns of imitation, with final search for identity and the emergence of expectations.

6125. Carrington, Lawrence D. Determining language education policy in Caribbean sociolinguistic complexes (LING, 175, 1976, p. 27-43, bibl.)

Although many studies have been written on languages of Caribbean area, there have been few statements on language education policies that prevail in territories where creole languages are media of oral communication among people. From Belize through the Guianas there are creole languages of English, French, Spanish-Portuguese, even Hindi. Carrington proposes six principles that may be applied to whether other than the official language of the territory should be used in school system involved. These six precepts are sociolinguistic in nature, and the most important consideration would seem to be that creole is first language of most of the people.

6126. Castillo Mathieu, Nicolás del. Léxico caribe en el Caribe negro de Honduras británica (ICC/T, 30:3, sept./dic. 1975, p. 401-470, bibl.)

Black slaves who were taken to Caribbean became in some cases part of American Indian communities, notably in San Vicente and ultimately in Belize and Guatemala, and mestizos that followed preserved customs and language of Indians. To such an extent did this happen to black caribs that only two African words have survived, *mutu* (people) and *pinda* (peanut). Writer lists some 158 terms from this language which he calls *caribe negro* and compares it to *caribe insular* (Dominica) and to South American Caribe terms. There seems to be general trait of voicing original voiceless in black Carib. Article has addendum of Katío words from work of Constancio Pinto García, *Los indios katíos* (Medellín, Colombia, 1974).

6127. Craig, Dennis R. Bidialectal education: creole and standard in the West Indies (LING, 175, 1976, p. 93-134, bibl.)

Writer states that bidialectal education situation can be considered to exist where natural language of children differs from "standard" language that is considered official by school system, but at same time is sufficiently related to this "standard" for there to be some amount of overlap in vocabulary and grammar. Standard language in many cases should be taught as second language. Increased study of creole language since 1950 has created better understanding of sociolinguistic factors involved. Good bibliography.

6128. Cuthberg, Marlene ed. Language and communication. Bridgetown, The Cedar Press [and] Caribbean Conferences of Churches, 1976. 103 p., bibl.

First published as text for English course at Univ. of the West Indies. Articles by several authors on contributions of linguistics and communications studies to study of English in area where language situation is complicated by presence of popular English creole languages for oral communication, while written material has to be in standard English.

6129. Lafebvre, Gilles-R. Les diglossies françaises dans la Caraïbe (*in* Programa Interamericano de Lingüística y Enseñanza de Idiomas (PILEI), VI, San Juan, P.R., 1971. Actas, informes y comunicaciones [see *HLAS 39:1730*] p. 50-67, bibl., tables)

In contrast with bilingualism, diglossia is concerned with two variants of same language, each one filling a different role in sociolinguistic structure. Of more than six million speakers of creole languages in Caribbean area, 5.6 million speak some variety of creole based on French. Deals with attitudes to creole, languages and social stratification, and several instances of diglossia. [A.C. Wares]

6130. Lichtveld, Lou. Linguistic problems in the Caribbean area (*in* Programa Interamericano de Lingüística y Enseñanza de Idiomas (PILEI). VI. San Juan, P.R., 1971. Actas informes y comunicaciones [see *HLAS 39:1730*] p. 42-49)

Sees establishment of national languages as major linguistic problem in Caribbean area, with need for investigation by psycholinguists and sociolinguists, but governments fail to appreciate that "language" is an all important factor in a nation's development. [A.C. Wares]

6131. Reinecke, John E. and others. A bibliography of pidgin and creole languages. Honolulu, The Univ. Press of Hawaii, 1975. 804 p. (Oceanic linguistics special publication, 14)

Widely inclusive and authoritative collection of materials. Research completed before 1971. Compilers first discuss general nature of creole and pidgin and then list about 100 kinds of creole, each with an introduction that explains the nature of historical and geopolitical circumstances involved. Includes section on black English, another on sign languages. Much of book amounts to good catalogue of materials on languages in contact. Fine index of periodicals in creole languages and author index.

6132. Solomon, Denis. A form-content approach to dialect of Trinidad: the problem of continuous texts (*in* Programa Interamericano de Lingüística y Enseñanza de Idiomas (PILEI), VI, San Juan, P.R., 1971. Comisión de Lingüística y Dialectología Iberoamericanas. Actas, informes y comunicaciones [see *HLAS 39:1730*] p. 208-219, bibl., tables)

Considers units of meaning plus units of form necessary for analysis of stylistic continuum in Caribbean linguistics. Finds Driver's theory of grammar convincing because it explains departure from randomness in distribution of forms in relation to messages conveyed. To test theory, considerable textual material is needed because "there must be increased reliance, for the conveyance of messages, on inference from context." [A.C. Wares]

6133. Taylor, Douglas. Languages of the West Indies. Foreword by Sidney W. Mintz and Dell Hymes. Baltimore, Md., The Johns Hopkins Univ. Press, 1977. 278 p., bibl. (Johns Hopkins studies in Atlantic history and culture)

Informative study of creole languages of West Indies, with emphasis on vestiges of Amerindian tongues. Island-Carib, originally of Dominica and St. Vincent, now of Central America, is analyzed, with depictions of its grammar and vocabulary and numerous texts. Other creoles are examined: Dutch, French, English, Iberian, and a look at loan words shows vast influence of Romance languages. Author and others apparently believe that some of first slaves of America were already *ladinos*.

6134. Valdman, Albert. La estandarización (sic) del criollo en Haití (*in* Programa Interamericano de Lingüística y Enseñanza de Idiomas (PILEI), VI, San Juan, P.R., 1971. Comisión de Lingüística y Dialectología Iberoamericanas. Actas, informes y comunicaciones [see *HLAS 39:1730*] p. 34-41)

Mentions ways in which creole French of Haiti, spoken by vast majority of population and even permitted in debates in National Assembly, is becoming accepted as standard language alongside French. [A.C. Wares]

6135. ———. The language situation in Haiti (*in* Rubin, Vera and Richard P.

Schaedel eds. The Haitian potential [see *HLAS 37:1288a*] p. 61-82, bibl., tables)

Authority on Haitian creole believes that central feature of language situation in Haiti is diglossia that characterizes country's élite, who speak standard French and creole, languages that are not mutually intelligible. Reviews works that have described language situation in Haiti to identify areas that need further study or re-examination. Tells of varieties of creole and of conditions that lead to creolization. Creole is a continuation of French just as French is a continuation of Latin.

6136. Warner, Keith Q. Creole languages and national identity in the Caribbean (CLA/J, 20:3, March 1977, p. 319-332)

Despite attempts of colonists to suppress languages of African slaves, a variety of dialects persist in Caribbean area. These have formed basis for local languages that have developed in every country. With roots firmly embedded in Caribbean history and culture these "creoles" are closely identified with masses, who use them exclusively, and are closely related to national identity. Author feels that "creoles" should be kept alive and strengthened as they are important to the masses who are not at ease in any other tongue. Further asserts that both standard language and creole have their place in the Caribbean; first as international communication, second as repository of national traditions and folklore. [N.M. Garrett]

6137. Winford, Donald. Teacher attitudes toward language varieites in a creole community (LING, 175, 1976, p. 45-75, bibl.)

Deals with educational problems of Caribbean creole communities—problems that are directly attributable to fact that a form of English creole is everyday language of majority of population. Recommends training in linguistics for all teachers, especially interference theory and social factors that influence language and language learning. Advocates teaching second system rather than correcting popular one.

JOURNAL ABBREVIATIONS

AAC/AJ	Anthropological Journal of Canada. Anthropological Association of Canada. Quebec, Canada.
AAL/B	Boletín de la Academia Argentina de Letras. B.A.
AATSP/H	Hispania. Univ. of Cincinnati *for the* American Association of Teachers of Spanish and Portuguese. Cincinnati, Ohio.
ACO/B	Boletín de la Academia Colombiana. Bogotá.
BRP	Beiträge zur Romanischen Philologie. Rütten & Loening. Berlin, FRG.
CDLA	Casa de las Américas. Instituto Cubano del Libro. La Habana.
CIDG/O	Orbis. Bulletin international de documentation linguistique. Centre International de Dialectologie Générale. Louvain, Belgium.
CIF/FA	Folklore Americano. Organización de los Estados Americanos, Instituto Panamericano de Geografía e Historia, Comisión de Historia, Comité Interamericano de Folklore. Lima. See IPGH/FA.
CLA/J	CLA Journal. Morgan State College *for the* College Language Association. Baltimore, Md.
CM/NRFH	Nueva Revista de Filología Hispánica. El Colegio de México [and] The Univ. of Texas. México.
FFCLM/A	Alfa. Univ. de São Paulo, Faculdade de Filosofia, Ciências e Letras. Marília, Brazil.
IAA	Ibero-Amerikanisches Archiv. Ibero-Amerikanisches Institut. Berlin, FRG.
ICC/T	Thesaurus. Instituto Caro y Cuervo. Bogotá.
IPGH/FA	Folklore Americano. Instituto Panamericano de Geografía e Historia, Comisión de Historia, Comité de Folklore. México. See also CIF/FA.
IU/AL	Anthropological Linguistics. Indiana Univ., Dept. of Anthropology *for the* Archives of the Languages of the World. Bloomington.
JGSWGL	Jahrbuch für Geschichte von Staat, Wirtschaft und Gesellschaft Lateinamerikas. Köln, FRG.
LING	Linguistics. An international review. Mouton. The Hague.
LINGUA	Lingua. North-Holland Publishing Co. Amsterdam.
MLTA/MLJ	Modern Language Journal. Univ. of Pittsburgh *for the* National Federation of Modern Language Teachers Association. Pittsburgh, Pa.

RIB	Revista Interamericana de Bibliografía (Inter-American Review of Bibliography). Organization of American States. Washington.
SBPL/RBL	Revista Brasileira de Lingüística. Sociedade Brasileira para Professores de Lingüística. São Paulo.
SIL	Studies in Linguistics. Southern Methodist Univ., Dept. of Anthropology. Dallas, Tex.
UBN/R	Revista de la Biblioteca Nacional. Ministerio de Instrucción Pública y Previsión Social. Montevideo.
UC/BF	Boletín de Filología. Univ. de Chile, Instituto de Filología. Santiago.
UCAB/M	Montalbán. Univ. Católica Andrés Bello, Facultad de Humanidades y Educación, Institutos Humanísticos de Investigación. Caracas.
UCLV/I	Islas. Univ. Central de las Villas. Santa Clara, Cuba.
UCP/IAP	Ibero-Americana Paragensia. Univ. Carolina de Praga, Centro de Estudios Ibero-Americanos. Prague.
UCP/RP	Romance Philology. Univ. of California Press. Berkeley.
UCR/RCS	Revista de Ciencias Sociales. Univ. de Costa Rica. San José.
UCV/S	Signos. Estudios de lengua y literatura. Univ. Católica de Valparaíso, Instituto de Literatura y Ciencia del Lenguaje. Valparaíso, Chile.
UFB/AA	Afro-Asia. Univ. Federal da Bahia, Centro de Estudos Afro-Orientais. Bahia, Brazil.
UFP/RL	Revista Letras. Univ. Federal do Paraná, Setor de Ciências Humanas, Letras e Artes. Curitiba, Brazil.
UH/RJ	Romanistisches Jahrbuch. Universität Hamburg, Ibero-Americanisches Forschungsinstitut, Romanisches Seminar. Hamburg, FRG.
UNAM/AL	Anuario de Letras. Univ. Nacional Autónoma de México, Facultad de Filosofía y Letras. México.
UNL/H	Humanitas. Univ. de Nuevo León, Centro de Estudios Humanísticos. Monterrey, Mex.
UNT/H	Humanitas. Univ. Nacional de Tucumán, Facultad de Filosofía y Letras. Tucumán, Arg.
USMLA/LA	La Antigua. Univ. de Santa María La Antigua, Oficina de Humanidades. Panamá.
USP/LL	Língua e Literatura. Univ. de São Paulo, Depto. de Letras, Faculdade de Filosofia, Letras e Ciências Humanas. São Paulo.
UTIEH/C	Caravelle. Cahiers du monde hispanique et luso-brésilien. Univ. de Toulouse, Institute d'Études Hispaniques, Hispano-Americaines et Luso-Bresíliennes. Toulouse, France.
UY/R	Revista de la Universidad de Yucatán. Mérida, Mex.
VOZES	Vozes. Revista de cultura. Editora Vozes. Petrópolis, Brazil.

LITERATURE

SPANISH AMERICA: COLONIAL PERIOD

DANIEL R. REEDY

Professor of Spanish
University of Kentucky

AS A RULE, BIBLIOGRAPHIC STUDIES of the literature of Spanish America during the colonial period lack the stimulation of the modern period in which there is the expectation of an exciting new writer on the scene or the publication of a new work which promises to become a classic; nonetheless, at regular intervals archives, libraries, and private collections around the world yield to the industrious investigator some new piece of material that was previously unknown, or if known, was unavailable in a reliable edition during 200 years or more. The article by Garciagómez (item 6419) on Pablo de Olavide y Jáuregui deals with exciting information about this Peruvian neoclassic writer's production as a novelist. Comments are based on some seven novels written before the end of the 18th century and published posthumously in 1828 in N.Y. Thanks primarily to Peru's Estuardo Núñez, a most capable researcher, these works have come to light and our future knowledge of them should dramatically change our view of Spanish American letters in the 18th century. Núñez has also uncovered new poems by the Peruvian pre-romantic, Mariano Melgar (item 6443). An autograph manuscript in Indiana Univ.'s Lilly Library has yielded a significant find—12 poetic compositions of which five were previously unknown.

Among other texts the anthology of poems of Antonio Bastidas and Jacinto de Evia (item 6440), two Ecuadorian poets from Guayaquil, is also a welcome addition, although its value would have been enhanced had all their poems been included rather than a selection. The publication of the complete text of Diego José Abad's *Poema heroico* (item 6438) is also worthy of note. This edition contains the complete Latin text and a prose Spanish translation of the work which first appeared in 1780. Of a similar nature is the edition of Bernardino de Llanos' *Egloga por la llegada de Antonio de Mendoza* . . . (item 6442), a poem first published in Latin in 1615 (Mexico). The present version contains the Latin original and facing Spanish translation. Two studies (items 6414 and 6421) deal with Rafael Landívar's *Rusticatio Mexicana* (Guatemala), which has also been translated into Spanish from the original Latin.

In 1973 Emilio Carilla published an excellent edition of Carrió de la Vandera's *Lazarillo de ciegos caminantes* (see *HLAS 38:6450*). This edition is now complemented by Carilla's book-length analysis and study of the text (item 6410). Other noteworthy studies have appeared: José Durand's volume of nine essays on the Inca

Garcilaso (item 6416) deals with a variety of topics related to the Inca's life and works. The article by Juan Durán Luzio (item 6415) is a good companion piece to the aforementioned volume since it compares ideas in the *Comentarios reales* with those of Thomas More. Silvia Benso's study of narrative techniques in Rodríguez Freile's *El carnero* (item 6406) is an excellent piece of scholarship in which the author deals with the 24 interpolated stories in the corpus of the *Carnero*. Two brief articles by Raquel Chang-Rodríguez on the same work also add to our knowledge of this subject.

The writings on Sor Juana Inés de la Cruz and her works are often very general or lacking in creative approach, but the articles by Sabat de Rivers (item 6434) on scientific ideas in the "Primero Sueño," by Lumsden-Kouvel and MacGregor (item 6426) on a section of the same poem, and the provocative study by Waldo Ross (item 6433) comparing aspects of the "Sueño" to Hindu polytheism are welcome additions as examples of sound scholarship on a difficult subject.

INDIVIDUAL FIGURES

6401. Abellán, José Luis. Los orígenes españoles del mito del "buen salvaje:" Fray Bartolomé de las Casas y su antropología utópica (IGFO/RI, 145/146, julio/dic. 1976. p. 157-179)

Chapter of a book, *Historia crítica del pensamiento español*, to be published later. Author finds that the concept of the "noble savage" was clearly formulated in Spanish thought early in the 16th century. Central focus of this article is Las Casas' *Brevísima relación de la destrucción de Indias* (1552). Information relates to subsequent concepts of *indianismo* and *indigenismo*.

6402. Anderson, Robert Roland. *La nueva cristiada* de Juan Manuel de Berriozábal: refundición romántica de la epopeya de Fray Diego de Hojeda (IILI/RI, 42:96/97, julio/dic. 1976, p. 329-348, bibl.)

Berriozábal, who edited Hojeda's *Cristiada* in Paris in 1837, subsequently rewrote the poem in his own version, publishing the *Nueva Cristiada* in Madrid in 1841. Author studies the two texts comparatively. Bibliographies on both writers are included.

6403. Aquila, August J. Ercilla's concept of the ideal soldier (AATSP/H, 60:1, March 1977, p. 68-75)

Both Indian and Spanish soldiers fit Ercilla's preconceived notion of the qualities which an ideal soldier should have. His concept of the ideal image is the product of clearly defined chivalric and moral norms whose origins may be traced to medieval literature. Well written and worthwhile.

6404. Atamoros de Pérez Martínez, Noemí. Sor Juana Inés de la Cruz y la ciudad de México. México, Depto. del Distrito Federal, Secretaría de Obras y Servicios, 1975. 109 p., illus., plate (Col. Popular ciudad de México, 25)

General information on Sor Juana from the time of her birth through the various moments of her life. Obviously intended for the reader with little knowledge of the life and works of the Monja mexicana.

6405. Baudot, Georges. Los últimos años de Fray Bernardino de Sahagún o la esperanza inaplazable (UTIEH/C, 23, 1974, p. 23-45)

Letters and other documents found in the Archivo General de Indias in Seville shed new light on the life of this important chronicler. Personal letters to the King or Consejo de Indias begin on 30 May 1586.

6406. Benso, Silvia. La técnica narrativa de Juan Rodríguez Freile (ICC/T, 32:1, enero/abril 1977, p. 95-165)

Excellent article, well-documented, which analyzes the 24 stories interpolated into the texts of *El carnero*. Fine example of how current theories and methodologies may be applied with success to 17th century texts.

6407. Bryant, William C. Sor Juana Inés de la Cruz y la literatura de cordel del siglo XVIII: noticias bibliográficas (UNAM/AL, 13, 1975, p. 273-276)

This note-length piece is of special interest to the bibliophile and specialist on Sor Juana. Lists works by the Monja in the Hispanic Society of N.Y. collection.

6408. Cáceres, María Leticia. La personalidad y obra de D. Juan del Valle y Caviedes. Arequipa, Peru, El Sol, 1975. 280 p., bibl.

Written in 1944, this study contains dated material. Bibliography has been updated. Deals with historical milieu of Caviedes' time, manuscripts of his works, and various aspects of his poetry.

6409. Carilla, Emilio. Irradiación bibliográfica de *El Lazarillo de ciegos caminantes* (*in* Homenaje al Instituto de Filología y Literaturas Hispánicas Dr. Amado Alonso en su cincuentenario, 1923-1973. B.A., Editorial Fernando García Cambeiro, 1975, p. 55-62)

Carilla traces the rich bibliographical history of the *Lazarillo de ciegos caminantes*. Well documented, but of primary interest to the specialist (see item 6410).

6410. ———. El libro de los "misterios:" *El Lazarillo de ciegos caminantes*. Madrid, Editorial Gredos, 1976. 189 p. (Biblioteca románica hispanica, 247)

Most complete study to date of Carrió de la Vandera's life and major work. Extensive analysis of the *Lazarillo de ciegos caminantes* plus information in appendices on the various editions, prior studies of the work, and an index of thematic materials.

6411. Chang-Rodríguez, Raquel. El "Prólogo al Lector" de *El carnero*: guía para su lectura (ICC/T, 29, 1974, p. 177-181)

Brief note showing the relationship of Rodríguez Freile's Prologue to the plan and structural composition of *El carnero*.

6412. ———. Realidad y fantasía en *El carnero* (*in* Yates, Donald A. ed. Otros mundos, otros fuegos: fantasía y realismo mágico en Iberoamérica; memoria del XVI Congreso Internacional de Literatura Iberoamericana. East Lansing, Michigan State Univ., Latin American Studies Center, 1975, p. 73-76)

Shows how Rodríguez Freile mixed history and imaginative fiction into his chronicle, *El carnero* (1636-38). Deals with selected facets of this 17th-century prose work.

6413. ———. and **Donald A. Yates** eds. Homage to Irving A. Leonard: essays on hispanic art, history and literature. East Lansing, Michigan State Univ., Latin American Studies Center, 1977, 230 p.

Consists of articles published in honor of Dr. Irving A. Leonard (who from 1936 to 1964 served as contributing editor for this section of *HLAS*). Several contain information on colonial Spanish American writers and works: Charles Gibson, "*Reconquista and Conquista*" (p. 19-28) is primarily of historical and cultural interest; Alfredo I. Roggiano, "Instalación del Barroco Hispánico en América: Bernardo de Balbuena (p. 61-74), comments on *La grandeza mexicana*; Raquel Chang-Rodríguez "Epístola Inédita de Pedro de Carvajal, Poeta de la Academia Antártica" (p. 83-92), reproduces Carvajal's first poetic contribution; William C. Bryant "Martín de León's *Historia del huérfano*, an Unpublished Narrative of Colonial Perú" (p. 93-104), includes a selection from a virtually unknown picaresque-type narrative written in 1621; Anthony M. Pasquariello "The Seventeenth-Century Interlude in the New World Secular Theater" (p. 105-113), deals with pieces by Sor Juana and Caviedes; John E. Englekirk "Another Look at the Legend of Ollantay" (p. 115-121), offers new arguments that Antonio Valdez was the author and not the translator of the *Ollantay*.

6414. Couttolenc Cortes, Gustavo. Federico Escobedo, traductor de Landívar: estudio crítico estilístico. México, Editorial Jus, 1973. 200 p., bibl.

Detailed study of Federico Escobedo's 1925 verse translation (*Geórgicas mexicanas*) of Landívar's Latin poem, *Rusticatio mexicana* (see item 6421). Of interest to the specialist.

6415. Durán Luzio, Juan. Sobre Tomás Moro en el Inca Garcilaso (IILI/RI, 42:96/27, julio/dic. 1976, p. 349-361)

Striking similarities are found between Thomas More's utopian concepts and Inca society as described by the Inca Garcilaso in his *Comentarios reales*. Where the former describes the ideal dream, the latter relates the truths he knew. Well written and documented.

6416. Durand, José. El Inca Garcilaso, clásico de América. México, Secretaría de Educación Pública, Dirección General de Divulgación, 1976. 170 p. (SepSetentas, 259)

Collection of nine essays previously published in several journals. Subjects include ideas related to Platonism, to the honor concept, to Humanism in the Inca's works as well as biographical data. Excellent volume of studies by one of the outstanding Inca Garcilaso scholars.

6417. Edmonson, Munro S. ed. The work of Sahagún. Albuquerque, Univ. of New Mexico Press, 1974. 292 p., bibl., tables.

Important volume of studies by various scholars on Sahagún's works, which are one of the prime sources of information on Indian culture in Central

Mexico at the time of the Conquest. Contains an excellent bibliography.

6418. Fuentes y Guzmán, Francisco Antonio de. Poesías en celebración del onomástico de Carlos II, 1674 (IAHG/AHG, 21:1/2, enero/dic. 1969, p. 45-70)

Description of two poems by Francisco Antonio de Fuentes Guzmán (1642-99) Guatemalan poet, chronicler, great-great-grandson of Bernal Díaz del Castillo. Poems, contained in a single volume, were published in Guatemala in 1675 to celebrate the 13th birthday of Carlos II. Texts of the two works are included.

6419. Garciagómez, Juan José. Pablo de Olavide: primer novelista en Hispanoamérica (UNL/H, 16, 1975, p. 231-246)

Valuable article dealing with aspects of the life and literary development of Peru's Pablo de Olavide. Especially interesting for the assessment of his role as novelist based on recently discovered works—some seven novels—published in 1828 after the author's death and virtually unknown until recent years.

6420. Giménez, Iris. L'élaboration de la *Historia general de las cosas de Nueva España* de Fray Bernardino de Sahagún: un exemple; les folios 82, 88 et 104 de l'Académie de l'Histoire de Madrid (UTIEH/C, 27, 1976, p. 171-187)

Brief but interesting essay on problems related to the manuscript tradition of Sahagún's *Historia general*. A comparison of representative texts from three sources follows the essay. Of importance for scholars interested in methods for establishing reliable texts of colonial works.

6421. Kerson, Arnold L. El concepto de utopía de Rafael Landívar en la *Rusticatio mexicana* (IILI/RI, 42:96/97, julio/dic. 1976, p. 363-379)

Well documented article on one of the rare works by a Guatemalan writer, Rafael Landívar (1731-93), a Jesuit. While covering many aspects of the work, the author centers on the work's idealized images and finds Landívar to be a precursor of the Enlightenment in the New World.

6422. Labandeira Fernández, Amancio. En torno a *El vasauro* de Pedro de Oña (IGFO/RI, julio/dic. 1976, p. 217-241)

General in nature but does provide an idea of the internal historical structure and chronology of *El vasauro* (written in 1635, but not published until 1941). Documentation is also of interest.

6423. Lerner, Isaías. El texto de *La araucana* de Alonso de Ercilla: observaciones a la edición de José Toribio Medina (IILI/RI, 42:94, enero/marzo 1976, p. 51-60)

Points out important variants between Medina's monumental edition of the *Araucana* (1910-18) and the original sources which utilized. Highly technical, but of great value to the specialist.

6424. Losada, Angel. Observaciones sobre "La Apología" de Fray Bartolomé de las Casas: respuesta a una consulta (CAM, 212:3, mayo/junio 1977, p. 152-162)

Adds additional information on the Sepúlveda/Las Casas debates as asserted by Zavala (see item 6437). Author confirms Zavala's findings that the "Apología" as seen in the Paris manuscript contains a concise view of Las Casas' ideas at mid-16th century.

6425. Lowe, Elizabeth. The Gongorist model in *El primero sueño* (UA/REH, 10:3, 1976, p. 409-427)

Article paraphrases the poem, comments on structure, themes, symbols, versification, rhyme, vocabulary and syntax, and rhetorical devices. Very general in nature and offers little new on the subject.

6426. Lumsden-Kouvel, Audrey and Alexander P. MacGregor. The enchantress *Almone* revealed: a note on Sor Juana Inés de la Cruz' use of a classical source in the *Primero sueño* (Revista Canadiense de Estudios Hispánicos [Univ. of Toronto, Canada] 2:1 otoño 1977, p. 65-71)

A convincing explanation of the puzzle which has surrounded lines 89-96 of the *Primero sueño* and the question of reading *Almone* (as earlier printed) or *Alcione* (as edited by Méndez Plancarte). The authors find a source for *Almone* in Cartari's *Il Flavio intorno ai Fasti volgari* (1553). Of interest to the specialist.

6427. Montes, Hugo. Estudios sobre *La araucana*. 3. ed., corregida y aumentada. Valparaiso, Chile, Univ. Católica de Valparaiso, Ediciones Universitarias, 1975. 122 p., bibl. (Col. Aula media, 7)

Third edition of a standard text and anthology of Ercilla's *Araucana*. Introductory essays are genera and provide an overview of literary trends in the

Literature: Spanish America, Colonial Period / 365

16th century plus historical framework in which the epic was written. Of little value for the specialist.

6428. Oviedo y Valdés, Gonzalo Fernández de. Las memorias de Gonzalo Fernández de Oviedo. Edited by Juan Bautista Avalle-Arce Chapel Hill, Univ. of North Carolina (U.N.C.), Dept. of Romance Languages, 1974. 2 v. (740 p.) (Continuous pagination) facsims. (North Carolina studies in romance languages and literatures. Texts, textual studies and translations, 1/2)

Selection of personal commentaries, excluding some portions of the text, by Oviedo in the autograph of *Las quincuagenas de la nobleza de España*, finished in 1556. Text provides great insight into the life and times of Oviedo.

6429. Pawlowski, John. *Periquillo* and *Catrín*: comparison and contrast (AATSP/H, 58:4, Dec. 1975, p. 830-842)

Comparative study of Fernández de Lizardi's *Periquillo* and *Don Catrín de la Fachenda* based on characterization, parallel passages, and novelistic techniques. No evaluative judgment is drawn.

6430. Pérez, María Esther. Lo americano en el teatro de Sor Juana Inés de la Cruz. Eastchester, N.Y., Eliseo Torres, 1975. 257 p., bibl. (Torres library and literary studies, 20)

Initial chapters deal with the theater prior to Sor Juana, observations on her life and personality, and an analysis of *Los empeños de una casa*. Others treat manifestations of her personality in her works, analyses of the *loas*, and comments on indigenous folklore elements which they contain. Seemingly well-documented and serious study.

6431. Pérez Botero, Luis. Contenidos barrocos de las *Elegías* de Juan de Castellanos (UCM/ALH, 3:4, 1975, p. 27-37)

Begins with stylistic comparisons of Castellanos to Camões and Tasso. Author sees Castellanos as an imitator of classical models who followed Renaissance and pre-Baroque precepts of Rhetoric, but whose work clearly shows his movement toward the aesthetics of the Baroque.

6432. Roggiano, Alfredo. Conocer y hacer en Sor Juana Inés de la Cruz (Caribe [Univ. of Hawaii at Manoa, Dept. of European Languages and Literature, Honolulu] 1:2, otoño 1976, p. 29-37)

Author sees a kind of existential drama in the concepts surrounding *saber* and *conocer* as they relate to the art and life of Sor Juana.

6433. Ross, Waldo. Las Maha-vidya-s y el *Sueño* de Sor Juana (UA/U, 48:184, enero/marzo 1972, p. 81-99)

Provocative article which examines parallels between the Maha-Vidya-s or great visions of Hindu polytheism and internal aspects of Sor Juana's *Primero Sueño*. Although some of the ideas may seem unusual, they do emphasize the universal nature of concepts found in the *Sueño*.

6434. Sabat de Rivers, Georgina. Sor Juana y su *Sueño*: antecedentes científicos en la poesía española del siglo de oro (CH, 310, abril 1976, p. 186-204)

Author compares scientific ideas in the *Primero Sueño* with those of a Benedictine, Fray Canales, whose work dealing with Aristotelian thought, *Compendio de toda la philosophia natural de Aristóteles traduzida en metro castellano*, was published in 1547. Comments are made also on Garcilaso and Fray Luis de León. Excellent article on the interrelated ideas of major Golden Age poets.

6435. Sáenz de Santa María, Carmelo. Los manuscritos de Pedro Cieza de León (IGFO/RI, dic. 1976, p. 181-215, bibl.)

Careful study of the manuscript sources of the various works of Cieza de León. Of particular interest of the author's discovery of a manuscript of the *Tercera parte de la Crónica del Perú*. Well documented and complemented by a brief bibliography. Author is at work on an edition of Cieza's complete works.

6436. Soons, Alan. Alonso Ramírez in an enchanted and a disenchanted world (Bulletin of Hispanic Studies [Liverpool, UK] 53:3, 1976, p. 201-205)

A brief but interesting study of a little noticed work, Sigüenza y Góngora's *Infortunios de Alonso Ramírez* (1690).

6437. Zavala, Silvio. Aspectos formales de la controversia entre Sepúlveda y Las Casas en Valladolid, a mediados del siglo XVI (CAM, 212:3, mayo/junio 1977, p. 137-151)

Author distinguishes two attitudes in the Sepúlveda/Las Casas polemics of 1550 and 1551: one as seen through the oral presentations and the second through the published texts later. Of interest to the specialist.

TEXTS

6438. Abad, Diego José. Poema heroico. Introducción, versión y aparato crítico de Benjamín Fernández Valenzuela. Noticia preliminar de Felipe Tena Ramírez. México, UNAM, Dirección General de Publicaciones, 1974. 781 p., bibl.

Complete text of the 6434 Latin hexameters of Mexican Diego José Abad's *Poema heroico* (first version and ed. 1773) with a prose translation in Spanish by Benjamín Fernández Valenzuela. Extensive introducción by Fernández Valenzuela provides details of interest on author and work. Valuable edition of a little known Latin text, made accessible to others in a Spanish version.

6439. Avila Echazu, Edgar. Literatura pre-hispánica y colonial. La Paz, Librería y Editorial Gisbert, 1974. 202 p., bibl.

Valuable book which treats precolumbian Aymara and Quechua culture as well as that of the colonial period. Limited geographically to Bolivia (Audiencia de Charcas), this volume deals with language, myths, art and literary production. An anthology of representative pieces of literature enhances the total value of this study.

6440. Bastidas, Antonio and Jacinto de Evia. Ramillete de varios flores poéticas recogidas y cultivadas en los primeros abriles de sus años. Introducción de Galo René Pérez. Quito, Casa de la Cultura Ecuatoriana, 1975. 267 p. (Col. Básica de escritores ecuatorianos, 1)

Selection and anthology of poems by the Jesuit Antonio Bastidas (1615-81) and his student, Jacinto de Evia, both from Guayaquil, whose original joint volume of *Ramillete de varias flores poéticas* was published in 1675. Texts are modernized. Complete edition would have been worthwhile.

6441. *El güegüense o macho ratón:* comedia-bailete anónima de la época colonial. Texto de Emilio Alvarez Lejarza. Edición de Jorge Eduardo Arellano. 16. ed. Managua, Univ. Centroamericana, Libreria, 1976. 48 p., illus., music, plates.

Folk-theater first published in 1883, but which shows clear evidence of pre-hispanic dramatic conventions. The 12. ed. in 13 years, surely a record for this kind of work. [F. Dauster]

6442. Llanos, Bernardino de. Égloga por la llegada del Padre Antonio de Mendoza representada en el Colegio de San Ildefonso, siglo XVI. Introducción, paleografía, versión rítmica y notas de José Quiñones Melgoza. México, UNAM, Instituto de Investigaciones Filológicas, 1975. 1 v. (Various pagings) (Col. Cuadernos del centro de estudios clásicos, 2)

Little known writer, Fray Bernardino de Llanos (1560-1639), a Jesuit, went to Mexico from Spain in 1584. Authored two dramatic eclogues in Latin as well as other minor poetic works in addition to the *Pro patris Antonii de Mendoza in collegio Divi Ildephonsi*. Facing texts of Latin original and Spanish translation are included together with a brief introduction to the author and comments on salient aspects of the poem. First published in Mexico in 1615, poem contains 468 lines.

6443. Núñez Hague, Estuardo. Un manuscrito autógrafo y desconocido de Mariano Melgar. Lima, P.L. Villanueva, 1971. 13 p., facsims. (Series literatura)

Five poems, previously unpublished, by Peru's Mariano Melgar, are presented in facsimile with printed texts. Source of the poems is an autographed manuscript in Indiana Univ.'s Lilly Collection. Textual variants in other works show need for a new edition of this important poet's works. Valuable study and text.

6444. Orduna, Germán ed. and *comp.* Selección de romances viejos de España y América. B.A. Editorial Kapelusz, 1976. 157 p., bibl. (Col. Grandes obras de la literatura universal, 121)

Contains introductory materials on versification, style, and possible classification of romance. Section on the *romancero viejo* in its oral tradition in Hispanic America is brief but interesting. Approximately 18 *romances* come from the New World oral traditions. Notes and a brief bibliography enhance the value of this anthology.

MISCELLANEOUS

6445. Aguirre, Mirta. El romance en Cuba y en otros países latinoamericanos (UCLV/I, 51, mayo/agosto 1975, p. 217-235, bibl.)

Treats peninsular antecedents of the *romance*; also shows how some subjects were continued and changed in the New World, with comments on the form to our days. Primary focus is on Cuba and selected other countries.

6446. Antelo, Antonio. El mito de la Edad de Oro en las letras hispanoamericanas del siglo XVI (ICC/T, 31:1, enero/abril 1975, p. 81-112, bibl.)

The classical myth of the Age of Gold is examined in the writings of historians, chroniclers, missionaries and others. Author treats ancient classical sources and prehispanic traditions of the myth. Important article whose value is enhanced by the rich bibliography.

6447. Arjona Santos, Angel. Quetzalcoatl: la historia y el mito (CH, 310, abril 1976, p. 94-123)

The myth of Quetzalcoatl forms the fundamental nucleus of precolumbian myth in Mesoamerica according to the author who discusses the historical sources (Sahagún, Mendiceta, Clavigero, Durán, and others) before providing a detailed study of the genesis and development of the myth. A valuable secondary source for other studies.

6448. Florián, Mario. La épica inkaika (CAM, 210:1, enero/feb. 1977, p. 131-141)

Brief but fascinating look at the precolumbian epic among the Incas. Author draws on sources from several *cronistas*. Of interest both to colonialists and critics of modern fiction.

6449. Gingerich, Willard P. A bibliographic introduction to twenty manuscripts of classical Nahuatl literature (LARR, 10:1, 1975, p. 105-125)

A guide to materials of interest to investigators of literature, ethnology, history, religion or linguistics. Detailed descriptions of the manuscripts are provided.

6450. Lida de Malkiel, María Rosa. Fantasía y realidad en la conquista de América (*in* Homenaje al Instituto de Filología y Literaturas Hispánicas Dr. Amado Alonso en su Cincuentenario, 1923-1973. B.A., Editorial Fernando García Cambeiro, 1975, p. 210-220)

Published almost two decades after the author's death, this article vividly depicts two opposing views of the New World through the works of chroniclers and writers of fiction. Well written and of interest to the specialist or generalist.

6451. Lohmann Villena, Guillermo. Los ministros de la Audiencia de Lima en el reinado de los Borbones 1700-1821: esquema de un estudio sobre un núcleo dirigente. Sevilla, Escuela de Estudios Hispano-Americanos, 1974. 200 p., illus., tables.

Primarily of historical interest, but worthwhile for secondary background information on the cultural history of 17th-century Perú. Appendix contains 51 sketches of members of the Audiencia de Lima.

6452. Méndez Plancarte, Alfonso. El barroco en Méjico (HM, 28:324, marzo 1975, p. 18, 78, plates)

An ennumeration of the various characteristics of the Baroque and their multiple manifestations. Emphasis on Góngora's influence and comments on his devotees in Mexico, especially Sor Juana and Sigüenza y Góngora. General in nature.

Perdomo Escobar, José Ignacio. El Archivo Musical de la Catedral de Bogotá. See item 9093.

6453. Rojas Garcidueñas, José. El teatro de Nueva España en el siglo XVI. 2. ed. México, Secretaría de Educación Pública, 1973. 191 p., bibl., facsims., map (SepSetentas)

Second ed. (first published in 1935) of Rojas Garcidueñas' study of the theater in New Spain during the 16th century. Text is composed of seven essays. Useful and updated bibliography is also included.

6454. Sánchez, Jean-Pierre. Sebastián de Covarrubias et l'Amérique (UTIEH/C, 27, 1976, p. 251-261)

Brief study of some of the New World lexical elements which entered the Spanish language through the earlier historians and chroniclers to Sebastián de Covarrubias' *Tesoro de la lengua castellana, o española* (1611).

6455. Vergara y Vergara, José María. Historia de la literatura en Nueva Granada. t. 1, 1538-1790; t. 2, 1790-1820. Con notas de Antonio Gómez Restrepo y Gustavo Otero Muñoz. Bogotá, Biblioteca Banco Popular, 1974. 2 v. (272, 343 p.) plate (Publicaciones, 63/64)

First published in 1867, this is a reedition of Vergara y Vergara's two volume history of the literature of New Granada. Vol. 1 covers the period 1538-1790; Vol. 2 from 1790-1820. Although occasionally lacking in methodology this history contains useful information.

6456. Villate S., German. El teatro aborígen precolombino a través de los cronistas de la época española (UM/R, 20, julio/sept. 1975, p. 29-44, illus.)

Aboriginal ceremonies, dances, songs and other dramatic spectacles are examined as examples of precolumbian theatre. Sources are selected historians and chroniclers: Fernández de Oviedo, Cobo, Betanzos, Sahagún, Inca Garcilaso, Poma de Ayala, and others. Study is a kind of preliminary sketch.

SPANISH AMERICA

19TH AND 20TH CENTURIES: GENERAL

HARVEY L. JOHNSON

Professor Emeritus of Spanish and Portuguese
University of Houston

IT IS OBVIOUS THAT THE CONTEMPORARY SPANISH AMERICAN novel has made an impact on world literature. A number of essays evaluate it. Numerous critics are interested in its remarkable character, so unlike that of the US or Europe; nonetheless, it has ceased to be excessively regional or totally national by breaking with the traditional vision of the previous generation. For the first time, it is possible to speak of a Latin American novelistic system. For substantial studies on the new novel, Adams (item 6458), Alegría (item 6460a) and Brushwood (see *HLAS 38:6478*) merit special recognition. A number of well edited texts of novels and short stories containing excellent introductions and illuminating notes are available. Incidentally, the compilations of short stories attain a superior quality and some of the tales rival in interest and artistry the best novels.

Numerous essays elevate literary criticism to a high level; they are more theoretical, more sophisticated and more professional than in the past. The studies address the esthetic quality of works rather than their value as social documents. Several articles are written by French and Brazilian critics. Sarmiento continues to attract attention; his *Facundo* (items 6543-6544, 6470 and 6472) seems to be as relevant today as when it was written. Scholarly editions of Rivera's (items 6532 and 6533) and Carrasquilla's works (items 6474 and 6475) attest genuine interest in their narratives. Bibliographies by Flores (item 6493), Marti (item 6513) and Robb (see *HLAS 38:6514*) are excellent research tools. The same can be said of David and Virginia Foster's compilation of critical commentaries (see *HLAS 38:6492*).

6457. Achury Valenzuela, Darí. Biografía de Santiago Pérez, 1830-1900 (ACO/B, 23:96, feb./marzo 1973, p. 32-47, plate)

Biographical sketch summarizes Santiago Pérez' life: career as educator, statesman, writer of poetry, plays, grammatical studies, journalistic activities, etc. Literary contribution of little importance.

6458. Adams, Michael Ian. Three authors of alienation: Bombal, Onetti, Carpentier. Austin, Univ. of Texas Press, 1975. 128 p., bibl. (Latin American monographs, 36)

Analyzes a central theme interpreted differently by three outstanding novelists: Bombal's and Onetti's characters feel alienation as a life experience while Carpentier's protagonist in *Los pasos perdidos* owes his loss of self to social conditions. Valuable study.

6459. Aguilar Vázquez, Carlos. Obras completas. v. 3, Prosa. Quito, Editorial Fray Jodoco Ricke, 1972. 590 p.

Compilation of wise sayings, sage advice, parables, lofty thoughts. Short essays on peoples, customs, regions of Ecuador; birds, animals, trees; Bolívar, Sucre, Olmedo, Montalvo; writers (Martí, Silva, *et al.*) and miscellaneous topics. Journalistic articles.

6460. Ainsa, Fernando. La espiral abierta de la novela latinoamericana (ICC/T, 28:2, mayo/agosto 1973, p. 224-260)

Studies elements that integrated, adjusted and readjusted enter into construction of novel of complex unity, which is no longer regional, Creole, Indianist, sociopolitical or a battle with nature. The two areas, ever interacting and intercommunicating are: a) narrative techniques—more autonomy in work with less intervention from author— and structural arrangement; b) themes deeply Latin American with incursions into realm of myth and symbol, yet universal and cosmopolitan. Also more preoccupation with time and space. It is now possible to speak of a Latin American novelistic system. Essay elucidates qualities of contemporary novel.

6460a. Alegría, Fernando. Literatura y revolución. México, Fondo de Cultura Económica, 1970. 243 p.

Ten essays on diverse topics, beginning with "Literature and Revolution" which gives the title to the collection. Alegría asserts writers are revolutionists through their images, symbols, language, etc., and their works may be as important as rifles. Other essays treat Miguel Asturias, a novelist of the Old and New Worlds; Alejo Carpentier and magic realism; César Vallejo and mestizo masks; antiliterature and antipoetry, etc.

6461. Andújar, Manuel. Narrativa del exilio español y literatura latinoamericana: recuerdos y textos (CH, 99:295, enero 1975, p. 63-86)

Profiles of Spanish writers exiled in Mexico because of Civil War and contemporary Mexican novelists. Comments of a personal nature about their narratives, cultural conditions in Mexico and effect of different environment on emigrés.

6462. Arguedas, José María. "Agua" y otros cuentos indígenas. Prólogo de Washington Delgado. Lima, Editorial Milla Batres, 1974. 168 p.

Contains seven stories written at different periods of time, mostly concerned with social injustices perpetrated against Peruvian Indians. Reveal intensity of Arguedas' writing, evolution in his thinking, basic characteristics of his literary production. Informative prologue by Washington Delgado Tresierra.

6463. ———. Cuentos olvidados. Notas críticas por José Luis Rouillon. Lima, Ediciones Imágenes y Letras, 1973. 138 p.

Contains five of Arguedas' stories published originally in newspapers and journals during 1934-35 and never before collected in a book. Examples of his early work. José Luis Rouillon's three articles, published previously in journals under the titles "Testigo del Perú," "El Mundo Mágico" and "El Espacio Mítico," constitute an excellent commentary on Arguedas' writings about the indigenous world of Perú.

6464. Azuela, Mariano. Páginas escogidas. Prólogo y selección: Luis Leal. México, UNAM, Dirección General de Publicaciones, 1973. 217 p. (Biblioteca del estudiante universitario, 97)

Leal's excellent prologue relates Azuela's biography stresses his importance in the evolution of Mexican fiction, and discusses his novels and influence on his successors. Anthology made up of parts from six of his principal novels, five short stories and two essays.

6465. Barriga López, Franklin and Leonardo Barriga López. Diccionario de la literatura ecuatoriana. Quito, Editorial Casa de la Cultura Ecuatoriana, 1973. 590 p.

Good dictionary of Ecuadorian writers. Quite detailed in listing of their works. Useful reference tool.

6466. Battilana, Beatriz G. de and Néstor Alfredo Noriega. 17 [i.e. Diecisiete] cuentos hispano-americanos. Santa Fe, Arg., Editorial APIS, 1974. 307 p. (Col. Hispanoamérica, 5. Biblioteca maestros del idioma, 18)

Introductory essay on evolution of Spanish American short story; bibliography of Spanish American short study in general followed by bibliographies of this genre in various countries. Each selection preceded by brief evaluation and bibliographic sketch of author. Notable writers (Borges, Mistral, Bosch, Darío, Carpentier, et al.) Practical exercises follow each narrative and helpful notes clarify difficult interpretations.

6467. Beardsell, Peter R. Güiraldes' role in the avant-garde of Buenos Aires (UPDRL/HR, 42:3, Summer 1974, p. 293-309)

Beardsell recognizes that every major element of the avant-garde is in *El cencerro de cristal* but demonstrates that it had few readers and little influence. He concludes that Güiraldes' close contact with young writers was his main contribution in stimulating the movement which he had gotten to know in France and from reading French authors.

6468. Bejarano Díaz, Horacio. La narrativa hispanoamericana (ACO/B, 23:98, junio/julio 1973, p. 231-254)

Discusses evolution of Spanish American narrative in following major divisions, each having subsections: romantic, modernist, post-modernist, vanguard. Indicates their characteristics, gives brief sketch of novelists with titles of their works, and ends each division with selective bibliography. A sort of skeleton with some flesh on it.

6469. Benedetti, Mario and others. Cuentos de la revolución 2. ed. Montevideo, Editorial Girón, 1972. 121 p. (Col. La invención, 2)

This anthology has five inedited short stories by the Uruguayans Benedetti, Galeano, Lago, Martínez Moreno, and Peri Rossi; although representatives of three distinct literary periods, they hold identical attitudes toward different revolutionary movements in their nation. Before each story, the author comments on its composition.

6470. Borello, Rodolfo A. *Facundo*: heterogeneidad y persuasión (CH, 263/264, mayo/junio 1972, p. 283-302)

The heterogeneity of *Facundo* is manifested in its distinct and dissimilar materials: dramatic skill in narration, sociological and cultural observations deduced from an example or story, sketches of customs, actual episodes, biographical tales and personal interpretations, general concepts based on something concrete, comprehensive grasp of national reality—all related with didactic verve and persuasive effectiveness, etc. These are the elements that attract and hold the attention of readers who in our time still find much that is relevant to conditions in Spanish American countries. Thought-provoking essay.

6471. Bratosevich, Nicolás A.S. El estilo de Horacio Quiroga en sus cuentos. Madrid, Editorial Gredos, 1973. 204 p. (Biblioteca románica hispánica)

Takes three approaches in appraising Quiroga's style: the expression of vital truth, the key to intensity and the mythic version of the world—all related to his life and search for new creations. In two appendices, Bratosevich offers critiques of *La insolación* and *Los desterrados*. Scholarly work with fresh ideas.

6472. Caillet-Bois, Julio. Naturaleza e historia, providencia y libertad en *Facundo* de Sarmiento (UB/BH, 75:3/4, juillet/déc. 1973, p. 329-354)

Sarmiento, influenced by 18th-century European thinkers, affirms in *Facundo* that nature and history are manifestations of the same providential design, that ignorance and despotism can only be temporary setbacks. Providence does not remain indifferent to the struggle for liberty of the enslaved; Facundo at his assassination was on the verge of joining the cause of civilization, so he was the symbol of nature redeemed by society.

6473. Campo, Angel del. Pueblo y canto. Prólogo y selección de Mauricio Magdaleno. 2. ed. México, UNAM, Dirección General de Publicaciones, 1973. 206 p. (Biblioteca del estudiante universitario, 9)

Stories selected from three books, chapter from a novel and articles on current topics and scenes of national life before 1910 show Micrós, author's pen name, to be a *costumbrista* of real artistry. Magdaleno's prologue contains brief account of historical and intellectual period in which Del Campo lived and wrote. Useful text.

6474. Carrasquilla, Tomás. Cuentos. La Habana, Casa de las Américas, 1973. 268 p. (Col. Literatura latinoamericana)

Ambrosio Fornet in his enlightening prologue discusses regionalism (Antioquia), language, and importance of religion in Carrasquilla's narratives; observes that they have similarities with contemporary fiction. Anthology contains five representative short stories plus an essay by Carrasquilla about his writings, a reproduction of Federico de Onís' splendid prologue published in the first ed. of Carrasquilla's complete works. Unusually good book.

6475. ———. La marquesa de Yolombó. Edición crítica de Kurt L. Levy. Bogotá, Instituto Caro y Cuervo, 1974. 630 p., facsims., plates (Biblioteca colombiana, 10)

Splendid critical edition of Carrasquilla's historical novel. Discerning introduction with discussion of novel's genesis and biographical elements, ambience, lack of precision in dates and chronology of events, numerous characters, language and style. Explanation of norms used for orthographical changes, punctuation and correction of errors. Facsimiles of dedication, pages of manuscript and printed editions. Scholarly work.

6476. Castillo, Eduardo. Aquella bella época. Bogotá, Editorial Revista Colombiana, 1973. 219 p. (Col. Populibro, 56)

Castillo's evocations have the value of testimonials, recalling poets (Julio Flórez, Rafael Pombo, Federico Martínez Rivas, *et al.*), humorous anecdotes, gatherings with recitations of poems, writers and their pseudonyms, i.e., the literary scene in the Bogotá of the early decades of this century. Second half paints detailed portrait of Guillermo Valencia.

6477. Castro Arenas, Mario *ed.* and *comp*. El cuento en Hispanoamérica. Lima, Librería Studium, 1974. 341 p., bibl.

Contemporary stories of this anthology chosen to show the balance in concern with style (influence of Modernism) and changes in mimetic realism of predecessors. Short biographies of authors who are from 11 Latin American countries including Brazil. Representative tales from some of most notable writers (Borges, Cortázar, García Márquez, Donoso, Rojas, Fuentes, Rulfo, Onetti, Vargas Llosa, Guimarães Rosa, *et al.*).

6478. Chaves, Flávio Loureiro *ed.* Ficção Latino-americana. Porto Alegre, Brazil, Univ. Federal do Rio Grande do Sul, 1973. 173 p., bibl.

Six concise studies, two concerned with Brazilian authors, and the remainder with Spanish Americans (Carpentier, Rulfo, García Márquez, and Kafka's influence on writers of the Plata countries). Original presentations and fresh perspectives.

6479. Conteris, Hiber. Notas para una sociología de la novela latinoamericana (UNAM/RMS, 35:3, julio/sept. 1973, p. 647-656)

Examination of the way through which a literary work becomes the source of acquaintance with the social reality.

6480. Cornejo Polar, Antonio. José María Arguedas: las nuevas dimensiones del indigenismo (INSULA, 29:332/333, julio/agosto 1974, p. 11, 22, plates)

New dimensions of *indigenismo* are manifest in Argueda's last novels. The Indian, upon leaving his Andean world, faces new problems, unforseen adjustments: integration into another social order, the retention of authenticity, etc., in a nation that is undergoing changes that erode even the insularity of the sierra. The traditional *novela indigenista* can no longer have validity because of the cultural upheavals occurring even in the most underdeveloped countries. For a more complete study on Arguedas by this author, see *HLAS 38:6483*.

6481. Covo, Jacqueline. Les idées d'Altamirano dans *La navidad en las montañas* (UTIEH/C, 19, 1972, p. 157-165)

Covo discovers in the low clergyman idealized by Altamirano in *La navidad en las montañas* the means of ameliorating the wretched conditions approved through the centuries by high authorities of the Church. In short, he makes of the humble priest an instrument for carrying out the reforms for which the liberals had waged the war. Covo detects in this attitude the influence of the utopians of the 18th century.

6482. Crespi, Roberto Simón. *La vorágine*: cincuenta años después (CDLA, 15:85, julio/agosto 1974, p. 43-50)

Half a century after the publication of *La vorágine*, the hero's nightmare has almost completely replaced the historical components of the novel with the consequent abandonment of Rivera's denunciation of deplorable conditions of the Colombian inferno.

6483. Cruz, Mary. Gertrudis Gómez de Avellaneda y su novela *Sab* (UNION, 12:1, marzo 1973, p. 116-149)

Provides facts about Avellaneda's early life and novel *Sab*; clears up some questions about her love affairs; evaluates the novel, indicates its sources, prohibition to its entry into Cuba; etc. Well documented study.

6484. Cuellar, José Tomás de. La linterna mágica. Selección y prólogo de Mauricio Magdaleno. México, UNAM, Dirección General de Publicaciones, 1973. 213 p., illus. (Biblioteca del estudiante universitario, 27)

From *La linterna mágica*, the title of Cuellar's collection of novels, are reprinted in this volume *Baile y cochino* and *La Noche Buena*, typical of his narratives with their types, moralizing, satire and Mexican ambience. *El aguador* is representative of his sketches of customs. The prologue furnishes information about the period in which the author lived.

6485. Cuervo, Rufino José. Epistolario de . . . con los miembros de la Academia Colombiana. Edición introducción, y notas de Mario Germán Romero. Bogotá, Instituto Caro y Cuervo, 1973. 416 p., facsims., plates (Archivo Epistolar Colombiano, 5)

Vol. 5 of series *Epistolario de Rufino José Cuervo*, it contains his correspondence (letters written and received) with members of the Colombian Academy, which celebrated in 1971 the centennial of its founding. The letters are arranged chronologically. A short summary relates the history of the Academy and its antecedents as well as Cuervo's relations with it. Biographic notes and portraits of the writers of the letters plus information about events mentioned in them add to the interest of the book.

6486. Cyrus, Stanley ed. El cuento negrista sudamericano. Antología. Quito, Editorial Casa de la Cultura Ecuatoriana, 1973. 215 p.

An anthology consisting of 12 short stories by eight writers from four South American nations. A brief introduction with information about each author precedes his tale or tales. Several of the best known narrators (José Diez-Canseco, Enrique López Albújar, Adalberto Ortíz, Ramón Díaz Sánchez, *et al.*) are represented in these stories of violence, anguish, mystery, customs, etc., with Negro characters.

6487. Delgado, Rafael. Cuentos. Prólogo y selección de Francisco Monterde. 2. ed. México, UNAM, Dirección General de Publicaciones, 1973. 203 p., illus. (Biblioteca del estudiante universitario, 39)

Twenty-one short stories in this collection attest Delgado's skill in this genre. They commonly treat of contemporary incidents set in scenes typical of the State of Veracruz and manifest some of the characteristics of his sketches of manners that are purposely excluded from this anthology. Monterde's prologue considers Delgado primarily as a writer of short stories.

6488. Dessau, A. La literatura peruana y la emancipación social en la segunda mitad del siglo XIX (*in* Congreso Internacional de Literatura Iberoamericana, XV, Lima, 1971. Literatura de la emancipación hispano-americana [see *HLAS 38:6412*], p. 85-90)

Discussion limited to three authors in period (1845-95). Palma in *Tradiciones peruanas* expresses feelings of citizens of Lima with ironical portrayal of oligarchy and clergy, using popular speech but no manifestation of social concern. Matto de Turner in *Aves sin nido* represents capitalists' points of view and their desire to dissolve semifeudal society of Cuzco along with social liberation of Indian. González Prada through his articles and poetry calls attention to debasement of people, employing a literary language inspired in coloquial speech.

6489. Diez, Luis A. Carpentier y Rulfo: dos largas ausencias (CH, 272, feb. 1973, p. 338-349)

Since 1962, Carpentier has been working on *El año 1959*, supposedly vol. 1 of a trilogy on the Cuban Revolution. Diez surmises the recentness of Castro's triumph may be the problem in finishing the work. Casa de las Américas has published a fragment of it. Rulfo, since 1955, has been writing *La cordillera*, a novel and *Días sin floresta*, collection of stories. In the meantime, two stories "El Día del Derrumbe" and "La Presencia de Matilde Arcángel," also titled "La Herencia de M.A.," have been published. Diez wonders if these will be in *Días sin floresta*. It is rumored that *La cordillera* has similarities with *Cien años de soledad*, perhaps the reason why Rulfo does not bring out his work. Part of this article just guesses.

6490. Dunham, Lowell. Rómulo Gallegos: an Oklahoma encounter and the writing of the last novel. Norman, Univ. of Oklahoma Press, 1974. 100 p.

Memories of Dunham's association with Gallegos, particularly during the latter's stay in Norman, Okla. where he wrote the first draft of *Tierra bajo los pies*, the novelist's last work. Very personal account.

6491. Echeverría, Esteban. El matadero y otras prosas. Edited, compiled and annotated by Nélida Salvador. B.A., Editorial Plus Ultra, 1975. 171 p., bibl. (Clásicos hispanoamericanos, 22)

In her bibliographic introduction, Nélida Salvador discusses the importance of Echeverría's poetry in Spanish American Romanticism; his literary prose, little appreciation of *El matadero*. Volume includes *El matadero* "Cartas a un Amigo" and other prose writings by Echeverría. Concludes with a few critiques by Argentinians. Useful as textbook.

6492. Fernández, Magalí. Rómulo Gallegos y Agustín Yáñez: dos ensayos sobre literatura hispanoamericana. N.Y., Iberama Publishing Co., 1972. 32 p., bibl.

The first essay offers a linguistic, anthropological and stylistic study of Gallego's novel *Sobre la misma tierra*. The second is a comparative analysis of Yáñez and Faulkner's novels with emphasis on *Al filo del agua* and *As I lay dying*. Interesting but too brief and superficial.

6493. Flores, Angel *comp*. Bibliografía de escritores hispanoamericanos (A Bibliography of Spanish-American writers): 1609-1974. N.Y., Gordian Press, 1975. 318 p., bibl.

Includes most notable authors, some 200, with information about principal editions of their works, bibliographic data (selective critical studies in form of books, essays, doctoral dissertations, reviews, etc.). Useful in research.

6494. Galiana, G.R. Letras de América (UC/A, 29:3/4, julio/dic. 1973, p. 147-205, plate)

Essay concerns language, the responsibility of the translator, Spanish of Spain and Spanish America, this language and several congresses of the Academies, unity of Spanish American literature, and Bernardo de Balbuena in México. Concise discussion.

6495. Giordano, Jaime A. Notas sobre Vasconcelos y el ensayo hispanoamericano del siglo veinte (UPDRL/HR, 41:3, Summer 1973, p. 541-554)

Vasconcelos pointed out the values of the Spanish American and his culture, espousing the theory that the mixing of races—far from causing degeneration—improves the human species; defends idealism, the enjoyment of beauty, and the esthetic existence as opposed to the regulated life, intellectual or practical. Recent thinkers neither refute nor reject Vasconcelos' views.

6496. Güiraldes, Ricardo. Don Segundo Sombra. With an introduction, notes and glossary by P.R. Beardsell. Oxford, U.K., Pergamon Press, 1973. 231 p. (The Commonwealth and international library. Pergamon Oxford Latin-American series)

New edition with a sound introduction that considers the novel from various points of view: historical and literary background; analysis of structural features—quite original—utilizing author's plan for novel; style and narrative technique; variety of interpretations; note on language. Also includes map and glossary of unusual expressions and words of local usage.

6497. Gutiérrez Nájera, Manuel. Cuentos, crónicas y ensayos. Prólogo y selección de Alfredo Maillefert, México, UNAM, Dirección General de Publicaciones, 1973. 171 p. (Biblioteca del estudiante universitario, 20)

A good bibliographic prologue by Maillefert precedes the selections of short stories, chronicles, articles of literary criticism and notes on travels-

—fresh, spontaneous, impressionistic, enriched with fantasy and expressed in poetic language—which demonstrate value of Gutiérrez Nájera's prose.

6498. Heredia, Nicolás. Leonela. La Habana, Instituto Cubano del Libro, 1972. 339 p. (Biblioteca básica de autores cubanos)

A novel that reflects Cuban life under Spanish rule at the end of the 19th century. It denounces colonial oppression and slavery, portrays picturesque types and offers pictures of towns and countryside. An interesting character is the Cuban formed in the US, who reverts to his true heritage upon returning to the island. An appraisal of Heredia as a writer appears in the appendix.

6499. Hidalgo R., Arturo. Binomios: ensayos idiomático-literarios. Quito, Editorial Casa de la Cultura Ecuatoriana, 1972. 387 p.

Linguistic articles about diverse topics; "tú y vos," "ser y estar," "leísmo y loísmo," etc. are somewhat amateurish; explanations would be improved with more scientific-academic knowledge. Literary and historical essays ("Prosa y Poesía," "Criticones y Criticados," "Juan Montalvo y el General Veintemilla," etc.) are considerably better.

6500. Huerta, David. Cuentos románticos. México, UNAM, Dirección General de Publicaciones, 1973. 258 p. (Biblioteca del estudiante universitario, 98)

Collection of stories published in Mexico between 1837-88. Number appeared originally in journals and hence not available up to now. Authors are some of best of the 19th century: Altamirano, Riva Palacio, Prieto, Sierra, Roa Bárcena, et al. Instructive prologue by David Huerta.

6501. Icaza, Jorge. Atrapados: Tríptico. Cuadro 1, El juramento. Cuadro 2, En la ficción. Cuadro 3, En la realidad. B.A., Editorial Losada, 1972. 3 v. (217, 252, 227 p.)

Icaza's most ambitious effort, it pictures Ecuador with despotic plantation owners who exploit Indians, a hypocritical Church, immoral mestizos, corrupt politicians, abject poor, and degenerates against a background of brutality and violence. It incorporates a novel, short plays and lenghty dialogues within the narrative. The speech is colloquial, crude at times, and has numerous Indian words. Much is autobiographical and symbolic. Differs in structure from Icaza's other novels.

6502. Issorel, Jacques. Seize lettres inédites de Xavier Villaurrutia à Alfonse Reyes (UTIEH/C, 23, 1974, p. 47-61)

Reflects friendship uniting two friends, doubts and anguishes of Villaurrutia, news of works and impressions of literary scene in Mexico, comfort and encouragement received from Reyes.

6503. Johnson, Harvey L. Literature (in Woodbridge, Hensley C. and Dan Newberry, co-eds. Basic list of Latin American materials in Spanish, Portuguese and French. Amherst, Univ. of Massachusetts, 1975, p. 101-150, bibl. [Seminar on the acquisition of Latin American library materials])

Sec. V, p. 101-150, covers area of Latin American literature (Brazilian and Spanish American) and is divided into: Reports of Conquest and Indian Civilizations, Manuals and Works on Culture, Studies on Short Story and Novel, Essay, Theatre, Poetry, National Literatures broken down into sections of Criticism and Creative Writing, and Periodicals. Includes 327 entries briefly annotated; material in English is omitted.

6504. Jozef, Bella. O espaço reconquistado: linguagem a criação no romance hispano-americano contemporâneo. Petrópolis, Brazil, Editora Vozes, 1974. 151 p., bibl. (Vozes do mundo moderno, 13)

Opening chapter summarizes the history of Spanish American narrative prior to the present era. Rest of book focuses on major writers (Asturias, Borges, Carpentier, Vargas Llosa, Cabrera Infante, et al.) with analyses of their works and reaching conclusions about their special characteristics. One of the best studies in Portuguese on the subject.

6505. Kuteishchikova, Vera Nikolaevna. Novyi latino-amerikanskii roman 50-60e gody; literaturo-kriticheskie ocherki (The new Latin American novel of the 1950-1960s; literary-critical essays). Moscow, Sovetskii pisatel, 1976. 368 p.

Soviet survey of recent novels, especially those of Miguel Angel Asturias, Carlos Fuentes, Augusto Roa Bastos, and others. Final chapter discusses reflection of the "revolutionary process" in Latin American literature. Lack of index or bibliography hampers use of this study.

6506. Lancelotti, Mario A. Teoría del cuento. B.A., Ministerio de Cultura y Educación, Ediciones Culturales Argentinas, 1973. 150 p.

A miscellany of short essays, most of them concerned with the short story; its brevity, form, style; the story and the novel; the story and the reader: etc. For illustrative purposes, Lancelotti draws on a number of authors of various nationalities and their stories.

6507. Leal, Luis. Imagen de la nueva novela hispanoamericana (EX, 6:2, verano 1972, p. 47-57)

Synthesis of opinions held by other critics of the merits and demerits and contribution of the new novel. Leal concludes, voicing his own opinion.

6508. List Arzubide, Germán. Tlatoani: vida del gran señor Nezahuacóyotl. México, Librería de Manuel Porrúa, 1975. 156 p. (Biblioteca mexicana, 51)

Charming in style, this book about the Indian chief, celebrated as sage, ruler and poet, mixes history with legend to paint a utopian picture of Indian life and customs prior to the discovery of America. The author draws on some of the most authentic sources.

6509. Luzián, Juan *ed.* and *comp.* López Osornio y Chascomús. La Plata, Arg., Ministerio de Educación de la Provincia de Buenos Aires, Subsecretaría de Educación, Instituto de Literatura, 1972. 70 p., bibl. (Cuadernos del Instituto de Literatura. Serie nuestra provincia, 16)

Four tales plus bibliography of López Osornio's writings, biographical sketch with comments on his contribution to Argentine regional literature through novels, plays, stories of a historical nature and studies about folk or traditional customs.

6510. Magdaleno, Mauricio. Las palabras perdidas. 2. ed. México, Manuel Porrúa Librería, 1976. 1 v. (Unpaged) (Biblioteca mexicana, 43)

Consists of 24 essays by Magdaleno. First ed. 1956. Discusses crucial events and circumstances following Obregón's assassination, emergence of Vasconcelos as the leader of opposition to oligarchy and his candidacy for the presidency and defeat. These essays, like Magdaleno's novels, short stories and plays are very Mexican in every respect.

6511. Martí, José. José Martí: ensayos sobre arte y literatura. Selección y prólogo de Roberto Fernández Retamar. La Habana, Instituto Cubano del Libro, 1972. 248 p. (Arte y sociedad)

Martí's principal essays written between 1875-94 about esthetic subjects treat a variety of topics: Flaubert, contemporary Spanish poets, Wilde, Emerson, Whitman, Twain, Heredia, Casal, Goya, etc. Demonstrate his criteria for evaluating art and literature: desire that they be authentic, especially with respect to creative products of this hemisphere, and give expression to his ideology.

6512. ———. Páginas escogidas. Con un estudio preliminar y bibliografía seleccionada por Benito Valera Jácome. Barcelona, Editorial Bruguera, 1973. 441 p., bibl. (Libro clásico, 120)

The study of Valera Jácome considers Martí's works from various points of view. Passages by Martí offer great diversity of subject matter: Indians; San Martín; Bolívar; politics and revolution in several countries; the North Americans; Flaubert; Wilde; Spencer; and fragments from his novel *Amistad funesta*.

6513. Martín, José Luis. Literatura hispanoamericana contemporánea con una biografía amplia e índices. Río Piedras, P.R., Editorial Edil, 1973. 393 p., bibl.

Divided into four parts: 1) Poetry before and after Neruda; 2) Theatre of River Plate and Mexico, the latter focused on Villarrutia and Usigli; 3) The essay before and after Reyes; 4) Narrative extending from social and psychological realism to magic realism. Rich bibliography of more than 1,000 entries.

6514. Matteson, Marianna M. Imagery in Díaz Rodríguez' *Sangre patricia* (AATSP/H, 56:4, Dec. 1973, p. 1014-1020)

Focuses on imagery in Díaz Rodríguez' novel *Sangre patricia*, a stylistic element that causes the work to be considered modernist. The examples of imagery involve some or all the senses and are complex. The factual type of image occurs with more frequency than the evocative which is indirect and involves interrelated comparisons.

6515. Matto de Turner, Clorinda. Indole. Introducción de Antonio Cornejo Polar. 2. ed. Lima, Instituto Nacional de Cultura, 1974. 275 p. (INC, 8)

Naturalistic novel of 19th century with condemnation of clergyman's infamy, setting in Andean region of Peru; recounts conflicts between the "notable" families, sketches Indian and mestizo customs. Informative introduction by Cornejo Polar. Good to have available the second ed.

6516. Mejía Duque, Jaime. Narrativa y neocolonialismo en América Latina (ESP, 122, abril 1972, p. 5-31)

Descriptions of nature in the romantic novel are idealistic, exalted, subjective, permeated by languid happiness or melancholy of the characters. The conquistadors look upon nature as a neutral or stubborn force from which to wrest gold or gems. The atmosphere is political and violent. In modern fiction, nature becomes tragic, destructive, a punishing force that thwarts man's wishes. *Machismo*, the self-sufficient man, changes little until the appearance of *Rayuela*. Mannish women appear in several works. For a longer version of this study, see *HLAS 38:6502*.

6517. Meyer-Minnemann, Klaus. Enrique Gómez Carrillo, *Del amor, del dolor y del vicio:* anotaciones en torno a una novela del modernismo hispanoamericano (CM/NRFH, 22:1, 1973, p. 61-77)

Essay offers good analysis of Gómez Carrillo's trivial novel *Del amor, del dolor y del vicio*, which falls into the category of literature read for pastime. Deeply influenced by Modernism and French fiction, it is set in Paris, in richly furnished rooms occupied by Bohemian characters given to voluptuousness and eroticism.

6518. Miró Quesada Sosa, Aurelio. Píura en las *Tradiciones* de Palma. Piura, Perú, Univ. de Piura, 1973. 36 p. (Col. Del algarrobo, 11)

The Peruvian prov. of Piura is the setting of more than 20 of Palma's *tradiciones*. In several more there are references to the port of Paita and other places in this province.

6519. Moix, Ana María. 24 × 24 [i.e. Veinticuatro por veinticuatro]: entrevistas. Fotos de Colita. Barcelona, Ediciones Península, 1973. 235 p., plates (Ediciones de bolsillo, 251)

Twenty-four refreshing interviews, published originally in a Barcelona newspaper. Reflect the personalities, tastes, comments, interests, reminiscences of García Márquez, Dalí, Aub, Vargas Llosa, Donoso, Matute, etc.

6520. Montaña Peláez, Servando. Nemesio Canales: lenguaje y situación. San Juan, Editorial Universitaria, Univ. de Puerto Rico, 1973. 254 p., bibl.

Analyzes articles by Canales which are less known but refer to fundamental conditions in the ambience or in the author's work. Their themes are: political, social, literary problems of Puerto Rico and character of its inhabitants; women's position in the world; problems of language, press and politics of Spanish America; violent character of humanity; force of nature; prostitution of human race; etc.

6521. Montoya, Alberto Angel. El hombre que se adelantó a su fantasma y otras prosas. Prólogo de Jorge Padilla. Bogotá, Talleres Gráficos del Banco Popular, 1974. 280 p., plates.

A number of Montoya's stories, some in the form of letters, have love of woman as their central theme. Articles on Colombian writers are personal in approach and impressionistic in conclusions—little genuine feeling in appraisals. Draws on written sources for much of his inspiration. Influenced by Modernism. Informative prologue by Jorge Padilla.

6522. Morales, Juan Bautista. *El Gallo Pitagórico*. Reproducción facsimilar de la edicion de 1845. México, Manuel Porrúa, 1975. 280 p., plates.

Satirical articles, published originally in the journal *El Siglo Diecinueve* between 1842-44 and collected in a volume with the title *El gallo pitagórico*. Pictures Mexico over a period of two years as corrupt, hypocritical, etc. Attractive book.

6523. Noble, Enrique. Literatura afrohispano-americana: poesía y prosa de ficción. Lexington, Mass., Xerox, 1973. 200 p.

Useful text for study of Afro-Spanish American poetry and prose. Themes of poetry concerned with slavery, ethnic, and social problems, dances, songs, religion, myths, etc. Stories and legends convey impressions of local customs, religious beliefs, culture, etc.

6524. Palanza, Ugo M. Profilo storico della letteratura sudamericana. Parma, Italy, C.E.M. Editrice, 1972. 105 p.

A profile of Spanish American letters for Italian readers. Focuses only on major writers, starting with precolumbian times and extending to middle of 20th century.

6525. Palma, Ricardo. Tradiciones en salsa verde. Lima, Ediciones de la Biblioteca Universitaria, 1973. 61 p.

These off-color tales of Palma have not appeared before in a book because of squeamishness about their language. Spicy in nature, they show human qualities of Bolívar, Sucre, clergymen, etc., not commonly known. These anecdotes neither add to nor detract from Palma's fame as a narrator.

6526. Pérez, Galo René. La novela indigenista hispanoamericana (RIB, 23:3, July/Sept. 1973, p. 302-318)

Survey of the principal *indigenista* novels; takes into account those by Matto de Turner, Arguedas, Vallejo, Alegría and Icaza, pointing out the characteristics of each narratives. Little material that is original.

6527. Pérez Triana, Santiago. Reminiscencias tudescas y Cuentos a Sonny. Bogotá, Biblioteca Banco Popular, 1972. 237 p., illus., plates (Publicación, 33)

Two collections of short stories with Leipzig and its university being the setting of tales of

Reminiscencias tudescas. Some of the *Cuentos a Sonny* have their source in history. Excellent prose; demonstrate author's rich culture.

6528. Pimentel y Vargas, Fermín de. Escenas de la gleba. Bogotá, Banco Popular, 1973. 219 p. (Biblioteca Banco Popular, 44)

Collection of stories and sketches of customs in rural Colombia—based on personal experiences. Pimentel y Vargas, a rural priest, draws lifelike pictures of his characters and gives pictorial impressions of the landscape. Language of his rustics authentic.

6529. Quiroga, Horacio. Sus mejores cuentos. Prólogo de Mario Rodríguez Fernández. Santiago, Editorial Nascimento, 1972. 152 p. (Biblioteca popular Nascimento)

Good prologue traces evolution in Quiroga's style, comments on settings of stories, influences of other authors and tragic episodes in his life. Stories representative and rank high among his works. For an excellent English translation of his stories by Margaret S. Peden, see *The decapitated chicken and other stories* (Austin, Univ. of Texas Press, 1976).

6530. Rabassa, Gregory. La nueva narrativa hispanoamericana en los Estados Unidos (EX, 6:1, primavera 1972, p. 55-59)

Observations on the comments of critics and readers of Spanish American authors whose novels he has translated into English. Notes a slow improvement in understanding and appreciation as demonstrated in the acclamation.

6531. Reyes, Alfonso. Prosa y poesía. Edición de James Willis Robb. Madrid, Ediciones Cátedra, 1975. 206 p. (Col. Letras hispánicas)

Collection of representative short stories, poetry and essays from the rich contribution of Reyes. In introduction, Robb speaks of the presence in Reyes of Monterrey, Mex., Spain, France, Argentina and Brazil. Discusses his library named "La Capilla Alfonsina," and the "Duende de la Alfonsina." This is a concise summary noting that a lot of his work remains unpublished.

6532. Rivera, José Eustasio. La vorágine. Introducción y selección de Fernando Curiel. México, Dirección General de Publicaciones, 1972. 268 p. (Nuestros clásicos, 35)

A popular ed. of this classic. The introduction by Curiel contains a short biography of Rivera and an appraisal of the novel. He notes that it is a condemnation of the cruel exploitation of the rubber workers and discusses the novel's form, structure, characters, the landscape (particularly the jungle), as well as the native tribes.

6533. ———. *La vorágine*: 1924-1974. Edición crítica por Luís Carlos Herrera Molina. Bogotá, Edición de la Caja de Crédito Agrario [and] Editorial Pax, 1974. 391 p., facsims., illus., maps, plates.

Critical, scholarly ed. of *La vorágine* designed to commemorate the 50th anniversary of the first 1924 ed. Introduction contains information on previous editions and translations into foreign languages; discusses structure, style, symbolism, Dantesque qualities. The editor Herrera Molina, incorporates almost 3,000 variants inserted by Rivera. A brief vocabulary of regionalisms prepared by Rivera is found at the end of the book.

6534. Rockland, Michael A. Domingo F. Sarmiento y Henry W. Longfellow (JEHM/R, 1:7, 1972, p. 155-158)

Sarmiento admired Longfellow, praised his command of the Spanish language, gave him Argentine books and had others sent to him, presented him copies of his own writings, persuaded him to translate into English a few verses of Juana Manso's poem about Lincoln, and had a bust of the poet. Longfellow planned to write a poem about Sarmiento, supported the petition to have Harvard grant him an honorary doctorate, not successfully realized, and sent to him in B.A. an autographed copy of his poem "Ultima Thule."

6535. Rodríguez Almodóvar, Antonio. Lecciones de narrativa hispanoamericana, siglo XX: orientación y crítica. Sevilla, Spain, Univ. de Sevilla, 1972. 119 p., bibl.

A series of short sketches on a number of topics related to contemporary Spanish American fiction. After a brief survey of the antecedents of the boom, Rodríguez Almodóvar devotes several pages to nine novelists of the 1960s, theorizes about the systematization of the present-day novel and then in brief essays discusses miscellaneous subjects: experiments in fiction, realism and reality, eroticism and sexology, time and death, etc. No depth here.

6536. Rodríguez Castelo, Hernán *ed.* Cuento ecuatoriano del siglo XIX y Timoleón Coloma. Guayaquil, Ecua., Publicaciones Educativas Ariel, 1974? 198 p. (Clásicos Ariel, 95)

The introduction by Rodríguez Castelo serves to trace the development of the Ecuadorian short story during its formative period of development. Each tale from the 10 writers is preceded by a brief bibliographic sketch. Useful for making the acquaintance of some of nation's best writers of the narrative.

6537. Rodríguez-Monegal, Emir. Latin American literature (*in* Ivask, Ivar and Gero von Wilpert *eds.* World literature since 1945: critical surveys of the contemporary literatures of Europe and the Americas. N.Y., Frederick Ungar, 1973, p. 416-448, bibl.)

Presents a panorama of contemporary Latin American literature, concentrating on major authors and their principal works. Observes that the literature is no longer a collection of individual works; takes into account the contributions of the writers' predecessors and Spanish émigrés, preparatory efforts in essay and lyric poetry, leadership in fiction, dividing novelists of the 20th century into four generations and pointing out briefly respective writers' contributions, experimentations, etc. Good survey.

6538. ———— and **Thomas Colchie** *eds.* The Borzoi anthology of Latin American literature. v. 1, From the time of Columbus to the twentieth century; v. 2, The twentieth century: from Borges and Paz to Guimarães Rosa and Donoso. N.Y., Alfred A. Knopf, 1977. 2 v. (982 p.) (Continuous pagination) (A Borzoi book)

Outstanding edition of Latin American writings that will probably become a classic for English-speaking audiences. It is especially noteworthy because of the quality of the translations (e.g., Samuel Beckett's renditions of Mexican Baroque poets) as well as for the comprehensive incorporation of Brazil and the Portuguese-American tradition (usually slighted in anthologies of this type). The short introductions that precede each author, period, or school make delightful reading. One wishes in fact, that this anthology were available in the Spanish and Portuguese originals. These volumes are highly recommended to the general reader and specialist alike. [Ed.]

6539. Rosa, João Guimarães and others. Los grandes cuentan. Antología. Montevideo, Ediciones América Nueva, 1974? 107 p. (Publicación, 1)

A collection of six splendid short stories by the eminent writers: Guimarães Rosa, Carpentier, Lezama Lima, Rulfo, Onetti, and Asturias. A brief bibliographic sketch of the author precedes each tale.

6540. Rouquié, Alain. La genése du nationalisme culturel dans l'oeuvre de Manuel Gálvez: 1904-1913 (UTIEH/C, 19, 1972, p. 7-34)

Thousands of immigrants entering Argentina in a short period of time, growth of materialism, change in social structure in B.A., increase in European influence motivated Gálvez to exalt an image rooted in traditionalism, provincialism, Spanish ancestry; attachment to oligarchy, authoritarian government, Catholic Church, etc. — ideas espoused in his mature works. Rouquié develops his theme logically and carefully.

6541. Salgado, J.A. César. *O Facundo* de Sarmiento e *Os sertões* de Euclides (APL/R, 30:81, julho 1973, p. 19-47)

Comparative study that begins by collating and contrasting incidents in lives of Sarmiento and Euclides da Cunha, similarities and dissimilarities of their personalities, successes and failures in love affairs, correspondences in objectives of their two masterpieces, likenesses in their interpretations of nature and land, resemblances and differences of their profiles of *gaucho* and *sertanejo*, parallel roles in Argentine and Brazilian literatures. Interesting article.

6542. Sánchez Mármol, Manuel. *Antón Pérez y Juanita Sousa.* Prólogo de Francisco J. Santamaría. Edición de Antonio Castro Leal. México, Editorial Porrúa, 1974. 326 p. (Col. De escritores mexicanos, 90)

Makes available two novels of which the first editions are scarce. *Antón Pérez* and *Juanita Sousa* have naturalistic scenes, some of the earliest in Mexican realistic fiction. The first work, based on historical episode, has for its background the years following the war against the Empire of Maximilian. Two letters about *Antón Pérez* shed light on its conception. Good edition.

6543. Sarmiento, Domingo Faustino. Facundo. Edición anotada y comentada por Jorge Luis Borges. B.A., Librería El Ateneo Editorial, 1974. 274 p., bibl., facsim. (Libros fundamentales comentados)

Borges' prologue offers pertinent comments about the gaucho and gaucho literature, the genesis of *Facundo* and concludes with thought-provoking statement about Argentina's most perceptive book: "Diré yo si lo hubiéramos canonizado como nuestro libro eiemplar, otra sería nuestra historia y mejor."

6544. ————. Facundo. Introducción y notas de Emma Susana Speratti Piñero. México, UNAM, Dirección General de Publicaciones, 1972. 283 p. (Nuestros clásicos, 2)

In her brief introduction, Speratti Piñero gives an account of Rosas' regime, Sarmiento's life supplemented by a helpful chronological table, and analyzes *Facundo*. Edition suitable for classes.

6545. Shaw, Donald. Gallegos' revision of *Doña Bárbara*, 1929-1930 (UPDRL/HR, 42:3, Summer 1974, p. 265-278)

Gallegos changed drastically in the 2. ed. the structure and characters of *Doña Bárbara*, altering the sequence of chapters and adding almost 20,000 words of new or rewritten material. He modified markedly the characters of Santos and Doña Bárbara, especially the latter whom he developed significantly. Splendid synthesis of the differences between 1. and 2. eds.

6546. Siles Guevara, Juan. Las cien obras capitales de la literatura boliviana. La Paz, Editorial Los Amigos del Libro, 1975. 513 p., bibl., facsims., plates.

Introduction contains comments on birth of various genres in Bolivia. Brief remarks on author, his works from which passages are selected, and list of editions form a unit. At end, there are indices of authors, subjects, and titles to facilitate use of book.

6547. Silva, Ricardo. Artículos de costumbres, Bogotá, Imprenta Banco Popular, 1973. 247 p. (Biblioteca Banco Popular, 45)

These sketches, slightly satirical in tone, were written by Ricardo Silva, father of José Asunción Silva; he describes in them types and scenes or incidents in daily life of Bogotá. Contains much dialogue with examples of colloquial speech.

6548. Silva de Rodríguez, Cecilia. Vida y obras de Ermilo Abreu Gómez. Fort Worth, Texas Christian Univ., 1975. 182 p. (Mexican monograph series, 2).

Considers Abreu Gómez' contribution to Mexican theatre, novel, short story, essay, bibliography, etc. Sound study, good selective bibliography.

6549. Stimson, Frederick S. and **Ricardo Navas-Ruiz** *eds.* Literatura de la América Hispánica: antología e historia. t. 3, La época contemporánea. N.Y., Dodd, Mead & Co., 1975. 504 p.

Vol. 3 concentrates on contemporary period which is divided into three parts that in turn are separated into narrative and poetry. Biographies of authors and analyses of movements and genres succinct but packed with information. Extensive footnotes and vocabulary. Good text for survey course.

6550. Tamayo Vargas, Augusto. Literatura en Hispanoamerica, v. 1/2. Lima, Ediciones Peisa, 1973. 2 v. (513 p.) (Continuous pagination)

Good survey of Spanish American literature from pre-columbian times to present. Focuses on major writers and their contribution to various genres. Vol. 2 is an anthology of the works discussed in vol. 1.

6551. Tapia y Rivera, Alejandro. Mis memorias. Río Piedras, P.R., Editorial Edil, 1973. 252 p.

Sort of autobiography of Tapia y Rivera (1826-82) with account of education, family life, experiences as a journalist, literary career, exile, trips to Spain, impressions of slavery, theatrical performances, political situation in Puerto Rico, etc. Personal in tone. Concludes with articles about him, his death, etc.

6552. Téllez, Hernando. Selección de prosas. pt. 1. Bogotá, Biblioteca Colombiana de Cultura, 1975? 254 p. (Col. De autores nacionales)

Collection of essays and sketches selected from five books by Téllez; originally appeared in journals; develop diverse themes: social, esthetic, etc. Thoughtful pieces.

6553. Tzitsikas, Helene. Dos revistas chilenas: *Los Diez* y *Artes y Letras*. Estudios, índices anotados y apéndices. Santiago, Editorial Nascimento, 1973. 240 p., bibl., illus., plates.

Thorough study of two Chilean journals *Los Diez* (1916-17) and its successor *Revista de Artes y Letras* (1918): annotations on the contents —literary criticism, short stories, plays, poems, essays, fragments of novels, comments on foreign writers, etc. Reprints in appendices of polemical articles about the controversial *Pequeña antología de poetas chilenos contemporáneos* (1917), published by *Los Diez*, and literary works, illustrations, and music selected from the two journals.

6554. Urrello, A. Antecedentes del neo-indigenismo (CH, 268, oct. 1972, p. 5-25)

Examination of literature about Indian from the time of discoverers and chroniclers through historians, novelists, poets and essayists up to José María Arguedas' *neoindigenismo*. Excellent synthesis and well documented.

6555. Uslar-Pietri, Arturo. Andrés Bello, el desterrado (CAM, 214:5, 1977, p. 147-158)

Reprint of the same article published 30 years before in CAM. An impressionistic view of Bello which dwells primarily on biographical details. [D.R. Reedy]

6556. Valdelomar, Abraham, *Conde de Lemos.* La aldea encantada. Cuentos. Presencia de Valdelomar por Ramón Barrenechea Vinatea. Lima, Ediciones Los Andes, 1973. 284 p., illus.

Collection of short sketches published originally in magazines, treating a variety of themes —several of a religious nature and practically all concerned with life in Perú. Last selection consists of Valdelomar's poetry.

6557. Villaverde, Cirilo. Cecilia Valdés. Estudio crítico por Raimundo Lazo. México, Editorial Porrúa, 1972. 301 p. (Col. Sepan cuantos, 227)

Scholarly introduction by Raimundo Lazo, which orients reader about Cuban colonial history and society, the quality of the narrative and characters, style. Makes available a novel, interesting for its reflection of local customs, lively dialogues with different patterns of speech and characters copied from real life.

PROSE FICTION

MEXICO

JUAN BRUCE-NOVOA

Assistant Professor of Spanish
Yale University

OF THE FICTION WORKS REVIEWED for this volume, Carlos Fuentes' monumental anti-historical novel *Terra nostra* (item 6573) overshadows the rest. However, other works of the first order are: Juan García Ponce's new short-story collection *Encuentros* (item 6577) and his 10th novel, *El gato* (item 6578); Julieta Campos' *Tiene los cabellos rojizos y se llama Sabina* (item 6564); and María Luisa Mendoza's *De Ausencia* (item 6582); these last four being poetic novels of erotic encounters. Sergio Fernández' *Segundo sueño* (item 6571) also falls under that category, though the love is homosexual. Onda literature, initiated by José Agustín and Gustavo Sainz over a decade ago, is being stretched to its thematic and linguistic extremes by Avilés in *Tantadel* (item 6560), Domínguez Aragón in *Donde el agua es blanca* (item 6568), and Mendiola in *y te sacaron los ojos* (item 6581). Luis Spota published a third title in his series on Mexican political intrigue. Of the newcomers, the most notable is León Roberto García with *Del cristal con que se mira* (item 6576), a mature work of depth and stylistic self-confidence. Other promising first publications include: *Los largos días* (item 6566) and Prieto's *Caracoles* (item 6584), both of which owe much to García Ponce's prose; Tita Valencia's *Minotauromaquia* (item 6590), another poetic novel; and Marcela del Río's *Proceso a Faubritten* (item 6586) which may well be Mexico's best science fiction novel to date. An extraordinary number of important anthologies were published during the last two years: Salvador Elizondo's *Antología personal* (item 6570) and vol. 1 of Fuentes' *Obras completas* (item 6572). In criticism, US journals continue to focus primarily on Rulfo and Fuentes. However, there is a growing body of criticism on lesser known writers of equal importance inside Mexico and this is reflected by items annotated in this section. Also, during these two years several good interviews have appeared with people such as Paz, Elizondo, García Ponce, Sainz, and even the reluctant Rulfo. Brushwood's article on literary periods (item 6597) and Durán's introduction to the *Antología de la Revista de los Contemporáneos* (item 6558) reflect a notable shift in the image of 20th-century Mexican prose. It seems as if we are finally recognizing that much discussed literature of the Revolution dominated by social concerns does not represent the main thrust of Mexican prose during the first seven decades of our century. Aesthetic innovation, cosmopolitanism, and art have been and are central preoccupations. A revindication of the Contemporáneos and their seminal role in Mexican letters is long overdue.

PROSE FICTION

6558. Antología de la revista *Contemporáneos*. Introducción, selección y notas de Manuel Durán. Mexico, Fondo de Cultura Económica. 1973. 430 p., bibl. (Letras mexicanas, 111)

Selection of poetry, fiction, and criticism from this seminal journal of the 1930s, including not only works of the *contemporáneos*, but of foreign authors and Mexicans not usually linked to them. The introduction places the group in clear perspective, disproving the opinion that they were narrow elitists. Indicates that their critical views, while unpopular at the time, have proved correct in almost every case. Good bibliography.

6559. Arreola, Juan José. Y ahora, la mujer . . . México, Utopía, Compañía Editorial, 1975. 151 p., plates.

Jorge Arturo Ojeda arranged 138 brief quotations and a letter into a fragmented statement by Arreola on women, love, art, and death. Oral tone derives from the fact that quotes were transcribed from interviews. Illuminates Arreola's pithy erotics and adds insight into his personality, but falls short of his previous books.

6560. Avilés Fabila, René. Tantadel. México, Fondo de Cultura Económica, 1975. 139 p. (Letras mexicanas, 114)

Another of Avilés' satirical shots at the middle class. A liberal young writer, who is actually still a pathetic macho, writes a novel to win back his estranged lover. Reader must be careful not to mistake narrator's clichés with Avilés' style, or the satire, and point, will be missed.

6561. Azuela, Arturo. Un tal José Salomé. México, Editorial Joaquín Mortiz, 1975. 222 p. (Nueva narrativa hispánica)

Highway construction brings progress and pernicious urbanization. In a treatment reminiscent of naturalism, author idealizes nature while also perceiving it as locked into fatal determinism. Thematic clichés are almost salvaged by the poetic tone of the writing. Arturo Azuela seems less modern than his famous grandfather, Mariano.

6562. Blixen, Hyalmar. Aquel año 3-Tochtli. Novela. Montevideo, Editorial Alfa, 1974. 248 p., map (Col. Tiempo y memoria)

Standard historical novel about the founding of the Aztec empire. Narrated by a warrior-adviser to king Netzahualcoyotl, the perspective is Texcocan, rather than Aztec. Interesting companion to Frances Gilmor's *Flute of the smoking mirror: a portrait of Nezahualcoyotl, poet-king of the Aztecs*.

6563. Camacho Morelos, Jesús. La bicicleta embarazada. México, Editorial Diana, 1976. 115 p., illus.

Onda (adolescent) literature (see item 6592) taken to its extreme, with hip Mexico City slang almost excluding readers from outside the age group or the region. Rock star goes insane and narrates the novel to his psychiatrist. Attempts to satirize the hippy generation and its eventual futility, but falls short of the same venture as achieved by Jose Agustín in *Se está haciendo tarde* (1973, see *HLAS 38:6522*).

6564. Campos, Julieta. Tiene los cabellos rojizos y se llama Sabina. México, Editorial Joaquín Mortiz, 1974. 179 p. (Nueva narrativa hispánica)

Through a series of evanescent images of Sabina, both as subject and object of perception, and the sea, a love story passes before us, impossible to hold, but suggestive. Intertextual play with Anais Nin's *A spy in the house of love*. Nin and Campos share literary orientation. Example of the poetic novel of recent years.

6565. Catorce mujeres escriben cuentos. Antología. Selección y presentación de Elsa de Llarena. México, Federación Editorial Mexicana, 1975. 190 p. (Col. Narración representativa, 25)

Anthology of 24 stories, many previously unpublished, by some of Mexico's leading women writers. The brief introduction and biographical notes are of little critical utility. No bibliography.

6566. Chacón, Joaquín Armando. Los largos días. México, Editorial Joaquín Mortiz, 1973. 144 p. (Nueva narrativa hispánica)

Novel about the writing of a novel about Julia, the narrator's departed lover who later commits suicide. Time is fragmented into small units and shuffled without any attempt to assist the reader, yet through the use of names clarity is maintained. Inclusion of the Tlatelolco massacre seems forced. Interesting as an example of García Ponce's influence in the younger generation. Ponce's story "Tajimara" (1963) is a constant echo in Chacón's novel.

6567. El cuento erótico en México. Recopilación y prólogo de Enrique Jaramillo Levi. México, Editorial Diana, 1975. 429 p.

Collection of 50 erotic short stories by the who's who of Mexico's last five generations. Demonstrates the wide ranging interest in eroticism, which has become a central thematic concern in Mexican letters. Excellent examples of the styles of Mexico's best contemporary writers. Highly recommended.

Literature: Prose Fiction, Mexico / 381

6568. Domínquez Aragonés, Edmundo. Donde el agua es blanca como el gis. México, Editorial Diana, 1973. 198 p. (Novelistas mexicanos, 17)

Mexicanization of Spanish refugees. Interesting European perspective on Mexico. The language is highly oral in tone, taking the Onda techniques of José Agustín (see item 6592) to an extreme. With all its brilliant linguistic pyrotechnics, it still seems ephemeral.

6569. Echeverría, Manuel. Un redoble muy largo. México, Editorial Joaquín Mortiz, 1974. 268 p. (Nueva narrativa hispánica)

History of two families, one rich, one poor, from the Díaz era to the 1940s. Notable for the objective, concise, purification of the material and absence of clichés characteristic of the novel of the Revolution. The material is strictly literary, aesthetic; reality derives from language, not from history.

6570. Elizondo, Salvador. Antología personal. México, Fondo de Cultura Económica, 1974. 107 p. (Archivo del fondo, 17)

Selected and arranged by Elizondo, the anthology omits his poetry, *El hipogeo secreto* (1968), and any example of his critical essays. Yet it provides a comprehensive overview of an author who deserves more recognition. No critical introduction or bibliography.

6571. Fernández, Sergio E. Segundo sueño. México, Editorial Joaquín Mortiz, 1976. 420 p. (Nueva narrativa hispánica)

Explores socially repressed love and sexuality, and their projection into art. Mirrors Sor Juana's *Primero sueño*: linguistic universe unable to capture the adored center, nor anything but the search; yet it constitutes the author's metaphorical body and spirit, seductively, though implicitly, layed bare.

6572. Fuentes, Carlos. Obras completas. t. 1. Prólogo de Fernando Benítez. México, Aguilar Editor, 1974. 1414 p., plates (Biblioteca de autores modernos)

Massive first volume which contains *La región más transparente*, *Las buenos conciencias*, *La muerte de Artemio Cruz*, and *Zona Sagrada*. With the exception of Benítez' tendentious prologue, the critical essays are available elsewhere. Reeve's bibliography is excellent.

6573. ———. Terra nostra. México, Editorial Joaquín Mortiz, 1975. 789 p. (Novelistas contemporáneos)

Fuentes has always been attracted to rewriting his reading of historical material. Here he takes Spanish history, especially as Américo Castro interpreted it, and creates a vast, expanding collage of distorted characters caught in multiple repetitions of the same events. Destroys the normal foundation of the historical novel—and thus the faith in written history itself—by eliminating all secure reference points in time. Every character is distorted into various others, thus negating individual identity. History must now derive its reality from literature, since the text is now liberated from time other than its own. Includes excellent segments, but somewhat tiresome on the whole.

6574. Galeana, Benita. Benita. México, Editorial Extemporáneos, 1974. 206 p.

First person narration of Benita's picaresque life from orphaned child to political activist during the first half of the 20th century. Probably re-released in the wake of the popularity of Elena Poniatowska's *Hasta no verte Jesús mío* (1969) which it resembles slightly. Proves the value of a good editor-novelist like Poniatowska. *Benita* has documentary value, but falls short of literature.

6575. Galindo, Sergio. El hombre de los hongos. México, Editorial Joaquín Mortiz, 1976. 173 p. (Nueva narrativa hispánica)

Behind the facade of a simple child's story, Galindo offers a fantasy of erotic awakening and the loss of the garden of innocence. Among the best of Galindo's many prose books.

6576. García, León Roberto. Del cristal con que se mira. México, Fondo de Cultura Económica, 1976. 393 p. (Col. Tezontle)

Four generations of a family are caught in the cyclical repetitions of Mexican history. The narrative flows from one time-space to another along channels of words, phrases, actions shared by the juxtaposed scenes. Like the kaleidoscope image which illustrates the cover, the time periods duplicate each other, thus serving as mirrors in which the narrator can see his past and, perhaps, his future.

6577. García Ponce, Juan. Encuentros. México, Fondo de Cultura Económica, 1972. 111 p. (Letras mexicanas, 106)

Characteristic Garciaponcesque prose in which "nothing" happens, yet in the end a definite poetic image remains. Three stories of human realization through impersonalization—a state similar to animals or objects, which are in the world and life without the disadvantages of rational alienation.

6578. ———. El gato. B.A., Editorial Sudamericana, 1974. 161 p. (Col. El espejo)

The presence of a cat in the relationship of two lovers facilitates the depersonalization of their encounters, allowing them to enter a more intense zone of love and eroticism. Written as is if the narrator were describing the actions as seen on a movie screen, the objectivity of the narration reflects the state of objectification reached by the protagonists.

6579. Guzmán, Humberto. Manuscrito anónimo llamado consigna idiota. México, Editorial Joaquín Mortiz, 1975. 104 p. (Serie del volador)

Four monologues à-la-Kafka/Beckett, connected by the surrealistic vision of grotesque, erotic fantasy. Improbable events flow logically within the language of the text which in no way attempts to relate to so-called reality.

6580. Laiter, Salomón. David. México, Editorial Joaquín Mortiz, 1976. 159 p. (Nueva narrativa hispánica)

Poorly developed story of a young Jewish Mexican's growth from childhood to adolescence. Attempts to portray anti-Semitism in both the US and Mexico after World War II, and the ideal of Israel as a new, positive alternative to the failure of the American dream. The Jewish diaspora in Mexico is a barely explored subject and it deserves better treatment.

6581. Mendiola, Salvador. . . . y te sacaron los ojos. México, Organización Editorial Novaro, 1974. 205 p.

Onda literature (adolescent literature) which takes issue with the 1960s ideals of the uncommitted, pop artists. Rock star hero sees the light (politically) and denounces social injustice. Recaptures the iconoclasm of early Onda works, but falls short of José Agustín or Gustavo Sainz, in its attempt at formulating a critical evaluation of such a cultural base.

6582. Mendoza, María Luisa. De ausencia. México, Editorial Joaquín Mortiz, 1974. 212 p. (Nueva narrativa hispánica)

Novel of sexual obsession and the struggle against relentless aging. Mendoza's prose is striking for its power and directness, and innovations which break down normal grammar.

6583. Ojeda, Jorge Arturo. Muchacho solo. México, Editorial Grijalbo, 1976. 154 p.

A photographic session with erotic interludes allows the author to practice a well written, though superficial, essayism on society and morals through the alternating voices of characters who never are more than ideal types. Examples of Mexico's recent intellectual eroticism, but not among the best.

6584. Prieto, Francisco. Caracoles. México, Editorial Joaquín Mortiz, 1975. 267 p. (Nueva narrativa hispánica)

Structured like a snail shell, the novel begins with a group of characters loosely related, spins into a party scene where they all come together, then spins out again. The group is made up of middle class Catholics in their early thirties, all struggling with personal alienation. Well written, though burdened with existentialistic clichés.

6585. Revueltas, José. Antología personal. México, Fondo de Cultura Económica, 1975. 111 p. (Archivo del fondo, 36)

Excerpting from novels usually damages, but in Revuelta's case it is flattering. Nine selections prove again that he was a good short story writer unable to sustain quality in longer works. His best work, *El apando* (1969) is not included. No critical essay or bibliography.

6586. Río, Marcela del. Proceso a Faubritten. México, Aguilar Editor, 1976. 351 p., plates (Col. Novela nueva)

Death takes a permanent holiday when Dr. Faubritten unleashes the L(ife) Bomb; life without death becomes hell. Science fiction with a Thomas Pynchon twist. Texts deny or explicate texts until the surprising ending, which leaves us at the unpredictable new beginning. Demonstrates great stylistic versatility.

6587. Spota, Luis. Palabras mayores. 10 ed. México, Editorial Grijalbo, 1976. 383 p. (Best sellers)

Second in series "La costumbre del poder" (see item 6588). Avila Puig, economist and friend of Olid Inc. Chairman M. Rebul, is chosen to be the next president. Describes the development of the president's Mexican style.

6588. ———. Retrato hablado. México, Editorial Grijalbo, 1975. 368 p. (Best sellers)

Around business magnate E. Olid's corpse, Spota spreads a series of flashbacks relating the mourners to the man and his company. Final flashback reveals how his assistant had stripped him of power. With this novel Spota began a series titled "La costumbre del poder," continued in *Palabras mayores* (item 6587) and *Sobre la marcha* (item 6589), on the power structure of Mexican politics. With a keen eye for subjects of mass interest, Spota continues to produce best sellers that manage to fall short of first-rate literature. The series is interesting but unmemorable.

6589. ———. Sobre la marcha. México, Editorial Grijalbo, 1976. 448 p. (Best sellers)

Third in the series "La costumbre del poder." Presidential candidate Avila Puig's pre-election tour turns into a scandalous attack on the corruption of his own party, which controls Mexico. He becomes his own man and a threat to the ruling oligarchy. Novel ends on election day with the ominous thoughts of a would-be assassin.

6590. Valencia, Tita. Minotauromaquia. Crónica de un desencuentro. México, Editorial Joaquín Mortiz, 1976. 209 p. (Nueva narrativa hispánica)

Lyrical account of a woman's voyage through the despair and madness of unrequited love. Value lies in lyricism and the implicit criticism of male-centered culture, which relegates women to passivity. Here, Theseus and Ariadne are one woman, liberated from the male Minotaur, left trapped in his static labyrinth.

6591. Vasconcelos, José. Cuentos. Nota de Pedro Guillén. México, Comunidad Latinoamericana de Escritores, 1976. 113 p. (Col. Casa de la cultura latinoamericana)

New edition of the collected stories of an author more known for his socio-political writings. Introduction places the stories in the context of Vasconcelos' complete works, but offers little critical evaluation. No bibliography.

LITERARY CRITICISM AND HISTORY

6592. Agustín, José. Cuál es la onda (Diálogos [El Colegio de México] 10:1[55] enero/feb. 1974, p. 11-13)

Statement on the origins and present situation of La Onda (youth movement) by the leading exponent of Onda literature. Emphasizes the central role of rock music. "Lo profundo, la onda, es entonces, el cambio; lo inalterable, el espíritu común que permite la transformación. Y lo superficial son las demás ondas: las manifestaciones de la transformación, lo transitorio; en este caso, el caló, la ropa, la mariguana, el pelo, etcétera." Important essay for students of recent Mexican fiction.

6593. Bastos, María Luisa and **Sylvia Molloy.** La estrella junto a la luna: variantes de la figura materna en *Pedro Páramo* (MLN, 92:2, March 1977, p. 246-268)

Convincing study of the central role of the mother —in varied guises—as catalyst and guide to both the action and the narrative. Mythological perspective.

6594. Brodman, Barbara L.C. The Mexican cult of death in myth and literature. Gainesville, The Univ. Presses of Florida, 1976. 89 p., bibl. (Univ. of Florida monographs. Humanities series, 44)

Succinct study of the backgrounds of the death cult of Aztec and Spanish cultures as seen in their poetry. Traces its presence in five contemporary writers. The last brief chapter on recent writers and the changing attitudes is not sufficiently developed.

6595. Bruce-Novoa, Juan. Entrevista con Salvador Elizonda (La Palabra y el Hombre [México] 16, oct./dic. 1975, p. 51-58)

Focuses on Elizondo's theory of novel as pure creation divorced from so-called reality, and the contrast between the realization of the theory in *Farabeuf* (1964) and *El hipogeo secreto* (1968).

6596. Brushwood, John S. Cuatro novelas de Juan García Ponce: imaginación e intelecto (*in* Alazraki, Jaime ed. Homenaje a Andrés Iduarte: ofrecido por sus amigos y discípulos. Clear Creek, Ind., American Hispanist, 1976, p. 51-63)

One of the few US studies of this leading Mexican novelist. Attempts to distinguish between novels dominated by intellectual preoccupations and those of a more creative vein.

6597. ———. Literary periods in twentieth-century Mexico: the transformation of reality (*in* International Congress of Mexican History, IV, Santa Monica, Calif., 1973. Contemporary Mexico: papers. Los Angeles, Univ. of California, Latin American Center, 1976, p. 671-683)

Succinct proposal for this division of 20th-century Mexican literature into periods by one of the most knowledgeable critics in the field. Indicates that contrary to general opinion, innovation and art have dominated Mexican literature for most of the modern era, and that the literature of the Revolution was an exception, not the rule.

6598. Castellanos, Rosario. El mar y sus pescaditos. México, Secretaría de Educación Pública, Dirección General de Divulgación, 1975. 198 p. (SepSetentas, 189)

Posthumous collection of well written and informative essays, all previously published separately. Although superficial from the perspective of literary criticism, they are useful for understanding Castellanos herself rather than the subjects and authors she discussed.

6599. Colina, José de la. Juan García Ponce: la narración ensimismada (Plural [México] 3:8, mayo 1974, p. 57-61)

Study of Ponce's poetic novels which are structured in rhythmic flows of intensity similar to music, that resolve into a total image. This expanding image coincides with the main characters' own search for an impersonal, permanent existence in the world, like that of a novel.

6600. Decker, David. The circles and obsessions of Gustavo Sainz (REVIEW 76 [N.Y.] 18, Fall 1976, p. 44-47)

Studies the tension between language and the protagonist in Sainz's three novels. Language itself, as a dynamic, self-propelled force, moves the narratives more than the usual catalysts of character and plot.

6601. Durán, Gloria. Carlos Fuentes Cumpleaños [Birthday]: a mythological interpretation of an ambiguous novel (LALR, 2:4, Spring/Summer 1974, p. 75-86)

Archetypal interpretation centered on the variable phases of the Goddess. More plausible than analyses of social themes, though it does not discount them.

6602. Fuentes, Carlos. Cervantes o la crítica de la lectura. México, Editorial Joaquín Mortiz, 1976. 114 p. (Cuadernos de Joaquín Mortiz, 42)

Cannot be read as serious criticism of Cervantes. Although derivative of Américo Castro and Borges, it remains at a simpler level. Useful both as a possible prep-school text on Spanish culture and as a notebook on *Terra nostra* (see item 6573).

6603. García Ponce, Juan. Teología y pornografía. Pierre Klossowski en su obra: una descripción. México, Biblioteca Era, 1975. 182 p.

Lucid and thorough interpretation of the difficult and little known literature of the French novelist Klossowski. Proves again that Ponce is a critic of the highest stature, willing to explore new areas and provide the reader with new, original insights. Important for Mexican letters in that in the recent past, Ponce's interest—such as Pavese, Musil, Bataille—have become influences among the younger writers.

6604. ———. Trazos. México, UNAM, Dirección General de Publicaciones, 1974. 294 p. (Col. Poemas y ensayos)

Collection of essays on literature and society, and a one-act play. The series of essays on drama in the mid 1950s and early 1960s offer valuable insights into Mexican theatre. Political essays reveal a side of Ponce most readers are unaware of. The play is Ponce's last theatre piece, an anti-realism work which declares theatre to be a free, literary space.

6605. Gonzales, Michael. Cambio de piel or the myth of literature. Glasgow, U.K., Univ. of Glasgow, Institute of Latin American Studies, n.d. 16 p., bibl. (Occasional papers, 10)

Perceptive Marxian analysis of Fuentes' novel, positing the contradiction between Fuentes' ideal response to alienation and the need for "real" action. Limited by the Marxian refusal to consider the reality of "ideal" orders and the power they exert in the "real" order, and that literature is the confluence of the two in what perhaps can be seen as a third.

6606. Gyurko, Lanin A. Identity and demonic self in two narratives by Fuentes (UPRM/RL, 6:21, marzo 1974, p. 87-118)

Detailed analysis of the mythological elements in the novel *Aura* and the story "Tlactocatzine, del Jardín de Flandes."

6607. ———. Social satire and the ancient Mexican gods in the narrative of Fuentes (IAA, 1, 1975, p. 113-150, bibl.)

Ancient god figures are used by Fuentes to criticize contemporary Mexico, yet they themselves are frustrated in a society which no longer grants them relevance.

6608. Leal, Luis. La feria de Juan José Arreola: tema y estructura (*in* Giacoman, Helmy ed. Perspectivas de nueva narrativa hispanoamericana: autores. Río Piedras, P.R., Ediciones Puerto, 1973, p. 245-258)

Study of Arreola's only novel. The central theme of the failure of social organization is structured into a labyrinth of apparently unrelated vignettes, whose order derives from the pervasive theme, the satirical tone, and the image of the fair.

6609. ———. El nuevo cuento mexicano (*in* Pupo-Walker, Enrique ed. El cuento hispanoamericano ante la crítica. Madrid, Editorial Castalia, 1973, p. 280-295)

After a concise review of the short story in Mexico up to the 1940s, Leal studies the contributions of Revueltas, Arreola, Rulfo, and Fuentes which established a new mode in the genre. However, the key to the change is the work of Efrén Hernández (1904-58), who brought about a "desplazamiento de lo anecdótico a lo ornamental, a lo ambiental, a lo inconsecuente." Names present-day writers who are leaders in the genre, but does not analyze their work, only stating that they differ from Fuentes in their lack of preoccupation with national identity.

6610. Michaelis, Pierre. Escritura y realidad en *Farabeuf* (Plural [México] 4:4, enero 1975, p. 63-68)

Study of the novel's structural elements—photograph—death / eroticism / religion—West / East—and their configuration around three signs: mirrow, dividing line, and simulacrum. Emphasizes the text's insistence on doubtful representation, which finally only represents itself. More illuminating than previous essays on *Farabeuf*.

6611. Ojeda, Jorge Arturo. *Gazapo* extraordinario (Diálogos [El Colegio de México] 13:2[74] marzo/abril 1977, p. 15-17)

Brief, but useful study on Gustavo Sainz' first novel. Emphasizes linguistic innovations through Anglicisma, phonetic transformations, *albures* or Mexican puns.

6612. Paley-Francescato, Martha. Gustavo Sáinz: entrevista (HISPA, 5:14, agosto 1976, p. 63-81)

Extensive interview with one of the two leading exponents of Onda literature in Mexico (see item 6592).

6613. Paz, Octavio. Vuelta a *El laberinto de la soledad* (UTIEII/C, 25, 1975, p. 171-189)

Retrospective interview in which Paz appraises key points from his first major sociological essay, as well as the influences on him at the time he wrote it.

6614. Peralta, Violeta and Liliana Befumo Boschi. Rulfo: la soledad creadora. B.A., Fernando García Cambeiro, 1975. 245 p., bibl. (Col. Estudios latinoamericanos)

Two monographs under one title. Though both critics draw from many critical sources, they show a marked preference for a mythostructuralist approach. Produce some valuable insights.

6615. Poniatowska, Elena. Entrevista a Salvador Elizondo (Plural [México] 4:9, junio 1975, p. 28-35)

Focus on Elizondo's solipsistic orientation which is taking him more towards personal isolation, and his literature from prose (*Farabeuf*, 1964; *El hipogeo secreto*, 1968) to poetry.

6616. Portal, Marta. Proceso narrativo de la Revolución Mexicana. Madrid, Ediciones Cultura Hispánica, 1977. 329 p.

Important study of the novel of the Revolution. Studies the literature as history passing into the narrative structure, then the latter's transformation into a new mythological structure. By tracing the Revolution as a literary image, Portal is not limited by arbitrary historical dates or periods, as is R. Rodríguez Coronel in his *Recopilación de textos sobre la novela de la Revolución mexicana* (item 6618), and can thus include works written as late as 1969. She structures the evolution of the image into three stages: 1) simple realism and personal testimony; 2) critical realism or the novel of social protest; and 3) aesthetic renovation of the symbolism. Weakness lies in her attempt to analyze all novels according to such set criteria which results in her forcing some into categories regardless of their literary merit.

6617. Robinson, Cecil. Mexico and the Hispanic Southwest in American literature. Tucson, The Univ. of Arizona Press, 1977. 391 p., bibl., illus.

Revised version of 1963 ed., *With the ears of strangers*. With what in most cases are brief additions, Robinson updates and improves his already superb study of the Mexican in U.S. literature. Notable are the images gleaned from the poets as well as from Denise Levertov and Carlos Castañeda. Most significant addition is the insightful ch. 10 on Chicano literature.

6618. Rodríguez Coronel, Rogelio *ed*. Recopilación de textos sobre la novela de la Revolución Mexicana. La Habana, Casa de las Américas, Centro de Investigaciones Literarias, 1975. 431 p. (Valoración múltiple)

Collection of the most important articles on the subject. Includes a general introduction and sections on Azuela, Guzmán, López y Fuentes. The work is useful if somewhat limited by the editor's Marxist approach. Includes bibliography.

6619. Ruffinelli, Jorge. Código y lenguaje en José Agustín (La Palabra y el Hombre [México] 13, enero/marzo 1975, p. 57-62)

Good resumé of the characteristics of the Mexican Onda (adolescent) literature (see item 6592). Studies how Agustín uses language to challenge established structures, follows the evolution of this use from the hip dialogue of early works to its inclusion in the narration of his latest novel.

6620. ———. La perversa candidez de Juan García Ponce (Plural [México] 4:3, dic. 1974, p. 23-30)

Comprehensive interview covering all the major fiction works of one of Mexico's most prolific major novelists. Explores the relationship between Ponce and authors such as Pavese, Musil, and Klossowski.

6621. Sommers, Joseph. Entrevista: Juan Rulfo (HISPA, 2:4/5, 1973, p. 103-107)

Rulfo breaks his infamous silence to briefly discuss his early readings, the non-autobiographical nature of *Pedro Páramo*, and the attack on certain social absolutes.

6622. Vidal, Hernán. El modo narrativo en *La muerto de Artemio Cruz* de Carlos Fuentes (ICC/T, 31:2, mayo/agosto 1976, p. 300-326)

Noteworthy attempt to view the novel as a total image, yet limited by the psychoanalytic term, "super-yo," which fixes the text in the character, instead of in itself as literary discourse, or in the totalizing act of reading and recall which is the novel as image.

CENTRAL AMERICA

THOMAS B. IRVING

Professor of Romance Languages
University of Tennessee
with the collaboration of Dr. Evelyn Uhrhan Irving
Tennessee Technological University

DURING THE PAST FEW YEARS literary expression has blossomed in all six countries that make up the Central American and Panamanian isthmus, and a full intellectual life is reflected in these publications. The difficulty lies in trying to make some sort of order out of such heterogeneous literature.

The research scholar and literary explorer will find a crop of recent anthologies, half a dozen of them: Acosta's *Alabanza de Honduras* (item 6624); Benítez Rojo's on the Panama Canal (item 6628); Alfonso Chase's *Narrativa contemporánea de Costa Rica* (item 6630); Quince Duncan on blacks in Costa Rica (item 6659); the Nicaraguan Sergio Ramírez with two collections, the first a two-volume set on the Central American short story, and the other on that in his own country (items 6646-6649); and finally a most welcome one on the great Costa Rican editor Joaquín García Monge, whose selections were chosen by his son (item 6634b).

In Central America, short stories are plentiful because most newspapers have literary supplements each weekend and small magazines also publish stories. One with sustained literary pretensions is *Revista Lotería* (item 6669) from Panama. The late Salvadoran author and artist Salarrué is commemorated by a beautifully illustrated re-edition of his *Cuentos de cípotes* or 'Kids' Stories' (item 6653).

The novel has likewise been productive in recent years, and surprisingly in Honduras, with some hitherto unpublished works. Amaya Amador contributes *Prisión verde* (item 6626) about the North coast of Honduras, in a diatribe against Tiburcio Carías, who was dictator there 40 years ago. Monteforte Toledo of Guatemala has come back with a fresh novel *Los desencontrados* (item 6639) after pursuing sociology during his long Mexican exile since his expulsion in 1954; an earlier novel of his *Entre la piedra y la cruz* (item 6660) is studied in an essay by Virginia de Fonseca. M.A. Flores writes *Los compañeros* (item 6634a) on the continuing tragedy of these Guatemalan exiles. P.R. Gutiérrez' *Una ciudad para Lena* describes the effect of the Nicaraguan earthquake of 1973; Sergio Ramírez' *Charles Atlas también muere* (item 6646) laments and satirizes American influence in that country; and Joaquín Gutiérrez follows a Costa Rican family through its changes in *Murámonos, Federico* (item 6635).

Literary criticism has been vigorous: Rodrigo Miró leads it with his history of Panamanian literature (item 6673); Guardia de Alfaro studies Rogelio Sinán of Panama (item 6664); and Burdiel de López does the same with Costa Rican novelist Carmen Naranjo (item 6656).

There is social criticism too: Johnson studies "The North American in Sandinista novels" (item 6665); Fonseca tells of life on a Panamanian prison island in "Pulga Acusa" (item 6661a) something like José Luis Sánchez' *La isla de los hombres solos* off Costa Rica, and *Prisión verde* (item 6626) inveighs against the dictatorship of Tiburcio Carías 30 years ago in Honduras. Marxist writers are Amaya Amador from Honduras (item 6626); Joaquín Gutiérrez from Costa Rica (item 6635); and a biography of the late C.L. Fallas of Costa Rica (author of *Mamita Yunai*) by Marín Cañas (item 6669a). Jaime Díaz is another Marxist writer who has published a serious study of the *Popol Vuh* (item 6658). Psychology is also a fad: Virginia de Fonseca shows this in her study of the prison island off Panama, and so does Regales with Panamanian society.

There is satire and humor too: like Tony Fergo's *¡Qué pobres somos los ricos!* (item 6633); Alfonso Chase's *Mirar con inocencia* (item 6629); and Ferrer Valdez' *La muerte de la ópera en la selva* (item 6634), which is hilarious. The Panama Canal is covered with M.R. Sepúlveda's *El tema del canal* (item 6674) which was published in two places.

A whole array of other themes are tackled: the jungle and banana plantations appear with Quince Duncan's *Los cuatro espejos* (item 6632) as well as *El negro* previously mentioned; and Amaya Amador's *Prisión verde* from Honduras. Lisandro Chávez' *Balsas* (item 6631) covers the urban jungle in Nicaragua. Sketches on sea life are Laguna Nova's *Cuando la vela coja viento* (item 6638) from along the Atlantic coast of eastern Panama; and Pitty's *Estación de navegantes* (item 6644) also from Panama.

There are many interviews: Torriente talks with Che Guevara; Jorge Campos with Jaramillo Levi of Panama; C. Meneses the Peruvian with Miguel Angel Asturias. Three other authors are concerned with the same Nobel Prize winner: F. Merrel on "Juan Girador;" and Raúl Leiva and Otto-Raúl González, two poets who knew Asturias in Guatemala during the 1940s and early 1950s.

PROSE FICTION

6623. Abaúnza Salinas, Ramiro. Un general sin estrellas. Novela. Ilustraciones de Luis Balladares Gurdian. León, Nic., Imprenta Hospicio, 1974. 238 p., illus.

A regionalistic or *costumbrista* novel illustrated with line drawings by Luis Balladares Gurdian is set in "Santiago," or the city of León, Nic. It moves to Managua, the capital, and we meet characters like the smuggler, a soldier, a barber, a prostitute, etc. A glossary is provided for Nicaraguan terms and slang.

6624. Acosta, Oscar *comp.* Alabanza de Honduras. Antología. Prólogo, selecciones y notas de . . . Madrid?, Ediciones Anaya, 1975. 271 p., bibl.

This full yet compact anthology covers Honduran culture from the 16th century and even before discovery till the present. The work is divided into themes, and includes writers in both prose and verse. These begin with Christopher and Hernando Columbus, and embrace most Honduran writers like Rafael Heliodoro Valle, Rómulo E. Durón, Medardo Mejía, Froylán Turcios, Ramón Rosa as well as foreigners like Rubén Darío, John Lloyd Stephens, José Martí, Rafael Arévalo Martínez. Their sources are not quoted. The book is well printed in Spain.

6625. Aldef [*pseud. for* **Leda Falconio**]. Cuentos de tierra y mar. San Salvador, Ministerio de Educación, Dirección de Publicaciones, 1974. 128 p. (Col. Narradores, 5)

This volume offers 26 short stories by the Italian writer now living in El Salvador. The range covers folklore ("El Tesoro de Frances [sic] Drake") and contemporary city life. The style is clear and direct. Well printed by the Salvadoran ministry of education.

6626. Amaya-Amador, Ramón. Prisión verde. Prólogo de Longino Becerra. 2. ed. Tegucigalpa, Editorial Ramón Amaya-Amador, 1974. 367 p., plate.

The theme of the Central American jungle runs through this long novel by this left-wing Honduran writer. The jungle is the north coast of Honduras and the drama lies in the workers' effort to stage a strike against the foreign company. First ed. was published in Mexico.

6627. Arroyo, Justo. Capricornio en gris. Cuentos. Panamá, Instituto Nacional de Cultura y Deportes, Dirección de Cultura, Depto. de Letras, Artes Escénico y Editorial, 1973. 117 p. (Col. Concurso literario Ricardo Miró. Sección cuento, 1972)

Ten sophisticated short stories by a professor of the Univ. of Panama. Quotations from contemporary Latin American and foreign writers show his broad experience and models.

6628. Benítez Rojo, Antonio *ed.* and *comp.* Canal: tres relatos panameños. La Habana, Casa de las Américas. 1974. 96 p. (Col. La honda)

Three well-known Panamanian authors in their three short stories present a topical picture of Life in Panama. Joaquín Beleño C. is represented by his story "Canal;" Carlos Francisco Changmarín, by "Faragual;" and the best known Rogelio Sinán, by "Bobby." Important because of their vision of the American presence in this area—how it created and fomented a life of prostitution, misery, disease, and a deep need to make the Canal Panama's. [EUI]

6629. Chase, Alfonso. Mirar con inocencia. Narraciones. San José, Editorial Costa Rica, 1975. 178 p., bibl., illus.

Costa Rica has a true humorist in Chase, whose score of amusing tales are matched by line drawings by Hugo Díaz. They cover many aspects of Costa Rican social life, and vary from thumbnail sketches to longer short stories. A short bibliography of the author's other works is also offered.

6630. ——— *ed.* Narrativa contemporánea de Costa Rica. Selección, estudio introductorio y notas de . . . San José, Ministerio de Cultura, Juventud y Deportes, Depto. de Publicaciones, 1975. 2 v. (467, 521 p.) (Serie estudios literarios, 1)

Panorama of 24 short-story writers from this century that covers all tendencies: *costumbrista*, naturalistic, whimsical, Marxist. Includes long critical introduction, thumb-nail sketch and individual bibliography of each author. General bibliographies are appended to vol. 2.

6631. Chávez Alfaro, Lizandro. Balsa de serpientes. México, Editorial Joaquín Mortiz, 1976. 159 p. (Col. Nueva narrativa hispánica)

Author is from the Atlantic coast of Nicaragua, and so knows the jungle life there. This adds to the symbolic or surrealistic themes in this novel of the urban jungle, possibly Mexico City where he has lived for the past 30 years.

6632. Duncan, Quince. Los cuatro espejos. Novela. San José, Editorial Costa Rica, 1973. 163 p.

Prize-winning novel by black Costa Rican writer. Describes life in the capital San José and reflections from the banana plantations on the Caribbean coast, along with the racial and economic problems that prevail in that area.

6633. Fergo, Tony. Que pobres somos los ricos. Novela costumbrista panameña. Panamá, Litho-Impresora Panamá, 1973. 100 p.

Short novel of farcical sketches satirizes the rich Panamanian. The *niños bien* who fill its pages can be found in any plutocratic society in Latin America. The humor is raw but funny.

6634. Ferrer Valdez, Manuel. La muerte de la opera en la selva. Panamá, Instituto Nacional de Cultura, 1975. 153 p. (Col. Múltiple. Serie, 6)

Long short story or short novel of the title is followed by seven other short stories plus one ("El Gallo Ciego") by Rodrigo Miró. One of them was first published in 1928; others continue to date. The edition is subsidized by the Panamanian National Cultural Institute.

6634a. Flores, Marco Antonio. Los compañeros. México, Editorial Joaquín Mortiz, 1976. 237 p. (Col. Nueva narrativa hispánica)

In 1954 many Guatemalans went into exile. This book, by one of them, offers his thoughts on their trials. Language is coarse and at times brutal, bearing witness to endless curiosity and unfinished education that their predicament and exile led to.

6634b. García Monge, Joaquín. Obras escogidas. Selección de Eugenio García Carrillo. Prólogo de Alfonso Chase. San José, Editorial Universitaria Centroamericana (EDUCA), 1974. 632 p., plates (Col. Séptimo día)

Anthology of works by distinguished Costa Rican journalist who edited *El Reportorio Americano* (segunda serie) for many years in San José. Almost 150 essays on numerous subjects plus several photographs document range of interests (selected by his son Eugenio).

6635. Gutiérrez, Joaquín. Murámonos, Federico. Novela. San José, Editorial Costa Rica, 1973. 228 p.

A Costa Rican family is followed through its slow and painful disintegration. The father (Federico) is a dreamer, the mother a *devota* who cannot face reality, who have three children. The eldest tells about

6636. Gutiérrez, Pedro Rafael. Una ciudad para Lena. 2. ed. Managua, Editorial y Litografía San José, 1974. 151 p. (Col. Nueva narrativa hispanoamericana)

Contemporary novel involving problems caused by the earthquake which destroyed Managua in 1972. It is full of bald humor and reasonable optimism. The book is dedicated to the author's family, and the last chapter to Ernesto Cardenal.

6637. Hurtado, Gerardo César. Los parques. San José, Editorial Costa Rica, 1975. 150 p.

Various parks offer the setting for some of the action and conversation of the protagonist and his friends (male and female) in this Costa Rican novel. The setting is universal with its themes of illicit love as the university-aged but rather mature individuals carry on their lives and low-key love affairs. Dialogue and description are interestingly interspersed. In some aspects the novel is reminiscent of Unamuno's *Niebla* although the general theme and its handling is part of the present scene. [EUI]

6638. Laguna Novas, Jorge. Cuando la vela coja viento. Novela. Panamá?, Impresora Geminis, 1976. 138 p.

This short novel tells of sailors and sea life in the Atlantic along the Panamanian border with Colombia. It is a romantic story with realistic parts revealing the harsh life of its characters.

6639. Monteforte Toledo, Mario. Los desencontrados. México, Editorial Joaquín Mortiz, 1976. 190 p. (Col. Nueva narrativa hispánica)

This consistent Guatemalan novelist, also a sociologist, now living in Mexico, takes up writing fiction again in this novel of Mexican life. He explores the many exiles who live in that hospitable country, and probes their joys and their sorrows. He has been in exile there during the past quarter of a century.

6640. Naranjo, Carmen. Diario de un multitud. San José, Editorial Universitaria Centroamericana (EDUCA), 1974. 297 p. (Col. Séptimo día)

Novel about modern man in egalitarian Costa Rica (where the author lives and writes) tries to find a meaning to his life in the midst of social problems and class distinctions. This is a concerned attempt by the novelist to make society more human and to show her sympathy for the common citizen.

6641. Oqueli, Arturo. Silbando al viento. Novela hondureña. Tegucigalpa, Oficina Central de Información de SECTIN, Asociación de Periodistas y Escritores Nacionales, 1976. 140 p., illus.

This Honduran novel remained unpublished for over 20 years. It concerns the life and ideals of a poor schoolteacher on the country's north coast.

6642. Oreamuno Q., Alfredo. El jardín de los locos. San José, Editorial Albur, 1975. 158 p.

The 17 previously unpublished short stories in this volume are described by the author as purely for entertainment and not a literary exercise. The topics concern daily life or the author's past; the style is simple, direct, and the length varies. For those interested in chronological data, the author has included a table of contents at the end of the anthology specifying the month and year of each short story. [EUI]

6643. Pinto, Julieta. A la vuelta de la esquina. San José, Editorial Conciencia Nueva, 1975. 121 p.

Collection of 18 short stories about life in Costa Rica which reflect Central American speech and incidents. The author is a well-known writer who is interested in life among the lower-classes in her country.

6644. Pitty, Dimas Lidio. Estación de navegantes. Panamá, Instituto Nacional de Cultura, Direccion Técnica de Extensión Cultural, Depto. de Publicaciones, 1975. 252 p. (Col. Concurso literario Ricardo Miró. Sección novela, 1974)

First novel by Panamanian writer living in Mexico aims for naturalism and uses the theme of the canal in Panamanian life. Although complaining of North American influence in society, Pitty has also succumbed to it in his manner of writing.

6645. Quijada Urías, Alfonso. Otras historias famosas. San Salvador, Ministerio de Educación, Dirrección de Publicaciones, 1976. 98 p. (Col. Nueva-palabras, 8)

A baker's dozen of charming stories from El Salvador fill this small volume. Quijada Urías, the author, is a member of the Group of Five who are active in Salvadoran letters.

6646. Ramírez, Sergio. Charles Atlas también muere. México, Editorial Joaquín Mortiz, 1976. 118 p. (Col. Serie del volador)

Six tales about Gringo cultural influence in the tropics by the Nicaraguan short-story writer. The language is standard Spanish for the book is published in Mexico with an international audience in view.

6647. ——. De tropeles y tropelias. 3. ed. Managua, Ediciones el Pez y la Serpiente, 1976. 108 p., illus.

We have 15 cynical fables on political life in Nicaragua, followed by a long code of behavior for such a republic. The work is illustrated by woodcuts of the animals depicting the various attributes which are censured. Although published in Managua, the book is printed in Costa Rica.

6648. —— ed. Antología del cuento centroamericano. v. 1/2. San José, Editorial Universitaria Centroamericana (EDUCA), 1973. 2 v. (680, 473 p.) bibl., table (Col. Séptimo día)

Remarkably balanced and sensitive collection of Central American short stories. Authors include: Ricardo Estrada, Hugo Lindo, Yolanda Oreamuno, Fabián Dobles, Ernesto Cardenal, Alvaro Menén Desleal, and the editor himself. Vol. 1 includes a 50-p. introduction in the form of an essay on Central American narrative, from the indigenous *Popol Vuh* to the present. Vol. 2 also contains several careful indices by authors, themes, countries and a long comparative table linking Central American writing with that of other Hispanic countries and the world in general. Also includes bibliography and list of journals. A most valuable work.

6649. —— ed. El cuento nicaragüense. Antología. Managua, Ediciones el Pez y la Serpiente, 1976. 267 p.

Consists of 34 short stories (five anonymous) by 16 authors, e.g., Rubén Darío, Pablo Antonio Cuadra, Ernesto Cardenal, Mariano Fiallos Gil. Each selection is preceded by brief discussion. Includes good introduction on the subject by the editor. [EUI]

6650. Retana, Marco. La nocha de los amadores. Cuentos. Ilustraciones de Rafael Fernández. San José, Editorial Costa Rica, 1975. 86 p., illus.

Consists of 12 short stories which offer a glimpse of simple Costa Rican country life. Retana spent a good part of his life in this countryside and can therefore reproduce it. He uses impressionistic language and plot, providing a unique vision of the *campesino*. Illustrations by Rafael Fernández accompany each short story. [EUI]

6651. Rodríguez, Victor Manuel. Al margen de la vía. Panamá, Univ. de Panamá, 1975. 26 p.

These four stories were awarded the 1974 University Prize. They are pictorial prose poems, evoking images expressed in onomatopoeic and experimental language. [EUI]

6652. Salarrué [*pseud. for* **Salvador Salazar Arrué**]. Catleya luna. Novela. San Salvador, Ministerio de Educación, Dirección de Publicaciones, 1974. 197 p.

Latest novel by the Salvadoran writer Salarrué on a native theme of the Pipil nation which occupied Cuscatlán or precolumbian Salvador. They were the "baby Aztecs" who brought Mexican folklore to Central America, which the novelist attempts to revive.

6653. —— [——]. Cuentos de cipotes. Ilustraciones de Maya Salarrué. 2. ed. San Salvador, Ministerio de Educación, Dirección de Publicaciones, 1974. 183 p., illus.

The late artist and author from El Salvador, Salarrué is honored with a reprinting of his classical collection of children's stories. It is illustrated in color by Maya Salarrué. The language, especially in the dialogs, is the characteristic street dialect of the urchins or *cipotes* it describes.

6654. Ulloa, Juan. El narrador. Cuentos y relatos. San Salvador, Ministerio de Educación, Dirección de Cultura, Dirección de Publicaciones, 1973. 168 p., illus.

Vignettes on Salvadoran life, in the capital and in the country along the Pacific coast. Each story is preceded by a black-and-white sketch to illustrate it. The language is not dialectal but provincial, with some of the Salvadoran attraction for theosophy, and also the US.

**LITERARY CRITICISM
and
HISTORY**

6655. Azofeifa, Isaac Felipe. Incomunicación y soledad en el mundo narrativo de Salazar Herrera (UCR/RHCLC, 1:1, julio/dic. 1974, p. 15-20)

Discussion of the style of Salazar Herrera, contemporary Costa Rican short-story writer. Notes prevalence of introspection and moods of loneliness in his tales.

6656. Burdiel de López, María Cruz. Estudio de tres cuentos de Carmen Naranjo (UCR/R, 41, julio 1975, p. 101-110)

Analysis of three stories by winner of the 1973 Costa Rican Prize: "Hoy es un Largo Día," "El Viaje de los Viajes" and "¿Para que Matar a la Condesa?" by Carmen Naranjo. This study exemplifies the useful criticism of native authors conducted at the national Univ. of Costa Rica.

6657. Campos, Jorge. "Duplicaciones" de Enrique Jaramillo Levi y otros narradores panameños (INSULA, 29:334, sept. 1974, p. 14)

Description and interview with young Panamanian writer, Enrique Jaramillo Levi. It bears on his book of short stories *Duplicaciones*, and the contemporary literary scene in Panama.

6658. Díaz Rozzotto, Jaime. El *Popol Vuh*: fuente estética del realismo mágico· de Miguel Angel Asturias (CAM, 201:4, julio/agosto 1975, p. 85-92)

The leftist Guatemalan critic and professor Díaz Rozzotto analyzes the influence of the Mayan classics on the writing of Miguel Angel Asturias. His interest is chiefly on how this provided the "magical realism" in Asturias' evocative long poem *Clarivigilia Primaveral*.

6659. Duncan, Quince ed. and *comp*. El negro en la literatura costarricense. Prólogo de Fabián Dobles. San José, Editorial Costa Rica, 1975. 190 p.

Two dozen excerpts and tales about Jamaicans brought to Costa Rica, chiefly to work on banana plantations along the Atlantic coast. Preface by Fabián Dobles, and a careful study of each author by the editor precedes the selections.

6660. Fonseca, Virginia de. *Entre la piedra y la cruz*: novela de espacio (UCR/RHCLC, 1:1, julio/dic. 1974, p. 51-77)

Analysis of an important novel by Mario Monteforte Toledo whose work has been overshadowed by his compatriot Asturias. This study of the Indian Lu or Pedro Matzar as he progresses from his native village near Lake Atitlán to "ladino" status in the capital of Guatemala via the teaching profession and the army is more convincing than many stories of this sort.

6661. ———. La estructura interna de *El árbol de los pañuelos* y sus niveles temporales (UCR/R, 37, julio 1974, p. 51-63)

Structural study of recent Honduran novel, *El árbol de los pañuelos* by Julio Escoto. Fonseca analyzes the mystery surrounding Balam Cano, the orphaned son of a witch doctor who was burned to death in 1843. The time sequence is strange, as are the differing points of view of several characters who consider Balam's role in their community.

6661a. ———. Pulga acusa (UCR/RHCLC, 1:2, enero/junio 1975, p. 111-119)

Life on a Panamanian island prison is seen here through the eyes of a dog called Pulga. Fonseca analyzes this short story, showing the psychological parallels and contrasts between human and canine characters in the short story, where dreary existence is relieved by humor.

6662. García Murillo, Guillermo. La vida en las minas de Abangares y la novela histórica *La colina del buey* de José León Sánchez (UCR/R, 38, julio 1974, p. 87-97)

Study of 1971 Costa Rican novel *La colina del buey* by José León Sánchez concerning life in the gold mines at turn of the century.

6662a. González, Luisa and **Carlos Luis Sáenz.** Carmen Lyra. San José, Ministerio de Cultura, Juventud y Deportes, Depto. de Publicaciones, 1972. 173 p., bibl., plates (Serie ¿Quién fue y qué hizo?, 4)

Two friends have written a short biography of great Costa Rican educator and poet, Carmen Lyra (*pseud. for* María Isabel Carvajal). Work describes her long and active life, and includes some tales for children, short skit called "Juguete" (or 'Plaything'), several photographs and detailed bibliography of her works. Luisa González and Carlos Luis Sáenz are to be congratulated for their labor of love.

6663. González, Otto-Raúl. Miguel Angel Asturias: el gran lengua (CAM, 196:5, sept./oct. 1974, p. 91-103)

Exiled Guatemalan poet offers a detailed survey of the work of his fellow countryman, including short comparisons with other Latin American writers. Otto-Raúl knows Guatemala and knew Asturias, so his observations are valid.

6664. Guardia de Alfaro, Gloria. Cuentos de Rogelio Sinán: una revisión de la vanguardia en Panamá. Panamá, Academia Panameña de la Lengua, 1974. 23 p.

Short but careful analysis of Sinán's short-story style and of the vanguardist movement which Sinán represents.

6665. Johnson, David D. The North American in Sandinista novels (SECOLAS/A, 8, March 1977, p. 30-37)

Short study of the literature evoked by the US Marines occupation of Nicaragua in the late 1920s and early 1930s. The nationalist here was Augusto

César Sandino, whose memory is still alive in Central America, largely through these novels.

6666. Kunzmann, Ulrich. Acerca de la concepción del realismo mágico en la novela *Hombre de maíz* de Miguel Angel Asturias (BRP, 12:1, 1973, p. 97-126)

Analysis of this important indigenous novel published after *El Señor Presidente* in 1949. He evaluates the "magic realism" of the setting as well as its native contribution.

6667. Leiva, Raúl. Las principales novelas de Miguel Angel Asturias (CAM, 196:5, sept./oct. 1974, p. 63-90, plates)

Examination of four major prose works: *Leyendas de Guatemala*, *El Señor Presidente*, *Hombres de maíz* and *El papa verde* which might be called novels. There are two photographs of the late Nobel prize winner during a visit to Mexico.

6668. López Alvarez, Luis. Conversaciones con Miguel Angel Asturias. Madrid, Editorial Magisterio Español, 1974. 215 p., bibl., illus., plates (Col. Novelas y cuentos, 155)

This small volume offers a concise biography of the Guatemalan poet and novelist who won the Nobel prize in 1967. It is based on conversations held with the author. Well illustrated with photographs and a few caricatures covering his life at home and abroad. Useful overview of the writer, his views of events and his books.

6669. *Lotería.* Lotería Nacional de Beneficencia. No. 250, dic. 1976- Panamá.

The National Lottery of Panama publishes a monthly magazine which permits literary figures to see their works in print. This Dec. 1976 issue includes poems by John Rayan, a short story and novel, a short skit, an essay on Panamanian blacks by Roberto de la Guardia, and reviews of current publications. These works won prizes in the 1976 contest named after Ricardo Miró.

6669a. Marín Cañas, José. Ensayos: 14 artículos, 9 ensayos, 1 réquiem. San José, Editorial Costa Rica, 1972. 254 p.

The 14 articles, 9 essays and a "réquiem" for the late Costa Rican writer Carlos Luis Fallas, published here have all previously appeared in print during 2 1/2 years of author's academic and journalistic career. Some appeared in *La Nación* of San José. Topics are diverse—music, people, democracy, communism. [EUI]

6670. La más antigua novela nicaragüense (UCR/RHCLC, 1:1, julio/dic. 1974, p. 93-98)

Quasi-anonymous article by F.C. which probes the earliest possible Nicaraguan novel: *La juventud de Bismark* by an Italian immigrant named Fabio Carnevalini, published in 1876 in literary supplements to the newspaper "El Porvenir." Little is said to recommend it.

6671. Meneses, Carlos. Miguel Angel Asturias. Madrid, Ediciones Jucar, 1975. 206 p., bibl., plates (Col. Los poetas. Serie, 14)

Peruvian critic offers short but detailed biography of the Guatemalan man of letters. His intention is to show his work as a poet and a teller of tales rather than as a novelist. Includes a 60-p. anthology of poems, a few short articles, one skit "Rayito de Estrella," and 16 photographs of Asturias at several stages. The result is brief yet vivid.

6672. Merrell, Floyd. La estructura de "Juan Girador" de Miguel Angel Asturias (HISPA, 3:9, 1975, p. 21-33)

Discussion of the structure of the poetic sketch by Miguel Angel Asturias. Shows its relation to Mayan myth, and especially the Volador dance which is still celebrated in Papantla, Veracruz, and Chichicastenango, Quiché. Several tables illustrate this structure.

6673. Miró, Rodrigo. La literatura panameña: origen y proceso. 3. ed. Panamá, Editorial Serviprensa, 1976. 336 p., bibl., facsims., illus., plates.

History of Panamanian literature 300 years in the making, which begins in the Iberian peninsula, discusses early Spanish explorers and colony, continues through growing Creole consciousness to the literary movements of the past century and the contemporary republic. Includes bibliography and index.

6674. Sepúlveda, Mélida Ruth. El tema del canal en la novelística panameña (UCAB/M, 4, 1975, p. 217-286, bibl.)

Long critical analysis of panamerican novels on the subject of the canal. Such a vital issue has had an overriding effect on the country and its society, and so become one of the most realistic themes in its literature.

HISPANIC CARIBBEAN

ROBERTO GONZALEZ ECHEVARRIA

Associate Professor of Spanish
Yale University

CARLOS R. HORTAS

Associate Professor of Spanish
Hunter College

LEZAMA'S DEATH ON 9 AUG. 1976, and the posthumous publication of *Oppiano Licario* (1977, see item 6690), were the dramatic highlights of two or three years in which the author of *Paradiso* was the object of increasing critical attention. Though criticism of Lezama is still at a somewhat elementary stage, it is safe to predict that it will eventually reach the level of sophistication that his works deserve.

The institutionalization of the Revolution in the past two or three years is already affecting the cultural area. The II Congress of the Unión Nacional de Escritores y Artistas de Cuba (UNEAC), which took place in Oct. 1977, is going to have long-range effects on literary production. The Congress emphasized the important role literature plays in a socialist society and laid down very liberal guidelines for literary activity. Such official normalization of literary production is bound to have a positive impact, particularly as younger critics, formed under established revolution, replace older types who still translate the instability of the early years of the regime into squeamish, "safe" and innocuous writing.

Other than the recognition of Lezama by critics in general, the most important news in the area of Cuban narrative continues to be the edition of forgotten classics in the Cuban tradition. This is an indication that the most notable progress made in the past few years has been in the area of academic criticism. The professionalism of scholars has increased remarkably and there are now debates underway among *investigadores* about topics such as the anti-slavery novel. Still, it is unfortunate that the criticism which is more widely disseminated is mostly ceremonial, ritualistic and fearful of risk (the death of Juan Marinello, whose rigor and imagination were without parallel among Cuban critics, left a void that will be very difficult to fill). Young scholars with training in critical theory have gravitated mostly to *La Gaceta de Cuba*, where some of the most interesting critical activity is taking place (a special issue, No. 100, under the direction of Desiderio Navarro, is devoted to "Problemas de la Crítica y la Ciencia Literaria").

In Puerto Rico René Marqués (items 6693-6694 and 6726) and Enrique Laguerre, continue actively writing and adding to their already important narrative work. Younger writers, notably Emilio Díaz Valcárcel (item 6685) and Luis Rafael Sánchez (item 6697) have established themselves with an identifiable *oeuvre*, and relative newcomers Rosario Ferré (item 6686) and Egberto Figueroa (items 6687 and 6688) are writers who have made important recent contributions. Although Puerto Rico has not participated fully in the so-called "Boom" of Latin American narrative, *La guaracha del macho Camacho* (item 6697) and *Papeles de Pandora* (item 6686) are excellent examples of innovations in language and structure that compare favorably with recent Latin American narrative.

Beginning with this year's volume, *HLAS 40*, Carlos R. Hortas will co-author this section. He is in charge of Puerto Rican literature.

PROSE FICTION

6675. Bueno, Salvador *ed. and comp.* Cuentos cubanos del siglo XX. Antología. La Habana, Editorial Arte y Literatura, 1975. 490 p.

Extremely useful anthology of short stories by recognized figures and others less known. Introductions report bare facts about each author, reliably nevertheless. Concludes with chart listing in parallel columns important events in authors' lives, and major events in Cuban world history. Bueno's introduction is conventional and rhetorical and he omits Lino

Novás Calvo and Guillermo Cabrera Infante. First was extremely influential as short-story writer before the Revolution and latter's *Así en la paz como en la guerra* was first important collection of short-stories published after Revolution. Both authors live outside of Cuba now.

6676. Cardoso, Onelio Jorge. El hilo y la cuerda. La Habana, Unión de Escritores y Artistas de Cuba, 1974. 90 p., illus.

Masterful stories by unjustly forgotten writer. Cardoso's mixture of realism with an intense, poetic prose is unique among today's Latin American writers.

6677. Carpentier, Alejo. Crónicas. Prólogo de José Antonio Portuondo, redacción por Omelio Ramos Mederos. La Habana, Editorial Arte y Literatura, 1975. 2 v. (919 p.) (Continuos pagination)

Truly important addition to Carpentier *corpus*. Vol. 1 contains all his articles from *Social* (save for those on fashion signed *Jacqueline*), while vol. 2 contains generous selection of pieces from *Carteles*. With these volumes, general public finally has access to nearly all of Carpentier's journalistic and essayistic production in 1920s, 1930s, and 1940s. Fascinating *crónicas* were influential in introducing European avant-garde into Cuba and Latin America. They still make profitable and entertaining reading. Unfortunately, Carpentier was allowed to have a hand in the selection. Portuondo in his useful prologue discretely prints a letter from Carpentier in which the writer offers some lame and squeamish excuses for his pieces of Parisian nightlife and a note at the beginning of vol. 2 explains that Carpentier regrouped pieces according to themes. Two significant series of articles from *Carteles*, published after Carpentier's return from Europe in 1939 were left out: "El Ocaso de Europa" and "La Habana Vista por un Turista Cubano."

6678. ———. Letra y Solfa. v. 1, Visión de América. Selección, prólogo y notas de Alexis Marquéz R. B.A., Ediciones Nemont, 1976. 134 p. (Col. Autores contemporáneos)

First ed. (all in one vol.) was published in 1975 by Síntesis Dosmil in Caracas. Márquez Rodríguez' introduction and selection are not very good and notes are scarce and generally useless. Instead of organizing Carpentier's articles in chronological order, editor follows a vaguely defined thematic division, and in this second ed. some articles lack date of publication. But since *El Nacional*, the Caracas newspaper where these brief pieces appeared during 1950s, is not easily available, book is useful to Carpentier specialist and others. It is regretful that the edition is not as scholarly as it could have been.

6679. ———. Razón de ser: conferencias. Caracas, Univ. Central de Venezuela, Ediciones del Rectorado, 1976. 120 p.

Preceded by a "Noticia sobre Este Libro" by Rafael José Neri and "Homenaje a Alejo Carpentier" by Alexis Márquez Rodríguez, neither of any interest, the four lectures by the Cuban novelist are important for specialists in his works. Also contains a "Conversación" between Carpentier and various journalists that is fairly uninteresting. In the lectures Carpentier goes back to topics that made up *Tientos y diferencias*: "conciencia e identidad de América," "lo barroco y lo real maravilloso," "problemática del tiempo y el idioma en la moderna novela latinoamericana," etc. The lecture entitled "Un Camino de Medio Siglo: An (other) Autobiographical Account" contains some fresh information. Carpentier repeats himself a good deal in lectures and as usual his statements are richer if viewed in relation to his fiction. Lectures are really talks, and from them a less formal Carpentier emerges.

6680. ———. El reino de este mundo. B.A., Librería del Colegio, 1975. 168 p. (Col. Narradores de nuestro mundo)

Re-ed. of Carpentier's 1949 masterpiece with long critical prologue that contains some insights, though it is generally uninformed.

6681. Chaple, Sergio. Hacia otra luz más pura. La Habana, Unión de Escritores y Artistas de Cuba, 1975. 90 p.

Chaple is a well-informed critic who writes short stories.

6682. El cuento en la revolución. Antología. La Habana, Unión de Escritores y Artistas de Cuba, 1975. 379 p.

Less ambitious project than Bueno's anthology, this volume contains some established figures, but also many not so well known. Prologue by Félix Pita Rodríguez is brief, but interesting, particularly for those who study his work.

6683. Cuentos modernos. Antología. Río Piedras, P.R., Editorial Edil, 1975. 188 p.

Short stories by eight young writers, previously published only in literary periodicals. Of some interest but lacking in stylistic vigor and maturity.

6684. Díaz Montero, Aníbal. Nico, el pinche: estampas jíbaras. San Juan, P.R., The Author, 1975. 123 p.

Short narrative pieces in *costumbrista* tradition by well-known Puerto Rican writer. Slices of island's country life.

6685. Díaz Valcárcel, Emilio. Inventario. Novela. Río Piedras, P.R., Editorial Cultural, 1975. 208 p.

Novel of a Puerto Rican insurance salesman working for a US firm in Puerto Rico. Flashbacks to protagonist's childhood and adolescence. When novel begins, Germán Ramos is approaching 60 years of age and is taking stock of his life—a life of incorrect choices and wasted moments. Excellent insights into problems and conflicts of middle-class Puerto Ricans.

6686. Ferré, Rosario. Papeles de pandora. México, Editorial Joaquín Mortiz, 1976. 207 p. (Nueva narrativa hispánica)

Rosario Ferré's first full-length book of 14 short stories and six narrative poems. Ferré is an excellent stylist and a superb story-teller. Poignant, stark, at times poetic, these are first-rate stories. Highly recommended.

6687. Figueroa, Egberto. Abrojos. Río Piedras, P.R., Editorial Edil, 1975. 154 p.

Fourteen short stories of uneven quality that demonstrate a fine literary sensitivity. Thematically, stories range from childhood memories to Vietnam War. Figueroa is a young writer still maturing, yet quite talented.

6688. ———. Mas allá de ti. Novela a favor del futuro. San Juan, P.R., The Author, 1975. 213 p.

Interesting and often humorous novel about life and loves of protagonist, Julián Lunares. Perspicacious look at contemporary Puerto Rican society, its follies and foibles. Valuable contribution to contemporary Puerto Rican narrative.

6689. García-Márquez, Gabriel. No se me ocurre ningún título (CDLA, 16:100, enero/feb. 1977, p. 84-89)

Delicious chapter of GGM's forthcoming book on Cuba, in which author tells of his first visit to the island shortly after the triumph of the Revolution.

6690. Lezama Lima, José. Oppiano Licario. México, Ediciones Era, 1977. 232 p.

Lezama's posthumous novel was incomplete when the writer died on 9 Aug. 1976. This edition is based on manuscript given by Lezama's widow to Era, according to note at book's beginning. There is another, Cuban, edition, with a prologue by distinguished historian Manuel Moreno Fraginals, but I have not been able to see it. In this novel, where characters from *Paradiso* reappear, Lezama unfolds theme of resurrection. Licario, who died in previous novel reappears now accompanied by sister Ynaca Eco. Ynaca has relations with both Cení and Fronesis and is impregnated by first, to whom she had delivered Licario's wisdom in a manuscript entitled *Súmula nunca infusa de excepciones morfológicas*. Though obviously not a breakthrough of the magnitude of *Paradiso*, *Oppiano Licario* is yet another major work by writer who may be the greatest in 20th-century Latin America.

6691. Loveira y Chirino, Carlos. Generales y doctores. La Habana, Ediciones Huracán, Instituto Cubano del Libro, 1972. 409 p.

Popular ed. of Loveira's bitter account of republic's first years. First published 1920, this novel together with *Juan Criollo*, deserves more critical attention. Forgotten because of the unjust criticism of *vanguardistas* and general apathy with which national literary figures were treated, Loveira might make a come-back now.

6692. Manzano, Juan Francisco. Autobiografía de un esclavo. Introducción, notas y actualización del texto de Ivan A. Schulman. Madrid, Ediciones Guadarrama, 1975. 117 p.

Careful, scholarly ed. of this bizarre book. A solid contribution to studies of 19th century Cuba.

6693. Marqués, René. Inmersos en el silencio. Cuentos. Introducción de José M. Lacomba. Río Piedras, P.R., Editorial Antillana, 1976. 171 p.

Selection of short stories written by Marqués between 1955-75. All have appeared previously, are accompanied here by useful introduction in which José M. Lacomba provides some background and an evaluation of each story.

6694. ———. La mirada. Novela. Río Piedras, P.R., Editorial Antillana, 1975. 100 p.

Novel of modern Puerto Rico, in which there is repeated reference to Greek gods Cronus and Gaea, and fate of protagonists is likened to that of House of Atreus. Explicit sexual episodes, some of which were excised by the Spanish censors. Puerto Rican origin myths are viewed within the framework of Greek mythology. Interesting and suggestive, this novel invites close reading and discussion.

6695. Portuondo, José A. Astrolabio. La Habana, Editorial de Arte y Literatura, 1973. 181 p. (Col. Astrolabio)

Portuondo collects series of minor pieces going back to 1930s. Author writes these off as *divertimentos*, but they help give a more rounded view of Portuondo, whose more ambitious work tends to be somewhat mechanical and schematic.

6696. Rodríguez, Luis Felipe. Ciénaga. Prólogo de César Leante. La Habana,

Editorial Arte y Literatura, Instituto Cubano del Libro,, 1975. 192 p. (Col. Biblioteca básica de literatura cubana)

Rodríguez' 1937 *Novela de la tierra* shares with its Latin American counterparts an allegorical tendency, as well as realistic design. Leante's prologue is contained in *El espacio real* (see item 6724). Volume closes with very useful chronology. Good popular ed.

6697. Sánchez, Luis Rafael. La guaracha del macho Camacho. B.A., Ediciones de la Flor, 1976. 256 p.

Scathing, humorous critique of modern Puerto Rican life and mores. Iris Chacon, traffic jams, US consumer products, public, political and historical figures all sway to El Macho Camacho's guaracha *La vida es una cosa fenomenal*. Perhaps Luis Rafael Sánchez' best work to date, this novel is an important contribution to Puerto Rican letters and to modern Latin American narrative.

6698. Soler, Rafael. Campamento de artillería. La Habana, Unión de Escritores y Artistas de Cuba, 1975. 150 p.

Stark narratives, depending mostly on dialogue, after the fashion of the *novela de testimonio*. Soler had (d. 1974, age 31), however, a gift for the unexpected poetic line: "Si en los días claros [thinks an anti-aircraft gunner] los aviones se metían en el sol para hacerse invisibles, había que tirarle al sol."

6699. Sorel, André *comp.* Cuentos de Cuba socialista. Madrid, ZERO, 1976. 190 p. (Col. Se hace camino al andar, 45. Serie: Guernica)

Extremely conventional anthology intended for Spanish market. Readers should beware that Andrés Sorel's general introduction is plagued with errors, as also are some introductions to individual authors.

6700. Stolk, Gloria. Cuentos del Caribe. Caracas, Monte Avila Editores, 1975. 164 p. (Col. Continente)

Short stories told in a traditional narrative style. Sad and tragic endings predominate. Few of literary value.

6701. Zeno Gandía, Manuel. La charca: crónicas de un mundo enfermo. Río Piedras, P.R., Editorial Edil, 1973. 220 p.

Inexpensive student ed. of classic naturalistic novel. Lacks any foreword, critical study, or introduction. The 1966 Instituto de Cultura Puertorriqueña ed. was superior in every respect.

LITERARY CRITICISM AND HISTORY

6702. Aguilar Mora, Jorge and others. Severo Sarduy. Selección y montaje por Julián Ríos. Madrid, Editorial Fundamentos, 1976. 202 p., plate (Col. Espiral)

Volume containing nearly all mature criticism on Sarduy: articles by Jorge Aguilar Mora, Roland Barthes, Jean Michel Fossey, Suzanne Jill Levine, Julio Ortega, Roberto González Echevarría (who also contributes a bibliography), Emir Rodríguez Monegal and Philippe Sollers. Also contains chapter from Sarduy's next novel and introduction by his mother.

6703. Barrera, Ernesto M. Philosophical transformations in contemporary Cuban literature (UCSD/NS, 5:1, 1975, p. 109-112, bibl.)

Wildly misinformed and simplistic. The alluring title will mislead many a scholar. The piece should never have been published.

6704. Bosch, Rafael. Análisis objetivo material del primer Carpentier: 1933-1962 (RCLL, 2:4, 1976, p. 81-102)

Author betrays tenets of his elementary Marxist approach by lack of attention to facts about Carpentier's life and works. His attempt to prove Carpentier's petit-bourgeois ideological basis is predictable and the analyses of the novels superficial and ill informed.

6705. Canales, Nemesio R. Paliques. Barcelona, Editorial Vosgos, 1974. 206 p. (Col. Grandes maestros, 75. Col. Universal, 77)

Inexpensive student ed. of short essays (Paliques) of Nemesio Canales, which initially appeared as newspaper articles in Puerto Rico. Well written and vigorous, they address social, political and other aspects of Puerto Rican life. Lacks critical study or any introduction.

6706. Cheuse, Alan. Hamlet in Haiti: style in Carpentier's *The kingdom of this world* (UWI/CQ, 21:4, Dec. 1975, p. 13-29)

Reasonably well-informed essay that English-speaking readers of Carpentier will find useful.

6707. Chiampi Cortez, Irlemar. A poética do realismo maravilhoso: *Los pasos* *perdidos*. São Paulo, Univ. de São Paulo, 1976. 429 p.

Most thorough and convincing structuralist approach to Carpentier to date based on vast knowledge of Carpentier's works. Very important effort in Latin American criticism even if there are debatable points concerning applicability of Greimasian theories to vaguely defined conceptual tag such as *real maravilhoso*.

6708. Documentos del Primer Congreso del Partido Comunista de Cuba sobre la Cultura Artística y Literaria: tesis, resolución (CDLA, 16:99, nov./dic. 1976, p. 5-25)

Wide-ranging document of great import in the history of the debate about artistic freedom and responsibilities in post-revolutionary Cuban society. Though it does not call for any radical changes in cultural policy, the document sets out, in systematic fashion, that policy. For instance, the duties of organizations such as UNEAC are spelled out, there is a call for the establishment of copyright in the intellectual field, etc.

6709. Fernández Retamar, Roberto. La contribución de las literaturas de la América Latina a la literatura universal en el siglo XX (RCLL, 2:4, 1976, p. 17-30)

Major essay that reconsiders all of Latin American literature from 1880s to present. Author maintains that Latin American literature does not begin to make a sustained contribution to world literature until 1960s, after the Cuban Revolution. There are many insights on the literary movements discussed and an attempt to integrate Brazil and English and French Caribbean into overall formulations. But premises of essay—furnished by organizer of a symposium—are questionable. Does Latin American literature make contributions to large and imposing category called *universal literature*? Or is *universal literature* abstraction invented in post-Enlightenment Europe? Essay moves in area somewhere between conventional idealist literary history and Marxist reassessment, but succeeds more as the former than latter. Essay should be seen in relation to author's previous work, particularly his well-known essay "Calibán."

6710. ———. Nuestra América y Occidente (CDLA, 16:98, sept./oct. 1976, p. 36-58)

Retamar's most important piece since "Calibán" this essay is a revision of the earlier, much-circulated and polemical antecedent. Retamar assumes here a more dialectical stance in his analysis of the relationship between the Western World and Latin America. He maintains that *Occidente* equals capitalism, which would then make Latin America *and* the oppressed within the Western World a unity. In this way Retamar bypasses the usual allegation that Marxism is as foreign to Latin America as any other imported ideology. Though such broad claims stand in need of further analysis, Retamar's essay is the most cogent to come out on the subject from Cuba, or Latin America, for that matter, in a long time.

6711. ———. Para una teoría de la literatura hispanoamericana y otras aproximaciones. La Habana, Casa de las Américas, 1975. 141 p. (Cuadernos casa, 16)

Book collects several pieces published earlier which, according to author "los une un propósito común: señalar la necesidad de que nuestra literatura sea abordada con respeto para su especificidad; de que no se le aplique, colonialmente, la ortopedia de conceptos que se modelaron sobre otros cuerpos." None of articles here collected can be read as theoretical breakthrough, together, however, they constitute a cogent *prise de position*. Implicitly and explicitly Retamar wishes to begin all theoretical formulations with Martí, from whose dispersed work one can gather another *prise de position*: that Latin American literature is unique and therefore must be dealt with by rules that it sets for itself. Important collection.

6712. Garzón Céspedes, Francisco. Cuba: el papel del género policíaco en la lucha ideológica (CDLA, 15:89, marzo/abril 1975, p. 159-162)

Positive appraisal of two recent detective novels published in Cuba, *La ronda de los rubíes* and *No es tiempo de ceremonias*. Though jargony and somewhat uncritical, this is an important piece on a literary phenomenon being promoted in Cuba.

6713. González, Eduardo. Baroque endings: Carpentier, Sarduy and some textual contingencies (MLN, 92:2, March 1977, p. 269-295)

Remarkable meditation on literature that begins with a gloss of Carpentier's "Viaje a la Semilla" and ends with a critique of Sarduy's *Barroco*. Dense style and variegated field of allusions make it difficult reading, but this is nonetheless an important essay on both Carpentier and Sarduy.

6714. González Bolaños, Aimée. Los cuentos de Montecallado (UCLV/I, 50, enero/abril 1975, p. 106-152)

Ponderously academic and wordy study of Félix Pita Rodríguez, who deserves more attention than he has received outside of Cuba.

6715. González Echevarría, Roberto. Alejo Carpentier: the pilgrim at home. Ithaca, N.Y., Cornell Univ. Press, 1977. 307 p., bibl.

Study of Carpentier's *oeuvre* and rewritings of his own life.

6716. ———. Relecturas: estudios de literatura cubana. Caracas, Monte Avila, 1976. 163 p.

Collection of previously published essays, slightly retouched, on Carpentier, Lezama Lima and Sarduy, plus an unpublished piece "José Arrom, Autor de la *Relación acerca de las antigüedades de los indios*: Picaresca e Historia."

6717. Goytisolo, Juan. Lectura cervantina de *Tres tristes tigres* (IILI/RI, 42:94, enero/marzo 1976, p. 1-18)

Academic Goytisolo is discovering a lot of what critics have known for a long time about Cervantes' masterpiece; his reading of *TTT* from such premises is somewhat mechanical, though at times insightful. Prefers Cabrera Infante over Cortázar.

6718. ———. La metáfora erótica: Góngora, Joaquín Belda y Lezama Lima (IILI/RI, 42:95, abril/junio 1976, p. 157-175)

Somewhat predictable analysis of Lezama and the "discovery" of a minor Spanish novelist. More interesting ultimately for those focusing on Goytisolo than on Lezama.

6719. Jitrik, Noé. Blanco, negro, ¿mulato?: una lectura de *El reino de este mundo*, de Alejo Carpentier (CELRG/A, 1975, p. 167-205)

Rambling, uninformed, occasionally insightful, grounded on an uncritical mixture of approaches that pretend to be structuralist, post-structuralist and Marxist all at once.

6720. Kadir, Djelal. Stalking the oxen of the sun and felling the sacred cows: Joyce's *Ulysses* and Cabrera Infante's *Three trapped tigers* (LALR, 4:8, Spring/Summer 1976, p. 15-22)

Fruitful comparison of *Ulysses* and *Three trapped tigers*, using as point of departure relationship of one episode in each with the twelfth book of the *Odyssey*. Author considers *TTT* to be latest in series of manifestations of the Spirit of Literature, a spirit whose main concern is self-mockery. There are many insights into *TTT*, though I think a more balanced view of question of its "sources" would have taken into account Lewis Carroll.

6721. King, Lloyd. Mr. Black in Cuba (ASAWI/B, 5, Dec. 1972, p. 21-26)

Though not scholarly, this brief piece gives a stark view of négritude and Afrocubanism, devoid of the usual sentimentality. King deals, in passing, with figures such as Fernando Ortíz, Palés Matos, Césaire, Guillén and Carpentier.

6722. Kuteischikova, Vera. El concepto del barroco en Alejo Carpentier y la nueva visión artístico-ideológica en la novela contemporánea de América Latina (CELRG/A, 1975, p. 121-128)

Superficial, sounds like a talk given at a symposium.

6723. Leante, César. Dos obras antiesclavistas cubanas (CAM, 35[207]:4, julio/agosto 1976, p. 175-188)

Reassessment of Manzano's *Autobiografía* and Suárez Romero's *Francisco* that assigns them more revolutionary value than Yero Pérez (or the Cuban film *El otro Francisco* would). Leante concludes that: "entre las cuchillas que incidieron en su extirpación [de la esclavitud] están las obras de Anselmo Suárez y Juan Francisco Manzano, que, por encima de toda limitación, han quedado como dos estremecedoras denuncias del régimen esclavista, como dos viriles acusaciones contra la servidumbre negra, como dos inestimables contribuciones a 'la causa más noble del mundo' en aquel tiempo."

6724. ———. El espacio real. La Hábana, Unión de Escritores y Artistas de Cuba (UNEAC), 1975. 182 p. (Contemporáneos)

César Leante, who with *El perseguido* and *Muelle de Caballerías* has taken a place among more important Cuban novelists, is also a good critic. In this book he devotes essays to Cuban prose-fiction writers such as Cirilo Villaverde, Carlos Loveira, Labrador Ruiz, Alejo Carpentier and Luis Felipe Rodríguez. There are two middle chapters on Quiroga and Gallegos, followed by several studies of French writers such as Hugo, Saint-Exupéry and Sartre. Leante is both haunted and repelled by novel of the *boom* and by impact of French letters on Latin America. But this latter worry is somewhat dated, since it concerns Sartre. In spite of limitations imposed by this time-lag Leante is an important writer.

6725. Levine, Suzanne Jill. Jorge Luis Borges and Severo Sarduy: two writers of the neo-Baroque (LALR, 2:4, Spring/Summer 1974, p. 25-37)

Against more obvious and significant differences between two authors, article endeavors to show that there is in Sarduy's Baroque "an osmotic reading of Borges." Acute.

6726. Marqués, René. The docile Puerto Rican. Translated with an introduction by Barbara Bockus Aponte. Philadelphia, Pa., Temple Univ. Press, 1976. 137 p.

Seven of Marqués' speeches, articles and prologues translated into English and highlighted by "The Docile Puerto Rican," Marqués' best known essay.

Backus Aponte's translation is at times stiff but very good in general. First published translation of Marqués' essays into English. For political scientist's comment see *HLAS 39:7264*.

6727. Marqués, Sarah. Arte y sociedad en las novelas de Carlos Loveira. Miami, Fla., Ediciones Universal, 1977. 240 p., bibl. (Col. Polymita)

Sedulously researched introduction to life-and-works of a novelist deserving much more attention than he has been accorded so far. Marqués' background of Cuban history and the Cuban novel and her knowledge of the intellectual relations between Cuba and Spain are a sound contribution, though she tends to be somewhat prolix and is not a particularly elegant writer. Analyses of novels are not high powered criticism but are convincing within their narrow academic scope. Though there are debatable points throughout, book is a solid contribution, soaring above level of what Ediciones Universal usually publishes.

6728. Martínez Laínez, Fernando. Palabra cubana. Madrid, Akal Editor, 1975. 317 p., bibl., plates (Serie Akal, 74:24)

Interviews with Cuban writers and critics: Nicolás Guillén, José Lezama Lima, Roberto Fernández Retamar, Antonio Benítez Rojo, Jesús Orta Ruiz, Sergio Chaple, José Antonio Portuondo, Hugo Chinea, Noel Návarro, Félix Pita Rodríguez and Onelio Jorge Cardoso. Some interviews are candid and revealing. Unfortunately, author, a Spanish journalist, does not know Cuban history and literature well and makes errors of fact in introductions. Still a useful book.

6729. Méndez, José Luis. Manipulación y fabricación de mitos en la subliteratura (CDLA, 15:89, marzo/abril 1975, p. 122-131, illus.)

Overview of topic centering on several recent books by Umberto Eco, Ariel Dorfmann and Armand Mattelart, Ludovico Silva, Francis Lacassin and others. Though not very original, it is a fairly good introduction to the topic.

6731. Molinero, Rita. La narrativa de Enrique Labrador Ruiz. Madrid, Nova Scholar, 1977. 262 p., bibl.

Though extremely conventional in approach, this book marks a good beginning to study of novelist unjustly neglected by criticism. Molinero's detailed account of his life and works is followed by very good bibliography. Work of serious scholar, book is somewhat marred by presumptuous and irresponsible prologue by one Carlos Alberto Montaner.

6732. On his seventieth birthday Alejo Carpentier answers seven questions (UWI/CQ, 21:1/2, March/June 1975, p. 88-90)

Carpentier reveals that "what I announced on several occasions as a trilogy begun with a volume entitled *The Year 59*, eventually became *The Rites of Spring [La consagración de la primavera]*, which is actually three novels in one."

6733. Peavler, Terry J. Edmundo Desnoes and Cuba's lost generation (LARR, 12:3, 1977, p. 129-135)

Platitudinous and ill-informed general introduction to the Cuban novel of the Revolution, followed by a study of Desnoes' novels whose merit is being the first to date.

6734. ———. Prose fiction criticism and theory in Cuban journals (UP/CSEC, 7:1, Jan. 1977, p. 58-118, bibl.)

Extremely useful piece of research, occasionally marred by inconsistencies in format and somewhat cryptic commentary on items listed. But given difficulties involved in researching Cuban materials, this bibliography is a must for all specialists.

6735. Rincón, Carlos. Sobre Carpentier y la poética de lo real maravilloso americano (CDLA, 15:89, marzo/abril 1975, p. 40-67, illus.)

Rincón's turgid style and the mutiplicity of topics he attempts to touch upon mar a considerable research effort. His article contains useful details and several interesting observations.

6737. Rodríguez, Iraida ed. Artículos de costumbres cubanas del siglo XIX. Antología. La Habana, Editorial de Arte y Literatura, Instituto Cubano del Libro, 1974. 255 p., bibl., tables.

Estampas by such figures as Gaspar Betancourt Cisneros, José M. Cárdenas y Rodríguez, José Victoriano Betancourt, Anselmo Suárez y Romero and Luis Victoriano Betancourt with useful preface and biographies. Important contribution.

6738. Rodríguez Monegal, Emir. Alejo Carpentier: lo real y lo maravilloso en *El reino de este mundo* (IILI/RI, 37:76/77, julio/dic. 1971, p. 619-649)

Best account yet on Carpentier's relation to avant-garde, particularly surrealism. But author misses importance of German thought as acquired through Ortega's *Revista de Occidente* in Carpentier's work. Reading of novel stresses convincingly counterpoint between Haitian and European magic.

6739. Rodríguez Ramos, Esther. Los cuentos de René Marqués. San Juan, Univ. de Puerto Rico, Editorial Universitaria, 1975. 202 p., bibl. (Col. Uprex. Serie estudios literarios, 46)

Needed and welcome study of short stories of René Marqués. Based on master's thesis, it nevertheless contributes useful information on effect of Marqués' life and political beliefs on his writings. Includes discussion of Marqués' style and narrative techniques.

6740. Sarduy, Severo. Oppiano Licario de José Lezama Lima (Vuelta [México], 18, mayo 1978, p. 31-35)

Brilliant review-article by Lezama's most distinguished disciple.

6741. ———. Todo por convencer (HISPA, 1:3, 1973, p. 38-43)

Brief but important essay that is obviously a stage in development of *Barroco*. Here Sarduy, writing on word *barroco* goes on to play with a Greimasian notion of analogy "que articula al referente con la forma del significante." He writes: "Se trata simplemente de una *conformidad* entre ese producto barroco ejemplar [El Santo Sudario de Guarini] y la palabra que lo designa, conformidad a nivel de la última, en dos planos: la forma de su expresión (la distribución de sus elementos conconánticos y vocálicos el grafismo de estos últimos) y el sitio simbólico de su surgimiento histórico (el vocabulario técnico de la joyería)."

6742. Souza, Raymond D. Major Cuban novelists: innovation and tradition. Columbia, Univ. of Missouri Press, 1976. 120 p., bibl.

Souza's very interesting introduction traces back to 1920s experiment to write a novel a *al alimón* by several Cuban writers, origins of avant-garde narrative in island. He then devotes chapters to Lezama, Carpentier and Cabrera Infante that deserve attention, even if the very notion of national tradition in avant-garde literature is more complex than Souza infers. Honest, serious book, that should be read by all those interested in contemporary Latin American novel.

6743. Ulloa, Justo C. and Leonor A. de Ulloa. Leyendo las huellas de Auxilio y Socorro (HISPA, 4:10, 1975, p. 9-24)

Useful, erudite decoding of some of allusions in Sarduy's *De donde son los cantantes*.

6744. Ureña, Pedro Henríquez. Obras completas. t. 1, 1899-1909. Selección y prólogo de Juan Jacobo de Lara. Santo Domingo, Univ. Nacional Pedro Henríquez Ureña, 1976. 384 p.

Vol. 1 in series that intends to gather, in chronological order all the writings by the distinguished Dominican humanist. Though volume and project are a needed contribution, compiler Lara does not make clear just how he established chronology. Preface is of little help in this and other matters.

6745. Vitier, Cintio. Ese sol del mundo moral para una historia de la eticidad cubana. México, Siglo XXI Editores, 1975. 200 p., bibl.

Cintio Vitier is one of the more serious and responsible intellectual figures in Cuba today. Known for his first-rate poetry and for his studies of Cuban poetry, Vitier launches a major effort in this book to trace the history of the idea and practice of justice in Cuba. This is a wide-ranging, engrossing book that all experts on Cuba should read.

6746. Weiss, Judith A. Casa de las Américas: an intellectual review in the Cuban Revolution. Chapel Hill, N.C., Estudios de Hispanófila, 1977. 171 p., bibl.

Based on a Yale dissertation, this is a scholarly contribution of merit, essential for the understanding of the background of much literature produced in Cuba after the Revolution.

6747. Yedra, Elena. La imagen de la mujer en la obra de Miguel de Carrión: *Las honradas* (UCLV/I, 51, mayo/agosto 1975, p. 121-152)

Academically solid work (obviously a thesis) about an unjustly forgotten author, from a Marxist and feminist perspective. Yedra concludes that Carrión is a puritan outraged because 'antes reinaba el desequilibrio de la represión [sexual], ahora reina el desequilibrio del desenfreno." Though Carrión, who delights in describing deviant sexuality is more interesting than is implied here, this is sound scholarship.

6748. Yero Pérez, Luis. El tema de la esclavitud en la narrativa cubana (UCLV/I, 49, sept./dic. 1974, p. 65-93, bibl.)

Reasonably thorough introduction to topic by someone very familiar with Cuban novel of 19th century, and particularly those produced by Domingo del Monte's group. First part of study describes Cuban society from the late 18th to mid-19th century, following, above all, Moreno Fraginals' *El ingenio*. Though based on a thesis, and lacking in critical sophistication, it is nevertheless an honest, well-documented introduction to the topic.

ANDEAN COUNTRIES

(BOLIVIA, COLOMBIA, ECUADOR, PERU, VENEZUELA)

JOSE MIGUEL OVIEDO
Professor of Spanish
Indiana University

DJELAL KADIR
Associate Professor of Spanish
and Comparative Literature
Purdue University

ALTHOUGH SEMIOTICS AND FORMALIST CRITICISM have made their impact on this region, its critical literature for the last two years has in fact followed two divergent courses: the interpretation of symbolic and conceptual planes of narrative, and the scrutiny of its connections with the social, historical and ideological ambit. While critics interested primarily in the literature of Colombia and Peru have rediscovered Northrop Frye, Goldman and Lukács, in Bolivia a rather unique phenomenon has come about: the introduction of the theory of formalist poetics, thanks to one of Bolivia's young novelists, Renato Prada Oropeza. The repercussion of this singular event in a country which, along with Ecuador, has been reticent to accept critical renovations are still impossible to assess. This is a considerable gain, at any rate.

As in previous years, native and foreign criticism has been concentrated on two of the most important novelists: Gabriel García Márquez and Mario Vargas Llosa. Interest in the first has been revived by the appearance of *El otoño del patriarca* (1975), and has yielded at least three new books—one of them, by George McMurray (item 6815), is the first to appear in English on the novelist—and a good many studies and articles in many journals. A considerable number of them has focused on searching for historical and literary antecedents to the author's novels, especially *Cien años de soledad*; others rummage through his initial phase as a journalist in search of the sources of his imaginary vision of Colombian reality. The numerous studies by Jacques Gilard in this respect (items 6808-6811) are especially significant. Even certain studies dedicated to other authors and works, such as the one on Alvaro Cepeda Samudio's *La casa grande* (item 6816) are motivated by the same zeal to discover the possible antecedents of García Márquez.

The criticism of Vargas Llosa's work has been increasing in the US as manifested by the publication of special issues, appearing almost simultaneously, of *World Literature Today* (item 6849) and *Texas Studies in Literature and Language* (item 6845), dedicated to pay homage and to study the work of the Peruvian novelist. They include contributions from critics in the US, Spanish America, Spain, and Europe. While García Márquez was the aim of almost all studies on Colombian narrative, research on Peruvian prose was not limited to Vargas Llosa. Studies on José María Arguedas (items 6836 and 6842), problems of "indigenismo" and Ciro Alegría (items 6828, 6831, 6837, 6844 and 6846), the narrative of Julio Ramón Ribeyro (item 6848), etc., attest to the variety of criticism on the literature of this country. Studies of Venezuelan and Ecuadorian narrative were scarce. Besides certain bibliographical items on Venezuelan literature (items 6851 and 6852) there is little to report. More significant were collections of primary sources edited and published by the Instituto Colombiano de Cultura on García Márquez (item 6807), the review *Voces* (item 6826), and the new literature by younger Colombian writers (item 6758).

However, the masterpiece of critical thought from this region during this period is a book which, alien to concerns of traditional criticism referred to above, is very difficult to classify. Nicolás Gómez Dávila's *Escolios a un texto implícito* (item 6812) is a type of essay written as a series of aphorisms but with conceptual coherence and systematic rigor. The author's boundless intellectual curiosity is not limited to pondering literary or esthetic phenomena. Indeed, his work aspires to become a *summa* of human knowledge, sifted in thousands of indelible but precise images.

Like all true works of thought, Gómez Dávila's book constitutes a feat of the imagination as unique as Borges' *Otras inquisiciones* or Alfonso Reyes' *La experiencia literaria*. [JMO]

Of the five countries in the Andean region covered by this section Colombia and Venezuela appear to be the most prolific in the publication of prose fiction. Monte Avila Editores of Caracas and the Instituto Colombiano de Cultura in Bogotá are in the forefront of the publication industry. Both publishing houses continue to bring out high quality fiction, traditional and experimental. Ecuador's Casa de la Cultura Ecuatoriana is also actively engaged in publishing older, more established authors, as well as some younger writers. The long and distinguished tradition of socially committed literature continues to dominate Ecuadorian letters, as is the case in Bolivia and, to a lesser extent, in Peru.

If any comprehensive statement on the literary production of this region can be ventured at this time, it would have to hark back to that constant dialectic between literature and history. The prose fiction of this area, as in the rest of the Hemisphere, finds its greatest antagonist (and, frequently, its collaborator) in history, that capricious construct which tries to impose its own version of the truth about past, present, and even future life of the region. For Latin American writers official history has always comprised another fiction, albeit one with perhaps more widely accepted, though still arbitrary, conventions. This phenomenon may perhaps explain in part the everpresent preoccupation in the works of these writers with the human condition, with official institutions and the underlying social order, which frequently mocks the selfserving chimeras of officialdom with bitter irony.

Because of the immense quantity of accumulated publications, I have limited my purview to works which have appeared primarily during the period of 1974 to 1976 leaving significant works, such as those by the Peruvians Bryce and Vargas Llosa and by the Colombians Alvarez Gardeazábal and Héctor Sánchez which have appeared subsequently for the next volume of *HLAS*. Within these parameters, I have tended to review new works rather than re-editions, attempting to highlight up and coming writers of the present generation.

The *boom* of the 1960s certainly has *not* been followed by a vacuum. A number of young writers, born mostly in the 1940s, are representative of those impressionable adolescents who came into the arena of letters, mostly as students and aspiring writers, at the time of the *boom* of the Latin American novel. While availing themselves of esthetic innovations and technical novelties introduced by the writers of the late 1950s, the decade of the 1960s, and early 1970s, the present generation of writers still clings to a vital American experience. The fears of some critics and literary historians that the Latin American novel would go the way of the sterile, formalistic road of the French new novel have proved unfounded. While ably managing very sophisticated stylistic and esthetic narrative modes, ultimately at the core of recent works lies the human condition and its peculiar American vicissitudes. Colombia's Gustavo Alvarez Gardeazábal (item 6744) and Fanny Buitrago (item 6757), Peruvians Marcos Yauri Montero (item 6785) and the already well established Julio Ramón Ribeyro (item 6782), Venezuela's Héctor de Lima (item 6793) and the older Vicente Ibarra (item 6791) and Miguel Otero Silva (item 6797) clearly exemplify the urgency to confront the infamy of history of national and hemispheric life with an alternate set of convincing literary conventions which effectively subvert the calumny of historical "truth."

In terms of experimental fiction, I wish to point to three very successful attempts: 1) Ecuador's Alsino Ramírez Estrada (item 6770) who converts the Spanish language and its tropological possibilities into a novelistic happening; 2) Peru's Marcos Yauri Montero (item 6785) whose notable interweaving of history, myth, indigenous cosmogony and superstition yields a highly complex, trying, but satisfying (for the persevering reader) novel; and 3) Venezuela's Francisco Massiani (item 6795) while not as radically innovative as the first two writers mentioned here, has managed to infuse the Venezuelan short story with a new charge. He is a very young writer and promises great things to come.

The legacy of the 1960s, its flower children, the new morality, and the general reappraisal of social values has also left its mark, particularly on those writers who were young enough to have lived in the 1960s and early 1970s with greatest intensity. In this respect the Peruvians Fernando Ampuero (item 6777) and Luis Felipe Sánchez Espinar (item 6784) are worthy of note. In Venezuela two young writers confront the readjustments of this period: Mercedes Carvajal de Arocha (item 6798) and Antonieta Madrid (item 6794). I should point out that the last two are very different from each other in their manner of approaching the epoch and its problems. In addition, the generic consciousness raising and sexual revolution have also left their mark in a very intelligently rendered work by the Colombian Héctor Martori (item 6761).

I wish, finally, to indicate a few anthologies which may prove very useful, short story anthologies for the most part: for Bolivia *Cuentos bolivianos contemporáneos: antología*, edited by Lijeron Alberdi and Pastor Poppe (item 6751); for Colombia *Obra en marcha 1: la nueva literatura colombiana* (item 6758); for Peru there are two collections: 1) Julio Ramón Ribeyro (item 6782), and 2) Harry Belevan's *Antología del cuento fantástico peruano* (item 6778) in which the reader will find one of the most erudite and perceptive discussions on the fantastic by the collection's editor. For Venezuela, the two volume collection *Cuentos venezolanos: antología* (item 6788) might be of some interest. [DjK]

PROSE FICTION

BOLIVIA

6749. Botelho Gosálvez, Raúl. Con la muerte a cuestas y otros cuentos: 12 cuentos. La Paz, Difusión, 1975. 195 p. (Col. Vereda. Series, 9)

Uneven collection. Title story, by far the most convincing, encapsulizes author's thematic preoccupations: indigenous Bolivian world *vis-à-vis* harsh realities of encroaching modernity and development. Twelve stories elaborate this theme in varied Bolivian settings: city, mountains, highlands, and jungle. Stylistically, works emerge as a peculiar brand of romantic realism. [DjK]

6750. Jaimes Freyre, Ricardo. Cuentos. La Paz, Instituto Boliviano de Cultura, 1975. 55 p.

Gathered here are stories: "Zoe," "Los Viajeros," "Zaghi, Mendigo," "En las Montañas," and "En un Hermoso Día de Verano" which were originally published between 1896-1907. These typical examples of Modernist prose are more frequently mentioned than actually read and interest of collection lies in this fact. At same time, it is a pity that Carlos Castañón Barrientos in his prologue does not take opportunity to study these stories, that no notes are furnished and that ed. is in such poor shape and appearance. [JMO]

6751. Lijeron Alberdi, Hugo and Ricardo Pastor Poppe eds. Cuentos bolivianos contemporáneos. Antología. La Paz, Ediciones Camarlinghi, 1975. 201 p., bibl.

Excellent anthology, first rate selections, and very useful editorial apparatus. Eleven writers are represented, each with a story, for most part written within decade preceding anthology's publication. Editors introduce each author with bio-bibliographical note, a synopsis of each story which unfortunately, steals the story's thunder at times, and general bibliography on Bolivian short story follows at end. [DjK]

6752. Soriano Badani, Armando ed. Antología del cuento boliviano. La Paz, Editorial Los Amigos del Libro, 1975. 438 p. (Col. Enciclopedia boliviana)

Extensive collection which attempts to cover period 1900-74, it is loosely organized in chronological order. While rather extensive in coverage of first 50 years, it is rather sparse for more recent period. Editor's attempt at critical ordering, periodization, and literary history emerges as rather naive and not very helpful. Literary historians may find the anthology useful. [DjK]

6753. Taboada Terán, Néstor ed. Bolivia en el cuento. Antología de ayer y de hoy. B.A., Editorial Convergencia, 1976. 119 p.

For those who wish to have summary and quick idea of Bolivian short story in this century, this is an opportune selection. Editor has ordered texts thematically: mines, Indian, war, politics, love. Prologue and notes are plagued by generalities and confused characterizations which detract greatly from value of the volume. [JMO]

6754. Viscarra Fabre, Guillermo ed. Antología del cuento chileno-boliviano. Santiago, Editorial Universitaria, 1975. 279 p.

While somewhat idiosyncratic, collection has merit. Unfortunately, it is more notable for omissions than inclusions. Editor makes no claims of completeness, however, and justifiably so. Hardly any recent writers are included. Each author is introduced with a brief bio-bibliographical note. [DjK]

COLOMBIA

6755. Alvarez Gardeazábal, Gustavo. La boba y el Buda. Barcelona, Ediciones Destino, 1975. 156 p. (Col. Ancora y delfín, 434)

Very closely knit collection of nine short stories and title story which is actually long enough to be considered a novella. Overriding concern here is "la violencia," that bloody period in Colombia's recent history which underlies a good deal of Colombian contemporary literature. Book could in fact be read as a fragmented novel. Characters, setting, animosities are common to all the stories. Alvarez Gardeazábal is an accomplished narrator. [DjK]

6756. Bastidas Padilla, Carlos. Las raíces de la ira. La Habana, Casa de las Américas, 1975. 124 p.

Collection of 22 snapshots portraying unmitigated brutality unleashed by wrath of some demonic god that occupies dark recesses of mans inhumanity. Bitter taste of irony belies detached narration of these slices of life randomly captured from the political life of a town with an equally ironic name, Puerto Ventura. Collection won the Casa de las Américas Short Story Prize in 1975. Bastidas Padilla's powerful narration is not for the fainthearted. The ire is contagious. [DjK]

6757. Buitrago, Fanny. Bahía sonora. Relatos de la isla. Bogotá, Instituto Colombiano de Cultura, Subdirección de Comunicaciones Culturales, División de Publicaciones, 1976. 159 p. (Biblioteca colombiana de cultura. Col. popular)

Collection of 15 short stories set in an island of Colombia's Caribbean coast. Buitrago ably juxtaposes island's haunting past with transience of progress and transient tourists and adventurers. Island is transformed into microcosm of "comedia humana." [DjK]

6758. Cobo Borda, J.G. ed. Obra en marcha 1: la nueva literatura colombiana. Bogotá, Instituto Colombiano de Cultura, Subdirección de comunicaciones Culturales, División de Publicaciones, 1975. 319 p. (Biblioteca colombiana de cultura. Col. Popular, 4)

In what editor promises to be first of two-vol. collection of young writers (under 40), 30 authors and all literary genres are represented. In terms of short prose fiction, literary future of Colombia looks very bright here indeed. Degree of experimental ambition is very high, as is the level of accomplishment in some instances. Some of these writers have already proved themselves as able novelists, e.g., Héctor Sánchez. Others (Jaime Manrique Ardila, Amalia Iriarte, Alonso Aristizábal, Roberto Burgos Cantor, Gustavo Majía) show much promise and should be watched very closely. Very valuable collection, it also includes bio-bibliographical note on each author. [DjK]

6759. Espinosa, Germán. Los doce infiernos. Bogotá, Instituto Colombiano de Cultura, Subdirección de Comunicaciones Culturales, División de Publicaciones, 1975. 161 p. (Biblioteca colombiana de cultura. Col. Popular, 16)

With but a couple of exceptions, the 12 short stories of this collection demonstrate Espinosa's success as prose narrator. He is already an accomplished poet. Futility of love (of all sorts) and human communion is stories' underlying theme. High quality lyricism and poignancy characterize author's narrations. [DjK]

6760. Lucena, Luis Fernando. El elegido. Bogotá, Editorial Bandera Roja, 1976. 74 p.

Roman è clef with a very big clef, Lucena's novella is sad, ludicrous, but true satire of Colombia's 1974 presidential elections. No facet of modern society escapes Lucena's caustic irreverence—motherhood, flower children, church, family, conservatives, liberals, rhetoric, ideals, the press. All receive their share of Lucena's satire. Accurate, though farcical, portrait of modern society and politics demonstrates that Colombia has come of age. [DjK]

6761. Martori, Héctor. Fragmentos de la vida de Paula. B.A., Ediciones Corregidor, 1976. 308 p.

Fundamentally serious, political novel, this is one of few works of fiction which confronts problem of sex, sexuality, and sociopolitical roles predicated on gender. Martori demonstrates a profound understanding and, therefore, a revolutionary one, of the unjust nature of a morality which oppresses human beings on the basis of their sex and/or sexual preferences. [DjK]

6762. Palacios Acero, Eduardo. Presencias de redención. Relatos. Armenia, Colombia, Editorial Quin-Gráficas, 1976. 257 p.

Collection of 27 short stories very closely linked thematically. The link: prostitution and prostitutes. This has to be one of the most complete "prostibularios" of the generation. While some stories do achieve technical excellence, thematic insistence does render collection monotonous at times, despite admirable narrative talent demonstrated by author. [DjK]

6763. Romero, Armando. El demonio y su mano. Caracas, Monte Avila Editores, 1975. 137 p. (Col. Donaire)

Collection of 10 short pieces that can not really be considered short stories in the traditional sense. Romero, who is a member of a group of young writers known as "nadaístas," transforms reality into a psychological state. By showing fluid and illusory nature of that state, he manages to render reality as insubstantial image. While not very innovative, the undertaking is an interesting exercise. [DjK]

6764. Salom Becerra, Alvaro. Un tal Bernabé Bernal. Bogotá, Ediciones Tercer Mundo, 1975. 182 p. (Col. Literaria)

Novelistic frame for the memoirs of a cultured, sensitive, honest bureaucrat whose idealism and pusillanimity make him a perfect victim of a morally, ethically, and politically bankrupt society. Through protagonist's tragicomic life, author portrays sociopolitical farce of Colombian life in past 60 years. As in his two previous novels, Salom Becerra demonstrates his acute social sensitivity and mastery of novelistic medium. [DjK]

ECUADOR

6765. Alvarado, Hipólito. La segunda voz. Cuentos. Guayaquil, Ecua., Casa de la Cultura Ecuatoriana, Núcleo del Guayas, 1975. 103 p. (Col. Letras del Ecuador, 5)

Collection of 11 short stories. Lyrical vein runs through all narratives which are thematically linked by love, guilt, generosity, and futile fate. Most poignant of stories are those dealing with *"éducation sentimentale,"* the coming of age of young protagonists when confronted with inexorable circumstances of life, death, and self-identity. [DjK]

6766. Calderón Chico, Carlos *ed.* Nuevos cuentistas del Ecuador. Prólogo de Hugo Salazar Tamariz. Guayaquil, Ecua., Casa de la Cultura Ecuatoriana, Núcleo del Guayas, 1975. 133 p., bibl. (Col. Letras del Ecuador, 9)

Good collection which anthologizes 14 writers with one selection from each. Bio-bibliographical note precedes each story and cursory bibliography is appended at end. Editor's introduction is lamentably useless for specialist and general reader. [DjK]

6767. Dávila Andrade, César. Cuentos. Cuenca, Ecua., Casa de la Cultura, Núcleo del Azuya, 1976. 243 p. (Col. Libros para el pueblo, 3)

Collection of 17 stories of varying quality. Thread of death and madness gives collection its thematic unity. Death and reincarnation, social entrapment, and schizophrenia dominate the collection. [DjK]

6768. Iglesias Mata, Dumar. El bulevar y otros cuentos. Guayaquil, Ecua., Casa de la Cultura Ecuatoriana, Núcleo del Guayas, 1976. 95 p. (Col. Letras del Ecuador, 35)

Iglesias Mata is in best tradition of Ecuadorian socially committed literature. The 10 short stories of this collection portray series of hapless victims up against overwhelming odds of nature and inhuman sociopolitical forces. While quite traditional in their stylistic conventions, stories emanate a lyrical sensibility. Young author (b. 1948) shows some potential as good narrator. [DjK]

6769. Martínez Queirolo, José. Cuentos y relatos. Guayaquil, Ecua., Casa de la Cultura Ecuatoriana, Núcleo del Guayas, 1976. 187 p. (Col. Letras del Ecuador, 12)

Eleven of 22 stories in this collection first appeared 1959 under title *La lluvia muere en silencio,* perhaps Martínez Queirolo's most powerful book. He is one of Ecuador's most able narrators with a penchant for the "outsider," intense psychic states, and personages of the lower-middle class. [DjK]

6770. Ramírez Estrada, Alsino. Ceremonial. Guayaquil, Ecua. Casa de la Cultura Ecuatoriana, Núcleo del Guayas, 1975. 113 p. (Col. Letras del Ecuador, 10)

An anti-novel of satirical irony and sarcastic rhetoric. Ramírez Estrada masterfully transforms the novel into a happening, a panegyric into literary discourse. A successful experimental work which confronts the nature of language, oratory, and the generic limits of the novel. [DjK]

6771. Ramón, Gonzalo. Guandal. Novela. v. 1. Quito, Editorial Casa de la Cultura Ecuatoriana, 1976. 347 p. (Col. Premios nacionales de literatura)

This is perhaps best specimen of stream-of-consciousness novel to come out of Ecuador. Novel, which won first prize for best novel in Ecuador in 1975 and was runnerup in 1974 International Prize of Madrid's "Editorial Alfaguara" competition, presents delirious utterances of marginal personality who has had a colorful career outside the law. An acute "diorama" of Ecuadorian society. [DjK]

6772. Rodríguez, Marco Antonio. Historia de un intruso. Quito, Editorial Casa de la Cultura Ecuatoriana, 1976. 147 p., illus.

Collection of 10 short stories, first of which is actually long enough (60 p.) to be a novella. Collection is tightly organized and follows linear progression towards psychic degeneration and, by the end, complete mental breakdown in the characters. Rodríguez is a masterful narrator of psychological projection and redoubling of personality. He handles theme of the double in a very original manner. [DjK]

6773. Taboada Terán, Néstor *ed.* Ecuador en el cuento. B.A., Editorial Convergencia, 1976. 127 p.

Anthology, rather scant, of major 20th-century short-story writers. Ten authors are represented by one story each, introduced with short bio-bibliographical note. Brief (three and a half p.) introduction on Ecuadorian short story presents the volume. [DjK]

6774. Tenen Ortega, Guillermo. De la duda y otros juegos. Cuentos. Guayaquil, Ecua., Casa de la Cultura Ecuatoriana, Núcleo del Guayas, 1975. 99 p. (Col. Letras del Ecuador, 3)

Sixteen "avantgarde" narratives of spurious *eros* and its hapless victims. Tenen Ortega, a witty and entertaining writer, seemingly considers foregoing of punctuation analogous to "vangardism." That idiosyncrasy aside, he is a delightfully sardonic parodist of social norms and human psychology. [DjK]

6775. Velasco Mackenzie, Jorge. De vuelta al paraíso. Cuentos. Guayaquil, Ecua., Casa de la Cultura Ecuatoriana, Núcleo del Guayas, 1975. 96 p. (Col. Letras del Ecuador, 4)

Ten short stories of diverse thematic concerns and of uneven quality. Author succeeds most convincingly in three pieces: "La Otra Cara del Tiempo;" "Una Visita a la Viuda;" and "Abrir y Cerrar los Ojos." First two are thematically linked, third is highly lyrical. [DjK]

6776. Vera, Pedro Jorge. Cuentos escogidos. Guayaquil, Ecua., Casa de la Cultura Ecuatoriana, Núcleo del Guayas, 1976. 189 p. (Col. Letras del Ecuador, 14)

Of socially committed writers of Ecuador, Vera is among most esthetically convincing. The 19 stories of this collection are unified by cruel and impeccable death. Fatal dementia of personal, social, and political nature permeates Vera's works and inevitably victimizes his protagonists. [DjK]

PERU

6777. Ampuero, Fernando. Deliremos juntos. Lima, Kosmos, 1975. 130 p. (Col. Literaria)

Better known for his earlier novel, *Mamotreto* (1974) young author (b. 1949) articulates lost and searching condition of his inarticulate generation: rebels, flower-children, rock, drug, and motorcycle crazed innocence in search of a center that will hold. These seven short narratives are of uneven quality, best one is entitled "Ambito Enano." Ampuero shows great potential as narrator. [DjK]

6778. Belevan, Harry *ed.* Antología del cuento fantástico peruano. Lima, Univ. Nacional Mayor de San Marcos, Dirección Universitaria de Biblioteca y Publicaciones, 1977. 192 p., illus., tables.

Very useful anthology with extremely erudite introduction by editor on the *genre* of the Fantastic. Collection includes works by 12 writers, presented with short bio-bibliographical note. Varied anthology that ranges from Clemente Palma (b. 1872) to Belevan himself (b. 1947). Selections are good and make this the most complete anthology of its kind for Peru. [DjK]

6779. Bendezú, Edmundo. Tres de octubre: crónica de fugitivos. Lima, Editorial Universo, 1976. 251 p. (Serie novela contemporánea, 1)

Unconvincing historical novel based on 1948 revolution which manages to historicize the novel rather than to novelize history. Book's construction is based on alternating chapters which are fictionalized testimonial and press clippings or actual historical statements by key political and intellectual figures of period. Socio-historians might find it useful. [DjK]

6780. Bouroncle Carreón, Alfonso. El viaje. Novela. Lima, Editorial Arequipa, 1976. 253 p.

Clearly ambitious first novel that attempts everything and which a good editor might have turned into a first-rate work. Both utopian and futuristic, it presents sardonic critique of contemporary society and officialdom from privileged perspective of marginal elements—petty criminals, dreamers, sailors, and farceures. Novel has flashes of technical and stylistic brilliance. [DjK]

6781. Martínez, Gregorio. Tierra de caléndula. Cuentos. Prólogo de Miguel Gutiérrez. Lima, Editorial Milla Batres, 1975. 144 p., map, plates.

Collection of 13 short stories with introduction by Miguel Gutiérrez in which he gives general appraisal of contemporary short story in Peru. Introduction might prove helpful to non-specialist. Stories, author's first book, are of varied stylistic mode and uneven quality. Young writer (b. 1942) shows great deal of potential. By far most accomplished of these narratives is "Antes de las Doce." [DjK]

6782. Ribeyro, Julio Ramón. La palabra del mudo. Cuentos: 1952-1972. v. 1/2. Lima, Editorial Milla-Batres, 1973. 2 v. (293, 291 p.)

One could claim with some justification that Ribeyro is to contemporary Peruvian short story what Mario Vargas Llosa is to contemporary Peruvian novel. This two-vol. anthology which includes 20 years of production in the short story genre is clearly indicative of Ribeyro's significance to the so-called 1950s generation. Two vols. include three books of short stories each: vol. 1, Ribeyro's *Los gallinazos sin plumas* (1955), *Cuentos de circunstancia* (1958), *Las botellas y los hombres* (1964); vol. 2 consists of *Tres historias sublevantes* (1964), *Los cautivos* (1972), and *El próximo mes me nivelo* (1972). Ribeyro's stories can be characterized as Kafkaesque, Pirandellian chronicles of modern life. Urban settings are predominant in these stories. Ribeyro demonstrates a penchant for psychological narrative, although his dexterity with a great variety of narrative techniques does not allow for any one particular pegging of this accomplished writer. [DjK]

6783. Rivera Saavedra, Juan. Cuentos sociales de ciencia-ficción. Diseños de Octavio Santa Cruz. Lima, Editorial Horizonte, 1976. 48 p., illus.

Interesting little book whose stories are more social than science fiction. Rivera Saavedra hyperbolizes socio-economic dichotomies by projecting them into futuristic setting thereby accentuating absurdity of contemporary social structures and economic-racial prejudices. The 31 pieces are all very brief and have a fable quality to them. [DjK]

6784. Sánchez Espinar, Luis Felipe. Le disparé al sheriff pero creo que no ha muerto. Relatos. Lima, Editorial Ari, 1974. 120 p. (Col. Literaria)

Collection of seven short stories which deal with turned-on generation of late 1960s and early 1970s. Sánchez Espinar, a member of that generation focuses on the recklessness of his contemporaries and

the banal actuality their defiance sought to subvert. Also focuses on another marginal group, the elderly, that defies traditional role of passiveness and discards of society.[DjK]

6785. Yauri Montero, Marcos. En otoño, después de mil años. La Habana, Casa de las Américas, 1974. 336 p.

Complex work which won the 1974 Casa de las Américas prize for best novel. Intricate weave of social concern and aesthetic experimentation which spans entire range of Peruvian history—from apocalyptic Inca vision to contemporary bourgeois urbanity and decadence, it makes for rewarding reading for those initiated in the intricacies of contemporary prose aesthetics. This is author's third novel, previous two having been relatively successful. [DjK]

6786. Zavaleta, Carlos Eduardo. El fuego y la rutina. Prólogo, selección y nota bibliográfica de Luis Fernando Vidal. Lima, Ediciones Peisa, 1976. 193 p., bibl. (Biblioteca peruana, 57)

Carlos Eduardo Zavaleta has been dominant voice in Peruvian letters since 1948. This particular collection of 10 short stories anthologizes pieces from different periods. Unifying thread which runs through stories is a social commitment which renders literature testimonial of social reality. Stylistically conventional, Zavaleta adheres to very traditional narrative techniques. Anthology's editor, Luis Fernando Vidal, furnishes useful bibliography of works by and about author. [DjK]

VENEZUELA

6787. Antillano, Laura. Un carro largo se llama tren. Caracas, Monte Avila Editores, 1975. 190 p. (Col. Donaire)

Collection of 19 short sketches which elude genre classification. Narrations range from lyrical reminiscences to cavilations of naïve sensibilities. While not accomplished prose fictions, an acute poetic strain runs through these sketches. [DjK]

6788. Castellanos, Rafael Ramón *ed*. Cuentos venezolanos. Antología. v. 1/2. Caracas, Publicaciones Españolas, 1975. 2 v. (143, 139 p.)

Two-vol. anthology covering period from Modernism to present. Collection follows generational, chronological scheme and presents 26 authors with selection from each. Brief bio-bibliographical note introduces each writer. In brief prologue, editor traces development of Venezuelan short story by interrelating history of certain key periodicals to publication of stories and rise of genre. [DjK]

6789. Chocrón, Isaac E. Rómpase en caso de incendio. Caracas, Monte Avila Editores, 1975. 352 p. (Col. Continente)

Novelization of personal identity crisis of Latin American Sephardic Jew who sets out to find his roots. This third novel of author has epistolary form and comprises protagonist's letters to those who, like himself, embody decadent fragments of faded past. Pilgrimage only reveals to protagonist his own mediocrity and ends fatally in Tangiers. Chocrón manages to capture predicament of cultural and psychological displacement and makes for fascinating reading. [DjK]

6790. González Paredes, Ramón. Números o el caballo amarrado. Novela. Caracas, Univ. Central de Venezuela, Dirección de Cultura, 1974. 326 p. (Col. Letras de Venezuela, 34)

Political novel on futility of revolutionary ardor. Narrated as flashback in oneiric sequences that flow from stream of consciousness of an "imprisoned" protagonist, Jorge Luna. Rather heavy on the didactic side, narrative is laden with obvious Biblical allusions. [DjK]

6791. Ibarra, Vicente. De la rotunda a la calle larga. Caracas, Editorial Fuentes, 1974. 262 p. (Col. La historia viva)

Historical novel that covers tumultuous period 1913-29. With great historical accuracy Ibarra relates events under Gómez' dictatorship (1908-35) which culminated in fated "Falke Invasion" of Cumaná in 1929. Side glances at French capital of 1920s capture era's madness and intrigue. Ibarra is an exciting narrator who has obviously researched history of period exhaustively. Successful rendering of history into fiction. [DjK]

6792. Liendo, Eduardo. Los topos. Novela, testimonio. Caracas, Monte Avila Editores, 1975. 185 p. (Col. Continente)

Fascinating account of guerrilla activity, armed confrontation, and imprisonment. Novel is based on author's experiences as activist, revolutionary, and prisoner. Inside story of idealism, defeat, prison conditions, and survival, present work is Liendo's second novel. He is a sophisticated narrator. [DjK]

6793. Lima, Héctor de. La noche de la derrota. Caracas, Monte Avila Editores, 1975. 128 p. (Col. Continente)

Polychromatic narrative with parallel and refracted narrative planes all of which ultimately emanate from one spatial source: Capatarida—a provincial town enshrouded in an air of decadence and mystery, a Venezuelan Luvina or Comala as Rulfo's readers will recognize. This is Lima's first novel and a very promising one indeed. While some of narrative parallels remain disembodied from whole, work has very strong linguistic consistency that compensates for this disembodiment. [DjK]

6794. Madrid, Antonieta. No es tiempo para rosas rojas. Novela. Caracas, Monte Avila Editores, 1975. 184 p. (Col. Continente)

Chronicle of 1960s narrated through intimate, confessional tone of protagonist who finds herself as much the victim of flowers, music, drugs, sex, love, and social revolution as of decaying social values that idealism of her generation tried to subvert. Moving poetic narrative, it shows acute sensitivity and technical finesse of its author. [DjK]

6795. Massiani, Francisco. El llanero solitario tiene la cabeza pelada como un cepillo de dientes. Relatos. Caracas, Monte Avila Editores, 1975. 179 p., table (Col. Donaire)

Ten short narrations which are linked by futility of incommunicative fates that plague individual characters. With a couple of exceptions, stories are consistently good. Title story and one called "Había una Vez un Tigre" are by far most accomplished, especially latter. Massiani is one of the best young writers on Venezuelan scene today. [DjK]

6796. Mata, Humberto *ed.* Distracciones. Antología del relato venezolano, 1960-1974. Caracas, Monte Avila Editores, 1974. 191 p.

Very uneven and unconvincing collection. While anthology covers very exciting period and includes short stories by 24 younger authors, the truly accomplished selections are very few (those of León, Massiani, Noguera, Quintero). Each writer is introduced by very brief bio-bibliographical note. [DjK]

6797. Otero Silva, Miguel. La muerte de Honorio. Caracas, Ariel y Seix Barral Venezolana, 1975. 194 p. (Col. Nueva narrativa hispánica)

Another excellent work by Barcelona-born Venezuelan. Novel relates political tortures of five activists just prior to 1958. Five narrative threads are masterfully interwoven by Otero Silva, especially in novel's second half which converges on Honorio, a young boy who emerges as symbol of their solidarity. Techniques of *montage* and superpositioning of narrative planes are ably executed. [DjK]

6798. Palacios, Lucila [*pseud. for* **Mercedes Carvajal de Arocha**]. Reducto de soledad. Novela. Caracas, Monte Avila Editores, 1975. 106 p. (Col. Continente)

Novel of identity crisis which documents dilemma of young man in London caught between traditional

Venezuelan family values, as represented by his dominant and dead father, and 1960s counter-culture values. Subjective, first-person narration, could be first-rate novella with the aid of good editor. [DjK]

6799. Quintero, Ednodio. Volveré con mis perros. Caracas, Monte Avila Editores, 1975. 182 p. (Col. Donaire)

Collection of 16 short pieces. Quintero is uneven. While some stories are highly poetic or gruesomely lyrical, others suffer from an all too personal vision hermetically sealed from reader. "Stories" evolve in dream-like, hallucinogenic atmosphere. If Quintero manages to overcome his solipsism, he will no doubt become a first rate narrator. Among better of the young writers (b. 1947), he shows great potential. [DjK]

6800. Urbaneja Achelpohl, Luis Manuel. Selección de cuentos. Compilación y prólogo de Gustavo Luis Carrera. Caracas, Monte Avila Editores, 1976. 170 p. (Col. Eldorado)

Collection of author's 15 best short stories published on occasion of 30th anniversary of his death. All stories originally appeared in Urbaneja Achelpohl's *El criollismo en Venezuela en cuentos y prédicas* (1945). Recognized as one of best criollistas and realism writers of Venezuela, author is presented by Gustavo Carrera Damas in a very informative critical introduction. Minimal bibliography on author is included. [DjK]

LITERARY CRITICISM AND HISTORY

BOLIVIA

6801. Echevarría, Evelio. Panorama y bibliografía de la novela social boliviana (RIB, 27:2, abril/junio 1977, p. 143-152, bibl.)

Pt. 1 of study is a succinct historical synthesis of genre from 1904, year of Alcides Arguedas' *Wuata Wuara*, to present in its various manifestations: Indigenista novel, novels of the mining region, of Chaco War, of Mestizo, etc. Pt. 2 contains bibliography proper, and is divided into two large periods: 1904-52; 1952-70. [JMO]

6802. Finot, Enrique. Historia de la literatura boliviana. 4. ed. complementada. Dibujos originales de José de Mesa y Teresa Gisbert. La Paz, Gisbert, 1975. 588 p., plates.

Fourth ed. of Bolivian literary classic history, first published 1944. Like analogous works by Luis Alberto Sánchez and Alberto Zum Felde for other parts of the continent, this work is a pioneering effort, an indispensible work of consultation, but full of defects and limitations, now more visible than ever. For this ed., work has been supplemented with two appendices (one for the colonial period, another for contemporary writers) which do not go beyond being mere catalogues of names and titles without slightest critical value. [JMO]

6803. Ortega, José. Bibliografía selecta de la literatura boliviana: 1969-1974 (RCLL, 1:1, 1975, p. 159-169, bibl.)

Brief review of literary process in Bolivia since *Raza de Bronce* (1924) by Alcides Arguedas up to more recent and younger writers. Author presents bibliography arranged by genre (prose fiction, poetry, theater, essay, and critical works on these) with brief annotations. Complements item 6801. [JMO]

Siles Guevara, Juan. Las cien obras capitales de la literatura boliviana. See item 6546.

COLOMBIA

6804. Arnau, Carmen. El mundo mitico de Gabriel García Márquez. 2. ed. Barcelona, Ediciones Península, 1975. 134 p., table (Ediciones de bolsillo)

Author purports to analyze certain constants in García Márquez' first four books: the banana company, civil wars, violence, military presence, and some other topics (time, death, myth) in *Cien años de soledad*, establishing each book as an element of a system. Unfortunately, lack of organization in the work (e.g., chapter devoted to "El Juego," studies incest and death) prevents her from meeting all her goals. This impression is further aggravated by a confused style and by many generalities (e.g., "G.M. intenta transmitir al lector sus impresiones, no es imparcial, su obra es eminentemente subjetiva," p. 65). [JMO]

6805. Carrillo, Germán Darío. La narrativa de Gabriel García Márquez: ensayos de interpretación. Madrid, Ediciones de Arte y Bibliofilia, 1975. 165 p., bibl.

Book is divided into two large sections: 1) dedicated to *Cien años de soledad*, with a part devoted to *Historia de un deicidio* (Mario Vargas Llosa's book on García Márquez); and 2) another section dedicated to the Colombian writer's short stories. Of greater interest is first section in which certain ideas of N. Frye and R.W.B. Lewis are applied in the study of such aspects as the presence of Biblical myths, the "inocencia de la caída," and the "caída afortunada." The level of criticism, however, is less than consistent when discussing the question of "magical realism," which is not properly clarified, and narrative modes in the novel, which again are not sufficiently or clearly examined. Includes dialogue between critic and Colombian novelist and brief bibliography whose first part appears under the title "Cronología de la Obra de G.M." [JMO]

6806. Gallo, Marta. El futuro perfecto de Macondo (HIUS/R, 38:3, 1974/1975, p. 115-135)

Concentrates on novel's first sentence subjecting it to intense linguistic analysis in order to demonstrate how novelist's use of future perfect tense is an attempt to abolish that very temporal dimension. Certain confusion in exposition not cleared by the overabundance of diagrams and tables makes for difficult reading. [JMO]

6807. García Márquez, Gabriel. Crónicas y reportajes. Bogotá, Instituto Colombiano de Cultura, 1976. 518 p. (Biblioteca colombiana de cultura. Col. Popular, 11)

Hefty volume gathers good number of newspaper articles that author wrote first as reporter for *El Espectador* between Feb. 1954-July 1955, and later as correspondent for same paper in Europe between July 1955-April 1956. Among these texts figure his chronicles on "La Marquesita de la Sierpe," which deal with witchcraft and superstition in the Atlantic coastal area of Colombia. In light of the short story "Los Funerales de la Mama Grande," this youthful discovery of the magical world of the jungle is significant to the reconstruction of the novelist's artistic evolution (see item 6811). [JMO]

6808. Gilard, Jacques. De *Los sangurimas* a *Cien años de soledad* (UM/R, 21, enero/marzo 1976, p. 183-196, illus.)

Comparative effort intended to demonstrate similarities between masterpieces of José de la Cuadra (see item 6827) and Gabriel García Márquez. Presence of certain mythical elements is highlighted, e.g., incest, crime, exodus, founding, apocalypsis, symbolic tree, etc. Does not suggest any direct influence but, rather, a mere "recurrencia estructural y temática." Study is more descriptive than evaluative. [JMO]

6809. ———. García Márquez, le groupe de Barranquilla et Faulkner (UTIEH/C, 27, 1976, p. 159-170)

Another study by this author on the novelist's formative period. In this instance, the time spent in the provinces as a newspaper reporter who also wrote short stories (see item 6810). The "Grupo de Barranquilla" has attracted critical attention since it introduced the novelist to the strongest influence on his initial work: William Faulkner. With ample and accurate documentation Gilard chronicles that encounter with the intellectuals of Barranquilla (José Féliz Fuenmayor, Alvaro Cepeda Samudio, and above all the Catalan Ramón Vinyes [see item 6826]). Author states that it "ne pouvait être le fait du hasard" as Vargas Llosa claimed, and offers exact dates. Among various Anglo-Saxon writers with whom García Márquez became familiar (Huxley, Virginia Woolf, Joyce, Hemingway), Faulkner was the dominant presence, another way in which García Márquez is indebted intellectually to Vinyes. [JMO]

6810. ———. García Márquez en 1950 et 1951: quelques données sur la genèse d'une oeuvre (UTIEH/C, 26, 1976, p. 123-146)

On the basis of abundant but hitherto unknown documentation, Gilard offers a detailed study of author's early pages. Clearly intended as narratives, they were written during period of title and were published in *El Heraldo* and *Crónica* of Barranquilla (see item 6809). Pieces in question are: *La hija del coronel; El hijo del coronel; La casa de los Buendía* (subtitled *Apuntes para una novela*) and *El regreso de Meme* (*Apuntes de una novela*). They are built around certain archetypal motifs: home, family, community. Last one became part of *La hojarasca*, while first three were fragments of a novel (*La casa*) which Colombian author never finished. Study is crucial for understanding author's initial period. [JMO]

6811. ———. La obra periodística de García Márquez: 1954-1956 (RCLL, 2:4, 1976, p. 151-176, bibl.)

Compilation and commentary on García Márquez news reporting activities first from Bogotá, later from Europe as correspondent for *El Espectador* and *El Independiente* (1954-56). Exhaustively researched work about this formative period in novelist's career. Verifies writer's chronology and apprenticeship of his style (see item 6807). [JMO]

6812. Gómez Davila, Nicolás. Escolios a un texto implícito. Bogotá. Instituto Colombiano de Cultura, 1977. 2 v. (477, 500 p.) (Col. Autores nacionales, 22)

Truly exceptional work in which this practically unknown author gathers thousands of aphorisms that synthesize in a lucid and precise manner his skeptic but wise vision of history, politics, art, thought, and human behavior. Totality of work is impressive not only because of mastery of wide range of knowledge it reveals, but because its impeccable style heralds a great writer. It is rare to find such a book in Spanish American letters. [JMO]

6813. Gutiérrez Girardot, Rafael. Horas de estudio. Bogotá, Instituto Colombiano de Cultura, Subdirección de Comunicaciones Culturales, 1976. 388 p. (Col. Autores nacionales, 17)

Consists of 20 essays and articles covering wide gamut of interests and themes: authors and problems of contemporary Spanish American literature, peninsular poetry, modern German literature, notes on European thinkers, etc. Most extensive and complete of these is study on Borges which appeared as a book in 1959. Study on Vallejo and "La Muerte de Dios" also contains valuable insights. Greatest contribution, however, is to be found in studies of a theoretical-polemical nature: notion of "modernidad" in new Spanish American narrative, problems of criticism, discussion of these of Hegel and Benjamin, social theory of literature, etc. Gutiérrez Girardot is a critic of very firm ideas and a very solid knowledge of German thought. This makes for a tone of intellectual arrogance that is unfortunate, e.g., the sharp attacks on a good part of criticism (from Juan Larrea to Bachelard, to Busoño). Moreover, style is overly heavy and grave, portentous sentences not infrequent. Nevertheless, a serious work. [JMO]

6814. Kooreman, Thomas E. Two novelistic views of the *bogotazo* (LALR, 3:5, Fall/Winter 1974, p. 129-134)

Subject of the *Bogotazo* (1948) is one among many themes of Colombia's "novela de violencia." Author examines it in: *El monstruo* (1955) by Carlos H. Pareja and *La calle 10* (1960) by Manuel Zapata Olivella. First is a crude political document, second attempts a more literary structure and technique without much success. [JMO]

6815. McMurray, George R. Gabriel García Márquez. N.Y., Frederick Ungar, 1977. 182 p., bibl. (Modern literature monographs)

First book-length study of author and an appropriate introduction to his work in English. Includes chapter on *El Otoño del patriarca*. In his novels, author notes a constant: presence of "the absurd hero," whom he defines as "the protagonist whose passion for life enables him to struggle unceasingly against overwhelming odds" (p. 25). Of particular interest and completeness are his analyses of *Cien años* . . . and *El otoño* . . . McMurray concludes that novelist has made a complete turn around "in his depiction of subjective states of mind reminiscent of surrealism" (p. 157) and that his world gives the impression of being concemned "either to imminent annihilation or to entropic stagnation and decay" (p. 161). Overall, this is a good study which also includes bibliography and thematic index. [JMO]

6816. Mena, Lucila Inés. *La casa grande*: el fracaso en un orden social (HISPA, 1:2, 1972, p. 3-17)

Proposes analysis of two levels of meaning on which this interesting novel of Alvaro Cepeda Samudio is structured: a) a psychological one which is central and on which the problem of family develops and b) a sociological one which serves as background. Perhaps, inadvertently, study inverts order after bringing forth some observations on the family (p. 6 and 7). Observes that one of the chief focal points of tension is hate and the dialectic of betrayal/rebellion; that author creates more than characters, archetypes, the Father, the Sister; that it frames political circumstance (the banana strike of 1928) in a mythical atmosphere where time does not flow and incest is insinuated. This is enough to consider the work a fairly direct precursor of certain pages of *Cien años de soledad* (see item 6818). [JMO]

6817. ———. *Cien años de soledad*: novela de "la violencia" (HISPA, 5:13, abril 1976, p. 3-23)

Attempts to show correspondence between novel and political history of Colombia and, generally, America and even Western man. Study focuses on numerous historical sources which reveal how novel's themes of repression and incest are rooted in Colombian reality. Author adds another contribution to establishment of nonliterary sources, precursors, and models for the well known novel (see also items 6816 and 6818). [JMO]

6818. ———. El General Rafael Uribe Uribe como modelo histórico del Coronel Aureliano Buendía en *Cien años de soledad* (RIB, 25:2, abril/junio 1975, p. 150-168)

The personality and public accomplishments of a hero of Liberal uprisings of the last century, Gen. Rafael Uribe Uribe, coincide to an extent with those of the character in García Márquez' work. For example, their response to lack of arms, is textually identical. Author concludes that although novelist seems at times to be offering "una exagerada deformación de la realidad, . . . está reproduciendo con considerable veracidad, la figura de un personaje que habita muchas páginas de la historia de Colombia." [JMO]

6819. Merrell, Floyd. José Arcadio Buendía's scientific paradigms: man in search of himself (LALR, 2:4, Spring/Summer 1974, p. 59-70)

Attempts to draw certain homologues "on broad historical/archetypal levels" between certain episodes of *One hundred years of solitude* engendered by José Arcadio Buendía's scientific curiosity and "the structural history of cientific philosophy in the Western World." Thus, Buendía's attitude towards the gypsies who visit Macondo "is favorably analogous to that of the Ionians when introduced to Eastern thought." While some homologues prove well founded and plausible, others (like the one about the dream of the infinite rooms and the discovery of quantum theory) remain unconvincing speculation. [JMO]

6820. Porras Collantes, Ernesto *comp*. Bibliografía de la novela en Colombia. Con notas de contenido y crítica de las obras y guías de comentarios sobre los autores. Bogotá, Instituto Caro y Cuervo, 1976. 888 p. (Serie bibliográfica, 11)

Important and rigorous bibliographical work which incorporates and completes (up to 1974) what was previously collected by Antonio Curcio Altamar in *Evolución de la novela en Colombia* (Bogotá, Instituto Caro y Cuervo, 1957). Entries are arranged in alphabetical order and are most comprehensive because in addition to bibliographical details, a synopsis of each novel and available critical references are included. Volume also lists pseudonyms and a chronological index. All of these features make consultation much easier. [JMO]

6821. Reid, Alastair. Basilisks' eggs (The New Yorker, 8 Nov. 1976. p. 175-208)

Although intended merely as a review of García Márquez' *El otoño del patriarca* (of its English translation in fact) article offers an intelligent and admiring overview of Colombian's *oeuvre*, as well as a quick panorama of contemporary Spanish American literature with particular reference to Borges, Neruda and Vargas Llosa, the latter as critic of García Márquez. Finally, author affirms that *The autumn of the patriarch* "is a formidable piece of invention, and pushes the discoveries of *One hundred years of solitude* further, closer to a contained whole." This must be the most comprehensive magazine review of this work to appear in the US. [JMO]

6822. *Revista de Literaturas Hispánicas.* Univ. Nacional de Rosario, Facultad de Filosofía, Instituto de Investigaciones Literarias. No. 10, 1970- Rosario, Arg.

Issue dedicated exclusively to an examination of Gabriel García Márquez' narrative. Only one piece (Edelweis Serra's "La Búsqueda de la Forma en G.G.M.") attempts a comprehensive vision of García Márquez' work. Remaining studies focus on specific works "Estructura y Estilo en *La prodigiosa tarde de Baltazar*" by Rosa Boldori de Baldussi; "Lectura de *Una tarde después del sábado*" by Inés Santa Cruz; "Anotaciones de Antroponimia en *Cien años de soledad*" by Evangelina Simón de Poggia; "Análisis del 'motivo' en *Los funerales de la Mamá Grande*" by María Delia Rasetti; and "Aspectos de *La hojarasca*" by Mónica Couzier de González del Cerro. Graciela Alvarez de Lalli furnishes a "Bibliografía Crítica sobre G.G.M." Articles, which range methodologically from stylistic studies to structural analysis, are of average critical value. [JMO]

6823. Roberts, Gemma. El sentido de lo cómico en *Cien años de soledad* (CH, 104:312, junio 1976, p. 708-722)

Convinced of the essential function of "el espíritu del desengaño" and "la ambigüedad de la ironía," in the novel, author studies the presence of humor in the novel, in the light of certain Kierkegaardian principles. He observes that "la comicidad en *Cien años de soledad* no elimina, sino refuerza, la seriedad fundamental del tema" and exercises a critical-parodic effect in our perception of reality. Although some observations are interesting and deserving of attention, article suffers from insufficient analysis and inconsistent exposition. [JMO]

6824. Sims, Robert L. García Márquez' "La Hojarasca:" paradigm of time and search for myth (AATSP/H, 59:4, Dec. 1976, p. 810-819)

Detailed study of novel's different temporal levels (e.g., continuous present, memory, subjective experience, circularity) which García Márquez interweaves in order to create "a timeless realm in which myth can exist." Author delineates two principal temporal planes of the present in the story: a "horizontal" one that is linear, and a "vertical" one which reveals the past by reversing the flow of normal time. Thus, the significance of memory in the novel, whose function "is to transfer the past events from a chronological time schema to a continuous present. Repetitive style of exposition lengthens article unnecessarily. [JMO]

6825. Tobin, Patricia. García Márquez and the subversion of the party line (LALR, 2:4, Spring/Summer 1974, p. 39-48)

Author notes triple subversion of linearity: a) "linearity of genealogy," the frenetic sexual activity of Macondo lacks meaning and ridicules paternal order; b) a negation of the rationalist concept of historical progress, positing prodigality as a value, as well as the superiority of novelty over utility; and finally c) a subversion of "the linearity of narrative structure" through the enumeration of heterogeneous or illogical elements. In all cases there is a distortion of causality and order which author compares to "the highly sophisticated Moebius strip." Study itself is highly sophisticated as well, assimilating ideas of Paul West, Barthes, and Todorov. [JMO]

6826. Vargas, Germán *ed.* and *comp. Voces*: 1917-1920. Bogotá, Instituto Colombiano de Cultura, Subdirección de Comunicaciones Culturales, 1977. 431 p. (Col. Autores nacionales. Serie las revistas)

Selection of best material published in this Barranquilla journal, founded and supported by Catalan writer Ramón Vinyes, who promoted Colombian literature during first quarter of century (José Félix Fuenmayor, León de Greiff, Luis Carlos López, etc.). Although its scope was national, *Voces* also published important Spanish American authors (Huidobro, Tablada, Valdelomar, all in this compilation). Journal also disseminated first manifestations of European avant-garde throughout the Americas. [JMO]

ECUADOR

Barriga López, Franklin and **Leonardo Barriga López.** Diccionario de la literatura ecuatoriana. See item 6465.

6827. Robles, Humberto E. Testimonio y tendencia mítica en la obra de José de la Cuadra. Quito, Editorial Casa de la Cultura Ecuatoriana, 1976. 264 p., bibl.

Covers greatly varying aspects of Ecuadorian author's life and work: literary development; involvement with the "Generación del 30;" years of apprenticeship; esthetics; *testimonial* and *lyric poles* that distinguish his narrative; presence of the extraordinary; mythical realism of *Los sangurimas*, considered his best work and a precursor of much contemporary fiction. This final part complements the comparative study on the novel by Jacques Gilard (see item 6808). The author's contribution is more appreciable for its store of information than for its methodology. [JMO]

PERU

6828. Alegría, Ciro. Mucha suerte con Harto Palo. Memorias. Ordenamiento, prólogo y notas de Dora Varona. B.A., Editorial Losada, 1976. 471 p., bibl. (Cristal del tiempo)

Collection of numerous loose texts of literary, testimonial, and journalistic nature through which author portrays himself, his work and time. Collection has been put together by Alegría's widow, Dora Varona, who included series of previously unpublished texts to complement these writings thus tracing a type of memoir which Alegría never got around to writing. For those interested in Alegría as literary figure, this collection of otherwise inaccessible materials is very useful. At end of collection is a bibliographical reference for each page included. [JMO]

6829. Bikfalvy, Péter. Contraste y paralelismo en *La ciudad y los perros* (Acta Litteraria [Academiae Scientiarum Hungaricae, Budapest] 17:1/2, 1975, p. 247-268, tables)

Detailed analysis of two fundamental constants already noted in author's first novel. Convinced that they are present at every level of the work, Bikfalvy examines them in characters, contents, relationships and situations, novelistic structure, narrative focii, and style. Study concludes that this double principle explains why Vargas Llosa's protagonists are psychologically contradictory and confront difficulties in forging genuine human relationships, especially when a third party is involved. Concludes with polemical commentary on novelist's position vis-à-vis Marxist esthetics and the technical repertory of the realistic novel. Article is rigorous and well founded, although it makes for rather dry reading. [JMO]

6830. Castro Klarén, Sara. Sobre preguntas de . . .: José María Arguedas (HISPA, 4:10, 1975, p. 45-54)

Author taped these testimonials in conversations with Peruvian novelist in Lima between 1966-67. Arguedas touches on all aspects of his childhood, family life, and the indigenous world, as well as the writing of some of his novels and on literary technique. [JMO]

6831. Cornejo Polar, Antonio. Para una interpretación de la novela indigenista (CDLA, 16:100, enero/feb. 1977, p. 40-48)

Author rates similarity between colonial chronicles and *indigenísta* novel in order to describe the latter. Discusses heterogeneity of "indigenismo," i.e., use of cultural elements from Western culture "para dar razón de otro sistema, el indígena" (p. 42); thus, its "excentric" character with respect to its social and cultural context. His proposal is polemic despite his academic language. Some of his theoretical assumptions such as that the novel as a form "no dispuesta para la representación de sociedades rurales" (p. 46), are not easy to accept. [JMO]

6832. Escobar, Alberto. La partida inconclusa o la lectura literaria. 2. ed. Lima, Instituto Nacional de Cultura, 1976. 259 p., bibl.

Work contains series of perspectives, theoretical discussions and methodological applications, which try to highlight "la interrelación entre el fenómeno lingüístico y el literario" and to point out the importance of "la *lectura* en tanto modalidad individual e histórica." Author's point of view is quite eclectic: he rejects fray of critical methods and refuses to accept any method which "se desentienda de lo formal [y] de lo histórico." Book, by virtue of its didactic and balanced tone, is a good instrument for teaching at university level. [JMO]

6833. Forgues, Roland. Lectura de "Los Cachorros" de Mario Vargas Llosa (HISPA, 5:13, abril 1976, p. 33-49)

Intended to study "la estructura del relato y el sistema de los personajes en sus relaciones conflictivas." Key point of author's argument is that the "complejo de castración" drives Cuéllar to homosexuality. In his search for evidence to substantiate this thesis author exaggerates a few symbolic interpretations, e.g., that Cuéllar's surname alludes to female genitals; the group's references to homosexuality (p. 41), etc. Despite repetitious observations this analysis helps illuminate this ambiguous story. [JMO]

6834. García Barron, Carlos. Diálogos literarios. Lima, Librería Studium Editores, 1976? 105 p.

Text of conversation between author and four Peruvian critics (Julio Ortega, José Miguel Oviedo, Antonio Cornejo Polar, and Alberto Escobar) about their respective works, methods, plans, and ideas of Peruvian culture. [JMO]

6835. Hancock, Joel. Animalization and chiaroscuro techniques: descriptive language en *La ciudad y los perros* (*The city and the dogs*) (LALR, 4:7, Fall/Winter 1975, p. 37-47)

Author reexamines two distinct themes in this study: the technique of "animalization," which consists of describing characters, their activities and behavior in non-human terms; the result is a caricaturesque effect comparable to Valle Inclán's *esperpento*. The second theme concerns the "chiaroscuro" process whereby changes of attitude are inferred and the reader's attention is focused on specific aspects producing grotesque effects. Article of considerable value and interest. [JMO]

6836. Larco, Juan ed. and comp. Recopilación de textos sobre José María Arguedas. La Habana, Casa de las Américas, Centro de Investigaciones Literarias, 1976. 498 p., bibl., illus. (Serie valoración múltiple)

Very useful collection of critical interpretations on the Peruvian novelist. Peruvian, Spanish-American and European critics examine relationship of Arguedas to: "indigenismo;" his overcoming of this trend; relationship between his narrative and social process in Andean environment; problems of ideology, language and myth posited by author's work; as well as other major aspects. Also includes brief testimonials, documents, and bibliography by and about Arguedas. Volume is a substantial contribution to knowledge and dissemination of author's work. [JMO]

6837. Losada Guido, Alejandro. Ciro Alegría como fundador de la realidad hispanoamericana (Acta Litteraria [Academiae Scientiarum Hungaricae, Budapest] 17:1/2, 1975, p. 71-92)

Extensive study poses interesting task of sociological criticism: the way in which Ciro Alegría creates "un sentido renovado de la existencia que cuestiona los modos habituales con que su sociedad se comprende en el mundo" (p. 71). Highlights fundamental points in author's novels: presentation of Indian environment as "un estilo cultural;" "objetivación del narrador;" autonomy of narrative world; mode of "composición aditiva," etc. Author's attempt falls short rather abruptly, however, he assumes a defensive stance by denying all perspectives other than his own. Moreover, study suffers from excessive rhetoric, conceptual confusion and author's tendency toward theoretical digression. [JMO]

6838. ———. Creación y praxis: la producción literaria como praxis social en Hispanoamérica y el Perú. Lima. Univ. Nacional Mayor de San Marcos, Dirección Universitaria de Biblioteca y Publicaciones, 1976. 289 p., bibl.

Study's attempt is not small: re-examination of Peruvian narrative of 20th century through five of its major figures (Arguedas, Vargas Llosa, Ribeyro, Bryce, and Scorza) and, subsequently, the narrative of Spanish America, trying to comprehend these narrative works as a form of "praxis social" which reflects certain ideological and class conditionings. Author avails himself of theses of Luckács and Goldman. His attempt, however, falls short because of incoherent assimilation of the vocabulary he uses, and further because of the confused language and prejudices implicit in an analysis which is more partisan than persuasive. [JMO]

6839. Luchting, Wolfgang Alexander. Alfredo Bryce: humores y malhumores. Lima, Editorial Milla Batres, 1975. 143 p. (Col. Perfil y tiempo)

Confusing title which refers to personal dispute between critic and author, a dispute emanating from critic's tenacious search. Volume contains mass of heterogeneous material. Despite their confused rendering, they include a couple of longer studies on the structure and narrative point of view of *Un mundo para Julius* which are of some interest, chiefly because of scarcity of studies on this novel. Rest of book does not go beyond the anecdotal. [JMO]

6840. Morino, Angelo. *Pantaleón y las visitadoras:* un caso di autoregolazione testuale (IUO/A, 18:2, luglio 1976, p. 163-185)

On the basis of a Vargas Llosa statement about his novel and availing himself of certain ideas of Barthes, Hjelmslev and Formalism, author studies three aspects of Vargas Llosa's verbal reality: 1) "la disintegrazione del tempo referente" through a number of different types of plural dialogues; 2) use of "un repertorio di linguaggi settoriali," in which each character is depicted by verbal traits of a specific social level; and 3) search for "l'autonomia della finzione" that Morino identifies with Flaubert (not with author of *Madame Bovary* but that of *Bouvard et Pécuchet*). One of more detailed studies on the new novelistic language of Vargas Llosa. [JMO]

6841. Ortega, Julio. La imaginación crítica: ensayos sobre la modernidad en el Perú. Prólogo de José Lezama Lima. Lima, Ediciones Peisa, 1974. (Biblioteca peruana)

Popular ed. gathers studies on poets and novelists of contemporary Peru (Eguren, Vallejo, Moro, Arguedas, and Vargas Llosa). Studies appeared previously in author's *La contemplación y la fiesta* (1969) and *Figuración de la persona* (1971), and are reissued here with some additions and amendations. Texts, which according to author "proponen un acceso analítico a quienes son los fundadores de la modernidad literaria en el Perú," tend to be very suggestive, personal, and pithy in addition to being written in a language attuned to various recent critical currents. Eulogistic prologue by José Lezama Lima. [JMO]

6842. Rens, Ivo. El suicidio de Arguedas: ensayo psico-político (CAM, 207:4, julio/agosto 1976, p. 79-127, bibl.)

Essay proposes absorbing and provocative interpretation of Peruvian writer's suicide by applying the Adlerian model of comparative individual psychology. Rens examines the case first in literary terms (concentrating on *El zorro de arriba y el zorro de abajo*) and, later in psychological terms Observes that in author's last novel predominate self-destructive and sexual impulses, an agonizing identification with nature, and a conflict-ridden relationship with society. This extreme case of Arguedas' "neurosis artística" was exacerbated by the particular political situation he faced as an intellectual: the military revolution of 1968 which constituted a moral challenge he could not withstand. Rens concludes not convincingly that Arguedas' suicide was "una traición política." [JMO]

6843. Ribeyro, Julio Ramón. La caza sutil: ensayos y artículos de crítica literaria. Bibliografía de Fernando Vidal. Lima, Editorial Milla Batres, 1976. 168 p., bibl. (Col. Perfil y tiempo)

Collection of 21 brief essays and articles written by Peruvian short-story writer between 1953-75. Themes are varied: French literature (past and present); a few Peruvian authors (well known, such as José María Arguedas and unknown, such as Leopoldo Chariarse); reflections on literary life ("Las Discusiones," "El Amor a los Libros," "Peruanos en París"); theoretical positions ("Problemas del Novelista Actual" and "Las Alternativas del Novelista"); and reflections on his own work. Critically, most valuable pieces are those on Arguedas and García Márquez' *El otoño del patriarca*. Intimate warmth of his style, tasteful discernment of his models and literary passions, coherence of his personal vision of narrative task make for captivating reading. Bibliography by Luis Fernando Vidal is appended. [JMO]

6844. Simposio Nacional sobre la Obra Narrativa de Ciro Alegría, *Arequipa, Perú, 1974.* La obra de Ciro Alegría: simposio realizado del 26 al 28 de julio de 1974 en Arequipa. Presentación de Jorge Cornejo Polar. Arequipa, Perú, Univ. Nacional de San Agustín (UNSA), Programa Académico de Literatura y Lenguas, 1976. 151 p.

Studies presented at this Symposium which are reproduced in this publication, only three hold any interest: "*Lazaro* y el problema de la Técnica Narrativa" by Edmundo Bendezú Aibar, "La Dinámica de la Realidad en las Dos Primeras Novelas de C.A." by Antonio Cornejo Polar; and "Notas sobre la Teoría Novelística de C.A." by Jorge Cornejo Polar. On the other hand, "social and ideological" analysis that Tito Cáceres Cuadros dedicates to the short story "Calixto Garmendia" is a model of incomprehension. [JMO]

6845. *Texas Studies in Literature and Language.* Univ. of Texas Press. Vol. 19, No. 4, Winter 1977-   . Austin.

Prof. Charles Rossman has edited this special issue devoted to the work of Mario Vargas Llosa. Together with *World Literature Today* (See item 6849) they constitute another serious attempt to stimulate and disseminate critical output in English of this Peruvian novelist. There are some interesting studies dedicated to specific works (Rilda L. Baker on *The time of the hero*, Michael Moody and Luis A. Díez on *Conversation in the cathedral*, Raymond L. Williams and William L. Siemens on *Pantalén y las visitadoras*), and others on more general themes and aspects of author's work (studies by Luis Harss, Malva E. Filer, Robert Brody, Joseph A. Feustle Jr., and Mary Davis). The "homenaje" is rounded out with poems by Robert de Lima and a dialogue with the author on his latest novel. [JMO]

6846. Točilovac, Goran. La comunidad indígena y Ciro Alegría: un estudio de *El mundo es ancho y ajeno.* Lima. Ediciones de la Biblioteca Universitaria, 1975. 123 p.

Publication consists of author's thesis (Univ. de San Marcos, Lima). Relying on rather conventional, sociological approach, work analyzes economic, political, and social aspects of community of Rumi in Alegría's above mentioned work. It also examines work's literary techniques with which Rumi is presented as superior model of human organization. Simplistic manner in which author utilizes sociological method and lack of consistent critical rigor limit significance of some interesting but partial observations. [JMO]

6847. Vargas Llosa, Mario. La novela. José María Arguedas. La novela y el problema de la expresión literaria en el Perú. Vicente López, Arg., América Nueva, 1974. 71 p.

Unauthorized ed. of recordings of two lectures by two greatest Peruvian novelists of recent years. Despite informal nature of their expositions, texts offer a couple of interesting analyses on authors' respective concepts of the novel, the creative experience and on their social significance. [JMO]

6848. Vidal, Luis Fernando. Ribeyro los espejos repetidos (RCLL, 1:1, 1975, p. 73-88, tables)

Attempts to bridge the literary and socio-cultural significance of this Peruvian writer by applying the concepts of Greimas, Todorov, and Formalism. To this end, author establishes a thematic and environmental classification based on whether Ribeyro's stories allude to Peru or not. In first instance he distinguishes texts of an inventive or evocative modality. He then notes that there are three human types in his texts (the assimilated, marginal, and uprooted), but barely develops these categories. What author attempts to state is well founded, even if less original than his critical language would suggest. Article's conclusion is excellent. [JMO]

6849. World Literature Today. A literary quarterly. Univ. of Oklahoma. Vol. 52, No. 1, Winter 1978- . Norman.

Special issue devoted to Mario Vargas Llosa. Comprises three principal sections: 1) introduction, with texts by editor Ivar Ivask, by author himself, and a chronology; 2) collection of nine essays of Spanish and Anglo-American critics on general or specific aspects of novelist's work; and 3) bibliography of works about and by Vargas Llosa. Also includes photographs documenting author's visit to Oklahoma, March 1977, to attend Symposium held by this journal. Important contribution comparable to the one by *Texas Studies in Literature and Language* (see item 6845). [JMO]

VENEZUELA

6850. Brushwood, John S. Cinco novelas de Salvador Garmendia: el impacto sobre los hábitos perceptivos (AATSP/H, 60:4, Dec. 1977, p. 884-890)

Studies three key aspects of Garmendia's work: 1) adjustment of language to atmosphere of alienation; 2) the activity of "fantasear en lugar de fabular;" and 3) "la introspección del narrador-protagonista-problema" (p. 885). Author notes that novels tend to end "en estado de suspensión más que en resolución" (p. 884) and that "los sentidos constituyen un factor básico en la experiencia" (p. 885). Value of this perspective on Garmendia is hampered by certain linguistic uncertainties in the exposition, possibly owing to faulty translation. [JMO]

6851. Cardozo, Lubio *comp*. Bibliografía de bibliografías sobre la literatura venezolana en las bibliotecas de Madrid; París y Londres. Maracaibo, Ven., Univ. del Zulia, Centro de Estudios Literarios [and] Univ. de los Andes, Centro de Investigaciones Literarias, 1975. 67 p., facsims.

Author writes: "están todas [bibliographies indicated in title], grandes y pequeñas, impresas y multigrafiadas, acompañadas de una breve nota caracterizante de su contenido con respecto a la literatura venezolana." Despite usefulness of compilation, work suffers from apparent haste and carelessness with which commentaries were written. [JMO]

6852. Larrazabal Henríquez, Osvaldo; Amaya Llebot; and Gustavo Luis Carrera *comps*. Bibliografía del cuento venezolano. Caracas, Univ. Central de Venezuela, Facultad de Humanidades y Educación, Instituto de Investigaciones Literarias, 1975. 313 p.

Useful compilation offering a very complete list of Venezuelan short story writers through a century (1875-1973), including authors of a single story. Other appendices (on existing anthologies and collections, chronology of the genre, indices of authors and titles, etc.) facilitate consultation. [JMO]

6853. Uslar Pietri, Arturo. Veinticinco ensayos. Antología. Caracas, Monte Avila Editores, 1969. 248 p. (Col. Prisma)

The volume is a kind of anthology of the Venezuelan author's essayistic works, culled from books that extend from *Las nubes* (1951) to *En busca del Nuevo Mundo* (1969). In these pages, in which Uslar Pietri deals practically with everything (literature, culture, society, history, art, voyages, trips, manners and customs, etc.), is a catalog of intellectual curiosity of the author's own world, his comprehensions and incomprehensions. The book reproduces as prologue some old pages (1945) by Mariano Picón Salas on the author. [JMO]

CHILE

CEDOMIL GOIC

Professor of Spanish American Literature
The University of Michigan, Ann Arbor

LA NOVELA CHILENA HA CONTINUADO, durante los años 1974 a 1976 su producción creciente. Una parte importante de esta novelística sigue encontrando su motivación en lo que se ha dado en llamar el proceso chileno, novelas que se ocupan de Chile bajo el gobierno de Salvador Allende y sus principales conflictos, sobre el país después del golpe militar del 11 de sept. de 1973, sobre otros acontecimientos políticos o sociales que se muestran vinculados a aquellos hechos. Las novelas en cuestión se ordenan en dos clases que corresponden a los puntos de vistas ideológicos en oposición. *Soñé que la nieve ardía*, de Antonio Skármeta (item 6872) pertenece a la serie de las novelas del proceso chileno que es más que una crónica de hechos la formulación de la persistencia y del vigor del sueño político. Las novelas de Waldo Vila o de Carlos Correa Iglesias (item 6864) o Carlos Morand (item 6869) ahondan en los antecedentes morales de la crisis política, la manipulación del terrorismo y los efectos del miedo.

Entre los hechos más destacados debe contarse con la publicación de *La Historia de María Griselda* de María Luisa Bombal (item 6859), que no había sido recogida en libro. La obra más innovadora es *La orquesta de cristal* de Enrique Lihn (item 6868) "nueva escritura" del género de narraciones que irrelizan la situación narrativa dando un lugar importante a las referencias metanarrativas y a desusados géneros de decir. Los nuevos nombres que aparecen son los de Adolfo Couve (item 6865), que define una personalidad literaria muy singular y Enrique Valdés (item 6783) más cerca de la realidad que de la fantasía, con una notable novela del mundo austral.

En el cuento destaca la colección de Miguel Arteche, *Mapas del otro mundo* (item 6856). El premio Casa de las Américas 1975 de cuento recayó en el joven escritor Leonardo Carvajal Barrios (item 6861) más por el contenido de sus cuentos—el proceso chileno—que por sus méritos literarios.

Un volumen considerable sigue alcanzando en la producción chilena el articulismo y la crónica periodísticas de diverso género. La reedicion de tradicionistas y memorialistas como Manuel Concha (item 6863) o Augusto D'Halmar (item 6866) se suma a las publicaciones recientes de artículos de Teófilo Cid (item 6862), Homero Bascuñan y, entre los más originales, de Guillermo Blanco (item 6858). Las memorias literarias de Alone (item 6875) pueden ponerse en esta misma tendencia.

La crítica aparece especialmente volcada al estudio de la obra de José Donoso, numerosos artículos y una compilación le están dedicados (items 6877, 6881, y 6884). Un libro se ocupa de la vida y obra de Nicomedes Guzmán (item 6886).

PROSE FICTION

6854. Aldunate B., Elena. Angélica y el delfín. Santiago, Ediciones Aconcagua, 1977? 130 p. (Col. Mistral)

Cuentos fantásticos cuyos asuntos van de lo maravilloso natural a la ciencia-ficción.

6855. Arteche, Miguel. La disparatada vida de Félix Palissa. Santiago, Zig-Zag, 1975. 256 p. (Libros de bolsillo Zig-Zag)

Es la tercera novela del autor. Novela policial contada desde el punto de vista del muerto quien con la ayuda de un perro sabueso ultramundano revive su último año de vida en busca del asesino. El último capítulo entrega un desenlace inesperado. El temple humorístico de la narración es uno de sus rasgos salientes.

6856. ———. Mapas del otro mundo. Introducción disparatada del autor. Santiago, Ediciones Aconcagua, 1977. 134 p. (Col. Mistral)

Primer libro de cuentos del conocido poeta y novelista. Cuentos de humor y fantasía con excelente dominio del género.

6857. Barros, Alvaro. Al sur del Beagle. Cuentos. Prólogo de Francisco Coloane. Santiago, Ediciones Aconcagua, 1976? 110 p., illus. (Col. Mistral)

Cuentos regionales del Archipiélago del Cabo de Hornos que animan la cultura y la lengua de los indígenas yámanas. Cuentos sencillos de anécdota elemental o ritual.

6858. Blanco, Guillermo. Placeres prohibidos. Santiago, Ediciones Aconcagua, 1976. 191 p. (Col. Mistral)

Compilación de las amenas crónicas de una sección de la revista *Ercilla* intitulada "La Vida Simplemente" que el periodista y narrador animó durante varios años. El humor irónico, a veces fustigante, es la característica principal de estas crónicas.

6859. Bombal, María Luisa. La historia de María Griselda. Quillota, Chile, Editorial El Observador, 1976. 91 p. (Col. Relámpago)

Primera edición en libro de esta novela corta publicada anteriormente en la revista *Sur* (B.A., 142, 1946). La edición lleva: unas "Palabras Previas" de Alone; el cuento "Trenzas;" una suerte de postfacio por Sara Vial "María Luisa Bombal Nuestra Abeja de Fuego;" y una cronología de María Luisa Bombal acompañada de una bibliografía sobre la autora.

6860. Brieba. Liborio. Episodios nacionales. Ilustraciones de Julio Palazuelos. Santiago, Editorial Andrés Bello, 1975. 3 v. (394, 453, 603 p.) illus.

Nueva edición de las novelas históricas folletinescas de Brieba. El autor, perteneciente a la generación de Alberto Blest Gana, ordena en 10 libros el asunto abarcado por las luchas de Independencia desde la Reconquista hasta la Patria Nueva.

6861. Carvajal Barrios, Leonardo. Definición del olvido. Cuentos. La Habana, Casa de las Américas, 1975. 119 p. (Premio Casa de las Américas 1975. Cuento)

Primer libro del joven autor, nacido en 1951. El conjunto de cuentos revela impericia y escasa originalidad. El premio parece justificarse por razones relacionadas con el proceso chileno que es el asunto común de las narraciones.

6862. Cid, Teófilo. ¡Hasta Mapocho no más . . .! Santiago, Editorial Nascimento, 1976. 423 p.

Teófilo Cid (1914-64), poeta y narrador, vinculado al grupo surrealista chileno La Mandrágora aparece en este volumen en una nueva dimensión, la del cronista. De las nutridas páginas de este libro destacan las dedicadas a su generación y a los surrealistas así como a la comprensión del surrealismo en nuestro continente.

6863. Concha, Manuel. Tradiciones serenenses. Santiago, Editorial Nascimento, 1975. 2 v. (231, 294 p.) (Biblioteca popular Nascimento)

Reedición de las tradiciones completas de Manuel Concha, el más importante tradicionista del siglo XIX. Es el Ricardo Palma chileno, sin el humor picante del peruano sino más suave aunque persistentemente satírico. Tipos y costumbres son ilustrados mediante una anécdota sencilla que contempla la vinculación del presente con el pasado histórico.

6864. Correa Iglesias, Carlos. Palitroques. Santiago, Ediciones Barcelona, 1975. 373 p.

Novela en clave, de fácil resolución, que refiere la historia de una atentado político fatal contra un expresidente de la república y de los grupos terroristas que lo ejecutaron. Novela que también dice relación con el llamado proceso chileno. Es una novela excelentemente escrita dentro de formas tradicionales. Una de las mejores que tienen por asunto los acontecimientos chilenos de los años 70.

6865. Couve, Adolfo. El tren de cuerda: el parque. Santiago, Ediciones de la Galería Epoca, 1976. 131 p.

Esta obra contribuye decididamente a definir al autor, nacido en 1940, como uno de los narradores más singulares de su generación. Novelas en las que la perspectiva de la sensibilidad—maravilla, decepción, ensueño, horror—es dominante junto con la aguda percepción de matices visuales. En esta obra Couve ha conquistado ya un lenguaje propio.

6866. D'Halmar, Augusto. Recuerdos olvidados. Prólogo de Alfonso Calderón. Santiago, Editorial Nascimento, 1975. 550 p. (Biblioteca popular Nascimento)

Memorias del autor publicadas originalmente en la prensa de Santiago, entre 1939-40 principalmente, y presentadas por un personaje ficticio, Cristián Delande. De gran interés para el conocimiento de la biografía del escritor y de su generación. Las memorias mezclan libremente la realidad y la ficción.

6867. Frías, Gustavo A. Pasaje al fondo de la tierra: los días de Arne Saknussem. Santiago, Editorial del Pacífico, 1975. 122 p.

Novela fantástica sin comparación en la novelística chilena contemporánea. Narración de un mito de pasaje o *descenso ad inferos* construida, parcialmente, mediante collages de textos de Julio Verne, Huizinga, Mircea Eliade y otros. En relación a estos textos se propone la novela como juego o acertijo adjudicando al lector un puntaje según acierte en su reconocimiento.

6868. Lihn, Enrique. La orquesta de cristal. B.A., Editorial Sudamericana, 1976. 153 p. (Col. El espejo)

Con esta obra el conocido poeta y cuentista irrumpe en el campo de la "nueva escritura" o de la destrucción del genero novelístico. La monografía musical, la crónica artística, la *causerie littéraire* y los *faits divers* son los géneros de decir en que se ven polémicamente envueltas cinco o seis voces. La irrealidad de los orquesta de cristal y de sus actuaciones se acompaña de la parodia verbal de la literatura simbolista y de sus epígonos y de la recreación de los principales temas del simbolismo poético y musical. La referencia bibliográfica fidedigna se confunde con la superchería o la invención. La irrealidad del objeto investigado confunde sus términos con referencias históricas efectivas que se prolongan hasta la Francia ocupada de los años cuarenta. La abundancia de referencias metanarrativas confunde los términos de la escritura real y de la escritura irreal.

6869. Morand, Carlos. Llegarán de noche. Santiago, Editora Nacional Gabriela Mistral, 1976. 210 p.

Es la segunda novela del autor (n. 1936) y uno de los más destacados narradores de su generación. En esta novela el proceso chileno es visto en las tensiones amenazantes del campo chileno en los años 70. Ironización de las situaciones que envuelven a dos parejas durante un fin de semana en el campo.

6870. Orrego Vicuña, Claudio. Las sorprendentes memorias de Baltazar. Cuento. Santiago, Ediciones Brocal, 1974. 105 p.

El conocido sociólogo y analista político escribe no un cuento, como subtitula su libro, sino una novela corta en la forma de unas memorias del oso polar, Baltazar, del zoológico santiaguino. Sus meditaciones, que adoptan la moral ingenua propia de la literatura infantil, se ocupan extensamente en la libertad interior y la extrañeza frente a los humanos.

6871. Rojas, Manuel. Mares libres. Selección, prólogo y notas de Norman Cortés L. Valparaíso, Chile, Univ. Católica de Valparaíso, 1975. 157 p. (Aula media, 6)

Excelente antología de cuentos que reúne lo mejor de la producción de Manuel Rojas. Cada cuento va cuidadosamente presentado, con orientación bibliográfica, un breve y preciso análisis y acompañado de útiles notas.

6872. Skármeta, Antonio. Soñé que la nieve ardía. Barcelona, Editorial Planeta, 1975. 228 p.

Esta es la primera novela publicada por el autor, considerado el más notable narrador de su generación por su obra cuentística. La novela ordena sin rigidez tres series narrativas diferentes que mezclan con desenfado la crónica y el irrealismo. Una fuerte perspectiva satírica deforma la primera serie caracterizada por las aspiraciones confusas de un joven futbolista que intenta triunfar en la capital. Envuelta en la crónica del proceso chileno de los años 70 hace converger la primera y la tercera series en la transformación del joven por el espíritu solidario de jóvenes militantes de la causa popular. La segunda parte tiene las marcas de irrealidad más acentuadas por el esquematismo caricaturesco de los personajes. Las aspiraciones de los personajes se modifican trágicamente o bien se realizan conforme a una moral ingenua. El título de la novela responde por la aspiración mítica e irrenunciable que constituye la perspectiva interpretativa dominante de la novela.

6873. Valdés, Enrique. Ventana al sur. Santiago, Zig-Zag, 1975. 166 p.

Premio Gabriela Mistral, 1974, es la primera novela del joven poeta (n. 1943). Una de las notables novelas de los últimos años. Es la nostálgica evocación del padre y de la vida pionera en las tierras australes de la provincia de Aysén. Notable calidad del lenguaje que oscila entre la poesía de la evocación y la lengua coloquial de rasgos regionales.

Viscarra Fabre, Guillermo *ed.* Antología del cuento chileno-boliviano. See item 6754.

LITERARY CRITICISM AND HISTORY

6874. Adams, Michael Ian. Three authors of alienation: Bombal, Onetti, Carpentier. Austin, Univ. of Texas Press, 1975. 128 p. (Latin American monographs, 36)

En el caso particular de la Bombal y de su novela *La última niebla*, el autor desarrolla las relaciones entre la alienación del personaje y la imagen poética de la niebla como dos modos diferentes de acceso a la interioridad del personaje o de su experiencia de la vida.

6875. Alone [*pseud. for* **Hernán Díaz Arrieta**]. Pretérito imperfecto. Memorias de un crítico literario. Santiago, Nascimento, 1976. 515 p.

Memorias del crítico literario que lleva 50 años de crítica periodística del país defendiendo las banderas del hedonismo y los modelos críticos de Saint-Beuve. Traen referencias de interés sobre escritores chilenos destacados como Huidobro, la Mistral, Neruda y muchos otros de menor figuración.

6876. Droguett, Carlos. Escrito en la aire. Valparaíso, Chile, Ediciones Universitarias de Valparaíso, 1972. 192 p. (Ensayos)

Crónicas literarias y de viaje. Extraordinariamente reveladoras de la personalidad del autor y del caudal de sus ideas y lecturas. Buena fuente de información para su biografía.

6877. Fraser, Howard M. Witchcraft in three stories of José Donoso (LALR, 4:7, Fall/Winter 1975, p. 3-8)

Buen análisis de los cuentos "Veraneo," "Paseo" y "Santelices" a la luz de distinciones poco convincentes que quedarían ilustradas por esos cuentos como combinación de asuntos nacionales y técnicas mágicas.

6878. Goić, Cedomil. La novela chilena. Los mitos degradados. 4. ed. Santiago, Editorial Universitaria, 1976. 214 p. (Teoría literaria, 1)

Agrega un "Prólogo a la Cuarta Edición" en que se da cuenta de la recepción del libro por la crítica chilena e hispanoamericana y por especialistas norteamericanos y europeos.

6879. ———. El surrealismo y la literatura iberoamericana (Revista Chilena de Literatura [Univ. de Chile, Depto. de Español, Santiago] 8, dic. 1977, p. 5-34)

Discusión de los límites y las características de la asunción del surrealismo en la literatura iberoamericana. El surrealismo y su étymon, la presencia histórica y lo surreal americano.

6880. Lastra, Pedro. Registro bibliográfico de antologías del cuento chileno: 1876-1976 (RCLL, 3:5, 1. semestre 1977, p. 89-111)

Completísimo registro que llena de modo excelente un vacío en la bibliografía chilena. Va precedido de una introducción que señala los criterios con que se ha ordenado el registro y una clasificación de antologías.

6881. Magnarelli, Sharon. El obsceno pájaro de la noche: fiction, monsters, and packages (UPDRL/HR, 45:4, Autumn 1977, p. 413-419)

Análisis de los aspectos del epígrafe a la luz de la Gramatología del filósofo francés Jacques Derrida como pura "escritura," como puro "significante." Ingenioso pero finalmente inadecuado.

6882. Massey, Kenneth W. From behind the bars of signifiers and signifieds (Dispositio [Univ. of Michigan, Dept. of Romance Languages, Ann Arbor] 2:4, invierno 1977, p. 87-92)

Estudio comparativo del proceso ritual de enajenación entre Zoom (México, Siglo XXI Editores, 1971) la segunda y más importante novela de Hernán Valdés y Tejas Verdes: diario de un campo de concentración en Chile (Barcelona, Ariel, 1974) como reflejado en un proceso de fetichización del lenguaje.

6883. Morand, Carlos. Los siete estados internos en "El Capanga" (Revista Chilena de Literatura [Univ. de Chile, Depto. de Español, Santiago] 7, dic. 1976, p. 69-76)

Excelente análisis del cuento de Jorge Guzmán.

6884. Ocanto, Nancy. Bio-bibliografía de José Donoso (Actualidades [Caracas] 2:2, 1977, p. 191-215)

Se suma a las contribuciones de George R. MacMurray y John Hasset et al completando los datos biográficos y bibliográficos y poniendolos al día hasta 1976.

6885. Ortega Luere, Marcela and **Leticia Hulsz Piccone.** Diálogo con Hernán Lavín Cerda (UNAM/FL, 3:4, julio/agosto 1977, p. 25-31)

Entrevista de valor informativo sober la obra y la concepción de la literatura del escritor, poeta y cuentista. Abundantes datos sobre sus antecedentes literarios y sobre su producción más reciente.

6886. Pearson, Lon. Nicomedes Guzmán: proletarian author in Chile's literary generation of 1938. Columbia, Univ. of Missouri Press, 1976. 285 p.

Monografía sobre la vida, las circunstancias generacionales y la obra de Nicomedes Guzmán (1914-64), uno de los destacados novelistas chilenos de este siglo. En ella, los conceptos de literatura proletaria o estilo proletario resultan inadecuados para la comprensión de este novelista. La generación del 38, por otra parte, no alcanza la elaboración propuesta por la crítica de la generación ni se adecúa a los criterios más exigentes.

6887. Promis Ojeda, José and others. José Donoso: la destrucción de un mundo. B.A., Fernando García Cambeiro, 1975. 170 p. (Col. Estudios latinoamericanos, 14)

Compilación de estudios dedicados principalmente a la novela de Donoso desde Coronación a Tres novelista burguesas. Destacan los trabajos de Promis, Antonio Cornejo Polar y Adriana Valdés (los otros son de Cedomil Goić, Raúl Bueno Chávez, Fernando Moreno Turner y Edmundo Bendezú).

6888. Revista Chilena de Literatura. Univ. de Chile, Depto. de Español. No. 7, dic. 1976- . Santiago.

Con este número se reanuda la publicación de la revista fundada en 1970.

6889. Rojo, Grínor. Una novela del proceso chileno. Soñé que la nieve ardía de Antonio Skármeta (CAM, 36:3, 1977, p. 238-261)

Buen análisis de la novela. Considera, con exceso, que esta novela responde a un supuesto impasse de la novela hispanoamericana actual que no habría sabido hasta ahora interpretar al proletariado como protagonista de la vida en América Latina.

6890. Santander, Carlos. El peso de la noche (Nueva Narrativa Hispánica [Madrid] 5, 1975, p. 159-178)

Extenso y pormenorizado análisis de la novela de Jorge Edwards. Considera la disposición de sus dos series alternas y su sentido paralelo en las dos direcciones contrapuestas en que se desarrollan. El título de la novela—una famosa frase de Diego Portales—vendría a cifrar una homología entre el mundo representado en la novela y el orden social del país.

Somoshegyi-Szokol, Gaston. Contemporary Chilean literature in the University Library at Berkeley: a bibliography with introduction, biographical notes and commentaries. See *HLAS 39:30*.

6891. Walker, John. *Páginas de un pobre diablo*: the light in the darkness (IAA, 3:1, 1977, p. 29-36)

Artículo que intenta situar este libro y en especial la novela corta que le da nombre en relación al resto de la obra de Barrios. Propone una revaloración a la luz de la importancia de su visión del mundo como vínculo entre las primeras y las últimas obras del narrador chileno.

6892. Wyers Weber, Frances. "La dinámica de la alegoría: *El Obsceno Pájaro de la Noche* de José Donoso" (HISPA, 11/12, 1975, p. 23-31)

La autora ve en la novela de Donoso una alegoría de la lucha por el poder que ocurre en todos los niveles y de la identidad prestada de la burguesía hispanoamericana. La novela podría considerarse como la exploración de todas las consecuencias del fracaso de autodefinición.

ARGENTINA AND URUGUAY*

EARL M. ALDRICH JR.

Professor of Spanish
University of Wisconsin, Madison

ALFRED J. MAC ADAM

Associate Professor of Spanish
University of Virginia

THE MAJORITY OF THE SHORT NARRATIVES and novels reviewed in this section were published between 1974-77. In Argentina the variety and quantity of this fiction is notable: predominant are experimental works which can be conveniently categorized under the heading of "new narrative;" however, the publication of fiction written in a more traditionally realistic mode continues unabated. Fantasy, an unabashed exploration of the unconventional and the seemingly inexplicable as well as moral, ideological, and regionalistic concerns inspire the authors.

The quality of the fiction is not consistently high; in particular, it is apparent that some of the writers have made a cult out of abstruseness and underestimate the need to communicate ideas as well as sensations. Poor imitation is also obvious. Unfortunately a mode or style cultivated successfully by an established craftsman may be trite when attempted by a less gifted writer. It should be emphasized, however, that there are a number of meritorious works reviewed here, including those of relatively young authors. For example, Griselda Gambaro's *Ganarse la muerte* (item 6910) is an extraordinary novel in which black humor is the device for expressing a profoundly felt truth. Enrique Medina is also a young novelist worth noting; *Transparente* (item 6928), published in 1974, *El Duke* (item 6925) 1976, and *Strip-tease* (item 6927) 1976 are not only controversial but original. The latter work, in particular, is an unusual and effective metaphor of evil of national degradation. Among the more established authors who deserve to be highlighted here are Haroldo Conti whose *Mascaró el cazador humano* (item 6901) was a co-winner of the Casa de las Américas novel prize for 1975 and Eduardo Gudiño Kieffer who published *Será por eso que la quiero tanto* (item 6914). *El beso de la mujer araña* (item 6938), Manuel Puig's fourth novel, shows him to be a writer with an uncanny ear for spoken language and a special ability to articulate delicately and imaginatively the structural elements of the novel.

The short story is similarly well-represented. Cortázar's latest collection, *Alguien que anda por ahí* (item 6902) blends simplicity and profundity and explores in artful

---

*Paraguayan novels and short stories will be reviewed in *HLAS 42* (only criticism is annotated in this volume).

fashion certain ineffable and ambiguous elements of life. Other short story collections worthy of note are Eduardo Mignoga's *Cuatrocasas* (item 6929), co-winner of the Casa de las Américas short story prize for 1976 and Marta Lynch's *Los dedos de la mano* (item 6922).

The quality and quantity of Uruguayan fiction continues to be disappointingly low. Only one work, Eduardo Galeano's *Canción de nosotros* (item 6950), co-winner of the Casa de las Américas novel prize for 1975, merits special notice. The theme, the shattered myth of Uruguay as a South American model of progress and well-being, is hardly new, but it is presented with subtle insight. [EMA Jr.]

The political realities of life in Argentina, Uruguay, and Paraguay have had in recent years a serious effect on literary criticism as it is practiced in that area. It is difficult for any intellectual there not to find himself "involved" in issues (whether he wants to be or not), and this of necessity distracts the attention of the critic: neither the text nor the author can be studied seriously when the society which produced both is in a state of crisis.

Naturally, for those critics who study the literature of these countries from without, these problems are not part of daily life, and it is certainly a pleasure to report sustained interest in those nations in Spain, France, Germany, the US, Brazil, and other Latin American countries.

No major trend dominates the criticism dedicated to Argentina, Paraguay and Uruguay: every form is practiced, and this in itself suggests that despite their current political unrest, these countries constitute one of the liveliest literary zones of Latin America. [AJMcA]

PROSE FICTION

ARGENTINA

6893. Angelind, Diego. Con otro sol. B.A., Ediciones Corregidor, 1976. 94 p.

In this excellent collection of ten short stories which have rural Argentina as the setting, death, violence, danger, and loneliness predominate. The author has been able to develop with consumate skill a narrow range of moods. Winner of *La Nación* literary prize.

6894. Asís, José. Fe de ratas. B.A., Sudamericana, 1976. 175 p.

Excellent collection of ten narratives which are linked together by the pervasive presence of sordidness and hostility. The characters, caught frequently in the most ordinary, drab situations, exist without really caring, seemingly devoid of morality. The style is noteworthy in that *porteño* slang is skillfully recreated—not, however, in a costumbristic manner. The author is not interested in simple documentary description but in language as art.

6895. Bioy Casares, Adolfo. Historias fantásticas. Madrid, Alianza Editorial, 1976. 307 p.

Collection contains 14 of Bioy Casares' best known fantastic short stories.

6896. Bosco, María Angélica. Cartas de mujeres. B.A., Emecé, 1975. 236 p.

Collection of 18 narratives written in epistolary form, and addressed by historical and literary women. Examples: Adán a Eva, Madame de Staël a Brigitte Bardot, la Papisa Juana a las mujeres de la Liberación. Full of subtle insights and good humor, these narratives challenge the excesses of feminism as well as the evils of male chauvinism.

6897. Bullrich, Silvina. Será justicia. B.A., Editorial Sudamericana, 1976. 159 p.

Novel composed of four letters through which the characters reveal the psychological crosscurrents that keep them in a state of conflict.

6898. ———. Te acordarás de Taorima. B.A., Emece, 1975. 253 p.

The first person narrator of this novel—a mother—reveals her fears, hopes, disappointments and evokes bitter-sweet memories in an intimate sort of soliloquy directed toward her daughter. Melancholy, irony, and resignation characterize this unusual revelation of a woman's feelings regarding the role thrust upon her by society and those closest to her.

6899. Castillo, Abelardo. Las panteras y el templo. B.A., Editorial Sudamericana, 1976. 168 p.

Collection of 11 carefully polished and elaborated stories which deal in a subtle, poetic manner with such topics as guilt, the confused, often tormented relationships between men and women, rationally inexplicable phenomena, and crime. Interesting narrative point of view. Effective use of imagery to establish mood.

6900. Conti, Haroldo. Cuentos y relatos. Selección, estudio preliminar y notas de Eduardo Romano. B.A., Editorial Kapelusz, 1975. 156 p.

An annotated anthology of selections from the novels *Sudeste, Alrededor de la jaula, En vida* plus several of Conti's stories. Useful introduction and notes by Romano.

6901. ———. Mascaró el cazador humano. La Habana, Casa de las Américas, 1975. 245 p.

Winner of a Casa de las Américas novel prize for 1975. A work in which the characters, who lack any depth or psychological development, seem to represent modern man alone in an incomprehensible universe. These characters, without substance, without personal identity, are destined to grope futilely within an environment which is to them foreign and hostile. The events and setting are presented with a deliberate vagueness so that ambiguity is maximized and efforts to approach the work extrinsically, to find referential meaning are frustrated.

6902. Cortázar, Julio. Alguien que anda por ahí. México, Editorial Hermes, 1977. 213 p.

New collection of 11 narratives by Cortázar which are reminiscent of his earlier short stories: favorite images of the past appear again as does the tendency toward structural disjunction; the unexpected ending is of fundamental importance; even the device used in "Las Babas del Diablo" is once more exploited with great effectiveness in one of the selections. All of this is not to say that Cortázar has merely returned to an early phase. Quite the contrary, he has taken certain elements from the past in order to develop them in a more delicate, simple, yet profound way. His special sense of humor is to be noted in "Reunión con un Círculo Rojo" which is dedicated to Borges. Only at the end does the reader discover that he refers to Jacobo Borges.

6903. ———. Vampiros multinacionales. México, Excelsior, 1975. 77 p., illus.

Cortázar's attempt to combine comic books and politics. The intentions are admirable, but the results never get beyond the level of the "cute." Cortázar fans are advised to see the text as one more step away from *Rayuela* toward a new political and, one hopes, literary maturity for Cortázar.

6904. Estrazulas, Enrique. Los viejísimos cielos. B.A., Editorial Sudamericana, 1975. 174 p.

Failure to grasp a delicate mystery, the conflict between the ideal and the real, the experience of loneliness and frustration are themes which are developed skillfully in the 13 stories of this collection.

6905. Ferreiro, M. Jorge. Ocurrió en Betín-Curá (y todo entre 1920 y 1930). B.A., Talleres Gráficos El Municipio, 1976. 142 p.

Costumbristic novel which takes place in the pampa. Example of rural-regional fiction which still continues to be written.

6906. Filloy, Juan. Vil & Vil (La gata parida). B.A., Macció Hermanos, 1975. 348 p.

Readers of Juan Filloy who have come to expect the unusual will not be disappointed by this novel which deals with the presence of political instability, revolution and military dictatorships in Latin America in satirical fashion.

6907. Foguet, Hugo. Frente al mar de timor. B.A., Gránica Editor, 1976. 155 p.

Novel in which author attempts to develop a special world of sophisticated irony and word games.

6908. Franzini, Haydée. Pueblo seco. B.A., Emecé, 1976. 239 p.

Novel depicts, in a series of vignettes which are both varied and complementary, the life of a community—its identity and its struggle to survive. Extraordinary use of language.

6909. Gallardo, Sara. Historia de los galgos. B.A., Editorial Alfa Argentina, 1975. 138 p.

An extraordinary novelette in which the main characters are dogs whose activities and relationships are interpreted through the eyes of a first-person narrator. It should be emphasized that the dogs, in a very subtle, effective way, are used to examine certain human characteristics such as love, loyalty, jealousy, betrayal.

6910. Gambaro, Griselda. Ganarse la muerte. B.A., Ediciones de la Flor, 1976. 194 p.

Despair, absurdity, and irony characterize this novel about a girl who suffers abandonment, exploitation, and brutality. Helpless against systematic, institutionalized forces of repression which are beyond her comprehension and control, she is, in fact, an archetypal victim. This essential theme is developed through an extraordinary style reminiscent in part of Kafka, and in part of American practitioners of black humor.

6911. Gorostiza, Carlos. Los cuartos oscuros. B.A., Editorial Sudamericana, 1976. 260 p.

The protagonist in this novel searches for self-identity, for a meaning to his existence and to the puzzling, enigmatic nature of the situations in which he finds himself. Interesting development of the tension that exists between the desire for revelation and the ability to grasp it.

6912. Grimani, Santiago. El fiat verde. B.A., Intersea, 1976. 94 p.

Collection of 12 short stories in which the author deals in a humorous way with certain aspects of modern culture and technological society.

6913. Gudiño Kieffer, Eduardo. La hora de María y el pájaro de oro. B.A., Losada, 1975. 165 p.

This collection of narratives is divided into three parts, the first and second containing very short pieces and the third devoted to one long selection. The subtle irony and suggestiveness of author's earlier work continues to be present but an additional element—the unexpected, the magical—is found also, as the reader is challenged by a new order of reality.

6914. ———. Será por eso que la quiero tanto. B.A., Emecé, 1975. 244 p.

This extraordinary novel deals with the experiences of a family which has recently moved from rural Argentina to B.A. In a series of 21 episodes divided into five major sections, the experiences of the family as it relates to the lower elements of the city are recounted. The action occurs in an urban environment where naïveté can prove fatal and promises illusory. Lurking behind the temptations of hope and excitement is the pervasive evil which corrupts and eventually destroys all it touches. Though the events and circumstances of the work have a social basis, this is essentially a metaphysical novel.

6915. Guido, Beatriz. Piedra libre. B.A., Editorial Galera, 1976. 203 p.

Collection of eight stories which combine elements of fantasy and realism. The title story was the basis of a Torre Nilson film. An interesting addition to this collection is the "línea argumental" of the film version of "Piedra Libre."

6916. Jofre Barroso, Haydee M. ed. Así escriben los argentinos. B.A., Ediciones Orión, 1975. 279 p.

Anthology of narratives and excerpts from longer works by 14 well-known Argentine authors, e.g., Sábato, Borges, Lynch.

6917. Jordán, Joaquín ed. Narrativa argentina '75. B.A., Lumen Latinoamericana, 1975. 246 p.

Anthology of short stories in which many of the principal contemporary Argentine writers are represented.

6918. Kordon, Bernardo. Bairestop. B.A., Losada, 1975. 111 p.

Kordon continues his interest in *porteño* customs in this work as he focuses on the aspirations and activities of lower-class city dwellers. The work is divided, effectively, into two parts, one portraying the blacks of B.A., at the time of Argentine independence and the other depicting *peronista* supporters of the early 1970s. The unity of the two parts is found in the common, fervently expressed hope for a better Argentine society.

6919. ———. Todos los cuentos. B.A., Ediciones Corregidor, 1975. 360 p.

Collection of 28 short costumbristic narratives, the earliest of which bears the date 1948 and the latest 1972.

6920. Lancelotti, Mario A. Las estatuas. B.A., Emecé, 1975. 226 p.

In this excellent collection of 21 brief narratives, the author has been able to infuse everyday events with the magical, lyrical qualities, and to isolate in a haunting manner subtle, unspoken desires, fears, forebodings. Extraordinary economy of style.

6921. Lastra, Héctor. Cuentos. B.A., Ediciones Corregidor, 1976. 160 p.

This collection of 22 short stories includes the first two works published by Lastra plus four of his previously unpublished narratives. With precision and extraordinary choice of words he is able to capture the most delicate nuances of feeling especially in the narratives that deal with the protagonists' attempts to cope with the emptiness and meaninglessness of their worlds.

6922. Lynch, Marta. Los dedos de la mano. B.A., Editorial Sudamericana, 1976. 235 p.

In the 13 stories of her latest collection, Lynch presents a series of characters who face cruel, often tragic circumstances. Some are victims of violence, others of injustices or forces beyond their control, but all are developed masterfully within the special limits of the stories. Particularly noteworthy is "Hotel Taorima" in which reality blends subtly into fantasy.

6923. Martínez Estrada, Ezequiel. Cuentos completos. Edición preparada por Roberto Yahni. Madrid, Alianza Editorial, 1975. 468 p.

Collection of Martínez Estrada's 20 stories. A very useful feature of this edition is the fact that the works are dated according to the time they were written as opposed to publication. Martínez Estrada's stories are interesting both in their own right and as a point of comparison to his essays.

6924. Mastrángelo, Carlos ed. Veinticinco cuentos argentinos magistrales. B.A., Plus Ultra, 1975. 334 p.

Critical anthology of stories by major authors beginning with Echevarría and ending with Cortázar. Useful prologue and notes.

6925. Medina, Enrique. El duke. B.A., Eskol, 1976. 188 p.

This novel records the interior monologue of an ex-prize fighter whose life has been filled with violence but little success. The interspersion of occasional narrative sequences add to the readers' understanding of a corrupt society which promotes immorality. The content could be described as crude—even exceedingly so—but it serves as an effective denunciation of moral failure.

6926. ———. Las hienas. B.A., Sudamericana, 1975. 215 p.

Reminiscent of Cortázar's narratives but not comparable to their qualities are the nine stories in this collection in which the author attempts to force us as readers to come to terms with unusual, uncanny, and shocking phenomena not part of our normal perception of reality. The title story of the collection is the most successful.

6927. ———. Strip-tease. B.A., Ediciones Corregidor, 1976. 520 p.

A provocative, controversial novel which presents the sordidness of life in the starkest sort of language. Through the perspective of the first person narrator, the reader is returned over and over again to shoddy, disgusting entertainment of cheap strip joints where performers and viewers alike are mutually exploited and dehumanized. The ultimate effect of the novel's constant, obsessive dwelling on human sexuality at its most degraded level is to convince the reader of evil. The work is emetic—intentionally so—rather than erotic.

6928. ———. Transparente. B.A., Editorial Sudamericana, 1974. 245 p.

Unusual, provocative novel in which the first-person narrator, a provincial woman, evokes her childhood and adult experiences in rural Argentina and B.A. Effectively juxtaposed are her recollections of family love, parental strength and concern, and the degrading experiences of city life. The illustrative, "family album type" and newspaper pictures which accompany the text provide the reader with a special sense of historical background.

6929. Mignoga, Eduardo. Cuatrocasas. La Habana, Casa de las Américas, 1976. 112 p.

Co-winner of the 1976 Casa de las Américas short-story prize. The background for the stories in this collection is a town called Cuatrocasas—a mythical place in which the lives of two major families are traced. Some of the characters appear in more than one story, thus giving the reader an insight into multiple aspects of their development. The author's attempt at giving coherence and relatedness to the stories is contrived but the overall effect is successful. The influence of García Márquez is notable, but the work is commendable for its humor—especially its irony—and the ingenious use of narrative point of view.

6930. Mujica Láinez, Manuel. Sergio. B.A., Sudamericana, 1976. 243 p.

This novel does not match author's previous works but offers flashes of the brilliant blend of satire and fantasy to which readers of Mujica have become accustomed. Sergio, the protagonist, cursed by his physical attractiveness, is the object of persecution during his picaresque wanderings through society.

6931. Mumpeu, Eduardo. La clave. B.A., Emecé, 1976. 243 p.

This collection of 14 short stories was given the Premio Emecé for 1975-76. All of the selections fall readily within the category of fantastic fiction as the author finds his inspiration in esoteric philosophies, alchemy, and mysterious apparitions.

6932. Navarro, Ana. Después del incendio. B.A., Stilcograf, 1975. 110 p.

In a straightforward, conventional fashion the author of this novel depicts the alienation of an Argentine social class which was not able to establish its identity firmly.

6933. Onega, Gladys S. ed. Los cuentistas de Rosario. Rosario, Arg., Editorial La Cachimba, 1975. 184 p.

An anthology which contains the stories of seven authors. The works, which are existential in nature, are unified by the common theme of "man alone" facing circumstances which overwhelm him.

6934. Orgambide, Pedro. Historias con tangos y corridos. La Habana, Casa de las Américas, 1976. 183 p.

Co-winner of the 1976 Casa de las Américas short story prize. Some of the stories in the collection are realistic, others could more appropriately be categorized as fantastic. Both rural and urban environments form the backgrounds for works which are not up to the artistic level of previous writings by the author.

6935. Peltzer, Federico. Un país y otro país. B.A., Emecé, 1976. 254 p.

The 17 short stories in this collection are divided into three categories: the first includes stories of a more traditionally realistic type; the second contains mythical, legendary selections; the third presents stories of a mysterious, fantastic nature.

6936. Piglia, Ricardo. Nombre falso. B.A., Siglo XXI Editores, 1975. 172 p.

The protagonists of the narratives in this collection have in common their confinement within the prison of failure or their experience with violence. The most interesting and original narrative is "Homenaje a Roberto Arlt" which combines elements of detective fiction with those of textual criticism.

6937. Pueyrredón, Victoria. Acabo de morir. B.A., Emecé, 1976. 161 p.

Many of the 17 stories of this collection contain unexpected, magical elements but they start from a base of conventional reality. Failure, the loss of illusions, and the loss of innocence are some of the themes developed.

6938. Puig, Manuel. El beso de la mujer araña. Barcelona, Seix Barral, 1976. 286 p.

Puig's fourth novel is based on a succession of dialogues between two prisoners—one a homosexual, the other a political activist—who share the same cell in a B.A. prison. Interspersed with their dialogues are impersonal documents in the form of footnotes which deal with theories of sexual orientation and interior monologues which provide unusual insights into the backgrounds of the two main characters. The dialogues, which consist largely of the recounting of old movies, serve as a significant corollary to the present reality of the prisoners, and as the novel evolves, the reader is witness to a subtle evolution in the attitudes of the two men. The style of the work, which is deceptively simple, reveals a mature writer, one with an uncanny ear for language and an unusual ability to articulate delicately and imaginatively the structural elements of a novel.

6939. Sánchez Sorondo, Fernando. Jardín de invierno. B.A., Editorial Sudamericana, 1976. 161 p.

A highly intellectualized novel in which the concept of the journey is fundamental. In this work the protagonist experiences both an exterior journey and one into himself in quest of personal meaning.

6940. Schóo, Ernesto. Función de gala. B.A., Editorial Sudamericana, 1976. 149 p. (Col. Espejo)

This novel is a representation of the B.A. of the 1920s and 1930s with particular emphasis on the selfish, decadent lifestyle of the characters depicted. At the same time it should be noted that the narrative is not simply an attempt to evoke a narrow slice of history. It is rather, an artistic endeavor with no referential pretentions. An interesting work worthy of critical attention.

6941. Seiguerman, Osvaldo. Todo puede ser peor. B.A., Ediciones de la Flor, 1973. 172 p.

An existential novel in which the first person narrator experiences the most profound alienation. The society he is trapped in is selfish, boring, valueless. Well aware that he shares fully in these negative characteristics, he experiences a completely meaningless existence.

6942. Sociedad Argentina de Escritores, *Buenos Aires.* Nuestros cuentos. Prólogo de Roger Plá. B.A., Talleres Literarios, 1975. 130 p.

Anthology of short stories by 18 Argentine authors most of whom have not published their fiction previously. Stories range from the fantastic, to the psychological, to the traditionally realistic. They are, as is to be expected, uneven in quality, but several show originality.

6943. Sorrentino, Fernando. El mejor de los mundos posibles. B.A., Plus Ultra, 1976. 206 p.

Collection of 11 narratives which satirize, often in brilliant fashion, such things as Latin American bureauracy, the self-importance of intellectuals, and the sometimes excessive concern for the rights of criminals.

6944. Tizón, Héctor. Sota de bastos, caballo de espadas. B.A., Crisis, 1975. 406 p.

This novel, which is set temporally in the colonial period, is reminiscent of the chronicles with its magical elements, its exaggerations, its unusual choice of details for elaboration, its strangely heroic and antiheroic characters.

6945. Togno, María Elena *ed.* Así escriben las mujeres. B.A., Ediciones Orión, 1975. 187 p.

Anthology of 13 narratives by Argentine women writers all of whom have published extensively. Among the better known are Silvina Ocampo, Marta Lynch, and Silvina Bullrich.

6946. Valenzuela, Luisa. Aquí pasan cosas raras. B.A., Ediciones de la Flor, 1975. 134 p.

Collection of 27 stories of varying lengths in which irreverent humor, irony, whimsy, and a profound sense of the absurd are prominent elements.

URUGUAY

6947. Banchero, Andersen. Triste calle cortada. Montevideo, Ediciones de la Banda Oriental, 1975. 79 p.

In this collection of seven stories, an atmosphere of melancholy is sustained not only through skillful use of imagery but through the fate of protagonists who have lacked the inner strength to cope with life or who have been overcome by circumstances beyond their control. The sad comprehension of human failure is most poignantly developed in the title story of the collection.

Benedetti, Mario and others. Cuentos de la revolución. See item 6469.

6948. Dinardi, Alberto. El hombre que fué payaso. Montevideo, Talleres Gráficos de la Comunidad del Sur, 1975. 74 p.

The five short stories in this book deal with problems of alienation, failure, unrealized dreams.

6949. Espínola, Francisco. Cuentos completos. Montevideo, Arca, 1975. 146 p.

This collection of Espínola's short stories will be of interest to students of Uruguayan literature. Basically a traditional realist, his stories give emphasis to the anecdotal. Especially in the stories with rural settings, an attempt is made to portray "typical" speech patterns through the characters.

6950. Galeano, Eduardo. Canción de nosotros. B.A., Sudamericana, 1975. 243 p.

Co-winner with *Mascaró el cazador americano* by Conti of the Casa de las Américas novel prize for 1975. This novel deals with the crisis of contemporary Uruguay. In a richly ironic fashion Galeano reveals the plight of his compatriots who face, without either hope or concrete solutions, a devastating social, political and economic situation. The shattered myth of Uruguay as the South American model of progress, democracy, and well-being is presented with subtle insight.

6951. Hierro Gambardella, Luis. El sórdido clamor y otros relatos. Montevideo, Geminis, 1974. 123 p.

The theme of *soledad* links the nine somber narratives of this collection.

6952. Luna, Angel María. Cuentos de los domingos. Montevideo, Arca, 1974. 126 p.

Collection of 30 stories which capture the solitude of rural Uruguay.

6953. Manini Ríos, Carlos. Romeo en los infiernos. Montevideo, Talleres de Imprenta Letras, 1973. 256 p.

A novel written in diary form in which the first-person narrator reveals his suffering, confusion, and failure.

6954. Mattos, Tomás de. Libros y perros. Montevideo, Ediciones de la Banda Oriental, 1975. 100 p.

Collection of four previously unpublished short stories in which suspense, the unusual ending, and the presence of mystery within the apparently commonplace are important ingredients.

6955. Moreira, Omar. Rosendo y sus manos. Montevideo, Ediciones de la Banda Oriental, 1976. 92 p.

A novelette based on the drought of 1942-43.

6956. Onetti, Juan Carlos. Tan triste como ellos y otros cuentos. Prólogo de Joaquín Marco. Barcelona, Editorial Lumen, 1976. 336 p.

Collection of 18 of Onetti's narratives—all previously published.

6957. Ricci, Julio. El grongo. Cuentos. Montevideo, Geminis, 1976. 155 p.

Ricci's second collection of short stories (the first entitled *Los maniáticos*, 1970) contains 12 selections which could be classified as psychological. The author is especially effective when dealing with his protagonists' dreams and illusions. Essentially characters that live within themselves, they are incapable of translating their thoughts into action or of adjusting to the reality that surrounds them.

LITERARY CRITICISM AND HISTORY

ARGENTINA

6958. Anderson Imbert, Enrique. El éxito de Borges (CAM, 208:5, sept./oct. 1976, p. 199p212)

A meditation, embellished with many personal anecdotes, on Borges' ambiguous fame. An interesting document in the "secret history" of Argentine literature by one of its great critics.

6959. Avellaneda, Andrés. Encuentro, pérdida, búsqueda en los cuentos de Daniel Moyano (HISPA, 1:3, 1973, p. 25-38)

Application of the methods of Tzvetan Todorov to a reading of Moyano's short stories. While interesting as a critical exercise, analysis of Moyano often gets entangled in the method. Should be made part of a larger text.

6960. ——— and others eds. Ocho escritores: Martínez Estrada, Marechal, Borges, Bioy Casares, Quiroga, Groussac Lugones, Macedonio Fernández por ocho periodistas. B.A., Timerman Editores, 1976. 127 p.

Important contribution to the history of Argentine literary journalism. Consists of essays and interviews which appeared in the supplement to *La Opinión* by Martínez Estrada, Marechal, Borges, Bioy, Macedonio Fernández, etc. Criteria applied in selection of examples is not included.

6961. Bastos, María Luisa. "Contorno", "Ciudad", "Gaceta Literaria": tres enfoques de una realidad (HISPA, 2:4/5, 1973, p. 49-64)

Essay in literary history— in the best sense of the word. Bastos studies three magazines which all set out to analyze and criticize the cultural and intellectual life of Argentina. The key names here are David Viñas, Noé Jitrik, Adolfo Prieto, and Juan José Sebrelli. Valuable document.

6962. Battistella, Ernesto H. El lenguaje extensional de "Funes el Memorioso" (USB/RVF, 5/6, 1976/1977, p. 7-17)

Interesting discussion of "Funes el Memorioso" within the context of language philosophy and structuralism. Its principal drawback is that it loses its object (Borges' story) in the process. Battistella might also have pointed out that Funes first appears in an essay on Joyce—as Joyce's ideal reader.

6963. Books Abroad. An international literary quarterly. Univ. of Oklahoma Press. Vol. 50, No. 3, Summer 1976- . Norman.

Entire issue devoted to Julio Cortázar reproduces papers delivered at conference in his honor held in Univ. of Oklahoma, Norman, Nov. 1975. For individual annotations, see items 6970, 6974, 6978, 6989 and 6994.

6964. Borges, Jorge Luis and Ernesto Sábato. Dialogos. B.A., Emecé Editores, 1976. 198 p.

While these seven dialogues between Borges and Sábato, organized, recorded, and edited by Orlando Barone, seem at times to have been written by Samuel Beckett, they contain fascinating remarks by both men. Important document in Argentine literary history.

6965. Borinsky, Alicia. Macedonio: su proyecto novelístico (HISPA, 1:1, 1972, p. 31-48)

Important presentation of Macedonio Fernández' anti-realist and humorous esthetics. Borinsky reveals his influence on later work of Borges, Cortázar, and Néstor Sánchez.

6966. Brody, Robert. Twos and threes in Cortázar's *Rayuela* (*in* Beck, Mary Ann and others. The analysis of Hispanic text: current trends in methodology. Jamaica, N.Y., CUNY, York College, Dept. of Foreign Languages [and] Bilingual Press Editorial Bilingüe, 1976, p. 113-129)

Meditation on the role of the numbers two and three in *Rayuela*. Brody refers in a footnote to René Girard's triangular desire and in his text to the desire expressed in *Rayuela* to transcend binary oppositions.

6967. Cantarino, Vicente. Borges, filósofo de Dios: *argumentum ornithologicum* (ICC/T, 31:2, mayo/agosto 1976, p. 288-299)

Ingenious attempt to relate Borges "Argumentum ornithologicum" (*El Hacedor*) to the corpus of scholastic thought concerned with deriving the existence of God. Cantarino notes that Borges begins his meditation by saying, "Cierro los ojos y veo...", but he does not pursue this paradox, which would have led him to the realm of imagination (and Bishop Berkeley) instead of the scholastics.

6968. Catania, Carlos. Sábato: entre la idea y la sangre. Prólogo de Isaac Felipe Azofeifa. San José, Editorial Costa Rica, 1973. 206 p. bibl.

Attempt at literary criticism by one who would not like to be defined as a literary critic. Passionate essay lacking in substance. No index, no bibliography.

6969. Coulson, Graciela. Leopoldo Marechal: la aventura metafísica (HISPA, 3:7, 1974, p. 29-39)

Study of *Adán Buenosayres* as an enactment of the theme of *homo viator* which is a close and thematic reading of Marechal's text and should be of use to Marechal critics. Coulson does not note Cortázar's review of the novel, in *Realidad* (1948), which would have provided a link between Marechal and the *Boom*.

6970. Filer, Malva E. The ambivalence of the hand in Cortázar's fiction (UO/BA, 50:3, Summer 1976, p. 595-599)

Catalogues appearance of hands in Cortázar's writings. While no startling conclusions are reached ("the hand in Cortázar's fiction is an ambivalent if not altogether threatening presence"), the essay is a useful delineation of a motif.

6971. Flint, J.M. Politics and society in the novels of Roberto Arlt (IAA, 2:2, 1976, p. 155-163, bibl.)

Intelligent attempt to define the ideological content of Arlt's writings. Flint does not take sides in the Boedo-Florida squabble concerning Arlt: he points out how much Arlt took from Dostoevsky and how his (Arlt's) writings define the problems of a society rather than the means to resolve those problems.

6972. Foster, David William. Literatura argentina y realidad política: David Viñas and sociological criticism in Argentina (IAA, 1, 1975, p. 253-277, bibl.)

Detailed examination of David Viñas' literary criticism with the intention of "locating" him in a tradition of sociological literary studies. Essay that is occasionally difficult to understand. Builds on earlier studies by Emir Rodríguez Monegal.

6973. Fuss, Albert. Ernesto Sábato, *Sobre héroes y tumbas* (UH/RJ, 26, 1975, p. 343-364)

A general consideration of Sábato's esthetics and writings with special emphasis on *Sobre héroes y tumbas*. Fuss investigates in detail Sábato's assertion that literature is closely related to dream and myth.

6974. González Echevarria, Roberto. Los *reyes*: Cortázar's mythology of writing (UO/BA, 50:3, Summer 1976, p. 548-557)

Excellent essay uses Cortázar's early text *Los reyes* as a model for deriving a theory of his aims as a writer. Interestingly, this theory runs somewhat against the grain of what Cortázar himself says of *Los reyes* in his interview with Luis Harss (*Los nuestros*).

6975. González Tuñón, Raúl. La literatura resplandeciente. B.A., Editorial Boedo-Silbalba, 1976. 237 p.

Journalistic pieces document important aspect of Argentine literary journalism: the reception of 20th-century (and earlier) literature and its interpretation for a mass-medium. González Tuñón's remarks on the Argentine avant-garde will be of special interest in this context. Unfortunately there is no list of sources indicating when and where these pieces appeared.

6976. Gossy, Hélène. L'itinéraire spirituel de Silvio, héros du roman *El juguete rabioso* de Roberto Arlt, 1926 (UR/EHLIA, 1973, p. 55-82)

Interesting "close-reading" of Arlt's early novel, with emphasis on sociological aspects of text. Gossy's title suggests a link with St. Bonaventure, but this is not pursued. No bibliographic references.

6977. Gyurko, Lanin A. Borges and the theme of the double (IAA, 2:3, 1976, p. 193-226, bibl.)

Literature: Prose Fiction, Argentina / 429

A catalogue of Borges' use of the double motif in stories, poems, and essays. Lacks references to the critical material on this subject and relies on intuition (as opposed to Freud or Jung or even Robert Rogers) to decipher this "enigma."

6978. Hernández, Ana María. Vampires and vampiresses: a reading of 62 (UO/BA, 50:3, Summer 1976, p. 570-576)

Interesting discussion of the vampire in Cortázar. This essay together with Cortázar's own note on the gothic (see *HLAS 38:6837*) should open a new chapter in Cortázar studies, including his translations of Poe.

6979. Jitrik, Noé. Hacia una lectura antinarcisista: *Matar a título* de Arturo Cerretani (RCLL, 1:1, 1975, p. 151-156)

Attempt to "locate" three novellas by Arturo Cerretani, Argentine writer whose career began in the 1930s, in the literary context of 1974, year of Roa Bastos' *Yo, El Supremo* and Carpentier's *El recurso del método*. Jitrik calls Cerretani's work a "prolongación ultrarrefinada" of Roberto Arlt's, a problematic study of the narrating "I."

6980. ———. La novela futura de Macedonio Fernández, con un retrato discontinuo, una antología y una bibliografía. Caracas, Univ. Central de Venezuela, Ediciones de la Biblioteca, 1973. 144 p., bibl. (Nuevos planteamientos, 11)

Useful introduction to Fernández' "novelistic" writing, and to Macedonio in general. Divided into: 1) portrait of Macedonio derived from quotations by and about him; 2) essay by Jitrik on Macedonio's "novela futura," and 3) bibliography by and on Macedonio by Horacio Jorge Becco.

6981. Lagmanovich, David *ed*. Estudios sobre los cuentos de Julio Cortázar. Barcelona, Ediciones Hispam, 1975. 227 p., bibl. (Col. Blanquerna)

Consists of 13 articles on different aspects of Cortázar's short stories: Jaime Alazraki's thematic comparison of Borges and Cortázar is excellent as is Alicia Borinsky's more speculative essay. A good collection of essays on the subject.

6982. ———. Rasgos distintivos de algunos cuentos de Julio Cortázar (HISPA, 1:1, 1972, p. 5-15, table)

Attempt to reduce Cortázar's stories to a limited number of models, using methods derived from linguistics. While the results are interesting, the apparatus is so difficult to use that one wonders if the effort was worthwhile. Supposedly, the preview of a larger study.

6983. Lewald, H. Ernest. Eduardo Mallea. Boston, Mass., Twayne Publishers, 1977. 118 p.

Solid general introduction to the life and works of Eduardo Mallea which is not a work of speculative criticism.

6984. Neyra, Joaquín. Ernesto Sábato. B.A., Ediciones Culturales Argentinas, Ministerio de Cultura y Educación, 1973. 170 p., illus., plates (Serie Argentinos en las letras)

Impressionistic "life-and-works" study. Includes useful selection of documents by Sábato on various subjects (from thermodynamics to Adolph Eichmann). No Index.

6985. Paley-Francescato, Martha. Entrevista: Adolfo Bioy Casares (HISPA, 3:9, 1975, p. 75-81)

Interviews with Bioy Casares (or Borges) are usually ironic farses—with the interviewer playing the part of straightman. Although this one is no exception, Bioy makes some interesting statements about himself, Borges, and literature in general.

6986. ———. Entrevista: Marta Lynch (HISPA, 4:10, 1975, p. 33-44)

Useful interview: Lynch speaks about the current Argentine political situation, feminism (in and outside of Argentina), and her work habits. Interesting remarks about her relations with other Argentine writers.

6987. Piglia, Ricardo. Roberto Arlt: la ficción del dinero (HISPA, 3:7, 1974, p. 25-28)

Short essay (part of larger text) on the role of money in Arlt's work, money taken as a symbol and money in its relation to the power of imagination. Interesting fragment which makes good use of the *Aguafuertes*.

6988. Pintor Genaro, Mercedes. Eduardo Mallea, novelista. San Juan, Editorial Universitaria, Univ. de Puerto Rico, 1976. 277 p., bibl. (Col. Mente y palabra)

Good general introduction to the life and works of Mallea. Useful notes and bibliography. Based on author's dissertation.

6989. Rabassa, Gregory. Lying to Athena: Cortázar and the art of fiction (UO/BA, 50:3, Summer 1976, p. 542-547)

"Open letter" to Cortázar's readers by one of his most important translators, "The approach to Cortázar's works, then, must be carried on in the same spirit as that with which they are written." Rabassa does not explain how this difficult approximation of reader and artist is to be brought about.

6990. Rasi, Humberto M. Jorge Luis Borges y la revista *Los Anales de Buenos Aires* (RIB, 27:2, abril/junio 1977, p. 135-141)

Summary which may surprise many Borges "scholars:" the contents of an important review directed by Borges in which he published (1946-48) material never gathered up in any volume.

6991. Rest, Jaime. Borges y el "pensamiento sistemático" (HISPA, 1:3, 1973, p. 3-23)

Rest documents Borges' fascination with systematic thought together with his skepticism. His conclusion that Borges, like Kafka (though without Kafka's despair), reminds us of our alienation from reality is not new. Worthwhile because of the energy of his readings of Borges' work.

6992. ———. Borges y el universo de los signos (HISPA, 3:7, 1974, p. 3-24)

Interesting reading of Borges in the light of 20th-century language philosophy which does not take into account the three collections of essays Borges published in the 1920s, all of which are concerned with language.

6993. Rodríguez Monegal, Emir. Borges, hacia una lectura poética. Madrid, Ediciones Guadarrama, 1976. 127 p. (Literatura)

The true title of this valuable contribution to Borges studies is *Borges, hacia una poética de la lectura*. Rodríguez Monegal gathers together here three texts first published in English and provides Borges' readers with essays on the relationship between Borges and Paz, on Borges as seen by contemporary French criticism, and on the relationship between Borges' criticism and his fiction.

6994. Safir, Margery A. An erotics of liberation: notes on transgressive behavior in *Rayuela* and *Libro de Manuel* (UO/BA, 50:3, Summer 1976, p. 558-570)

Links "erotic transgressions" in Cortázar's last two novels to "the Western tradition of descent, death and resurrection." An interesting, well-documented study, sometimes tangled in its own jargon.

6995. Sorrentino, Fernando. Siete conversaciones con Jorge Luis Borges. B.A., Casa Prado, 1973. 162 p.

Extremely useful series of interviews: Borges repeats much of what he has been saying for many years, but adds information not found elsewhere. Valuable biographical material as well as information concerning Argentine writers of the early 20th century.

6996. Sosnowski, Saúl. Entrevista: Jorge Luis Borges (HISPA, 3:8, 1974, p. 55-60)

Interviews with Borges must be read by Borges critics, even if they are all, ultimately, exercises in futility. Borges answers questions in ways unrelated to the question, i.e. dialogue of the deaf. This one is useful because of Borges' references to his current style and Macedonio Fernández.

6997. ———. Entrevista: Manuel Puig (HISPA, 1:3, 1973, p. 69-80)

Excellent interview with Puig, who here recounts his life and his literary career. Important summary for readers and critics of Puig and contemporary Argentine literature.

6998. ———. Julio Cortázar (HISPA, 5:13, abril 1976, p. 51-68)

In this interview, Cortázar shows enormous consistency despite the changes, particularly political changes, he has undergone. His life-long desire to change humanity through literature has taken on new vitality as a result of political commitment.

6999. Speck, Paula. *Las fuerzas extrañas:* Leopoldo Lugones y las raíces de la literatura fantástica en el Río de la Plata (IILI/RI, 42:96/97, julio/dic. 1976, p. 411-426)

Excellent review of Lugones' collection of short stories, first published in 1926. Speck uses formalist techniques (Propp) in order to present new aspects of Lugones' work and situates him in the context of River Plate "fantastic literature."

7000. Speratti Piñero, Emma Susana. Judas en la obra de Borges (*in* Homenaje al Instituto de Filología y Literaturas Hispánicas Dr. Amado Alonso en su Cincuentenario, 1923-1973. B.A., Editorial Fernando García Cambeiro, 1975, p. 401-409)

Well-documented summary of Borges' use of the theme of the traitor, with special emphasis on Judas.

7001. Szichman, Mario. Entrevista: David Viñas (HISPA, 1:1, 1972, p. 61-67)

In this interview, David Viñas speaks of his participation in the theater and of his writings in general. His opinions of Cortázar and Sábato are not intended to please followers of those two authors.

7002. Verbitsky, Bernardo. Literatura y conciencia nacional. B.A., Editorial Paidos, 1975. 106 p. (Biblioteca del hombre contemporáneo, 295)

Unsuccessful attempt to demonstrate the existence of an Argentine literary heritage (hence the title) through disconnected essays on Güiraldes, Eduardo Gutiérrez, Mansilla, José Hernández, and Leopoldo Marechal. Of greatest interest is the section on Marechal (nearly half the volume) since it contains biographical data.

7003. Viñas, David. Literatura argentina y realidad política. v. 2, Apogeo de la oligarquía. B.A., Ediciones Siglo Veinte, 1975. 190 p.

By one of Argentina's most important novelists of social consciousness, this collection of essays attempts a sociology of the "generación del ochenta" (Mansilla, Cané, and Martel in particular). It also includes chapters on Florencio Sánchez and Gerchunoff. Important study of the *porteño Zeitgeist* of the late 19th and early 20th centuries. For vol. 1, *De Sarmiento a Cortázar*, see *HLAS* 34:2821.

PARAGUAY

7004. Aldana, Adelfo L. La cuentística de Augusto Roa Bastos. Montevideo, Ediciones Geminis, 1975. 218 p., bibl. (Col. Novus orbis)

General introduction to Roa Bastos' short story writing: Aldana first locates Roa Bastos in the context of Paraguayan writing, then considers the ways in which Roa Bastos deals with that tradition (mixing social criticism with modern narrative techniques) and then analyzes Roa Bastos' short stories in terms of style and structure. Useful guide, although critically unsophisticated.

7005. Andreu, Jean L. Aventurisme, sadisme et révolution: notes sur un personage de *Yo, El Supremo* (UTIEH/C, 27, 1976, p. 11-20)

Essay on the figure of Charles Andreu-Legard in the context of Roa Bastos' novel. By means of isolating this particular figure, Andreu gains access to this perplexing text. Good introduction.

7006. Bareiro Saguier, Rubén. El tema del exilio en la narrativa paraguaya contemporánea (UTIEH/C, 14, 1970, p. 79-96)

Excellent introduction to the phenomenon of exile in Paraguayan life and letters. Bareiro Saguier traces the historical process of exile since the Chaco War (1932-35) until the present and then shows how it functions in literature, with particular emphasis on the works of Roa Bastos and Gabriel Casaccia.

7007. Foster, David William. Augusto Roa Bastos' *I, the Supreme*: the image of the dictator (LALR, 4:7, Fall/Winter 1975, p. 31-36)

Review of Roa Bastos' difficult novel. Foster includes an "anatomy" of the text which may serve as a guide to other readers.

7008. Miliani, Domingo. El dictador: objeto narrativo de *Yo, El Supremo* (RCLL, 2:4, 1976, p. 103-119)

Attempt to use linguistic techniques, some taken from Max Bense, to analyze Roa Bastos' complex novel about the reign of Dr. Francia. More an outline than an essay, this text, while very interesting, ought to be enlarged and transformed into a unity.

7009. Rodríguez Alcalá de González Oddone, Beatriz; Ramiro Domínguez; Adriano Irala Burgos; and Josefina Plá. Comentarios sobre *Yo, El Supremo*. Asunción, Ediciones Club del Libro No. 1, 1975. 66 p., illus.

Good collection of essays on this novel. Of particular interest is Ramiro Domínguez' applications of recent linguistic techniques in his analysis of the text.

7010. Zokner, Cecilia Teixeira de Oliveira. A palabra *tierra* e o vocabulário sócio-hierárquico em *Hijo de hombre*; relações (UFP/RL, 23, 1975, p. 71-80, bibl.)

Utilization of the most recent linguistic techniques in literary analysis (Greimas, Ulrich Ricken) in order to see how Roa Bastos' social "message" corresponds to his literary style. Interesting technique and interesting because this is a Brazilian studying a Spanish-American literary text.

URUGUAY

7011. Ludmer, Josefina. Onetti: "La Novia (carta) Robada," a Faulkner (HISPA, 3:9, 1974, p. 3-19)

Important study of intertextuality in the work of Juan Carlos Onetti. "La Novia Robada" is juxtaposed to Faulkner's "A Rose for Emily." Ludmer utilizes Lacanian techniques to reveal the hidden patterns in Onetti's text and how they echo Faulkner. Dense but fascinating.

7012. Mathieu, Corina S. and Víctor C. Dahl. The contemporary Uruguayan novel: reflections of a society in crisis (LALR, 4:8, Spring/Summer 1976, p. 57-66)

Assessment of contemporary Uruguayan literature in the light of the political crisis of that country. A well-intentioned, sincere essay that nevertheless remains on the surface of these matters.

7013. Onetti, Juan Carlos. Requiem for Faulkner. Montevideo. Arca Editorial, 1976? 235 p., bibl. (Col. Arca/calicanto, 8)

The modest "J.R." who compiled this collection of Onetti's contributions to *Marcha*, (literary articles published 1953-71; interviews, 1966-75) has done all readers of Onetti a service. This volume fills in many blank spaces in the career of a great writer. One might hope for some explanatory notes in a subsequent edition.

7014. Torres Fierro, Danubio. Recent Uruguayan literature: an assessment (UCSD/NS, 5:1, 1975, p. 113-116)

A short essay which constitutes an *aggiornamento* with regard to Uruguay. Torres Fierro concentrates on writers born (in the main) in the early 1930s and shows how the current crisis in Uruguayan politics has led these writers to take a political stance in their work.

7015. Verani, Hugo J. Los comienzos: tres cuentos de Juan Carlos Onetti anteriores a *El Pozo* (HISPA, 1:2, 1972, p. 27-34)

Extremely useful note on Onetti's earliest writings. This essay points out the need to have these stories and Onetti's journalistic writings somehow added to his *Obras completas*. Verani emphasizes the unity of Onetti's *oeuvre*.

POETRY

HUMBERTO M. RASI

Dean, School of Graduate Studies
Andrews University

RUBEN A. GAMBOA

Assistant Professor of Spanish
Department of Foreign Languages
Mills College

PEDRO LASTRA

Professor of Spanish
Department of Hispanic Languages
State University of New York at
Stony Brook

ESTHER PEREYRA-SUAREZ

Professor of Spanish
Department of Foreign Languages
San Jose State University

BETTY TYREE OSIEK

Professor of Spanish
Department of Foreign Languages
Southern Illinois University at
Edwardsville

CAROLYN MORROW

Associate Professor of Spanish
Department of Languages
University of Utah

OSCAR HAHN

Assistant Professor of Spanish
Department of Spanish and Portuguese
University of Iowa

CORINA MATHIEU-HIGGINBOTHAM

Associate Professor of Spanish
Department of Foreign Languages
University of Nevada, Las Vegas

ELIANA RIVERO

Associate Professor of Spanish
Department of Romance Languages
University of Arizona

EL CRECIENTE VOLUMEN DE LA PRODUCCION poética hispanoamericana y de su contorno crítico ha aconsejado una reorganización de las tareas propias de esta sección. Nueve son los colaboradores que han reseñado publicaciones recientes de creación o análisis correspondientes a los siglos XIX y XX: México (C. Morrow); América Central y Panamá (R.A. Gamboa); Antillas hispanas (E. Rivero); Colombia y Venezuela (B.T. Osiek); Ecuador, Perú y Bolivia (P. Lastra); Chile (O. Hahn); Uruguay y Paraguay (E. Pereyra-Suárez); Argentina (C. Mathieu-Higginbotham); coordinación y estudios generales (H.M. Rasi). Las acotaciones que siguen tienen el propósito de subrayar nombres, rasgos y tendencias que se destacan entre los trabajos analizados.
ANTOLOGIAS: Merecen mención las antologías dedicadas a la poesía de Argentina (item 7023), Colombia (items 7016 y 7031), Cuba (items 7019 y 7021), Ecuador (item 7024), El Salvador (item 7022), y Panamá (item 7027); así también como una selección de poesía afroantillana (item 7028) y una muestra de poetas peruanos contemporáneos (item 7030).
LIBROS DE POESIA: Sobresalen algunos volúmenes sustanciales que reúnen la obra de poetas conocidos como Mariano Melgar (item 7116); Luis Carlos López (item 7108); Vicente Huidobro (item 7095); León de Greiff (item 7081); Jorge Carrera Andrade (item 7056); Germán Pardo García (item 7131); Otto-Raúl González (item 7078); Ricardo E. Molinari (item 7120); Ernesto Mejía Sánchez (item 7115); Alvaro Figueredo (item 7069); Juan Gelman (item 7073); y Javier Heraud (item 7090).
ESTUDIOS: Gracias al análisis cuidadoso de various críticos, el perfil literario de varios poetas se percibe ahora con más nitidez o resulta más accesible para el estudioso. Contribuyen a ello los trabajos centrados en la obra de Rafael Pombo (item 7208), María Eugenia Vaz Ferreira (item 7215), Guillermo Valencia (item 7227), Julio Herrera y Reissig (item 7212), Andrés Eloy Blanco (item 7224), Delmira Agustini (item 7222), César Vallejo (items 7191 y 7221), León de Greiff (item 7214), Jorge Luis Borges (item 7177), Xavier Villaurrutia (items 7190 y 7207), Nicolás Guillén (item 7203), Pablo Neruda (item 7220), Martín Adán (item 7230), y Octavio Paz (item 7189).

POETAS: Tres poetas establecidos han publicado obras de importancia durante el período considerado: Octavio Paz, *Vuelta*; Enrique Lihn, *París: situación irregular*; y Gonzalo Rojas, *Oscuro*. Entre los poetas de promociones más próximas, varios se encuentran en trayectoria ascendente: César Calvo, Hugo Gutiérrez Vega, Oscar Hahn, Waldo Rojas, Juan Gonzalo Rose, Claudio Ross, Desiderio Macías Silva y Manuel Silva [HMR].

BALANCE: *México*: Se advierte una disminución de las preocupaciones sociopolíticas y una creciente influencia del surrealismo, especialmente de André Breton [CM]. *Antillas hispanas*: La nueva poesía caribeña sigue dominada por la forma conversacional que la producción lírica de Cuba ha impuesto desde la década del 1960, a excepción de las formas experimentales de la poesía dominicana (grupo de la "Poesía Sorprendida"). Lo más significativo de la poesía puertorriqueña es la producción de textos de protesta "niuyorriqueños," ya dentro de la literatura étnica de los Estados Unidos. La preferencia de los críticos continúa girando en torno a las figuras clásicas: Martí, Guillén y Casal. Se echan de menos trabajos sobre otros poetas destacados, como Julia de Burgos. Se mantiene el interés crítico y antológico por la poesía afroantillana y negrista. El poeta de mayor influencia es, sin duda, Nicolás Guillén. Con la muerte de José Lezama Lima (1912-76) desaparece un importante poeta, ensayista y novelista [ER]. *Colombia y Venezuela*: Con escasas excepciones, las antologías populares y los estudios generales evaluados tienden a la mediocridad. Sería recomendable que las editoriales exigieran más rigor por parte de los poetas y los investigadores. Entre éstos se destaca, por la calidad sobresaliente de sus trabajos, el crítico colombiano Héctor Orjuela. La muerte del innovador León de Greiff (1895-1976) ha concitado considerable interés en su poesía. Los nuevos poetas reflejan preocupaciones básicas—amor, muerte, sentido de la existencia—expresadas frecuentemente con un tono pesimista o melancólico y un lenguaje desarticulado que sólo en contados casos alcanza calidad arítistica [BTO]. *Ecuador, Perú y Bolivia*: El proceso literario del Perú vive un momento extraordinario dentro de la región. La vitalidad pujante de su poesía, así también como la alta calidad de las ediciones y los estudios críticos, son dignas de encarecimiento. A la imaginación y rigor de los investigadores se suma el notable auge editorial que experimenta el país. Es marcado el esfuerzo por valorar y difundir las obras de autores del siglo XIX. El Instituto Nacional de Cultura ha asumido la publicación, en ediciones cuidadas y atractivas, de escritores más o menos jóvenes junto a la obra de autores ya consagrados. El trabajo de varias editoriales privadas continúa mejorando en presentación y se ha intensificado también de manera apreciable [PL]. *Chile*: El golpe militar de 1973 influyó fundamentalmente en las direcciones que tomó la poesía chilena de los últimos años. La mayoría de los poetas significativos se encuentra en exilio, lo que produjo diversas consecuencias. Varios de ellos consideraron que este acontecimiento cancelaba una etapa de su producción y publicaron en el extranjero libros en los que incluyeron su obra completa. En el plano temático, incorporaron la protesta contra la situación de Chile y también temas no políticos, relacionados con el país de exilio. En lo formal hubo cierta desorientación con respecto al camino a seguir. En todo caso, la poesía de Nicanor Parra dejó de ser un modelo de escritura para la mayoría. Dos poetas chilenos obtuvieron el premio Casa de las Américas: Omar Lara (1975) y Hernán Miranda (1976). Por otra parte, los poetas residentes en Chile sufrieron los efectos de la censura y la autocensura, al tiempo que la actividad editorial alcanzaba uno de los puntos más bajos en la historia del país [OH]. *Argentina*: El panorama poético no presenta cambios marcados. Los temas tradicionales—el amor, el interrogante metafísico, la historia nacional—sigue teniendo un gran número de cultores. Los críticos se concentraron en estudios generacionales, sin olvidar el centenario del nacimiento de Leopoldo Lugones. El vivo interés por la vida y obra de Alfonsina Storni es un reflejo de las actividades del movimiento feminista [CMH].

ANTHOLOGIES

7016. Abril Rojas, Gilberto *ed.* Poesía joven de Colombia. México, Siglo XXI Editores, 1975. 143 p. (Col. Mínima, 71)

Five to nine poems each from 12 Colombian poets, majority of whom were born in 1940s. Selections from Miguel Méndez Camacho, Juan Gustavo Cobo Borda, Gilberto Abril Rojas, Jaime Jaramillo Escobar, Jaime García Maffla and Mariamercedes Carranza are most representative of the distinctive talents of the young poets. Includes also Giovanni Quessep, Elkin Restrepo, William Agudelo, Henry Luque Muñoz, David Bonells Rovira and Joaquín Peña Gutiérrez. [BTO]

7017. Acosta, Oscar *ed.* Los premios nacionales de literatura Ramón Rosa: 1951-1972. Antología. Prólogo de J. Napoleón Alcerro. Tegucigalpa, Ministerio de Educación Publica, Dirección General de Educación Artística y Extensión Cultural, 1973. 246 p.

Incluye poemas de Luis Andrés Zúñiga, Guillermo Bustillo Reina, Claudia Barrera, Jacobo Bárcamo, Daniel Laínez, Argentina Díaz Lozano, Clementina Suárez, Medardo Mejía y Roberto Sosa. [RG]

7018. Adet, Walter *ed.* Poetas y prosistas salteños: 1582-1973. Salta, Arg., Editorial Eco, 1973. 315 p.

Generosa y exhaustiva recopilación de escritores de la provincia de Salta, con un prólogo que concluye con un conmovido homenaje a Juan Carlos Dávalos. [CMH]

7019. Aray, Edmundo *ed.* Poesía de Cuba. Antología viva. Caracas, Univ. de Carabobo, Dirección de Cultura, 1976. 355 p.

Volumen publicado casi simultáneamente al de Cardenal (véase item 7021) que reúne una selección mucho más reducida (28 poetas), pero abarca más textos de cada uno (6-10). La introducción da una visión generacional de la poesía después de 1959, aunando crítica previa (véase *HLAS 36:4247*) a la acostumbrada información. Ciertas exclusiones inexplicables: Belkis Cuza Malé, Nancy Morejon. [ER]

7020. Becco, Horacio Jorge *ed.* Poetas argentinos contemporáneos. B.A., Extensión Cultural Dos Muñecos, 1974. 123 p., bibl.

Breve antología de 21 poetas entre los que se incluyen a Juan Gelman, Alberto Girri, Aldo Pellegrini, Alejandra Pizarnik y César Fernández Moreno. Es lamentable que el volumen carezca de una introducción. [CMH]

7021. Cardenal, Ernesto *ed.* Poesía cubana de la revolución. México, Editorial Extemporáneos, 1976. 334 p. (Col. A pleno sol, 50)

Una de las dos más recientes antologías de poesía cubano (véase item 7019) que incorpora muestras de la obra de autores desconocidos ("novísimos") y consagrados para completar un total de 54 poetas y 112 textos. El prólogo de Cardenal es un tanto ingenuo pero las notas biobibliográficas ayudan al investigador. Edición manuable y selección representativa. [ER]

7022. Cea, José Roberto *ed.* Antología general de la poesía en El Salvador. San Salvador, Editorial Universitaria de El Salvador, 1971. 482 p., plates.

Larga nómina de poetas con abundante muestra de su labor lírica. José Roberto Cea incluye a aquellos poetas que, según su criterio, han contribuído a la creación del pensamiento poética salvadoreño. [RG]

7023. Crogliano, María Eugenia *ed.* Antología de la poesía argentina: siglos XIX y XX. B.A., Editorial Kapelusz, 1975. 181 p. (Biblioteca grandes obras de la literatura universal, 122)

A pesar de la condensación que impone una obra de esta índole, el antólogo ha logrado presentar con acierto un bosquejo de la poesía argentina. El estudio preliminar es sucinto pero menciona figuras y hechos sobresalientes, así como también define y explica con claridad las tendencias literarias. Buena guía. [CMH]

7024. Garcés Larrea, Cristóbal *ed.* Madrugada: una antología de la poesía ecuatoriana. Quito, Casa de la Cultura Ecuatoriana, 1976. 202 p. (Col. Letras de Ecuador, 16)

Muestras de 15 poetas que integran la promoción ecuatoriana que surgió hacia 1944 en torno a la revista quiteña *Madrugada*. El prólogo y las notas son informativos, aunque el autor ha prescindido de mayores precisiones bibliográficas. El punto más alto de la antología es, sin duda, el extenso poema de César Dávila Andrade, "Boletín y Elegía de las Mitas." [PL]

7025. Hahn, Oscar and **Waldo Rojas** *eds.* Muestra chilena: 1961-1973 (HISPA, 9, 1975, p. 55-73)

Incluye poetas nacidos entre 1935 y 1950, miembros todos de la misma generación. La muestra se basa en un corpus de poemas escritos antes del golpe militar de 1973 y quiere ser el registro de un período cancelado por ese acontecimiento. Los autores considerados son, entre otros: Floridor Pérez, Hernán Lavín Cerda, Federico Schopf, Omar Lara, Jaime Quezada, Manuel Silva y Gonzalo Millán. [OH]

7026. Madrid-Malo, Néstor ed. 50 [i.e. Cincuenta] años de poesía colombiana: 1924-1974. Bogotá, Ediciones Tercer Mundo, 1973. 139 p. (Serie verde. Cuadernitos que despierte el leñador, 18)

With one poem from each of 57 contributors, including one of his own, it is difficult to judge the itinerary of Colombian poetry as editor hopes. Introduction (15 p.) catalogues names and periods with few instances of penetrating critical judgment. Shows excessive reverence for certain poets. [BTO]

7027. Miró, Rodrigo ed. Itinerario de la poesía en Panamá: 1502-1974. Panamá, Editorial Universitaria, 1974. 735 p., bibl.

Antología mayor. Miró hace meticuloso recuento de poetas desde la colonia hasta el presente, ofreciendo generosa muestra de la obra de cada uno de ellos. Es una valiosa aportación al estudio de la lírica panameña. [RG]

7028. Morales, Jorge Luis ed. Poesía afroantillana y negrista: Puerto Rico, República Dominicana, Cuba. Río Piedras, Univ. de Puerto Rico, 1976. 269 p.

Util antología. Prólogo idealizador de la "negritud," que podría completarse con la lectura de un trabajo objetivo (veáse item 7195). [ER]

7029. Nueva antología de la poesía nicaragüense. Managua, Ediciones *El Pez y la Serpiente,* 1972. 261 p.

La antología incluye demasiados nombres. La exigua muestra de la labor de cada una de ellos no permite formarse una idea cabal ni de su labor creadors ni del desarrollo de la lírica en Nicaragua. [RG]

7030. Oviedo, José Miguel ed. Estos 13: Manuel Morales/Antonio Cillóniz/ Jorge Nájar/José Watanabe/Oscar Málaga/Elqui Burgos/Juan Ramírez Ruiz/Abelardo Sánchez León/Feliciano Mejía/Tulio Mora/José Rosas Ribeyro/ José Cerna/Enrique Verástegui. Poemas, documentos. Lima, Mosca Azul Editores, 1973, 189 p.

Más que una antología, este libro es un documento probatorio de la vitalidad de la poesía peruana. En él, Oviedo ofrece textos poéticos y testimoniales que ilustran el fervor de la búsqueda, de las adhesiones y rechazos de una promoción de veras significativa: la que empezó a manifestarse hacia fines de la década del 60 en los movimientos "Hora Zero" y "Estacíon Reunida." Se trata de una promoción fuertemente polémica y hasta agresiva, actitud que registra con largueza la sección documental del volumen.

También es generosa la muestra poética, que da una idea bastante clara de las direcciones que sigue este novedoso y dinámico proceso. Libro de importancia considerable. [PL]

7031. Pacheco Quintero, Jorge ed. Antología de la poesía en Colombia. t. 1, Epoca colonial, períodos renacentista y barroco. t. 2, El neoclasicismo, los romances tradicionales. Bogotá, Instituto Caro y Cuervo, 1970. 2 v. (595, 549 p.) (Publicaciones, 14)

Fruit of 20 years of research and culling poetry from Colombian archives, this anthology is arranged in chronological order. Admitting that work has some lacunae, still an excellent effort. Gives short, biographical sketches and notes. [BTO]

7032. Rojas, Jorge ed. *Cuadernos de Piedra y Cielo*: 1939-1940. Bogotá, Ministerio de Educación Nacional, Instituto Colombiano de Cultura, 1972. 164 p. (Biblioteca colombiana de cultura. Col. Popular, 122)

Reproduction of first several numbers of bi-monthly *Cuadernos de Piedra y Cielo,* containing poems of seven writers of *Piedra y Cielo* group. [BTO]

7033. Salas, Horacio ed. Generación poética del sesenta. B.A., Ministerio de Cultura y Educación, Secretaría de Estado de Cultura, Ediciones Culturales Argentinos, 1975. 209 p. (Col. Movimientos literarios argentinos)

Salas, miembro él mismo de la generación del 60, preparó esta antología con breve introducción. Los autores incluídos son aquellos que publicaron su primer libro antes de 1966. Sigue la metodología propuesta por Cambours Ocampo en 1963 para las generaciones literarias argentinas. [CMH]

7034. Subero, Efraín ed. El mar en la literatura venezolana. v. 1, Poesía. Caracas, Ediciones del Congreso de la República, 1974. 1 v. (Unpaged)

Well conceived collection with several poems on the sea by each author anthologized. Introduction outlines constancy of theme in Venezuelan poetry and reflects comprehensive knowledge of poet-editor. Attractive volume also gives sources of poems included. Vol. 2 contains prose on the same theme. [BTO]

7035. Valdivia, Manuel Rafael and **Artemio Peraltilla Díaz** eds. Lira arequipeña. Colección de las más selectas poesías de los vates antiguos y modernos. t. 1/2. Arequipa, Perú, Imprenta Editorial El Sol, 1972. 2 v. (365, 365 p.)

Es reedición del volumen publicado en 1889 por M.R. Valdivia, dispuesta ahora por A. Peraltilla Díaz. Muestras de 66 poetas de Arequipa, desde Mariano Melgar (1790-1815) hasta Hipólito Renato Morales (1867-1909) y otros escritores de ese tiempo. Las adiciones biográficas del reeditor no acrecientan el módico interés local e histórico del libro. [PL]

BOOKS OF VERSE

7036. Alberto, Eliseo. Importará el trueno. Poesía. La Habana, Unión de Escritores y Artistas de Cuba (UNEAC), 1975. 74 p. (Col. David)

Buena muestra de la actual poesía testimonial de Cuba: directa y lírica sin dejar lo anecdótico, sea amatoria o introspectiva. Primer libro de un joven poeta, hijo del consagrado Eliseo Diego. [ER]

7037. Arellano, Jesús. El canto del gallo: poelectrones. 2. ed. aumentada. México, UNAM, Dirección General de Publicaciones, 1975. 117 p. (Col. Poemas y ensayos)

Showing occasionally a fine wit, Arellano experiments here with language and with the union of the conceptual and the visual. Result is uneven, with format making it difficult to read more than a few poems at a time. Themes of work are largely social and political. [CM]

7038. Argüelles Bringas, Roberto. Fuerza y dolor. Antología poética. Prólogo, selección y bibliografía de Serge I. Zaïtzeff. México, Secretaría de Educación Pública, Dirección General de Divulgación, 1975. 191 p., bibl. (SepSetentas, 181)

First ed. of complete works of minor Mexican writer, the *modernista* Argüelles Bringas (1875-1915), who also wrote patriotic verse. [CM]

7039. Avilés, Alejandro. Los claros días. México, Editorial Jus, 1975. 58 p. (Col. Poesía, 5)

Delicate poems on the passing of life, solitude, and author's profound religious faith. [CM]

7040. Benarós, León. Carmencita Puch. B.A., Cuadernos de la Banderita, 1973. 17 p.

Una vez más el poeta encuentra inspiración en momentos y personajes históricos; este vez, en la abnegada esposa de Martín Güemes. [CMH]

7041. ———. La mano y los destinos. B.A., Editorial Antares, 1973. 93 p.

Con acentos panteístas el poeta analiza el significado de las manos en la historia humana incorporando mitos y supersticiones ancestrales. [CM]

7042. Benavides, Wáshington. Hokusai. Montevideo, Ediciones de La Banda Oriental, 1975. 69 p. (Col. Acuarimantima)

Este poemario está dividido en tres partes: 1) "Fragmentos," una serie de 13 poemas permeados de lo peor de los instintos humanos, con descripciones punzantes y deprimentes; 2) "Hokusai," en que el autor detalla la vida del pintor acuarelista del siglo XIX, nacido en lo que hoy es Tokio; y 3) "Cautelas," que incluye 18 poemas sobre el amor erótico, el amor idílico, la desilusión amorosa, la frustración del artista creador frente a la incomprensión de su arte y la pobreza. Poesía sin estrofas, sin puntuación, arrítmica, de verso y pensamiento libre . . . Hay partes en que su libertad bordea en libertinaje ofensivo. [EPS]

7043. Berenguer, Amanda. Composición de lugar. Montevideo, Editorial Arca, 1976. 82 p.

Esta poesía cinética expresa la complejidad de los tiempos contemporáneos: la ciencia, la tecnología, la desorganización psicológica que anhela la conquista del espacio. Parece un rompecabezas litográfico. Unas palabras, escritas en mayúsculas, captan más la vista que las escritas en minúsculas. Hay que leer vertical y horizontalmente con espacios entre palabras. No hay renglones; se forman líneas y figuras geométricas. [EPS]

7044. Binetti, Mario. Perfil de niebla. Elegía filial. B.A., Francisco A. Colombo, 1973. 97 p.

Con gran ternura y sencillez el poeta recrea la atmósfera hogareña homenajeando a la madre fallecida. [CMH]

7045. Blanco, Andrés Eloy. Poesía de *Barco de piedra* a *La juanbimbada*. v. 2. Pórtico de Pedro Beroes. Caracas, Ediciones Centauro, 1976. 266 p.

Includes 52-p. analysis of Blanco's epoch. Evaluation of his works by poet-critic Pedro Beroes is followed by reproduction of poems from editions published 1928-38. [BTO]

7046. ———. Poesía de *Tierras que me oyeron* a *Baedeker 2000*. v. 1. Pórtico de Juan Ramón Medina. Caracas, Ediciones Centauro, 1976. 252 p.

Juan Ramón Medina has written sensitive prologue to vol. I by poet who d. 1955 in automobile accident while exiled in Mexico. This is a reedition of vol. 1 of his *Poesías: obras completas* (Caracas, Ediciones del Congreso de la República Caracas, 1973). Includes poems from 1917-29. A poet of profound emotion who took his vocation seriously, post-Modernist Blanco is simple, direct and expressive. Uses language of the people and his themes show his moral preoccupation with humankind and feelings of solidarity. [BTO]

7047. Bonifaz Nuño, Rubén. La flama en el espejo. México, Fondo de Cultura Económica, 1971. 91 p. (Letras mexicanas, 104)

Introduced with quote from *Paradiso*, this is a collection of dense thought and language. Bonifaz Nuño has abandoned the more approachable and personal world of *El ala del tigre* (*HLAS 32:4174*) for a metaphorical realm reminiscent of Dante. Rewarding journey for the determined reader. [CM]

7048. Borges, Jorge Luis. La moneda de hierro. B.A., Emecé, 1976. 162 p.

Sonetos y poemas de versificación libre escritos en East Lansing y en Argentina durante 1976. Los símbolos no han cambiado, pero el poeta presente cada vez más el fin de sus días. [CMH]

7049. Brenes Mesén, Roberto. Poesías. Prólogo de José Basileo Acuña. San José, Editorial Costa Rica, 1975. 391 p.

Reimpresión de la obra del poeta costarricense que pone al alcance del estudioso un importante jalón de poesía modernista. [RG]

7050. Cáceres Carenzo, Raúl. Para decir la noche. México, UNAM, Dirección General de Publicaciones, 1973. 114 p. (Col. Poemas y ensayos)

Interesting first book on great variety of topics, among them friendship, poetry and the poet, love, social injustice, and political events. There are echoes of several of Cáceres Carenzo's *compatriotas*, especially Pellicer, Huerta, and Arellano. [CM]

7051. Calderón, Alfonso. Isla de los bienaventurados. Santiago, Nascimento, 1977. 189 p.

El hablante básico transita por la música, por la literatura, por el cine, por la pintura, por la historia y por la cultura *pop*. Su mérito es la impecable factura de los poemas; su peligro, cierta falta de tensión, cierta falta de sombra en la claridad y en el rigor de los diseños. [OH]

7052. Calvo, César. Pedestal para nadie. Prólogo de Alberto Escobar. Lima, Instituto Nacional de Cultura, 1975. 293 p., bibl. (Col. Año de la mujer peruana)

Recopilación de la obra completa realizada hasta aquí por César Calvo (n. 1940), una de las figuras prestigiosas de la promoción poética surgida a principios de los años 60. El prólogo de Escobar—"El Vértigo de la Palabra"—abunda en aciertos descriptivos y valorativos, y es un excelente acercamiento a esta poesía. Incluye: *Poemas bajo tierra* y *Ensayo a dos voces* (escrito en colaboración con J. Heraud, 1961); *Ausencias y retardos* (1963); *El cetro de los jóvenes* (1967); *Pedestal para nadie* (1970), y sus más recientes poemas y canciones. [PL]

7053. Campo, Xorge del. Animal de amor. México, UNAM, Dirección General de Publicaciones, 1972. 142 p. (Col. Poemas y ensayos)

Erotic verse with moments of great appeal. [CM]

7054. Carballo, Emmanuel. Eso es todo. México, Editorial Diógenes, 1972. 175 p.

Frequent commentator on contemporary Mexican culture, Carballo presents here 166 three-line poems on the dissolution of a love affair. Although many are sensitive and humorous, the form wears thin before the end of the work. [CM]

7055. Carranza, Eduardo. Epístola mortal y otras soledades. Bogotá, Corporación Financiera (COFINATURA), 1975. 1 v. (Unpaged)

Sentimental, but sensual and original, with subtle symbols and original metaphors. Writes of his own personal, lyrical, dreamworld. Never pessimistic but melancholic, poems reflecting agony and solitude about those who have died. Sometimes repetitious, but nevertheless, a good, mature craftsman. [BTO]

7056. Carrera Andrade, Jorge. Obra poética completa. Quito, Editorial Casa de la Cultura Ecuatoriana, 1976. 596 p.

Libro necesario, que contiene la sostenida y valiosa producción lírica de Carrera Andrade (Ecuador, 1902), durante 1917-72. El carácter comprensivo de la edición permite seguir la trayectoria de un poeta que se singulariza por un designio constante de claridad y rigor expresivos (ver *HLAS 36:6522* y *HLAS 36:6669*). [PL]

7057. Casal, Julián del. The poetry of . . .: a critical edition. v. 1. Edited by Jay Glickman. Gainesville, The Univ. Presses of Florida, 1976. 287 p.

Colección de 144 poemas de *Hojas al viento*, *Nieve* y *Rimas*, y 13 composiciones sueltas (*Varia*); vol. 1 de tres que prometen ser la edición definitiva de las obras líricas del cubano. Importante contribución a la fijación del *corpus* de textos modernistas hispanoamericanos. [ER]

7058. Castillo. Otto René. Informe de una injusticia. Antología poética.

7058. Introducción de Roque Dalton y Humberto Alvarado. San José, Editorial Universitaria Centroamericana (EDUCA), 1975. 419 p., bibl. (Col. Séptimo día)

La poesía de Castillo (1936-67) constituye alto testimonio de vocación revolucionaria. Castillo poetizó el exilio, su amor a una Guatemala desgarrada, su angustia, su lucha agónica, su aliento visionario. Los estudios por Roque Dalton y Alfonso Chase calan en la época y la obra del autor. [RG]

7059. Cisneros, Antonio. Como higuera en un campo de golf. Lima, Instituto Nacional de Cultura, 1972. 146 p.

Libro que confirma los reconocidos valores de la obra de Cisneros: también aquí su trabajo poético revela la felicidad de la experimentación y la lucidez de la búsqueda de un lenguaje y de una sintaxis auténticamente anticonvencionales. [PL]

7060. Cócaro, Nicolás. Las esquinas del mundo. B.A., Emecé, 1975. 123 p.

La patria continuá siendo el tema fundamental en la obra lírica de Cócaro. El poeta se detiene a observar detalles de la gran urbe—B.A.—aunque también aparecen poemas relacionados con el pasado histórico de la patria y otros de índole general. [CMH]

7061. Corcuera, Arturo. Puente de los suspiros. Lima, Ediciones Arte/Reda, 1976. 18 p., illus. (Col. Cantos rodados)

Poesía de situaciones, que la mirada recrea en una exploración irónica de la sensibilidad amorosa. La sutileza de estos textos breves y precisos, situados en la tradición del epigrama, encubre y corroe a la vez la nostalgia del hablante. [PL]

7062. Correa Vásquez, Pedro. Principio de oscura sinfonía. Panamá, Univ. de Panamá, 1975. 60 p.

Tercera entrega de este nuevo poeta panameño. Correa Vásquez corre el riesgo de dejarse controlar más por la disposición tipográfica que por el genuino pensamiento poético. [RG]

7063. Cote Lamus, Eduardo. Obra literaria. Bogotá, Instituto Colombiano de Cultura, Subdirección de Comunicaciones Culturales, 1976. 435 p., bibl. (Biblioteca básica colombiana, 15)

Attractively edited complete works of imagist poet who concentrated at first on erotic, life as a dream and death, and later, on time and destiny of humans. Prologue analyzes chronological development until his premature accidental death. Final work attains a more universal expression. [BTO]

7064. Dal Vera, Juan. Poemas desde una casa para locos. Panamá, Instituto Nacional de Cultura, Dirección Técnica de Extensión Cultural, Depto. de Publicaciones, 1975. 104 p.

Poemario de gran fuerza expresiva que pone al desnudo la imagen misma de la alienación. Esta obra recibió el Premio Ricardo Miró de poesía en 1975. [RG]

7065. Debravo, Jorge. Vórtices. San José, Editorial Costa Rica, 1975. 71 p.

En poemas escritos a los 21 años—y que dejó inéditos—, Debravo hace el inventario de las cosas sencillas para hacernos descubrir su esencia y su pureza. [RG]

7066. Diego, Eliseo. Nombrar las cosas. La Habana, Bolsilibros Unión, 1973. 364 p.

Recopilación antológica del poeta del grupo *Orígenes*, que incluye entre sus mejores muestras el texto íntegro de *En la Calzada de Jesús del Monte* (1947) y *El oscuro esplendor* (1966), y una breve selección de *Muestrario del mundo o Libro de las maravillas de Boloña* (1968). Edición manuable. [ER]

7067. Eielson, Jorge Eduardo. Reinos. n.p., Ediciones de la Clepsidra, 1973. 1 v. (Unpaged) illus.

Edición de 16 textos poéticos, parcialmente conocidos desde 1945, y que instituyeron el prestigio del autor en la literatura de su país. Poesía del asombro, generadora de transformaciones de materias y hechos fuertemente interiorizados. [PL]

7068. Espinosa Altamirano, Horacio. Apocalipsis apócrifo. México, Ediciones Universo, 1975. 54 p., illus.

Scatological trip through Hell. [CM]

7069. Figueredo, Alvaro. Poesía. Maldonado, Uru., The Author, 1974. 130 p.

Selección de poemas de uno de los mayores poetas uruguayos (1907-66), realizada por su viuda, Amalia de Figueredo. Incluye poesías histórico-regionales ("Descubrimiento del Uruguay," "Exaltación de Bartolomé Hidalgo," "Romance de la Declaratoria de la Independencia"); poemas del libro *Mundo a la vez* (1956); y también poemas posteriores sobre poetas uruguayos: Julio Herrera y Reissig, Delmira Agustini y Bartolomé Hidalgo, entre otros. El mundo poético de Alvaro Figueredo está lleno de un apasionado sentimiento de lo terrestre que él siente incorporado a su propia vida. [EPS]

7070. Florián, Mario. Anuario de la oligarquía latifundista dominante y de la clase trabajadora dominada, de una provincia andina, correspondiente a 1955. Lima, Imprenta-Editorial Fidel Ramírez Lazo, 1976. 34 p.

La estructura contrastante de estos poemas suele disolverse en un dictado esquemático, pero algunos textos que escapan al estereotipo insinúan las posibilidades de la modalidad ensayada aquí por Florián. [PL]

7071. Gaitán Durán, Jorge. Obra literaria, poesía y prosa. Recopilación y prólogo por Pedro Gómez Valderrama. Bogotá, Instituto Colombiano de Cultura, Subdirección de Comunicaciones Culturales, 1975. 453 p. (Biblioteca básica colombiana)

Premature accidental death of Jorge Gaitán Durán in 1962 stimulated collection of his works. Their merit is more apparent in completed form than when volumes were scattered. Writes intimately and profoundly of desolation. Obsessed in philosophical way with love as a harbinger of death, with time and the joys of life which he feels are fleeting, racing toward nothingness. Contains his inimitable prose writings including travel diary, political analysis of Colombia, short stories, prose poems and critical articles. [BTO]

7072. García Saldaña, Parménides. Mediodía. México, Editorial Joaquín Mortiz, 1975. 112 p. (Serie del volador)

Preoccupations of youth of the late 1960s and 1970s. Written in verse with many ties to rock music. [CM]

7073. Gelman, Juan. Obra poética. B.A., Ediciones Corregidor, 1975. 410 p.

Este volumen reúne todo el itinerano poético del escritor. Gelman delata una ambiciosa búsqueda de un lenguaje trascendente en el cual se deja sentir la influencia de Vallejo. Esporádicamente la aventura verbal, aunada a un realismo crítico en su manera de ver al mundo se conjuga exitosamente. Sin embargo, el compromiso social y político tiende a convertirse en lastre innecesario. [CMH]

7074. Giovanetti Viola, Hugo. París póstumo. Montevideo, Ediciones de la Balanza, 1976. 46 p. (Serie poesía)

Primer volumen poético de Giovanetti Viola (n. 1948). Sus versos parecen frescos y espontáneos, sin elaboración. "Arte Poética en Carta Familiar" impresiona como el poema de más hondos sentimientos. Acosado por la preocupación de la muerte, el poeta pide que su vida continúe hasta lograr sus anhelos amorosos, descifrar sus incógnitas metafísicas y comunicar su mensaje social a los hombres. [EPS]

7075. Girri, Alberto. Girri + Sabat: galería personal. B.A., Sudamericana, 1975. 71 p.

El poeta, conjuntamente con Hermenegildo Sabat, dibujante, ofrece un museo ideal. Girri ha reunido una serie de poemas sobre pintores (Modigliani, Klee, etc.) para revelar hasta qué punto son inagotables los significados del arte. Las tendencias surrealistas del poeta se avienen magníficamente a la tarea. [CMH]

7076. Godoy, Emma. Poemas. Del torrente; pausas y arena. México, Editorial Jus, 1975. 114 p. (Col. Poesía, 4)

In Del Torrente one finds delicate verses of love and others of a profound religious feeling. Pausas y arena is a further development of religious themes. [CM]

7077. González, Oscar. Hoguera sobre el agua. México, Fondo de Cultura Económica, 1972. 95 p. (Letras mexicanas)

As in his first book, Tiempo adentro (1970), González writes thoughtful and sensitive verse on a number of topics. [CM]

7078. González, Otto-Raúl. Poesía fundamental: 1943-1967. Guatemala, Univ. de San Carlos de Guatemala, Editorial Universitaria, 1973. 523 p. (Col. Creación literaria, 2)

Valiosa recopilación de la labor lírica de uno de los representantes de la generación del 40 en Guatemala. [RG]

7079. González Prada, Manuel. Letrillas. t. 1. Introducción y edición de Luis Alberto Sánchez. Lima, Editorial Milla Batres, 1975. 210 p.

Es el primero de los tres tomos de la obra inédita de González Prada (los siguientes serán: t. 2., Ortometría y t. 3, Cantos del otro siglo). Agudezas de ingenio como instrumento de crítica costumbrista mordaz o simplemente picaresca, estos poemas muestran un aspecto, poco conocido de la personalidad del autor. El prólogo de Sánchez se refiere a los tres libros inéditos. [PL]

7080. González Rojo, Enrique. El quíntuple balar de mis sentidos o el monstruo y otros mariposas. México, Editorial Joaquín Mortiz, 1976. 69 p. (Las dos orillas)

Curious book joining echoes of Baudelaire ("L'Ennemi") and social concerns. [CM]

7081. Greiff, León de. Obras completas. t. 1/2. Prólogo de Jorge Zalamea. Bogotá, Tercer Mundo, 1975. 2 v. (418, 446 p.) facsim., plates.

Lithographic reproduction of first ed. of De Greiff's Obras completas (Medellín, Colombia, 1960) with same prologue by Jorge Zalamea. Also contains reproduction of *Nova et Vetera* (Bogotá, 1974). De Greiff (d. 1976) used Spanish language from all epochs in his poems, mixing it freely, according to sound and sense. He displayed an unbelievable richness of language and poetic form, and as other Modernists, he tore down and set up idols of past literary periods. In spite of hermetic rhetorical imagery, he never lost tenuous and delicate music, original and varied rhythm. Ironic and satiric, he conveyed much depth of feeling in some more serious poems. [BTO]

7082. ———. Selección de poemas. Prólogo de Fernando Garavito. Bogotá, Ministerio de Educación Nacional, Instituto Colombiano de Cultura, 1972. 126 p. (Biblioteca colombiana de cultura. Col. Popular, 52)

Short, intuitive and well-judged analysis of De Greiff by Fernando Garavito precedes this undistinguished popular ed. of some of poet's least hermetic poems. Taken from 1960 ed. of his *Obras completas*. [BTO]

7083. Guevara, Pablo. Hotel del Cuzco y otras provincias del Perú. Lima, Instituto Nacional de Cultura, 1971. 91 p.

Libro de gran interés, y uno de los pocos en la poesía latinoamericana donde la naturaleza del asunto ("la lectura del pasado y la historia social") no impide un tratamiento noble de esos materiales. Se explica que algunos de los escritores jóvenes congregados por J.M. Oviedo en *Estos 13* (véase item 7030) hayan reconocido la línea poética de Guevara como verdaderamente productiva para su propio trabajo. [PL]

7084. Guillén, Nicolás. El corazón con que vivo. La Habana, Unión de Escritores y Artistas de Cuba (UNEAC), 1975. 67 p. (Manjuarí poesía)

Pequeño volumen de poemas de amor, seleccionados por el propio poeta de entre todos los de su vasta obra. [ER]

7085. ———. Poemas manuables. La Habana, Unión de Escritores y Artistas de Cuba (UNEAC), 1975. 348 p. (Contemporáneos)

Acertada presentación de una amplia muestra de la poesía de Guillén, dirigida al lector no especializado. División en grupos temáticos: poemas "mulatos," sociales y políticos, festivos, satíricos, de amor, para niños y varios ("El Aeroplano y otros Poemas"). Útil libro de texto. [ER]

7086. Gutiérrez, Ernesto. Antología. Selección de Carlos Martínez and Sergio Ramírez. San José, Editorial Universitaria Centroamericana (EDUCA), 1976. 151 p. (Col. Séptimo día. Serie Mayor)

Recoge la antología poemas publicados entre 1953-73. Gutiérrez pertenece a la generación de poetas nicaragüenses que se comienza a afirmar en la década de los 50. Su poemática se bifurca en vertientes ya intimistas, ya abiertamente comprometidas. [RG]

7087. Gutiérrez Vega, Hugo. Cuando el placer termine. México, Editorial Joaquín Mortiz, 1977. 82 p.

Winner of Premio Nacional de Poesía in 1976, this book offers sensitive verse on death, love, and the art of poetry among other topics. Author's fifth volume of poetry. [CM]

7088. Hahn, Oscar. Arte de morir. Prólogo de Enrique Lihn. B.A., Ediciones Hispamérica 1977. 180 p.

Manifestación intensa y lograda de lo que se ha definido como una experiencia visionaria. Su tema constante (la finitud del hombre y de la especie, la transitoriedad del ser y de las cosas) y el rigor de una escritura que acoge y reactualiza múltiples posibilidades formales, vinculan estos poemas con el mejor legado de la tradición, desde las danzas medievales de la muerte. *Arte de morir* incluye toda la producción de Hahn y deberá considerarse como su primer libro: la suma que lo constituye explora y ordena un tema y se ofrece aquí como un ciclo unitario, cuya apertura hacia otras indagaciones de expresión y de sentido se insinúa sin embargo en "Tractatus de Sortilegiis," texto final de esta obra notable de la poesía hispanoamericana actual. [PL]

7089. Heraud, Javier. Poesías completas. 2. ed. Lima, Campodónico-*ediciones*, 1973. 382 p., facsims., illus., plates.

Hermosa reedición de unas de las expresiones más valiosas de la poesía peruana contemporánea. A diez años de la muerte de su autor, ella representa el condigno homenaje a "una obra poética perdurable." Contiene los dos libros publicados por Heraud, *El río* (1960) y *El viaje* (1961), los poemas de *Estación reunida* y otras piezas inéditas que integraron la primera edición de *Poesías completas y homenaje* (1964), además de las cartas y nuevos textos. Una útil antología de estudios sobre este poeta incluye trabajos de José Miguel Oviedo, Washington Delgado, Jorge Cornejo Polar y Gerardo Mario Goloboff. [PL]

7090. ———. Poesías completas y cartas. Lima, Ediciones Peisa, 1976. 248 p., bibl. (Biblioteca peruana)

Edición popular igual a la de 1973 (Heraud, *Poesías completas*. Lima, Campodónicoeditores), menos el estudio de J.M. Oviedo. [PL]

7091. Hernández Gómez, Jorge. Palabra en el tiempo. Bogotá, Ediciones Tercer Mundo, 1976. 70 p.

Terse poems with some outstanding ones reflecting emotional depth and a conscious control of poetic ideas and concepts. Conveyed in free verse, with rhythmical and musical qualities. Preoccupied with death. [BTO]

7092. Herrera y Ressig, Julio. Poesías. Selección, prólogo y notas de Mario Alvarez Rodríguez. Montevideo, Ediciones de La Banda Oriental, 1975. 124 p.

En la introducción, Alvarez Rodríguez examina las tendencias del modernismo para ubicar al poeta en un contexto literario e histórico. Analiza las tres etapas fundamentales de su obra y señala las constantes estilísticas y temáticas. Incluye una ficha biográfica y una bibliografía mínima. Esta edición comprende una selección de *Los éxtasis de la montaña, Sonetos vascos, Los parques abandonados, El laurel rosa, La torre de las esfinges* (en forma íntegra), *Las clepsidras* y *Berceuse blanca*. [EPS]

7093. Huerta, David. El jardín de la luz. México, UNAM, Dirección General de Publicaciones, 1972. 105 p. (Col. Poemas y ensayos)

Author's first book, one of serene and luminous verse, shows much promise. Herta (b. 1949, Mexico) writes of love, nature, the sea, and the city. [CM]

7094. Huerta, Efraín. Circuito interior. México, Editorial Joaquín Mortiz, 1976. 90 p. (Las dos orillas)

Another collection from prolific Mexican writer. It is divided into four parts, last of which gives title to the whole. Third section, "Pausa Mínima," continues his *poemínimos* of *Los eróticos y otros poemas* (see *HLAS 38:6964*). As in earlier works, Huerta combines personal and social themes. His tone is initially bitter, then humorous. Among poems are moving elegies to Roque Dalton, José Revueltas, and Pablo Neruda. [CM]

7095. Huidobro, Vicente. Obras completas. Prólogo y edición de Hugo Montes. Santiago, Editorial Andrés Bello, 1976. 2 v. (910, 765 p.)

La nueva edición de las obras de Huidobro hace honor a su título, en cuanto agrega los libros *Pasando y pasando* y *Finis Britannia* e incorpora poemas y artículos impresos en revistas de difícil obtención. Este material no fue recogido en las *Obras completas* (Santiago, Editorial Zig-Zag, 1964). El t. 1 incluye el prólogo de Montes, la totalidad de los libros de poemas, las composiciones desestimadas en esos volúmenes, los ensayos y dos "cuentos diminutos." El t. 2 contiene las creaciones novelescas, el teatro y una guía bibliográfica de la obra huidobriana, ordenada por Nicholas Hey. Falta en cambio una bibliografía *sobre* Huidobro. Tanto en su aspecto material como en su contenido, la edición de H. Montes representa un evidente progreso con respecto a la realizada por Braulio Arenas para la Editorial Zig-Zag. [OH]

7096. Isla, Carlos. Maquinaciones. México, Editorial Joaquín Mortiz, 1975. 65 p., illus. (Las dos orillas)

First half of book contains prosaic, often witty poems about incongruencies of life. Second part, a series of pages with rectangles to be cut out and folded, seems to be a game author is playing on his reader. [CM]

7097. Jaramillo, Carlos Eduardo. Crónicas de la casa, los árboles y el río. Quito, Editorial Casa de la Cultura Ecuatoriana, 1973. 96 p. (Col. Poetas del Ecuador, 1)

El título declara con sobriedad los contenidos de mundo de los poemas que integran la primera parte del libro. La transparencia de los símbolos es aquí manifiesta. La segunda parte—"Viaje al Planeta Eurídice"—es un intento novedoso y sugestivo de reactualización del mito de Orfeo, correlato de ricas posibilidades que Jaramillo aprovecha parcialmente. [PL]

7098. ———. Una vez, la felicidad. Guayaquil, Ecua., Casa de la Cultura Ecuatoriana. Núcleo del Guayas, 1972. 122 p.

Poesía que intuye un lenguaje y cuestiona la realidad desde un sentimiento genuino de la incertidumbre. Suele conspirar contra su eficacia cierta tendencia a la conceptualización, que no siempre enriquece al ámbito del poema y más bien debilita su intensidad. [PL]

7099. Juárez, Salvador Antonio. Al otro lado del espejo. San Salvador, Ministerio de Educación, Dirección de Cultura, Dirección de Publicaciones, 1973. 92 p. (Nuevapalabra, 7)

Suárez se vale de la expresión popular, del giro crudo como método para calar la realidad y para hacernos sentir el mundo absurdo en que vivimos. [RG]

7100. Junco, Alfonso. Poesía completa. México, Editorial Jus, 1975. 273 p. (Col. Poesía, 2)

Complete works of minor Mexican poet. Written between 1917-58, their principal subject matter is religious. [CM]

7101. Lameda, Alí. Sonetos del viajero enlutado. Caracas, Monte Avila Editores, 1975. 180 p.

Book of 154 sonnets, written during Lameda's travel abroad. Has perspicacious introduction by poet José

Ramón Medina. Poems are in a brutal, denunciating tone, fairly clear in their message but with some very personal images. Strong, energetic and authentic but pessimistic. [BTO]

7102. Lara, Omar. Oh buenas maneras. La Habana, Casa de las Américas, 1975. 76 p.

Poemas breves, a veces epigramáticos, impregnados de lirismo, enunciados por un hablante crítico de la sociedad actual y sobre todo del Chile posterior al golpe militar. Reparos: cierta ocasional impericia sintáctica y cierta inseguridad en el manejo de los niveles connotativos. [OH]

7103. Lastra, Pedro. Y éramos inmortales. Santiago, Editorial Universitaria, 1974. 63 p. (Col. Los presentes, 9)

La poesía de Lastra hace honor a la siguiente observación de Emil Staiger: "El pasado como tema de lo lírico es un tesoro del recuerdo." El recuerdo aparece en ella como forma pura y temple de ánimo que sobrepasa a sus propios contenidos y distancia lo recordado. Su virtud consiste en que es capaz de sintonizar al lector en la misma frecuencia de ese temple, no por acción de las figuras (ya que está exenta de ellas), sino por aquello que Amado Alonso denominaba "los encantos de la voz," y también por la intensidad de las vivencias configuradas verbalmente. [OH]

7104. Lavín Cerda, Hernán. Ciegamente los ojos. México, UNAM, 1977. 302 p. (Col. Poemas y ensayos)

Reordenación de la poesía de Lavín Cerda, realizada a base de composiciones inéditas y principalmente de libros publicados entre 1962-76. Se caracteriza por el empleo de un lenguaje coloquial sujeto a control, que mediante el humor y el ingenio intenta desacralizar los temas ligados a las preocupaciones del hombre contemporáneo. El relajamiento del hablante, fruto de su deliberada soltura, redunda a veces en una falta de tensión lírica, perceptible sobre todo en los finales de algunos poemas. [OH]

7105. Leyva, Daniel. Crispal. México, Editorial Joaquín Mortiz, 1975. 111 p. (Las dos orillas)

Curious book dominated by a surrealistic approach that is sometimes successful, sometimes not. [CM]

7106. Lihn, Enrique. París, situación irregular. Santiago, Ediciones Aconcagua, 1977. 93 p. (Col. Mistral)

En estos poemas el sujeto del texto, provisto de un cuaderno, se pasea por París y anota todo lo que se le pasa por la cabeza y lo que escapa a la autocensura. Al mismo tiempo, se imitan distintos tipos de discursos no prestigiados por la poesía: la oratoria académica, el gesto del emisor de noticias, la gesticulación sintáctica del que escribe una carta o hace una rápida anotación en su agenda. Libro importantísimo como propuesta de nuevas direcciones para la poesía hispanoamericana. [OH]

7107. ———. Por fuerza mayor. Barcelona, Barral Editores, 1975. 80 p. (Col. Ocnos, 49)

Como gran parte de la última narrativa de Lihn—y con la maestría de siempre—, varios de los poemas claves del libro implican una reflexión sobre los alcances de la escritura. En otras composiciones retorna a uno de sus temas favoritos: el enfoque de la relación amorosa desde una perspectiva existencial. El núcleo de la obra está constituido por cuatro secciones de sonetos, a través de los cuales crea distintos tipos de hablantes. Entre ellos sobresale "el energúmeno," personaje que en la tradición del Quevedo más corrosivo, refuerza la agresividad de las referencias con la sonoridad de los significantes. [OH]

7108. López, Luis Carlos. Obra poética. Compilación y estudio crítico de Guillermo Alberto Arévalo. Bogotá, Ediciones del Banco de la República, 1976. 585 p., bibl., facsim., illus.

Introduction of eight short chapters (95 p.) presents superior critical analysis with original interpretations of López' life and works. Although admittedly not containing all of his work, this most complete ed. contains 201 poems, several previously published. Also includes two interviews, correspondence, 16 essays about him, occasional pieces, prologues to previous editions, and few truly analytical articles. Lists errors in four different collections of his poems. [BTO]

7109. Marchena, Julián. Alas en fuga. Poesía. 5. ed. San José, Editorial Costa Rica, 1975. 117 p.

Nueva edición del poemario publicado originalmente en 1941. Uno de los grandes valores de la lírica costarricense. [RG]

7110. Martín Adan [*pseud. for* **Rafael de la Fuente Benavides**]. Diario de poeta. Lima, Ediciones Inti-Sol, 1975. 95 p. (Col. Jacarandá, 1)

Conjunto de 46 poemas rigurosamente trabajados (algunos de ellos son sonetos memorables), que revelan otra vertiente de la tenaz meditación existencial de Martín Adán. Seis de los sonetos de este libro aparecieron en 1971 en la edición de la *Obra poética* (véase *HLAS 38:6913* e item 7230). [PL]

7111. Martínez, David. Enrique Banchs, poeta del sentimiento humano: seguido de antología viva de sus poesía. B.A., Editorial Plus Ultra, 1975. 155 p. (Col. Ensayos, 10)

Breve antología que incluye selecciones de sus cinco obras, entre ellas *La urna*, colección de sonetos considerada la culminación de su obra. La introducción señala los aspectos más importantes de la obra del excelente aunque poco difundido poeta. [CMH]

7112. Maya, Rafael. El retablo del sacrificio y de la gloria. Bogotá, Ediciones de la Revista *Ximénez de Quesada*, n.d. 44 p., illus. (Biblioteca del Instituto colombiano de cultura hispánica, 7)

Unfortunately, Maya's classic and serene poetic expression here is too academic, too traditional in theme as well as mode of expression. [BTO]

7113. ———. El tiempo recobrado. Poemas. Bogotá, Instituto Caro y Cuervo, 1974. 87 p. (Serie la granada entreabierta, 5)

The octogenerian Maya regains in some lines his depth of lyrical expression in these poems of return to childhood. Their lyrical grace is marred by narrative, overly prosaic and rhetorical description. His critical knowledge may be a disadvantage to him by stifling his poetic sensibility. [BTO]

7114. Medina Romero, Jesús. Orfeo 71. México, Ediciones Cuadernos Americanos, 1973. 76 p.

Poems written in 1970 and 1971 that are of a much more traditional nature than most. Although sometimes awkward, they show a moving sincerity. Medina Romero's concerns are diverse: life, death, love, poetry and the poet, and the passing of time. [CM]

7115. Mejía Sánchez, Ernesto. Recolección. León, Nic., Univ. Nacional Autonoma de Nicaragua, 1972. 204 p., illus. (Col. Poesía, 7)

Antología que pone al alcance del estudioso la obra completa de uno de los grandes valores de la lírica nicaragüense. Además de reproducir—en facsímil—todos los libros publicados anteriormente, esta edición recoge *Impureza* (Premio Nacional Rubén Darío, 1951), que había permanecido inédito. [RG]

7116. Melgar, Mariano. Antología poética. Prólogo y selección de Antonio Cornejo Polar. Lima, Editorial Universo, 1975. 136 p. (Col. Autores peruanos, 50)

En un prólogo excelente por su precisión, Cornejo Polar discute el sentido, la ubicación y el valor fundacionales de la obra poética de Melgar en el proceso de la literatura peruana. La antología—ceñida y bien dispuesta—confirma eficazmente las afirmaciones sustentadas en el prólogo. [PL]

7117. Menéndez Franco, Alvaro. La nueva voz de los antiguos ríos. Panamá, Univ. de Panamá, 1974. 88 p.

Colección presentada al Concurso "Ricardo Miró" de 1951, en el que obtuvo tercer lugar. La obra, no obstante, había quedado inédita. Poeta postvanguardista, Menéndez Franco perfecciona la biografía poética como instrumento de protesta social. [RG]

7118. Mir, Pedro. El huracán Neruda: elegía con una canción desesperada. Santo Domingo, Ediciones de Taller, 1975. 1 v. (Unpaged)

Largo poema a la muerte de Pablo Neruda, escrito en el estilo conversacional de los nuevos textos líricos hispanoamericanos. Edición de formato y tipografía interesantes. [ER]

7119. Miranda, Hernán. La moneda y otros poemas. La Habana, Casa de las Américas, 1976. 51 p.

El libro (Premio Casa de las Américas 1976) está dividido en dos secciones: 1) que recoge 16 poemas relacionados con la situación socio-política chilena y su efecto en la vida personal del sujeto lírico; y 2) una sola composición extensa titulada "La Moneda," que muestra diversas imágenes de la casa presidencial, primero como cuna de la oligarquía y luego como sede del gobierno popular. Poesía clara, sencilla, coloquial, que linda a veces con la nota periodística, pero que entrega siempre su protesta sin aspavientos ni declamaciones. [OH]

7120. Molinari, Ricardo E. Los sombras del pájaro tostado. Obra poética: 1923-1973. B.A., El Mangrullo, 1975. 511 p.

Amplia selección, realizada por el poeta, de la obra escrita a lo largo de medio siglo. [CMH]

7121. Monge, Carlos Francisco. Población del asombro. San José, Editorial Costa Rica, 1975. 85 p.

Después de una corta etapa preparatoria—"jornadas"—, el poeta se concentra en las meditaciones de "En nuestra casa:" ritual, honda celebración del hogar incipiente. [RG]

7122. Montero, José Antonio. Apelaciones y exhalaciones. México, UNAM, Dirección General de Publicaciones, 1972. 58 p. (Col. Poemas y ensayos)

In this first book Montero writes sensitively of city and province, love, identity, his family, and his craft. Uses colloquial language and simple poetic forms. Work shows the influence of Paz, Bonifaz Nuño, Quasimodo, and Breton. [CM]

7123. Montero Vega, Arturo. Poemas escogidos. San José, Editorial Costa Rica, 1975. 181 p.

La angustia del hombre da origen a la emoción lírica, en tanto que la sobriedad de estilo nos hace participar, directa y activamente, de los matices del sentimiento. Montero Vega entrega poesía comprometida sin comprometer la poesía. [RG]

7124. Morena, H.A. El águila que desaparece. B.A., Editorial Alfa, 1975. 1 v. (Unpaged)

Breves poemas de contenido conceptual que replantean los problemas del ser. [CMH]

7125. Mutis, Alvaro. Maqroll el gaviero. Bogotá, Instituto Colombiano de Cultura, Subdirección de Comunicaciones Culturales, División de Publicaciones, 1975. 143 p. (Biblioteca colombiana de cultura. Col. Autores nacionales, 5)

Rigorous craftsman, Mutis produces poems which show an effort to attain subtle, high-quality poems where he dominates language. His nihilistic world is a disintegrating, decomposing punishment through which men and women must live somehow, and which the poet must portray in all his pessimism with honesty and clarity. [BTO]

7126. Nájar, Jorge. Malas maneras. Editado por Fernando Sánchez Vela. Pucallpa, Perú, Editorial Impetu, 1973. 53 p. (Col. Contra viento y marea)

Primer libro—no demasiado precoz—de uno de los polémicos integrantes de *Estos 13* (véase item 7030). El desenfado de un discurso escéptico hasta de sí mismo le confiere especial interés, aunque la audacia de esta palabra no renuncia del todo a la peligrosa vecindad de otros convencionalismos. [PL]

7127. Nandino, Elías. Eternidad del polvo. México, Editorial Joaquín Mortiz, 1970. 89 p. (Las dos orillas)

In first section, which gives title to book, Nandino meditates at length on death. Other themes are love, resignation, and solitude. As in his earlier works, the poet's tone is often one of anguish. [CM]

7128. Nieto, Manuel Orestes. Dar la cara. La Habana, Casa de las Américas, 1975. 116 p.

Nieto le levanta enconado proceso a la Zona del Canal y, por extensión, al imperialismo norteamericano. Al poeta le duele profundamente esa presencia y de su dolor surgen el impulso poético y el poema. [RG]

7129. ———. Reconstrucción de los hechos. Panamá, Editora de la Nación, 1973. 91 p.

La carga vivencial se convierte en eje de estos poemas. Nieto reconstruye los límites del vivir cotidiano, para erigir la angustia que le dicta su fuerte conciencia social. Esta obra recibió el Premio Ricardo Miró de Poesía en 1972. [RG]

7130. Odio, Eunice. Territorio del alba y otros poemas. San José, Editorial Universitaria Centroamericana (EDUCA), 1974. 247 p. (Col. Séptimo día)

Recoge esta antología póstuma poemas escritos entre 1946-72. No cabe duda de que el sostenido vuelo de "Tránsito de Fuego" es suficiente para labrarle a Eunice Odio un importante nicho dentro de la lírica costarricense e hispanoamericana. [RG]

7131. Pardo García, Germán. Apolo Pankrátor: 1915-1975. México, Editorial Libros de México, 1977. 1364 p., plates.

Presents from six to around 50 poems from each of 32 different vols. A most revealing mini-autobiography outlines (36 p.) his perceptions of formative events of his life. Although his poetry is often maligned or ignored, Pardo García has written numerous good and some excellent poems. [BTO]

7132. Parra, Violeta. Décimas. Barcelona, Editorial Pomaire, 1976. 181 p.

Relación autobiográfica correspondiente al género épico-lírico (análoga al Romancero español o al *Martín Fierro*), escrita en la estrofa de mayor raigambre en el pueblo chileno: la décima. Colmados de esa sabiduría que sólo se aprende en contacto directo con una realidad a la vez cambiante y tradicional, estos notables poemas trascienden la historia personal y se convierten en la expresión de una sensibilidad colectiva. [OH]

7133. Paz, Octavio. Vuelta. México, Editorial Seix Barral, 1976. 92 p. (Biblioteca breve)

Important collection of the writer's poetry from the years 1969-74. Paz continues to develop many of his familiar themes. The focus is on Mexico here rather than on the Orient, as in *Ladera este* (see *HLAS 36:6587*), his collected poems of 1962-68. [CM]

7134. Paz Soldán y Unanue, Pedro [*pseud. for* **Juan de Arona**]. Poesías completas. v. 1. Recopilación, prólogo y notas de Estuardo Núñez. Lima, Academia Peruana de la Lengua, 1975. 624 p., plate (Clásicos peruanos, 2)

Importante ed. de la obra poética de un escritor muy representativo del siglo XIX. Este volumen incluye los libros *Ruinas* (1863) y *Cuadros y episodios peruanos* (1867), levemente redispuestos según el orden sugerido por la incorporación de una parte del primero en la publicación de 1867. En un prólogo documentado y riguroso, Estuardo Núñez reseña las varias facetas de la poesía de Juan de Arona (lírica, satírica y regional), plantea la necesidad de reexamen y enjuiciamiento definitivos de "la proteica figura" del autor, e indica el contenido del o de los volúmenes siguientes: los ocho "Poemas Mayores," el libro inédito Rimas del Rímac, otros textos posteriores a 1891 y las numerosas traducciones realizadas por Arona. [PL]

7135. Pietri, Pedro. Puerto Rican obituary. N.Y., Monthly Review Press, 1973. 109 p.

Importante texto de poesía boricua de N.Y., que destaca la agonía vital en un ghetto latino. Rítmica, directa y políticamente fuerte; estilo asimilado a la nueva poesía norteamericana de protesta. [ER]

7136. Posternak, Dora. Piedras sobre piedra. Montevideo, Ediciones Fesela, 1976. 59 p., illus.

La primera parte de esta antología de poemas es un testimonio personal, una reflexión de su ascendencia hebraica. La segunda parte, con más acento israelí, se refiere a los sufrimientos, alegrías, esperanza y muerte de su pueblo. Gracias a su habilidad de despertar emociones, su gente y su ascendencia se hacen nuestras. [EPS]

7137. Quesada, José Luis. Porque no espero nunca más volver. San José, Ministerio de Cultura, Juventud y Deportes, Depto. de Publicaciones, 1974. 31 p. (Serie los premios)

La ciudad aporta imágenes cortantes y la alienación cobra cuerpo. El lenguaje, consistentemente sombrío, crea el tono justo de la angustia. Quesada enriquece la lírica hondureña con esta entrega. [RG]

7138. Quirós, Rodrigo. Abismo sitiado. San José, Editorial Costa Rica, 1973. 85 p.

Ágil y sonora se yergue la palabra en el poema de Rodrigo Quirós; y la voz lírica va plasmando un itinerario personal, una búsqueda, una visión. [RG]

7139. Reyes, Jaime. Isla de raíz amarga, insomne raíz. México, Ediciones Era, 1976. 119 p. (Alacena)

Poems of protest filled with pain, fury, and frustration. Language is angry and tone sarcastically bitter except for some descriptions of passion at the end of collection. [CM]

7140. Riquelme de Molinas, Yula. Los moradores del córtice. Poemas. n.p., n.p., 1976. 77 p.

Preocupada por la pérdida de los valores morales. la autora pinta en los primeros 23 poemas los diversos vicios que aprisionan al hombre. En los tres últimos, da la esperanza de la salvación gracias al arrepentimiento y la expiación. Presenta la Fe, la Esperanza y la Caridad como armas con las cuales luchar contra el pecado. [EPS]

7141. Rodríguez Castillos, Osiris. Canto y poesía. Montevideo, Arca Editorial, 1974. 164 p. (Bolsilibro, 96)

Antología que recoge las majores producciones del poeta y presenta también sus últimas e inéditas obras. Poesía de raíz criollista y telúrica, de gran acercamiento al hombre de la tierra. Canto comunitario que expresa lo colectivo; gestas de la independencia y de las convulsiones revolucionarias. Usa a veces el lenguaje culto y otras veces el habla popular. [EPS]

7142. Rojas, Gonzalo. Oscuro. Caracas, Editorial Monte Avila, 1977. 214 p. (Col. Altazor)

Colección de composiciones inéditas y de otras publicadas previamente, que se estatuye no como una muestra antológica sino como una suma poética. Algunos de los textos son de índole metafísica; otros se refieren a la intensidad del sentimiento amoroso; otros, a la vivencia del tiempo y de la muerte; y otros, a la realidad social latinoamericana. Todos ellos poseen emotividad y gran rigor artesanal. *Oscuro* confirma a Gonzalo Rojas como una de las figuras más significativas de la poesía contemporánea en lengua española. [OH]

7143. Rojas, Waldo. El puente oculto y otros poemas. Jalisco, Mex., Gobierno de Jalisco, Depto. de Bellas Artes, 1976. 70 p. (Col. Textos latinoamericanos)

Quebrado el puente de unión entre el sujeto lírico y el mundo objetivo, los hablantes de estos poemas deambulan por los aledaños del pasado, en busca de un nuevo vínculo que les permita acceder a los códigos ocultos de una realidad trabajosamente sondeada por el lenguaje. Sin duda uno de los libros más significativos de la última poesía chilena. [OH]

7144. Romero, Elvio. Destierro y atardecer. B.A., Editorial Losada, 1975. 96 p. (Poetas de ayer y de hoy)

El poeta lejos de su patria, en el atardecer, añora su tierra nunca olvidada y canta, ruega. Como le está vedado regresar a su país, Romero usa el recuerdo y espera "en la orilla opuesta del gran río." [EPS]

7145. Romualdo, Alejandro. En la extensión de la palabra. Lima, Ediciones Viva Voz, 1974. 39 p.

Esta búsqueda de un "espacio libre abierto" para instalar una nueva palabra poética es uno de los intentos más audaces en la poesía peruana de hoy. El experimento realizado por Romualdo queda bien definido en las observaciones de Alberto Escobar, que en la nota final del volumen pondera las virtualidades renovadoras de una tendencia ¡que se inspira en la relación dialéctica entre unidades completas ... que desborda los límites del libro y reclama relaciones significadores," multiplicando las lecturas posibles. [PL]

7146. ———. Poemas. La Habana, Casa de las Américas, 1975. 161 p. (Col. La honda)

Selección preparada por el autor, que dispone en orden cronológico variados textos de sus libros anteriores, desde *La torre de los alucinados* (1949) hasta *En la extensión de la palabra* (1974, véase item 7145). [PL]

7147. Rose, Juan Gonzalo. Obra poética. Estudio preliminar de Alberto Escobar. Lima, Instituto Nacional de Cultura, 1974. 425 p.

Contiene los libros *Cantos desde lejos* (1957), *Simple canción* (1960), *Las comarcas* (1964), *Informe al rey y otros libros secretos* (1967) y numerosos textos no recogidos en volúmenes unitarios o independientes hasta ahora. En un prólogo iluminador "Juan Gonzalo o la Poética de la Anti-Poesía," Alberto Escobar sitúa la notable obra de Rose en el proceso de la poesía peruana y valora la significación mayor de su quehacer, sobre todo a partir de 1967. [PL]

7148. Ross, Claudio. Equinoccio del miedo. Prólogo de Clara Silva. Montevideo?, Editorial Aire 8, 1976. 29 p. (Serie poesía)

El autor es un joven de 23 años cuya expresión original e intensidad lírica prometen mucho. Sus versos arquitecturados como sonetos, aunque no lo sean realmente ("casi sonetos") descubren un mundo triste que se nutre de llanto y las modificaciones que introduce (versos de distinta medida, rimas asonantes y consonantes, alternadas indistintamente) responden a su convencimiento de que la forma no es "un elemento de ahogo del espíritu sino todo lo contrario." [EPS]

7149. Rueda, Manuel. Con el tambor de las islas: pluralemas. Santo Domingo, Editora Taller, 1975. 161 p.

Fascinante volumen de poesía visual, en la tradición del concretismo y los topoemas; los textos múltiples integran música, dibujo y fotografía. Apéndices con comentarios y un interesante manifiesto del "Movimiento Pluralista" en la República Dominicana. [ER]

7150. Schvartzman, Celia de. Un después de amor. Concepción del Uruguay, Arg., Ediciones de Haor, 1975. 61 p., illus.

Motivos principales de su poesía: la gestación de la vida con su misterio e incertidumbre, la problemática del hombre, su sed de justicia y anhelos de eternidad. Su canto se nutre de imágenes bíblicas. La Sulamita en búsqueda del Amado; Ana, la triunfadora de su esterilidad; Débora, Raquel y Ruth se pasean por sus versos. [EPS]

7151. Silva, Desiderio Macias. Ascuario. México, Editorial Joaquín Mortiz, 1973. 113 p.

Winner of the Premio Nacional de Poesía in 1972, this work shows much promise. Author writes sensitively of man's emotions, primarily love. [CM]

7152. Silva Acevedo, Manuel. Lobos y ovejas. Santiago, Galería Paulina Waugh, 1972. 1 v. (Unpaged)

A pesar del manido simbolismo al que remiten las menciones del título, este pequeño libro consigue despegar de lo obvio y se instala en los dominios de la poesía, gracias al temblor emotivo que despiertan sus configuraciones verbales y a la autenticidad que despliegan sus contenidos como signos de la condición humana. [OH]

7153. Skell, Otto. Poemas. n.p., Fondo Editor Paraguayo, 1976. 1 v. (Unpaged)

Poesía religiosa, fuerte, viril. Preguntas trascendentes sin respuestas. Skell describe los males de la tecnología moderna y lamenta la destrucción humana. [EPS]

7154. Sologuren, Javier. Surcando el aire oscuro. Edited by Carlos Milla Batres. Madrid, Carlos Milla Batres Ediciones, 1970. 46 p. illus. (Col. Ernesto Che Guevara)

Textos de notable factura, sabiamente controlados y de gran poder de sugerencia, que demuestran una vez más la eficacia del arte de Sologuren, que podría definirse como poética de la alusión. [PL]

7155. Talayer, Felipe. Cardos y chircas: poesía gaucha, coplas nativas, rimas ciudadanas. Montevideo, El Siglo Ilustrado, 1976. 126 p.

En este libro se puede apreciar la rica temática gauchesca que como el autor dice, "me seduce y me atrae como un buen hijo de tierra adentro que soy." Se presenta al gaucho como una persona heroica, patriótica, pobre pero libre e independiente. El uno es alegre y sencillo. [EPS]

7156. ———. Ombúes y ñandubays: surcos sembrados de versos y episodios nativos, páginas líricas. n.p., n.p., 1976. 92 p.

Homenaje en tres partes a los gestores de la patria al cumplirse el sesquicentenario de la Epopeya Nacional de 1825: 1) contiene poemas de temas nacionalistas: sus personajes son José G. Artigas, Juan Antonio Lavalleja, Fructuoso Rivera y los 33 Orientales; 2) hay poemas de la tierra, de los pájaros y de los ríos del Uruguay; y 3) incluye títulos como "El Llanto que Nunca Lloré," y "Tristeza," más sentimentales que los anteriores. [EPS]

7157. **Tejada Gómez, Armando.** Canto popular de las comidas. La Habana, Casa de las Américas, 1974. 118 p.

Colección de originales poemas sobre los pueblos y sus comidas típicas; textos de corte narrativista y conversacional. Una "geopoética del hambre" en América, con admitida inspiración en Pablo de Rokha y Pablo Neruda. [ER]

7158. **Tello, Jaime.** Geometría del espacio y otros poemas. Caracas, Editorial Arte, 1971. 137 p.

Poems are better than title indicates, original and somewhat intellectual but poetic in concept and tone. Sometimes derivative, reflecting his travels in Europe and his readings, yet often coolly humorous and at times ironical, with philosophical touches. [BTO]

7159. **Terán, Ana Enriqueta.** Libro de los oficios. Poemas, 1967. Caracas, Monte Avila Editores, 1975. 76 p. (Col. Altazor)

Harsh poetry of thought and vocabulary, reflecting a controlled desperation, but original in concept. Oneiric at times, but stirring. [BTO]

7160. **Torres-García, Joaquín** and **Esther de Cáceres.** Plástica y poesía. Dibujos de Joaquín Torres García. Presentación de Arturo Sergio Visca. Montevideo, Asociación de Impresores del Uruguay, 1976. 1 v. (Unpaged) illus.

Contiene siete grabados del pintor uruguayo Joaquín Torres García y once poemas de Esther de Cáceres que la conocida poetisa denominó *Cantata*. El carácter religioso de la obra está indicado por el título—*Cruz y éxtasis de la Pasión*—y las citas de Santa Teresa de Jesús y Miguel de Unamuno. Lo poético y lo plástico están integrados como si todas las manifestaciones estéticas tuvieran una raíz común, a pesar de la delimitación de sus formas expresivas. [EPS]

7161. **Urquiza, Concha.** Poemas. Antología. México, Editorial Jus, 1975. 60 p. (Col. Poesía, 1)

Selection of 28 poems by the Morelian writer who died in 1945. She expresses her varied themes (mystical, regional, erotic) in elegant language and traditional poetic forms. Urquiza has many ties with the past, particularly San Juan de la Cruz and Fray Luis de León. [CM]

7162. **Uslar-Pietri, Arturo.** Manoa. Caracas, Editorial Arte, 1972. 111 p.

Six epigraphs precede 37 poems by Uslar-Pietri. Some have the sound and rhythms of folk-songs. His expression is original and forceful, yet at times he appears to be searching yet to find his own voice. There is a prosaic simplicity which at times seems deliberate. [BTO]

7163. **Vallejo, César.** César Vallejo. Prólogo, selección y notas de Carlos Luis Altamirano. San José, Ministerio de Cultura, Juventud y Deportes, Depto. de Publicaciones, 1975. 245 p., bibl., plates (Serie pensamiento de América, 3)

Antología rigurosa y bien meditada, precedida por un extenso estudio que sitúa la obra de Vallejo en su contexto histórico y cultural. Son sugestivos los apartados III y IV del prólogo, en los que el autor examina algunos de los recursos estilísticos que caracterizan el sistema expresivo vallejiano. Libro recomendable como texto introductorio, por su claridad y por la adecuada utilización de la bibliografía. Incluye las cinco cartas de Vallejo al poeta trujillano Oscar Imaña. [PL]

7164. **Viel Temperly, Héctor.** Carta de marear. B.A., Juárez Editor, 1976. 51 p.

Tres brevísimas colecciones de vibrante dinamismo y con una estructura metafórica surrealista. [CMH]

7165. **Walsh, María Elena.** Cancionero contra el mal de ojo. B.A., Editorial Sudamericana, 1976. 99 p.

Poesía de carácter popular que refleja preocupaciones con acontecimientos de actualidad. Un número apreciable de las composiciones son también canciones. [CMH]

GENERAL STUDIES

7166. **Baeza Flores, Alberto.** La poesía dominicana en el siglo XX: historia, crítica, estudio comparativo y estilístico; modernismo, Vedrinismo, Postumismo y Los Triálogos, 1883-1943. Prólogo de Héctor Incháustegui Cabral. Santiago, R.D., Univ. Católica Madre y Maestra, 1976. 671 p. (Col. Estudios, 22)

De interés porque trata de establecer nexos entre la hispanidad y esa literatura tan "insular" (e.g., entre el Postumismo y la vanguardia española); también por el panorama detallado de una materia tan poco tratada. Enfoque histórico-estilístico a ratos abrumador; útil al especialista. [ER]

7167. Charry Lara, Fernando. Lector de poesía. Bogotá, Instituto Colombiano de Cultura, Subdirección de Comunicaciones Culturales, División de Publicaciones, 1975. 169 p. (Biblioteca colombiana de cultura. Col. Autores nacionales, 3)

Eighteen articles and critical essays by noted Colombian poet-critic have been collected from various periodicals in which they appeared. Divided into sections on Colombian poetry, colonial poetry in Spanish America, on the Generation of 1927 in Spain and on later Latin American poetry. [BTO]

7168. Concha, Jaime. La poésie chilienne d'aujourd'hui (EUR, 570, oct. 1976, p. 107-155)

Visión panorámica de la poesía chilena desde Huidobro hasta "los nuevos," seguida de una antología de poemas traducidos al francés, en la que están representados los siguientes autores: Gonzalo Rojas, Enrique Lihn, Efraín Barquero, Armando Uribe, Luis A. Faúndez, Jorge Teillier, Jaime Giordano, Oscar Hahn, Omar Lara, Waldo Rojas, Gonzalo Millán, Fernando Quilodrán y Eloy Diego. Completa la muestra una interesantísima selección de poemas escritos por prisioneros políticos chilenos. [OH]

7169. Dolz Henry, Inés. Los romances tradicionales chilenos. Santiago, Editorial Nascimento, 1976. 270 p.

Interesante estudio temático y técnico de la poesía tradicional chilena y fundamentalmente del Romancero local. La autora examina y compara los romances sobrenaturales, eróticos y novelescos y llega a la conclusión de que aunque esas composiciones tienen claros antecedentes en la poesía popular española, revelan sin embargo la idiosincracia del pueblo, que recrea los diversos elementos heredados de la tradición peninsular. [OH]

7170. Fernández Spencer, Antonio. Lo universal en la poesía dominicana del siglo XX (UNPHU/A, 3:10/11, julio/dic. 1974, p. 11-83)

Extenso artículo que precisa el ámbito y las características de la "Poesía Sorprendida" y de los poetas que componen este grupo. Interesante visión histórico-crítica. [ER]

7171. Ibañez Langlois, José Miguel. Poesía chilena e hispanoamericana actual. Santiago, Editorial Nascimento, 1975. 399 p. (Biblioteca popular)

Recopilación de los artículos sobre poesía publicados por Ibañez Langlois en las columnas dominicales de El Mercurio (1967-74) bajo el seudónimo de Ignacio Valente. Muchas veces lúcidas, algunas veces arbitrarias, estas notas ofrecen una muestra viva de los avatares de la poesía chilena de los últimos años, sobre el telón de fondo de la poesía hispanoamericana. [OH]

7172. Partida, Armando. Acerca del modernismo (VME/R, 34:2218, julio/sept. 1975, p. 41-52, bibl.)

El autor intenta rectificar lo que considera errores acerca del movimiento modernista. Según José O. Jiménez. el modernismo "es un movimiento integral ... expresivo del angustioso conflicto espiritual del hombre contemporáneo ... que conoció una veta hispánica y preocupada, complementaria de la afrancesada y frívola a que se le ha querido reducir ..." Los verdaderos iniciadores de este movimiento son José Martí y Manuel Gutiérrez Nájera, y no Rubén Darío. Este llega a sustituir los elementos de las viejas formas, pero no a romper ni a rechazar, dado que utiliza los mismos recursos a los que da un giro moderno, hasta alcanzar su forma de finitiva en Cantos de vida y esperanza. [EPS]

7173. Portuondo, José Antonio. Concepto de la poesía y otros ensayos. Prólogo de Roberto Fernández Retamar. México, Editorial Grijalbo, 1974. 209 p., bibl. (Col. Teoría y praxis, 7)

Enfoque marxista de la explicación del fenómeno poético; contiene, además del titular, otros sobre teoría literaria. De particular interés al estudioso es la evaluación de Wellek y Warren y del New Criticism anglo-sajón. [ER]

7174. Santana, Francisco. Evolución de la poesía chilena. Santiago, Editorial Nascimento, 1976. 342 p.

Este estudio se propone trazar el desarrollo de la poesía chilena desde el siglo XVI hasta los años 70 del siglo XX; pero como tal empresa no está fundada en principios metodológicos rigurosos, el resultado es la mera yuxtaposición de notas impresionistas o periodísticas sobre autores y movimientos. Sin embargo el esfuerzo de Santana es encomiable por las útiles informaciones que proporciona sobre revistas especializadas, galardones, datos biográficos y primeras ediciones. [OH]

7175. Uribe Echevarría, Juan. El tema del juicio final en la poesía popular traditional de Chile (UC/BF, 23/24, 1972/1973, p. 315-381, illus.)

Estudio y exposición de textos sobre los signos previos al Juicio Final y sobre el tema del "Acabo de Mundo" a consecuencia de catástrofes naturales, en los cantos a lo divino de la poesía popular chilena, como prolongación y reelaboración de temas análogos, procedentes de la tradición medieval española. [OH]

SPECIAL STUDIES

7176. Abayubá Olave, Carlos. Andrés Héctor Lerena Acevedo: angustia y soledad (UBN/R, 14, marzo 1976, p. 125-141)

Conferencia pronunciada en la Biblioteca Nacional de Montevideo, para rendirle un homenaje póstumo al poeta. El crítico señala como partes definidas en su poética: una dulce sensación de delectación en la vida y en el colorido, paisajes que muestran una nueva apreciación de retratos sencillos y descripciones de la naturaleza agreste. Su tristeza romántica la identifica con paisajes, la melancolía la proyecta en sensaciones de vacío y estos estados se funden con la naturaleza, que a veces adquiere carácter religioso. [EPS]

7177. Alazraki, Jaime. Jorge Luis Borges: el escritor y la crítica. Madrid, Ediciones Taurus, 1976. 363 p.

Colección de estudios críticos sobre la obra de Borges en la cual se han incluído también artículos de críticos norteamericanos. La cuidadosa selección incluye trabajos de prestigiosos hispanistas como Pedro Henríquez Ureña, Amado Alonso y Raimundo Lida. [CMH]

7178. Andino, Alberto. Notas a propósito de *Tabaré* y el velatorio de Caracé (CH, 105:313, julio 1976, p. 179-191)

El autor mantiene que Zorrilla de San Martín linda con el modernismo en sus imágenes repletas de color y de sonido. Da ejemplos de impresiones auditivas, ópticas, táctiles, gustativas y olfativas y muestra juegos lumínicos, contrastes de sombra y la luz. También se refiere a escenas de realismo mágico en que la visión está distorsionada por la ingestión constante de chicha y por la superstición. Concluye que es como un caleidoscopio lo que el poeta nos ofece, "como uno de esos recursos muy modernos de fotografía cinematográfica." [EPS]

7179. Armand, Octavio. La poesía de Juan Sánchez Peláez: un discurso contra el método (CONAC/RNC, 227, dic. 1976, p. 109-119, plate)

Illustrates poet's efforts to solve eternal enigmas, through themes such as death and eroticism. Judges that for the poet the name of something is not really the thing itself and that naming does not give possession or complete knowing. Venezuelan poet is considered to reflect man's vacillation and uncertainty and to use those characteristics in conjunction with contradictions, with a technique of dissolving the contradictions implied by the contiguous placement of opposite ideas. [BTO]

7180. Augier, Angel. Alusiones africanas en la poesía de Nicolás Guillén (UCLV/I, 39/40, mayo/dic. 1971, p. 127-137)

Corto estudio de la significación negrista de Guillén por un conocido intérprete de su obra. [ER]

7181. Blanco Aguinaga, Carlos. Crítica marxista y poesía: lectura de un poema de Julián del Casal (*in* Beck, Mary Ann and others. The analysis of Hispanic text: current trends in methodology. Jamaica, N.Y., CUNY, York College, Dept. of Foreign Languages, Bilingual Press/Editorial Bilingue, 1976, p. 191-205)

Análisis textual de la obra basado en sus relaciones con la ideología del capitalismo y la sociedad de consumo (los objetos-fetiches del "interior urbano"), y de sus nexos con los modelos europeos imperantes. Estudio de la visión de mundo que arroja el poema, y de sus fundamentos sociales. [ER]

Brodman, Barbara L.C. The Mexican cult of death in myth and literature. See item 6594.

7182. Chavez, Fermîn. Un nuevo diálogo gauchesco sobre Rosas: el poeta Bernardo Echevarría; vida y obra. B.A., Ediciones Theoria, 1975. 85 p.

Este volumen es el producto de un estudio sistemático de la vida cultural durante los tiempos de Rosas. Con la obra de Echevarría, porteño y federal, Chavez añade al panorama literario del siglo XIX un interesante ejemplo de literatura rosista. El diálogo entre el paisano Justo Calandria y Perico Bienteveo merece ser incorporado al parnaso gauchesco. [CMH]

7183. Cornejo, Justino. Olmedo y sus críticos contemporáneos. Guayaquil, Ecua., Junta Cívica de Guayaquil, 1975. 84 p., illus. (Col. Equinoccial, 4)

Comenta los juicios de S. Bolívar, A. Bello, Vicente Solano y el propio Olmedo sobre el poema *La victoria de Junín: canto a Bolívar*. El tema es interesante, pero el tratamiento superficial que aquí tiene—a través de un lenguaje crítico desarticulado y enfadoso—lo deja prácticamente intocado. [PL]

7184. Debarbieri Casagrande, César A. Los personajes en la poética de José María Eguren. Lima, Univ. del Pacífico, Depto. de Humanidades, 1975. 274 p.

La carencia de estudios críticos sobre la poesía de J.M. Eguren empieza a inquietar en buena hora a los investigadores peruanos. Ejemplo de esta preocupación es el ensayo de Debarbieri, que aborda el examen de la poética de Eguren a partir del análisis de una actitud sin precedentes en la literatura peruana: "la aparición de la poesía simbólica, reflejada en sus personajes, sucedáneos del símbolo." Las verificaciones textuales son minuciosas y las conclusiones resultan sugerentes. [PL]

7185. Di Candia, Alcides J. Ayudando a leer el Martín Fierro. Montevideo, Publicaciones de la Comisión Nacional de Homenaje del Sesquicentenario de los Hechos Históricos de 1825, 1975. 224 p.

Detallada explicación de texto que incorpora las opiniones de una serie de críticos rioplatenses. Las referencias a los acontecimientos políticos del momento que inspiraron a Hernández son abundantes, así como también los ataques al *Facundo* y a la posición de Sarmiento. [CMH]

7186. En torno a José Martí: coloquio internacional celebrado bajo los auspicios de Sala José Martí de la Biblioteca Nacional de Cuba; José Martí Foundation de Estados Unidos; Institut d'Études Ibériques et Ibéro-Américaines; de l'Université de Bordeaux III. Bordeaux, Éditions Bière. 1974. 547 p.

Importante volumen de crítica martiana que contiene los siguientes trabajos: "Contenido Profético del Epistolario Martiano" de Manuel Pedro González; "La Irrupción Americana en la Obra de Martí" de Cintio Vitier; "Fuentes y Raíces del Pensamiento Antimperialista de José Martí" de Juan Marinello; "Historia Colectiva e Individual en la Obra de José Martí" de Ivan A. Schulman; "Nuestra América o la Plena Libertad" de Jaime Díaz Rozzoto; "José Martí y la Independencia Hispanoamericana" de Charles Lancha; "Le Thème Argentin Chez Martí" de André Joucla-Ruau; "Carácter Específico de la Militancia Revolucionaria en la Vida y Obra de José Martí" de Andrés Sorel; "Un 'Socialista' Mexicano: José Martí" de Paul Estrade; "'Teoría Martiana del Partido Revolucionario" de José Antonio Portuondo; "José Martí en la Literatura Latino-Americana" de Adalbert Dassau; "La Sencilla Poesía de Martí en México" de Alfonso Herrera Franyutti; "Apuntes para un Estudio sobre el Realismo Mágico en la Prosa Política de José Martí" de Luis Amado-Blanco; "El Tiempo en la Crónica Norteamericana de Martí" de Fina García Marruz; "Sobre la Idea de Naturaleza en José Martí" de Jean Lamore; "En Torno al Idealismo de José Martí" de Noël Salomon; "José Martí y Gabriela Mistral" de Juan Loveluck; "Algunas Notas sobre la Estructura General de los 'Versos Sencillos'" de Margot Arce de Vázquez; "José Martí y Antonio Machado" de Carmen C. de Rodríguez-Puértolas; "Martí y Francia" de Alejo Carpentier; "Una Investigación por Hacer: 'José Martí y la Raza Negra'" de René Durand. Apéndice con homenajes de diversos autores. [ER]

7187. Fernández Alonso, María del Rosario. Angustia existencial en la poesía de María Eugenia Vaz Ferreira: breve homenaje en el centenario de su nacimiento, 1875-1924 (CH, 303, sept. 1975, p. 634-653)

Este artículo trata el tema de la muerte y la angustia existencial de una vida infecunda. Analiza a fondo el poema "El Regreso" de *La isla de los cánticos* (1925), obra póstuma de M.E.V.F., en el cual el aniquilamiento total se vuelve liberación porque es descanso. Concluye la autora que esta poesía puede sentirse próxima, por su temática y su momento, al canto de Antonio Machado en la lírica española. [EPS]

7188. Figueira, Gastón. Herrera y Reissig en su centenario (RIB, 25:3, julio/sept. 1975, p. 241-255)

De Herrera y Reissig se puede decir que es un poeta únicamente, integralmente modernista, en tanto que el modernismo no fue para él—como lo fue para Darío y Lugones—una etapa en su evolución. Figueira estudia las influencias parnasianas, simbolistas y decadentes en la obra del poeta uruguayo. [EPS]

7189. Flores, Angel *ed*, Aproximaciones a Octavio Paz. México, Editorial Joaquín Mortiz, 1974. 279 p., bibl. (Confrontaciones: los críticos)

Important collection of critical writings. Pt. 1) "Recursos Expresivos y Temática," contains perceptive essays on general topics by Juan García Ponce, Ramón Xirau, Carlos Fuentes, Julio Requena, Jean Franco, Manuel Durán, and Luis Alfonso Díez. Pt. 2) "Crítica de su Obra y Análisis de Textos," includes thoughtful contributions from Luis Mario Schneider, Eduardo González Lanuza, Luis Leal, Carlos H. Magis, Ramón Xirau, John M. Fein, Tomás Segovia, José Emilio Pacheco, E. Caracciolo Trejo, Roberta Seabrook, Julio Ortega, Octavio Armand, Javier Sologuren, Guillermo Sucre, Enrique Pezzoni and Saúl Yurkievich. Also includes useful bibliography by and on the writer and brief eulogistic piece "Homenaje a una Estrella de Mar" by Julio Cortázar. [CM]

7190. Forster, Merlin H. Fire and ice: the poetry of Xavier Villaurrutia. Chapel Hill, Univ. of North Carolina, Dept. of Romance Languages, 1976. 176 p. (North Carolina studies in the romance languages and literatures. Essays, 11)

Valuable study of well-known Mexican poet, a member of the "Contemporáneos" group. Chapters on lexicon and syntax, sound and form, and imagery and symbol are followed by more general comments on Villaurrutia's themes and overall importance. Detailed outline of earlier scholarships opens book. [CM]

7191. Franco, Jean. César Vallejo: the dialects of poetry and silence. Cambridge, U.K., Cambridge Univ. Press, 1976. 296 p., bibl.

Estudio documentado que significa una contribución a las investigaciones vallejianas. Es ponderable la coherencia del punto de vista metodológico, que funde las varias dimensiones textuales y contextuales del examen. Libro de enterés para el especialista. Incluye una bibliografía concisamente anotada y un buen índice analítico. [PL]

7192. González, Manuel Pedro. Amor y mito en Juana Borrero. Montevideo, Centro de Estudios Latinoamericanos, 1973. 86 p.

Estudio del epistolario de la malograda poeta cubana del XIX, que interesa por la exploración de sus nexos con los escritores Julián del Casal y Carlos Pío Uhrbach. De valor a un enfoque histórico del modernismo finisecular. [ER]

7193. Guevara, Darío. Olmedo: poeta e insurgente. Quito, Editorial Casa de la Cultura Ecuatoriana, 1971. 154 p., illus.

Crónica biográfica entusiasta, dedicada a "La Juventud de América." El estilo es adjetival y abunda en lugares comunes. Prescindible para el especialista. [PL]

7194. Hernández de Mendoza, Cecilia. La poesía de Greiff. Bogotá, Instituto Colombiano de Cultura, 1974. 69 p., plates (Biblioteca colombiana de cultura. Col. Autores nacionales)

Collection of essays of exegesis of selected poems from León de Greiff's works. Previously published in Colombian periodicals. Deserves commendation for her perspicacity since some articles are from as early as 1945 when De Greiff was not yet considered an important writer. [BTO]

7195. Hernández Novás, Raúl. Luis Palés Matos: poeta antillano (CDLA, 15:89, marzo/abril 1975, p. 28-39, illus.)

Breve pero medular estudio que ofrece una perspectiva ideológica de la visión negrista del poeta, y la distingue dentro del marco popular y realista de autores como Nicolás Guillén. Justa e interesante valoración del "negrismo" literario y de específicamente puertorriqueño. [ER]

7196. Instituto Cubano del Libro, La Habana. Bibliografía de Nicolás Guillén. La Habana, Biblioteca Nacional José Martí [and] Editorial Orbe, 1975. 379 p., bibl., plate.

Excelente obra de consulta, que muestra la variadísima extensión de la obra en verso y prosa de Guillén (libros, folletos, colaboraciones periodísticas) así como una gama de guilleniana: prólogos, traducciones, partituras, discos. La bibliografía pasiva consta de 685 fichas, pero sólo abarca hasta 1972; Ruscalleda Bercedóniz (item 7216) añade otras entre 1972-74, en especial el trabajo de Nancy Morejón, Recopilación de textos sobre Nicolás Guillén (La Habana, Casa de las Américas, 1974). [ER]

7197. Irazusta, Julio. Leopoldo Lugones en el centenario de su nacimiento (ANH/B, 47, 1974, p. 211-217)

Presenta una valorización objetiva de la obra histórica de Lugones, en especial de la Historia de Sarmiento. [CMH]

7198. Laguna-Díaz, Elpidio. The phenomenology of nothingness in the poetry of Julia de Burgos (in Ivette E. Miller and Charles M. Tatum eds. Latin American women writers: yesterday and today. With an introduction by Ivette E. Miller. Pittsburgh, Pa., Latin American Literary Review, 1977, p. 127-133)

Muy breve trabajo sobre una importante poeta puertorriqueña, a veces ignorada. El mérito del artículo consiste en apuntar y "redescubrir" un motivo vital a la producción de Julia de Burgos, si bien el enfoque crítico y la extensión dejan que desear. [ER]

7199. Leiva, Raúl. Introducción a Sor Juana: sueño y realidad. México, UNAM, Instituto de Investigaciones Filológicas, Centro de Estudios Literarios, 1975. 158 p. (Letras del XVI al XVIII. Textos y estudios, 1)

Important critical study of Mexican colonial writer. Leiva examines her poetry, particularly "Primero Sueño," in book's first section and her thought in general in second. Third sec. evaluates in detail earlier analyses of Sor Juana by Ezequiel A. Chávez, Francisco López Cámara, Irving A. Leonard, Ludwig Pfandl, and Anita Arroyo. [CM]

7200. Lemaître, Monique J. Octavio Paz: poesía y poética. México, UNAM, Dirección General de Publicaciones, 1976. 127 p., bibl. (Col. Poemas y ensayos)

Thoughtful analysis of Paz' verse and of his many statements on the nature of poetry. Lemaître presents in addition a useful survey of the varied sources that have influenced the Mexican writer. [CM]

7201. Lewkowic, Lidia F. Generación poética del treinta. B.A., Ministerio de Cultura y Educación, Secretaría de Estado de Cultura, Ediciones Culturales Argentinas, 1974. 291 p. (Col. Movimientos literarios argentinos)

Por medio de este breviario se trata de documentar y reconstruir las actividades de la Novísima Generación. La introducción consigna algunas particularidades a través de las cuales se presiente porqué nació dicha promoción. Antología poética a continuación de la introducción. [CMH]

7202. Madrid-Malo, Néstor. El mar en el poesía colombiana (RIB, 26:3, julio/sept. 1976. p. 269-281)

Poet-critic gives short overview of poetry on theme of ocean. Summary analysis precedes one poem by each writer on that theme up until the 1960s. [BTO]

7203. Martínez Estrada, Ezequiel. La poesía de Nicolás Guillén: seguido de un antología del poeta por Horacio Salas. B.A., Calicanto Editorial, 1977. 151 p.

Novedoso enfoque de la poesía del conocido autor cubano, fundamentándola en su cubanidad "glandular:" la esencia de su ancestro, hibridación de lo negrotelúrico y lo europeo-cultural. Interesante análisis del lenguaje. [ER]

7204. Miller, Beth *comp*. Ensayos contemporáneos sobre Jaime Torres Bodet. México, UNAM, Dirección General de Publicaciones, 1976. 131 p. (Col. Poemas y ensayos)

Collection of essays on Torres Bodet as a "Contemporáneo," his books *La casa* and *Los días*, his prose works, his other poetry, and his death. Some selections are critical, others not. Authors of essays are: José Emilio Pacheco, Salvador Elizondo, Estelle Irizarry, E.J. Mullen, Merlin H. Forster, Sonja Karsen, Beth Miller, Antonio Castro Leal and Rafael Solana. [CM]

7205. Moffett, Oren E. Lautreamont en el Uruguay (UBN/R, 14, marzo 1976, p. 143-152)

Lautréamont no dejó ninguna información autobiográfica con respecto a su vida en el Uruguay. Para descifrar el enigma que rodea su niñez y primeros años de su adolescencia, el autor de este artículo aclara unos cuantos datos significativos: la fecha del bautismo del poeta (16 nov. 1847), posterior en más de un año y medio a la de su nacimiento (4 abril 1846); la teoría de la muerte por suicidio de la madre del poeta; la epidemia de fiebre amarilla, en 1857, que provocó 851 muertes en Montevideo; el interés de Lautréamont en la Historia Natural, y finalmente su presunto regreso al Uruguay entre 1865 y 1867. [EPS]

7206. Mohler, Stephen Charles. El estilo poético de León de Greiff. Bogotá, Ediciones Tercer Mundo, 1975. 145 p., bibl. (Col. Literaria)

Based on author's doctoral dissertation (1969). This study of poet's life and works concentrates on metaphor. Classifies De Greiff as a vanguardista, chronologically and in essence, because of poet's lack of interest in the real world and its problems. Studies influences of poets and musicians upon De Greiff. Catalogues many image and metaphor techniques. In chapter on Structural Techniques writer actually treats metrics, rhythm and rhyme. [BTO]

7207. Moretta, Eugene Lawrence. La poesía de Xavier Villaurrutia. México, Fondo de Cultura Económica, 1976. 227 p. (Sección de lengua y estudios literarios)

Detailed examination of Villaurrutia's works of poetry followed by brief final chapter on poet's concept of artistic creation. Sections on *Nostalgia de la muerte* (1938) are most thorough. [CM]

7208. Orjuela, Héctor H. La obra poética de Rafael Pombo. Bogotá, Instituto Caro y Cuervo, 1975. 457 p., bibl. (Publicaciones, 34)

Appropriate sequel to Colombian critic's two-volume collection of previously scattered poems by Pombo (see *HLAS 34:3845*). In this thorough study of Pombo's complete poetic works, Orjuela continues to publish his meticulous research and surprisingly complete bibliographies on Colombian poets and criticism. Work is fruit of 10 or more years study on Pombo, beginning with doctoral dissertation on his prose and poetry. Introduction is concise and critically apt characterization of Romanticism in Colombia. [BTO]

Paz, Octavio. Vuelta a *El laberinto de la soledad*. See item 6613.

7209. Phillips, Rachel. Alfonsina Storni: from poetess to poet. London, Tamesis Books, 1975. 131 p.

Estudio detallado de la obra de Storni que comprende análisis de su prosa y creaciones teatrales. La agresiva actitud feminista que adopta la autora en ciertos pasajes para encarar el tema le quita seriedad al trabajo. [CMH]

7210. *Quaderni di Letteratura Americane*. Cattedra di Letteratura Ispano-Americana. No. 1, set. 1976- . Venezia, Italia.

Número dedicado al estudio de la poesía de Neruda, a cargo de tres especialistas italianos. En "Per una Lettura Ritmemica di una Poesia de Neruda," Giussepe Tavani analiza el poema "Los Perdidos del Bosque;" Giussepe Bellini examina los ocho libros publicados después de la muerte del poeta y los relaciona con su producción anterior. Y Giovanni Battista De Cesare, en "Funzione del 'Canto' nelle 'Nuevas Odas Elementales'," indica que en ellas el yo poético es rebasado—aunque no anulado—por la finalidad histórico-social de los poemas. [OH]

7211. Ramón Medina, José. Juan Beroes y su obra en el proceso contemporáneo de la poesía venezolana (CELRG/A, 1975, p. 129-145)

Reproduction, as a gesture of homage, of excellent prologue written for *Antología poética* by Juan Beroes (d. 1975). Critic summarizes previous investigation on poet and displays his own superior depth of knowledge and insight concerning Beroes' work. [BTO]

7212. *Revista de la Biblioteca Nacional.* Ministerio de Educación y Cultura. No. 13, abril 1976- . Montevideo.

Número especial dedicado a Herrera y Reissig, contiene excelentes artículos. Incluye: 1) Un homenaje lírico al poeta por Carlos Sabat Ercasty y Martín C. Martínez; 2) Perspectivas críticas: "La Torre de los Panoramas" de Roberto Ibáñez, "Presencia Lírica de J.H. y R." de Ildefonso Pereda Valdés, "El Paisaje en los *Extasis de la montaña*," de Susana de Jaureguy, y "La Poesía Amatoria de J.H. y R.," de Magda Olivier; 3) Correspondencia: Selección epistolar de corresponsales varios, Cartas de J.H. y R. a Edmundo Montagne y la correspondencia de Julio y Julieta. Según Pereda Valdés, en su poesía se observa la influencia de Rubén Darío y en forma más directa la de Teófilo Gautier. También hay influencias románticas francesas y simbolistas. Su originalidad frente a sus modelos consiste en la renovación de los temas, por la forma personal de tratarlos, subjetivándolos. El amor es un tema fundamental; emplea también profusamente el tema exótico y tropical de evocaciones hinduistas. Hay claridad y sencillez en su expresión, como asimismo una oscuridad de lenguaje y de pensamiento que lo convierte en un poeta barroco y surrealista o creacionista precursor de las nuevas líricas. Para Susana de Jaureguy, el paisaje de Minas influyó en el poeta. Pero este paisaje serrano está trasmutado en un intento de exotismo, volviéndolo un típico paisaje español. Magda Olivier opina que *Los parques abandonados* constituyen la concesión mayor que el modernismo de Herrera y Reissig hace al romanticismo y al simbolismo. Esta obra no representa lo más logrado de su poesía pero vale por su estilo personalísimo y su prodigioso dominio verbal. Aunque el único tema es el amor, éste cubre una innumerable cantidad de situaciones en la que toda la gama del sentimiento se hace presente: amor feliz, sufrimiento, orgullo, celos, desprecio y olvido. [EPS]

7213. Reyes Nevares, Beatriz. Rosario Castellanos. México, Secretaría de la Presidencia, Depto. Editorial, 1976. 64 p., illus.

Mixture of biographical, critical, and eulogistic remarks on the late Mexican writer. Useful for its data on her youth in Chiapas. [CM]

7214. Rodríguez-Sardiñas, Orlando. León de Greiff: una poética de vanguardia. Madrid, Playor, 1975. 186 p., bibl. (Col. Nova scholar)

Aptly qualifies Colombian literary criticism of León de Greiff as unfortunate. Author wisely chose the poet as subject because of fame he is gaining among the young of Spanish America. Somewhat perfunctory and giving a too wide-ranging treatment to other authors in Colombian literature, but on the whole, an excellent and welcome work with a solid critical approach to a difficult writer. Studies theme and motif, images, figures of rhetoric, rhythm and rhyme as he investigates the writer's ties with past literary movements and clarifies his place with the vanguardistas. [BTO]

7215. Rubinstein Moreira. Aproximación a María Eugenia Vaz Ferreira. Montevideo, Editorial Montesexto, 1976. 108 p., bibl.

Libro importante por su análisis valorativo crítico de la vida y obra de una mujer singularmente original, contradictoria y compleja. Se estudian sus ideas estéticas, filosóficas y religiosas asimismo como los tres períodos en su trayectoria poética. Para un mejor conocimiento de la múltiple personalidad de María Eugenia, se añade un aspecto hasta ahora no explorado, el epistolar. Contiene bibliografía. [EPS]

7216. Ruscalleda Bercedóniz, Jorge María. La poesía de Nicolás Guillén: cuatro elementos sustanciales. Río Piedras, Univ. de Puerto Rico, Editorial Universitaria, 1975. 310 p., bibl., tables (Col. Mente y palabra)

Estudio exhaustivo del tema (tesis, 1972). De corte estilístico, apunta lo sustancial en Guillén: lo popular, lo social, lo político y lo entrañablemente lírico. Aunque limitado por su visión simplista, es útil al lector no especializado por la totalidad del enfoque biográfico-crítico, y al especialista por el aparato bibliográfico que contiene. [ER]

7217. Salas, Horacio. Conversaciones con Raúl González Tuñón. B.A., Ediciones La Bastilla, 1975. 183 p.

Extenso diálogo con el poeta de Boedo que ilumina toda una época del acontecer literario argentino. González Tuñón evoca su juventud y nos brinda chispeantes comentarios sobre Güiraldes, Borges, Nalé Roxlo, Pondal Ríos y otros. [CMH]

7218. Schopf, Federico. La poesía de Waldo Rojas (ECO, 187, 1977, p. 61-79)

Tomando la poesía de Waldo Rojas como centro irradiador de significados, Federico Schopf revela con lucidez ejemplar el sentido y el sinsentido de la generación de poetas chilenos nacidos entre 1935 y

1950, y el desenfoque de la crítica al juzgar sus vinculaciones con la realidad socio-política chilena de 1970. [OH]

7219. Schulman, Ivan A. Casal's Cuban counterpoint of art and reality (LARR, 11:2, 1976, p. 113-128, illus.)

Revaloración del "escapismo" del poeta modernista, en un lúcido análisis de las fuerzas polares que pugnan en su visión (realidad vs. irrealidad). Estudio de imágenes y motivos como *frío, brumas, infinito* y *hastío*, que reflejan las reacciones psicológicas del poeta a las iniquidades de la sociedad colonial. [ER]

7220. Simposio Pablo Neruda, *Columbia, S.C., .1974.* Actas. Edited by Isaac Lévy and Juan Loveluck. Columbia, Univ. of South Carolina, Dept. of Foreign Languages and Literature, 1974. 427 p. (Hispanic studies series)

Actas del evento organizado por la Univ. of South Carolina (Nov. 1974) en homenaje a Neruda. Incluye una introducción, los textos leídos en la sesión inaugural, los saludos y tributos, las intervenciones de los participantes en la mesa redonda y las exégesis presentadas. Ellas son: Jaime Alazraki "Para una Poética de la Poesía Póstuma de Pablo Neruda;" Eliana Suárez Rivero "La Estética Esencial en una Oda Nerudiana;" Carlos Cortínez "Lectura de 'Madrigal Escrito en Invierno';" Jaime Concha "Observaciones sobre Algunas Imágenes de *Residencia en la tierra*;" Manuel Durán "Sobre la Poesía de Neruda, la Tradición Simbolista y la Desintegración del Yo;" Alain Sicard "Soledad, Muerte y Conciencia Histórica en la Poesía Reciente de Pablo Neruda;" Nelson Osorio "El Problema del Hablante Poético en *Canto general*;" Emir Rodríguez Monegal "Pablo Neruda: las *Memorias* y las Vidas del Poeta;" "El Navío de Eros: *Viente poemas de amor* . . . número nueve;" Donald A. Yates "Neruda and Borges;" Alfredo Roggiano "Ser y Poesía en Pablo Neruda;" Jean Franco "Orfeo en Utopía: el Poeta y la Colectividad en el *Canto general*;" Enrique Anderson Imbert "La Prosa Vanguardista de Neruda;" Fernando Alegría "Neruda: Reflexiones y Reminiscencias;" John Felstiner "A Feminist Reading of Neruda;" Hernan Loyola "Lectura de *Veinte poemas de amor* . . .;" Enrico-Mario Santí "Fuentes para el Conocimiento de Pablo Neruda, 1967-1974;" y Saúl Yurkievich "El Génesis Oceánico." [OH]

7221. Sobrevilla, David. La investigación peruana sobre la poesía de Vallejo: 1971-1974 (RCLL, 1:1, 1975, p. 99-150)

Ensayo ejemplar de una crítica de la crítica, referida a la exegética de la poesía vallejiana. El autor considera cuatro libros de investigadores peruanos publicados entre 1971-74, a través de un certero examen del método empleado en cada uno de ellos, y del consiguiente juicio sobre el planteo expuesto, la coherencia mantenida y el conocimiento del estado de la cuestión. Los libros reseñados por Sobrevilla son los siguientes: Alejandro Lora Risco, *Hacia la voz del hombre: ensayo sobre César Vallejo* (1971); Américo Ferrari, *El universo poético de César Vallejo* (1974); Enrique Ballón Aguirre, *Vallejo como paradigma: un caso especial de escritura* (1974, véase *HLAS 38:7047*), y Alberto Escobar, *Cómo leer a Vallejo* (1973, véase *HLAS 38:7076*). El apartado seis resume los resultados del análisis y propone algunas tareas importantes para la futura investigación vallejiana. [PL]

7222. Stephens, Doris T. Delmira Agustini and the quest for transcendence. Montevideo, Ediciones Geminis, 1975. 220 p., bibl.

El propósito de este excelente estudio crítico de la obra de Delmira Agustini es mostrar la búsqueda de la transcendencia, tema unificante de su creación poética. En la primera parte la profesora Stephens analiza las influencias románticas y modernistas como también las influencias de Charles Baudelaire y Paul Verlaine, la de Edgar Allan Poe y la de Francisco Villaespesa. En la segunda parte estudia la búsqueda de transcendencia a través de la poesía, de los sueños, del amor y de la muerte de la poetisa. Concluye la crítica que, aunque Delmira nunca satisfizo en vida su deseo de más allá, en su poesía logró una transcendencia con la cual nunca siquiera había soñado. Al final de la obra se incluye una bibliografía selecta de y sobre la poetisa uruguaya. [EPS]

7223. Subero, Efraín. El sentido espiritual metafísico en la poesía de Fernando Paz Castillo (UCAB/M, 4, 1975, p. 663-686)

Well-constructed study of Paz Castillo's metaphysical poetry. Considers following constants in his poetry: the search for the eternal in man's mortal life, enigma which is human life here on earth; relation of human beings to omnipotent God versus an increasingly closer, more human deity; and growth of death within humans who strive to accept and understand its constant presence. [BTO]

7224. ———— ed. Apreciaciones críticas sobre la vida y la obra de Andrés Eloy Blanco. 2. ed. Caracas, Univ. Católica Andrés Bello, Centro de Investigaciones Literarias, Institutos Humanísticos de Investigación, 1974. 568 p., bibl.

Consists of 51 critical essays, eulogiac pieces, and addresses concerning Andrés Eloy Blanco. Most notable contributors: Rómulo Gallegos, Efraín Subero, José Ramón Medina, Alfonso Reyes, Juan Liscano, Miguel Otero Silva. [BTO]

7225. Sucre, Guillermo; Ida Vitale; Saul Yurkievich; and **Alejandro Paternain.** Acerca de Octavio Paz. Montevideo,

Fundación de Cultura Universitaria, 1974. 102 p. (Cuadernos de literatura, 26)

Thoughtful essays on different aspects of Paz' poetry. Sucre's "La Fijeza y el Vértigo" has already appeared in *Revista Iberoamericana* (Pittsburgh, Pa., 37:74, enero/marzo 1971, p. 47-72). Vitale examines briefly Paz' poetic development leading up to *Blanco*. Yurkievich's "Octavio Paz, Indagador de la Palabra," has been published earlier in the same issue (p. 73-95). Paternain's work originally appeared in *Cuadernos Hispanoamericanos*, (Madrid, 276, junio 1973, p. 427-440). [CM]

7226. Titiev, Janice Geasler. Alfonsina Storni's *Mundo de siete pozos*: form, freedom and fantasy (UK/KRQ, 23:2, 1976, p. 185-197)

En este penúltimo libro, publicado en 1934, la forma es más importante para Alfonsina que el contenido. En *Mundo de siete pozos* no hay un tema predominante, pero sí una forma predominante que da unidad al libro. A través de toda su obra, la poetisa fluctuó entre libertad y limitación estructural y ambas son evidentes en este volumen, desigual en calidad. La atmósfera íntima, que ha sido parte integral de su poética, desaparece y se nota una naturaleza filosófica y un sentimiento pesimista de la vida. [EPS]

7227. Torres, Hernán ed. Estudios: edición en homenaje a Guillermo Valencia, 1873-1973. Cali, Colombia, Carvajal, 1976. 438 p., bibl., plate.

Volume in commemoration of first centenary of Guillermo Valencia's birth. Contains one poem on Valencia, critical essays in pt. 1, and addresses in pt. 2. Superior to most homage studies, the following critical essays are included: Robert Jay Glickman "Guillermo Valencia: Aspectos de la Cosmografía Simbólica de *Ritos*;" Gerardo Valencia "La Creación Poética en *Catay*;" Iván A. Schulman "La 'Salomé' de Julián del Casal y Guillermo Valencia: Trasposición y Werden;" Otto Olivera "El Dolor de Vivir en Guillermo Valencia;" Eugenio Florit "Apostillas a Algunos Versos de Guillermo Valencia;" Alan S. Trueblood "Wilde y Valencia; 'La Balada de la Cárcel Reading;' " Martha LaFollette Miller "Dos Poemas de Guillermo Valencia: 'Palemón el Estilita,' y 'San Antonio el Centauro;' " Reinaldo Ayerbe Chaux "Guillermo Valencia, Modernista Comprometido;" Dianne Coon de Torres "La Visión de Popayán en Guillermo Valencia." [BTO]

7228. Villavicencio, Laura N. de. La distorsión de las imágenes en la poesía de Julio Herrera y Reissig (CH, 309, marzo 1975, p. 389-402)

Artículo interesante mantiene que la ruptura de la armonía mediante la irrupción de alusiones dislocadas y extrañas a los temas básicos es una constante en la poesía de J.H. y R. Esta tendencia a la distorsión se traduce en imágenes auditivas o visuales, muchas veces lúgubres y morbosas. Las referencias a la liturgia católica son una preferencia expresiva cuya obsesiva incidencia no puede atribuirse a un convencional rasgo de escuela. A veces la simbiosis entre los motivos religiosos y eróticos es completa. Las alusiones satánicas delatan una peculiar actitud ante los temas sagrados que quizá responde a una angustiada visión interior que conduce al poeta a la dislocación de la realidad externa. [EPS]

7229. Villegas, Juan. Estructuras míticas y arquetipos en el Canto General de Neruda. Barcelona, Editorial Planeta, 1976. 209 p.

Juan Villegas se aboca a la interpretación del *Canto* como construcción lingüística, a la develación de su estructura y al análisis del proceso de mitificación del hablante lírico. Describe y explica la función de los héroes, la visión demoníaca de América y de los antihéroes, y el rol del bestiario, para concluir mostrando la presencia de un espacio mitificado, como asiento del desarrollo histórico de América Latina. [OH]

7230. Weller, Hubert P. Bibliografía analítica y anotada de y sobre Martín Adán (Rafael de la Fuente Benavides): 1927-1974. Bibliografía de Martín Adán. Lima, Instituto Nacional de Cultura, 1975. 139 p.

Bibliografía exhaustiva de uno de los poetas más significativos del Perú y de Hispanoamérica, cuya obra no ha tenido aún la repercusión que merece. Las anotaciones de Weller a las referencias sobre el autor describen con propiedad su objeto y resultan siempre orientadoras. [PL]

MISCELLANEOUS
(Bibliographies, Letters, Memoirs, etc.)

7231. Dill, Hans-Otto. El ideario literario y estético de José Martí. La Habana, Casa de las Américas, 1975. 204 p.

Tema ya estudiado extensamente, y revalorado aquí a la luz de la base antimperialista que cimenta la producción artística del escritor cubano. Dirigido principalmente al lector europeo, expone la relevancia del ideario cultural en la lucha revolucionaria de Martí y el interés que su obra ofrece a los hispanistas del campo socialista. [ER]

7232. Guillén, Nicolás. Prosa de prisa: 1929-1972. t. 1/2. La Habana, Instituto Cubano del Libro, Editorial Arte y Literatura, 1975. 2 v. (427, 456 p.)

Un prólogo esclarecedor de Angel Augier abre esta valiosa colección de crónicas y comentarios. Hay en ella 43 años de artículos periodísticos sobre temas tan diversos como el sitio de Madrid (1937), el

Reader's Digest (1941), la represión policíaca (1952), la literatura como oficio (1960). Los textos son de fascinante temática, lectura amena, y demuestran el acertado talento del escritor que—aquí como *chroniqueur*—capta el vivir diario de su pueblo y el desarrollo de su propia vocación literaria y política. [ER]

7233. Laurencio, Angel Aparicio. Bibliografía de José María Heredia (RIB, 26:2, abril/junio 1976, p. 177-196)

Util obra de referencia, que pone al día la dispersa bibliografía del poeta cubano. Incorpora los más recientes trabajos de Fermín Peraza y de la Biblioteca Nacional de Cuba. [ER]

7234. Neruda, Pablo. Confieso que he vivido. Memorias. B.A., Editorial Losada, 1974. 497 p.

Tomando como base las memorias publicadas por la revista *O Cruzeiro de Sao Paulo* (1962), y materiales de distinta procedencia, Neruda se abocó en 1973 a la tarea de componer sus nuevas memorias. Para ello realizó un montaje de los textos antiguos—con los ajustes necesarios—y de los recién escritos, y produjo esta obra que narra "las vidas" del poeta, desde su infancia en Temuco hasta el golpe militar de septiembre de 1973. Dividido en 12 cuadernos autobiográficos, entre los cuales se intercalan pasajes de prosa poética, el libro es interesantísimo, sobre todo porque revela aspectos inéditos de la personalidad nerudiana. [OH]

7235. Vallejo, César. Cartas: 114 de . . . a Pablo Abril de Vivero, 37 de Pablo Abril de Vivero a . . . Lima, Librería Editorial Juan Mejía Baca, 1975. 173 p., facsim.

Importante epistolario, que ilustra un momento central de la vida de César Vallejo en Europa (1924-34). Su interés para la investigación literaria es considerable por muchas razones. Una de ellas: la intensidad con que se revela en estas páginas la cercanía entre la peripecia biográfica y el sentimiento de orfandad proyectado en la obra poética de Vallejo. [PL]

DRAMA

FRANK DAUSTER

Professor of Romance Languages
Rutgers University

THIS WAS A PARTICULARLY PRODUCTIVE PERIOD; the number of plays published, including anthologies, reeditions and new works, must be a record. There were useful reeditions of such standard authors as Discépolo, Sánchez and Barros Grez, in addition to new editions of important plays by Beneke, Luis Rafael Sánchez, Galich, Carballido, Carlos Gorostiza, Cossa, Lizárraga and the multi-author *Avión negro*. Puerto Rico, Mexico and the Cuban *bufo* were represented in anthologies. There is also a remarkable harvest of new plays. Established playwrights with important new works are Lizárraga, his first in many years, Carballido, Luisa Josefina Hernández, Chocrón, Talesnik, Gorostiza and Sieveking. Of special note are José de Jesús Martínez *El caso Dios* (item 7288) and the works of Eduardo Pavlosky (items 7294-7297) who has emerged as a major dramatist in a dramatic idiom of chilling power. Monti and Vilalta confirmed their earlier promise in strong new works (items 7290 and 7316).

New dramatists of note are largely Argentine. Filippis, Peña and Antonietto (items 7239, 7261 and 7298) all present a cruel and guilty world based on obsessive falsification. Goldenberg and Maldonado Pérez (items 7266 and 7287) in different ways, find technical answers to the problem of creating dramatic tension in political works. The collective creation concept continues to flourish, producing plays which are militant, committed and frequently non-dramatic, preferring other, more didactic, ends. The centennial of Sánchez birth produced a number of items, although none of major import. Usigli, at last, is beginning to receive serious analytical attention, and there is a growing interest in Freudian and Jungian criticism. There are useful new overviews for Peru, Guatemala and Venezuela, and the Lyday-Woodyard bibliography is a research tool of major importance (item 7353).

ORIGINAL PLAYS

7236. Adellach, Alberto. Teatro. Homo dramaticus. Esa canción es un pájaro lastimado. Chau, Papá. B.A., Ediciones del Tablado, 1974. 171 p.

Homo dramaticus consists of three one-acters which show man's innate playacting on different levels. Esa canción . . . is an often delightful, often menacing but drastically overlong vision of the same; Chau, papá is a black humor view of the middle class which sets some sort of record for a new low in taste. Adellach is undeniably talented, but his work is undisciplined.

7237. Ankerman, Jorge and **Guillermo Ankerman.** Entremeses. La Segunda República reformada. Las cosas de Cuba. Todo por el honor (UCLV/I, 51, mayo/agosto 1975, p. 81-120)

Three previously unpublished examples of the bufo by one of the genre's most important creative teams.

7238. Antología colombiana del teatro de vanguardia. Bogotá, Biblioteca Colombiana de Cultura, Instituto Colombiano de Cultura, 1975. 242 p. (Col. Popular, 5)

Gilberto Martínez Arango's El grito de los ahorcados is a long and uninspired historical melodrama of the Independence; Sebastián Ospina's La huelga is equally political but with a leavening of theater. Best is Jairo Aníbal Niño's El Monte Calvo, a bitter ritualized vision of war. None of the three is really very avantgarde.

7239. Antonietto, Elena. Mea culpa. B.A., Talía, n.d. 48 p.

Shattering vision of a family whose lies and defenses are eroded by a group of mysterious workmen, leaving the family naked with their guilt, individual and collective. A strong and stunning play.

7240. Azar, Héctor. Teatro breve. México, Editorial Jus, 1975. 187 p.

Five short works, all but El premio de excelencia previously published. They all show Azar's personal mix of popular themes with surreal or miraculous atmosphere. Includes El premio, La appassionata, El alfarero, El milagro y su retablo, El corrido de Pablo Damián.

7241. Balla, Andrés. Los que respondieron al fuego: drama en tres actos. B.A., Autores Argentinos Asociados, 1975. 77 p.

Refugees from an unspecified tropical civil war caught in a jungle which is their own egocentricity and, in a large scale, man's selfishness and violence. Needs careful direction because of Balla's tendency toward declamation, but could be very effective.

7242. Barros Grez, Daniel. Teatro. Como en Santiago. Cada oveja con su pareja. En ensayo de la comedia. El vividor. Prólogo y notas bibliográficas de Ignacio Ossa Galdames. Santiago, Chile, Editorial Nascimiento, 1975. 319 p.

One of the best of the 19th century costumbristas in a careful and useful edition.

7243. Belaval, Emilio. Hay que decir la verdad (PRAAC/B, 8:2/3, abril/sept. 1972, p. 162-199)

Atypical bit of farcical froth by a Puerto Rican pioneer usually more given to committed theater.

7244. Beneke, Walter. El paraíso de los imprudentes. Pieza en 3 actos. Funeral home. Pieza en 3 actos. 2. ed. San Salvador, Ministerio de Educación, Dirección de Publicaciones, 1974. 235 p.

Originally published in 1956 (Paraíso) and 1959 and highly praised, both now seen intellectualized and stuffily verbose, especially Paraíso. Funeral home retains considerable power but both dialogue and some attitudes seem dated.

7245. Britto García, Luis. El tirano Aguirre o la conquista de El Dorado. Suena el teléfono. Caracas, Gobernación del Distrito Federal, Dirección Nacional de Cultura, 1976. 90 p. (Cuadernos de difusión. Serie teatro, 6)

Extremely curious melange of scenes from Aguirre's life, quotes from him and from all sorts of other Golden Age sources, all in verse and with characters such as don Pablos, don Juan and Sancho. With firm direction might just be very theatrical, although as a dramatic text it is stilted and nearly parodic. Suena el teléfono is an overlong one-actor which effectively unveils the fear and isolation within which we live.

7246. ———. Venezuela tuya. Así es la cosa. Teatro. Caracas, Editorial Tiempo Nuevo, 1973. 104 p.

Venezuela was a hit in 1971; it is a satirical political text composed of pop songs, excerpts from historical texts and newspaper columns, etc. Así es la cosa, unstaged as of 1973, begins much like Talesnik's La fiaca but becomes a political document, composed mostly of excerpts. Both depend on shock impact and visual and aural elements.

7247. Cañas, Alberto F. La segua y otras piezas. 2. ed. San José, Editorial Universitaria Centroamericana (EDUCA), 1976. 227 p. (Col. Séptimo día)

Cañas is preoccupied with fantasy and pathological emotional states; his characters all seem to be on the edge of another existence. They are often seemingly unmotivated in a normal sense and their behavior is odd within the author's realistic idiom, but he does create interesting dramatic situations. First published 1974.

7248. Carballido, Emilio. La Fonda de las Siete Cabrillas (Revista de Bellas Artes [México] 19, enero/feb. 1975, p. 50-64)

Adaptation of Gorostiza's *Don Bonifacio* which gives Carballido free rein to develop his characteristic theme and his fondness for alternative actions. Delightful theater.

7249. ———. Por si alguna vez soñamos (Caribe [Honolulu, Hawaii] 1:2, otoño 1976, p. 5-19)

Provocative short vision of the implications of dreams, which lends itself to various interpretations.

7250. ———. Teatro. El relojero de Córdoba. Medusa. Rosalba y los llaveros. El día que se soltaron los leones. México, Fondo de Cultura Económica, 1976. 273 p. (Col. Popular, 159)

Welcome reedition of long out-of-print plays by a major dramatist.

7251. Carrero, Jaime. Flag inside (CDLA/CO, 25, julio/sept. 1975, p. 20-48)

Standard realism and the impact on a Puerto Rican family of a son's death in Viet Nam. Betrays some technical uncertainty, but the characters come alive.

7252. Castellanos, Rosario. El eterno femenino. México, Fondo de Cultura Económica, 1975. 204 p. (Col. Popular, 144)

Witty and often hilarious spoof on the war between the sexes in a male-dominant society by a brilliant novelist and poet dead too soon. The play is long and would probably need some cutting, but the humor and the cutting edge it never hides have great potential.

7253. ———. Poesía no eres tú. México, Fondo de Cultura Económica, 1972. 1 v. (Unpaged)

Includes *Salomé* and *Judith*, poetic dramas with Biblical resonances, which take place in the author's native Chiapas. More poems than drama, but with proper direction and staging could be effective.

7254. Chocrón, Isaac. La máxima felicidad. Caracas, Monte Avila, 1974. 96 p.

Abrasive triangular relationship which is also an experiment in communal life and love and a search for an adoptive family which is more real than inherited relationships. Chocrón has become one of the best at letting his characters abrade themselves into understanding.

7255. Conjunto. Revista de teatro latinoamericano. Comité Permanente de Festivales. Casa de las Américas. Vol. 24, abril/junio 1975- . La Habana.

Devoted to children's theater of all sorts. Includes several articles, original plays by Javier Villafañe (*La calle de los fantasmas*), Manuel Galich (*Miel amarga o el oso colmenero*), Carlos José Reyes (*La fiesta de los muñecos*), Rómulo Loredo (*La guarandinga de Arroyo Blanco*) and information about the plays.

7256. ———. ———. No. 29, julio/sept. 1976- . La Habana.

In addition to usual news on productions, prizes, etc., includes several items on preconquest theater; Manuel Galich's *Puedelotodo vencido o El Gran Gukup-Cakish*, based on a section of the *Popol Vuh*; an adaptation of Brecht's *El proceso de Lucullus* entitled *El proceso al señor Gobernador*, by Colombian Gilberto Martínez and notes on *Guadalupe, años sin cuenta* (Premio Teatro Casa de las Américas 1974) and Esteban Navajas Cortés' *La agonía del difunto*, co-prizewinner for 1976.

7257. Cossa, Roberto M.; Germán Rozenmacher; Carlos Somigliana; and **Ricardo Talesnik.** El avión negro. B.A., Talía, 1970. 56 p. (Col. Grupo de autores, 1)

Series of sketches presenting the effect on various social levels of the rumored return of Perón. An agile, imaginative and incisive play. Also published in *Tres obras* (La Habana, Casa de las Américas, 1970, see *HLAS 34:4051*).

7258. Diaz, Jorge and **Francisco Uriz.** Mear contra el viento (CDLA/CO, 21, julio/sept. 1974, p. 8-50)

Script of a semi-documentary on the ITT involvement in Chile prepared for Swedish television. Formally traditional and understandably partisan, but with no real dramatic impact.

7259. Discépolo, Armando. Mateo-Stéfano. Estudio preliminar y notas de Beatriz de Nóbile. B.A., Editorial Kapelusz, 1976. 109 p. (Grandes obras de la literatura universal, 132)

Two of Discépolo's best works, with an introduction providing a concise summary of the originality of his *grotescos*.

7260. Estrella, Ulises *ed*. "S S 41," sobre la dominación petrolera y la Guerra 1941. Teatro documental. Creación colectiva del grupo "Ollantay" de la Escuela Politécnica Nacional (CDLA/CO, 22 oct,/dic. 1974, p. 59-66)

An Ecuadorian group which has toured with this, which is hardly *documental*; it presents the 1941 war with Peru as provoked by Anglo-American interests, and is a pretext for violent political satire. Whatever its value in political terms, as theater it is haphazard.

7261. Filippis, Jorge. Los hijos de un drama. B.A., Ediciones Kargieman, 1975. 43 p.

Imaginative and shocking work in which adult actors portray children who are playing at being adults, with disastrous results. The resolution is melodramatic, but the play is potentially brilliant.

7262. Florit, Eugenio. Una mujer sola (EX, 7:4, Invierno 1973, p. 73-179)

Unpretentious and gentle vignette of an old woman living on dreams, premiered at Barnard College in 1956.

7263. Galich, Manuel. Míster John Ténor y yo (CDLA/CO, abril/junio 1976, p. 27-111)

Long verse adaptation of *Don Juan Tenorio* into contemporary political terms.

7264. ———. Ortaet ed apor, o para leer al revés (CDLA/CO, 26, enero/marzo 1976, p. 77-93)

One-act children's play, better than most, with some nice touches. Accompanied by Francisco Garzón Céspedes' "Una Excepcional Historia de Amor Creada para los Jovenes."

7265. ———. El último cargo (CDLA/CO, 20, abril/junio 1974, p. 83-102)

Even if having a revolutionary leader, the head of the repressive police and a double agent all in the same family were convincing the characters are so stereotyped as to remove any dramatic interest.

García Ponce, Juan. Trazos. See item 6604.

7266. Goldenberg, Jorge. Relevo 1923. La Habana, Casa de las Américas, 1975. 96 p.

Political assassination of 1921 with its corollary of murders and revenge. Goldenberg uses recreations and alternative versions of individual acts to create a work of great dramatic tension, proof that political theater does not have to be simplistic. Shared the 1975 Premio Teatro de la Casa de las Américas with Sieveking's *Pequeños animales abatidos*.

7267. González de Cascorro, Raúl. El hijo de Arturo Estévez. La Habana, Unión de Escritores y Artistas de Cuba (UNEAC), 1975. 107 p.

Counterinsurgency and heroism in the Escambray, winner of the Premio UNEAC de Teatro 1974. There are a few moments of humanity, chiefly involving the female characters, but this is the kind of thing normally associated with Hollywood's idea of the war effort, ca. 1943.

7268. González Freire, Natividad *ed.* and *comp*. Teatro cubano del siglo XIX. Antología. t. 2. La Habana, Editorial Arte y Literatura, Instituto Cubano del Libro, 1975. 411 p. (Biblioteca básica de literatura cubana)

Includes Gómez de Avellaneda's *Munio Alonso, Baltasar* and *Tres amores,* and Martí's *Amor con amor se paga* and *Abdala*.

7269. Gorostiza, Carlos. La clave encantada. B.A., Talía, 1970. 47 p.

Puppet plays for children of varying degrees of interest and sophistication, worth noting because they reflect a new side of an important dramatist.

7270. ———. Juan y Pedro. Caracas, Monte Avila, 1976. 85 p. (Col. Teatro)

An absorbing parable of man's rejection of cowardice and assumption of responsibility. Would probably be stronger and equally mordant if the ending had avoided a suddenly political dimension, but still a powerful and trenchant work. Gorostiza continues to experiment and grow.

7271. ——— and **Roberto M. Cossa.** El puente. Nuestro fin de semana. Estudio preliminar y notas de Julia Elena Sagaseta y Amelia Lourdes Figueiredo. B.A., Kapelusz, 1977. 220 p.

Useful reedition of two plays which were very influential in the development of Argentine theater over the last quarter century. The introduction points out Gorostiza's seminal influence on Cossa and others of the 1960s movement.

7272. Gregorio, Jesús. Canción para un día de julio (CDLA/CO, 16, abril/junio 1973, p. 41-75)

Collage of fragments from diverse texts giving an orthodox left-wing interpretation of the Moncada attack and other political events. Although there is a theatrical element, the end result is static and aimed largely at the cult of the leader.

7273. Grupo Aleph. Erase una vez un rey (CDLA/CO, 21, julio/sept. 1974, p. 68-83, illus.)

Sardonic fable of man's drive to power and need for cooperation by a Chilean collective group. Funny and effective.

7274. Grupo La Candelaria. La ciudad dorada (CDLA/CO, 20 abril/junio 1974, p. 42-69)

A much-raised Colombian collective group in some straightforward social protest, composed of a series of loosely-connected scenes. Theatrically not very sophisticated.

7275. ——. Guadalupe años sin cuenta. Creación colectiva del . . . La Habana, Casa de las Américas, 1976. 108 p.

Thoroughly one-sided view of the first years of the Colombian *violencia*, but theatrically impressive for the use of song and different perspectives of the key event. A 2. ed. appeared in 1977 (Bogotá, Ediciones Alcaraván, 108 p.)

7276. Hernández, Luisa Josefina. La pavana de Aranzazú (Tramoya [Univ. Veracruzana, Xalapa, Mex.] 1, oct./dic. 1975, p. 13-37, illus.)

Subtitled "auto sacramental," and the sacrament is marriage, but more importantly, love, human and divine. Seemingly simple play which is in reality a complex exposition of a religious attitude.

7277. Herzfeld, Anita and Teresa Cajiao Salas. Teatro de hoy en Costa Rica. San José, Editorial Costa Rica, 1973. 1 v. (Unpaged)

Useful critical anthology of the 1960-70 period. Includes Alberto Cañas' *Algo más que dos sueños*, Samuel Rovinski's *El laberinto*, Daniel Gallegos' *La colina*, and two works by younger authors, Antonio Yglesias' *Las hormigas*, and William Reuben's *Teófilo Amadeo: una biografía*. Both are political and use antirealistic forms, both are fairly obvious The Cañas is a pleasant trifle, the Gallegos is one of the best plays done in Costa Rica, the Rovinski is an odd combination of blatant political pamphlet and provocative questioning of reality.

7278. Kraly, Néstor. Balada maleva. B.A., Talía, 1972. 55 p.

Kraly is trying to get at the roots of moral decay in B.A., but the parade of sexual corruption and economic deceit does not convince. People change too abruptly to be effective within the realistic framework which author has chosen.

7279. Lauten, Flora. Los hermanos: creación colectiva del Teatro La Yaya (CDLA/CO, 27, enero/marzo 1976, p. 19-38)

Attack on the Testigos de Jehová and their alleged antirevolutionary activities. Unsavory example of popular theater used in a directed campaign against a religious group.

7280. Leal, Rine ed and comp. Teatro bufo siglo XIX. Antología. v. 1/2. La Habana, Editorial Arte y Literatura, 1975. 2 v. (380, 346 p.) bibl. (Biblioteca básica de literatura cubana)

Useful collection of unpublished or out-of-print examples of the *bufo*, a folk theater which became commercially successful. Leal's comments deal primarily with the historical context and the clearly ethnic content and implications, skimping the appreciation as theater.

7281. Lizárraga, Andrés. Santa Juana de América. 2. ed. La Habana, Casa de las Américas, 1975. 150 p.

Second ed. of the 1960 Premio Teatro play (there is also a 1968 not listed here). One of the earliest and best efforts at epic theater in Spanish América (see *HLAS 24:5619*).

7282. ——. El torturador (CDLA/CO, 15, enero/marzo 1973, p. 95-121)

Clash of conceptions of justice among political prisoners. Complicated system of flashbacks needs careful handling.

7283. Magaña-Esquivel, Antonio ed. Teatro mexicano 1968. Mexico, Aguilar, 1974. 299 p., illus.

Includes Rafael Solana's *El día del juicio* (see *HLAS 31:4480*), a busy imaginative drama; Héctor Azar's very theatrical *Higiene de los placeres y de los dolores* (see *HLAS 32:4403*); Vicente Leñero's effective version of the Father Lemercier case, *Pueblo rechazado* (see *HLAS 32:4448*); and Emilio Carballido's fine tragedy *Medusa*, finally staged in Spanish long after its English premiere (published 1960; 2. ed. 1976).

7284. —— ed. Teatro mexicano 1970. Mexico, Aguilar, 1973. 353 p., illus.

Includes Maruxa Vilalta's powerful *Esta noche juntos, amándonos tanto* (see *HLAS 34:4055*), Federico S. Inclán's heavyhanded *Frida Kahlo* (see *HLAS 38:7177*) and Vicente Leñero's complex *Compañero* (see *HLAS 36:6776*). Also Marcela del Rio's *El pulpo*, an elaborate, fanciful and ultimately simplistic attempt at documentary theater which explains the presidency and death of John Kennedy in terms of his struggle with the economic octopus of big business.

7285. ——— ed. Teatro mexicano 1971. Mexico, Aguilar, 1974. 277 p., illus.

Includes Vicente Leñero's *La carpa*, an imaginative version of his novel *Estudio Q*; Alejandro Galindo's ... *Y la mujer hizo al hombre*, a superficial dated comedy; Fernando Sánchez Mayans' *Un extraño laberinto*, a "relevant" version of the Theseus myth turned parable for today's youth, and very wordy; and Luisa Josefina Hernández' exercise in choreographic theater, the brilliant *Danza del urogallo múltiple*.

7286. ——— ed. Teatro mexicano 1972. Mexico, Aguilar, 1975. 285 p., illus.

Includes Salvador Novo's bravura farse *In Ticitezcatl o El espejo encantado*, Willebaldo López' *Yo soy Juárez*, an attempt to get at the real man behind the mythology, and two new plays: Carlos Olmos' *Juegos fatuos* and Héctor Azar's *Inmaculada*. *Juegos fatuos* examines the deliberate withdrawal of two provincial women in a fashion recalling Marqués and Arrufat, although less successfully than either; *Inmaculada* is another of Azar's individual mixtures of high comedy, low punning and idiosyncratic semisurrealist visions of the human animal.

7287. Maldonado Pérez, Guillermo. Por estos santos latifundios. La Habana, Casa de las Américas, 1975. 75 p. (Premio Teatro, 1975)

Distinguished from other routine versions of land takeover by a degree of human individualization of peasants (the *latifundistas* are typified and stereotyped) and by a simplicity which lends some freshness to the work. Conscious allegorization helps to make the work more abstract and less immediate.

7288. Martínez, José de Jesús. El caso Dios. Panamá, Ediciones Tareas, 1975. 59 p.

The trial of God, accused of responsibility for cruelty and death. One actor handles all the roles in a text which is witty, incisive and the author's best. One of the best plays in a long while; had it been written in Paris or London, it would be an international cause célèbre.

7289. Mauricio, Julio. La depresión. B.A., Talía, 1970. 5 p.

Mauricio is essentially a realist who is widely regarded in some circles. *La depresión* is a serio-comic look at middle-aged foibles, much in the vein of Neil Simon, although less witty and with more dark corners of the soul showing. First performed 1970.

7290. Monti, Ricardo. Historia tendenciosa de la clase media argentina, de los extraños sucesos en que se vieron envueltos algunos hombres públicos, su completa dilucidación y otras escandalosas revelaciones. B.A., Talía, 1972. 53 p.

A 1972 play, closer to the sketch or to Esteve's *La gran histeria nacional* than to Monti's *Una noche con el Sr. Magnus e hijos*, in its bitter vision of Argentine history and the use of rapid and sometimes almost unrelated scenes.

7291. Navajas Cortés, Esteban. La agonía del difunto. La Habana, Casa de las Américas, 1976. 58 p.

Peasant revenge on a murderous landowner expressed in political realism which often becomes grotesque and is reminiscent of the traditional *paso*. Often obvious, and the peasants occasionally demonstrate a ludicrous control of dialectic, but potentially a vivid piece of political theater. Premio Teatro Casa de las Américas for 1976.

7292. Oves, Santiago Carlos. La toma: creación colectiva del Grupo Octubre (CDLA/CO, 23, enero/marzo 1975, p. 36-77)

Argentine strikers and the taking of a factory. Political and one-sided, like virtually all collective theater, although there is some rudimentary human dimension. Cannot be judged by any normal criteria for theater.

7293. Palant, Jorge. Las visitas. Griselda en la cuerda. Vine a verte, Papá. B.A., Ediciones Kargieman, 1975. 88 p.

Las visitas and *Griselda en la cuerda* make effective use of two-person situations to underline the desperation of daily living. *Vine a verte, papá* is more complex; a difficult personal situation suddenly becomes an ugly evocation of cowardice and compromise. Palant has a feeling for creating people who have been defeated and defiled by life.

7294. Pavlovsky, Eduardo A. La mueca. B.A., Talía, 1971? 37 p.

A stunning example of ritual theater. A young middle class couple are subjected to degrading but ultimately liberating experiences by a group of what might be called emotional terrorists. There are a number of unresolved ambiguities—the real nature of the terrorists, the implications of the ending—but the play is striking. Also published in *Tres obras* (La Habana, Casa de las Américas, 1970, see *HLAS 34:4051*).

7295. ———. El señor Galíndez (Primer Acto [Madrid] 179/181, Verano 1975, p. 62-73)

Chilling portrait of torture and torturers which subtly makes the double point that the torturer is both an ordinary being and part of a dehumanized system.

7296. ———. Telarañas. B.A., Ediciones Búsqueda, 1976. 69 p. (Col. Teatro de hoy)

Highly imaginative view of the real nature of family tensions by a psychoanalyst who is one of Spanish America's most acute and acerbic dramatists. The form of the sketch, which is extremely popular in Argentina, permits him to cut deeply and wittily without needing to concern himself with standard dramatic or psychological creation.

7297. ——— and **Juan Carlos Herme.** Ultimo match. B.A., Talía, 1970. 45 p.

Impressionist-absurdist vision of life as perpetual boxing match in which we are all champions doomed to final defeat. A bitter and vivid text which a skilled director could make into brilliant theater. First performed 1970.

7298. Peña, Edilio. Resistencia: o un extraño sueño sobre la tortura de Pablo Rojas. El círculo. Caracas, Monte Avila Editores, 1975. 98 p. (Col. Teatro)

Resistencia (1974) is a highly theatrical vision of a cruel and obsessive world; El círculo (1975) presents the ultimate falsity of normal life, again using imaginative conventions. Peña (b. 1951) has great promise.

7299. Ramírez Farías, Carlos. Palito y Godsuno. Caracas, Ediciones MAPA, 1976. 100 p.

Beckettian encounter of two grave-diggers whose function is to make more room for the new dead created by incessant war. The overall tone is political but not partisan; the play is often interesting but overlong.

7300. Rengifo, César. La sonata del alba. Una medalla para las conejitas (CDLA/CO, 22, oct./dic. 1974, p. 10-42)

Sonata is a 1948 vision of the poor with an inspiring if unconvincing ending; Medalla (1973) is the sort of propaganda which its supporters would have trouble taking seriously. Accompanied by Manuel Galich's "Venezuela en el Teatro de César Rengifo," a favorable overview (p. 2-9).

7301. Rial, José Antonio. La muerte de García Lorca. Caracas, Monte Avila, 1976? 133 p., bibl. (Col. Teatro)

Very complicated partisan view of the events leading to Lorca's death, weakened by unnecessary elements. The original interesting notion of confronting proposed theories of the murder in the persons of their authors, gets lost somewhat. Author is a Spaniard long active in Venezuelan theater.

7302. Ribeyro, Julio Ramón. Teatro. Lima, Instituto Nacional de Cultura, 1975. 260 p.

Seven pieces by a highly-regarded novelist. Most are obviously social and overdone. Exceptions are Santiago el pajarero (1960), an effective tragic farse of an 18th-century visionary, and El último cliente, a sensitive portrait of pathetic innocence betrayed.

7303. Ripoll, Carlos and **Andrés Valdespino.** Teatro hispanoamericano. Antología crítica: siglo XIX. N.Y., Anaya Book Co., 1973. 603 p.

Useful collection covering the century. Includes Cruz Varela, Dido; Gorostiza, Contigo pan y cebolla; Rodríguez Galván, Muñoz, visitador de México; Gómez de Avellaneda, La hija de las flores and Baltasar; Segura, El sargento Canuto; Méndez Quiñones, Los jíbaros progresistas; Sánchez, La gringa, Barranca abajo and Los muertos.

7304. Rovinski, Samuel. Las fisgonas de paso ancho. Teatro. San José, Editorial Costa Rica, 1975. 45 p., plates.

Rovinski's best yet and a hit in 1971, Las fisgonas is a satire on Costa Rican institutions, popular and otherwise, in the line of the pasos and entremeses. Spirited, rapid and funny.

7305. ———. Un modelo para Rosaura o la manera de acomodar una historia a nuestro gusto: tragicomedia burguesa en dos actos. San José, Editorial Costa Rica, 1975. 125 p.

Straightforward parody on vacuous bourgeoisie abruptly becomes obviously Pirandellian and then jumps to a finale based on Orestes. Rovinski has talent but needs control.

7306. Sánchez, Florencio. Teatro completo. t. 1. Introducción y notas por Fernando García Esteban. Montevideo, Editorial Salamandra, 1975. 244 p.

García Esteban has attempted to restore Sánchez' notoriously corrupted texts to their original state insofar as possible. The introduction and discussion of individual plays is valuable for this kind of textual information.

7307. Sánchez, Luis Rafael. Los angeles se han fatigado. Río Piedras, P.R., Editorial Cultural, 1976. 35 p.

Two-act monodrama previously published in 1960 and 1962. Tour-de-force requiring bravura acting; would benefit from cutting to one act. From a period when Sánchez was heavily influenced by Marqués.

7308. ———. Farsa del amor compradito. Río Piedras, P.R., Editorial Cultural, 1976. 109 p.

Very Lorquian farse originally published in 1960, agile, perhaps too long and a good deal of fun.

7309. ———. La hiel nuestra de cada día. Río Piedras, P.R., Editorial Cultural, 1976. 65 p.

Aging couple's collapse into poverty and despair which now, 15 years after first publication in 1962, seems far more ritualistic and consciously stylized.

7310. Sieveking, Alejandro. Pequeños animales abatidos. La Habana, Casa de las Américas, 1975. 107 p. (Premio Teatro 1975)

The days prior to the overthrow of Allende with a curious counterpoint provided by a pair of ghosts who are presumably symptomatic of the fall of the bourgeoisie over the last 60 years. Even when overtly political, Sieveking creates gentle, human characters, including a lead character who is memorable.

7311. Talesnik, Ricardo. Cien veces no debo. B.A., Talía, 1972. 40 p.

Bitter denunciation of the conformism and superficiality of a middle-class family which pays lip service to its own myths of behavior. Evidence that Talesnik can do more than the comedy of *La fiaca*.

7312. Teatro puertorriqueño. Décimo festival. San Juan, Instituto de Cultura Puertorriqueña, 1971? 348 p., illus.

The 1967 festival including Gerard Paul Marín's *Retablo y guiñol de Juan Canelo*, an agile and diverting use of popular elements; Roberto Rodríguez Suárez' *Las ventanas*, a drama of the pitfalls of transculturation in N.Y. which becomes repetitious and one-dimensional and Alejandro Tapia y Rivera's *La cuarterona*, a 19th-century Romantic drama which achieves some degree of sobriety. Presented here in its original form rather than in the adaptation by Piri Fernández, which was actually staged.

7313. Teatro puertorriqueño. Undécimo festival. San Juan, Instituto de Cultura Puertorriqueña, 1971? 488 p., illus.

Roberto Rodríguez Suárez' *El casorio* deals with the frustrations of village life; Manuel Méndez Ballester's *Arriba las mujeres* is a satirical caricature of the upper-middle class. *El hombre terrible del 87* presents a crucial moment of Puerto Rican history in a curious mixture of melodrama and imaginative styling. Star of the volume is Luis Rafael Sánchez' *La pasión según Antigona Pérez* (see *HLAS 34:4043*).

7314. Teatro 70. B.A., Comuna Baires, 1970? 211 p.

Includes Osvaldo Dragún's *Historias para ser contadas* and *Los de la mesa diez* and Guillermo Gentile's *Hablemos a calzón quitado*, all previously commented on. New plays include Alberto Adellach's *Chau papá* (see item 7236), black humor which is sometimes excoriating, sometimes merely crude; Walter Oporto's *Ceremonia al pie del obelisco*, reminiscent of *Marat-Sade* and fairly obvious, and Renzo Casali's *Maximiliano diez años después*, a curious and ambiguous but stimulating work which seems to be an ironic-serious version of a Nativity play. Publication of a radical alternative commune.

7315. 3 [i.e. Tres] obras de teatro vanguardia nicaragüense. Managua, Editorial Unión, 1975. 180 p. (Ediciones el pez y la serpiente)

Three plays important in the attempt to create a popular theater 40 years ago. *Chinfonía* and *Petenera* use similar popular sources; the latter is gentler and less strained, the former linguistically daring in its exaggeration. *Por los caminos . . .* is moderately successful social drama. *Petenera* is previously unpublished in book form.

7316. Vilalta, Maruxa. Nada como el piso 16. México, Joaquín Mortiz, 1977. 104 p., illus. (Teatro del volador)

Three people play out a parable of power and domination, of the sacrifices necessary to triumph. A strong, often startling play by a dramatist who has rapidly emerged as one of Mexico's best. Chosen best play of 1975 by the Asociación Mexicana de Críticos de Teatro and the Unión de Críticos.

7317. Zarlenga, Ethel Gladys. Por la calle: comedia operística en dos actos. Tucuman, Arg., Editorial Atenas, 1973. 83 p.

Libretto for a comic operetta; frivolous fun and unexpectedly amusing. With acute direction, could be a stage success.

CRITICISM

7318. Arriví, Francisco. El décimocuarto festival de teatro puertorriqueño (ICP/R, 16:58, enero/marzo 1973, p. 7-15, illus.)

The 1971 festival, featuring Arriví's *Sirena*, Belaval's *La muerte*, Marques' *Un niño azul para esa sombra* and a premiere, Luis Rechani Agrait's *Llora en el atardecer la fuente*.

7319. Beardsell, Peter R. Insanity and poetic justice in Usigli's *Corona de sombra* (UK/LATR, 10:1, Fall 1976, p. 5-14)

Intelligent analysis of Usigli's deviation from history and its reasons: the use of Carlota to awaken the audience's nationalistic feelings. Beardsell's approach to tragedy is Golden Age-oriented, which provides for some unusual insights into the tragic process of Carlota.

7320. Ben-Ur, Lorraine Elena. Myth montage in a contemporary Puerto Rican tragedy: *La pasión según Antígona Pérez* (*The passion according to Antigone Pérez*) (LALR, 4:7, Fall/Winter 1975, p. 15-22)

Analysis of the elements of classical, sacrificial and "metapolitical" myth in a complex play. An illuminating study.

7321. Bogdanich, Esteban Carlos. Leónidas Barletta y el teatro del pueblo (CDLA/CO, 26, enero/marzo 1976, p. 94-98)

Interesting because of a brief interview with Barletta, (d. 1975), an important director in the 1930s and early 1940s, and direct ancestor of much of today's committed theater.

7322. *Boletín de la Academia de Artes y Ciencias de Puerto Rico.* Vol. 8, Nos. 2/3, abril/sept. 1972- . San Juan.

Devoted to Emilio Belaval, a pioneer of Puerto Rican theater. Includes prose fiction, critical writings, a play *Hay que decir la verdad* (see item 7243) and iconography.

7323. Brownell, Virginia A. The eucharistic image as a symbol of the downfall of modern man (UK/LATR, 10:1, Fall 1976, p. 37-43)

Studies the inverted use of Eucharistic imagery to communicate man's isolation in three works by Triana, Fuentes and Cuzzani.

7324. Caballero, Juan. El teatro de Sebastian Salazar Bondy. Balconcillo?, Perú, Editor García Ribeyro, 1975. 151 p.

Examines social concerns in Salazar Bondy's theater. Includes *Solo una rosa*, a previously unpublished one-acter of a dominant mother, a recurrent theme.

7325. Campa, Román V. de la. Entrevista con el dramaturgo argentino Osvaldo Dragún (AR, 3:4, 1977, p. 46-49, illus.)

Interesting interview which provides light on Cuban theater of the early 1960s and on Dragún's view of Latin American drama.

7326. Castagnino, Raúl H. Escritores hispanoamericanos, desde otros ángulos de simpatía. B.A., Editorial Novoa, 1971. 365 p. (Biblioteca arte y ciencia de la expresión)

Includes "Evocación de Armando Moock" (p. 207-269), a biographical memoir of the Chilean dramatist, and "Sentido de lo Universal en el Teatro de Armando Moock" (p. 271-289). The latter points out that Moock, at least, considered himself a Chilean despite his long Argentine residence, and that his works deal with universal human passions, although the characters are never really archetypical.

7327. Castedo-Ellerman, Elena. Variantes de Egon Wolff: fórmulas dramática y social (HISPA, 5:15, dic. 1976, p. 15-38)

Sees Wolff's work as basically stylized realism treating the conflict of social caste.

7328. Cerutti, Franco. Bosquejo a vuela pluma del teatro guatemalteco (UCR/RHCLC, 1:2, enero/junio 1975, p. 5-43)

Considerable amount of useful historical information, preceded by some acute observations on the nature and limitations of national as opposed to regional literary movements.

7329. *Cuba Review.* Cuba Resource Center. Vol. 7, No. 4, Dec. 1977- . N.Y.

Interviews and articles reflecting the official point of view about development of a popular theater.

7330. Cypess, Sandra Messinger. Physical imagery in the works of Griselda Gambaro (Modern Drama [Lawrence, Kans.] 18:4, Dec. 1975, p. 356-363)

Discusses Gambaro's Artaudian use of physical imagery—both action and object.

Daneri, Alberto. Carta abierta de un peronista a un confundido. See *HLAS 39:7653*.

7331. Dauster, Frank. Lo prehispánico en el teatro de Salvador Novo (Reflexión [Carleton Univ., Ottawa] 2:3/4 [2. época] 1974/1975, p. 17-23)

Examination of prehispanic themes throughout Novo's theater, stressing the authentic interest in a past which the author considered still vital in Mexican life.

7332. Defelitto, Ana María and **Eithel Orbit Negri.** *Narcisa Garay, mujer* *para llorar*: semiótica de la escenografía (UK/LATR, 9:2, Spring 1976, p. 31-41)

Analysis of scene, set, etc., pointing out its relevance to the dramatic action. Well done, but it is hard to see that the semiotics is any more than a technical vocabulary not necessary to the analysis.

7333. Delgado, Lenelina. Los realizadores cuestionan la crítica (Escena [Caracas] 5/6, agosto /nov. 1975, p. 45-48)

Interviews with four directors who are deeply critical of Venezuelan theater criticism. Followed by "Los críticos tienen la palabra" (p. 49-60) an *encuesta* with six critics. Interesting sidelight on seldom-discussed aspect of the field.

7334. *Escena*. Revista nacional de teatro y del espectáculo. Consejo Nacional de la Cultura, Dirección de Artes Escénicas. No. 3, feb./abril 1975- , Caracas.

Handsome new journal devoted to entertainment in general, with a good deal on opera, dance and theater, usually short articles. Included in this issue: Fradie Zerán's "Libre Teatro de Córdoba" (p. 10-11); Pablo Antillano's "El Desaffo del Teatro Banal," remarks on the current success of frivolous theater in Caracas (p. 12-15); "Cuando Caracas es Verona," (p. 16-17), on Alvaro de Rosson and Miguel Otero Silva's adaptation of *Romeo and Juliet*; one-page notes on Rodolfo Santana and César Rengifo; Orlando Rodríguez' "El Teatro Cubano: Un Teatro para una Revolución" (p. 30-33), on present activity; Haydée Ascanio's "Quien es Quien en el Teatro para Niños" (p. 51-63); and a review of Talesnik's *Los japoneses no esperan* by Antillano. Other issues of interest are: No. 4, 5/6, 7 and 8.

7335. Espinosa Domínguez, Carlos. La Yaya: el teatro en manos del pueblo (CDLA/CO, 27, enero/marzo 1976, p. 2-18)

Sensible discussion of a group composed of non-professionals, including interview with their director and founder (1973), the actress Flora Lauten. An example of the positive side of this kind of theater.

7336. ———. Entrevista con César Rengifo (CDLA/CO, 26, oct./dic. 1975, p. 69-82)

Venezuelan dramatist speaks of his work and ideology, Brecht and theater in Venezuela and Latin America.

7337. Foster, David William. Roberto Arlt's *La isla desierta*: a structural analysis (UK/LATR, 11:1, Fall 1977, p. 25-34)

Examines language textures as evidence of Arlt's neoexpressionist technique.

7338. Foster, Virginia Ramos. Variations on Latin American Third world drama (LALR, 2:3, Fall/Winter 1973, p. 35-43)

Posits general tendencies of the radical theater and adds brief comments on a variety of manifestations.

7339. Garzón Céspedes, Francisco. Hablan los jurados de teatro (CDLA/CO, 20, abril/junio 1974, p. 4-37)

Interview with Julio Mauricio, Carlos José Reyes and Herminia Sánchez, plus articles by Mauricio and Reyes about theater in Argentina and Colombia. All three insist on the need for artistic quality as well as ideological integrity.

7340. González del Valle, Luis and **Antolín González del Valle.** El teatro visto como teatro: una entrevista con el dramaturgo argentino Alberto Wainer (RIB, 25:1, enero/marzo 1975, p. 24-34)

Informative comments by an interesting and little-known dramatist.

7341. González Freire, Nati. Festival del Caribe 1972 (CDLA/CO, 26, oct./dic. 1975, p. 3-13)

Background and information on the 1972 Carifesta. Accompanied by Manuel Galich's "Una Nota sobre Walcott y su Obra" (p. 10-13) and a translation into Spanish by Antonio Benítez Rojo of Derek Walcott's *Drums and colours*.

7342. Grossman, Lois. *Los albañiles*, novel and play: a two-time winner (UK/LATR, 9:2, Spring 1976, p. 5-12)

Points out the technical and contentual differences between the novel and theater versions, differences which are more significant than sometimes realized.

7343. Grupo de teatro Aty-ñe'e (Cadernos de Teatro [Sociedade Brasileira de Autores Teatrais, Rio] 67, out./dez. 1975, p. 37-40)

Paraguayan group which since 1974 has been doing theater in Guaraní in rural areas.

7344. Gyurko, Lanin A. The vindication of La Malinche in Fuentes' *Todos los gatos son pardos* (IAA, 3:3, 1977, p. 233-266)

Examines the mythic shadows behind the historical characters of the play and sees La Malinche as a national voice and a visionary figure.

7345. Hinds, Harold E., Jr. and **Charles Tatum.** José María Samper's costumbrista play *Un alcalde a la antigua* (UK/LATR, 10:1, Fall 1976, p. 53-61)

A highly successful 1856 comedy remarkable because it is a vehicle for progressive notions.

7346. Holzapfel, Tamara. *Pueblo rechazado*: educating the public through reportage (UK/LATR, 10:1, Fall 1976, p. 15-21)

Discusses Leñero's use of and rationale for the documentary form.

7347. Horcasitas, Fernando. El teatro popular en Náhuatl y una danza de Santiago (UNAM/RUM, 29:5, enero 1975, p. 1-9)

Discusses several texts still staged in 20th century and presents Spanish version of *La danza de Alcharriones*, a version of *moros y critianos* probably written in large part in Mexico and still staged in the state of Mexico in 1930.

7348. Kronik, John. Usigli's *El gesticulador* and the fiction of truth (UK/LATR, 11:1, Fall 1977, p. 5-16)

Intricate reading inspired by Abel's concept of metatheater, which sees *El gesticulador* as a structure of linguistic ambiguities which reflect the ambiguities of history and reality. A healthy antidote to the usual sociological reading of Usigli.

7349. *Latin American Theatre Review*. A journal devoted to the theatre and drama of Spanish and Portuguese America. Univ. of Kansas, Center of Latin American Studies. Vol. 9, No. 2, Spring 1976- . Lawrence.

In addition to articles by Defelitto and Negri, Grossman, Martin, Morris, Muncy, and Watson Espener (see items 7332, 7342, 7356, 7365-7367 and 7404), includes articles on "A Situação Social da Mulher" in Consuelo de Castro and Leilah Assunção and Coelho Neto, and notes on theater in Paraguay, Lima, Colombia, two notes on Chicano theater and reviews of Luzuriaga and Reeve, Ripoll and Valdespino, Orjuela, Manuel del Cabral and Néstor Madrid-Malo. Other issues with articles of interest are 9:2 Spring 1976; 10:1, Fall 1976; 10:2 Spring 1977; and 11:1 Fall 1977.

7350. Leal, Rine. Acerca de una bibliografía de teatro cubano (BNJM/R, 14:2 [3. época] mayo/agosto 1972, p. 164-172)

Review essay on Antuña and García Carranza's "Bibliografía del Teatro Cubano" which appeared in *Revista de la Biblioteca Nacional José Martí* (13:3, sept./dic. 1971, p. 97-154). Points out some existing supplementary sources and some areas still to be investigated.

7351. Lindstrom, Naomi Eva. The world's illogic in two plays by Argentine expressionists (LALR, 4:8, Spring/Summer 1976, p. 83-88)

Sees Arlt's *El desierto entra a la ciudad* and Discépolo's *Entre el hierro* as typical plays of expressionism, which Lindstrom takes to be the reasonable presentation of the failure of reason in an irrational world.

7352. López, Oswaldo A. Crítica a las limitaciones del individuo (Explicación de Textos Literarios [California State Univ., Sacramento] 3:2, 1974/1975, p. 151-159)

Rather schematic examination of the characters of Carballido's *El día que se soltaron los leones*, stressing the problem of variant solutions to individual liberty and the implicit social criticism.

7353. Lyday, Leon F. and **George W. Woodyard** comps. A bibliography of Latin American theater criticism: 1940-1974. Austin, Univ. of Texas, Institute of Latin American Studies, 1976. 243 p. (Guides and bibliographies series, 10)

Indispensable research tool for anyone working in the field.

7354. Magaña-Esquivel, Antonio. José Peón Contreras: dramaturgo mexicano (RIB, 26:2, abril/junio 1976, p. 162-176)

Useful overview of work of 19th-century romantic-realist.

7355. Marco, Susana; Abel Posadas; Marta Speroni; and **Griselda Vignolo.** Teoría del género chico criollo. B.A., Editorial Universitaria de Buenos Aires (EUDEBA), 1975. 455 p.

Lengthy examination of the historical origins, characteristics, typology and social milieu of the *sainete* and related forms. Treated exclusively as a social document relating to a specific social class, which makes the rare esthetic judgments, such as the blanket condemnation of early Modernismo, untrustworthy. Very rigid in typology and analysis.

7356. Martin, Eleanor J. *Calígula* and *La muerte no entrará en palacio*: a study in characterization (UK/LATR, 9:2, Spring 1976, p. 21-30)

Finds considerable similarities which are not always convincing to this editor. Many of them seem built-in to the plays' structures.

7357. Maruxa Vilalta, grande autora teatral (Nivel [Gaceta de cultura, México] 160, abril 30, p. 1-2)

Collection of excerpts from reviews of her latest. *Nada como el piso 16.* Useful as a source for work on a dramatist generating considerable interest.

7358. Mejía Duque, Jaime. El nuevo teatro en Colombia: 1960-1975 (UTIEH/C, 26, 1976, p. 159-169)

One-sided but informative account of the causes and characteristics of the radicalization of Colombian theater and its emphasis on collective creation.

7359. Monasterios, Rubén. Un enfoque crítico del teatro venezolano. Caracas, Monte Avila, 1975. 128 p.

Dedicated primarily to the period since 1950. Monasterios is an acute critic with a pronounced point of view, which sometimes leads him into judgments which seem forced, such as his comments on Chocrón. Informative and stimulating work.

7360. Monleón, José. Con Ariel Betancurt y Luis Molina (Primer Acto [Madrid] 173, oct. 1974, p. 65-68)

Interview with a Colombian and a Puerto Rican director, remarkable chiefly because it shows the extent of politization of most Latin American theater festivals. It is odd to find them believing that there is a special national kind of political dramatic technique for each area.

7361. ———. Diálogo con "Teatro del 60" (Primer Acto [Madrid] 178, marzo 1975, p. 50-54)

Interview with members of the group which attracted attention with *Puerto Rico Fua* The group is obviously trying to develop in its own fashion; Monleón (and others) keep carping about their lack of "ideological precision."

7362. ———. Festival de Caracas (Primer Acto [Madrid] 173, oct. 1974, p. 56-64)

Discussion of the participants in the 1974 Caracas Festival. Monleón's point of view is political, but he is critical of the routine demagogy which seems to have dominated much of the Festival.

7363. Montes Huidobro, Matías. El caso Dorr: el autor en el vórtice del compromiso (UK/LATR, 11:1, Fall 1977, p. 35-43)

Examines *El agitado pleito entre un autor y un ángel* in terms of Dorr's development to political commitment. A sensitive analysis of a complex problem.

7364. ———. El teatro de Milanés y la formación de la conciencia cubana (UCM/ALH, 2/3, 1973/1974, p. 223-240)

Studies Milanés' *El conde Alarcos* and *Un poeta en la corte* as expressions of a personality, individual and national, not yet clear as to its national situation and commitment.

7365. Morris, Robert J. The contemporary Peruvian theater. Lubbock, Texas Technical Univ., 1977. 98 p. (Graduate studies, 15)

Conscientious survey covering the late 1940s to 1970. Fills a longstanding need.

7366. Muncy, Michèle. Entrevista con Luisa Josefina Hernández (UK/LATR, 9:2, Spring 1976, p. 69-77)

Interesting exposition of Hernández' views on religion, the role of women in México, and her own work.

7367. ———. Teatro de Salvador Novo. 2. ed. México, Instituto Nacional de Bellas Artes, 1976. 188 p. (Col. De teatro, 3)

Second ed. of work first published in 1971 (see *HLAS 34:4094*) Still the only full-length study of a major dramatist.

7368. Nigro, Kirsten F. *La noche de los asesinos*: playscript and stage enactment (UK/LATR, 11:1, Fall 1977, p. 45-57)

Reading of the text in terms of its potential for staging and the impact of such staging on the meanings of the text. Nigro knows that theater is theater, happily.

7369. Ordaz, Luis and **Erminio G. Neglia.** Repertorio selecto del teatro hispanoamericano contemporáneo. Caracas, n.p., 1975. 1 v. (Unpaged)

A listing of plays, published and unpublished, by selected dramatists. Useful, but needs a careful revision to eliminate errors, which are numerous.

7370. Orenstein, Gloria. The theater of the marvellous. N.Y., New York Univ. Press, 1975. 315 p., illus.

Book-length study of surrealist theater which includes subsections on Paz, Díaz, Teófilo Cid, Leonora Carrington, Garro, Cortázar, Jodorowsky. Some interesting work, but Orenstein tends to see only surrealism and not other aspects. Some important playwrights are missing: Carballido, Hernández, Arrufat, and others who are as surrealist as Garro. etc.

7371. **Palls, Terry I.** The theater of the absurd in Cuba after 1959 (LALR, 4:7, Fall/Winter 1975, p. 67-72)

Sees the absurd in Cuba as the expression of a search for individual stability, which Palls sees as a "revolutionary reality," and therefore another kind of revolutionary theater. There is a point at which the term "absurd" becomes almost all-inclusive and the dramatists mentioned have all apparently ceased writing.

7372. Panorama de teatro cubano (CDLA/CO, 21, julio/sept. 1974, p. 111-126)

Play by play comments by various critics on the 1974 Panorama festival. Includes: Ignacio Gutiérrez, *Los chapuzones* and *Llevame al la pelota*; Joaquín Lorenzo Luaces, *El fantasmón de Aravaca*; an anthological selection, *Lo mejor del bufo*; Freddy Artiles, *Adriana en dos tiempos*; Paco Alfonso, *Cañaveral*; Raúl Macías, *Brigada 2506*; Gómez de Avellaneda, *La hija de las flores*; Héctor Quintero, *Si llueve te mojas como los demás*; Nicolás Dorr, *La chacota*; Herminia Sánchez, *Amante y penol*.

7373. **Peden, Margaret Sayers.** Kindergarten: a new play by Egon Wolff (UK/LATR, 10:2, Spring 1977, p. 5-10)

In his first play since 1970, Wolff presents three old people who, in the meaningless present, return to the games of their childhood. Peden acutely points out the continuity in Wolff's work of the struggle between external and internal forces, physically and psychically.

7374. **Pereira Salas, Eugenio.** Historia del teatro en Chile desde sus orígenes hasta la muerte de Juan Casacuberta: 1849. Santiago, Univ. de Chile, 1974. 440 p., illus., facsim., tables.

Detailed examination of the historical setting, lists of plays, etc. Of little interest for analytical purposes, but a mine of factual information.

7375. **Perri, Dennis.** *La colina* and the theatre of Daniel Gallegos (UK/LATR. 10:1, Fall 1976, p. 45-52)

Sees *La colina* as the culmination of Gallegos' earlier work; stresses the ritual structure leading to a reexamination of spiritual values.

7376. **Petersen, Gerald W.** El mundo circular de Rodolfo Usigli (Explicación de Textos Literarios [California State Univ., Sacramento] 6:1, 1977/1978, p. 105-108)

One of the few efforts to do something with Usigli beside pick his prologues for ideas. Petersen's use of "circular" seems to mean different things, but he suggests a rich field for further study, the use of recurrent dramatic forms and the persistence of archetypes.

7377. **Peterson, Karen.** Essential irony in three Carballido plays (UK/LATR, 10:2, Spring 1977, p. 29-35)

Sees *Medusa, Teseo* and *Las estatuas de marfil* as variants on the existential theme of the impossibility of escaping the circumstance through choice or role-playing.

7378. **Phillips, Rachel.** Alfonsina Storni: from poetess to poet. London. Tamesis, 1975. 131 p.

Includes a sympathetic and perceptive chapter on Storni's theater, an interesting and little-known aspect of her work.

7379. **Pilditch, Charles.** René Marqués: a study of his fiction. N.Y., Plus Ultra, 1976? 245 p.

Useful introduction to the corpus of Marqués fiction and theater through the mid-1960s.

7380. **Posani, Clara.** Dos dramaturgos en el Nuevo Grupo (Escena [Caracas] 4, junio/julio 1975, p. 32-36)

Interviews with Isaac Chocrón and Elisa Lerner about their own work and the "Nuevo Grupo" with which they are affiliated.

7381. **Quackenbush, L.H.** The Magian Kings: religious drama in Latin American theater (LALR, 2:4, Spring/Summer 1974, p. 139-148)

After preliminary remarks about colonial variants and folk survivals of the *Reyes Magos* theme, comments briefly on Heiremans. Interesting theme which should be worked further.

7382. **Rabassa, Clementina.** Hacia la négritude: las ediciones *variorum* de *Dientes blancos* (*in* Alazraki, Jaime; Roland Grass; and Russell O. Salmon eds. Homenaje a Andrés Iduarte. Clear Creek, Ind., The American Hispanist, 1976, p. 285-300)

Discusses variants in the texts of different editions and relates the play's attitudes to those of writers of the *negrista* movement in English, French and Spanish.

7383. Ramón y Rivera, Luis Felipe. El tema del negro en el teatro español: su proyección en América (UCV/CA, 1:1, 1975, p. 49-102, bibl., illus., scores)

Reproduces two unpublished dramatic *canciones*, one of this century and one of unknown origin, gathered in Venezuela, and shows their formal and thematic relationships with the Spanish *entremés* in its origins, and with theater in the rest of Spanish America.

7384. *Revista Biblioteca Nacional.* Ministerio de Educación y Cultura. No. 11, oct. 1975-   . Montevideo.

Devoted to Florencio Sánchez on the centennial of his birth. Includes Roberto Ibañez' "Aportes y Enmiendas a su Biografía," A. Rosell's "El Lenguaje en Sánchez," Inés Lizaso's "Las Capas Medias Urbanas en el Teatro de Sánchez," and a selection of letters and periodical writings.

7385. Richards, Katharine C. The Mexican existentialism of Solórzano's *Los fantoches* (LALR, 4:9, Fall/Winter 1976, p. 63-69)

Suggests French existentialism and Mexican popular attitudes as sources for the play, which is not exactly new. It would be valuable to examine to what extent the existentialism of the play is indeed "Mexican."

7386. Richardson, Ruth. Florencio Sánchez and the Argentine theater. N.Y., Gordon Press, 1975. 243 p., bibl.

Although nowhere so labeled, this is a reprint of 1933 ed., now outdated, but one of first serious efforts at Latin American theater criticism in the US.

7387. Riva Buglio, Hugo. Valoración de Florencio Sánchez en el teatro latinoamericano. Montevideo, Asociación General de Autores del Uruguay (AGADU), 1976. 55 p. (Publicaciones AGADU)

Winner of the Concurso of the Asociación General de Autores del Uruguay, in connection with Sánchez centenary, but says little or nothing new. Sánchez still needs a full-scale study using contemporary methodology.

7388. Rodríguez B., Orlando. El teatro cubano: un teatro para una revolución (Escena [Caracas] 3, feb./abril 1975, p. 30-33)

Discussion of the various principal theater groups active in Cuba, particularly those operating in the provinces and among workers.

7389. Rojo, Grinor. Orígenes del teatro hispanoamericano contemporáneo. Valparaíso, Chile. Univ. Católica de Valparaíso, 1972. 227 p.

Deals primarily with the "imaginative" and "neopsychological" wings of recent theater, exemplified by Nalé Roxlo and Villaurrutia. Also includes an appendix examining the various histories of contemporary Latin American theater, and an introduction in which Rojo justifies his adoption of Goić's generational methodology. The chief problem is that Rojo sees theater as a branch of literature in general, which is fine, but that he then tries to force his chronology to fit; i.e., he sees the theater movement of the 1920s as an aspect of the general renovation about 1920, a dubious proposition.

7390. Rosell, Avenir. El lenguaje en Florencio Sánchez. Prólogo de Arturo Sergio Visca. Montevideo, Comisión Nacional de Homenaje del Sesquicentenario de los Hechos Históricos de 1825, 1975. 269 p., bibl.

Primarily a study of the language of Sánchez and his characters: dialect, vocabulary, etc. Sections devoted to more strictly theatrical matters are of little interest.

7391. Shaw, Donald L. Dramatic technique in Usigli's *El gesticulador* (Theater Research International [Glasgow, U.K.] 1:2 [new series] 1976, p. 125-133)

Discusses the technical component of this ambiguous and complex work, including the author's pretension to having created a formal tragedy. Usigli needs more of this sort of analytical treatment.

7392. Sterne, Richard C. Hawthorne transformed: Octavio Paz's La hija de Rappacini (Comparative Literature Studies [Univ. of Maryland, College Park] 13:3, Sept. 1976, p. 230-239)

Compares Paz' recreation with Hawthorne's original, and finds that Paz' *Beatriz* seeks spiritual reintegration with higher meaning through erotic love, which Sterne sees as a constant in Paz' recent work.

7393. Suárez Radillo, Carlos Miguel. El teatro experimental penitenciario uruguayo . . . (UCM/ALH, 4, 1975, p. 249-263)

Program of theater by inmates, including interviews with long-time prisoner participants. The focus is more sociological than theatrical, but the potential of such activity is considerable.

7394. El teatro puertorriqueño dentro del nuevo teatro latinoamericano: Colectivo Nacional de Teatro de Puerto Rico (CDLA/CO, 26, oct./dic. 1975, p. 62-68)

New travelling political theater group, outgrowth of previous groups Anamú and Moriviví. An example of their work, which closely resembles agit-prop of the 1930s, is *Bahía sucia, bahía negra* (see *Conjunto*, 25, julio/sept. 1975, 49-54).

7395. Troiano, James J. The grotesque tradition and the interplay of fantasy and reality in the plays of Roberto Arlt (LALR, 4:8, Spring/Summer 1976, p. 7-14)

Concludes that for Arlt reality is relative, that life is harsh and the escape into fantasy extremely dangerous.

7396. ———. The grotesque tradition in *Medusa* by Emilio Carballido (Inti [Univ. of Connecticut, Storrs] 5/6, Primavera/Otoño 1977, p. 151-156)

Interesting because the methodology provides unexpected insights into a fine play.

7397. Las últimas experiencias del Teatro Experimental de Cali ... (CDLA/CO, 14, sept./dic. 1972, p. 94-100)

Brief but illuminating comments on TEC's collective creative process.

7398. Urquiza-Almande, Oscar F. El teatro en Buenos Aires en la época de la emancipación: 1810-1820 (UK/LATR, 10:2, Spring 1977, p. 11-28)

Discusses in detail the productions in the period, pointing out that the usual statement that the theater became politicized immediately in 1810 is incorrect, and that only in 1816 did it become militant.

7399. Uruguay. Ministerio de Educación y Cultura. Biblioteca Nacional. Florencio Sánchez: centenario de su nacimiento, 1875-1975; bibliografía. Montevideo, 1975. 53 p.

Bibliography of the exposition commemorating Sánchez birth.

7400. Usigli, Rodolfo. Mexico in the theater. Translated with an introduction by Wilder P. Scott. Univ. of Mississippi, 1976. 220 p., plates (Romance monographs, 18)

Usigli's still useful classic *México en el teatro*, first published in 1932.

7401. Vázquez Pérez, Eduardo. El teatro argentino: Julio Mauricio y *Los retratos* (CDLA/CO, 16, abril/junio 1973, p. 86-94)

Overview of an often-praised but little-studied Argentine whose works are social but formally traditional.

7402. Vidal, Hernán. Dos brasas: trasfondo de excremento para una sátira social (Explicación de Textos Literarios [California State Univ., Sacramento] 4:1, 1975/1976, p. 3-9)

Rigidly Freudian analysis which sees capitalism, as Eichelbaum presents it, as an expression of anal-erotic retentionism, and assumes that this is universally applicable to capitalist estructures.

7403. ———. Los invasores: Egon Wolff y la responsabilidad del artista católico (HISP, 55, sept. 1975, p. 87-97)

Suggests that Wolff was deeply influenced by the esthetics of Maritain, and sees the play as a Jungian dream by the protagonist Meyer.

7404. Vodanovic, Sergio. Theater in society in Latin America (UM/JIAS, 18:4, Nov. 1976, p. 495-504)

Important dramatist uses the Woodyard and Lyday *Dramatists in revolt*, about which he has some curious misconceptions, as a pretext to push for a notion of Latin American theater as necessarily regional and political.

7405. Watson Espener, Maida. Enrique Buenaventura's theory of the committed theatre (UK/LATR, 9:2, Spring 1976, p. 43-47)

Short but concise summary of Buenaventura's revolutionary esthetics.

BRAZILIAN LITERATURE
NOVELS

ALEXANDRINO E. SEVERINO

Chairman
Department of Spanish and Portuguese
Vanderbilt University

THE MOST MOMENTOUS EVENT of the past two years, as far as the Brazilian novel is concerned, is the death of Clarice Lispector on 9 Dec. 1977. She was 52 years old. Having published her first novel, *Perto de coração selvagem* (1944), at the age of 18, she went on to establish a reputation as a first rate novelist and as a master of the short story. At the time of her death, she shared with Guimarães Rosa (d. 1967) the distinction of being the foremost literary figure of the post-modernist period. Both the Modern Language Association and the American Association of Teachers of Spanish and Portuguese are planning to honor Clarice Lispector at their 1978 Annual Convention by devoting one of the Portuguese-Brazilian sessions to the study of her work.

Among the novels reviewed here, those written by well-established novelists are the most deserving of a brief comment. *A Hora da estrela*, Clarice Lispector's last novel (item 7417) published a little more than a month before she died, is both a disquieting foreboding of imminent death and a condemnation of social inequity and injustice. It is a curious departure, for an author known especially for the universality of her themes. A similar departure, just as surprising, is found in Osman Lins' *A Rainha dos cárceres da Grécia* (item 7416). Here, too, the technical complexities focus on the plight of a Northeastern girl at odds with government bureaucracy. Autran Dourado's *Novelário de Donga Novais* (item 7411) provides another panel to the saga of a small town in Minas Gerais. The subject matter and the use of stream-of-consciousness and point of view to describe eccentric human behavior are reminiscent of Faulkner's Yoknapatawpha County transposed to its Brazilian regional counterpart.

Several excellent novels have been written in an allegorical vein by accomplished novelists who are obviously preoccupied with the advent of a post- "1984" society. In Herberto Sales' *O fruto do vosso ventre* (item 7423) technocratic efficiency has taken the form of compulsory abortion to curtail population growth. The protagonist in Maria Alice Barroso's *Um dia vamos rir disso tudo* (item 7406) identifies the human frailties that have led to the dominance of the computer and the tube, while in José J. Veiga's *Os pecados da tribo* (item 7427) human civilization, having barely survived the last conflict, is bent on restraining human freedoms once more, inviting a second holocaust. A different kind of allegory with a message closer to home is portrayed in Hermilo Borba Filho's *Os ambulantes de Deus* (item 7407), published posthumously. The loss of human values and the implementation of rigid controls on the citizenry are the basic elements shared by the allegorical novels reviewed.

Other types of novels represented in this section, which deserve special mention, deal with the socio-political situation, the urban milieu, and international intrigue. Antonio Callado's *Reflexos do baile* (item 7409) is the third in a series dedicated to the political events taking place before and after the 1964 military takeover. Although the urban novel appears to be thriving, judging from its considerable output, no particular distinction may be ascribed to this category. The city outcast and the sordid world he inhabits are depicted in such novels as Plínio Marcos' *Uma reportagem maldita* (item 7418a) and Antônio Torres' *Um cão uivando para a lua* (item 7425). Another kind of urban novel portrays an inconsequential cultural elite as well as the very rich, all leading purposeless lives, best exemplified by Antonio Olinto's

Copacabana (item 7422). A most enjoyable experience has been provided by a story of international intrigue written masterfully by Plínio Cabral; *Ticonderoga* (item 7408) is a successful blend of the detective story and the psychological novel.

No example of the backland novel exists among the works examined for review. This is most surprising, for ever since the superior example set by João Guimarães Rosa's work, the literary production under this category has been both plentiful and of a high caliber. To partially fill this gap, however, we are happy to report the well-received publication in English of João Ubaldo Ribeiro's *Sergeant Getúlio* (1977).

An important literary event occurred with the admittance into the Brazilian Academy of Letters of Rachel de Queiroz, the first woman to be so honored.

Alceu Amoroso Lima (Tristão de Athayde) won the XI National Contest—the Brasília Prize for Literature—in 1977, while in 1978 the recipient of the same prize was Dinah Silveira de Queiroz. The Heliodoro Valle Prize, awarded by Mexico's National Library, went to the Brazilian novelist, Autran Dourado.

Other deaths to be noted during this period are those of José Geraldo Vieira (1977) and Rosário Fusco (1977). Osman Lins died 8 July 1978. He was 54 years old.

7406. Barroso, Maria Alice. Um dia vamos rir disso tudo. Rio, Editora Nova Fronteira, 1976. 173 p.

Tender love story between a girl journalist and a nature-loving athlete set in a world grown imperceptibly more impersonal because of a dominant technocratic state and the use of mass communication to stifle individual expression. The story is narrated 30 years later by the girl protagonist. The book is a protest against the milieu as well as an admission of regret. It was the repudiation of those values represented by her lover that had helped to bring about the new society. Excellent.

7407. Borba, Hermilo. Os ambulantes de Deus. Novela. Rio, Civilização Brasileira, 1976. 145 p. (Col. Vera Cruz: literatura brasileira, 221)

There is little plot but lots of fantasy and allegory in this posthumous novel written by one of Brazil's most important contemporary novelists who died in the summer of 1976. The adventures of the five travellers adrift on a raft for five years on an impossible river are an allegory of Brazil's social ills. Although the parallels are difficult to identify, the book makes delightful reading because of the allusions to Northeastern folklore and because of the popular, colloquial language in which it is written.

7408. Cabral, Plínio. Ticonderoga. São Paulo, Summus Editorial, 1976. 216 p.

Novel of international intrigue. Good, suspenseful drama, written by an accomplished, even if occasional, story teller. While trying to find the reason for his father's murder, Valdo comes upon his father's world of women and international crime. The title symbolizes the father's hidden life, not a particular place but the far-off regions of the human personality. Excellent.

7409. Callado, Antonio. Reflexos do baile. Rio, Editora Paz e Terra, 1976. 140 p. (Col. Literatura e teoria literaria, 10)

Third in series of novels written to describe political events which took place before and after the revolution in 1964. Makes references to the late 1960s, a time of diplomatic kidnappings and student unrest. Written in the form of letters, diaries and other testimonials, the novel attains a greater artistic autonomy than the others which read more like treatises than fiction. Still, this work will be read more for its political than for its artistic content.

7410. Cardoso, Lúcio. O viajante: obra póstuma de ... Nota de Adauto Lúcio Cardoso. Introdução de Octavio de Faria. Rio, Livraria José Olympio Editora, 1973. 305 p., plate.

Left unfinished, this novel written by important novelist of post-modernist period is difficult to assess, mainly because of several gaps within narrative. Recommended especially to those interested in study of author's work or in modern Brazilian psychological novel (1944-55).

7411. Dourado, Waldomiro Autran, Novelário de Donga Novais. Rio, Difusão Editorial (DIFEL), 1976. 152 p.

Brazil's greatest contemporary novelist writes about the same city as *Opera dos mortos*. There are references to Rosalina and her father, Coronel João Capistrano Honório da Costa. It is Dourado's Yoknapatawpha country. Lelena's infidelities are narrated by Donga, an old neighbor. Time and events do not follow a logical sequence. Low in plot, but high on technique.

7412. Faria, Octávio de. O indigno. Rio, Pallas Editora [and] Instituto Nacional do Livro, 1976. 471 p. (Tragédia burguesa, 12)

Em este romance da série *Tragédia Burguesa*, o autor retoma o problema principal apresentado em um dos romances anteriores, *O Senhor do Mundo*, VII: A culpabilidade do Padre Luís, a quem uma jovem antes de morrer acusara de a ter violentado e engravidado. Muito embora o romance trate com convicção dos mesmos problemas ontológicos que caracterizam os romances anteriores, as interferências diretas do narrador-autor, que têm uma função didática, interferem no desenvolvimento da ação e diminuem o prazer da leitura.

7413. França Júnior, Oswaldo. Os dois irmãos. Romance. Rio, Editora Rocco, 1976. 131 p.

Author's sixth novel represents a welcome departure from urban situations. Tells the story in the form of a parable without a moral, in a Biblical style, and it treats the need to know others, or the *other*, in order to best know ourselves. Deserves consideration.

7414. ———. O homen de Macacão. Rio, Editora Sabiá, 1972. 121 p.

Routine fiction, this novel of the Brazilian working class is notable because of its colloquial, pornographic dialogue.

7415. ———. A volta para Marilda. Romance. Rio, Livraria José Olympio Editôra, 1974. 107 p.

Author appears oblivious to major technical advances of contemporary Brazilian fiction. This story of the Brazilian lower-middle and working classes, unfolds from beginning to end in a straight line. Useful as a guide to sociological urban trends and speech habits.

7416. Lins, Osman. A rainha dos cárceres da Grécia. São Paulo, Edições Melhoramentos, 1976. 218 p.

The thin, translucent line which divides fiction and reality is theme of this novel written by one of Brazil's most important current novelists. Narrator is led by feelings toward Julia Enone to commentary on her posthumous novel, which, in turn, depicts story of Maria de França who, like Julia, had been victimized by government bureaucracy. Relationship between actor and text, interaction between the two, are basis for technical innovations present in novel. Indispensable for study of "aesthetic revolution" in contemporary Brazilian prose fiction.

7417. Lispector, Clarice. A hora da estrela. Rio, Livraria José Olympio Editora, 1977. 104 p.

Lispector's last novel, published little more than a month before she died, may be seen as departure from previous work. There is implied social commitment, an implicit cry of protest in portrayal of this Northeastern girl, condemned by early environment to life of misery and early death. More important, however, are recognizable Lispector traits: the surprising word, the novel expression, the inquiring mind, the attempt to define the undefinable. With Lispector's death, an incomparable, original voice is stilled. Excellent.

7418. Lobato, Manoel. A verdadeira vida do Irmão Leovegildo. Romance. Belo Horizonte, Brazil, Interlivros, 1976. 120 p.

Novel by well-known short-story writer. Portrays world of outcasts and dejected (prostitutes, homosexuals, the mentally ill) of Belo Horizonte. Among them is brother Leovegildo, a lay brother who left the seminary to find his *true* calling among the unfortunate whose lives he shares. Undistinguished as a work of art but valuable portrayal of social conditions in Brazil.

7418a. Marcos, Plínio. Uma reportagem maldita: querô. Romance. São Paulo, Edições Símbolo, 1976? 98 p.

O mundo dos marginais e das prostitutas e homosexuais, com toda a sua brutalidade e rudeza, ditadas pela condição em que vivem, continua a ser o assunto preferido do paulista Plínio Marcos. O romance é escrito em uma linguagem subterrânea peculiar ao autor. O romance vale mais como documento linguístico do que como ficção.

7419. Monteiro, Benedicto. O minossauro. Rio, Novacultura Editora, 1975. 191 p.

Vol. 3 of author's Amazon trilogy which includes *Verde vagamundo* and *Terceira margem*. In the tradition of Guimarães Rosa, this work unites the regional and universal. Includes vivid transcription of regional speech. Consists of short pieces on political events throughout the world, with special emphasis on American economic interference. A good novel, deserving to be read.

7420. Nascimento, Esdras do. Paixão bem temperada. Romance. Rio, Civilização Brasileira, 1970. 243 p. (Col. Vera Cruz: literatura brasileira, 148)

Another urban novel about the lives of "lost" city (Porto Alegre) souls seeking solace from their ills in prostitutes, adultery, drink, and occasional social protest. Although well written, with excellent dialogue, it is undistinguishable from many novels on this subject.

7421. Novaes, Carlos Eduardo. A história de Cândido Urbano Urubu. Ilustrações de Vilmar Rodrigues. Rio, Editorial Nórdica, 1975. 141 p., illus. (Col. Humor para humoristas)

De prazerosa leitura, este livro de um urubú citadino, desconsoladamente perdido no mundo dos homens, porém com maiores probabilidades de sobrevivência, apresenta uma crítica contundente e mordaz à sociedade contemporânea. Vale pela ironia e pela graça de certos trocadilhos de linguagem.

7422. Olinto, Antonio. Copacabana. Romance. São Paulo, Livros Irradiantes, 1975. 197 p.

Urban novel of the Brazilian upper-middle class set in fabled world of Copacabana, with its endless parties, pseudosophisticated liberalism and loose morals. Story takes place during three days in June 1970, when Brazil won the Soccer World Cup for the third time. The feat accomplished by players from the lower classes contrasts with the inconsequential liberalism of the Copacabana crowd. Among these, Mario and Sílvia stand out. He is a sometime soccer player drained of his manhood by the inconstant, sexually insatiable Sílvia. Recommended.

7423. Sales, Herberto. O fruto do vosso ventre. Romance. Rio, Civilização Brasileira, 1976. 192 p. (Col. Vera Cruz: literatura brasileira, 223)

Novel in the form of a timely allegory by one of Brazil's most accomplished novelists. Portrays a technocratic state that stifles individual expression and where, in order to limit population, abortion becomes mandatory and use of the pill required. Concludes with part written in Biblical style wherein Joseph, a carpenter, and his wife Mary, defy the state and bring forth a child. Sardonic humor of first and second parts leads to lofty end where hope is restored. Excellent.

7424. Spalding, Tassilo Orpheu. O livro dos demônios. São Paulo, Editorial Tanagra, 1974. 196 p.

Este livro tenta reproduzir a sociedade medieval do século quinze. Superstições, bruxarias, deboches, sobretudo os praticados pelos padres são aqui representados, assim como as práticas de feitiçaria e pactos com o demônio alta noite em densas florestas. Livro curioso, insólito, escrito por alguém que obviamente está familiarizado com a sociedade medieval.

7425. Torres, Antônio. Um cão uivando para a lua. Rio, Edições Gernasa, 1972. 126 p.

Um dos muitos romances urbanos que estão sendo escritos atualmente no Brasil. Trata do insucessos de um paulistano perdido na grande cidade. A solidão trazida pelo progresso material gera o desamor, o desemprego, o desespero, e finalmente a loucura. As citações tiradas da obra de F. Scott Fitzgerald se por um lado ajudam a compreender a solidão triste do protagonista, por outro lado detraem da originalidade da obra, vinculando-a à do escritor norte-americano.

7426. Vallaça, Antonio Carlos. Monsenhor. Rio. Editora Brasília, 1975. 127 p.

Composite of several genre (autobiography, memoirs, fiction) this novel by a Catholic writer examines the present state of the Church as well as the meaning of life in a Catholic context. Villaça brings to the portrayal of the monsignor personal recollections of real people and references to true places and real events in a style characterized by discernment and sensibility. Worth reading, especially for the style of one of Brazil's finest writers.

7427. Veiga, José J. Os pecadoa da tribo. Rio, Civilização Brasileira, 1976. 122 p. (Col. Vera Cruz: literatura brasileira, 220)

Novel where reality and fantasy blend together to form an allegory. The tribe lives on after the present civilization has perished. However, man has not changed. The old sins are still there—lack of freedom, censorship, power politics. The story is direct and to the point while the colloquial speech helps to drive the fable to its rightful Brazilian setting. Excellent novel by an accomplished writer.

SHORT STORIES

MARIA ANGELICA GUIMARAES LOPES DEAN

Lecturer in the Humanities
University of Wisconsin, Parkside

IN THE BEGINNING OF THE DECADE the basic directions of the short story were psychological and regional (see *HLAS 38*, p. 498-499). From 1975 to 1977, though, the former waxed while the latter waned. One can say that now psychological dimension often permeates, and even supplants regionalism. Minor tendencies are magic realism and political allegory, often combining both psychological and regional elements. Constant printing of story collections, and numerous literary contests of national scope prove the vitality of the genre in Brazil.

The shadow of Guimarães Rosa, who so effectively united introspection and regionalism, still looms large. Almost single-handedly he set new syntactical and lexical paths; moreover, he sharpened the psychological approach by introducing a metaphysical dimension to it. Unlike many predecessors, Rosa conquered new territory: the complex psyche of peasant and villager, whom he saw as human beings, and not as caricatures. Much of exciting story writing now is indebted to this master: Grossman's tight, convoluted prose conveys the magic of frighteningly beautiful incidents and emotions; Lobo's play on words follows both his and Sousândrade's; Colônia's collection is the work of a poet possessing enviable sureness of hand. Poetical ambiguity, however, muddled in its execution, detracts from otherwise successful collections, such as Areas' and Mora Fuentes'. Others, like Costa's, convey complexity and psychological wealth in finely structured stories.

Good regionalism, again, is rare these days, but it exists, often stressing picturesque geographical landscapes side by side with psychological ones. While some writers focus on the city (D. Trevisan on Curitiba, João Antônio on Rio, and D. Silva on mythical Sanga da Amizade), others prefer the country and hamlet (Borda Filho, Carvalho, the two Valles, and Pellegrini).

The psychological direction, the main one, stylistically runs the gamut from journalistic, matter of fact prose (Gomes in *Verde suicida*, Gouvêia, Lobato, Martins, João Antônio, Tross) to intricate language (Arêas, Grossmann, Mora Fuentes, Lobo) as noted above. Both often succeed. Thematically, stories of an introspective bend touch upon the pains of growing up, of sickness, and death (Abreu, Dauster, Martins, Lobato, Tross, Gomes); upon the difficulties of communication among human beings (Carvalho, Arêas Coutinho, Colônia, Soares, Nader, Grossman, Denser, Abreu); and upon the inhumanity of the cities and the times (Coutinho, Nader, Carvalho, Martins, Grossman, Lobato). Irony underlies the majority of these collections, as exemplified by Denser, Martins, Coutinho, Guterres, Mora Fuentes, Rey, and Zwetsch. One psychological approach deals with the relatively recent phenomenon of the "liberated woman," which expectedly interests women, although in different modes: ribald (Denser), matter of fact (Dauster), anguished (Coutinho) and more serene (Colônia).

Important literary prizes, such as those of the Concurso de Contos do Paraná, and the Fernando Chinaglia from the prestigious União Brasileira de Escritores, as well as extensive endeavors from publishing houses, have not only stimulated good authors, old and new, but also eased some of these writers' more pressing material problems. The result is a number of fine collections. Notwithstanding such activities, one is shocked to know that at the end of 1977, Clarice Lispector, a master well-known in her own country, and translated abroad, was saved from penury before her death only through the assistance of a friend, Minister Nascimento Silva.

An effort is being made to reprint important authors: Valdomiro Silveira and João Alphonsus de Guimaraens are having their work reissued by Civilização Brasileira and Imago Editora, respectively. Machado de Assis' early *Histórias fluminenses* were issued as vol. 1 of a critical edition of his *Obras completas*. Carlos Drummond de Andrade's *Contos de aprendiz* was reprinted for the 15th time by José Olympio in 1977—a clear proof that after 50 years of literary activity our national poet is still a now writer, and in prose, to boot. São Paulo's Ática continues to reissue fine works such as Lispector's admirable *A legio estrangeira* (1964), as well as to publish stories by more recent writers. Ática's books include excellent illustrations by artists of Elifas Andreato's caliber.

In conclusion, the short-story genre, peculiarly suited to the national ethos, thrives in Brazil.

7428. Amado, Jorge and others. Gente boa. Prefacio de Antônio Houaiss. Rio, Editora Brasília, 1975. 145 p. bibl.

Book offers varied fare: short stories, "crônicas," interviews, newspaper articles, poetry, "literatura de cordel," and political commentary. Its only three short stories are not representative either of the excellence or the importance of the genre in Brazil.

7429. Antônio, João. Malhação do Judas Carioca. Rio, Civilização Brasileira, 1975. 140 p.

Author continues underworld chronicle in his powerful, moving style. In this, an homage to the great Lima Barreto, and the social and spiritual underdogs of Rio, João Antônio treads the fine line between journalism and literature, often sacrificing latter to former. Should be read.

7430. Arêas, Vilma. Partidas. Rio, Francisco Alves, 1976. 140 p.

Solid start by forceful writer has short stories with mysterious characters performing incomprehensible acts in magical settings: tightrope walker's body spider-like weaves its own rope; man kills fiancées to collect photographs; princes chew gum in girl's garden, or naked, resemble shell-less tortoises and snails. Poetry marred by hermeticism, though.

7431. Colônia, Regina Célia. Canção para o totem. Rio, Civilização Brasileira, 1975. 161 p. plates.

One of the most distinguished recent collections, book offers varied formats, themes, characters, and especially, high literary level. Successful experimental techniques and poetry transposed into prose create a "sexto continente" of language (Teles' use of author's title in perceptive essay.) Well deserves prestigious prizes. Author previously acclaimed as poet of *Sumaimana*.

7432. Costa, Flávio Moreira da. Os espectadores. Contos, texto, drama. São Paulo, Edições Simbolo, 1976. 100 p.

Taut, muscular language conveys perception, imagination and irony. Pt. 1) brief, varied stories; pt.2) texts, a unit, mingle actual and fictional movie characters in scenarios reminiscent of Hollywood oldies and New Wave movies; pt. 3) another parody, is absurd play, with actors as spectators and social commentators. Outstanding.

7433. Coutinho, Sônia. Uma certa felicidade. Rio, Francisco Alves, 1976. 120 p.

Superbly written morality tales convey confusion and despair of "modern," educated young women who left the province for Rio. With the best of themselves behind, they are unable to find even "uma certa felicidade" in a city they love and hate. Marvelous language that is poetical and balanced.

7434. Dauster, Bluma. Estoriário. Rio, Imago Editora, 1976. 99 p. (Série ficção Imago)

Competent collection by young author offers variety to formats and themes—from mediaeval prose "Cantiga de Amigo" to stream of consciousness monologue. Mainly deals with contemporary ambiguities pursued and explored. Strong plotting. Effective narrative and dialogue. Esthetic stories which capture mystery of moment, and create seemingly undefinable moods.

7435. Denser, Márcia M. Tango fantasma. Contos. São Paulo, Editora Alfa-Omega, 1976. 108 p.

Author, a moralist, succeeds in showing "mulher [precipitada] nos labirintos de si mesma . . . [porque] sua libertação sexual é puramente anatômica . . ." in effective prose: an amalgam of slant, obscenities, artistic and philosophical considerations. Unusual in Brazilian literature: female narrator relates her amorous adventures with apparent cynicism and profound bitterness, often producing comical effect.

7436. Fuentes, José Luis Mora. O cordeiro da casa. Ficções. São Paulo, Edições Quiron, 1974. 147 p. (Col. Jogral. Ficção contemporânea, 4)

Book has enviable narrative powers, breadth, and irony. Best stories are carefully scaffolded and suspenseful: "E Rebanhos, e Cardumes . . .," "Um Dia antes do Parlamento, Entrar no Minguante," "Gentil Senilidade," and "Amigos." Young author fulfills his ambition for collection as revealed in one story: "remota unidade de romance" through "prismas diferentes."

7437. Gomes, Duílio. O nascimento dos leões. Belo Horizonte, Brazil, Interlivros de Minas Gerais, 1975. 191 p.

"Punch and poetry," the *sine qua* of a good story according to O'Faolain, are evident in the clear language and able scaffolding of these stories. Situations are often dramatic, introducing diverse characters examined in a flash or through a period of time. Collection deserves all praise accorded.

7438. ———. Verde suicida. São Paulo, Editora Ática, 1977. 94 p., illus. (Col. De autores brasileiros, 8)

Based on premise that "life is a murderous smile awaiting us around each corner." Incisive, accomplished stories show human beings are predatory: adults seduce children, psychoanalysts persecute patients, fathers and sons fight a "Holy War"—title of one story. A bitterly ironic book, less poetical than *O nascimento dos leões* (see item 7437).

7439. Gouveia, Jaime Prado. Dorinha Dorê. Roteiros para a classe média. Belo Horizonte, Brazil, Interlivros de Minas Gerais, 1975. 168 p.

Disguised as humble paperback, collection offers variety and literary technique. Includes excellent monologues by diverse characters: charismatic guitarrist gone mad ("Angel"), obsessed chief of police ("Dois Olhos Claros"), and young girl dreaming ("Dorinha Dorê"). One successful story format is list: of passengers on bus, horoscope, and "Roteiros para a Classe Média."

7440. Guimaraens, João Alphonsus de. Contos e novelas. Rio, Imago, Editora, 1976. 249 p.

After a decade, a reprint of the three collections of one of our best short-story writers. "Escritor Miudo" (A. Coutinho) focuses on middle-class of then quiet Belo Horizonte—a microcosm. Stories: direct product of Modernismo, but even after 40 years, language remains supple, vivid.

7441. Guterres, Sérgio dos Santos. Contos mínimos. Rio, Editora Artenova, 1976. 35 p.

Most of these brief stories verge on prose poems, sometimes marred by obscurity. Lightly sketched characters are evanescent, and almost inseparable from atmosphere. Fine language and elusive mood accord book its literary distinction.

7442. Lobato, Manoel. Flecha em repouso. São Paulo, Editora Ática, 1977. 76 p., illus. (Col. De autores brasileiros, 9)

Like the sick and downtrodden to whose needs author ministers, as pharmacist, these characters are fate's victims. Lobato's stories have become sparser, more stringent since previous collection (see *HLAS 38:7373*). Title story exploits parallels successfully. Book represents same bitter outlook on life as his colleagues Gomes' and Tross', simultaneously published (see item 7438 and 7453).

7443. Lobo, Luíza. Por trás dos muros: arte-fábulas. Rio, Editora Brasília, 1976. (Col. Literatura)

In these "arte-fábulas" rich, dense texts convey, through "reflexão/refração/reflexos" another reality: blindman's, madman's, magician's. Reader is invited to collaborate, to "aprender/apreender" "shattered pieces of reality." "Words play with words, mingle, marry, give birth to other words. Poetry? Prose? Though occasionally hermetic, well worth reading.

7444. Machado de Assis, Joaquim Maria. Obras. v. 1, Contos fluminenses. Edições críticas, texto estabelecido pela Comissão Machado de Assis. Rio, Civilização Brasileira, 1975. 265 p.

Vol. 1 of critical edition of Machado's work. The unrepresentative and mediocre first stories were carefully prepared by illustrious machadianos, with all the bibliographical apparatus. A must for students of Machado.

7445. Nader, Vladyr. Cafarnaum. São Paulo, Vertente Editora, 1976. 112 p.

Distinguished collection offers dramatic interior monologues and confessions, in which introspective, dissatisfied, modern "paulista" Hamlet is able to see but unable to act. Economic style and direct approach are reminiscent of Graciliano Ramos, whose words "alegre como um desgraçado" are used as epigraph.

7446. Pellegrini Júnior, Domingos. O homem vermelho. Contos. Rio, Civilização Brasileira, 1977. 122 p.

Justly acclaimed work of young new writer, book was recipient of two major prizes. Subject matter is plight of the exploited proles: truck drivers and small farmers in Paraná; electricians of Rio-Niteroi Bridge. All told in dramatic monologues and malleable language. "Red man" emerges as anonymous hero, winner over oppressors.

7447. Silva, Deonísio da. Exposição de motivos. Rio, Editora Artenova, 1976. 160 p.

With sure hand, supple language and spicy humor, Silva creates Sanga de Amizade, Paraná—a contrast to gigantic São Paulo, to which some "sangaenses" emigrate. In both, clay feet of "Religião, Pátria e Família" are soon exposed, in stories couched in a variety of formats: inquests, reports, dialogues. An exciting book.

7448. Silveira, Valdomiro. Mixuangos. Contos. 2. ed. Rio, Civilização Brasileira [and] Instituto Nacional do Livro, Brasília, 1975. 139 p. (Vera Cruz, 200)

This reprint of *Mixuangos* and five other story collections commemorates centennial of one of Brazil's foremost regionalist. Besides Silveira's glossary, book includes biographical notes and fine prefatory article. Moving, often dramatic stories still read well—quaintness is merely superficial. Effective contrast between classical diction and country patois.

7449. Soares, Murilo César. Anaflor, uma noite. Contos. Prefácio de Paulo Rangel. São Paulo, Edições Símbolo, 1976. 109 p.

Well crafted stories won second prize of 1975 Fernando Chinaglia Contest. Author in his mid-20s seldom shows novice's hand, expressing obliqueness in language classical in its simplicity. Also noteworthy: gamut ranges from realism to fantasy. Title story is a gem.

7450. Souza, Hugo de A. Globo da morte. Belo Horizonte, Brazil, Edição Alternativa, 1975. 90 p. (Col. Os novos, 1)

Very young writer offers perceptive, brief stories (monologues, dialogues, narratives, and a radio-interview) in auspicious debut—this collection —awarded the Honorable Mention from the respected Fernando Chinaglia Prize of the União Brasileira de Escritores.

7451. Trevisan, Dalton. Abismo de rosas. Rio, Civilização Brasileira, 1976. 123 p.

In reversed fairy-tale world without happy endings, João and Maria torture each other, and "are unhappy for the rest of their lives." Here, arena gets smaller for "miniaturist" Trevisan—in Lara Resende's words—paralleled by emphasis on small size of characters and abundant diminutives. Fine Trevisan, though occasionally repetitious.

7452. Trevisan, João Silvério. Testamento de Jônatas deixado a David. Contos. São Paulo, Editora Brasiliense, 1976. 150 p.

Uneven collection with many good stories. Majority deal with male homosexuality and its impact on family, friends. Author intent on revealing this "zona crepuscular de semirrealidade" (Paz' epigraph) through several angles: comic, tragic, burlesque, pathetic. Plastic language and dramatic situations. Influenced by contemporary Spanish American writers. Title story: outstanding.

7453. Tross, Sérgio. Garfo e água fresca. São Paulo, Editora Atica, 1977. 78 p., illus. (Col. De autores brasileiros, 10)

Collection conveys apparently disenchanted vision of life underscored by atmosphere of blood and death. Still, underlying one can sense young author's faith in humanity: "acredito muito em muita gente." Astringent, often brutal stories in terse language. An impressive, dramatic book.

7454. Valle, Dinorath do. O vestido amarelo. Contos. Rio, Editora Artenova, 1976. 183 p.

Winner of several literary prizes, collection of effective stories. Most expose joys and ugly side of life, in country and village, through eyes of young narrator, which gives continuity to book. Marred by awkward transitions in interior monologues.

7455. Valle, Roberto do. As leopardas. São Paulo, Edições Símbolo, 1976. 95 p.

Most of these stories won prizes at the 1972 Paraná Short Story Contest. Themes are evil passions, as they influence country people's lives. Through keen powers of observation and able characterization, author conveys psychological complexities.

7456. Vieira, Emanuel Medeiros *ed.* Assim ascrevem os catarinenses. São Paulo, Editora Alfa-Omega, 1976. 192 p.

Collection designed to prove that "catarinenses" write well. Wide gamut of styles, subject matters, moods. Best stories are by Cardozo, Bell, Hoffman, and Menezes. Noteworthy is previously unpublished "Se Lembra de Stela," by Osmard de Andrade, in which language cadence follows rhythm of character's remembrances.

7457. Viggiano, Alan. O exilado. Belo Horizonte, Brazil, Editora Comunicação [and] Instituto Nacional do Livro, Brasília, 1976. 77 p.

Alceu Amoroso Lima, in awarding this volume his vote for the 1973 Afonso Arinos Prize of the Brazilian Academy of Letters, describes the content thus: "Oscila dentro de uma grande variedade de temas ... desde o quadro rústico e popular do sertão até elucubrações apocalípticas de um fim do mundo em que a humanidade volta à condição de arborícola." [R.E. Dimmick]

7458. Zwetsch, Valdir. O fabricante de sonhos. Contos. Prefácio de Ignácio de Loyola Brandão. São Paulo, Edições Símbolo, 1976. 110 p.

Tight, Kafkaesque short short stories about strange metamorphoses and inexplicable facts by capable young author with fine sense of humor.

CRÔNICAS

GERALD M. MOSER

Professor of Spanish and Portuguese
The Pennsylvania State University

THE PERIODICAL COLUMN known as the *crônica* continues to be widely cultivated in Brazil by several writers outstanding in other genres, as well as by numerous competent journalists. As a result, it is possible to apply to it the high standards set by the best authors ever since the days of França Júnior and Machado de Assis over 100 years ago.

Each generation that is now alive has its masters of the genre, and they are well represented among the new collections of *crônicas*. In the older generation, Rachel de Queiroz delights with nostalgic sketches of her youth in Ceará, to be found in *As menininhas* (see item 7483). Carlos Drummond de Andrade still strikes sparks of poetic whimsy in *Os dias lindos* (see item 7483). Some *crônicas* were resurrected from old newspaper files, e.g. Mário de Andrade's *Taxi* series (1927-32, item 7461) or were anthologized, as was the case of the articles of "Stanislaw Ponte Preta" (item 7481).

In the intermediate generation, Fernando Sabino cultivates his witty manner of taking candid "snapshots" of the ridiculous human animal (including himself in the species) in *Deixaio Alfredo falar!* (item 7485), while João Antônio gathered poignant, well-documented reports in *Casa de loucos* (item 7462) that went far beyond the ephemeral nature of run-of-the-mill commentaries. Another thoughtful contribution coming from this intermediate generation was Margarida Sabóia de Carvalho's posthumously collected meditations (item 7465). She was one of several authors —others are Rachel de Queiroz, Ciro Colares and Carmelita Setúbal—who lead one to the conclusion that the northeastern state of Ceará is a fertile breeding ground of good *cronistas*. The younger generation is coming to the fore with two excellent humorists, the *gaúcho* Luís Fernando Veríssimo, as funny as a cartoonist as he is a bitingly satirical *cronista* in *A grande mulher nua* (item 7487), a clear advance over his earlier collections, and the *fluminense* Carlos Eduardo Novaes, who justifies his growing popularity with *O caos nosso de cada dia* (item 7478).

The genre, polymorphous as it is, has been expanded into the realm of medicine and spiritualism (see items 7473 and 7477). Another specialized variant, the sports commentary, was singled out by Ivan Cavalcanti Proença for a school anthology (item 7482). Does that mean that the impish *crônica* has become academically respectable? In spite of such a threat, the genre can be said to be thriving. And while it remains for most authors an unpretentious way to entertain distracted readers or, at most, make them reflect sentimentally for a moment, a few courageous cronistas among the best have managed, in a subtle way, to challenge the political leadership of the country with commentaries on such sticky subjects as military rule, film and press censorship, industrial pollution, elections, the "death squad," and the arbitrary use of police power.

7459. Aiala, Luís [*pseud. for* **Luís Gonzaga Gusmão de Andrade**]. O sábado e o curió. Crônicas. Prefácio de Sócrates Times de Carvalho and Mauro Mota. Recife, Brazil, Associação de Imprensa de Pernambuco, 1975. 142 p.

Posthumous selection of sketches by an irreverent, consumptive and bohemian journalist from Olinda, made from *Último dia* and *O sonho e a ilha*. Yet, these selections are anything but irreverent; they are the musings of a lonely man, expressing his somber moods in moving, sincere prose.

7460. Andrade, Carlos Drummond de. Os dias lindos. Rio, Livraria José Olympio Editora, 1977. 145 p., bibl.

Crônicas make up the smaller part of the volume. They deal e.g. with communicating the joy of a beautiful day (whence the title). They supplement four lengthy tales, six shorter stories, and 14 language games, e.g. an article composed entirely of exclamations. The whimsical approach exists throughout. Even the wordiest pieces are lit up by flashes of poetic imagination.

7461. Andrade, Mário de. Táxi e crônicas no *Diário Nacional*. Edited by Telê Porto Ancona-Lopez. São Paulo, Livraria Duas Cidades *em convênio com a* Secretaria da Cultura, Ciência e Tecnologia, 1976. 604 p., illus.

Like his friends Manuel Bandeira and Câmara Cascudo, the liveliest of the Brazilian Modernists contributed *crônicas* to the *Diário Nacional* of São Paulo, in which he discussed ideas, politics, language and literature very critically and yet very engagingly. First published between 1927-32, they have now been collected and intelligently annotated.

7462. Antônio [de Andrade Ferreira], João. Casa de loucos. Rio, Civilização Brasileira, 1976. 137 p. (Col. Vera Cruz. Literatura brasileira, 219)

Contains 12 interviews and reports, penetratingly constructed by story writer who admires Lima Barreto. The last, "Drama: Casa de Loucos," serves as a reminder and a metaphor. The first, "Protesto: Olá, Professor, há Quanto Tempo!," sets the intrepid tone with a protest against police surveillance. Popular musicians and the exploitation of soccer players furnish themes to the diverse and eloquent collection.

7463. Boal, Augusto. Crônicas de nuestra América. Rio, Editora Codecri, 1977. 167 p., illus. (Col. Edições do pasquim, 10)

Boal sent the ten farcical stories to *O Pasquim* from his exile in B.A. Laid in countries from the Falkland Islands to Venezuela, they are much too long and elaborate to be true *crônicas*. Brazil is the scene of a biting satire on newspaper editors, "Acabou a Censura."

7464. Carvalho, Luciano de. Prosa leve. Crônicas, ensaios, contos. Prefácio de José Tavares de Miranda. São Paulo, IBREX, 1975. 205 p.

Author served in the state government of São Paulo. His sketches of travels in Europe and northern Brazil occupy about a third of the volume, having appeared first in the *Folha de S. Paulo* (1974-75).

The rest are articles on Brazilian problems (without any levity) and a few faintly humorous stories.

7465. Carvalho, Margarida Sabóia de. Crônicas. Prefácio de Sânzio de Azevedo. Fortaleza, Brazil, Terra de Sol, 1976. 218 p.

The articles appeared in *Diário do Povo* and *Tribuna do Ceará* from 1951 on. They were collected in the year of her death. Many are meditations about the human condition. Marked by the "disillusions, pains and upsets of life," she possessed a wisdom, refined by a classical education, which is rarely found among commentators.

7466. Colares, Ciro. 100 [i.e. Cem] crônicas escolhidas. Seleção de Jáder de Carvalho. Fortaleza, Brazil, Univ. Federal do Ceará, 1976. 239 p.

Articles originally written for the *Tribuna do Ceará* and selected from six books were published 1965-73. They share a playful, lyrical tone and a mildly sensual, frank, natural style.

7467. Cristaldo, Janer. A força dos mitos. Crônicas. São Paulo, Editora Alfa-Omega, 1976. 168 p. (Biblioteca Alfa-Omega de cultura universal, 2:5)

Sketches first published in the *Folha da Manhã* (Porto Alegre, 1975-76) and named after one which discusses two "pretty words," democracy and love, enriched by the author's Scandinavian experience. He excels in Swiftian satire, e.g., against the literary establishment, absolute power, lurid advertising, or youth cults.

7468. Dapena, Ortênsia Muradás. Adeus ao mundo. Crônicas. Prefácio de Maria Dinorah. Porto Alegre, Brazil, Editora Bels, 1975. 133 p.

Emotional, even passionate sketches, written 1953-75, protesting with a sense of futility in the first, important section against the devastation of the environment in her adopted town, Cruz Alta, and other parts of Brazil. It includes an illustrated *crônica* of the poisoning of a hummingbird by pesticides.

7469. Espinheiro Filho, Ruy. Sob o último sol de fevereiro. Crônicas. Rio, Editora Civilização Brasileira, 1975. 110 p.

Escapist fantasies first published by the Bahian poet in *Tribuna da Bahia* (1969-75). The title is taken from the last sketch, in which the author typically rides with a companion on the back of a marine monster out into the open sea.

7470. Franco, Sérgio da Costa. Quarta página. Crônicas. 2. ed. Porto Alegre,

Brazil, Editora Movimento, 1975. 79 p. (Col. Rio Grande, 13)

Originally published in *Correio do Povo* (1970-73), p. 4). Most sketches reproduce scenes observed in the city of Porto Alegre, some, nostalgic memories of life in a country town, appealing eloquently to middle-class readers' compassion for the poor.

7471. Gabaglia, Marisa Raja. Meu dia-a-dia. Crônicas. Prefácio de Humberto Vieira. Rio, Livraria José Olympio Editora, 1976. 175 p.

Sketches written by successful young woman journalist. Her indiscreet account of big little worries of society girl and TV personality, transplanted from Rio to São Paulo, have snob appeal. She does write amusing, slangy banter, rarely succumbing to depressions. They read like pages from a diary, but they are a far cry from Eleanor Roosevelt's "My Day."

7472. Galeno, Cândida and others. Quinteto em ritmo de crônica. Fortaleza, Brazil, Editora Henriqueta Galeno, 1975. 158 p.

Intermingled sketches by five women: Cândida Maria Santiago Galeno exalts compatriots she has known. Carmelita Setúbal contributes poems in prose about unique characters and places in Ceará; Maria de Lourdes de Araújo is more prosaic but handles heterogeneous themes skillfully; Olga Monte Barroso's subjects are religion and ethics; Risette Cabral Fernandes, the youngest, is the sentimental dreamer.

7473. Grinbaum, Emílio. Crônicas de um médico. Prefácio de Magda Leward. Belo Horizonte, Brazil, Escola Alberto Einstein, 1975. 64 p.

Articles written by cardiologist for the *Jornal de Minas* (1972-75) to defend medicine from dehumanizing effects of technology. Although their literary quality is low, they aim at drawing public attention to perplexing health problems, thus opening a new territory for the *crônica*.

7474. Meireles, Cecília. Ilusões do mundo. Crônicas. Prefácio de Darcy Damasceno. Rio, Editora Nova Aguilar, 1976. 128 p., bibl. (Biblioteca manancial, 50)

Written 1961-63 for radio program and for the most part published among her *Inéditos* in 1967. Rich in experience and feeling, these *crônicas* are superbly written, though steeped in the melancholy thought that the good life is giving way to barbarity.

7475. Messias, Ney [Cassiano Ricardo]. O construtor de mistérios. Seleção e prefácio de Janer Cristaldo. Porto Alegre, Brazil, Editora Garatuja, 1975. 153 p.

Posthumously edited selections from columns published in *Folha de Tarde* and *Folha Esportiva* by poet (d. 1970). He brings sense of mystery, terror, irrational forces to bear on his observations.

7476. Monteiro, Mozart. Histórias da vida real. Fortaleza, Brazil, Editora Henriqueta Galeno, 1975? 135 p.

Although the author is a history teacher he harbors illusions about the objectivity of a story teller like himself. He rivals Ripley's "Believe it or not" in reporting short items of human oddity, paradox and diversity. Surprisingly, almost none of the examples are Brazilian.

7477. Neiva, Lauro. Os mortos ensinam aos vivos: obra póstuma. Rio, Editora Artenova, 1975. 175 p.

Posthumously published articles by psychiatrist who turned to spiritualism. Includes several lengthy essays in defense of spiritualism as aid to psychiatry as well as nine shorter pieces which qualify as *crônicas*. Although they vary widely, from a lovers' tale to recollections of Getúlio and Darcy Vargas and a professional visit to Montreal, they have a psychiatric angle in common.

7478. Novaes, Carlos Eduardo. O caos nosso de cada dia. Prefácio de Sérgio Augusto. Rio, Editorial Nórdica, 1974. 172 p., ilus.

Humorous sketches written for the *Jornal do Brasil* (Rio). Author's acknowledged model is the droll Sérgio Porto. His best one (about congested traffic in Rio, to which title alludes) makes him most entertaining as well as the most instructive Brazilian humorist alive.

7479. Ouro Preto, Maluh [Maria Luisa] de. Ardentia. Crônicas. Rio, Editora Nova Fronteira, 1975. 263 p., illus.

Articles written (1948-75) and grouped according to themes, such as seaside vacations, air travels, paintings, etc. Sensitive to living creatures, colors, sounds, author describes life as a beautiful spectacle, tinged at times with a melancholy that saves her from facility.

7480. Pereira, Maura de Senna. Nós e o mundo. Crônicas, resenhas, artigos. Rio, Livraria São José, 1976. 149 p.

Sketches originally published in the *Gazeta de Notícias* (Rio). Many are brief and friendly notices of new books. The few real *crônicas* are comments on "the drama of time" in human life. Some evoke eminent men of science, some call for preservation of historic landmarks.

7481. Pôrto, Sérgio [*pseud. for* **Stanislaw Ponte Preta**]. O melhor de Stanislaw. Crônicas escolhidas. Seleção e organização de Valdemar Cavalcanti. Ilustações de Jaguar. Rio, Livraria José Olympio Editora, 1976. 228 p., illus.

Selections from seven collections published under name of author's famous buffonish character, surrounded by other originals, such as Aunt Zulmira, an old belle as bright and irreverent a *carioca* as her creator. The often slightly risqué "historinhas" cleverly allude to the mores of his Rio and his Brazil.

7482. Proença, Ivan Cavalcanti *ed.* Nelson Rodrigues e Joao Saldanha, a crônica e o futebol: ensaios e textos comentados sobre autores contemporâneos brasileiros e portugueses. Rio, Educação e Comunicação Editora (EDUCOM), 1976. 174 p. (Col. Autores contemporâneos. Série brasilera, 1)

Annotated school anthology of soccer columns, originally published in newspapers of the 1960s and 1970s. Proença points out the passionate subjectivity, love of hyperbole and invented characters in the articles by N.R., the former playwright, and the colloquial *carioca* lingo and familiarity with the underlying conditions in the articles of J.S., the former coach.

7483. Queiroz, Rachel de. As menininhas e outras crônicas. Rio, Livraria José Olympio Editora, 1976. 177 p., bibl., illus.

Written 1971-75. The worldly comments of "a velha senhora" zero in on the decline she observes in the quality of western life, e.g., her reactions to the women libbers or to the machine age. Most appealing are the autobiographical *crônicas* about the Ceará of her youth. Like some other writers, she—oh, so gently—breaks lances for a return to democracy.

7484. Ribeiro, Antônio Carlos. Vivência. Crônicas. Prefácio de J.A. Pio de Almeida. Porto Alegre, Brazil, Editora Movimento *em convênio com o* Instituto Estadual do Livro (IEL), Depto. de Assuntos Culturais (DAC), Secretaria de Educação e Cultura do Rio Grande do Sul (SEC), 1975. 80 p. (Col. Rio Grande, 16)

Rapid, breezy commentaries, which rarely rise above commonplaces, by journalist who hails from Érico Veríssimo's hometown Cruz Alta, Rio Grande do Sul. He publishes his weekly column in the *Correio do Povo* (Porto Alegre) and, being one of the editors, takes care not to offend anyone.

7485. Sabino, Fernando. Deixa o Alfredo falar! Rio, Distribuidora Record, 1976. 213 p.

"Snapshots of daily life," spiced with anecdotes, in Sabino's usually humorous manner, cultivated since writing about N.Y.C. in *A cidade vazia* (1950). They include the *crônica* of the title (about the art of the Brazilian bate-papo), another on the more difficult art of keeping quiet, his adventures as a broadcaster and a filmmaker and his confessions as a writer: "Facing the Mirror."

7486. Salles, Waldemar Batista de. Uma voz dentro da noite. Crônicas. Manaus, Brazil, Estado Amazonas, Imprensa Oficial, 1974. 138 p.

Many of the sketches are short and complacent book reviews. The style is journalese, full of clichés. The collection presents some interest because so few books are published in the state of Amazonas. But only a few of the sketches refer to Amazonian topics.

7487. Veríssimo, Luís Fernando. A grande mulher nua. Crônicas. Rio, Livraria José Olympio Editora, 1975. 149 p., illus.

Veríssimo's myth-making imagination turns the world as we know it topsy-turvy, both in his prose and his cartoons, which are additions, not illustrations. He derives unorthodox psychological conclusions from animals—spiders, praying mantises, whales and sloths—as well as from humans, sexual mores, movies and even—in Brazil!—from politics. No doubt, he is becoming one of the country's best humorists.

POETRY

RALPH E. DIMMICK

*General Secretariat
Organization of American States*

VERSE CONTINUES TO BE PRODUCED IN QUANTITY, but there is little to record in the way of novelty for the period here covered, save for Paulo Augusto's treatment (item 7569) of a theme previously taboo. Well-known figures such as Carlos Drummond de Andrade (item 7494), Walmir Ayala (item 7499), Geir Campos (item 7510), Ferreira Gullar (item 7529), Homero Homem (item 7532), Henriqueta Lisboa (item 7541), Thiago de Mello (item 7554), João Cabral de Melo Neto (item 7556), Geraldo Pinto Rodrigues (item 7579), Gilberto Mendonça Teles (item 7594), and Armindo Trevisan (item 7596) produced new works in their usual manners, the most rewarding being that by the first mentioned. There were a number of reprints of collected or selected verse, both by figures still living—Carlos Drummond de Andrade (item 7495), Haroldo de Campos (item 7511), Lêdo Ivo (item 7533), Mauro Mota (item 7561), and Afonso Félix de Sousa (item 7592)—and by ones of the recent or more remote past—Augusto dos Anjos (item 7496), Raimundo Correia (item 7516), Junqueira Freire (item 7525), Jorge de Lima (item 7538), Murilo Mendes (item 7557), Artur de Sales (item 7582), Augusto Frederico Schmidt (item 7587), and Da Costa e Silva (item 7588). The Schmidt item is of special interest, in that it contains a sizable body of previously unpublished material. The one "new" name is that of Waldemar Lopes, who, after long decades of silence, produced three volumes (items 7544-7546) of unusual distinction.

7488. Agra, [Antônio José] Figueirêdo. Tempos da noite. Rio, Livraria São José, 1975. 101 p.

All life for Agra is part of a universal and eternal process of dying.

7489. ———. Vida flauta. n.p., Iterplan, 1974. 93 p.

Agra has much to say about what poetry should be and how words should be used ("Valem as palavras no poema/quanto não sejam só palavras/ e confundam em suas sílabas/ vida, tensão, a essência e seu travo") but his own style is generally flat and sententious.

7490. Albuquerque, Terêza Tenório de. O círculo e a pirâmide. São Paulo, Edições Quíron *em convênio com a* Secretaria de Educação e Cultura, Prefeitura Municipal do Recife, 1976. 75 p. (Col. Sélesis, 8)

Drawing inspiration from classic myth and Christian religion, ancient epic and the travels of present-day astronauts, poet writes well-structured verse expressive of mystical vision.

7491. Almeida, Guilherme de [Andrade]. Raça. 2. ed. Rio, Livraria José Olympio Editora, 1972. 52 p. (Col. Sagarana, 88)

Reissue of a classic of the nationalistic aspect of Brazilian Modernism, with a biographical sketch by Frederico Pessoa de Barros; critical articles by Lêdo Ivo, Tristão de Athayde [Alceu Amoroso Lima], Agrippino Grieco, and Sérgio Milliet; and bibliographical notes.

7492. Almeida, Prisciliana Duarte de. Antologia poética. Prefácio e seleção de Oliveira Ribeiro Neto. São Paulo, Secretaria da Cultura, Ciência e Tecnologia, Conselho Estadual de Cultura, 1976. 125 p. (Col. Poesia, 11)

Selected compositions by a turn-of-the-century poet, conventional, but pleasingly sincere in verse inspired by the death of her husband.

7493. Anchieta, José de. Poemas eucarísticos e outros. De eucaristia et aliis. Poemata varia. Originais latinos, acompanhados de tradução portuguesa, introdução e notas pelo Armando Cardoso. São Paulo, Edições Loyola, 1975. 243 p. (Obras completas, 2)

Primarily of historical interest, for the study of one of the first intellectual figures associated with Brazil.

7494. Andrade, Carlos Drummond de. Menino antigo: boitempo-II. Rio, Livraria José Olympio Editora *em convênio com o* Ministério da Educação e Cultura, Instituto Nacional do Livro, 1973. 176 p.

Like an album of daguerreotypes, this collection recaptures in sharp detail a past that is dead and gone. And from it transpires a sense of the poet's inner revolt against the excessive rigors of the patriarchal semirural society into which he was born.

7495. ———. Poesia completa e prosa. Introdução geral, nota editorial de Afrânio Coutinho. As várias faces de uma poesia de Emanuel de Moraes. Fortuna crítica de Mário de Andrade, Otto Maria Carpeaux, Álvaro Lins, Sérgio Buarque de Holanda, Haroldo de Campos, João Gaspar Simões, Rubem Braga. Cronologia da vida e da obra. 3. ed. Rio, José Aguilar Editora, 1973. 1315 p., bibl.

Updated, much enlarged (by 232 p.) third edition of work first issued in 1964 (see *HLAS 28:2662a*) with the change in title due to omission of some crônicas. Wealth of critical and bio-bibliographical material in addition to complete, carefully edited text makes this volume invaluable for the study of one of the greatest of contemporary poets.

7496. Anjos, Augusto [de Carvalho Rodrigues] dos. Toda a poesia. Com um estudo crítico de Ferreira Gullar: Augusto dos Anjos ou vida e morte nordestina. Rio, Editora Paz e Terra, 1976. 201 p.

"Essa necessidade de não de desprender do vivido, de não traí-lo, de não disfarçá-lo com delicadezas, de erguê-lo de sua vulgaridade à condição de poesia por força da palavra é que determina a originalidade desse poeta e o salto que sua obra significa naquele momento de nossa poesia." So writes Ferreira Gullar in his excellent and extended critical study of a poet who, despite his insistence on morbid themes and excessive use of scientific vocabulary, has known singular public success: this is the 31st reprinting of the single work published during his lifetime.

7497. Anjos, Ricardo Augusto [Pena] dos. Agrolírica. São Paulo, Edições Quíron *em convênio com o* Ministério da Educação e Cultura, Instituto Nacional do Livro, 1974. 63 p. (Col. Sélesis, 1)

A celebration of sensual love, in which the beloved is often identified with the earth.

7498. Augusto, Eudoro. A vida alheia. Rio, The Author, 1975. 1 v. (Unpaged) plates.

These descendants of the *poema-piada* of Modernism possess genuinely humorous and lyrical qualities.

7499. Ayala, Walmir. A pedra iluminada. Rio, Pallas Editora *em convênio com o* Ministério da Educação e Cultura, Instituto Nacional do Livro, 1976. 89 p.

Love and death are Ayala's most frequently recurring themes but neither seems of much concern to him in these graceful but impersonal lyrics.

7500. Baraúna, Alberto Luiz. Quarenta quase sonetos e uma sextantina hexagonal para viola d'amore. Obra dedicada ao geômetra do raro e ruivo isóceles perfeito entoada aos anjos de Jorge de Lima. Salvador, Brazil, Edições Macunaima, 1975. 21 l., illus.

Influenced by Lima's *Invenção de Orfeu*, classical in language and allusions, these compositions are highly obscure as regards meaning.

7501. Barbosa, Cláudio Tavares. As raízes. Rio, Editora Rio *em convênio com as* Faculdades Integradas Estácio de Sá, 1976. 84 p.

Barbosa's "O fazer poético" gives an excellent idea both of his procedure and his manner: "Repensar e recomeçar,/ . . . /Inventar, e na invenção/ superar-se, recriar na criação./ /Fiar o verso e a vida, lento,/ fundir, e refundindo sempre,/apascentar o frêmito . . ."

7502. Bastos, Hermenegildo. A coisa comum. Rio, Imago Editora *em convênio com o* Ministério da Educação e Cultura, Instituto Nacional do Livro, 1976. 108 p. (Série poesia Imago)

One of the few clear statements in this collection is "a poesia é o sonho em demasia/outros os sonhos possíveis." In general, words for Bastos have become an end in themselves; syntax all but disappears. The general effect is rather like that of the aleatory music with which certain contemporary composers are mystifying audiences.

7503. Bell, Lindolf. Incorporação. São Paulo, Edições Quíron, 1974. 211 p., illus. (Col. Sélesis, 3)

This collection reprints works written between 1962-72 and shows Bell primarily as a manipulator of words. The summation of his poem on the death of Manuel Bandeira "Manuelancolia" provides one sample of his technique, which is also characterized by parallelistic and repetitive devices. A recent activity, exemplified in the illustrations, is the printing of poems on T-shirts—the "corpoema."

7504. Benevides, Artur Eduardo. Elegias de outono e canções de muito amar e de adeus. Fortaleza, Brazil, The Author, 1974. 168 p.

Benevides has much to say about the art of poetry but, save in the section devoted to his birthplace, Pacatuba, he writes conventional verse on commonplace themes.

7505. ———. Viola de andarilho. Fortaleza, Brazil, THEMA-Publicigráfica, 1974. 84 p.

Sonnets on the death of the poet's grandson exhibit genuine feeling; the flatness of the other compositions is exemplified by these lines from "Domingo no Brasil:" "Há defeitos e incultura./ Muita ciência vazia./ Isso vem da conjuntura./ Seremos grandes um dia."

7506. Beznos, Clóvis. Outros poemas. São Paulo, Massao Ohno, 1973. 1 v. (Unpaged) illus.

Like the paintings of de Chirico, Beznos' compositions have a harmonious, neoclassical quality, but seem empty of feeling.

7507. Branco, Joaquim. Consumito. Poemas & processos. Belo Horizonte, Brazil, Imprensa Oficial, 1975. 1 v. (Unpaged) illus.

Poemas in the Concretist manner are accompanied by "processes"—collages, diagrams, rebuses, graphs, etc.

7508. Caliman, Plínio. O rio da minha aldeia. pt. 1, Ciropédia. Rio, Livraria Editora Cátedra, 1976. 69 p.

A small town in Espírito Santo, as seen through the eyes of a child 40 years ago, described in picturesque rural language.

7509. Campos, Augusto de. Poetamenos. São Paulo, Edições Invenção, 1973. 1 v. (Unpaged)

To the other graphic tricks of Concretist poetry, Campos adds type of varying color, with the aim of enhancing "chromatic" effect.

7510. Campos, Geir [Nuffer de]. Canto de peixe & outros cantos. Rio, Civilização Brasileira, 1977. 94 p. (Col, Vera Cruz. Literatura brasileira, 239)

Concern for freedom and human rights is expressed to better literary effect in discreetly symbolic compositions than in such blatant declamations as the "Canto ao Homem da ONU."

7511. Campos, Haroldo de. Xadrez de estrelas. Percurso textual 1949-1974. São Paulo, Editora Perspectiva, 1976. 248 p., illus. (Col. Signos, 4)

Anthology illustrating Campos' evolution from conventional, neoclassical beginnings to the role of a leading exponent of Concretist poetry.

7512. Carlos, Helio Lima. Manequins no sobrado. Rio, Lídio Ferreira Júnior Artes Gráficas e Editora, 1975? 67 p.

A sexagenarian, reflecting on life, seeks to distinguish what is real from what is mere appearance, the ephemeral from the permanent.

7513. Caruso, Raimundo C. Poema para certa canção. Curitiba, Brazil, Editora Cooperativa de Escritores, 1976? 126 p.

Caruso declares that poetry's mission is to speak to men's hearts and needs; however, despite expressed sympathy for popular causes, it is doubtful that verse so hermetic as his can touch a public of any size.

7514. Castro, Nei Leandro de. Feira livre. Rio, Editora Put'zig, 1975? 71 p., plates.

Humorously philosophic verse inspired by produce for sale at an open-air market.

7515. Celso Japiassu [pseud. for Celso Almir Japiassu Lins Falcão]. A região dos mitos. Rio, Folhetim Livraria Editora, 1975. 69 p.

The poet's highly evocative verses resemble the shots by which a movie director builds atmosphere for a coming event, but frustrate the reader by omitting the happening.

7516. Correia, Raimundo [da Mota de Azevedo]. Poesias. Rio, Editora Nova Aguilar em convênio com o Ministério da Educação e Cultura, Instituto Nacional do Livro, 1976. 156 p. (Biblioteca manancial, 63)

Pessimistic, sensual, indulging in occasional mystic flights of singular beauty, Correia was the most accomplished verse artist of the Parnassian period.

Reproducing the Portuguese ed. of 1898, this selection represents his own choice of his best work. Introductory note by Alphonsus de Guimaraens Filho; essay on Correia by Manuel Bandeira; chronology of the poet's life and work; bibliographies of works by and about him.

7517. Dias, Ruy. São sete conchas douradas no colar de Yemanjá. Poesia. Prefácio de José Cândido de Carvalho. Rio, Livraria José Olympio Editora *em convênio com o* Ministério da Educação e Cultura, Instituto Nacional do Livro, 1975. 150 p., illus.

Poems in the popular manner, largely on Afro-Brazilian themes, that seem conceived to be sung to guitar accompaniment.

7518. Dobal [Teixeira], H[indemburgo]. A província deserta. Rio, Editora Artenova, 1974. 62 p.

The gallery of wry provincial portraits making up the central third of this volume ("A Serra das Confusões") constitutes a Brazilian *Spoon river anthology*.

7519. Fernandes, Anna Maria. Seiva e sumo. Rio, Editora Artenova *em convênio com o* Ministério da Educação e Cultura, Instituto Nacional do Livro, 1975. 46 p.

In obscure but refreshingly imaginative language (*e.g.* "aramista fiando luz") the poet seeks to capture her varying emotional states.

7520. Fernandes, Millôr. Papáverum Millôr. Rio, Editorial Nórdica, 1974. 181 p., illus.

In light verse, written between 1949 and 1973, Fernandes comments humorously on human foibles, some universal, many peculiar to his contemporary compatriots.

7521. Ferreira, Celina. Espelho convexo. Porto Alegre, Brazil, Editora Movimento *em convênio com o* Ministério da Educação e Cultura, Instituto Nacional do Livro, 1973. 34 p.

The mirror of Ferreira's verse reflects reality from unexpected and thought-provoking angles.

7522. Ferreira, Jurandir. O tocador de requinta. Poços de Caldas, Brazil, Editora Candeia, n.d. 50 l., illus.

Conventional lyrics, marked at times by depth of sensual feeling and skillful use of musical effects.

7523. Fonseca, José Paulo Moreira da. A noite o mar o sol. Rio, Livraria AGIR Editora, 1975. 55 p.

In a long nocturnal walk the poet's sense of loneliness and mortality gives way to consciousness of human solidarity and thought of rebirth with the coming of day.

7524. Fonseca, Yone Giannetti. Rosa dialética. São Paulo, Edições Quíron, 1975. 80 p. (Col. Sélesis, 5)

A curious mélange composed of rather commonplace verse inspired by grandmotherly affection for children, word games, compositions whose conciseness and evocative power bring to mind haiku, and a few lyrics remarkable for the intensity of the passion they convey.

7525. Freire, [Luís José] Junqueira. Desespero na solidão. Rio, Editora Nova Aguilar *em convênio com o* Ministério da Educação e Cultura, Instituto Nacional do Livro, 1976. 138 p., bibl. (Biblioteca manancial, 51)

The inner struggle of a monk without vocation, vacillating between mysticism and eroticism, is reflected in these selections by a "Romantic of the Second Generation." Introduction and chronology by Antônio Carlos Villaça; bibliography of works by and about the author.

7526. Freto, Diderto. Microcosmos. Sonetos com versos monossilábicos. Rio, Gráfica Portinho Cavalcanti, 1975. 44 p.

A mere curiosity, this volume contains 222 one- or two-syllable line sonnets, 34 without verbs and 21 featuring prominently the words "tique taque."

7527. Giglio, Maria José. 3 [i.e. Três] motivos + 1. São Paulo, Editora do Escritor, 1976. 1 v. (Unpaged) illus. (Col. Do poeta, 14)

Personal reactions to, rather than reworkings of, Chinese and classic Greek motifs. Poems accompanied by comments of the author on their origin and form.

7528. Guimarães, Júlio Castañon. Vertentes. Rio, Editora Fon-Fon e Seleta, 1975. 46 p.

Brief (in some cases one-line) poems exhibiting an effective "contraponto de concretude e sonho."

7529. Gullar, Ferreira [*pseud. for* **José Ribamar Ferreira**]. Poema sujo. Rio,

Civilização Brasileira, 1976. 103 p. (Col. Vera Cruz. Literatura brasileira, 231)

In a long stream-of-consciousness poem the author recreates in memory the São Luís de Maranhão of his young days. Particularly successful is the description of a train ride, which is directed to be sung to the music of Villa-Lobos' "Trenzinho do Caipira."

7530. Hein, Ronaldo [Alberto]. A noite das almôndegas. Prefácio de Álvaro Alves de Faria. São Paulo, Editora Alfa Omega, 1975. 92 p., illus.

If these compositions exhibit the irreverence and lack of sense of direction one might expect of a writer barely 20, they also show genuine poetic talent and a gift for capturing human types in humorous style ("Bonitinha," "O carioca de Cracóvia").

7531. Holanda [Cavalcanti de Albuquerque], Celina de. A mão extrema. São Paulo, Edições Quíron em convênio com a Prefeitura Municipal do Recife, 1976. 67 p.

Deeply conscious of the "tristeza/de sermos o que somos e não/como queriam que fôssemos os que amamos," this poet of exquisite sensibility and unusual power of suggestion accepts both life and death with quiet resignation.

7532. Homem [de Siqueira Cavalcanti], Homero. O assessor do dia. Poesia. Rio, Novacultura em convênio com o Ministério da Educação e Cultura, Instituto Nacional do Livro, 1976. 90 p.

Tributes to friends and public figures. Outstanding are the cycle on the death of Jackson de Figueiredo and the "Auto do Imperador Lucius Menênio Sextio a caminho do ostracismo" dedicated to President Castelo Branco.

7533. Ivo, Lêdo. Central poética. Poemas escolhidos. Rio, Editora Nova Aguilar em convênio com o Ministério da Educação e Cultura, Instituto Nacional do Livro, 1976. 249 p. (Biblioteca manancial, 48)

Anthology drawn from works published 1940-70 by an outstanding contemporary poet. Contains a critical essay by Mário Chamie, a biographical chronology, and bibliographies of works by and about Ivo.

7534. Jordão, Yolanda. Biografia do edifício. Brasília, Clube de Poesia de Brasília, 1975. 17 p., illus.

Newspaper-size, deluxe ed. of the title composition of item 7535.

7535. ———. Biografia do edifício e anexos. Rio, Imago Editora em convênio com o Ministério da Educação e Cultura, Instituto Nacional do Livro, 1976. 88 p. (Série poesia Imago)

The apartment building whose "biography" constitutes the principal piece in this collection may well be taken as symbolic of Jordão's poetry: an imposing formal structure, adorned with carefully sculptured imagery, echoing with human existence, but essentially untouched by human emotion.

7536. Krause, Gustavo. Pálpebra. Rio, Gráfica Editora Lidador, 1975. 1 v. (Unpaged) illus.

Aimless youthful revolt against the ugliness and unfairness of the world as it is, more eloquently expressed in Chico Calmon's photographs than in Krause's verse.

7537. Lima, Jorge de. Jorge 80 anos. Trabalho organizado por Rubens Jardim. n.p., n.p., 1973? 1 v. (Unpaged)

Selections from the poet's verse, accompanied by statements made by him regarding his life and work drawn from various sources, arranged as if constituting his replies to an interviewer.

7538. ———. Poesias completas. Rio, José Aguilar Editora em convênio com o Ministério da Educação e Cultura, Instituto Nacional do Livro, 1974. 4 v. (181, 204, 295, 203 p.) bibl. (Biblioteca manancial, 25/28)

Reprints poetry, a few essays, and some of the critical appreciations from the one-volume Aguilar edition of the Obra completa. Indicative of continuing interest in a major figure of Modernism.

7539. Lima, Regina Helena Cunha. Venham borboletas esta pequena mariposa me enjoa. Venham borboletas azuis verdes indecentes. Venham me sobrevoem suavemente. São Paulo, Massao Ohno, 1976. 1 v. (Unpaged) illus.

Poems of a nocturnal dream world, in which the poet awaits the dawn.

7540. Lisboa, Henriqueta. O menino poeta. Belo Horizonte, Brazil. Imprensa Oficial, 1975. 213 p., illus.

Less verse for children than an adult's poetic interpretation of children's voices. First published in 1943. Contains a didactic introduction on interpretation of poetry by Alaíde Lisboa de Oliveira and a critical essay on Henriqueta Lisboa's poetry for children by Gabriela Mistral.

7541. ———. Miradouro e outros poemas. Rio, Editora Nova Aguilar *em convênio o com o* Ministério da Educação e Cultura, Instituto Nacional do Livro, 1976. 164 p. (Biblioteca manancial, 49)

A flower, a bird in flight, the notes of a viola—such are the inspirations for Lisboa's newest lyrics, which have the delicate, but pale and evanescent quality of watercolors. Contains selections from previous collections, an introductory essay by Maria José de Queiroz, and a bibliography of works by and about the poet.

7542. **Litrento, Oliveiros** [Lessa]. 100 [i.e. Cem] sonetos de amor. Rio, Editora Rio, 1974. 60 p.

Obsessed with his beloved, the poet identifies her with every aspect of existence—to the point that she possesses no corporeal reality for the reader of these well-made, conventionally worded, unrhymed sonnets.

7543. **Lombardi, Bruna.** No ritmo dessa festa. São Paulo, Edições Símbolo, 1976? 159 p.

The sensual aspects of love form the principal material of these poems, in which, curiously, the author takes a masculine viewpoint as often as a feminine one.

7544. **Lopes, Waldemar.** Inventário do tempo. Rio, Lia Editor, 1974. 43 p.

Inclusion of 10 early compositions (1928-33) permits the reader to appreciate Lopes' remarkable evolution from rather conventional beginnings to the extraordinarily personal style exhibited in more recent tributes to friends (e.g. *Manuel Bandeira*) and places (e.g. *Brasília*).

7545. ———. Os pássaros da noite. Brasília, Clube de Poesia de Brasília, 1974. 49 p. (Série Buriti, 1)

"Dádiva de beleza para sempre/ em seu breve milagre de poesia:" Lopes' lines to a tree of the *planalto* well betoken the worth of this handful of sonnets, exceptional for their musical grace and the evocative power of their highly imaginative conceptions.

7546. ———. Sonetos do tempo perdido. Rio, Editorial Palmares, 1970. 142 p.

Lopes' remembrances of things past, uncertainly reflected in the light of the present, have a tantalizingly elusive character, well suggested by the verses "a poesia da tarde, fugitiva,/ mas eterna no instante em que foi bela."

7547. **Luiz Raimundo** [*pseud. for* **Luiz Raimundo Batista de Carvalho**]. Amanhecerá. Prefácio de Alceu Amoroso Lima. Rio, Livraria Editora Cátedra, 1976. 84 p.

Social questions were the main concern of this young man, dead at 25 in a madhouse ("Sou poeta do meu tempo:/ minha palavra deixará/ de ser desespero, espanto/ quando a noite se acabar"), but his best lyrics touch on such simple themes as bird songs and juvenile love.

7548. **Machado, Nauro.** Os parreirais de Deus. Poesia. São Luís, Brazil, Fundação Cultural do Maranhão, 1975. 124 p.

A prey to loneliness ("a condição da vida é sermos sós") and preoccupied with death (the poet sees himself stand "cego, sozinho em frente a Deus"), Machado finds a creative effort his sole justification for existence ("um verso é tudo que a vida me arranca").

7549. **Madureira, Pedro Paulo de Sena.** Devastação. Mordaças e revelações. Rio, Imago Editora, 1976. 129 p. (Série poesia Imago)

The density and intensity of Sena Madureira's opening section "Mordaças" is well suggested by the lines "toda literatura é opaca/ até que venhas e risques/ na página enfurecida/ mero poema,/ simples rasura." Rather more accessible is the second part, "Revelações," tributes to a number of other poets, Brazilian and foreign, each composition in a manner suggestive of the honoree's style and character.

7550. **Maranhão, Heloisa.** Castelo interior e moradas. Rio, Edições Porta de Livraria, 1974. 106 p. (Série poesia, 19)

Delirious monologues, partly in pseudo-antique Portuguese seasoned with snatches of Spanish and Latin, in which the speaker imagines herself Inês de Castro, Sor Mariana, Saint Isabel of Portugal and other personages—well justifying her observation "Sou um mosaico."

7551. **Marques, Núbia N.** Geometria do abandono. São Paulo, Editora do Escritor, 1975. 62 p. (Col. Do poeta, 10)

The best of these lyrics (e.g. "Rastro Rabisco," "Cinza-Concreto") might be classified as impressionistic, moods and images being created by the sound of words rather than their meaning, by their harmony rather than their syntactical relationship.

7552. **Martins, Max.** O risco subscrito. Belém, Brazil, Mayr Editor, 1976. 1 v. (Unpaged)

The relation of word to word is here more a matter of sound than of syntax; the effect, at best, is that of a vocalise.

7553. **Meireles, Cecília.** Poesia. [Organizada por] Darcy Damasceno.

Rio, Livraria AGIR Editora, 1974. 74 p., illus. (Col. Nossos clássicos, 107)

Good selection and perceptive introduction by Damasceno; biographical and bibliographical notes; brief quotes from leading critics on Meireles' work. Didactically useful.

7554. Mello, Thiago de. Poesia comprometida com a minha e a tua vida. Pequena história natural no fim que vem vindo do século vinte. Rio, Civilização Brasileira, 1975. 87 p. (Col. Vera Cruz. Literatura brasileira, 197)

Part elegy for the tragic end of the Allende adventure in Chile, part affirmation of faith in the common man, this collection is impressive both for its sincerity and for the truly poetic terms in which Mello deals with political subjects.

7555. Melo, Maria do Carmo Barreto Campello de. Verdevida: o tempo simultâneo. São Paulo, Edições Quíron em convênio com a Secretaria de Educação e Cultura de Pernambuco, 1976. 166 p., illus. (Col. Sélesis, 10)

To a sense of existence as walled solitude Melo opposes the feeling of need for communication with others—to be "menos solitários, mais solidários."

7556. Melo Neto, João Cabral de. Museu de tudo. Poesia: 1966-1974. Rio, Livraria José Olympio Editora, 1975. 96 p.

This collection is more of a photograph album than a museum. Its short pieces are essentially snapshot impressions of places from Mauritania to Recife, and of persons from Proust to Marques Rebelo, all evidencing the author's keen power of perception and his inimitably concise style.

7557. Mendes, Murilo [Monteiro]. Antologia poética. Seleção de João Cabral de Melo Neto. Introdução de José Guilherme Merquior. Brasília, Editora Fontana em convênio com o Ministério de Educação e Cultura, Instituto Nacional do Livro, 1976. 150 p., illus.

Excellent selection from the work of a poet who evolved from the prosaic-humoristic style of early Modernism, through a period of mystic lyricism, to a neoclassic manner. In Merquior's view "seus melhores poemas são como que fragmentos de um cântico dos cânticos ao mesmo tempo fortemente social, sexual e anímico."

7558. Milhomem, Wolney. A morte da tempestade. Líricas. São Paulo, Italo-Latino-Americana Palma, 1975. 86 p. (Col. Poesia do Brasil de hoje)

"Meus olhos/pousam/ no vexame do futuro,/ cujo timão/ desapareceu" writes Milhomem in a characteristic expression of the torment of doubt that infuses his lyrics.

7559. Monteiro, Clodomir. Derroteiro de rotinas. São Paulo, Edições Quíron [and] Práxis, 1976. 125 p. (Col. Sélesis, 11)

Word games, intended to suggest a variety of possible meanings rather than any specific message from the poet to the reader.

7560. Morais, Régis de. Queda de areia: 1971-1974. São Paulo, Cortez & Moraes, 1976. 82 p.

Though perplexed by the contradictions of daily existence, the poet, through faith, hopes for the ultimate synthesis of eternal life.

7561. Mota [e Albuquerque], Mauro [Ramos da]. Itinerário. Poesia de Mauro Mota. Prefácio de Fausto Cunha. Rio, José Olympio em convênio com o Ministério da Educação e Cultura, Instituto Nacional do Livro, 1975. 100 p.

Selected compositions (including early contributions to provincial newspapers) by a modern master who, fusing classical, Parnassian, Symbolist, and Modernist elements into a style peculiarly his own, fashions upon the most commonplace of themes poetry remarkable for insight, depth of feeling, and eloquence of expression. Contains biographic and bibliographic notes, and a critical study by Fausto Cunha.

7562. Motta, Maurício. Viagem. Poemas. Prefácio de Gilberto Freyre. Recife, Brazil, Univ. Federal de Pernambuco, 1975. 46 p.

Brief, graceful lyrics, expressive more of the mood of a moment than of ideas or sentiments.

7563. Nunes, Cassiano. Madrugada. Poemas a Edson Nery da Fonseca. Recife, Brazil, Pool Editorial, 1975. 1 v. (Unpaged)

Unpretentious, discreetly sensuous compositions with an underlying message of "carpe diem."

7564. Oliveira, Denise Cabral de. Luz própria. Rio, Livraria São José, 1975. 58 p., illus.

Life must be experienced by all the senses if it is to linger in the memory, according to Oliveira's sensuous compositions.

7565. Oliveira, Marly de. Contato. Rio, Imago Editora, 1975. 127 p. (Série poesia Imago)

For Oliveira, existence is identified with personal experience ("o que vivi me vive"), which is timeless ("impossível excluir do eterno instante/ o que há de vir e aquilo que houve sido:/ que é tudo o refluir da mesma água"). Reprints the earlier "A Vida Natural" and "O Sangue na Veia" (see *HLAS 36:7110*).

7566. Osório, Laci. A canção vem do rio. Porto Alegre, Brazil, Editora Movimento, 1976. 83 p.

Treating folk material of Rio Grande do Sul with sophistication and social and political issues without demagoguery, Osório writes verse lively with movement and rich in power of suggestion.

7567. ———. Música e semente. Porto Alegre, Brazil, Editora Movimento, 1974. 75 p. (Col. Poesiasul, 9)

Rhapsodic poems expressing sympathy for leftist causes mingle with simpler lyrics inspired by love for children.

7568. Pallottini, Renata. Coração americano. São Paulo, META Editora de Letras e Artes, 1976. 1 v. (Unpaged)

Quietly eloquent protest against the stifling of liberty under authoritarian regimes in South America.

7569. Paulo Augusto [*pseud. for* **Paulo Augusto da Silva**]. Falo. Rio, The Author, 1977. 61 p.

An eloquent celebration of homosexual love, with wry comment on its unacceptability to society.

7570. Pena Filho, Carlos. Livro geral. Olinda, Brazil, Gráfica Vitória, 1973. 1 v. (Unpaged) illus.

The best of this somewhat conventional verse captures picturesque aspects of the Northeast, particularly Recife.

7571. Peres, Fernando da Rocha. Poemas bissextos: 1955-1972. Salvador, Brazil, Edições Macunaíma, 1972. 43 p.

The high quality of this "leap-year poetry" is well exemplified by a composition such as "TEMPO / Objeto I," devoted to the "Moringa, ausente/ companheira/ de tardes avarandadas."

7572. Perticarati, Jane Arduino. Tritão e Nereida. São Paulo, Editora do Escritor, 1973. 28 p. (Col. Do poeta, 6)

A Dutch-door page arrangement permits reading these short but pretentious compositions in varying order—to no perceptible advantage.

7573. Pinheiro, Paulo Benedicto. Organização das horas. São Paulo, Conselho Estadual de Cultura, Secretaria de Cultura, Esportes e Turismo, 1974. 61 p. (Col. Poesia, 10)

Pinheiro describes the poetic method thus: "Só importa reter a consciência/ viva das coisas passageiras/ . . . da vida freqüentada a vida inteira./ E assim a prisão repetitiva/ extraindo da posse os objetos/ fará do que se der a grande novidade . . ." Awarded the "Prêmio Governador do Estado" for 1973.

7574. Pinto, Antísthenes. Angústia numeral. Poesia. Manaus, Brazil, Edição Prefeitura Municipal de Manaus, 1976. 83 p., illus.

Some of Pinto's tropes are highly effective ("os olhos da negra e velha gata feitos de telhas e silêncio"), others are wildly eccentric and meaningless in their combination one with another ("As flores se povoam azuis e ouro no ânus desse jardim em galope").

7575. Placer, Xavier. Notícias da viagem. Rio, Livraria São José, 1976. 37 p.

Brief meditations on chance thoughts that have occurred to the writer, expressed as prose poems.

7576. Prade, Péricles. Nos limites do fogo. São Paulo, Editora do Escritor, 1976. 67 p., illus. (Col. Do poeta, 13)

A "cantor dos infernos" cultivates flowers of evil in the "jardim enfermo do sonho."

7577. Quintana, Mário. Apontamentos de história sobrenatural. Porto Alegre, Brazil, Editora Globo *em convênio com o* Instituto Estadual do Livro, Depto. de Assuntos Culturais e Secretaria de Educação e Cultura, 1976. 167 p. (Col. Sagitário)

Poetry in the popular vein by a man with a gift for capturing the spirit of a moment, past or present, whose attempts at philosophizing, however, never reach beyond banalities.

7578. Reis, Marcos Konder. Sol dos tristes. Caporal douradinho. São Paulo, Livraria Martins Editora *em convênio com o* Ministério da Educação e Cultura, Instituto Nacional do Livro, 1976. 262 p.

Poetic prose and verse, much based on fragmentary recollections of the author's early years.

7579. Rodrigues, Geraldo Pinto. Os verdes matinais. São Paulo, Clube de Poesia de São Paulo, 1975. 81 p.

Whether reminiscing on his childhood, meditating on the thoughts that come with dawn, or recording amatory experiences, Rodrigues writes with a dignity, restraint, formality, and elevation of language that brings to mind such classic French poets as Corneille and Racine.

7580. Rodrigues, José Mário. Os motivos. Rio, Livraria Editora Cátedra, 1975. 42 p.

The conflict between high aspiration and cruel necessity ("Ah imensa vontade do ser e desesperada exigência do ter") constitutes the leitmotif of these noble lyrics.

7581. Sá, Carlos A. de. Canto tentado. Rio, Bloch Editores, 1972. 104 p.

If Sá's themes (love, recollections of childhood, human solitude) are traditional, his handling of them is personal and the feeling expressed is sincere. Lacking however are qualities of rhythm and music. All in all, a promising debut.

7582. Sales, Artur de. Obra poética. Salvador, Brazil, Secretaria de Educação de Cultura, 1973. 464 p.

Collected poetic works (including a translation of *Macbeth*) of a provincial writer of the early part of the century in whom one finds carried to an extreme the Parnassian love of formalism and erudite vocabulary.

7583. Sales, Luís. Pássaro sôfrego. São Luís, Brazil, Fundação Cultural do Maranhão, 1975. 57 p.

Sales' intention and degree of achievement are well indicated by his description of himself as a "pássaro sôfrego/ flutuando no vazio incomunicável/ à procura da verdade transcendental."

7584. Sampaio, Walter M. A rosa e o enigma. Poemas. São Paulo, Editora H, 1976. 44 p., illus.

Well-meaning but undistinguished poems written between 1942-52, expressive of the social and humanitarian concerns of that period.

7585. Sant'Anna, Affonso Romano de. Poesia sobre poesia. Rio, Imago Editora, 1975. 246 p. (Série poesia Imago)

Sant'Anna calls the poet of today a "confuso devedor" to his predecessors—in his own case, to Eliot, Pound, and Dante, to name but three. The use he makes of his heritage is indeed confusing in effect, to the point that he often finds it necessary to provide extensive notes explaining allusions, foreign expressions, etc., many of which are employed with considerable inaccuracy.

7586. Santa Rosa, F. Affonso. O artesão. Experiência poética. n.p., The Author, n.d. 34 p., illus.

Pleasing short lyrics on traditional themes—recollections of childhood, thoughts on death, etc.

7587. Schmidt, Augusto Frederico. Eu te direi as grandes palavras. Poemas escolhidos e versos inéditos. Rio, José Aguilar Editora *em convênio com o* Ministério da Educação e Cultura, Instituto Nacional do Livro, 1975. 150 p., bibl. (Biblioteca manancial, 22)

Though a contemporary of the Modernists, Schmidt was an unabashed Romantic, distinguished by his use of Biblical imagery and his mysterious, prophetic tone. His verse, highly uneven in quality, is best read in a selection such as this by Alphonsus de Guimaraens Filho, who includes a surprisingly large number of previously unpublished compositions and provides a perceptive introduction and bibliographies of works by and about Schmidt.

7588. Silva, [Antônio Francisco] da Costa e. Poesias completas. 2. ed. rev. e anotado por Alberto da Costa e Silva. Rio, Livraria Editora Cátedra *em convênio com o* Ministério da Educação e Cultura, Instituto Nacional do Livro, 1976. 449 p., bibl.

Collected verse of a regrettably neglected Symbolist, active in the first three decades of this century. Extensive biographical and critical introduction by his son; variants; bibliography of works by and about the poet.

7589. Silva, Domingos Carvalho da. Vida prática. Rio, Imago Editora *em convênio com o* Ministério da Educação e Cultura, Instituto Nacional do Livro, 1976. 69 p. (Série poesia Imago)

Silva views poetry as part inspiration ("Este poema há tanto tempo morto/ no meu chão, renasce como um grito . . . e no papel projeta o seu caminho") and part effort ("salário e suor do meu rostro"). The present collection smacks more of the latter than the former, coming from the head rather than the heart, but reflects, often with charm, the wisdom age has brought to the writer.

7590. Silva, Rolando Roque da. Ato de presença. São Paulo, Milton Godoy Campos Editor, 1971. 61 p.

Silva speaks out for freedom but his verse is pedestrian.

7591. ———. Poesia preferencial. Antologia. São Paulo, HUCITEC, 1976. 112 p. (Col. Artur Neves, 1)

Selected verse—conventional, but pleasing—by a poet of limited feeling and personality.

7592. Sousa, Afonso Felix de. Pretérito imperfeito. 25 anos de poesia. Rio, Civilização Brasileira *em convênio com o* Ministério da Educação e Cultura, Instituto Nacional do Livro, 1976. 302 p. (Col. Vera Cruz. Literatura brasileira, 214)

Nostalgia for childhood, the frustrations of love, and folk motives encountered in travels at home and abroad provide subject matter for a poet notable for clarity, versatility, and felicity in expression, who lacks withal a distinguishing mark of originality (his collected works span 1945-69).

7593. Tavares, Odorico. Livro de Luciano. Salvador, Brazil, Edições Macunaima, 1975. 1 v. (Unpaged) illus.

Tavares' rather prosaic compositions, largely on the art of being a grandfather, scarcely seem to justify this *édition de luxe*.

7594. Teles, Gilberto Mendonça. Arte de armar. Rio, Imago Editora, 1977. 87 p.

Conscious of his skill with words ("sei da fala/ e do ato de lavrá-la na falavra"), Teles is equally aware of the difficulty of making them give adequate expression to deeply felt emotion ("Quanto mais se torna claro/ o espaço das nossas mágoas,/ tanto mais aumenta o escuro/ do texto, na despedida").

7595. Torres, Ivo. Encadernação do pasmo. Rio, The Author, 1974. 1 v. (Unpaged)

Concern for the H bomb and social preoccupations are the chief themes of these Concretist word games.

7596. Trevisan, Armindo. O abajur de Píndaro: a fabricação do real. São Paulo, Edições Quíron *em convênio com o* Ministério da Educação e Cultura, Instituto Nacional do Livro, 1975. 98 p., illus. (Col. Sélesis, 4)

The poet seeks, through intuition, to escape to an extrasensorial world, "um país no qual a língua mantém as coisas em ordem," but is always led back to the ultimate reality of sensual love ("Profunda é a pele!/ A alma, menos profunda"), which he celebrates in a style reminiscent of the Song of Songs.

7597. Unger, Edyla Mangabeira. Solidão visitada. Salvador, Brazil, Oficinas Gráficas da Editora Beneditina, 1975. 29 p.

Unger unquestionably possesses lyric talent, but this volume is too brief to present any picture of a poetic personality.

7598. Val, Chagas. Chão e pedra. Poesia. São Luis? Brazil, SIOGE, 1973. 45 p.

Variations on the cycle of nature: all creatures and processes attain their end only to begin again.

7599. Villaça, Alcides. O tempo e outros remorsos. São Paulo, Editora Ática, 1975. 95 p., illus.

Villaça's attempt to capture the ephemeral in human existence and relationships is well conveyed by a quatrain from "Lembrança:" "Beijo a nascer primeiro/ que seu dono, envelhecido/ nos lábios de algum fantasma/ única forma de vida."

7600. Werk, Alcides. Da noite do rio. Poesia. Manaus, Brazil, Casa Editora Madrugada, 1974. 92 p., illus.

Werk's intentions are good, but, whether writing verse with a social message or describing his native Amazon region, his efforts fall flat.

7601. Wrigg, Ivan. Cemitério geral. Rio, Livraria Editora Cátedra, 1974. 109 p.

Beneath the surface of Wrigg's wry comments on the world of today there lurks an ache at its indifference to individual feeling.

7602. Zuccolotto, Afrânio. Retrato do artista remanescente. São Paulo, Clube de Poesia de São Paulo, 1976. 1 v. (Unpaged)

Delightfully humorous verse portrait of a member of the older generation who maintains the standards of his youth in opposition to those of the present.

DRAMA

BENJAMIN M. WOODBRIDGE, JR.

Professor of Portuguese
University of California, Berkeley

ONCE AGAIN THERE ARE NO PARTICULARLY exciting developments to report. Censorship is frequently blamed for the doldrums; it may be at least in part responsible for the production of musical spectaculars more effective on stage than in print, but it can hardly explain the generally lack-luster quality of most playwriting. Indeed one is not surprised at the banning of certain plays that flaunt poor taste in language and situation (see item 7635). On the other hand Gianfrancesco Guarnieri continues to express social protest successfully, this time in an atemporal play (item 7624). Farce, well handled, points another way out (item 7628), as does the use of folklore motifs (item 7617). Experimentation does go on, but at best it is groping and results in no really moving theater.

The Serviço Nacional de Teatro, with the support of Shell Oil Company, has published more out-of-print titles in the *Dramaturgia brasileira* series; as before, they are most welcome, but again one can only lament that the texts are not free of errors. The Serviço has also helped keep drama alive by publishing new plays.

It is plays for children that constitute the most attractive theater listed in the present report. In varying degrees and according to various formulas the authors make fancy probable and in the process delight adults as well as youngsters (see items 7609 and 7625).

Of miscellaneous works with a collateral interest for literature, Almeida Prado's monograph on João Caetano (item 7656) deserves special mention as a fine piece of research, a sample of the best in Brazilian scholarship. Athos Damasceno and his collaborators also merit an accolade for their highly readable account of the Teatro São Pedro (item 7652).

To be noted with regret is the death in 1976, at the age of 58, of Hermilo Borba Filho (item 7612), director, dramatist, and critic of note. In the same year died Paulo Pontes, Chico Buarque de Hollanda's collaborator in *Gota d'água* (item 7626).

ORIGINAL PLAYS

7603. Aguiar, Cláudio. Flor destruída. Drama. São Paulo, Editora do Escritor *em convênio com a* Prefeitura Municipal, Secretaria da Educação e Cultura, Recife, Brazil, 1976. 83 p. (Col. De teatro, 3)

External happenings rather than character determine course of events in this drama of poverty. Claimed symbolism of undying flower of hope hardly comes through.

7604. Almeida, Abílio Pereira de. Santa Marta Fabril sociedade anônima. Comédia em 3 atos. Rio, Ministério da Educação e Cultura, Serviço Nacional de Teatro, 1973. 63 p. (Col. Dramaturgia brasileira)

Varying generational attitudes are manifested in a family that owns a large manufacturing plant; author's social sympathies are clear in this play of 1955. For original ed. see *HLAS 22:5524*.

7605. Anchieta, José de. Auto representado na festa de São Lourenço. Livre adaptação de Walmir Ayala. Rio, Ministério da Educação e Cultura, Serviço Nacional de Teatro, 1973. 41 p. (Col. Dramaturgia brasileira)

Original (ca. 1583) was written in Portuguese, Spanish, and Tupi; present version, all in Portuguese, is an abridgment. Lively drama of devils, Roman emperors, and Christian saints ends in long sermon on Christian living.

7606. Andrade, Jorge. O telescópio. Peça em 1 ato. Rio, Ministério da Educação e Cultura, Serviço Nacional de Teatro, 1973. 51 p. (Col. Dramaturgia brasileira)

In this early play author's preoccupation with dissolution of patriarchal society and with lack of communication between generations already appears.

7607. Aranha, José Pereira da Graça. Malazarte. Peça em 1 ato. Rio, Ministério da Educação e Cultura, Serviço Nacional de Teatro, 1973. 47 p. (Col. Dramaturgia brasileira)

Play of 1911 represents author's attempt to dramatize his ideas on the essential life force; result is more discussion than drama.

7608. Arinos, Afonso. O contratador dos diamantes. Peça em 3 atos. Rio, Ministério da Educação e Cultura, Serviço Nacional de Teatro, 1973. 56 p. (Col. Dramaturgia brasileira)

Pageantry and patriotism characterize this 1917 historical drama of oppression and resistance in mid-18th-century Minas Gerais.

7609. Bender, Ivo. Teatro escolhido, incluindo peças infantis. Ensaios introdutórios de Regina Levin Zilberman, Maria da Glória Bordini, and Ana Mariza Ribeiro Filipouski. Porto Alegre, Brazil Editora Bels [and] Secretaria da Educação e Cultura (SEC), Dept. de Assuntos Culturais (DAC), Instituto Estadual do Livro, 1975..143 p.

Touted as theater of the fantastic, the first two plays seem more like theater of nonsense. More successful and truly fanciful are the plays for children.

7610. Bezerra Filho, José. Canudos. n.p., n.p., n.d. 51 p.

Interpretation of drama of Canudos in which Antônio Conselheiro dies disillusioned amidst followers who believe fervently in his messianic mission.

7611. Boal, Augusto. Tres obras de teatro. B.A., Ediciones Noé, 1973. 217 p.

Acting versions in Spanish of three plays presumably written in Portuguese by an important Brazilian now in exile. *Torquemada* (1972) was written in jail; it is a sensitive and humane document of suffering. *El gran acuerdo internacional del Tío Patilludo* (1971) and *Revolución en América del Sur* (1973) are radical propaganda; the latter makes interesting use of elements of popular theater. [F. Dauster]

7612. Borba Filho, Hermilo. Sobrados e mocambos: uma peça segundo o sugestões da obra de Gilberto Freyre nem sempre seguidas pelo autor. Prefácio de Gilberto Freyre. Rio, Civilização Brasileira, 1972. 167 p.

More of a pageant than a play, this piece illustrates various aspects of Brazilian society through the centuries; tropical lushness pervades the successive manifestations of social organization. Freyre's preface outlines differences between his points of view and Borba's.

7613. Botelho de Oliveira, Manuel. Hay amigo para amigo. Comedia famosa y nueva. Rio, Ministério da Educação e Cultura, Serviço Nacional de Teatro, 1973. 57 p. (Col. Dramaturgia brasileira)

There is much of what a prosaic comic character calls "gongorática poesía" in this play written in Spanish and published in 1705. The title is presumably a counterpart of Rojas Zorrilla's *No hay amigo para amigo* (published 1640); the plot is different, but almost as convoluted. Each play illustrates in its own fashion the motto of the title.

7614. Camargo, Joracy. Deus lhe pague. Figueira do inferno. Um corpo de luz. Apresentacão de R. Magalhães Júnior. Introdução de Afrânio Coutinho. Rio, Edições de Ouro, n.d. 250 p., illus. (Col. Prestígio)

Contrived situations, simplistic characters, and wooden dialogue damage these message-laden plays—1932, 1954, and 1945 (as *Bonita demais*) respectively.

7615. Campos, Geir. Castro Alves ou O canto da esperança. Teatro. Rio, Leitura [and] Instituto Nacional do Livro, 1972. 124 p.

Rise and fall of poet's love affair with actress Eugênia Câmara serves as framework for recitation of a fair amount of his verse, with stress on poet's faith in the future.

7616. Cardoso, Lúcio. O escravo. Peça em 3 atos. Rio, Ministério da Educação e Cultura, Serviço Nacional de Teatro, 1973. 56 p. (Col. Dramaturgia brasileira)

Written in 1937 and first published in 1945, this play is imbued with the dark psychological atmosphere of author's novels. Enslaved by forces beyond his control, the slave escapes from them by suicide, using a razor symbolic of those forces. For first ed., see *HLAS 11:3443*.

7617. Cardozo, Joaquim. De um noite de festa; bumba meu boi. Rio, Livraria Agir Editora, 1971. 150 p. (Teatro moderno, 23)

Folklore elements combine, in this diffuse play, with themes suggested by medieval theater to satirize certain aspects of contemporary society and in the end deliver a message of hope based on faith. For other plays by the author, see *HLAS 28:2650* and *HLAS 38:7533*.

7618. Emery, Milton de Moraes. O começo é sempre fácil o difícil é depois. Rio, Serviço Nacional do Teatro, 1968. 71 p.

Skillfully-handled two-act dialogue between man and wife, given to constant bickering, comes to a too abrupt end when women's liberation takes over and the woman leaves.

7619. Figueiredo, Guilherme. Um deus dormiu lá em casa. Peça em 3 atos. Rio, Ministério da Educação e Cultura, Serviço Nacional de Teatro, 1973. 42 p. (Col. Dramaturgia brasileira)

Sardonic, tongue-in-cheek version of the Amphytrion legend. For earlier ed., see *HLAS 30:4206*.

7620. França Júnior, Joaquim José da. Caiu o ministério. Comédia em três atos. Rio, Ministério da Educação e Cultura, Serviço Nacional de Teatro, 1972. 46 p. (Col. Dramaturgia brasileira)

Light-hearted satire (1884) on rise and fall of a ministry and fawning intrigue that besets those in power. For earlier reprint, see *HLAS 28:2656*.

7621. Garcia, Maria de. Teatro na escola. 5 peças infantis. Prefácio de Vieira de Melo. Rio, Coisas da Mente, 1975. 70 p., illus.

Light-hearted drawings by Maria Eduarda accompany these short plays, in which reality and imagination somewhat self-consciously coexist.

7622. Gomes, Roberto. A casa fechada. Peça em 1 ato. Rio, Ministério da Educação e Cultura, Serviço Nacional de Teatro, 1973. 17 p. (Col. Dramaturgia brasileira)

Tension rises inexorably in this undated play (author d. 1922) about diverse attitudes in a small town toward a woman banished for infidelity to a brutish husband.

7623. Grisolli, Paulo Affonso. A trilogia do avatar. Rio, Editora Rio, 1975. 127 p.

Each of the plays constitutes a variation on the theme of human behavior under the stress of fear.

7624. Guarnieri, Gianfrancesco. Ponto de partida. Fábula em um ato, com música de Sérgio Ricardo. São Paulo, Editora Brasiliense, 1976. 78 p.

The Establishment murders a non-conforming idealist but cannot kill the spirit of joy in life and of challenge to authority that he represented.

7625. Have, Hilton. Loja de brinquedos. Prefácio de Miroel Silveira. Apresentação de Nívea Gordo. São Paulo, Edições Símbolo, 1976? 103 p.

Two delightful plays in which children's imagination creates a new reality.

7626. Hollanda, Chico Buarque de and **Paulo Pontes.** Gota d'água. Rio, Editora Civilização Brasileira, 1975. 168 p. (Col. Teatro hoje, 28)

Grafts elements of legend of Jason and Medea onto a musical on the exploitation of the poor by the rich. Language is popular, at times vulgarly realistic, and the end luridly melodramatic.

7627. Jacintha, Maria [pseud. for **Maria Jacintha Trovão da Costa Campos**]. Intermezzo da imortal esperança. Peça em três atos. Rio, Ministério da Educação e Cultura, Serviço Nacional de Teatro, 1973. 74 p.

As is usual with Maria Jacintha (see *HLAS 32:4873*), there is more talk than action in this play about idealistic survivors of a presumably nuclear holocaust who organize a new world of peace in a secluded valley.

7628. Lima, Edy. A farsa da esposa perfeita. Porto Alegre, Brazil, Editora Garatuja [and] Secretaría de Educação e Cultura, Depto. de Assuntos Culturais, Instituto Estadual do Livro, 1976. 64 p.

Merry farce in which wife achieves perfection by betraying her happily unsuspecting husband in order to improve his material situation.

7629. Lins, Osman. Santa, automóvel e soldado. Teatro. São Paulo, Brazil, Livraria Duas Cidades, 1975. 100 p.

Three plays experimental in technique: one actor takes several parts, each identified by a different mask. Two of the pieces revolve around integrity, artistic in one case, moral in the other; the third is a fantasy of a rebellion of cyclists and pedestrians against the all-pervading automobile, seen from a policeman's point of view.

7630. Macedo, Joaquim Manoel de. O novo Otelo. Comedia em 1 ato. Rio, Ministério da Educação e Cultura, Serviço Nacional de Teatro, 1972. 17 p. (Col. Dramaturgia brasileira)

In this comedy of 1860, an amateur actor, taking his part of Othello too literally, creates a ludicrous situation with his real-life fiancée (for an earlier reprint see *HLAS 28:2656*).

7631. Machado de Assis, Joaquim Maria. Quase ministro. Comédia em um ato. Rio, Ministério da Educação e Cultura, Serviço Nacional de Teatro, 1972. 20 p.

In this urbane drawing-room satire of 1863, fawning parasites descend on a deputy rumored to be in line for a ministerial position and then swiftly abandon him when they learn that he was not appointed.

7632. Magalhães, Gonçalves de. O poeta e a inquisição. Drama em 5 atos. Rio, Ministério da Educação e Cultura, Serviço Nacional de Teatro, 1972. 62 p.

Originally titled *Antônio José ou o poeta e a Inquisição*, this play of 1838 chronicles the lurid fate of the 18th-century playwright against a background of Romantic love, hate, and repentance. The text is not free of error, it is also unfortunate that the revealing preface is not included.

7633. Maranhão, José. Os trigais de São Paulo. São Paulo, Empresa Gráfica da Revista dos Tribunais, 1972. 62 p.

In the form of stilted dialogue, a confused hymn to love and peace and progress.

7634. Maranhão Filho, Luiz. Espanta gato: os da esquerda são devotos de Santo Antônio. Comédia em 3 atos. Rio, Ministério da Educação e Cultura, Serviço Nacional de Teatro, n.d. 78 p.

Rivalry between two music bands creates potentially explosive situations in small town, but author sees to it that they explode only into the hilarious and unexpected.

7635. Marcos, Plínio. Barrela. Peça em 1 ato. Teatro brasileiro. São Paulo, Edições Símbolo, 1976. 60 p., illus.

Lurid scene of a night in a prison ward.

7636. Marinuzzi, Raul. O hydromel dos avatares. Belo Horizonte, Brazil, Informac Editora Gráfica, 1975. 64 p., illus.

Lyrical conversation on Mt. Olympus: each of four religious figures, mythical and historical, attempts to define God; a humble beggar outdoes them all.

7637. Nunes, Carlos Alberto. Estácio. Drama. Precedido de um ensaio sobre a natureza do drama. São Paulo, Edições Melhoramentos, 1971. 84 p.

Greek tragedy serves as a mold, and prosaic decasyllabic blank verse as a vehicle, for a drama on 16th-century hero Estácio de Sá.

7638. Nunes, Cassiano. As luvas de Ema. Drama em um ato e quatro quadros. Rio, Livraria São José, 1973. 57 p.

Diffuse play whose meaning is hardly clear. The gloves seem to symbolize love of luxury at the expense of morality.

7639. Paraná (state), *Brazil*. Governo do Estado do Paraná. Secretaria de Estado da Educação e da Cultura. Fundação Teatro Guaíra. Cinco textos para teatro infantil. Coletânea das peças premiadas no Concurso Nacional de Textos para Teatro Infantil. Curitiba, Brazil, 1975. 206 p., music.

These plays by Sílvia Ortoff, Benjamin Santos, Jorge Argemiro da Silva, Ilo Krugli, and Maria Luíza Lacerda, different among themselves, are distinguished by the absence of shallow didacticism and a wealth of free wheeling imagination. The delightful cover was done by a 10-year-old girl.

7640. Pedroso, Bráulio. Teatro de ... v. 1/2. Rio, Pallas, 1975. 2 v. (215, 199 p.)

Seven plays (1966-75) which portray, at times in the vein of a light-weight musical, seriously disturbed or at least marginal characters. For earliest piece see *HLAS 32:4876*.

7641. Queiroz, Rachel de. A beata Maria do Egito. Peça em 3 atos e 4 quadros. Rio, Ministério da Educação e Cultura, Serviço Nacional de Teatro, 1973. 41 p. (Col. Dramaturgia brasileira)

Stress on taut psychological situations rather than on the resulting actions mark this play of 1958. Uses as its epigraph Manuel Bandeira's "Balada de Santa Maria Egipcíaca" and chronicles an episode in the life of a devoted nun leading supporters of Padre Cícero. For first ed., see *HLAS 21:4330*.

7642. *Revista de Teatro.* Sociedade Brasileira de Autores Teatrais (SBAT). No. 389, set./out. 1972 [through] Nos. 413/414, set./dez. 1976- . Rio.

Excellent journal which includes: texts of plays, news and comments of professional interest, interviews, etc. Among the more notable plays are: Ronaldo Radde's *Transe* (No. 389); the hilarious *O crime da cabra* by Renata Pallotini (No. 394); César Vieria's *O Evangelho segundo Zebedeu* (No. 404) and *Rei Momo* (No. 411); Raimundo Alberto's *Os mansos da terra* (No. 406); Antônio Bivar's moving *Cordélia Brasil* (No. 413); and Pedro Bloch's *Karla, valeu a pena?* (No. 414).

7643. Rio, João do [*pseud.* for **Paulo Barreto**]. A bela Madame Vargas. Peça em 3 atos. Rio, Ministério da Educação e Cultura, Serviço Nacional de Teatro, 1973. 68 p. (Col. Dramaturgia brasileira)

Clever dialogue à-la-Oscar-Wilde and a melodramatic plot in which villain threatens happiness of distraught heroine until very end, when he is unmasked—such are the characteristics of this long-drawn-out 1912 play.

7644. Sampaio, José da Silveira. Flagrantes do Rio. Espetáculo composto de 3 peças em 1 ato. Rio, Ministério da Educação e Cultura, Serviço Nacional de Teatro, 1973. 41 p. (Col. Dramaturgia brasileira)

Witty, sophisticated dialogue and situations characterize these sketches of urban life (*Treco nos cabos, A vigarista*, and *Triângulao escaleno*. On the last see *HLAS* 20:4422).

7645. Silva, Francisco Pereira da. O vaso suspirado. Peça em 1 ato. Rio, Ministério da Educação e Cultura, Serviço Nacional de Teatro, 1973. 12 p. (Col. Dramaturgia brasileira)

In this amusing comedy (1963) a wise old bishop, using the chamber pot his two fanatical maidservants covet as a memento of him, teaches them a lesson about saints and miracles.

7646. Silva, Hélcio Pereira da. Um galho ilustre dos Cubas. Peça em três atos. Uma interpretação do romance *Memórias póstumas de Brás Cubas*, de Machado de Assis. Rio, Ministério da Educação e Cultura, Serviço Nacional de Teatro, 1973. 66 p.

The interpretation is awkward at best, hardly dramatic at worst. For another attempt by the author to dramatize Machado de Assis, see *HLAS* 38:7572.

7647. Vicente, José. Hoje é dia de rock; roteiro para um espetáculo em estílo de romance. Rio, Lia, 1972. 59 p. (Col. Teatro Ipanema, 1)

Disintegration of a family that moves from the country to a town.

DRAMA CRITICISM, HISTORY, AND MISCELLANEOUS

Braga, Genesino. Restauração do Teatro Amazonas. See item 490.

7648. Brazil. Ministério da Educação e Cultura. Sociedade de Cultura Artística de Sergipe. Serviço Nacional de Teatro. Plano nacional de difusão do teatro: projeto, especificações e detalhamento de Unidade Cultural. Rio, 1974. 55 p., tables.

Detailed plans, including specifications and budgets, for the construction of small cultural centers (the theaters would seat 168 to 320 spectators) in Brazilian cities for multiple uses.

7649. Brito, Moema Renart de. Cartilhas de teatro. v. 3. Manual de administração teatral. Rio, Ministério da Educação e Cultura, Serviço Nacional de Teatro, 1972. 145 p., bibl.

A step-by-step guide to the formidable obligations, frustrations, and administrative red tape that beset those engaged in producing theatrical spectacles in Brazil.

7650. *Cadernos de Teatro*. O Tablado. Nos. 68/69, jan./junho 1976- Rio.

Articles reprinted from various sources on aspects of the theater, data on actors and directors of note, translations (Strindberg, Ghelderode, *Maître Pathelin*, e.g.), lists of prize-winning plays and of plays in production in Rio and São Paulo.

7651. Costa, Beatriz. Sem papas na língua. Prefácio de Jorge Amado. Rio, Civilização Brasileira, 1975. 301 p. (Col. Tempo e contratempo, 3)

Anecdotal recollections of a Portuguese actress, much of whose success was obtained in Brazil. Of some interest for the history of the Brazilian state. [R.E. Dimmick]

7652. Damasceno, Athos; Guilhermino Cesar; Paulo Antônio Moritz; and Herbert Caro. O Teatro São Pedro na vida cultural do Rio Grande do Sul. Porto Alegre, Brazil, Secretaria da Cultura e Educação, Dept. de Assuntos Culturais, 1975. 408 p., plates.

Lively and detailed interpretive history of the activities (drama, opera, light opera, dance, music) of

Literature: Brazilian, Drama, Criticism / 499

the Porto Alegre theater, founded in 1858, to its closing for repairs in 1973.

7653. Figueiredo, Guilherme. Cartilhas de teatro, VI. Como escrever peças de teatro. Oito diálogos e conselhos sobre a criação dramática. Rio, Ministério da Educação e Cultura, Serviço Nacional de Teatro, 1973. 102 p.

Well-read, sophisticated, and wise practicing playwright distills his experience, buttressed with numerous specific examples. For first ed. (1957), see *HLAS 24:5711*.

7654. Gonçalves, Alice Ramos and others comps. Bibliografia sobre teatro paulista. Edição preliminar. Apresentação de Zilda Machado Taveira. São Paulo, Univ. de São Paulo, Escola de Comunicações e Artes, Depto. de Biblioteconomia e Documentação, 1972. 103 l. (Série biblioteconomia e documentação, 2)

Annotated bibliography of critical articles in books, journals, newspapers, and collections. The items are arranged alphabetically by authors' names; a cross-index by play title facilitates reference to given items.

7655. Gonçalves, Augusto de Freitas Lopes. Dicionário histórico e literário do teatro no Brasil. v. 1, Letra A. Prefácio de Guilherme Figueiredo. Rio, Livraria Editora Cátedra, 1975. 338 p.

Alphabetical listing of plays, operas, authors, composers, translators, actors, singers, dancers, maestros—both Brazilian and foreign—that have had some connection with Brazilian theatrical production from the beginnings to 1968. Biobibliographical data, as well as dates and details of staging, are given when known. Based on 20 years of research. No bibliography.

7656. Prado, Décio de Almeida. João Caetano: o ator, o empresário, o repertório. São Paulo, Editora da Univ. de São Paulo [and] Editora Perspectiva, 1972. 245 p., illus., plates (Col. Estudos, 11)

Scholarly and judicious assessment of the career of Brazil's greatest 19th-century actor (1808-63).

7657. Teatro paulista 1968. São Paulo, Editora Gráfica Niamar, n.d. 1 v. (Unpaged) plates.

Article by prize-winning director Heleny Guariba on the theory of theatrical communication is followed by photographs from productions; lists of plays presented and actors involved, prizes awarded, lecture series, schools of dramatic art; excerpts from criticism; a roster of authors, directors, actors, theaters, amateur groups.

7658. Tito, A. Praça Aquidabã, sem número. Revisão de Salvador Pittaro. Rio, Editora Artenova, 1975. 158 p., table.

Year-by-year log of the ups-and-downs of the Teatro 4 de Setembro (1894-   ) in Terezina, capital of Piauí state.

7659. Valladares, Clarival do Prado. Renovation and restoration of the Teatro Amazonas. Preface by João Walter de Andrade. English version by Richard J. Spock and Janni Contopoulos. Manaus, Brazil?, Governo do Estado de Amazonas, 1974. 63 p.

A meandering report on the original artists and the 1974 renovation appears in an awkward English version shorn of the notes of the Portuguese original.

7660. Wanderley, Jaime dos G. Sandoval Wanderley: um homem de teatro. Natal, Brazil, Secretaria Municipal de Educação e Cultura do Estado do Rio Grande do Norte, 1973. 12 p. (Col. Literatura, 2)

Tribute to idealistic and courageous Rio Grande do Norte journalist, public servant, author, and theater director (1893-1972). The Natal Municipal Theater now bears his name.

LITERARY CRITICISM AND HISTORY

WILSON MARTINS

Professor of Portuguese
New York University

THE AVANT-GARDE OF BRAZILIAN literary criticism is nowadays essentially *formalist* in the technical sense of the word, meaning that it derives from and adheres to so-called Russian Formalism, generally read and known through French translations, comments, and practice. At present, formalism is equated with the avant-garde in both the literary and political spheres, without any apparent awareness that both concepts are reactionary by definition. Writing from a leftist perspective many years ago, L. Trotsky remarked that Russian Formalism was the only theory which opposed Marxism in Soviet Russia. He went on to denounce its "reactionary character" while admitting that "confined within legitimate limits" Formalism might "help clarify the artistic and psychological peculiarities of form" or rather that "the methods of formal analysis are necessary but insufficient" (see David Craig's *Marxists on literature*, 1975, p. 363 ff.). The fact remains that although Formalism was banned in the name of revolutionary purity and replaced by Zhdanovism, its current resurgence clearly presages a turn toward the intellectual right. And one need not be Trotskyite to perceive this.

The problem lies in determining what are the "legitimate limits" of any doctrine one wishes to apply to literature, theoretical systems, and ideas that are not merely diverse but which spring from entirely different historical and cultural circumstances. Brazilian critics have been subjected to an endless barrage of conflicting theories that range from New Criticism through Structuralism and Russian Formalism to Semiotics without having the time necessary to assimilate and organize them into a coherent intellectual system. A similar phenomenon occurred in Italy where, according to Maria Corti and Cesare Segre, critics skipped the intermediate stages of development, a lack that generated a type of literary criticism that can be best described as a trailblazing exercise in futility. Such doctrines, some more than 40 years old, others as recent as this morning's newspapers, were adopted at the same time by many critics not equipped to discriminate among their different potentials for literary interpretation. The result was considerable confusion and obfuscation (see *I Metodi attuali della critica in Italia*, 1970).

Still, one should welcome the positive effects of such a variety of opposing systems which, to paraphrase Corti and Segre, have awakened consciousness of the exceptional possibilities of criticism for integrating methods and tools into a total and exhaustive investigation of problems in a work of art.

That this goal, at present, is more of a hope than a reality is exemplified by the fact that none of the formalist works listed below (in all of their variety, scope and purpose) can be included among the five more important books of the period. Instead, these are in my view: the reprint of José Veríssimo's *Estudos de literatura brasileira* (item 7700); Frederick G. Williams' *Sousândrade: vida e obra* (item 7764); Josué Montello's *Aluísio Azevedo e a polêmica d'O Mulato* (item 7725); Flávio Loureiro Chaves' *Érico Veríssimo: realismo e sociedade* (item 7708); and the reprinting of Gilberto Freyre's *Manifesto regionalista* (item 7681). These works are singled out for specific reasons mentioned in their annotations.

Moreover, those interested in the intellectual life of Brazil cannot ignore these additional studies: Plínio Doyle's *História de revistas e jornais literários* (item 7678); Celuta Moreira Gomes' *O conto brasileiro e sua crítica* (item 7715); Andrade Muricy's *Panorama do movimento simbolista brasileiro* (item 7749); Oliveira Lima's

Estudos literários (item 7697); J. Galante de Sousa's *Em torno do poeta Bento Teixeira* (item 7757); and Wilson Martins' *História da inteligência brasileira* (item 7692).

GENERAL

7661. Amaral, Amadeu. Obras. Letras floridas. O elogio da mediocridade: estudos e notas de literatura. Ensaios e conferências. São Paulo, Secretaria da Cultura, Ciência e Tecnologia do Estado de São Paulo, 1976. 3 v. (162, 205, 197 p.)

These *Obras* consist of separate volumes that are not numbered. The one entitled *O elogio da mediocridade* is a small classic by a minor critic. The other two contain material for Amaral's intellectual biography.

7662. Avila, Affonso ed. **O modernismo.** São Paulo, Editora Perspectiva, 1975. 227 p., bibl., facsims., illus., table (Col. Stylus, 1)

Collected papers of the VI Festival de Inverno (Ouro Preto, Minas Gerais, 1972), commemorating the 50th anniversary of the Week of Modern Art.

7663. Azevedo, Manuel Antônio Alvares de. Cartas de Alvares de Azevedo. Comentários de Vicente de Azevedo. São Paulo, Academia Paulista de Letras, 1976. 253 p., illus. (Biblioteca academia paulista de letras, 1)

Of strictly biographical interest.

7664. Azevedo, Rafael Sânzio de. Literatura cearense. Fortaleza, Brazil, Academia Cearense de Letras, 1976. 597 p., bibl. (Col. Antônio Sales, 3)

Literary history through the texts; very useful for data concerning writers born in Ceará and who lived there; the ones born elsewhere but who worked in Ceará, and finally "cearenses" that have lived in different States.

7665. Benevides, Artur Eduardo. Evolução da poesia e do romance cearenses. Fortaleza, Brazil, Univ. Federal do Ceará, 1976. 96 p., bibl., tables.

Proposes as "cearenses" all the works which reflect the region's spirit or life. Very useful, although somewhat overenthusiastic and bibliographically defective.

7666. Brasil, Assis. A nova literatura. v. 3, O conto; v. 5, O modernismo. Rio, Companhia Editora Americana [and] Pallas *em convenio com o* Ministério da Educação e Cultura (MEC), Instituto Nacional do Livro (INL), 1975/1976. 2 v. (158, 148 p.) bibl. (História crítica da literatura brasileira)

Like other volumes in the series (see *HLAS 38:7592*) v. 5 is shallow, hasty and capricious. V. 3 provides a brief panorama of the Brazilian short story.

7667. Brazil. Biblioteca Nacional. Movimentos de vanguarda na Europa e modernismo brasileiro, 1909-1924: catálogo da exposição organizada pela seção de exposições e inaugurada em março de 1976. Apresentação de Wilson Lousada. Rio, Divisão de Publicações e Divulgação, 1976. 83 p., plates.

Very useful.

7668. ———. Conselho Federal de Cultura. História da cultura brasileira. v. 1/2. Rio, Conselho Federal de Cultura (CFC) [and] Fundação Nacional de Material Escolar (FENAME), 1973-1976. 2 v. (213, 392 p.) bibl., plates.

Written by group of intellectuals whose contributions neither relate to each other nor follow a coherent pattern of development. Vol. 1 deals with "O Meio e o Homem" and "As Instituições e Modos de Vida;" vol. 2 covers "O Desenvolvimento da Cultura and "A Transmissão da Cultura" during the 18th century. Presumably other volumes will follow.

7669. Carvalhal, Tania Franco. O crítico à sombra da estante: levantamento e análise da obra de Augusto Meyer. Apresentação de Moysés Vellinho. Porto Alegre, Brazil, Editora Globo *em co-edição com a* Secretaria de Educação e Cultura do Rio Grande do Sul, Depto. de Assuntos Culturais, Instituto Estadual do Livro, 1976. 154 p., bibl. (Col. Literatura, teoria & crítica)

First thorough study of minor critic by author who also tends to overestimate his work.

7670. Castello, José Aderaldo ed. and comp. O movimento academicista no Brasil, 1641-1820/22. v. 3, t. 1/2, Festejos públicos comemorativos. São Paulo, Conselho Estadual de Cultura, 1974-1975. 2 v. (228, 284 p.) (Col. Textos e documentos, 25/26)

When papers of the 17th-century literary academies were still buried in the archives, everyone longed for their publication. Now that they are available, one wonders if the effort was worthwhile. In any case, no self-respecting library could do without them for possible consultations. They certainly will never be reprinted again.

7671. Castro, Sílvio. A revolução da palavra: origens e estrutura da literatura brasileira moderna. Petrópolis, Brazil, Editora Vozes, 1976. 279 p., bibl.

From Symbolism to Concrete poetry, the author presents this book as a history of Brazilian Modernismo.

7672. Chalmers, Vera M. 3 [i.e. Três] linhas e 4 verdades: o jornalismo de Oswald de Andrade. Revisão de Tereza R. Guilares. São Paulo, Livraria Duas Cidades *em coedição com a* Secretaria da Cultura, Ciência e Tecnologia do Estado do São Paulo, 1976. 224 p., bibl., tables.

First analysis and evaluation of Oswald de Andrade's newspaper columns.

7673. Colares, Otacílio. Lembrados e esquecidos: ensaios sobre literatura cearense. v. 1/3. Fortaleza, Brazil, Univ. Federal do Ceará, 1975-1977. 3 v. (204, 212, 212 p.) plates.

Essays about books and authors related to Ceará, including a few forgotten ones. Useful, if not innovative.

7674. Congresso Brasileiro de Língua e Literatura, *VI, Rio, 1974.* Sexto congresso brasileiro de língua e literatura. Rio, Edições Gernasa [and] Novacultura Editora, 1975. 168 p., bibl., tables.

Interesting because of Antônio Sérgio Mendonça's paper on the avant-garde, which adds to the current historical evaluation of concretismo (for more on this subject, see items 7706 and 7762).

7675. Coutinho, Afrânio. Conceito de literatura brasileira. Rio, Pallas *em co-edição com o* Ministério da Educação e Cultura (MEC), Instituto Nacional do Livro (INL), 1976. 201 p.

Reprint of original title (1. ed. 1960) together with a number of author's essays (e.g., "Euclides, Capistrano e Araripe," published 1959).

7676. ———. Notas de teoria literária. Rio, Civilização Brasileira, 1976. 99 p., bibl., table.

Brief introduction to literary theory for the benefit of college students.

7677. ———. Visão da ficção brasileira contemporânea (Via [Univ. of California, Office of Student Activities, Berkeley] 1, May 1976, p. 48-54)

Uneven survey, of contemporary Brazilian literature.

7678. Doyle, Plínio. História de revistas e jornais literários. v. 1. Apresentação de Homero Senna. Rio, Ministério da Educação e Cultura, Fundação Casa de Rui Barbosa, 1976. 206 p., facsims. (Col. De estudos bibliográficos, 1)

Valuable bibliographic description of literary periodicals, most of them extremely rare; e.g., *Niterói, Revista da Sociedade Fênix Literária, Gazeta Literária, Revista Sul-Americana, A Nova Revista, Klaxon, Estética, A Revista, Festa, Verde, Revista de Antropofagia, Revista Nova,* and *Literatura* (see also item 7753).

7679. Duarte, Pablo. Amadeu Amaral. São Paulo, Secretaria de Cultura e Tecnologia do Estado de São Paulo, Humanismo Ciência e Tecnologia (HUCITEC), 1976. 183 p.

Compilation in bookform of author's scattered writings about Amadeu Amaral.

7680. Escrita. Revista mensal de literatura. Vertente Editora. Anos 1/2, Nos. 7/15, 1976- . São Paulo.

Good periodical.

7681. Freyre, Gilberto. Manifesto regionalista. 6. ed. Introdução de Manuel Diégues Júnior. Recife, Brazil, Instituto Joaquim Nabuco de Pesquisas Sociais, 1976. 80 p., plate.

Reprint of famous text on 50th anniversary of publication. However, as a result of evidence unearthed by recent research (see *HLAS 38:7619*), author admits that: a) the Regionalist movement of 1926 in Recife did not have any national repercussions: b) the Manifesto was only "oral;" and c) it was first published in 1952.

7682. Girão, Raimundo. A Academia de 1894. Fortaleza, Brazil, Academia Cearense de Letras, 1975. 263 p., plates.

Factual history of Academia Cearense de Letras which includes valuable data.

7683. Inojosa, Joaquim. Os Andrades e outros aspectos do modernismo. Rio, Editora Civilização Brasileira *em co-edição com o* Ministério da Educação e Cultura (MEC), Instituto Nacional do Livro (INL), 1975. 284 p. (Col. Vera Cruz. Literatura brasileira, 211)

Compilation of literary columns culled from periodicals. The Andrades are Mário, Oswald and Carlos Drummond in addition to other writers.

7684. ———. A arte moderna, 1924-1974. O Brasil brasileiro, 1925-1975. Rio, Editora Meio-Dia, 1977. 177 p., plates.

Commemorative reprint of classical text of Modernismo (1. ed. 1924). Marks introduction of new literary school into the Northeast.

7685. ———. Notícia de bibliográfica de . . . Rio, Editora Meio-Dia, 1975. 92 p., plates.

Valuable information about the writer who first brought Modernismo to the Northeast.

7686. Lara, Cecília de. *Klaxon* et *Lumière* (UTIEH/C, 25, 1975, p. 77-102)

Examines the relationship of two modernist literary reviews. For a more thorough study of the topic by this author, see item 7687.

7687. ———. *Klaxon & Terra Roxa e outras terras:* dois periódicos modernistas de São Paulo. São Paulo, Univ. de São Paulo (USP), Instituto de Estudos Brasileiros, 1972. 307 p., bibls. (Publicações, 19)

The Instituto de Estudos Brasileiros is encouraging its students to conduct systematic research into rare and out-of-print periodicals. This is a descriptive and careful study of two of them.

7688. Lins, Osman. Do ideal e da glória: problemas inculturais brasileiros. São Paulo, Summus, 1977. 189 p.

Polemical articles on various aspects of Brazilian intellectual life, from textbooks to the national representation at the book fair of Frankfurt.

7689. Litrento, Oliveiros. Apresentação da literatura brasileira. t. 1, História literária; t. 2, Antologia. Rio, Biblioteca do Exército Editora [and] Forense Univ., Rio, 1974. 2 v. (323, 458 p.) bibl. (Biblioteca do Exército, 439. Col. General Benício, 116/117)

Textbook, more didactic than critical, which was precisely the author's purpose.

7690. Lucas, Fábio. Poesia e prosa no Brasil. Belo Horizonte, Brazil, Interlivros de Minas Gerais, 1976. 133 p., bibl., table (Ensaio)

Four papers on Clarice Lispector, Tomás António Gonzaga, Machado de Assis and Murilo Mendes, originally intended for a foreign audience. Routine.

7691. Martins, Eduardo. Carlos D. Fernandes: notícia biobibliográfica. João Pessoa, Brazil, A União, 1976. 231 p., plates.

Useful bibliography of an author relatively forgotten but deserving more attention.

7692. Martins, Wilson. História da inteligência brasileira. v. 1. 1550-1794; v. 2, 1794-1855;v. 3, 1855-1877; v. 4, 1877-1896; v. 5, 1897-1914; v. 6, 1915-1933. São Paulo, Editora Cultrix [and] Editora da Univ. de São Paulo, 1976-1978. 6 v. (585, 546, 554, 570 p.) (p. for 5/6 unavailable) plates.

Intellectual history of Brazil, from 16th century to present. Vol. 7 is scheduled for publication in 1978. For historian's comment, see item 3996.

7693. Merquior, José Guilherme. De Anchieta a Euclides. v. 1, Breve história da literatura brasileira. Rio, Livraria José Olympio Editora, 1977. 248 p., bibl., plate (Col. Documentos brasileiros, 182)

Only includes "main authors." Merquior follows pattern established by Ronald de Carvalho of introducing chapter with large section on world literature of the period. Marred by number of errors.

7694. Moraes, Carlos Dante de. Alguns estudos e um fragmento de autobiografia. Prefácio de Guilhermino César. Porto Alegre, Brazil, Editora Metrópole *em convênio com a* Secretaria de Educação e Cultura (SEC), Depto. de Assuntos Culturais, Instituto Estadual do Livro, 1975. 198 p.

Pt. 1 concerns Brazilian writers (Machado de Assis, Euclides da Cunha, Drummond, etc.); pt. 2, foreign ones (Rimbaud, Baudelaire); pt. 3 consists of autobiographic segment. Entire book written in the subjective, impressionistic style characteristic of this author.

7695. Moraes, Jomar. Apontamentos de literatura maranhense: uma abordagem contextual que leva em conta os fatores políticos, sociais e econômicos. 2. ed. aumentada. São Luis, Brazil, Edições SIOGE, 1977. 273 p., bibl.

Particularly valuable because of the copious information on books and writers from Maranhão.

7696. Nogueira, Hamilton. Jackson de Figueiredo. 2. ed. Rio, Livraria Hachette [and] Edições Loyola, São Paulo, 1976. 145 p., bibl. (Col. Brasil sempre. Série documentos, 3)

Indispensable for the history of reactionary thought in Brazil.

7697. Oliveira Lima, Manuel de. Estudos literários. Reunidos e selecionados por Barbosa Lima Sobrinho. Rio, Imprensa Nacional, 1975. 296 p.

Important and useful collection of articles previously scattered in several periodicals and other sources of difficult access.

7698. Portella, Eduardo and others. Teoria literária. 2. ed. Rio, Tempo Brasileiro, 1976. 190 p., bibl.

Textbook.

7699. Prado, Yan de Almeida. A grande semana de arte moderna: depoimento e subsídios para a cultura brasileira. São Paulo, São Paulo Livraria Editora, 1976. 141 p.

Polemical view.

7700. Veríssimo de Mattos, José. Estudos de literatura brasileira. v. 1, Introdução de João Alexandre Barbosa; v. 2, Introdução de Vivaldi Moreira; v. 3, Introdução de Oscar Mendes. Belo Horizonte, Brazil, Editora Itatiaia [and] Univ. de São Paulo, 1976. 3 v. (179, 161, 166 p.) (Biblioteca de estudos brasileiros, 11/13)

Long overdue reprint of a fundamental collection of critical essays (see *HLAS 38:7585*).

7701. Weber, João Hernesto. Do modernismo à nova narrativa. Porto Alegre, Brazil, Editora Metrópole *em co-edição com a* Secretaria de Educação e Cultura (SEC), Depto. de Assuntos Culturais, Instituto Estadual do Livro, 1976. 96 p., bibl.

Two essays on the sociology of literature, applying to Mário Palmério and Modernismo the now fashionable concept of "dependence."

7702. Xavier, Livio. O elmo de Mambrino de . . . Rio, Livraria José Olympio Editora *em contrato com a* Secretaria de Estado da Cultura, Ciência e Tecnologia da São Paulo (SECCT), 1975. 155 p., illus.

Selective compilation of reviews published in several periodicals over a span of more than 40 years by an ingenious, if minor, literary critic. Of interest because he served as witness and recorder of the ebb and flow of literary reputations, some of which have endured.

FICTION

7703. Bagby, Alberto I., Jr. *Iaiá Garcia*: more optimism in Machado de Assis (RIB, 25:3, julio/sept. 1975, p. 271-284, bibl.)

Reevaluates *Iaiá Garcia* among Machado's novels; proposes seeing him rather as a realist than a pessimist.

7704. Bruyas, Jean-Paul. Técnicas, estruturas e visão em *Grande sertão: veredas* (USP/RIEB, 18, 1976, p. 75-92)

Another intelligent reading of *Grande sertão: veredas*, in spite of author's assumption that only by miracle could a great novel come into existence today.

7705. Camargo, Suzana. *Macunaíma*: ruptura e tradição. São Paulo, Massao Ohno [and] João Farkas, 1977. 147 p., bibl.

Based on second-hand knowledge of so-called Menippean satire (through the works of Russian critic Mikhail Bakhtin), author believes that *Macunaíma* exactly fits that model and that it is a parody of Rabelais.

7706. Campos, Augusto de; Décio Pignatari; and **Haroldo de Campos.** Teoria da poesia concreta: textos críticos e manifestos, 1950-1960. 2. ed. São Paulo, Livraria Duas Cidades, 1975. 207 p., tables.

Now that Concretismo is a thing of the past, this reprint of a 1965 collection of manifestoes and pamphlets is useful.

7707. Campos, Maria Consuelo Cunha. Sobre o conto brasileiro. Rio, Editora Gradus, 1977. 76 p., bibl., table.

Panoramic view of modern short story in Brazil.

7708. Chaves, Flávio Loureiro. Erico Veríssimo: realismo e sociedade. Porto Alegre, Brazil, Editora Globo [and] Secretaria de Educação e Cultura do Rio Grande do Sul, Depto. de Assuntos Culturais, Instituto Estadual do Livro, 1976. 185 p., bibl. (Col. Literatura. Teoria & crítica)

Excellent first full-length study of the novelist and his work.

7709. Coelho, Nelly Novaes and Ivana Versiani. Guimarães Rosa: dois estudos. São Paulo, Edições Quíron [and] Ministério da Educação e Cultura (MEC), Instituto Nacional do Livro (INL), Brasília, 1975. 142 p., bibl., illus. (Col. Escritores de hoje, 4)

Two independent studies: Guimarães Rosa as a fiction writer (Nelly Novaes Coelho), and his stylistic usage of the subjunctive (Ivana Versiani).

7710. Colares, Octacílio. A rainha do ignoto. Romance cearense, pioneiro do fantástico no Brasil? Fortaleza, Brazil, Editora Henriqueta Galeno, 1977. 36 p.

Somewhat overenthusiastic notice of minor writer's 19th-century forgotten novel. Reprint from revista *Aspectos* (Secretaria de Cultura, Desporte e Promoção Social, No. 11).

7711. Davis, William Myron. Japanese elements in *Grande sertão: veredas* (UCP/RP, 29:4, May 1976, p. 409-434)

Although the idea of Nipponisms in Guimarães Rosa is not improbable in itself, the examples marshalled here are scarcely convincing.

7712. Dourado, Waldomiro Autran. Uma poética de romance: matéria de carpintaria. 2. ed. rev. e aumentada. São Paulo, Difel/Difusão Editorial, 1976. 187 p., tables.

Convinced that literary critics did not do justice to his novel, *O risco do bordado*, author explains its subtleties and intricacies. Indispensable, not only for the study of this particular novel but for understanding author's work as whole.

7713. Faro, Arnaldo. Eça e o Brasil. Préfacio de Miécio Táti. São Paulo, Companhia Editora Nacional [and] Editora da Univ. de São Paulo, 1977. 281 p. (Brasiliana, 358)

Valuable study for those interested in comparative literature.

7714. Galvão, Walnice Nogueira. Saco de gatos. Ensaios críticos. Revisão de Tereza R. Guilares. São Paulo, Livraria Duas Cidades *em co-edição com a* Secretaria da Cultura, Ciência e Tecnologia do Estado de São Paulo (SCCT), 1976. 146 p.

Essays on various literary subjects of greater and lesser interest and importance. Noteworthy because of severe "revision" (or re-vision) of Jorge Amado and his work.

7715. Gomes, Celuta Moreira. O conto brasileiro e sua crítica: bibliografia, 1841-1974. v. 1, A-L. v. 2, M-Z. Rio, Biblioteca Nacional, 1977. 2 v. (656 p.) (Continuous pagination)

Indispensable and invaluable study of the Brazilian short story.

7716. Gomes, Eugênio. Machado de Assis: influências inglesas. Rio, Pallas *em convênio com o* Ministério da Educação e Cultura (MEC), Instituto Nacional do Livro (INL), 1976. 123 p.

This is a reprint of author's first eight chapters in *Espelho contra espelho* (1949) without reference to this fact. For some inexplicable editorial reason Victor Hugo is included among English influences.

7717. Hill, Amariles Guimarães. A crise da diferença: leitura das *Memórias póstumas de Brás Cubas*. Rio, Livraria Editora Cátedra *em convênio com o* Ministério da Educação e Cultura (MEC), Instituto Nacional do Livro (INL), 1976. 141 p., bibl.

Rereading of the novel, presented not surprisingly as a document of Machado de Assis' intellectual maturity.

7718. Lepecki, Maria Lúcia. *Autran Dourado*: uma leitura mítica. São Paulo, Edições Quíron [and]

Ministério da Educação e Cultura (MEC), Instituto Nacional do Livro (INL), 1976. 256 p., bibl., fold. table, illus. (Col. Escritores de hoje, 5)

Although all of the puzzle's pieces are here, author fails to organize them into a coherent pattern.

7719. Lima, Luiz Costa. A perversão do trapezista: O romance em Cornélio Penna. Rio, Imago, 1976. 199 p., bibl., (Série logoteca)

Rereading of Cornélio Pena "from a specific theoretical standpoint," which the author refuses to identify as "structuralist or neo-structuralist."

7720. Lins, Osman. Lima Barreto e o espaço romanesco. São Paulo, Edições Ática, 1976. 154 p., bibl.

Proposes a rather impressionistic rereading of Lima Barreto based on author's Ph. D. dissertation.

7721. Machado, Alvaro Manuel. Osman Lins e a nova cosmogonia latinoamericana (COLOQ, 33, sept. 1976, p. 30-39)

Enthusiastic and occasionally questionable, but still good introduction to a modern experimentalist in fiction.

7722. Machado, Ana Maria. Recado do nome: leitura de Guimarães Rosa à luz du nome de seus personagens. Rio, Imago Editora, 1976. 200 p., bibl. (Série logoteca)

Exhaustive analysis of all proper names in Guimarães Rosa's work.

7723. Malard, Leticia. Ensaio de literatura brasileira: ideologia e realidade em Graciliano Ramos. Belo Horizonte, Brazil, Editora Itatiaia, 1976? 164 p., bibls., tables (Col. Universidade viva, 1)

Incisive usage of modern techniques in the literary analysis of Graciliano Ramos' work.

7724. Martins, Heitor *ed.* The Brazilian novel. Bloomington, Indiana Univ., 1976. 76 p.

Essays by Jon M. Tolman, Ivana Versiani, Jack E. Tomlins, Jon S. Vincent and Wilson Martins on the historical development of the Brazilian novel and some of its representative authors (e.g., Machado de Assis, Graciliano Ramos, Guimarães Rosa).

7725. Montello, Josué. Aluísio Azevedo e a polêmica d' *O mulato*. Rio, Livraria José Olympio Editora *em convênio com o* Ministério da Educação e Cultura (MEC), Instituto Nacional do Livro (INL), 1975. 335 p., bibl., facsims., illus. (Col. Documentos brasileiros, 167)

Interesting research showing that the novel *O mulato* has been conceived as a weapon in the anticlerical struggle. Indispensable study because of the new perspective it offers.

7726. Olival, Moema de Castro e Silva. O processo sintagmático na obra literária. Apresentação de Rolando Morel Pinto. Prefácio de Alfredo Bosi. Goiânia, Brazil, Oriente, 1976. 221 p., bibl., tables.

Laborious stylistic analysis of Bernardo Élis' short stories.

7727. Pozenato, José Clemente. O regional e o universal na literatura gaúcha. Prefácio de Guilhermino César. Porto Alegre, Brazil, Editora Movimento, 1974. 62 p., bibl. (Col. Augusto Meyer, 4)

Studies on Simões Lopes Neto, Érico Veríssimo and the early regionalists of Rio Grande do Sul.

7728. Prado, Antônio Arnoni. Lima Barreto: o crítico e a crise. Rio, Cátedra [and] Instituto Nacional do Livro, Brasília, 1976. 123 p., bibl.

Rereading of an author allegedly forgotten or underrated by critics. Current studies on the subject do not support this view.

7729. Salles, David. O ficcionista Xavier Marques: um estudo da "transição" ornamental. Rio, Civilização Brasileira *em convênio com o* Instituto Nacional do Livro, Brasília, 1977. 223 p., bibl.

Good analysis of forgotten novelist now eliciting critical attention.

7730. Schwarz, Roberto. Ao vencedor as batatas: forma literária e processo social nos inícios do romance brasileiro. São Paulo, Livraria Duas Cidades, 1977. 169 p.

First part of study of Machado de Assis. Its central theme (as suggested by the title) is not quite clear.

7731. Sovereign, Marie F. Proust and modern Brazilian writers (AATSP/H, 59:3, Sept. 1976, p. 460-464)

First account for a foreign audience of Proust's and *Nouvelle Revue Française*'s early penetration in Brazil.

7732. Sperber, Suzi Frankl. Caos e cosmos: leituras de Guimarães Rosa Revisão de Tereza R. Guilares. São Paulo, Livraria Duas Cidades em co-edição com a Secretaria da Cultura, Ciência e Tecnologia do Estado de São Paulo (SCCT), 1976. 210 p., bibl.

Study of the spiritual sources in Guimarães Rosa (Esoterism, the Old and New Testaments, Plato, Plotinus, Oriental mystics, Christian Science, etc.).

POETRY

7733. Bernardini, Aurora F. M. de Andrade, A. Soffici, V. Maiakovski: estudo comparativo (USP/RIEB, 18, 1976, p. 65-74, bibl.)

Good study about some of Mário de Andrade's theoretical sources.

7734. Brayner, Sônia comp. Carlos Drummond de Andrade. Rio, Civilização Brasileira em convênio com o Ministério da Educação e Cultura (MEC), Instituto Nacional do Livro (INL), Brasília, 1977. 282 p.

Useful and practical guide for the study of the poet's "fortuna crítica."

7735. Brito, Mário da Silva. Breve informação sobre "O Santeiro do Mangue" (VIA, 1, May 1976, p. 68-73)

Notice about Oswald de Andrade's unfinished poem, a piece for a museum of literary oddities.

7736. Busatto, Luiz. Montagem como processo de composição em Jorge de Lima (UC/V, 31:3, set. 1975, p. 69-82, bibl.)

Increasingly, "Invenção de Orfeu" is regarded as an example of montage. Here, author points to obvious Virgilian sources.

7737. Campos, Haroldo de. Morfologia do *Macunaíma*. São Paulo, Editora Perspectiva, 1973. 303 p., facsims., illus., maps (Col. Estudos, 19)

According to author, *Macunaíma* follows structural patterns established by Vladimir Propp in *Morphology of the folktale*.

7738. Carvalho, Ronald de. O espelho de Ariel e poemas escolhidos. Nota editorial de Antonio Carlos Villaça. Rio, Editora Nova Aguilar em convênio com o Instituto Nacional do Livro (INL), Ministério da Educação e Cultura (MEC), 1976. 205 p. (Biblioteca manancial, 44)

Reprints odd assemblage of poetry and critical essays by an undeservedly semi-forgotten author.

7739. Cirne, Moacy. Vanguarda: um projeto semiológico. Petrópolis, Brazil, Editora Vozes, 1975. 141 p., illus. (Vozes do mundo moderno, 14)

Perceives literary avant-garde as an esthetic rather than historical entity which ranges from Concrete and Processo poetry to the more recent experiments in creativity.

7740. Dantas, Antonio Arruda. Gustavo Teixeira: o poeta da solidão e da renúncia, 1955. São Paulo, Editora Pannartz, 1977. 128 p., bibl., illus.

Worthless as literary criticism but contains factual data about minor and forgotten Parnassian poet.

7741. Emorine, Jacques and **Neroaldo Pontes de Azevedo.** Uma interpretação do tempo em *Paulicéia Desvairada* (UTIEH/C, 27, 1970, p. 97-107, bibl., tables)

Linguistic analysis based on the frequency lists organized by the Center of Lexicology, Toulouse Univ., France (see item 7754).

7742. Frota, Francisco Marialva Mont'Alverne. Sousandrade: o último périplo. São Luis, Brazil, Sioge, 1977. 36 p.

Add this item to the routine bibliography about the poet.

7743. Helena, Lúcia. A cosmo-agonia de Augusto dos Anjos. Rio, Tempo Brasileiro, 1977. 132 p., bibl.

Like Lima Barreto, Guimarães Rosa and Cornélio Pena, the poet Augusto dos Anjos is now a fashionable subject of rereadings, most of them, as this one, more ambitious than critically rewarding.

7744. Houaiss, Antônio. Drummond mais seis poetas e um problema. Revisão de José Carlos Campanha. Rio, Imago Editora, 1976. 259 p. (Série logoteca)

Reprints texts published elsewhere, since 1947; e.g., Drummond, Silva Alvarenga, Gonçalves Dias, Augusto dos Anjos, Joaquim Cardoso and João Cabral. The "problem" of the title is Concrete poetry (article of 1957).

7745. Ivo, Lêdo. Teoria e celebração. Ensaios. Revisão de Herbene Mattióli, Cristina Chaer and Valéria C. Salles. São Paulo, Livraria Duas Cidades *em co-edição com a* Secretaria da Cultura, Ciência e Tecnologia do Estado de São Paulo (SCCT), 1976. 147 p.

Memoirs of life and literature by one of the leading poets of the Generation of 1945.

7746. Linhares, Temístocles. Diálogos sobre a poesia brasileira. São Paulo, Melhoramentos *em convênio com o* Instituto Nacional do Livro (INL), 1976. 280 p.

Critical appraisal of young Brazilian poets through author's Socratic and dialectic method.

7747. Magalhães Júnior, R. Poesia e vida de Augusto dos Anjos. Rio, Civilização Brasileira, *em convênio com o* Instituto Nacional do Livro (INL), 1977. 328 p.

Another biography by a reputed master of biographies; somewhat less satisfactory when venturing into literary analysis.

7748. Moisés, Carlos Felipe. Poesia e realidade: ensaios acerca de poesia brasileira e portuguesa. São Paulo, Editora Cultrix [and] Secretaria da Cultura, Ciência e Tecnologia (SCCT), 1977. 213 p.

Essays on Fernando Pessoa, João Cabral, Antero de Quental, Álvares de Azevedo, Raul de Leôni, and others by sensitive young critic and poet.

7749. Muricy, José Cândido de Andrade. Panorama do movimento simbolista brasileiro. v. 1/2. 2. ed. Brasília, Ministério da Educação e Cultura (MEC), Instituto Nacional do Livro (INL), 1973. 2 v. (1290 p.) (Continuous pagination) plates (Col. De literatura brasileira, 12)

First published in 3 vols. (1952), this is the expanded and updated edition of the most authoritative book about Symbolism in Brazil; indispensable and rewarding.

7750. Nunes, Benedito. João Cabral de Melo Neto. Nota biográfica, introdução crítica, antologia [and] bibliografia. Petrópolis, Brazil, Editora Vozes *em convênio com o* Instituto Nacional do Livro (INL), Brasília, 1971. 217 p., bibl., illus., plates (Col. Poetas modernos do Brasil, 1)

Excellent critical study precedes this anthology.

7751. Paes, José Paulo. Pavão, Parlenda, Paraíso: uma tentativa de descrição crítica da poesia de Sosígenes Costa. São Paulo, Editora Cultrix *em convênio com o* Clube Grapiúna do Livro, Projeto de Atividades Culturais Cacau (PACCE), Itabuna, Brazil, 1977. 119 p.

Attempt to rescue a forgotten poet, from oblivion.

7752. Parker, John M. The poetry of Lupe Cotrim Garaude: 1933-1970 (IAA, 1, 1975, p. 39-60)

First (and last?) thorough study of a minor poet.

7753. *Revista de Antropofagia.* Editora Abril [and] Metal Leve. 1975- São Paulo.

Facsimile edition of legendary periodical. Indispensable. The original was published in São Paulo (May 1928-Aug. 1929). This reprint includes an introduction by Augusto de Campos.

7754. Roche, Jean. Sur le vocabulaire préférentiel de la poésie au Portugal et au Brésil du XVIe and XXe siècle (UTIEH/C, 27, 1976, p. 239-250, tables)

Linguistic study based on frequency lists established by the Center of Lexicology, created in 1967-68 at the Univ. of Toulouse, France (see also item 7741).

7755. Santiago, Silviano. Carlos Drummond de Andrade. Petrópolis, Brazil, Editora Vozes, 1976. 131 p., bibl., illus., plates (Col. Poetas modernos do Brasil, 4)

Another analysis of the most analyzed poet in contemporary Brazil.

7756. Silva, Aristides Monteiro de Carvalho e. Panorama da poesia em Campinas até 1920. Apresentação e notas de Hilton Federici. Campinas, Brazil, Academia Campinense de Letras, 1976. 89 p. (Publicações, 34)

Faithful to its title; very informative.

7757. Sousa, J. Galante de. Em tôrno do poeta Bento Teixeira. São Paulo, Univ. de São Paulo, Instituto de Estudos Brasileiros, 1972. 113 p. (Publicação, 24)

Updates what is known about the poet, corrects persistent biographical and editorial errors. An indispensable study.

7758. Souza, Antônio Cândido de Melo e. A autobiografia poética e ficcional na literatura de Minas (*in* Seminário de Estudos Mineiros, IV, Belo Horizonte, Brazil, 1976. Quarto seminário de estudos mineiros. Belo Horizonte, Brazil, Univ. Federal de Minas Gerais, 1977. p. 41-70)

Interesting study of autobiography as a literary art form in Carlos Drummond de Andrade, Murilo Mendes, and Pedro Nava.

7759. Tolman, Jon M. Augusto Frederico Schmidt. Tradução de Laís Corrêa de Araújo. São Paulo, Edições Quíron em convênio com o Ministério de Educação e Cultura (MEC), Instituto Nacional do Livro (INL), 1976. 273 p., bibl., illus. (Col. Escritores de hoje, 6)

Assuming that Augusto Frederico Schmidt has been underrated by Brazilian criticism, author attempts to redress this wrong not very successfully.

7760. ———. Castro Alves, poeta amoroso (USP/RIEB, 17, 1975, p. 27-49)

Good interpretation of Castro Alves that is somewhat overeager in its dismissal of previous ones.

7761. Vilhena, Maria da Conceição. As duas cantigas medievais de Manuel Bandeira (USP/RIEB, 17, 1975, p. 51-66)

Interesting study of medieval lyrical techniques and sources of a modern poet.

7762. *Vozes.* Revista de cultura. Editora Vozes. Ano 71, Vol. 71, No. 1, jan./fev. 1977- . Petrópolis, Brazil.

Another balance sheet of Concretismo as it recedes into history. Important because of the personal memoirs of participants (see item 7706).

7763. Wanke, Eno Teodoro. A trova literária: história da quadra setissilábica autônoma, especialmente na literatura brasileira. Carta de recomendação de Luís da Câmara Cascudo. Rio, Folha Carioca Editora, 1976. 363 p.

Useful, if awkward survey of an endangered literary species.

7764. Williams, Frederick G. Sousândrade: vida e obra. Introdução de Jorge de Sena. São Luis, Brazil, Edições SIOGE, 1976. 277 p., bibl. (Col. Gonçalves Dias, 2)

Somewhat more balanced and well documented evaluation, after the critical overestimations of the 1960s.

**MISCELLANEOUS
(Bibliographies, Letters, Memoirs, etc.)**

7765. Almeida, José Américo de. Memórias: antes que me esqueça. Rio, Livraria Francisco Alves Editora, 1976. 171 p.

With their vivid, concise depictions of turn-of-the-century individuals and customs, poetic turns of language, and all-pervading air of freshness, these delightful childhood memoirs of a distinguished politician and man of letters seem anything but the work of a man approaching 90. [R.E. Dimmick]

7766. Antologia brasileira de humor. v. 1/2. Porto Alegre, Brazil, L & PM Editores, 1976. 254 p., illus.

Cartoons and short prose pieces by 84 different hands which would seem to indicate that black humor is the order of the day in Brazil. [R.E. Dimmick]

7767. Brito, Mário da Silva. Diario intemporal. Rio, Civilização Brasileira, 1970. 191 p. (Col. Vera Cruz. Literatura brasileira, 140)

Along with his customary random reflections and *boutades* Brito provides interesting personal recollections of Oswald de Andrade, Monteiro Lobato, and Mário de Andrade. [R.E. Dimmick]

7768. Cannabrava, Euryalo. Meu fabulário infantil: livro de imagens. Belo Horizonte, Brazil, Imprensa Oficial, 1973. 226 p.

The reader is alternately attracted by the power Cannabrava exhibits in revoking the individuals who peopled his childhood and repelled by the pomposity of his reflections on his discovery of the world. [R.E. Dimmick]

7769. Cardoso, Maria Helena. Vida-vida. Memória. Nota de Clarice Lispector.

Rio, Livraria José Olympio Editora [and] Instituto Nacional do Livro, Brasília, 1973. 385 p.

A *journal intime* of the years from the novelist Lúcio Cardoso's stroke to his death, written by his sister and companion; reflective, but not very revealing. [R.E. Dimmick]

7770. Ciclo de Debates da Cultura Contemporânea, *I, Rio, 1975*. Ciclo de debates do Teatro Casa Grande. Ilustrações de Hermenegildo Sabat. Rio, Editora Inúbia, 1976. 238 p. (Col. Opinião)

Proceedings of series of round-table discussions (1975) on the state of cinema, theater, popular music, the plastic arts, television, journalism, literature, and publicity in Brazil. Questions from the audience and responses by the panelists are also recorded. The woes of censorship and of foreign influences are recurring themes. Notable for historical perspective and dispassionate analysis is the section on literature (Alceu Amoroso Lima, Antônio Houaiss, Affonso Romano de Santanna, Antônio Callado, Antônio Cândido de Mello e Souza). Hermenegildo Sabat's caricatures of the panelists are a delight. [B.M. Woodbridge]

7771. Conrado, Raul. Pequeno dicionário diferente. Rio, Editora Pongetti, 1974. 86 p.

As the author of a "devil's dictionary," Conrado shows some of Bierce's wit but little of his bite. A sample definition: "CAUDILHO—Um, seguido duma fileira de zeros." [R.E. Dimmick]

7772. Duarte, Paulo. Memórias. v. 1, As raízes profundas; v. 2, A inteligência da fome; v. 3, Selva oscura; v. 4, Os mortos de Seabrook. Apresentação de Erico Veríssimo. São Paulo, Humanismo, Ciência e Tecnologia (HUITEC), 1974/1976. 4 v. (257, 328, 389, 436 p.) illus.

At times lively reading, at times tediously detailed, these memoirs of a journalist, polemicist, politician, ethnologist, magazine director, and writer on an abundance of themes are a treasure trove of information on public life in São Paulo, in which Duarte has figured prominently for half a century. Alternation between early and late events is somewhat confusing, and lack of index hinders use as a source book. [R.E. Dimmick]

7773. Lima, Alceu Amoroso. Memórias improvisadas. Diálogos com Cláudio Medeiros Lima. Prefácio de Antônio Houaiss. Petrópolis, Brazil, Editora Vozes, 1973. 343 p.

Transcriptions of tape-recorded interviews with Medeiros Lima, who says: "É este um livro em que dados biográficos e memória se misturam, acrescidos de impressões sobre acontecimentos e pessoas, além de definições de caráter político, religioso e filosófico. Tudo isto expresso em tom coloquial e sem a menor preocupação de método ou de seguimento cronológico." Short on "facts" but invaluable for the view it gives of an outstanding 20th-century intellectual—critic, teacher, and Catholic lay leader. Contains index of proper names. [R.E. Dimmick]

7774. Lima, Hermes. Travessia. Memórias. Rio, Livraria José Olympio Editora, 1974. 297 p. (Col. Documentos brasileiros, 163)

Though the author belongs to the Brazilian Academy of Letters, his memoirs are primarily of interest to historians, as notes on political developments in Brazil since 1930 and the country's position in international organizations since World War II. [R.E. Dimmick]

7775. Nabuco, Carolina. Oito décadas. Rio, Livraria José Olympio Editora, 1973. 221 p., plates.

These memoirs of a distinguished biographer and novelist and member of one of Brazil's most illustrious diplomatic families are disappointingly superficial and impersonal—discreet to a degree that only an honor graduate of the Instituto Rio Branco could bring himself to admire. [R.E. Dimmick]

FRENCH AND ENGLISH WEST INDIES AND THE GUIANAS

NAOMI M. GARRETT

Visiting Professor
Denison University

THERE HAS BEEN A CONSIDERABLE INCREASE in the literary production of the French and English West Indies during the past few years. While a slight growth is noted in the volumes of poetry and prose fiction appearing in this section, the greatest increase has been in studies of writers and their works, especially in the

French language area. The 18 items presented do not include all that have appeared recently; only those available in time to be reviewed for this issue.

As in the last report from this region, studies on the Martinican poet and dramatist, Aimé Césaire, lead the list of subjects. Items 7797, 7799, 7805 and 7807 focus their attention entirely on Césaire while item 7791a discusses him along with other writers; his work is included in item 7825. Copies of four issues of *Cahiers Césairiens* edited by Professor Thomas Hale of Pennsylvania State University arrived too late to be discussed here. They will appear in *HLAS 42*. The importance attached to the Martinican writer in this country is further witnessed by the Seminar on Césaire held at the annual meeting of the Modern Language Association in N.Y. in 1974.

Haiti still produces the greatest number of poetic contributions and many of the writers are quite young and promising. Eight poets published individual volumes; one of these· is a woman making her first appearance (item 7786). Four other young Haitians published a volume together (item 7789).

Although there has been little recently from French Guiana to gain wide circulation, note must be made of the work of a young poet who shows potential (item 7791).

Interest in dramatic works, both full dramas and short plays, is attested to by items 7779-7781, 7810 and 7813. French and English language writings are included.

It is a pleasure to see collections from several well established English West Indian poets in this section. Of special importance are Edward Brathwaite (item 7814), John Figueroa (item 7816) and Arthur Seymour (items 7821 and 7822), whom we hope will be included in future articles along with many of their younger colleagues. One of the promising newer poets has two small volumes (item 7818a and 7819) reviewed in this issue.

The literary world has been saddened by the recent loss of two writers whose works have often appeared here. Philippe Thoby-Marcelin, the Haitian novelist and poet, died in N.Y. two years ago. León-Gontran Damas, a poet from French Guiana and one of the founders of Négritude, died in Jan. 1978. Both will be missed. A re-edition of folk tales by Damas (item 7776a) and a special study of his poetry (item 7806) appear in this issue. He is also included in other studies.

The growing interest in this country in the general area of the West Indies is evident in the number of works being published in the US. This growth is further reflected in the number of institutions of higher learning now offering courses in literature from the region. It is hoped that this developing interest will bring these important works to the attention of a wider public.

FRENCH WEST INDIES

PROSE FICTION

7776. Courtois, Félix. Les nuits de Port-au-Prince (IFH/C, 127/128, déc. 1975, p. 75-100)

Narrator of this "nouvelle" recollects his youth, nocturnal meanderings through streets and alleys of poorer sections of his native city. Sights, sounds and odors bring nostalgic memories. The main part of the story is the narrative of a sad love affair by an unusual man encountered by the writer.

7776a. Damas, León-G. Veillées noires. 2. ed. Ottawa, Canada, Editions Leméac, 1972. 181 p.

New ed. of volume first published in 1943. Stories of animals and humans as characters reveal qualities of some of the best tales found in many folkloric traditions. All are humorous and have a particularly Antillean flavor. Author uses the device of the expert old story-teller.

7777. Lherisson, Justin. La famille des Pitite-Caille: les fortunes de chez nous. 2. ed. Port-au-Prince, Editions Fardin, 1975. 120 p.

Reproduction of original 2. ed., Paris, Typographie Firmin-Didot et Cia., 1929. Recent ed. of novel first published 1905. Satiric yet sympathetic account of rise and fall of Haitian family during 19th century, e.g., problems, pretensions and customs of Port-au-Prince. Lherrison criticizes political and social climate indicating how to survive both.

7778. Magloire, Nadine. Autopsie a vivo. Le sexe mythique: récit. Port-au-Prince, Editions do Verseau, 1975. 58 p.

Story of liberated young Haitian woman who refuses to remain inferior to males even in her sex life. Author injects her views on equal rights. Condemns complacency of Haitian women and their dependence and subjugation to males.

DRAMA

7779. Condé, Maryse. Dieu nous l'a donné... Pièce en 5 actes. Avant-propos de Guy Tirolien. Préface de Lilyan Kesteloot. Paris, Editions Pierre Jean Oswald, 1972. 75 p. (Théâtre africain)

Ambitious young doctor arrives on imaginary Caribbean island with intention of starting revolution which will create better life for inhabitants. Islanders show little interest in his idealistic, and somewhat selfish, plans. Drama describes protagonist's methods in attempting to foment revolution based on a traditional mystique and to develop a sense of national unity and pride. Lack of organization and the absence of well defined plans cause the failure of his project and lead to his death.

7780. Guérin, Mona. Chambre 26. Pièce en 4 actes. Les cinq chéris: théâtre pour adolescents; comédie en 3 actes. Port-au-Prince, Deschamps, 1973? 200 p., illus. plates.

First play concerns young girl hospitalized for an illness caused mainly by her unhappy home life with an unkind stepmother. The girl falls in love with her doctor from whom she receives love and affection for the first time. Second play is light, amusing comedy involving young girl who becomes infatuated with attractive cousin who comes to spend his vacation with her family.

7781. Philoctête, René. Monsieur de Vastey. Théâtre. Port-au-Prince, Les Editions Fardin, 1975. 121 l.

Drama in five acts about Baron de Vastey, secretary and favorite of Haiti's King Henri Christophe. While others curry favor with President Boyer, Vastey alone remains faithful to the king's memory.

POETRY

7782. Antoine, Yves. Les sabots de la nuit. n.p., Imprimerie Gasparo, 1974. 76 p.

Author of Au gré des heures (see *HLAS 36:7176*) presents fourth collection of verse. Nostalgia for Haiti, grief caused by exile, memories of traditions and customs of his homeland run through much of the poetry. Though tone is largely pessimistic, hope persists as if awaiting a miracle. Very sensitive, highly condensed verse.

7783. Berrou, F. Raphaël. Miroir de poète. Port-au-Prince, Imprimerie Centrale, 1974. 59 p.

Collection of 26 poems dedicated to author's former students who furnished inspiration for much of the work. Variety in form: ballad, sonnet, dialogue, alexandrine, free verse. Themes vary. Though often philosophic and religious, verse is highly colored by nature and daily life on the island.

7784. Casirir, Berard. Pour un monde. Port-au-Prince, The Author, 1976. 1 v. (Unpaged)

Collection of 37 poems by promising young poet in two sections. First is inspired by love of a real or dream girl. Second contains 22 poems about nature, the underprivileged, search for identity.

7785. Charles, Jean-Claude. Negotiations. Poémes. Suivis d'une étude par Gérard Campfort. Paris, Editions Pierre Jean Oswald, 1972. 108 p. (J'exige la parole)

Six long poems by talented young Haitian. Themes: childhood full of magic and illusion, problems confronting compatriots, wretched conditions of the underprivileged, social and moral decay. Decries emphasis on modern technology at the expense of human needs. Lyric and rhythmic poetry, at times elliptical and obscure. Reminiscent of Magloire Saint Aude whose works provide the inspiration for the last poem.

7786. Colimon, Marie-Thérèse. Mon cahier d'écriture numéro. I. Port-au-Prince, Atelier Fardin, 1973. 29 p.

New female poet finds inspiration in Haiti, love, personal reflections. Written over a number of years.

7787. Dauphin, Marcel. Flammeches. Port-au-Prince, Editions Fardin, 1976. 186 p.

Nature, twilight, street scenes, personal sentiments and reflections are the themes. Many poems were written in exile and portray nostalgic longing for Haiti.

7788. Garçon, Jean Dieudonné. Poèmes pour trois continents: suivi de Pour qui le tocsin? Paris, Editions Pierre Jean Oswald, 1972. 132 p. (J'exige la parole)

Poems with social mission, revolutionary in tone. Author, expressing sympathy for black Americans and for the Vietnamese, sees himself as the voice for the underprivileged and deprived masses. Laments conditions in his native Haiti but in a note of optimism predicts a better day for his country.

7789. Saint Vil, Jean-Claude; Jean Gary Charles; Benjamin Joseph; and Marc Allan Déronvil. Les melodies de Pharilon. Port-au-Prince, Imprimerie M. Rodríguez, 1974. 40 p., plate.

First efforts by four young poets still in their teens. Themes: parents, Haiti, sentiments of love and thoughts of the divine. Verse is commendable if not great.

7790. Soucougnan. La troisième île. Paris, Editions Pierre Jean Oswald, 1973. 51 p. (Voix nouvelles)

Title of this volume is same as that of largest section. Poet describes daily life and conditions in the islands, life in metropolis and problems of exiles. Verse is sensuous and musical, much of it imitating rhythms of the blues and the bolero. Many titles are in English.

7791. Stephenson, Elie. Une flèche pour le pays à l'encan. Poèmes. Préface de Serge Patient. Paris, Pierre Jean Oswald, 1975. 90 p. (J'exige la parole)

First volume by young poet from French Guiana gives promise of considerable talent. There is a variety of themes: homage to his ancestors, slavery, the evils of colonialism, the wretchedness of the deprived mass in La Guyane and other French possessions in the New World. Verse has a sustained lyric quality which heightens its artistic value. This reviewer hopes to read more from this promising young writer, probably the first from his country to come to wide attention since Léon G. Damas

SPECIAL STUDIES

7791a. Bansart, Andrés *ed.* Poesía negro-africana. Santiago? Univ. Católica de Chile, Vicerrectoría de Comunicaciones, Ediciones Nueva Universidad, 1971. 63 p.

Five poets from the French West Indies are included in this vol.: Césaire from Martinique; Damas from French Guiana; Niger and Tirolien from Guadeloupe; and Roumain from Haiti. Selections from their verse support the author's thesis that though these poets differ in style, they and all other black writers express similar sentiments because of their African ancestry and their experience of suffering and despair. Editor sees a cry for freedom and hope in their verse.

7792. Berrou, F. Raphaël. *Gouverneurs de la Rosée* ou le testament de Jacques Roumain (IFH/C, 133, mars/avril 1977, p. 61-83)

Scholarly study sees Roumain's novel as his last testament, a message of love to his compatriots and country. Critic singles out examples of various types of love in novel. Stresses artistic qualities, language, images, description, symbolism. Hails as best legacy Roumain could have left.

7793. Charles, Christophe. Dix nouveaux poètes et écrivains haïtiens. Port-au-Prince, Union Nationale Haïtienne des Travailleurs Intellectuels, 1974. 116 p., plates (Col. UNHTI)

All young writers discussed began publishing after 1960. Inspired, by the ideas of Jacques Roumain, Jean Brierre, René Depestre and others, most have continued to follow their predecessors, but giving, at times, a new tone to their verse. Most talented of the group left country between 1963 and 1966 or ceased writing. Short biography of each writer precedes discussion of work.

7794. Dash, J. Michael. Marvellous realism-the way out of négritude (UPR/CS, 13:4, Jan. 1974, p. 57-70)

Study contends that the idea of Négritude, deemed necessary and important to racially dispossessed black intellectuals early in this century, is being replaced by a realism which takes into account all elements in a person's background. In the case of Caribbean writers, these include traits from their West Indian past as well as those from Africa and Europe. Négritude is based on the erroneous idea that the African experience was a total loss. Instead, author maintains that diverse influences in each national group have fused and synthesized to form a new and specific national culture.

7795. Gindine, Ivette. Satire and the birth of Haitian fiction, 1901-1905 (UWI/CQ, 21:3, Sept. 1975, p. 30-37)

Author notes how Marcelin, Lherisson and Hibbert, creators of the Haitian novel, exposed the anarchy as well as the greed and corruption of politicians that were ravaging their society. Their satires enriched the island's cultural patrimony and inaugurated a new phase in its literature.

7796. Gouraige, Ghislain. La Diaspora d'Haïti et l'Afrique. Ottawa, Canada, Editions Naaman, 1974. 196 p., bibl.

Interesting attempt by critic, essayist and novelist to explain the complexity of Haitian character. While all blacks in this hemisphere were subjected to a variety of social, geographical and cultural influences, he contends that Haitians had the additional experience of conducting the only successful slave revolt in history and causing the first defeat of modern colonialism. Haitian character was also shaped by country's isolated location in a racially and geographically hostile environment and by the indignities suffered during the American Occupation. He ridicules the elite in his country for their idea of race and their preference for the European rather than the African elements in their culture. Author hopes that this study will help young Haitians discover their true identity.

7797. Harris, Rodney E. L'humanisme dans le théâtre d'Aimé Césaire; étude de trois tragédies: *Et les chiens se taisaient, La tragédie du Roi Christophe, Une saison au Congo.* Préface de Thomas Cassirer. Ottawa, Canada, Editions Naaman, 1973. 170 p., bibl. (Col. Etudes, 3)

More than 40 studies on Césaire's tragedies since 1964 show widespread interest in the Martinican poet. Connected by theme, structure and history, these works link African roots with black man's present situation. Césaire's hero is a leader who is misunderstood by his people but who fights for them. He is condemned to solitude and eventual death for his intransigence but his idealism survives. While treating the problem of the black man, Césaire reflects on the dignity of man in general.

7798. Hoffman, Léon-François. En marge du premier roman Haitien: *Stella* d'Eméric Bergeaud (IFH/C, 131, nov. 1976. p. 75-102)

Study of work published in 1859 which critic labels first Haitian novel. Story of cruel, ruthless plantation owner who has had a young slave woman, mother of his son, Remus, beaten to death. Romulus, an older son by her husband an African chief, and Remus vow to avenge mother's brutal death. Led and inspired by Stella, a young French woman who, also, has been mistreated by the cruel master, they obtain their revenge. Then the three, representing the island's white, mulatto and black elements, join in their country's fight for freedom, independence and progress. Critic notes that novel, while idealistic, presents many of the realities in Haiti's history.

7799. Knight, Vere. The West Indian attitude to tragedy: the example of Aimé Césaire (ASAWI/B, 5, dec. 1972, p. 61-69)

Author asserts that Aimé Césaire's notion of tragic hero adds to traditional Aristotelian concept an aspect that seems peculiarly Caribbean. Describes this modification as admixture of admiration and derision, an element of mockery which emphasizes hero's flaws and leads to his ruin. Draws examples from Césaire's *La tragédie du Roi Christophe, Une saison au Congo* and *Et les chiens se taisaient.*

7800. Laroche, Maximilien. *Dézafe* de Franketiénne: un tournant de la littérature haitienne (IFH/C, 131, nov. 1976, p. 107-119)

Defense of Franketiénne's theme of the zombi and his use of créole in *Dézafé*. Critic maintains that character or myth of zombi is strictly a Haitian phenomenon and that popular language, therefore, is the natural vehicle for treating the subject. He believes that *Dézafé* remains closer to oral tradition by use of créole and mixture of songs, proverbs, riddles and puns found in his work.

7801. ———. La figure du sujet dans le *Roi Moko* de Rassoul Labuchin (IFH/C, 127/128, déc. 1975, p. 57-74, bibl.)

Explanation of use and significance of personal pronoun forms in Haitian créole. Examples are given from Labuchin's *Roi Moko* to illustrate pronoun usage and to demonstrate poet's artistic techniques.

7802. Marc, Jules André. Regard sur la littérature haïtienne. t. 2, 1804-1973. Port-au-Prince, n.p., 1974? 76 p. (Col. Les sambas caraïbéens, 4)

Vol. 2 of study prepared for students in Haitian schools. Though the author covers long period and many writers, there is little attention to detail. Nine of author's contemporaries (1960-73) are discussed while equally important writers of the period 1920-60 are entirely omitted. Includes helpful section on French versification for beginners.

7803. Mullen, Edward J. ed. Langston Hughes in the hispanic world and Haiti. Hamden, Conn., Shoe String Press, 1977. 193 p.

Two articles by Hughes concern Haiti. First depicts the Black Republic as it appeared to visitor during the American Occupation. Second is an appeal to writers and artists to protest the imprisonment of Jacques Roumain who was incarcerated for circulating a French magazine of Negro liberation.

7804. Papailler, Hubert. Carl Brouard, the poet of humble love (CLA/J, 21:2, dec. 1977, p. 312-320)

Writer lauds Carl Brouard, one of the founders of Haiti's "mouvement indigéniste", as best interpreter of the soul of his country's lower classes. Leaving his upper-class, well-to-do home, Brouard elected to live among the culturally and materially impoverished in the capital city. He found inspiration for his beautiful love poems in prostitutes and other persons of low moral character among whom he enjoyed life and companionship.

7805. Simmons, Ruth J.S. Aimé Césaire: colonialism and the poetics of authenticity (CLA/J, 19:3, March 1976, p. 382-388)

Analysis of Césaire's ideas of the effects of assimilation on colonized people. The Martinican maintains that Caribbean natives, instead of being passively assimilated into European culture, should cultivate those traits which are solely attributable to their Afro-Antillean heritage. The poet can help in this endeavor and, at the same time, achieve authenticity in his verse by choosing his images from his background and using language unique to his experience.

7806. Warner, Keith Q. Léon Damas and the calypso (CLA/J, 19:3, March 1976, p. 374-381)

Study of Damas' poetry showing that while utilizing certain techniques from French literary tradition, the poet also chose elements from calypso and jazz. Examples: his frequent use of the call/response technique" where a chorus not only supports the calypsonian but adds ideas. Damas' humorous satire in poems combined with a surprise ending shows close affinity with the calypso tradition.

7807. Williams, Lorna V. The image of King Christophe (CLA/J, 22:3, March 1977, p. 333-340)

Comparison of image of Haiti's King Christophe in Alejo Carpentier's novel *El reino de este mundo* and Aimé Césaire's drama *La tragédie du Roi Christophe*, shows that Carpentier's hero lacks depth. He is perceived only in externals and novel fails to provide sufficient motives for his actions. Césaire's king, on the other hand, assumes specificity and his intentions and plans are clearly delineated. Author affirms that the character of Césaire's hero emerges in action whereas Carpentier's remains static. The latter's king shows little desire for the power which affects history while Césaire's tragic hero fights and builds for his country.

ENGLISH WEST INDIES

PROSE FICTION

Angrosino, Michael V. V.S. Naipaul and the colonial image. See *HLAS 39:1175*.

7808. Anthony, Michael. Cricket in the road. London, André Deutsch, 1973. 143 p.

Collection of 20 stories, many of which had appeared earlier in *Bim*, the Barbadian literary magazine. Most are set in Mayaro, a seaport in southeast Trinidad. The stories, some tragic, others comic, describe life, childhood experiences and adolescence while presenting cultural elements found in the multifaceted population of Trinidad.

7809. Carnegie, James. Wages paid. La Habana, Casa de las Américas, 1976. 104 p.

Story covering a single day's actions on slave plantation in Jamaica. Mary, head cook and discarded mistress of slave master, devises plan, with aid of plantation Obeah-man, to get revenge on master as well as on the estate stud who, too, had begun to spurn her. Plan ends in tragedy for both men as well as for the stud's young daughter. An expression of female retaliation against exploitation and abuse.

7810. López, Basil. In another's house. Spanish Town, Jam., Press Box Printers, 1973. 135 p.

Drama of problems and conflicts of three generations of racially mixed Jamaican family. Importance of color and social mobility causes much of their trouble. Whole gamut of concerns, including Obeah, adultery, homosexuality and involvement with the Rastafarians, touches family members. Incongruous deaths of most of the main characters render conclusion illogical.

7811. Patterson, Horace Orlando. Die the long day. N.Y., William Morrow, 1972. 253 p.

Novel of life on Jamaican sugar plantation in 18th century gives insight into subtleties of master-slave relationships and thus better understanding of contemporary West Indian society. Conflict develops when slave-woman Quasheba attempts to prevent her beautiful mulatto daughter from becoming mistress of diseased plantation owner. Mother's subsequent death, at the hands of maroons who are sent to capture her, causes many slaves to reflect upon tragedy of their existence.

7812. Sadeek, Sheik M. Across the green fields and five other stories. Georgetown, The Author, 1974. 37 p.

Collection of stories on life in Guyana, among sugar plantation workers. Stories are interesting and well told, giving glimpses into life and customs of East Indians and blacks.

DRAMA

7813. Sadeek, Sheik M. Goodbye Corentyne. Georgetown, The Author, 1973. 22 p.

One-act play in which the arranged marriage of a young East Indian couple is about to be terminated because of the wife's desire for an education. An unforeseen incident causes the couple to come to terms with themselves, they discover that they love each other and save their marriage.

POETRY

7814. Brathwaite, Edward. Days and nights. Mona, Jam., Caldwell Press, 1975. 1 v. (Unpaged)

Two long poems in dialect treating race relations and daily life in small locality in Jamaica. Example of use of folk language by major poet.

7815. Dawes, Neville and **Anthony McNeill** eds. The Caribbean poem. An anthology of 50 Caribbean voices. With a foreword by A.J. Seymour. n.p., Carifesta, 1976. 112 p.

Consists of 115 poems by many outstanding and lesser-known English-language writers of the Caribbean, most of whom find inspiration in their own cultural or personal background. They use variety of forms: rhymed dialect, free verse, long prose poems. Ten of the 50 poets are women.

7816. Figueroa, John. Ignoring hurts. Poems. Introduction by Frank Getlein. Washington, Three Continents Press, 1976. 121 p.

Vol. 3 of poetry by Figueroa contains much original verse as well as selections from early collections. Though a light, jesting tone is present, poems are classical, revealing religious and philosophical inspiration. While cosmopolitan in theme, style and interest, poet's verse is often flavored by history and life of his native Jamaica.

7817. For the fighting front. An anthology of revolutionary poems. A special edition for the P.Y.O. [Progressive Youth Organization] Festival Congress, 13-15 April 1974. Annandale, Guyana, n.p., 1974. 24 p.

Twelve poems written to renew spirit of protest in Guyanese youth against government then in power. They call for unity of blacks and East Indians and demand that a socialistic program be instituted by the government. Publication sponsored by National Student Committee.

7818. Keens-Douglas, Paul. When moon shine. Port-of-Spain, Moko Enterprises, 1975. 59 p.

Consists of 22 poems in dialect and standard English. Title of volume comes from first poem which describes joyous activities on moonlight nights.

7818a. Prasad, Krishna. Childhood days: a collection of poems. Demerara, Guyana, The Author, 1976. 16 p.

Collection of 13 poems written for and about children. Some appear to stem from childhood memories; others grow out of the observation of children's activities today.

7819. ———. Dawning days. Demerara, Guyana, The Author, 1976. 36 p.

First verse of young Guyanese poet. Deeply moved by injustice and suffering, he pleads for better life for less fortunate and against conditions that divide two of the more deprived groups, blacks and the East Indians.

7820. Prince, Maureen. Birth of a dream. n.p., Guyana Printers, n.d. 9 p.

Small pamphlet contains four poems in standard English and three-scene play in local dialect. Verse draws inspiration from natural beauty of Guyana and is greatly influenced by country's socialist tendencies. First attempt by young poet.

7821. Seymour, Arthur J. Italic. Georgetown, Press of the Labour Advocate, 1974. 18 p.

These 11 poems by talented poet on variety of themes make interesting reading.

7822. ———. Love song. Georgetown, Labour Advocate, 1975. 21 p.

Consists of 23 poems of love with images drawn largely from nature and history. There is variety in form, style and technique. Several are outstanding.

7823. Winston, Joe Bacchus. The murmurings of Aschak. n.p., Scope Publishing Co. Caribbean, 1976. 56 p.

Includes poems from two earlier collections, *On carnival* and *Future shock*. Personal reflections on daily life characterize most of the verse. Author adapts type of speech to occasion and social class depicted.

7824. Zide's fifty drops of blood. Georgetown, Labour Advocate, n.d. 16 p.

Harold A. Bascom wrote brief introduction for this small volume of short poems. Verse by youthful writer inspired, generally, by love, black awareness and a desire for unity of the youth.

SPECIAL STUDIES

7825. Hearne, John ed. Carifesta forum. An anthology of 20 Caribbean voices. Kingston, Times Printery, 1976. 248 p.

Among 20 Caribbean writers in this volume, 14 are from English and French-speaking areas. Each writer attempts to define or explain an aspect of his culture and to describe the formation of the Caribbean spirit. John Hearne writes the introduction for this collection of well selected essays and excerpts from longer works. Includes biographical notes on authors.

7826. Lawrence, Leota S. Three West Indian heroines: an analysis (CLA/J, 21:2, Dec. 1977, p. 238-250)

Study of heroines in three West Indian novels: Bita in Claude McKay's *Banana bottom*, Maisie in C.L.R. James' *Minty Alley* and Tee (Cynthia) in Merle Hodge's *Crick crack monkey*. From different areas, but all from impoverished cultures, each escapes from her environment in order to find herself. Author views McKay's heroine as romanticized version of West Indian womanhood while James' Maisie and Hodge's Tee are more realistic.

McDowell, Robert Eugene. Bibliography of literature from Guyana. See *HLAS 39:25*.

7827. Sander, Reinhard W. *ed.* and *comp.* An index to Bim: 1942-1972. With a foreword by Esmond D. Ramesar, an introduction by Edward Baugh, and an interview with Frank Collymore. St. Augustine, T. and T., Univ. of the West Indies, Extra-Mural Studies Unit, 1973. 86 p. (Art & civilisation, 2)

Vol. 1 of this Art & Civilization series commemorated President of Senegal Léopold-Sedar Senghor's visit to the Univ. of the West Indies. This vol. commemorates 80th birthday of Barbadian poet Frank Collymore and 30th anniversary of *Bim*, the literary journal which he founded. This complete index of *Bim* (1942-72) is divided into: fiction, drama, poetry, articles, reviews and editorial comments. Shows that writers from all English language countries and occasionally from French language areas contributed to this important review. The Foreword, Introduction and Interview with Collymore give insight into the development of writing in the West Indies. Useful work for students and other interested in the literature of this area.

TRANSLATIONS

MARGARET SAYERS PEDEN

Professor of Spanish
University of Missouri, Columbia

STATE OF THE ART: Translation is flourishing as never before. Increasingly, universities are offering programs, or simply courses, in translation—Columbia Univ., the Univ. of Arkansas, the SUNY system, among some dozen others. SUNY-Binghamton, Columbia, and the Univ. of Texas at Dallas offer clearinghouse services. Two organizations are working for translators' rights and the dissemination of information of interest to translators, The American Translators' Association (Croton-on-Hudson, N.Y., which is primarily organized for scientific and commercial translators, but which also shelters literary translators), and the American Literary Translators' Association (Univ. of Texas-Dallas). An enormous Index for Translations is being compiled, designed as a companion volume to *The Literary Marketplace*. *Review*, published by the Center for Inter-American Relations, is an excellent journal devoted exclusively to matters concerning Latin American translation. Its success speaks of the high interest in the field. In addition, Latin American literature in translation is constantly more visible in most national magazines and book reviews. Slowly, and laboriously, the academic community is coming to recognize the scholarly aspect of translation. Sections on translation are appearing on programs of both creative and scholarly organizations. Sewanee Univ. sponsored a conference on the art of translation in 1977. A 1977 blockbuster was the *encontro* between North American and Brazilian literary communities. And in 1977, for the first time, the National Endowment for the Humanities formalized its recognition of translation by adding to its list a number of fellowships for literary translation. The current scene is one of a great deal of activity, a great deal of interest, and a great deal of accomplishment.

QUALITY OF THE ART: Amazingly high if one considers the small rewards offered the average translator. Quality has improved noticeably in the last decade. More translators are being trained, more qualified people are being attracted to the practice of translation, and, apparently, publishers are becoming more sophisticated in editing translations. While some bad translations still appear, more are at least competent, few an embarrassment. Beyond the competently average, there are peaks of consistent excellence. Among the outstanding translations of the decade are Rabassa's *One hundred years of solitude* (item 7898), some of Helen Lane's and Jill

Levine's prose translations, Di Giovanni's Borges, Reid's Neruda, and Bishop's Brazilian poetry. Stellar names, like magnets, have attracted numbers of translations; some poems have been translated six or seven times (even though they may not yet have found their definitive translations). Quality is more than ever the norm, especially if one is willing to abandon the word-for-word search for specific errors that so delights some critics, and to adopt the ultimately more important criteria of tone and flow (always acknowledging the need for basic accuracy).

SELECTION: Because of space limitations, only book-length works are considered for this first section on translations in *HLAS 40*. For the same reasons, only books published between 1968-78, an arbitrary selection of dates that is workable, but that also displays the vitality and variety of translations. Most genres are represented, with the exception of criticism. Most significant authors, and some not as well known, but every reader will lament the omission of some favorite. A few omissions occurred because they were unavailable in any of the three good libraries used in this study. It is to be hoped that major omissions can be rectified in future volumes of the *Handbook*.

In sum, the English-speaking world now has access to a wealth of literature formerly unknown or unavailable. Barriers have been breached and beachheads established. In 1977, to a large degree *because of* translations into English, Latin American literature is acknowledged as a major literature in the US.

ANTHOLOGIES OF TRANSLATIONS FROM SPANISH AND PORTUGUESE

POETRY

7828. Ahern, Maureen and David Tipton *eds.* and *trans.* Peru: the new poetry. With an introduction by David Tipton. London, London Magazine Editions, 1970. 128 p.

Impressive collection of poetry not as widely studied as it might be. Some familiar names, among them, Sebastian Salazar Bondy, Antonio Cisneros, Julio Ortega, others not so familiar, but vital. Translations are natural (unless one is anti—ampersand) and provoking. In his brief comment Cisneros states, "We've always been influenced by . . . others. In a sense we're translators." Many of these voices are original.

7829. Benson, Rachel *trans.* Nine latin-american poets: José Gorostiza Vicente Huidobro, Pablo Neruda, Luis Pales Matos, Octavio Paz, Carlos Pellicer, Alfonsina Storni, Cesar Vallejo and Xavier Villaurrutia. N.Y., Las Americas, 1968. 359 p. (A Cypress book)

Many of these poems are *not* commonly anthologized. Choice of poets, too, is not ordinary, but based on personal preferences. Individually, translations read accurately; one's reservation is that overall tone doesn't change among voices of different poets. (Incidentally, choice of italics for all texts seems unfortunate.) *En face.*

7830. Bishop, Elizabeth and Emanuel Brasil *eds.* An anthology of twentieth-century Brazilian poetry. Middletown, Conn., Wesleyan Univ. Press, 1972. 181 p.

Book sponsored by Academy of American Poets with notes on editors and translators. Excellent introduction touches on all aspects of poetry in Brazil—history, language, attitudes. The 14 poets included represent, in the opinions, of the editors, the most representative and best-loved Brazilian poets. One cannot say too much for the line-up of translators, among them the most distinguished of contemporary North American poets. To point to only one, Miss Bishop (who lived for years in Brazil) has made beautiful translations. A basic Brazilian poetry reader. *En face.*

7831. Brotherston, Gordon and Edward Dorn *eds.* and *trans.* Our word: guerilla poems from Latin America (Palabra del guerrillero: poesía guerrillera de Latinoamérica). London, Cape Goliard, 1968. 1 v. (Unpaged)

Proposal of editors is to present collection of poems "by and about guerillas." Most of them are published for the first time; some poets have achieved recognition, but Che is the only one whose name is universally recognized. Collection is strangely poignant; the fact that some of the writers were killed in their struggles adds to that poignancy. The translations are inconsistent, at times too formal, at times self-consciously colloquial. *En face.*

7832. Caracciolo-Trejo, E. *ed.* The Penguin book of Latin American verse.

With an introduction by Henry Gifford. With plain prose translations by Tom Raworth and others. Harmondsworth, U.K., Penguin Books, 1971. 425 p. (The penguin poets)

Excellent selection of poets and poems. This is, actually, an edition of poetry in Spanish, but each poem is translated, as title page states, in "plain prose" in small type at bottom of each page. Translations are obviously intended as a guide to inexpert reader of Spanish and make no pretension of poetic translation. Volume could be of interest, however, for specific purposes, such as an intermediate reader, or for the nonspecialist. Includes an appendix which is an explanatory guide to movements in Latin American poetry.

7833. Carlisle, Charles Richard *ed*. Beyond the rivers. Anthology of twentieth century Paraguayan poetry. Berkeley, Calif., Thorp Springs Press, 1977. 72 p., bibl.

Really laudable undertaking, the presentation of the "state of the art" in contemporary Paraguayan poetry. Interesting and informed introduction by Carlisle. Regrettably, the poetry does not seem to be at the level of many national anthologies. Too, since many of the works are difficult to obtain in the original, one misses the opportunity to read the original Spanish.

7834. Durán, Cheli *ed*. and *trans*. The yellow canary whose eye is so black. N.Y., Macmillan, 1977. 348 p., bibl.

Collection has flavor of personal favorites—which they are, from Sor Juana and Gabriela, to Nahual and Quechua pieces, to Martín Fierro, Tablada, Vallejo, Borges, and Parra. There is a welcome accuracy in Ms. Durán's translations, but those in verse often strain that facet of her versions. Not to detract from the collection; Spanish rhymed poetry strains in English lines. *En face*.

7835. Fitts, Dudley *ed*. and *comp*. Anthology of contemporary Latin-American poetry (Antología de la poesía americana contemporánea). Westport, Conn., Greenwood Press, 1976. 677 p., bibl.

Fitts' stance on translation is obdurate: "our versions are not poetry, except accidentally." He insists upon an *ad litteram expressa*. Biographical and bibliographical notes. List (only) of translators. Selection reflects the time of original ed. (Norfolk, Conn., New Directions, 1947).

7836. Jaén, Didier Tisdel *comp*. and *trans*. Homage to Walt Whitman: a collection of poems in Spanish. With a foreword by Jorge Luis Borges. University, Univ. of Alabama Press, 1969. 87 p.

As title indicates, poems by Latin American and Spanish poets dedicated or addressed to Walt Whitman: Borges, León Felipe, Lugones, Darío, Martínez Estrada, Cardona Peña, García Lorca, Pedro Mir, and Pablo Neruda. Except for occasional over-dependence on cognates and the precise poetic line, the translations are very good. Includes appendices on José Martí and notes on poets and poems. *En face*.

7837. Lowenfels, Walter *ed*. and *comp*. For Neruda, for Chile: an international anthology. Boston, Mass., Beacon Press, 1975. 249 p.

Joint homage to Neruda and Allende, and through them, "to millions of people moved by the Chilean tragedy." Contributions by 140 poets from 27 countries. If quality of offerings varies greatly, there is no mistaking the genuine grief for the loss of a great poet. A remarkable volume. One cannot actually judge the quality of translations from Spanish, as some originals are not available. Includes appendix with Neruda chronology and some dates in Chilean history.

7838. Márquez, Robert *ed*. Latin American revolutionary poetry (Poesía revolucionaria latinoamericana). N.Y., Monthly Review Press, 1974. 505 p.

"Revolutionary" poetry stylistically as well as politically. Some expected names, Lihn, Guillén, Cardenal, Benedetti, some less well-known, one or two powerful anonymous pieces. Márquez translates, David Arthur McMurray, Elinor Randall, among others. As in any collection of this kind there is variation in the quality of translation, but overall, rather high than low.

7839. Strand, Mark *ed*. New poetry of Mexico. Selected with notes by Octavio Paz; Ali Chumacero; José Emilio Pacheco; and Homero Aridjis. London, Secker & Warburg, 1972. 187 p.

American edition sizeably reduced from Mexican edition, necessitated by Strand's insistence on "quality of the translations." Poems and translators were chosen well. Poets are representative of modern Mexican poetry, and with few exceptions, translation is fine. *En face*.

7840. Tarn, Nathaniel *ed*. Con Cuba. Anthology of Cuban poetry of the last sixty years. London, Cape Goliard, 1969. 143 p.

This volume results "haphazardly" from a trip to Cuba and a "desire to share . . . poems . . . discovered and read with pleasure." A number of the poems were previously included in the (unfortunately) defunct *Corno Emplumado* formerly edited by Margaret Randall. Tarn has re-translated few of the pieces, some are translated by other established names, like Kerrigan, Gardner Reynolds, and Elinor and Margaret Randall. Good selection, from personal to political. En face.

SHORT STORIES

7842. Howes, Barbara ed. The eye of the heart. Short stories from Latin America. Notes on contributors & notes on translators. Indianapolis, Ind., Bobbs-Merrill, 1973. 415 p.

To date the most ambitious compilation of Latin American short stories in translation, ranging from 1880s to 1970s. Some of the classic anthology pieces are here ("The Beautiful Soul of Don Damián," "The Switchman," "The Piano"), as well as brief fictions by most contemporary authors. Except for a couple of dubious choices which really cannot be labeled short stories, a very good and representative selection. Various translators. (Interesting bibliographical note: how writers play with their published pieces. Compare "A Nest of Sparrows on the Awning," by Cabrera Infante, to "Next, Door, Neighbors" in Mancini's anthology of stories, see item 7844.)

7843. Lawaetz, Gudie ed. Spanish short stories 2 (Cuentos hispánicos 2). Harmondsworth, U.K., Penguin, 1972. 216 p.

Edition follows format of first (1966) Penguin collection of Hispanic short stories. As in first collection, seven of these stories are from Latin Americans (Jorge Edwards, Vargas Llosa, Onetti, Carlos Fuentes, García Márquez, and Cortázar). Biographical notes on authors. Footnotes, happily, are found at the end of the book, not in the text. An interesting idea, an *en face*, prose edition. Translations are specifically British, not North American. En face.

7844. Mancini, Pat McNees ed. Contemporary Latin American short stories. Greenwich, Conn., Fawcett Publications, 1974. 479 p. (A Fawcett premier book)

In such anthologies one is constantly struck by the incredible range of Latin American literature, the contrast, for example, between the universality of a piece like Benedetti's "Gloria's Sunday," and the specific Mexicanity of Rulfo's "Talpa." There is no intent in this collection of unanimity of tone—compare Quiroga's fable for children, "How the Flamingoes Got Their Stockings," to Cabrera Infante's sophisticated word play in "Next, Door, Neighbors"—rather, of demonstrating the scope of the literature. In this sense, an excellent collection. Various translators. Includes further readings.

POETRY AND PROSE

7845. Bierhorst, John and others eds. and trans. Four masterpieces of American Indian literature. Translated from the Náhuatl and Maya. N.Y., Farrar, Straus & Giroux, 1974. 371 p.

"This volume is intended as a first step toward establishing a body of standard works, a canon, of native American literature." It is an important scholarly/literary achievement. The translation is carefully documented and footnoted. Of the four works translated, two are North American in origin, two Spanish American: "Quetzalcoatl, An Aztec Hero Myth," and "Cuceb, A Maya Prophecy."

7846. Bobín, María Teresa and **Stan Steiner** eds. Borinquen. Anthology of Puerto Rican literature. Translated from the Spanish by Barry Luby. N.Y., Knopf, 1974. 516 p.

Monumental undertaking—dating from conquest to present, encompassing most genres, spanning the bridge between Island and N.Y.C. Editors have compiled an impressive if uneven collection.

7847. Carpentier, Hortense and **Janet Brof** eds. and comps. Doors and mirrors. Fiction and poetry from Spanish America: 1920-1970. With biographical notes and an index of translators. N.Y., The Viking Press, 1972. 451 p.

Prose and poetry. The editors have compiled an interesting collection, but *not* "an historical survey of these fifty years of Spanish American literature." As a rough estimate, 80 percent of the material must date from the last 20 years. And it's good material, generally. Better in prose (except, where is Carlos Fuentes?) than poetry—some of the poems included are questionable in importance and lasting value. The interesting epilogue is the text of Vargas Llosa's acceptance speech on accepting the 1967 Rómulo Gallegos Prize. As in all such anthologies, the quality of the translation varies greatly.

7848. Donoso, José and **William A. Henkin** eds. The *Tri-Quarterly* anthology of contemporary Latin American literature. N.Y., E.P. Dutton, 1969. 496 p., illus.

One of the first, and major, instances of a special issue of a quarterly devoted exclusively to Latin American literature. Short stories, excerpts from novels, poems, art, all preceded by a timely essay by Paz, "A Literature of Foundations," which begins, "Is there such a thing as Spanish American literature?" All English, no original texts. No notes on translators.

7849. *Nimrod.* Latin American voices. University of Oklahoma. Vol. 18, No. 1, Fall/Winter 1973- . Tulsa.

Poetry (Neruda, Cardenal, Carío, Paz), fiction (Puig), criticism (Hugh Fox on Salazar Bondy), interview (Rita Guibert on García Márquez), a good sampling of what was going on in the early 1970s. Various translators. Quality of translation varies.

7850. Romano-V., Octavio Ignacio *ed.* El espejo (The mirror). Selected Mexican-American literature. Berkeley, Calif., Quinto Sol Publicaciones, 1969. 241 p.

Collection of works, all genres from a group of writers from the Southwest known primarily in the world of Chicano-Riqueño literature, as yet not incorporated into the mainstream of Spanish American literature. Some pieces appear in Spanish and then their English translation, some appear in English only, a few in a combination of languages.

7851. Troupe, Quincy and Rainer Schulte *eds.* and *comps.* Giant talk. Anthology of Third World writings. N.Y., Vintage Books, 1975. 546 p., bibl.

As one would suspect from the title, Latin American writers are well represented in this anthology containing both prose pieces and poems. Volume is divided into various sections ranging from "Oppression and Protest" through "Ritual and Magic" to "The Conceptual Voyage." Stunning representation of what must be the most exciting literature on the contemporary scene. No originals (all English); no notes on translators. Includes biographical notes.

7851a. Williams, Miller *ed.* Chile. Anthology of new writing. Kent, Ohio, Kent State Univ. Press, 1968. 1 v. (Unpaged)

Introduction of a post-Neruda generation of Chilean writers; poems, short fiction, an interview, a play. Most translations by Williams, a recent recipient of the Prix de Rome for poetry. *En face.*

PLAYS

7852. Colecchia, Francesca and Julio Matas *eds.* and *trans.* Selected Latin American one-act plays. Pittsburgh, Pa., Univ. of Pittsburgh Press, 1973. 204 p.

The one-act play is often awkward, a difficult form (in same way that novella is neither short story or novel), but the works here are well selected, both as drama and as representative works of theater from Spanish America (Mexico, Argentina, Guatemala, Colombia, Cuba, Chile and Venezuela). Among the plays, the most interesting new voice is that of Gustavo Andrade Rivera from Colombia. The translations alternate between an overly formal tone and good, relaxed dialogue. (But why Americanize names, as in the Garro piece?) Includes brief notes on authors.

7853. Jones, Willis Knapp *ed.* and *trans.* Men and angels. Three South American comedies. Foreword by J. Cary Davis. Carbondale, Southern Illinois Univ. Press, 1970. 191 p. (Contemporary Latin American classics)

Includes *The quack doctor* by Juan Fernando Camilo Darthés and Carlos S. Damel; *The fate of Chipí Gonzáles* by José María Rivarola Matto; and *The man of the century* by Miguel Frank. Jones is a pioneer in the field of Spanish American theater, and greatly to be admired. These plays, however, are by second-rate playwrights. The translation is good.

7854. Luzuriaga, Gerardo and Robert S. Rudder *eds.* and *trans.* The orgy. Modern one-act plays from Latin America. Los Angeles, Univ. of California, Latin American Center, 1974. 180 p., plates (Latin American studies, 25)

Includes some standard names, Jorge Díaz, Osvaldo Dragún, Marco Denevi, Enrique Buenaventura, and others less well-known. *Black light*, the title play, *The orgy*, and *The eve of the execution* are the most interesting pieces. The collection demonstrates the vitality of contemporary Spanish American theater. Translations are good. Includes brief biographical notes.

7855. Oliver, William I. *ed.* and *trans.* Voices of change in the Spanish American theater. Anthology. Austin, Univ. of Texas Press, 1971. 294 p. (The Texas Pan American series book)

Six plays by important Spanish American playwrights, from the chilling *The camp* (Gambaro) to socially commited humor of *The day they let the lions loose*. Translated very well by a professor and director who knows the importance of free-flowing dialogue.

7855a. Woodyard, George *ed.* The modern stage in Latin America: six plays. N.Y., E.P. Dutton, 1971. 331 p.

Represented here are Marqués, Dias Gomes, Dragún, Díaz, Triana, and Carballido. Along with William Oliver's *Voices of change* (item 7855) this collection offers English speakers a good idea of what's going on in Spanish American theater. Marqués is competent, but the others here are first-rate talents. Various translators, generally good.

TRANSLATIONS FROM SPANISH

POETRY

7856. Aridjis, Homero. Blue spaces. Selected poems. Edited and with an introduction by Kenneth Rexroth. N.Y., Seabury Press, 1974. 191 p. (A continuum book)

Blue spaces, says critic John Fandel, is that space "wherein a distinction between what is so and what is said is increasingly erased." This volume also includes poems from two collections other than *Los espacios azules*. Distinguished translators (among them, Merwin, Weinberger, Tarn), consistently good translations.

7857. Borges, Jorge Luis. In praise of darkness. Translated from the Spanish by Norman Thomas di Giovanni. N.Y., E.P. Dutton, 1974. 142 p., bibl.

From the beginning, Borges' poems have been less intellectual, more accessible, more *human*, than his prose (a strange inversion?). This, one of his most recent collections of poems, along with a few brief prose pieces, intensifies the sense of the man (from "Plain Things:" "Past our oblivion they will live on,/ familiar, blind, not knowing we have gone;" from "In Praise of Darkness:" "Soon I shall know who I am"). Includes preface by Borges. Di Giovanni's translations are excellent, but increasingly in his translations, one feels the emergence of the personality of the *translator*. Borges is enough.

7858. Cardenal, Ernesto. Homage to the American Indians. Translated from the Spanish by Monique Altschul and Carlos Altschul. Baltimore, Md., John Hopkins Univ. Press, 1973. 116 p., illus.

In his prologue to the Spanish ed. (omitted here) José Miguel Oviedo speaks of the "lack of metaphor in Cardenal's poetry," the quality of "spare expression, humbly narrative, almost anecdotal." The translators are generally faithful to this tone, with only occasional lapses of specific word choices.

7859. Carrera Andrade, Jorge. Selected poems. Translated and with an introduction by H.R. Hays. Albany, State Univ. of New York Press, 1972. 259 p., plate.

This selection reflects the trajectory of a principal Ecuadorian poet, from surrealist to Americanist. Translations are almost literal, and reliable as an introduction to the North American reader, but lack the spark of poetry. *En face*.

7860. Cisneros, Antonio. The spider hangs too far from the ground. Translated from the Spanish by Maureen Ahern, William Rowe and David Tipton. N.Y., Cape Goliard Press, 1970. 1 v. (Unpaged)

Extremely interesting young poet, Peruvian, but not specifically Peruvian except in the instance of some poems with historical references. Perhaps it's a prejudice for *en face* editions of poetry, but the Spanish original is sorely missed, for although adequate, something, as they say, is lost . . .

7861. Cuadra, Pablo Antonio. El jaguar y la luna (The Jaguar and the moon). Translated by Thomas Merton. Greensboro, N.C., Unicorn Press, 1974. 38 p., illus.

Very handsome volume. Merton, who also has translated Cardenal, was obviously attracted by the subject matter, "the grim and vital Indian present." Very spare lines, nicely translated. Merton's introduction to and translations from *El jaguar y la luna* were originally published in *Emblems of a season of fury* (N.Y., New Directions, 1963).

7862. Fraire, Isabel. Poems. Translated and with an introduction by Thomas Hoeksema. Athens, Ohio, Mundus Artium Press, 1975. 99 p.

Hoeksema's excellent introduction details the pervading metaphors of light (and its absence) in these very personal (no, not feminine!) poems. Poetry, Fraire has said, is the attempt to "give flesh to light" [Hoeksema]. The translations read like poems. *En face*.

7863. Guillén, Nicolás. Man-making words. Selected poems. Translated from the Spanish, and with an introduction, by Robert Márquez and David Arthur McMurray. Amherst, Univ. of Massachusetts Press, 1972. 214 p.

Admirable edition, excellent introduction, very helpful glossary and notes, good selection. One receives a tremendous shock of recognition from the poem "My Last Name:" "My roots and the roots/ of my roots . . . Am I Yelofe?/ Maybe Guillén Banguila?/ or Kumbá?" Some of the sounds of Guillén's many voices are difficult to capture, but the translators have done a creditable job. *En face*.

7864. ———. ¡Patria o muerte!: the "Great Zoo" and other poems. Translated, edited and with an introduction by Robert Márquez. N.Y., Monthly Review Press, 1972. 222 p.

Márquez' states that volume is "concerned primarily with Guillén's poetry of social protest." Half the collection consists of the powerful satire of the "Zoo" poems "K.K.K., this quadruped originates/ in Joplin, Missouri./ Carnivorous./ It howls long in the night/ without its usual diet of roast Negro."), the second half of selected poems from works written between 1925-69. Márquez' approach to the translation was carefully considered, and results in a consistent voice. *En face.*

7865. Hernández, José. The gaucho Martín Fierro. Translated from the Spanish by Frank G. Carrino, Alberto J. Carlos, and Norman Mangouni. With an introduction by Carrino. N.Y., Delmar, 1974. 78 p., bibl., facsims.

Format and concept are excellent. Brief introduction, translation, brief bibliography, facsimile reproduction of 1872 La Pampa publication. But the problems have not been met. The translation captures neither rhythm, tone, nor language of the original.

7866. Lihn, Enrique. This endless malice. Twenty-five poems. Selected and translated by William Witherup and Serge Echeverría. Northwood Narrows, N.H., Lillabulero Press, 1969. 82 p.

As Witherup notes in a very brief foreword, Lihn is a difficult poet. These poems come from two of his collections, *La pieza oscura* and *Poesía de paso*, from the late 1960s. Surprisingly, perhaps? since the translators seem not to have been in contact with Lihn, a number of their translations are really fine, particularly one or two of the more transparent pieces. *En face.*

7867. Neruda, Pablo. The captain's verses. Translated from the Spanish, and with a brief introduction by Donald D. Walsh. N.Y., New Directions, 1972. 151 p. (A new directions book)

Poems in the vein of *Veinte poemas* . . . and *Cien sonetos*, first published anonymously, in honor of Matilde Urrutia: ("I shall scratch the earth to make you a cave/ and there your Captain/ will wait for you with flowers in the bed.") Flowers, and some anguish. Perhaps Walsh's best Neruda translation.

7868. ———. Extravagaria. Translated from the Spanish by Alastair Reid. With a translator's note. London, Cape, 1972. 303 p.

A little of everything (a concrete poem, a poem with commentary, one of his most anthologized poems, "Fábula de la Sirena y los Borrachos," the refutation of a refrán, "Por Boca Cerrada Entran las Moscas"). This collection enjoys an overall sunniness and good nature. Reid says he has refined these translations. The sensitivity of the lines reflects this dedication. *En face.*

7869. ———. Five decades: 1925-1970. Translated from the Spanish, and with an introduction by Ben Belitt. N.Y., Grove Press, 1974. 431 p.

An anthology meant to have been "festive," marking the 70th birthday of Neruda, was instead posthumous. In spite of the tragedy of his death, the book fulfills its purpose, "to reflect the continuum of five decades" of his work. The Neruda translations have undoubtedly been the most controversial of the decade, the translators, the most contentious. And Belitt, probably the most criticized. Primarily, for basic errors in reading the Spanish, ultimately, and more importantly, for his interpretation, rather than his translation, of the poems. This anthology has the virtues of presenting a wide spectrum of Neruda.

7870. ———. Fully empowered. Translated from the Spanish by Alastair Reid. N.Y., Farrar, Straus & Giroux, 1975. 135 p.

Poems of his beloved Isla Negra, friends, sea, man, flower, stone, in other words, act of creation. Seven of the poems of this translation appeared in *Selected poems* edited by Nathaniel Tarn, but they have been substantially revised, primarily in the direction of simplification. A fine translation. *En face.*

7871. ———. A new decade. Poems: 1958-1967. Edited and with an introduction by Ben Belitt. Translations from the Spanish by Ben Belitt and Alastair Reid. N.Y., Grove Press, 1958. 274 p.

Includes a number of the translations available elsewhere (notably the Reid translation of *Estravagaria*, here called *Book of vagaries*) and *Fully Empowered* (here called *Full power*). A major introduction by Belitt, but translating honors go to Reid.

7872. ———. New poems: 1968-1970. Edited, translated from the Spanish and with an introduction by Ben Belitt. N.Y., Grove Press, 1972. 153 p.

Selections from *Las manos del día* (1968), *Fin de mundo* (1969), and *Las piedras del cielo* (1970). In his introduction, Belitt makes the important point that the reader cannot expect to pin Neruda down; as Neruda said, the poet must "change his furniture," but not his soul. While it seems that Belitt understands Neruda well, and appreciates him, these are not the ultimate Neruda translations. *En face.*

7873. ———. Residence on earth. Translated from the Spanish and with a brief introduction by Donald Walsh. N.Y., New Directions, 1973. 359 p.

Landmark in the voluminous *obra* of Neruda. There is a lot of poetic movement in this work (from the "hermetic" to the humanitarian," to use Alexander Coleman's words). Therefore, the language of the translation should also move, but instead, the "voice" remains constant throughout the translations. Again, the fatal over-reliance on cognates, so common in Spanish-English translations. (Certain of these poems are among Neruda's most translated pieces. A natural exercise for classes or workshops in translation.) *En face.*

7874. ———. Selected poems: a bilingual edition. Edited and with a brief introduction by Nathaniel Tarn. Translations from the Spanish by Nathaniel Tarn; Anthony Kerrigan; W.S. Merwin; and Alastair Reid. N.Y., Delacorte Press, 1972. 509 p. (A Delta book)

Representative selection of Neruda's work through 1967. To date, the best *selection* available in English. A stellar array of translators, however, a North American ear detects a certain British tone to the translations—which is to be expected. There are superb moments, as well as occasional lapses. Reid's translations are probably most consistently superior, but overall, especially considering the differing "voices," the quality is good. The basic Neruda English reader. *En face.*

7875. ———. Song of protest. Translated and with an introduction by Miguel Alagarín. N.Y., William Morrow, 1976. 118 p.

Introduction, "The Politics of Poetry," explains the importance of Neruda's political poetry to a New Yorker of Puerto Rican family. The poems, written by Neruda in praise of the Castro revolution, are well-translated. The Spanish originals would be welcome.

7876. Parra, Nicanor. Emergency poems. Translated from the Spanish and with an introduction by Miller Williams. N.Y., New Directions, 1972. 154 p.

Parra's innovative poems, characterized by the translator as consisting of "dark humor, disjointed logic, flatness of tone, directness of statement, suspicion of many of the stock poetical devices," and which Edith Grossman similarly suggests consists of the insistence "that antipoetry depend on the common-place in all its ramifications," are beautifully translated here. Very close, indeed to the original. *En face.*

7877. Paz, Octavio. ¿Aguila o sol? (Eagle or sun?). Translated from the Spanish by Eliot Weinberger. N.Y., New Directions, 1976. 121 p. (A new directions book)

This new ed. is a revised version of earlier publications of the same materials. Prose poems, fragments, impressions, memories, inventions, these poems of the late 1940s and early 1950s offer special problems to the translator. Weinberger has met the challenge of word play, alliteration and language convincingly.

(The title has always bothered me, even though it is explained in the first piece: ¿*Cara o cruz, águila o sol?/Heads or tails? eagle or sun?*) *En face.*

7878. ———. Configurations. With an introduction by Muriel Rukeyser. Various translators. N.Y., New Directions, 1971. 198 p.

Important collection of Paz' poetry, spanning the years between the landmark poems "Piedra de Sol/Sun Stone" (1959) and "Blanco" (1966). The Rukeyser and Kemp translations are the best, others, of varying quality. *En face.*

7879. Renga: a chain of poems. Translation by Charles Tomlinson. With an introduction by Claude Roy. N.Y., George Brazilier, 1972. 95 p.

Complex, ritualistic, elegant exercise. Primarily the concept of Paz (with an assist by Roy), this collective poem has four authors: Paz, Jacques Roubaud, Edoardo Sanguineti, and the translator Charles Tomlinson. Roubaud offers the rules of the Renga, Tomlinson describes the process of composition. Paz' comments alone (including those on translation, "Our century is the century of translations") are worth the price of the book. Tomlinson's translation is a tour de force. *En face.*

7880. Vallejo, César. Human poems. Translated from the Spanish and with an introduction by Clayton Eshleman. N.Y., Grove Press, 1968. 326 p.

Eshleman worked valiantly to put an order to the poems of this collection, Vallejo's most powerful poems, as well as some of the most moving poems of Latin American literature. The translator can capture a line or a phrase with great feeling, but at the same time defeats occasionally the lines by choosing a cognate out of tune with the tone of the Spanish. A moving collection. *En face.*

7881. ———. Spain, let this cup pass from me. Translated from the Spanish by Alvaro Cardona-Hines. Fairfax, Calif., Red Hill Press, 1972. 51 p.

Surreal and shattering, these poems rank among the most expressive resulting from the Spanish Civil War. They offer grave problems to a translator, some of which may never be solved. Cardona-Hines apologizes for the literalness of his translations, believing that "any attempt to correct these would have taken him too far from the terse meaning of the original." Actually, the opposite is true, literalness moves the English farther away from the original. (An index would be helpful.) *En face.*

NOVELS

7882. Asturias, Miguel Angel. Men of maize. Translated from the Spanish by

Gerald Martin. N.Y., Delacorte Press/Seymour Lawrence, 1975. 337 p. (A Merloyd Lawrence book)

This is—as aficionados of magical realism are aware—Asturias at his most mythic—and most difficult. The puns and orthographic devices, the highly local vocabulary, all pose serious problems. The translation really doesn't capture the original. Contains a helpful glossary.

7883. ———. Strong wind. Translated from the Spanish by Gregory Rabassa. N.Y., Delacorte Press, 1968. 242 p. (Seymour Lawrence books)

Asturias himself believes that *Strong wind* "marks the beginning of a new method of writing novels." Not as mythic as his *Leyendas* or *Men of maize*, the language still presents enormous problems for a translator. "'For a translator," Asturias says, "to put himself into my books is as difficult as for a European who has never seen America to understand our landscape." Even Rabassa, the best of Asturias' translators, is not up to par here.

7884. Benedetti, Mario. The truce. Translated from the Spanish by Benjamin Graham. N.Y., Harper & Row, 1969. 184 p.

"A statement not just about a single man, but about the Uruguayan people." (John S. Brushwood); "The vehicle of a vision of life" (Arthur Gold), this brief, well-structured novel by a lesser-known author recounts a temporary "truce" in a lonely life, which the diary format makes very personal. Good translation.

7885. Benítez, Fernando. Poisoned water. Translated from the Spanish by Mary E. Ellsworth. With brief foreword by J. Cary Davis. Carbondale, Southern Illinois Univ. Press, 1973. 152 p.

One more in what is one of Latin America's most persistent sub-genres, the novel of the political boss. Supposedly based on real events. Author, a professional journalist and author of many non-fiction books on all aspects of Mexican life, narrates from the point of view of a parish priest. Translation is occasionally stiff.

7886. Cabrera Infante, Guillermo. Three trapped tigers. Translated from the Cuban by Donald Gardner and Suzanne Jill Levine in collaboration with the author. N.Y., Harper & Row, 1971. 487 p., illus.

A gallery of voices, Cabrera Infante has said of his novel, written in a Cuban he expected no one other than the residents of a few square blocks in Havana to be able to understand. The translation is one of the most interesting of the decade. In collaboration with the author, Gardner and Levine have re-written TTT. It was the only way; nothing else would have approached the text, which is 50 percent word play, game, and linguistic satire. The result is very effective. The most noticeable lapses occur in monologues in which the tone is not completely established.

7887. Carballido, Emilio. The norther. Translated from the Spanish by Margaret Sayers Peden. With an introduction by the translator. Austin, Univ. of Texas Press, 1968. 101 p. (A Texas Pan American series book)

7888. Carpentier, Alejo. Reasons of state. Translated from the Spanish by Frances Partridge. N.Y., Knopf, 1976. 308 p.

The novel of the *caudillo* is alive and well, universalized, at the same time it is Americanized, here by Carpentier. Erudite, baroque, self-parodying, encompassing—as seen in the epilogue: ". . . the Earth is all one and that the earth of the Earth is earth of the Earth everywhere." Fine translation (*could* anything be done with *El recurso del método*?).

7889. ———. War of time. Translated from the Spanish by Frances Partridge. N.Y., Knopf, 1970. 179 p.

Alan Cheuse has called the "High Road of St. James," one of the five stories contained here, a brilliant short novel. The collection as a whole enjoyed a rather good critical reception. "Manhunt," from the Spanish edition, has not been included. Competent translation.

7890. Cortázar, Julio. A model kit, 62. Translated from the Spanish by Gregory Rabassa. N.Y., Pantheon Books, 1972. 281 p.

Continuation of *Hopscotch* in more ways than the fact it evolves from chap. 62 of that novel, the model kit, as Cortázar states "is the book he (the reader) has chosen to read." Excellent translation.

7891. Díaz Sánchez, Ramón. Cumboto. Translated from the Spanish by John Upton. Illustrated by Kermit Oliver. Austin, Univ. of Texas Press, 1969. 273 p., illus. (The Texas Pan American series book)

Cumboto was chosen by the Ibero-American Novel Project of the William Faulkner Foundation as the most notable novel published in Ibero-America between 1945-62. One might have thought this novel Brazilian rather than Venezuelan, if not for the nationality of the author. A saga of the estate Cumboto, the intermingling of white and black blood lines, magic, treasure, the deterioration of the white man in hostile tropics. Told through the person of Natividad, and very convincingly translated by Upton.

7892. Donoso, José. The obscene bird of night. Translated from the Spanish by Hardie St. Martin and Leonard Mades. N.Y., Knopf, 1973. 448 p.

A major novel by Chile's principal novelist in a translation called "brilliant and savage" (*The New Yorker*). As in so many contemporary Latin American novels, a virtuoso performance is demanded on the part of the translator (here, translators). St. Martin and Mades won the PEN prize for translation (1974) for their fine work.

7893. ———. Sacred families. Three novelas. Translated from the Spanish by Andrée Conrad. N.Y., Knopf, 1977. 206 p. (A Borzoi book)

One of three translations of Donoso works in 1977, these three novellas portray the emptiness of bourgeois life—a fact made more evident by the original title: *Tres novelitas burguesas*. Good Donoso, good translation.

7894. Fuentes, Carlos. A change of skin. Translated from the Spanish by Sam Hileman. N.Y., Farrar, Straus & Giroux, 1968. 462 p.

Sixth of Fuentes' nine novels this may be his most controversial book. The Italian critical reception was probably the warmest. In the US, the translation was questioned, probably because it is more an "improvisation" (Raymond West) than a translation—though it reads very well. The omission of sizeable portions of the original is puzzling.

7895. ———. Terra nostra. Translated from the Spanish by Margaret S. Peden. N.Y., Farrar, Straus & Giroux, 1976. 778 p.

7896. Galindo, Sergio. The precipice. Translated from the Spanish by John Brushwood and Carolyn Brushwood. With drawings by Luis Eades. Austin, Univ. of Texas Press, 1969. 185 p., illus. (A Texas Pan American series book)

Family saga by writer often eclipsed by his countryman Carlos Fuentes. Brushwood (critic and co-translator) has pointed out that although the novel is specifically Mexican, the main thrust is on character, not local color. Good translation by the Brushwood team.

7897. García Márquez, Gabriel. The autumn of the patriarch. Translated from the Spanish by Gregory Rabassa. N.Y., Harper & Row, 1976. 269 p.

A major novel, of course. And the second major Rabassa (García Márquez) translation of the decade (a large section was published in *The New Yorker* prior to book publication). An almost uninterrupted flow from first to final page, Rabassa recreates "the time of eternity" of the original. Deserving recipient of the 1977 PEN translation prize.

7898. ———. One hundred years of solitude. Translated from the Spanish by Gregory Rabassa. N.Y., Harper & Row, 1970. 422 p.

Without question, the single most important translation of the decade. The influence, and wide recognition, of this novel is without parallel. "With a single bound," as John Leonard said, García Márquez is an established figure to English language readers and critics. Probably Rabassa's best translation.

7899. Goldenberg, Isaac. The fragmented life of Don Jacobo Lerner. Translated from the Spanish by Robert S. Picciotto. N.Y., Persea Books, 1976. 186 p.

Echoing the title, fragmented technique of narrating fragmented lives; the theme is that of the Diaspora. The author is Peruvian, and novel follows flight of Russian Jew to a new life in Peru. Skillful translation.

7900. Lezama Lima, José. Paradiso. Translated from the Spanish by Gregory Rabassa. With a publishers' thanks to Mercedes Cortázar and the Center for Inter-American Relations. N.Y., Farrar, Straus & Giroux, 1974. 466 p.

There will of course not be another novel from Lezama Lima, and this stands as his master work. Baroquest of the baroque, the autobiographical overtones of the work (undoubtedly, its intricacy as well) have brought inevitable comparisons to Joyce and Proust. This denseness presents real difficulty to translation, which may explain why this is not the best of Rabassa's efforts.

7901. López Portillo y Pacheco, José. Quetzalcoátl. Translated from the Spanish by Eliot Weinberger and Diana S. Goodrich. N.Y., The Seabury Press, 1976. 151 p. (A continuum book)

This novel by the President of Mexico is a fictionalized version of the Quetzalcoátl (Plumed Serpent) legend. In an author's note, López Portillo states that he deals "with a human figure of mysterious character and ... the philosophical principle with which he is identified in the Indian Theogony." Good translation; captures satisfactorily the difficult mythical tone.

7902. Mujica-Láinez, Manuel. Bomarzo. Translated from the Spanish by Gregory Rabassa. N.Y., Simon and Schuster, 1969. 573 p.

Not a "Spanish American novel," but an historical novel by a Spanish American (Argentine) author. The novel is set in 16th-century Italy, its protagonist, Pier Francesco Orsini, Duke of Bomarzo. First person narrative, very rich in description. Good Rabassa.

7903. Onetti, Juan Carlos. A brief life. Translated from the Spanish by Hortense Carpentier. N.Y., Viking, 1976. 280 p.

A work years ahead of its time, *A brief life* was variously received by English reviewers as "a work of insurmountable obscurity," and "a remarkable novel," a "virtuosic" performance. The Brausen, Díaz Grey, Arce persona, labyrinthine interior passages, all make it a milestone on the way to the contemporary Spanish American novel. Fortunately, the translation is not bad, but it is not of the level of the original.

7904. Puig, Manuel. Betrayed by Rita Hayworth. Translated from the Spanish by Suzanne Jill Levine. N.Y., E.P. Dutton, 1971. 222 p.

Puig has said he never wanted to write, he had planned a career in film; and *Betrayed by Rita Hayworth*, he says, was simply the account of his personal limitations. He is too modest, this novel of provincial Argentine life is real to a generation who grew up with Hollywood heroes. Good translation.

7905. ———. The Buenos Aires affair: a detective novel. Translated from the Spanish by Suzanne Jill Levine. N.Y., E.P. Dutton, 1976. 259 p.

Third of Puig's novels, *The Buenos Aires affair* continues his experimentation with form and his self-confessed love affair with movies. Perhaps the darkest of his four novels. Levine is a first-rate translator.

7906. ———. Heartbreak tango, a serial. Translated from the Spanish by Suzanne Jill Levine. N.Y., E.P. Dutton, 1975. 224 p.

Puig is one of contemporary literature's great satirists; the soap opera and Saturday matinee raised to the level of moving literature. And he is one of the few who is funny. Humor is not a constant in the literature of contemporary Latin America.

7907. Sainz, Gustavo. Gazapo. Translated from the Spanish by Hardie St. Martin. N.Y., Farrar, Straus & Giroux, 1968. 179 p.

Sainz makes the now-familiar demands upon the reader, demanding that he sort out the details of this boy-girl-in-love story from the many narrative devices. (One sees, too, Sainz' interest in film, an influence shared by most contemporaries.) Great reliance is placed on everyday speech, and the translation does not capture the colloquial tone.

7908. Vargas Llosa, Mario. Conversation in the cathedral. Translated from the Spanish by Gregory Rabassa. N.Y., Harper & Row, 1975. 601 p.

Vargas Llosa's most complex novel stylistically, this barroom "conservation" is revolutionary is the now time-worn cliché of contemporary Latin American literature, both politically and novelistically. Rabassa does occasionally make mistakes, but one must look for them carefully. More important is the whole, and that, as usual, is excellent.

7909. ———. The green house. Translated from the Spanish by Gregory Rabassa. N.Y., Harper & Row, 1968. 383 p.

"There's nothing like the jungle," says one of the characters in this very exotic novel. Typical of Vargas Llosa's narrative style, the reader struggles through jungle liana and desert sand to untangle the many narrative lines, but the trip is worthwhile. Rabassa has made one of his best translations here.

7910. Yáñez, Agustín. The lean lands. Translated from the Spanish by Ethel Brinton. Illustrated by Alberto Beltrán. Austin, Univ. of Texas Press, 1968. 328 p., illus. (A Texas Pan American series book)

Not as important as *The edge of the storm*, this novel, nevertheless, illustrates the qualities that cause critics to consider Yáñez as the immediate Mexican precursor to the authors of the current Boom. Brinton's translation tends towards the formal.

SHORT STORIES AND MISCELLANEOUS PROSE

7911. Borges, Jorge Luis. The Aleph and other stories: 1933-1969. Edited and translated from the Spanish by Norman Thomas di Giovanni in collaboration with the author. N.Y., E.P. Dutton, 1970. 286 p., bibl.

Stated purpose of this collection is "to make available in English all my previously untranslated older stories, as well as to offer a sampling from my latest work in this form." The brief preface (jointly signed J.L.B./N.T. diG) addresses the problems of translation, the desire of author and translator to "rethink every sentence in English words." Rights to retranslate some of the author's most important stories was denied. Lástima. This should be the ultimately ideal situation for translation, and results are fine.

7912. ——. The book of sand. Translated from the Spanish by Norman Thomas di Giovanni. N.Y., E.P. Dutton, 1977. 125 p.

Thirteen new stories; perhaps of most interest to the totally dedicated fan or student is a Borges oddity: a love story. "The theme of love is quite common in my poems but not in my prose, which offers no other example than 'Ulrike'." Perhaps the best piece is the title story. A good translation. Includes author's note and afterword.

7913. ——. Doctor Brodie's report. Translated from the Spanish by Norman Thomas di Giovanni. N.Y., E.P. Dutton, 1972. 128 p.

Borges' afterword states, "Since 1953, after a longish interval of composing only poems and short prose pieces, these are the first stories I have written." Though they lack the diversity of earlier fictions, these "stories" are identifiably Borges. And though the content varies, there is a sameness about the format—most are attributed to a second person who is the "teller." Among the most interesting pages are those of the preface to the first edition and the new afterword. Translated almost simultaneously to the writing by Borges' long-time translator.

7914. ——. A universal history of infamy. Translated from the Spanish by Norman Thomas di Giovanni. With two brief introductions (1954 and 1935 editions) by the author. N.Y., E.P. Dutton, 1972. 146 p.

Though Borges himself has repudiated his earlier writings, among them this supposed chronicle of cruel individuals throughout history (which he calls "the irresponsible games of a shy young man who dared not write stories"), the pieces in this collection are nonetheless among those that created his reputation. The translation, resulting from the Borges/Di Giovanni collaboration, which lasted several years, is excellent.

7915. —— and **Adolfo Bioy-Casares.** Chronicles of Bustos Domencq. Translated from the Spanish by Norman Thomas di Giovanni. N.Y., E.P. Dutton, 1976. 143 p.

Not very important Borges. Though not terribly far removed from the spoof of a piece like "Tlön Uqbar," by comparison these pieces seem forced and self-conscious. The translation is fine, one more of the Borges-Di Giovanni collaboration.

7916. —— and ——. Extraordinary tales. Edited, translated and with foreword by Anthony Kerrigan. N.Y., Herder and Herder, 1971. 144 p.

As Kerrigan states, "an anthology of 'nightmares of great consequence' and of sheer moments of blinding insomniac consequence/inconsequence." A bizarre collection of fragments which Borges and Bioy Casares call "narratives." Stultifying *and* mind-boggling. Excellent translation. Includes foreword, note on the original texts and preliminary note. Original ed. titled *Cuentos breves y extraordinarios* (B.A., Editorial Santiago Rueda, 1967).

7917. Cortázar, Julio. All fires the fire. Translated from the Spanish by Suzanne Jill Levine. N.Y., Pantheon Books, 1973. 152 p.

Much more conventional in *form* than his novels, Cortázar's stories are unlimited insofar as content, ranging freely through time and space. And there are those who believe he is a better short story writer than novelist. At any rate, this is an excellent collection, excellently translated.

7918. ——. Cronopios and famas. Translated from the Spanish by Paul Blackburn. N.Y., Pantheon, 1969. 161 p., illus.

In a recent interview with Frank MacShane, Cortázar speaks of his pleasure when Cuban *guerrilleros* told him that when recovering from exhaustion they "like to read from . . . *Cronopios y famas*," not Lenin or Marx. Good advice for exhaustion. A fine translation.

7919. García Márquez, Gabriel. Leaf storm, and other stories. Translated from the Spanish by Gregory Rabassa. N.Y., Harper & Row, 1972. 146 p.

The publication of this collection postdates the monumental translation of *A hundred years of solitude*, but the Macondo of the novella *Leaf storm* predates that creation. A number of the stories, however, notably "The Handsomest Drowned Man in the World," "A Very Old Man with Enormous Wings," and "The Last Voyage of the Ghost Ship" belong to the logical illogic of the world of *A hundred years . . .* Though García Márquez the short story writer has been over-shadowed by García Márquez the novelist, we would have known his name well if the stories were all we had.

7920. Levine, Suzanne Jill and **Hallie D. Taylor** *eds.* and *trans.* Triple cross. Holy place [by] Carlos Fuentes. Hell has no limits [by] José Donoso. From Cuba with a song [by] Severo Sarduy.

Translated from the Spanish by Suzanne Jill Levine and Hallie D. Taylor. N.Y., E.P. Dutton, 1972. 329 p.

Three novellas that work very well together. (The subtitle here should be *Study in the Baroque*). *Holy place* deserves more attention, and it is good to see it translated. *From Cuba with a song*, one might have thought untranslatable; it's done very well, though even the Spanish reader misses a great deal unless he's a student of African religion. *Hell has no limits* is Donoso on the way to *The obscene bird of night*, transvestitism and illusion. Each of the three is obsessed with shifting identities. The translator(s) have captured the many voices.

7921. Martínez Estrada, Ezequiel. X-ray of the pampa. Translated from the Spanish by Alain Swietlicki. With an introduction by Thomas F. McGann. Austin, Univ. of Texas Press, 1971. 415 p. (A Texas Pan American series book)

Martin S. Stabb called these essays "merciless." Thomas F. McGann, in his introduction, defines them as "part history, part essay in social psychology, part prophecy." They are not widely read, but should be required reading for any individual who wants to know Argentina, (in the same way that one who wants to know Mexico must read *Labyrinth of solitude*). Alain Swietlicki has penetrated Martínez Estrada's dense style in an excellent translation.

7922. Monterroso, Augusto. The black sheep and other fables. Translated from the Spanish by Walter I. Bradbury. N.Y., Doubleday, 1974. 113 p., illus.

Described by his translator as a writer with a profound sense of humor, not a humorist, Monterroso, like all good fabulists, displays a delicious sense of satire ("It is said that once upon a time, a long time ago, there was a catholic ... who, assailed by doubts, began to think seriously of becoming a Christian"). A handsome and entertaining volume well-translated by distinguished editor-here-turned-translator, Walter Bradbury.

7923. Neruda, Pablo. Memorias. Translated from the Spanish by Hardie St. Martin. N.Y., Farrar, Straus & Giroux, 1977. 370 p.

There are few specific comments here about his works (rather people, places, events in his life), yet these words say everything about Neruda's writing. We are fortunate he lived to write his *Memoirs* (life, often, is not so tidy). There are delights here: from these pages fall "yellow leaves on their way to death, and grapes that will find new life in the sacred wine." A good translation. For comment on Spanish original, see item 7234.

7924. Paz, Octavio. Alternating current. Translated from the Spanish by Helen R. Lane. N.Y., Viking Press, 1973. 215 p. (A Richard Seaver book)

"A tissue of relations," Paz says; if so, a beautiful tissue. Thoughts, meditations, really, by this incomparable poet/philosopher. Grouped by Paz from journal publications into three sections: 1) What Does Poetry Name?; 2) Knowledge, Drugs, Inspiration; and 3) Revolt, Revolution, Rebellion. Paz is fortunate in Helen Lane's translations.

7925. ———. Conjunctions and disjunctions. Translated from the Spanish by Helen R. Lane. N.Y., The Viking Press, 1974. 148 p., plate (A Richard Seaver book)

Paz' remarkable series of essays on love and sexuality ("The Metaphor," "Conjugations," "Eve and Prajnaparamita," "Order and Accident") contrasting and juxtaposing Orient and Occident, sexuality and politics, concluding with the perception of a "new time" glimpsed in the alliance of poetry and rebellion. Helen Lane's translation of this dense prose is, as usual, excellent.

7926. ———. The siren & the seashell, and other essays on poets and poetry. Translated from the Spanish by Lysander Kemp and Margaret Sayers Peden. Illustrated by Barry Moser. Austin, Univ. of Texas Prss, 1976. 188 p., illus. (A Texas Pan American series book)

7927. Quiroga, Horacio. The decapitated chicken and other stories. Selected and translated from the Spanish by Margaret Sayers Peden, introduction by George D. Schade. Illustrated by Ed Lindloff. Austin, Univ. of Texas Press, 1976. 176 p., illus. (A Texas Pan American series book)

7928. Soto, Pedro Juan. Spiks. Translated from the Spanish, and with an introduction by Victoria Ortiz. N.Y., Monthly Review Press, 1973. 92 p.

Stories, and fragments called "miniatures," that document the despair of N.Y.'s Puerto Rican ghettos. Biting, bitter humor. An interesting talent. The translations have the sound of authentic street language.

7929. Valenzuela, Luisa. Clara. Thirteen short stories and a novel. Translated from the Spanish by Hortense Carpentier and J. Jorge Castello. N.Y., Harcourt, Brace & Jovanovich, 1976. 233 p.

These stories and novella by a young Argentine writer are primarily about women, and love—or, more accurately, about the search for or the loss of love. The interest is in character studies; setting and plot are of lesser importance. The novel, particularly is well translated.

PLAYS

7930. Carballido, Emilio. The golden thread and other plays. Translated from the Spanish by Margaret Sayers Peden. With an introduction by the translator. Austin, Univ. of Texas Press, 1970. 224 p.

7931. Neruda, Pablo. Splendor and death of Joaquín Murieta. Translated from the Spanish by Ben Belitt. N.Y., Farrar, Straus & Giroux, 1972. 182 p.

Neruda's Chilean hero drawn to California gold, a section, he says, that galloped out of The Barcarole. Belitt justifies, rightly, the need for certain liberties in the California setting: "The *yanqui* reader, however . . . has a right to expect an American 'sound' not present in the inflection of Neruda." However, as usual, the translation comes out with a large dose of Belitt and not enough Neruda. Incidentally, the *en face* correlation becomes very annoying.

7932. Wolff, Egon. Paper flowers: a play in six scenes. Translated from the Spanish by Margaret Sayers Peden. With an introduction by the translator. Columbia, Univ. of Missouri Press, 1971. 78 p.

TRANSLATIONS FROM PORTUGUESE

POETRY

7934. Andrade, Mário de. Hallucinated city. Translated from the Portuguese by Jack E. Tomlins. With an introduction by the translator. Nashville, Tenn., Vanderbilt Univ. Press, 1968. 100 p.

Author is the so-called "Pope of Futurism," father of Brazilian Modernist poetry. These 22 poems addressed to São Paulo are filled with humor and conscious extravagance. The translation is literal, overly indebted to cognates, but dependable. Helpful introduction.

7935. Barge, Ernest J. and **Jan Feidel** *trans.* The warriors: *peleja* between Joaquim Jaquiera and Manoel Barra Mansa. Illustrated by Donald Canzana. N.Y., Grossman, 1972. 131 p., illus. (A Mushinsha book)

There was a time in Brazilian literature when the ethnographers were absorbing "popular literature." Has that been reserved? This *desafio* (whose origins may be in the similar Baroque *glosa*) is popular literature at its most entertaining. The translators are shackled by the demands of the text, but are generally satisfying. *En face*.

NOVELS

7936. Amado, Jorge. Dona Flor and her two husbands: a moral and amorous tale. Translated from the Portuguese by Harriet de Onís. N.Y., Knopf, 1969. 576 p.

Appreciated for its exhuberance and sensuality, its evocation of Bahia, this robust and zestful novel has enjoyed an unusual success in the US. One of De Onís' better translations, but not as good as Shelby on Amado. Brief glossary.

7937. Azevedo, Aluizio. A Brazilian tenement. Translated from the Portuguese by Harry W. Brown. N.Y., Howard Fertig, 1976. 320 p., illus.

Aluizio Azevedo is the father of Brazilian realism/naturalism and this novel (*O cortiço*) is considered to be his major work. The translation, however, is flawed from the beginning because of the decision to omit certain "incidents" and "details" because of the "squeamish sensibilities of our reading public." Reprint of first ed. (N.Y., R.M. McBride, 1926).

7938. Callado, Antonio. Don Juan's bar. Translated from the Portuguese by Barbara Shelby. N.Y., Knopf, 1972. 271 p.

In the same political vein as his more widely-known *Quarup*. A good translation except for an occasional old-fashioned turn of phrase.

7939. Castro, Josue de. Of men and crabs. With "a rather generous" preface by . . . Translated from the Portuguese by Susan Hertelendy. N.Y., Vanguard Press, 1970. 190 p.

Fictionalized bibliography, reminiscence, fiction, this book by a specialist on world hunger is a very moving protrait of his homeland in Recife, and the resemblances and relationships between crab and man. The translation is very smooth and easy and appropriate to the original.

7940. Machado de Assis, Joaquim Maria. Counselor Ayres' memorial. Translated from the Portuguese by Helen Caldwell. With an introduction by the translator. Berkeley, Univ. of California Press, 1972. 196 p.

Machado de Assis probably has the greatest immediate recognition to a North American reader of any Brazilian writer. His major novels have all been translated. This is the last, and the most recent translation. Again translated by Helen Caldwell, who devoted a career to studying and translating this author's works.

7941. ——. The hand and the glove. Translated from the Portuguese by Albert I. Bagby, Jr. With an introduction by the translator. Foreword by Helen Caldwell. Lexington, The Univ. Press of Kentucky, 1970. 116 p.

This small novel is from the first of the author's two periods, the Romantic phase which is not as highly regarded critically as his later work. The translation of period novels raises serious questions, never satisfactorily resolved: to what degree does the translator "modernize" (or in this case, "de-Romanticize") the text? The translator has, I believe, erred in favor of maintaining the period, to the detriment of universality.

7942. Pereira, Antonio Olavo. Marcoré. Translated from the Portuguese by Alfred Hower and John Saunders. With an introduction by Alfred Hower. Illustrated by Newton Cavalcanti. Austin, Univ. of Texas Press, 1969. 234 p., illus.

Critical and popular success, a simple, straightforward story expressed through first person narrative. Very well-crafted characters. The translation is smooth, and appropriate to the tone of the novel.

SHORT STORIES

7943. Grossman, William L. *ed.* and *trans*. Modern Brazilian short stories. Berkeley, Univ. of California Press, 1968. 167 p.

"Almost all the authors of these stories," writes the translator, "manifest in varying degree the nationalistic tendency of modernism." The stories do seem a representative selection. ("The Piano," at least, has been anthologized previously.) Some are memorable (Guimarães Rosa's "The Third Bank of the River," for example). Generally good translation, with some awkwardness in passages of dialogue.

7944. Machado de Assis, Joaquim Maria. The devil's church and other stories. Translated from the Portuguese by Jack Schmitt and Lorie Ishimatsu. With an introduction by the translators. Austin, Univ. of Texas Press, 1977. 152 p., illus. (The Texas Pan American series)

A few of these stories have been previously translated, but the majority appear for the first time, an addition to the body of work available to the English reader who wants to study this well-known Brazilian writer. Primarily concerned with plot, these pieces can be read as social commentary. Translations are generally good, but occasionally waver slightly, primarily because of questions of how to maintain the tone of the time.

7945. Trevisan, Dalton. The vampire of Curitiba and other stories. Translated from the Portuguese and with an introduction by Gregory Rabassa. N.Y., Knopf, 1972. 267 p.

Tales from four collections of brief fiction; some pieces are almost fragments. For those who don't know Trevisan, he is an amazing discovery. Rabassa, in an excellent introduction, cites Trevisan's response to those who await his novel: his movement is not towards the long fictional form, but towards the sonnet, and from there, the haiku. Trevisan may have been joking, but these pieces are in accord with the remark. Fine translation.

JOURNAL ABBREVIATIONS

AATSP/H	Hispania. American Association of Teachers of Spanish and Portuguese. Univ. of Cincinnati. Cincinnati, Ohio.
ACO/B	Boletín de la Academia Colombiana. Bogotá.
ANH/B	Boletín de la Academia Nacional de Historia. B.A.
APL/R	Revista da Academia Paulista de Letras. São Paulo.
AR	Areito. Areíto, Inc. N.Y.
ASAWI/B	Bulletin. African Studies Association of the West Indies. Kingston.
BNJM/R	Revista de la Biblioteca Nacional José Martí. La Habana.
BRP	Beiträge zur Romanischen Philologie. Rütten & Loening. Berlin, FRG.
CAM	Cuadernos Americanos. México.
CDLA	Casa de las Américas. Instituto Cubano del Libro. La Habana.
CDLA/CO	Conjunto. Revista de teatro latinoamericano. Casa de las Américas *for the* Comité Permanente de Festivales. La Habana.
CELRG/A	Araisa. Anuario del Centro de Estudios Latinoamericanos Rómulo Gallegos. Caracas.
CH	Cuadernos Hispanoamericanos. Instituto de Cultura Hispánica. Madrid.
CLA/J	CLA Journal. The College Language Association. Morgan State College. Baltimore, Md.
CM/NRFH	Nueva Revista de Filología Hispánica. El Colegio de México [and] the Univ. of Texas. México.
COLOQ	Colóquio. Revista de artes e letras. Fundação Calouste Gulbenkian. Lisbon.
CONAC/RNC	Revista Nacional de Cultura. Consejo Nacional de Cultura. Caracas. See VME/R.
ESP	Espiral. Revista mensual de artes y letras. Editorial Iqueima. Bogotá.
EUR	Europe. Revue mensuelle. Paris.
EX	Exilio. N.Y.
HISP	Hispanófila. Univ. of North Carolina. Chapel Hill.
HISPA	Hispamérica. Revista de literatura. Takoma Park, Md.
HIUS/R	Revista Hispánica Moderna. Columbia Univ., Hispanic Institute in the United States. N.Y.
HM	Harper's Magazine. Harper Brothers Publishers. N.Y.
HR	Hispanic Review. A quarterly devoted to research in the Hispanic languages and literatures. Univ. of Pennsylvania, Dept. of Romance Languages. Philadelphia.
IAA	Ibero-Amerikanisches Archiv. Ibero-Amerikanisches Institut. Berlin, FRG.
IAHG/AHG	Antropología e Historia de Guatemala. Instituto de Antropología e Historia de Guatemala. Guatemala.
ICC/T	Thesaurus. Instituto Caro y Cuervo. Bogotá.
ICP/R	Revista del Instituto de Cultura Puertorriqueña. San Juan.
IFH/C	Conjonction. Institut Français d'Haïti. Port-au-Prince.
IGFO/RI	Revista de Indias. Instituto Gonzalo Fernández de Oviedo [and] Consejo Superior de Investigaciones Científicas. Madrid.
IILI/RI	Revista Iberoamericana. Univ. of Pittsburgh *for the* Instituto Internacional de Literatura Iberoamericana. Pittsburgh, Pa.
INSULA	Insula. Madrid.
IUO/A	Annali. Istituto Universitario Orientale. Sezione Romanza. Napoli, Italy.
JEHM/R	Revista de la Junta de Estudios Históricos de Mendoza. Mendoza, Arg.
LALR	Latin American Literary Review. Carnegie-Mellon Univ., Dept. of Modern Languages. Pittsburgh, Pa.
LARR	Latin American Research Review. Univ. of North Carolina Press *for the* Latin American Studies Association. Chapel Hill.
MLN	Modern Language Notes. The Johns Hopkins Univ. Press. Baltimore, Md.
PRAAC/B	Boletín de la Academia de Artes y Ciencias de Puerto Rico. San Juan.
RCLL	Revista de Crítica Literaria Latinoamericana. Latinoamericana Editores. Lima.

REVIEW	Review 72, 73, etc. Center for Inter-American Relations. N.Y.
RIB	Revista Interamericana de Bibliografía [Inter-American Review of Bibliography]. Organization of American States. Washington.
SECOLAS/A	Annals of the Southeastern Conference on Latin American Studies. West Georgia College. Carrollton.
UA/REH	Revista de Estudios Hispánicos. Univ. of Alabama, Dept. of Romance Languages, Office of International Studies and Programs. University.
UA/U	Universidad. Univ. de Antioquia. Medellín, Colombia.
UB/BH	Bulletin Hispanique. Univ. de Bordeaux *avec le concours du* Centre National de la Recherche Scientifique. Bordeaux, France.
UBN/R	Revista de la Biblioteca Nacional. Ministerio de Instrucción Pública y Previsión Social. Montevideo.
UC/A	Anales de la Universidad de Cuenca. Cuenca, Ecua.
UC/BF	Boletín de Filología. Univ. de Chile, Instituto de Filología. Santiago.
UC/V	Verbum. Univ. Católica. Rio.
UCAB/M	Montalbán. Univ. Católica Andrés Bello, Facultad de Humanidades y Educación, Institutos Humanísticos de Investigación. Caracas.
UCLV/I	Islas. Univ. Central de las Villas. Santa Clara, Cuba.
UCM/ALH	Anales de Literatura Hispanoamericana. Univ. Complutense de Madrid. Madrid.
UCP/RP	Romance Philology. Univ. of California Press. Berkeley.
UCR/R	Revista de la Universidad de Costa Rica. San José.
UCR/RHCLC	Revista Histórico-Crítica de Literatura Centroamericana. Univ. de Costa Rica [and] Ministerio de Cultura, Juventud y Deporte. San José.
UCSD/NS	The New Scholar. Univ. of California, Center for Iberian and Latin American Studies, Institute of Chicano Urban Affairs [and] John Muir College. San Diego.
UCV/CA	Cuadernos Afro-Americanos. Univ. Central de Venezuela, Consejo de Desarrollo Científico y Humanístico, Facultad de Humanidades y Educación, Instituto de Antropología e Historia. Caracas.
UFP/RL	Revista Letras. Univ. Federal do Paraná, Setor de Ciências Humanas, Letras e Artes. Curitiba, Brazil.
UH/RJ	Romanistisches Jahrbuch. Romanisches Seminar, Ibero-Americanisches Forschungsinstitut der Universität Hamburg. Hamburg, FRG.
UK/KRQ	Kentucky Romance Quarterly. Univ. of Kentucky. Lexington.
UK/LATR	Latin American Theatre Review. A journal devoted to the theatre and drama of Spanish and Portuguese America. Univ. of Kansas, Center of Latin American Studies. Lawrence.
UM/JIAS	Journal of Inter-American Studies and World Affairs. Univ. of Miami Press *for the* Center for Advanced International Studies. Coral Gables, Fla.
UM/R	Revista Universidad de Medellín. Univ. de Medellín, Centro de Estudios de Posgrado. Medellín, Colombia.
UNAM/AL	Anuario de Letras. Univ. Nacional Autónoma de México, Facultad de Filosofía y Letras. México.
UNAM/FL	Filosofía y Letras. Univ. Nacional Autónoma de México, Facultad de Filosofía y Letras. México.
UNAM/RMS	Revista Mexicana de Sociología. Univ. Nacional Autónoma de México, Instituto de Investigaciones Sociales. México.
UNAM/RUM	Revista de la Universidad de México. Univ. Nacional Autónoma de México. México.
UNION	Unión. Unión de Escritores y Artistas de Cuba. La Habana.
UNL/H	Humanitas. Univ. de Nuevo León, Centro de Estudios Humanísticos. Monterrey, Mex.
UNPHU/A	Aula. Univ. Nacional Pedro Henríquez Ureña. Santo Domingo.
UO/BA	Books Abroad. An international literary quarterly. Univ. of Oklahoma. Norman.
UP/CSEC	Cuban Studies/Estudios Cubanos. Univ. of Pittsburgh, Univ. Center for International Studies, Center for Latin American Studies. Pittsburgh, Pa.

UPDRL/HR	See HR.
UPR/CS	Caribbean Studies. Univ. of Puerto Rico, Institute of Caribbean Studies. Río Piedras.
UPRM/RL	Revista de Letras. Univ. de Puerto Rico en Mayagüez, Facultad de Artes y Ciencias. Mayagüez.
UR/EHLIA	Études d'Histoire et de Littérature Ibéro-Américaines. Univ. de Rouen, Centre de Recherches Ibéro-Américaines. Rouen, France.
USB/RVF	Revista Venezolana de Filosofía. Univ. Simón Bolívar [and] Sociedad Venezolana de Filosofía. Caracas.
USP/RIEB	Revista do Instituto de Estudos Brasileiros. Univ. de São Paulo, Instituto de Estudos Brasileiros. São Paulo.
UTIEH/C	Caravelle. Cahiers du monde hispanique et luso-brésilien. Univ. de Toulouse, Institute d'Études Hispaniques, Hispano-Americaines et Luso-Brésiliennes. Toulouse, France.
UWI/CQ	Caribbean Quarterly. Univ. of the West Indies. Mona, Jam.
VIA	Via. Univ. of California, Office of Student Activities. Berkeley.
VME/R	Revista Nacional de Cultura. Ministerio de Educación, Instituto Nacional de Cultura y Bellas Artes. Caracas. *See* CONAC/RNC.

MUSIC

ROBERT STEVENSON

Professor of Music
University of California, Los Angeles

THE PUBLISHING EVENT OF THE BIENNIUM was Monseñor José Ignacio Perdomo Escobar's superb catalogue of the Bogotá cathedral music archive (see item 9093). As a new departure, he published all the texts of the vernacular music in the archive, thus making the catalogue equally indispensable to the musicologist and the student of Baroque literature. Another extremely handsome volume that rates as indispensable to both the literary and music historian published during the biennium (see item 9132) contained the text of Pedro Calderón de la Barca's 1660 *representación música, La púrpura de la rosa*, set musically in 1701 by the Lima Cathedral chapel-master, Tomás de Torrejón y Velasco (b. 1644, d. 1728).

Testifying to the excellence of Torrejón y Velasco's 1701 music, Donald Jay Grout wrote as follows in a letter dated at Berkeley 10 March 1976: "The music of *La púrpura de la rosa* is charming. It should make a very attractive feature of a national AMS [American Musicological Society] meeting, some year." The music, like Juan Hidalgo's setting of Calderón de la Barca's other opera libretto of 1660, *Celos aún del aire matan*, survives in a manuscript containing only voice parts and mostly unfigured instrumental continuo. Thus, like Brünnhilde, this 1701 opera score awaits the kiss of a Leppard to awaken it to new life. But again according to Grout, the Leppard who makes a realization of the continuo and adds instrumentation should be not the editor but the conductor. "A conductor who couldn't do these things—and wouldn't prefer to do them himself—ought not to be conducting this kind of work."

The periodicals that continued doing the most for Latin American music during the biennium were *Revista Musical Chilena* edited with unflagging zeal, accuracy, and timeliness by Luis Merino, Director, and María Ester Grebe, Assistant Director (whose merits were successively recognized in 1976 and 1977 by Guggenheim fellowships), and *Heterofonía*, a private enterprise captained by the unique Esperanza Pulido. As during previous editorships, the continuing merits of the Chilean magazine were largely due to Magdalena Vicuña Lyon. The editor of the Mexican bi-monthly was the subject of a glowing tribute published in Havana (see item 9117).

Ficta Difusora de Música Antigua, directed by Sergio S. Simonovich and managed by Jorge V. González (México 1208, B.A. 1097), reached 64, 80, and 76 pages in the first three numbers of tomo I (Nov. 1976, March 1977, June 1977). Lavishly illustrated with plates, music examples, and charts, this welcomed quarterly included in both second and third numbers an article on a New World colonial composer (Araujo, Lienas). After falling two years behind the cover year, the *Yearbook of the Inter-American Institute for Music Research* ceased publication with volume 11. Although cover-dated 1975, the last volume included at least one major contribution not written until mid-1976 (see item 9002). Despite the announcement that annuals were always to be obtained from the Institute of Latin American Studies, approximately half the feature articles in volumes 6-10 published after the *Yearbook* moved to the Univ. of Texas at Austin dealt with US topics. By contrast, the feature articles in volumes 1-5 edited at Tulane Univ. were heavily weighted in Latin America's favor.

Another journal testifying to the recent chronic plight of Latin America in mixed journals, even with an area specialist for editor, was *Ethnomusicology*. Among 52 feature articles in Sept. 1974 through Sept. 1977 issues, the two that were overtly Latin American in theme (see items 9032 and 9068) dealt with extra-musical associations of the Argentine tango and communicative events during La Rose singing on St. Lucia island. Dena J. Epstein's history of the folk banjo in an issue guest-edited by Portia K. Maultsby (item 9066) contained welcomed new data from the non-Spanish-speaking Caribbean islands.

A hitherto neglected aspect of Latin American music that for the first time elicited the full-length book coverage that it obviously merits—even if in this instance realization failed to match expectation—was *Popular music in Mexico* (item 9109). In a welcomed book on Carlos Gardel (b. 1887, d. 1935, item 9028) the tango hero's discography and film credits were itemized with the same care that should now be shown several more recent idols of the urban masses.

No facet of Latin American music more urgently awaits bibliographic control than the popular product fed urban radio, television, and concert-going publics. Folk music and ethnic interests enjoy the consistently enlightened patronage of the outstanding team heading the Instituto Interamericano de Etnomusicología y Folklore at Caracas, Dr. Isabel Aretz and Don Luis Felipe Ramón y Rivera—whose publications in article or book form are always major events. However, writing on such popular themes as contemporary Argentine rock require enormously time-consuming searches through B.A. newspapers (items 9022a-9022c). Any items thus recovered can be listed in *HLAS* only as sporadic examples. Yet it is the popular products that constitute the reality of Latin American music to millions (items 9048 and 9059)—not the sequestered folk music of the Mískitos on the Honduras coast (item 9070) nor the art music of a Danião Barbosa de Araújo (b. 1778, d. 1856, item 9043).

GENERAL

9001. Baron, Robert. Syncretism and ideology: Latin New York *salsa* musicians (CFS/WF, 36:3, July 1977, p. 209-225)

Salsa, Cuban dance music played in NYC by immigrants from Latin urban areas, is passing through an identity crisis. What can the *salsa* player retain from Havana days in a commercialized loud crossover product capable of attracting the mass American audience? This lengthy article relays tentative answers from a wide group of unidentified informants interviewed in NYC during May/Oct. 1975.

9002. Béhague, Gerard. Latin American music: an annotated bibliography of recent publications (UT/YIMR, 11, 1975 [i.e. 1977] p. 190-218)

Although published in the 1975 *Yearbook*, this 128-item bibliography also lists and comments on articles published in 1976.

9003. Claro Valdés, Samuel. Discos (UCIEM/R, 31:137, enero/marzo 1977, p. 57-61)

Extremely valuable analysis of the four-album Qualiton (B.A.) series issued 1973-75 (Archivo Colonial de América Latina) written with his customary sagacity by the present-day leading authority on this repertory.

9004. Correa, Manuel *brother* and others. Vilancicos portugueses. Transcrição e estudo de Robert Stevenson. Lisbon, Fundação Calouste Gulbenkian, 1976. 161 p., music (Portugaliae musica, série A)

Gaspar Fernandes (d. 1629 at Puebla, Mex.) composed two of the earliest Portuguese-text villancicos in this volume. The manuscripts of six of the 18 works herein transcribed and commented on were found in Oaxaca, Guatemala City, Bogotá, and Cuzco.

9005. **Kuss, Malena.** Latin America (*in* Orrey, Leslie *ed*. The encyclopedia of opera [see item 9013] p. 196-199)

Authoritative synopsis of operatic developments in Argentina, Brazil, Colombia, Cuba, Mexico, Peru and Uruguay, written by a recognized specialist whose doctoral thesis (1976) treated of "Nativistic Strains in Argentine Operas Premiered in the Teatro Colón: 1908-1972."

9006. ———. Latin American music in contemporary reference sources: a study session. Paramount, Calif., Academy Printing and Publishing Co., 1976. 19 p., bibl.

Valuable summary of a study session at the national meeting of the American Musicological Society, Washington, Oct. 31-Nov. 2, 1974, devoted to Latin American music reference materials. Eleven participants' contributions are here synopsized (alphabetical order): Gerard Béhague, Lester D. Brothers, Gilbert Chase, Isabel Pope Conant, Malena Kuss, Arthur La Brew, Luis Merino, Juan Orrego Salas, Charles Seeger, Carleton Sprague Smith, and Donald Thompson.

9007. **Lange, Francisco Curt.** O progresso da musicologia na América Latina: um balanço (USP/RH, 55:109, jan./março 1977, p. 228-229)

After a half-century at the forefront of Latin American musicology, Dr. Lange compares the courses offered in German universities with those in Latin America, surveys the present state of musicological and ethnomusicological studies in Argentina, Brazil, Venezuela, Mexico, and other OAS nations, remarks on the condition of musical museums, and assesses the contributions of various individual scholars. He concludes with an apt quotation from Dr. Roberto Lehmann-Nitsche (letter dated 13 May 1933) congratulating him on his enthusiasm but warning him that "joy in published research results will have to compensate" for ingratitude, incomprehension, and penury.

9008. **Lemmon, Alfred E.** Los jesuitas y la música de los negros (HET, 10:6, nov./dic. 1977, p. 5-9)

From New Spain to Paraguay blacks attached to Jesuit missions displayed singular musical aptitude. Guaraní Indians taught music to the blacks sent to Paraguay. Like the other articles in this excellent series, it is authoritatively documented.

9009. **Livingstone, William.** A Latin postscript (Stereo Review [Chicago, Ill.] 30:5, May 1973, p. 82-84, illus.)

Carlos Gardel (1887-1935) still remains popular with the buying public. Libertad Lamarque, a later Argentine singer, recorded everything—boleros, rumbas, rancheras, folk songs of the Peruvian Andes, Cuban theater music—but nothing more convincingly than tangos. Other stars discussed or mentioned: Trío los Panchos ("who have produced some of the happiest sounds ever recorded"), Miguel Aceves Mejía ("his records are the best introduction to rancheras"), Cuco Sánchez and the Dueto América, Imperio Argentina, Sarita Montiel, Nati Mistral, Leonardo Favio, Julio Iglesias, Camilo Sesto, António Carlos Jobim, Luiz Bonfá.

9010. **Merino, Luis.** Festival of early Latin American music (UCIEM/R, 30:133, enero/marzo 1976, p. 78-79)

Roger Wagner's interpretations of works by Cristóbal de Belsayaga, Manuel Blasco, Antonio Durán de la Mota, Gutierre Fernández Hidalgo, José Maurício Nunes Garcia, Francisco López Capillas, and Domenico Zipoli, confirm the strong impression of the Latin American Colonial repertory left by his interpretations in *Salve Regina* (Angel S-36003 [1966]).

9011. ———. Perspectivas latinoamericanas (UCIEM/R, 30:133, enero/marzo 1976, p. 71-74)

Reflections of the offhanded treatment of Latin America in *The New Oxford History of Music*, vol. 10 (1974), in contrast with the more appreciative role accorded music in *HLAS 36*.

9012. ———. Presencia de Joseph Haydn en Latinoamérica colonial y decimonónica: "Las Siete Ultimas Palabras de Cristo en la Cruz", y dos fuentes en Chile (UCIEM/R, 30:135/136, oct./dic. 1976, p. 5-21, bibl.)

Magisterial study of the spread of F.J. Haydn's reputation and works in Latin America. Among many Haydn imprints in Chile, two in the library of Isidora Zegers escaped the notice of Anthony van Hoboken: Ariane a Naxos (early Paris edition), and "Forgive me" (English words by P.L. Courtier adapted to No. 19 of Haydn's *24 Lieder von verschiedenen Dichtern: 1781-1784*).

9013. **Orrey, Leslie** *ed*. The encyclopedia of opera. N.Y., Charles Scribner's Sons, 1976. 376 p., col. plates.

For the first time an international opera lexicon gives Latin America its due in a series of distinguished articles by Malena Kuss (biography at p. 8) on Argentina, *Beatrix Cenci*, Arturo Beruti, *Bomarzo*, Brazil, Buenos Aires, *Don Rodrigo*, Alberto Ginastera, António Carlos Gomes, *Il Guarany*, Latin America, and Rio de Janeiro. Color plate opposite p. 51 of the sumptuous opera house built at the apex of the rubber boom and opened 31 Dec. 1896 at Manaus, Brazil, should be labeled Teatro Amazonas.

9014. Palarea, Álvaro Fernaud. Comportamiento musical, educación musical y folklore en América Latina (IPGH/FA, 22, dic. 1976, p. 153-155)

In this paper read by the Venezuelan subdirector of INIDEF (Instituto Interamericano de Etnomusicología y Folklore, Caracas) at the V International Seminar on Music Education Research (Mexico City, 3-10 Sept. 1975), the author laments the almost complete submission of urban Latin American youth to commercial repertories and styles exported via television and radio from the US and Europe. Nothing individual or significant emerges because urban youth has now become a sort of blotting paper that absorbs the latest foreign fads.

9015. Stevenson, Robert. *Latin American Music Treasures from the Sixteenth, Seventeenth, and Eighteenth Centuries* [liner notes]. Conducted by Roger Wagner. Los Angeles, Univ. of California, Latin American Center, 1977. 1 v. (Unpaged) (Eldorado S:2)

Liner notes issued with sound recording of same name which includes vernacular pieces by Juan de Araujo, José de Orejón y Aparicio, Gaspar Fernandes, Caetano de Mello Jesus, and Manuel Zumaya (Bolivia, Peru, Guatemala, Brazil, and Mexico), Latin-text works by Gutierre Fernández Hidalgo, Pedro Bermúdez, Fernandes, and Araujo, and an organ tiento by Estacio de la Serna.

9016. ———. Music in Aztec & Inca territory. Berkeley, Univ. of California Press, 1976. 378 p., bibl., music, plates.

Slightly revised version, with additional plates of *HLAS 30:4526.*

9017. ———. Nuevos recursos para el estudio de la música latinoamericana (HET, 10:1, enero/feb. 1977, p. 15-24)

Summaries of the dissertations listed in *HLAS 38*, p. 546.

9018. ———. Rumbos de la investigación sobre música colonial latinoamericana (UCIEM/R, 30:134, abril/sept. 1976, p. 3-8)

Wills and capitular acts define composers' lives, but only extant music studied in tandem with biography can convince outsiders that the colonial Latin American music legacy merits worldwide applause. See *HLAS 38:9024*, for an earlier version of this same essay.

9019. ———. The South American lyric stage to 1800 (OAS/IMB, 87, July/Oct. 1973 [i.e. 1974] p. 1-27)

Opera history highlighting Torrejón y Velasco, Ceruti, and Massa.

9020. ———. Visión musical norteamericana de las otras Américas hacia 1900 (UCIEM/R, 31:137, enero/marzo 1977, p. 5-35, music notations)

Latin American music, authentic and pseudo-, published in the US before 1900. Operas on Latin American subjects. US visits, some short, some prolonged, by celebrities such as António Carlos Gomes and Teresa Carreño.

9021. Valenti Ferro, Enzo. Congreso de críticos musicales y Festival Interamericano de Música en Washington (BAM, 31:486, junio 1976, p. 1, 5)

From 18-22 May 1976 the Asociación Interamericana de Críticos de Música (organized in 1973) met during a first congress that coincided with the VII Festival Interamericano de Música, 17-24 May. Among the invited guests were critics representing 10 Latin American countries. In his valuable summary, Valenti Ferro records the highlights of both the critics' congress and the Festival. Apart from him as president the other Latin American officers elected by the critics' association were: Federico Heinlein (Chile, first vice-president), Raúl Cosío (Mexico, treasurer), Washington Roldán (Uruguay, secretary general), and Esperanza Pulido (Mexico, assistant treasurer).

9022. Vance, Joel. The Latin connection (Stereo Review [Chicago, Ill.] 30:5, May 1973, p. 78-81, illus.)

A knowledgeable survey of Latin music heard in N.Y. "A direct emotional communication that makes you forget your troubles and gives you an identity that makes you comfortable and proud is now pretty much the exclusive property of Latin music." Artists mentioned include: Tito Puente, the "Duke Ellington of Latin Music" ("his compositions and arrangements are the most colorful, his orchestra is tightly disciplined, and it swings simply ferociously"), La Lupe, the "Tina Turner of Latin music," Celia Cruz, Santos Colón, Roberto Roena, Airto Moreira, Eddie Palmiere, Cándido and Mongo Santamaría.

ARGENTINA

9022a. Andrés, Jorge Héctor. El mito de Carlos Gardel (La Opinión [B.A.] 24 junio 1975, n.a.)

40th-anniversary tribute by a leading Argentine authority on popular culture. For his reaction to Julio

De Caro and a new interpretation of his works, see La Opinión [B.A.], 12 abril 1975. On Julio De Caro, Pedro Maffia, Enrique Delfino, three masters of classic tango, see La Opinión, 21 March 1973. His report on Dino Saluzzi, a new tango composer, 15 julio 1972; on the legacy of Ángel Vargas, tango vocalist, 31 agosto 1971; comeback of Eduardo Rivero, veteran innovator of tango, 31 julio 1971.

9022b. ———. Reunión de Astor Piazzolla (La Opinión [B.A.] 19 agosto 1975, n.a.)

Rated by the author as Argentina's most important pop musician, Piazzolla joined in 1975 with Gerry Mulligan, master jazz saxophonist. For author's enthusiastic report on Piazzolla's Concierto para quinteto, see La Opinión, 21 julio 1971.

9022c. ———. Zona de desastre (Correo de la Semana [B.A.] 17 oct. 1975, n.a.)

Report on Argentine rock. For author's earlier overall report on rock in B.A., see La Opinión [B.A.], 9 feb. 1973; reaction to rock artist Litto Nebbia in La Opinión, 11 sept. 1973; report on rock version of La Biblia, 3 agosto 1974.

9023. Centrángolo, Aníbal E. La misa a cinco voces de Juan de Lienas en el códice mexicano del convento de Nuestra Señora del Carmen (Ficta [B.A.] 1:3, junio 1977, p. 179-190, music, plates)

Excellent analysis of Lienas' mass with the head-motive *fa re ut fa sol la* (hard hexachord) first published in *Tesoro de la música polifónica en México* (1952). Written by the founder-director of Ars Nova and Cantoria del Buen Ayre, who in 1977 also taught in the Collegium Musicum and conducted the Dante Alighieri choir, this article concludes with five pages of music (Kyrie-Christe-Kyrie). Concerning the putative Gregorian sources of the head-motive, John R. Bryden and David G. Hughes, *An index of Gregorian chant* (Harvard Univ. Press, 1969, Ch. II, p. 18-19) list some other more appealing possibilities than the Palm Sunday antiphon *Pueri hebraeorum*—which begins not with the required *fa re ut fa sol la* but with *re fa re ut fa sol fa la*. The question of Lienas' ever having been a Carmelite remains open if indeed he married—as his works imply (contained in the Newberry Case MS VM 2147 C36, v. 1/3 and 6). Also see *HLAS 36:9172*. The almost invariable "Don" before his name implies his being a cacique.

9024. Epstein, Ernesto. Carlos Guastavino (MGG [Supplement] 150/151, 1975, p. 550-551, bibl.)

Unsympathetic biography with partial works list.

9025. Guinzburg, Juana. Alberto Ginastera en el Festival de Lucerne (BAM, 32:495, abril 1977, p. 5)

In an interview with Ginastera and Marta Casals-Istomin before the European premiere of his *Glosses sobre temes de Pau Casals* (op. 46, 1976), the composer exactly specifies Casals' themes borrowed in the three movements of a tribute (introducción, romance, cauto) composed for a string orchestra and distant quintet of solo strings. Also mentioned in this useful article: European premieres of *Don Rodrigo* sung in French and *Bomarzo* in English, festivities associated with Ginastera's 60th birthday, recordings of his second piano concerto and quintet for piano and strings (Hilde Somer, pianist).

9026. Jurafsky, Abraham. Carlos López Buchardo (Anuario I [Academia Nacional de Bellas Artes, B.A.] 1973, p. 13-20, music, plate)

An abridgment of the author's encomiastic 56-p. *Carlos López Buchardo* [1881-1948] (B.A., Ediciones Culturales Argentinas, 1966).

9027. Kuss, Malena. Argentina (*in* Orrey, Leslie *ed*. The encyclopedia of opera [see item 9013] p. 23-24)

Excellent survey of opera in the country with "the strongest tradition of native opera in Latin America."

9028. Morena, Miguel Ángel. Historia artística de Carlos Gardel: estudio cronológico. B.A., Editorial Freeland, 1976. 256 p., bibl., discography.

Year-by-year chronological account of the life of Charles Romuald Gardes (b. at Toulouse 11 Dec. 1887, d. in an airplane accident 24 June 1935 at Medellín, Colombia) emphasizing facets of his professional career. Appendices list his 11 films, and provide an exhaustive discography divided under recording companies and titles recorded (p. 163-243). As a documentary record of a star whose legendary fame continues, this book is invaluable. His Argentine citizenship awarded 1 May 1923 rested on a fraudulent certificate of birth at Tacuarembó, Uru., 11 Dec. 1887, granted him by the Uruguayan consul at B.A. 4 Oct. 1920 (p. 147-149).

9029. Recuperación de Julián Bautista (BAM, 32:495, abril 1977, p. 3)

Unsigned article lengthily quoting Tomás Marco, critic for *Ya* (Madrid) on the successful performance of Bautista's *Sinfonía Breve* (1956) and his mounting reputation in Spain. B. 21 April 1901 in Madrid, Bautista emigrated to Argentina in 1940 and lived mostly in B.A. until his death there 8 July 1961.

9030. Sargent, David H. The twelve-tone row in technique of Juan Carlos Paz (UT/YIMR, 11, 1975 [i.e. 1977] p. 81-105, music notations)

Article extracted from the author's D.M.A. dissertation, "Juan Carlos Paz, Self-Taught Twelve Tonalist and Innovative Argentine Composer" (University of Illinois, 1975). Using as documents Paz' *3ª Composición en los 12 Tonos* for clarinet and piano, *4ª composición* for violin and piano, *Balada II* for piano, and *Diez piezas sobre una serie en los doce tonos*, Sargent argues Paz' independence from Schoenberg—despite numerous previous labelings of Paz as a "Schoenberg disciple."

9031. Stevenson, Robert. Roberto García Morillo (MGG [Supplement] 150/151, 1975, p. 415-416, bibl.)

Biography with works list.

9032. Taylor, Julie M. Tango: theme of class and nation (Ethnomusicology [Society for Ethnomusicology, Middleton, Conn.] 20:2, May 1976, p. 273-292)

Sociological history of the tango, with special emphasis on the Gardel myth. Around 1900 the *bandoneón*, a German relative of the accordion, began replacing the guitar and by 1930 was "considered the quintessential instrument of the tango and tragedy" (p. 283).

9033. Turró, Ricardo. La novia del hereje, merecido homenaje (BAM, 31:490, oct. 1976, p. 1)

At the age of 96 Pascual de Rogatis appeared at the Teatro Colón to acknowledge the ovation accorded the revival there of his opera (libretto by Tomás Allende Iragorri after Vicente Fidel López' novel) premiered 13 June 1935 and mounted at the Teatro Colón 18 times since then.

BOLIVIA

9034. Auza León, Aliliano. Melodías y canciones de Tarija: IV centenario, 1574-1974. Tarija, Bol., Comité de Obras Públicas y Desarrollo de Tarija La Comercial, 1974. 44 p., music.

Piano-vocal scores of 40 historically popular songs edited by a leading Bolivian composer (b. Sucre, 1928; studied with Alberto Ginastera in B.A. in 1965).

9035. Fernández de la Fuente, Amalia and **Susana Caballero de Cortés.** 100 [i.e. Cien] danzas folklóricas y populares de Bolivia. Sucre, Bol., Tupac Katari, 1972. 158 p., music.

Piano arrangements of 100 regionally popular dances.

9036. García Muñoz, Carmen. Juan de Araujo: un compositor en la América colonial (Ficta [B.A.] 1:2, marzo 1977, p. 115-124, music notations, plates)

Transcription of an "eighth-tone" Christmas villancico *a 3* with continuo, *Cayósele el Alba*, by the "great composer" Juan de Araujo—as the distinguished author rightly qualifies the maestro who directed music at the cathedral in Sucre, 1680-1712. Preceded by introductory analysis, the transcription halving note-values and retaining original pitches was made from the original sheets in the music archive of Sucre Cathedral.

9037. Jaime Laredo (BAM, 31:488, agosto 1976, p. 2)

Under auspices of the Organización Elías Grapa the 35-year old Bolivian violinist triumphed at the B.A. Coliseo in a program of sonatas by Brahms (Op. 108), Ravel and Beethoven (Op. 47).

9038. Malitzke-Goes, Ana Rosa de. Música folklórica boliviana (UY/R, 18:105, mayo/junio 1976, p. 89-94, bibl.)

Superficial organological survey culled from Antonio González Bravo (see *HLAS 14:3359*) and Ernesto Cavour (b. La Paz, 1940), author of a 43-p. instructional manual *Aprenda a tocar charango* (La Paz, 1973).

9039. Olsen, Dale A. Música vesperal Mojo en San Miguel de Isidoro, Bolivia (UCIEM/R, 30:133, enero/marzo 1976, p. 28-46, bibl., music, plates)

Experienced ethnomusicological analysis of the indigenous elements still prevailing in the music for vespers of St. Michael recorded 28 Sept. 1968 *in situ* by Dori Reeks, anthropology graduate of UCLA. Then in Bolivia as a Peace Corps volunteer, she also gathered much of the historical data on the Mojos used by Olsen as a prelude to the valuable music transcriptions and analysis.

9040. Tichauer, Werner Guttentag. Bibliografía boliviana del año 1972. Cochabamba, Bol., n.p., 1973. 139 p.

In this bibliography, Nos. 45, 54, and 95 list three Christian hymnals (with music) published at Cochabamba in 1972, the texts in Quechua, Aymara, and Chipaya, respectively. Other recent annual issues of this same bibliography itemize a 213-p. music text published at Sucre (1972 [1973] No. 194), instructional manuals for charango, guitar, and quena published at La Paz; popular dances and hymns arranged for accordion (1973 [1974], Nos. 120-123; 239-240), Christmas music (1974 [1975], No. 184), and patriotic anthems and marches arranged for accordion (1975 [1976], No. 1). Although not eligible for *HLAS* annotations, these music publications credited to Cochabamba, La Paz, Oruro, and Sucre valuably illustrate the kinds of vocal and instrumental music presently being disseminated in Bolivia.

BRAZIL

9041. Ayatai, Desidério. O sistema tonal do canto xavante (MP/R, 1975, p. 65-83, bibl., music notations)

The only melodic instrument of the Shavante Indians in Mato Grosso is a gourd-flute, *umreñiduruture*, emitting three sounds. Of the three songs transcribed in this article, the first consists of the notes *re mi fa la*; the second starts with *re fa* but drops a semi-tone in the second through fifth incises to include what are transcribable as flatted *ut re mi fa*. In the third Shavante song the incises alternate between triadic notes of the C and C flat chords. The author specifies an informant named Waritinodze recording in 1961 for the second song, and specifies 1974 as the year when the third song was recorded. The force of his arguments would grow if he were able to give more exact information on when and how and why the recordings were made, and if he could give present cataloguing details. His acquaintance with Nettl, McAllester, and List has taught him proper method, but he seems at times chary of applying it.

9042. Béhague, Gerard. Correntes regionais e nacionais na música do candomblé baiano (UFB/AA, 12, junho 1976, p. 129-140, music)

Although previous anthropological research stressed African retentions, "'national' cult currents (Cabloco, Umbanda) exert a substantial influence on the religious musical practices of hundreds of small cult centers in Salvador." The first musical example is a Gêge song transcribed and published by Alan P. Merriam in 1963, the second is a *cantiga para Exu* (*Ketu*) transcribed by Robert Witmer and the author. The texts of both are "purposely" omitted.

9043. Brazil. Ministério da Educação e Cultura. Departamento de Assuntos Culturais. Plano de Ação Cultural. *Compositores da Bahia 3* [liner notes]. *Compositores da Bahia 4* [liner notes]. Bahia, Brazil, Univ. Federal da Bahia, Coordenação Central de Extensão, Escola de Música e Artes Cênicas, 1975. 2 v. (1, 2 p.) (UFBA, 1002/1003)

Under the direction of Piero Bastianelli (b. Pisa, Italy, 1935) and Ernst Widmer (b. Aarau, Switzerland, 1927), O conjunto de Música Nova and the Orquestra Sinfonica e Madrigal da UFBA recorded two albums containing three contemporary works and Memento Baiano (UFBA-1002 Side A) by Damião Barbosa de Araújo (1778-1856). Araújo (b. Itaparica Island, Bahia) played violin first at the Teatro Guadalupe, then the Ópera Velha in Bahia, before transferring to Rio during John VI's residency there. Around 1828 he returned to Bahia, and from 1830-36 belonged to the Academia de Música (d. Salvador 20 April 1856). The contemporary composers whose data enhance the usefulness of the liner notes are Agnaldo Ribeiro (1943), Lindemberque Cardoso (1939), and Jamary Oliveira (1944).

9044. Chaves Júnior, Edgard de Brito. Wagner e o Brasil. Rio, Companhia Editora Americana, 1976. 64 p., illus.

Lohengrin was premiered 19 Sept. 1883, in the Teatro D. Pedro II (later renamed Lyrico); *Tannhäuser* (30 Sept. 1892; *Die Mesitersinger* 3 Aug. 1905; *Tristan und Isolde* 27 May; *Die Walküre* 2 Sept. 1913; *Parsifal* 9 Sept. 1913; *Das Rheingold* 15 Sept. 1922; *Seigfried* 26 Sept. 1922; *Götterdämmerung* 6 Oct. 1922; and *Die fleigende Holländer* 8 Aug. 1952, in the Teatro Municipal of Rio de Janeiro. From 1913, São Paulo usually heard the same operas given in its Teatro Municipal by the same visiting companies. This excellent monograph also lists artists. The first chapter, based on an article by Carlos H. Hunsche in Humboldt (No. 23, 1961) corrects Wagner's misstatements in his autobiography of 1864 relative to his correspondence with Ernesto Ferreira França in 1857. Wagner's 1857 letters to Ferreira França reveal that he seriously considered dedicating *Tristan und Isolde* to D. Pedro II and visiting Rio for the production there of his operas translated into Italian.

9045. Duprat, Régis. Música na Matriz e Sé de São Paulo colonial (UT/YIMR, 11, 1975 [i.e. 1977] p. 8-69, plates)

Condensed revision of the author's nonpareil doctoral dissertation (1963). Among new data he reveals that António Manso continued at São Paulo from 1772 until at least 1811, not 1778 (p. 29). Numerous footnotes in the dissertation are drastically reduced or omitted. Important dissertation data on the surviving plainchant imprints at São Paulo Cathedral (p. 24) and corresponding plates are sacrificed. The author's dissertation tribute to Lange is forfeited (p. 58, No. 6). Considering the unique worth of much of the excised material, the scholar will still profit from having at hand both the printed reduction and the microfilmed dissertation. The running together of many of Duprat's paragraphs and the failure to observe his double-indented distinction of quoted documents save space at the expense of easy understanding.

9046. França, Eurico Nogueira. A evolução de Villa-Lobos na música de câmara. Rio, Ministério da Educação e Cultura, Museu Villa-Lobos, 1976. 98 p., music, plate, portrait.

Analytical essays on 19 chamber works liberally interspersed with musical examples. This monograph needs a table of contents and an index. It received the Prémio Villa-Lobos, II Concurso Nacional sobre o Estilo Técnico, Estético e Analítico 1976.

9047. Golfeder, Miriam. A cultura musical na década de 50: um análise ideologica (VOZES, 20:8, out. 1976. p. 70-72)

During the 1950s Rádio Nacional foisted on the lower working class Emilinha Borba as the ideal

Brazilian woman. Fan clubs gave her iceboxes and washing machines. Her rival was Marlene who sang mostly songs of Brazilian origin—whereas Emilinha sang an international repertory that included tangos and boleros. According to the author, these idols created by the mass media are symbols of the manipulation of the masses by the ruling circles.

9048. Jambeiro, Othon. Canção de massa as condições de produção. São Paulo, Livraria Pioneira Editora, 1975. 156 p.

Music for the masses viewed not as art but as business. Valuable insights into the Brazilian record-producing industry.

9049. Kiefer, Bruno. História da música brasileira, dos primórdios ao início do séc. XX. Porto Alegre, Brazil, Editora Movimento, 1976. 140 p., illus. (Col. Luís Cosme, 9)

Despite the author's wide acquaintance with recent literature, this textbook history of Brazilian music to 1900 lacks a bibliography and adequate footnotes. Although in his *preâmbulo* he defends expounding his own opinions on the esthetic value of various monuments of Brazilian music, the space taken by his idiosyncratic opinions could have been devoted to the documentation. For laudatory review, see *Heterofonía* (10:3, mayo/junio 1977, p. 27-29).

9050. Kuss, Malena. Brazil (*in* Orrey, Leslie *ed*. The encyclopedia of opera [see item 9013] p. 56-57)

Synopsis of opera developments centered chiefly at Rio, from the mid-19th century to the 1960s.

9051. Lange, Francisco Curt. Um fabuloso redescobrimento: para justificação da existencia de música erudita no período colonial brasileiro (USP/RH, 54:107, julho/set. 1976, p. 45-67, bibl.)

Beginning in 1944 the author uncovered the Brazilian Baroque as it flowered in the works of numerous mulatto composers in Minas Gerais, among them José Joaquim Emérico Lobo de Mesquita, Francisco Gomes da Rocha, Ignácio Parreiras Neves, Marcos Coelho Netto, and Manoel Dias de Oliveira. All told, the author has given over 2000 lectures or courses on the Minas Gerais school in 23 European nations and throughout the Western Hemisphere, stimulating performances in the most renowned world centers. Caetano de Mello [de] Jesus, a native of Bahia and longtime cathedral chapelmaster there, sent to Portugal for printing a treatise copied in 1758-59 but written before 1740 that attests superlative musical learning. The manuscript at Évora Biblioteca Pública attracted the attention of Ernesto Vieira, who mentioned it in his *Diccionário biográphico de músicos portuguezes* (1900), but was misplaced on the Évora library shelves until rediscovered by Canon José Augusto Alegria. Lange asks for a microfilm and for the privilege of editing the treatise, the two extant volumes of which number 613 and 630 p.

9052. Machado, Cristina de Miranda Mata. Contribuição ao estudo das rodas infantis em Minas, Brasil (IPGH/FA, 20, junio/dic. 1975, p. 83-101, bibl., music)

Updated and improved version of the essay with the same title published in *Revista da Universidad Federal de Minas Gerais* (18, dez. 1968/1969, p. 225-244). See *HLAS 34:5042*, where it is noted that "rounds" is not a suitable English transation for *rodas*.

9053. Mariz, Vasco. Heitor Villa-Lobos compositor brasileiro. 5. ed. Rio, Ministério da Educação e Cultura, Museu Villa-Lobos, 1977. 174 p., bibl., music, plates.

Definitive and final version of the landmark biography first published in 1949 by the present (1978) distinguished Brazilian ambassador to Israel. For comment on prior editions, see *HLAS 15:2805; HLAS 26:2192; HLAS 30:4572;* and *HLAS 34:5045*.

9054. Mendunni, Teresinha Rosa Principe. Viola, guitarra e violão: suas características, semelhanças e diferenças, levando em conta sua evolução, e sua presença na casa brasileira da época da independencia e atualmente, na cultura espontánea da cidade de São Paulo (Boletim [Secretaria de Cultura, Esportes e Turismo, Seminários do Museu da Casa Brasileira, São Paulo] 2, feb. 1975, p. 53-75)

Author differentiates the terms viola, violão, guitarra, guitarra portuguesa (Lisbon versus Coimbra tunings), as they are understood by popular performers interviewed in São Paulo. Among them were Zé do Rancho, José Ferreira da Rosa, Manuel Marques Pereira de Oliveira, Joaquim Duarte, José Joaquim Martins, and various Spanish guitar players at the Casa de Galícia. This essay contains valuable data on morphology and tunings but is poorly organized and very unattractively presented.

9055. Neves, Guilherme Santos. Variações sobre o tangolomango (CDFB/RBF, 14:41, maio/agôsto 1976, p. 13-36, bibl., music notations)

In *O folk-lore: estudos de literatura popular*, João Ribeiro (1860-1934) defined tangolo-mango as "a demonic force conjured by witchcraft, divination, or exorcism to annihilate individuals by progressive steps." Children sing songs about this demonic force, as for instance when used by an old hag to kill off her nine daughters one by one or her ten sons one by one. The three musical notations of children's songs contain some careless copying errors.

9056. Peppercorn, Lisa M. Foreign influences in Villa-Lobos' music (IAA, 3:1, 1977, p. 37-51)

During his first year in Paris 1923-24, Villa-Lobos—then in his late 30s—realized that to capture worldwide attention he had to develop an idiosyncratic personal style that foreigners could label "Brazilian." Earlier at Rio he had absorbed Wagner, the Russian Five, Tchaikovsky, Puccini, and Debussy, through hearing and performing their works while an orchestral cellist. The author who is a recognized specialist (see *HLAS 34:5053*) cites chapter-and-verse to prove her well-made points.

9057. ———. Le influenze del folklore brasiliano nella musica di Villa-Lobos (Nuova Rivista Musicale Italiana [Torino, Italy] 10:2, aprile/giugno 1976, p. 179-184, music notation)

In Villa-Lobos' piano piece *Sul América* (23 March 1925) he for the first time consciously incorporated folkloric elements. Edgard Roquette Pinto (1884-1954) who in 1912 had traveled to Mato Grosso and Amazonas and who from 1926 to 1935 administered the National Museum introduced him to Spix and Martius' *Brasilianische Volkslieder und indianische Melodien* (Munich, 1831), called his attention to Jean de Léry's Tupynambá melodies collected in 1557 (published at Geneva in 1585), and gave him a personally collected melody *Nozani-ná* that both he (*Chôros*, No. 3 [1925] and *Chansons typiques bresiliennes*) and Oscar Lorenzo Fernández (*Imbapara*) used to great advantage. Villa-Lobos' term Chôros derives ultimately from African xolo, converted by Brazilian blacks into xoro (St. John's Day dance or other festivity).

9058. Rezende, Carlos Penteado de. Mocidade de um compositor dos tempos do império no interior paulista (IHGSP/R, 72, 1975, p. 145-154)

Youth of Emilio [Correa] do Lago (b. at França in 1837, not at Mogi-Mirim in 1835 or 1838, as hitherto erroneously stated)—to whom Carlos Gomes dedicated *Tão longe de mim distante*, his modinha inspired by Ambrosina, Emilio's sister (not daughter, as heretofore reported). For a "sequel" to the present excellent article, see Rezende's "Casamento de Emilio do Lago" in *Revista do Arquivo Municipal* (181, 1970, p. 89-99).

9059. O Som do Pasquim: grandes entrevistas com os astros da música popular brasileira. Rio, Editora Codecri, 1976. 206 p., illus. (Edições do Pasquim, 6)

Lively, often malicious, interviews with 13 stars: Chico Buarque de Holanda, Waldick Soriano, Maria Bethânia, Lupicinio Rodrigues, António Carlos Jobim, Luiz Gonzaga, Caetano Veloso, Martinho da Vila, Ângela Maria, Roberto Carlos, Moreira da Silva, Raul Seixas, and Agnaldo Timóteo.

9060. Veiga, Manuel. Bruno Kiefer (HET, 10:3, mayo/junio 1977, p. 27-29)

Appreciative comments by the leading Bahia musicologist, together with important additional data omitted from Kiefer's well-intentioned 1976 history of Brazilian music (see item 9049).

9061. Vendramini, Maria do Carmo. A dança de São Gonçalo em Ibiúna (CDFB/RBF, 14:41, maio/agôsto 1976, p. 45-74, bibl., music, plates)

The data for this study was collected chiefly the night of 30 Nov. 1975 during the dance honoring São Gonçalo, protector of guitarists and patron of late marriages, at Ibiúna (São Paulo). The transcribed vocal music, mostly duets in thirds, is entirely 19th-century European in character.

THE CARIBBEAN (EXCEPT CUBA)

9062. Austin, Roy L. Understanding calypso content: a critique and an alternative explanation (UWI/CQ, 22:2/3, June/Sept. 1976, p. 74-83, bibl.)

In contrast with calipso texts analyzed by J.D. Elder in 1968, the put-down of women has declined in those composed more recently, perhaps as the result of a widening of interests of the lower classes who support calypsonians. Nonetheless, satire on local incidents and characters continues to typify present-day calypso's content.

9063. Coore, Rita. Music in society (NHAC/K, 14, July 1976, p. 78-82)

An invited address given at Carifesta '72 by a leading Jamaican music teacher (1952-72). From the wealth of her experience she offers several valuable insights. "The late Mrs. Vera Moody and I once did a survey of the concert going public in Jamaica and we found that there were only about 500 people who were regular concert goers, collected records and had some idea of what to look for in terms of style, expression and technique in a performance." She also believes that folk music is no longer attractive to the broad masses of Jamaica. The young were attracted during the 1960s by pop music "almost entirely imported from the U.S.A." More recently Jamaicans have developed reggae and Rastafarian songs, which while "heavily influenced by American themes and rhythms," begin to show a more local flavor.

9064. Cortés, Féliz; Angel Falcón; and Juan Flores. The cultural expression of

Puerto Ricans in New York: a theoretical perspective and critical review (LAP, 3[10]:3, Summer 1976, p. 117-152, bibl., illus.)

Turgid and often redundant theoretical prose heavily weights this lengthy essay. The more helpful comments include the following (p. 126-127): "The musical experience of the Puerto Rican in New York today is dominated by the commercial music controlled by a corrupt, multi-million dollar industry . . . Salsa, the catchall denomination for the commercial and popular rhythms of Latin music, developed in New York. It stems from Cuban music with its wealth of African elements . . . The New York setting allowed for changes on the original Cuban rhythms. The most significant innovation in the last ten years has been the amplification of the musical instruments producing the large, at times overwhelming, sound characteristics of rock and soul. Just as significant, although also characteristics of the popular music in Cuba, has been the increasing tempo given to the original Cuban music. Other particular features of salsa were introduced by Puerto Rican musicians—the central role given the trombone by Eddie Palmieri and Willie Colón's integration of traditional Puerto Rican and other Caribbean rhythms with this music."

9065. Dower, Catherine A. Libraries with music collections in the Caribbean Islands (Notes of the Music Library Association [Washington] 34:1, Sept. 1977, p. 27-38)

Valuable list of libraries in Aruba, Barbados, Bermuda, Cuba, Curaçao, Haiti, Jamaica, Martinique, Puerto Rico, Trinidad, and Virgin Islands. Data collected during author's personal visits (except Cuba). Unfortunately, the library holdings are often meager and, except for Cuba, include nothing that was in the islands before 1800.

9066. Epstein, Dena J. The folk banjo: a documentary history (Ethnomusicology [Society for Ethnomusicology, Middleton, Conn.] 19:3, Sept. 1975, p. 347-371, bibl., plates)

With exemplary skill the author collected and annotated 33 Caribbean references to the banjo (and cognate terms). Found mostly in travel literature dealing with Antigua, Barbados, Guadeloupe, Jamaica, Martinique, St. Croix, St. Kitts, Trinidad, and other unspecified West Indies, these references range chronologically from 1678 (Martinique) to 1849 (Trinidad). The term started as banza, then became bangil in Jamaica (1708-40) and banjar in Barbados (1788, 1796).

9067. Lizardo, Fradrique. Instrumentos musicales indígenas dominicanos. Santo Domingo, Editora Alfa y Omega, 1975 [i.e. 1976]. 109 p., bibl., illus. (Ediciones cultural nacional)

Dedicated to Isabel Aretz, this profusely illustrated volume lists (p. 29) 16 indigenous idiophones, each coded by authors mentioning the instrument. It itemizes (p. 67) six types of aerophone, similarly coded, and adds (p. 101-105) a compendious bibliography. The section on *espátulas vomicas sonajeras* (p. 12-26) is by the archaeologist Manuel A. García Arévalo. The author, b. in Santo Domingo, 4 Aug. 1930, studied folklore with Argeliers León and María Teresa Linares de León in 1961, and with Luis Felipe Ramón y Rivera and Isabel Aretz in 1964 and 1975. In 1976 he was director of the *Revista Dominicana de Folklore* and Secretary General of the Sociedad Folklórica Dominicana. This pioneering study deserves warm praise.

9068. Midgett, Douglas K. Performance roles and musical change in a Caribbean society (Ethnomusicology [Society for Ethnomusicology, Middleton, Conn.] 21:1, Jan. 1977, p. 55-73, bibl., plates)

The singing of La Rose Society members on St. Lucia island culminates at the Aug. 30 celebration of the patron saint's day (St. Rose of Lima). Rosette, or "Mamma Rose," the society's head *shatwèl* (solo singer), claims to be the best anywhere. Annie and Paula, her nearest competitors, each boasts special skills, Annie on "hot" numbers, Paula as an adapter of country and western hits. For ethnologist's comment, see *HLAS 39:1233*.

9069. Thompson, Donald. A new world mbira: The Caribbean Marímbula (African Music [Roodepoort, South Africa] 5:4, 1975/1976, p. 140-148, plates)

Reprinted with new title and slight revisions from *Yearbook for Inter-American Musical Research* (7. 1971, p. 103-116).

CENTRAL AMERICA

9070. Agerkop, Terry. Música de los mískitos de Honduras (IPGH/FA, 23, junio 1977, p. 7-37, bibl., music)

Between 1 Oct. and 15 Dec. 1973, the author, a native of Suriname resident in Caracas, visited the Honduras coastal area between the Wans Coco, Segovia and Patuca rivers to gather data for INIDEF (Instituto Interamericano de Etnomusicología y Folklore, Caracas) on Mískito singing. He was accompanied by a Honduras folklorist with area experience Ronny Velázquez, and a Mískito, Nathan Pravia Lacayo, who traveled with them as guide and interpreter. Although acknowledging the paramount musical influence of Moravian and other missionary groups, the author deals solely with the two types of Mískito song least contaminated by European inroads, the weeping *inanka* and the love *tune* (songs sung by men with guitar). Two tunings of the guitar prevail: mi-la-re-sol-si-mi and sol-re-sol-si-re-fa. Includes 10 musical examples, translated texts, and valuable commentary.

9071. Arosemena Moreno, Julio. Danza de la Montezuma Española en la villa de Los Santos (INC/RNC, 1:1, oct./dic. 1975, p. 34-52, bibl., music, plates)

The Panamanian version of the widely diffused Montezuma Española dance enlists 10 personages, half of whom do not match the actors in the Mexican version. The music is performed by violinist, guitarist, and player of triangle and military drum. As danced at Los Santos, a village on the Azuero peninsula near Chitré, the drama ends with Montezuma's being sent captive to Spain. The music for the introit and Danza de la Montezuma (p. 37-38) was transcribed with acumen and skill by Leslie George, "etnomusicólogo panameño."

9072. Hadel, Richard. Black Carib folk music (UWI/CQ, 22:2/2, June/Sept. 1976, p. 84-96, bibl.)

Informed description of Black Carib dance songs, such as *púnta, hüngü(hü)ngü, wanáragua* (= John Canoe), and non-dance such as *bérusu* and *abaímahani*, with five sample song-texts and translations. The author who spent a year at Sein Bight, British Honduras, corrects various misapprehensions in Emory C. Whipple's 1971 article "The Music of the Black Caribs of Honduras." For ethnologist's comment see *HLAS 39:1215*.

9073. Kuss, Malena. Julio Fontana (MGG [Supplement] 148/149, 1974, p. 325-326, bibl.)

Biography and works list of a chief Costa Rican composer of the 20th century.

9074. McCosker, Sandra. San Blas Cuna Indian lullabies: a means of informal learning (*in* Wilbert, Johannes *ed.* Enculturation in Latin America: an anthology. Los Angeles, Univ. of California, Latin American Center, 1976, p. 29-66, bibl., music, plates)

Cuna lullabies involve improvised texts sung by mother, sister, or female cousin, as she swings a hammock and shakes a rattle. Behavioral patterns are taught via these texts, 13 of which with English translations are printed in Appendix II. Melodic patterns involve do-re-mi in a typical lullaby (No. 35).

9075. Stevenson, Robert. Guatemala Stadt (MGG [Supplement] 150/151, 1975, p. 551-555, bibl.)

Musical developments at Kaminaljuyú and the various sites that served as capital of Guatemala from aboriginal times to the present.

9076. Zárate, Dora P. de. Siempre sobre nuestros tambores panameños (Música [La Habana] 53, julio/agosto 1975, p. 10-15, illus.)

Description of drums (and sticks, when used)—differentiating those of European and African origin (illustrated with line drawings of nine drums).

CHILE

9077. Aisthesis. Revista chilena de investigaciones estéticas. Univ. Católica de Chile, Instituto de Estética. No. 8, 1974- . Santiago.

Special issue entitled "La música y sus problemas en Chile." 15 essays by 12 authors ranging in subject matter from esthetic theory, music in Chile, personal experiences of three Chilean composers, to lists of courses in the four depts. that comprised the institute in 1974. Of special interest are the following chapters: Tomás Lefever "Tres Maestros Chilenos" (Soro, Allende, Leng, p. 201-240); Alfonso Letelier Llona "Consideraciones sobre la Música Chilena (p. 241-254); Roberto Escobar "Estilo y Tendencia de los Compositores Chilenos (p. 255-261); and Manuel Dannemann "Estudios sobre Música Folklórica Chilena" (p. 269-305).

9078. Amenábar, Juan. Algunos rasgos de la personalidad docente de Jorge Urrutia Blondel (UCIEM/R, 31:138, abril/junio 1977, p. 33-38)

Urrutia Blondel, trained first for a legal career, departed for Europe on a government grant in Sept. 1928. On returning to teach in Chile (where he began composition classes in 1940) he did not try to impose the value judgments of the school he followed.

9079. Bustos, Raquel. Enrique Soro (UCIEM/R, 30:135/136, oct./dic. 1976, p. 39-73, bibl., music notations)

Enrique Soro Barriga (b. Concepción 15 July 1884; d. Santiago 3 Dec. 1954) was the most published, performed, and honored Chilean composer of his immediate time, the initiator of the Chilean symphony, and a transcendental national cultural figure. In this definitive essay the author traces his career, analyzes his style (with abundant musical examples), lists newspaper and magazine articles on Soro, and meticulously catalogues his works.

9080. Claro Valdés, Samuel. Las artes musicales y coreográficas en Chile (Cultura Chilena [Univ. de Chile, Facultad de Ciencias Humanas, Depto. de Ciencias Antropológicas y Arqueológicas, Santiago] 1977, p. 241-270, bibl.)

This excellent bird's-eye view of music and dance from earliest times written by the nation's leading authority goes beyond a mere summary of previously available data. From documents discovered by him at the Archive of the Indies, Claro established 5 Jan. 1775 as the date that Barcelona-b. José de Campderrós (1742-1842) left Cádiz for Callao. In Lima he worked both as a merchant and a maestro de capilla before coming to Chile. Every paragraph of this summary is densely packed with precise facts. The survey of present musical entities at work in Santiago, Concepción, Valdivia, Valparaíso, Osorio, and Temuca includes schools, orchestras, bands, choruses, and is most useful. The section on dance is a model of historical summary.

9081. ———. La musicología y la historia: una perspectiva de colaboración científica (ACH/B, 87, 1973, p. 53-96, bibl.)

Address read at his reception as *académico de número* of the Chilean Academy of History (3 May 1973) as successor to Alfonso Bulnes Calvo (1885-1970), former president of the Academy. To illustrate the importance of music in Chilean history Claro reviews the musical allusions in several classic Chilean historians and analysts before discussing the political content of various songs sung in Santiago Cathedral on the eve of Independence. The speech of reception by Eugenio Pereira Salas (p. 85-90), president of the Academy in 1973, outlines Claro's eminent career. Claro's musicological bibliography (p. 91-96) is exceedingly rich.

9082. ———. La tertulia musical como antecedente de los compositores decimales (*in* "Los Diez" en el arte chileno del siglo XX. Santiago, Editorial Universitaria, 1976, p. 39-49, plates)

"Los Diez" are best known as a confraternity of visual artists whose paintings and sculpture were exhibited in 1916 in El Mercurio salon and are commemorated in this handsome 60th-anniversary booklet (83 p.) which includes this excellent article. "Los Diez" also encouraged musicians such as Alfonso Leng, Alberto and Eduardo García Guerrero to attend meetings in the house of Luis Arrieta and José Miguel Besoain. In a reunion held on 20 April 1908, Enrique Soro played two movements of his C sharp minor piano sonata. Acario Cotapos started coming 20 Jan. 1914. Claro traces the antecedents of such artistic gatherings in fine Chilean houses back to 1770. Among later outgrowths of such private salons, Claro lists the Sociedad de Música Clásica founded in 1879, the Sociedad Cuarteto in 1885, the Sociedad Bach, and many more musical clubs in Santiago and outside (at Copiapó, Ovalle, Valparaíso, Concepción, and Osorno).

9083. "Los días de Dios" oratorio de Juan Orrego-Salas (UCIEM/R, 30:135/136, oct./dic. 1976, p. 100-107, music notations)

Authoritative analysis of *The Days of God* (Opus 73) premiered at Kennedy Center, Washington, 2-3 Nov. 1976 (National Symphony led by Antal Dorati). This bicentenially commissioned work was Orrego-Salas' fifth and largest choral masterpiece composed 1965-74.

9084. Grebe, María Ester. Aportes de Jorge Urrutia Blondel a la literatura musical chilena (UCIEM/R, 31:138, abril/junio 1977, p. 39-54, bibl.)

Valuable analysis of Urrutia Blondel's 39 published writings, 1925-73, with a complete listing. There are 23 items that deal with Chilean music, erudite and traditional.

9085. In memoriam: Josefina Pelizzari de Brazioli, 1887-1977 (UCIEM/R, 31:138, abril/junio 1977, p. 94-96)

Biography of the distinguished harpist resident in Chile since 1907, awarded the Order of Merit 6 June 1957 after a half-century of teaching and concertizing.

9086. Letelier Llona, Alfonso. Jorge Urrutia Blondel: sus obras sinfónicas (UCIEM/R, 31:138, abril/junio 1977, p. 22-32, music notations)

Informed analysis of composer's major orchestral works, *Pastoral de Alhué* (Homenaje a Ravel, 1937); *La Guitarra del Diablo* (1942); *Música para un Cuento de Antaño* (1948).

9087. Merino, Luis. Catálogo de la obra musical de Jorge Urrutia Blondel (UCIEM/R, 31:138, abril/junio 1977, p. 55-72)

A model catalogue of the musical compositions arranged under the following categories: chamber, symphonic, and choral, with dates of creation and premiere (when ascertainable).

9088. Santa Cruz, Domingo. El compositor Jorge Urrutia Blondel (UCIEM/R, 31:138, abril/junio 1977, p. 17-21)

Urrutia Blondel follows Flaubert's path in "correcting, correcting, correcting."

9089. Subercaseaux, Bernardo and **Jaime Londoño.** Gracias a la vida: Violeta Parra, testimonio. B.A., Editorial Galerna, 1976. 139 p.

Interviews with friends, family, and associates of the folksinger (1917-67) who worked on the forefront of Chilean communism. Violeta was the younger sister of the poet Nicanor Parra and the mother of Ángel Parra.

9090. Urrutia Blondel, Jorge. Ensayo de una síntesis autobiográfica (UCIEM/R, 31:138, abril/junio 1977, p. 5-16)

Recollections of Nadia Boulanger, Charles Koechlin, Paul Dukas. Activities as Eugenio Pereira Salas' successor in heading the Instituto de Investigaciones Musicales of the Univ. of Chile music faculty. Compositions entitling him to the Premio Nacional de Arte 1976.

COLOMBIA

9091. Billip, Jim. *Sacred and profane music of the Ika* [liner notes]. N.Y., Folkways Record & Service Corp., 1977. 4 p., plates (Ethnic folkways album, FE 4055)

Some 2000 Ika live in an isolated mountain mass in north Colombia. Notes on music recorded during and after their annual Fiesta de San Juan in 1976 at the village of San Sebastián de Rábago. The chicotes played on an accordion, some with guacharaca (rasp) accompaniment on Side 1, on a German harmonica on Side 2, are two-step rollicking dance music. Author stresses the decline of Ika traditions.

9092. Escobar, Luis Antonio. *Aspectos de la música colonial en Colombia: anexo al disco "Obras Corales de Colombia"* [record booklet]. Bogotá, Telecom, 1973 [i.e. 1974]. 16 p., plate (Archivo musical colombiano, LAES-0001)

In this booklet accompanying the disk *Obras Corales de Colombia*, the author selects Gutierre Fernández Hidalgo and José Cascante as twin peaks of the colonial period and outlines the development of the Baroque villancico. Side 1 of the disk contains also a Christmas villancico by Matías Durango and a Magnificat Septimi toni by Sebastián Aguilera de Heredia. Side 2 of the disk contains nine of Escobar's own *Cánticas Colombianas* and a lullaby dedicated to the newborn daughter of the conductor of the Grupo Ballestrinque that recorded the album. The liner notes inside the album augment data in the booklet.

9093. Perdomo Escobar, José Ignacio. El archivo musical de la Catedral de Bogotá. Bogotá, Instituto Caro y Cuervo, 1976. 819 p., bibl., discography, facsims., music, plates (Publicación, 37)

This superb catalogue itemizes all the historic music manuscripts and imprints in the South American cathedral with the richest archive of Renaissance and Baroque works. In addition Monseñor Perdomo Escobar has transcribed all the villancico texts (p. 123-635), making this volume indispensable for any student of South American colonial poetry. The first two chapters, written with his customary magisterial authority, deal with the history of Bogotá cathedral music to about 1800, and identify the qualifying characteristics of the Baroque villancico. In its kind, this catalogue compares favorably with Pedrell's monumental Barcelona *Catàlech* of 1908-09 and the Anglés-Subirá Madrid catalogue of 1946-51. To date only Granada, among cathedrals in Spain, has inspired a more luxurious publication.

9093a. Piñeros Corpas, Joaquín. Historia de la música colombiana: la llave del tesoro (El Tiempo [Bogotá] 21 May 1977, n.a.)

Among contemporary Colombians who have helped rescue the nation's musical past Rodolfo Pérez (director of the Coltejer coro in Antioquia), Luis Antonio Escobar (editor of a volume containing Cascante's works; see *HLAS 38:9113*), María Cristina Sánchez de Vesga (leader of the Grupo Ballestrinque), and Amalia Samper (conductor of the Univ. de Los Andes coro) have each made signal contributions. However the paladin has been José Ignacio Perdomo Escobar, national historian *par excellence*.

CUBA

9094. Borbolla, Carlos. El son, exclusividad de Cuba (UT/YIMR, 11, 1975 [i.e. 1977] p. 152-156, music notations)

The identifying characteristic of the Cuban son, the typology of which was consolidated between 1920 and 1940, is constant syncopation with the two tied notes in the syncope (whether eighths or sixteenths) being obligatorily of equal value. Pt. 2 of the danzón *El Combate* (1883) by the trombonist Raimundo Valenzuela (1848-1905) anticipated the Cuban son. It was he also who enlarged the danzón from two to three parts. Borbolla closes this provocative and informative essay with the assurance that neither Manuel Saumell (1817-70) nor Ignacio Cervantes (1847-1905) foresaw the son—except in pt. 1 of the latter's danza *Zig-Zags*.

Brouwer, Leo. *Lucía* en tres movimientos. See *HLAS 39:5010*.

———. La música, lo cubano y la innovación. See *HLAS 39:5011*.

———. La música en el cine cubano: un año de experimentación. See *HLAS 39:5012*.

9095. Concierto conmemorativo 250 años del nacimiento de Esteban Salas (Boletín UNESCO [Comisión Nacional Cubana de la UNESCO, La Habana] 15:62, marzo/abril 1976, p. 12-15, plates)

At the close of 1971 Hilario González moved to Santiago where he painstakingly continued the scholarly investigations begun by Pablo Hernández Balaguer (d. 1966). After herculean efforts, González prepared 106 works for performance during the Festival de Coros, 1975. Throughout that year, Salas' birth at Havana was commemorated therein with a series of events culminating in a concert on Dec. 25, his 250th birthday. Salas' father was a garrison soldier from the Canary Islands, who d. shortly after 1725. In 1733 Salas became a choirboy in the Havana parochial church where he learned Gregorian chant, violin playing, and organ. At 15 he entered San Carlos Seminary (founded at Havana in 1729) where he studied theology and canon law. His chief music teacher was probably the Catalonian Cayetano Pagueras. In 1763 on Bishop Agustín Morell de Santa Cruz' invitation he went to Santiago where he spent the rest of his life as cathedral chapelmaster.

Entrevistas con directores de largometrajes, fotografía, escritores y músicos. See *HLAS* 39:5034.

9096. González, Hilario. Algunas tesis sobre las raíces de nuestra música sinfónica (BNJM/R, 18[67]:3, sept./dic. 1976, p. 151-162)

This paper was read in the Sala White at Matanzas during the V Encuentro de Rumba, 19-25 April 1976, by an acknowledged expert on Esteban Salas. According to the author, Félix Martín de Arrate erred in supposing that the Cuban indigenes were annihilated in the 16th century. Therefore black and indigenous mixed to form the Cuban musical psyche. In the search for Cuban symphonic roots, he mentions Juan Casamitjana's pioneer *Cocuyé* for band written at Santiago in 1836; Manuel Ubeda's transcription of Laureano Fuentes' *Potpourri de aires cubanos* of 1847; and Julián Reyno's highly successful *Cocuyé* of 1849. After Gottschalk's seminal pieces, the author proposes as other precursors of Alejandro García Caturla's *Obertura Cubana* various sections in operas by Eduardo Sánchez de Fuentes, whom he vigorously defends against charges of racism. The author wishes also to rehabilitate the *areito de Anacaona* as much more authentically indigenous melody than is now generally supposed.

9097. Hernandez López, Rházes. Violinistas en Caracas (Música [La Habana] 63, marzo/abril 1977, p. 3-7, plate)

Both Claudio Brindis de Salas (1852-1911) and José White (1836-1918)—world-famous black cuban violinists—successfully concertized in Caracas. *El Zancudo* (issues of 3 Dec. 1876 and 11 March 1877) published their biographies. This fine article by a leading Venezuelan musicologist includes facsimiles of the appropriate pages. But the exalted social position ascribed to Brindis de Salas *père* (1800-72) in the *El Zancudo* biography (rich nobleman, court favorite of Queen Isabel II, decorated by other foreign governments) is a mere fabrication. White dedicated his *Danza Cubana* composed at Caracas 22 April 1877 to Ramón de la Plaza, Venezuela's paramount 19th-century music historian.

9097a. Marsans, Luis Felipe. Elogian el concierto sinfónico dirigido por Hernández Lizaso en el Gusman Hall (Diario Las Américas [Miami, Fla.] 30 June 1977, n.a.)

Glowing interview with Aurelio de la Vega (province of La Habana, 28 Nov. 1925) concerning music heard at the 1977 Reencuentro Cubano, sponsored by National Endowment for the Arts, Univ. of Miami, and other entities. Conductor of the 25 June concert given by the Orquesta Filarmónica de Miami was Antonio Hernández-Lizaso (La Habana, 14 May 1933) whose program included a portion of his own *Perichoresis* (1970), Julián Orbón's *Pavana* and *Xilófono* (1953), Alejandro García Caturla's *Tres danzas cubanas* (1926), and De la Vega's *Obertura a una farsa seria* (1950).

9098. Stevenson, Robert. Esteban Salas y Castro primer compositor nativo de Cuba (HET, 10:4, julio/agosto 1977, p. 4-7)

Surviving works—some in print, the rest in manuscript—by Salas y Castro (1725-1803), maestro de capilla at Santiago de Cuba from 1763 to his death, entitle him to first-class honors in hemispheric music history.

ECUADOR

9099. Coba, Carlos. Nuevos planteamientos a la etnomúsica y al folklore (Sarance [Instituto Otavaleño de Antropología, Otavalo, Ecua.] 2:3, agosto 1976, p. 50-62)

Author contends that Samuel Martí's "scales" for archaeological ocarinas and flutes are defective. Advocates the terms *chaqui* or *tushug* for an indigenous group dancing or a group of indigenous dances honoring a divinity. More gristle than lean meat in this essay.

9100. Muriel, Inés. Contribución a la cultura musical de los indios jívaros del Ecuador (Música [La Habana] 60, sept./dic. 1976, p. 3-19, bibl., music notations)

Painstaking survey of Jívaro music based on 26 melodies collected by the Ecuadorian missionary priest Raimundo M. Monteros and published at Quito in 1942 (*Música autóctona del oriente* ecuatoriano; see HLAS 8:4798) and an unstated number of melodies recorded by Philippe Luzuy for the Musée de l'Homme in 1958. Unfortunately, Monteros was no trained ethnomusicologist and Luzuy's ability to separate the authentic from the fake has been questioned (see HLAS 23:700). Five songs printed in this article using exclusively notes in major triads are exhaustively analyzed.

Whitten, Norman E., Jr. Musical contexts in the Pacific lowlands of Colombia and Ecuador. See HLAS 39:1578.

Vol. 7 (1973) contains articles on Candelario Haízar (p. 97), Julio Ituarte (p. 362), Jarabe (p. 456), Agustín Lara (p. 591-592); vol. 8 (1974) on Tomás León (p. 50-51), Samuel Martí (p. 296), Vicente T. Mendoza (p. 437-438), and Carlos J. Meneses (p. 439-440); and vol. 9 (1975) on Melesio Morales (p. 183), música (p. 288-301), and Jaime Nunó (p. 457-458). Although Manuel Jorge de Elías (Mexico City, 5 June 1939, see HLAS 38:9152) wrote the general article on *música* this and the unsigned entries lack the detail and bibliographical precision of articles on Mexican subjects in *Die Musik in Geschichte und Gegenwart* and *Riemann* (see HLAS 38:9017).

MEXICO

9101. Alcázar, Miguel. *Tablatura mexicana para guitarra barroca* [liner notes]. México, Discos Capitol de México, 1975. 2 p., facsims., plates (Angel SAM-35029)

The 18th-century MS 1560 at the Biblioteca Nacional containing numerous pieces that recall Santiago de Marcia provided the virtuoso guitarist who recorded this one-disk album with 12 pieces and four sonata movements. The painting reproduced on the front cover of the album shows a Mexico City street procession in the epoch of Viceroy Revilla Gigedo (1746-55), to which approximate period the source manuscript belongs. Four of the recorded items are minuets, one is a guitar version of Corelli's folia. This is an album of music played, not made, in Mexico.

9102. Alderson, Richard. *Modern Mayan: the Indian music of Chiapas, Mexico, v. 2* [liner notes]. N.Y., Folkways Record & Service Corp., 1977. 4 p., music, plates (Ethnic folkways album, FE 4379)

The author, a NYC recording engineer, recorded the festival music in this album *in situ* between 1972 and 1974 at Venustiano Carranza (Fiesta de San Bartolo), Petalcingo (Ascensión [Asunción]), Tila (Santa Lucía), Huistan (San Miguel), and other village communities near San Cristóbal de las Casas. The guitars, violins, mandolin, as well as three-hole flutes and trumpets, on which the instrumentalists play frequently betray local manufacture. The one transcribed selection (Side 2, Band 3) is tonic-dominant music changing implied chords with the regularity of a fandango. Misspellings in the notes, Spanish and English (*custumbre* for *costumbre*, subtley), imply hasty preparation.

9103. Alvarez, José Regilio ed. Enciclopedia de México. v. 7/9. México, Enciclopedia de México, 1973-1975. 3 v. (596, 612, 620 p.) maps, plates, tables.

9104. Biggs, Johns. *California mission music performed by The John Biggs Consort* [liner notes]. Berkeley, Univ. of California, Univ. Extension and Extension Media Center, 1974. 1 v. (Unpaged) (KSK recording 75217-75218)

Liner notes issued with two-disk sound recording of an *ensalada* by Mateo Flecha *el Viejo*, Credo from Cristóbal de Morales' *Missa Si bona suscepimus*, Magnificat by Francisco López Capillas, vernacular Christmas music by Juan Gutiérrez de Padilla, and other selections. Among factual lapses, the Flecha in question is incorrectly identified and López Capillas worked at Puebla (not Mexico City) in the 1640s; however, the honorable intentions of the album and liner notes compensate for occasional errors of fact in a pioneering venture of this magnitude.

9105. Cabello Moreno, Antonio. Panorama musical de la Ciudad de México. México, Talleres Gráficas de la Nación, 1975. 190 p., illus. (Col. Popular Ciudad de México, 32)

Published 650 years after the traditional founding year of Tenochtitlan, this school text stresses prehispanic culture (123 p.). The author (b. Saltillo 1911) joined the Instituto Mexicana del Seguro Social as an *abogado* in 1946 and in 1963 became editor of the *Revista Cultural de la Casa de Coahuila*. His honorable intentions are largely frustrated in this undocumented panorama by what seems to be complete innocence of pertinent literature by Estrada, Horcasitas, Lemmon, Saldívar, Spell, and others.

9106. Carmen Sordo Sodi en Cuba (Música [La Habana] 61, nov./dic. 1976, p. 30)

Director of the Mexican CENIDIM (Centro Nacional de Investigación, Documentación e Información Musical), Carmen Sordo Sodi visited Cuba during Sept./Oct. 1976 as "distinguished guest of the Second Meeting of Musical Researchers." This is a record of her activities in the island.

9107. Collins, Anne C. The *maestros cantores* in Yucatán (*in* Jones, Grant D. ed. Anthropology and history in Yucatán. Austin, Univ. of Texas Press, 1977, p. 233-247, maps, tables)

This essay contains a useful outline history of Franciscan missionary endeavor in colonial Yucatán explaining why lay native adjutants were indispensable. The maestro de capilla, maestro cantor, and maestro de escuela of colonial Yucatán inherited many functions of the Ah Kin Mai, who were the Mayan keys of learning and guardians of religious ceremony. After independence these lay maestros continued functioning not only as ceremonial and musical leaders but also as surrogates for priests when none was available. There regious leadership functions permitted maestros cantores' performing baptisms and marriages, and during the Caste War of 1847-53 of intervening with advice that purported to be God's will.

9108. Estrada, Julio. *Manuel M. Ponce* [liner notes]. México, UNAM, Dirección General de Difusión Cultural, 1976. 6 p., music (Voz viva de México, Serie música nueva, VV-MN-14)

Biographical synopsis, career data and brief analyses of Ponce's piano *Concerto in F sharp minor* (1910) premiered by the composer at Mexico City (7 July 1912) and guitar *Concierto del Sur* premiered by Andrés Segovia at Montevideo (4 Oct. 1941). In each recording Eduardo Mata conducts the Orquesta Filarmónica de la UNAM, with María Teresa Rodríguez as pianist and Alfonso Moreno as guitarist in their respective concertos (the piano concerto includes Ponce's last revisions that shortened it and eliminated pauses between the three movements).

9109. Geijerstam, Claes af. Popular music in Mexico. Albuquerque, Univ. of New Mexico Press, 1976. 187 p., bibl., music, plates.

Written by a Swedish visitor who enlisted the aid of Carmen Sordo Sodi and Juan S. Garrido (the latter a popular musician from Chile resident in Mexico City since 1932). Subject headings include: mariachi, norteño and marimba ensembles, corrido, canción, modern dance rhythms. Includes chapter by Elizabeth H. Heist on "Border Music of the 1970s in the Southwestern United States." Critical reaction to this first and "only" book-length English-language study of popular music in Mexico has been almost without exception adverse (see *HLAS 38:9141*). Includes index.

9110. ———. Respuesta a Mark Fogelquist (HET, 10:1, enero/feb. 1977, p. 28-30)

While admitting some lapses, the author of *Popular Music in Mexico* (see item 9109) defends his choice of informants and his concentration on commercial music in the capital.

9111. Gutiérrez Heras, Joaquín. *Pablo Moncayo Huapango; Carlos Chávez; Corrido El sol; Silvestre Revueltas Redes* [liner notes]. México, UNAM, Dirección General de Difusión Cultural, 1974. 1 p. (Voz viva de México. Série música nueva, VV MN-7)

Conducted by Eduardo Mata, the Orquesta Filarmónica de la UNAM (with Coro de la UNAM in Chávez' *El sol*) here recorded three masterworks from the "best period of Mexican nationalism." Valuable data concerning the works.

9112. Lemmon, Alfred E. Los jesuitas y la música colonial en México (HET, 10:2, marzo/abril 1977, p. 7-10; 10:3, mayo/junio 1977, p. 31-32)

Recognizing that artistic singing was a principal occupation of Indian nobility, the Jesuits from their first entry in 1572 emphasized music instruction. At the reception of relics in 1578 Hernando Franco—"unique in the art" and of exemplary character—conducted the music. Numerous colonial Jesuits were performers and musical enthusiasts, including Francisco Javier Clavigero. The documentation for this fundamental article is a paragon.

9113. ———. Los jesuitas y la música de Baja California (HET, 10:4, julio/agosto 1977, p. 13-17; 10:5, sept./oct. 1977, p. 14-17)

Outstanding article, richly documented, on the musical side of the Jesuit mission in Lower California.

9114. ———. Jesuits and music in Mexico (AHSI, 46:91, Jan./June 1977, p. 191-198)

Definitive version of items 9112 and 9113. This epoch-making study based on prime documents is enhanced by added footnotes and a continuous proofread text. An example of the valuable novelties in Latin American musicology is the case of Juan María Salvatierra (1644-1717) of Milan who became an expert lute player during four years in the Collegio de Nobili at Parma and later emigrated to Lower California where he taught the Indians.

9115. Provost, Paul Jean and **Alan R. Sandstrom.** *Sacred guitar & violin music of the modern Aztecs* [liner notes] N.Y., Folkways Records & Service Corp., 1977. 7 p., illus., map (Ethnic folkways library album, FE 4358)

Description of the winter solstice ceremonial music of a Nahua enclave in the remote village of Puyecaco, Municipio de Ixhuatlan de Madero, Veracruz, recorded live by the authors in 1972. Although admitting their syncretic nature, the authors minimize the Roman Catholic elements in the rituals and downplay the European components of the music.

The misleading word "Aztecs" in the album title undoubtedly "sells" the album but as the authors themselves admit is by no means a scientifically appropriate term. The violin pictured on the album cover was a cheap mass-produced instrument bought in the village marketplace.

9116. Pulido, Esperanza. Muerte de José Yves Limantour (HET, 10:1, enero/feb. 1977, p. 3-9, plates)

Highlights of the musical career of the homonym grandson of a famous Porfirian *científico*. B. at Paris 9 August 1919, Limantour conducted the Xalapa orchestra 1944-53 during which period Arrau, Uninski, Angélica Morales, Carmela Castillo Betancourt and others played with it. On Szeryng's recommendation he then accepted a three-year contract with the Bilbao symphony.

9117. Una revista de música (Música [La Habana] 61, nov./dic. 1976, p. 35)

Glowing tribute to Esperanza Pulido, "eminente musicóloga mexicana," and to the bimonthly *Heterofonía* founded by her in 1968. This unique Mexican periodical offers not only musicological articles, but also publishes letters to the editor, interviews, reports on contemporary concert life, composers' biographies, and reviews of records and books.

9118. Ruiz Carvalho de Baqueiro, Eloisa. Tradiciones, folklore, música y músicos de Campeche. Campeche, Mex., Talleres gráficos del Gobierno del Estado, 1970. 147 p., bibl., music, plates (Publicaciones del Gobierno del Estado de Campeche, 14)

Includes extremely valuable chapters for local history on professional music in the 19th century; theater; the Sociedad Filarmónica (p. 71-101); and popular song in Campeche (p. 105-136). The biography of the author's husband, the noted musician Gerónimo Baqueiro Fóster (p. 98-101), is also most useful.

9119. Sordo Sodi, Carmen. El folclor en la Ciudad de México en la época de Juárez (Música [La Habana] 53, julio/agosto 1975, p. 3-15, music notations)

Text of a lecture read at the Casa de las Américas, La Habana, 21 Sept. 1976.

9120. Stevenson, Robert. Acentos folklóricos en la música mexicana temprana (HET, 10:2, marzo/abril 1977, p. 5-7)

Musical characteristics of Latin American Baroque villancicos classed in archival sources as *negros, negrillas, guineos, gitanillas, gallegos*.

9121. ———. Blas Galindo Dimas (MGG [Supplement] 150/151, 1975, p. 402-403, bibl.)

Biographical article with works list.

9122. ———. Directores nativos de México en Texas (HET, 10:6, nov./dic. 1977, p. 4-5)

Eduardo Mata at Dallas, Abraham Chávez, Jr. at El Paso.

9123. ———. Francisco López Capillas (MGG [Supplement] 154/155, 1977, p. 1157-1158, bibl.)

Biography with works list; see *HLAS 38:9134*, concerning this composer.

9124. ———. Jaime Nunó despúes de 1854 (HET, 11:1, enero/feb. 1978, p. 3-13)

After the premiere of Nunó's music for the Mexican national anthem 15 Sept. 1854, he remained in Mexico City another 13 months. When Antonio López de Santa Anna's departed in 9 Aug. 1855 (sailed for Havana 14 Aug.) Nunó was left without a protector. He went first to N.Y. where he conducted the orchestra at Thalberg's sensational debut. During the next 14 years he conducted orchestras traveling with opera stars such as the Polish-b. Felicità Vestvali. In 1869 be settled at Buffalo where with some significant interruptions he remained until death at Bayside (now part of Queens in N.Y.C.) 18 July 1908. The present detailed account of his career 1854-1908 (and subsequent reburial in Mexico City) draws on contemporary newspapers, city directories, census returns, exposition programs, and a wide variety of secondary sources.

9125. ———. Melesio Morales (MGG [Supplement] 154/155, 1977, p. 1290, bibl.)

Biography with works list correcting previous encyclopedia articles on Mexico's most prolific composer of operas.

9126. ———. Mexiko Stadt (MGG [Supplement] 154/155, 1977, p. 1270-1274, bibl.)

Musical developments at Tenochtitlan during Aztec times and at Mexico City from its Spanish capture to the present.

9127. ———. Primeros compositores nativos de México (HET, 10:3, mayo/junio 1977, p. 4-5)

New biographical data extracted from wills and libros de defunciones.

9128. Summers, William. Music of the California missions: 1769-1836 (Soundings [Univ. of California, Santa Barbara] 9:1, June 1977, p. 13-30, music, plates)

Excellent synopsis of scholarly advances since Owen da Silva's *California mission music* (Santa Barbara, 1941), accompanied by facsimiles of music theory book title pages dated 1606-1848, a catalogue of mission music manuscripts in 10 archives, and an illuminating commentary.

9129. Williams G., Roberto. Falleció la máxima autoridad de la investigación musical precolombina (Boletín del Departamento de Investigación de las Tradiciones Populares [México] 2, oct. 1975, p. 117-119, bibl., plate)

Samuel Martí, b. El Paso, Texas, 18 May 1906, d. Tepoztlán, Morelos, 29 March 1975. During his last months he was subsidized by the Secretaría de Educación Pública to prepare a music text for classroom use.

PARAGUAY

9130. Ruiz Rivas de Domínguez, Celia. Danzas tradicionales paraguayas: método de enseñanza, reseña histórica de la danza en el Paraguay y nociones sobre el folklore. Asunción, Imprenta Makrografic, 1976. 2 v. (324, 32 p.)

Although primarily designed for the use of dance instructor in schools and assemblies, this manual opens with a historical chapter (p. 33-70) containing valuable data on dance developments in Paraguay. Vol. 2, *Album musical suplemento*, consists of music for 16 dances transcribed for piano by Eldo Gladys Galeano and cued by page-number to the choreographic descriptions in vol. 1. The music examples illustrate the following dance types: cielito chopí, palomita, golondrina, Londón Karapé, pericón, solito, el cazador, cuadrilla, cuadrilla boliviana, chotis, montonero, malagueño.

PERU

9131. El estreno de dos obras peruanos (Música [La Habana] 61, nov./dic. 1976, p. 32)

At the seventh winter concert of the Orquesta Sinfónica Nacional were premiered the Cuzco-b. (1927) Armando Guevara Ochoa's Violin concerto (Federico Britos, soloist) and Enrique Pinilla's *Evoluciones II* for percussion and orchestra (Manuel Mujica, soloist).

9132. Peru. Instituto Nacional de Cultura. Biblioteca Nacional. La Púrpura de la Rosa composed by Tomás de Torrejón y Velasco. Libretto by Pedro Calderón de la Barca. Estudio preliminar y transcripción de la música por Robert Stevenson. Lima, P.L. Villanueva, 1976. 134 p., bibl., music, plate.

Estuardo Nuñez Hague and Javier Malagón Barceló wrote the introduction to this volume, Maestro Guillermo Espinosa the preface. Graciela Sánchez Cerro initiated the idea of the edition, Lucila Valderrama oversaw it, Rodolfo Barbacci served as *asesor*. Octavio Santa Cruz designed the cover. Apart from an OAS $3,000 subvention, the heavy publication costs of 1000 copies of this extremely handsome volume commemorating the sesquicentennial of Peruvian independence were met with subsidies from the Banco Central de Reserva del Perú, the Banco de la Vivienda del Perú, the Compañía de Seguros y Reaseguros Peruanó-Suiza, the Banco Peruano de la Construcción and the Banco de la Nación—"a collective financial action in Peru rarely met within the strictly cultural realm," as wrote Dr. Nuñez Hague in his introduction. Portions of the loa as well as the nymphs' chorus *a 7* from this opera—now the largest monument of New World Baroque music in print—were recorded in 1966 by the Roger Wagner Chorale (Salve Regina, Angel Recording S36008).

9133. Stevenson, Robert. Celso Garrido-Lecca (MGG [Supplement] 150/151, 1975, p. 419-420, bibl.)

Biography with works list.

9134. ———. José de Orejón y Aparicio (MGG [Supplement] 154/155, 1977, p. 1442-1443, bibl.)

Biography with works list of Peru's most important native-b. composer before 1800.

9135. ———. Lima (MGG [Supplement] 152/153, 1976, p. 1138-1139, bibl.)

Musical history of Lima from 1535 to the present.

9136. Wistrand Robinson, Lila. Cashibo song poetry (UT/YIMR, 11, 1975, [i.e. 1977] p. 137-151, bibl., music notations)

Authoritative analysis of 43 tape-recorded songs collected by the author in 1958-64 while representing the Summer Institute of Linguistics among the approximately 1000 Cashibo-speaking Indians in the central Peruvian *montaña* (banks of the Aguaytia, San Alejandro, and Sungaruyacu rivers). A model study of texts and melodies.

URUGUAY

9137. Roldán, Washington. Realismo y sensatez de la composición uruguaya (HET, 10:2, marzo/abril 1977, p. 18-20)

Valuable listing of important new Uruguayan works heard at Montevideo during the 1976 season, with dated excerpts from the author's reviews in *El País* (Montevideo).

VENEZUELA

9138. Asuaje de Rugeles, Ana Mercedes. *Antología del madrigal venezolano* [liner notes]. Caracas, Fundación Mito Juan Pro-Musica, 1975. 20 p., plates, texts (Schola cantorum de Caracas, MJ-07[1-2])

History of the choral movement in Caracas that began in 1927 with the visit of the Ukranian choir, that continued with the Orfeón Lamas organized by Vicente Emilio Sojo (first concert in the Teatro Nacional 15 July 1930; first national tours outside Caracas to Valencia and Barquisimeto in 1937; first international tour to Bogotá for the IV Centenario in 1938), and that after Sojo's death proliferated in such other groups as the Schola Cantorum directed by Alberto Grau. This choral movement stimulated the large Venezuelan repertory of *a cappella* gems by José Antonio Calcaño, Evencio Castellanos, Antonio Lauro, Juan Bautista Plaza, and Sojo recorded in MJ-07[1] and of Inocente Carreño, Gonzalo Castellanos, Antonio Estévez, Moisés Moleiro, and Angel Sauce recorded in MJ-07[2]—each disk in a pressing of 4000 copies.

9139. Bendahan, Daniel. Reynaldo Hahn: su vida y su obra. Caracas, Italgráfica, 1973. 115 p., bibl., index, plates.

Biography plus a succinct discussion of the works of a composer b. Caracas 9 Aug. 1874 and taken to France at age three. The author, first to record in Venezuela an LP of Hahn's songs, graduated 1947 with a Ph.D. in Political Science from the Univ. Central of Caracas and subsequently occupied high administrative posts with the Creole Petroleum Corp. and the Compañía Shell de Venezuela. The luxury of the illustrations (seven full-page color plates), the paper, and binding qualify this as the most sumptuous book thus far published on a composer born in Latin America.

9140. Comerlatti, Marila. Venezuela tiene ya un sitio digno en la historia musical latinoamericano (El Nacional [Caracas] 4 agosto 1977, p. C-4m plate)

Venezuela almost alone among Latin American nations has continuously respected and cultivated its colonial heritage. Plaza's *Ensayos* (Caracas, 1883, see item 9146) initiated Latin American musicology, both historical and ethnic. The balance of the two aspects continues alive today in Venezuela where in 1977 were published Luis Felipe Ramón y Rivera's *La música popular en Venezuela* and José Antonio Calcaño's *El Atalaya*. Venezuela composers, thanks to the economic situation, can more easily hear their orchestral works performed than composers in many other less prosperous Latin American nations.

9141. Hernández López, Rházes. *Virginia ópera en cuatro actos y seis escenas del compositor venezolano José Ángel Montero (1832-1881) sobre el libreto de Domenico Bancalari (1809-1879)* [liner notes]. Caracas, Instituto Nacional de Cultura y Bellas Artes, Dirección de Artes Auditivas, 1976. 2 p., facsims., plate.

Liner notes issued with sound recording. Singers and technical personnel are listed. Primo Casale updated the score for its revival, which was sparked by Hernández López' discerning enthusiasm. For comments on the importance of this opera, see *HLAS 38:9194*.

9142. Lamas, José Ángel. Gran miserere. Caracas, Ministerio de Educación Dirección General, Depto. de Publicaciones, 1973. 92 p., music (Col. Cuadernos de música, 4)

Psalm 50=51 set sectionally for mixed chorus, paired oboes and horns in F, and strings. This masterwork by the prince of Venezuelan colonial composers (1775-1814) belongs in every substantial music library. Vicente Emilio Sojo wrote the one-page introduction.

9143. Lares, Oswaldo. *"Música de Venezuela," Indio Figueredo* [liner notes]. Caracas, Grabaciones Continente, 1975. 12 p., map, plates (OLP-1/2)

A 75th-birthday tribute, this two-disk reissued album contains 24 popular selections—chiefly joropos—performed by the Venezuelan diatonic harp virtuoso Ignacio Figueredo (b. at El Cajón de Arauca, Apure, 31 July 1900) with the assistance of members of his family playing cuatro and maracas. Except for four songs, the texts are by him, other Figueredos, or are anonymous.

9144. Liendo, Miguel Ángel. Localizada en Mérida la Primera Ópera Escrita en el País: su autor es el caraqueño José María Osorio, nacido en 1803 (El Nacional [Caracas] 9 agosto 1977, p. C-12, plates)

Working outside the capital, as National Library investigators, José Peñín Cachón and Walter Guido found a descendant of José María Osorio at Mérida, Josefina Bernal, who showed them leaves of an opera buffa *El Maestro Rufo* (1884) and of a *Directorio Coral*, both lithographed in Mérida where Osorio had settled.

9145. Páez, José Antonio. La flor del retiro. Caracas, Ministerio de Educación, Dirección General, Depto. de Publicaciones, 1973. 4 p., music, plate (Col. Cuadernos de música, 1)

Choral arrangement by Evencio Castellanos of a song for tenor solo and piano composed at B.A. about 1868 by the exiled ex-president of Venezuela.

9146. Plaza, Ramón de la. Ensayos sobre el arte en Venezuela. [Introductions by] Luis García Morales, Alfredo Boulton, José Antonio Calcaño. Caracas, Imprenta Nacional, 1977. 261 p., facsims., music, plates (Col. Clásicos venezolanos, 6)

Facsimile of original ed. (Caracas, Imprenta al Vapor "La Opinión Nacional," 1883). Published the same year as the first history of music in the US, this one published in a Latin American country, was a masterpiece for its time. Calcaño, the chief South American-born musicologist of his generation (b. 1900), greatly enhances the usefulness of this facsimile ed. by itemizing specific errors in Plaza's text that have been copied by such authors as Chase

For a review of this important work, see *Notes of the Music Library Association* (35:3, March 1978).

9147. Velázquez, José Francisco (El Viejo). Los cielos destilaban alegría. Caracas, Ministerio de Educación, Dirección General, Depto. de Publicaciones, 1973. 16 p., music (Col. Cuadernos de música, 3)

Claudio García Lazo wrote the preface to this A Major Christmas villancico by the elder Velázquez (1756-1805). Scored for two tiples accompanied by paired oboes, horns in A, and strings.

9148. Venezuela. Biblioteca Nacional. Fondo No Bibliográfico. Inventario de manuscritos musicales propiedad de la Biblioteca Nacional. Caracas, 1977. 202 p.

Compiled under the intelligent supervision of Ingrid Hernández Mantellini aided by Jorge Escobar Rago, this extremely useful preliminary catalogue of 1046 manuscript items in the Edificio Macanao, Calle París de Las Mercedes, ranges from late 18th-century tonadillas by the Spaniard Blas Lacerna to early 20th-century Venezuelan composers. However the strength of the collection resides in sacred and secular works by the chief 19th-century Venezuelan composers, among them José Ángel Lamas, Juan Meserón and seven members of the Montero clan (especially José Ángel Montero).

JOURNAL ABBREVIATIONS

ACH/B	Boletín de la Academia Chilena de la Historia. Santiago.
AHSI	Archivum Historicum Societatis Iesu. Rome.
BAM	Buenos Aires Musical. B.A.
BNJM/R	Revista de la Biblioteca Nacional José Martí. La Habana.
CDFB/RBF	Revista Brasileira de Folclore. Ministério da Educação e Cultura, Campanha de Defesa do Folclore Brasileiro. Rio.
CFS/WF	Western Folklore. Univ. of California Press *for the* California Folklore Society. Berkeley, Calif.
HET	Heterofonía. Revista musical bimestral. México.
IAA	Ibero-Amerikanisches Archiv. Ibero-Amerikanisches Institut. Berlin, FRG.
IHGSP/R	Revista do Instituto Histórico e Geográfico de São Paulo. São Paulo.
INC/RNC	Revista Nacional de Cultura. Instituto Nacional de Cultura. Panama.
IPGH/FA	Folklore Americano. Instituto Panamericano de Geografia e Historia, Comisión de Historia, Comité de Folklore. México.
LAP	Latin American Perspectives. Univ. of California. Riverside.
MGG	Die Musik in Geschichte und Gegenwart. Kassel. Wilhelmshöhe, FRG.
MP/R	Revista do Museu Paulista. São Paulo.
NHAC/K	Kaie. National History and Arts Council of Guyana. Georgetown.
OAS/IMB	Inter-American Music Bulletin. Organization of American States. Washington.
UCIEM/R	Revista Musical Chilena. Univ. de Chile, Instituto de Extensión Musical. Santiago.

UFB/AA	Afro-Asia. Univ. Federal da Bahia, Centro de Estudos Afro-Orientais. Bahia, Bra.
USP/RH	Revista de História. Univ. de São Paulo, Faculdade de Filosofia, Ciências e Letras, Depto. de História [and] Sociedade de Estudos Históricos. São Paulo.
UT/YIMR	Yearbook for Inter-American Musical Research/Anuario Interamericano de Investigación Musical. Univ. of Texas, Institute of Latin American Studies [and] College of Fine Arts, Dept. of Music. Austin.
UWI/CQ	Caribbean Quarterly. Univ. of the West Indies. Mona, Jam.
UY/R	Revista de la Universidad de Yucatán. Mérida, Mex.
VOZES	Vozes. Revista de cultura. Editora Vozes. Petrópolis, Bra.

PHILOSOPHY

JUAN CARLOS TORCHIA-ESTRADA

General Secretariat
Organization of American States

SALVO SITUACIONES EXCEPCIONALES, los cambios de dirección en la filosofía latinoamericana ocurren a un ritmo que exige mucho más de dos años—la periodicidad propia del *Handbook*—para apreciar modificaciones fundamentales. Más apropiado parece—además de señalar los puntos salientes del material de cada número—mantener una reflexión constante sobre la actualidad filosófica latinoamericana, destacando en cada oportunidad diferentes aspectos. Así como desde el punto de vista del material recogido no se puede tener una buena visión de conjunto más que abarcando varios números (cada uno de por sí es resultado de un corte temporal demasiado rígido), así también el comentario es de alguna manera el producto de períodos más amplios. Por ese carácter "abierto" de la información y el comentario, no dudamos en incorporar materiales anteriormente omitidos ni en repensar situaciones del pasado inmediato.

La actividad filosófica en Iberoamérica se realiza casi exclusivamente en las Universidades. De allí la importancia que, para dar el tomo a la producción filosófica, tienen la orientación de las cátedras, las publicaciones y revistas universitarias y, en algunos casos, el apoyo oficial a la investigación. Por ello, dada la importancia de las Universidades estatales, ocurre que ciertos cambios en la vida de un país pueden convertirse, en la superficie al menos, en cambios de la orientación filosófica. Complementariamente, los cambios que resultan de nuevas (o distintas) preferencias filosóficas tienden a manifestarse también mediante aquellos signos externos: orientación de las cátedras, contenido de las revistas universitarias, etc. Teoría y praxis frecuentemente andan mezcladas en el cambio filosófico-institucional, que suele ser el más ostensible, si bien no siempre el más profundo.

En sus grandes líneas, las corrientes que predominan en la filosofía latinoamericana no han variado. La producción inspirada en la fenomenología, el pensamiento de Heidegger o el neotomismo no ofrece mayores cambios. La presencia del marxismo está más extendida en algunos medios universitarios y por eso mismo en muchos casos aparece más "institucionalizado," es decir, con menos aire de combate. Podría decirse que está más extendida la filosofía analítica, si bien a veces lo que se acepta en realidad es el "estilo analítico" en filosofía. Ocurre con esta tendencia lo que ocurrió en otra época con la fenomenología: se acepta el método o la modalidad, aunque no siempre el contenido estricto.[1] Por último, la "filosofía de la liberación" renueva el impulso que animó al "americanismo filosófico," que tuvo su mayor auge

---

[1] Esto coincidiría con lo afirmado por Ferrater Mora, cuando, al referirse al "giro analítico" en la filosofía reciente, dice que "no debe considerarse como una moda filosófica, . . . sino como un instrumento de trabajo." (José Ferrater Mora, *Cambio de marcha en filosofía*, Madrid, Alianza, 1974, p. 115).

en México a partir de la década del 40. Como un eje que une el ayer y el hoy dentro de la tendencia americanista, se mantiene constante la obra de Leopoldo Zea.

Si se excluyen los extremos "comprometidos," en los cuales colocaríamos al marxismo, la filosofía de la liberación y formas combinadas en las que predomina el interés político, ideológico o de cambio social, la corriente central está compuesta por lo que a falta de mejor expresión llamaríamos la filosofía profesional, que se expresa en publicaciones como *Cuadernos de Filosofía* y *Revista Latinoamericana de Filosofía* (Argentina), *Revista Venezolana de Filosofía*, *Revista Brasileira de Filosofía*, *Diánoia* (México), *Diálogos* (Puerto Rico) y *Crítica* (México)—las dos últimas, más "analíticas"—, además de otras de más irregular aparición. *Latinoamérica* (México) y *Revista de Filosofía Latinoamericana* (Argentina) son la mayor expresión del "americanismo," sea en la forma que lo entiende Zea y su grupo o como filosofía de la liberación.

En la vida filosófica latinoamericana de hoy no puede dejar de señalarse una marcada elevación en el nivel del rigor filosófico. La exigencia de rigor y profesionalización está muy generalizada en muchos de quienes se encuentran en la etapa más productiva y también en generaciones más jóvenes. Ello se fleja en el uso de instrumentos metodológicos más afinados y se manifiesta, entre otras cosas, en una más profesional dedicación a la historia de la filosofía, campo en el que ya se producen trabajos que pueden ser una contribucíon a la bibliografía mundial.

Los indudables beneficios que trae la rigurosa profesionalización de la filosofía tienen también su contraparte, por comparación con la época anterior de los "fundadores" o "patriarcas." Por ejemplo, predominando la comunicación técnica y la monografía sobre el ensayo tradicional, hay menos preocupación por el estilo de la exposición escrita. La inserción del pensador en su sociedad es menor o menos directa que en el caso de los grandes pensadores individuales de otra época. Por último, al no ser la filosofía algo que se cultiva *a pesar de* ciertas dificultades, deja de tener, en el que la ejercita, el tono de "sabiduría heroica" de otros tiempos, para participar, en ocasiones, de *la petit histoire* propia del ejercicio de un medio de vida. Independientemente de estas características, que caen más bien en el campo de la "sociología de la filosofía," puede aventurarse que esta modalidad "profesional" será la predominante en el futuro filosófico latinoamericano, si la politización del pensamiento (que no es lo mismo que la aplicación del pensamiento a la política) no le impide su desarrollo.

De los materiales recogidos en esta entrega, entre las obras de carácter instrumental o didáctico destacamos una nueva reimpresión del ya clásico y admirable *Diccionario de Filosofía* de Ferrater Mora (item 9414) y una cuidadosa obra de iniciacion filosófica a cargo de Luis O. Gómez y Roberto Torreti, publicada por la Editorial Universitaria de la Univ. de Puerto Rico (item 9417).

Entre los textos que agrupamos bajo el título de "Fuentes," y donde recogemos ediciones de autores filosóficos latinoamericanos que podrían denominarse "clásicos," encontramos nuevos volúmenes de las *Obras* de Antonio Caso (item 9448), que se agregan a las incluidas en el *HLAS 36* (item 5038-5040) y *HLAS 38* (item 9451). Otro tanto ocurre con Coriolano Alberini: en este número incluimos sus *Escritos de metafísica* (item 9446) que se añaden a los *Escritos de ética* (*HLAS 36:5036*) y los *Escritos de filosofía de la educación* (ver *HLAS 38:9450*). En el caso de Brasil hay que señalar la edición, en dos volúmenes, de escritos filosóficos de Clóvis Bevilaqua (item 9447) y una nueva colección de textos clásicos del pensamiento brasileño que ha comenzado a editar la Pontificia Univ. Católica de Rio de Janeiro.

El interés histórico-crítico por el pensamiento filosófico latinoamericano no decrece. En materia de bibliografías destacamos la muy útil de W.B. Redmond sobre filosofía colonial en Iberoamérica (item 9482) y la realizada por Antonio Paim sobre literatura filosófica brasileña desde 1931 a 1971 (item 9479). Entre los panoramas nacionales o regionales deben señalarse: la reedición del clásico libro de Gallegos Rocafull sobre el pensamiento mexicano de los siglos XVI y XVII (item 9461); *La filosofía en Chile*, de Roberto Escobar (item 9459); la reedición aumentada de la obra de Pinheiro Machado sobre la fiosofía en Brasil (item 9470); el ensayo de Michael Weinstein sobre el pensamiento filosófico mexicano reciente (item 9490); el número de *Cuadernos de Filosofía* (Buenos Aires), dedicado a la filosofía argentina (item 9456); la reedición ampliada de la obra de Miguel Reale sobre la filosofía en São Paulo (item 9481); y el libro de Solomon Lipp, *Three Chilean philosophers* (item 9469). Por su procedencia europea señalamos también la obra colectiva *Le temps et la morte dans la philosophie contemporaine d'Amérique Latine* (item 9487) y un ambicioso panorama del pensamiento filosófico hispanoamericano contemporáneo, publicado recientemente en Italia, del cual es autor Sergio Sarti (item 9485).

Un tema que sigue gozando de vitalidad es el del "problema" de la filosofía latinoamericana. Este tema tiene antecedentes en el siglo XIX, en el pensamiento de Juan Bautista Alberdi. Entre los "fundadores" o "patriarcas," Korn y Vasconcelos se vinculan también al asunto. El problema cobró mayor vigencia al desarrollarse en México la "filosofía de lo mexicano," la cual, bajo el liderazgo de Leopoldo Zea, tenía en la base una posición "americanista" en la concepción de la filosofía que debía hacerse en América Latina. Esta posición engendró una polémica largamente sostenida con sectores que reivindicaban el carácter "universalista" de la filosofía en general y por ende de la que debiera practicarse en Latinoamérica.

Acallados los ecos de esta polémica, la cuestión vino a ser renovada por la utilización, en el plano filosófico, de la teoría de la dependencia, combinada con la generalización de la problemática del desarrollo (el caso de Salazar Bondy, por ejemplo) y la identificación de América Latina con el Tercer Mundo ("filosofía de la liberación").

Entre los trabajos aquí recogidos y orientados en la línea de la filosofía de la liberación, destacamos: el volumen colectivo *Cultura popular y filosofía de la liberación* (item 9402); un numero especial de la revista *Nuevo Mundo,* de Argentina (item 9478); y artículos de Arturo A. Roig (item 9483), Enrique Dussel (item 9458) y Leopoldo Zea (item 9491). Helio Gallardo, por su parte, ha examinado las posiciones de Augusto Salazar Bondy y Leopoldo Zea ante el problema de la filosofía latinoamericana, en su ensayo "El Pensar en América Latina" (item 9450). Mención especial dentro de este asunto merecen varios trabajos de Francisco Miró Quesada. En primer lugar, su libro *Despertar y proyecto del filosofar latinoamericano* (item 9474); pero también un artículo que viene a resultar complementario de dicho libro, titulado "Posibilidad y Límites de una Filosofía Latinoamericana" (item 9476). Por último, se vinculan también a este tema las palabras pronunciadas por Ernesto Mayz Vallenilla al instalar el IX Congreso Interamericano de Filosofía (item 9472).

En esta entrega, igual que en la anterior, sorprende el número de trabajos sobre el ensayista peruano José Carlos Mariátegui, de quien se ha vuelto a reeditar recientemente su libro *La escena contemporánea,* originalmente aparecido en 1925 (item 9512).

En materia de historiografía de las ideas en Hispanoamérica, dos artículos resultan de particular interés: el de Arturo Ardao, "La Historia de la Historiografía de las Ideas en Latinoamérica" (item 9494) y el de Leopoldo Zea, "De la Historia de las Ideas a la Filosofía de la Historia (item 9527).

Aunque no todos los volúmenes están directamente vinculados con la filosofía, sino que caen más bien en el orden más general de la "historia de las ideas," recientemente se han publicado en Buenos Aires varias obras del llamado "nacionalismo" argentino, caracterizado por su antiliberalismo y su catolicismo hispanista. En esta entrega registramos obras de Carlos Ibarguren (item 9510), Leonardo Castellani (item 9498), Jordán Bruno Genta (item 9504) y Juan Carlos Goyeneche (item 9505). A ello hay que agregar una compilación de artículos periodísticos realizada por Julio Irazusta, miembro del mismo grupo (item 9511). Siempre en el campo de la historia de las ideas, debe recordarse la antología de Genevois y Le Godinec,

Aspects de la pensée hispano-americaine (item 9503), que recoge textos del ensayo hispanoamericano entre 1898 y 1930.

La literatura critica sobre historia de la filosofía constituye una parte muy considerable de la produccion filosófica latinoamericana. Como dijimos más arriba, el aumento de la calidad técnica de algunos de estos trabajos es evidente en comparación con épocas anteriores, aunque no faltan los artículos ocasionales y algunos de nivel inferior. Entre los libros de crítica recogidos en este número es sin duda uno de los mejores el de Bernabé Navarro, *El desarrollo fichteano del idealismo trascendental de Kant* (item 9593). Siempre citando libros únicamente, recordaremos: Angel J. Cappelletti, *La teoría aristotélica de la visión* y *Diógenes de Apolonia y la segunda filosofía jónica* (items 9537 y 9533); Octavio N. Derisi, *Santo Tomás de Aquino y la filosofía actual* (item 9540); H. Malo González, *El hábito en la filosofía de Félix Ravaisson* (item 9586); Luis Villoro, *Estudios sobre Husserl* (item 9640); Th. R. Giles, *História do existencialismo e da fenomenologia* (item 9618); y R. Murrillo Zamora, *Antonio Machado: ensayo sobre su pensamiento filosófico* (item 9627).

En Ernildo Stein, *Melancolia: ensaios sobre a finitude no pensamento occidental* (item 9735) nos parece entrever el comienzo de un pensamiento filosófico personal de valor, aunque todavía envuelto en el ropaje de la crítica. Por último, en *Introducción a los problemas fundamentales del hombre* (item 9676a), Risieri Frondizi extiende a un más amplio contexto antropológico sus continuadas reflexiones sobre el problema del valor.

En junio de 1977, organizado por la Sociedad Interamericana de Filosofía y la Sociedad Venezolana de Filosofía tuvo lugar en Caracas el IX Congreso Interamericano de Filosofía (VI de la Sociedad Interamericana). Fué su Presidente el Dr. Ernesto Mayz Vallenilla. Se resolvió que el próximo Congreso Interamericano de Filosofía se realice en Estados Unidos.

El temario estuvo dividido en dos grandes grupos: I. "La Realidad Latinoamericana como Problema para el Pensar Filosófico;" y II. "Las Tendencias Actuales de la Filosofía en el Continente Americano." Cada uno de ellos comprendió a su vez tres temas. Los del primero fueron: 1) "Enseñanza de la Filosofía en América Latina;" 2) "Historia y Evolución de las Ideas Filosóficas en América Latina;" y 3) "Posibilidades y Límites de una Filosofía Latinoamericana." Los del segundo: 1) "Filosofía de la Ciencia y Filosofía Analítica;" 2) "Filosofía de la Praxis;" y 3) "Fenomenología y Filosofía Existencial." Los temas del primer grupo fueron tratados en las sesiones plenarias y en comisiones de trabajo; los del segundo en comisiones de trabajo solamente.

Una vez más fué asunto saliente el problema de la filosofía latinoamericana. Una vez más, también, a la posición que busca en la realidad latinoamericana la única fuente del filosofar propio se opuso la corriente que no quiere renunciar a una posición universalista para la filosofía. También parece haberse notado cierta incomunicación entre los grandes grupos: existencialismo y fenomenología, filosofía analítica, marxismo, etc., lo cual sin duda no está reflejando una peculiaridad latinoamericana, sino una característica general de la filosofía actual.

En este bibliografía se incluyen libros y artículos de autores latinoamericanos, cualquiera sea el tema filosófico de que se ocupen, y de autores no latinoamericanos, siempre que traten asuntos relativos al pensamiento y la filosofía de América Latina.

En el presente número, aproximadamente las dos terceras partes de las entradas corresponden a trabajos publicados entre 1974 y 1977. El resto, a los años inmediatos anteriores.

En la subsección "Obras Generales y Didácticas" se agrupan los trabajos que responden a ese título, pero también otros que, por su número, no justificarían una subsección independiente. También se incluyen allí libros o artículos que se refieren a Latinoamérica en general, como tema o problema.

Bajo la designación de "Pensamiento Latinoamericano" recogemos tres tipos de escritos: las reediciones de "clásicos" del pensamiento latinoamericano ("Fuentes"); los estudios críticos sobre la filosofía en América Latina ("Filosofía Latinoamericana"); y los estudios históricos no estrictamente filosóficos pero vinculados a la filosofía, que agrupamos bajo el título de "Historia de las Ideas."

Las divisiones de los trabajos sobre historia de la filosofía no requieren aclaraciones, excepto la imprecisa línea divisoria entre la filosofía "moderna" y la "contemporánea" en lo que se refiere a las últimas décadas del siglo XIX. Tendemos a colocar bajo "Filosofía Contemporánea" a los autores que desarrollaron su obra—o lo principal de ella—en nuestro siglo.

La división por disciplinas filosóficas se atiene a los criterios más generalizados, aunque los casos en que un trabajo puede caer bajo más de un título son inevitables.

OBRAS GENERALES Y DIDACTICAS

9401. Ardiles, Osvaldo M. Contribuciones para una elaboración filosófica de las mediaciones histórico-sociales en el proceso de liberación latinoamericana (Stromata [Univ. del Salvador, Facultades de Filosofía y Teología, San Miguel, Arg.] 28:3, enero/junio 1972, p. 351-370)

Partiendo de la pregunta inicial, "¿por qué hay que hacer la Revolución?", concluye que "la tarea de un pensar genuino consiste en elucidar las contradiciones objetivo-estructurales del actual sistema socioeconómico que determina nuestra situación de dependencia.."

9402. ———— and others. Cultura popular y filosofía de la liberación: una perspectiva latinoamericana. B.A., Fernando García Cambeiro, 1975. 270 p. (Col. Estudios latinoamericanos)

Aproximadamente el mismo grupo de autores que colaboraron en el primer número de la *Revista de Filosofía Latinoamericana* (véase *HLAS 38*, p. 567) y en el número especial de la revista *Nuevo Mundo* (véase item 9478) reitera aquí la temática del tercermundismo y la liberación.
Contiene:
Osvaldo Ardiles "Ethos, Cultura y Liberación" p. 9-32
Mario Carlos Casalla "Algunas Precisiones en Torno al Concepto de Pueblo" p. 33-69
Máximo R. Chaparro "Dominación y Cultura" p. 71-86
Julio D. de Zan "Para una Filosofía de la Cultura y una Filosofía Política Nacional" p. 87-139
Enrique D. Dussel "Hacia una Pedagógica de la Cultura Popular: Eticidad y Moralidad de la Conducta Cultural p. 141-180
Antonio Enrique Kiner "Tercer Mundo: Precisiones para una Reflexión Filosófica" p. 181-202
Rodolfo Kusch "Dos Reflexiones sobre la Cultura" p. 203-219
Alberto Parisí "Pueblo, Cultura y Situación de Clase" p. 221-239
Juan Carlos Scannone "Teología, Cultura Popular y Discernimiento: hacia una Teología que Acompañe a los Pueblos Latinoamericanos en su Proceso de Liberación" p. 241-270.

9403. Arróspide de la Flor, César. Cultura y liberación. Lima, Instituto Nacional de Cultura, 1975. 225 p.

Aunque recoge artículos publicados en periódicos, el nivel está por encima de lo periodístico. Las meditaciones que contiene quieren servir al proceso de la revolución peruana, en el orden de la cultura. El esquema básico está dado por la teoría de la dependencia, de la que surge la consiguiente "liberación." Los dos primeros capítulos se dedican al concepto de cultura, para llegar al final de lo específico del tema peruano y de la política cultural del Estado. Gran parte de las reflexiones se dedican al tema del arte y la función del artista en la creación de una nueva sociedad. El capitalismo se identifica con el individualismo egoísta, y a éste se contrapone el espíritu colectivo, con la siguiente exaltación de la cultura del pueblo.

9404. Basave Fernández del Valle, Agustín. Estructura e sentido da filosofia da religião (Convivium [São Paulo] 11:6, nov./dez. 1972. p. 515-532)

Después de examinar el hecho religioso, la naturaleza de lo sagrado, la estructura de la fe, etc., establece que por existir en el hombre un afán de plenitud sustancial se comprueba que existe un Ser Pleno, "existente en sí y por sí".

9405. Bordón, Nellibe Judith. Aproximaciones a la imagen bíblica del hombre: el hombre, un misterio para sí mismo (UNT/H, 18:24, 1977, p. 61-75)

Intenta encontrar una respuesta a la cuestión de la naturaleza del hombre en el texto bíblico (*Génesis* y partes del *Nuevo Testamento*).

9406. Cappelletti, Angel J. Lao-tse y Chuang-tse. Caracas, Gobernación del Distrito Federal [and] Centro Simón Bolívar, 1976. 110 p. (Cuadernos de difusión, 8)

Esta obra de difusión sobre el taoísmo se originó en dos trabajos recogidos anteriormente en la obra del autor, *La filosofía china del período clásico* (Puebla, Mex., 1966).

9407. Caturelli, Alberto. El II Congreso Nacional de Filosofía (UNC/RH, 13/14, julio 1971, p. 149-169)

Crónica comentada de los orígenes y el desarrollo del II Congreso Argentino de Filosofía (1971). Tiene valor documental.

9408. Corbisier, Rolando. Conceitos de universo (VOZES, 68:5, junho/julho 1974, p. 375-382)

Sobre el concepto y la evolución de la idea de "universo."

9409. Costa, João Cruz. Mi encuentro con Zea (UNAM/L, 10, 1977, p. 79-82)

El autor, historiador de las ideas en Brasil, rememora su primer encuentro con Zea en 1945 y aprecia la labor realizada por este último.

9410. Encuentro Latinoamericano de Espiritualidad, III, Quito, 1974. Hacia una espiritualidad latinoamericana: teología, espiritualidad de la liberación. Bogotá, Editorial Kelly, 1974? 268 p.

Reunión de representantes de la Orden de Carmelitas Descalzos, que tuvo lugar en 1974. Si se deja de lado, en las propuestas de los participantes, las connotaciones teológico-religiosas, el tema central de aquellas es la injusticia que pesa sobre las clases desposeídas de América Latina y la necesidad de remediarlas. Algunos autores reiteran los esquemas de la teoría de la dependencia.

9411. *Estudios de Filosofía y Religiones del Oriente.* Univ. de Buenos Aires, Facultad de Filosofía y Letras, Centro de Estudios de Filosofía Oriental. Vol. 1, No. 1, 1971-   . B.A.

Esta revista, sobre cuya continuidad más allá de su primer número no tenemos noticia, constituye una excepción en el ámbito filosófico latinoamericano, dado que en él los estudios orientales no están muy desarrollados. El artículo que abre el volumen (A. Asti Vera "Fundamentos Metafísicos del Simbolismo Oriental" p. 5-30), intenta señalar las características propias de la metafísica oriental en general y advertir sobre los equívocos a que conduce, en su interpretación, la aplicación de los conceptos de la filosofía occidental. Además explica la función del simbolismo en aquella metafísica. Los restantes trabajos versan sobre temas más específicos: J. Severino Croatto "Simbolismo Mítico y Creatividad" p. 31-47); Fernando Tola "El Simbolismo en el Tantrismo" (p. 49-77); O. Machado Mouret "El Simbolismo en el Pensamiento Místico de los Sufíes" (p. 79-90); F. García Bazán "El Simbolismo Maniqueo" (p. 91-104); Carlos A. Benito "El Simbolismo, Vida y Muerte en las Religiones de la Antigua Mesopotamia" (p. 105-114); N. Altuchow "El Lenguaje Simbólico del Vedanta" (p. 115-122). El volumen reproduce también *La Upanishad del aislamiento*, en texto original y traducción.

9412. *Estudios Filosóficos.* Sociedad Venezolana de Filosofía. No. 1, 1974-   . Caracas.

Contiene las siguientes conferencias, organizadas por la Sociedad Venezolana de Filosofía: Francisco Bravo "La Dialéctica en Teilhard de Chardin" (sobre el problema del conocimiento en este autor); Rafael Carias "El Conocimiento de Dios en Max Scheler" (sobre *Vom Ewigen im Menschen*); Angel J. Cappelletti "El Fuego y el Logos en la Filosofía de Heráclito"; Víctor Li Carrillo "Estructuralismo y Antihumanismo" (véase *HLAS 32:6107*); y tres artículos de Alberto Rosales, en gran parte dedicados al problema de la verdad en Heidegger: "Martín Heidegger y la Crisis de la Filosofía Trascendental"; "La Crítica de Heidegger al Idealismo Moderno"; y "El Giro del Pensamiento de Heidegger."

9413. Fernández Méndez, Eugenio ed. Antología del pensamiento puertorriqueño: 1900-1970. 2 v. Hato Rey, Univ. de Puerto Rico, 1975. 1306 p.

Recoge textos de unos 90 autores sobre el tema de la cultura—en sentido amplio—de Puerto Rico.

9414. Ferrater Mora, José. Diccionario de filosofía. 5. ed. B.A., Sudamericana, 1975, 2 v. (1072, 1005 p.)

Esta obra, monumental para ser escrita por una sola persona, apareció por primera vez en 1941 y fué creciendo considerablemente, edicion tras edición. El presente es el texto de la 5a. edición (1969). Da idea del crecimiento de la obra el hecho de que para esta edición se hayan escrito 546 artículos nuevos, en tanto la anterior había incorporado 762 de la misma índole, sin contar ampliciones y reelaboraciones. Continúa siendo un instrumento de trabajo fundamental, en cualquier idioma, y expresión de un portentoso saber filosófico individual, probablemente el máximo conocido en el idioma del autor. No es uno de los menores méritos de la obra el manejarse con la misma soltura con conceptos y autores de la tradición europeo-continental—la más frecuentada históricamente en España e Iberoamerica—y de la orientación filosófica predominante en los países de habla inglesa.

9415. García, Guadalupe and Carlos Sabino. Dictadura de la tecnocracia. B.A., Proyección, 1974. 199 p.

El título resulta restringido con respecto al contenido del libro. Como muchas obras semejantes, se basa en una actitud teórica—y emotiva—que tiene su punto de partida en la afirmación de la dependencia de los países latinoamericanos y que utiliza el marxismo como método. Sin embargo, los autores muestran una mayor amplitud de lo que suele ser común en este tipo de literatura. Ilustrativo resulta, por ejemplo, que quieran complementar la relación marxista "infraestructura-superestructura" con aplicaciones de la teoría de la cultura. La obra se origina y concluye en preocupaciones de praxis política (o "revolucionaria"). En cuanto a su contenido es básicamente un análisis del capitalismo y el socialismo en relación con dichas preocupaciones.

9416. Genovesi, Antonio. As instituções de lógica. Introdução de Antonio Paim. Rio, Pontificia Univ. Católica [and] Conselho Federal de Cultura, Editora Documentario, 1977. 127 p. (Textos didáticos do pensamento brasileiro, 4)

Esta obra de Genovesi (1713-69), autor italiano, fué impuesta como texto en Portugal bajo las reformas ilustradas del Ministro Pombal, e influyó tambien en Brasil. El texto de este volumen es el de la traducción portuguesa que se utilizó para ese propósito. Contiene además una presentación de Celina Junqueira, una Introducción de Antonio Paim y una nota de Capone Braga sobre Genovesi.

9417. Gómez, Luis O. and Roberto Torretti. Problemas de la filosofía: textos filosóficos clásicos y contempóraneos. Hato Rey, Univ. de Puerto Rico, Editorial Universitaria, 1975. 768 p.

Antología de textos filosóficos, destinada a la enseñanza, realizada con todo el cuidado técnico. Contiene introducciones a los diferentes temas, bibliografías e índices. La agrupación de textos por grandes temas es la siguiente: problemas metafísicos, problemas del conocimiento, el problema moral, filosofía de la historia, filosofías orientales. Aunque por el carácter altamente selectivo de una obra de esta naturaleza pueden existir diversos criterios para componerla, la presente es representativa y posiblemente sea la mejor en su género publicada en Hispanoamerica.

9418. Guzmán Valdivia, Isaac. La civilización actual contra el destino del hombre: notas y comentarios. México, Editorial Tradición, 1974. 192 p., bibl. (Col. De estudios políticos, 5)

Reflexiones sobre la situación de la vida contemporánea que parten del contraste entre el adelanto científico-tecnológico y el estancamiento en el plano moral, y que proponen como salida una visión teocéntrica del mundo y de la existencia humana.

9419. Jalfen, Luis Jorge. Ideología y filosofía. B.A. Ediciones Noé, 1975. 182 p. (Col. Los lanzallamas)

Libro de meditaciones, más que obra orgánica. El tema de filosofía e ideología se trata, entre otros, en la primera parte de la obra. La segunda está compuesta por "testimonios," expresiones de un pensar en plena búsqueda.

9420. Láscaris-Comneno, Teodoro. Introducción al filosofar y filosofía griega. Valencia, Ven., Univ. de Carabobo, Ediciones de la Dirección de Cultura, 1975. 158 p.

Se trata, en realidad, de dos libros introductorios yuxtapuestos: uno de iniciación a la filosofía y otro de introducción a la filosofía griega, de los presocráticos a Aristóteles.

9421. Naranjo Villegas, Abel. Una filosofía proyectiva (ACO/B, 21:86, 1971, p. 33-37)

9422. Pérez, Jorge Osvaldo. La filosofía en la historia de Occidente. v. 1, Pensamiento grecolatino. B.A. Editorial Abaco de Rodolfo Depalma, 1975. 2 v. (700 p.) (Continuous pagination)

Obra de intención didáctica y primera parte de una historia general de la filosofía. Infrecuente como intento originalmente escrito en castellano. Contiene capítulos que sitúan el pensamiento filosófico en la historia general de las respectivas épocas. Abarca desde los comienzos de la filosofía griega hasta el fin del mundo antiguo.

9423. Pescador Prudencio, Augusto. Filosofía de la vida y la vida en la filosofía (Cuadernos de Filosofía [Univ. de Concepción, Instituto Central de Filosofía, Chile] 3/4, 1974/1975, p. 105-116)

Reflexiones filosóficas sobre la vida humana.

9424. Pescador Sarget, Augusto. La importancia de lo inútil en el mundo de la técnica (UC/AT, 429/430, 1974, p. 117-160)

Extenso ensayo que toca numerosos temas, desde el uso del tiempo libre hasta la muerte humana. Una de las opiniones más centrales es que la utilidad es una categoría que no puede aplicarse a todas las actividades del hombre. Así, por ejemplo, la filosofía es importante y a la vez "inútil."

9425. Pesce, Hugo. El factor religioso. Lima, Editora Amauta, 1975. 166 p. (Presencia y proyección de los siete ensayos, 4)

La obra versa sobre "el factor religioso y su influencia en el Perú" y es parte de una serie en que se desean ampliar los temas tratados por Mariátegui en los *Siete ensayos*. El prólogo de Alberto Tauro está dedicado al análisis del problema religioso en Mariátegui y a la figura del autor del presente libro.

9426. Pilotto, Erasmo. Obras. v. 1. Pequenos ensaios. Para um humanismo individualista. Temas da educação de nosso tempo. Direito à educação. Curitiba, Brazil, n.p., 1973. 522 p.

Contiene algunos temas filosóficos tratados de modo ensayístico. La filosofía aparece también en el libro *Temas da educação de nosso tempo* (1. ed. 1954; 2 ed. 1973) incluido en este volumen.

9427. Ponce, Anibal. Obras completas. v. 1/4. Revisadas y anotadas por Héctor P. Agosti. B.A., Cartago, 1974. 4 v. (438, 686, 557, 734 p.)

Oportuna edición de las *Obras completas* de Aníbal Ponce (1898-1938), escritor, ensayista y psicólogo argentino, que fuera discípulo de José Ingenieros. Además de un extenso estudio sobre Ponce, del cual es autor el editor de estas *Obras*, y que abre el vol. 1, el contenido es el siguiente: Vol. 1: Para una historia de Ingenieros; La Vejez de Sarmiento; Sarmiento; constructor de la nueva Argentina. Vol. 2: La gramática de los sentimientos; Estudios de psicología; Problemas de psicología infantil; Ambición y angustia de los adolescentes; Diario íntimo de una adolescente. Vol. 3: Un cuaderno de croquis; Apuntes de viaje; Educación y lucha de clases; Humanismo burgués y humanismo proletario. Vol. 4: Los autores y los libros; Apuntes dispersos; Notas de México; Apéndice precoz; Bibliografía general de Aníbal Ponce.

9428. Ribeiro, Darcy. La cultura latinoamericana (UNAM/L, 9, 1976, p. 9-89)

El enfoque participa de lo antropológico, lo político, lo ideológico y lo histórico. Con base en trabajos anteriores del autor, el análisis de América Latina se realiza en función de "procesos civilizatorios" determinados principalmente por cambios tecnológicos, que a su vez generan dos clases de "pueblos:" "pueblos autónomos" y "pueblos dependientes" (entre los que desde luego son incluidos los latinoamericanos). En términos de clasificación dentro de América Latina, distingue tres grandes "configuraciones histórico-culturales:" "pueblos testimonio" (México, Guatemala, Bolivia, Perú, Ecuador); "pueblos nuevos" Brasil, Venezuela, Colombia); y "pueblos trasplantados" (Argentina, Uruguay). La última parte está dedicada a examinar las condiciones de las culturas en situación de dependencia y a aplicar los resultados a la comprensión de la cultura latinoamericana. Al final de este extenso trabajo, el anuncio de una nueva civilización, de carácter ecuménico, se avala con una cita de Fidel Castro.

9429. Ron, José. Realidad actual de la cultura ecuatoriana (UCE/A, 353, 1975, p. 28-38)

Una afirmación que permite filiar la orientación de este ensayo (parte de un próximo libro) es la siguiente: la cultura ecuatoriana es una cultura alienada, producto de la colonización y el sistema capitalista.

9430. Schirato, Sérgio José. Homem 70. São Paulo, Edições Loyola, 1975. 80 p., bibl.

Reflexiones sobre el hombre contemporáneo, sin intención de obra filosófica elaborada.

9431. Soler, Ricaurte and **José de J. Martínez.** Estudios filosóficos. Panamá, Incude, 1974. 157 p. (Concurso literario Ricardo Miró. Sección ensayo, 1971)

Contiene los siguientes trabajos: de Ricaurte Soler: "Modelo Mecanicista y Método Dialéctico;" "Causalidad en el Mecanicismo y Casualidad en la Dialéctica;" y "Dialéctica de Universales e Individuales." De José de J. Martínez: "Sobre el Humanismo en la Edad Media y en el Renacimiento;" y "Sobre el Problema de la Muerte."

9432. Versiani Velloso, Arthur. Informação sobre o idealismo (UMGFF/K, 20:67, 1973/1974, p. 60-122)

Proporciona, en efecto, información sobre cómo ha sido entendido el idealismo por diversos autores.

9433. Zea, Leopoldo. La cultura en las dos Américas (VME/R, 30:196, enero/marzo 1971, p. 3-12)

Presentación sintética de las diferencias entre la América anglosajona y la América ibérica, en lo que se refiere a sus respectivos modos de valorar el mundo y la vida, (y por consiguiente de comportarse ante ellos), diferencias que se remontan a las distintas modalidades de la colonización original en cada una de las Américas. Se señalan las consecuencias para algunos aspectos de las respectivas culturas.

9434. ———. Dialéctica de la conciencia americana. Mexico, Alianza Editorial Mexicana, 1976. 354 p. (Biblioteca iberoamericana, 1)

Análisis de la situación de América Latina en el siglo XX. El autor ha tratado de continuar la labor que desarrolló en obras anteriores sobre el siglo XIX, consistente en una combinación de historia de las ideas y filosofía de la historia. Una de las tesis principales, reiterada en otros escritos de Zea, es la de que los pueblos que han constituido la avanzada de la civilización sentaron principios de liberación y dignidad humanas que no pusieron en práctica en su relación con otros pueblos, especialmente de América Latina, Asia y Africa. Esta tesis se ilustra en el libro con la relación entre Estados Unidos y América Latina, la cual ocupa gran parte de la obra. Algunas opiniones sobre acontecimientos recientes (sobre la revolución cubana, por ejemplo), muestran tal vez que no es posible una "filosofía de la historia" con cierto grado de objetividad cuando se trata de hechos del pasado inmediato, en los cuales el que analiza está comprometido con sus simpatías.

9435. ———. La integración cultural y social latinoamericana (UNAM/L, 8, 1975, p. 9-25)

La nueva dependencia hace de la filosofía latinoamericana una filosofía de la liberación. La conciencia del propio pasado es necesaria para que las formas culturales ajenas que se asimilen sean verdaderamente propias y no meramente yuxtapuestas.

TEORIA DE LA FILOSOFIA

9436. **Derisi, Octavio N.** El problema fundamental de la filosofía (UNL/H, 17, 1976, p. 173-192)

"El problema fundamental y primero de la filosofía reside en señalar con precisión el objeto formal de la inteligencia." El éxito del tomismo ha sido su acierto al tratar este problema. El artículo es un intento de demostrar esta última proposición, principalmente mediante el examen del asunto en Santo Tomás.

9437. **Herra, Rafael A.** Filosofía de la falsa conciencia, falsa conciencia de la filosofía (UCR/RF, 12:35, julio/dic. 1974, p. 115-120)

Propone un concepto de filosofía entendida como "ideología crítica" y se pregunta por el sentido del quehacer filosófico en su propio país (Costa Rica).

9438. **Katz, Chaim Samuel.** Níveis e dimensão no sistema filosófico: uma visão estrutural (TEMBRAS, 15/16, 1973, p. 221-229)

El artículo se propone ser un enfoque de la historia de la filosofía y de lo que es un sistema filosófico desde un punto de vista estructuralista.

9439. **Macedo, Ubiratan de.** Da interpretação em história da filosofia (Convivium [São Paulo] 11:5, set./out. 1972, p. 439-450)

Se presentan varios tipos de interpretación de una obra filosófica: por reducción a sus fuentes; según bases socioeconómicas (Marxismo); por intuición (propuesta por Bergson); interpretación estructural (Martial Guéroult y Víctor Goldschmidt); e interpretación existencial-histórica (entre otros, Ortega y Gasset).

9440. ———. O problema do ponto de partida da filosofia (Convivium [São Paulo] 11:6, nov./dez. 1972, p. 549-559)

Se compone de tres temas: una crítica al punto de partida de la filosofía tal como lo entiende la fenomenología; la distinción de tres posibles puntos de partida (noético, cosmológico y ontológico); y la presentación de una serie de aporías con respecto al problema del punto de partida.

9441. **Murquía, Adolfo.** De la búsqueda filosófica (UBAFFL/C, 14:21, enero/junio 1974, p. 107-118)

Ensayo que, partiendo de lo que actualmente se considera crisis o peligro de desaparición de la filosofía, afirma la función de ésta como búsqueda de la verdad.

9442. **Pucciarelli, Eugenio.** El lenguaje de los filósofos (UBAFFL/C, 14:21, enero/junio 1974, p. 133-159)

Además de lo que tiene de valioso para quien quiera introducirse en el tema, lo más personal del artículo es la afirmación de la imposibilidad de un lenguaje universal de la filosofía, asunto que trata con profundidad y amplitud de saber filosófico.

9443. ———. Unidade da filosofia e pluralidade das doutrinas (Convivium [São Paulo] 12:4, julho/agôsto 1973, p. 283-290)

Este ensayo, bajo la apariencia de tratar un tema frecuentemente analizado, alcanza la altura de un "credo" filosófico, no sólo por el contenido, sino por el tono, salvaguardado en otro idioma por una oportuna traducción. Viene a decir que la eterna contienda de las escuelas filosóficas es la manifestación del impulso de superación que anima la vida del espíritu, y que el sentido de ese constante esfuerzo de superación tal vez no sea otro que "la defensa de la vida humana, su redención por la conciencia de su espontaneidad ciega y versátil y la exaltación de su dignidad por la certeza de su libertad."

9444. **Salmerón, Fernando.** La filosofía, la educación y la crítica (UNAM/RUM, 26:9, mayo 1972, p. 1-6)

La filosofía es análisis crítico, y toda educación culmina en la enseñanza de la filosofía, asi entendida. Dentro de este marco se analizan las características y requisitos de la enseñanza de la filosofía.

9445. **Saltor, Jorge E.** La utilidad de la filosofía (UNT/H, 18:24, 1977, p. 43-51)

Entendiendo que la categoría de "utilidad" se aplica exclusivamente "al poder humano de manipulación y transformación de la materia," la filosofía (que aquí se identifica con la metafísica) estaría en el nivel de la "suprautilidad," en el sentido que dió a este término maritain.

PENSAMIENTO LATINOAMERICANO
Fuentes

9446. **Alberini, Coriolano.** Escritos de metafísica. Mendoza, Arg., Facultad de Filosofía y Letras, Univ. Nacional de Cuyo, Instituto de Filosofía, 1973.

260 p. (Col. De historia de la filosofía argentina. Serie documental, 2)

Esta obra complementa otra anterior, también reunión de escritos de Coriolano Alberini (1886-1960): *Escritos de ética* (véase *HLAS 36:5036*) y es tan oportuna como ella. Entre los artículos incluidos se encuentran: "Interpretación Idealista del Bergsonismo," extenso ensayo de 1919, inédito hasta ahora; "Croce y la Metafísica de la Libertad Histórica" (1953); "La Teoría Kantiana del Juicio Sintético a Priori", temprano trabajo de 1907; y otros trabajos críticos de tema epistemológico. Precede a la recopilación un buen estudio de Diego F. Pró, "La Metafísica de Alberini."

9447. Bevilaqua, Clóvis. Obra filosófica. v. 1, Filosofía geral; v. 2, Filosofía social e jurídica. Apresentação de Ubiratan de Macedo. Introdução de San Thiago Dantas. São Paulo, Editora da Univ. de São Paulo [and] Editorial Grijalbo, 1975. 2 v. (148, 259 p.) (Estante do pensamento brasileiro)

Clóvis Bevilaqua (1859-1944) perteneció a la llamada Escuela de Recife, junto con Sylvio Romero, Tobías Barreto y Arthur Orlando. La mayor parte de los artículos contenidos en el vol. 1 están tomados de *Esboços y fragmentos* (1899) y representan la posición filosófica general del autor. El vol. 2 contiene trabajos de filosofía jurídica y social, campo en el cual Bevilaqua desarrolló su mayor acción. Estos últimos estudios están tomados de varios libros, aparecidos entre 1886 y 1940.

9448. Caso, Antonio. Obras completas. v. 3, La existencia como economía, como desinterés y como caridad; v. 7, El acto ideatorio y la filosofía de Husserl. Positivismo, neopositivismo y fenomenología; v. 8, La persona humana y el Estado totalitario. El peligro del hombre. Prólogos de José Gaos [v. 1], Luis Villoro [v. 2], y Mario de la Cueva [v. 3]. Compilación de Rosa Krauze de Kolteniuk. México, UNAM, Dirección General de Publicaciones, 1972/1975. 3 v. (200, 242, 445 p.) (Nueva Biblioteca Mexicana, 15-19/20)

El vol. 1, *La existencia como economía, como desinterés y como caridad*, la principal obra filosófica de Caso, comenzó siendo un folleto de 1916. La edición definitiva es de 1943. Aquí se reproducen esta última y el mencionado folleto. Un índice cronológico da idea de la procedencia de los materiales, antes de 1916, en la edición de ese año, en la de 1919 y en la de 1943. El fallecimiento de José Gaos impidió que pudiera concluir el prólogo que se le había solicitado para esta edición. A causa de ello, se reproduce el trabajo "El Sistema de Caso", que el maestro Gaos publicó en la revista *Luminar* en 1946. Son atinentes a esta obra algunos comentarios del estudio preliminar de Luis Villoro al vol. 7 que reproduce *El acto ideatorio y la filosofía de Husserl*, edición de 1946 que reunió dos libros de 1934, y *Positivismo, neopositivismo y fenomenología*, de 1941. En apéndice se agregan varios artículos periodísticos relacionados con los temas de esos tres libros. La procedencia de los materiales se indica en un útil índice cronológico. La introducción de Villoro da una idea general de estas obras; pero, sobre todo, desde la perspectiva de una generación filosóficamente más informada, muestra el efecto de la fenomenología sobre Caso, cuyo pensamiento se hallaba avanzado cuando conoció las primeras obras de Husserl. El vol. 8 contiene *La persona humana y el Estado totalitario* (1941) y *El peligro del hombre* (1942). Mario de la Cueva analiza en el prólogo las ideas políticas y sociales de Caso. Otros volúmenes de las *Obras completas* se han reseñado en *HLAS 36:5038-5040* y *HLAS 38:9451*.

9449. Fernández, Macedonio. Teoría. Obras completas. v. 3. Ordenación y notas de Adolfo de Obieta. B.A., Ediciones Corregidor, 1974. 308 p.

Macedonio Fernández, escritor argentino, además de literato fué autor de escritos filosóficos, como *No toda es vigilia la de los ojos abiertos*. En este volumen, bajo el título general de *Teorías*, se agrupan páginas inéditas escritas entre 1908 y 1940.

9450. Pinheiro Ferreira, Silvestre. Idéias políticas: cartas sobre a revolução de Brasil; memórias políticas sobre os abusos gerais; manual do cidadão em um governo representativo. Introdução de Vicente Barreto. Rio, Pontifícia Univ. Católica [and] Conselho Federal de Cultura, Editora Documentario, 1976. 176 p. (Textos didáticos do pensamento brasileiro, 7)

De Silvestre Pinheiro Ferreira (1769-1846), intelectual y hombre público portugués que estuvo en Brasil desde 1809 a 1821, se había publicado hace unos años sus *Preleções filosóficas* (véase *HLAS 34:5154*). Se incluyen aquí, completos, *Memórias políticas sobre os abusos gerais* y *Cartas sobre a revolução do Brasil*, y en forma parcial, *Manual do cidadão em um governo representativo*. Vicente Barreto en su introducción afirma que este autor fué el primero que desarrolló sistemáticamente, en lengua portuguesa, la teoría del Estado liberal constitucional.

Filosofía Latinoamericana

9451. Ardao, Arturo. El descubrimiento de América y la idea del cosmos, en Humboldt (UNAM/L, 8, 1975, p. 27-39)

Sobre la influencia que el descubrimiento de América tuvo en lo obra de Alejandro de Humboldt, *Cosmos*, especialmente en lo que ésta tiene de filosofía de la historia.

9452. Caturelli, Alberto. Orígenes doctrinales de la tercera escolástica en la filosofía argentina del siglo XIX (UCA/S, 26:100/102, abril/dic. 1971, p. 291-322)

Expone una serie de autores de orientación católica, la mayoría de segundo orden o poco estudiados (con excepción, por ejemplo, de José Manuel Estrada), que oscilan entre el tradicionalismo, la apologética y el escolasticismo. Es mérito del artículo la cantidad de datos poco divulgados que contiene.

9453. ———. Presente y futuro de la filosofía en la Argentina. Córdoba, Arg., Univ. Nacional de Córdoba, Facultad de Filosofía y Humanidades, 1972. 83 p.

Originalmente apareció en la revista *Eidos* (véase HLAS 38:9484).

9454. *Convivium.* Revista de investigação e cultura. Vol. 11, No. 3, maio/junho 1972- . São Paulo.

Este número especial "O Pensamento de Vicente Ferreira da Silva" sobre el filósofo brasileño, desaparecido a los 47 años en 1963, se divide en dos partes: "Testimonios" y "Estudios." En la primera colaboran Julián Marías "Uma Vocação filosófica" (p. 183-18); Dora Ferreira da Silva, esposa del filósofo "Fim e Começo" (p. 189-193); Milton Vargas "O Jovem Vicente Ferreira da Silva", (p. 194-201); y Ernesto Grassi "Recordação e Metáfora" (p. 202-204). Los estudios sobre Ferreira da Silva son los siguientes: Heraldo Barbuy "Subjetividade e Interioridade" (p. 205-214); Efraim Tomás Bó "O Portador dos Segredos" (p. 215-225); Adolpho Crippa "Origem e Natureza da Cultura", (p. 226-245); Agostinho da Silva "Vicente: Filosofia e Vida" (p. 246-251); Luigi Bagolini "Consciência Humana e Mistério" (p. 252-258); Gilberto de Mello Kujawski "O Signo de Dionisos" (p. 259-271); José Francisco Coelho "A Desmitização" (p. 272-290); Diva Ribeiro de Toledo Plaza "Um Novo Conceito do Homem" (p. 291-296); Vilém Flusser "Da Responsabilidade do Intelectual" (p. 297-30) artículo a la vez discrepante, respetuoso y apreciativo; Joaquim Montezuma de Carvalho "Vicente Ferreira da Silva, Filósofo da Liberdade" (p. 304-313) muestra semejanzas del pensador brasileño con el pensamiento de Francisco Romero; y Euryalo Cannabrava "Estrutura Metalingüística da Lógica" (p. 314-325) sobre la primera época de Ferreira da Silva, dedicada a problemas lógicos.

9455. Cordero, Rodrigo *ed.* Moisés Vincenzi. San José, Ministerio de Cultura, Juventud y Deportes, Depto. de Publicaciones, 1975. 307 p. (Serie del creador analizado, 3)

Antología de escritos filosóficos, literarios y políticos de Moisés Vincenzi (1895-1964), autor costarricense considerado por Constantino Láscaris (*Desarrollo de las ideas filosóficas en Costa Rica*, 1964) como "el filósofo más maduro, completo y original que ha producido Centroamerica." Precede a los textos un estudio de Rodrigo Cordero.

9456. *Cuadernos de Filosofía.* Univ. Nacional de Buenos Aires, Facultad de Filosofía y Letras. Vol. 15, Nos. 22/23, enero/dic. 1975- . B.A.

Número especial dedicado a la filosofía en la Argentina.

Contiene:
Eugenio Pucciarelli "Problemas del Pensamiento Argentino" (p. 7-28): revisa los intentos historiográficos sobre el pensamiento argentino y las interpretaciones de la realidad argentina realizada por algunos pensadores del país.
Vicente Fatone "Cinco Sonetos Religiosos de Alejandro Korn" (p. 29-33): este artículo se publicó por primera vez en 1943. Contiene una interpretación del pensamiento religioso de Korn y reproduce cinco sonetos de este filósofo.
Norberto Rodríguez Bustamante "Teoría Filosófica, Sociedad y Cultura en la Obra de Alejandro Korn" (p. 35-57): presenta una visión expositivo-crítica de la filosofía de Korn, destacando la vinculación de su pensamiento con los problemas de la realidad argentina.
Arturo García Astrada "Alberto Rougès y el Problema del Tiempo" (p. 59-67): examina un tema clave en el pensamiento de Rougès.
Alberto Caturelli "El pensamiento de Saúl Taborda" (p. 69-88): útil visión de conjunto que destaca en este pensador sus ideas pedagógicas y su concepto de "lo facúndico".
Diego F. Pró "Coriolano Alberini" (p. 89-136): amplia síntesis por quien más detalladamente ha estudiado la obra de Alberini.
Juan Carlos Torchia Estrada "Un Texto Inédito de Francisco Romero: *La decadencia del espíritu teórico en la filosofía*" (p. 137-155): después de una breve presentación, reproduce el texto mencionado de Romero, escrito en 1955, al cual considera una especie de "testamento filosófico."
Eugenio Pucciarelli "Francisco Romero en la Cátedra Universitaria" (p. 157-169): da testimonio de la labor de cátedra de Romero—especialmente en los primeros años—, de las novedades que introdujo y del estilo de profesor que era.
Adolfo Ruiz Díaz "Luis Juan Guerrero y su Estética Operatoria" (p. 171-182): examina la obra
Rodolfo M. Agoglia "Luis Juan Guerrero, Intérprete del pensamiento Argentino" (p. 183-200): oportuna exposición de un aspecto poco conocido de la enseñanza y la obra de Guerrero.
Aldo Prior "Tres Fragmentos sobre Carlos Astrada" (p. 201-213): traza una silueta filosófica de Astrada de mayor valor de lo que hace pensar la modestia del título.
Arturo Andrés Roig "El neo-platonismo Aporético de Miguel Angel Virasoro" (p. 215-234): posiblemente el mejor trabajo sobre Visoro.
Rafael Virasoro "Subjetividad y Trascendencia en la filosofía de Angel Vassallo" (p. 235-245): sobre la significación de la subjetividad y la ética en la filosofía de Vassallo.

Eugenio Pucciarelli "Saber y Ser en el Pensamiento de Angel Vassallo" (p. 247-254): fino ensayo que traza una semblanza de Vassallo como filósofo y señala el núcleo de su pensamiento.

José Vilanova "Carlos Cossio y la Teoría Egológica" (p. 255-269): sobre la filosofía del derecho—o de la ciencia del derecho—del conocido jusfilósofo argentino.

Francisco García Bazán "Vicente Fatone: el Pensador y el Orientalista a Través de las Obras de su Madurez" (p. 271-292); analiza la veta orientalista de Fatone, explica la calificación de "pensador" que le atribuye y compulsa otros juicios emitidos sobre Fatone y su obra.

Francisco José Olivieri "Vicente Fatone" (p. 293-306): palabras pronunciadas en un homenaje, que trazan la silueta personal y filosófica de Fatone. Acompaña una excelente bibliografía de escritos filosóficos de Fatone.

9457. De Beer, Gabriela. La raza cósmica: an ethical and scientific consideration (RIB, 25:1, enero/marzo 1975, p. 35-40)

Muestra que la teoría de la "raza cósmica" de Vasconcelos no se sostiene científicamente, a la vez que señala su fondo ético loable (el ideal de reunir a las razas).

9458. Dussel, Enrique. Filosofía y liberación latinoamericana (UNAM/L, 10, 1977, p. 83-91)

Este artículo, especie de autoexposición o capítulo de autobiografía intelectual, será de interés para quien se interese por los orígenes y la marcha de la llamada "filosofía de la liberación." El autor es uno de sus representantes más importantes y de mayor productividad intelectual.

9459. Escobar, Roberto. La filosofía en Chile. Santiago, Editorial Univ. Técnica del Estado, 1976. 157 p.

Es la única obra de conjunto sobre la filosofía en Chile. En breves páginas se cubre el período 1592-1810 y, proporcionalmente, otro tanto podría decirse del siglo que va de 1810 a 1918 (el capítulo sobre el positivismo tiene cuatro páginas). La pt. 3 "La Apertura a la Filosofía Contemporánea (1918-1950)," está representada principalmente por Enrique Molina, Osvaldo Lira y Clarence Finlayson. Aproximadamente la mitad del libro está dedicada al período 1950-75 y, naturalmente, incluye un elevado número de autores. Originalmente esta obra había sido encargada al autor por la Secretaría General de la OEA.

9460. Gallardo, Helio. El pensar en América Latina. Introducción al problema de la conformación de nuestra conciencia: A. Salazar Bondy y L. Zea (UCR/RF, 12:35, julio/dic. 1974, p. 183-210)

Examen bastante detallado de dos obras: Augusto Salazar Bondy, ¿Existe una filosofía de nuestra América? (véase HLAS 32:6054) y Leopoldo Zea, La filosofía americana como filosofía sin más, (1969, véase HLAS 34:5177). Al final se extiende en consideraciones, más bien de tono inquisitivo, sobre el problema de la filosofía latinoamericana, con tendencia a vincularlo con la situación de América Latina en la situación político-económica del mundo actual. Contiene bibliografía.

9461. Gallegos Rocafull, José M. El pensamiento mexicano en los siglos XVI y XVII. México, UNAM, 1974. 380 p.

La primera edición de este libro, fundamental para el tema, es de 1951. Se presenta en reedición no modificada.

9462. Gomes, Roberto. Crítica da razão tupiniquim (VOZES, 68:5, junho/julho 1974, p. 13-20)

Ensayo que busca establecer las condiciones de posibilidad de una filosofía auténtica en Brasil. Relaciona esa posibilidad con la asunción del modo de ser brasileño, sin inhibiciones.

9463. Grand Ruiz, Beatriz Hilda. Reflexiones en torno a la estructuración de una filosofía latinoamericana (RIB, 27:4, oct./dic. 1977, p. 365-371)

Para contestar las preguntas "¿que somos?" y "¿como estamos siendo?", "se sugiere un análisis existencial-fenomenológico de la realidad en el rico entrecruzamiento de los procesos nacionales y latinoamericanos."

9464. Guandique, José Salvador. Perfiles sobre Caso y Vasconcelos: pt. 2 (UNL/H, 17, 1976, p. 215-265)

Continuando un trabajo anterior sobre Antonio Caso (véase HLAS 38:9471), y dentro del mismo estilo de más o menos libre comentario, se exponen aspectos de la acción y la obra escrita de Vasconcelos. Se utiliza abundantemente la obra de Basave F. del Valle sobre Vasconcelos.

9465. Herrera R., Daniel. El proceso filosófico en Colombia y sus condicionamientos socio-políticos (USB/F, 18:52, enero/abril 1976, p. 5-14)

Visión breve y pesimista del desarrollo de la filosofía en Colombia, desde la colonia hasta hoy, vinculándola a las circunstancias históricas y políticas.

9466. Himelblau, Jack. A. O. Deustua on the dilemma of order vs. liberty in occidental thought (RIB, 26:1, enero/marzo 1976, p. 60-78)

Exposición de la obra de Deustua, *Las ideas de orden y libertad en la historia del pensamiento humano*.

9467. Kourim, Zdeněk. Dos emancipadores de la filosofía en México: Caso y Vasconcelos (UNL/H, 17, 1976, p. 139-160)

Apreciación de conjunto de los pensadores mexicanos, sin que falte el comentario crítico, especialmente en el caso de Vasconcelos.

9468. Ladusāns, Stanislav *ed.* Rumos da filosofia atual no Brasil. v. 1, Em auto-retratos. São Paulo, Edições Loyola, 1976. 533 p.

Contiene 27 autoexposiciones de autores brasileños actuales. Predominan los de orientación católica. Entre los más conocidos figuran: Alcântara Nogueira, Carlos Lopes de Mattos, Cruz Costa, Fernando Arruda Campos, H.C. de Lima Vaz, J.C. de Oliveira Torres, Leonardo van Acker, Luis Washington Vita, Miguel Reale, Ubiratan Macedo y Vilém Flusser.

9469. Lipp, Solomon. Three Chilean thinkers. Waterloo, Canada, McGill Univ., 1975. 160 p., bibl.

Con la misma estructura que su libro anterior (*Three Argentine thinkers*, véase *HLAS 32:6043*) y después de una introducción general expone tres pensadores representativos. Francisco Dilbao (1823-65), Valentín Letelier (1852-1919) y Enrique Molina (1871-1964).

9470. Machado, Geraldo Pinheiro. A filosofia no Brasil. 3. ed. São Paulo, Cortez e Moraes, 1976. 121 p.

Aunque la presente es la 3. ed., es la primera vez que se publica como volumen independiente. Anteriormente figuró como parte de la traducción portuguesa de la *Historia de la filosofía* de Johannes Hirschberger. Aunque en forma compendiada, abarca desde la colonia hasta el presente. La mayor parte de la obra está dedicada a los siglos XIX y XX, con una división en dos períodos: hasta la Primera Guerra Mundial (eclecticismo, tomismo, positivismo y evolucionismo—en este capítulo incluida, sin embargo, la reacción "antimaterialista" de Farias Brito—); y después de dicha Guerra. Un *addendum* más bien bibliográfico se refiere a la situación actual de la filosofía en Brasil.

9471. Martins, José Salgado. Breve história das idéias no Rio Grande do Sul: século XIX e princípios do atual. Porto Alegre, Brazil, Ministério da Educação e Cultura, Instituto Nacional de Estudos Pedagógicos [and] Centro Regional de Pesquisas Educacionais do Rio Grande do Sul, 1972. 18 p.

Breve pero útil trabajo que expone las resonancias del pensamiento filosófico europeo en Rio Grande do Sul, especialmente el positivismo y el evolucionismo.

Martins, Wilson. História da inteligência brasileira. See items 3996 and 7692.

9472. Mayz Vallenilla, Ernesto. Palabras del Presidente del IX Congreso Interamericano de Filosofía y VI de la Sociedad Interamericana de Filosofía en el acto de instalación (RIB, 27:4, oct./dic. 1977, p. 339-342)

Con prosa de pulcritud infrecuente, el autor llama la atención sobre "¿que deseamos hacer con la filosofía?", dadas las circunstancias del mundo actual, los impedimentos a la libertad de expresión y el cuestionamiento de la filosofía por el avance de las ciencias sociales. Sostiene que "la filosofía no es un mero ejercicio intelectual, sino una actitud ante la historia," y que el filósofo latinoamericano tiene la obligación de usar sus instrumentos intelectuales "para lograr que sus ideas se incorporen en aquellas decisiones humanas que influyen sobre el destino de su propia comunidad y perfilan el sentido de la historia."

Mercadante, Paulo. A consciência conservadora no Brasil. See *HLAS 39:7588*.

9473. Miliani, Domingo. Conciencia vigilante de América Latina (UNAM/L, 10, 1977, p. 93-101)

Como "conciencia vigilante de América Latina" califica el autor a Leopoldo Zea. El artículo destaca el significado de la obra de este último.

9474. Miró Quesada, Francisco. Despertar y proyecto del filosofar latinoamericano. México, Fondo de Cultura Económica, 1974. 238 p. (Col. Tierra firme. Historia de las ideas en América, 9)

Aunque algunas partes de la obra parecen escritas hace una o dos décadas, y a pesar de ciertas objeciones que inspira, indudablemente se trata de una de las obras más serias y válidas que se han escrito sobre el tema. Temáticamente se compone de dos partes: 1) una interpretación del desarrollo histórico de la filosofía en América Latina (en la que el autor resalta demasiado, a nuestro juicio, las limitaciones que ha sufrido el pensador latinoamericano para hacer filosofía); y 2) una serie de trabajos críticos: dos ensayos sobre Francisco Romero (en los que se hace justicia a la función de éste en la formación de una conciencia filosófica latinoamericana); un trabajo sobre varios pensadores peruanos; y otro sobre la obra de Leopoldo Zea. El lector interesado en este tema y en la posición de Miró Quesada frente a él debe complementar esta obra con un artículo reciente (item 9476).

9475. ———. La filosofía de lo americano: treinta años después (UNAM/L, 10, 1977, p. 11-23)

Traza un cuadro muy útil y en sus grandes líneas correcto de la "filosofía de lo americano:" desde las primeras producciones historiográficas de Leopoldo Zea hasta la filosofía del Tercer Mundo y la liberación, pasando por la "filosofía de lo mexicano" y la transición, en la obra de Zea, de la historia de las ideas a la filosofía de la historia. Es un trabajo no prescindible como visión sintética para quien se interese por el asunto.

9476. ———. Posibilidad y límites de una filosofía latinoamericana (RIB, 27:4, oct./dic. 1977, p. 353-363)

Este trabajo es uno de los más claros y definitivos (podría decirse, también, de los más conciliadores) que se han escrito sobre un tema cuyo interés no sólo no ha decrecido sino que se ha renovado con variantes de su contenido. Con optimismo mayor que el expresado en su obra *Despertar y proyecto del filosofar latinoamericano,* el autor afirma ahora: "Creemos que la filosofía latinoamericana no sólo es una posibilidad, sino una realidad. En el momento actual, está en pleno florecimiento. Se está realizando en el doble sentido de pensamiento que contribuye a la marcha de la filosofía universal y a la constitución de una filosofía de lo americano. Analiza la vieja polémica entre la posición "americanista" y la "universalista"; la cuestión más reciente de la "cultura de la dominación"; la orientación actual, según corrientes y tendencias; y los límites de la filosofía latinoamericana, que estima son los de cualquier filosofía.

9477. Moreno Davis, Julio César. La vida, obra y pensamiento vivo de Isaías García Aponte: 1927-1968. Panamá, INAC, 1975. 537 p. (Concurso literario Ricardo Miró. Sección ensayo, 1974)

Isaías García Aponte (1927-68) profesor panameño orientado primero hacia el marxismo y luego hacia la fenomenología, el existencialismo y algunas manifestaciones de la filosofía francesa del presente siglo, es tratado aquí con una gran extensión. La obra contiene: la biografía de García Aponte, el análisis de sus escritos, observaciones sobre la situación de la filosofía en Panamá y un apéndice documental donde, además de documentos, se reproducen textos del autor estudiado.

9478. *Nuevo Mundo.* Biblioteca Fray Mamerto Esquiú. Vol. 3, No. 1, enero/junio 1973-   . San Antonio de Padua, Arg.

En general, la mayoría de los artículos de este número especial reitera el tema de la dependencia de América Latina y las consecuencias de esa situación para la filosofía, la cultura, el pensamiento político, etc. Consiguientemente, la filosofía latinoamericana se concibe como una "filosofía de la liberación." Algunos artículos, sin embargo, versan sobre temas históricos o de crítica. El contenido es el siguiente: Osvaldo Ardiles "Bases para una destrucción de la historia de la filosofía en la América indoibérica. Prolegómenos para una filosofía de la liberación" (p. 5-24);
Hugo Assmann "Presupuestos políticos de una filosofía latinoamericana" (p. 25-35);
Mario M. Casalla "Filosofía y cultura nacional en la situación latinoamericana contemporánea" (p. 36-50);
Horacio V. Cerrutti Guldberg "Para una filosofía política indo-iberoamericana: América en las utopías del Renacimiento" (p. 51-89);
Carlos Cullen "El descubrimiento de la nación y la liberación de la filosofía" (p. 90-102);
Julio de Zan "La dialéctica en el centro y en la periferia" (p. 103-115);
Enrique Dussel "El método analéctico y la filosofía latinoamericana" (p. 116-135);
Aníbal Fornari "Política liberadora, educación y filosofía" (p. 136-162);
Daniel E. Guillot "La mala conciencia del filósofo latinoamericano" (p. 163-169);
Rodolfo Kusch "Una lógica de la negación para comprender a América" (p. 170-178);
Diego F. Pró "Americanismo y europeísmo en Alberdi y Groussac" (p. 179-201);
Arturo Andrés Roig "El problema de la "alteridad" en la ontología de Nimio de Anquín" (p. 202-220);
Juan Carlos Scannone "Trascendencia, praxis liberadora y lenguaje. Hacia una filosofía de la religión postmoderna y latinoamericanamente situada" (p. 221-245).

9479. Organization of American States. General Secretariat. Bibliografía filosófica brasileira: período contemporâneo; 1931-1971. v. 1, Libros, opúsculos e teses acadêmicos. Rio, Pontifícia Univ. Católica do Rio de Janeiro, 1972. 218 p. (Bibliografias básicas, 10)

El trabajo fué dirigido por Antonio Paim y se realizó en el Depto. de Filosofia de la Pontificia Univ. Católica de Rio de Janeiro. Es parte de la serie *Bibliografías básicas* (v. 10) de la Secretaría General de la OEA, si bien aparece como separata de la revista *Verbum* (v. 29, Nos. 3/4, set./dez. 1972). Por su carácter único, su utilidad es indudable. Contiene también traducciones aparecidas en Brasil.

9480. Paim, Antônio. O ciclo de formação da corrente eclética: 1833-1848 (IBF/RBF, 26:104, out./dez. 1976, p. 468-475)

Identifica los autores que introdujeron el eclecticismo en Brasil, antes de la obra madura de Monte Alverne, Gonçalves de Magalhães y Ferreira Franca. Sitúa los orígenes de dicha corriente entre otras tendencias de la época.

9481. Reale, Miguel. Filosofía em São Paulo. 2. ed. revista e reestruturada.

São Paulo, Editora da Univ. de São Paulo [and] Editorial Grijalbo, 1976. 176 p.

La 1. ed. de esta obra apareció en 1962. La presente agrega tres estudios. Los seis que ahora componen el volumen son los siguientes: "Momentos Olvidados do Pensamento Brasileiro;" "O Kantismo do Padre Diogo António Feijó;" "Avelar Brotero, ou a Ideologia sob as Arcadas;" "Escolástica e Praxismo na Obra de João Mendes Júnior;" "Pedro Lessa e a Filosofia Positiva em São Paulo;" y "Preliminares a Metafísica de Vicente Ferreira da Silva Filho."

9482. Redmond, Walter Bernard. Bibliography of the philosophy in the Iberian colonies of America. The Hague, Martinus Nijhoff, 1972. 174 p. (International archives of the history of ideas, 51)

Obra utilísima. Contiene un catálogo de más de 800 entradas de manuscritos y obras impresas de filosofía de la época colonial. En Apéndice incluye obras del mismo tipo, pero que se han extraviado. Se complementa con una excelente bibliografía de literatura secundaria sobre el tema.

9483. Roig, Arturo Andrés. De la historia de las ideas a la filosofía de la liberación (UNAM/L, 10, 1977, p. 45-72)

Aunque no expresamente delimitados, este trabajo consta de dos partes: la primera es un repaso de los principales momentos de la historia de la historiografía filosófica latinoamericana (y en especial argentina); la segunda resume la trayectoria intelectual del autor, que ha contribuido considerablemente a esa historiografía. Se acepten o no sus posiciones, es un artículo de real interés.

9484. Sampay, Arturo E. La crítica de Monseñor Derisi a la ciencia política empírica (UCA/S, 26:100/102, abril/dic. 1971, p. 423-436)

Especialmente sobre un escrito de Derisi (filósofo neotomista argentino) de 1970. Exegésis escrita desde un punto de vista afín al autor estudiado.

9485. Sarti, Sergio. Panorama della filosofia ispanoamericana contemporanea. Milano, Italy, Cisalpino-Goliardica, 1976. 738 p.

Después de una Introducción que da una visión general desde la escolástica colonial hasta el positivismo, el cuerpo propiamente dicho del libro estudia el siglo XX, dividido en dos partes: hasta 1950 y desde 1950 hasta 1970. El autor es discípulo de M.F. Sciacca y su enfoque es semejante al que ese autor diera, desde el espiritualismo cristiano, al examen de la filosofía latinoamericana en *La filosofia oggi*. La tarea de abarcar el pensamiento latinoamericano del presente siglo es de por sí muy ambiciosa y tiene especial significación que haya sido intentada por un autor europeo con tanto detalle. Sin embargo, en una futura reedición sería conveniente remediar algunas omisiones y utilizar más ciertos sectores de la bibliografía crítica sobre el tema que no parecen debidamente aprovechados. El balance o proporción relativa de la extensión concedida a los distintos autores también podría mejorarse, aun admitiendo el margen de subjetividad que pueda haber en juicios de esta naturaleza.

9486. Téllez, Freddy. Emilio de Ipola y la teoría de la ideología o Marx contra Marx (UN/IV, 42/45. 1973/1975, p. 39-60)

Crítica a Emilio de Ipola, por su cercanía a las doctrinas del Althusser.

9487. Le temps et la morte dans la philosophie contemporaine d' Amérique Latine: ouvrage collectif de l'equipe de recherche associée au C.N.R.S. sur la philosophie des langues espagnole et portugaise. Tolouse, France, Univ. de Toulouse-Le Mirail, 1971. 212 p.

Los autores representados en esta antología son: María do Carmo Tavares de Miranda, Miguel León-Portilla, Luis Abad Carretero, Francisco Romero, Vicente Ferreira de Silva, Luis Farré, Juan E. Bolzán, Agustín Basave y Francesc Botey. Los textos se reproducen en francés y van precedidos de una presentación escrita por uno de los miembros del equipo de trabajo. Entre éstos ese encuentra el conocido hispanista de la Univ. de Toulouse, Alain Guy.

9488. Terán Mata, Juan Manuel. El pensamiento filosófico en la ciudad de México: épocas precortesiana y colonial. México, Depto. del Distrito Federal, Secretaría de Obras y Servicios, 1975. 110 p. (Col. Popular ciudad de México, 31)

Pequeño volumen de divulgación. Expone sintéticamente la visión del mundo de la civilización precolombina en la región del valle de México, su encuentro con la filosofía europea y la escolástica en la Nueva España hasta el siglo XVIII.

9489. Vera y Cuspinera, Margarita. José Vasconcelos, profeta de la "raza cósmica" (UNAM/L, 8, 1975, p. 191-202)

Exposición de la idea vasconceliana de una "raza" síntesis.

9490. Weistein, Michael A. The polarity of Mexican thought: instrumentalism and finalism. Philadelphia, Univ. of Pennsylvania Press, 1976. 128 p.

En un sentido muy básico puede decirse que la obra trata del positivismo en México y la reacción que frente a él comenzaron Caso y Vasconcelos. "Instrumentalismo" sería una designación general para el positivismo y las formas sociales y culturales que impregnó. "Finalismo" sería una expresión que englobaría a las distintas manifestaciones antipositivistas. La obra, por lo tanto, estudia a los dos filósofos mexicanos antes mencionados y también a Ramos, Zea, Uranga, Basave Fernández del Valle, al sociólogo Mendieta y Núñez y al escritor Octavio Paz. El autor se propone mostrar "una visión de la existencia humana" en la obra de los autores mencionados, a pesar de sus divergencias. El "finalismo" que encuentra en ellos le parece relevante como crítica a ciertos aspectos de la civilización moderna.

9491. Zea, Leopoldo. Dependencia y liberación en la filosofía latinoamericana (UNAM/D, 20, 1974, p. 172-188)

Afirma el autor que tanto la "filosofía de la liberación," según la exponen Salazar Bondy y E. Dussel, como la posición "moderna" y "profesional" que representa en México, por ejemplo, Luis Villoro, niegan el pasado pero no lo asimilan o asumen para una construcción distinta. "La filosofía de la liberación ha de ser filosofía que salve al hombre ... de la enajenación impuesta o autoimpuesta. Que lo salve como totalidad, sin amputación del pasado ni del futuro."

Historia de las Ideas

9492. Alvarez Curbello, Silvia. Vicisitudes del nacionalismo argentino (UNAM/L, 4, 1971, p. 71-90)

Se examinan aspectos de la vida argentina entre mediados del siglo XIX y la Segunda Guerra Mundial. Se destacan los aspectos de dependencia externa. Las fuentes utilizadas son las que participan de la preocupación por ese tema.

9493. Anastasia, Luis V. Pedro Figari, americano integral. Montevideo, Publicaciones de la Comisión Nacional de Homenaje del Sesquicentenario de los Hechos Históricos de 1825, 1975. 241 p.

Destaca los aspectos de la obra de Figari (1861-1938) como filósofo y especialmente como educador. Figari fué, además, uno de los más importantes pintores latinoamericanos de su época.

9494. Ardao, Arturo. La historia de la historiografía de las ideas en Latinoamérica (UNAM/L, 10, 1977, p. 25-38)

Util resumen de lo aportado a la historia de las ideas (especialmente filosóficas) latinoamericanas en las décadas del 40 y del 50, pero sin limitarse exclusivamente a ese período.

9495. Arteaga Calderón, Marco. Cinco razones para aceptar a Mariátegui. Lima, Empresa Editora Amauta, 1976. 121 p.

Ensayo definido por su autor como "acotaciones de lectura." Parte de considerar a Mariátegui totalmente actual, en lo ideológico, lo político y lo social. Los cinco temas tratados son: el problema educativo; la cuestión indígena; el antiimperialismo; la organización popular; y "la alternativa de Latinoamérica."

9496. Blasi, Alberto. Un conflicto de ideas en el ensayo argentino (RIB, 27:3, julio/set. 1977, p. 255-261)

Repasa con rápidos comentarios obras de un grupo de ensayistas comprendidas entre las fechas indicadas en el título.

9497. Carrión, Benjamin. José Carlos Mariátegui: el precursor, el anticipador, el suscitador. México, Secretaría de Educación Pública, 1976. 183 p. (SepSetentas, 238)

Aproximadamente la mitad del libro es un libre ensayo—comentario sobre Mariátegui. La otra mitad es una antología del autor peruano, en la que se reproduce parte de *Siete ensayos de interpretación de la realidad peruana*.

9498. Castellani, Leonardo. Lugones: esencia del liberalismo; nueva crítica literaria. B.A., Ediciones Dictio, 1976. 567 p., plate (Biblioteca del pensamiento nacionalista argentino, 8)

El P. Castellani es probablemente el más polémico del grupo representado en esta colección. Esta recopilación consta de tres libros: *Lugones*, 2. ed. ampliada; *Esencia del liberalismo*; 4. ed.; y *Nueva crítica literaria*, que aparece aquí por primera vez. Esta última obra está compuesta por artículos críticos en general breves. A pesar del título, contiene también crítica filosófica, si bien en el estilo nada "académico" del autor.

9499. Cid G., Francisco Javier *ed.* El humanismo de Manuel Larraín. 3 v. Santiago, Instituto Chileno de Estudios, 1975. 3 v. (238, 233, 230 p.)

Los tres volúmenes recogen escritos del P. Manuel Larraín, S.J. (1921-74), sobre temas políticos, sociales y universitarios. En la mayoría de los casos resultan de comentar asuntos de actualidad. Preceden a cada volumen breves comentarios del compilador, escritos con simpatía, pero sin llegar a constituir un estudio formal.

Costa, Carlos. O problema da sociologia como ciência e outros estudos. See *HLAS 39:9018*.

9500. Dessau, Adalbert. Literatura y sociedad en las obras de José Carlos Mariátegui (CDLA, 14:84, mayo/junio 1974, p. 19-39)

Análisis encomiástico de la crítica literaria de Mariátegui en el contexto de su posición marxista (que el autor estima marxista-leninista) y su actuación política. Una nota aclara que se trata de una versión abreviada y actualizada de un ensayo aparecido en el libro de Melis, Dessau y Kossok, *Mariátegui* (véase *HLAS 38:9522*).

9501. Escobar Valenzuela, Gustavo. En torno a la historia de las ideas en México (UNAM/L, 10, 1977, p. 103-124)

Reseña la aportación de José Gaos, Samuel Ramos, Leopoldo Zea y Abelardo Villegas a la historia de las ideas en México.

9502. Ferreira, João-Francisco. Rumo à utopia: uma introdução ao pensamento americanista de Ureña. Porto Alegre, Brazil, Hythlodaeus, 1974. 101 p.

Excelente ensayo sobre Henríquez Ureña: su vida, su obra, su significado y su preocupación americanista. Obra bien informada y bien escrita, con útil bibliografía.

9503. Genevois, Danièle and **Bernard Le Gonidec.** Aspects de la pensée hispano-américaine, 1898-1930. Rennes, France, Centre d'Etudes Hispaniques et Hispano-américaines, 1974. 254 p., bibl. (Publications de l'Univ. d'Haute-Bretagne)

Se trata de una antología del ensayo hispanoamericano entre las fechas señaladas en el título. El conjunto de autores es representativo. En la primera parte, las obras seleccionadas se comentan, con abundantes citas en castellano. Vienen luego indicaciones bibliográficas sobre los autores seleccionados. Al final, está la antología propiamente dicha.

9504. Genta, Jordán B. Acerca de la libertad de enseñar y de la enseñanza de la libertad. Libre examen y comunismo. Guerra contrarrevolucionaria. B.A., Ediciones Dictio, 1976. 580 p., bibl. (Biblioteca del pensamiento nacionalista argentino, 7)

Recoge tres libros del autor, uno de los representantes del nacionalismo católico, hispanista y antiliberal argentino más cercanos a la temática filosófica. Los tres libros son los siguientes: *Acerca de la libertad de enseñar y de la enseñanza de la libertad* (1. ed., 1945), al cual se agrega aquí el texto "Rehabilitación de la inteligencia" (1950); *Libre examen y comunismo* (1. ed. 1960); y *Guerra contrarrevolucionaria* (1. ed. 1964; 2a., 1965; 3a. 1971). Contiene bibliografía completa del autor.

9505. Goyeneche, Juan Carlos. Ensayos, artículos, discursos. B.A., Ediciones Dictio, 1976. 614 p. (Biblioteca del pensamiento nacionalista argentino, 9)

Reúne en un volumen lo escrito por el autor, uno de los principales representantes del nacionalismo argentino del presente siglo.

9506. Hale, Charles A. The reconstruction of nineteenth-century politics in Spanish America: a case for the history of ideas (LARR, 8:2, Summer 1973, p. 53-73)

Reivindica el valor de la historia de las ideas para comprender el proceso de la historia política hispano-americana. El artículo interesa también para el problema del liberalismo en Hispanoamérica.

9507. El humanismo de Alberto Hurtado. Santiago, Instituto Chileno de Estudios Humanísticos, 1975. 82 p.

Volumen compañero de otros dos, sobre Manuel Larraín (item 9508) y Francisco Vives (item 9509), respectivamente. El presente es una antología de textos del P. Alberto Hurtado (1901-52), representante del pensamiento católico chileno.

9508. El humanismo de Manuel Larraín. Santiago, Instituto Chileno de Estudios Humanísticos, 1975. 104 p.

Selección de textos de Monseñor Larraín (1921-74), sacerdote chileno preocupado por los problemas sociales desde su punto de vista cristiano.

9509. El humanismo social de Francisco Vives. Santiago, Instituto Chileno de Estudios Humanísticos, 1975. 82 p.

Antología de escritos de Francisco Vives, representante del pensamiento cristiano en Chile en el presente siglo. Los textos están tomados de sus libros *Filosofía del derecho* y *Principios de sociología cristiana*.

9510. Ibarguren, Carlos. La inquietud de esta hora. Historia del tiempo clásico. La reforma constitucional, sus fundamentos y su estructura. Escritos políticos e históricopolíticos. B.A., Ediciones Dictio, 1975. 456 p., bibl. (Biblioteca del pensamiento nacionalista argentino, 6)

Las críticas a la democracia liberal y las simpatías por el Estado corporativo, típicas de los autores nacionalistas representados en esta colección, se hacen evidentes en *La inquietud de esta hora*. Liberalismo, corporativismo, nacionalismo, que Ibarguren (1877-1956) publicó en 1934. *Historias del tiempo clásico* (un tema de historia romana) apareció por primera vez en 1924. *La reforma constitucional, sus fundamentos y su estructura*, fué una contribución a la reforma de la Constitución argentina que tuvo lugar en 1949, durante el primer gobierno de Perón. Los textos recogidos bajo el título de "Escritos políticos e histórico políticos" se publican por primera vez. El texto se completa con una reseña biográfica y una bibliografía del autor.

9511. Irazusta, Julio ed. and comp. El pensamiento político nacionalista. v. 1, De Alvear a Yrigoyen; v. 2, La revolución de 1930. B.A., Obligado Editora, 1975. 2 v. (82, 192 p.)

Recoge artículos periodísticos aparecidos, principalmente, en *La Nueva República*, desde 1927 a 1931. Entre los colaboradores figuran Rodolfo y Julio Irazusta, Ernesto Palacio y César E. Pico. La documentación es de interés para la historia del pensamiento nacionalista (católico-hispanista) argentino, en especial en relación con su participación doctrinaria en la Revolución de 1930, que derrocó al Presidente Yrigoyen.

Isaacson, José ed. El populismo en la Argentina. See *HLAS 39:9273*.

9512. Mariátegui, José Carlos. La escena contemporánea. 7. ed. Lima, Editora Amauta, 1976. 174 p. (Obras completas de José Carlos Mariátegui)

La primera edición apareció en 1925. Otras de esta misma editorial han sido de 1959, 1964, 1970, 1972 y 1975. Esta edición contiene un breve estudio preliminar del profesor italiano Antonio Melis. El tema de la obra es la actualidad política europea de la época.

9513. Morsella, Astur. Martínez Estrada. B.A., Plus Ultra, 1973. 134 p., bibl. (Esquemas ensayos, 1)

Ensayo escrito con simpatía, sobre el autor de *Radiografía de la Pampa*. El principal tema de libro es la interpretación de Martínez Estrada sobre la realidad argentina. Contiene útil bibliografía.

9514. Nahmad, Salomón. Las ideas sociales del positivismo en el indigenismo de la época pre-revolucionaria en México (III/AI, 33:4, oct./dic. 1973, p. 1169-1182, bibl.)

Basado en una bibliografía limitada, concluye que, en México, el positivismo sirvió de base a ideas conservadoras, a la justificación de la dictadura y a la defensa de la burguesía terrateniente. Comte y Spencer habrían servido para justificar el racismo, en razón del cual los indígenas fueron considerados como miembros de una raza inferior. Es interesante comparar este artículo con el del W.A. Raat, "Los Intelectuales, el Positivismo y la Cuestión Indígena" (véase *HLAS 38:9529*).

9515. París de Oddone, Blanca. En torno a la historia de las ideas filosóficas en Uruguay (UNAM/L, 10, 1977, p. 39-43)

Como era de esperar, el artículo está centrado en la capital contribución de Arturo Ardao a la historia de las ideas en el Uruguay.

9516. Peralta, José. La naturaleza ante la teología y la ciencia: apuntes científicos. Cuenca, Ecua. n.p., 1974. 206 p. (Obras completas de José Peralta)

Peralta, hombre público y escritor ecuatoriano, nació en 1859 y actuó en la política de su país hacia fines del siglo XIX y comienzos del XX. En esta obra se revela influido por el krausismo de Tiberghien, a quien cita, al igual que a Nicolás Salmerón. Aunque está contra la Iglesia y la revelación bíblica, es a la vez antimaterialista y defensor de la existencia de Dios. La obra es evidentemente una reedición de la 1. ed. de 1914 publicada en Lima, pero no trae la menor indicación crítica. Parece ser parte de las *Obras completas* del autor. La única breve nota del "editor" (no se sabe si esto alude a la editorial que publica o a alguien que preparó la edición) indica que esta obra y otra titulada *Teorías del universo* se complementan.

9517. Pino Iturrieta, Elías. La nueva generación de historiadores de las ideas: una breve noticia (UNAM/L, 10, 1977, p. 73-77)

Sobre las más recientes promociones de estudiosos de la historia de las ideas en América Latina, bajo la guía de José Gaos y Leopoldo Zea.

9518. Podestá, Bruno. Pensamiento político de González Prada. Lima, Instituto Nacional de Cultura, 1975. 223 p., bibl.

Se trata de una antología del pensamiento político de González Prada (1848-1918), poeta y ensayista peruano. Los textos son principalmente de los últimos años del autor y están extraídos de sus libros *Anarquía, Horas de lucha y El tonel de Diógenes*. Contiene una presentación o estudio del compilador y una útil bibliografía sobre González Prada.

9519. Posada Zarate, Francisco. Los orígenes del pensamiento marxista en Latinoamérica. Bogotá, Nuevas Ediciones, 1977. 65 p.

A pesar de la generalidad del título, se trata de un ensayo sobre José Carlos Mariátegui. Sobre una base de simpatía ideológica, el tono es de comentario crítico.

9520. Rama, Carlos M. El nacionalismo cultural argentino (UNAM/L, 9, 1976, p. 139-167)

Aunque no se percibe una tesis central claramente presentada, contiene útiles indicaciones, especialmente en lo que se refiere a las manifestaciones historiográficas argentinas que se engloban bajo el llamado "revisionismo histórico."

9521. Real de Azúa, Carlos. Filosofía de la historia e imperialismo (UNAM/L, 9, 1976, p. 191-210)

A pesar del título, se trata de un extenso comentario crítico-analítico del libro de Leopoldo Zea, *América en la historia* (véase item 9522).

9522. ———. Historia visible e historia esotérica: personajes y claves del debate latinoamericano. Montevideo, Arca/Calicanto, 1975, 173 p.

Se compone de siete ensayos: "Los Males Latinoamericanos y su Clave: Etapas de una Reflexión" (sobre las causas que se han buscado históricamente a los males latinoamericanos); "Filosofía de la Historia e Imperialismo" (sobre: Leopoldo Zea, *América en la historia);* "El Desarraigo Rioplatense: Mafud y el Martinezestradismo;" "Memoria Tardía de un Gran Americano" (sobre José Vasconcelos); "El Inventor del Arielismo: Luis Alberto Sánchez;" El Problema de la Valoración de Rodó;" y "Ariel, Libro Porteño." Participa de la historia intelectual, la historia de las ideas y el ensayo de interpretación de conjunto de América Latina.

9523. Roig, Arturo Andrés. Los ideales bolivarianos y la propuesta de una Universidad Latinoamericana Continental (UNAM/L, 9, 1976, p. 231-245)

Expone y documenta dos intentos de crear una universidad continental latinoamericana: una iniciativa de Francisco Bilbao, de 1856, y otra de Julio Ricardo Barcos (n. 1883), educador argentino vinculado a la Reforma Universitaria de 1918 y simpatizante de las ideas anarquistas. En ambos casos se trataba de destacar y mantener viva la cultura de los países hispanoamericanos y de fomentar la unidad de éstos.

9524. Rouillon D., Guillermo. La creación heroica de José Carlos Mariátegui. t. l, La edad de piedra: 1894-1919. Lima, Editorial Arica, 1975. 341 p.

Muy detallada biografía de los primeros 25 años de José Carlos Mariátegui, es decir, antes de su viaje a Europa, que marca un hito clave en su vida intelectual. El autor prepara la continuación de la obra y ha redactado esta primera parte en base a numerosos testimonios.

9525. Valcárcel, Luis E. El problema del indio. El proceso de la instrucción pública: estudio de Augusto Salazar Bondy. El proceso de la literatura: estudio de Augusto Tamayo Vargas. Lima, Biblioteca Amauta, 1976. 90 p. (Presencia y proyección de los 7 ensayos, 5)

Los tres trabajos versan sobre José Carlos Mariátegui (1894-1930), autor de *Siete ensayos de interpretación de la realidad peruana*.

9526. Vanden, Harry E. Mariátegui: influencias en su formación ideológica. Lima, Biblioteca Amauta, 1975. 145 p. (Serie presencia y proyección de la obra de Mariátegui)

Trabajo monográfico que rastrea los autores y obras que habrían influido en Mariátegui. Una de las fuentes utilizadas es la biblioteca personal del autor peruano, que Vanden trata de reconstruir en un apéndice documental de la presente obra. Naturalmente, se presta la mayor atención a autores europeos (especialmente franceses e italianos) que Mariátegui conoció durante su viaje a Europa. El autor tiende a destacar la influencia directa de Marx y Lenin sobre Mariátegui, frente a la opinión de otros críticos.

9527. Zea, Leopoldo. De la historia de las ideas a la filosofía de la historia (UNAM/L, 10, 1977, p. 125-137)

El autor expresa su concepción de la historia de las ideas en América Latina y su relación con una filosofía de la historia de la región. Tal vez lo más interesante del artículo sea la respuesta de Zea a algunos de sus críticos norteamericanos. Con alguna variante, este artículo fué reproducido en *Revista Interamericana de Bibliografía* (27:4, oct./dic., 1977).

HISTORIA DE LA FILOSOFIA
Filosofía Antigua y Medieval

9528. Argerami, Omar. El infinito actual en Santo Tomás (UCA/S, 26:100/102, abril/dic. 1971, p. 217-232)

Examen, a través de los textos originales, de las variadas opiniones de Santo Tomás sobre el tema. Para el autor, Santo Tomás no habría resuelto el problema del infinito de modo unívoco.

9529. Barata Viana, Sylvio. Sobre Pitágoras e pitagóricos (UMGFF/K, 20:67, 1973/1974, p. 1-22)

Exposición general de la doctrina pitagórica.

9530. Calderón Bouchet, R. Marsilio de Padua: un idéologo del siglo XIV (IFP/E, 1, 1973, p. 293-310)

Exposición de conjunto del autor del *Defensor Pacis*. Se destaca este juicio del autor: "Marsilio fué, con Ockham, el prototipo del intelectual al servicio del poder. Sus ideas fueron medios para lograr determinados objetivos políticos. Por esta condición de su pensamiento lo consideramos un ideólogo."

9531. Camacho, Luis. Isomorfismo, inmaterialidad y conocimiento sensible: planteamiento de una dificultad (UCR/RF, 13/36, enero/junio 1975, p. 73-80)

Comentario y variante de una argumentación crítica de W.F. Sellars a la doctrina tomista del conocimiento sensible.

9532. Cappelletti, Angel J. Diógenes de Apolonia y la autoconciencia del monismo jónico (UZ/H, 1:1/2, 1974, p. 83-116)

Trabajo global sobre Diógenes de Apolonia que se incorporó a la obra del autor *Diógenes de Apolonia y la segunda filosofía jónica* (véase item 9533).

9533. ———. Diógenes de Apolonia y la segunda filosofía jónica. Maracaibo, Ven., Univ. del Zulia, 1976? 112 p. (Biblioteca de textos filosóficos)

Además de un estudio sobre Diógenes de Apolonia, contiene otros sobre Arquelao de Mileto, Hipón de Samos e Ideo de Himera. Sobre Diógenes de Apolonia véase del mismo autor, *HLAS 38:9543*.

9534. ———. Etica, política y bien común en Aristóteles (Atlántida [Univ. Simón Bolívar, División de Ciencias Sociales y Humanidades, Caracas] 3:5, feb. 1976, p. 28-32)

Trata la interrelación de ética y política en diversos textos de Aristóteles y señala las consecuencias de desigualdad que resultan de un Estado concebido desde esas bases.

9535. ———. Naturaleza y funciones del tacto, según Aristóteles (USB/RVF, 4, 1976, p. 19-51)

Trabajo monográfico, bien elaborado, basado principal pero no exclusivamente en los pasajes pertinentes del *De Anima* (véase tambien item 9537).

9536. ———. El problema de la eternidad del mundo en Tomás de Aquino (Atlántida [Univ. Simón Bolívar, División de Ciencias Sociales y Humanidades, Caracas] 2:2, feb. 1975, p. 29-38)

En primer lugar, coloca el tema en el momento histórico de Santo Tomás, situado entre la "derecha" tradicionalista que veía con desconfianza la incorporación de la doctrina aristotélica, y la "izquierda" averroísta. Expone la posición de Santo Tomás en *De aeternitate mundi* (Dios pudo crear al mundo desde siempre), pero antes examina antecedentes del tema, desde los presocraticos hasta el siglo XIII.

9537. ———. La teoría aristotélica de la visión. Caracas. Sociedad Venezolana de Ciencias Humanas, 1977. 97 p.

Monografía sobre la teoría de la sensación, de la visión y de los colores en Aristóteles.

9538. Castañeda, Héctor-Neri. El análisis de Platón de las relaciones y de los hechos relacionales en el *Fedón* (UPR/D, 26, abril 1974, p. 7-15)

Véase *HLAS 38:9544*.

9539. Cordero, Néstor Luis. Acerca de tres pasajes del Poema de Parménides (CIF/RLF, 1:3, nov. 1975, p. 237-243)

Exégesis detallada de los pasajes seleccionados.

9540. Derisi, Octavio N. Santo Tomás de Aquino y la filosofía actual. B.A., Univ. Católica Argentina, 1975. 506 p.

Escritos originados en el VII Centenario de la muerte de Santo Tomás y otros anteriores se reúnen en este volumen. Además de la Introducción ("Santo Tomás de Aquino en el VII Centenario de su Muerte"), contiene trabajos agrupados en cuatro secciones: 1) Actualidad del tomismo; 2) El intelectualismo tomista frente a las distintas posiciones de la filosofía actual; 3) La metafísica tomista frente a la fenomenología existencial contemporánea; y 4) Axiología y moral en el tomismo. Es intención del autor profundizar los principios tomistas, "para reelaborar con ellos una solución a los problemas actuales de la filosofía."

9541. Disandro, Carlos A. Filosofía y poesía en el pensar griego. La Plata, Arg., Ediciones Hostería Volante, 1974. 356 p. (Veterum Sapientia, 5)

Continuación de los temas tratados en un libro anterior: *Tránsito del mythos al logos* (1969). "La fisonomía doctrinal de Anaxágoras, Demócrito, Empédocles nos interesa ... como típica modulación de un vínculo ... entre las dos laderas del lenguaje griego: el lenguaje de la inmediatez numinosa (*mythos*), el lenguaje de la perspectiva analítica y selectiva (*logos*)."

9542. Eggers Lan, Conrado. El sol, la línea y la caverna. B.A., Editorial Universitaria de Buenos Aires. 1975. 146 p. (Temas de EUDEBA)

Las alegorías del sol, la línea y la caverna aparecen en los libros VI y VII de la *República* de Platón. Aquí se reproducen, en castellano, los textos platónicos correspondientes, con un capítulo introductorio y varios posteriores que analizan dichos textos en función de los problemas que presentan y de la bibliografía sobre el asunto, pero sobre todo con intención didáctica.

9544. García Máynez, Eduardo. Tesis del *Critón* sobre el deber de obediencia a las leyes del estado y las sentencias de sus jueces (UNAM/D, 20, 1974, p. 10-22)

Después de comentar la parte pertinente del diálogo platónico, lo relaciona con teorías modernas sobre la seguridad jurídica y el reconocimiento de la obligatoriedad de las leyes.

9545. Gómez C., Jaime and **Víctor Peñuela C.** De las cuatro direcciones en el nombrar del Oscuro de Efeso (Escritos [Univ. Pontificia Bolivariana, Facultad de Filosofía y Letras, Medellín, Colombia] 2:5, feb. 1977, p. 17-35)

Primera parte de una tesis de grado.

9546. Gómez-Lobo, Alfonso. Sobre "lo que es en cuanto es" en Aristóteles (CIF/RLF, 2:1, marzo 1976, p. 19-26)

Una de las principales conclusiones de este trabajo sobre la expresión aristotélica *tò òn hê ón*, es: "Aristóteles no distingue ni hace temático el uso existencial del verbo "ser." Por ende, su Filosofía Primera es una ciencia concebida básicamente como una indagación del principio y la causa por la cual los atributos esenciales pertenecen a sus sujetos"

9547. Guariglia, Osvaldo N. Orden social jerárquico y norma consuetudinaria en el pensamiento ético-político de Aristóteles (CIF/RLF, 2:2, julio 1976, p. 121-166)

Extenso y minucioso trabajo en el cual el pensamiento ético-político de Aristóteles es examinado en sus textos y en relación con la sociedad griega.

9548. Laje, Enrique. La propiedad en la *Suma teológica* (IFP/E, 1, 1973, p. 81-91)

Destacamos sólo una de las conclusiones de este trabajo, breve pero minucioso: el derecho natural indica que todo hombre tiene derecho a poseer, pero no determina cuál debe ser la propiedad de cada uno; esta determinación, según Santo Tomás, se realiza por derecho positivo.

9549. Láscaris, Constantino *ed.* and *trans.* Parménides: sobre la naturaleza (UCR/RF, 13:36, enero/junio 1975, p. 3-55)

Edición bilingüe. El texto griego se toma de la edición de Diels-Kranz. Además de la exposición del contenido del poema o paráfrasis, agrega una bibliografía. De indudable utilidad.

9550. Lértora Mendoza, Celina A. La *Summa Physicorum* y la filosofía natural de Grosseteste (UCA/S, 26:100/102, abril/dic. 1971, p. 199-216)

Comparando la *Summa in VIII Libros Physicorum* con el *Commentarius in VIII Libros Physicorum Aristotelis* y otras obras de Grosseteste, se inclina por la opinión de que la *Summa* no es atribuible a dicho autor. El cuerpo del trabajo se dedica a esas comparaciones.

9551. Maciel, Jarbas. Atualidade da cosmología platónica (IBF/RBF, 26:104, out./dez. 1976, p. 436-459)

Apoyándose en una reciente declaración de Heisemberg sobre la relación de la doctrina platónica con la estructura de la explicación física de la materia, examina sumariamente la naturaleza y el origen de la cosmología platónica.

9552. Mas Herrera, Oscar E. Algunos aspectos de la teoría del conocimiento en Santo Tomás de Aquino: introducción a la doctrina de la iluminación de la inteligencia en el sistema tomista (UCR/RF, 13:36, enero/junio 1975, p. 57-71)

Sobre la teoría tomista del conocimiento en relación con la tradición agustiniana.

9553. ———. La doctrina de la iluminación de la inteligencia y del hombre interior en San Agustín (UCR/RF, 14:39, julio/dic. 1976, p. 63-73)

Sobre la doctrina contenida en el diálogo *De Magistro*, de San Agustín.

9554. Napolitano, Antonio. Reflexión epistemológica: teoría del conocimiento en Santo Tomás y en la ciencia contemporánea. Caracas, Univ. Católica Andrés Bello, Dirección de Cultura, 1972. 44 p. (Escuela de filosofía, 1)

La conclusión final del autor es la siguiente: "fundamentalmente la problemática actual de la epistemología científica gira en torno a las mismas notas cognoscitivas que la de Santo Tomás."

9555. Navarro, Bernabé. Apuntes para una revisión de la gnoseología platónica (UNAM/D, 20, 1974, p. 23-37)

La interpretación tradicional habla de la existencia.

transcendente de las ideas en Platón ("realismo de las idesas"). Pero, para el autor, "la doctrina de la separación o existencia separada de las ideas ... no es en su verdadero fondo sino la independencia y la validez por sí mismas de las estructuras mental-objetivas del espíritu; la doctrina sobre ellas como seres individuales concretos es sólo la conclusión lógica de una interpretación errónea sobre la existencia separada."

9556. **Pascuali, Antonio.** La ética de Demócrito (UZ/H, 1:1/2, 1974, p. 185)

Extensá monografía sobre la doctrina ética de Demócrito, usualmente más reconocido por su atomismo y su "física."

9557. **Ponferrada, Gustavo Eloy.** Tomás de Aquino en la Universidad de París (UCA/S, 26:100/102, abril/dic. 1971, p. 233-262)

Interesante narración, bien documentada, sobre el destino del aristotelismo en la Univ. de París (siglo XIII), las disputas—filosóficas y humanas—en la universidad y los comienzos de la carrera docente de Santo Tomás.

9558. **Prado de Mendonça, Eduardo.** Santo Tomás e o pensamento contemporâneo (VOZES, 68:5, junho/julho 1974, p. 5-12)

Con algunos ejemplos quiere mostrar que Santo Tomás estudiado con profundidad puede ser "una presencia en nuestros días."

9559. **Raffo Magnasco, Benito.** Volición y voluntad en Aristóteles (UCA/S, 26:100/102, abril/dic. 1971, p. 137-150)

La pregunta que se plantea el trabajo, y que se busca responder acudiendo a los textos propios de Aristóteles, es si para éste existe una facultad como la voluntad, distinta de la razón. La respuesta es que "no obstante la falta de claridad y las dificultades que provoca el modo cómo el Estagirita toca la cuestión de la voluntad, ésta existió en su pensamiento como una facultad distinta realmente del entendimiento..."

9560. **Sacheri, Carlos A.** Aspectos lógicos del discurso deliberativo (IFP/E, 1, 1973, p. 175-191)

Análisis de la "deliberación" (*consilium*) en Santo Tomás, según la Ia-IIae, q. 14.

9561. **Saxe Fernández, Eduardo.** Reflexión y autoritarismo en Parménides y Platón (UCR/RF, 14:39, julio/dic. 1976, p. 47-62)

Afirma intentar una interpretación psicoanalítica de la noción de "auto-constitución primaria."

9562. **Schmidt Osmanczik, Ute** *ed.*

Platón, Menón. México, UNAM, 1975. lcix, 43 p. (Biblioteca scriptorum graecorum et romanorum mexicana)

Debe destacarse en esta obra que es una edición bilingüe, con estudio preliminar y bibliografía. Asimismo, que es el noveno diálogo de Platón incluido en esta colección.

9563. **Souza, Eudoro de.** Dioniso em Creta e outros ensaios: estudos de mitologia e filosofia da Grécia antiga. São Paulo, Livraria Duas Cidades, 1973. 333 p. (Série universidade, 1)

Estudios minuciosos, bien caracterizados por el subtítulo del libro, y más dedicados a la religión que a la filosofía griegas.

9564. **Xirau, Ramón.** Nuevamente Heráclito (UNAM/D, 20, 1974, p. 38-43)

Sobre el *logos* en Heráclito y a propósito de la obra de Clémence Ramnoux. *Héraclite ou l'homme entre les choses et les mots* (1968).

Filosofía Moderna

9565. **Antonietta, Eduardo.** La sexta meditación cartesiana (UNT/H, 18:24, 1977, p. 11-29)

Trabajo de naturaleza expositiva.

9566. **Arias A., Edison.** El problema de la libertad en Descartes (Cuadernos de Filosofía [Univ. de Concepción, Instituto Central de Filosofía, Chile] 3/4, 1974/1975, p. 83-95)

Exposición del tema acudiendo a los textos de Descartes y eludiendo las interpretaciones extremas de Gilson, *La liberté chez Descartes et la théologie* y de Laporte, *La liberté selon Descartes*.

9567. **Arnaudo, Florencio José.** Las principales tesis marxistas. B.A., Pleamar, 1975. 171 p.

Desde un punto de vista no marxista, se procede a una tarea sistemática: se toman las principales tesis marxistas en filosofía, sociología, economía y política se reproducen textos que las explicitan y se realiza una crítica, de las mismas. Entre otros, se analizan los conceptos de materialismo, dialéctica, teoría del valor y de la plusvalía, Estado, revolución socialista, etc.

9568. **Betancur R., John Jairo.** Nietzsche: hacia una nueva sensibilidad (Escritos [Univ. Pontificia Bolivariana, Facultad de Filosofía y Letras, Medellín, Colombia] 1:1, julio 1974, p. 48-58)

Sobre las relaciones entre vida y verdad en Nietzsche, sin tesis definida.

9569. **Braun, Rafael.** La teoría de la guerra en los *Elements of law* de Hobbes (CIF/RLF, 1:2, 1975, p. 81-107)

Favoreciendo una interpretación histórica de los sucesivos textos de la teoría política de Hobbes, se examina en detalle, en *The elements of law, natural and politic*, la guerra en el estado de naturaleza y la guerra internacional.

9570. **Cappelleti, Angel J.** La pedagogía de Condillac (Educación [Ministerio de Educación, Caracas] 37:153/154, dic. 1974, p. 157-171)

Cómo Condillac aplicó a la pedagogía su teoría sensualista del conocimiento.

9571. **Celli, Bruni.** La evolución de Descartes en la presentación de su método (UZ/H, 1:1/2, 1974, p. 57-81)

Se examina el método cartesiano en dos obras: el *Discurso del método* y las *Meditaciones metafísicas*.

9572. **Chaves, Eduardo Oscar de Campos.** David Hume e a questão básica da *Crítica da razão prática* (CIF/RLF, 2:3, nov. 1976, p. 215-241)

El tema del trabajo es la filosofía moral de Kant. Sostiene la tesis de que dicha filosofía resulta de un "desafío" que le impuso a Kant la doctrina de Hume. Este, pues, no habría influido solamente en la filosofía teórica de Kant, como usualmente es reconocido.

9573. **Da Costa Leiva, Miguel.** El fenomenismo de David Hume (Cuadernos de Filosofía [Univ. de Concepción, Instituto Central de Filosofía, Chile] 3/4, 1974/1975, p. 39-81)

Trabajo monográfico sobre la teoría del conocimiento de Hume.

9574. **Dascal, Marcelo.** La razón y los misterios de la fe según Leibniz (CIF/RLF, 1:3, nov. 1975, p. 193-226)

Contribución a la filosofía de la religión de Leibniz y de hecho también a la estructura del discurso religioso, especialmente sus componentes epistemológicos y semánticos.

9575. **Díaz A., Jorge Aurelio.** ¿Qué es la fenomenología del espíritu? (UN/IV, 42/45, 1973/1975, p. 203-226)

En base a ciertos textos que señalan lo que es la *Fenomenología del espíritu*, se trata de desentrañar "el sentido en que Hegal mismo desarrolló su obra y la intención que lo movió a escribirla."

9576. **Estiú, Emilio.** Leonardo y la ciencia de la pintura (CIF/RLF, 2:1, marzo 1976, p. 3-17)

Principalmente sobre las relaciones entre las matemáticas y la pintura en el Renacimiento.

9577. **Finol de Jiménez, Mary.** Sobre la *Crítica de la razón práctica* y sus implicaciones éticas (Boletín de Filosofía [Univ. del Zulia, Facultad de Humanidades y Educación, Centro de Estudios Filosóficos, Maracaibo. Ven.] 1972, p. 27-117)

Extensa exposición del contenido de la *Crítica de la razón práctica*, de Kant.

9578. **García Bacca, Juan David.** El concepto de naturaleza en el Renacimiento y en nuestros días (UNL/H, 17, 1976, p. 161-171)

Más que de una comparación, como sugiere el título, se trata de una aguda reflexión general sobre el sentido de la naturaleza y de la técnica, y de la personalidad humana en medio de ellas.

9579. **Guerrero, Arturo.** Feuerbach: una crítica a medio camino, a propósito de *La esencia del cristianismo* (USB/F, 18:52, enero/abril 1976, p. 103-112)

Siguiendo a Engels, sostiene que Feuerbach se quedó a medio camino en la crítica al idealismo hegeliano.

9580. **Ingianna M., Yolanda.** El ideal trascendental en la *Crítica de la razón pura* de Kant: una interpretación histórico-crítica (UCR/RF, 13:36, enero/junio 1975, p. 101-107)

Sobre el paso de la etapa pre-crítica a la *Crítica de la razón pura*.

9581. **Iturralde Colombres, Carlos A.** La ontología modificada (UCA/S, 26:100/102, abril/dic. 1971, p. 389-410)

Crítica a la interpretación heideggeriana de Kant.

9582. **Jarauta Marión, Francisco.** Kierkegaard: los límites de la dialéctica del individuo. Cali, Colombia, Univ. del Valle, División de Humanidades, 1975? 139 p., bibl. (Cuadernos del valle, 9)

El autor caracteriza su trabajo como "una aproximación crítica a la problemática kierkegaardiana acerca de la subjetividad: su fundamentacion, su estructura y dialéctica." Es uno de los escasos trabajos en castellano sobre Kierkegaard que tratan el tema con cierto detalle y se basan en las fuentes originales. Contiene también útil bibliografía.

9583. ———. Kierkegaard y Schleiermacher: nota sobre su concepción de lo religioso (UA/RF, 33/34, dic. 1973, p. 46-58)

Expone primero la concepción de la religión en Schleiermacher y luego la relación de Kierkegaard con aquél. Con E. Hirsch afirma que Kierkegaard fue "el único auténtico discípulo de Schleiermacher de toda su generación."

9584. Leal A., Fernando. La función de la experiencia posible en el pensamiento kantiano (UCR/RF, 13:36, enero/junio 1975, p. 87-100)

Sobre uno de los aspectos de la relación entre lo *a priori* y lo sensible en la *Crítica de la razón pura*.

9585. Lopez Martín, Alfonso. El estoicismo en el pensamiento kantiano (UCR/RF, 14:39, julio/dic. 1976, p. 85-98)

Intenta rastrear los rasgos estoicos en la ética kantiana.

9586. Malo González, Hernán. El hábito en la filosofía de Félix Ravaisson. Quito, Pontificia Univ. Católica del Ecuador, Centro de Publicaciones, 1976. 282 p., bibl.

Contiene la traducción castellana de *De l'habitude* (1838) de Ravaisson, precedida de un estudio que suponemos es el más completo en castellano. Se complementa con una útil bibliografía.

9587. Martínez González, Humberto. En tono a la metodología trascendental de Kant (UNL/H, 12, 1971, p. 53-71)

La intención metafísica de Kant se percibe más claramente si tanto la Estética como la Analítica trascendentales (de la *Crítica de la razón pura*) se estudian en función de la Metodología trascendental (de la misma obra).

9588. Mateo, Martha S. El hombre, su realización moral y su destino según Pascal (UNT/H, 18:24, 1977, p. 53-60)

Comentarios a los *Pensamientos* de Pascal sobre los temas del título.

9589. Mattos, Carlos Lopes de. Espinosa (IBF/RBF, 26:104, out./dez. 1976, p. 427-435)

Parte de un libro inédito, expone sintéticamente el desarrollo biográfico-intelectual de Spinoza.

9590. Matute, Alvaro. Lorenzo Boturini y el pensamiento histórico de Vico. México, UNAM, Instituto de Investigaciones Históricas, 1976. 88 p., bibl.

Boturini (1702-1755) escribió una *Idea de una nueva historia general de la América Septentrional* (1746), en la que aplicó las teorías de Vico. En esta bien elaborada monografía se trata la vida y la obra de Boturini, los juicios que mereció, la filosofía de la historia de Vico, la relación de ésta con el mencionado libro de Boturini, etc. Contiene útil bibliografía.

9591. Monteiro, João Paulo. Indução natural (CIF/RLF, 2:3, nov. 1976, p. 243-256)

Sobre la teoría de la inducción en Hume.

9592. Museo Judío de Buenos Aires, Argentina. Homenaje a Baruch Spinoza: con motivo del tricentenario de su muerte. B.A., 1976. 254 p.

Volumen colectivo, la mayor parte de las contribuciones son tributos al filósofo de la *Etica*. Entre las más extensas destacaríamos: Jacobo Kogan "La Imaginación en la Filosofía de Spinoza;" Francisco Miró Quesada "Spinoza y la Racionalidad de la Praxis;" Rodolfo Mondolfo "La Contribución de Spinoza a la Concepción Historicista;" Ezequiel de Olaso "Spinoza y Nosotros;" y Eugenio Pucciarelli "Tiempo y Eternidad en Spinoza."

9593. Navarro, Bernabé. El desarrollo fichteano del idealismo trascendental de Kant. México, Fondo de Cultura Económica [and] UNAM, 1975. 244 p. (Publicaciones de *Diánoia*)

El trabajo contribuye a un movimiento reciente de revaloración de Fichte, que tiene lugar en Alemania. El objetivo es mostrar, desde una cuidadosa perspectiva, la relación de Fichte con Kant. Más concretamente, se dirige a "demostrar la coincidencia fundamental del pensamiento de Fichte con el de Kant desde el punto de vista de la filosofía trascendental." Por ello, el autor estima que su obra es "una exposición sistemática del paralelo y enlace hechos por Fichte mismo en innumerables pasajes entre su pensamiento y el de Kant." El trabajo es expresivo de la modalidad latinoamericana más bien reciente de realizar estudios críticos que, en lo que respecta a la técnica de investigación, no desmerecen de los que se hacen en los mejores centros del mundo.

9594. Núñez Tenorio, J.R. Problemas de la teoría y el método de la economía política marxista. Caracas, Univ. Central de Venezuela, Facultad de Ciencias Económicas y Sociales, División de Publicaciones, 1976. 501 p. (Col. Libros)

Extensa tesis doctoral, de difícil resumen. Para el autor, la filosofía no es ciencia, sino crítica ideológica. Su ensayo "participa de la lucha ideológica contemporánea como expresión de la lucha de clases." Lo concibe, además, como una "crítica ideológica" al "humanismo historicista representado por Sartre y al neoepistemologismo teoricista representado por Althusser." El tema específico del libro se desarrolla en un contexto mucho más amplio: relaciones de la ciencia con la ideología, método científico, conocimiento histórico, etc. La parte tercera "El Problema Filosófico," es de hecho un libro aparte que se agregó al texto de la tesis. El objetivo final de la obra sería, partiendo del marxismo, contribuir a "una filosofía científica del conocimiento y de las ciencias."

9595. Orlando, Carlos Alberto. Fundamentos de la crítica de Feuerbach (UBAFFL/C, 14:21, enero/junio 1974, p. 101-106)

Sobre la crítica a la religión en *La esencia del Cristianismo*, de Feuerbach.

9596. Pagallo, Julio F. Positividad y "Saber absoluto" en el joven Hegel (UZ/H, 1:1/2, 1974, p. 41-56)

Trabajo expositivo, basado en la consulta directa de las obras de juventud de Hegel.

9597. Pucciarelli, Eugenio. Tiempo y eternidad en Hegel (Revista de la Facultad de Filosofía y Letras [Univ. de Morón, Arg.] 2, 1971, p. 9-18)

La exposición se basa, principal pero no exclusivamente, en los pasajes que Hegel dedica al tiempo en la *Enciclopedia*.

9598. Puchet. Enrique. La pedagogía de Kant (USB/RVF, 4, 1976, p. 85-121)

De hecho, el trabajo abarca no sólo las ideas pedagógicas de Kant, sino también sus ideas sobre el hombre y la historia.

9599. Queiroz, Paulo Edmur de Souza. Considerações sobre a vontade geral de Rousseau (Convivium [São Paulo] 12:4, julho/agôsto 1973, p. 311-329)

Comentarios a la concepción del hombre de Rousseau y su doctrina de la voluntad general, desde una perspectiva "existencial."

9600. Quintero V., Magello. La enajenación en Marx (Boletín de Filosofía [Univ. del Zulia, Facultad de Humanidades y Educación, Centro de Estudios Filosóficos, Maracaibo, Ven.] 1972, p. 151-185)

La primera part expone los orígenes del concepto de alienación. La segunda trata de la enajenación en Marx, concebida como "alienación del trabajo tal como aparece en la sociedad capitalista" y por lo tanto susceptible de superación al suprimir la propiedad privada. El estilo de la exposición es deficiente.

9601. Serrano Caldera, Alejandro. Introducción al pensamiento dialéctico. Mexico, Fondo de Cultura Económica, 1976. 93 p. (Archivo del fondo, 68)

Para el autor, el "pensamiento dialéctico" se constituye en un proceso que se inicia con Descartes y culmina en Marx, pasando por Rousseau y Hegel. La obra dedica sendos capítulos a esos filósofos.

9602. Soriano G., José. La cosmovisión de Malebranche y el hombre contemporáneo (Boletín de Filosofía [Univ. del Zulia, Facultad de Humanidades y Educación, Centro de Estudios Filosóficos, Maracaibo, Ven.] 1972, p. 187-261)

Trata de establecer una relación "lógica e histórico-cultural" entre la cosmovisión de Malebranche y la del "hombre contemporáneo."

9603. Soto Badilla, José Alberto. El *a priori* en los prefacios de la *Crítica de la razón pura*: 1781-1787 (UCR/RF, 13:36, enero/junio 1975, p. 109-110)

Sobre los dos Prefacios a la *Crítica*. Al final esboza "una crítica metafísica al Criticismo," basado en Rosmini.

9604. Truyol y Serra, Antonio. Grocio y Leibniz desde una perspectiva actual (UCV/P, 1, 1972, p. 121-136)

Paralelo entre Grocio y Leibniz, especialmente en aspectos de su trayectoria intelectual y en lo que concierne al derecho internacional.

9605. Vaz, Henrique C. de Lima. Cultura e ideologia. Sobre a interpretação do cap. VI da *fenomenologia do espírito* (UMGFF/K, 20:67, 1973/1976, p. 23-59)

Exposición monográfica basada en fuentes de primera mano.

Filosofía Contemporánea

9606. Abdala, Nayib. La acción en la ética de Max Scheler (UA/RF, 33/34, dic. 1973, p. 3-30)

Exposición de la parte pertinente de *Der Formalismus in der Ethik* . . . y su polémica con Kant.

9607. Battistella, Ernesto H. Interpretación del atomismo lógico del *Tractatus* mediante la lógica modal relativa de von Wright (USB/RVF, 4, 1976, p. 7-18)

Se intenta probar en el artículo que "el sistema [de lógica modal] de von Wright es un marco adecuado para caracterizar el atomismo lógico (en su versión wittgensteiniana)."

9608. Casasus, Fernando Rafael. Gabriel Marcel (UNL/H, 12, 1971, p. 83-94)

Imagen de conjunto del pensador francés.

9609. Castañeda, Héctor-Neri. El atomismo sintáctico en la filosofía posterior de Wittgenstein y la naturaleza de las cuestiones filosóficas (CIF/RLF, 2:2, julio 1976, p. 103-120)

Según el autor, en la filosofía de habla inglesa hubo dos "revoluciones": en la década del 50, la producida por las *Philosophical Investigations* de Wittgenstein; en la década del 60, la de la filosofía del lenguaje ordinario. Este interesante artículo expone por qué ambos movimientos han sido superados, atendiendo no tanto a factores externos como a la lógica interna del desarrollo de las ideas filosóficas. Interesa también la apreciación final del autor sobre la situación actual de la filosofía de habla inglesa.

9610. Cordi, Cassiano Agostino. A comunicação em Max Scheler (VOZES, 68:5, junho/julho 1974, p. 357-364)

Principalmente sobre *Wesen und Formen der Sympathie*, de Max Scheler.

9611. Cordua, Carla. La teoría de los elementos últimos en Wittgenstein (CIF/RLF, 2:3, nov. 1976, p. 197-214)

El artículo tiende a mostrar que la crítica ha magnificado las diferencias entre la primera etapa de Wittgenstein (el *Tractatus*) y la segunda (las *Investigaciones filosóficas*), en lo que se refiere a la doctrina de los elementos últimos. Señala asimismo la importancia de este tema para comprender la evolución de dicho autor.

9612. Cossio, Carlos. La descripción en el propósito descriptivo de la fenomenología (UNL/H, 17, 1976, p. 93-112)

Sobre el carácter básico y fundante de la descripción fenomenológica, frente a la naturaleza explicativa de la ciencia.

9613. De Panasewicz, Nitsche. El integracionismo en relación con el problema de la muerte en la filosofía de José Ferrater Mora (Boletín de Filosofía [Univ. del Zulia, Facultad de Humanidades y Educación, Centro de Estudos Filosóficos, Maracaibo, Ven.] 1972, p. 127-149)

La exposición del "integracionismo" de Ferrater Mora se hace en base a una de sus obras: *El ser y la muerte*. Destaca con justicia que la filosofía de Ferrater no tiene el reconocimiento y la difusión que su calidad merece.

9614. Derisi, Octavio N. El ámbito del objeto de la fenomenología en E. Husserl (UCA/S, 26:100/102, abril/dic. 1971, p. 273-290)

La teoría del conocimiento de Husserl vista desde el ángulo del realismo tomista.

9615. Domínguez H., Javier. El pensar moderno y las tareas del pensar según Martín Heidegger (Escritos [Univ. Pontificia Boliviariana, Facultad de Filosofía y Letras, Medellín, Colombia] 2:5, feb. 1977, p. 3-13)

Primera parte de una tesis de licenciatura. El tema es la evolución del pensamiento de Heidegger en relación con el pensamiento moderno.

9616. Escribar Wicks, Ana. Consideraciones en torno al alcance filosófico de la obra teilhardiana (Cuadernos de Filosofía [Univ. de Concepción, Instituto Central de Filosofía, Chile] 3/4, 1974/1975, p. 151-167)

Principalmente sobre el concepto de materia en Teilhard de Chardin y su libro *Le phénomene humaine*.

9617. Francis C., Esther. La rebelión un estudio sobre Albert Camus. Caracas, Univ. Católica Andrés Bello, Dirección de Cultura, 1972. 114 p. (Escuela de filosofía, 2)

Expone los principales temas de orden filosófico que se encuentran en la obra de Camus, especialmente en *Le mythe de Sisyphe y L'homme révolté*, con frecuente apelación a los textos originales.

9618. Giles, Thomas Ransom. História do existencialismo e da fenomenologia. v. 1/2. São Paulo, Editora da Univ. de São Paulo, 1975. 2 v. (302, 370 p.)

Extensa exposición, subdividida por autores. El primer volumen se ocupa de Kierkegaard, Nietzsche, Husserl y Heidegger. El segundo, de Scheler, Buber, Jaspers y Sartre.

9619. Giordani, Mário Curtis. Iniciação ao existencialismo. Rio, Livraria Freitas Bastos, 1976. 143 p.

La intención expresa de la obra es examinar el existencialismo en tanto doctrina que pone en peligro los principios del pensamiento católico. Después de una introducción general se dedican capítulos a Kierkegaard, Jaspers, Heidegger, Sartre y Marcel.

9620. Illanes Maestre, José Luis. El testimonio de Maritain (ISTMO, 88, set./oct. 1973, p. 52-55)

Breve exposición del modo de entender Maritain la filosofía y el ejercicio filosófico.

9621. Macedo, Ubiratan de. A epistemologia do neopositivismo (Convivium [São Paulo] 12:4, julho/agosto 1973, p. 291-300)

Breve pero claro resumen del desarrollo histórico del llamado neopositivismo y de sus principales tesis.

9622. Montemayor, Alfredo. Pensamiento político de Maritain. Lima, Univ. del Pacífico, Depto. de Ciencias Sociales y Políticas, 1975. 210 p. (Serie departamentos académicos, 3)

Contiene un ensayo introductorio titulado "Permanencia de Jacques Maritain," una antología del pensamiento político de dicho autor y una bibliografía de y sobre Maritain.

9623. Montemayor Salazar, Jorge. El tema de la libertad en la filosofía de Karl Jaspers (UNL/H, 12, 1971, p. 37-51)

Trabajo de índole expositiva, basado en la obra de Jaspers, *Filosofía*.

9624. Moulines, Carlos Ulises. Bertrand Russell: la infatigable búsqueda de certeza (VME/R, 30:196, enero/marzo 1971, p. 52-59)

Breve pero clara exposición de los principales momentos de la evolución filosófica de Russell en función de su búsqueda de un conocimiento indudablemente cierto. Señala también la significación de Russell para la filosofía contemporánea.

9625. Munguía, Adolfo. La pregunta fundamental de la metafísica según Heidegger (VMD/R, 30:196, enero/marzo 1971, p. 60-79)

Agil comentario al tema de la pregunta por el ser, en Heidegger.

9626. Munita R., Enrique. La realidad viviente humana: introducción al pensamiento de Ortega y Gasset (Cuadernos de Filosofía [Univ. de Concepción, Instituto Central de Filosofía, Chile] 3/4, 1974/1975, p. 121-138)

Síntesis de las principales ideas de Ortega sobre la vida como realidad radical y, consecuentemente, sobre las creencias, la verdad, el perspectivismo, etc.

9627. Murillo Zamora, Roberto. Antonio Machado: ensayo sobre su pensamiento filosófico. San José, Editorial Fernández-Arce, 1975. 281 p.

Comentario amplio y bien elaborado de los aspectos filosóficos del poeta español.

9628. Núñez Crisosto, Eduardo. De las estructuras centradas a las estructuras acéntricas (Cuadernos de Filosofía [Univ. de Concepción, Instituto Central de Filosofía, Chile] 3/4, 1974/1975, p. 117-120)

Sobre dos trabajos de Jacques Derrida.

9629. Pacheco, Francisco Antonio. El derecho en el pensamiento de Ortega y Gasset (UCR/RF, 14:39, julio/dic. 1976, p. 139-190)

Extensa monografía que analiza el Derecho en Ortega sobre el trasfondo de su teoría de lo social. Precisamente una de las conclusiones es que la idea orteguiana del Derecho es sociológica.

9630. Presas, Mario A. Corporalidad e historia en Husserl (CIF/RLF, 2:2, julio 1976, p. 167-177)

Se discute el tema, comentando una interpretación de Ludwig Landgrebe en *El camino de la fenomenología*.

9631. ———. Interpretación existencial de la enfermedad en Karl Jaspers (ISTMO, 88, set./oct. 1973, p. 56-64)

Jaspers, afectado por una enfermedad crónica, escribió su propia historia clínica. El artículo extrae el significado de ese escrito para la biografía y la filosofía de Jaspers y su interpretación.

9632. Pucciarelli, Eugenio. Hombre e historia en la obra filosófica de Rodolfo Mondolfo (Nuovi Quaderni Italiani [Istituto Italiano di Cultura, B.A.] 7, dic. 1975, p. 37-56)

Palabras leídas al incorporarse el célebre historiador de la filosofía Rodolfo Mondolfo a la Academia Nacional de Ciencias de B.A. Traza las principales líneas de las ideas de Mondolfo sobre la filosofía, el hombre, la historia y los supuestos de su labor historiográfica.

9633. Rabossi, Eduardo A. *El Tractatus* y la filosofía crítica (CIF/RLF, 1:2, julio 1975, p. 109-132)

En un trabajo que es modelo de pulcritud expositiva, la dificultad que presentan los dos "componentes" del *Tractatus* (el "lógico" y el "místico"), tiende a ser solucionada reconduciendo esta primera obra de Wittgenstein al "modelo kantiano." Lo dicho por ninguna manera hace justicia a la riqueza informativa del ensayo.

9634. *Revista de Filosofía de la Universidad de Costa Rica.* Vol. 6, no. 32, enero/junio 1973- . San José.

Número especial dedicado al estructuralismo. Contiene: Alfonso López Martín "El Estructuralismo Lingüístico" (p. 3-11); Guillermo Malavassi V. "Bricolage sobre Naturaleza y Estructura" (p. 13-31); Adelita Aguilar de Alfaro "Los Métodos Estructuralistas en Algunas Ciencias Sociales" (p. 33-52); Carmen María de Hernández "Origen y Significado de las Estructuras en Lévi-Strauss" (p. 53-82); Jorge Enrique Guier "Incesto, Matrimonio y Derecho" (p. 83-116); Rodrigo Cordero "Mito y Totemismo en Sigmund Freud y Claude Lévi-Strauss" (p. 117-162); Fernando Mora "Estructuralismo y Derecho" (p. 163-180).

9635. Robles, José A. Teoría de relaciones y universales en Bertrand Russell (UNAM/D, 20, 1974, p. 86-97)

Sobre el problema de los universales en Russell, complementando puntos de vista de Alan Donagan en "Universales and Metaphysical Realism" (1963).

9636. Rotella, Oscar S. Wittgenstein, Ockham y Santo Tomás (UNT/H, 18:24, 1977, p. 31-43)

El autor resume así su tarea: "Vamos a poner de relieve una serie de actitudes que muestran cómo en el primer Wittgenstein hay un acercamiento a Ockham y al nominalismo que lo aleja en los puntos fundamentales de Santo Tomás. Para ello expondremos la concepción del ser, del pensamiento y del lenguaje en el primer Wittgenstein, en Ockham, en el nominalismo, en Santo Tomás, y finalizaremos con algunas consideraciones sobre la vía mística."

9637. Sierra Mejía, Rubén. La filosofía de Bertrand Russell (UN [Univ. Nacional de Colombia, Dirección de Divulgación Cultural, Bogotá] 11, oct. 1972, p. 185-192)

Homenaje a Russell en el centenario de su nacimiento. El propósito es divulgar el concepto de filosofía en Russell y sus principales contribuciones al pensamiento filosófico contemporáneo.

9638. Ugarte Corcuera, Francisco. La filosofía como actitud vital (ISTMO, 76, set./oct. 1971, p. 15-10)

Comentario general sobre la "filosofía existencial."

9639. Vallejos, M.A. Raúl. Sobre Kierkegaard y el existencialismo (UNL/U, 83, set./dic. 1975, p. 13-22)

Exposición de carácter general.

9640. Villoro, Luis. Estudios sobre Husserl. México, UNAM, 1975. 179 p. (Col. Opúsculos, 83. Serie investigación)

Recoge trabajos publicados entre 1959 y 1966. Contiene los estudios: "Los Antecedentes de la Reducción Fenomenológica;" "La Reducción a la Inmanencia;" "La Constitución de la Realidad en la Ciencia Pura" (examen del segundo tomo de las *Ideas*); "Ciencia Radical y Sabiduría;" y dos notas críticas: una sobre la segunda parte de *Erste Philosophie* y otra sobre el libro de J.N. Mohanty, *Edmund Husserl's theory of meaning*.

LOGICA, GNOSEOLOGIA Y FILOSOFIA DE LA CIENCIA

9641. Angelelli, Ignacio. La jerarquía de clases de Johann Caspar Sulzer: 1755 (UBAFFL/C, 14:21, enero/junio 1974, p. 90-94)

Análisis de un texto del autor mencionado en el título del artículo, que opera con la noción de clase y aun construye una jerarquía de clases. Contribución a la historia de la lógica en el siglo XVIII.

9642. Basave Fernández del Valle, Agustín. Filosofía de las ciencias (UNL/H, 12, 1971, p. 13-35)

Consideraciones físico-cosmológicas desde una perspectiva teísta.

9643. Battistella, Ernesto H. Las ideas básicas de los teoremas de Gödel (Boletín de Filosofía [Univ. del Zulia, Facultad de Humanidades y Educación, Centro de Estudios Filosóficos, Maracaibo, Ven.] 1972, p. 7-25)

El propósito del artículo es didáctico. Sin requerir del lector más que el conocimiento de la notación simbólica, expone el contenido de los teoremas de Gödel, previa aclaración de conceptos básicos para comprender esa exposición.

9644. Bolzán, J.E. Individuación, analogía y participación en el plano físico (UCA/S, 26:100/102, abril/dic. 1971, p. 173-198)

Primera parte de un trabajo más extenso. El tema es el individuo en el orden natural, desde un punto de vista—en lo filosófico—tomista.

9645. ———. Lugar y ubicación

(UNL/H, 17, 1976, p. 207-214)

El concepto de "ubicación," que se discute en el trabajo, sería propio de la filosofía natural. "Lugar," como ente de razón, pertenecería al plano de la ciencia.

9646. Cardozo Biritos, Dennis F. Las paradojas lógicas y la teoría de la predicación. Mendoza, Arg., Univ. Nacional de Cuyo, Facultad de Ciencias Políticas y Sociales, Instituto de Ciencias Políticas, 1976. 23 p. (Serie de cuadernos, 42)

Las paradojas son examinadas desde el punto de vista de la lógica escolástica (especialmente la teoría de la suplencia), por contraposición al tratamiento que le da la "lógica positivista" (la lógica moderna que, según el autor, se reduce a un análisis del lenguaje).

9647. Coffa, Alberto J. Notas para un esquema de la filosofía de la ciencia contemporánea (UNAM/C, 6:16/17, enero/mayo 1972, p. 15-51)

Tomando como base la filosofía de la ciencia vigente hacia 1950 (Popper, Carnap) presenta el pensamiento aproximadamente posterior a esa fecha. Los autores expuestos con mayor extensión son Sellars y Kuhn. Hacia el final, se extraen consecuencias para el problema de la verdad. Trabajo útil, dada la complejidad del tema y de las posiciones involucradas.

9648. D'Alessio, Juan Carlos. Hacia una ontología de los colores (UBAFFL/C, 14:21, enero/junio 1974, p. 75-78)

Los colores y los términos que los expresan serían no disposicionales.

9649. Furlán, Augusto. La subordinación de la lógica a la ciencia (UCA/S, 26:100/102, abril/dic. 1971, p. 121-136)

El propósito del trabajo es "mostrar en qué modo, según el tomismo, la lógica se orienta en todas sus ramas a cooperar en la adquisición de la ciencia."

9650. Gómez, Orlando Danián. Contribución bachelardiana al pensamiento científico (USB/F, 18:52, enero/abril 1976, p. 15-56)

Se propone una "relectura" de la obra de Gastón Bachelard. Se divide en tres partes: "El Pensamiento Científico de Bachelard;" "Filosofía del Espíritu Científico;" y "Psicoanálisis del Conocimiento Objetivo."

9651. González Asenjo, Florencio. Algunos temas y aplicaciones de la lógica matemática actual (UBAFFL/C, 14:21, enero/junio 1974, p. 57-74)

Una de las conclusiones del autor es que si bien la lógica matemática no puede enriquecer el contenido de una teoría, debido a su carácter neutral o instrumental, sin embargo demuestra "su mayor poderío ... en la manera precisa en que articula una concepción original rica."

9652. Gortari, Eli de. Propiedades del razonamiento por analogía (UNAM/D, 20, 1974, p. 57-84)

El propósito del artículo es "establecer las bases para la formulación rigurosa del razonamiento por analogía y la determinación de sus propiedades." Después de recordar los orígenes de la analogía en el pensamiento griego, se dan definiciones y se desenvuelven inferencias utilizando notación simbólico-matemática.

9653. Japiassu, Hilton Ferreira. Introdução ao pensamento epistemológico. Rio, Livraria Francisco Alves Editora, 1975. 112 p.

Excluyendo intencionalmente la filosofía de la ciencia que origina el empirismo lógico, expone, con propósito introductorio, el pensamiento epistemológico de Piaget, Bachelard y Foucault. También se ocupa de algunos aspectos del pensamiento de la Escuela de Frankfurt sobre el asunto (Habermas). Concluye con reflexiones sobre la situación actual de la epistemología y la filosofía de la ciencia.

9654. Klimovsky, Gregorio and others. Ideología, ciencia y política científica. Montevideo, Fundación de Cultura Universitaria, 1972. 56 p. (Cuadernos de ciencias sociales, 5)

La base de este cuaderno es un reportaje a Gregorio Klimovsky sobre ciencia e ideología. Este profesor y T.M. Simpson defienden—en esencia—la posibilidad de la objetividad científica, negada radicalmente por O. Varsavsky (sobre este autor véase *HLAS 38:9667*). Hay también colaboraciones de R. García y J. Schvarzer. Polémica típica del ambiente intelectual argentino en el momento en que apareció la publicación. Destacamos el trabajo de T.M. Simpson.

9655. Lahud, Michel. "Egocentric particulars;" os deiticos na concepção de Russell (CIF/RLF, 2:1, março 1976, p. 43-55)

El tema se examina en la obra de Bertrand Russell, *An inquiry into meaning and truth*.

9656. Maliandi, Ricardo and Jorge Alfredo Roetti. La paradoja de la "inmutabilidad del móvil" (UBAFFL/C, 14:21, enero/junio 1974, p. 38-56)

La paradoja de "la inmutabilidad del móvil" o de "la inmovilidad de lo cambiante," expresada por

Antonio Machado en su *Juan de Mairena*, es analizada desde el punto de vista lógico y, apoyándose en Nicolai Hartmann, desde el punto de vista ontológico. Se discute al final la opinión de Machado de que la aprehensión del ser es extralógica.

9657. Miró Quesada, Francisco. Sobre el concepto de razón (CIF/RLF, 1:3, nov. 1975, p. 183-191)

La proliferación de diversos tipos de lógica y el desarrollo de la investigación metateórica han llevado a negar el concepto tradicional de razón. El artículo muestra que a pesar de esa diversidad existen elementos comunes, los cuales constituyen una estructura que debe considerarse racional, si bien el concepto clásico de razón resultaría ampliado. "Comprender a fondo cómo es esta dinámica de la razón, y cuál es su unidad dentro de una diversidad que se realiza sin término, es la meta más importante de una filosofía del conocimiento que pretenda comprender lo que está sucediendo en el moderno conocimiento científico."

9658. Orayen, Raúl. Una paradoja en las doctrinas filosóficas de Frege (UBAFFL/C, 14:21, enero/junio 1974, p. 79-89)

Discute dificultades que surgen de la concepción de Frege según la cual las entidades del universo son o bien funciones o bien objetos. La paradoja en cuestión "está basada en una extrapolación de consecuencias ontológicas a partir de observaciones lingüísticas."

9659. Pescador Sarget, Augusto. El problema de la modalidad y los fundamentos ónticos de la lógica (Cuadernos de Filosofía [Univ. de Concepción, Instituto Central de Filosofía, Chile] 3/4, 1974/1975, p. 7-37)

La modalidad óntica es el fundamento de la modalidad lógica. "El estudio de las modalidades del ser tiene el carácter de un prolegómeno a la lógica modal."

9661. Silva, M. Rocha e. A evolução do pensamento científico. São Paulo, Editora de Humanismo, Ciência e Tecnologia, 1972. 374 p.

Como lo indica el propio autor, no es una historia orgánica, sino una serie de trabajos que tratan algunos momentos principales de la historia del pensamiento científico. Pero hay también capítulos sobre la relación del lenguaje con la ciencia y sobre la creatividad científica.

9662. Soler, Ricaurte. Causalidad en el mecanicismo y casualidad en la dialéctica (LNB/L, 193, dic. 1971, p. 1-7)

Sostiene que el mecanicismo necesita negar la realidad de lo contingente (el autor dice 'casual'). Afirmando que algunos filósofos marxistas mantienen un "mecanicismo vergonzante," el trabajo aboga por reconocer la "realidad ontológica del azar."

9663. Stahl, Gerold. Preguntas con exigencias numéricas y de totalidad (UBAFFL/C, 14:21, enero/junio 1974, p. 95-100)

Contribución a la discusión que origina la lógica de las preguntas y continuación de un trabajo anterior del autor, "Preguntas y Premisas" publicado en *Revista de Filosofía* (Santiago, 1961).

AXIOLOGIA Y ETICA

9664. Basso, Domingo. Experiencia, ciencia y conducta (IFP/E, 1, 1973, p. 145-174)

Dentro de la orientación aristotélico-tomista, el trabajo tiene dos objetivos: encontrar "las vinculaciones entre la ciencia y el hábito de los primeros principios;" y determinar "los alcances normativos de la ciencia ... que es como examinar el puente tendido por Santo Tomás entre el orden especulativo y el práctico."

9665. Bueno, Miguel. La filosofía como axiología (UNAM/D, 20, 1974, p. 98-125)

La tesis básica del autor, que dice adherir al criticismo, es que la filosofía es axiología (formal), o que "la axiología es la única filosofía posible en esta época."

9666. Cárdenas, Rodolfo Marcelo. El hombre: ¿alienado o culpable? B.A., Plus Ultra, 1976. 125 p. (Col. Mundo presente, psicología, 7)

Trata el problema del libre albedrío y sus consecuencias para la ética, con la intención de comprender la naturaleza de las acciones morales (o inmorales) del hombre. Aunque no está elaborado con la más refinada técnica filosófica, es un intento de pensar el tema por cuenta propia y basándose en realidades concretas. No pretende tanto el establecimiento de una doctrina como aclarar el tema y denunciar simplificaciones. Con ese fin se analizan algunos elementos de la tradición griega, del cristianismo, del liberalismo, del marxismo, de lo expresado por el Concilio Vaticano II, etc. Una de las conclusiones es que el libre albedrío no sería algo individual, sino un logro de la humanidad a través de la historia.

9667. Gracia, Jorge J.E. El valor como cualidad relacional (UNAM/D, 19, 1973, p. 173-188)

Elaboración teórica del concepto de valor definido como "la cualidad que adquiere lo deseable cuando es deseado en una situación determinada." Igualmente apartado del objetivismo y del subjetivismo, sostiene que el valor es una cualidad relacional.

9668. Hartmann, Robert S. La estructura axiológica de la personalidad (UNAM/D, 19, 1973, p. 64-88)

Reconoce tres dimensiones axiológicas (sistémica, extrínseca e intrínseca) e intenta aplicarlas a la personalidad. El calor humano de ciertos pasajes contrasta con la intención formalizadora.

9669. Maliandi, Ricardo. Experiencia axiológica y experiencia del conflicto (CIF/RLF, 2:1, marzo 1976, p. 27-41)

El problema que se plantea el artículo es si existe una experiencia que se adquiere a través de valoraciones. Ni las formas de objetivismo ni las de subjetivismo en teoría de los valores captan el fenómeno valorativo en su integridad. Al preguntar qué se experimenta en la experiencia axiológica el autor elabora el concepto de "negación axiológica," el cual permite comprender aquella experiencia como conciencia de límites y como conflicto. "Lo que el hombre capta en la 'experiencia axiológica' es la *realidad*."

9670. Rabossi, Eduardo A. Análisis filosófico y teorías éticas (IFP/E, 1, 1973, p. 193-210)

El propósito del trabajo es establecer una classificación de los distintos tipos de teorías éticas, no como mero interés taxonómico o didáctico, sino para determinar "las presuposiciones y los objetivos" de esas teorías. La base de tal clasificación es lingüística. Las dos principales categorías que se reconocen (con varias subdivisiones) son las de "teorías descriptivistas" y "teorías no descriptivistas," siguiendo las terminología de R.M. Hare.

9671. Soaje Ramos, G. Elaboración del problema del valor (IFP/E. 1, 1973, p. 105-143)

Capítulo de una obra en preparación: *Introducción sistemática a la filosofía del derecho*. Se consideran con cierto detalle las diversas posiciones que resultan de las contraposiciones objetivismo-subjetivismo y relativismo-no relativismo. Luego se estudia la índole y estructura de la estimación y se concluye con extensas consideraciones sobre "metafísica del valor."

ANTROPOLOGIA FILOSOFICA Y CIENCIAS HUMANAS

9672. Barriocanal, Eusebio Angel. La nueva ciencia política y los aportes del enciclopedismo. B.A., Plus Ultra, 1975. 139 p.

Contiene sumarias indicaciones sobre la obra y la significación de D'Alembert, Voltaire, Rousseau, Montesquieu, etc., sin una tesis definida. Se refiere también a la influencia del iluminismo en América.

9673. Bueno, Miguel. El sincretismo psicológico (UNAM/D, 19, 1973, p. 145-172)

Distingue diversas orientaciones del saber psicológico y propone sistematizar y aprovechar esa variedad en un enfoque sincrético.

9674. Carmo, Raymundo Evangelista do. Antropologia filosófica geral. Belo Horizonte, Brazil, Editora o Lutador, 1976. 180 p.

Obra didáctica, de introducción al tema. Es segunda edición reelaborada de un libro anterior, con la misma finalidad: *O mistério da existência* (1972).

9675. Castañeda, Héctor-Neri. Sobre la fenomenológica del yo (UPR/D, 8:23, nov. 1972, p. 23-31)

Análisis lógico del yo. En lo que se refiere a yo y mundo, la conclusión es: "El yo no es ... una entidad en el mundo, sino una entidad 'fuera' del mundo que debe ser identificable en términos de entidades en el mundo."

9676. Chiavegato, Augusto José comp. Homem hoje. 2. ed. São Paulo, Cortez & Moraes, 1976. 130 p.

Se compone de "los textos fundamentales que orientan los trabajos pedagógicos de la cátedra de Problemas Filosóficos y Teológicos del Hombre Contemporáneo" de la Univ. Católica de São Paulo. Se examina el hombre en relación con la ciudad, el trabajo, la familia, el fenómeno religioso y la educación. Siguen exposiciones de las opiniones de Mounier, Fromm y Marcuse sobre la sociedad contemporánea.

9676a. Frondizi, Risieri, Introducción a los problemas fundamentales del hombre. México, Fondo de Cultura Económica, 1977. 1 v. (Unpaged) (Breviarios, 260)

Poniendo el origen de la filosofía en las preocupaciones vivas del hombre, y no en las teorías, la obra se estructura según problemas: el problema moral; la libertad; el problema del yo; la vida humana y los valores. A la vez que obra de introducción, sirve al autor para expresar su posición filosófica personal, especialmente ampliando las ideas expuestas en su obra anterior. *¿Que son los valores?* y constituyendo, sobre todo, los fundamentos de una ética.

9677. Granell, Manuel. Existencia y cultura (UZ/H, 1:1/2, 1974, p. 117-128)

Con la limitada extensión de una ponencia a un Congreso, es fundamentalmente una concepción de la *existencia* como el hecho radical de lo humano. Aunque la orientación en general reconoce cierta familiaridad con las ideas de Ortega y Gasset y el Heidegger de *Ser y tiempo*, es un trabajo muy personal. Apareció también en *Cuadernos de Filosofía* (B.A., 14:21, enero/junio 1974).

9678. Japiassu, Hilton Ferreira. Introdução à epistemologia da psicologia. Rio, Imago Editora, 1975. 174 p. (Série logoteca)

Después de consideraciones sobre el proceso de constitución de las ciencias humanas en general, se estudia la formación de la psicología científica a partir del positivismo. Luego se contraponen el behaviorismo y la psicología introspectiva y se examinan otras formas de psicología, especialmente el psicoanálisis y las doctrinas de Foucault, Lacan, Politzer, etc. Concluye con consideraciones sobre la práctica de la psicología en la actualidad.

9679. Karlic, Estanislao and others. Hacia un nuevo humanismo. B.A., Editorial Bonum, 1974. 300 p. (Enfoques latinoamericanos, 11)

La publicación es el resultado de un seminario entre representantes de universidades católicas y estatales de América Latina y Alemania Occidental, que tuvo lugar en Argentina, durante 1973. El tema básico es la problemática de la situación del mundo contemporáneo en relación con un nuevo humanismo. Destacamos algunas contribuciones de autores latinoamericanos:

Héctor D. Mandrioni "Reflexiones en Torno a un Humanismo Nuevo" p. 33-37
Francisco Interdonato "La Teología Antropológica como Humanismo Latinoamericano" p. 38-74
Ricardo Antoncich "Ideologías, Fe y Realidad Latinoamericana" p. 97-121
Néstor A. Corona "El Ente, el Hombre y lo Abierto" p. 156-161
Carlos L. Ceriotto "Cuestiones para Humanismo Nuevo" p. 162-165
Juan R. Sepich-Lange "Hechos, Situaciones, Método" p. 170-182
Eduardo Briancesco "¿Libertad o Liberación?" p. 230-240
Alberto Cupani "Filosofía y Educación Humanística en la Transformación de América Latina" p. 269-272
Luis Noussan-Lettry "Sobre las Humanidades en Latinoamérica" p. 273-281.

9680. Legaz Lacambra, Luis. Humanismo, estructuralismo y marxismo (ISTMO, 88, set./oct. 1973, p. 5-20)

El tema del artículo es en realidad el humanismo, y cómo es afectado por la filosofía estructuralista, en su costado cientificista (Foucault, Lévi-Strauss) o marxista (Althusser). También se toma en cuenta la posición del último Sartre.

9681. Lértora, Adolfo C. Estructura del hombre. B.A., Ediciones Silaba, 1974. 257 p.

Desde un estricto punto de vista marxista se tratan temas como psicogénesis y dialéctica, el lenguaje, la personalidad, el inconsciente, medicina y estructura del hombre, etc.

9682. Miguelez, Roberto. Conflicto de paradigmas y análisis filosófico de las ciencias sociales (CIF/RLF, 1:3, nov. 1975, p. 227-235)

Se refiere a la aplicación del concepto de paradigma," propuesto por Kuhn en *The structure of scientific revolutions*, al campo de las ciencias sociales. En especial trata de los conflictos de paradigmas. Destaca que no deben tomarse en cuenta solamente los factores internos (lógicos y metodológicos, por ejemplo), sino también los externos a la práctica científica (política, ideología, etc.).

9683. Njaim, Humberto. La concepción empírico-analítica de las ciencias sociales (UCV/P, 1, 1972, p. 57-88)

Util exposición de la concepción empírico-analítica de las ciencias sociales, o filosofía analítica de la ciencia, tal como es representada por autores como G.C. Hempel, E. Nagel, K. Popper, Hans Albert y Ernst Topitsch. Al tratar el tema de la neutralidad axiológica de las ciencias sociales se comenta la polémica de los autores mencionados con los representantes "dialécticos" de la Escuela de Frankfurt.

9684. Nudler, Oscar. Crítica a la concepción piagetiana de lo mental (CIF/RLF, 2:1, marzo 1976. p. 57-69)

El propósito del trabajo es examinar críticamente la concepción de la mente en Piaget, mostrando que es en realidad una teoría del desarrollo de lo mental de enfoque que el autor denomina "logicista."

9685. Quiles, Ismael. El hombre según las filosofías de Oriente y Occidente (UNL/H, 17, 1976, p. 193-206)

Reconociendo las diferencias entre Oriente y Occidente en lo que se refiere a la concepción del hombre, busca "la base de una síntesis," la plataforma común de ambos modos de pensar. Reconocer o destacar asos puntos de coincidencia puede abrir "una nueva perspectiva para el estudio comparado de las filosofías de Oriente y Occidente."

9686. Subercaseaux, Benjamin. Una nueva interpretación del hombre: teoría de la desnaturación antropológica. Santiago, Editorial Andrés Bello, 1972. 519 p.

La obra es condensación de dos anteriores: *Historia inhumana del hombre* y *El hombre inconcluso*. En la segunda se había expuesto la "teoría de la desnaturación" del hombre, que se reitera en este libro. Según dicha teoría, existirían ."dos tipos de hombres, psicológicamente diferenciados y que solamente se habrían dado en el *Homo Sapiens*." Uno de ellos, por una supuesta mutación, "habría logrado una autonomía suficiente que lo colocó . . . fuera del dominio de la naturaleza" (desnaturación). El otro tipo humano sería un "animal superior," "sometido a un proceso de *limitación dirigida* enseñanza, tradición, etc.), que lo hace actuar bajo un 'disfraz de hombre', por obra del otro tipo humano . . ."

FILOSOFIA DEL DERECHO Y FILOSOFIA POLITICA

9687. Alzate P., Alberto. El encubrimiento como arma ideológica (USB/F, 18:53, mayo/agosto 1976, p. 169-237)

Toda teoría y toda práctica responden a un trasfondo de intereses ideológicos que es "ocultado habilidosamente" por quienes tienen el poder. Por ello se habla en el título de encubrimiento como arma ideológica. Después de consideraciones sobre la ideología en general, se trata de "develar" ese encubrimiento en: 1) los "aparatos significantes" (planificación, educación, comunicaciones); 2) los "discursos y prácticas significantes" (ciencia, historia, positivismo, psicología conductista, etc.): 3) la educación en especial.

9688. Arruda Campos, Fernando. O tomismo atual no dialogo com o marxismo a respeito do problema de Deus (IBF/RBF, 26:104, out./dez. 1976, p. 411-426)

Paralelo de las dos posiciones, en lo que respecta al problema elegido. El único punto de contacto parece estar en el concepto de 'alienación', aunque tiene distinto significado en Marx y en el tomismo (si éste adoptara aquel término).

9689. Cappelletti, Angel J. El ateísmo de Bakunin Ruta [Publicación ácrata, Caracas] 7:28, 1 junio 1976, p. 8-21)

Expone las ideas de Bakunin sobre la religión y el ateísmo. Antes se refiere a la evolución del pensamiento de dicho autor, que no fue ateísta desde un principio: "Su negación de Dios no se da . . . sino después de o . . . junto con la negación del capitalismo y del Estado."

9690. Caturelli, Alberto. La política de Maurras y la filosofía cristiana. B.A., Nuevo Orden, 1975. 86 p.

Se exponen los principales aspectos de la filosofía política de Maurras, en especial su crítica a la democracia liberal y su corporativismo, y se examinan críticamente sus ideas desde el punto de vista de una filosofía cristiana. En la Tercera Parte se señala la influencia de Maurras en autores argentinos como los hermanos Irazusta, el P. Menvielle, Ernesto Palacio, etc.

9691. Esquivel, Javier. La concepción del derecho en la obra de Maquiavelo (UNAM/D, 20, 1974, p. 44-56)

La intención del trabajo es extraer de la obra de Maquiavelo (especialmente *El principe* y los *Discursos*) su concepción del derecho, que no se encuentra sistemáticamente expuesta en el pensador florentino. Después de detallado análisis, concluye que puede considerarse a Maquiavelo un precursor del positivismo jurídico.

9692. Harnecker, Marta. Los conceptos elementales del materialismo histórico. B.A., Siglo XXI Editores, 1975. 341 p.

Este manual, de orientación althusseriana, ha tenido gran difusión, como lo prueba el número de ediciones. Aparentemente se trata del texto ampliado y revisado correspondiente a la 6. ed., y lleva una presentación del propio Althusser. Los tres principales temas de la obra son: la estructura social -producción, infraestructura y superestructura, ideología-; las clases sociales; y la teoría marxista de la historia.

9693. ———— and Nicos Poulantzas. Lucha de clases, poder política, Estado. Bogotá, Editor Rojo, 1972. 82 p.

Contiene el trabajo de Marta Harnecker "Política y Clases Sociales en Poulantzas," sobre el libro de este autor: *Pouvoir politique et classes sociales*. Además, incluye un texto de Poulantzas: "Sobre el Concepto de Política." Marta Harnecker se orienta en el marxismo en la dirección de Althusser.

9694. Lanz, Rigoberto. Dialéctica de la ideología. Caracas, Univ. Central de Venezuela, Facultad de Ciencias Económicas y Sociales, División de Publicaciones, 1975. 127 p., bibl.

En lenguaje a ratos poco inteligible, y desde un punto de vista marxista, se desea "llamar la atención sobre el estado actual de la discusión sobre el problema central de la ideología." Hacia el final del libro se impugnan igualmente el estructuralismo de Althusser y el "neopositivismo." Contiene abundante bibliografía.

9695. Mandrioni, Héctor Delfor. Filosofía y política. B.A., Guadalupe, 1975. 91 p. (Col. Esta hora del cambio)

Propuesta de un "habitar creador" como actitud del hombre para convivir en sociedad, donde ésta elimine las alienaciones y otros defectos que tienen los modelos de sociedad actualmente vigentes.

9696. Millas, Jorge. Derecho y sociedad de masas (UC/A, 429/430, 1974, p. 71-89)

El trabajo tiende a contestar las siguientes preguntas: "¿como afecta el fenómeno de masificación al orden jurídico?" y "¿qué misión cumple realizar al derecho como recurso de acción frente al desafío de la sociedad de masas?" Expresado en terminos exageradamente simples, el principal problema es, para el autor, el avance del poder del Estado sobre el individuo.

9697. Motta, Benedito. Filosofia e história do direito. São Paulo, Bushatsky, 1976. 194 p. (Col. Jurídica, 15)

Escrito bajo la influencia de la obra de Miguel Reale, se compone de dos partes: "La Interpretación Analógica en la Teoría Tridimensional" y "El Fenómeno del Derecho Vulgar."

9698. Nuño, Juan A. El marxismo y las nacionalidades: el planteamiento de la cuestíon judía en el marxismo clásico. Bogotá, Ediciones Tercer Mundo, 1972. 92 p. (Cuadernitos que despierte el lenãdor, 14)

Aunque se examinan tesis del marxismo clásico y soviético sobre la cuestión de las nacionalidades, el libro es fundamentalmente un ataque a la política de la Unión Soviética sobre su población judía.

9699. Ortoneda, Baldomero. Principios fundamentales del marxismo-leninismo. Unidad y lucha de contrarios. Paso de cantidad a calidad. Negación de la negación. México, n.p., 1974. 738 p.

Detalladísima exposición y crítica de las tres leyes fundamentales de la dialéctica sostenidas por el marxismo-leninismo y mencionadas en el subtítulo del libro. Básicamente se compone de dos partes: la exposición de las leyes de la dialéctica y su crítica (o refutación) pormenorizada con ejemplos tomados de la física, la química, la biología, etc. La exposición de cada punto está ilustrada con ejemplos de textos de autores marxista-leninistas, clásicos y actuales, por donde la obra viene a resultar también una especie de enciclopedia de afirmaciones de autores de dicha tendencia. Contiene abundante bibliografía, especialmente de autores soviéticos.

9700. Pucciarelli, Eugenio. Las funciones sociales de la ideología (Boletín de la Escuela de Guerra Naval [B.A.?] 6, 1974. p. 117-137)

Después de exponer temas como las diversas maneras en que se ha entendido el concepto de 'ideología;' el llamado "fin de las ideologías;" e ideología y ciencia; y tras dar ejemplos de ideologías como programas de acción político-social, se refiere a la función de la ideología como factor de cohesión e integración del cuerpo social, exponiendo a la vez las ideas de Gramsci sobre este asunto. Al intelectual compete la elaboración de ideologías para el mantenimiento del orden de la sociedad o para facilitar su cambio.

9701. Recaséns Siches, Luis. Derecho y poder (UNAM/D, 19, 1973, p. 120-144)

Después de estudiar las aportaciones hechas al tema por Theodor Geiger y Carl J. Friedrich, resume su posición en estas proposiciones: No hay intrínsecamente una oposición entre derecho y poder; lo que se opone es el poder injusto al poder justo; todo derecho, para realizarse, necesita un poder; el poder al servicio del derecho y de la justicia constituye un valor.

9702. ———. Los derechos humanos (UNAM/D, 20, 1974, p. 126-146)

Aunque admite que hay dimensiones contingentes en la concepción de los derechos humanos (época, cultura), les asigna una fuente iusnaturalista: "son principios ... de estimativa jurídica ... [que tienen] una validez en sí y por sí, porque constituyen la proyección sobre el mundo del derecho, de la esencia mismo de lo humano."

9703. *Revista de la Facultad de Derecho de México.* Univ. Nacional Autónoma de México. Vol. 12, Nos. 87/88, julio/dic. 1972- . Mexico.

Se trata de un número especial, en homenaje al jurista y filósofo mexicano del derecho, Eduardo García Máynez. Entre los artículos de autores latinoamericanos de mayor contenido filosófico destacamos:
Leandro Azuara Pérez "Los Conceptos Jurídicos Fundamentales" (análisis del tema en función de los grandes autores y tratadistas) p. 363-404;
Agustín Basave F. del Valle "La Dimensión Jurídica del Hombre: Fundamentos de Antropología Jurídica" (el Derecho visto "como una forma antropológica de convivencia") p. 411-434;
Carlos Cossio "La Lógica Jurídica y su Denominación" (sobre los aportes realizados al tema por el propio Cossio y su escuela egológica, Kelsen y von Wright) p. 447-470;
Javier Esquivel "Algunas Consideraciones sobre la Cientificidad de la Axiología" (examen de la cuestión en Scheler-Hartmann, el neotomismo y la filosofía analítica) p. 471-480;
Héctor González Uribe "El Personalismo en la Axiología Jurídica y Política" (expresión del personalismo cristiano que frente al liberalismo y al socialismo defiende un "humanismo social") p. 553-585;
Luis Recasens Siches "El Problema de 'la Naturaleza de las Cosas'" (la "naturaleza de las cosas" no permite extraer consecuencias axiológicas o de "deber ser") p. 643-651;
Manuel Terán Mata "La Estructura Lógica y Ética de la Jurisprudencia y del Derecho" p. 709-721;
Hay también estudios y comentarios sobre la obra de García Máynez:
Víctor Carlos García Moreno "Ensayo Bibliográfico de la Obra del Doctor Eduardo García Máynez" (sobre bibliografía de García Máynez véase también *HLAS 36:5005*) p. 515-527;

Francisco González Díaz Lombardo "Doctor Eduardo García Máynez" p. 541-553;
Abelardo Rojas Roldán "La Concepción Multirelacional del Derecho de Eduardo García Máynez" p. 665-684;
Leonardo van Acker "Una Interpretación Tomista del Perspectivismo" p. 723-732;
Miguel Villoro Toranzo "Reflexión sobre la Lógica Jurídica de García Máynez" p. 733-762.

9704. *Revista Mexicana de Ciencia Política.* Univ. Nacional Autónoma de México, Facultad de Filosofía y Ciencias Sociales. Vol. 20, No. 78, oct./dic. 1974- . México.

Este número se titula "Filosofía y Política." Además de otros artículos de doctrina marxista de autores europeos, contiene una serie de trabajos que analizan el libro de Lenin, *Materialismo y empiriocriticismo.* Son los siguientes:
Raúl Olmedo "Presentación: Leer *Materialismo y empiriocriticismo*" p. 71-77;
Guillermo Knochenhaver Müller "La Relación entre la Filosofía, la Ciencia y la Política" p. 79-87;
Margarita Barrientos Lavín "La Categoría Filosófica de Materia" p. 89-94;
Eduardo Barraza González "El Criterio de la Práctica" p. 95-99
Martha Múgica "Verdad Relativa y Verdad Absoluta" p. 101-110;
Marco Antonio González Gómez "La Crítica al Agnosticismo Marxista" p. 111-116;
Víctor Manuel Muñoz "La Dialéctica" p. 117-121;
Agustín Cueva "Sobre la Filosofía y el Método Marxista" p. 123-130;
Patricio Marcos "Tractatus Metodológico-Marxista" p. 131-150.

9705. Sacheri, Carlos A. El orden natural. B.A., Instituto de Promoción Social Argentina, 1975. 188 p.

Conjunto sistemático de trabajos de breve extensión, aparecidos en el periódico de Bahía Blanca (Arg.), *La Nueva Provincia*, con el título general de "La Iglesia y lo Social."

9706. Sánchez Vasquez, Adolfo. Del socialismo científico al socialismo utópico (*in* Kolakowsky, Leszek and others. Crítica de la utopía. México, UNAM, Facultad de Ciencias Políticas y Sociales, 1971. p. 93-142 [Serie estudios, 25])

Desde un punto de vista marxista amplio, examina el utopismo socialista anterior a Marx; destaca elementos utópicos en el propio Marx y en Lenin; y señala los elementos de la situación contemporánea que favorecen o dificultan el paso al socialismo.

9707. Seminario Nacional de Filosofía, *I, Bogotá, 1975.* Filosofía y sociedad. Bogotá, Centro de Investigación y Acción Social, 1975. 278 p.

Trabajos resultantes del seminario dedicado al tema "Filosofía y Sociedad." Las ponencias fueron:
Francisco Jarauta M. "La Práctica Filosófica" (orientado en el pensamiento epistemológico francés actual) p. 41-57;
Jaime Barrera P. "La Metafísica como Saber del Todo y las Ciencias Humanas como Conocimiento de las Partes" p. 59-67;
Magdalena Holguín F. "Sentido del Mito como Estructura Social desde el Pensamiento de Heidegger" p. 69-81;
Luis E. Orozco S. "Marxismo y Compromiso Cristiano" (franco intento de aprovechar lo asimilable del marxismo para los cristianos comprometidos con la "liberación" de América Latina) p. 83-128;
Fabio Vélez U. "Consideraciones para una Interpretación Cristiana de la Historia" p. 129-142;
John Jairo Betancur "Filosofía y Política" (defensa de la objetividad e independencia de la filosofía) p. 143-160;
Guillermo Hoyos V. "Sociedad Nueva y Ética" (sobre el lugar de la ética en la política, partiendo de la contraposición Popper-Marcuse) p. 161-197;
Carlos Bendaña "La Producción Intelectual en América Latina" p. 199-240;
Luis J. Ortiz V. "Cómo Incide la Dependencia Cultural en las Estructuras Mentales del Pueblo Latinoamericano" p. 241-258;
Javier Domínguez "Funciones del Filósofo en Nuestra Sociedad Actual" p. 259-278.

9708. Sepich-Lange, Juan R. El derecho en la filosofía del espíritu (IFP/E, 1, 1973, p. 245-262)

En lo que se refiere a la filosofía del derecho, en nuestro tiempo se enfrentan dos actitudes: el formalismo racionalista (herencia de la Ilustración) y el "pensamiento nuevo," que se origina en Hegel. Es al hilo del pensamiento de éste que se desarrollan las reflexiones del ensayo.

9709. Serrano, A.E. La filosofía del derecho, hoy. Textos básicos para su estudio. Maracaibo, Ven., Univ. del Zulia, Facultad de Humanidades y Educación, Escuela de Filosofía, 1973. 401 p. (Biblioteca de textos filosóficos)

Los autores representados en esta antología son los siguientes: Stammler, Kelsen, Lask, Radbruch, Mayer, del Vecchio, Messner, Reinach, Schapp, Schreier, Cossio, Recasens Siches, Frank, Ross, Hart, Pound y Levy-Bruhl. Lamentablemente no contiene introducciones ni bibliografías.

9710. Silva, Ludovico. Anti-manual para uso de marxistas, marxólogos y marxianos. 2. ed. Caracas, Monte Avila, 1976. 273 p. (Col. Estudios)

El autor propone una revaloración crítica y libre del marxismo, a la altura de las circunstancias actuales. Para ello le parece necesario revisar los conceptos fundamentales de dicha doctrina y componer una especie de diccionario, combatiendo el anquilosamiento que, a su juicio, denotan los manuales marxistas, especialmente los soviéticos. Gran parte del contenido de la obra es, precisamente, el examen de conceptos marxistas básicos como dialéctica, materialismo, alienación, ideología, etc. La primera edición apareció en 1975.

9711. Soriano, Graciela. Aspectos políticos en el pensamiento de Adam Ferguson (UCV/P, 1, 1972, p. 137-174)

Sobre la obra de Ferguson, *An essay on the history of civil society* (1767).

FILOSOFIA DE LA HISTORIA Y DE LA CULTURA

9712. Basave Fernández del Valle, Agustín. Filosofía de la cultura (UNL/H, 17, 1976, p. 13-22)

Caracterización de la cultura; la cultura en la vida y el mundo humanos; la cultura en relación con Dios: tales algunos de los temas del artículo.

9713. Crippa, Adolpho. Cultura e transcendencia (Convivium [Sáo Paulo] 12:1, jan./fev. 1973, p. 3-20)

Se refiere principalmente al cristianismo en su relación con la cultural occidental.

9714. Escobar, Carlos Henrique de. A psicanálise e a ciência da história (VOZES, 65:6, agôsto 1971, p. 451-458)

La aproximación del psicoanálisis a una "ciencia de la historia" se haría mediante el análisis combinado de los conceptos de 'inconsciente' en Freud y de 'modo de producción' en Marx.

9715. Labarca P., Domingo A. Esbozo para un análisis científico de la cultura (Boletín de Filosofía [Univ. del Zulia, Facultad de Humanidades y Educación, Centro de Estudios Filosóficos, Maracaibo, Ven.] 1972, p. 119-126)

A pesar del título, viene a decir que las ideas de Malinowski sobre la cultura fueron anticipadas por Marx y Engles en *La ideología alemana*.

9716. Rionda Arreguín, Luis. Spengler, Toynbee, Senghor y la proyección de sus conceptos fundamentales (UNL/H, 17, 1976, p. 79-91)

Toynbee y Spengler se relacionan por los puntos básicos de sus respectivas filosofías de la historia. Mucho menos clara se ve la relación con Senghor.

9717. Vázquez, Eduardo. La historia como progreso (UZ/H, 1:1/2, 1974, p. 9-40)

Fundamentalmente se refiere al asunto del tema en Hegel y Marx.

ESTETICA Y FILOSOFIA DEL ARTE

9718. Balzer, Carmen. Arte, fantasía y mundo. B.A., Plus Ultra, 1975. 271 p.

El tema de la obra es, en realidad, la fantasía, la cual se examina en relación con el juego, el sueño, el azar y el lenguaje. Otros temas del libro son: arte y locura y el arte y lo demoníaco.

9719. Galeffi, Romano. Arte e comunicação (Convivium [São Paulo] 12:1, jan./fev. 1973, p. 51-62)

Ponencia al VIII Congreso Interamericano de Filosofía. Concluye: "Toda obra de arte y todo acto creador artístico implica un indispensable acto de comunicación."

9720. Lyra, Pedro. Utiludismo. A socialidade da arte: ensaio. Rio, Tempo Brasileiro, 1976. 117 p. (Temas de todo tempo, 19)

El tema principal es la relación entre el arte y la sociedad, poniendo especial énfasis en la situación del mundo contemporáneo.

9721. Merquior, José Guilherme. A estética de Lévi-Strauss. Rio, Editora Univ. de Brasília [and] Tempo Brasileiro, 1975. 114 p. (Biblioteca tempo universitário, 40)

El texto se preparó originalmente en francés y fue leído en 1969 en un Seminario dirigido por Lévi-Strauss en el Collège de France. No pretende realizar una interpretación global de la estética estructuralista, sino que se refiere específicamente a ciertos escritos del antropólogo francés relacionados con el arte.

9722. Mosquera, Juan José Mouriño. Psicologia da arte. 2. ed. revista e ampliada. Porto Alegre, Brazil, Sulina, 1976. 142 p., bibl.

Esta obra, de carácter didáctico, de hecho va más allá de una *psicología* del arte. Son temas del libro el arte como creación, la dinámica del arte, los tipos de personalidades artísticas creadoras, arte y educación y las concepciones estéticas de Eco y Read. Para concebir la creación artística se utilizan las ideas de Koestler en *The act of creation*. Contiene amplia bibliografía.

9723. Tinajero, Fernando. Notas sobre la posibilidad de una estética científica (UCE/A, 353, 1975, p. 39-53)

La tesis principal es que, a diferencia del irracionalismo de la "filosofía burguesa," el marxismo es la única doctrina capaz de fundar y constituir una estética científica.

FILOSOFIA DEL LENGUAJE

9724. Delago, F.R. Un ejemplo de análisis filo-lógico-psíquico (UNL/H, 12, 1971, p. 73-82)

Exaltación del valor humanístico de la filología.

9725. García Caffarena, Judith G. Norma y uso (UNL/H, 17, 1976, p. 285-295)

Comenta obras de Hjelmslev, Coseriu y Rona sobre el problema de la relación entre norma y uso lingüísticos.

9726. Li Carrillo, Víctor. Las tres lingüísticas (USB/RVF, 4, 1976, p. 53-84)

Después de trazar las grandes líneas del desarrollo actual de la lingüística a partir de Saussure, y encontrando que la riqueza de teorías y escuelas ha llegado a un punto crítico, propone una división del trabajo lingüístico en tres esferas: lingüística descriptiva, lingüística teórica y lingüística matemática. Estudio serio y bien informado.

9727. Mendonça, Antônio Sérgio. Por uma filosofía da linguagem (VOZES, 65:5, junho/julho 1971, p. 31-38)

El objeto de la lingüística es la lengua articulada. El de la semiología, el discurso ideológico. La teoría del lenguaje estudia la articulación entre el nivel ideológico contextual y el del lenguaje específico de un discurso.

9728. Ravera, Rosa María. Estética y lingüística (UBAFFL/C, 14:21, enero/junio 1974, p. 119-132)

Se refiere "a la proyección de algunos aportes de la lingüística contemporánea (y derivados de ella) en la problemática estética, con particular relación a las artes plásticas."

METAFISICA

9729. Cruz Vélez, Danilo. Tres ensayos metafísicos (Boletín Cultural y Bibliográfico [Banco de la República, Biblioteca Luis-Angel Arango, Bogotá] 3:2, 1972, p. 22-76)

Los tres ensayos son los siguientes: "Metafísica del Hombre y de la Cultura;" "Metafísica y Teología;" y La Metafísica y las Ciencias del Lenguage." Los dos últimos son los más elaborados y parecen más acordes con la posición actual del autor que el primero, en el cual se afirma la existencia de tres principios metafísicos: lo inorgánico, el principio vital y el espíritu. Precede a estos tres textos la transcripción de una entrevista con el autor ("Diálogo con Danilo Cruz Vélez," p. 5-21), que contiene pasajes interesantes como testimonio.

9730. González Salas, Carlos. Dios y las pruebas de su existencia en la filosofía (UNL/H, 17, 1976, p. 41-77)

El tema es examinado en Pascal, Kant, Bergson, William James, Xubiri, Nietzsche y Sartre.

9731. Kogan, Jacobo. Literatura y metafísica. B.A., Editorial Nova, 1971. 108 p.

La evolución futura del hombre se desarrollará en el ámbito del espíritu, el cual consiste en elevarse desde la naturaleza "a un plano de libertad y creación." Siendo el arte fundamental para la realización humana, aporta datos esenciales a la metafísica, en tanto ésta busca esclarecer el sentido de la realidad en general. Se exponen las doctrinas de Schelling, Whitehead y Heidegger sobre el arte. En oposición al tercero, insiste en que el arte no tiene carácter cognoscitivo.

9732. Nicol, Eduardo. Fenomenología y dialéctica (UNAM/D, 19, 1973, p. 40-63)

Recoge anotaciones de un seminario de Metafísica (1971-72). El tema del trabajo es la relación entre el ser y el tiempo. Su desarrollo se desenvuelve en gran parte en el examen del pensamiento griego, partiendo de que está todavía por realizarse la "destrucción" de la ontología programada por Heidegger. Una de las principales discrepancias con Heidegger es considerar al ser como patente.

9733. Rosales, Alberto. El problema de la negatividad (USB/RVF, 4, 1976, p. 123-174)

Según manifiesta el propio autor, las meditaciones contenidas en este trabajo "despliegan el problema de la negatividad en la perspectiva de las obras tempranas de Martín Heidegger." La intención, sin embargo, va más allá de la mera exégesis. El presente estudio extiende consideraciones iniciadas en el libro del autor, *Transzendenz und Differenz* (1970) y son parte de una obra futura, *Verdad y no verdad*.

9734. Sanabria, José Rubén. El punto de partida de la metafísica: ¿abstracción o intuición? (UCA/S, 26:100/102, abril/dic. 1971, p. 347-368)

Postulando la necesidad de un tomismo abierto, sostiene la tesis de que la intuición del ser es el punto de partida de la metafísica.

9735. Stein, Ernildo. Melancolia. Ensaios sobre a finitude no pensamento ocidental. Porto Alegre, Brazil, Editora Movimento, 1976. 125 p. (Col. Dialética, 4)

El concepto de *melancolía* no lo entiende el autor en el sentido puramente psicológico, sino en el plano "ontológico-existencial." El tema del libro es, en realidad, la relación entre finitud y trascendencia. Se compone de ensayos escritos entre 1968 y 1976, que constituyen el comienzo de un pensamiento filosófico personal.

JOURNAL ABBREVIATIONS

ACO/B	Boletín de la Academia Colombiana. Bogotá.
CDLA	Casa de las Américas. Instituto Cubano del Libro. La Habana.
CIF/RLF	Revista Latinoamericana de Filosofía. Centro de Investigaciones Filosóficas. B.A.
IBF/RBF	Revista Brasileira de Filosofia. Instituto Brasileiro de Filosofia. São Paulo.
IFP/E	Ethos. Revista de filosofía práctica. Instituto de Filosofía Práctica. B.A.
III/AI	América Indígena. Instituto Indigenista Inter-americano. México.
ISTMO	Istmo. Revista del pensamiento actual. México.
LARR	Latin American Research Review. Univ. of North Carolina Press *for the* Latin American Studies Association. Chapel Hill.
LNB/L	Lotería. Lotería Nacional de Beneficencia. Panamá.
RIB	Revista Interamericana de Bibliografía [Inter-American Review of Bibliography]. Organization of American States. Washington.
TEMBRAS	Tempo Brasileiro. Revista de cultura. Rio.
UA/RF	Razón y Fabula. Univ. de los Andes. Bogotá.
UBAFFL/C	Cuadernos de Filosofía. Univ. de Buenos Aires, Facultad de Filosofía y Letras. B.A.
UC/A	Anales de la Universidad de Cuenca. Cuenca, Ecua.
UC/AT	Atenea. Revista de ciencias, letras y artes. Univ. de Concepción. Concepción, Chile.
UCA/S	Sapientia. Univ. Católica Argentina Santa María de los Buenos Aires, Facultad de Filosofía. B.A.
UCE/A	Anales de la Universidad Central del Ecuador. Quito.
UCR/RF	Revista de la Filosofía de la Universidad de Costa Rica. San José.
UCV/P	Politeia. Univ. Central de Venezuela, Facultad de Derecho, Instituto de Estudios Políticos. Caracas.
UMGFF/K	Kriterion. Univ. de Minas Gerais, Faculdade de Filosofia. Belo Horizonte, Brazil.
UN/IV	Ideas y Valores. Univ. Nacional, Instituto de Filosofía y Letras. Bogotá.
UNAM/C	Crítica. Revista hispanoamericana de filosofía. Univ. Nacional Autónoma de México, Instituto de Investigaciones Filosóficas. México.
UNAM/D	Diánoia. Univ. Autónoma de México, Centro de Estudios Filosóficos. México.
UNAM/L	Latinoamérica. Anuario de estudios latinoamericanos. Univ. Nacional Autónoma de México, Facultad de Filosofía y Letras, Centro de Estudios Latinoamericanos. México.
UNAM/RUM	Revista de la Universidad de México. México.
UNC/RH	Revista de Humanidades. Univ. Nacional de Córdoba, Facultad de Filosofía. Córdoba, Arg.
UNL/H	Humanitas. Univ. de Nuevo León, Centro de Estudios Humanísticos. Monterrey, Mex.

UNL/U	Universidad. Univ. Nacional del Litoral. Santa Fe, Arg.
UNT/H	Humanitas. Univ. Nacional de Tucumán, Facultad de Filosofía y Letras. Tucumán, Arg.
UPR/D	Diálogos. Univ. de Puerto Rico. Río Piedras.
USB/F	Franciscanum. Revista de las ciencias del espíritu. Univ. de San Buenaventura. Bogotá.
USB/RVF	Revista Venezolana de Filosofía. Univ. Simón Bolívar [and] Sociedad Venezolana de Filosofía. Caracas.
UZ/H	Hermeneia. Univ. del Zulia, Escuela de Filosofía, Maracaibo, Ven. [and] Univ. Central de Venezuela, Escuela de Filosofía. Caracas.
VME/R	Revista Nacional de Cultura. Ministerio de Educación, Instituto Nacional de Cultura y Bellas Artes. Caracas.
VOZES	Vozes. Revista de cultura. Editora Vozes. Petrópolis, Brazil.

INDEXES

SHADOWS

ABBREVIATIONS AND ACRONYMS*

a.	annual
ABC	Argentina, Brazil, Chile
A.C.	antes de Cristo ·
ACAR	Associação de Crédito e Assistência Rural, Brazil
AD	Anno Domini
A.D.	Acción Democrática, Venezuela
ADESG	Associação dos Diplomados de Escola Superior de Guerra, Brazil
AGI	Archivo General de Indias, Sevilla
AGN	Archivo General de la Nación
AID	Agency for International Development
Ala.	Alabama
ALALC	Asociación Latinoamericana de Libre Comercio
ANAPO	Alianza Nacional Popular, Colombia
ANCARSE	Associação Nordestina de Crédito e Assistência Rural de Sergipe, Brazil
ANCOM	Andean Common Market
ANDI	Asociación Nacional de Industriales, Colombia
APRA	Alianza Popular Revolucionaria Americana
Arg.	Argentina
Ariz.	Arizona
Ark.	Arkansas
ASSEPLAN	Assesoria de Planejamente e Acompanhamento, Recife, Brazil
Assn.	Association
Aufl.	Auflage (edition, edición)
AUFS	American Universities Field Staff Reports, Hanover, N.H.
Aug.	August, Augustan
b.	born (nacido)
B.A.	Buenos Aires
Bar.	Barbados
BBE	Bibliografia Brasileira de Educação
BC	Before Christ
bibl.	bibliography
BID	Banco Interamericano de Desarrollo
BNDE	Banco Nacional de Desenvolvimento Econômico
Bol.	Bolivia
BP	before present
b/w	black-and-white
C14	Carbon 14
ca.	circa
C.A.	Centro América, Central America
CACM	Central American Common Market
CADE	Conferencia Anual de Ejecutivos de Empresas, Peru
CAEM	Centro de Altos Estudios Militares, Peru
Calif.	California
CARC	Centro de Arte y Comunicación
CARICOM	Caribbean Common Market

*Except for journal acronyms which are listed at: a) the end of each major disciplinary section (e.g. History, Literature, etc.); and b) after each serial title in the *Title List of Journals Indexed*, p. 607.

CARIFTA	Caribbean Free Trade Association
CBD	central business district
CD	Christian Democrats, Chile
CDI	Conselho de Desenvolvimento Industrial
CEBRAP	Centro Brasileiro de Pesquisas, São Paulo
CECORA	Central de Cooperativas de la Reforma Agraria, Colombia
CEDAL	Centro de Estudios Democráticos de América Latina, Costa Rica
CEDE	Centro de Estudios sobre Desarrollo Económico, Univ. de los Andes, Bogotá
CEDEPLAR	Centro de Desenvolvimento e Planejamento Regional, Belo Horizonte, Brazil
CEDES	Centro de Estudios de Estado y Sociedad, Buenos Aires
CELADE	Centro Latinoamericano de Demografía
CEMLA	Centro de Estudios Monetarios Latinoamericanos, México
CENDES	Centro de Estudios del Desarrollo, Venezuela
CENIDIM	Centro Nacional de Información, Documentación e Investigación Musicales, Mexico
CEPADE	Centro Paraguayo de Estudios de Desarrollo Económico y Social
CEPA-SE	Comissão Estadual de Planejamento Agrícola, Sergipe, Brazil
CEPAL	See ECLA.
CES	constant elasticity of substitution
cf.	compare
CFI	Consejo Federal de Inversiones, B.A.
CGE	Confederación General Económica, Argentina
CGTP	Confederación General de Trabajadores del Perú
ch., chap.	chapter
CHEAR	Council on Higher Education in the American Republics
Cía.	compañía
CIA	Central Intelligence Agency
CIDA	Comité Interamericano de Desarrollo Agrícola
CIE	Centro de Investigaciones Económicas, Buenos Aires
CIP	Conselho Interministerial de Preços
CLACSO	Consejo Latinoamericano de Ciencias Sociales, Secretaría Ejecutiva, Buenos Aires
CLASC	Confederación Latinoamericana Sindical Cristiana
CLE	Comunidad Latinoamericana de Escritores, México
cm	centimeter
CNI	Confederação Nacional da Industria, Brazil
Co.	company
COBAL	Companhia Brasileira de Alimentos
Col.	collection, colección, coleção
Colo.	Colorado
COMCORDE	Comisión Coordinadora para el Desarrollo Económico, Uruguay
comp.	compiler
CONDESE	Conselho de Desenvolvimento Econômico de Sergipe, Brazil
Conn.	Connecticut
COPEI	Comité Organizador Pro-Elecciones Independientes, Venezuela
CORFO	Corporación de Fomento de la Producción, Chile
CORP	Corporación para el Fomento de Investigaciones Económicas, Colombia
Corp.	Corporation
C.R.	Costa Rica
CUNY	City University of New York
CVG	Corporación Venezolana de Guayana
d.	died
DANE	Departamento Nacional de Estadística, Colombia
DC	Demócratas Cristianos, Chile
d.C.	después de Cristo
Dec.	December, décembre
Del.	Delaware
dept.	department
depto.	departamento

Abbreviations and Acronyms / 601

dez.	dezembro
dic.	diciembre
DNOCS	Departamento Nacional de Obras Contra as Sêcas, Brazil
D.R.	Dominican Republic
Dra.	Doctora
ECLA	Economic Comission for Latin America
ECOSOC	UN Dept. of Economic and Social Affairs
Ecua.	Ecuador
ed(s).	edition(s), edición(es), editor(s)
EDEME	Editora Emprendimentos Educacionais Florianópolis, Brazil
Edo.	Estado
EEC	European Economic Community
EFTA	European Free Trade Association
e.g.	exempio gratia [for example]
El Sal.	El Salvador
ELN	Ejército de Liberación Nacional, Colombia
estr.	estrenado
et al	et alia [and others]
ETENE	Escritório Técnico de Estudios Econômicos do Nordeste, Brazil
ETEPE	Escritório Técnico de Planejamento, Brazil
EUDEBA	Editorial Universitaria de Buenos Aires
EWG	Europaische Wirtschaftsgemeinschaft. *See* EEC.
facsim.	facsimile
FAO	Food and Agriculture Organization of the United Nations
feb.	February, febrero
FEDECAFE	Federación Nacional de Cafeteros, Colombia
fev.	fevreiro, février
ff.	following
FGV	Fundação Getúlio Vargas
FIEL	Fundación de Investigaciones Económicas Latinoamericanas, Argentina
film.	filmography
fl.	flourished, floresció
Fla.	Florida
FLACSO	Facultad Latinoamericana de Ciencias Sociales, Buenos Aires
fold. map	folded map
folded table	fold. table
fols.	folios
FRG	Federal Republic of Germany
ft.	foot, feet
FUAR	Frente Unido de Acción Revolucionaria, Colombia
Ga.	Georgia
GAO	General Accounting Office, Washington
GATT	General Agreement on Tariffs and Trade
GDP	gross domestic product
GDR	German Democratic Republic
Gen.	General
GMT	Greenwich Meridian Time
GPA	grade point average
GPO	Government Printing Office
Guat.	Guatemala
h.	hijo
HLAS	*Handbook of Latin American Studies*
HMAI	*Handbook of Middle American Indians*
Hond.	Honduras
IBBD	Instituto Brasileiro de Bibliografia e Documentação
IBRD	International Bank of Reconstruction and Development
ICA	Instituto Colombiano Agropecuario
ICAIC	Instituto Cubano del Arte e Industria Cinematográficas
ICCE	Instituto Colombiano de Construcción Escolar
ICSS	Instituto Colombiano de Seguridad Social
ICT	Instituto de Crédito Territorial, Colombia

IDB	Inter-American Development Bank
i.e.	id est [that is]
IEL	Instituto Euvaldo Lodi, Brazil
IEP	Instituto de Estudios Peruanos
IERAC	Instituto Ecuatoriano de Reforma Agraria y Colonización
III	Instituto Indigenista Interamericano, Mexico
IIN	Instituto Indigenista Nacional, Guatemala
Ill.	Illinois
illus.	illustration(s)
ILO	International Labour Organization, Geneva
IMES	Instituto Mexicano de Estudios Sociales
in.	inches
INAH	Instituto Nacional de Antropología e Historia, México
INBA	Instituto Nacional de Bellas Artes, México
Inc.	incorporated
INCORA	Instituto Colombiano de Reforma Agraria
Ind.	Indiana
INEP	Instituto Nacional de Estudos Pedagógicos, Brazil
INI	Instituto Nacional Indigenista, Mexico
INIT	Instituto Nacional de Industria Turística, Cuba
INPES/IPEA	Instituto de Planejamento Econômico e Social, Instituto de Pesquisas, Brazil
IPA	Instituto de Pastoral Andina, Univ. de San Antonio de Abad, Seminario de Antropología, Cuzco, Peru
IPEA	Instituto de Pesquisa Econômico-Social Aplicada, Brazil
IPES/GB	Instituto de Pesquisas e Estudos Sociais, Guanabara, Brazil
ir.	irregular
ITT	International Telephone and Telegraph
Jam.	Jamaica
jan.	January, janeiro, Janvier
JLP	Jamaican Labour Party
JUCEPLAN	Junta Central de Planificación, Cuba
Jul.	juli
Jun.	Juni
Kans.	Kansas
km	kilometers, kilómetros
Ky.	Kentucky
l.	leaves, hojas (páginas impresas por una sola cara)
La.	Louisiana
LASA	Latin American Studies Association
LDC	less developed country
Ltda.	Limitada
m	meters, metros, monthly
M	mille, mil, thousand
MAPU	Movimiento de Acción Popular Unitario, Chile
MARI	Middle American Research Institute, Tulane University, New Orleans
Mass.	Massachusetts
MCC	Mercado Común Centro-Americano
Md.	Maryland
MDC	more developed countries
MEC	Ministério de Educação e Cultura, Brazil
Mex.	Mexico
Mich.	Michigan
mimeo	mimeographed, mimeografiado
min.	minutes, minutos
Minn.	Minnesota
MIR	Movimiento de Izquierda Revolucionaria, Chile
Miss.	Mississippi
MIT	Massachusetts Institute of Technology
mm.	millimeter
MCN	multinational corporation

Abbreviations and Acronyms / 603

MNR	Movimiento Nacionalista Revolucionario, Bolivia
Mo.	Missouri
MOIR	Movimiento Obrero Independiente y Revolucionario, Colombia
MRL	Movimiento Revolucionario Liberal, Colombia
ms.	manuscript
msl	mean sea level
n.	nacido (born)
N.C.	North Carolina
n.d.	no date
N. Dak.	North Dakota
Nebr.	Nebraska
neubearb.	neurbearbeitet (revised, corregida)
Nev.	Nevada
n.f.	neue Folge
N.H.	New Hampshire
Nic.	Nicaragua
N.J.	New Jersey
N. Mex.	New Mexico
no(s).	number(s), número(s)
NOSALF	Scandinavian Committee for Research in Latin America
Nov.	noviembre, November, novembre, novembro
n.p.	no place, no publisher
NSF	National Science Foundation
NY	New York
NYC	New York City
OAS	Organization of American States
oct.	October, octubre
ODEPLAN	Oficina de Planificación Nacional, Chile
OEA	Organización de los Estados Americanos
OIT	*See* ILO.
Okla.	Oklahoma
Okt.	Oktober
op.	opus
OPEC	Organization of Petroleum Exporting Countries
OPEP	Organización de Países Exportadores de Petróleo
OPIC	Overseas Investment Corporation
Oreg.	Oregon
ORIT	Organización Regional Interamericana del Trabajo
out.	outubro
p.	page
Pa.	Pennsylvania
Pan.	Panama
PAN	Partido Acción Nacional, Mexico
Par.	Paraguay
PC	partido comunista
PCR	Partido Comunista Revolucionario, Chile and Argentina
PCV	Partido Comunista de Venezuela
PDC	Partido Demócrata Cristiano, Chile
PEMEX	Petróleos Mexicanos
PETROBRAS	Petróleo Brasileiro
PIP	Partido Independiente de Puerto Rico
PLANAVE	Engenharia e Planejamento Limitada, Brazil
PLANO	Planejamento e Assesoria Limitada, Brazil
PLN	Partido Liberación Nacional, Costa Rica
PNM	People's National Movement, Trinidad and Tobago
PNP	People's National Party, Jamaica
pop.	population
PPP	purchasing power parities
P.R.	Puerto Rico
PRI	Partido Revolucionario Institucional, Mexico
PROABRIL	Centro de Projetos Industriais, Brazil

Prof.	Professor
PRONAPA	Programa Nacional de Pesquisas Arqueológicas, Brazil
prov.	province, provincia
PS	Partido Socialista, Chile
pseud.	pseudonym, pseudónimo
pt(s).	part(s), parte(s)
PUC	Pontificia Universidade Católica, Rio
PURSC	Partido Unido de la Revolución Socialista de Cuba
q.	quarterly
R.D.	República Dominicana
rev.	revisada, revista, revised
R.I.	Rhode Island
Rio	Rio de Janeiro
S.a.	semiannual
SALALM	Seminar on the Acquisition of Latin American Library Materials
S.C.	South Carolina
sd.	sound
S. Dak.	South Dakota
SDR	special drawing rights
Sec.	section, sección
SELA	Sistema Económico Latinoamericano
SENAC	Serviço Nacional de Aprendizagem Comercial, Rio
SENAI	Serviço Nacional de Aprendizagem Industrial, São Paulo
Sept.	September, septiembre, septembre
SES	socio-economic status
SESI	Serviço Social de Industria, Brazil
set.	setembre
SIECA	Secretaría Permanente del Tratado General de Integración Centroamericana
SIL	Summer Institute of Linguistics
SINAMOS	Sistema Nacional de Apoyo a la Movilización Social, Peru
S.J.	Society of Jesus
SNA	Sociedad Nacional de Agricultura, Chile
SPVEA	Superintendência do Plano de Valorização Econômica da Amazônia, Brazil
sq.	square
SUDAM	Superintendência do Desenvolvimento da Amazônia, Brazil
SUDENE	Superintendência do Desenvolvimento do Nordeste, Brazil
SUFRAMA	Superintendência da Zona Franca de Manaus, Brazil
SUNY	State Universities of New York
t.	tomo, tome
T. and T.	Trinidad & Tobago
TAT	Thematic Apperception Test
TB	tuberculosis
Tenn.	Tennessee
Tex.	Texas
TG	transformational generative
TL	Thermoluminescent
TNP	Tratado de No Proliferación
trans.	translator
U.K.	United Kingdom
UN	United Nations
UNAM	Universidad Nacional Autónoma de México
UNCTAD	United Nations Conference on Trade and Development
UNDP	UN Development Programme
UNEAC	Unión de Escritores y Artistas de Cuba
UNESCO	United Nations Educational, Scientific and Cultural Organization
univ.	university, universidad, universidade, université, universität
uniw.	uniwersytet
UP	Unidad Popular, Chile
URD	Unidad Revolucionaria Democrática

URSS	Unión de Repúblicas Soviéticas Socialistas
Uru.	Uruguay
US	United States of America
USIA	United States Information Agency, Washington
USSR	Union of Soviet Socialist Republics
UTM	Universal Transverse Mercator
v.; vol.	volume, volumen
Va.	Virginia
Ven.	Venezuela
V.I.	Virgin Islands
vs.	versus
Vt.	Vermont
W.I.	West Indies
Wis.	Wisconsin
Wyo.	Wyoming
yr.	the younger, el joven, year

TITLE LIST OF JOURNALS INDEXED*

Acta Litteraria. Academiae Scientiarum Hungaricae. Budapest.
Actualidades. Caracas.
African Music. Roodepoort, South Africa
Afro-Asia. Univ. Federal da Bahia, Centro de Estudos Afro-Orientais. Bahia, Brazil. (UFB/AA)
Agricultural History. The quarterly journal for the Agricultural History Society by the Univ. of California Press. Berkeley. (AHS/AH)
Aisthesis. Revista chilena de investigaciones estéticas. Univ. Católica de Chile, Instituto de Estética. Santiago.
Alfa. Univ. de São Paulo, Faculdad de Filosofia, Ciências e Letras. Marília, Brazil. (FFCLM/A)
América. Revista cuatrimestral de asuntos históricos. B.A.
América Indígena. Instituto Indigenista Interamericano. México. (III/AI)
América Latina. Academia de Ciencias de la URSS [Unión de Repúblicas Soviéticas Socialistas]. Moscú. (URSS/AL)
American Historical Review. American Historical Association. Washington. (AHA/R)
The American Journal of Economics and Sociology. Francis Neilson Fund [and] Robert Schalkenbach Foundation. N.Y. (AJES)
American Journal of Political Science. Midwest Political Science Association. Detroit, Mich.
American Speech. Columbia Univ. Press. N.Y.
Américas. Organization of American States. Washington. (OAS/AM)
The Americas. A quarterly publication of inter-American cultural history.

Academy of American Franciscan History. Washington. (AAFH/TAM)
Anais da Biblioteca Nacional. Rio.
Anais do Museu Histórico Nacional. Ministério da Educação e Cultura. Rio. (BMHN/A)
Anales Científicos de la Univ. del Centro del Perú. Huancayo, Peru. (UNCP/AC)
Anales de Antropología. Univ. Nacional Autónoma de México. Instituto de Investigaciones Históricas. Mexico. (UNAM/AA)
Anales de la Sociedad de Geografía e Historia de Guatemala. Guatemala. (SGHC/A)
Anales de la Sociedad Rural Argentina. Revista pastoril y agrícola. B.A. (SRA/A)
Anales de la Universidad Central del Ecuador. Quito. (UCE/A)
Anales de la Universidad de Cuenca. Cuenca, Ecua. (UC/A)
Anales de la Universidad del Norte. Antofagasta, Chile. (UN/A)
Anales de Literatura Hispanoamerica. Univ. Complutense de Madrid. Madrid. (UCM/ALH)
Anales del Instituto de Investigaciones Estéticas. Univ. Autónoma de México. México.
Análisis. Cuadernos de investigación. Lima. (ANA)
Anglia. Anuario/estudios angloamericanos. Univ. Autónoma de México, Facultad de Filosofía y Letras. México. (UNAM/A)
Annali. Instituto Universitario Orientale. Sezione Romanza. Napoli, Italy. (IUO/A)
Annali della Fondazione Luigi Einaudi. Torino, Italy.

*Journals that have been included in the *Handbook* as individual items are listed alphabetically by title in the Author Index.

Annals of the Association of American Geographers. Lawrence, Kans. (AAG/A)
Annals of the New York Academy of Sciences. N.Y. (NYAS/A)
Annals of the Southeastern Conference on Latin American Studies. West Georgia College. Carrollton. (SECOLAS/A)
L'Année Sociologique. Presses Universitaires de France. Paris. (PUF/AS)
Anthropological Journal of Canada. Anthropological Association of Canada. Quebec, Canada. (AAC/AJ)
Anthropological Linguistics. Indiana Univ., Dept. of Anthropology for the Archives of the Languages of the World. Bloomington. (IU/AL)
Anthropos. Anthropos-Institut. Psoieux, Switzerland. (AI/A)
La Antigua. Univ. de Santa María La Antigua, Oficina de Humanidades. Panamá. (USMLA/LA)
Antiquity. A quarterly review of archaeology. The Antiquity Trust. Cambridge, U.K. (AT/A)
Antropología Andina. Cuzco, Peru.
Antropología e Historia de Guatemala. Instituto de Antropología e Historia de Guatemala. Guatemala. (IAHG/AHG)
Anuario. Academia Nacional de Bellas Artes. B.A.
Anuario. Univ. Central de Venezuela, Instituto de Estudios Hispanoamericanos. Caracas. (IEH/A)
Anuario de Estudios Americanos. Consejo Superior de Investigaciones Científicas [and] Univ. de Sevilla, Escuela de Estudios Hispano-Americanos. Sevilla. (EEHA/AEA)
Anuario de Historia. Univ. Nacional Autónoma de México. México. (UNAM/AH)
Anuario de Letras. Univ. Nacional Autónoma de México, Facultad de Filosofía y Letras. México. (UNAM/AL)
Anuario Histórico Jurídico Ecuatoriano. Corporación de Estudios y Publicaciones. Quito.
Apuntes. Revista de teatro de la Univ. Católica de Chile. Santiago. (UCCH/A)
Apuntes. Univ. del Pacífico, Centro de Investigación. Lima. (UP/A)
Araisa. Anuario del Centro de Estudios Lationoamericanos Rómulo Gallegos. Caracas. (CELRG/A)
Arbor. Madrid. (ARBOR)
Archives Internationales de Sociologie de la Coopération et du Développement. Paris. (AISCD)
Archivo Ibero-Americano. Los Padres Franciscanos. Madrid. (PF/AIA)
Archivum Historicum Societatis Iesu. Roma. (AHSI)
Areito. Arieto, Inc. N.Y. (AR)
Argentina Outreach. Argentine Information Service Center. Berkeley, Calif.
Arizona and the West. Univ. of Arizona. Tucson. (UA/AW)
Arquitectura México. México.
The Art Gallery. The international magazine of art and culture. Hollycroft, Ivoryton, Conn.
Art News. N.Y.
Asclepio. Consejo Superior de Investigaciones Científicas, Instituto Arnau de Vilanova de Historia de la Medicina, Archivo Iberoamericano de Historia de la Medicina y Antropología Médica. Madrid. (CSIC/A)
Atenea. Revista de ciencias, letras y artes. Univ. de Concepción. Concepción, Chile. (UC/AT)
Atlántida. Univ. Simón Bolívar, División de Ciencias Sociales y Humanidades. Caracas.
Aula. Univ. Nacional Pedro Henríquez Ureña. Santo Domingo. (UNPHU/A)
Ausgewählte neuere Literatur. Institut für Iberoamerika-Kunde, Dokumentations-Leitstelle Lateinamerika. Hamburg, FRG.
Avances. Revista boliviana de estudios históricos y sociales. La Paz.
Avances de Investigación. Univ. de Costa Rica, Facultad de Ciencias Sociales, Instituto de Investigaciones Sociales. San José.

Beiträge zur Romanischen Philologie. Rütten & Loening. Berlin, FRG. (BRP)
Bibliografía Ecuatoriana. Quito.
Boletim. Secretaria de Cultura, Esportes e Turismo, Seminários do Museu da Casa Brasileira. São Paulo.
Boletim Bibliográfico da Biblioteca Na-

cional. Ministério da Educação e Cultura, Depto. de Assuntos Culturais, Biblioteca Nacional. Rio.
Boletín Bibliográfico de Antropología Americana. Instituto Panamericano de Geografía e Historia, Comisión de Historia. México. (BBAA)
Boletín Cultural y Bibliográfico. Banco de la República, Biblioteca Luis-Angel Arango. Bogotá.
Boletín de Estudios Latinoamericanos. Centro de Estudios y Documentación Latinoamericanos. Amsterdam. (CEDLA/B)
Boletín de Filología. Univ. de Chile, Instituto de Filología. Santiago. (UC/BF)
Boletín de Filosofía. Univ. del Zulia, Facultad de Humanidades y Educación, Centro de Estudios Filosóficos. Maracaibo, Ven.
Boletín de Historia y Antigüedades. Academia Colombiana de la Historia. Bogotá. (ACH/BHA)
Boletín de la Academia Argentina de Letras. B.A. (AAL/B)
Boletín de la Academia Chilena de la Historia. Santiago. (ACH/B)
Boletín de la Academia Colombiana. Bogotá. (ACO/B)
Boletín de la Academia de Artes y Ciencias de Puerto Rico. San Juan. (PRAAC/B)
Boletín de la Academia Nacional de Historia. B.A. (ANH/B)
Boletín de la Academia Nacional de la Historia. Caracas. (VANH/B)
Boletín de la Biblioteca del Congreso de la Nación. B.A.
Boletín de la Escuela de Guerra Naval. B.A.
Boletín de la Facultad de Derecho y Ciencias Sociales. Univ. Nacional de Córdoba. Córdoba, Arg.
Boletín del Archivo General de la Nación. Secretaría de Gobernación. México. (MAGN/B)
Boletín del Archivo Histórico de Miraflores. Presidencia de la República, Secretaría General. Caracas. (AHM/B)
Boletín del Archivo Nacional de Historia. Casa de la Cultura Ecuatoriana. Quito. (EANH/B)
Boletín del Departamento de Investigación de las Tradiciones Populares. México.
Boletín del Instituto Nacional de Antropología e Historia. Secretaría de Educación Pública. México. (INAH/B)
Boletín del Instituto Riva-Agüero. Pontificia Univ. Católica del Perú. Lima. (IRA/B)
Boletín Histórico. Fundación John Boulton. Caracas. (FJB/BH)
Boletín Histórico del Estado Mayor General del Ejército. Sección Historia y Archivo. Montevideo. (EMGE/BH)
Boletín Informativo del Archivo Nacional de Panamá. Ministerio de Gobierno y Justicia. Archivo Nacional de Panamá. Panamá.
Boletín Nicaragüense de Bibliografía y Documentación. Banco Central de Nicaragua, Biblioteca. Managua. (BNBD)
Boletín UNESCO. Comisión Nacional Cubana de la UNESCO. La Habana.
Books Abroad. An international literary quarterly. Univ. of Oklahoma Press. Norman. [For issues published after 1977 see new title, *World Literature Today*] (UO/BA)
Buenos Aires Musical. B.A. (BAM)
Bulletin. African Studies Association of the West Indies. Kingston. (ASAWI/B)
Bulletin de la Société d'Histoire de la Guadeloupe. Archives Départementales *avec le concours du* Conseil Général de la Guadeloupe. Basse-Terre, W.I. (SHG/B)
Bulletin de l'Institut Français d'Études Andines. Lima. (IFEA/B)
Bulletin Hispanique. Univ. de Bordeaux *avec le concours du* Centre National de la Recherche Scientifique. Bordeaux, France. (UB/BH)
Bulletin of Eastern Caribbean Affairs. Univ. of the West Indies, Institute of Social & Economic Research (Eastern Caribbean). Cave Hill, Barbados.
Bulletin of Hispanic Studies. Liverpool, U.K.
Business History Review. Harvard Univ., Graduate School of Business Administration. Boston, Mass. (HLL/BHR)

Cadernos de Teatro. Sociedade Brasileira de Autores Teatrais. Rio.
Cahiers des Amériques Latines, Paris. (CDAL)
Cahiers du Cinéma. Paris.
El Caimán Barbudo. La Habana.
The California Geographer. Annual publication of the California Council of Geography Teachers. Long Beach. (CCGT/CG)
Caravelle. Cahiers du monde hispanique et luso-brésilien. Univ. de Toulouse, Institute d'Études Hispaniques, Hispano Americaines et Luso-Bresíliennes. Toulouse, France. (UTIEH/C)
Caribbean Quarterly. Univ. of the West Indies. Mona, Jam. (UWI/CQ)
Caribbean Studies. Univ. of Puerto Rico, Institute of Caribbean Studies. Río Piedras. (UPR/CS)
Caribe. Univ. of Hawaii at Manoa, Dept. of European Languages and Literature. Honolulu.
Casa de las Américas. Instituto Cubano del Libro. La Habana. (CDLA)
Centromidca. Centro Taller Regional de Restauración y Microfilmación de Documentos para el Caribe y Centroamérica. Santo Domingo.
Chungara. Univ. del Norte, Depto. de Antropología. Arica, Chile.
Ciencia. Univ. Autónoma de Santo Domingo. Santo Domingo.
Ciência e Cultura. Sociedade Brasileira para o Progresso da Ciência. São Paulo. (SBPC/CC)
Ciencias Administrativas. Univ. Nacional de La Plata, Facultad de Ciencias Económicas, Instituto de Investigaciones de Ciencias Administrativas. La Plata, Arg. (UNLP/CA)
Cine al Día. Caracas.
Cine Cubano. Instituto Cubano del Arte e Industria Cinematográfica. La Habana. (ICAIC/CC)
Cinematógrafo: Revista de Cultura Cinematográfica. Lima.
CLA Journal. Morgan State College for the College Language Association. Baltimore, Md. (CLA/J)
CLASE: Citas Latinoamericanas en Sociología y Economía. Univ. Nacional Autónoma de México, Centro de Información Científica y Humanística. México.
Colóquio. Revista de artes e letras. Fundação Calouste Gulbenkian. Lisboa. (COLOQ)
Comparative Literature Studies. Univ. of Maryland. College Park.
Comparative Studies in Society and History. An international quarterly. Society for the Comparative Study of Society and History. The Hague. (CSSH)
Comunicación y Cultura. La comunicación masiva en el proceso político latinoamericano. Editorial Galerna. B.A. y Santiago. (CYC)
Comunicaciones Proyecto Puebla-Tlaxcala. Fundación Alemana para la Investigación Científica. Puebla, Mex. (FAIC/CPPT)
Comunidad. Revista de la U.I.A. Cuadernos de difusión cultural. Univ. Iberoamericana. México. (UIA/C)
Conjonction. Institut Français d'Haïti. Port-au-Prince. (IFH/C)
Conjunto: Revista de teatro latinoamericano. Casa de las Américas for the Comité Permanente de Festivales. La Habana. (CDLA/CO)
Convivium. Revista de investigação e cultura. São Paulo.
Correo de la Semana. B.A.
Crítica. Revista hispanoamericana de filosofía. Univ. Nacional Autónoma de México, Instituto de Investigaciones Filosóficas. México. (UNAM/C)
Croissance des Jeunes Nations. Paris. (CJN)
Cuadernos Afro-Americanos. Univ. Central de Venezuela, Consejo de Desarrollo Científico y Humanístico, Facultad de Humanidades y Educación, Instituto de Antropología e Historia. Caracas. (UCV/CA)
Cuadernos Americanos. México. (CAM)
Cuadernos de Filosofía. Univ. de Buenos Aires, Facultad de Filosofía y Letras. B.A. (UBAFFL/C)
Cuadernos de Filosofía. Univ. de Concepción, Instituto Central de Filosofía. Concepción, Chile.
Cuadernos de Historia y Arqueología. Casa de la Cultura Ecuatoriana, Núcleo del Guayas. Guayaquil, Ecua. (CCE/CHA)
Cuadernos del Seminario de Historia.

Pontificia Univ. Católica del Perú, Instituto Riva-Agüero. Lima. (PUCP/CSH)
Cuadernos Hispanoamericanos. Instituto de Cultura Hispánica, Madrid. (CH)
Cuadernos Prehispánicos. Univ. de Valladolid, Seminario Americanista. Valladolid, Spain.
Cuba Review. Cuba Resource Center. N.Y.
Cuban Studies/Estudios Cubanos. Univ. de Pittsburgh, Univ. Center for International Studies, Center for Latin American Studies. Pittsburgh, Pa. (UP/CSEC)
Cultura. Ministério da Educação e Cultura, Diretoria de Documentação e Divulgação. Brasília. (MEC/C)
Cultura Chilena. Univ. de Chile, Facultad de Ciencias Humanas, Depto. de Ciencias Antropológicas y Arqueológicas. Santiago.
Current Anthropology. Univ. of Chicago. Chicago, Ill. (UC/CA)
Current History. A monthly magazine of world affairs. Philadelphia, Pa. (CUH)

Dados. Publicação semestral do Instituto Universitário de Pesquisas do Rio de Janeiro. Rio. (IUP/D)
Desarrollo Económico. Instituto de Desarrollo Económico y Social. B.A. (IDES/DE)
Diálogos. El Colegio de México. México.
Diálogos. Univ. de Puerto Rico. Río Piedras. (UPR/D)
Diánoia. Univ. Autónoma de México, Centro de Estudios Filosóficos. México. (UNAM/D)
Diario Las Américas. Miami, Fla.
Dispositio. Univ. of Michigan, Dept. of Romance Languages. Ann Arbor.

Economía. Revista del Instituto de Investigaciones Económicas y Sociales. Univ. de San Carlos de Guatemala, Facultad de Ciencias Económicas. Guatemala. (USCG/E)
Ecran. Paris.
Educación. Ministerio de Educación. Caracas.
Encuentro. Revista de la Univ. Centroamericana. Managua.
Erdkunde. Archiv für Wissenschaftliche Geographie. Univ. Bonn, Geographisches Institut. Bonn, FRG. (UBGI/E)
Escena. Revista nacional de teatro y del espectáculo. Consejo Nacional de la Cultura, Dirección de Artes Escénicas. Caracas.
Escrita. Revista mensual de literatura. Vertente Editora. São Paulo.
Escritos. Univ. Pontificia Bolivariana, Facultad de Filosofía y Letras. Medellín, Colombia.
Espiral. Revista mensual de artes y letras. Editorial Iqueima. Bogotá. (ESP)
Estrategia. Instituto Argentino de Estudios Estratégicos y de las Relaciones Internacionales. B.A. (IAEERI/E)
Estudios Andinos. Univ. of Pittsburgh, Latin American Studies Center. Pittsburgh, Pa. (UP/EA)
Estudios de Arqueología. Salta, Arg.
Estudios de Filosofía y Religiones del Oriente. Univ. de Buenos Aires, Facultad de Filosofía y Letras, Centro de Estudios de Filosofía Oriental. B.A.
Estudios Filosóficos. Sociedad Venezolana de Filosofía. Caracas.
Estudios Latinoamericanos. Polaka Akademia Nauk (Academia de Ciencias de Polonia). Instytut Historii (Instituto de Historia). Warszawa. (PAN/ES)
Estudios Paraguayos. Univ. Católica Nuestra Señora de la Asunción. Asunción. (UCNSA/EP)
Estudios Sociales Centroamericanos. Consejo Superior de Universidades Centroamericanas, Confederación Universitaria Centroamericana, Programa Centroamericano de Ciencias Sociales. San José. (CSUCA/ESC)
Estudos Históricos. Facultad de Filosofía, Ciências e Letras, Depto. de História. Marília, Brazil. (FFCLM/EH)
Ethnology. Univ. of Pittsburgh. Pittsburgh, Pa. (UP/E)
Ethnomusicology. Society for Ethnomusicology. Middleton, Conn.
Ethos. Revista de filosofía práctica. Instituto de Filosofía Práctica. B.A. (IFP/E)
Etudes d'Histoire et de Littérature Ibéro-Américaines. Univ. de Rouen,

Centre de Recherches Ibéro-Américaines. Rouen, France. (UR/EHLIA)
Etudes Hispano-Américaines. Univ. de Haute Bretagne, Centre d'Etudes Hispaniques, Hispano-Américaines et Luso-Brésiliennes. Rennes, France. (UHB/EHA)
Europe. Revue mensuelle. Paris. (EUR)
Exilio. N.Y. (EX)
Explicación de Textos Literarios. California State Univ. Sacramento.

Ficta. B.A.
Film Comment. N.Y.
Film Quarterly. Univ. of California Press. Berkeley.
Filosofía y Letras. Univ. Nacional Autónoma de México, Facultad de Filosofía y Letras. México. (UNAM/FL)
The Florida Historical Quarterly. The Florida Historical Society. Jacksonville. (FHS/FHQ)
Folklore Americano. Instituto Panamericano de Geografía e Historia, Comisión de Historia, Comité de Folklore. México. (IPGH/FA)
Foreign Affairs. Council on Foreign Relations. N.Y. (CFR/FA)
Formato 16. Panamá.
Foro Internacional. El Colegio de México. (CM/FI)
Franciscanum. Revista de las ciencias del espíritu. Univ. de San Buenaventura. Bogotá. (USB/F)
French Historical Studies. Society for French Historical Studies. Columbus, Ohio.

Gaceta. Bogotá.
Graphis. Zürich, Switzerland.

Hablemos de Cine. Lima.
Harper's Magazine. N.Y. (HM)
Hermeneia. Univ. del Zulia, Escuela de Filosofía, Maracaibo, Ven. [and] Univ. Central de Venezuela, Escuela de Filosofía. Caracas. (UZ/H)
Heterofonía. Revista musical bimestral. México. (HET)
Hispamérica. Revista de literatura. Takoma Park, Md. (HISPA)
Hispania. Univ. of Cincinnati *for the* American Association of Teachers of Spanish and Portuguese. Cincinnati, Ohio. (AATSP/H)
Hispanic American Historical Review. Duke Univ. Press *for the* Conference on Latin American History of the American Historical Association. Durham, N.C. (HAHR)
Hispanic Review. A quarterly devoted to research in the Hispanic languages and literatures. Univ. of Pennsylvania, Dept. of Romance Languages. Philadelphia. (HR)
Hispanófila. Univ. of North Carolina. Chapel Hill. (HISP)
Historia. Univ. Católica de Chile, Instituto de Historia. Santiago. (UCCIH/H)
Historia. Univ. Nacional de San Agustín, Depto. Académico de Historia, Geografía y Antropología. Arequipa, Peru. (UNSA/H)
Historia Marítima del Ecuador, Documentación y Estudios. Marina del Ecuador, Depto. de Historia. Quito.
Historia Mexicana. El Colegio de México. México. (CM/HM)
Historia y Cultura. Museo Nacional de Historia. Lima. (PMNH/HC)
The Historian. A journal of history. Phi Alpha Theta, National Honor Society in History. Univ. of Pennsylvania. University Park, Pa. (PAT/TH)
Histórica. Pontificia Univ. Católica del Perú. Depto. de Humanidades. Lima. (PUCP/H)
Histórica. Univ. Autónoma del Estado de México, Instituto de Investigaciones Históricas. México. (UAEM/H)
Historiografía y Bibliografía Americanista. Escuela de Estudios Hispano-Americanos de Sevilla. Sevilla. (EEHA/HBA)
History of Religions. International journal for comparative historical studies. Univ. of Chicago. Chicago, Ill. (UC/HR)
Hombre y Cultura. Revista del Centro de Investigaciones Antropológicas de la Univ. Nacional. Panamá. (UNCIA/HC)
Human Biology. Official publication of the Human Biology Council. Wayne State Univ., School of Medicine. De-

troit, Mich. (WSU/HB)
Humanitas. Univ. de Nuevo León, Centro de Estudios Humanísticos. Monterrey, Mex. (UNL/H)
Humanitas. Univ. Nacional de Tucumán, Facultad de Filosofía y Letras. Tucumán, Arg. (UNT/H)

Ibero-Americana. Research news and principal acquisitions of documentation on Latin America in Denmark, Finland, Norway and Sweden. Latinamerika Instituet. Stockholm. (LI/IA)
Ibero-Americana Pragensia. Univ. Carolina de Praga, Centro de Estudios Ibero-Americanos. Praha. (UCP/IAP)
Ibero-Amerikanisches Archiv. Ibero-Amerikanisches Institut. Berlin, FRG. (IAA)
Ideas y Valores. Univ. Nacional, Instituto de Filosofía y Letras. Bogotá. (UN/IV)
Illimani. La Paz.
L'Information d'Histoire de l'Art. J.B. Bailliere et fils. Paris. (INHA)
Insula. Madrid. (INSULA)
Inter-American Economic Affairs. Washington. (IAMEA)
Inter-American Music Bulletin. Organization of American States. Washington. (OAS/IMB)
Inti. Univ. of Connecticut. Storrs.
Investigaciones y Ensayos. Academia Nacional de la Historia. B.A. (ANH/IE)
Islas. Univ. Central de las Villas. Santa Clara, Cuba. (UCLV/I)
ISSO. Pré Estréia. Aconselhável para maiores de 16 anos. Porto Alegre, Brazil.
Istmo. Revista del pensamiento actual. México. (ESTMO)
Isto É. São Paulo.

Jahrbuch für Geschichte von Staat, Wirtschaft und Gesselschaft Lateinamerikas. Köln, FRG. (JGSWGL)
Journal de la Société des Américanistes. Paris. (SA/J)
Journal of Anthropological Research. Univ. of New Mexico, Depto. de Anthropology. Albuquerque, N. Mex. (UNM/JAR)
Journal of Arizona History. Arizona Historical Society. Tucson.
Journal of Belizean Affairs. Belize City. (JBA)
A Journal of Church and State. Baylor Univ., J.M. Dawson Studies in Church and State. Waco, Tex. (BU/JCS)
The Journal of Developing Areas. Western Illinois Univ. Press. Macomb, Ill. (JDA)
Journal of Economic History. New York Univ., Graduate School of Business Administration *for* The Economic History Association. Rensselaer, N.Y. (EHA/J)
The Journal of European Economic History. Roma.
Journal of Inter-American Studies and World Affairs. Univ. of Miami Press *for the* Center for Advanced International Studies. Coral Gables, Fla. (UM/JIAS)
The Journal of Interdisciplinary History. The MIT Press. Cambridge, Mass. (JIH)
Journal of International Affairs. Columbia Univ., School of International Affairs. N.Y. (CU/JIA)
Journal of Latin American Lore. Univ. of California, Latin American Center. Los Angeles. (UCLA/JLAL)
Journal of Latin American Studies. Centers or institutes of Latin American studies at the universities of Cambridge, Glasgow, Liverpool, London and Oxford. Cambridge Univ. Press. London. (JLAS)
The Journal of Politics. The Southern Political Science Association *in cooperation with the* Univ. of Florida. Gainesville, Fla. (SPSA/JP)
The Journal of San Diego History. The San Diego Historical Society. San Diego, Calif. (SDHS/J)
The Journal of the Barbados Museum and Historical Society. Bridgetown, W.I. (BMHS/J)
Journal of the West. Los Angeles, Calif. (JW)
Jump/Cut: A Review of Contemporary Cinema. Chicago, Ill.

Kaie. National History and Arts Council of Guyana. Georgetown. (NHAC/K)
Kentucky Romance Quarterly. Univ. of

Kentucky. Lexington. (UK/KRQ)
The Kiva. Arizona Archaeological and Historical Society. Tucson. (AAHS/K)
Kriterion. Univ. of Minas Gerais, Faculdade de Filosofia. Belo Horizonte, Brazil. (UMGFF/K)

Labor History. Tamiment Institute. N.Y.
Latin American Index. Latin American Research Group. Washington.
Latin American Literary Review. Carnegie-Mellon Univ., Dept. of Modern Languages. Pittsburgh, Pa. (LALR)
Latin American Perspectives. Univ. of California. Riverside. (LAP)
Latin American Research Review. Univ. of North Carolina Press *for the* Latin American Studies Association. Chapel Hill. (LARR)
Latin American Theatre Review. A journal devoted to the theatre and drama of Spanish and Portuguese America. Univ. of Kansas, Center for Latin American Studies. Lawrence. (UK/LATR)
Latin American Yearly Review. American College in Paris. Paris.
Latinoamérica. Anuario de estudios latinoamericanos. Univ. Nacional Autónoma de México, Facultad de Filosofía y Letras, Centro de Estudios Latinoamericanos. México. (UNAM/L)
Lingua. North-Holland Publishing Co. Amsterdam. (LINGUA)
Língua e Literatura. Univ. de São Paulo, Depto. de Letras, Faculdade de Filosofia, Letras e Ciências Humanas. São Paulo. (USP/LL)
Linguistics. An international review. Mouton. The Hague. (LING)
Logos. Univ. del Valle, Depto. de Humanidades. Cali, Colombia. (UV/L)
Lotería. Lotería Nacional de Beneficencia. Panamá. (LNB/L)
Luso-Brazilian Review. Univ. of Wisconsin Press. Madison, Wis. (UW/LBR)

Military History of Texas and the Southwest. Military History Press. Austin.

Missionalia Hispanica. Instituto Santo Toribio de Mogrovejo [and] Consejo Superior de Investigaciones Científicas. Madrid. (ISTM/MH)
Modern Drama. Lawrence, Kans.
Modern Language Journal. Univ. of Pittsburgh *for the* National Federation of Modern Language Teachers Association. Pittsburgh, Pa. (MLTA/MLJ)
Modern Language Notes. The Johns Hopkins Univ. Press. Baltimore, Md. (MLN)
Módulo. Revista de arquitetura, urbanismo e artes. Avenir Editora. Rio.
Montalbán. Univ. Católica Andrés Bello, Facultad de Humanidades y Educación, Institutos Humaníticos de Investigación. Caracas. (UCAB/M)
Monthly Review. An independent Socialist magazine. N.Y. (MR)
Mundo Hispánico. Madrid. (MH)
Música. La Habana.
Kie Musik in Geschichte und Gegenwart. Kassel, Wilhelmshöhe, FRG. (MGG)

El Nacional. Caracas.
Nebraska History. Nebraska State Historical Society. Lincoln.
New Mexico Historical Review. Published jointly by the Historical Society of New Mexico [and] the Univ. of New Mexico. Albuquerque. (UNM/NMHR)
The New Scholar. Univ. of California, Center for Iberian and Latin American Studies, Institute of Chicano Urban Affairs [and] John Muir College. San Diego. (UCSD/NS)
The New Yorker. N.Y.
Nimrod. Latin American voices. Univ. of Oklahoma. Tulsa.
Nivel. Gaceta de cultura. México.
Norte. Revista hispano-americana. Frente de Afirmación Hispanista. México. (FAH/N)
Norte Grande. Revista de estudios integrados referentes a comunidades humanas del Norte Grande de Chile, en una perspectiva geográfica e histórico-cultural. Univ. Católica de Chile, Instituto de Geografía, Depto. de Geografía de Chile, Taller Norte Grande. Santiago. (UCC/NG)

Notes et Études Documentaires. Direction de la Documentation. Paris. (FDD/NED)
Notes of the Music Library Association. Washington.
Nuestra Historia. Centro de Estudios de Historia Argentina. B.A. (CEHA/NH)
Nueva Antropología. México.
Nueva Narrativa Hispánica. Madrid.
Nueva Revista de Filología Hispánica. El Colegio de México [and] The Univ. of Texas. México. (CM/NRFH)
Nuevo Día del Perú. Semanario. Trujillo, Peru.
Nuevo Mundo. Biblioteca Fray Mamerto Esquiú. San Antonio de Padua, Arg.
Numen. International review for the history of religions. International Association for the History of Religions. Leiden, The Netherlands. (IAHR/N)
Nuova Rivista Musicale Italiana. Torino, Italy.
Nuovi Quaderni Italiani. Istituto Italiano di Cultura. B.A.

Octubre. México.
L'Oeil. Revue d'art mensuelle. Novelle Sedo. Lausanne, Switzerland. (OEIL)
Ojo al Cine. Cali, Colombia.
La Opinión. B.A.
Orbis. Bulletin international de documentation linguistique. Centre International de Dialectologie Générale. Louvain, Belgium. (CIDG/O)
Orbis. A journal of world affairs. Foreign Policy Research Institute, Philadelphia, Pa. *in association with* Tufts. Univ., Fletcher School of Law and Diplomacy, Medford, Mass. (FPRI/O)
Otrocine. México.

Pacific Historian. Univ. of the Pacific. Stockton, Calif. (UP/PH)
The Pacific Historical Review. Univ. of California Press. Los Angeles. (UC/PHR)
La Palabra y el Hombre. México.
El Palacio. School of American Research; Museum of New Mexico; [and] Archaeological Society of New Mexico. Santa Fe, N. Mex. (SAR/P)
Papel Periódico Ilustrado. Bogotá.
Past and Present. London. (PP)

Peasant Studies Newsletter. Univ. of Pittsburgh, Center for International Studies [and] Dept. of History. Pittsburgh, Pa. (UP/PSN)
Pensamiento Político. Cultura y ciencia política. México. (PPO)
Plural. México.
Politeia. Univ. Central de Venezuela, Facultad de Derecho, Instituto de Estudios Políticos. Caracas. (UCV/P)
Política y Sociedad. Univ. de San Carlos de Guatemala, Facultad de Ciencias Jurídicas y Sociales, Escuela de Ciencia Política, Instituto de Investigaciones Políticas y Sociales. Guatemala. (USCG/PS)
Primer Acto. Madrid.
Proceedings of the American Philosophical Society. Philadelphia, Pa. (APS/P)
Proceedings of the Pacific Coast Council on Latin American Studies. Univ. of California. Los Angeles. (PCCLAS/P)
Punto. Caracas.

Quaderni di Letteratura Americane. Cattedra di Letteratura Ispano-Americana. Venezia, Italy.
Quitumbe. Pontificia Univ. Católica del Ecuador, Facultad de Pedagogía, Depto. de Historia. Quito.

Razón y Fabula. Univ. de los Andes. Bogotá. (UA/RF)
Reflexión. Carleton Univ. Ottawa, Canada.
Repertorio Boyacense. Tunja, Colombia.
Review 72, 73, etc. Center for Inter-American Relations. N.Y. (REVIEW)
Revista Biblioteca Nacional. Ministerio de Educación y Cultura. Montevideo.
Revista Brasileira de Filosofia. Instituto Brasileiro de Filosofia. São Paulo. (IBF/RBF)
Revista Brasileira de Folclore. Ministério da Educação e Cultura, Campanha de Defesa do Folclore Brasileiro. Rio. (CDFB/RBF)
Revista Brasileira de Geografia. Conselho Nacional de Geografia, Instituto Brasileiro de Geografia e Estatística. Rio. (EBGE/R)
Revista Brasileira de Lingüística. Sociedade Brasileira para Professores de Lingüística. São Paulo. (SBPL/RBL)

Revista Canadiense de Estudios Hispánicos. Univ. of Toronto. Toronto.
Revista Chilena de Historia y Geografía. Sociedad Chilena de Historia y Geografía. Santiago. (SCHG/R)
Revista Chilena de Literatura. Univ. de Chile, Depto. de Español. Santiago.
Revista da Academia Paulista de Letras. São Paulo. (APL/R)
Revista de Antropofagia. Editora Abril [and] Metal Leve. São Paulo.
Revista de Bellas Artes. México.
Revista de Biblioteconomia de Brasília. Associação dos Bibliotecários do Distrito Federal [and] Univ. de Brasília, Faculdade de Estudos Sociais Aplicados, Depto. de Biblioteconomia. Brasília.
Revista de Ciencias Sociales. Univ. de Costa Rica. San José. (UCR/RCS)
Revista de Costa Rica. Ministerio de Cultura, Juventud y Deportes. San José. (RCR)
Revista de Crítica Literaria Latinoamericana. Latinoamericana Editores. Lima. (RCLL)
Revista de Estudios Hispánicos. Univ. de Alabama, Dept. of Romance Languages, Office of International Studies and Programs. University. (UA/REH)
Revista de Historia. Univ. de Concepción, Instituto de Antropología, Instituto de Antropología, Historia y Geografía. Concepción, Chile.
Revista de História. Univ. de São Paulo, Faculdade de Filosofia, Ciências e Letras, Depto. de História [and] Sociedade de Estudos Históricos. São Paulo. (USP/RH)
Revista de Historia. Univ. Nacional de Costa Rica, Escuela de Historia. Heredia, C.R. (UNCR/R)
Revista de Historia de América. Instituto Panamericano de Geografía e Historia, Comisión de Historia. México. (PAIGH/H)
Revista de Historia Militar. Servicio Histórico Militar. Madrid. (SHM/RHM)
Revista de Humanidades. Univ. Nacional de Córdoba, Facultad de Filosofía. Córdoba, Arg. (UNC/RH)
Revista de Indias. Instituto Gonzalo Fernández de Oviedo [and] Consejo Superior de Investigaciones Científicas. Madrid. (IGFO/RI)
Revista de la Academia Hondureña de Geografía e Historia. Tegucigalpa. (AHGH/R)
Revista de la Biblioteca Nacional. Ministerio de Instrucción Pública y Previsión Social. Montevideo. (UBN/R)
Revista de la Biblioteca Nacional José Martí. La Habana. (BNJM/R)
Revista de la Facultad de Derecho de México. Univ. Nacional Autónoma de México. México.
Revista de la Facultad de Filosofía y Letras. Univ. de Morón. Morón, Arg.
Revista de la Filosofía de la Universidad de Costa Rica. San José. (UCR/RF)
Revista de la Junta de Estudios Históricos de Mendoza. Mendoza, Arg. (JEHM/R)
Revista de la Universidad Católica. Lima.
Revista de la Universidad de Costa Rica. San José. (UCR/R)
Revista de la Universidad de México. Univ. Nacional Autónoma de México. México. (UNAM/RUM)
Revista de la Universidad de Yucatán. Mérida, Mex. (UY/R)
Revista de Letras. Univ. de Puerto Rico en Mayagüez, Facultad de Artes y Ciencias. Mayagüez. (UPRM/RL)
Revista de Literaturas Hispánicas. Univ. Nacional de Rosario, Facultad de Filosofía, Instituto de Investigaciones Literarias. Rosario, Arg.
Revista de Teatro. Sociedade Brasileira de Autores Teatrais (SBAT). Rio.
Revista del Archivo General de la Nación. B.A.
Revista del Archivo General de la Nación. Instituto Nacional de Cultura. Lima. (PEAGN/R)
Revista del Archivo Histórico del Guayas. Guayaquil, Ecua. (AHG/R)
Revista del Archivo Nacional. Instituto Colombiano de Cultura, Subdirección de Patrimonio Cultural, División de Archivo Nacional. Bogotá.
Revista del Archivo Nacional. San José. (CRAN/R)
Revista del Instituto de Cultura Puertorriqueña. San Juan. (ICP/R)
Revista del Instituto Peruano de Investigaciones Genealógicas. Lima.

Revista del Museo Nacional. Casa de la Cultura del Perú, Museo Nacional de la Cultura Peruana. Lima. (PEMN/R)

Revista del Pensamiento Centroamericano. Centro de Investigaciones y Actividades Culturales. Managua. (RCPC)

Revista do Instituto de Estudos Brasileiros, Univ. de São Paulo, Instituto de Estudos Brasileiros. São Paulo. (USP/RIEB)

Revista do Instituto do Ceará. Fortaleza, Brazil. (EC/R)

Revista do Instituto Histórico e Geográfico. Instituto Histórico e Geográfico, Guarujá/Bertiago. São Paulo. (IHGSP/R)

Revista do Instituto Histórico e Geográfico Brasileiro. Rio. (IHGB/R)

Revista do Museu Paulista. São Paulo. (MP/R)

Revista Dominicana de Antropología e Historia. Univ. Autónoma de Santo Domingo, Facultad de Humanidades, Depto. de Historia y Antropología, Instituto de Investigaciones Antropológicas, Santo Domingo. (UASD/R)

Revista Eme-Eme. Estudios dominicanos. Univ. Católica Madre y Maestra. Santiago de los Caballeros, R.D. (EME)

Revista Geográfica. Instituto Panamericano de Geografía e História, Comissão de Geografia. Rio. (PAIGH/G)

Revista Hispánica Moderna. Columbia Univ., Hispanic Institute in the United States. N.Y. (HIUS/R)

Revista Histórica. Museo Histórico Nacional. Montevideo. (UMHN/RH)

Revista Histórico-Crítica de Literatura Centroamericana. Univ. de Costa Rica [and] Ministerio de Cultura, Juventud y Deporte. San José. (UCR/RHCLC)

Revista Iberoamericana. Univ. of Pittsburgh *for the* Instituto Internacional de Literatura Iberoamericana. Pittsburgh, Pa. (IILI/RI)

Revista Interamericana de Bibliografía (Inter-American Review of Bibliography). Organization of American States. Washington. (RIB)

Revista Latinoamericana de Filosofía. Centro de Investigaciones Filosóficas. B.A. (CIF/RLF)

Revista Letras. Univ. Federal do Paraná, Setor de Ciências Humanas, Letras e Artes. Curitiba, Brazil. (UFP/RL)

Revista Mexicana de Ciencias Políticas y Sociales. Univ. Nacional Autónoma de México, Facultad de Ciencias Políticas y Sociales. México. (UNAM/RMCPS)

Revista Mexicana de Sociología. Univ. Nacional Autónoma de México, Instituto de Investigaciones Sociales. México. (UNAM/RMS)

Revista Musical Chilena. Univ. de Chile, Instituto de Extensión Musical. Santiago. (UCIEM/R)

Revista Nacional de Cultura. Consejo Nacional de Cultura. Caracas. (CONAC/RNC)

Revista Nacional de Cultura. Instituto Nacional de Cultura. Panamá. (INC/RNC)

Revista Paraguaya de Sociología. Centro Paraguayo de Estudios Sociológicos. Asunción. (CPES/RPS)

Revista Universidad de Medellín. Univ. de Medellín, Centro de Estudios de Posgrado. Medellín, Colombia. (UM/R)

Revista Venezolana de Filosofía. Univ. Simón Bolívar [and] Sociedad Venezolana de Filosofía. Caracas. (USB/RVF)

La Revue du Cinema: Image et Son. Paris.

Revue Française de l'Élite Européenne. Paris. (RFEE)

Revue Historique. Presses Universitaires de France. Paris. (PUF/RH)

Romance Philology. Univ. of California Press. Berkeley. (UCP/RP)

Romanistisches Jahrbuch. Univ. Hamburg, Romanisches Seminar, Ibero-Amerikanisches Forschungsinstitut, Hamburg, FRG. (UH/RJ)

Ruta. Publicación ácrata. Caracas.

Sapientia. Univ. Católica Argentina Santa María de los Buenos Aires, Facultad de Filosofía. B.A. (UCA/S)

Sarance. Instituto Otavaleño de Antropología. Otavalo, Ecua.

Science. American Association for the Advancement of Science. Washington. (AAAS/S)

Science and Society. N.Y. (SS)
Sight & Sound. London
Signos. Estudios de lengua y literatura. Univ. Católica de Valparaíso, Instituto de Literatura y Ciencia del Lenguaje. Valparaíso, Chile. (UCV/S)
Signs. Chicago, Ill.
Social and Economic Studies. Univ. of the West Indies, Institute of Social and Economic Research. Mona, Jam. (UWI/SES)
Social Sciences. USSR Academy of Sciences, Section of the Social Sciences. Moscow. (USSR/SS)
Socialist Review. Oakland, Calif.
Sociologie du Travail. Association pour le Développement de la Sociologie du Travail. Paris. (ADST/SDT)
Soundings. Univ. of California. Santa Barbara.
South Atlantic Urban Studies. College of Charleston, Urban Studies Center [and] Univ. of South Carolina Press. Charleston.
Southwestern Historical Quarterly. Texas State Historical Association. Austin. (TSHA/SHQ)
Stereo Review. Chicago, Ill.
Stromata. Univ. del Salvador, Facultades de Filosofía y Teología. San Miguel, Arg.
Studies in Linguistics. Southern Methodist Univ., Dept. of Anthropology. Dallas, Tex. (SIL)

Tempo Brasileiro. Revista de cultura. Rio. (TEMBRAS)
The Texas Quarterly. Austin.
Texas Studies in Literature and Language. Univ. of Texas Press. Austin.
Theater Research International. Glasgow, U.K.
Thesaurus. Instituto Caro y Cuervo. Bogotá. (ICC/T)
El Tiempo. Bogotá.
La Torre. Univ. de Puerto Rico. Río Piedras. (UPR/LT)
Tramoya. Univ. Veracruzana. Xalapa, Mex.
Trimestre Político. Publicación trimestral del Fondo de Cultura Económica. México. (FCE/TP)

UN. Univ. Nacional de Colombia, Dirección de Divulgación Cultura. Bogotá.
UNESCO Bulletin for Libraries. United Nations Educational, Scientific and Cultural Organization. Paris. (UNESCO/BL)
Unión. Unión de Escritores y Artistas de Cuba (UNEAC). La Habana. (UNION)
Universidad. Univ. de Antioquia. Medellín, Colombia. (UA/U)
Universidad. Univ. Nacional del Litoral. Santa Fe, Arg. (UNL/U)
Universitas Humanistica. Pontificia Univ. Javeriana, Facultad de Filosofía y Letras. Bogotá. (PUJ/UH)
L'Universo. Rivista bimestrale dell'Instituto Geografico Militare. Firenze, Italy. (IGM/U)
Utah Historical Quarterly. Utah State Historical Society. Salt Lake City.

Veja. São Paulo.
Verbum. Univ. Católica. Rio. (UC/V)
Veritas. Pontificia Univ. Católica do Rio Grande do Sul. Porto Alegre, Brazil. (PUC/V)
Via. Univ. of California, Office of Student Activities. Berkeley. (VIA)
Visión Boliviana. La Paz.
Vozes. Revista de cultura. Editora Vozes. Petrópolis, Brazil. (VOZES)
Vuelta. México.

Western Folklore. Univ. of California Press *for the* California Folklore Society. Berkeley. (CFS/WF)
The Western Historical Quarterly. Western History Assn., Utah State Univ. Logan. (WHQ)
Wissenschaftliche Zeitschrift der Humboldt Univ. Gesellschafts- und Sprachwissenschaft- liche Reihe. Berlin, FRG. (WZHUB)
World Archaeology. London.
World Development. Pergamon Press. Oxford, U.K. (WD)
World Literature Today. Univ. of Oklahoma Press. Norman. [For issues published prior to 1977 see *Books Abroad*]. (WLT)

Yearbook for Inter-American Musical Research/Anuario Interamericano de Investigación Musical. Univ. of Texas, Institute of Latin American

Studies [and] College of Fine Arts, Dept. of Music. Austin. (UT/YIMR)

Zeitschrift für Ethnologie. Deutschen Gesellschaft für Völkerkunde. Braunschweig, FRG. (DGV/ZE)

Zeitschrift für Lateinamerika Wien. Osterreichisches Lateinamerika-Institut. Wien. (OLI/ZLW)

Zeitschrift für Missionswissenschaft und Religionswissenschaft. Lucerne, Switzerland. (ZMR)

SUBJECT INDEX

Bibliography and General Works (1-134)
Art (251-536)
Film (951-1048)
History (1951-4190)
Language (6001-6137)
Literature (6401-7945)
Music (9001-9148)
Philosophy (9401-9735)

Abela, Eduardo, 339.
ABOLITION. See also Slavery and
  Slave Trade. *Brazil*, 2141, 4082-4129,
  4139, 4147. *British West Indies*, 3002.
  Cuba, 2998-2999. *Danish Antilles*,
  2982. *Dominican Republic*, 3004.
  Dutch Antilles, 2997. *Haiti*, 3000.
  Jamaica, 2983. *Latin America*, 2149.
  Puerto Rico, 2994-2996, 3003.
  Venezuela, 2990.
Abreu Gómez, Ermilo, 6548.
Abularach, Rodolfo, 333.
Acevedo, Lerena, 7176.
Africa and Latin American Relations,
  3040.
Afro-American Studies, 2383.
Afro-Brazilians. See Blacks.
Afro-Cubans. See Blacks.
Afro-Panamanians. See Blacks.
AGRARIAN REFORM. See also
  Cooperatives; Land Tenure.
  Argentina. 3773, 3794. *Bibliography*,
  2126. *and the Catholic Church*, 2622.
  Chile, 3640. *Colombia*, 3135a-3136,
  3144. *Colonial Period*, 3135a-3136,
  3144. *Ecuador*, 3467. *Guatemala*,
  2926. *Latin America*, 2126, 2380.
  Mexico, 2622, 2682, 2704, 2714, 2717,
  2730, 2744, 2755, 2764, 2775, 2777,
  2779, 2785. *Panama*, 2793. *Peru*, 3212,
  3225, 3512, 3520, 3528, 3532, 3545,
  3547, 3550, 3565, 3568.

AGRICULTURE. See also Agrarian
  Reform; Cooperatives; Imports and
  Exports; Irrigation; Land Tenure;
  Labor; Plantations; Rural Settlement.
  Agronomy, 2322. *Andean Area*, 2046.
  Argentina, 3277, 3718, 3740, 3756,
  3773. *Bananas*, 2820, 2925.
  Bibliography, 30. *Brazil*, 2252, 2958,
  4024, 4126, 4131. *Cacao*, 2252, 3172,
  4024. *Camelids*, 2040. *Cattle Raising*,
  2527, 2744, 2970, 3265, 3270, 3533,
  3891, 3927, 4126. *Cereals* 3756. *Chile*,
  3245, 3257, 3642. *Coffee*, 2886, 2898,
  2916-2917, 3038, 3424, 4131. *Colombia*,
  3424. *Colonial*, 2256. *Corn*, 2419,
  2515. *Costa Rica*, 2799, 2806, 2868,
  2886, 2916-2917, 2925. *Cotton*, 2523,
  2853, 3509. *Cuba*, 2958, 2970,
  2985-2986, 3032, 3064. *Dominican
  Republic*, 2944, 2987, 3055-3056.
  Economics, 2419, 2500. *Ecuador*,
  3172, *El Salvador*, 2791, 2917. *French
  Guiana*, 2958. *Guatemala*, 2898, 2917.
  Haiti, 30. *Henequen*, 2594. *History*,
  2357, 2420, 3296-3297, 3299, 3301-3302.
  Honduras, 2820, 2925. *Latin America*,
  2386. *Mexico*, 2420, 2478, 2491, 2500,
  2502, 2523, 2603, 2630, 2744.
  Nicaragua, 2853. *Panama*, 2925.
  Paraguay, 3891. *Peru*, 3231, 3482,
  3489, 3497, 3502, 3509, 3531, 3533,
  3540-3542. *Portuguese Dictionary*,

6114. *Precolumbian*, 2112. *Puerto Rico*, 8, 3046. *Sheep*, 3489. *Sugar*, 2256, 2478, 2958, 2985-2987, 3032, 3055-3056, 3064, 3482, 3497, 3531. *Tobacco*, 2806, 2812, 2944. *Uruguay*, 3927, 3940. *Venezuela*, 3099, 3101, 3350. *Wheat*, 3231.
Agustín, José, 6619.
Alamán, Lucas, 2592.
Alberdi, Juan Bautista, 3813, 3824, 3887.
Alberini, Cariolano, 9446, 9456.
Alcohol and Alcoholism. *Colonial Period*, 3147a.
Alegría, Ciro, 6526, 6837, 6844, 6846.
Alfaro, Eloy, 3475.
Allende, Salvador, 3612, 7310, 7554, 7837.
Alliance for Progress. See US and Latin American Relations.
Almazán, Juan Andreu, 2788.
Almeida, José Américo de, 7765.
Alvarado, Pedro de, 1979.
Alvarado, Salvador, 2761, 2775.
Alves, Castro, 7760.
Amado, Jorge, 7714.
Amaral, Amadeu, 7661, 7679.
AMAZONIA (region).
  History, 3170, 4011, 4024-4025.
  Literature.
    Prose Fiction, 7419, 7486.
    Poetry, 7600.
American Revolution. *Brazilian Revolution Contrasted*, 4044. *Caribbean Area*, 2362-2363, 2942. *French Participation*, 2570. *Impact on Latin American*, 2223, 3364. *Spanish Participation*, 2570, 2577.
ANDEAN AREA. See also specific countries.
  Art, 251.
  History, 2340, 3845.
    Ethnohistory, 2028, 2030-2031, 2036, 2039, 2045-2046, 2048-2049, 2056, 2067, 2069-2070, 2073, 2076, 2078-2079, 2081, 2083-2084, 2090-2094, 2096-2097, 2099-2101, 2103, 2108-2109, 2112, 2115, 2117-2124, 2262.
Andersen Alfredo, 456.
Andrade, Carlos Drummond, 7683, 7734, 7755.
Andrade, João Batista de, 996.
Andrade, Mário, 7683, 7733, 7767.
Andrade, Oswald de, 7672, 7683, 7735,
7767.
Andrade Rivera, Gustavo, 7852.
Angel, Félix, 367.
Anjos, Augusto de, 7743-7744, 7747.
ANTARCTICA (region).
  History, 3617.
Antequera, José de, 3300.
Anthropology. See also Archaeology; Ethnohistory; Linguistics. *Bolivia*, 965, 3589. *Brazil*, 77. *Film*, 965. *Latin America*, 9428. *Mexico*, 2599, 2730. Philosophical works, 9671-9686.
ANTIGUA.
  Music, 9066.
Antillano, Pablo, 393.
ANTILLES. See also Lesser or Greater Antilles.
  History, 3145.
    Ethnohistory, 3145.
Araujo, Guido, 996.
Araujo, Juan de, 9036.
Archaeology. See also Calendrics; Codices; Monuments; Precolumbian Cultures. *Andean Area*, 2036. *Archaeologists*, 2071. *Bolivia*, 3580, 3589, *Chile*, 2025. *Mexico*, 278. *Techniques*, 2087. *Theory*, 2036, 2085.
Architects. See also names of individual architects. *Bolivia*, 257. *Brazil*, 389, 431, 487, 489. *Chile*, 362. *Mexico*, 329. *Venezuela*, 399.
ARCHITECTURE. See also Architects; Urban Planning. *Bibliography*, 272, 306, 493. *Brazil*, 425, 428, 430-431, 439-440, 451, 470, 488, 493-503, 4110. *Catholic Church*, 261, 264-265, 277, 280, 286, 293, 297-299, 306, 428, 438, 490-491, 494. *Chile*, 268, 366. *Colombia*, 269, 274-275. *Cuba*, 340-341. *Dictionary*, 6078. *Dominican Republic*, 261-263. *Fortification*, 267. *Journals*, 498. *History*, 493. *Mexico*, 252, 277, 279-281, 284-290, 292, 329. *Panama*, 267. *Paraguay*, 293. *Peru*, 297-299, 301. *Precolumbian*, 1951. *Puerto Rico*, 117. *Trinidad*, 336. *Uruguay*, 302. *Venezuela*, 305-306, 399, 404. *16th Century*, 263-264, 286. *17th Centruy*, 299, 301, 495. *18th Century*, 268, 276, 488, 495. *19th Century*, 274, 451, 488.
ARCHIVES. See also Libraries and Library Services; Manuscripts. *Archivists*, 34. *Archives Nationales de*

Subject Index

Archives—Art / 623

Paris, 3523. *Archivo de Corona de Aragón (Spain)*, 62. *Archivo de la Confederación (Argentina)*, 63. *Archivo del Congreso de la Nación (Argentina)*, 63. *Archivo del Ministerio de Asuntos Exteriores (Spain)*, 62. *Archivo del Ministerio de Relaciones Exteriores (Argentina)*, 63. *Archivo General de la Nación (Argentina)*, 61-63. *Archivo General de la Nación (Peru)*, 3220, 3536. *Archivo General de Indias (Spain)*, 62, 87, 2293, 3244, 3292, 6405. *Archivo Histórico del Ministerio de Hacienda (Peru)*, 3536. *Archivo Histórico Nacional (Colombia)*, 3160. *Archivo Histórico Nacional (Spain)*, 62. *Argentina*, 3699, 3745, 3800. *Austria*, 2372. *Brazil*, 2179 4046. *Caribbean*, 64. *Central America*, 64. *Chile*, 3621. *Colombia*, 3085, 9093. *Dictionary of Archival Terms*, 45. *Diplomatic*, 62. *Ecuador*, 3189, 3468-3469. *Europe*, 2186. *France*, 2372, 4028. *Guide for Quito, Ecuador*, 3189. *Guyana*, 2148. *Instituto Nacional de Antropología e Historia (Mexico)*, 71. *Italy*, 2372. *Journals*, 3166. *Lesser Antilles*, 2148. *Mexico*, 2430, 2442, 2765. *Music*, 9093. *National Archives (US)*, 74, 2240. *Paraguay*, 113. *Patiño Co. (Bolivia)*, 3595. *Peru*, 3513. *Peruvian Ministry of Foreign Relations*, 3593. *Portugal*, 4032. *Researchers*, 2237. *Spain*, 62, 2237, 2362, 2372, 2379, 6405. *Surinam*, 2148. *United Kingdom*, 3549. *Univ. of London*, 3549. *Uruguay*, 3414. *US*, 2240. *USSR*, 3988. *Venezuela*, 35, 3446.
Area Handbook for, *Colombia*, 119. *Trinidad and Tobago*, 118.
ARGENTINA. See also Antarctica; Patagonia; possessions.
Bibliography and General Works, 12, 41, 57, 128.
Art, 255-256, 344-361, 3737.
Film, 952-953, 960-961, 968-973.
History, 2128, 2145-2146, 2150, 2156, 2248, 2306, 2343, 2359, 2386, 2393, 3070, 3258, 3268, 3273, 3277, 3280, 3283, 3285-3286, 3309, 3617, 3674-3888, 3937.
Ethnohistory, 2037, 2068.
Language, 6034-6035, 6045, 6059, 6067, 6084, 6116.
Literature.
  Prose Fiction, 6084, 6467, 6470, 6472, 6496, 6509, 6540-6541, 6543-6544, 6717, 6893-6946, 6958-7003, 7018, 7020, 7023, 7033, 7209, 7890, 7902, 7904-7906, 7911-7918, 7921, 7929.
  Poetry, 6491, 7018, 7040-7041, 7044, 7048, 7060, 7075, 7088, 7111, 7120, 7124, 7144, 7150, 7164-7165, 7182, 7197, 7201, 7217, 7226, 7865.
  Drama, 7236, 7239, 7241, 7257, 7259, 7261, 7269, 7271, 7278, 7289-7290, 7292-7297, 7311, 7314, 7333, 7339-7340, 7351, 7386, 7398, 7933.
  Music, 9005, 9007, 9013, 9022a-9033.
  Philosophy, 9446, 9449, 9452-9453, 9456, 9484, 9492, 9496, 9498, 9504-9505, 9510-9511, 9513, 9654, 9690.
Argentina and Germany Relations, 2401.
Arguedas, Alcides, 6803.
Arguedas, José María, 2097, 6462-6463, 6480, 6554, 6830, 6836, 6838, 6841-6843, 6847.
Arizona. See Borderlands.
Arlt, Roberto, 6971, 6976, 6979, 6987, 7337, 7351, 7395.
Armed Forces. See Military.
Arms. See also Military. *Argentina*, 2358. *Brazil*, 2358. *Chile*, 2358. *Mexico*, 2700. *Panama*, 2929.
Arreola, Juan José, 6608-6609.
Arria, Diego, 393.
ART (items 251-536). See also Architects; Architecture; costumbrismo; Crafts; Dictionaries, art; Film; Folk Art; Iconography; Mass Media, cartoons; Monuments; Museums and Museology; Painters; Sculptors; Sculpture, specific countries and regions. *Abstract*, 455. *Antiques*, 535. *Art Noveau*, 319. *Awards*, 347. *Bibliography*, 266, 311, 334, 338, 528. *Catholic Church*, 252-254, 256, 291, 294-295, 297-299, 423, 427, 433-434, 436, 439, 535. *Criticism*, 330, 376, 413, 418-419, 507. *Curator*, 448. *Drawings*, 313, 345, 347, 379, 384, 447, 452, 458, 466, 468, 472, 477, 480, 483, 486, 512, 531. *Education*, 443. *Eroticism*, 395. *Exhibits*, 477-479, 505. *Fashion Designing*, 526. *Furniture*, 430, 437.

Government Regulations and Legislation, 266, 289. *History*, 363, 405, 407, 465. *Illustrators*, 205. *Impressionism*, 383, 473, 484. *Journals*, 406, 460. *and Latin American Society*, 311. *Lithographs*, 444, 449, 7081. *Marxist*, 365. *Murals*, 326. *Patrons*, 378, 453, 530. *Philosophy of*, 9718-9722. *Photography*, 532, 534. *and Politics*, 316, 325, 343, 370. *Primitivism*, 392. *Prints and Printmakers*, 372, 394-395, 406, 421, 452, 454, 465-466, 477-478, 481, 510, 7160. *Private Collections*, 446, 453, 505. *Realism*, 402. *Symbolism*, 319. *Socialism*, 395. *Surrealism*, 318. *Symposiums*, 310, 312. *Textbooks*, 415. *16th Century*, 255, 291, 298, 424, 435. *17th Century*, 251, 255, 298, 416, 424, 435, 438-439. *18th Century*, 251, 255, 282, 414, 416, 423-424, 432, 436-439, 504. *19th Century*, 414, 416, 432, 442, 444-445, 449, 531. *20th Century*, 344, 356, 417-419, 531.
Artigas, José Gervasio, 3410, 3414, 3416.
Artists. See Architects; Art, prints and printmakers; Crafts, artisans; Dramatists; Musicians; Novelists; Painters; Poets; Sculptors.
ARUBA.
Bibliography and General Works, 6.
Music, 9065.
Arze, José Antonio, 2093.
Assassination. *Mexico*, 2722.
Astrada, Carlos, 9456.
Astronautics. *Portuguese dictionary*, 6117.
Astronomy. *Astronomers*, 88. *Chile*, 3608. *Inca*, 2119, 2124. *Portuguese dictionary*, 6117.
Asturias, Miguel Angel, 6658, 6663, 6666-6668, 6671-6672.
Atahualpa, 3194.
Audiencias. See History, Colonial.
Augustini, Delmira, 7222.
Austria and Latin American Relations, 2359.
Austrians in Latin America, 2612.
Avellaneda, Gertrudis Gómez de, 6438.
Avellaneda, Nicolás, 3844.
Aviation, 3799, 3944, 4056.
Avila Camacho, Manuel, 2788.
Azevedo, Manuel Antônio Alvares, 7663.
Aztec Language. See Indigenous Languages, Náhuatl.
Aztecs, 1957, 1959, 1975, 1978, 1989, 2007, 2024, 2262, 6447, 6594, 9126.
Azuela, Mariano, 6464, 6618.

Back, Sílvio, 996.
Bagé Group. See Brazil, art.
Baja California. See Borderlands.
Balance of Payments. *Chile*, 3632.
Baliño, Carlos, 2965.
Bandeira, Manuel, 7761.
Banditry, 3818.
BANKING AND FINANCE. See also Commerce; Debt; Fiscal Policy.
Acronyms dictionary, 101. *Argentina*, 3769, 3844, 3864, 3875, 3878. *Brazil*, 4005, 4177. *Colombia*, 3433. *Colonial*, 2255, 2321, 3096. *Dominican Republic*, 2933. *Ecuador*, 3465. *and Exploration*, 2339. *Honduras*, 2792. *House of Welser*, 2321. *Mexico*, 2602. *Panama*, 2865. *Peru*, 3511, 3514. *Uruguay*, 3940.
BARBADOS. See also Lesser Antilles.
Bibliography and General Works, 40, 52.
History, 2201, 2954, 2966.
Music, 9065-9066.
Barbosa, Rui, 4116-4117.
Barletta, Leónidas, 7321.
Barreto, Lima, 7720, 7728.
Barrientos, René, 3694.
Barrios, Alvaro, 373.
Barrios, Justo Rufino, 2871.
Bartolache, José Ignacio, 2524.
Basques in Latin America, 2155, 3505.
Bassols, Narciso, 2777.
Bastidas, Antonio, 6440.
Batlle, José, 3927.
Battles. *Ayacucho*, 3371, 3376. *Boquerón*, 3918. *Boyacá*, 3359. *Carabobo*, 3352. *Chacabuco*, 3329. *Junín*, 3376. *El Carmen*, 3893. *Llano del Carrillo*, 3363. *Pichincha*, 3369. *San Carlos*, 3837. *Sarandí*, 3954.
Bautista, Julián, 9029.
Bay of Pigs Invasion, 2216, 3007, 3017.
Belaval, Emilio S., 7318, 7322.
Belgians in Latin America, 2160.
BELIZE.
Bibliography and General Works, 9.
History, 2790, 2840, 2857, 2883, 2919.

Language, 6125-6126.
Belken, Arnold, 312.
Bello, Andrés, 2370, 6001, 6555.
Benedetti, Mario, 7844.
Benítez Rono, Antonio, 6728.
BERMUDA.
 Music, 9065.
Berni, Antonio, 355.
Berriozábal, Juan Manuel de, 6402.
Berrueco, Luis, 277.
Betancurt, Ariel, 7360.
Bevilaqua, Clóvis, 9447.
Bianchetti, Glênio, 454.
BIBLIOGRAPHY AND GENERAL WORKS (items 1-134). See also Archives; Biographies; Catalogs; Dictionaries; Dissertations and Theses; Encyclopedias; Government Documents; Latin American Studies; Libraries and Library Services; Library and Information Science; Manuscripts; National Bibliographies; Research; specific disciplines, specific countries. *Bibliographers*, 34. *Caribbean Bibliography*, 9. *General References on Latin America*, 103, 2407. *Social Science Bibliography*, 8. *World Bank/Fund Bibliography on Developing Areas*, 70.
Bilbao, Francisco, 3667, 9469.
Bilingualism. *Paraguay*, 6028, 6032, 6055, 6064. *Peru*, 6039. *Spanish/Guaraní*, 6028, 6055, 6064. *Spanish/Quechua*, 6039.
Billinghurst, Guillermo, 3490.
Biographies. See also Genealogy; specific discipline, occupation or name of the individual. *Argentina*, 106, 3754-3755. *Autobiography as an art form*, 7758. *Biographers*, 7775. *Brazil*, 1, 108, 3959, 3967, 3983, 4020, 4058, 4060, 4076. *Chile*, 3252, 3619, 3628, 3652. *Colombia*, 3418. *Costa Rica*, 2875. *Cuba*, 3060. *Dominican Republic*, 3023. *El Salvador*, 2900. *Guatemala*, 2846. *Honduras*, 2800. *Latin America*, 3087. *Latin Americans in Washington, D.C.*, 129. *Mexico*, 112, 2502, 2531, 2536, 2543, 2550, 2580, 2657. *Panama*, 2789, 2795, 2927. *Paraguay*, 107. *Peru*, 3548. *Puerto Rico*, 117, 133, 3059. *Uruguay*, 3928, 3941, 3948-3949. *Venezuela*, 35, 121.
Biological Sciences. *Biologists*, 88.

Black Legend, 2291, 2294.
BLACKS. See also Abolition; Caribs; Negritude; Race and Race Relations; Slavery and Slave Trade. *Afro-Brazilian*, 511-512, 514, 6094. *Afro-Panamanian*, 2810. *Afro-Cuban*, 6042a, 6086, 6721. *Argentina*, 3760, 3767. *Bibliography*, 22. *Brazil*, 22, 2181, 2214, 4000. *Caribbean*, 2946, 7805. *Colombia*, 3437. *Contributions*, 2342. *Costa Rica*, 2214, 2802. *Cuba*, 2181. *Ecuador*, 3163. *Haiti*, 7796-7797, 7803. *Honduras*, 2214. *Jamaica*, 2991. *Language Usage*, 6042a, 6046-6047, 6086. *Latin America*, 2227, 2242, 2267. *in Literature*, 7812. *Maroons*, 3001. *Mexico*, 2490, 2513. *Music*, 9057, 9069. *Nicaragua*, 2214. *Panama*, 6669. *Paraguay*, 3924, 9008. *Population*, 3924, 4000. *West Indies*, 2181.
Blanes, Juan Manuel, 383.
Boggio, Emilio, 397.
Bogotazo, 6814.
Bolívar, Simón, 2207, 2249, 2350, 3310, 3312, 3326-3327, 3330-3332, 3343, 3345a-3346, 3353, 3368, 3372, 3377, 3380-3381, 3445, 6525.
BOLIVIA. See also Andean Area. Bibliography and General Works, 12, 128.
 Art, 251, 257-259.
 Film, 952-953, 960-961, 965, 974-979.
 Literature.
  Prose Fiction, 3589, 6546, 6749-6754, 6801-6803.
  Poetry, 6803.
 History, 61, 87, 2388, 3048, 3072, 3088, 3238-3244, 3330, 3571, 3573-3606, 3694.
  Ethnohistory. See also Andean Area. 2032, 2102.
 Language, 6072, 6080.
 Music, 9015, 9034-9040.
Bolivia and Chile Relations, 3554.
Bolivia and Germany Relations, 2401.
Bolivia and Peru Relations, 3571, 3593, 3618.
Bolivian Revolution. See also Political Organization and Political Parties; Revolution and Revolutionary Movements. 2158, 2228, 2382, 3584, 3587, 3591.
Bombal, María Luisa, 6458, 6859, 6874.
BORDERLANDS.

Bibliography and General Works, 86, 2672.
History, 2443, 2468, 2543, 2547-2549, 2551, 2555-2557, 2565-2566, 2568, 2570-2571, 2573, 2576, 2578, 2581-2585, 2625, 2642, 2646, 2672, 2684, 2746, 2759, 3644.
Borges, Jacobo, 359, 388, 398, 6902.
Borges, Jorge Luís, 6725, 6813, 6821, 6916, 6958, 6964, 6977, 6985, 6990-6993, 6995-6996, 7000, 7177, 7217, 7836.
Borrero, Juana, 7192.
Botany. *History*, 2322. *Maya*, 2010.
Botero, Fernando, 374.
Boundary Disputes. *Argentina*, 3685, 3857. *Bibliography*, 16. *Ecuador/Peru*, 2462, 3474, 3480. *Chile/Peru*, 3488, 3561. *Colombia/Peru*, 3561. *Ecuador/Peru*, 3561. *Honduras/El Salvador*, 2896. *Portuguese/Spanish Boundary in New World*, 3273. *US*, 2624. *Venezuela/Colombia*, 16.
Brain Drain, 2409.
BRAZIL. See also Amazonia; Northeast, Brazil (region).
Bibliography and General Works, 1, 4, 7, 12, 14, 47, 50, 60, 128, 130, 134.
Art, 405-536, 3996.
Film, 460, 953, 961, 963, 980-999, 7770.
History, 70a, 77, 130, 428, 2146, 2156, 2201, 2252, 2256, 2307, 2343, 2359, 2386, 2388, 2393, 2406, 2730, 2958, 3793, 3886, 3956-4190, 7692.
Language, 6037-6038, 6087-6120.
Literature.
  Prose Fiction, 70a, 536, 992, 995, 3996, 6541, 7406-7487, 7661-7732, 7770, 7936-7945.
  Poetry, 7448-7602, 7733-7764, 7934-7935.
  Drama, 7603-7660, 7770.
Music, 3, 407, 536, 3996, 7770, 9005, 9007, 9013, 9015, 9041-9061.
Philosophy, 9454, 9462, 9467, 9470, 9479-9481.
Brazil and Austria Relations, 4155.
Brazil and Belgium Relations, 4177.
Brazil and France Relations, 4028.
Brazilian Studies, 4013.
Brazilians in Africa, 2153.
BRITISH GUIANA.
History, 3035.

BRITISH HONDURAS. See Belize.
BRITISH VIRGIN ISLANDS. See Tortola; US Virgin Islands.
BRITISH WEST INDIES. See Bahamas; Barbados; British Virgin Islands; Dominica; Jamaica; Tortola; Trinidad and Tobago.
Brouard, Carl, 7804.
Brown, Guillermo, 3316.
Brown, Hugo Blair, 3426.
Buenaventura, Enrique, 7405, 7854.
Bullrich, Silvina, 6945.
Burgos, Julia de, 7198.
Bustamante, Juan, 3567.
Bustamante, William Alexander Clark, 3051.
Butler, Tubal Uriah Buzz, 3021.

Caballero, Luís, 373.
Cabrera, Luís, 2690, 2748, 2776.
Cabrera, Miguel, 284.
Cabrera Infante, Guillermo, 955, 6718, 6742, 7842, 7844.
Caciques, 2028, 2032, 2034, 2079. *Ecuador*, 3185. *Mexico*, 2509. *Peru*, 3198.
Caldeira, Osvaldo, 996.
Calendrics. *Andean Area*, 2123-2124. *Aztec Calendar Stone*, 2022. *Mesoamerica*, 1956, 1982.
California. See Borderlands.
Callejas, Rodrigo, 367.
Calles, Plutarco Elías, 2740, 2781, 2788.
Calzadilla, Juan, 393.
Câmara, Eugênia, 7615.
Camargo, Sergio, 459.
Campenella, Tomás, 2291.
Campesinos. See Peasants.
Campos, Haroldo de, 7511.
Canada and Latin American Relations. *History*, 2206.
Candeias, Ozualdo, 996.
Cannabrava, Euryalo, 7768.
Capitalism, 2164. *Mexico*, 2473, 2737. in *Philosophy*, 9415. in *Theater*, 7402. *Puerto Rico*, 2947.
Carballido, Emilio, 7352, 7377, 7396, 7933.
Cárdenas, Lázaro, 2697, 2788.
Cárdenas, Santiago, 373.
Cardona Peña, Alfredo, 7836.
Cardoso, Joaquim, 487.
Cardoso, Lúcio, 7769.
Cardoso, Onelio Jorge, 6728.

CARIBBEAN. See also specific countries; Lesser Antilles; West Indies.
Bibliography and General Works, 6, 12, 43, 85, 128.
Art, 260-263, 336-337.
History, 64, 2156, 2306, 2405, 2930-3064.
Ethnohistory, 2117, 2279, 2383.
Language, 6121-6137.
Literature.
Prose Fiction, 6675-6748, 7825.
Poetry, 7805, 7815.
Drama, 7341, 7779.
Music, 9062-9069.
Caribbean and Europe Relations, 2190.
Caribs. *Guyana*, 2033. *Language*, 6126. *Music*, 9072. *Venezuela*, 2033.
Carlota Joaquina de Borbón y Parma, *princess*, 3392.
Caro, Miguel Antonio, 6009.
Carpentier, Alejo, 6458, 6460a, 6489, 6679, 6704, 6706-6707, 6713, 6715-6716, 6719, 6722, 6732, 6735, 6738, 6742, 6874.
Carranza, Venustiano, 2715, 2760, 2764-2765, 2767, 2769-2771.
Carrasquilla, Tomás, 6474-6475.
Carrió de la Vandera, Alonso, 6409-6410.
Carrión, Miguel de, 6747.
Cartography. See Maps and Cartography.
Cartoons. See Mass Media, cartoons; Government and Politics, cartoons.
Carvaja, María Isabel. See Lyra, Carmen.
Casaccia, Gabriel, 7006.
Casal, Julián del, 7181.
Casas, Bartolomé de las, 2088, 2125, 2202, 2211, 2251, 2269-2270, 2278, 2296, 2298, 2302, 2310, 2320, 2335, 6401, 6424, 6437.
Caso, Antonio, 9448, 9464, 9467, 9490.
Caspicara [*pseud. for* Manuel Chili] 276.
Cassa, Roberto, 3054.
Castañeda, Carlos, 6617.
Castellanos, Juan de, 6431.
Castellanos, Rosario, 6598, 7213.
Castles, John, 367, 373.
Castro, Cipriano, 37, 3440-3442, 3458.
Castro, Fidel, 3006, 3008.
Catalogs, Card and Book. *Biblioteca Luis Angel Arango (Colombia) Supplement*, 65. *Ibero-Amerikanisches Institut (Berlin, FRG) Subject Catalog*, 69. *Periodical Holdings in Costa Rican Libraries*, 82. *Periodical Holdings in Mexican Libraries*, 66. *Periodical Holdings in Peruvian Libraries*, 89. *Universidad Nacional Autónoma de México*, 109. *Universidad Nacional de Colombia Publications Catalog*, 68. *Universidad Nacional del Sur Publications Catalog*, 84. *University of Miami, Cuba and Caribbean Library*, 85.
CATHOLIC CHURCH. See also Art; Architecture; Religion. *Argentina*, 2691, 3265, 3297-3298, 3402, 3768, 3836. *Bolivia*, 3287, 3385. *Brazil*, 3966, 3969, 3979, 4022-4023, 4027, 4030, 4048, 4073, 4092, 4128, 4182, 4186, 4190. *Capuchins*, 3120, 4027, 4190. *Carmelites*, 2476, 3969. *Chile*, 3084, 3621, 3673. *Clergy*, 95, 112, 2006, 2299, 2574, 2584, 2649, 2781, 2845, 2902, 3112, 3148, 3362, 3476, 3836, 3979. *Colombia*, 3112, 3137, 3141, 3143, 3148, 3362, 9093. *Conferences*, 9410. *Consejo, Episcopal Latinoamericano (CELAM)*, 95. *Costa Rica*, 2877. *Cuba*, 2970. *Dominicans*, 2540. *Ecuador*, 3470, 3476. *Franciscans*, 2442, 2444, 2456, 2483-2484, 3065, 3071, 3105, 3111, 3278, 3287, 3297, 4022-4023. *Guyana*, 3106. *History*, 433, 2146a. *and Indians*, 2006, 2510, 3141, 3148, 4030. *Jesuits*, 2105, 2217, 2424, 2471, 2482, 2488, 2491, 2497, 2519-2521, 2537, 2550, 2558, 3119, 3263, 3265, 3269, 3278, 3282, 3303, 3908. *Journals*, 3476. *Latin America*, 17, 2157, 2267, 2345. *and Literature*, 7725. *Mexico*, 112, 2456, 2469, 2471, 2476, 2482-2484, 2510, 2512-2513, 2534, 2547, 2552, 2558, 2561, 2574, 2616, 2649, 2730, 2781. *Missionaries and Missions*, 2127, 2206, 2272, 2290, 2432, 2438, 2483-2484, 2536, 2547, 2555, 2558, 2571, 3148, 3298, 3698, 3966, 4022-4023. *Paraguay*, 3290, 3303, 3908, 9008. *Peru*, 3300, 3527, 3529. *Puerto Rico*, 2956, 2992. *and Society*, 2534. *Venezuela*, 3105, 3107, 3111, 3126, 3457.
Caviedes, Juan del Valle y, 6408.

Censorship. *Books*, 115. *Brazil*, 998-999. *Chile*, 1003. *Cuba*, 6483, 6708. *Film*, 954, 999, 1003, 1044. *Freedom of Speech*, 9504. *Haiti*, 7803. *Literature*, 6483, 6708. *Mexico*, 2653. *Venezuela*, 1044.
Census. *Argentina*, 3406. *Colombia*, 3421. *Ecuador*, 3469. *Paraguay*, 3924. *Peru*, 3504, 3555-3556.
CENTRAL AMERICA. See also specific countries.
Bibliography and General Works, 12, 55, 85, 128.
Art, 264-267, 331-335.
History, 64, 2674, 2789-2929.
Ethnohistory, 2279.
Language, 6041, 6133.
Literature.
Prose Fiction, 6623-6674.
Music, 9070-9076.
Cepeda Samudio, Alvaro, 6816.
Ceramics. *Brazil*, 429, 460, 474, 513. *Tiles*, 429.
Cerretani, Arturo, 6979.
Césaire, Aimé, 7797, 7799, 7805.
Chaco War (1934), 3577, 3581, 3587, 3596, 3601, 3892, 3896, 3898-3899, 3902-3903, 3915. *in Literature*, 7006.
Chambi, Manuel, 1034.
Chaple, Sergio, 6728.
Chaves, Lucrecia, 390.
Chicanos. See also Labor, US; Migrations. *Bibliography*, 6014. *Language*, 6071. *Literature*, 6617, 7850. *Movement*, 2730, 2746. *Music*, 9122. *Theater*, 7349.
Chilam Balam, 1985, 1990.
Children. *Brazil*, 4160. *Literature*. 6653. *Music*, 9052, 9055. *Poetry*, 7818a. *Speech*, 6103. *Theater*, 7264, 7269, 7609.
CHILE. See also Antarctica; Patagonia; possessions.
Bibliography and General Works, 12, 128.
Art, 268, 362-366.
Film, 952-953, 960-961, 963, 1000-1007, 7258.
History, 2145, 2150, 2156, 2216, 2306, 2340, 2359, 2386, 2388, 2393, 2404, 3084, 3086, 3089, 3245-3257, 3286, 3294, 3309-3310, 3315, 3321, 3390-3397, 3607-3673, 3882, 7837.
Ethnohistory, 2025, 2037.
Language, 6052, 6066a.
Literature.
Prose Fiction, 6854-6892, 7841, 7892-7893, 7920, 7923.
Poetry, 7025, 7051, 7095, 7103, 7106-7107, 7132, 7143, 7152, 7168-7169, 7171, 7174-7175, 7218, 7234, 7837, 7841.
Drama, 7242, 7273, 7373-7374.
Music, 9077-9090.
Phliosophy, 9459, 9469, 9499.
Chile and Bolivia Relations, 3554.
Chile and Germany Relations, 2401.
Chile and Mexico Relations, 2731.
Chile and Peru Relations, 3548, 3554.
Chili, Manuel, 276.
CHILOE (island, Chile).
History, 3630.
Chinea, Hugo, 6728.
Chinese in Latin America, 2861, 3030, 3513, 3544-3545.
Chirinos, Rafael, 390.
Chocrón, Isaac, 7380.
Chomsky, Noam, 6024-6025, 6091, 6096.
Christian Democratic Parties. See Political Organization and Political Parties.
CIA. See US Central Intelligence Agency.
Ciccillo [*pseud. for* Francisco Matarrazzo] 527.
Cienfuegos, Camilo, 3014.
Cinema. See Film.
City Planning. See Urban Planning.
CLASS STRUCTURE. See also Peasants; Social Organization.
Argentina, 3690, 3757, 3760. *Barbados*, 2954. *Bolivia*, 3591. *Brazil*, 3980, 4119, 4140, 4151, 4168, 4175, 4189. *Caribbean*, 2941, 2967. *Chile*, 3249, 3254, 3620, 3622, 3660. *Dominican Republic*, 3029, 3056. *Latin America*, 2304, 2396, 2967. *Mexico*, 2465, 2486-2487, 2528, 2530, 2539, 2544, 2783. *Panama*, 2820, 2920. *Peru*, 3195, 3224, 3501, 3532, 3557. *Precolumbian*, 1954, 1959, 1965-1966, 1968, 1972, 1981, 1986, 1992, 2001, 2013, 2028. *Puerto Rico*, 3038. *Quiché*, 1962-1963. *Trinidad*, 2931, 3045.
Clavijero, Francisco Javier, 2471a.
Cochrane, Tomás Alejandro, 2376.
Codices. See also Manuscripts. *Aztec*, 1957-1958, 1971, 2011. *Borbonicus*,

1982. *Campos*, 2015. *Florentine*, 2012.
Ixtlilxochitl, 1971. *Magliabechiano*,
1971. *Maya*, 29, 1980. *Nahua*, 1953.
Coffee. See Agriculture; Industry,
Museums; Plantations.
Collymore, Frank, 7827.
COLUMBIA. See also Amazonia,
Andean Area.
Bibliography and General Works, 12,
48, 85, 114, 118, 128.
Art, 205, 251, 269-275, 367-376.
Film, 953-954, 960-961, 1008-1011.
History, 2156, 2340, 2386, 2404, 2654,
2660, 3073, 3082, 3085, 3109, 3112,
3129-3162, 3336, 3417.
 Ethnohistory, 2027, 2063, 2074,
 2113, 3134-3135.
Language, 6027, 6040, 6047,
6049a-6051, 6058, 6073.
Literature.
 Prose Fiction, 122, 6474-6476, 6485,
 6528, 6547, 6755-6764, 6804-6826,
 7071, 7897-7898, 7919.
 Poetry, 7016, 7026, 7031-7032, 7055,
 7063, 7071, 7081-7082, 7091, 7108,
 7112-7113, 7125, 7166, 7194, 7202,
 7206, 7208, 7214.
 Drama, 7238, 7274-7275, 7339, 7358,
 7397.
Music, 9005, 9091-9093a.
Philosophy, 9465.
Colonization. See also Rural Settlement.
Argentina, 3698, 3740, 3871,
3883-3884. *Belize*, 2857. *Bibliography*,
27. *Brazil*, 3977, 4137, 4143-4144, 4163,
4170. *New World*, 2282, 2329.
Columbus, Christopher, 2271, 2275,
2291, 2304, 2306, 2315, 2324, 6007.
COMMERCE. See also Banking and
Finance; Illegal Trade; Imports and
Exports; Marketing and Product
Distribution; Tariffs and Trade
Protection; Transportation. *Andean
Area*, 2040. *Argentina*, 2359, 3706,
3733, 3757, 3788, 3875. *Associations*,
4162. *Brazil*, 108, 2252, 2359, 3994,
4047, 4131-4132, 4162, 4181, 4289.
Businessmen, 108, 4132, 4181. *Central
America*, 2848. *Chile*, 2359, 3395.
Colonial, 2027, 2032, 2081-2082, 2084,
2099, 2107, 2255, 2257, 2295, 2311,
2321, 2329, 2331, 2338, 2514, 2516,
2530, 3118, 3131, 3146, 3167, 3172,
3176, 3199, 3210, 3226, 3235, 3293.
Colombia, 2654, 3131, 3421, 3437.
Costa Rica, 2918. *Cuba*, 2970.
Ecuador, 2252, 3167-3168, 3172, 3176,
3465, 3470. *Guyana*, 123, 3356.
Independence Period, 2353-2354.
Jamaica, 2949. *Latin America*, 2386.
Mexico, 2441, 2473, 2496, 2499, 2501,
2514, 2516, 2530, 2616, 2644, 2654,
2675. *Nineteenth Century*, 2367.
Paraguay, 3306. *Peru*, 3199, 3210,
3226, 3235, 3496-3497, 3515. *Puerto
Rico*, 3046. *Surinam*, 2252. *Uruguay*,
3293, 3940. *Venezuela*, 2252, 3118.
West Indies, 2252, 2978. *World
Industrial Expositions*, 2675. *World
Trade*, 2197, 2239.
Commodities. See Agriculture; Industry;
Plantations; specific commodities.
*Government Basic Commodities
Corporation (Mexico)*, 2719, 2721.
Communication. See also Language;
Mass Media. *Oral*, 6128. *Written*,
6099.
COMMUNISM AND COMMUNIST
PARTIES. See also Marxism;
Socialism. *Argentina*, 3675, 3763.
Paraguay, 3275. *Venezuela*, 3449.
Community Development. *Peru*, 3546.
Compadrazgo. See Kinship.
COMPOSERS AND CONDUCTORS.
See also names of individuals.
Argentina, 9022a, 9024-9026,
9029-9031. *Bolivia*, 9015, 9034, 9036.
Brazil, 7656, 9015, 9043, 9046, 9051,
9053, 9056-9058. *Chicanos*, 9122.
Chile, 9012, 9077-9079, 9083-9084,
9088, 9090. *Costa Rica*, 9073. *Cuba*,
9095, 9098. *Guatemala*, 9015. *Latin
America*, 9018, 9022. *Mexico*, 9015,
9108, 9116-9117, 9121, 9123-9125, 9127.
Peru, 9131, 9133-9134. *Venezuela*,
9139-9140, 9142, 9148.
Computers and Computerization. See
also Library and Information Science.
Biblioteca Nacional (Brazil), 47.
Social Science Index, 94. *Universidad
Nacional Autónoma de México*, 109.
CONASUPO (Compañía Nacional de
Subsistencias Populares). See
Commodities, Government Basic
Commodities Corporation, (Mexico).
Conflict. See Battles; Boundary
Disputes; Revolution and
Revolutionary Movements, specific

wars.
Concolorcorvo [*pseud. for* Carrío de la Vandera, Alonso] 6409-6410.
Conferences. See specific disciplines.
Conquest. See also Exploration and Expeditions; Explorers. *Chile*, 3294. *Colombia*, 3135, 3140. *Costa Rica*, 2822. *Ecuador*, 3169, 3179, 3181-3183. *Florida*, 2551. *Guatemala*, 2837. *Mexico*, 2426, 2439, 2540-2542. *New World*, 2273, 2284, 2309, 2333-2334, 6450, 6503. *Original Sources*, 2054. *Peru*, 3098, 3212, 3510, 3527. *Puerto Rico*, 2973.
Conquistadores. See Explorers.
Conselheiro, Antônio [*pseud. for* Antonio Vicente Mendes Maciel] 7610.
Constitutional History. *Chile*, 3623. *Guatemala*, 2824, 2850. *Latin America*, 2162. *Mexico*, 2645, 2768.
Contestado Rebellion. See Revolution and Revolutionary Movements, Brazil.
Contremaestre, Carlos, 390.
Cooperatives. See also Agrarian Reform; Land Tenure; Peasants. *Honduras*, 2897. *Mexico*, 2711, 2745, 2779-2780. *Peru*, 3509.
Cornejo, Enrique, 3526.
Corporatism. See also Dictatorships. 2730, 2782, 9510.
Corral, Ramón, 2626.
Correia, Raimundo da Mota de Azevedo, 7516.
Cortázar, Julio, 6717, 6924, 6963, 6966, 6970, 6974, 6978, 6981-6982, 6989, 6994, 6998, 7001, 7843.
Cortés, Fernando, 2506, 2522.
Cosmology. *Andean*, 2090. *Inca*, 2123. *Maya*, 2019. *Nahua Indians (Mexico)*, 1973.
Cossío, Carlos, 9456.
Cossío Villegas, Daniel, 2726, 2751.
Costa, Lúcio, 487.
COSTA RICA.
Bibliography and General Works, 12, 55, 128.
Art, 265, 334.
History, 2156, 2388, 2404, 2796-2797, 2799, 2801-2802, 2804, 2806, 2809, 2812, 2818, 2820-2822, 2829-2830, 2834, 2849, 2852-2854, 2868, 2873, 2875, 2877, 2880-2881. 2884, 2886, 2903-2904, 2914, 2916-2918.
Language, 6042, 6065.
Literature.
Prose Fiction, 6629-6630, 6632, 6634b-6635, 6637, 6640, 6655-6656, 6659, 6662, 6665, 6669a.
Poetry, 7049, 7058, 7065, 7086, 7109, 7121, 7123, 7130, 7137-7138.
Drama, 7247, 7277, 7304-7305.
Music, 9073.
Philosophy, 9437, 9455.
Costa Rica and Europe Relations, 2918.
Costumbrismo. *in Art*, 323, 379. *in Film*, 972. *in Literature*, 2656, 6473, 6484, 6496, 6509, 6543-6544, 6623, 6630, 6633, 6684, 6905, 6919. *in Theater*, 7242, 7345.
COUP D'ETAT. *Argentina* (1930), 3808. (1966), 3846. (1976), 3689. *Brazil* (1889), 4096. (1937), 4091. (1964), 4172. *Chile* (1973), 2403, 3639, 7310. *Costa Rica*, 2873. *Guatemala*, 2874. *Latin America*, 2232, 2394. *Peru* (1968), 3572.
Crafts. See also Art, folk; Ceramics. *Argentina*, 3280, 3298. *Artisans*, 303, 315. *Brazil*, 463, 474, 513. *El Salvador*, 309. *Embroidery*, 308. *Goldsmithing*, 303. *Guatemala*, 308-309. *Mexico*, 308, 315. *Silversmithing*, 3280. *Tapestry*, 463, 474. *Uruguay*, 463. *Weaving*, 309. *18th Century*, 303.
Creoles, 2819, 6121-6137.
Crime. *Colonial Period*, 3110.
Cristero Rebellion. See Mexican Revolution.
Croix, Charles, 2464.
Croix, Theodore, 2464.
Crônicas. See Prose Fiction, *crónicas*.
Cruz, Juana Inés de la, *Sor*. See Juana Inés de la Cruz, *Sor*.
Cuadra, José de la, 6808, 6827.
Cuauhtémoc, 2460.
CUBA.
Bibliography and General Works, 12, 23, 74, 116, 128.
Art, 260, 338-343.
Film, 961, 963, 1012-1016.
History, 74, 2150, 2201, 2216, 2248, 2343, 2347, 2388, 2405, 2934, 2940, 2943, 2952, 2958, 2961, 2970, 2980, 2998-2999, 3006-3014, 3016-3019, 3032-3033, 3037, 3040, 3043-3044, 3060-3061, 3063-3064, 6557.
Language, 6036, 6042a, 6060, 6063,

6086, 6094.
Literature.
  Prose Fiction, 97, 6445, 6460a, 6483, 6489, 6498, 6511-6512, 6557, 6675-6682, 6690-6692, 6695-6696, 6703-6704, 6706-6708, 6712-6725, 6727, 6730, 6732, 6742-6743, 6748, 7231, 7232, 7886, 7888-7889, 7900, 7920.
  Poetry, 7019, 7021, 7036, 7066, 7084, 7102, 7128, 7157, 7172, 7186, 7192, 7203, 7216, 7233, 7840, 7863, 7875.
  Drama, 7237, 7266-7268, 7280-7281, 7287, 7291, 7310, 7350, 7364, 7372, 7388.
  Music, 9001, 9005, 9065, 9094-9098.
  Philosophy, 6745.
Cuba and Spain Relations in Africa, 3040.
Cuban Americans. *Bibliography*, 24. *Political Exiles*, 2951.
Cuban Revolution. See also Bay of Pigs Invasion. 2228, 2382, 3006, 3010-3014, 3018, 6689, 6730, 6746, 7875.
Cuervo, Rufino José, 6006, 6009, 6485.
Cuevas, José Luis, 312, 322.
Cultural Development and Evolution, 2220, 2337, 3510, 9408, 9415, 9418, 9423, 9428, 9430, 9433, 9435, 9478, 9712.
Cultural Identity. *Belize*, 2840. *Bolivia*, 3554. *Colombia*, 3430. *Ecuador*, 3478, 3554. *Latin America*, 6012. *Mexico*, 2418, 2433, 2466-2467, 2471a, 2615, 2666, 2692, 2730, 2784. *Peru*, 3554.
Cunha, Euclides da, 6541.
CURAÇAO.
  Bibliography and General Works, 6.
  Music, 9065.
Czechs in Latin America, 2217, 3796.

Damas, León, 7806.
Damel, Carlos S., 7853.
Dance. *Bolivia*, 9035, 9040. *Calypso*, 7806. *Chile*, 9080. *Colombia*, 9091. *Cuba*, 9094. *Dancers*, 7655. *Ecuador*, 9099. *Journals*, 7334. *Panama*, 9071. *Paraguay*, 9130. *Volador*, 6672.
Darío, Rubén, 7188, 7836.
Darthés, Juan Fernando Camilo, 7853.
Death. See also Mortality and Morbidity Patterns. *Brazil*, 4026. *in Literature*, 6594, 6767. *in Philosophy*, 9431.

Debt. *Peru*, 3496, 3514, 3544. *Spain*, 2529. *Uruguay*, 3940. *Venezuela*, 3452.
Deities. See Religion.
Delgado, Rafael, 6487.
DEMOGRAPHY. See also Colonization; Family Planning; Migrations; Mortality and Morbidity Patterns; Rural Settlements; Urbanization. *Andean Area*, 2078. *Argentina*, 3304, 3767, 3811. *Bolivia*, 3385. *Borderlands*, 2555. *Brazil*, 3958, 4004, 4184. *Central America*, 2820. *Chile*, 3247, 3621. *Colombia*, 3073, 3437. *Colonial Period*, 2029, 2101, 2106, 2113, 2122, 2258, 3113, 3152, 3200-3201, 3221, 3243. *Costa Rica*, 2868. *Cuba*, 2970. *Ecuador*, 2065, 3170, 3174. *History*, 2357, 3284. *Indians*, 2059, 3145-3146, 3152, 3221, 3243. *Latin America*, 2114, 2231, 2243, 2386, 2396, 2406. *Lesser Antilles*, 2148. *Methodology*, 2258. *Mexico*, 2507, 2517, 2525, 2571, 2578. *Paraguay*, 3284, 3289, 3307. *Peru*, 2029, 2037-2039, 2062, 3200-3202, 3221, 3224-3225, 3516, 3527, 3536, 3541. *Precolumbian*, 1989, 2104, 2525. *Social Organization*, 3289. *Venezuela*, 3113, 3350.
Denevi, Marco, 7854.
Dependency. *Andean Area*, 3554. *Argentina*, 3851. *Brazil*, 4099, 4173. *Chile*, 3622. *Costa Rica*, 2916. *Dominican Republic*, 3056. *Latin America*, 2174, 2191, 2218, 2239, 2375, 2400, 9410, 9415, 9491-9492. *Mexico*, 2602, 2730, 2766. *Peru*, 3556, 9403. *Philosophy*, 9478. *Teaching*, 2142. *Uruguay*, 3927. *Venezuela*, 3449, 3458.
Derisi, Octavio Nicolás *Monseñor*, 9484.
Desnoes, Edmundo, 6733.
Development. See Community Development; Cultural Development and Evolution; Economic Development; Political Development.
D'Halmar, Augusto, 6866.
Díaz, Félix, 2610.
Días, Jorge, 7854, 7933.
Díaz, Porfirio, 2600-2603, 2608, 2632, 2662, 2664, 2669, 2675, 2770.
Díaz del Castillo, Bernal, 2541.
Dictatorships. See also Corporatism; Military. *Ecuador*, 3463. *El Salvador*, 2907. *Guatemala*, 2858, 2876. *Latin*

America, 2199. 2768.
DICTIONARIES. See also Biographies.
Acronyms, 101. *Agricultural Portuguese*, 6114. *Architecture Portuguese*, 6078. *Archival Terms*, 45. *Argentinisms*, 3302, 6067, 6069. *Art*, 410, 414. *Astronautics*, 6117. *Astronomy*, 6117. *Brazil*, 6069. *Colombianisms*, 6058. *Costaricanisms*, 6042. Diccionario de la lengua castellana, 3250. *English/Portuguese, Portuguese/English*, 6109. *English/Spanish Onomatopoeic*, 6077. *Idioms*, 6081, 6083. *Library and Information Science Terms*, 45. *Linguistics*, 6115. *Lunfardo*, 6045. *Historical* 3093, 3485. Historical Dictionary of Brazil, 3960. Historical Dictionary of Colombia, 3423. Historical Dictionary of Costa Rica, 2796. Historical Dictionary of Haiti, 2950. Historical Dictionary of Honduras, 2803. Historical Dictionary of Peru, 3548. Historical Dictionary of Puerto Rico, 2938. *Humorous*, 7771. *Marketing Portuguese*, 6120. *Peru*, 3485. *Peruvianisms*, 6054. *Philosophy*, 9414. *Portuguese*, 96, 6110. *Quotations Portuguese*, 6119. *Remote Sensing*, 6085. *Soccer*, 6111. *Social Sciences*, 6074. *Spanish*, 3250, 6079. *Spanish/Portuguese, Portuguese/Spanish*, 6108. *Technical Portuguese/English*, 6107. *Tourism Portuguese*, 6112.
Di Cavalcanti, Emiliano, 461.
DIPLOMATIC HISTORY. See also Archives; Manuscripts; Treaties; specific countries. *Argentina*, 3403, 3787, 3800. *Bolivia*, 3573, 3588, 3593, 3596. *Brazil*, 3904, 3967, 4028, 4175. *Chile*, 3633-3634. *Colombia*, 2654, 3338, 3341-3342, 3420, 3439. *Diplomats*, 36, 2875, 2923, 3476a, 3488, 3573, 3588, 3616, 3634, 3800, 4175. *Ecuador*, 3468, 3476a-3477, 3480. *Germany*, 2928. *Guatemala*, 2923. *Guide*, 2379. *Methodology*, 2161. *Mexico*, 2443, 2566, 2611, 2639, 2651, 2658, 2705, 2718, 2722, 2730. *Paraguay*, 3904, 3916. *Peru*, 3314, 3486-3488, 3505, 3508, 3561, 3593-3594. *Spain*, 21, 2564. *United Kingdom*, 2356, 3496. *US*, 2361, 2390, 2397, 2399, 2651, 2658, 2705, 2718, 2760,
2878, 3031, 3554, 3561, 3603, 3616, 3633, 3967. *Uruguay*, 3938, 3947. *Venezuela*, 3452.
Discépolo, Armando, 7259, 7351.
Diseases. *of Conquistadores*, 2285. *Diglossia*, 6129, 6135. *of Indians*, 2425. *Malaria*, 3652. *Tuberculosis*, 3450. *Venereal*, 2324.
Dissertations and Theses. See also specific disciplines. *Brazil*, 4, 60, 75, 111. *Caribbean*, 6, 67. *Haitian*, 92. *Humanities*, 67. *Latin America*, 67. *Social Sciences*, 60, 67. *Venezuela*, 83.
Divorce. See Family Relationships.
Djanira. See Silva, Djanira da Mota e.
DOMINICA.
Bibliography and General Works, 6.
History, 3001.
Language, 6133.
DOMINICAN REPUBLIC.
Bibliography and General Works, 12, 128.
Art, 261-263.
History, 2201, 2942, 2948, 2955, 2969, 2971, 2975, 2977, 2981, 3004, 3015, 3020, 3026, 3029, 3036, 3041, 3050, 3053.
Language, 6060.
Literature.
  Prose Fiction, 6744.
  Poetry, 7118, 7149, 7166, 7170.
Music, 9067.
Philosophy, 9502.
Dom Pedro I, 4155.
Dom Pedro II, 522, 4069, 4075, 4155.
Domínguez, Francisco Atanasio, 2543, 2581.
Donoso, José, 6519, 6877, 6884, 6887, 6892.
Dorfman, Ariel, 6729.
Dorr, Nicolás, 7363.
Dragún, Osvaldo, 7325, 7854, 7933.
DRAMA (items 7236-7405, 7603-7660). See also Dramatic Criticism; Dramatists; Plays; Translation. *Actors*, 6513, 7001, 7317. *Black*, 7383. *Bolivia*, 6803. *Brazil*, 7349. *Colombia*, 7349. *Colonial Period*, 6430, 6441, 6453. *Cuba*, 7272, 7350. *Experimental Theater*, 7393, 7397. *Existentialism*, 7385. *Folk Theater*, 7280, 7617. *Journals*, 7255-7256, 7322, 7329, 7334, 7349, 7384, 7650, 7827. *Latin America*, 6503, 7338. *Mexico*, 6513, 7541, 7548,

6604, 9118. *Paraguay*, 6513, 7349. *use in Penitenciary*, 7393. *Political*, 7260, 7266, 7272, 7360, 7394. *Precolumbian*, 6456. *Production*, 7649, 7653. *Puerto Rico*, 117. *Religious*, 7381, 7636. *Revolutionary*, 7405. *Schools*, 7657. *Surrealism*, 7370. *Theater of the Absurd*, 7371. *Theaters*, 490, 7648, 7652, 7658-7659, 9033. *Uruguay*, 6513. *Vanguard*, 7238. *Venezuela*, 3122. *West Indies*, 7813.
DRAMATIC CRITICISM (items 7318-7390). See also Drama; Dramatists. *Anthologies*, 7303. *Argentina*, 7333-7334, 7339-7340, 7351, 7386, 7398. *Bibliography*, 7353. *Brazil*, 7648-7660. *Chile*, 7374. *Colombia*, 7339, 7358, 7397. *Cuba*, 7334, 7364, 7372, 7388. *Guatamala*, 7328. *Latin America*, 7353. *Mexico*, 7319, 7331, 7344, 7346-7347, 7352, 7376-7377, 7385, 7391-7392, 7400. *Paraguay*, 7343. *Peru*, 7365. *Puerto Rico*, 7318, 7320, 7322, 7361, 7394. *Uruguay*, 7387, 7390. *Venezuela*, 7334, 7359, 7362.
Dramatists. See also names of individual dramatists. *Argentina*, 7259, 7325, 7330, 7333, 7337, 7378, 7384, 7395, 7401, 7854. *Brazil*, 7650, 7655, 7657. *Chile*, 7326-7327, 7373, 7403, 7854. *Colombia*, 7345, 7360, 7405, 7852. *Costa Rica*, 7375. *Cuba*, 7268, 7363, 7372. *Guatemala*, 7341. *Haiti*, 7797. *Latin America*, 7404, 7854. *Mexico*, 7346, 7354, 7357, 7366, 7391, 7396. *Peru*, 7324. *Puerto Rico*, 7321, 7360. *Uruguay*, 7384, 7399. *Venezuela*, 7336, 7380.
Droguett, Carlos, 6876.
Duarte, Juan Pablo, 3024, 3039.
Duarte, Paulo, 7772.
Dussell, Enrique, 9458, 9491.
Dutary, Alberto, 402.

Earthquakes. See Natural Disasters.
East Indians in Latin America, 3030, 3035.
Ecco, Humberto, 6729.
Echevarría, Bernardo, 7182.
Echeverría, Luis, 1017, 2682, 2713, 2720, 2731, 2747, 2750, 2755, 2774.
ECOLOGY. See Fish and Fishing Industry; Flora and Fauna; Marine Resources; Natural Resources. *Chile*, 3248. *Deforestation*, 3248.
Economic Assistance to Latin America, 2197.
ECONOMIC DEVELOPMENT. See Banking and Finance; Commerce; Dependency; Imports and Exports. *Argentina*, 2150, 3695, 3716, 3770, 3779, 3787. *Aztec*, 1961. *Bolivia*, 3580, 3587. *Brazil*, 3922, 4099, 4113, 4170-4171, 6095a. *Chile*, 2150, 3662. *Colonial Period*, 2095, 2234. *Cuba*, 2150. *Ecuador*, 3172. *Haiti*, 126. *History*, 2166, 2245. *Inca*, 2086. *Journals*, 89. *Language Usage*, 6095a. *Latin America*, 10, 2166, 2191, 2241, 2385-2386. *and Law*, 2183. *Mexico*, 2150, 2436, 2473, 2530, 2606, 2616, 2640, 2663, 2686, 2730, 2741. *Peru*, 89, 2150, 3496, 3514, 3537, 3550. *Uruguay*, 3931. *Venezuela*, 3453.
ECONOMICS. See Banking and Finance; Economic Development; Debt; Fiscal Policy; History, economic; Imports and Exports; Income Distribution; Investment; Multinational Corporations; Taxation. *Argentina*, 2248. *Brazil*, 130. *Cuba*, 2248. *Journals*, 103. *Journal Indexes*, 94,109. *Mexico*, 2248. *Puerto Rico*, 117.
ECUADOR. See also Amazonia; Andean Area.
Bibliography and General Works, 12, 39, 128.
Art, 251, 276.
History, 2252, 3079, 3163-3193, 3367, 3370.
  Ethnohistory, 2063, 2065, 2075, 2089, 3163, 3176, 3178-3179.
Language, 6029.
Literature.
  Prose Fiction, 6465, 6501, 6526, 6536, 6765, 6776, 6827.
  Poetry, 7024, 7056, 7097-7098, 7183, 7193, 7859.
  Drama, 7260.
Music, 9099-9100.
Philosophy, 9429, 9516.
Education. See also Public Policy; Students; Universities; specific disciplines. *Argentina*, 3252, 3737, 3811, 3866. *Brazil*, 3966-3967, 4051, 4116-4117, 4160, 4189. *Caribbean*, 6137. *Chile*, 3252, 3628. *Colombia*,

3421-3422. *Colonial*, 3104, 3222. *Costa Rica*, 2868. *Educators*, 4128, 4160, 6001, 9523. *Guyana*, 123. *Institutions*, 2423, 2481, 2508, 2521. *Mexico*, 2423, 2458, 2481, 2681, 2692, 2694, 2758, 2777, 2783. *Peru*, 3198, 3521-3522. *Puerto Rico*, 117, 3046. *Technical*, 3628. *West Indies*, 6127. *Venezuela*, 3104, 3119, 3357.
Edwards, Jorge, 6890, 7843.
Ejido. See cooperatives, Mexico.
EL CHACO. See also Chaco War.
Ethnic Geography, 2080.
Elections and Electoral Traditions. *Columbia*, 3419. *Peru*, 3527.
Elites. See Catholic Church; Class Structure; Military; Social Organization.
Elizondo, Salvador, 6615.
Eloy Blanco, Andrés, 7224.
EL SALVADOR.
Bibliography and General Works, 12, 85, 128.
Art, 334.
History, 2343, 2791, 2831, 2872, 2895-2896, 2900, 2907, 2915, 2917, 2921.
Language, 6043.
Literature.
Prose Fiction, 6625, 6645, 6652-6654.
Poetry, 7022, 7099.
Drama, 7244.
El Salvador and Honduras Relations. See Boundary Disputes, Honduras/El Salvador.
Emigration. See Migrations.
Encomienda, 2039, 2062, 2066, 2340, 2490. *Argentina*, 3733. *Chile*, 3253. *Colombia*, 3129, 3156. *Colonial Period*, 3146. *Encomenderos*, 3195, 3249. *Guatemala*, 2837. *Mexico*, 2505, 2522, 2542. *Nicaragua*, 2826. *Peru*, 3230, 3497.
Encyclopedias. *Colombia*, 3433. *Cuba*, 116. *Fashion*, 3433. *Latin America*, 2152. *Mexico*, 9103. *Puerto Rico*, 117.
Energy Sources. *Brazil*, 4173.
Enríquez, Carlos, 339.
Epstein, Isidoro, 2623.
Equino, Antonio, 975.
Ercilla y Zúñiga, Alonso de, 6403, 6423.
Escobedo, Federico, 6414.
Estancia. See Plantation.

ETHNOHISTORY (items 1051-2124).
See also specific country or region; Mesoamerica; Precolumbian Cultures.
Historical development, 1994. *South America*, 2025-2124. *Theory*, 2085.
Ethnomusicology. *Argentina*, 9032. *Bolivia*, 9038-9039. *Caribbean*, 9066-9068, 9072, 9074. *Ecuador*, 9099-9100. *Latin America*, 9007. *Honduras*, 9070. *Panama*, 9071.
Europeans in Latin America. See also specific nationalities. 2413.
EUSTATIUS.
Bibliography and General Works, 6.
History, 3042.
EXPLORATION AND EXPEDITIONS. See also Conquest; Travel and Tourism, travel accounts.
Argentina, 3286, 3309, 3761. *Borderlands*, 2551, 2557, 2573. *Brazil*, 3963, 3975, 3987, 4025, 4027, 4054. *Chile*, 3286, 3648, 3563, 3671. *Coronado Expedition*, 2560. *Domínquez-Escalante Expedition*, 2543, 2581. *Filibustering Expeditions*, 2560. *Flores Expedition*, 3473. *French*, 2962. *Gillis Expedition*, 3608. *Langsdorff Expedition*, 3987. *Magallan-Elcano Expedition*, 2281. *Mexico*, 2671. *New World*, 2313, 3097. *Orellana Expedition*, 4025. *Panama*, 2817. *Peru*, 3071. *Precolumbian*, 2330. *La Ravardiere Expedition*, 4027. *Río de la Plata*, 3408. *Royal Botanical Expedition*, 3138. *Russian*, 3987. *San Martín Expeditions*, 3315, 3319, 3324. *South America*, 2253, 2339. *Spanish*, 3286.
Explorers. See also Columbus; Cortés; Humboldt; Pizarro; etc. *Andean Area*, 2066, 3182. *Argentina*, 3753. *Florida*, 2551. *Guatemala*, 1979. *Illness*, 2284. *Italians*, 2165. *Language Usage*, 6007, 6010. *Latin America*, 2208. *New World*, 2268, 2271, 2277, 2286, 2506. *Peru*, 2072. *Russians*, 2373. *South America*, 2263. *US*, 3563. *World*, 2308.
Exports. See Imports and Exports.

Fascism, 3559.
Fages, Pedro, 2572.
Falcón, Francisco, 2067.
FALKLAND ISLANDS. See Malvinas, Islas.

Fallas, Carlos Luis, 6669a.
Family Planning. See also Children; Mortality and Morbidity Patterns; Women. 2243, 3804.
Family Relationships. See also Kinship. *Argentina*, 3872. *Barbados*, 2966. *Brazil*, 3958, 4073. *Divorce*, 2589. *Government Regulations & Legislation*, 2966. *Marriage*, 3457, 3872, 3958, 4073. *Mexico*, 1964, 2554, 2589, 2730. *Peru*, 3506. *Venezuela*, 3124. *and Women*, 2213.
Fatone, Vicente, 9456.
Fazendas. See Plantations.
Federalism, 2146, 3736.
Fernandes, Carlos D., 7691.
Fernández, Albino, 353.
Fernández, León, 2821.
Fernández, Macedonio, 6960, 6965, 6980, 6996.
Fernández de Bonilla, Alonso, 2040.
Fernández Retamar, Roberto, 6728.
Ferrari, Juan Manuel, 386-387.
Festivals. See also Music, festivals. *Inca*, 2115.
Fierro, Pancho, 379.
Figari, Pedro, 9493.
Figueiredo, Jackson de, 7696.
Figueres, José, 2891.
Filibustering Expeditions. See Exploration and Expeditions.
FILM (items 951-1048). See also Censorship, film; Filmmakers; Mass Media; specific countries. *Actors*, 1016. *Awards*, 988, 1012. *Bibliography*, 956, 962, 964, 998, 1002. *Brazil*, 4087. *Cinema Novo*, 983, 986-987, 990, 993, 999. *Criticism*, 987, 994, 997, 1002, 1006, 1010, 1012-1013, 1015. *Distribution*, 1047. *Documentaries*, 973, 1027. *Experimental University Film Group*, *Panama*, 1031-1032. *Filmmaking*, 960, 966-967, 979, 986, 989, 1000, 1005, 1007-1008, 1011, 1018-1020, 1021-1023, 1036, 1046, 1048. *Filmography*, 958-959, 961, 969, 971, 977, 1002, 1010, 1037, 1041. *Government Legislation and Regulations*, 971, 1011. *History*, 969-971, 977, 980, 983, 985, 988-989, 998, 1005, 1007, 1013, 1018, 1021, 1026, 1029-1030, 1033, 1038, 1042, 1046. *Institutes*, 1012, 1026, 1045. *Journals*, 986, 991, 1028. *and Literature*, 955, 992, 995. *Marxist*, 963. *and Novelists*, 7907. *and Politics*, 951, 953, 957, 964, 999, 1001, 1004, 1013. *Screenings and Exhibits*, 984, 1008. *and Student Movements*, 1028.
Filmmakers. *Argentina*, 952, 968, 973, 1039. *Bolivia*, 982, 987, 990-991, 996-997. *Chile*, 952, 1000-1004, 1006. *Colombia*, 957, 1009. *Cuba*, 957. *International*, 988, 1008. *Latin America*, 959. *Mexico*, 957, 1024. *Panama*, 1032-1033. *Peru*, 1034-1036. *Uruguay*, 1043. *Venezuela*, 1045.
Fiscal Policy. *Argentina*, 2248. *Brazil*, 4109. *Central America*, 2848. *Colombia*, 3443. *Cuba*, 2248, 2970. *for Industrialization*, 2167. *Mexico*, 2248.
Fish and Fishing Industry. *Peru*, 3532. *New World*, 2281.
Flora and Fauna. *Argentina*, 3775. *Barbados*, 2966. *Mexico*, 1971, 2489. *New World*, 2281. *Puerto Rico*, 117. *Royal Botanical Expedition*, 3138.
Florida. See Borderlands.
Florence, Hercules, 447.
Flores, Paulo Osório, 455.
Flores Magón, Ricardo, 2687.
Folk Art. *Brazil*, 504-510. *Mexico*, 307-309. *Woodcuts*, 510.
Folklore. See also Costumbrismo; Ethnomusicology; Folk Art; Indigenismo, in literature; Music, folk. *Argentina*, 2170. *Brazil*, 3970, 7776a, 4021. *Chile*, 2170. *Cuba*, 2170. *El Salvador*, 6625. *and Language*, 6066. *Latin America*, 9014. *Mexico*, 1955, 9119. *Panama*, 2170. *Peru*, 6066. *Puerto Rico*, 8, 117.
Fonseca, José Paulo Moreira da, 464.
Food. See Agriculture; Nutrition.
Foreign Aid. See Economic Assistance; Military Assistance.
Foreign Investment. See Investment.
Foreign Policy. See Diplomatic History; International Relations; specific countries.
Foulché-Delbosc, Raymond, 6006.
Francia, Aldo, 1000.
Francia, José Gaspar Rodíguez de, 3889, 3909-3910, 3920-3921, 3947.
Frank, Miguel, 7853.
Frankétienne, 7800.
Freemasonry, 2283, 2709, 2953, 3441, 3818, 3982, 4182.

Frei, Eduardo, 238.
Freire, Luis José Junqueira, 7525.
FRENCH GUIANA.
 Bibliography and General Works, 6.
 History, 2958, 3058.
 Literature.
  Poetry, 7791-7791a.
French in Latin America, 2190, 2591, 2611, 3866.
FRENCH WEST INDIES. See Guadeloupe; Haiti; Martinique.
Freyre, Gilberto, 7612.
Fuenmayor, José Félix, 6826.
Fuentes, Carlos, 955, 6601, 6605, 6607, 6609, 6618, 6622, 7344, 7843.
Funston, Frederick, 2961.
Future Studies, 2405, 2410, 2412.

Gaitán, Jorge Eliécer, 3436.
Galich, Manuel, 7341.
Gallegos, Daniel, 7375.
Gallegos, Rómulo, 6490, 6492, 6545.
Gálvez, Bernardo de, 2548, 2556, 2574.
Gálvez, Manuel, 6540.
Gambaro, Griselda, 7330.
Gamero, Manuel, 2871.
Gaos, José, 9501, 9517.
Garaude, Lupe Cotrim, 7752.
García, José, 1040.
García, Linda Burk, 1040.
García Aponte, Isaías, 9477.
García Diego y Moreno, Francisco, 2584.
García Márquez, Gabriel, 318, 955, 6519, 6689, 6804-6805, 6808-6811, 6815, 6817-6819, 6821-6825, 6843, 6929, 7843.
García Miranda, Nelson, 1035-1036.
García Moreno, Gabriel, 32.
García Morillo, Roberto, 9031.
García Ponce, Juan, 6596, 6599, 6603, 6620.
Garcilaso de la Vega (El Inca), 2557, 6415-6416.
Gardel, Carlos, 9009, 9022a, 9028, 9032.
Garmendia, Salvador, 6850.
Garrido-Lecca, Celso, 9133.
GENEALOGY. *Andean*, 2090. *Argentina*, 3873, 3875. *Brazil*, 3958, 4019, 4066, 4168. *Mexico*, 1965, 2422, 2431, 2554, 2580, 2730. *Paraguay*, 3912. *Peru*, 3236, 3506, 3539.
Genta, Jordán B., 9504.
Geography. See also Flora and Fauna; Geology; Maps and Cartography; Natural Resources; Travel and Tourism. *Bolivia*, 3580, 3589. *Brazil*, 77, 130. *Geographers*. 3563. *Mexico*, 2439. *Place Names*, 4054. *Venezuela*, 3350.
Geology. See also Minerals and Mining; Paleontology. 3991. *Geologists*, 88.
Germans in Latin America. *Argentina*, 3821. *Brazil*, 2180, 3991, 4057, 4066, 4144, 4163, 4170. *Ecuador*, 3090. *Guatemala*, 2798. *Honduras*, 2928. *Nicaragua*, 2888.
Germany and Latin American Relations, 2399, 2401, 2918.
Getino, Octavio, 1039.
Ginastera, Alberto, 9025.
Gómez, Juan Vicente, 3440-3442, 3450, 3458.
Gómez, Ramiro, 373.
Gómez Cornet, Ramón, 344.
Gómez de Avellaneda, Gertrudis, 7268.
Gómez Farías, Valentín, 2607.
Gompers, Samuel, 2787.
Gonçalves, Danúbio Villamil, 454.
Góngora, Leonel, 312.
González, Beatriz, 373.
González, Carmelo, 395.
González, Manuel, 2605-2606.
González Prada, Manuel, 3529, 3562, 6488, 9518.
González Tuñón, Raúl, 7217.
Gorostiza, José, 7829.
Government and Politics. See also Boundary Disputes; Coup d'Etat; Dependency; Government Regulations and Legislation under specific subjects; Guerrillas; Labor and Unions; Military; Political Organization and Political Parties; Revolution and Revolutionary Movements; Thinkers and Philosophers. *Argentina*, 2248, 6971, 6986, 7003. *Brazil*, 3980, 4080, 4180. *Cartoons*, 516. *Colombia*, 7071. *Cuba*, 2248, 6689. *Guatemala*, 6634a. *Journals*, 103. *Latin America*, 2396. *in Literature*, 6971-6972, 6986, 7003, 7014. *Mexico*, 2248, 2605, 2628, 2645, 2674, 2708, 2721, 2730, 2739, 2741, 2747, 2768, 6522. *Nicaragua*, 6647. *Nueva Granada*, 3359. *Peru*, 3543. *Philosophy*, 9654, 9672. *Puerto Rico*, 8. *US*, 2951. *Uruguay*, 7014.
Government Documents. *Brazil*, 78

Brazilian State Gazettes, 104. *Federal Senate (Brazil)*, 76. *US on Latin America*, 2247.
Graciano, Clóvis, 467.
Gramajo Gutiérrez, Alfredo, 396.
Granados, Omar, 390.
Grande, Emilio Alejandro, 348.
Grases, Pedro, 3451.
Grassman, Marcelo, 468.
GREATER ANTILLES. See also Cuba; Dominican Republic; Haiti; Jamaica; Puerto Rico; West Indies.
  Language, 6124.
Grieff, León de, 6826, 7194, 7206, 7214.
GUADELOUPE.
  Bibliography and General Works, 6.
  History, 2955.
  Literature.
    Poetry, 7791a.
  Music, 9066.
Gual, Pedro, 3340.
Guano. See Natural Resources.
Guastavino, Carlos, 9025.
GUATEMALA.
  Bibliography and General Works, 12, 128.
  Art, 264.
  History, 2798, 2805, 2811, 2819-2820, 2823-2824, 2827-2828, 2837-2839, 2846-2847, 2850, 2858-2859, 2863, 2866-2867, 2871, 2874, 2876, 2885, 2890, 2898, 2913, 2915, 2917, 2923.
  Ethnohistory. See Mesoamerica.
  Language, 6126.
  Literature.
    Prose Fiction, 6634a, 6658, 6663, 6667, 7882-7883.
    Poetry, 7078.
    Drama, 7328.
  Music, 9015, 9074.
Güiraldes, Ricardo, 6467, 7217.
Guerrero, Alfredo, 373.
Guerrero, Luis Juan, 9456.
Guerrero Galván, Jesús, 328.
Guerrillas. See also Revolution and Revolutionary Movements; specific guerrilla leaders. *Bolivia*, 3585. *Chile*, 3661. *Mexico*, 2669. *Nicaragua*, 6665. *Peru*, 3379. *Poetry*, 7831. *in Theater*, 7294. *US*, 2961.
Guevara, Ernesto "Che", 3585.
Guevara, Roberto, 393.
GUIANAS. See French Guiana; Guyana; Surinam.
Bibliography and General Works, 85.
Language, 6125.
Guignard, Alberto da Veiga, 472.
Guillén, Nicolás, 6721, 6728, 7180, 7196, 7216.
Gutiérrez, Alfredo Gramajo. See Gramajo Gutiérrez, Alfredo.
GUYANA.
  Bibliography and General Works, 6, 12, 123.
  History, 2148, 3106, 3356, 3747.
    Ethnohistory, 2033.
  Literature.
    Prose Fiction, 7812.
    Poetry, 7817, 7818a-7822, 7824.
    Drama, 7813, 7820.
Guzmán, Jorge, 6883.
Gúzman, Nicomedes, 6886.
Guzmán, Patricio, 1004, 1006.
Guzmán Blanco, Antonio, 3452.

Haciendas. See Plantations.
Hahn, Reynaldo, 9139.
HAITI.
  Bibliography and General Works, 12, 30, 92, 128.
  History, 126, 2950, 2971, 3015, 3050.
    Ethnohistory, 2383.
  Language, 6094, 6123, 6134-6135.
  Literature.
    Prose Fiction, 6738, 7776-7778, 7792, 7795-7796, 7798, 7800, 7802.
    Poetry, 7782-7790, 7791a, 7793, 7801, 7806.
    Drama, 7780-7781.
  Music, 9065.
Handler, Mario, 1043.
Haya de la Torre, Víctor Raúl, 3420, 3526, 3543, 3557, 3566.
Héctor, Andrés, 7176.
Heegaard, Anna, 2982.
Henríquez Ureña, Camila, 3041.
Henríquez Ureña, Pedro, 9502.
Heredia, José, 7233.
Heredia, Nicolás, 6498.
Hernández, Luisa Josefina, 7366.
Hernández Martínez, Maximiliano, 2907.
Herrán, Saturnino, 330.
Herrera y Reissig, Julio, 7188, 7212, 7228.
Herskovits, M.J., 2383.
Heyn, Piet, 2300.
Highways. See Transportation.
HISPANIOLA. See Dominican

Republic; Haiti.
Historiography, 2134, 2143, 2164, 9494. *Argentina*, 2159, 3738, 3784, 3888, 9520. *Black Legend*, 2202. *Brazil*, 2159, 2179, 3989-3990, 3999, 4009, 4039, 4178. *Caribbean*, 2937. *Chile*, 2159, 3624, 3673. *Colombia*, 3082. *Dominican Republic*, 3024. *Eastern European on Latin American Independence*, 3323. *Mexico*, 2159, 2673, 2677, 2679, 2730. *New World*, 2305. *Paraguay*, 3275. *Venezuela*, 3444-3445.
History of Ideas. See Intellectual History; Thinkers of Philosophers.
HISTORY (items 1051-4190). See also Archives; Constitutional History; Dictionaries; Diplomatic History; Ethnohistory, Government and Politics; History, colonial; History, independence; History, 19th and 20th Century; Intellectual History; Maritime History; Monuments; Oral History; Political Leaders/ Administrations; Political Organization and Political Parties; specific disciplines; specific countries. *General*, 2125-2249. *Annual Conference of Caribbean Historians*, 6th, Río Piedras, Puerto Rico (1974), 2931. *Anthologies*, 2751. *Bibliography*, 2145, 2148, 2576, 3067, 3080. *Congreso Centroamericano de Historia Demográfica, Económica y Social*, 1st, Santa Barbara, Costa Rica (1973), 2820. *Congreso de Historia Argentina, Regional*, 2nd, Comodoro Rivadavia, Arg. (1973), 3070. *Congreso de la Historia de los Pueblos de la Provincia de Buenos Aires*, 2nd, Tandil, Arg. (1972), 3732. *Dissertations*, 2173. *Economic*, 2257, 2440, 2491-2492, 2514, 2537, 2547, 2558, 2943, 3073, 3196, 3218, 3289, 3304, 3315, 3465, 3496, 3785, 3886, 3934. *English Language Histories on Latin America*, 2178. *Historians and Researchers*, 2091-2092, 2151, 2156, 2237, 2329, 2843, 3250-3251, 3451, 3574, 3607, 3613, 3641, 3657, 3663, 3673, 3786, 3862, 3984, 3997, 4013, 4039, 4064, 9517. *Indexes*, 2135. *International Congress of Mexican History*, 4th, Mexico (1973), 2730.

Journals, 2706, 2726, 2806-2808, 2834, 2850, 2955, 2966, 3076, 3085, 3166, 3271, 3373, 3434, 3400-3442, 3476, 3527, 3845, 3870, 3875, 3946. *Methodology*, 2142-2143, 2179, 2212. *Philosophy of*, 3121, 9451, 9527. *Teaching Latin American History*, 2138. *Textbooks*, 3981. *Universal*, 2233.
HISTORY, COLONIAL. See also Archives; Art; Encomienda; Plantation; Travel and Tourism, travel accounts; specific countries. *General*, 2250-2342. *Alto Peru*, 3238-3244. *Argentina*, See Rio de la Plata. *Audiencia de Buenos Aires*, 3285. *Audiencia de Caracas*, 3110, 3116. *Audiencia de Santo Domingo*, 3102. *Audiencias*, 2265, 2287, 2292, 2332, 3094, 3178, 3180, 3184, 6451. *Bolivia*, See Alto Peru. *Borderlands*, 2549, 2567. *Brazil*, 4024, 4055. *Cabildos*, 3305. *Caracas*, 3094, 3099-3128. *Caribbean*, 2955-2978. *Central America*, 2812-2848. *Chile*, 3245-3257, 3286. *Colombia*, See Nueva Granada. *Cortes de Cádiz*, 2351, 2364, 3285. *Costa Rica*, 3020. *Council of Indies*, 2261-2262, 2264, 2472, 2511, 3260. *Defense*, 3192-3193. *Dominican Republic*, 2977. *Economic*, 3100, 3102, 4024, 4047. *Ecuador*, See Quito. *Guatemala*, 2844. *Lexicon*, 6070. *Mexico*, 2293, 2427, 2436, 2450-2586. *Nueva Barcelona*, 3117, 3128. *Nueva Granada*, 2129-2162. *Paraguay*, See Rio de la Plata. *Peru*, 2293, 3065, 3194-3237, 3300, 3497, 3510. *Quito*, 3163-3193, 3464, 3472. *Research Manual*, 2569. *Revolt of the Comuneros*, 3151. *Rio de la Plata*, 3258-3309, 3862. *Semana de Estudos Históricos*, 1st, Ponte Nova, Brazil (1972), 4050. *Spanish South America*, 3065-3309. *Textbook*, 4036. *Uruguay*, See Rio de la Plata. *Venezuela*, See Caracas. *Viceroys and Colonial Officials*, 2293, 2326, 2344, 2461-2462, 3142, 3147a, 3155, 3158, 3164, 3173, 3192, 3219, 3235, 3260, 3262, 3267, 3304, 4031. *Visitas*, 2039-2040, 2053, 2055, 2112-2113, 2122, 2259, 2325, 3094, 3102-3103, 3150, 3157, 3208, 3210, 3237. *West Indies*, 2266, 2299,

2314, 2968.
HISTORY, INDEPENDENCE. See also Battles; Military Leaders; Revolution and Revolutionary Movements. *General*, 2132, 2148, 2223-2224, 2344, 2353-2354, 2362, 2371-2372, 2377, 3310-3334. *Alto Peru*, 61, 3330, 3382-3389, 3598. *Argentina*, See Rio de la Plata. *Bibliographies*, 2374, 3320, 3384. *Blacks*, 2227. *Bolivia*, See Alto Peru. *Brazil*, 3961, 3966, 3971-3972, 3974, 4002, 4020, 4044, 4071, 4149, 4179. *Caribbean*, 3019-3024. *Chile*, 3310, 3315, 3321, 3390-3397, 3661. *Colombia*, See Gran Colombia and Nueva Granada. *Congresso de História da Indepêndencia do Brasil*, Río (1972), 3967. *Ecuador*, See Quito. *Gran Colombia*, 3336-3345a. *Mexico*, 2426, 2436. See Mexican Revolution. *Nueva Granada*, 3359-3366. *Paraguay*, See Río de la Plata. *Patriots and Martyrs*, 3340, 3383, 3409, 3598. *Peru*, 3068, 3319, 3321, 3324, 3330, 3371-3381, 3497, 3510. *Quito*, 3169, 3316, 3318, 3367-3370, 3464, 3477. *Rio de la Plata*, 2378, 3398-3416, 3761, 3862, 3911, 3932. *Royalists*, 3363, 3397, 3404-3405, 3413. *Uruguay*, See Río de la Plata. *Venezuela*, 3340, 3346-3358, 3453.

History, National. See History, Independence or History, 19th and 20th Centuries.

HISTORY, 19TH AND 20TH CENTURIES. See also Archives; Art, 19th and 20th centuries; History, Independence; specific countries. 2343, 2345-2417. *Argentina*, 3610, 3674-3888, 3937. *Bibliography*, 2386, 3524, 3784. *Bolivia*, 3573-3606. *Brazil*, 3793, 3886, 3956-4023, 4056-4190. *Caribbean*, 3025-3064. *Central America*, 2849-2929. *Chile*, 3607-3673, 3882. *Colombia*, 3417-3439. *Cuba*, 74, 3043-3044. *Economic*, 2386, 3992, 3998, 4011, 4133. *Ecuador*, 3461-3480. *Mexico*, 2587-2788, 3793. *Paraguay*, 3899-3921. *Peru*, 3481-3572, 3594. *Uruguay*, 3882, 3925-3956. *Venezuela*, 3440-3460.

Hojeda, Diego de, 6402.

HONDURAS.
Bibliography and General Works, 12, 128.
Art, 334.
History, 2792, 2800, 2803, 2808, 2820, 2862, 2869, 2871, 2896-2987, 2904, 2911.
Literature.
Prose Fiction, 6624, 6626, 6641, 6661.
Poetry, 6624, 7017.
Music, 9070.

Hostos, Eugenio María de, 2995.
Hoyos, Ana Mercedes, 373.
Huayna Capac, 2028, 2079.
Huidobro, Vicente, 6875, 7829.
Humanities. See Art; Film; History; Language; Literature; Music; Philosophy; Research Aids; specific countries. *Bibliography*, 20.
Human Rights. See also Political Prisoners. *Argentina*, 3688. *in the Inter-American System*, 2193. *Philosophy*, 9702.
Humboldt, Alexander von, 2208, 9451.
Humor. *Brazil*, 981.
Hungarians in Latin America, 2343.
Hurtado, Alberto, 9507.

Inanelli, Thomaz, 470.
Icaza, Ernesto, 328.
Icaza, Jorge, 33, 6501, 6526.
Iconography. *Andean Area*, 251. *Brazil*, 452. *18th Century*, 253.
Iglesia, Ramón, 2751.
Illegal Trade. *Cuba*, 2970. *Dominican Republic*, 2981. *Ecuador*, 3318. *Latin America*, 3005. *Mexico*, 2662. *Piracy*, 2300, 2326, 3169, 3317. *Smuggling*, 2326, 2662. *Venezuela*, 3118. *West Indies*, 3158.
Immigration. See Migrations.
Imperialism, 2169, 2245, 3769, 3816.
Imports and Exports. *Barbados*, 2966. *Brazil*, 4173. *Chile*, 3632. *Costa Rica*, 2868. *Cuba*, 3064. *Jamaica*, 3052. *Peru*, 3495, 3498, 3514-3515, 3517, 3544, 3560.
Incas, 1989, 2044, 2047-2049, 2056-2057, 2060, 2068, 2075, 2086, 2089, 2093, 2095, 2098, 2103, 2115, 2262, 3590.
Income Distribution. *Haiti*, 30. *Latin America*, 2163.
Independence. See History, Independence.
INDIANS. See also Bilingualism;

Caribs; Encomienda; Indigenismo;
Indigenous Languages; Labor;
Precolumbian Cultures; Public Policy;
Race and Race Relations. *Andean
Area*, 2070, 2121. *Araucanians (Chile)*,
3294. *Argentina*, 3265, 3296, 3695,
3733, 3739, 3758, 3838, 3841, 3852,
3863. *Aymara (Bolivia/Peru)*, 2107.
Bibliography, 2154. *Borderlands*, 2425,
2438. *Brazil*, 513, 4041. *Cañaris
(Ecuador/Peru)*, 2089, 3179, 3183,
3223. *Capchas (Bolivia/Peru)*, 3239.
Caribbean, 6126. *Cashibo (Peru)*,
9136. *Colombia*, 2063, 3135a-3136,
3140, 3144-3145, 3147, 3152, 3430.
Colonial Period, 2027, 2298, 2545,
3073, 3129, 3144-3145. *Costa Rica*,
2812. *Cuna (Panama)*, 2924, 9074.
Ecuador, 2063, 3170, 3175, 3178, 3186.
Education, 9525. *Ethnocide*, 2182.
*Government Regulations and
Legislation*, 2648. *Guaraní
(Paraguay)*, 107, 3276, 3278, 3284,
3291. *Guatemala*, 2827, 2847, 2898.
Ika (Colombia), 9091. *Indian Fighter*,
3739, 3838, 3841. *Indian Protectors*,
2127, 2335, 2574, 4041. *Jívaros
(Ecuador)*, 9100. *Kariña (Venezuela)*,
2033. *Latin America*, 2170, 2279. *Maya
(Mexico)*, 9102. *Mexico*, 1963, 2154,
2457, 2463, 2470, 2472, 2490, 2494,
2505, 2510, 2516-2517, 2528, 2538,
2648. *Mískitos (Honduras)*, 9070.
Mojos (Bolivia), 9039. *Moxos
(Bolivia)*, 2343. *Música (Colombia)*,
2027. *Music*, 9057, 9070, 9091, 9100,
9102. *Nahua (Mexico)*, 1991.
Nicaragua, 2826, 2833. *Ona (Chile)*,
3648. *Panama*, 2793, 2833. *Panches
(Colombia)*, 3134. *Paraguay*, 3890.
Peru, 2067, 2833, 3229, 3232-3233,
3235, 6462-6463. *Pijao (Colombia)*,
2074. *Population*, 2059, 2426, 2827,
3278, 3281, 3291, 3890. *and Positivism*,
9514. *Qolla (Peru)*, 2027. *Ranquel
(Arg.)*, 3692. *Resistance*, 2309, 2463,
2563, 2617, 2820, 2828, 2834,
3178-3179, 3196-3197, 3229, 3253, 3296,
3307. *Rights*, 2127, 2298. *Shavante
(Brazil)*, 9041. *Spanish Policy*,
2545-2546, 2565. *Uruguay*, 3270, 3281.
Venezuela, 3107. *Yuayos (Peru)*, 3207.
Zambos-Mosquitos (Costa Rica),
2834.

Indigenismo. *Andean Area*, 2070, 3430.
in Literature, 2773, 6401, 6417,
6462-6463, 6480, 6488, 6501, 6515,
6526, 6554, 6666-6667, 6801, 6830-6831,
6836-6837. *Mexico*, 2470, 2471a. *Peru*,
3484, 3529.

Indigenous Civilizations. See Aztecs;
Incas; Mayas; Precolumbian Cultures;
Toltecs; Zapotecs.

Indigenous Languages. See also
Bilingualism; Codices; specific
countries. *Andean Area*, 2071.
Aymara, 6439, 9040. *Aztec*, 7845.
Chipaya, 9040. *Chocó*, 6049a.
Colombia, 6051. *Colonial Period*,
2105. *Guaraní*, 6113. *Maya*, 6048,
7845. *Náhuatl*, 1953, 1971, 6003, 6043,
6449, 7347, 7834. *Panama*, 6057.
Poetry, 7834. *Quechua*, 2042, 2061,
2118, 6044, 7834, 9040. *Tupi*, 7605.

INDUSTRY AND INDUSTRIAL-
IZATION. See also Agriculture;
specific commodities. *Argentina*, 3779,
3798, 3822, 3853. *Bibliography*, 2739.
Brazil, 4102, 4037, 4113, 4158, 4170.
Chile, 3666. *Coffee*, 4118. *Costa Rica*,
2868. *and Fiscal Policy*, 2167.
Guyana, 123. *Industrialists*, 2686,
3628, 3666, 3798. *Latin America*, 2386,
2405. *Mexico*, 2616, 2664, 2685-2686,
2788. *Peru*, 3493-3494, 3496, 3500,
3516-3517, 3532. *Rubber*, 3494, 3496,
3516-3517, 4161. *Steel*, 2686, 3493.
Sugar, 3531, 3779, 3853, 4037, 4158.
Uruguay, 3940.

Ingenieros, José, 3868-3869, 9427.

Inojosa, Joaquim, 7685.

Inquisition, 2283. *Mexico*, 2452. *Peru*,
3191.

Insurance. *Latin America*, 2147. *Mexico*,
2147.

Insurgente, María, 2629.

Intellectual History. See also
Philosophy; Thinkers and
Philosophers. *Argentina*, 3710, 3714,
3738, 3764. *Bolivia*, 3586. *Brazil*, 3996,
4058, 4128, 7692, 9450. *Chile*, 3393.
Colombia, 3162. *Dominican Republic*,
3041. *Ecuador*, 3478. *Latin America*,
9707. *Mexico*, 2471, 2524, 2623, 2650,
2706, 2736, 2770. *Peru*, 3222, 3488,
3557.

International Relations. See also
Diplomatic History; specific countries

or regions. *Colombia*, 2654. *Latin America*, 2387. *Mexico*, 2654.
Invasions. See also Bay of Pigs
Invasion. *Argentina*, 3815. *British in Rio de la Plata*, 3268, 3401, 3939. *British in Venezuela*, 3354. *French in Argentina*, 3752.
Investment. *Argentina*, 3740, 3886. *Brazil*, 3886, 4131. *British*, 2222, 3886. *Colombia*, 3437. *Latin America*, 2386. *Mexico*, 2150, 2632, 2658, 2663. *Peru*, 3495, 3501.
Ipola, Emilio de, 9486.
Irish in Latin America, 3426.
Irrigation. *Andean Area*, 2046. *Chile*, 3257. *Mexico*, 2256. *Peru*, 3218, 3503, 3533. *Precolumbian*, 2003.
Italians in Latin America, 106, 2128, 2165, 2349, 2413, 3069, 3506, 4062, 4086-4087, 4093, 4105, 4107-4108, 4127, 4190, 6007.
Iturbide, Agustín de, 2674.
Ivo, Lêdo, 7533, 7745.
Ixcue, Nora, 1035-1036.
Ixtlilxochitl, 1987.

JAMAICA.
  Bibliography and General Works, 6, 12, 52, 128.
  History, 2939, 2949, 2953, 2955, 2960, 2983, 2988, 3052.
  Literature.
    Prose Fiction, 7809-7811.
    Poetry, 7814, 7816.
  Music, 9063, 9065-9066.
Japanese in Latin America, 3545.
Jaramillo, Oscar, 367.
Jaramillo Levi, Enrique, 6657.
Jews in Latin America, 2260, 2267, 2393, 3743, 3865-3866, 4153, 4188.
Jitrik, Noé, 6961.
Journalism. See Press.
Journals. See specific disciplines.
Juana Inés de la Cruz, Sor, 6404, 6407, 6426, 6430, 6432-6434, 6452, 7199, 7281, 7834.
Juárez, Benito, 2610, 2616, 2631.
Justicialism. See Perón and Peronism.
Justo, Juan Bautista, 3734.

Kahlo, Frida, 320.
Kennedy, John F., 3566.
King Christophe, 7807.
Kinship. See also Family Relationships.
Indian, 2120. *Mexico*, 1964. *Peru*, 3536.
Korn, Alejandro, 9456.

LABOR AND UNIONS. See also Encomienda; Peasants; Slavery and Slave Trade; Strikes; Unemployment.
Agricultural, 3547, 4114. *Argentina*, 2408, 3277, 3687, 3773, 3777-3778, 3783, 3787, 3792-3793, 3826, 3846, 3852, 3881. *Barbados*, 2954. *Blacks*, 3437. *Bolivia*, 2403, 2408, 3591, 3595. *Brazil*, 2408, 3792, 3994, 4001, 4074, 4089, 4098, 4112, 4114, 4130. *Caribbean*, 3030. *Chile*, 3612, 3645. *Chinese*, 3544-3545. *Colombia*, 3427, 3437. *Colonial*, 2005, 2256, 2327. *Confederación de Trabajadores (CTM), Mexico*, 2774. *Cuba*, 2403, 2408, 3063-3064. *Exploitation of Indians*, 2058. *Foreign*, 2413. *Government Regulations and Legislation*, 3563. *Guadeloupe*, 3030. *History*, 2219, 2403, 2408. *Indians*, 2005, 2058, 2072, 2340, 2425, 2515, 2531, 3156, 3207, 3240. *Industrial*, 3563. *Jamaica*, 2988. *Japanese*, 3544-3545. *Latin America*, 2156. *Leaders*, 2784, 3490, 3564, 3867. *Mexico*, 2408, 2419-2421, 2473, 2587, 2593, 2621, 2698-2699, 2701, 2729-2730, 2762, 2764, 2771, 2774, 2782, 2787, 3792. *Movements*, 2219, 2403, 2408, 2701, 2712, 2729, 2771, 2782, 3021, 3062-3063. *National Confederation of Industrial Communities (Peru)*, 3563. *Occupations*, 3555. *Paraguay*, 3897. *Peru*, 2403, 3218, 3482, 3493, 3507, 3511, 3516, 3531-3533, 3544, 3547, 3555, 3563-3564. *Precolumbian*, 2104. *Puerto Rico*, 8, 3038, 3046, 3062. *Steelworkers*, 3493. *Trinidad*, 3021. *US*, 2728, 2763. *Wages*, 3437, 3669, 4074. *Worker Participation*, 3563.
Labrador Ruiz, Enrique, 6731.
Labuchin, Rassoul, 7801.
Lacassin, Francis, 6729.
Ladinos, 2827, 6057, 6133.
Lam, Wifredo, 338.
Lamarque, Libertad, 9009.
Land and Labor. See Agrarian Reform; Land Tenure; History, Colonial; Labor; Plantations; Social Organization.

LAND TENURE. See also Agrarian Reform; Cooperatives; Plantations. *Andean Area*, 2050. *Argentina*, 3719. *Aztec*, 1961. *Borderlands*, 2567. *Brazil*, 2958. *Caribbean*, 3030. *Chile*, 2404, 3254, 3612, 3645. *Colombia*, 2404, 3147, 3424, 3439. *Colonial Period*, 3135a-3136, 3144, 3152. *Costa Rica*, 2404, 2829. *Cuba*, 2958. *El Salvador*, 2791. *French Guiana*, 2958. *Government Regulations and Legislation*, 3545. *Guadeloupe*, 3030. *Incas*, 2079. *Mexico*, 1963-1964, 2419-2421, 2428, 2434, 2473, 2477, 2500-2501, 2515, 2521, 2544, 2546, 2568, 2592-2593, 2630. *Peru*, 2041, 2047, 2404, 3203, 3219, 3497-3498, 3502-3504, 3536, 3545, 3568. *West Indies*, 2958.
Landi, Antônio José, 431
Landívar, Rafael, 6421
LANGUAGE (items 6001-6137). See also Bilingualism; Creole; Dictionaries; Indigenous Languages; Linguistics; Literature; Portuguese Language; Public Policy; Spanish Language; Translation; specific countries. *Basque*, 6014a. *Catalan*, 6014a. *Colonial Period*, 2105. *Conferences*, 7674. *Institutes*, 6058, 6485, 6494. *Papiamento*, 6122. *Philosophy of*, 9724, 9727. *Pidgin*, 6131. *Teaching Languages*, 102, 6088, 6092, 6137. *Urban*, 6049.
Larraín Errázuriz, Manuel, 3643, 9499, 9507-9508.
LATIN AMERICA. See specific region or country.
Latin American Library Collections. See Libraries and Library Services; Catalogs.
Latin American Studies in. See also Brazilian Studies. *Czechoslovakia*, 3012. *Federal Republic of Germany*, 69, 90. *France*, 2730. *International Approach*, 2200. *Italy*, 100. *Latin Americanists*, 102. *Latin Americanists in Europe*, 113. *Texas*, 49, 102. *United Kingdom*, 127. *USSR*, 2171, 2192, 3011, 3605, 3889, 3987-3988.
Lavrín Cerda, Hernán, 6885.
Law. See also Government Regulations and Legislation under specific subject terms; Law of the Sea; Territorial Law. *Colonial*, 2250, 2254, 2266. *Death Penalty*, 3483. *and Development*, 2183. *History*, 9697. *Peru*, 3483. *Philosophy of*, 9687, 9696, 9701-9703, 9708-9709. *Puerto Rico*, 118. *West Indies*, 2957.
Law of the Sea. *Bibliography*, 28, 2411. *Legislation*, 2411.
El Lazarillo de ciegos caminantes, 6409.
Leguía, Augusto, 3501.
Leñero, Vicente, 7346.
León, Pedro Cieza de, 6435.
León Sánchez, José, 6662.
Leonard, Irving A., 6413.
Lerner, Elisa, 7380.
LESSER ANTILLES. See also Aruba; Barbados; Curaçao; Dominica; Eustatius; Guadeloupe; Martinique; Montserrat; St. Kitts; St. Lucia; St. Vincent; Tortola; Trinidad and Tobago; US Virgin Islands; West Indies.
Bibliography and General Works, 6, 12, 2148.
History, 2148, 2974.
Language, 6124.
Letelier, Valentín, 9469.
Levertov, Denise, 6617.
Lévi-Strauss, Claude, 9634, 9721.
Lezama Lima, José, 6716, 6728, 6740, 6742.
Libraries and Library Services. See also Archives; Catalogs; Computers and Computerization; Library and Information Science; Publishing Industry; Research Aids. *Argentina*, 57. *Barbados*, 52. *Biblioteca Jesuíta (Ecuador)*, 3165. *Biblioteca Nacional (Brazil)*, 2-5, 47. *Biblioteca Nacional (Colombia)*, 48. *Biblioteca Nacional (Peru)*, 44, 3536. *Biblioteca Nacional (Venezuela)*, 58. *Biblioteca Nacional José Martí, (Cuba)*, 98. *Brazil*, 46, 70a, 528. *Caribbean*, 9065. *Central America*, 55. *Centro de Documentación Patagónica*, 72. *Colombia*, 65. *Colonial Period*, 3154, 3241. *Costa Rica*, 55. *Cuba*, 81. *Ecuador*, 3165. *France*, 1978. *Fundaço Movimento Brasileiro de Alfabetização (MOBRAL) Library*, 54. *Guide to Argentine University Libraries*, 57. *Guide to Peruvian University Libraries*, 53. *Hispanic Society (US)*, 6407. *Instituto*

Subject Index — Libraries and Library Service—Literature / 643

do Ceará (Brazil), 77. *Institut für Ibero-Amerika Kunde (Hamburg, FRG)*, 90. *Jamaica*, 52. *Library of Congress (US)*, 50. *Library of Congress Acquisitions from Brazil*, 70a. *Music*, 9065. *Nicaragua*, 55. *Panama*, 55. *Rare Book Collecting and Brazil*, 73. *Spain*, 2305. *Universidad Nacional Autónoma de México*, 109. *University*, 46. *University of Texas Latin American Collection*, 49. *US Virgin Islands*, 59.

Library and Information Science. See also Archives; Computers and Computerization; Libraries and Library Services. *Annual Conference of the Association of Caribbean University and Research Libraries (ACURIL)*, 4th, San Juan, P.R. (1972), 43. *Dictionary*, 45. *Journals*, 98. *Librarians*, 48-49, 56. *Library Associations*, 59. *Mexico*, 56. *Reunión de Estudio Centro Catalográfico Centroamericano*, San José, C.R. (1976), 55.

Lima, Cláudio Medeiros, 7773.
Lima Hermes, 7774.
Lima, Jorge de, 7537.
Limantour, José Yves, 9116.
LINGUISTICS. See also Codices; Dictionaries; Indigenious Languages; Language; Philology; Portuguese Language; Spanish Language. *and Anthropology*, 6094. *Applied*, 6008, 6100. *Bibliography*, 6013, 6014a. *Comparative*, 6096. *Historical*, 6096. *Institutes*, 6100. *Paraguay*, 3276. *and Poetry*, 7754. *Theory*, 6008, 6091, 6106, 9726, 9728. *and Translation*, 6092.
Lins, Osman, 7721.
Lisboa, Henriqueta, 7541.
Literacy and Illiteracy. *Brazil*, 54. *Haiti*, 6123. *Indian*, 2105. *Mexico*, 2768. *Venezuela*, 3450.
LITERARY CRITICISM. *Argentine works*, 6717, 6958-7003. *Bolivia*, 6801-6803. *Brazilian works*, 7661-7732. *Caribbean works*, 7805. *Central American works*, 6655. *Chilean works*, 6874-6892. *Colombian works*, 6804-6826. *Costa Rican works*, 6655-6656, 6659, 6662, 6665. *Critics*, 6834, 7669, 7702. *Cuban works*, 6703-6704, 6706-6707, 6712-6713, 6715-6728, 6730, 6732-6738, 6742-6743, 6747-6748. *Ecuadorian works*, 6827. *Guatemalan works*, 6658, 6660, 6663, 6666-6667, 6671-6672. *Haitian works*, 7795, 7798, 7800. *Hispanic Caribbean works*, 6702-6748. *Mexico*, 6592-6622. *Nicaragua*, 6670. *Novels*, 6593, 6595-6596, 6599-6601, 6605-6606, 6608, 6610, 6616, 6619-6620, 6622, 6661-6662, 6665-6667, 6670, 6674, 6712-6713, 6722, 6724-6728, 6730-6732, 6742-6743, 6747, 6801, 6804-6806, 6809-6812, 6814-6815, 6817-6825, 6829-6831, 6835-6842, 6844-6847, 6849-6850, 6874, 6878, 6882, 6886-6892, 6966, 6971, 6973-6974, 6976, 6979-6980, 6994, 7005, 7007-7010, 7012, 7703-7705, 7710, 7712, 7714, 7716, 7719, 7721-7724, 7795, 7798. *Panamanian works*, 6657, 6661a, 6664, 6674. *Paraguayan works*, 7004-7010. *Peruvian works*, 6828-6849. *Poetry*, 6671-6672. *Puerto Rican works*, 6705, 6739. *Reviews*, 7702. *Short Stories*, 6655-6657, 6659, 6661a, 6664, 6705, 6713-6714, 6739, 6805, 6807, 6833, 6843, 6848, 6852, 6877, 6880, 6883, 6959, 6962, 6981-6982, 6987, 6999, 7004, 7006, 7011, 7013, 7015, 7666, 7707, 7715, 7726. *Uruguayan works*, 7011-7015. *Venezuelan works*, 6850-6853.

Literatura de Cordel, 6407.
LITERATURE (items 6401-7945). See also Costumbrismo; Drama; Film; Indigenismo; Language; Literary Criticism; Novelists; Poetry; Poets; Prose Fiction; Short Story Writers; Translation; specific countries. *Adolescent*, 6592, 6612, 6619. *Alienation*, 6874, 6932, 6941, 6948. *Avant-garde*, 6467, 7674. *Aymra*, 6439. *Aztecs*, 6594. *Bibliography*, 19, 6493, 6503, 6801-6803, 6851-6852. *Black*, 6486, 6523, 6632. *Bolivia*, 6802. *Chicano*, 6617. *Children*, 6653. *Colonial*, 6401-6456. *Comparative*, 7713. *Conferences*, 7674. *Eroticism*, 6567, 6575, 6578-6579, 6582-6584. *History*, 6802. *Inca*, 6447-6448. *Journals*, 91, 132, 6503, 6553, 6558, 6734, 6822, 6826, 6845, 6849, 6888, 6961, 6963, 7678, 7680, 7687, 7808, 7827. *Journal Indexes*, 97-98. *Latin*

America, 6513, 6537, 6709. *Literary Academies*, 7670, 7682, 7774. *Magic Realism*, 6658, 6666-6667, 6735, 6738. *Maya*, 6658. *Memoirs*, 7765, 7769, 7772-7775. *Mexico*, 6495. *Modern*, 6457-6557. *Modernism*, 6514, 6517, 7662, 7667, 7671, 7683-7684, 7686-7687, 7701. *Quechua*, 6439. *Regionalism*, 7663-7665, 7681, 7727. *and Revolution*, 6460a, 6469, 6596, 6616, 6618, 6682, 6708, 6723, 6730, 6746, 7021. *Surrealism*, 6879. *Teaching Literature*, 102. *Textbooks and Anthologies*, 6491, 6538-6539, 6549-6550, 6648-6649, 6682-6683, 6758, 6766, 6778, 6788, 6796, 6853, 6900, 6917, 6933, 7688-7689, 7698,7802. *Theory*, 6709-6711, 6832, 7676. *Vanguardist Movement*, 6664.
Littín, Miguel, 1000, 1004.
Lizardi, José Joaquín Fernández de, 6429.
Llanos, Bernardino de, 6442.
Lleras Camargo, Alberto, 3431.
Lleras Restrepo, Carlos, 3432
Lobato, José Bento Monteiro, 7767.
Lombardi, Francisco José, 1035-1036.
López, Francisco Solano, 3900, 3907, 3909.
López, Luis Carlos, 6826.
López Buchardo, Carlos, 9026.
López Osornio, Mario E., 6509.
Louisiana. See Borderlands.
Loveira, Carlos, 6727.
Lugones, Leopoldo, 6960, 6999, 7188, 7197, 7836, 9498.
Lunfardo, 6034, 6045.
Luperón, Gregorio, 3023.
Lynch, Marta, 6916, 6945, 6986.
Lyra, Carmen [*pseud. for* María Isabel Carvajal], 6662a.

Mabe, Manabu, 398.
Macedonio, Fernández, 9449.
Machado de Assis, Joaquim María, 7716-7717, 7730.
Madero, Francisco, 2691, 2722.
Madrid, José Fernández, 2347
Magalhães, Solange, 471
Magellan, Ferdinand, 2277.
Maldonado, Eduardo, 1024
Mallea, Eduardo, 6983, 6988.
Malnutrition. See also Nutrition. *Latin America*, 2197.

MALVINAS, ISLAS.
History, 3797, 3819, 3875.
Manuel, Víctor, 339.
MANUSCRIPTS. See also Archives; Music. *Aztec*, 1978. *Bolivian*, 61. *Brazil*, 4046. *Latin America*, 80. *Mexico*, 2442, 2444. *Náhuatl Literature*, 6449. *Peru*, 80, 3220. *Philip H. & A.S.W. Rosenbach Foundation*, 80. *Quechua*, 2118. *Sources for Latin American History*, 113, 2100, 2442, 2444, 2939, 3199, 3384, 3470, 4046.
Maps and Cartography. *Atlases*, 16. *Brazil*, 1, 3, 4055. *Colonial*, 1967, 1995, 3175. *Ecuador*, 3175. *Haiti*, 126. *Puerto Rico*, 8. *Remote Sensing*, 6085. *Venezuela/Colombia*, 16. *World*, 2308, 2550.
Marechal, Leopoldo, 6960, 6969, 7002.
Mariátegui, José Carlos, 3529, 9425, 9495, 9497, 9500, 9512, 9519, 9524-9526.
Marín, Alvaro, 367.
Marine Resources. *Bibliography*, 28.
Maritime History, 3399, 3508, 3523, 3646.
MARKETING AND PRODUCT DISTRIBUTION. *Andean Area*, 2081. *Argentina*, 3706. *Aztec*, 1961. *Chile*, 3612, 3625. *CONASUPO*, 2719, 2721. *Haiti*, 30. *Latin America*, 2398. *Mexico*, 2527, 2533, 2594, 2719. *Peru*, 3509, 3568. *Portuguese Dictionary*, 6120.
Marques, René, 6739, 7379, 7933.
Marques, Xavier, 7729.
Márquez, Gabriel. See García Márquez, Gabriel.
Marriage. See Family Relationships.
Martí, José, 2934, 2940, 3033, 7186, 7231.
Martín Fierro, 361, 7834, 7865.
Martínez, José de J., 9431.
Martínez, Raymundo, 328.
Martínez, Ricardo, 328.
Martínez Estrada, Ezequiel, 6960, 7836, 9513.
Martínez Villena, Rubén, 3060.
MARTINIQUE.
Bibliographic and General Work, 6.
Poetry, 7791a.
Music, 9065-9066.
Marx, Roberto Burle, 475.
Marxism, 9567, 9594, 9600, 9680,

9698-9699, 9704, 9706, 9710.
MASS MEDIA. See also Censorship;
Film; Press; Publishing Industry;
Radio; Television. *Brazil*, 515-525,
529, 980, 7766, 9047. *Cartoons*, 412,
515-525, 529, 6903, 7766. *Cuba*, 1014.
and Literature, 6975. *Peru*, 3519.
Recording Industry, 9048.
Matarazza, Francisco, 527.
Matías Moreno, José, 2625.
Matta, Roberto, 398.
Mattelart, Armand, 6729.
Matto de Turner, Clorinda, 6526.
Mauricio, Julio, 7401.
Mauro, Humberto, 991.
Maximilian and the French Intervention
in Mexico, 2611-2612, 2618, 2644,
2657, 2667.
Mayas, 1976, 1979-1980, 1983, 1993,
2019, 2857.
Medicine. See also Diseases; Public
Health. *Brazil*, 4016-4017, 4038, 4175.
Colonial Period, 2031, 2549. *Doctors*,
4175. *Ecuador*, 3461, 3466. *Medical
Profession*, 2260. *Nahua Indians*,
1991. *Paraguay*, 3901. *Precolumbian*,
1991.
Medrano, Salvador M., 2845.
Meiriles, Cecília, 7553.
Melgar, Mariano, 6443.
Mena y Medrano, Pedro de, 295.
Menéndez, Francisco, 2872.
Mérida, Carlos, 328, 398.
MESOAMERICA. See also
Precolumbian Cultures; specific
countries.
History, 2417, 2426.
Ethnohistory, 1951-2024, 2117, 2262,
2279.
Methodology. See specific discipline.
Mexican Americans. See Chicanos.
Mexican Revolution. See also Literature,
and revolution, 2158, 2228, 2382, 2390,
2621, 2664, 2680, 2683, 2687,
2690-2691, 2695, 2698, 2700, 2703-2704,
2707, 2710, 2717, 2724-2725, 2732,
2734-2736, 2742, 2753-2759, 2773, 2778,
2786. *Cristero Rebellion*, 2723, 2752.
Mexican War, 2633.
MEXICO.
Bibliography and General Works, 12,
56, 71, 85-86, 124, 128.
Art, 252-254, 277-292, 307-308,
314-330.
Film, 960-961, 1017-1030, 6048, 6052.
History, 71, 2145-2146, 2150, 2154,
2156, 2201, 2216, 2248, 2256, 2293,
2306, 2340, 2343-2344, 2386, 2388,
2418-2788, 3048, 3793.
Ethnohistory. See Mesoamerica.
Language, 6030, 6033, 6056, 6080.
Literature.
Prose Fiction, 99, 316, 6452, 6461,
6464, 6484, 6487, 6489, 6492, 6495,
6497, 6500, 6502, 6510, 6522, 6542,
6548, 6558-6622, 7885, 7887,
7894-7896, 7901, 7910, 7920,
7924-7926.
Poetry, 7037-7039, 7047, 7050,
7053-7054, 7068, 7072, 7076-7077,
7087, 7093-7094, 7096, 7100,
7104-7105, 7114, 7122, 7127, 7131,
7133, 7139, 7151, 7161, 7190,
7199-7200, 7207, 7213, 7225, 7839,
7877-7878.
Drama, 6604, 7240, 7252-7253, 7276,
7283-7286, 7316, 7319, 7331, 7344,
7346-7347, 7352, 7354, 7357,
7366-7367, 7376-7377, 7385,
7391-7392, 7400, 7930, 7933.
Music, 9005, 9007, 9015, 9023,
9101-9129.
Philosophy, 9448, 9457, 9460-9461,
9464, 9467, 9473, 9475, 9488,
9489-9491, 9501, 9527.
Mexico and Chile Relations, 2731.
Mexico and Spain Relations, 2749.
Meza, Guillermo, 328.
MIDDLE AMERICA. See
Mesoamerica.
MIGRATIONS. See also specific
nationalities, ethnic groups. *Andean
Area*, 2048-2049. *Argentina*, 2128,
2160, 2188, 2343, 2413, 3678, 3742,
3780, 3821, 3871. *Brazil*, 2160, 2180,
2188, 2343, 4112, 4114, 4137, 4153,
4169, 4176. *British Guiana*, 3035.
Canary Islands/Latin America, 2357,
2987. *Caribbean*, 3030. *Chile*, 2404,
3614. *Colombia*, 2404. *Colonial*, 2288.
Costa Rica, 2404, 2802. *Cuba*, 2343.
Dominican Republic, 2971. *Ecuador*,
3170. *El Salvador*, 2343. *Guatemala*,
2160, 2898. *Latin America*, 2187, 2217,
2238, 2349, 2369. *Mexico*, 2343, 2420,
2597, 2598, 2662, 2730. *Mexico/US*,
2698-2699, 2727, 2746, 2763. *Peru*,
2404, 3556. *Puerto Rico*, 3057.

US/Mexico, 2712. *West Indies*, 2261, 2969.
Milanés, José Jacinto, 7364.
MILITARY. See also Arms; Battles; Coup d'Etat; Exploration and Expeditions; Invasions; Maritime History; Military Leaders; Police. *Argentina*, 3403, 3692-3693, 3704, 3724, 3739, 3791, 3799, 3815, 3837, 3838, 3841, 3846. *Bolivia*, 3088, 3577, 3596-3597. *Brazil*, 3986, 4079, 4088, 4096, 4122-4124, 4142, 4152. *Chile*, 2414, 3256, 3395, 3609, 3627, 3635, 3654. *Colonial Period*, 2252, 2280, 2292, 3068, 3192-3193, 3256. *Cuba*, 3037. *Dominican Republic*, 2971. *Ecuador*, 3169, 3464. *El Salvador*, 2895-2896. *Guatemala*, 2885. *History*, 2669, 2683, 2772, 3464, 3570, 3596, 3654, 3693, 3704, 3893, 3913, 3954, 3986. *History of Engineering*, 3604. *Latin America*, 2394, 2396. *Mexico*, 2414, 2475, 2547, 2552, 2572, 2619, 2669, 2683, 2693, 2730, 2753, 2772, 2788. *Nicaragua*, 2901. *Panama*, 2929. *Paraguay*, 3923. *Peru*, 3068, 3088, 3510, 3529, 3538, 3543,3553, 3570, 3572. *and Politics*., 2394. *Precolumbian*, 2002, 2016. *Uruguay*, 3272, 3274, 3944, 3954.
Military Assistance from United States to Mexico, 2590.
Military Leaders. See also Explorers; specific names. *Argentina*, 3315, 3319, 3324, 3367, 3411, 3689. *Bolivia*, 3320, 3322, 3330, 3333, 3368-3369. *Chile*, 3329, 3390-3391, 3670. *Colombia*, 3365, 3426. *Peru*, 3334, 3375, 3538. *Uruguay*, 3410, 3935. *Venezuela*, 2207, 2249, 2350, 3310, 3312, 3326-3327, 3330-3332, 3343, 3345a-3346, 3349, 3353, 3355, 3368, 3372, 3377, 3380-3381, 6525.
Mindlin, Henrique Ephim, 489.
MINERALS AND MINING INDUSTRY. *Bolivia*, 3238-3240, 3242, 3595. *Borderlands*, 2562, 2627, 2646. *Brazil*, 4006. *California*, 3644. *Chile*, 3245, 3248, 3625, 3632, 3664, 3668. *Colonial Period*, 2084, 3131, 3146. *Colombia*, 3131, 3240. *Copper*, 2150, 3632. *Cuba*, 2970. *Gold*, 3159, 4006. *Government Regulations and Legislation*, 3238. *Jade*, 2018. *Latin America*, 2386. *Metallurgy*, 2322. *Mexico*, 2473, 2477, 2503. *Nitrates*, 2150, 3625. *Peru*, 3204-3205, 3218, 3518, 3533, 3549-3550. *Salt*, 2562. *Silver*, 2150, 2311, 2477, 3204-3205, 3242, 3550. *Tin*, 3242, 3595.
Mir, Pedro, 7836.
Miranda, Francisco de, 2132, 2224, 3343.
Missionaries. See Catholic Church; Protestant Churches.
Mistral, Gabriela, 6875, 7834.
Mörner, Magnus, 2156.
Molina, Enrique, 9469.
Molina, Juan Ignacio, 3251.
Molina, Luis, 7360.
Monleón, José, 7361-7362.
Monroe Doctrine. See US and Latin America Relations.
MONTSERRAT.
Bibliography and General Works, 6.
Monuments. *Argentina*, 3845. *Brazil*, 450, 488. *Eustatius*, 3042. *Paraguay*, 377. *Uruguay*, 302, 387.
Moock, Armando, 7326.
Moore, Philip, 337.
Moraes, Carlos Dante de, 7694.
Morales, Darío, 373.
Morra Fernández, Juan, 2880.
Morretes, Fredrico Lange de, 441.
Mortality and Morbidity Patterns. *Brazil*, 4026. *Colonial Period*, 2037. *Jamaica*, 3052. *Mexico*, 2517.
Moving pictures. See Film.
Moyano, Daniel, 6959.
MULTINATIONAL CORPORATIONS. See also Industry and Industrialization; Nationalization; specific industries. *International Harvester*, 2594, 2705. *Latin America*, 2389, 2394. *International Petroleum Co.*, 3552. *Peru*, 3514, 3517, 3549, 3552. *US Brands Co. (formerly United Fruit Co.)*, 2905, 2925, 2928, 3439. *Venezuela*, 3454. *W.R. Grace & Co.*, 3549.
Muñoz Marín, Luis, 3059.
Muñoz Rivera, Luiz, 2932.
Murta, Genesco, 473.
Museums and Museology. *Art*, 258-259, 270-271, 297, 369, 378, 398-399, 416, 436, 448, 459, 472, 474-475, 984. *Bolivia*, 258-259. *Brazil*, 416, 436, 448, 459, 472, 474-475, 500, 502, 984. *Coffee*, 502. *Colombia*, 270-271, 369.

Cuba, 81. *Dominican Republic*, 263. *Mexico*, 1958. *Music*, 9007. *Paraguay*, 378. *Peru*, 297. *Restoration*, 448. *Venezuela*, 398-399.

MUSIC (items 9001-9148). See also Composers and Conductors; Ethnomusicology; Mass Media; Musical Instruments; Musicians; Opera; Religion, music; Singers; Songs; Theaters; specific countries. *Academies*, 9043, 9077, 9080, 9090. *American Musiological Society meeting*, 9006. *Aztec*, 9016, 9126. *Baroque*, 9132. *Bibliography*, 9002, 9040. *Choral*, 9138, 9142, 9145. *Colonial*, 9003-9004, 9010, 9018, 9036, 9044, 9051, 9092, 9107, 9112. *Critics*, 9021. *Dissertations*, 9017, 9044. *Education*, 9014. *Festivals*, 9010, 9021, 9025, 9061. *Folk*, 9038, 9063, 9077, 9089. *Gregorian*, 9023. *History*, 9049, 9080-9081, 9093a, 9135, 9140, 9146. *Inca*, 9016. *International Seminar on Music Education Research*, 9014. *Journals*, 9077, 9117. *Libraries*, 9065. *Manuscripts*, 9004. *Musicologists*, 9060, 9117, 9129, 9146. *Musicology*, 9007. *Onomatopeic Sounds of Instruments*, 6077. *Political*, 9081. *Popular*, 9109-9110, 9118. *Reference works*, 9006, 9011. *Rock*, 9022c. *Salsa*, 9001, 9064. *Symphonies*, 9096, 9097a. *Tangos*, 9009, 9022a, 9032. *Textbooks*, 9105.

Musical Instruments. *Accordian*, 9040. *Bandoneón*, 9032. *Bango*, 9066. *Bolivia*, 9040. *Caribbean*, 9066. *Charago*, 9038, 9040. *Cuatro*, 9143. *Cuba*, 9097. *Dominican Republic*, 9067. *Drums*, 9076. *Flutes*, 9099, 9102. *Gourd-flute*, 9041. *Guitar*, 9040, 9054, 9101-9102, 9115. *Harp*, 9143. *Lute*, 9114. *Mandolin*, 9102. *Manuscripts*, 9148. *Maracas*, 9143. *Marimba*, 9109. *Ocarina*, 9099. *Quena*, 9040. *Trumpets*, 9102. *Viola*, 9054. *Violin*, 9102, 9115.

Musicians. See also names of individual musicians. *Argentina*, 9022b. *Bolivia*, 9037. *Brazil*, 9054, 9059. *Chile*, 362, 9083, 9085. *Mexico*, 9101, 9108, 9118. *Puerto Rico*, 9064. *Venezuela*, 9143.

Mythology. *Andean Area*, 2052. *Aztec*, 6447. *Inca*, 2097. *Paraguay*, 3276.

Naranjo, Carmen, 6656.
National Bibliographies. *Argentina*, 41, *Barbados*, 40. *Ecuador*, 39. *and International Standard Book Description*, 51. *Venezuela*, 42.
National Culture. See Cultural Identity.
Nationalism. *Argentina*, 3888, 6540, 9505, 9510-9511. *Costa Rica*, 2914. *Latin America*, 2174, 2239. *Mexico*, 2418, 2466-2467, 2764.
Nationalization. *Argentina*, 3808. *Bolivia*, 3595. *International Petroleum Co.*, 3572. *Peru*, 3538, 3572. *Petroleum*, 3538, 3808. *Tin*, 3595.
Natural Disasters. *Colonial Period*, 3147a. *Droughts*, 2744. *Earthquakes*, 2595, 3253, 3440, 6636. *Mexico*, 2595. *Nicaragua*, 6636.
Natural Resources. See also Energy Sources; Irrigation; Marine Resources; Minerals and Mining. *Argentina*, 3730. *Forests*, 3730. *Guano*, 3544. *Latin America*, 2239.
Nava, Homero, 390.
Navarro, Noel, 6728.
Negret, Edgar, 368.
Negritude, 7028, 7794. *Drama*, 7382.
Negroes. See Blacks.
Nemirovsky, José, 476.
Neruda, Pablo, 389, 6821, 6875, 7118, 7210, 7220, 7229, 7234, 7829, 7836-7837.
Neto, Simões Lopes, 7727.
New Granada, Viceroyalty of. See History, Colonial.
New Mexico. See Borderlands.
New Spain, Viceroyalty of. See History, Colonial.
Newspapers. See Press.
NICARAGUA.
  Bibliography and General Works, 12, 55, 128.
  Art, 332, 334.
  History, 2813, 2826, 2833, 2851, 2856, 2870, 2894, 2901-2902, 2905.
  Literature.
    Prose Fiction, 6631, 6636, 6646, 6649, 6670.
    Poetry, 7029, 7115-7116, 7172.
    Drama, 7315.
Niemeyer, Oscar, 389, 498.
NORTHEAST, BRAZIL (region).
  Art, 505, 510.
  History, 4029, 4063, 4115, 4133.

Language, 6095a.
Literature.
  Prose Fiction 7417, 7684-7685.
  Poetry, 7570.
Novelists. See also names of individual novelists. *Argentina*, 955, 6467, 6504, 6874, 6916, 6963, 7003. *Brazil*, 7708-7709, 7711, 7714, 7716, 7769, 7775. *Chile*, 6458, 6519, 6874. *Colombia*, 318, 955, 6689, 6758, 6811. *Colonial Period*, 6419, 6429. *Cuba*, 955, 6458, 6460a, 6483, 6489, 6498, 6504, 6679, 6715, 6721-6722, 6724, 6728, 6733, 6742-6743, 6747. *Ecuador*, 33, 6501. *Guatemala*, 6504-6505, 6639. *Latin America* 15, 6468, 6519. *Mexico*, 955, 6461, 6464, 6505, 6548, 6598. *Paraguay*, 6505, 7007-7010. *Peru*, 6480, 6504, 6519, 6830, 6836-6838, 6840-6842, 6845-6847, 6849. *Uruguay*, 6458. *Venezuela*, 42, 6490, 6806.
Novels. See Prose Fiction.
Novo, Salvador, 7367.
Numismatics, 2139, 2792, 2805, 3074, 3096, 3864.
Núñez, Enrique Bernardo, 36.
Núñez Cabeza de Vaca, Alvar, 2557.
Nutrition. See also Malnutrition. *Brazil*, 2406. *Chile*, 3255. *Colonial Period*, 2331, 3231, 3255. *Haiti*, 30, *Indians*, 2425.

Obregón, Alejandro, 312.
Obregón, Alvaro, 6510.
Ocampo, Melchor, 2588.
Ocampo, Silvina, 6945.
O'Gorman, Edmundo, 2751.
O'Gorman, Juan, 329.
O'Higgins, Bernardo, 3329, 3394, 3396, 3635, 3670.
Oil. See Petroleum and Petrochemical Industry.
Olavide, Pablo de, 6419.
Oliveira, André Luiz, 996.
Oña, Pedro de, 6422.
Onetti, Juan Carlos, 6458, 6874, 7011, 7013, 7015, 7843.
OPEC. See Organization of Petroleum Exporting Countries.
OPERA. *Argentina*, 9009, 9013, 9027, 9033. *Brazil*, 9009, 9013, 9044, 9050. *Encyclopedias*, 9005, 9013. *Houses*, 490, 9013. *Latin America*, 9019-9020. *Mexico*, 9125. *Venezuela*, 9141, 9144.

Oral History, 2415.
Orejón y Aparicio, José de, 9134.
Organization of American States (OAS). *Library Services*, 55.
Organization of Petroleum Exporting Countries (OPEC), 2410.
Orozco Romero, Carlos, 328.
Orta Ruíz, Jesús, 6728.
Ortíz, Fernando, 6721.
Otero, Alejandro, 389, 398.
Ovalla, Alonso de, 3250.
Oviedo, Gonzalo Fernández de, 6428.

Páez, José de, 282.
PAINTERS. See also names of individual painters. *Argentina*, 344-346, 348-350, 352-353, 357-361. *Brazil*, 398, 419-420, 422, 441, 447, 452-457, 461-462, 464, 466-467, 470-473, 475-476, 478-479, 482-486, 506, 533-534. *Chile*, 362-363, 398, 9083. *Colombia*, 312, 367-368, 371, 373-375. *Cuba*, 338-339, 342-343. *Guatemala*, 333. *Latin America*, 312, 7075. *Mexico*, 277, 282, 284, 312, 314, 316-317, 319-323, 325, 327-328, 330, 343. *Peru*, 300, 379-381. *Russia*, 2373. *Uruguay*, 38, 383-385, 9493. *Venezuela*, 304, 388, 390-393, 398, 400-403.
Palacios, Aliria, 394.
Paleontology. *Bibliography*, 31.
Palés Matos, Luis, 7195, 7829.
Pampas. See Argentina; Patagonia.
PANAMA.
  Bibliography and General Works, 12, 55, 128.
  Art, 267.
  Film, 1031-1033.
  History, 2789, 2793, 2795, 2816, 2825, 2840-2841, 2843, 2855, 2864-2865, 2882, 2887, 2905, 2908, 2920, 2927, 2929, 3325.
    Ethnohistory, 2924.
  Language, 6057.
  Literature.
    Prose Fiction 6627, 6634, 6638, 6644, 6657, 6664, 6669, 6673-6674.
    Poetry, 6651, 6669, 7027, 7062, 7064, 7117, 7129.
    Drama, 7288.
  Music, 9071, 9074, 9076.
  Philosophy, 9477.
Panama and Colombia Relations, 2882.

PANAMA CANAL ZONE. See also
  US and Panama Relations.
  History, 2196, 2215, 2855, 2860, 2889,
  2893, 2899, 2910, 3439.
  Literature.
    Prose Fiction, 6628, 6644.
Panama Congress, 2207, 2249, 2345-2346,
  2350, 2368, 3325, 3341.
Pan-Americanism. See also Panama
  Congress; Organization of American
  States. 2249.
PARAGUAY.
  Bibliography and General Work,
    12-13, 113, 128.
  Art, 293-294, 377-378.
  History, 107, 2340, 3091, 3263, 3266,
    3271, 3275-3276, 3278, 3282, 3284,
    3288-3291, 3303, 3305-3307, 3889.
    Ethnohistory, 2080.
  Language, 6028, 6029a, 6031-6032,
    6055, 6064.
  Literature.
    Prose Fiction, 7004-7010.
    Poetry, 7153, 7833.
    Drama, 7343.
  Music, 9008, 9130.
Paraguay and Austro-Hungarian Empire
  Relations, 3904.
Paraguayan War (War of the Triple
  Alliance), 3728, 3860, 3887, 3895, 3900,
  3906-3907, 3913, 3919-3920.
Pardo Tovar, Andrés, 9420.
PATAGONIA.
  History, 3070, 3309, 3563, 3669, 3674,
    3698, 3717, 3723, 3729, 3753, 3759,
    3797, 3802, 3806-3807, 3836, 3863,
    3883-3884.
Paz, Juan Carlos, 9030.
Paz, Octavio, 316, 6613, 7189, 7200,
  7225, 7392, 7829, 7879.
Paz Castillo, Fernando, 7223.
PEASANTS. See also Agrarian Reform;
  Cooperatives; Indians; Land Tenure.
  Andean Area, 2056, *Argentina*, 3852,
  3855. *Bolivia*, 3048, 3584. *Brazil*, 4063,
  4170. *Chile*, 3645. *Colombia*, 2074,
  3424, 3427, 3437. *El Salvador*, 2915.
  Guatemala, 2926. *Latin America*,
  2156, 2398. *Leaders*, 3567. *Mexico*,
  2649, 2730, 2734, 2755, 2780,
  2785-2786, 3048. *Movements*, 3512,
  3528, 3546-3547, 3567, 3584. *Peru*,
  2403, 3489, 3512, 3520, 3546-3547,
  3565. *Trinidad*, 3045.

Pellicer, Carlos, 7829.
Penna, Cornélio, 7719.
Penteado, Olivia Guedes, 530.
Peón Contreras, José, 7354.
Peralta, José, 9516.
Pereira Salas, Eugenio, 3631.
Pérez, Carlos Andrés, 3454.
Pérez, Santiago, 6457.
Pérez de Alesio, Mateo, 300.
Pérez Jiménez, Marcos, 3448.
Periodicals. See specific disciplines.
Peron and Peronism, 3676, 3683, 3708,
  3721, 3735, 3751, 3782, 3785,
  3789-3790, 3805, 3814, 3833-3834, 3855,
  3861, 3885, 3905.
Perón, Eva Duarte, 3744, 3820.
Perón, María Estela Martínez de, 3880.
PERU. See also Amazonia; Andean
  Area.
  Bibliography and General Works, 12,
    44, 53, 128, 132.
  Art, 251, 295-301, 379-382.
  Film, 953, 960-961, 1034-1039.
  History, 2150, 2156, 2201, 2293, 2306,
    2344, 2386, 2404, 3065-3068, 3071-3072,
    3077, 3081, 3083, 3088, 3194-3237,
    3300, 3319, 3321, 3324, 3330,
    3371-3381, 3594, 6451.
    Ethnohistory. See also Andean
      Area. 2027, 2029, 2035, 2037-2044,
      2047, 2053-2060, 2062, 2066,
      2071-2072, 2082, 2095, 2098, 2110,
      3202, 3223, 3232-3233, 3510.
  Language, 6038-6039, 6054, 6066.
  Literature.
    Prose Fiction, 6460a, 6480, 6488,
      6515, 6518, 6525-6526, 6554-6555,
      6777-6786, 6828-6849, 7899,
      7908-7909.
    Poetry, 7030, 7035, 7052, 7059, 7061,
      7070, 7079, 7089-7090, 7110, 7116,
      7126, 7134, 7145-7147, 7163, 7184,
      7191, 7221, 7230, 7235, 7828, 7860,
      7880.
    Drama, 7302, 7324, 7365.
  Music, 9005, 9015, 9131-9136.
  Philosophy, 9423, 9460, 9495, 9500,
    9518-9519, 9524.
Peru and Bolivia Relations, 3571, 3593,
  3618.
Peru and Chile Relations, 3548, 3554.
Peru, Viceroyalty of. See History,
  Colonial.
Peruvian Revolution, 9403.

Petroleum and Petrochemical Industry.
See also Organization of Petroleum of
Exporting Countries. *Argentina*, 3686,
3808, 3879. *Gas*, 3686. *International
Petroleum Co.*, 3552. *Mexico*, 2395,
2397, 2688, 2760. *Paraguay*, 3896.
Peru, 3503, 3572. *Standard Oil Co.*,
3896. *Trinidad*, 3021. *Venezuela*, 3449,
3454.
Pettoruti, Emilio, 344, 346.
Philology. *Portuguese*, 6090, 6095, 6101.
Psychic, 9724.
PHILOSOPHY (items 9401-9735). See
also Corporatism; Cultural
Development and Evolution;
Intellectual History; Marxism;
Positivism; Thinkers and Philosophers;
specific subjects and countries.
Argentina, 6967. *Anthologies*, 9487,
9503. *Axiologia*, 9665, 9668-9669.
Bibliography, 9479, 9482. *Colonial*,
9433, 9482, 9485, 9488. *Conferences*,
9412, 9472, 9707. *Cuba*, 6745.
Darwinism, 2635. *Eastern*, 9411, 9685.
Epistomology, 9653, 9707. *Esthetics*,
9721, 9723. *Ethics*, 9670, 9676. *Greek*,
9420. *Historiography of*, 9483.
History, 9422, 9439, 9517, 9528-9640.
Humanism, 9426-9427, 9431, 9499,
9507, 9679-9680. *Idealism*, 9432.
Instruction, 9444. *Journals*, 9454,
9456. *Juridic*, 9447. *Latin American
Thought*, 9446-9527. *Liberalism*, 9506,
9510. *Logic*, 9416, 9646, 9649, 9659,
9663. *Metaphysics*, 9446, 9729-9735.
Phenomenology, 9440, 9448, 9463,
9612, 9640, 9675. *Political*, 9693, 9704,
9707, 9711. *Semantics*, 6106.
Scholasticism, 9485. *Social*, 9447.
Structuralism, 9438, 9634, 9680, 9721.
Terminology, 9442. *Texts*, 9417.
Theory, 9436-9445. *Western*, 9422,
9685.
Photographic Research Materials.
Argentina, 3937. *Dominican Republic*,
2945, 3054. *Venezuela*, 3456.
Piazzolla, Astor, 9022b.
Pinheiro Ferreira, Silvestre, 9450.
Pinto, Estevão, 487.
Pita Rodríguez, Félix, 6714, 6728.
Pizarro, Francisco, 2066, 2072, 2089.
El Plan Inca. See Economic
Development, Peru.
Plantations. See also Agriculture.
Argentina, 2156, 3265, 3277, 3718,
3778. *Banana*, 6632, 6659. *Belize*,
2790. *Brazil*, 500, 502, 3957, 4089,
4097, 4114. *Caribbean Societies*,
2979-3005, *Chile*, 3640. *Coffee*, 502,
2916, 4089, 4114. *Colombia*, 2156,
3161. *Costa Rica*, 2829, 2916, 6632.
Cotton, 3535. *Cuba*, 2980. *Dominican
Republic*, 3036. *Guyana*, 7812.
Jamaica, 2960, 3052, 7811. *Latin
America*, 2185, 2303. *Mesoamerica*,
2417. *Mexico*, 2419-2421, 2428, 2431,
2445, 2478-2479, 2491, 2504, 2515,
2519-2520, 2522, 2532, 2535, 2537,
2539, 2575, 2661, 2779. *Peru*, 2156,
3218, 3224, 3482, 3497-3498, 3533-3535,
3542, 3546. *Sugar*, 500, 2478, 2960,
3036, 3482, 3530, 3534, 3957, 4097.
West Indies, 2417.
PLAYS (items 7236-7317). See also
Drama; Dramatic Criticism;
Translation. *Anthologies*, 7238.
Argentina, 7236, 7239, 7257, 7259,
7261, 7269, 7271, 7278, 7289-7290,
7292-7294, 7311, 7314. *Brazil*,
7603-7647, 7650, 7654-7655, 7657.
Caribbean, 7779. *Children*, 7264, 7269,
7609. *Chile*, 7242, 7273, 7374.
Colombia, 7238, 7274-7275. *Costa
Rica*, 7247, 7277, 7304-7305. *Cuba*,
7237, 7266-7268, 7280-7281, 7287, 7291,
7310. *Ecuador*, 7260. *El Salvador*,
7244. *Guyana*, 7813, 7820. *Haiti*,
7780-7781, 7797. *Historical*, 7608.
Latin America, 7303, 7369. *Mexico*,
7240, 7252-7253, 7276, 7283-7286, 7316.
Nicaragua, 7315. *Panama*, 7288. *Peru*,
2042, 7302. *Puerto Rico*, 7243, 7251,
7307-7309, 7312-7313. *Uruguay*, 7306.
Venezuela, 3122, 7245-7246, 7254,
7270, 7298-7301.
Poetic Criticism. Brazil, 7733-7764.
POETRY (items 7016-7235, 7488-7602).
See also Poets; Translation; specific
countries. *Anthologies*, 7016-7035,
7086, 7111, 7115-7116, 7161, 7167,
7511, 7749, 7815. *Argentina*, 6491,
7018, 7020, 7023, 7033, 7040-7041,
7044, 7048, 7060, 7075, 7088, 7111,
7120, 7124, 7144, 7150, 7164-7165,
7182, 7201, 7217, 7226. *Aztec*, 6594.
Black, 6523, 7028, 7180, 7195, 7791.
Books of Verse, 7036-7165. *Brazil*,
7488-7602. *Caribbean*, 7815. *Children*,

7818a. *Chile*, 7025, 7051, 7095, 7103, 7106-7107, 7132, 7143, 7152, 7168-7169, 7171, 7174-7175, 7234. *Colombia*, 7016, 7026, 7031, 7055, 7063, 7071, 7081-7082, 7091, 7108, 7112-7113, 7125, 7167, 7194, 7202. *Colonial Period*, 6425, 6438, 6440, 6442-6443. *Concretist*, 7507, 7509, 7511, 7595, 7671, 7706, 7739, 7744, 7762. *Costa Rica*, 7049, 7058, 7065, 7086, 7109, 7121, 7123, 7130, 7137-7138. *Cuba*, 7019, 7021, 7036, 7066, 7084-7085, 7102, 7128, 7157, 7186, 7192, 7203, 7216, 7219, 7233. *Dominican Republic*, 7118, 7149, 7166, 7170. *Ecuador*, 7024, 7056, 7097-7098, 7183, 7193. *El Salvador*, 7022, 7099. *English West Indies*, 7814-7827. *French Guiana*, 7791. *French West Indies*, 7782-7791. *Guatemala*, 7078. *Guyana*, 7817, 7818a-7822, 7824. *Haiti*, 7782-7790, 7801, 7806. *Honduras*, 6624, 7017. *Jamaica*, 7814, 7816. *Journals*, 6669, 7032, 7210, 7753, 7762, 7827, 7849. *Latin America*, 6503, 6513, 6537, 6549, 7083, 7189. *Linguistic Study*, 7754. *Mexico*, 6531, 7037, 7047, 7050, 7053-7054, 7068, 7072, 7076-7077, 7087, 7093-7094, 7096, 7100, 7104-7105, 7114, 7122, 7127, 7131, 7133, 7139, 7151, 7161, 7190, 7200. *Modernism*, 7172, 7178, 7188, 7192, 7212, 7219, 7491-7498, 7538. *Nicaragua*, 7029, 7115-7116. *Panama*, 6651, 6669, 7027, 7061, 7064, 7117, 7129. *Paraguay*, 7153. *Peru*, 6556, 7030, 7035, 7052, 7059, 7062, 7070, 7079, 7089-7090, 7110, 7116, 7126, 7134, 7145-7147, 7163, 7184, 7191, 7221, 7230, 7235. *Political*, 7554, 7566-7568. *Puerto Rico*, 117, 7195. *Revolutionary*, 7817, 7838. *Surrealism*, 7075, 7164-7165. *Symbolism*, 7749. *Theory*, 7733. *Trinidad*, 7818. *Trovas*, 7763. *Uruguay*, 7042-7043, 7069, 7074, 7092, 7136, 7141, 7148, 7155, 7185, 7188, 7212, 7222, 7228. *Venezuela*, 7034, 7045-7046, 7101, 7142, 7158-7159, 7162, 7211, 7224.

Poets. See also names of individual poets. *Argentina*, 6467, 7182, 7197, 7209, 7226. *Barbadian*, 7827. *Brazil*, 464, 510, 4134, 4175, 7511, 7516, 7533, 7537, 7541, 7553, 7587-7588, 7683, 7690, 7734-7735, 7740, 7742-7743, 7745-7748, 7751, 7755, 7757, 7759-7761, 7764, 7767. *Caribbean*, 7805, 7815. *Chile*, 389, 6553, 6875, 6885, 7218, 7234. *Colombia*, 6476, 7194, 7206, 7208, 7214. *Colonial Period*, 6402-6404, 6407-6408, 6413, 6418, 6423, 6426-6427, 6434, 6440, 6442. *Costa Rica*, 2875, 6662a, 7836. *Cuba*, 3060-3061, 7172, 7192, 7196, 7216, 7233. *French West Indies*, 7791a. *Guatemala*, 6668, 6671. *Haiti*, 7791a, 7793, 7801, 7804, 7806. *Latin America*, 7830, 7879. *Mexico*, 316, 7190, 7199, 7204, 7207, 7213, 7225. *Nicaragua*, 7172, 7188. *Panama*, 6669. *Peru*, 6460a, 6488, 6841, 7235. *Puerto Rico*, 7198. *Uruguay*, 7187-7188, 7205, 7212, 7215, 7228, 7722. *Venezuela*, 7179, 7188, 7224.

Poles in Latin America, 4176, 4183-4185.

Police. *Argentina*, 3848. *Brazil*, 4142, 4152. *Chile*, 3629.

Political Cartoons. See Government and Politics, cartoons.

Political Development. *Brazil*, 6095a, 4121. *Chile*, 3615, 3626-3627, 3654, 3658-3659. *Colombia*, 3417. *Language Usage*, 6095a. *Venezuela*, 3440, 3447.

Political Exiles. *from Cuba*, 2951. *from Guatemala*, 6634a. *from Haiti*, 7782, 7787, 7790. *from Mexico*, 2660. *from Peru*, 3420. *from Venezuela*, 3441.

POLITICAL LEADERS/ ADMINISTRATIONS. See also Caciques; names of individual leaders. *Anarchists*, 3969. *Argentina*, 972, 3399, 3679-3681, 3696-3697, 3707, 3709, 3722, 3724, 3734, 3742, 3761, 3788, 3803, 3810, 3812, 3832, 3840, 3843-3844, 3863, 3867, 3874, 3878, 6001. *Bolivia*, 3578, 3582, 3590, 3606, 3694. *Brazil*, 522, 4059, 4061, 4068-4069, 4072, 4074-4075, 4100, 4116-4117, 4120, 4134-4135, 4146, 4155, 4159, 4167, 4172, 7765. *Caudillos*, 3602, 3679, 3697, 3722, 3930, 3942. *Chile*, 1000, 3611, 3634, 3637, 3650, 3665, 3667. *Colombia*, 3428-3429, 3431-3432, 3436. *Cuba*, 2970, 3006, 3009, 3060. *Dominican Republic*, 3024, 3026. *Ecuador*, 32, 3463, 3471, 3475, 3477, 3479. *El Salvador*, 2872, 2900, 2907. *Guatemala*, 2850, 2867. *Haiti*, 7807.

Inca, 2083. Jamaica, 3051. Latin America, 2241. Mexico, 1017, 2390, 2444, 2448, 2474, 2480, 2495, 2528, 2586, 2588, 2600-2603, 2605-2608, 2610, 2614, 2616, 2625-2626, 2631-2632, 2651, 2664-2665, 2674, 2675, 2682, 2691, 2696-2697, 2705, 2713, 2720, 2731, 2740, 2747, 2750, 2755, 2760-2761, 2764-2765, 2767, 2769-2771, 2774-2775, 2781, 2788, 6510. Nicaragua, 2853, 2856, 2901. Panama, 2855, 2864. Paraguay, 3889, 3900, 3905, 3907, 3909-3910, 3920-3921. Peru, 3491, 3526, 3543, 3562. Portugal, 3392. Puerto Rico, 3059. United States, 2361, 2390-2391, 2397, 2651, 2705, 3566. Uruguay, 3410, 3927, 3930, 3933, 3942. Venezuela, 37, 3440-3442, 3448, 3450, 3456, 3458, 3460, 3947.

POLITICAL ORGANIZATION AND POLITICAL PARTIES. See also Communism and Communist Parties; Fascism; Marxism; Political Development; Political Leaders / Administrations; Rastafarism; Socialism and Socialist Parties. *Alianza Popular Revolucionaria Americana (APRA, Peru)*, 3526, 3529-3530, 3547, 3564, 3569. *Andean Area*, 2100. *Argentina*, 3714, 3720, 3731, 3743, 3746, 3766, 9505. *Aztec*, 1960, 1974, 1989, 2024. *Brazil*, 4090, 4130, 4150. *Chile*, 3627, 3659. *Christian Democratic Party (Chile)*, 3650-3651. *Colombia*, 3419, 3432. *Colorado Party (Paraguay)*, 3905, 3922. *Conservative Party (Chile)*, 3655. *Inca*, 1989, 2034, 2057, 2060, 2072, 2075, 2079, 2083, 2088, 2095, 2103-2104. *Indian*, 1963. *Latin America*, 2241. *Maya*, 1993. *Movimiento Nacional Revolucionario (MNR, Bolivia)*, 3603. *Partido Revolucionario de los Trabajadores (PRT, Argentina)*, 3828. *Partido Revolucionario Dominicano (PRD, Dominican Republic)*, 3053. *Partido Revolucionario Institucional (PRI, Mexico)*, 2730, 2750, 2774. *Peru*, 3490, 3500-3501, 3510, 3532, 3543, 3551, 3553, 3564, 3572. *Popular Participation*, 3553. *Puerto Rico*, 8. *Qolla*, 2027. *Quiché*, 1962. *Tarascan*, 1981. *União Democratica Nacional (UDN, Brazil)*, 4123. *Unidad Popular (UP, Chile)*, 3609, 3639, 3651, 3658-3660. *Venezuela*, 3449, 3460.
Political Prisoners. Bolivia, 3599.
Political Science. See Government and Politics.
Poma, Guaman, 2091, 2092.
Pombo, Rafael, 7208.
Ponce, Aníbal, 9427.
Ponce de León, Cristobal, 2039.
Popul Vuh, 1997, 2019, 6658.
Population. See Demography.
Populism, 3490. Bolivia, 3591.
Porras, Camilo A., 2908.
Porras, Demetrio Augusto, 2864.
Portuguese in Latin America, 2144, 4111, 4169.
PORTUGUESE LANGUAGE (items 6087-6120) See also Dictionaries; Linguistics; Literature; Translation. *Dialectology and Sociolinguistics*, 6037, 6087, 6105, 6113. *Lexicon and Semantics*, 6097, 6106, 6118-6119. *Phonology and Grammar*, 6088, 6089, 6093, 6098-6099, 6102, 6104. *Style Manual*, 6099.
Portuondo, José Antonio, 6728.
Positivism, 2650, 2652, 2751, 4140-4141, 9448, 9481, 9485, 9490, 9514.
Pottery. See Ceramics.
Pradt, Domingo de, 2345.
PRECOLUMBIAN CULTURES. See also Aztecs; Incas; Mayas, Quiché; Toltecs; Zapotecs. *Acculturation*, 2433. *Andean Area*, 2051, 2053, 2055, 2069. *Latin America*, 6503. *and Literature*, 6508, 6652. *Mesoamerica*, 1965, 1988. *Music*, 9126. *Origin*, 2289. *Space*, 1951. *Tarascans*, 1981.
Prelorán, Jorge, 973.
Prescott, Wilham Hickling, 2151.
Press. See also Censorship. *Argentina*, 3694. *Brazil*, 131, 4070, 4102, 4164-4165, 7672, 7770. *British Press on Mexican War*, 2638. *Chile*, 3637. *Colombia*, 110, 122, 205. *History*, 3351. *Illustrators*, 205. *Independence Period*, 3327. *Journalists*, 4059, 4095, 4164-4165. *Latin America*, 2241, 2670. *Mexico*, 2653, 2730. *Newspaper Indexes*, 110. *Panama*, 2789. *Printing*, 131. *US on Latin America*, 103, 2670. *Venezuela*, 3351.
Prieto, Adolfo, 6961.

Subject Index

Printing, *Colonial Period*, 2341. *Mexico*, 2536.
Prisons. *Brazil*, 4177. in Theater, 7635.
PROSE FICTION (items 6401-7015, 7406-7775). See also Literary Criticism; Novelists; Short Story Writers; Translation. *Argentine works*, 6467, 6470, 6472, 6491, 6496, 6504, 6541, 6543, 6544, 6893-6946. *Autobiography*, 7758. *Bolivian works*, 6546, 6749-6754. *Brazilian works*, 6541, 7406-7487. *Caribbean*, 7825. *Chilean works*, 6854-6892. *Colombian works*, 6474-6476, 6485, 6528, 6547, 6755-6764, 7071. *Costa Rican works*, 6629-6630, 6634b, 6635, 6637, 6640, 6650, 6669a. *Crônicas*, 7459-7487. *Cuban works*, 6483, 6489, 6498, 6504, 6511-6512, 6557, 6679-6682, 6690-6692, 6695-6696, 6698-6699, 6723-6725, 6727, 7231-7232. *Dominican works*, 6744. *Ecuadorian works*, 6465, 6501, 6536, 6765-6776. *English West Indies*, 7808-7812, 7825. *French West Indies works*, 7776-7781, 7825. *Guatemalan works*, 6504-6505, 6639. *Guyanese works*, 7812. *Haitian works*, 6738, 7776-7778, 7792, 7796, 7802. *Hispanic Caribbean*, 6675-6748. *Honduran works*, 6624, 6626, 6641. *Jamaican works*, 7809-7811. *Latin American Prose Writers*, 6465, 6477, 6513, 6521, 6549, 6551, 6555, 6662a, 6668, 6671, 6737, 6758, 6778, 6875-6876, 6884, 7003, 7448, 7483, 7485, 7491, 7495, 7661, 7663-7664, 7685, 7747. *Mexican works*, 6464, 6484, 6487, 6492, 6495, 6497, 6500, 6502, 6505, 6510, 6522, 6542, 6548, 6558-6622. *Nicaraguan works*, 6623, 6631, 6636, 6646-6647, 6649. *Novels*, 2773, 6464, 6475, 6478-6484, 6492, 6496, 6501, 6503-6505, 6507, 6514, 6516, 6519, 6526, 6532-6533, 6535, 6537, 6540, 6542-6545, 6548, 6560-6564, 6566, 6568-6574, 6578, 6582-6584, 6586-6590, 6623, 6626, 6631-6632, 6634a, 6635-6641, 6644, 6652, 6685, 6688, 6690-6691, 6694, 6696-6698, 6701, 6724-6727, 6758, 6760-6761, 6764, 6770-6771, 6779-6780, 6785, 6789-6794, 6797-6798, 6855, 6859-6861, 6864, 6867-6870, 6873, 6897-6898, 6900-6901, 6905-6911, 6914-6915, 6925, 6927-6928, 6930, 6932, 6938-6941, 6944, 6950, 6953, 6955-6956, 7406-7427, 7776, 7777, 7792, 7826. *Panamanian works*, 6627-6628, 6638, 6644, 6673. *Paraguayan works*, 6505, 7004-7010. *Peruvian works*, 6480, 6488, 6504, 6515, 6518, 6525, 6554, 6556, 6777-6786. *Puerto Rican works*, 117, 6520, 6683-6688, 6693-6694, 6697, 6701, 6726, 7379. *Salvadoran works*, 6625, 6645, 6652, 6653-6654. *Science Fiction*, 6586. *Short Stories*, 6462-6463, 6466, 6469, 6471, 6473-6474, 6477, 6486-6487, 6497-6498, 6500, 6503, 6506, 6527-6529, 6531, 6535, 6539, 6548, 6554, 6565, 6567, 6577, 6585, 6591, 6625, 6627, 6630, 6634, 6642-6643, 6645-6650, 6653-6654, 6675-6678, 6681, 6683-6684, 6686-6687, 6693-6694, 6699-6700, 6749-6757, 6759, 6762-6763, 6765-6769, 6772-6778, 6781-6784, 6786-6788, 6795-6796, 6799-6800, 6854, 6856-6858, 6862-6871, 6893-6896, 6899, 6902, 6904, 6912, 6917, 6919-6924, 6926, 6929, 6931-6937, 6942-6943, 6945-6949, 6951-6952, 6954, 6957, 7428-7458, 7776a, 7778, 7808-7812. *Trinidadian works*, 7808. *Uruguayan works*, 6469, 6471, 6529, 6947-6957. *Venezuelan works*, 6490, 6492, 6545, 6787-6800. *West Indian works*, 7826.
Prostitution. in Literature, 6762.
Protestant Churches. Baptists, 2206. Bibliography, 2235. Chile, 3656. Honduras, 9070. Latin America, 2235. Missionaries, 2206, 3656. Moravians, 9070.
Psychiatry. *Brazil*, 7477. in *Literature*, 7477.
Psychology, 9427, 9678.
Public Health. See also Diseases; Malnutrition; Nutrition. *Brazil*, 4007, 4017, 4104. *Chile*, 3652. *Colombia*, 3421. *Ecuador*, 3466. *Puerto Rico*, 3046.
Public Policy. See also Fiscal Policy. *Economic*, 2720. *Education*, 6125. *Indians*, 2067, 2438, 2775. *Mexico*, 2720. *Official Languages*, 6130. *Urbanization*, 2385.
Publishing Industry. See also Censorship; Press; Printing. *Argentina*, 3877. *Bookbinding*, 3877. *Bookdealers*, 79. *Brazil*, 93, 120, 7688. *Cuba*, 3018. *Dictionary of Book*

Dealers/Printers Terms, 45. *Frankfurt Book Fair*, 7688. *Mexico*, 79. *Spanish Language Material*, 115.
PUERTO RICO.
Bibliography and General Works, 8, 12, 133.
Art, 117.
Film, 1040-1042.
History, 8, 117, 2935-2936, 2938, 2947, 2971, 2973, 2989, 2992, 2994-2996, 3003, 3015, 3022, 3025, 3028, 3031, 3038, 3046-3047, 3049, 3057, 3062.
Language, 6056, 6060.
Literature.
  Prose Fiction, 117, 6520, 6551, 6683-6688, 6693-6694, 6697, 6701, 6726, 6739, 7379, 7928.
  Poetry, 7028, 7195, 7198.
  Drama, 7243, 7251, 7307, 7309, 7312-7313, 7318, 7320, 7322, 7361, 7379, 7394, 7933.
Music, 117, 9064-9065.
Philosophy, 8, 9413.
Puerto Rico and Spain Relations, 3049.
Puig, Manuel, 955, 6997.

Quetzalcoatl, 1954.
Quiché, 1962.
Quiroga, Horacio, 6471, 6960, 7844.

Race and Race Relations. See also specific ethnic groups, nationalities, and races. *Brazil*, 4070, 4102, 4124. *Colonial Period*, 2278. *Cuba*, 2986. *Language Usage*, 6076. *Latin America*, 2201, 2267, 2304, 2336. *Mexico*, 2486-2487. *Racism*, 2230. *Venezuela*, 3124.
Radicalism, 3809.
Radio. *Brazil*, 7474, 9047. *Language Usage*, 6004. *Latin America*, 2241, 9014.
Ramírez, Alejandro, 2839.
Ramírez, Dora, 367.
Ramos, Domingo, 342.
Ramos, Graciliano, 7723.
Ramos, María Elena, 393.
Ramos, Samuel, 9501.
Ras Tafarism. *Jamaica*, 7811. *Music*, 9063.
Rayan, John, 6669.
Rayo, Omar, 371, 374.
Real State. *Mexico*, 2634. *Panama*, 2820.
Rebolledo, Carlos, 1045.

RELIGION. See also Catholic Church; Freemasonary; Inquisition; Protestant Churches; Spiritualism; Witchcraft. *Andean Area*, 2045, 2067, 2073, 2076, 3077. *Artifacts*, 514. *Aztec*, 1959, 1975, 2004. *Bibliography on Theology*, 17. *Brazil*, 512, 514, 3970, 4101. *Dances*, 512. *Deities*, 1955, 1971, 1976, 1982, 1996, 1998-1999, 2017, 2021, 2026. *Eastern*, 9411. *Festivals*, 508. *Inca*, 2044. *Literature*, 6433. *Maya*, 1976, 1983, 2008. *Mesoamerica*, 1998, 2016. *Mexico*, 2497, 2597, 2704, 2708. *Music*, 9023, 9042, 9093, 9107, 9112-9114, 9128. *Philosophy of*, 9404-9405, 9690, 9705, 9713. *Puerto Rico*, 8. *Santería*, 504. *Theologians*, 2291. *Toltec*, 2023. *Venezuela*, 3126.
Remote Sensing. See Maps and Cartography.
Rengifo, César, 400, 7336.
Repatriation. *Mexico*, 2698, 2702.
Repression. *Latin America*, 2388.
Research Aids. See Archives; Catalogs; Dissertations and Theses; Future Studies; Government Documents; Libraries and Library Services; Manuscripts; Maps and Cartography; Photographic Research Materials; specific disciplines, methodology; specific subjects, journals.
Restrepo, Antonio José, 3429.
Restrepo, Javier, 373.
Retablo. See Sculpture.
Reveron, Armando, 388, 391, 401.
REVOLUTION AND REVOLUTIONARY MOVEMENTS. See also Bolivian Revolution; Cuban Revolution; Literature, and revolution; Mexican Revolution; Peruvian Revolution. *Argentina*, 3733, 3755, 3776. *Bolivia*, 2176a, 3313, 3386-3387. *Brazil*, 2176a, 2228, 4034, 4042, 4053, 4063, 4079, 4081, 4088, 4091, 4094, 4100, 4103, 4125, 4141, 4148, 4167, 4171, 9450. *Chile*, 3661. *Colombia*, 2228. *Comunero Revolt (New Granada)*, 3282. *Comunero Revolt (Paraguay)*, 3300. *Costa Rica*, 2849. *Guatemala*, 2382, 2850, 2859, 2863, 2866, 2885, 2926. *Haiti*, 3015. *Honduras*, 2228. *Independence Period*, 3313. *Latin America*, 2169. *Mexico*, 2176a, 2676,

2678-2679, 2704, 2715. *Paraguay*, 3282, 3412, 3912. *Peru*, 3527. *Philosophy of*, 9401. *Rio de la Plata*, 3400, 3404. *Venezuela*, 2176a, 3458.
Reyes, Antonio de los, 2574.
Reyes, Bernardo, 2600.
Ribera, Lucas, 2776.
Ribeyro, Julio Ramón, 6848.
Río de la Plata, Viceroyalty of. See History, Colonial.
Rivarola Matto, José María, 7853.
Rivera, Pedro, 1032-1033.
Roa Bastos, Augusto, 7004-7010.
Road Maps. *Inca*, 2068.
Roca, Julio, 3847, 3874.
Rocafuerte, Vicente, 3477.
Rocha, Glauber, 982, 990, 997.
Roda, Juan Antonio, 372, 374.
Rodrigues, Clauco, 454.
Rodríguez, Mariano, 343.
Rodríguez, Marta, 1009.
Rodríguez, Freile, Juan, 6406, 6411-6412.
Rodríguez Juárez, Juan, 284.
Rojas, Carlos, 373.
Rojas, Miguel Angel, 373.
Rojas, Waldo, 7218.
Romero, Francisco, 9456.
Rosa Guimarães, João, 7709, 7711, 7722, 7732.
Rosas Juan Manuel de, 972, 3680, 3684, 3707, 3709, 3713, 3716, 3727, 3742, 3761, 3788, 3843, 3854, 3858, 3863, 7182.
Roubaud, Jacques, 7879.
Rougès, Alberto, 9456.
Roumain, Jacques, 7803.
Rubber. See Industry and Industrialization.
Ruelas, Julio, 319.
Ruíz, Raúl, 1000, 1004.
Ruíz, Tomás, 2813, 2902.
Rulfo, Juan, 6489, 6609, 6614, 6621, 7844.
Rural Settlement. *Bibliography*, 27, 3257, 3388, 4185.
Russians in Latin America. *Argentina*, 2188. *Brazil*, 2188.

Saavedra, Francisco de, 3114.
Sábato, Ernesto de, 6916, 6964, 6968, 6973, 7001.
Sabel, Miguel, 2314.
Sabogal, José, 381.
Sahagún, Bernardino, 2012, 6405, 6417, 6420.
St. Christopher. See St. Kitts.
ST. KITTS.
Bibliography and General Works, 6.
Music, 9066.
ST. LUCIA.
Bibliography and General Works, 6.
Music, 9068.
ST. VINCENT.
Bibliography and General Works, 6.
Language, 6133.
Saínz, Gustavo, 6600, 6611.
Salazar, Braulio, 403.
Salazar Bondy, Augusto, 9460, 9491.
Salazar Bondy, Sebastián, 7324.
Salazar Herrera, Carlos M., 6655.
Saldívar, Jaime, 328.
Samper, José María, 7345.
SAN BLAS ISLANDS (PANAMA).
Music, 9074.
Sánchez, Delfino, 2923.
Sánchez, Florencio, 7384, 7386-7387, 7390, 7399.
Sánchez, Luis Alberto, 9522.
Sánchez Peláez, Juan, 7179.
Sandino, Augusto César, 6665.
Sanguineti, Edoardo, 7879.
Sanjinés, Jorge, 974, 976, 978-979.
San Martín, José de, 3367, 3411, 3947. *Expeditions*, 3315, 3319, 3324, 3727.
Santa Anna, Antonio López de, 2607, 2660.
Santa Cruz, Andrés, 3088.
Santana, Pedro, 3026.
Santería. See Religion.
Santo Domingo. See Dominican Republic.
Santos Zelaya, José, 2856.
Sarduy, Severo, 6702, 6713, 6716, 6725, 6736, 6743.
Sarmiento, Domingo Faustino, 3712, 3775, 3829, 3835, 3847, 3860, 6001, 6472, 6534, 6541, 7185, 9427.
Sarubi, Valdir, 481.
Scandinavians in Latin America, 2238.
Schmidt, Augusto Frederico, 7587, 7759.
Scholasticism, 2352.
Science and Technology. *Argentina*, 3737. *Bolivia*, 3604. *Brazil*, 4017. *Chile*, 3668. *Engineering*, 3418, 3604, 3669. *History*, 2322. *Latin America*, 2410. *Mexico*, 2721. *Paraguay*, 3923. *Philosophy of*, 9647, 9657, 9661. *Scientists*, 88, 2524, 2556.

Scots in Latin America, 2814-2815.
Scott, Winfield, 2671.
Sculptors. *Brazil*, 420, 422, 452, 459. *Chile*, 362, 9083. *Ecuador*, 276. *Guyana*, 337. *Mexico*, 314, 324. *Peru*, 295. *Uruguay*, 386-387. *Venezuela*, 389.
SCULPTURE. See also Monuments; Sculptors. *Abstract*, 469. *Brazil*, 469, 474, 498. *Costa Rica*, 266. *Ecuador*, 276. *Outdoor*, 469. *Peru*, 295. *Retablo*, 295. *Venezuela*, 304.
Sebreli, Juan José, 6961.
Seoane Ros, Enrique, 357.
Sepúlveda, Fidel, 6437.
Sepúlveda, G.J. de, 2302.
Sex and Sexual Relations. See also Prostitution. *Aztec*, 2004.
Short Stories. See Prose Fiction.
Short Story Writers. *Argentina*, 6916, 6924, 6933, 6942, 6945. *Chile*, 6885. *Colombia*, 6474-6475. *Ecuador*, 6766. *Latin America*, 6630, 7843. *Mexico*, 955, 6464, 6487, 6489, 6548. *Paraguay*, 7004, 7006. *Peru*, 6462-6463, 6786. *Puerto Rico*, 6739. *Uruguay*, 6471, 7015. *Venezuela*, 6796.
Sibellino, Antonio, 354.
Sigüenza y Góngora, Carlos de, 6436, 6452.
Silva, Antônio Francisco da Costa, 7588.
Silva, Djanira da Mota e, 462.
Silva, Jorge, 1009.
Silva, Ludovico, 6729.
Silveira, Vadomiro, 7448.
Sinán, Rogelio, 6664.
Sinclair, Arturo, 1036.
Siqueiros, David Alfaro, 316-317, 321, 325, 328.
Sinclair, Henry, 2313.
Singers. See also names of individual singers. *Argentina*, 9009, 9022a, 9028, 9032. *Brazil*, 9047, 9059. *Chile*, 9089. *Latin America*, 9009, 9022. *Mexico*, 9104. *Venezuela*, 9138.
Skármeta, Antonio, 6889.
SLAVERY AND SLAVE TRADE. See also Abolition. *Andean Area*, 2340. *Argentina*, 3277, 3767, 3855. *Belize*, 2790. *Brazil*, 2141, 2156, 2181, 2256, 3965, 3973, 3978, 3985, 4012, 4019, 4029, 4035, 4049, 4082, 4124, 4129, 4147. *Caribbean*, 2979, 3030. *Colombia*, 2156, 2214, 3130-3131, 3159, 3437. *Colonial Period*, 2278, 2327. *Costa Rica*, 2812, 2835. *Cuba*, 2181, 3040, 6086, 6723, 6748. *Dominican Republic*, 2975, 2987. *Ecuador*, 2214. *Government Regulations and Legislation*, 2959. *Guadeloupe*, 3030. *Guatemala*, 2823. *Haiti*, 2987, 7796, 7798. *Jamaica*, 2939, 2983, 2991, 7811. *Latin America*, 2201, 2210, 2227, 2242, 2267, 2984, 3005. *and Literature*, 6498, 6523, 6692, 6723, 6748, 7616, 7791, 7798. *Mexico*, 2485, 2513. *Nicaragua*, 2210, 2826, 2833. *Oral History*, 2214. *Panama*, 2210, 2825, 2840. *Peru*, 2210, 3203, 3209, 3211, 3218. *Precolumbian*, 1984. *Puerto Rico*, 2989, 2992. *Trinidad*, 2156. *Uprisings*, 3978, 4035, 4082, 4147. *Uruguay*, 3279. *Venezuela*, 3358. *West Indies*, 2181.
Sordo Sordi, Carmen, 9105.
SOCIAL ORGANIZATION. See also Class Structure. *Andean Area*, 2078. *Argentina*, 3280. *Aymara*, 2107. *Aztec*, 2024. *Caribbean*, 2967. *Dominica*, 3001. *Latin America*, 2398. *Mexico*, 2426, 2501, 2531, 2538. *Precolumbian*, 2110-2112.
SOCIAL SCIENCES. See also Anthropology; Dissertations and Theses; Economics; Education; Film; Geography; Government and Politics; History; Research Aids; Sociology; specific countries. *Bibliography*, 8. *Brazil*, 111. *Brazilian Acquisitions by the Library of Congress*, 70a. *Brazilian Dissertations*, 60. *and Catholic Church*, 17. *Computer-generated Index*, 94. *Latin America*, 2405. *Peruvian Journals*, 132. *Philosophy of*, 9682-9683. *Research*, 111. *Teaching*, 2730.
Social Security. Mexico, 2730.
SOCIALISM AND SOCIALIST PARTIES. See also Political Organization and Political Parties. *Argentina*, 3795-3796, 3868-3870, 3881. *Latin America*, 2133, 3558, 9415. *Peru*, 3558.
Society of Jesus. See Catholic Church, Jesuits.
Sociology. *Bolivia*, 3580. *Cuba*, 3013. *Journal Indexes*, 94, 109.
Soler, Ricaurte, 9431.
Soler, Xul, 344.

Solórzano, Carlos, 7385.
Somoza, Antonio, 2853, 2901.
SONGS. *Bolivia*, 9034. *Brazil*, 9041, 9048, 9052. *Calypso*, 9062. *Carib*, 9073. *Christmas Carols*, 9004, 9036. *Cuna*, 9074. *Hymns*, 9040. *Mexico*, 9120. *Panama*, 9074. *Peru*, 9136. *Venezuela*, 9147. *West Indies*, 9062.
Soria, Oscar, 975.
Soto, Helvio, 1000, 1003-1004.
Soto, Hernando de, 2551.
Soto, Marco A., 2871.
Sousandrade. See Souza de Andrade, Joaquim de.
South America. See specific region or country.
SOUTHERN CONE. See Argentina; Chile; Paraguay; Uruguay.
Souza de Andrade, Joaquim de, 7742, 7764.
Spaniards in Latin America. See also Explorers. 2204, 2261, 2288, 2369. *Language Usage*, 6001, 6011.
SPANISH LANGUAGE (items 6001-6086). See also Dictionaries; Linguistics; Literature; Translation. *Bibliography*, 6012. *Children's Speech*, 6082. *Dialectology and Sociolinguistics*, 6005, 6018, 6027-6066a. *Lexicon and Semantics*, 6067-6086, 6454. Loan words, 6003, 6044. *Phonology and Grammar*, 6015-6026. *Theory*, 6002-6003. *in the US*, 6013, 6071.
Spiritualism. *Brazil*, 7477. *in Literature*, 7477.
Sports. *Puerto Rico*, 117. *Soccer*, 7482. *Soccer* Lingo, 6111.
Statistics. *Bibliography*, 70. *Colombia*, 3421. *Latin America*, 2416.
Statisticians, 88.
Stockinger, Francisco, 453.
Storni, Alfonsina, 7209, 7226, 7378, 7829.
Strikes. *Argentina*, 3773, 3792-3793. *Mexico*, 2643. *Peru*, 3493. *Rio Blanco*, 2643.
Students. *Argentina*, 3252. *Brazil*, 4065. *Guyana*, 7817. *Latin America*, 2405. *Law*, 4065. *Mexico*, 2695, 2774, 6592. *Movements*, 6592.
Sucre, Antonio José de, 3320, 3322, 3333, 3368-3369, 6525.
Sugar. See Agriculture; Industry and Industrialization; Plantations.

SURINAM.
Bibliography and General Works, 6.
History, 2148, 2252.

Taborda, Saúl, 9456.
Takaoka, Yoshiya, 482.
Tamayo, Rufino, 328.
Tapía y Rivera, Alejandro, 6551.
Tariffs and Trade Protection. *Chile*, 3662. *Mexico*, 2733.
Taxation. *Bolivia*, 3385. *Borderlands*, 2646. *Central America*, 2848. *Chile*, 3246, 3612, 3662. *Colonial Period*, 2099, 3229, 3246. *Guatemala*, 2874. *Mexico*, 2473. *Peru*, 3229. *Puerto Rico*, 3046.
Taylor, Paul S., 2728.
Taylor, Zachary, 2671.
Teaching. See specific discipline.
Technology Transfer. *Belgium/Latin America*, 2409.
Teixeira, Bento, 7757.
Teixeira, Gustavo, 7740.
Television. *Bibliography*, 962. *Brazil*, 7770. *Cuba*, 1014-1015. *Language Usage*, 6004. *Latin America*, 2241, 9014. *in Sweden on Chile*, 7258.
Telles, Augusto C. de Silva, 487.
Telles, Sérgio, 483.
Territorial Law. See also Boundary Disputes; Law of the Sea. *Colombia*, 3442. *Mexico*, 2632.
Terrorists. See Guerillas.
Textile Industry. See also Crafts. *Argentina*, 3265. *Calendars*, 2124. *Colombia*, 3433. *Indigo*, 2832, 2838. *Peru*, 3489, 3515. *Precolumbian*, 1952. *Wool*, 3489, 3496, 3515.
Theaters. See Drama; Opera, houses.
THINKERS AND PHILOSOPHERS. See also Intellectual History; individual names. *Argentina*, 3813, 3824, 9427-9428, 9446, 9448, 9456, 9484, 9498, 9504, 9513. *Brazil*, 9447, 9450. *Chile*, 3251, 9469, 9499, 9507-9509. *Colombia*, 3149, 9420, 9486. *Dominican Republic*, 9502. *Ecuador*, 3171, 9516. *Mexico*, 2471-2471a, 2690, 9409, 9460, 9464, 9467, 9473, 9475, 9489-9491, 9501, 9521-9522, 9527. *Panama*, 9431. *Peru*, 9425, 9460, 9491, 9495, 9497, 9500, 9512, 9518-9519. *Puerto Rico*, 2995. *Uruguay*, 9493. *Venezuela*, 3119.

Third World. *European Intellectual Domination*, 2229. *Philosophy*, 9402, 9475. *Theater*, 7338.
TOBAGO. See Trinidad and Tobago.
Tobar Doctrine, 2921.
Toltecs, 1969, 2014, 2023.
Torres Bodet, Jaime, 7204.
Torres García, Joaquín, 38, 383-384, 7160.
Torrijos, Omar, 2855.
TORTOLA.
  Bibliography and General Works, 6.
Tourism. See Travel and Tourism.
Tovar y Tovar, Martin, 388.
TRANSLATION of Latin American literary works into English (items 7828-7945). *Argentina works*, 7852, 7865, 7890, 7902, 7904-7906, 7911-7918, 7921, 7929, 7933. *Brazilian works*, 7830, 7934-7945. *Chicano literature*, 7850. *Chilean works*, 7841, 7852, 7867-7876, 7892-7893, 7920, 7923, 7931-7932. *Colombian works*, 7852, 7897-7898, 7919. *Colonial Period*, 6414. *Cuban works*, 7840, 7852, 7863-7864, 7886, 7888-7889, 7900, 7920. *Ecuadorian works*, 7859. *Guatemalan works*, 7852, 7882-7883. *Indigenous Literature*, 2026, 7845. *and Literature*, 6092. *Mexican works*, 7839, 7852, 7877-7878, 7885, 7887, 7894-7896, 7901, 7910, 7920, 7924-7926, 7930, 7933. *Novels*, 7848, 7882-7910, 7936-7942. *Paraguayan works*, 7833. *Peruvian works*, 7828, 7860, 7880, 7899, 7908-7909. *Plays*, 7852-7855, 7930-7933. *Poetry*, 7828-7841, 7847-7849, 7851, 7856-7876, 7934-7935. *Prose Fiction*, 7847, 7851. *Puerto Rican works*, 7846, 7928, 7933. *Short Stories*, 7842-7844, 7848, 7911-7929, 7943-7945. *Theory*, 6494. *Translators*, 6530, 7655, 7830, 7842, 7849, 7857, 7861-7862, 7869, 7879, 7883. *Uruguayan works*, 7884, 7903, 7927. *Venezuelan works*, 7852, 7891.
Transportation. See also Commerce; Road Maps. *Airways*, 2384. *Argentina*, 2150, 3295, 3610, 3770, 3781, 3875. *Brazil*, 3886, 4131, 4173. *Carriages*, 426. *Carts*, 2799. *Chile*, 2150, 3610, 3669. *Colonial Period*, 3132. *Colombia*, 3132. *Costa Rica*, 2914. *Cuba*, 2150. *Guatemala*, 2913.
Highways, 2441, 3610. *Inca Roads*, 2068. *Latin America*, 2386. *Mexico*, 2150, 2441, 2604. *Paraguay*, 3306, 3913. *Peru*, 2150, 3550. *Railroads*, 2441, 2604, 2913-2914, 3295, 3550, 3669, 3770, 3781, 3875, 3886, 3913, 4131. *Venezuela*, 3459.
TRAVEL AND TOURISM. See also Exploration and Expeditions; Maps and Cartography; Transportation. *Argentina*, 3301, 3309, 3723, 3845. *Barbados*, 2966. *Belize*, 2919. *Brazil*, 3985, 4052, 4083. *Central America*, 2844. *Colombia*, 3109, 3336. *Costa Rica*, 2801. *Ecuador*, 3470. *Guatemala*, 125. *Guyana*, 123. *Malvinas*, 3797. *Mexico*, 2437, 2459, 2553, 2620, 2642, 2665, 2844. *Nicaragua*, 2888, 2906. *Patagonia*, 3797. *Puerto Rico*, 2963. *Travel Accounts*, 2553, 2556, 2642, 2665, 2801, 2844, 2906, 2963, 2966, 3109, 3270, 3301, 3309, 3336, 3455, 3723, 3797, 3845, 3985, 4052, 4083. *Uruguay*, 3270. *US*, 2677-2678. *Venezuela*, 3109, 3336, 3455.
Treaties. *Bolivia/Chile*, 3583. *Herrán-Hay*, 2922. *Roca-Runciman*, 3878.
TRINIDAD AND TOBAGO.
  Bibliography and General Works, 6, 12, 118.
  History 2156, 2931, 3021, 3045.
  Language, 6132.
  Literature.
    Prose Fiction, 7808.
    Poetry, 7818.
  Music, 9065-9066.
Truss, Ned, 373.
Tupac, Amaru, 3197.

Ubico, Jorge, 2858.
Ulive, Ugo, 1045.
Unda, José Vicente de, 3075.
Unemployment. *Argentina*, 3678. *Cuba*, 3064.
United Kingdom and Argentina Relations, 3842.
United Kingdom and Chile Relations, 3630.
United Kingdom and Mexico Relations, 2718.
United Kingdom and Paraguay Relations, 3909.

United Kingdom and Peru Relations, 3496, 3549.
United Kingdom and Uruguay Relations, 3939, 3955-3956.
US and Argentina Relations, 3882.
US and Bolivia Relations, 3554, 3582.
US and Caribbean Relations, 2190.
US and Chile Relations, 3633, 3649, 3882. *Project Camelot*, 3636.
US and Colombia Relations, 2922.
US and Costa Rica Relations, 2918.
US and Cuba Relations. See also Bay of Pigs Invasion. 3007, 3043-3044.
US and Ecuador Relations, 3554.
US and El Salvador Relations, 2895.
US and Europe Relations in the Caribbean, 3034.
US and Latin American Relations, 2361, 2363, 2367, 2371, 2381-2382, 2391, 2394, 2396, 2405, 2408, 3554, 3566. *Alliance for Progress*, 3537, 3649. *Bibliography*, 2374. *Monroe Doctrine*, 2190.
US and Mexico Relations. See also Mexican War. 2190, 2390, 2395, 2397, 2446, 2633, 2647, 2651, 2658, 2670, 2684, 2698-2699, 2702, 2705, 2712-2713, 2718, 2730, 2760.
US and Nicaragua Relations, 2853, 2870, 2901, 6665.
US and Panama Relations. See also Panama Canal Zone. 2929.
US and Peru Relations, 3495, 3554.
US and Puerto Rico Relations, 2935, 3047.
US and Spain Relations, 2362.
US and Uruguay, 3882.
US Central Intelligence Agency, 2216, 3905.
US VIRGIN ISLANDS.
Bibliography and General Works, 59.
Music, 9065-9066.
Universities. *Brazil*, 3993. *Colombia*, 3112. *Costa Rica*, 2854. *Cuba*, 81. *History*, 2323, 2851, 2854. *Latin America*, 9523. *Mexico*, 2695, 2743. *Nicaragua*, 2851.
University Reform. *Peru*, 3488.
Urbanization. *Argentina*, 3299, 3865, 3871. *Chile*, 3248. *Colombia*, 3137. *Ecuador*, 3167-3168, 3177. *Latin America*, 2385, 2410. *Mexico*, 2533, 2599, 2689, 2730. *Peru*, 3556. *Venezuela*, 3459.

Urban Planning. *Brazil*, 440, 487, 492, 498-499.
Urban Studies. *Bibliography*, 18. *Latin America*, 2218, 2385. *Mexico*, 2636.
Urquiza, Justo José de, 3788.
Uriarte, Carlos, 360.
Uribe, Juan, 367.
Uricoechea, Ezequiel, 6009.
Urrea, Blas, 2776.
Urrusti, Lucinda, 327.
Urrutia, Matilde, 7867.
URUGUAY.
Bibliography and General Works, 10, 12, 128, 3946.
Art, 302, 383-387.
Film, 960, 1043.
History, 2393, 3259, 3270, 3279, 3293, 3308, 3882, 3925-3956.
Language, 6037-6038, 6116.
Literature.
Prose Fiction, 6469, 6471, 6529, 6947, 6957, 7011-7015, 7884, 7903, 7927.
Poetry, 7042-7043, 7069, 7074, 7092, 7136, 7141, 7148, 7155, 7185, 7188, 7205, 7212, 7215, 7222.
Drama, 7306, 7387, 7390, 7393, 7399.
Music, 9005, 9137.
Philosophy, 9515.
Usigli, Rodolfo, 7319, 7348, 7476, 7391.
USSR and Brazil Relations, 3962.
USSR and Latin American Relations, 2394.

Valderrama, Francisco, 367.
Valdés, Hernán, 6882.
Valencia, Guillermo, 7227.
Vallejo, Aníbal, 367, 7834.
Vallejo, César, 6526, 6813, 6841, 7073, 7191, 7221, 7235, 7829.
Vallejo, Gerardo, 968.
Vanzo, Julio, 352, 361.
Vargas, Getúlio, 4172, 4186.
Vargas Llosa, Mario, 6519, 6821, 6838, 6840-6841, 6845, 6847, 6849, 7843.
Vasconcellos, Sylvio de, 487.
Vasconcelos, José María, 2814, 2692, 2783, 6495, 6510, 9457, 9464, 9467, 9489-9491, 9522.
Vassallo, Angel, 9456.
Vaz Ferreira, María Eugenia, 7187, 7215.
Vega, Garcilaso de la. See Garcilaso de

la Vega (El Inca).
Vega, Jorge de la, 350.
Velasco Ibarra, José María, 3463, 3479.
Vélez, Marta Helena, 367.
Vélez de Escalante, Silvestre, 2543, 2581.
Vellojín, Manolo, 373.
VENEZUELA.
  Bibliography and General Works, 9, 11-12, 19, 25-26, 42, 58, 85, 91, 128.
  Art, 303-306, 388-404.
  Film, 954, 961, 1044-1048.
  History, 11, 25, 35, 37, 2146, 2252, 2340, 2990, 3080, 3099-3128, 3340, 3346-3358.
    Ethnohistory, 2033.
  Language, 6061-6062.
  Literature.
    Prose Fiction, 11, 19, 91, 6492, 6545, 6787-6800, 6850-6853, 7891.
    Poetry, 7034, 7045-7046, 7101, 7142, 7158-7159, 7162, 7211, 7224.
    Drama, 7245-7246, 7254, 7270, 7298-7301, 7334, 7336, 7359, 7362.
  Music, 9007, 9138-9148.
Verísimo, Erico, 7708, 7727.
Vespucci, Américo, 2286.
Viconti, Eliseu, 484.
Victorica, Miguel Carlos, 344-345.
Vidal, Luis Fernando, 6786.
Vilalta, Maruxa, 7357.
Villa, Pancho, 2759.
Villanueva, Carlos Raúl, 399.
Villar, Hernando del, 373.
Villaurrutia, Xavier, 6502, 7190, 7207, 7829.
Villegas, Abelardo, 9501.
Viñas, David, 6961, 6972, 7001.
Vincenzi, Moisés, 9455.
Violence. *Latin America*, 2388.
La Violencia. *in Literature*, 6755. *in Theater*, 7275.
Virasoro, Miguel Angel, 9456.
Virmond, Frederico Guilherme, 441.
Visitas. See History, Colonial.
Vives, Francisco, 9507, 9509.
Vizcaíno, Sebastián, 2301.
Volpi, Alfredo, 453, 476, 485.

Wages. See Labor and Unions.
Wainer, Alberto, 7340.
Walker, William, 2879, 2903, 2909, 2912.
Wanderly, Sandoval, 7660.
War of Pacific, 3554, 3594, 3600, 3606, 3618.
Weissman, Franz, 453.
Welsh in Latin America, 3883-3884.
WEST INDIES. See also British West Indies; Cuba; Dominican Republic; French West Indies; Haiti; Jamaica; Lesser Antilles; Puerto Rico.
  Bibliography and General Works, 6, 12, 128.
  History, 2252, 2261, 2266, 2417, 2930-3064.
  Language, 6127-6128. 6133.
  Literature.
    Prose Fiction, 7776-7781, 7808-7812, 7825-7826.
    Poetry, 7782-7791, 7814-7827.
    Drama, 7813.
  Music, 9065-9066.
Witchcraft. *in Literature*, 6877. *Music*, 9055. *Shamanism*, 1998-1999.
Wolff, Egon, 7327, 7373, 7403.
Women. See also Family Relationship; Prostitution. *Argentina*, 3783, 3804, 3820. *Bibliographies*, 2392. *Brazil*, 4045, 4156-4157, 7483. *Colonial Period*, 2030. *Cuba*, 5064. *Current Research*, 2392. *and Development*, 2402. *Dominican Republic*, 3041. *Federação Brasileira pelo Progresso Feminino, Brazil*, 4156. *Honduras*, 2808. *Indian*, 2030, 2493. *Latin America*, 2172, 2213, 2236. *in Literature*, 6747, 7433, 7628, 7778. *Mexico*, 2429, 2435, 2449, 2493, 2531, 2589, 2609, 7366. *Panama*, 2927. *Paraguay*, 107, 3913. *Peru*, 3492, 3522. *and Politics*, 2402. *in Theater*, 7618, 7622. *Women's Studies Methodology*, 2236.
World War I. *Argentina*, 3772. *Chile*, 3625. *Peru*, 3560.
World War II. *Argentina*, 3842. *Brazil*, 4153. *Chile*, 3633.

Yáñez, Agustín, 6492.
Ydigoras Fuentes, Miguel, 2867.
Youth. *Inca*, 2115.
Yrigoyen, Hipólito, 3840, 3878.

Zanini, Mário, 486.
Zapotecs, 2021.
Zea, Leopoldo, 9409, 9460, 9473, 9475, 9501, 9517, 9521-9522, 9527.
Zuñiga, Adolfo, 2911.

AUTHOR INDEX

Abad, Diego José, 6438
Abad de Santillán, Diego, 6067
Abadie-Aicardi, Aníbal, 3258-3259, 3413
Abaúnza Salinas, Ramiro, 6623
Abayubá Olave, Carlos, 7176
Abdala, Nayib, 9606
Abecia Baldivieso, Valentín, 3382
Abeijón, Asencio, 3674
Abellán, José Luis, 6401
Abril Rojas, Gilberto, 7016
Academia de Ciências do Estado de São Paulo, *São Paulo*, 88
Academia de Geografía e Historia de Costa Rica, *San José*, 2812
Acevedo, Oscar, 2125
Achury Valenzuela, Darío, 6457
Acosta, Evalina, 2250
Acosta, Leonardo, 260
Acosta, Oscar, 6624, 7017
Actuaciones del cabildo de Tunja después de la Batalla de Boyacá, 3359
Actualidad de Bartolomé de las Casas, 2251
Adams, Eleanor B., 2543
Adams, Michael Ian, 6458, 6874
Adelaida de Juan: Venezuela en su pintura, 388
Adellach, Alberto, 7236
Ades, Dawn, 1951
Adet, Walter, 7018
Affonso, João, 526
Agerdop, Terry, 9070
Agosti, Héctor Pablo, 3675
Agra, [Antônio José] Figueirêdo, 7488-7489
Agrupación de Bibliotecas para la Integración de la Información Socio-Económica (ABIISE), *Lima*, 89
Agudelo Villa, Hernando, 3417
Aguiar, Cláudio, 7603
Aguiar, Manoel Pinto de, 4056
Aguilar, Francisco de, 2450
Aguilar, José Angel, 2680

Aguilar Bulgarelli, Oscar R., 2849
Aguilar Camín, Héctor, 2418, 2681
Aguilar Mora, Jorge, 6702
Aguilar Vázquez, Carlos, 6459
Aguilera, Francisco Vicente, 3019
Aguilera Gómez, Manuel, 2682
Aguirre, Mirta, 6445
Agustín, José, 6592
Ahern, Maureen, 7828, 7860
Aiala, Luís [*pseud. for* Luís Gonzaga Gusmão de Andrade], 7459
Ainsa, Fernando, 6460
Aisthesis, 9077
Aizcorbe, Roberto, 3676
Alagarín, Miguel *trans.*, 7875
Alamillo Flores, Luis, 2683
Alamos V., María Ignacia, 3607
Alanís Boyso, José Luis, 2474
Alazraki, Jaime, 7177
Alba, Víctor, 3481
Alberini, Coriolano, 9446
Albert, Bill, 3482
Alberto, Eliseo, 7036
Albino Zagonel, Carlos. See Zagonel, Carlos Albino.
Albor, Hugo R., 6027
Albuquerque, Celina de Holanda Cavalcanti de. See Holanda [Cavalcanti de Albuquerque], Celina de.
Albuquerque, Mauro Ramos da Mota e. See Mota [e Albuquerque], Mauro [Ramos da].
Albuquerque, Terêza Tenório de, 7490
Alcalá de González Oddone, Beatriz Rodríguez. See Rodríguez Alcalá de González Oddone, Beatriz.
Alcázar, Miguel, 9101
Alcina Franch, José, 3163
Aldana, Adelfo L., 7004
Aldef [*pseud. for* Leda Falconio], 6625
Alden, Dauril, 2252, 4024
Alderson, Richard, 9102
Aldunate B., Elena, 6854

Aldunate Phillips, Arturo, 3608
Alegría, Ciro, 6828
Alegría, Fernando, 6460a
Alejandro Otero, 389
Alen Lascano, Luis C., 3398, 3677-3680
Ales, Oreste Carlos, 3681
Alexander, María Teresa, 257
Alexander, Robert J., 2380
Alfaro, Ricardo Joaquín, 2789
Alfaro Vallejos, Florinda Julia, 3506
Ali, Manuel Said. See Said Ali, Manuel.
Allen, Hubert Raymond, 2930
Allen, Michael J.B., 2276
Alleyne, Mervyn C., 6121
Almeida, Abílio Pereira de, 7604
Almeida, Fernando Azevedo de, 527
Almeida, Guilherme de [Andrade], 7491
Almeida, João de, 6105
Almeida, José Américo de, 7765
Almeida, Paulo Mendes de, 405
Almeida, Prisciliana Duarte de, 7492
Almeida Prado, Décio de. See Prado, Décio de Almeida.
Almeida Prado, João Fernandes de. See Prado, João Fernandes de Almeida.
Almeida Prado, Yan de. See Prado, Yan de Almeida.
Almeida Santos, José de. See Santos, José de Almeida.
Alone [pseud. for Hernán Díaz Arrieta], 6875
Alonso Piñeiro, Armando, 3682
Al 'perovich, Moisei Samuilovich, 3889
Altamirano, Carlos, 3609
Altman, Ida, 2451, 2544
Altschul, Carlos trans., 7858
Altschul, Monique trans., 7858
Alurralde, Nicanor, 2253
Alvarado, Hipólito, 6765
Alvarado Garaicoa, Teodoro, 2254
Alvares de Azevedo, Manuel Antônio. See Azevedo, Manuel Antônio Alvares de.
Alvarez, Carlos, 1008
Alvarez, José Regilio, 9103
Alvarez, Raúl, 3890
Alvarez Curbello, Silvia, 9492
Alvarez Díaz, Enrique, 269
Alvarez Ganoza, Pedro L., 3483
Alvarez Gardeazábal, Gustavo, 6755
Alvarez Nazario, Manuel, 2989
Alvarez Romero, José María, 3260
Alvarez Salas, Juan, 3190
Alvaro Goicochea, 3555
Alves, Marieta, 422

Alves dos Santos, Francisco. See Santos, Francisco Alves dos.
Alzate P., Alberto, 9687
Amado, Janaina, 4057
Amado, Jorge, 7428, 7936
Amador, María Luisa, 1030
Amaral, Amadeu, 6087
Amaral, Aracy A., 452
Amaral, Francisco Pacífico do, 4058
Amaral, Hílton, 6106
Amaral, Pedro Ferraz do, 4059
Amaral, Raúl, 13
Amaral Lapa, José Roberto do. See Lapa, José Roberto do Amaral.
Amaral Rébula, Angela María. See Rébula, Angela María Amaral.
Amaral von Schmeling, Gila do. See Schmeling, Gila do Amaral von.
Amaya-Amador, Ramón, 6626
Amenábar, Juan, 9078
Ames, Charles R., 2684
Amich, José, 3065
Amoroso Lima, Alceu. See Lima, Alceu Amoroso.
Ampuero, Fernando, 6777
Ampuerto B., Gonzalo, 2025
Anais da Biblioteca Nacional, 406
Anales de la Sociedad de Geografía e Historia de Guatemala, 2850
Anales de la Universidad de Cuenca, 3461
Anales del Instituto de Investigaciones Estéticas, 277
Anastasia, Luis V., 9493
Anawalt, Patricia, 1952
Anchieta, José de, 7493, 7605
Anda Aguirre, Alfonso, 3164
Anderle, Adam, 2343
Anderson, Arthur J.O., 1953
Anderson, Robert Roland, 6402
Anderson, Rodney D., 2587
Anderson, Teresa J., 2126
Anderson Imbert, Enrique, 6958
Andino, Alberto, 7178
Andino, Osvaldo R., 3808
Andrade, Carlos Drummond de, 7460, 7494-7495
Andrade, Diva, 60
Andrade, Jorge, 7606
Andrade, Luís Gonzaga Gusmão de. See Aiala, Luís [pseud, for Luís Gonzaga Gusmão de Andrade].
Andrade, Manoel Correira de, 3957
Andrade, Mário de, 7461, 7934
Andrade, Víctor, 3573

Andrade Almeida, Guilherme de. *See* Almeida, Guilherme de [Andrade].
Andrade Brandão, Wilson de. *See* Brandão, Wilson de Andrade.
Andrade Ferreira, João Antônio de. *See* Antônio [de Andrade Ferreira], João.
Andrade Muricy, José Cândido de. *See* Muricy, José Cândido de Andrade.
André-Vincent, Philippe, 2127
Andrés, Jorge Héctor, 9022a-9022c
Andreu, Jean L., 7005
Andrews, George Reid, 2685
Andújar, Manuel, 6461
Angel, Félix, 367
Angelelli, Ignacio, 9641
Angelind, Diego, 6893
Anguiano, Marina, 1954
Anjos, Augusto [de Carvalho Rodrigues] dos, 7496
Anjos, Ricardo Augusto [Pena] dos, 7497
Ankerman, Guillermo, 7237
Ankerman, Jorge, 7237
Anna, Timothy E., 2344
Annals of the New York Academy of Sciences, 2979
Annino, Antonio, 2128
Annual Conference of the Association of Caribbean University and Research Libraries (ACURIL), *IV, San Juan, P.R., 1972*, 43
Annual Conference on Caribbean Historians, *IV, Río Piedras, P.R., 1974*, 2931
Antelo, Antonio, 6446
Antezana, José, 3485
Anthony, Michael, 7808
Antillano, Laura, 6787
Antione, Yves, 7782
Antología brasileira de humor, 7766
Antología colombiana del teatro de vanguardia, 7238
Antología de la revista Contemporáneos, 6558
Antonietta, Eduardo, 9565
Antonietto, Elena, 7239
Antônio, João, 7429
Antonio, Jorge, 3683
Antônio [de Andrade Ferreira], João, 7462
Antuña, Vicentina, 3041
Aprile-Gniset, Jacques, 114
Aquésolo Castro, Manuel, 3484
Aquila, August J., 6403
Arad, Irene S. de, 3891

Arana-Soto, Salvador, 2932, 3025
Aranha, José Pereira da Graça, 7607
Aráoz de la Madrid, Gregorio, 3684
Araújo, Antonio Gomes de, 3958
Araújo, Avelino [de Pina], 6107
Araújo, Maria de Lourdes de, 7472
Araújo, Vicente de Paula, 980
Araujo Subieta, Mario, 3574
Aray, Edmundo, 7019
Arbeláez, Ramiro, 1010
Arboleda, José Rafael, 2345
Arbulú, Ricardo, 44
Arce, Facundo A., 3685
Archer, Christon I., 2475, 2545
Archibald, Robert R., 2546-2547
Archivo Histórico de Tucumán, *Arg.*, 3261
Arcila Farías, Eduardo, 2990, 3099-3101
Arciniegas, Germán, 2129-2131
Arcocha, Carlos Enrique, 3686
Ardao, Arturo, 2132, 9451, 9494
Ardiles, Osvaldo M., 9401-9402
Arean, Carlos, 344
Arêas, Vilma, 7430
Arellano, Jesús, 7037
Arellano, Jorge Eduardo, 2813, 2851
Arellano Moreno, Antonio, 3102
Arestizábal, Irma, 507
Argentina. Academia Nacional de la Historia, 3262
Argentina. Consejo Nacional de Investigaciones Científicas y Técnicas. Centro de Estudios e Investigaciones Laborales (CEIL), 3687
Argentina Outreach, 3688
Argentine: chronologie de la Présidence de Perón; la prise du poufoir par la Junte Militaire, chronique de coup d'état, 34-31 mars 1976, 3689
Argerami, Omar, 9528
Arguedas, José María, 2026, 6462-6463, 6847
Argüelles Bringas, Roberto, 7038
Argüello Mora, Manuel, 2852
Argul, José Pedro, 383
Arias A., Edison, 9566
Aridjis, Homero, 7856
Arinos, Afonso, 7608
Arismendi, Rodney, 3925
Arjona Santos, Angel, 1955, 6447
Armand, Octavio, 7179
Armani, Alberto, 3263
Arnau, Carmen, 6804
Arnaudo, Florencio José, 9567
Arnaudo, Kidia, 3690

Arona, Juan de [pseud. *for* Paz Soldán y Unanué, Pedro], 6054, 7134
Arosemena, Marcia A. de, 2814
Arosemena Moreno, Julio, 9071
Arquitetura civil II, 487
Arreola, Juan José, 6559
Arreola Cortés, Raúl, 2588
Arriví, Francisco, 7318
Arrom, Silvia M., 2589
Arróspide de la Flor, César, 9403
Arroyo, Justo, 6627
Arroyo Cabello, Mary, 115
Arruda Campos, Fernando, 9688
Arruda Dantas, Antonio. *See* Dantas, Antonio Arruda.
Arte brasileira, 407
Arte sacra em Minas Gerais no século XVIII: acervo Geraldo Parreiras, 423
Arteaga Calderón, Marco, 9495
Arteche, Miguel, 6855-6856
Artes y letras de Mérida, 390
Arthur, Don, 278
Os artistas e a Olivetti: Exposição, 15 de abril a 15 de maio 1976, 453
Artistas plásticas, Mexico 75, 314
Arze Aguirre, René, 31, 3385
Arze Quiroga, Eduardo, 61
Aschiero, Hipólito R., 6068
Asiaín Marquez, Carlos, 6069
Asís, José, 6894
Assef, Alberto E., 3264
Assis, Joaquim Maria Machado de. *See* Machado de Assis, Joaquim Maria.
Assis, José Eugênio de Paula, 4061
Assumpção, Clovis, 454-455
Astesano, Eduardo B., 2133
Asturias, Miguel Angel, 7882-7883
Asuaje de Rugeles, Ana Mercedes, 9138
Atamoros de Pérez Martínez, Noemí, 6404
Atilio Palacio, Rubén, 345
Attema, Ypie, 3042
Augier, Angel, 7180
Augusto, Eudoro, 7498
Ausgewählte neuerer Literatur, 90
Austin, Roy L., 9062
Austos de la Revolución del Paraguay del 15 de mayo de 1811, 3412
Autran Dourado, Waldomiro. *See* Dourado, Waldomiro Autran.
Auza Lión, Aliliano, 9034
Avalle-Arce, Juan Bautista, 6428
Avances de Investigación, 2853
Avelino, Yvone Dias, 2255

Avellá Cháfer, Francisco, 3691
Avellaneda, Andrés, 6959-6960
Avellar, José Carlos, 981
Avila, Affonso, 7662
Avila Echazu, Edgar, 6439
Avila Martel, Alamiro de, 3310, 3390
Avilés, Alejandro, 7039
Avilés Fabila, René, 6560
Ayala, Walmir, 7499
Ayala Blanco, Jorge, 1017
Ayala Queirolo, Víctor, 3892
Ayala Z., Alfredo, 3575
Ayatai, Desidério, 9041
Azar, Héctor, 7240
Azevedo, Aluizio, 7937
Azevêdo, Eliane S., 4019
Azevedo, Manuel Antônio Alvares de, 7663
Azevedo, Milton Mariano, 6088-6089
Azevedo, Neroaldo Pontes de, 7741
Azevedo, Rafael Sânzio de, 7664
Azevedo, Thales de, 4062
Azevedo Correia, Raimundo da Mota de. *See* Correia, Raimundo [da Mota de Azevedo].
Azevedo de Almeida, Fernando. *See* Almeida, Fernando Azevedo de.
Azevedo Filho, Leodegário A. de, 6090
Azevedo Saes, Décio, *marquês de. See* Saes, Décio Azevedo, *marquês de*.
Azofeifa, Isaac Felipe, 6655
Azuela, Arturo, 6561
Azuela, Mariano, 6464

Báez, Vicente, 116-117
Báez Macías, Eduardo, 2476
Baeza Flores, Alberto, 7166
Bagby, Alberto I., Jr., 7703, 7941
Bahia (state), *Brazil*. Conselho Estadual de Cultura. Secretaria de Educação e Cultura, 3959
Bahia (state), *Brazil*. Coordenação de Fomento ao Turismo, 488
Baigorria, Manuel, 3692
Baily, Samuel L., 2381
Baker, George T., 2590
Baker, Maury, 2548
Balbuena Rojas, Dionisio, 3893
Balcácer, Juan Daniel, 3026
Baldrich, J. Amadeo, 3693
Balla, Andrés, 7241
Ballario Yoshida, Celia, 489
Ballé, Catherine, 2686
Balseiro, José Agustín 2549
Balzer, Carmen, 9718

Author Index

Banchero, Andersen, 6947
Banco de Desenvolvimento do Paraná (BADEP), *Curitiba, Brazil*, 441, 456
Banco de la República, *Bogotá*, 3336-3337
Bandecchi, Brasil, 3960
Bansart, Andrés, 7791a
Baptista Gumucio, Mariano, 3576-3578, 3587
Baptiste Debret, Jean. *See* Debret, Jean Baptist.
Barahona Jiménez, Luis, 2854
Barata, Mário, 442, 3961
Barata Viana, Sylvio, 9529
Baraúna, Alberto Luiz, 7500
Barbara, Leila, 6091
Barbón Rodríguez, José A., 6001
Barbosa, Cláudio Tavares, 7501
Barbosa Lima, Alexandre José. *See* Lima, Alexandre José Barbosa.
Barboza Mello, José. *See* Mello, José Barboza.
Barcelo Sifontes, Lyll, 91, 2346
Bardi, P.M., 424
Bareiro Saguier, Rubén, 6028, 7006
Barge, Ernest J., 7935
Barker, Nancy Nichols, 2591
Barman, Jean, 4065
Barman, Roderick J., 4063-4065
Barnadas, Josep M., 3165
Barnes, Thomas C., 2569
Barocke Malerei aus den Anden: Gemälde des 17. und 18, 251
Baron, Robert, 9001
Barrán, José Pedro, 3926-3927
Barrera, Ernesto M., 6703
Barrera V., Humberto, 3610
Barreto, Abeillard, 1
Barreto, Paulo, *See* Rio, João do [*pseud.* for Paulo Barreto].
Barrett, Ward J., 2256, 2478
Barrientos, José P., 3694
Barriga López, Franklin, 6465
Barriga López, Leonardo, 6465
Barriocanal, Eusebio Angel, 9672
Barrios, D. Walter, 3485
Barrios Pintos, Aníbal, 3928
Barros, Alvaro, 3695, 6857
Barros, Manoel Souza, 408
Barros Grez, Daniel, 7242
Barros Jarpa, Ernesto, 3611
Barroso, Maria Alice, 7406
Barroso, Olga Monte, 7472
Barthel, Thomas S., 1956
Bartley, Russell H., 2134, 3962
Bartra, Armando, 2687

Basadre, Jorge, 3486-3488
Basave Fernández del Valle, Agustín, 9404, 9642, 9712
Basseches, Bruno, 14
Basso, Domingo, 9664
Bastidas, Antonio, 6440
Bastidas Padilla, Carlos, 6756
Bastidas Urresty, Edgar, 3360
Bastos, Hermenegildo, 7502
Bastos, María Luisa, 6593, 6961
Bastos, Wilson de Lima, 4066
Basurto, Jorge, 2688
Bataillon, Claude, 2689
Bateman, Alfredo D., 2347, 3418
Batista de Carvalho, Luiz Raimundo. *See* Luiz Raimundo [*pseud. for* Luiz Raimundo Batista de Carvalho].
Batista de Salles, Waldemar. *See* Salles, Waldemar Batista de.
Battilana, Beatriz G. de, 6466
Battistella, Ernesto H., 6962, 9607, 9643
Baudot, Georges, 6405
Bauer, Arnold, 3612
Baum, Paul, 6122
Bautista Avalle-Arce, Juan. *See* Avalle-Arce, Juan Bautista.
Bautista Morales, Juan. *See* Morales, Juan Bautista.
Bayer, Osvaldo, 3696
Bayón, Damián, 310-311
Bazán, Raúl, 3697
Bazant, Jan, 2592-2593
Bazin, Germain, 409
Beardsell, Peter R., 6467, 7319
Beaujón, Oscar, 3346
Becco, Horacio Jorge, 7020
Beceyro, Raúl, 951
Becker, Félix, 2135
Becker, Idel, 6108
Bedoya Ballicián, Mario, 3383
Beer, Gabriella de, 2690
Beeson, Margaret E., 15
Beezley, William H., 2691
Befumo Boschi, Liliana, 6614
Béhague, Gerard, 9002, 9042
Behocaray Albero, Solange, 2452
Beiguelman, Paula, 4067
Beirão, Nirlando, 982
Bejarano Díaz, Horacio, 6468
Belaval, Emilio, 7243
Belevan, Harry, 6778
Belitt, Ben *trans*., 7869, 7871-7872, 7931
Bell, Lindolf, 7503
Beltrán, Ulises, 2479
Belza, Juan E., 3698

Ben-Ur, Lorraine Elena, 7320
Benarós, León, 7040-7041
Benavides, Wáshington, 7042
Benavides M., Julio, 3579
Bendahan, Daniel, 9139
Bender, Ivo, 7609
Bendezú, Edmundo, 6779
Benecia, Julio Arturo, 3699
Benedetti, Mario, 6469, 7884
Beneke, Walter, 7244
Benevides, Artur Eduardo, 7504-7505, 7665
Beni, Mário, 4068
Benites Vinueza, Leopoldo, 4025
Benítez, Fernando, 7885
Benítez Rojo, Antonio, 6628
Benjamin, Jules Robert, 3043-3044
Benjamin, Thomas, 2594
Bennassar, Bartolomé, 3700
Bennett, E. Fay, 2595
Benso, Silvia, 6406
Benson, Rachel, 7829
Benson, Robert L., 2276
Berdan, Frances Frei, 1953, 1957
Berenguer, Amanda, 7043
Berge, Dennis E., 2596
Bergquist, Charles W., 3419
Bermúdez, Oscar, 3245
Bernabo, Héctor Júlio Páride. See Carybé [pseud. for Héctor Júlio Páride Bernabo].
Bernales Ballesteros, Jorge, 295
Bernardet, Jean-Claude, 983
Bernardini, Aurora F., 7733
Bernasconi, Carlos Leonel, 3944
Berninger, Dieter G., 2597-2598
Berrou, F. Raphaël, 7783, 7792
Berry, Paul, 6123
Bertram, Geoff, 3489
Besouchet, Lídia, 4069
Bessa Lins, Maria Inês de. See Lins, Maria Iñes de Bessa.
Betances, Ramón Emeterio, 3027
Betancur R., John Jairo, 9568
Bevilaqua, Clovis, 9447
Bezerra Filho, José, 7610
Beznos, Clóvis, 7506
Bibliografía de y sobre Gabriel García Moreno, 32
Bibliografía Ecuatoriana, 39
Bibliografía histórica peruana: 1968-1970, 3066
Bibliografía histórica peruana: 1970-1973, 3067
Bibliografía sobre la frontera entre Venezuela y Colombia, 16
Bibliografía teológica comentada del área iberoamericana, 17
Bibliographie: les travaux de recherches a l'Université d'Etat d'Haiti, 92
Bibliography: recent urban studies on Latin America, 1974-1976, 18
Biblioteca Nacional, *Rio.* Divisão de Publicações e Divulgação, 528
Biedermann, Hans, 1958
Biedma, José Juan, 3701
Bierhorst, John, 7845
Biggs, John, 9104
Bikfalvy, Péter, 6829
Bilbao, Jon, 2155
Billip, Jim, 9091
Bills, Garland D., 6013
Binetti, Mario, 7044
Bioy Casares, Adolfo, 6895, 7915-7916
Birabent, Mauricio, 3702
Birckel, Maurice, 3191
Bischoff, Efraín U., 3703-3704
Bishop, Elizabeth, 7830
Biskind, Peter, 952
Biso, Luiz Carlos. See Caco [pseud. for Luiz Carlos Biso].
Bitar Letayf, Marcelo, 2257
Blaas, Richard, 3963
Black, Jan Knippers, 118
Blackburn, Paul *trans.,* 7918
Blakewell, Peter J., 2477
Blanc Renard, Neville, 3613
Blanchard, Peter, 3490
Blanco, Andrés Eloy, 7045-7046
Blanco, Guillermo, 6858
Blanco, José Joaquín, 2692
Blanco, José María, 3491
Blanco Aguinaga, Carlos, 7181
Blancpain, Jean-Pierre, 3614
Blasco, Concepción, 2518
Blasi, Alberto, 9496
Blasier, Cole, 2382
Blixen, Hyalmar, 6562
Blouet, Brian, 3045
Blutstein, Howard I., 118-119
Boal, Augusto, 7463, 7611
Bobín, María Teresa, 7846
Bodganich, Esteban Carlos, 7321
Bogotá: museos/museums, 270
Boils, Guillermo, 2693
Boletim Bibliográfico da Biblioteca Nacional, 2-5
Boletín de la Academia de Artes y Ciencias de Puerto Rico, 7322

Boletín del Archivo Histórico de Miraflores, 3440-3442
Boletín del Archivo Nacional de Historia, 3166
Boletín Informativo del Archivo Nacional de Panamá, 2855
Boletín Nicaraguense de Bibliografía y Documentación, 2856
Bolinger, Dwight, 6015
Bolivia. Comité Nacional del Sesquicentenario de la República, 3580
Bolland, O. Nigel, 2790, 2857
Bolo Hidalgo, Salomón, 3492
Bolsi, A.S., 3284
Bolzán, J.E., 9644-9645
Bolzoni, Francesco, 1000
Bombal, María Luisa, 6859
Bonfiglio, Giovanni, 3493
Bonfil Batalla, Guillermo, 2599
Bonifaz Nuño, Rubén, 7047
Bonilla, Heraclio, 3494-3496
Books Abroad, 6963
Borah, Woodrow, 2258, 2453
Borba, Hermilo, 7407
Borba de Moraes, Rubens. See Moraes, Rubens Borba de.
Borba Filho, Hermilo, 7612
Borbolla, Carlos, 9094
Bordenave, Maria Candida Rocha de Diaz, 6092
Bordón, F. Arturo, 3894
Bordón, Nellibe Judith, 9405
Borello, Rodolfo A., 6470
Borges, Analola, 2259
Borges, Jorge Luis, 6964, 7048, 7857, 7911-7916
Borinsky, Alicia, 6965
Borland, Francis, 2815
Borón, Atilio Alberto, 3615
Borrego Pla, María del Carmen, 3129-3130
Bosch, Rafael, 6704
Bosco, María Angélica, 6896
Bossano, Guillermo, 3462
Botelho de Oliveira, Manuel, 7613
Botelho Gosálvez, Raúl, 6749
Bothwell, Reece B., 3028
Boulton, Alfredo, 391
Bouroncle Carreón, Alfonso, 6780
Bouysse-Cassagne, Thérése, 2027
Bowers, Claude G., 3616
Bowman, Charles H., Jr., 3338
Boxer, C.R., 2260
Boyd-Bowman, Peter, 2261, 6070

Boyer, Richard, 2454
Bradbury, Walter I. *trans.*, 7922
Brading, David A., 2419-2421, 2480
Bradley, Peter T., 3192-3193
Braga, Genesino, 490
Brakel, C. Arthur, Jr., 6093
Brañas, Balbino, 3705
Branco, Joaquim, 7507
Branco Rangel, Leyla Castello. See Rangel, Leyla Castello Branco.
Brandão, Wilson de Andrade, 3964
Brasil, Assis, 7666
Brasil, Emanuel, 7830
Brathwaite, Edward Kamau, 2383, 6124, 7814
Bratosevich, Nicolás A.S., 6471
Bratzel, John F., 4070
Braun, Rafael, 9569
Braun Menéndez, Armando, 3617
Bravo Guerreira, María Concepción, 2028, 3194
Bravo Ramírez, Francisco J., 315
Brayner, Sônia, 7734
Brazil. Assembléia Constituinte e Legislativa, 4071
Brazil. Biblioteca Nacional, 7667
Brazil. Congresso. Câmara dos Deputados. Centro de Documentação e Informação, 93, 4072
Brazil. Conselho Federal de Cultura, 7668
Brazil. Ministério da Educação e Cultura (MEC). Departamento de Assuntos Culturais, 457, 9043
Brownell, Virginia A., 7323
Browning, David G., 2029, 2791
Browning, Harley L., 2218
Bruand, Yves, 443, 491-492
Bruce-Novoa, Juan, 6595
Brugada Guanes, Alejandro, 293
Bruna, Paulo J.V., 493
Brundage, Bun Cartwright, 2262
Brushwood, Carolyn *trans.*, 7896
Brushwood, John S., 6596-6597, 6850, 7896
Bruyas, Jean-Paul, 7704
Bryan, Anthony T., 2600-2601
Bryant, William C., 6407
Buarque de Hollanda, Chico. See Hollanda, Chico Buarque de.
Bueno, Miguel, 9665, 9673
Bueno, Salvador, 6675
Buenos Aires (prov.), *Arg.* Gobernación. Ministerio de Educación. Subsecretaría de Cultura, 3707

Buescu, Mircea, 3965, 4074
Buisseret, David, 2949
Buitrago, Fanny, 6757
Bulletin de la Société d'Histoire de la Guadeloupe, 2955
Bullrich, Silvina, 6897-6898
Bulnes, Gonzalo, 3618
Bunster, Enrique, 2263, 3619
Buonocore, Domingo, 45
Burden, William A.M., 2384
Burdiel de López, María Cruz, 6656
Burga, Manuel, 3196, 3497-3498
Burgos, Adriano Irala. *See* Irala Burgos, Adriano.
Buria Pérez, Lázaro, 1013
Burke, Michael E., 2695
Burke, William, 2348, 3311
Burkett, Elinor, 2030
Burkholder, Mark A., 2264-2265
Burlamáqui Köpke, Carlos. *See* Köpke, Carlos Burlamáqui
Burns, E. Bradford, 985, 2137-2138
Burrus, Ernest J., 2550
Burton, Julianne, 953-956, 1001
Busatto, Luiz, 7736
Bushnell, David, 3339
Busto Duthurburu, José Antonio del, 2551
Bustos, Raquel, 9079
Buttrey, Theodore V., Jr., 2139

Caballero, José María, 3361
Caballero, Juan, 7324
Caballero de Cortés, Susana, 9035
Cabello Moreno, Antonio, 9105
Cabral, Plínio, 7408
Cabral, Salvador, 3399
Cabral de Melo Neto, João. *See* Melo Neto, João Cabral de.
Cabral de Oliveira, Denise. *See* Oliveira, Denise Cabral de.
Cabral Fernandes, Risette. *See* Fernandes, Risette Cabral.
Cabrera Infante, Guillermo, 7886
Cabrera y Piña de Corsi, Matilde, 2422
Cáceres, Esther de, 7160
Cáceres, María Leticia, 6408
Cáceres Carenzo, Raúl, 7050
Cacho Vázquez, Xavier, 2482
Caco [*pseud. for* Luiz Carlos Biso], 515
Cadenhead, Ivie E., 2858
Cadernos de Teatro, 7650
Caicedo Castilla, José Joaquín, 3420
Caillet-Bois, Julio, 6472
Cairo, Angel, 3708
Cajiao Salas, Teresa, 7277
Calabrese, Humberto, 3709
Caldas Júnior, Waltércio, 458
Calderón, Alfonso, 7051
Calderón Bouchet, R., 9530
Calderón Chico, Carlos, 6766
Calderón Quijano, José Antonio, 2140
Caldwell, Helen *trans.*, 7940
Calgaro, Orlando Florencio, 3710
Caliman, Plínio, 7508
Callado, Antonio, 7409, 7938
Calloni, Stella, 1031
Calmon, Pedro, 4075
Calnek, Edward E., 1960-1961
Calvo, César, 7052
Calzadilla, Juan, 392
Camacho, Luis, 9531
Camacho Morelos, Jesús, 6563
Câmara, Jaime, 4076
Câmara Cascudo, Luís. *See* Cascudo, Luís da Câmara.
Camargo, Joracy, 7614
Camargo, Sergio, 459
Camargo, Suzana, 7705
Cambranes, J.C., 2859
Camello, Maurílio José de Oliveira, 3966
Camp, Roderic Ai, 316, 2696
Campa, Román V. de la, 7325
Campana antiguo, 3711
Campbell, Leon G., 2552, 3068, 3197
Campbell, Mavis Christine, 2991
Campello de Melo, Maria do Carmo Barreto. *See* Melo, Maria do Carmo Barreto Campello de.
Campo, Angel del, 6473
Campo, José Rodolfo del, 3499
Campo, Xorge del, 7053
Campo Lacasa, Cristina, 2956
Campobassi, José Salvador, 3712
Campos, Augusto de, 7509, 7706
Campos, Geir [Nuffer de], 7510, 7615
Campos, Haroldo de, 7511, 7706, 7737
Campos, Jorge, 6657
Campos, Julieta, 6564
Campos, Maria Consuelo Cunha, 7707
Campos, Maria Jacintha Trovão da Costa. *See* Jacintha, Maria [*pseud. for* Maria Jacintha Trovão da Costa Campos].
Campos Chaves, Eduardo Oscar de. *See* Chaves, Eduardo Oscar de Campos.
Campos da Silva, Zander. *See* Silva, Zander Campos da.
Camusso, Guillermina G. de, 3713
Canales, Nemesio R., 6705

Author Index

Cañas, Alberto F., 7247
Candido, Salvatore, 2349
Canedo, Lino Gómez, 62, 261, 2290, 2483-2484, 2553, 3104-3106
Canessa de Sanguinetti, Marta, 3929
Cañete y Domínguez, Pedro Vicente, 2266
Cannabrava, Euryalo, 7768
Cantarino, Vicente, 6967
Canto Hernández, Rosendo, 3006
Capela, José, 2141
Cappelletti, Angel J., 9406, 9532-9537, 9570, 9689
Capriles, Oswaldo, 1044
Caracas/Venezuela, 393
Caracciolo-Trejo, E., 7832
Carámbula de Barreiro, Margarita, 3400
Caravaglia, Juan Carlos, 3265
Caravedo Molinari, Baltazar, 3500-3501
Carballido, Emilio, 7248-7250, 7887, 7930
Carballo, Emmanuel, 7054
Carbone Mora, Pablo V., 3502
Carbonell, Galaor, 368
Cardenal, Ernesto, 7021, 7858
Cárdenas, Eduardo J., 3714
Cárdenas, Felipe, 3715
Cárdenas, Felipe, h., 3716
Cárdenas, Lázaro, 2697
Cárdenas, Manuel, 2957
Cárdenas, Rodolfo Marcelo, 9666
Cárdenas Ayaipoma, Mario, 3198
Cardero García, María Elena, 2602
Cardona-Hines, Alvaro *trans.*, 7881
Cardoso, Ciro Flamarion S., 2142-2143, 2958
Cardoso, Lawrence A., 2698-2699
Cardoso, Lúcio, 7410, 7616
Cardoso, Maria Helena, 7769
Cardoso, Onelio Jorge, 6676
Cardoza y Aragón, Luis, 317
Cardozo, Efraim, 3895
Cardozo, Joaquim, 7617
Cardozo, Lubio, 19-20, 6851
Cardozo, Manoel da Silveira Soares, 2144
Cardozo Biritos, Dennis F., 9646
Carew, Jan, 2267
Carilla, Emilio, 6409-6510
Carise, Iracy, 511
Carlés, Rubén Darío, 2816, 2860
Carletti, Francesco, 2268
Carlin Arce, Jorge, 3503-3504
Carlino, Carlos, 3717
Carlisle, Charles Richard, 7833
Carlos, Alberto J. *trans.*, 7865

Carlos, Helio Lima, 7512
Carmack, Robert M., 1962
Carmagnani, Marcello, 2145, 2168, 3069
Carman, Michael Dennis, 2700
Carmen Sordo Sodi en Cuba, 9106
Carmo, Raymundo Evangelista do, 9674
Carnegie, James, 7809
Carneiro, Newton I. da Silva, 444, 529
Carneiro da Silva, Euclides. *See* Silva, Euclides Carneiro da.
Caro, Herbert, 7652
Caro, Miguel Antonio, 6002, 6016
Caro Alvarez, José A., 262
Caro Costas, Aida R., 2959
Carone, Edgard, 4077-4079
Carpentier, Alejo, 6677-6680, 7888-789
Carpentier, Hortense, 7847, 7903, 7929
Carpizo, Jorge, 2146
Carr, Barry, 2701
Carranza, Eduardo, 7055
Carranza, María Mercedes, 122
Carrasco, Pedro, 1963-1966
Carrasquilla, Tomás, 6474-6475
Carrasquilla Botero, Juan, 48
Carré Lazcano, Elio, 3007
Carreño, Virginia 3718
Carrera, Gustavo Luis, 6852
Carrera, José Miguel, 3391
Carrera Andrade, Jorge, 7056, 7859
Carrera Damas, Germán, 3312, 3347-3348, 3444-3445
Carreras de Velasco, Mercedes, 2702
Carrero, Jaime, 7251
Carretero, Andrés M., 3719-3720
Carrière, Jean, 3620
Carrillo, Germán Darío, 6805
Carrillo Batalla, Tomás Enrique, 3443
Carrillo y Gariel, Abelardo, 279
Carrington, Lawrence D., 6125
Carrino, Frank G. *trans.*, 7865
Carrión, Benjamín, 2703, 9497
Carrocera, Buenaventura de, 2146a, 3107
Carroll, Patrick J., 2485
Caruso, Raimundo C., 7513
Carvajal Barrios, Leonardo, 6861
Carvajal de Arocha, Mercedes. *See* Palacios, Lucila [*pseud. for* Mercedes Carvajal de Arocha].
Carvalhal, Tania Franco, 7669
Carvalho, Luciano de, 7464
Carvalho, Luiz Raimundo Batista de. *See* Luiz Raimundo [*pseud. for* Luiz Raimundo Batista de Carvalho].
Carvalho, Margarida Sabóia de, 7465
Carvalho, Ronald de, 7738

Carvalho da Silva, Domingos. *See* Silva, Domingos Carvalho da.
Carvalho de Baqueiro, Eloisa Ruiz. *See* Ruiz Carvalho de Baqueiro, Eloisa.
Carvalho e Silva, Aristides Monteiro de. *See* Silva, Aristides Monteiro de Carvalho e.
Carvalho-Neto, Paulo de, 6029
Carybé [*pseud. for* Héctor Júlio Páride Bernabo], 512
Casal, Julian del, 7057
Casas, Bartolomé de las, 2269-2270
Casasús, Fernando Rafael, 9608
Casco, Marcos, 3721
Cascudo, Luís de Câmara, 4080
Casey, Jeffrey J., 2861
Casirir, Berard, 7784
Caso, Antonio, 9448
Cassano, Paul V., 6003, 6029a-6032
Casassas Canto, José María, 3246, 3621
Castagnino, Raúl H., 7326
Castañeda, Héctor-Neri, 9538, 9609, 9675
Castañeda García, Carmen, 2423
Castañon Guimarães, Júlio. *See* Guimarães, Júlio Castañon.
Castedo-Ellerman, Elena, 7327
Castellani, Leonardo, 9498
Castellanos, Alfredo Raúl, 302, 3930-3932
Castellanos, Rafael Ramón, 3340, 6788
Castellanos, Rosario, 6598, 7252-7253
Castello, J. Jorge *trans.*, 7929
Castello, José Aderaldo, 7670
Castello Branco Rangel, Leyla. *See* Rangel, Leyla Castello Branco.
Castelo, Julio, 2147
Castillero, Ernesto J., 2817
Castillero Reyes, Ernesto de Jesús, 2350
Castillo, Abelardo, 6899
Castillo, Eduardo, 6476
Castillo, Guido, 384
Castillo, Otto René, 7058
Castillo Flores, Arturo, 2792
Castillo Lara, Lucas G., 3349
Castillo Mathieu, Nicolás del, 2271, 6126
Castro, Jeanne Berrance de, 4081
Castro, Josue de, 7939
Castro, Nei Leandro de, 7514
Castro, Sílvio, 7671
Castro, Yeda Pessoa de, 6094
Castro Arenas, Mario, 6477
Castro Díaz, Alejandro, 2862
Castro Klarén, Sara, 6830
Castro Memória Ribeiro, Antonia Mota de. *See* Ribeiro, Antonia Mota de Castro Memória.
Castro Nevares, Federico, 63
Castro Rebello, Edgardo de. *See* Rebello, Edgardo de Castro.
Castro Santos Filho, Lycurgo de. *See* Santos Filho, Lycurgo de Castro.
Castro Seoane, José, 2272
Castro Souza, Luiz de. *See* Souza, Luiz de Castro.
Catania, Carlos, 6968
Catorce mujeres escriben cuentos, 6565
Caturelli, Alberto, 9407, 9452-9453, 9690
Los caudillos de este siglo, 3722
Cavalcanti, Carlos, 410
Cavalcanti, Emiliano di. *See* Di Cavalcanti, Emiliano.
Cavalcanti, Homero Homem de Siqueira. *See* Homem [de Siqueira Cavalcanti], Homero.
Cavalcanti Proença, Ivan. *See* Proença, Ivan Cavalcanti.
Cavallini de Arauz, Ligia, 2818
Cavarozzi, Marcilo, 3622
Cavazos Garza, Israel, 6033
Cavelier, Germán, 3341
Cea, José Roberto, 7022
Cea Egaña, José Juis, 3623
Cedran, Lourdes, 504
Celli, Bruni, 9571
Celorio, Gonzalo, 318
Celso, Angel T. lo. *See* Lo Celso, Angel T.
Celso Japiassu [*pseud. for* Celso Almir Japiassu Lins Falcão], 75-15
Celso Pinheiro, Lina. *See* Pinheiro, Lina Celso.
Centrángolo, Aníbal E., 9023
Centromidca, 64
Cerda Catalán, Alfonso, 3505
Cerqueim Lemos, Carlos Alberto. *See* Lemos, Carlos Alberto Cerqueim.
Cerutti, Franco, 7328
Cervo, Amado Luiz, 2273
Cesar, Guilhermino, 7652
Céspedes, Augusto, 3581-3582
Céspedes, Guillermo, 2274, 3092
Cevallos García, Gabriel, 2275
Chacón, Joaquín Armando, 6566
Chalmers, Vera M., 7672
Chambi, Manuel, 1034
Chanan, Michael, 1002
Chance, John K., 2486-2487
Chandler, Dewitt S., 2265, 2819
Chang-Rodríguez, Raquel, 6411-6413

Chapa, Matilde, 1954
Chaple, Sergio, 6681
Charles, Christophe, 7793
Charles, Jean-Claude, 7785
Charles, Jean Gary, 7789
Charry Lara, Fernando, 7167
Chartrain, François, 3896-3897
Chase, Alfonso, 6629-6630
Chatwin, Bruce, 3723
Chaurand, Susana, 1024
Chaves, Eduardo Oscar de Campos, 9572
Cháves, Fermín, 3724-3727, 7182
Chaves, Flávio Loureiro, 6478, 7708
Chaves, Osvaldo, 3266
Chaves Júnior, Edgard de Brito, 9044
Chávez Alfaro, Lizandro, 6631
Chávez Velásquez, Nancy, 2031
Cherubini, Humberto, 4107
Cheuse, Alan, 6706
Chevalier, François, 2148, 2704
Chiampi Cortez, Irlemar, 6707
Chianelli, Trinidad Delia, 3728
Chiappelli, Fredi, 2276
Chiavegato, Augusto José, 9676
Chinchilla Aguilar, Ernesto, 2794
Chipman, Donald, 2554
Chocrón, Isaac E., 6789, 7254
Choque Canqui, Roberto, 2032
Chueca Posadas, Susana, 3506
Chumbita, Hugo, 3729
Cichero Pitré, Aníbal, 3730
Ciclo de Debates da Cultura Contemporânea, *I, Rio, 1975*, 7770
Cid, Teófilo, 6862
Cid G., Francisco Javier, 9499
Cigliuti, Carlos Walter, 3933
Cine con la película debajo del brazo, 1045
Cine latinoamericano y lucha revolucionaria hoy, 957
Cine militante en Argentina: entrevista con Gerardo Vallejo, Grupo Cine Liberación, 968
Cine nacional: encuesta, 1035
Cine peruano: ¿Barrón y cuenta nueva?, 1036
Cinema chilien: entretien avec Helvio Soto, 1003
Le cinéma de l'Unité Populaire: bilan d'une expérience: interview with Patricio Guzmán, Miguel Littín, R. Ruiz, H. Soto, 1004
Cinéma mexicain, 1018
Cinemateca de Cuba, La Habana. Sección de Cine Cubano, 1012
Ciria, Alberto, 3731
Cirne, Moacy, 7739
Cisneros, Antonio, 7059, 7860
Cisneros Sánchez, Manuel, 379
Civrieux, Marc de, 2033
Clark, Victor Selden, 3046
Claro Valdés, Samuel, 9003, 9080-9082
CLASE: Citas Latinoamericanas en Sociología y Economía, 94
Clayton, Lawrence A., 3199
Clegern, Wayne M., 2863
Clemente Pozenato, José. *See* Pozenato, José Clemente.
Clementi, Hebe, 2149
Clements, Kendrick A., 2705
Cleveland, Donald, Jr., 4082
Coatsworth, John H., 2603-2604
Coba, Carlos, 9099
Cobo Borda, J.G., 6758
Cócaro, Nicolás, 7060
Cock C., Guillermo, 2034
Coelho, Ceres Pisani, 411
Coelho, Nelly Novaes, 7709
Coelho, Salvador José Correia, 4083
Coelho dos Santos, Silvio. *See* Santos, Silvio Coelho dos.
Coelho Frota, Lélia. *See* Frota, Lélia Coelho.
Coerver, Don M., 2605-2606
Coffa, Alberto J., 9647
Coiscou Henríquez, Máximo, 3020
Coke, Van Deren, 307
Colares, Ciro, 7466
Colares, Otacílio, 7673, 7710
Colchie, Thomas, 6538
Colecchia, Francesca, 7852
Colección *Banco Cafetero*, 369
Coleti, Giandomenico, 3093
Colimon, Marie-Thérèse, 7786
Colina, José de la, 1028, 6599
Coll y Toste, Cayetano, 3047
Collapiña, Supno, 2035
Collier, Simon, 3624
Collins, Anne C., 9107
Colmenares, Germán, 3131
Colombia. Banco de la República. Biblioteca Luis Angel Arango, 65
Colombia. Departamento Administrativo Nacional de Estadística, 3421
Colônia, Regina Célia, 7431
Colóquio Luso-Espanhol de História Ultramarina, *II, Lisboa, 1973*. Centro de Estudos de Cartografia Antiga, 2277

Colque Valladares, Víctor, 3507
Coltharp, Lurline H., 6071
Comadrán Ruiz, Jorge, 3267
Comas, Juan, 2278
Comerlatti, Marila, 9104
Comisión para Escribir la Historia Marítima del Perú, *Lima*, 3508
Comitas, Lambros, 6
Os Comités de Defesa da Revolução, 3009
La Compañía de Jesús en México: cuatro siglos de labor cultural, 1572-1972, 2424
Conceição Vilhena, Maria de. *See* Vilhena, Maria da Conceição.
Concha, Jaime, 7168
Concha, Manuel, 6863
Concierto conmemorativo 250 años del nacimiento de Esteban Salas, 9095
Condarco Morales, Ramiro, 2036
Condé, Maryse, 7779
Conde, Teresa del, 319-320
Congreso Centroamericano de Historia Demográfica, Económica y Social, *I, Santa Bárbara, C.R., 1973*, 2820
Congreso de Historia de los Pueblos de la Provincia de Buenos Aires, *II, Tandil, Arg., 1972*, 3732
Congreso de la Historia Argentina y Regional, *II, Comodoro Rivadavia, Arg., 1973*, 3070
Congreso Venezolano de Historia, *II, Caracas, 1974*, 3094
Congresso Brasileiro de Língua e Literatura, *VI, Rio, 1974*, 7674
Congresso de História da Independência do Brasil, *Rio, 1972*, 3967
Conjunto, 7255-7256
Coniff, Michael, 3167
Conrad, Andrée *trans.*, 7893
Conrado, Raul, 7771
Consejo Episcopal Latinoamericano (CELAM), *Bogotá*. Secretariado General, 95
Consejo Nacional de Ciencia y Tecnología, *México*. Departamento de Sistemas de Información, 66
Conte Porras, J., 2795, 2864-2865
Conteris, Hiber, 6479
Conti, Haroldo, 6900-6901
Conto de Magalhães, José Vieira. *See* Magalhães, José Vieira Conto de.
Contreras A., Juan, 3247
Contreras D., Milagros, 3108
Contreras Torres, Miguel, 1019
Contreras Vélez, Alvaro, 2866
Converso, Félix, 3733
Convivium, 9454
Cook, Noble David, 2037-2039, 3200-3201
Cook, Sherburne F., 2425
Cook de Leonard, Carmen, 1967
Coore, Rita, 9063
Corbière, Emilio J., 3734
Corbisier, Rolando, 9408
Corcuera, Arturo, 7061
Cordero, Néstor Luis, 9539
Cordero, Rodrigo, 9455
Cordi, Cassiano Agostino, 9610
Córdoba, Tomás, 3735
Córdova Iturburu, C., 346
Cordua, Carla, 9611
Cornejo, Justino, 7183
Cornejo Polar, Antonio, 6480, 6831
Cornelius, Wayne A., 2385
Corona Sánchez, Eduardo, 1968
Correa, Manuel *brother*, 9004
Corrêa de Araujo, Antonio Amaury. *See* Araujo, Antonio Amaury Corrêa de.
Corrêa Filho, José, 4085
Correa Iglesias, Carlos, 6864
Correa Vásquez, Pedro, 7062
Correas, Edmundo, 3736
Correia, Raimundo [da Mota de Azevedo], 7516
Correia Coelho, Salvador Josê. *See* Coelho, Salvador José Correia.
Correira de Andrade, Manoel. *See* Andrade, Manoel Correira de.
Cortada, James W., 21
Cortázar, Julio, 6902-6903, 7890, 7917-7918
Cortés, Félix, 9064
Cortés Conde, Roberto, 2150, 2386
Cortometrajes y cine nacional, balance y perspectivas, 1037
Cosío Villegas, Daniel, 2426, 2706
Cosmelli Ibáñez, José Luis, 3737
Cospín, Miguel Angel, 2867
Cossa, Roberto M., 7257
Cossio, Carlos, 9612
Costa, Beatriz, 7651
Costa, Flávio Moreira da, 7432
Costa, Francisco Augusto Pereira da, 3968-3969
Costa, Iraci del Nero da, 4026
Costa, João Cruz, 9409
Costa, Joaquim Ribeiro, 3970
Costa, Lúcio, 494
Costa, Rovílio, 4086

Costa Campos, Maria Jacintha Trovão da. *See* Jacintha, Maria [*pseud.* for Maria Jacintha Trovão da Costa Campos].
Costa de la Torre, Arturo, 3313, 3384
Costa e Silva, Antônio Francisco da. *See* Silva, [Antônio Francisco] da Costa e.
Costa Ferreira, Orlando da. *See* Ferreira, Orlando da Costa.
Costa Franco, Sérgio da. *See* Franco, Sérgio da Costa.
Costa Leiva, Miguel da. *See* Da Costa Leiva, Miguel.
Costa Lima, Luiz. *See* Lima, Luiz Costa.
Costa Maciel, Alba. *See* Maciel, Alba Costa.
Costa Porto, José da. *See* Porto, José da Costa.
Costa Rica. Ministerio de Economía, Industria y Comercio. Dirección General de Estadística y Censos. Sección de Publicaciones, 2868
Costella, Irineu, 4086
Costello, Julia, 278
Costeloe, Michael P., 2427, 2607
Cote Lamus, Eduardo, 7063
Couceiro, Solange Martins, 22
Coulson, Graciela, 6969
Courtois, Félix, 7776
Coutinho, Afrânio, 7675-7677
Coutinho, Sônia, 7433
Couttolenc Cortes, Gustavo, 6414
Couturier, Edith Boorstein, 2428
Couve, Adolfo, 6865
Couyoumdjian, Ricardo, 3625
Covo, Jacqueline, 6481
Craddock, Jerry R., 6013
Craig, Alan K., 3071
Craig, Dennis R., 6127
Craton, Michael, 2960
Creedman, Theodore S., 2796
Crespi, Roberto Simón, 6482
Crespo, Auan Carlos, 2040, 3202
Crespo de la Serna, J., 321
Crespo Gutiérrez, Alberto, 3583
Crespo R., Alberto, 3385
Crippa, Adolpho, 9713
Cristaldo, Janer, 7467
Crogliano, María Eugenia, 7023
Crouch, Thomas W., 2961
Crouse, Nellis M., 2962
Cruz, Ernesto Horácio da, 425
Cruz, Francisco Santiago, 2488

Cruz, Mary, 6483
Cruz Costa, João. *See* Costa, João Cruz.
Cruz Gouvêa, Fernando da. *See* Gouvêa, Fernando da Cruz.
Cruz Hermosilla, Emilio de la, 2351
Cruz Monclova, Lidio, 3028
Cruz Vélez, Danilo, 9729
Cuadernos de Filosofía, 9456
Cuadra, Pablo Antonio, 7861
Cuadros, Juan José, 2041
Cuba Review, 7329
Cuccorese, Horacio Juan, 3738
Cuche, Denys, 3509
Cuellar, José Tomás de, 6484
Cuéllar Abaroa, Crisanto, 2707
El cuento en la revolución, 6682
El cuento erótico en México, 6567
Cuentos modernos, 6683
Cuervo, Rufino José, 6485
Cultura, 460, 986
Cunha, Lygia da Fonseca Fernandes da, 445
Cunha Campos, Maria Consuelo. *See* Campos, Maria Consuelo Cunha.
Cunha Lima, Regina Helena. *See* Lima, Regina Helena Cunha.
Cunhill Grau, Pedro, 3248, 3350
Cupello, Francisco, 4087
Curi, Marcos, 347
Cuthberg, Marlene, 6128
Cuvi, Pablo, 3463
Cypess, Sandra Messinger, 7330
Cyr, Helen W., 958
Cyrus, Stanley, 6486

D'Abbeville, Claude, 4027
Da Costa Deiva, Miguel, 9573
Da Costa e Silva, Antônio Francisco. *See* Silva, [Antônio Francisco] da Costa e.
Dahl, Víctor C., 7012
Dal Vera, Juan, 7064
D'Alessio, Juan Carlos, 9648
Damas, León G., 776a
Damasceno, Athos, 7652
Dandler, Jorge, 3584
Dantas, Antonio Arruda, 530, 7740
Dantas, José Ibarê, 4088
Dante de Moraes, Carlos. *See* Moraes, Carlos Dante de.
Dapena, Ortênsia Muradás, 7468
D'Arc, Hélène Rivière, 2689
Darnell, Donald G., 2151
Dascal, Marcelo, 9574
Dash, J. Michael, 7794

Da Silva, Deonísio. See Silva, Deonísio da.
Da Silva, Domingos Carvalho. See Silva, Domingos Carvalho da.
Da Silva, Francisco Pereira. See Silva, Francisco Pereira da.
Da Silva, Hélcio Pereira. See Silva, Hélcio Pereira da.
Da Silva, Paulo Augusto. See Paulo Augusto [pseud. for Paulo Augusto da Silva].
Da Silva, Rolando Roque. See Silva, Rolando Roque da.
Dauphin, Marcel, 7787
Dauster, Bluma, 7434
Dauster, Frank, 7331
Davies, Keith, 3203
Davies, Nigel, 1969
Dávila, Arturo V., 2963, 2992-2993
Dávila, Mauro, 3446
Dávila Andrade, César, 6767
Davis, Charles L., 2708
Davis, Harold Eugene, 2387
Davis, Natalie Y., 280
Davis, Robert H., 3422-3423
Davis, Thomas B., 2709
Davis, William Myron, 7711
Dawes, Neville, 7815
Daza, José S., 3739
Deal, Carl W., 67
Dean, Warren, 4089
Deas, Malcolm, 3424
Debarbieri Casagrande, César A., 7184
O debate político no processo da independência, 3971
De Beer, Gabriela, 9457
Debes, Célio, 4090
Debravo, Jorge, 7065
Debray, Régis, 3585
Debret, Jean Baptiste, 4466
Decker, David, 6600
Deeds, Susan M., 2710
Defelitto, Ana María, 7332
De Grande, Eugenia, 348
De Greiff, León. See Greiff, León de.
Delago, F.R., 9724
Deler, J.P., 3168
Delgado, Lenelina, 7333
Delgado, Luiz, 4091
Delgado, Rafael, 6487
Delich, Francisco J., 3740
Della Cava, Ralph, 4092
Delpar, Helen, 2152
Denevan, William M., 2279
Denis, Dohou Codjo, 2153

Denser, Márcia M., 7435
De Panasewicz, Nitsche, 9613
Derenzi, Luiz Serafim, 4093
Derisi, Octavio N., 9436, 9540, 9614
Déronvil, Marc Allan, 7789
Deschamps Chapeaux, Pedro, 2980
Dessau, Adalbert, 6488, 9500
Destéfani, Laurio Hedelvio, 3268, 3401, 3741
D'Halmar, Augusto, 6866
Dias, Cicero, 4028
Dias, Ruy, 7517
"Los días de Dios" oratorio de Juan Orrego-Salas, 9083
Dias Lopes, José Antonio. See Lopes, José Antonio Dias.
Dias Tavares, Luís Henrique. See Tavares, Luís Henrique Dias.
Díaz, Benito, 3742
Diaz, Jorge, 7258
Díaz, Lilia, 2489
Díaz, Marco, 281
Díaz, Pío P., 2068
Díaz A., Jorge Aurelio, 9575
Díaz Arrieta, Hernán. See Alone [pseud. for Hernán Díaz Arrieta].
Diaz Bordenave, Maria Candida Rocha de. See Bordenave, Maria Candida Rocha de Diaz.
Díaz Chávez, Filander, 2869
Díaz Montero, Aníbal, 6684
Díaz Polanco, Héctor, 3048
Díaz Rodríguez, Rolando, 1013
Díaz Rozzotto, Jaime, 6658
Díaz Sánchez, Ramón, 7891
Díaz Soler, Luis M., 2994-2995
Díaz Suárez, Rosa, 3547
Díaz Valcárcel, Emilio, 6685
Di Candia, Alcides J., 7185
Di Cavalcanti, Emiliano, 461
Dicionário inglês-português ilustrado, 6109
Diego, Eliseo, 7066
Diégues Júnior, Manuel, 3972
Dieli, Robert F., 2711
Dietmann, Alfonso, 3973
Diez, Luis A., 6489
"Los Diez" en el arte chileno del siglo XX, 362
Di Giovanni, Norman Thomas trans., 7857, 7911-7915
Dill, Hans-Otto, 7231
Dinardi, Alberto, 6948
Dinwoodie, D.H., 2712
Dis, Emilio, 6034

Author Index

Disandro, Carlos A., 3269, 9541
Discépolo, Armando, 7259
Djanira, 462
Dobal [Teixeira], H[indemburgo], 7518
Dobkin de Ríos, Marlene, 1970
Dobyns, Henry F., 2154, 2555, 3510
Documentos del Primer Congreso del Partido Comunista de Cuba sobre la Cultura Artística y Literaria: tesis, resolución, 6708
Documentos inéditos de José Ives Limantour: apuntes relativos a una conversación habida con el Sr. Presidente en presencia de los Sres. Ramón Corral y Olegario Molina, Mayo 13 de 1908, 2608
Dodd, Thomas J., 2870
Doll, Ramón, 3743
Dolz Henry, Inés, 7169
Domínguez, Jaime, 3029
Domínguez, Ramiro, 7009
Domínguez Aragonés, Edmundo, 6568
Domínguez Compañy, Francisco, 2280
Domínguez H., Javier, 9615
Donni de Mirande, Nélida Esther, 6035
Donoso, José, 7848, 7892-7893
Donoso, Ricardo, 3626
Donoso-Barros, Roberto, 2281
Donoso Letelier, Crescente, 3627
Dore, Elizabeth, 3511
Dorn, Edward, 7831
Dos Anjos, Augusto de Carvalho Rodrigues. *See* Anjos, August [de Carvalho Rodrigues] dos.
Dos Anjos, Ricardo Augusto [Pena]. *See* Anjos, Ricardo Augusto [Pena] dos.
Dos Santos, José Martins. *See* Santos, José Martins dos.
Dos Santos Guterres, Sérgio. *See* Guterres, Sérgio dos Santos.
Dos Santos Jota, Zélio. *See* Jota, Zélio dos Santos.
Doucet, Gastón Gabriel, 3402
Doughty, Paul L., 3510
Douglas, William A., 2155
Dourado, Ângelo, 4094
Dourado, Waldomiro Autran, 7411, 7712
Dower, Catherine A., 9065
Doyle, Plinio, 7678
Drougett, Carlos, 6876
Drummond de Andrade, Carlos. *See* Andrade, Carlos Drummond de.
Duarte, Abelardo, 3974
Duarte, Carlos F., 303-304
Duarte, Erminda, 3744

Duarte, Paulo, 4095, 7679, 7772
Duarte de Almeida, Prisciliana. *See* Almeida, Prisciliana Duarte de.
Dubsky, Josef, 6036
Dudley, William S., 4096
Dueñas C., J. Armando, 2900
Duff, Ernest A., 2388
Dumézil, Georges, 2042
Duncan, Kenneth, 2156
Duncan, Quince, 2802, 6632, 6659
Dunham, Lowell, 6490
Duprat, Régis, 9045
Duque Botero, Guillermo, 3425
Durán, Cheli, 7834
Durán, Gloria, 6601
Durán Luzio, Juan, 6415
Durand, José, 6416
Durand Flórez, Guillermo, 3314
Durand-Forest, Jacqueline de, 1971
Dussan de Reichel, Alicia, 271
Dussel, Enrique, 2157, 9458
Duviols, Jean-Paul, 3109, 3270
Duviols, Pierre, 2042-2046
Dyckerhoff, Ursula, 1972
Dysart, Jane, 2429, 2609
Dzuibiński, Andrzej, 3342

Echevarría, Evelio, 6801
Echeverri M., Aquiles, 3426
Echeverría, Esteban, 6491
Echeverría, Juan María, 2352
Echeverría, Manuel, 6569
Echeverría, Serge *trans.*, 7866
Eckstein, Susan, 2158
Ecuador. Fuerzas Armadas. Estado Mayor Conjunto. Dirección de Historia y Militar, 3464
Ecuador. Fuerzas Armadas [and] Dirección de Historia y Geografía Militar del Estado Mayor, 3169
Editoriales de *La Voz del Nuevo Mundo*: Honduras-Guatemala, 2871
Edmondson, Munro S., 6417
Edwards, Agustín, 3628
Eggers Lan, Conrado, 9542
Ehlke, Cyro, 3975
Eielson, Jorge Eduardo, 7067
Eisenberg, Peter L., 4097
Eliá, Oscar Horacio, 3315
Elia, Sílvio, 6095
Eliezer Galvão, Maria Rita. *See* Galvão, Maria Rita Eliezer.
Elizaincín, Adolfo, 6037-6038
Elizalde, Rufino de, 3745
Elizondo, Salvador, 6570

Ellsworth, Mary E. trans., 7885
El Salvador. Archivo General de la Nación, 2872
Elsey, Wayne, 1973
La emancipación americana en Bolivia y Perú, 3072
Emery, Milton de Moraes, 7618
Emorine, Jacques, 7741
En torno a José Martí: coloquio internacional celebrado bajo los auspicios de Sala José Martí de la Biblioteca Nacional de Cuba, 7186
Encina, Eulogio, 3898
Encuentro de Tapicería Uruguayo Brasileño, I, Montevideo, 1975, 463
Encuentro Latinoamericano de Espiritualidad, III, Quito, 1974, 9410
Una encuesta: cineastas frente al tercer cine, 1048
Engstrand, Iris Wilson, 2556
Entretien avec Jorge Sanjinés (Interview with Jorge Sanjinés), 974
Entrevista con Jorge Silva y Marta Rodríguez, 1009
Epstein, Dena J., 9066
Epstein, Ernesto, 9024
Erdheim, Mario, 1974
Erickson, Kenneth Paul, 4098
Erminy, Peran, 1044
Ermolaiev, V.I., 2159
Escala Escobar, Manuel, 3629
Escena, 7334
Eschmann, Anncharlott, 1975
Escobar, Alberto, 6039, 6832
Escobar, Carlos Henrique de, 9714
Escobar, Luis Antonio, 9092
Escobar, Roberto, 9459
Escobar Valenzuela, Gustavo, 9501
Escovar Salom, Ramón, 3447
Escribar Wicks, Ana, 9616
Escrita, 7680
Eshleman, Clayton trans., 7880
Espejo-Ponce Hunt, Marta, 2490
Espinheiro Filho, Ruy, 7469
Espínola, Francisco, 6949
Espinosa, Germán, 6759
Espinosa Altamirano, Horacio, 7068
Espinosa Domínguez, Carlos, 7335-7336
Espinosa Soriano, Waldemar, 2047-2050
O espírito criador do povo brasileiro, através da coleção da Abelardo Rodrigues do Recife: exposição, Palácio do Itamaraty, Brasília, julho e agosto 1972, 505
Esquivel, Javier, 9691

Estado y política agraria: cuatro ensayos, 3512
Estellé Méndez, Patricio, 3089, 3392, 3630
Estéve, Michel, 987
Estevez, Alfredo, 3315
Estevez, Fred, 985
Estiú, Emilio, 9576
Estrada Ycaza, Julio, 3316, 3465-3466, 9108
Estrazulas, Enrique, 6904
Estrella, Julio C., 2933
Estrellan Ulises, 7260
El estreno de dos obras peruanos, 9131
Estudios de Filosofía y Religiones del Oriente, 9411
Estudios Filosóficos, 9412
Estudios Paraguayos, 3271
Etchepareborda, Roberto, 3746-3747
Eugenio Martínez, María Angeles, 3132-3133
Evangelista do Carmo, Raymundo. See Carmo, Raymundo Evangelista do.
Evans, Peter B., 4099
Everaert, John, 2160
Evia, Jacinto de, 6440
Ewald, Ursula, 2491
Ewald Filho, Rubens, 988
Ewell, Judith, 3448
Los excéntricos, 3748
Exposição-Feira de Artesanato do Pará, Belem, Brazil, 513
Ezquerra, Ramón, 2282

Fagalde, Lauro, 3749
Fagan, Brian, 278
Fagen, Richard R., 2713
Fajardo Terán, Florencia, 3272
Falcão, Celso Almir Japiassu Lins. See Celso Japaissu [pseud. for Celso Almir Japiassu Lins Falcão].
Falcón, Angel, 9064
Falcón, Romana, 2714
Falcone, Frank S., 2610
Falconio, Leda. See Aldef [pseud. for Leda Falconio].
Fallas Barrantes, Marco Antonio, 2873
Fallas Monge, Carlos Luis, 2874
Fallope, J., 3030
Fals Borda, Orlando, 3073
Faraone, Roque, 3934
Faria, Octávio de, 7412
Faro, Arnaldo, 7713
Fatemi, Nasrollah S., 2389
Febres Cordero, Julio, 3351

Author Index

Feidel, Jan, 7935
Feldman, Lawrence H., 1976-1977
Feliú Cruz, Guillermo, 3631
Fellman Velarde, José, 3586
Fergo, Tony, 6633
Ferguson, Yale H., 2161
Fernandes, Anchieta, 412
Fernandes, Anna Maria, 7519
Fernandes, Francisco, 6110
Fernandes, Maria do Carmo Leite de Oliveira, 6111
Fernandes, Millôr, 7520
Fernandes, Risette Cabral, 7472
Fernandes da Cunha, Lygia da Fonseca. *See* Cunha, Lygia da Fonseca Fernandes de.
Fernández, Carlos José, 3899
Fernández, Emilio, 3386
Fernández, José B., 2557
Fernández, León, 2821
Fernández, Macedonio, 9449
Fernández, Magalí, 6492
Fernández, Matilde, 3134
Fernández, Sergio E., 6571
Fernández Alonso, María del Rosario, 7187
Fernández Balzano, Oscar Alberto, 3750
Fernández Cabrelli, Alfonso, 3935
Fernández de Avila, Rafael Camon, 2353
Fernández de la Fuente, Amalia, 9035
Fernández de Piedrahita, Lucas, 3135
Fernández Guardia, Ricardo, 2797, 2822
Fernández Méndez, Eugenio, 9413
Fernández Montagne, Ernesto, 3513
Fernández Naranjo,; Nicolás, 6072
Fernández Retamar, Roberto, 2934, 6709-6711
Fernández Robaina, Tomás, 23
Fernández Spencer, Antonio, 7170
Ferrater Mora, José, 9414
Ferraz, Geraldo, 413
Ferraz do Amaral, Pedro. *See* Amaral, Pedro Ferraz do.
Ferré, Rosario, 6686
Ferreira, Arnaldo Amado, 3900
Ferreira, Arthur, 3976, 4100
Ferreira, Aurelio Buarque de Holanda, 96
Ferreira, Celina, 7521
Ferreira, Fernando Luiz Vieira, 6112
Ferreira, Gilda Pires, 46
Ferreira, João Antônio de Andrade. *See* Antônio [de Andrade Ferreira], João.
Ferreira, João-Francisco, 9502
Ferreira, José Ribamar. *See* Gullar, Ferreira [*pseud. for* José Ribamar Ferreira].
Ferreira, Jurandir, 7522
Ferreira, Orlando da Costa, 531
Ferreira, Silvestre Pinheiro. *See* Pinheiro Ferreira, Silvestre.
Ferreira Japiassu, Hilton. *See* Japiassu, Hilton Ferreira.
Ferreira Lima, Heitor. *See* Lima, Heitor Ferreira.
Ferreira Reis, Arthur Cesar. *See* Reis, Arthur Cesar Ferreira.
Ferreira Santos, Célia Regina. *See* Santos, Célia Regina Ferreira.
Ferreiro, M. Jorge, 6905
Ferrer Benimeli, José Antonio, 2283
Ferrer Valdez, Manuel, 6634
Ferrero, Roberto A., 3751
Ferrez, Gilberto, 3977
Ferri, Gino, 4101
Ferro, Carlos A., 3367
Ffrench-Davis, Ricardo, 3632
Fichandler, Joseph B., 3249
Fichrer, Thomas, 2823
Fidente, Enrico, 3273
Figueira, Gastón, 7188
Figueiredo, Guilherme, 7619, 7653
Figueirêdo Agra, Antônio José. *See* Agra, [Antônio José] Figueirêdo.
Figueredo, Alvaro, 7069
Figueroa, Egberto, 6687-6688
Figueroa, John, 7816
Figueroa, Loida, 2935, 3031
Filer, Malva E., 6970
Filipak, Francisco, 6113
Filippis, Jorge, 7261
Filloy, Juan, 6906
Filmografía, 959
Finol de Jiménez, Mary, 9577
Finot, Enrique, 3587, 6802
Fisher, John R., 3204-3205, 3550
Fishman, César, 3074
Fitte, Ernesto J., 3317, 3752
Fitts, Dudley, 7835
Fitzgerald, E.V.K., 3514
Fitzgibbon, Russell H., 2162
Fleck, Anne, 985
Flint, J.M., 6971
Flinter, Jorge D., 2996
Florence, Hercules, 447
Flores, Angel, 6493, 7189
Flores, Juan, 9064
Flores, Marco Antonio, 6634a
Flores, Moacyr, 426
Flores Galindo, Alberto, 3196, 3515

Flores Marín, José A., 3516
Flores Pirán, Eduardo Ventura, 3850
Florescano, Enrique, 2436, 2455, 2492. 2558
Flórez, Luis, 6004, 6040
Flórez Estrada, Alvaro, 2354
Flórez-Tascón, Francisco José, 2284
Florián, Mario, 6448, 7070
Florit, Eugenio, 7262
Flory, Thomas, 4102
Foguet, Hugo, 6907
Fonseca, Fernando L., 427-428
Fonseca, José Paulo Moreira da, 464, 7523
Fonseca, Nair de Teffé Hermas, 4103
Fonseca, Virginia S. de., 2875, 6660-6661a
Fonseca, Yone Giannetti, 7524
Fontanella de Weinberg, María Beatriz, 6041
Foppa, Alaíde, 322
For the fighting front, 7817
Forgues, Roland, 6833
Fornet, Ambrosio, 2964
Forster, Merlin H., 7190
Foster, David William, 6972, 7007, 7337
Foster, Virginia Ramos, 7338
Fouchet, Max-Pol, 338
Foxley, Alejandro, 2163
Fraga, Clementino, 4104
Fraire, Isable, 7862
França, Dirceu Pinho, 448
França, Eurico Nogueira, 9046
França Júnior, Joaquim José da, 7620
França Júnior, Oswaldo, 7413-7415
France. Bibliothèque Nationale, 1978
Francis, Michael J., 3633
Francis C., Esther, 9617
Franco, Jean, 7191
Franco, Sérgio da Costa, 7470
Franco, Víctor I., 3901
Franco Carvalhal, Tania. *See* Carvalhal, Tania Franco.
Francovich, Guillermo, 3588
Frank, André Gunder, 2164
Frank, Darl Anton, 1979
Franqui, Carlos, 3010
Franzini, Haydée, 6908
Fraser, Howard M., 6877
Freile Granizo, Juan, 3318
Freire, [Luís José] Junqueira, 7525
Freitas, Décio, 3978
Freto, Diderto, 7526
Freyre, Gilberto, 7681
Freyre, Ricardo Jaimes. *See* Jaimes

Freyre, Ricardo.
Freyre J., Iris, 3517
Frías, Gustavo A., 6867
Frías, Isaac León, 1038
Frías y Soto, Hilarión, 323
Friedl Zapata, José, 3589
Frison, Bruno, 264
Frondizi, Risieri, 9676a
Frost, Elsa Cecilia, 2456
Frostin, Charles, 2981
Frota, Francisco Marialva Mont'Alverne, 7742
Frota, José Tupinambá da, 3979
Frota, Lélia Coelho, 506
Fuenmayor, Juan Bautista, 3449
Fuente Benavides, Rafael de la. *See* Martín Adan [*pseud. for* Rafael de la Fuente Benavides].
Fuentes, Carlos, 6572-6573, 6602, 7894-7895
Fuentes, José Luis Mora, 7436
Fuentes-Figueroa Rodríguez, Julián, 3368
Fuentes Mares, José, 2611
Fuentes Rueda, Helard L., 3206
Fuentes y Guzmán, Francisco Antonio de, 6418
Fuenzalida Vollmar, Fernando, 2052
Fulvi, Fulvio, 2165
Fundação Bienal de São Paulo, 465
Furlán, Augusto, 9649
Furlong, Guillermo, 3753
Furtado, Celso, 2166
Fuss, Albert, 6973

Gabaglia, Marisa Raja, 7471
Gacharná G., Gladys M., 68
Gadea, Juan Alberto, 3414
Gärtner, Eberhard, 6095a
Gagini, Carlos, 6042
Gaínza, Gastón, 6017
Gaioso, Raimundo José de Sousa, 3980
Gaitán, Gloria, 3427
Gaitán Durán, Jorge, 7071
Galante de Sousa, J. *See* Sousa, J. Galante.
Galarza Zavala, Jaime, 3467
Galasso, Norberto, 3754
Galaz C., Gaspar, 363
Galdós Rodríguez, Guillermo, 2053
Galeana, Benita, 6574
Galeano, Eduardo, 6950
Galeazzi, Pio Vitírio, 4105
Galeffi, Romano, 9719
Galeno, Cândida, 7472

Galiana, G.R., 6494
Galich, Manuel, 7263-7265
Galindo, Alejandro, 1020
Galindo, Sergio, 6575, 7896
Gallardo, Guillermo, 3755
Gallardo, Helio, 9460
Gallardo, Sara, 6909
Gallegos Ortiz, Rafael, 3450
Gallegos Rocafull, José M., 9461
Gallo, Ezequiel, 3756
Gallo, Marta, 6806
Galloway, J. H., 4029
Galmarini, Hugo Raúl, 3757
Galvão, Maria Rita Eliezer, 989
Galvão, Walnice Nogueira, 4106, 7714
Gálvez, Manuel, 3758
Galvis Galvis, Alejandro, 3428
Gambaro, Griselda, 6910
Gamilscheg, Felix, 2612
Gammalsson, Hialmar Edmundo, 3274
Gandía, Enrique de, 2285-2286, 3403
Gandulfo Arce de Ballor, Josefina, 3759
Garay, Blas, 3275
Garcés Contreras, Guillermo, 1980
Garcés Larrea, Cristóbal, 7024
Garcia, Albert, 2054
García, Flavio A., 3415, 3936
García, Genaro, 2613
García, Guadalupe, 9415
García, León Roberto, 6576
Garcia, Maria de, 7621
García Alcaraz, Agustín, 1981
García Bacca, Juan David, 9578
García Barron, Carlos, 6834
García Belsunce, César A., 3760
García Bernal, Manuela Cristina, 2493
García Caffarena, Judith G., 9725
García Carranza, Araceli, 97-98
García Chuecos, Héctor, 3075
García del Pino, César, 2965
García Espinosa, Julio, 1014
García-Gallo, Alfonso, 2287
García González, José, 6042a
García-Herreros, Guillermo Ramón, 3160
García Laguardia, Jorge Mario, 2824, 2876
García-Márquez, Gabriel, 6689, 6807, 7897-7898, 7919
García Máynez, Eduardo, 9544
García Méndez, Emilio A., 3816
García Molina, Fernando, 3808
García Monge, Joaquín, 6634b
García Moreno, Gabriel, 3468
García Muñoz, Carmen, 9036

García Murillo, Guillermo, 6662
García Ponce, Juan, 324, 6577-6578, 6603-6604
García Riera, Emilio, 1021-1022, 1028
García Saiz, Concepción, 2457
García Saiz, María del Carmen, 282
García Saldaña, Parménides, 7072
García Santana, Alicia, 336
García-Sayań, Diego, 3518
Garciagómez, Juan José, 6419
Garçon, Jean Dieudonné, 7788
Gardner, Donald trans., 7886
Gargurevich, Juan, 3519
Garmendia, Arturo, 1028
Garretón, Juan Antonio, 3761
Garrido Aranda, Antonio, 2458
Garzón Céspedes, Francisco, 6712, 7339
Gasman, Lydinéa, 3981
Gaspar Stork, Juan, 2877
Gaxiola, Francisco Javier, 2614
Geandré, 516
Géigel Polanco, Vicente, 2936
Geijerstam, Claes af, 9109-9110
Geithman, David T., 2167
Gelman, Juan, 7073
Gemelli Careri, Giovanni Francesco, 2459
Genevois, Danièle, 9503
Genovesi, Antonio, 9416
Genta, Jordán B., 9504
Gentile Lafaille, Margarita E., 2055, 3207
Geoffroy Rivas, Pedro, 6043
Gerber, Raquel, 990
Gerhard, Peter, 2494
Gerome, Frank, 2878
Gerson, Noel Bertram, 2879
Getino, Octavio, 1039
Gèze, François, 3762
Ghioldi, Rodolfo, 3763
Giacomel, Fortunato, 4107
Gianello, Leoncio, 3764
Gianetti Fonseca, Yone. See Fonseca, Yone Gianetti.
Gibson, Charles, 2168
Giglio, Maria José, 7527
Gil, Isabel, 2492, 2558
Gil-Bermejo García, Juana, 2288
Gilard, Jacques, 6808-6811
Gilderhus, Mark T., 2390, 2715
Giles, Thomas Ransom, 9618
Gilonne, Michel, 1982
Giménes Vega, Elías S., 3765
Giménez, Iris, 6420
Giménez Apaiola, Marcos, 3766

Giménez de Arcondo, Floraligia, 3110
Gindine, Ivette, 7795
Gingerich, Willard P., 6449
Giordani, Mário Curtis, 9619
Giordano, Jaime A., 6495
Giovanette Viola, Hugo, 7074
Giovanni, Norman Thomas di. *See* Di Giovanni, Norman Thomas.
Girão, Raimundo, 7682
Giron, Loraine Slomp, 4108
Giron, Nicole, 2615
Girri, Alberto, 7075
Gisbert, Teresa, 258-259, 299-300
Giudici, Alberto, 969
Glinkin, Anatoli, 2169
Gliozzi, Guiliano, 2289
Gnerre, Maurizio, 6044
Gobello, José, 6045
Godoy, Emma, 7076
Godoy Quesada, Mario, 1005
Góes Monteiro, Norma de. *See* Monteiro, Norma de Góes.
Goić, Cedomil, 6878-6879
Goldberg, Marta B., 3767
Goldenberg, Isaac, 7899
Goldenberg, Jorge, 7266
Goldfeder, Miriam, 9047
Gollob, Hedwig, 1983
Golte, Jürgen, 2056-2057
Gomes, Celuta Moreira, 7715
Gomes, Duílio, 7437-7438
Gomes, Eugênio, 7716
Gomes, H.E., 51
Gomes, Manoel, 3982
Gomes, Paulo Emílio Salles, 991
Gomes, Roberto, 7622, 9462
Gomes de Araújo, Antonio. *See* Araújo, Antonio Gomes de.
Gomes de Matos, Francisco. *See* Matos, Francisco Gomes de.
Gómez, Eugenio, 3590
Gómez, Luis O., 9417
Gómez, Orlando Danián, 9650
Gómez, Thomas, 2027
Gómez, Tomás, 2058
Gómez Acevedo, Labor, 3049
Gómez C., Jaime, 9545
Gómez Canedo, Lino. *See* Canedo, Lino Gómez.
Gómez Dávila, Nicolás, 6812
Gómez Ferreyra, Avelino Ignacio, 3768
Gómez-Lobo, Alfonso, 9546
Gómez Parente, Odilo, 3111-3112
Gómez Picón, Alirio, 3429
Gómez Rifas, José, 385
Gómez Rodríguez, Juan de la Cruz, 3520
Gómez U., Carmen Lila, 2880
Gonçalves, Alice Ramos, 7654
Gonçalves, Augusto de Freitas Lopes, 7655
Gonçalves, Danúbio, 466
Góngora, Mario, 2291
Gonidec, Bernard le. *See* Le Gonidec, Bernard.
Gonsalves de Mello, José Antonio. *See* Mello, José Antonio Gonsalves de.
Gonzales, Michael, 6605
Gonzales, Olga, 394
González, Alfonso, 99
González, Antonio E., 3902
González, Eduardo, 6713
González, Esther B., 24
González, Hilario, 9096
González, Juan Natalicio, 3276
González, Juan R., 339
González, Luis, 2616, 2716
González, Luisa, 6662a
González, Manuel Pedro, 7192
González, Margarita, 3135a
González, Oscar, 7077
González, Otto-Raúl, 6663, 7078
González Arzac, Alberto Ricardo, 3769
González Asenjo, Florencio, 9651
González Bolaños, Aimée, 6714
González Climent, Anselmo, 3769a
González de Cascorro, Raúl, 7267
González del Valle, Antolín, 7340
González del Valle, Luis, 7340
González Echenique, Javier, 3319
González Echevarría, Roberto, 6715-6716, 6974
González Freire, Natividad, 7268, 7341
González González, Alfonso, 2292
González-Goyri, Roberto, 331
González Jiménez, José Miguel, 340
González Luna, María Dolores, 3136
González Navarro, Moisés, 2617
González Oddone, Beatriz Rodríguez Alcalá de. *See* Rodríguez Alcalá de González Oddone, Beatriz.
González Paredes, Ramón, 6790
González-Polo, Ignacio, 2495
González Ponce, Enrique B., 2430
González Prada, Manuel, 7079
González Roa, Fernando, 2717
González Rodríguez, Luis, 2559
González Rojo, Enrique, 7080
González Salas, Carlos, 9730
González Torres, Yolotl, 1984
González Tuñón, Raúl, 6975

González Videla, Gabriel, 3634
González Vigil, Francisco de Paula, 3521-3522
Goodman, Frances Schaill, 308
Goodrich, Diana S. *trans.*, 7901
Goodwin, Paul B., Jr., 3770
Gorostiza, Carlos, 6911, 7269-7271
Gortari, Eli de, 9652
Gosálvez, Raúl Botelho. *See* Botelho Gosálvez, Raúl.
Goslinga, Cornelius Christiaan, 272
Goss, Robert C., 252-253, 280
Gossy, Hélène, 6976
Gouraige, Ghislain, 7796
Gouvêa, Fernando da Cruz, 3983
Gouveia, Jaime Prado, 7439
Goyeneche, Juan Carlos, 9505
Goytía, Víctor Florencio, 2170, 2881-2882
Goytisolo, Juan, 6717-6718
Grabados de Carmelo González, 395
Graça Aranha, José Pereira da. *See* Aranha, José Pereira da Graça.
Gracia, Jorge J.E., 9667
Graciano, Clóvis, 467
Graff, Gary W., 3137
Graham, Benjamin *trans.*, 7884
Graham, Richard, 4109
Grajales, Gloria, 2618
Gramajo Gutiérrez, Alfredo, 396
Grand Ruiz, Beatriz Hilda, 9463
Granda, Germán de, 6046-6047, 6073
Granda Alva, Germán, 3513
Grande, Eugenia de. *See* De Grande, Eugenia.
Grande São Paulo/76: exposição, 532
Los grandes negociados, 3771
Granell, Manuel, 9677
Granier Chirveches, Juan, 364
Grant, Cedric Hilburn, 2883
Grases, Pedro, 3320, 3451
Grassmann, Marcelo, 468
Gravil, Roger, 3772
Grebe, María Ester, 9084
Green, Michael Robert, 2619
Green, William A., 2937
Gregorio, Jesús, 7272
Greiff, León de, 7081-7082
Grela, Plácido, 3773-3774
Greñas Morales, Rosa, 2884
Grenón, Pedro, 3404
Grieb, Kenneth J., 2391, 2885, 2718
Grigulevich, Iosif, 2171
Grimani, Santiago, 6912
Grinbaum, Emílio, 7473
Grindle, Merilee S., 2719-2721
Grinevich, Emiliia Andreevna, 3011
Grisanti, Angel, 3371
Grisolli, Paulo Affonso, 7623
Grohs, Waltraud, 2059, 3170
Grossman, Lois, 7342
Grossman, William L., 7943
Grupo Aleph, 7273
Grupo de teatro Aty-ñe'e, 7343
Grupo de Trabajo de Desarrollo Cultural, 6074
Grupo La Candelaria, 7274-7275
Guandique, José Salvador, 9464
Guanes, Alejo H., 3903
Guarda Geywitz, Gabriel, 3321
Guardia, Roberto de la, 2825
Guardia de Alfaro, Gloria, 6664
Guariglia, Osvaldo N., 9547
Guarnieri, Gianfrancesco, 7624
Gudiño Kieffer, Eduardo, 6913-6914
Gudmundson K., Lowell, 3591
El güegüense o macho ratón: comedia-bailete anónima de la época colonial, 6441
Güiraldes, Ricardo, 6496
Guérin, Mona, 7780
Guerra, Flávio, 4110
Guerra, José Augusto, 47
Guerra B., Samuel M., 3171
Guerra M., Margarita, 3523
Guerrero, Arturo, 9579
Guerrero, César H., 3775
Guerrero Yoacham, Cristián, 2722
Guevara, Darío, 7193
Guevara, Pablo, 7083
Guido, Beatriz, 6915
Guido, Horacio J.M., 3776
Guilhermina, Maria, 469
Guillén, Nicolás, 7084-7085, 7232, 7863-7864
Guillén, Pedro, 325
Guillén Guillén, Edmundo, 2060
Guimaraens, João Alphonsus de, 7440
Guimarães, Júlio Castañon, 7528
Guimarães Hill, Amariles. *See* Hill, Amariles Guimarães.
Guimarães Rosa, João. *See* Rosa, João Guimarães.
Guinzburg, Juana, 9025
Guízar Oceguera, José, 2723
Gullar, Ferreira [*pseud.* *for* José Ribamar Ferreira], 7529
Gurría Lacroix, Jorge, 2460
Gushina, N., 6075
Gusmão de Andrade, Luís Gonzaga. *See*

Aiala, Luís [pseud. for Luís Gonzaga Gusmão de Andrade].
Guterres, Sérgio dos Santos, 7441
Gutiérrez, Ernesto, 7086
Gutiérrez, Guillermo, 3777
Gutiérrez, Joaquín, 6635
Gutiérrez, Laura, 3524
Gutiérrez, Pedro Rafael, 6636
Gutiérrez, Ramón, 3295
Gutiérrez Girardot, Rafael, 6813
Gutiérrez Heras, Joaquín, 9111
Gutiérrez Mesa, Virgen, 3014
Gutiérrez Muñoz, César, 31
Gutiérrez Nájera, Manuel, 6497
Gutiérrez Vega, Hugo, 7087
Gutiérrez Z., Ramón, 377
Guy, Donna J., 3778-3779
Guyana handbook: 1976, industry, tourism, commerce, 123
Guzmán, Gaspar H., 3697
Guzmán, Humberto, 6579
Guzmán, Patricio, 1006
Guzmán Valdivia, Isaac, 9418
Gyurko, Lanin A., 6606-6607, 6977, 7344

Haas, Margaret Bissler, 2538
Haber, Abraham, 349
Hadel, Richard, 9072
Hahn, Oscar, 7025, 7088
Hahner, June E., 2172, 4111
Halasz, Piri, 312
Hale, Charles A., 9506
Halil, Kiamran, 6076
Hall, Carolyn, 2886
Hall, Linda B., 2724
Hall, Michael M., 4112
Hall, N.A.T., 2982
Halmar, Augusto d'. See D'Halmar, Augusto.
Halperin-Donghi, Tulio, 3277, 3780
Hamerly, Michael T., 3172, 3469
Hamilton, Roland C., 2061
Hammarström, Göran, 6018
Hammond, George Peter, 2560
Hamnett, Brian R., 2496, 3362
Hancock, Joel, 6835
Hanisch Espíndola, Walter, 3250-3251, 3393
Hanke, Lewis, 2293, 2461, 3208
Hanrahan, Gene S., 2725
Hanson, Carl A., 2173
Harding, Colin, 2156
Harding, Timothy F., 2174
Hardoy, Jorge F., 2175
Hardy, R.W.H., 2620

Harnecker, Marta, 9692-9693
Harris, Charles H., 2431
Harris, Rodney E., 7797
Harrison, John P., 2240
Hart, John M., 2621
Harth-Terré, Emilio, 3209
Hartig, Pauline, 1985
Hartmann, Robert S., 9668
Haseloff, Bernd Kurt, 6114
Hauben, Paul J., 2294
Have, Hilton, 7625
Hayes, Robert A., 3986
Hays, H.R. trans., 7859
Hazard, Samuel, 3050
Hearne, John, 7825
Hein, Ronaldo [Alberto], 7530
Heise González, Julio, 3394, 3635
Helena, Lúcia, 7743
Helguera, J. León, 3430
Hellman, Ronald G., 2176
Henkin, William A., 7848
Hennebelle, Guy, 960
Henríquez Ureña, Pedro. See Ureña, Pedro Henríquez.
Heraud, Javier, 7089-7090
Heredia, Edmundo A., 2355-2356, 3405
Heredia, Nicolás, 6498
Heredia Herrera, Antonio 2462
Herme, Juan Carlos, 7297
Hernández, Ana María, 6978
Hernández, Angel Santos, 3278
Hernández, Eduardo, 2138
Hernández, José, 7865
Hernández, Luisa Josefina, 7276
Hernández de Alba, Guillermo, 48, 3138
Hernández de Mendoza, Cecilia, 7194
Hernández García, Julio, 2357
Hernández Gómez, Jorge, 7091
Hernández López, Rházes, 9097, 9141
Hernández Novás, Raúl, 7195
Herra, Rafael A., 9437
Herrera, Luis Alberto, 3938
Herrera R., Daniel, 9465
Herrera y Ressig, Julio, 7092
Herrero, Carmen, 2362
Herrick, Paul B., Jr., 3525
Hers, Marie-Areti, 2497
Hersch, Robert, 2358
Hertelendy, Susan trans., 7939
Herzfild, Anita, 7277
Heuer, Federico, 1023
Heysen, Luis E., 3526
Hicks, Frederick, 1986
Hidalgo L., Jorge, 2025
Hidalgo R., Arturo, 6499

Hierro Gambardella, Luis, 6951
Higman, B.W., 2983
Hileman, Sam *trans*., 7894
Hill, Amariles Guimarães, 7717
Hill, Frank, 3051
Hilton, Stanley E., 4113
Himelblau, Jack, 9466
Hinds, Harold E., Jr., 7345
Hiram, Allan K., 2887
Hirst, Lloyd, 3939
Historia, 3076
História de la evolución de Campana: centenario de la ciudad municipalidad de Campana, 1875-1895, 3781
Historia Mexicana, 2726
Histórica, 3077, 3527
Hoberman, Louisa Schell, 2498-2499
Hodges, Donald C., 3782
Hoeksema, Thomas *trans*., 7862
Hoernel, Robert B., 3032
Hoetink, Harmannus, 2997
Hoffman, Abraham, 2727-2728
Hoffman, Léon-François, 7798
Holanda [Cavalcanti de Albuquerque], Celina de, 7531
Holanda Ferreira, Aurelio Buarque de. *See* Ferreira, Aurelio Buarque de Holanda.
Holguín Callo, Oswaldo, 3210
Hollanda, Chico Buarque de, 7626
Hollander, Nancy Caro, 3783
Holloway, Thomas H., 4114
Holzapfel, Tamara, 7346
Homem [de Siqueira Cavalcanti], Homero, 7532
Honour, Hugh, 2177
Hood, Miriam, 3452
Hoornaert, Eduardo, 4030
Hoover, John P., 3322
Horcasitas, Fernando, 7347
Horowitz, Irving Louis, 3636
Hostos, Adolfo de, 2938
Houaiss, António, 7744
Houwald, Goetz von, 2888
Hower, Alfred *trans*., 7942
Howes, Barbara, 7842
Hoyos Andrade, Rafael M., 6005
Huamanga: una larga historia, 3078
Hüper Argüello, William, 2826
Huerta, David, 6500, 7093
Huerta, Efraín, 7094
Huerta, María Teresa, 2463
Huertas Vallego, Lorenzo, 2062
Huidobro, Vicente, 7095
Huitrón, Jacinto, 2729

Hulsz Piccone, Leticia, 6885
Hum, D., 3052
El humanismo de Alberto Hurtado, 9507
El humanismo de Manuel Larraín, 9508
El humanismo social de Francisco Vives, 9509
Humbert, Marc, 124
Humphreys, R.A., 125, 2178, 3984
Hurtado, Gerardo César, 6637
Hurtado, Osvaldo, 3079
Hurtado López, Flor de María, 2500
Hussey, Roland Dennis, 2295
Hutter, Lucy Maffei, 4143

Ianelli, Thomaz, 470
Ibañez Langlois, José Miguel, 7171
Ibarê Dantas, José. *See* Dantas, José Ibarê.
Ibarguren, Carlos, 9510
Ibarra, Vicente, 6791
Ibero-Amerikanisches Archiv, 2296
Ibero-Amerikanisches Institut, *Berlin, FRG*, 69
Icaza, Jorge, 6501
Iglesias, Francisco, 2179
Iglesias Mata, Dumar, 6768
Ilg, Karl, 2180
Illanes Maestre, José Luis, 9620
In memoriam: Josefina Pelizzari de Grazioli: 1887-1977, 9085
La independencia nacional: conferencias dictadas por encargo de la Comisión Nacional del Sesquicentenario de la Independencia del Perú; tercer ciclo, 3372
Infante, Leonardo, 3344
Infante Barros, Marta, 3637
Ingianna M., Yolanda, 9580
Ingram, Kenneth E., 2939
Inojosa, Joaquim, 7683-7685
Instituto Bibliográfico Antonio Zinny, *Buenos Aires*, 3784
Instituto Cubano del Libro, *La Habana*, 7196
Instituto de Estudios Sociales, *Buenos Aires*, 3785
Instituto Histórico e Geográfico de Alagoas, *Maceió, Brazil*. Museu, 514
Instituto Italo-Latinoamericano: Roma, 1966-1976, 100
Inter-American Development Bank (IDB), *Washington*. Office of the Controller. Management Services Office. Reports Management Section, 101

International Bank for Reconstruction and Development (IBRD), *Washington*. Joint Bank-Fund Library, 70
International Congress of Mexican History, *IV, Santa Monica, Calif., 1973*, 2730
International Monetary Fund (IMF), *Washington*. Joint Bank-Fund Library, 70
Introducción histórico-social a la obra de Icaza, 33
Irala Burgos, Adriano, 7009
Irazusta, Julio, 3786-3788, 7197, 9511
Irwin, Graham W., 2181, 2984
Ishimatsu, Lorie *trans*., 7944
Isla, Carlos, 7096
Isola, Ema, 3279
ISSO, 517
Issorel, Jacques, 6502
Iturralde Colombres, Carlos A., 9581
Ivelic, Milan, 363
Ivo, Lêdo, 7533, 7745
Ixtlilxóchitl, Fernando de Alva, 1987
Izaguirre, Rodolfo, 1044, 1046
Izard, Miguel, 3453
Izquierdo Fernández, Gonzalo, 3638

Jacintha, Maria [*pseud. for* Maria Jacintha Trovão da Costa Campos], 7627
Jacob, Raúl, 3940
Jacobs, W. Richard, 3021
Jaén, Didier Tisdel, 7836
Jaime Laredo, 9037
Jaimes Freyre, Ricardo, 6750
Jalfen, Luis Forge, 9419
Jambeiro, Othon, 9048
James, Daniel, 3789
Jansen, André, 2297, 2464
Japiassu, Hilton Ferreira, 9653, 9678
Jara Hantke, Alvaro, 283
Jaramillo, Carlos Eduardo, 7097-7098
Jaramillo Levi, Enrique, 2889
Jarauta Marión, Francisco, 9582-9583
Jassén, Raúl, 3790
Jaulin, Robert, 2182
Jauretche, Arturo, 3791
Jelin, Elizabeth, 3792-3793
Jijón y Caamaño, Jacinto, 2063
Jiménez S., Tomás E., 1988
Jitrik, Noé, 6719, 6979-6980
Joffily, Geraldo Ireneo, 4115
Jofre Barroso, Haydée M., 6916
Johnson, Ann Hagerman, 3612
Johnson, David D., 6665

Johnson, Harvey L., 6503
Johnson, Lyman L., 3280
Johnson, Phil Brian, 4116-4117
Johnston, Kathryn Therese, 118
Jóia Pereira, Uilcon. *See* Pereira, Uilcon Jóia.
Jonas, Susanne, 2890
Jones, Errol D., 2731
Jones, Willis Knapp, 7853
Jongh Osborne, Lilly de, 125
Jordán, Joaquín, 6917
Jordão, Yolanda, 7534-7535
Jorge de la Vega: 1930-1971, 350
Jornadas Americanistas, *III, Valladolid, Spain, 1974*, 2298
José Aleixo, *brother*, 4118
Joseph, Benjamin, 7789
Joseph, Gilbert M., 2732
Jota, Zélio dos Santos, 6115
The Journal of the Barbados Museum and Historical Society, 2966
Jouve, Marta Luisa, 3794
Jozef, Bella, 6504
Juárez, Salvador Antonio, 7099
Juárez A., Bárbara, 71
Judde, Gabriel, 3470
Junco, Alfonso, 7100
Junqueira Freire, Luís José. *See* Freire [Luís José] Junqueira.
Junyent, Albert, 397
Jurafsky, Abraham, 9026

Kadir, Djelal, 6720
Kahle, Günther, 3904
Kahler, Mary Ellis, 49
Kantor, Harry, 2891
Kapsoli E., Wilfredo, 3211, 3528
Karasch, Mary C., 2138, 3985
Karlic, Estanislao, 9679
Karnes, Thomas L., 2892
Karst, Kenneth L., 2183
Kasevich, Hugo, 3817
Katinsky, Julio Roberto, 495
Katz, Bernard S., 2733
Katz, Chaim Samuel, 9438
Katz, Friedrich, 1989, 2734
Kay, Cristóbal, 2184, 3639-3640Keel, Erich, 975
Keens-Douglas, Paul, 7818
Keith, Henry H., 3986
Keith, Robert G., 2185, 3212
Kellenbenz, Hermann, 2186-2187
Kelsey, Vera, 126
Kemp, Lysander *trans*., 7926
Kerig, Dorothy Pierson, 2735

Kerrigan, Anthony *trans.*, 7874, 7916
Kerson, Arnold L., 6421
Kessell, John L., 2432
Kiefer, Bruno, 9049
Killea, Lucy, 2561
King, Arden R., 2798
King, Lloyd, 6721
Kirk, John M., 2940, 3033
Klaiber, Jeffrey L., 3529
Klaren, Peter F., 3530-3531
Klein, Herbert S., 2998
Kleinmann, Hans-Otto, 2359
Klíma, Jan, 3795-3796
Klimovsky, Gregorio, 9654
Klintowitz, Jacob, 518
Kloe, Donald R., 6077
Knaster, Meri, 2392
Kneese de Mello, Eduardo. *See* Mello, Eduardo Kneese de.
Knight, Franklin W., 2941, 2967
Knight, Vere, 7799
Knoff, Udo, 429
Knowlton, Robert J., 2622
Köpke, Carlos Burlamáqui, 6096
Kogan, Jacobo, 9731
Komissarov, Boris N., 3987-3988
Konder Reis, Marcos. *See* Reis, Marcos Konder.
Kooreman, Thomas E., 6814
Kordon, Bernardo, 6918-6919
Kossok, Manfred, 2360, 3323
Korolev, Nicolai, 2188
Kourim, Zdeněk, 9467
Kovanda, Jan, 2189
Kraemer, Paul M., .562
Kraly, Néstor, 7278
Krause, Corinne Azen, 2623
Krause, Gustavo, 7536
Krauze, Enrique, 2736
Krebs Wilckens, Ricardo, 3641
Kronik, John, 7348
Kryzanek, Michael J., 3053
Kubánská revoluce: bibliografická, a biografická pomucka, 3012
Kubitschek, Juscelino, 4119
Kunzmann, Ulrich, 6666
Kuss, Malena, 9005-9006, 9027, 9050, 9073
Kuteishchikova, Vera Nikolaevna, 6505, 6722
Kvavik, Karen H., 6019

Labandeira Fernández, Amancio, 6422
Labarca P., Domingo A., 9715
Labrousse, Alain, 3762

Laclau, Ernesto, 2164
Lacombe, Lourenço Luiz, 4120
Lacombe, Robert, 127
Lacroix, Federico, 3797
Ladd, Doris M, 2465
Ladusāns, Stanislav, 9468
Lafaye, Jacques, 2466-2467
Lafebvre, Gilles-R., 6129
Lafrance, David, 2731
Lagmanovich, David, 6981-6982
Laguarda Trias, Rolando A. *See* Trias, Rolando A. Laguarda.
Laguna-Díaz, Elpidio, 7198
Laguna Novas, Jorge, 6638
Lahud, Michel, 9655
Laiter, Salomón, 6580
Laje, Enrique, 9548
Lamas, José Ángel, 9142
Lamb, Ursula, 2968
Lambert, Charles James, 3642
Lambert, Eric T.D., 3352
Lameda, Alí, 7101
Lamego, Alberto, 430
Lamounier, Bolivar, 4121
Lancelotti, Mario A., 6506, 6920
Landazuri Camacho, Carlos, 3173
Landeraf Piccolo, Helga Iracema. *See* Piccolo, Helga Iracema Landeraf.
Lane, Helen R. *trans.*, 7924-7925
Lange, Francisco Curt, 9007, 9051
Langley, Lester D., 2190, 2361, 3034
Lanuza, Alberto, 2894
Lanz, Rigoberto, 9694
La Orden Miracle, Ernesto, *padre*, 265, 332
Lapa, José Roberto do Amaral, 3989-3990
Lara, Cecília de, 7686-7687
Lara, Jesús, 2064
Lara, Omar, 7102
Larco, Juan, 6836
Lares, Oldo, 9143
Laroche, Maximilien, 7800-7801
Laroche, W.E., 386
Larraín Barros, Horacio, 2065-2066, 3174
Larraín Errázuriz, Manuel, 3643
Larrazabal Henríquez, Osvaldo, 6852
Larrea, Carlos Manuel, 3175, 3471
Larrea Alba, Luis, 3369
Láscaris, Constantino, 2799, 9549
Láscaris-Comneno, Teodoro, 9420
Lastra, Héctor, 6921
Lastra, Pedro, 6880, 7103
Lateinamerika: Die Entwicklung der Unterentwicklung, 2191

Latin American area specialist at Texas colleges and universities, 102
Latin American Index, 103
Latin American Perspectives, 3532
Latin American studies in Great Britain: an autobiographical fragment, 127
Latin American Theatre Review, 7349
Latin American Yearly Review, 128
Lauer, Mirko, 380
Laurencio, Angel Aparicio, 7233
Laurent, Gérard M., 2942
Lauten, Flora, 7279
Lavenère-Wanderley, Nelson Freire, 4122
Lavín Cerda, Hernán, 7104
Lavradio, Luis de Almeida Soares Portugal Alarcão Eça de Melo, marquês de, 4031
Lavrov, Nikolái, 2192
Lawaetz, Gudie, 7843
Lawrence, Leota S., 7826
Lazo Carcía, 3213
Leal, Hamilton, 4123
Leal, Juan Felipe, 2737-2739
Leal, Luis, 6507, 6608-6609
Leal, Rine, 7280, 7350
Leal, Wills, 992
Leal A., Fernando, 9584
Leante, César, 6723-6724
LeBland, Lawrence J., 2193
Lechín Suárez, Juan, 3324
Le Clézio, J.M.G., 1990
LeFeber, Walter, 2893
Legaz Lacambra, Luis, 9680
Le Gonidec, Bernard, 9503
Lehnertz, Jay, 3214
Leitman, Spencer L., 4124
Leiva, Miguel da Costa. See Da Costa Leiva, Miguel.
Leiva, Raúl, 6667, 7199
Lemaitre, Eduardo, 273
Lemaître, Monique J., 7200
Lemmon, Alfred E., 9008, 9112-9114
Lemos, Carlos Alberto Cerqueim, 496
Lemus, Juan de Luigi, 34
León Borja, Dora, 3176, 3186-3187
León de Palacios, Ana María, 2740
León-Portilla, Miguel, 2433, 2468
León Tello, Pilar, 2362
Leonard, Glen M., 2624
Leonardos, Othon Henry, 3991
Lepecki, Maria Lúcia, 7718
Le Riverend, Julio, 2943
Lerner, Isaías, 6423
Lerner, Nathan, 2393
Lerner, Victoria, 2741
Lértora, Adolfo C., 9681
Lértora Mendoza, Celina A., 9550
Leselbaum, Charles, 6006
Lessa Litrento, Oliveiros. See Litrento, Oliveiros
Letelier Llona, Alfonso, 9086
Levine, Robert M., 2742
Levine, Suzanne Jill, 6725, 7920, 7886, 7904-7906, 7917
Levitt, James H., 2835
Lewald, H. Ernest, 6983
Lewis, Leslie, 2501
Lewis, Oscar, 3013
Lewkowic, Lidia F., 7201
Leyva, Daniel, 7105
Lezama Lima, José, 6690, 7900
Lherisson, Justin, 7777
Li Carrillo, Víctor, 9726
El libro azul, 3054
Libro segundo de Cabildos de Cuenca: 1563-1569-3177
Lichtveld, Lou, 6130
Lida de Malkiel, María Rosa, 6450
Liebman, Seymour B., 2194
Liendo, Eduardo, 6792
Liendo, Miguel Ángel, 9144
Lihn, Enrique, 6868, 7106-7107, 7866
Lijeron Alberdi, Hugo, 6751
Lima, Alceu Amoroso, 7773
Lima, Alexandre José Barbosa, 4125
Lima, Edy, 7628
Lima, Héctor de, 6793
Lima, Heitor Ferreira, 3992
Lima, Hermes, 7774
Lima, Jorge de, 7537-7538
Lima, Luiz Costa, 7719
Lima, Manuel de Oliveira. See Oliveira Lima, Manuel de.
Lima, Regina Helena Cunha, 7539
Lima Bastos, Wilson de. See Bastos, Wilson de Lima.
Lima Carlos, Helio. See Carlos, Helio Lima.
Lima Vaz, Henrique C. de. See Vaz, Henrique C. de Lima.
Lindenboim, Javier, 3798
Lindstrom, Naomi Era, 7351
Lines, Jorge A., 266
Linhares, Temístocles, 7746
Lins, Maria Inês de Bessa, 104
Lins, Osman, 7416, 7629, 7688, 7720
Lins Falcão, Celso Almir Japiassu. See Celso Japiassu [pseud. for Celso Almir Japaissu Lins Falcão].

Lipp, Solomon, 9469
Lira Montt, Luis, 3252
Lironi, Julio Víctor, 3799
Lisboa, Henriqueta, 7540-7541
Lisboa, João Francisco, 4032
Lispector, Clarice, 7417
Liss, Peggy K., 2363
List Arzubide, Germán, 6508
Litrento, Oliveiros [Lessa], 7542, 7689
Livingstone, William, 9009
Lizardo, Fradrique, 9067
Lizárraga, Andrés, 7281-7282
Llanos, Bernardino de, 6442
Llebot, Amaya, 6852
Lleras Camargo, Alberto, 3431
Lleras Restrepo, Carlos, 3432
Llosa, Jorge Guillermo, 2195
Lluberes Navarro, Antonio, 2944
Lobato, Manoel, 7418, 7442
Lobdell, R., 3052
Lobo, Luíza, 7443
Lo Celso, Angel T., 351
Locker, Zvi, 2696
Lockhart, James, 1953, 2299, 2451, 2502
Lockhart, Washington, 3281, 3941-3942
Locria, Carlos Ignacio, 3800
Lohmann Villena, Guillermo, 2067, 3215-3216, 6451
Lombardi, Bruna, 7543
Lombardi, John V., 3113
Lomnitz, Larissa, 2743
Londoño, Jaime, 9089
Long, Robert W., 2625
Loor Moreira, Wilfrido, 3370
Lope Blanch, Juan M., 6048-6049
Lopes, Edward, 6097
Lopes, José Antonio Dias, 4126
Lopes, Waldemar, 7544-7546
Lopes Gonçalves, Augusto de Freitas. *See* Gonçalves, Augusto de Freitas Lopes.
López, Adalberto, 3282
López, Basil, 7810
López, José Ramón, 3055
López, Luis Carlos, 7108
López, Oswaldo A., 7352
López Alvarez, Luis, 6668
López Austin, Alfredo, 1991
López Cantos, Angel, 3114
López Martín, Alfonso, 9585
López Miramontes, Alvaro, 2503
López Portillo y Pacheco, José, 7901
López Rosas, José Rafael, 3801
López Sarrelangue, Delfina, 2504
López Soria, José Ignacio, 3217

López-Trejo, Roberto, 2895
López Urrutia, Carlos, 3644
Lorenzi, Mónica de, 2068
Lorenzo Sanz, Eufemio, 2505
Lorenzoni, Júlio, 4127
Losada, Angel, 6424
Losada Guido, Alejandro, 6837-6838
Lotería, 2910, 3325, 6669
Lourdes de Araújo, Maria de. *See* Araújo, Maria de Lourdes de.
Loureiro, María Amélia Salgado, 3993
Loureiro Chaves, Flávo. *See* Chaves, Flávio Loureiro.
Love, Robert William, Jr., 2999
Loveira y Chirino, Carlos, 6691
Loveman, Brian, 3645
Lovera de Sola, R.J., 25, 3080
Lovo Castelar, Luis, 2896
Lowe, Elizabeth, 6425
Lowenfels, Walter, 7837
Lowenthal, Abraham F., 2394
Lozano, Wilfredo, 3056
Luby, Barry *trans.*, 7846
Lucas, Fábio, 7690
Lucena, Clemencia, 370
Lucena, Luis Fernando, 6760
Lucena Salmoral, Manuel, 2069, 3139-3140, 3353
Luchting, Wolfgang Alexander, 6839
Ludmer, Josefina, 7011
Luiz Raimundo [*pseud. for* Luiz Raimundo Batista de Carvalho], 7547
Luján Muñoz, Jorge, 2827
Lumsden-Kouvel, Audrey, 6426
Luna, Andrés, 1024
Luna, Angel María, 6952
Luna, Jesús, 2626
Luque Colombres, Carlos, 3283
Lustosa, Eduardo Magalhães, 4128
Luzián, Juan, 6509
Luzuriaga, Gerardo, 7854
Lyday, Leon F., 7353
Lynch, Marta, 6922
Lyra, Pedro, 9720

McCamant, John F., 2388
McCosker, Sandra, 9074
McCreery, David J., 2898
McCullough, David, 2196, 2899
Macedo, Joaquim Manoel de, 7630
Macedo, Ubiratan de, 9439-9440, 9621
Macera, Pablo, 296, 2070-2071, 3218, 3533-3536
MacGregor, Alexander P., 6426
Machado, Alvaro Manuel, 7721

Machado, Ana Maria, 7722
Machado, Cristina de Miranda Mata, 9052
Machado, Geraldo Pinheiro, 9470
Machado, Manuel A., Jr., 2744
Machado, Nauro, 7548
Machado de Assis, Joaquim Maria, 6731, 7444, 7940-7941, 7944
McHenry, Dean E., Jr., 2745
Maciel, Alba Costa, 60
Maciel, Jarbas, 9551
MacKinnon, Richard M., 2627
McMorris, David S., 118
McMurray, David Arthur *trans*., 7863
McMurray, George R., 6815
McNees Mancini, Pat. *See* Mancini, Pat McNees.
McNeill, Anthony, 7815
MacNutt, Francis Augustus, 2506
Macune, Charles W., Jr., 2628
Mades, Leonard *trans*., 7892
Madrid, Antonieta, 6794
Madrid-Malo, Néstor, 7026, 7202
Madsen, Andreas, 3802
Madureira, Pedro Paulo de Sena, 7549
Maeder, Ernesto J.A., 3284
Maffei Hutter, Lucy. *See* Hutter, Lucy Maffei.
Magalhães, Gisela, 507
Magalhães, Gonçalves de, 7632
Magalhães, José Vieira Conto de, 4128a
Magalhães, Solange, 471
Magalhães Júnior, R., 7747
Magaña-Esquivel, Antonio, 7283-7286, 7354
Magdaleno, Mauricio, 6510
Magloire, Nadine, 7778
Magnarelli, Sharon, 6881
Mahieu, José Agustín, 970
Maia, Jerônimo Vingt-Un Rosado, 4129
Maidique Patricio, Hilda, 3014
Maillat, Philippe, 976
Majewski, Teresita, 1992
Málaga Medina, Alejandro, 2072, 3219-3221
Malard, Leticia, 7723
Malavassi, Guillermo, 2799
Maldonado, José Luis, 297
Maldonado-Denis, Manuel, 3057
Maldonado Pérez, Guillermo, 7287
Maliandi, Ricardo, 9656, 9669
Malitzke-Goes, Ana Rosa de, 9038
Malo González, Hernán, 9586
Malpica Silva Santisteban, Carlos, 3537
Mancini, Pat McNees, 7844

Mandeville, Peter B., 2507
Mandrioni, Héctor Delfor, 9695
Mangabeira Unger, Edyla. *See* Unger, Edyla Mangabeira.
Mangouni, Norman *trans*., 7865
Manigat, Leslie F., 3000
Manini Ríos, Carlos, 6953
Manning, Diana H., 2197
Manns, Patricio, 3646
Mantelli, Giovanna, 3069
Mantilla, Gabriel, 129
Manzano, Juan Francisco, 6692
Manzi, Homero, 972
Maram, Sheldon L., 4130
Maranhão, Heloisa, 7550
Maranhão, José, 7633
Maranhão, Marcos, 4033
Maranhão, Ricardo, 4036
Maranhão Filho, Luiz, 7634
Marc, Jules André, 7802
Marcelo, Carmen, 365
Marchena, Julián, 7109
Marco, Susana, 7355
Marcorelles, Louis, 1025
Marcos, Plínio, 7418a, 7635
Marcus, Joyce, 1993
Marianetti, Benito, 3803
Mariátegui, José Carlos, 9512
Mariátegui Oliva, Ricardo, 298
Mariluz Urquijo, José María, 3285
Marín Cañas, José, 6669a
Marini, Ana María, 3804
Marinuzzi, Raul, 7636
El Mariscal Benavides: su vida y su obra, 3538
Mariz, Vasco, 9053
Marques, Núbia N., 7551
Marqués, René, 6693-6694, 6726
Márques, Sarah, 6727
Marqués Rodiles, Ignacio, 326
Márquez, Robert, 7838, 7863-7864
Marrero, Levi, 2970
Marsans, Luis Felipe, 9097a
Marshall, Bernard A., 3001
Martí, José, 6511-6512
Martin, Eleanor J., 7356
Martin, Gerald *trans*., 7882
Martin, John, 6098
Martín, Jorge Abel, 971
Martín, José Carlos, 3539
Martín, José Luis, 6513
Martín, Luis, 3222
Martín, María Haydée, 3406
Martín Adan [*pseud*. *for* Rafael de la Fuente Benavides], 7110

Martín de Codoni, Elvira Luisa, 3407
Martinet, Jean Baptiste H., 3540-3541
Martínez, David, 7111
Martínez, Fernando, 1043
Martínez, Gregorio, 6781
Martínez, José de Jesús, 7288, 9431
Martínez, José Francisco, 2800
Martínez, Oscar J., 2746
Martínez, Pedro Santos, 3805
Martínez-Alier, Juan, 3542
Martínez B., Juan Ramón, 2897
Martínez de la Vega, Francisco, 2747-2750
Martínez Estrada, Ezequiel, 6923, 7203, 7921
Martínez González, Humberto, 9587
Martínez Laínez, Fernando, 6728
Martínez Marín, Carlos, 1994
Martínez Masdeu, Edgar, 133
Martínez Peláez, Severo, 2828
Martínez Queirolo, José, 6769
Martínez P., Marcos A., 2945
Martínez Ruiz, Bernabé, 3806
Martínez Salas, Rafael, 305
Martínez Torres, Augusto, 961
Martinho, Lenira Menezes, 3994
Martinic Beros, Mateo, 3286, 3647-3648
Martins, Antônio Egídio, 3995
Martins, Dileta Silveira, 6099
Martins, Eduardo, 7691
Martins, Heitor, 7724
Martins, José Salgado, 9471
Martins, Judith, 414
Martins, Max, 7552
Martins, Wilson, 3996, 7692
Martins Couceiro, Solange. *See* Couceiro, Solange Martins.
Martire, Eduardo, 3238-3239
Martius, Karl Friedrich Philipp von, 4052
Martori, Héctor, 6761
Maruxa Vilalta, grande autora teatral, 7357
Marx, Robert F., 2300
Marzal, Manuel M., 2073
La más antigua novela nicaragüense, 6670
Mas Herrera, Oscar E., 9552-9553
Massey, Kenneth W., 6882
Massiani, Francisco, 6795
Masterson, Daniel M., 3543, 4070
Mastrángelo, Carlos, 6924
Mata, Humberto, 6796
Mata Machado, Cristina de Miranda. *See* Machado, Cristina de Miranda

Mata.
Matas, Julio, 7852
Mateo, Martha S., 9588
Mateos, Francisco, 3141
Mathes, W. Michael, 2301
Mathew, W.M., 3544
Mathieu, Corina S., 7012
Matijevic, Nicolás, 72, 3807
Matos, Francisco Gomes de, 6100
Matos, Odilon Nogueira de, 3997
Matos Mar, José, 3545-3546
Matta Rodríguez-Caso, Enrique de la, 3142
Matteson, Marianna M., 6514
Matto de Turner, Clorinda, 6515
Mattoon, Robert H., Jr., 4131
Mattos, Carlos Lopes de, 9589
Mattos, Florisvaldo, 4034
Mattos, José Veríssimo de. *See* Veríssimo de Mattos, José.
Mattos, Tomás de, 6954
Mattoso, Katia M. Queiróz, 3997a
Matute, Alvaro, 2751, 9590
Mauá, Irineu Evangelista de Sousa, 4132
Mauricio, Julio, 7289
Mauro, Frédéric, 2198, 3998
Maximiliano Ibañez, Francisco, 3685
Maya, Rafael, 7112-7113
Mayo, Carlos A., 3808
Mayolo, Carlos, 1010
Mayz Vallenilla, Ernesto, 9472
Maza, Francisco de la, 284
Mazo, Gabriel del, 3809-3810
Mechoulan, Henri, 2302
Medeiros dos Santos, Corcino. *See* Santos, Corcino Medeiros dos.
Medeiros Vieira, Emanuel. *See* Vieira, Emanuel Medeiros.
Medina, Enrique, 6925-6928
Medina, José Ramón, 7211
Medina Ascensio, Luis, 2508
Medina Romero, Jesús, 7114
Meier, Matt S., 2629
Meira Penna, J.O. de. *See* Penna, J.O. de Meira.
Meireles, Cecília, 7474, 7553
Mejía, José Manuel, 3547
Mejía, Leonardo, 3472
Mejía Duque, Jaime, 6516, 7358
Mejía Lequerica, José, 2364
Mejía Sánchez, Ernesto, 7115
Meléndez Chaverri, Carlos, 2801-2802, 2829-2830
Melgar, Mariano, 7116
Melgar Callejas, José María, 2900

Melgarejo Vivanco, José Luis, 1995
Mellafe Rojas, Rolando, 3253
Melli, Oscar Ricardo, 3811
Mello, Eduardo Kneese de, 497
Mello, José Antonio Gonsalves de, 4133
Mello, Thiago de, 7554
Mello Júnior, Donato, 431
Melo, Carlos R., 3812
Melo, José Barboza, 4035
Melo, Maria do Carmo Barreto Campello de, 7555
Melo e Souza, Antônio Cândido de. See Souza, Antônio Cândido de Melo e.
Melo Neto, Joâo Cabral de, 7556
Melo Souza, José Ignacio de. See Souza, José Ignacio de Melo.
Melogno, Tabaré, 3416
Melón de Díaz, Esther, 133
Memória Ribeiro, Antonia Mota de Castro. See Ribeiro, Antonia Mota de Castro Memória.
Mena, Lucila Inés, 6816-6818
Mendes, Candido, 2199
Mendes, Murilo [Monteiro], 7557
Mendes de Almeida, Paulo. See Almeida, Paulo Mendes de.
Mendes Júnior, Antonio, 4036
Méndez, José Luis, 6729
Méndez Acebal, Ramón, 3813
Méndez Fleytas, Epifanio, 3905
Méndez Plancarte, Alfonso, 6452
Méndez Vives, Enrique, 3943
Mendiburu, Manuel de, 3548
Mendieta, Gerónimo de, 2469
Mendiola, Salvador, 6581
Mendonça, Antônio Sérgio, 9727
Mendonça, Eduardo Prado de. See Prado de Mendonça, Eduardo.
Mendonça, Rubens de, 7
Mendonça Teles, Gilberto. See Teles, Gilberto Mendonça.
Mendoza, Angela, 2074
Mendoza, Cristóbal L. 3326
Mendoza, Diego de, 3287
Mendoza, María Luisa, 6582
Mendunni, Teresinha Rosa Principe, 9054
Menéndez, Concepción, 2362
Menéndez, Elisabeth, 1996
Menéndez Franco, Alvaro, 7117
Meneses, Carlos, 6671
Menezes, Jayme de Sá, 4134
Menezes, Raimundo de, 4135
Menezes Martinho, Lenira. See Martinho, Lenira Menezes.

Menton, Seymour, 6730
Mercier Vega, Luis, 3814
Meregalli, Jaime, 3944
Merino, Luis, 9010-9012, 9087
Merquior, José Guilherme, 7693, 9721
Merrel, Floyd, 6672, 6819
Mertens, Hans-Günther, 2630
Merton, Thomas *trans.*, 7861
Merwin, W.S. *trans.*, 7874
Mesa, Carlos E., 3143
Mesa, José de, 258-259, 299-300
Mesa G., Carlos D., 977
Messeas, Ney [Cassiano Ricardo], 7475
Metzgar, Joseph V., 2434
Meurer, Carmen Torelly, 50
Mexico. Secretaría de la Presidencia. Dirección General de Estudios Administrativos, 2631
México. Secretaría del Patrimonio Nacional, 6078
Meyer, Eugenia, 1026
Meyer, Harvey Kessler, 2803
Meyer, Jean A., 2752-2753
Meyer, Lorenzo, 2395
Meyer-Minnemann, Klaus, 6517
Meyers, Albert, 2075
Meyers, William K., 2632
Meza Lopehandia, Juan N., 3144
Meza Villalobos, Néstor, 3145, 3240
Micciché, Lino, 993
Michaele, Faris Antonio S., 6116
Michaelis, Pierre, 6610
Michaels, Albert L., 3649
Midgett, Douglas K., 9068
Mieres, Antonio, 3327
Mignoga, Eduardo, 6929
Miguelez, Roberto, 9682
Milani, Virgil I., 6007
Milhomem, Wolney, 7558
Miliani, Domingo, 7008, 9473
Millares Carlo, Agustin, 35
Millas, Jorge, 9696
Miller, Beth, 7204
Miller, Rory, 3549-3550
Miller, William, 3328
Millet, Richard, 2901
Millones, Luis, 2076
Miño Grijalva, Manuel, 3223
Mintz, Sidney Wilfred, 2417, 2946
Minutolo, Cristina V., 3815
Mir, Pedro, 7118
Mirafuentes Galván, José Luis, 2563
Miranda, Hernán, 7119
Miranda Vásquez, Trinidad, 3146
Miri, Héctor F., 6079

Miró, Rodrigo, 6673, 7027
Miró Quesada, Francisco, 6008, 9474-9476, 9657
Miró Quesada Sosa, Aurelio, 6518
Mitry, Jean, 962
Moch de Martínez Mezquida, Raquel, 2435
Módulo, 498
Mörner, Magnus, 2077, 2200-2201, 2303-2304, 2365, 3224-3225, 3473
Moffett, Oren E., 7205
Mohler, Stephen Charles, 7206
Moisés, Carlos Felipe, 7748
Moix, Ana María, 6519
Molina, Carlos A., 3816
Molina de Lines, María, 266
Molina Lemus, Leonardo, 3363
Molina-Muñoz, Stella-Maris, 3408
Molina Silva, Sergio, 3650
Molinari, Ricardo E., 7120
Molinero, Rita, 6731
Molloy, Sylvia, 6593
Moloynik, J.R., 994
Mols, Manfred Heinrich, 2754-2755
Monasterios, Rubén, 7359
Monbeig, Pierre, 130
Mondain, Pierre, 3906
Money, Mary, 3385
Monge, Carlos Francisco, 7121
Monge Alfaro, Carlos, 2804
Monjarás-Ruiz, Jesús, 2756-2757
Monleón, José, 7360-7362
Monroy Huitrón, Guadalupe, 2758
Montaigne, Sanford H., 2633
Mont 'Alegre, Omen, 4037
Mont' Alverne Frota, Francisco Marialva. *See* Frota, Francisco Marialva Mont' Alverne.
Montaña Peláez, Servando, 6520
Monte Barroso, Olga. *See* Barroso, Olga Monte.
Monte-Mór, Jannice, 51
Montecinos, Hernán B., 366
Monteforte Toledo, Mario, 6639
Monteiro, Benedicto, 7419
Monteiro, Clodomir, 7559
Monteiro, Duglas Teixeira, 4136
Monteiro, João Paulo, 9591
Monteiro, Mozart, 7476
Monteiro, Norma de Góes, 4137
Monteiro Mendes, Murilo. *See* Mendes, Murilo [Monteiro].
Montejano y Aguiñaga, Rafael, 285
Montello, Josué, 7725
Montemayor, Alfredo, 9622
Montemayor Salazar, Jorge, 9623
Montenegro, Armando, 3592
Montero, José Antonio, 7122
Montero Vega, Arturo, 7123
Monterroso, Augusto, 7922
Montes, Hugo, 6427
Montes Giraldo, José Joaquín, 6049a-6051
Montes Huidobro, Matías, 7363-7364
Monti, Ricardo, 7290
Montoya, Alberto Angel, 6521
Moore, Brian L., 3035
Moore, John Preston, 2564
Moore, Robert J., 3002
Moorhead, Max L., 2565
Mora, Orlando, 1011
Mora Fuentes, José Luis. *See* Fuentes, José Luis Mora.
Mora Mérida, José Luis, 3288-3291
Moraes, Carlos Dante de, 7694
Moraes, Jomar, 7695
Moraes, Maia Augusta de Sant 'anna, 4003
Moraes, Rubens Borba de, 73
Moraes Emery, Milton de. *See* Emery, Milton de Moraes.
Morais, Frederico, 472
Morais, Régis de, 7560
Morales, Adolfo de, 2079
Morales, Francisco, 2202
Morales, Jorge Luis, 7028
Morales, Juan Bautista, 6522
Morales, María Dolores, 2634
Morales Carrión, Arturo, 2947, 2971, 3003, 3015
Morales P., Félix, 6052
Morand, Carlos, 6869
Morão, Simão Pinheiro, 4038
Moreira, Omar, 6955
Moreira da Costa, Flávio. *See* Costa, Flávio Moreira de.
Moreira da Fonseca, José Paulo. *See* Fonseca, José Paulo Moreira da.
Moreira Gomes, Celuta. *See* Gomes, Celuta Moreira.
Morena, H.A., 7124
Morena, Miguel Ángel, 9028
Moreno, Alvaro J., 6080
Moreno, Dennys, 341
Moreno, Fulgencio R., 2080
Moreno, Gabriel René, 3081
Moreno, Nahuel, 3817
Moreno, Roberto, 2470, 2635
Moreno Cebrián, Alfredo, 2081-2082, 3226

Moreno Davis, Julio César, 9477
Moreno de Alba, José G., 6053
Moreno Fraginals, Manuel, 2985
Moreno Proaño, Agustín, 276
Moreno Toscano, Alejandra, 2436, 2636
Moreno Yañez, Segundo, 3178
Moretta, Eugene Lawrence, 7207
Morino, Angelo, 6840
Moritz, Paulo António, 7652
Morley, Morris, 3454
Moron, Guillermo, 2203, 2366
Morris, Robert J., 7365
Morsella, Astur, 9513
Mosley, Edward H., 2637
Mosquera, Juan José Mouriño, 9722
Mota, Carlos Guilherme, 3999
Mota, Mauro. See Mota [e Albuquerque], Mauro [Ramos da].
Mota [e Albuquerque], Mauro [Ramos da], 7561
Motín en La Soledad, 3354
Mott, Luiz R.B., 4000
Motta, Benedito, 9697
Motta, Flavio L., 415
Motta, Maurício, 7562
Moulines, Carlos Ulises, 9624
Moura, Carlos Francisco, 432
Moura, Ismar de, 4138
Mouriño Mosquera, Juan José. See Mosquera, Juan José Mouriño.
Moya, Casimiro N. de, 2948
Moya Pons, Frank, 3004
Moyano, Ángela, 2437
Müller, Gene A., 2902
Mugaburu, Josephe de, 3227
Mujica Barreda, Elías, 3228
Mujica Láinez, Manuel, 6930, 7902
Mullen, Edward J., 7803
Mullen, Robert J., 286
Mullins, William H., 2638
Mumpeu, Eduardo, 6931
Munch G., Guido, 2509
Muncy, Michèle, 7366-7367
Munguía, Adolfo, 9625
Munita R., Enrique, 9626
Muñoz, Juan Bautista, 2305
Muratore, Joseph R., 2306
Murialdo Laport, Hugo, 963
Muricy, José Cândido de Andrade, 7749
Muriel, Inés, 9100
Murillo Garaycochea, Percy, 3551
Murillo Zamora, Roberto, 9627
Muro Romero, Fernando, 2083
Murquía, Adolfo, 9441
Murra, John V., 2084-2087

Murta, Genesco, 473
Murtil, Pierre-Albert, 3058
Musalem, José, 3651
El Museo de Bellas Artes de Caracas y algunas de sus obras, 398
Museo Judío de Buenos Aires, *Argentina*, 9592
Museu de Arte Moderna da Bahia, 474
Museu de Arte Moderna da Bahia, *Salvador, Brazil*. Comissão do Sesquicentenário da Independência da Bahia, 533
Museu de Arte Moderna de Prefeitura de Belo Horizonte, 475
Museu do Açúcar, *Recife, Brazil*, 4001
Museu Nacional de Belas Artes, *Rio*, 416
Musso Ambrosi, Luis Alberto, 3292
Mustapha, Monique, 2088
Mutis, Alvaro, 7125

Nabucao, Carolina, 7775
Nabuco, Joaquim, 4139
Nachman, Robert G., 4140-4141
Nader, Vladyr, 7445
Nahmad, Salomón, 9514
Nahum, Benjamín, 3927
Nájar, Jorge, 7126
Nandino, Elías, 7127
Napolitano, Antonio, 9554
Naranjo, Carmen, 6640
Naranjo Villegas, Abel, 9421
Nario, Hugo, 3818
Narssiso de Santa María Escobedo, Antonio 3256
Nasatir, Abraham F., 2566
Nascimento, Esdras do, 7420
Natal, Carmelo Rosario, 3059
Natella, Arthur A., Jr., 2204
The National Bibliography of Barbados, 40
Nava, Juan Carlos, 3819
Navajas Cortés, Esteban, 7291
Navarro, Ana, 6932
Navarro, Bernabé, 9555, 9593
Navarro, Marysa, 3820
Navarro García, Luis, 2307, 2510
Navarro Tomás, Tomás, 6020
Navas-Ruiz, Ricardo, 6549
Navilouca: almanaque dos aqua-loucos, 534
Naylor, Thomas H., 2569, 2759
Naziazene, Ademar, 4142
Nebrija, Antonio de, 6021
Needler, Martin C., 2396

Neghme, Amador, 3652
Neglia, Ermino G., 7369
Negri, Eithel Orbit, 7332
Nehemkis, Peter, 2205
Neiva, Lauro, 7477
Nelken, Margarita, 327
Nelson, Ralph, 1997
Nemby, Eric, 2308
Nemirovsky, José, 476
Neri, Michael C., 2438
Nero da Costa, Iraci del. *See* Costa, Iraci del Nero da.
Nerrou, F. Raphaël, 7783
Neruda, Pablo, 7234, 7867-7875, 7923, 7931
Neumann, Frank J., 1998-1999,
Neuvillate Ortíz, Alfonso de, 328
Neves, Abdias, 4002
Neves, Guilherme Santos, 9055
Newson, Linda A., 2972
Newton, Ronald C., 3821
Newton, Velma, 52
Neyra, Joaquín, 6984
Nicholson, Joe, Jr., 3016
Nickel, Herbert J., 287
Nicodemos, José Pedro, 4039
Nicol, Eduardo, 9732
Nicolau, Juan Carlos, 3822
Niemeyer, E. V., Jr., 3653
Nieto, Manuel Orestes, 7128-7129
Nigro, Kirsten F., 7368
Nimrod, 7849
Nizza da Silva, Maria Beatriz. *See* Silva, Maria Beatriz Nizza da.
Njaim, Humberto, 9683
Noble, Enrique, 6523
Nogueira, Arlinda Rocha, 4143
Nogueira, Hamilton, 7696
Nogueira de Matos, Odilon. *See* Matos, Odilon Nogueira de.
Nogueira França, Eurico. *See* França, Eurico Nogueira.
Nogueira Galvão, Walnice. See Galvão, Walnice Nogueira.
Noguera, María Luz de, 3433
Noriega, Néstor Alfredo, 6466
Notas sobre el Virreinato del Río de la Plata, 3293
Novaes, Carlos Eduardo, 7421, 7478
Novaes Coelho, Nelly. *See* Coelho, Nelly Novaes.
Nowotny, Karl A., 2000
Noyola, Antonio, 1027
Nudler, Oscar, 9684
Nueva antología de la poesía nicaragüense, 7029
Nuevo Día del Perú, 3373
Nuevo edificio del Museo de Bellas Artes de Caracas, 399
Nuevo Mundo, 9478
Nuffer de Campos, Geir. *See* Campos, Geir [Nuffer de].
Nunes, Benedito, 7750
Nunes, Cassiano, 7563, 7638
Núñez, Armindo, 1040
Núñez, M., 3823
Núñez Crisosto, Eduardo, 9628
Núñez Hague, Estuardo, 6443
Núñez Machín, Ana, 3060
Núñez Ortega, Angel, 2639
Núñez Tenorio, J. R., 9594
Nunn, Charles F., 2511
Nunn, Frederick M., 3654
Nuño, Juan A., 9698

Oberacker, Carlos H., Jr., 4144
Oberem, Udo, 2089, 3179
Obregón, Gonzalo, 288
Obregón Loria, Rafael, 2903
O'Brien, Dennis J., 2397, 2760
O'Brien, Thomas F., 3249
Ocampo López, Javier, 3082, 3343, 3364
Ocanto, Nancy, 6884
Ochoa Granados, Humberto, 2471
Ochoa O., Octavio, 3474
Oddone, Juan, 2168
Odio, Eunice, 7130
O'Donnell, Francisco Talaia, 4145
Official release of the 1763 monument, 337
Ogelsby, J. C. M., 2206
O'Gorman, Juan, 329
O'Grady de Paiva, Jorge. *See* Paiva, Jorge O'Grady de.
Ojeda, Jorge Arturo, 6583, 6611
Olaechea, R., 2512
O'Leary, Juan Emiliano, 3907
Olinto, Antonio, 7422
Oliva de Coll, Josefina, 2309
Olival, Moema de Castro e Silva, 7726
Oliveira, Denise Cabral de, 7564
Oliveira, Luiz Carlos de, 417
Oliveira, Manuel Botelho de. *See* Botelho de Oliveira, Manuel.
Oliveira, Marly de, 7565
Oliveira Camello, Maurílio José de. *See* Camello, Maurílio José de Oliveira.
Oliveira Fernandes, Maria do Carmo Leite de. *See* Fernandes, Maria do Carmo Leite de Oliveira.

Oliveira Lima, Manuel de, 7697
Oliveira Ribeiro Neto, Pedro Antônio de. *See* Ribeiro Neto, Pedro Antônio de Oliveira.
Oliveira Zokner, Cecilia Teixeira de. *See* Zokner, Cecilia Teixeira de Oliveira.
Oliver, Juan Pablo, 3824
Oliver, William I., 7855
Olivera, Mercedes, 2001
Olliff, Donathon C., 2640
Olmos, Ramón R., 3697
Olsen, Dale A., 9039
On his seventieth birthday Alejo Carpentier answers seven questions, 6732
Onega, Gladys S., 6933
Onetti, Juan Carlos, 6956, 7013, 7903
Onís, Harriet de *trans*., 7936
O'Phelan Godoy, Scarlett, 3229
Oqueli, Arturo, 6641
Orayen, Raúl, 9658
Ordaz, Luis, 7369
Orden Miracle, Ernesto la, *padre*. *See* La Orden Miracle, Ernesto, *padre*.
Ordenanças del señor doctor Antonio González y del señor Miguel de Ybarra, 3147
Ordenanças Reales de la Real Audiencia de Quito, 3180
Orduna, Germán, 6444
Oreamuno Q., Alfredo, 6642
Orenstein, Glorida, 7370
Orestes Nieto, Manuel. *See* Nieto, Manuel Orestes.
Orgambide, Pedro, 6934
Organization of American States. General Secretariat, 9479
The original and its reproduction: a Melhoramentos project, 477
Orjuela, Hector H., 7208
Orlando, Carlos Alberto, 9595
Ornstein, Leopoldo R., 3329
Orrego Vicuña, Claudio, 3253a, 3655, 6870
Orrey, Leslie, 9013
Ortega, Ezequiel César, 3825
Ortega, José, 6803
Ortega, Julio, 6841
Ortega Diaz, Pedro, 2207
Ortega Luere, Marcela, 6885
Ortega Ricaurte, Carmen, 105
Ortega y Medina, Juan A., 2208
Ortiz, Helen, 3036
Ortiz, Sergio Elías, 3147a
Ortiz, Victoria *trans*., 7928
Ortoneda, Baldomero, 9699

Osborne, Jongh, 309
Osborne, Lilly, 126, 309
Osório, Laci, 7566-7567
Ossio, Juan, 2090-2092
Otaduy, Ernesto, 306
Otero Silva, Miguel, 6797
Otte, Enrique, 2299
Ouro Preto, Maluh [Maria Luisa] de, 7479
Oved, Iaacov, 3826
Oves, Santiago Carlos, 7292
Oviedo, Jose Miguel, 7030
Oviedo y Valdés, Gonzalo Fernández de, 2973, 6428

Pacheco, Francisco Antonio, 9629
Pacheco, José Emilio, 2471a
Pacheco, Juan Manuel, 3148-3149
Pacheco, León, 2904
Pacheco Quintero, Jorge, 7031
Paço das Artes, *São Paulo*, 478
Padgug, Robert A., 2209
Paes, José Paulo, 7751
Páez, José Antonio, 9145
Páez de la Torre, Carlos, 3827
Pagallo, Julio F., 9596
Paim, Antônio, 9480
Paiva, Jorge O' Grady de, 6117
Palacin, Luis, 4003
Palacios, Lucila [*pseud. for* Mercedes Carvajal de Arocha], 6798
Palacios, Patricia, 2463
Palacios Acero, Eduardo, 6762
Palant, Jorge, 7293
Palanza, Ugo M., 6524
Palarea, Álvaro Fernaud, 9014
Paley-Francescato, Martha, 6612, 6985-6986
Pallottini, Renata, 7568
Palls, Terry I., 7371
Palma, Ricardo, 6525
Palmer, Colin A., 2513
Panamá y La Frutera: anális de un confrontación económico-fiscal, 2905
Panasewicz, Nitsche de. *See* De Panasewicz, Nitsche.
Panizza Pons, Carlos, 3308
Panorama de teatro cubano, 7372
Papailler, Hubert, 7804
Papel Periódico Ilustrado, 3434
Paraná (state), *Brazil*. Governo do Estado do Paraná. Secretaria de Estado da Educação e de Cultura. Fundação Teatro Guaíra, 7639
Pardo, Isaac J., 3115

Pardo D., Cruz, 3174
Pardo García, Germán, 7131
Paredes, Raymond A., 2642
Paredes-Candia, Antonio, 6081
Páride Bernabo, Héctor Júlio. See Carybé [pseud. for Héctor Júlio Páride Bernabo].
París de Oddone, Blanca, 9515
Parish, Helen Rand, 2310
Parker, Franklin D., 2906
Parker, John M., 7752
Parola, Luis, 3908
Parra, Nicanor, 7876
Parra, Violeta, 7132
Parry, J.H., 2472
Partida, Armando, 7172
Partido Revolucionario de los Trabajadores, *Buenos Aires*, 3828
Partridge, Frances trans., 7888-7889
Pascuali, Antonio, 9556
Pasquel, Leonardo, 2643
Pastor, Rodolfo, 2514
Pastor Poppe, Ricardo, 6751
Patch, Robert, 2515
Paternain, Alejandro, 7225
Patrick, Elizabeth Nelson, 2567
Patterson, Horace Orlando, 7811
Patton, Elda Clayton, 3829
Paul, Irven, 3656
Paula, Alberto S.J. de. 3295
Paula Assis, José Eugênio de. See Assis, José Eugênio de Paula.
Pauli, Evaldo, 4004, 4146
Paulo Augusto [pseud. for Paulo Augusto da Silva], 7569
Pavlovsky, Eduardo A., 7294-7297
Pawlowski, John, 6429
Pawson, Michael, 2949
Payá, Carlos M., 3714
Paz, Octavio, 6613, 7133, 7877-7878, 7924-7926
Paz Ballivián, Danilo, 2093
Paz Soldán y Unanué, Pedro. See Arona, Juan de [pseud. for Paz Soldán y Unanué, Pedro].
Pearson, Lon, 6886
Pease G.Y., Franklin, 2094-2098, 3374
Peavler, Terry J., 6733-6734
Peccorini Letona, Francisco, 2831
Peden, Margaret Sayers trans., 7373, 7887, 7895, 7926-7927, 7930, 7932
Pedrero, Gloria, 2661
Pedrosa, Mário, 418
Pedroso, Bráulio, 7640
Peers de Perkins, Carmen, 3830

Peláez, Carlos Manuel, 4005
Pellegrini, Enrique, 3831
Pellegrini Júnior, Domingos, 7446
Peltzer, Federico, 6935
Peña, Edilio, 7298
Peña, Miguel, 3344
Pena dos Anjos, Ricardo Augusto. See Anjos, Ricardo Augusto [Pena] dos.
Pena Filho, Carlos, 7570
Peña Kampy, Alberto, 2907
Peniche Vallado, Leopoldo, 2761
Penna, J.O. de Meira, 499
Penor, J., 2644
Penteado de Rezende, Carlos. See Rezende, Carlos Penteado de.
Peñuela C., Víctor, 9545
Peppercorn, Lisa M., 9056-9057
Peralta, José, 2210, 3475, 9516
Peralta, Violeta, 6614
Peraltilla Díaz, Artemio, 7035
Perazzo, Nicolás, 3375
Perdigão, Paulo, 995
Perdomo Escobar, José Ignacio, 9093
Pereira, Antonio Olavo, 7942
Pereira, Maura de Senna, 7480
Pereira, Ruy, 519
Pereira, Uilcon Jóia, 419
Pereira da Costa, Francisco Augusto. See Costa, Francisco Augusto Pereira da.
Pereira da Silva, Francisco. See Silva, Francisco Pereira da.
Pereira da Silva, Hélcio. See Silva, Hélcio Pereira da.
Pereira de Almeida, Abílio. See Almeida, Abílio Pereira de.
Pereira Salas, Eugenio, 3657
Pereña Vicente, Luciano, 2211, 3230
Peres, Fernando da Rocha, 7571
Pereyra, Mario Luis, 3832
Pereyra Plasencia, Hugo, 3376
Pérez, Galo René, 6526
Pérez, Jorge Osvaldo, 9422
Pérez, Louis A., Jr., 74, 3037
Pérez, María Esther, 6430
Pérez Botero, Luis, 6431
Pérez Brignoli, Héctor, 2142-2143, 2212
Pérez de la Riva, Juan, 2980
Pérez de Tudela y Bueso, Juan, 3150
Pérez Estremera, Manuel, 961
Pérez Fuentes, Gerardo, 3697
Pérez Martínez, Noemí Atamoros de. See Atamoros de Pérez Martínez, Noemí.
Pérez Moris, José, 3022

Pérez Triana, Santiago, 6427
Pérez Turrent, Tomás, 1028
Pernambuco (state), *Brazil*. Conselho Estadual de Cultura, 4040
Perón, Juan Domingo, 3833
Peronard Th., Marianne, 6082
El peronismo, 3834
Perri, Dennis, 7375
Perry, Laurens Ballard, 2645
Perticarati, Jane Arduino, 7572
Peru. Consejo Nacional de la Universidad Peruana (CONUP). Dirección de Evaluación de Universidades. Oficina de Evaluación, 53.
Peru. Instituto Nacional de Cultura. Biblioteca Nacional, 9132
Peru. Ministerio de Relaciones Exteriores, 3593
Perusse, Roland I., 2950
Pescador Sarget, Augusto, 9424, 9659
Pescador Prudencio, Augusto, 9423
Pescatello, Ann M., 2213-2214, 4147
Pesce, Hugo, 9425
Pessoa de Castro, Yeda. *See* Castro, Yeda Pessoa de.
Pestana, Francisco Rangel, 4148
Peterson, Gerald W., 7376
Peterson, Harold F., 2215
Peterson, Karen, 7377
Peterson, Mendel L., 2311
Peterson, Richard H., 2646
Petit de Murat, Ulises, 972
Petras, James F., 3454
Petriella, Dionisio, 106
Petrone, Maria Theresa Schorer, 4149
Pettus, Jo Ann Geurin, 3222
Phelan, John L., 2312
Philip, George, 3552-3553
Phillips, David Atlee, 2216
Phillips, Rachel, 7209, 7378
Philoctête, René, 7781
Picciotto, Robert S. *trans*., 7899
Piccirilli, Ricardo, 3835
Piccolo, Helga Iracema Landeraf, 4150
Picó, Fernando, 3038
Pietri, Pedro, 7135
Pietschmann, Horst, 2135, 2516
Piglia, Ricardo, 6936, 6987
Pignatari, Décio, 7706
Piho, Virve, 2002
Pike, Fredrick B., 3554
Pilditch, Charles, 7379
Piló, Conceição, 508
Pilotto, Erasmo, 9426
Pilotto, Osvaldo, 131

Pimentel y Vargas, Fermín de, 6528
Pina, Pedro Alejandrino, 3039
Pina Araújo, Avelino de. *See* Araújo, Avelino [de Pina].
Pinedo Nava, Angel Genaro, 3455
Piñera Ramírez, David, 2568
Piñeros Corpas, Joaquín, 9093a
Pinheiro, Lina Celso, 4152
Pinheiro, Paulo Benedicto, 7573
Pinheiro, Paulo Sérgio de M.S., 4151
Pinheiro Ferreira, Silvestre, 9450
Pinheiro Filho, Celso, 4152
Pinheiro Marão, Simão. *See* Morão, Simão Pinheiro.
Pinho França, Dirceu. *See* França, Dirceu Pinho.
Pinkuss, Fritz, 4153
Pino, Amalia del, 3836
Pino Iturrieta, Elías, 9517
Pino Santos, Oscar, 3061
Pinto, Antísthenes, 7574
Pinto, G. Hércules, 4041
Pinto, Honorio, 3555
Pinto, Julieta, 6643
Pinto, Luis, 4006
Pinto, Manuel, 3355
Pinto de Aguiar, Manoel. *See* Aguiar, Manoel Pinto de.
Pinto Escobar, Inés, 3151
Pinto Rodrigues, Geraldo. *See* Rodrigues, Carlos Pinto.
Pintor Genaro, Mercedes, 6988
Pintores de Rosario: Benvenuto, Cochet, Musto, Ouvrard, Schiavoni, Vanzo, 352
Pintos Carbajal, Mireya, 3945-3946
Pio, Fernando, 433
Piossek Prebisch, Teresa, 3296
Pires Ferreira, Gilda. *See* Ferreira, Gilda Pires.
Pisani Coelho, Ceres. *See* Coelho, Ceres Pisani.
Pistoia, Benito Honorato, 3297
Pitty, Dimas Lidio, 1032, 6644
Pizarro, Agueda, 333
Plá, Josefina, 294, 378, 3298, 3909, 6055, 7009
Placer, Zavier, 7575
Platt, Tristan, 2099-2100
Plaza, Ramón de la, 9146
Pletcher, David M., 2367, 2647
Podestá, Bruno, 132, 9518
Poggi, Rinaldo Alberto, 3837
Pohl, Frederick J., 2313
Pohl, Hans, 2630

Polesso, Hermenegildo, 4107
Polisenský, Josef, 2217, 2314
Pollak, Michael, 2315
Pollak-Eltz, Angelina, 26
Polo Figueroa, Nicolás, 6022
Polzer, Charles William, 254, 2569
Pommerin, Reiner, 2399
Pompa y Pompa, Antonio, 2316
Ponce, Anibal, 9427
Ponce, Fernando, 3083, 3556
Ponce Sanginés, Carlos, 2101-2103, 3594
Ponferrada, Gustavo Eloy, 9557
Poniatowska, Elena, 6615
Ponte Preta, Stanislaw. See Pôrto, Sérgio [pseud. for Stanislaw Ponte Preta].
Pontes, Paulo, 7626
Pontes de Azevedo, Neroaldo. See Azevedo, Neroaldo Pontes de.
Pontificia Universidade Católica, Rio. Vice-Reitoria para Assuntos Acadêmicos, 75
Porras, Camilo A., 2908
Porras Collantes, Ernesto, 6820
Portal, Marta, 6616
Portella, Eduardo, 7698
Portes, Alejandro, 2218
Porto, Carlos Eugênio, 4007
Porto, José da Costa, 4154
Pôrto, Sérgio [pseud. for Stanislaw Ponte Preta], 7481
Portocarrero M., Felipe, 3557
Portuondo, José Antonio, 6695, 7173
Posada Zarate, Francisco, 9519
Posadas, Abel, 7355
Posani, Clara, 3456, 7380
Posternak, Dora, 7136
Poulantzas, Nicos, 9693
Powell, Philip Wayne, 2317
Powell, T.G., 2648-2649
Poyo, Gerald E., 2951
Pozas Horcasitas, Ricardo, 2762
Pozenato, José Clemente, 7727
Prade, Péricles, 7576
Prado, Antônio Arnoni, 7728
Prado, Décio de Almeida, 7656
Prado, João Fernandes de Almeida, 420
Prado, Manuel, 3838
Prado, Yan de Almeida, 7699
Prado de Mendonça, Eduardo, 9558
Prado Gouveia, Jaime. See Gouveia, Jaime Prado.
Prado Valladares, Clarival do. See Valladares, Clarival do Prado.
Pradt, Dominique Georges Frédéric de Riom de Prolhiac de Fourt de, 2368

Prantner, Johanna, 4155
Prasad, Krishna, 7818a-7819
Prem, Hanns J., 1972, 2003
Prendes, Alvaro, 3017
Presas, Juan Antonio, 3839
Presas, Mario A., 9630-9631
Préstamos y donaciones de patriotas, españoles y portugueses vecinos de Mendoza en los años 1813 a 1817, 3409
Preta, Stanislaw Ponte. See Pôrto, Sérgio [pseud. for Stanislaw Ponte Preta].
Preto, Maluh [Maria Luisa] de Ouro. See Ouro Preto, Maluh [Maria Luisa] de.
Price, Richard, 2946
Prieto, Alejandro, 2439
Prieto, Francisco, 6584
Prince, Maureen, 7820
Princep, John, 3356
Principe Mendunni, Teresinha Rosa. See Mendunni, Teresinha Rosa Principe.
Probanza de Diego de Sandoval, 19.XI.1539, 3181
Probanza de meritos de Martín Ramírez de Guzmán, Quito, 12.XI.1574, 3182
Prober, Jurt, 2805
Proctor, Samuel, 2318
Proença, Ivan Cavalcanti, 7482
Programa de trabajo de la Dirección del Patrimonio Cultural y Artístico del Estado de México: documentos, 289
Promis Ojeda, José, 6887
Provost, Paul Jean, 9115
Pucciarelli, Eugenio, 9442-9443, 9597, 9632, 9700
Puchet, Enrique, 9598
Pueyrredón, Victoria, 6937
Puhle, Hans-Jürgen, 2400
Puig, Manuel, 6938, 7904-7906
Puiggrós, Rodolfo, 2164
Pulido, Esperanza, 9116
El puntero apuntado con apuntes breves, 2832

Quackenbush, L.H., 7381
Quaderni di Letteratura Americane, 7210
Quatrefages, René, 2570
Queiroz, Paulo Edmur de Souza, 9599
Queiroz, Rachel de, 7483, 7641
Queiróz Mattoso, Katia M. See Mattoso, Katia M. Queiróz.
Querejazu Calvo, Roberto, 3595-3596
Quesada, José Luis, 7137
Quezada, Noemí, 2004-2005
Quijada Urías, Alfonso, 6645

Quiles, Ismael, 9685
Quinn, David B., 2319
Quiñonero Gálvez, Juan, 2320
Quintana, Mário, 7577
Quintero, Ednodio, 6799
Quintero, José Humberto, 3457
Quintero Rivera, Angel, 3062
Quintero V., Magello, 9600
Quiroga, Horacio, 6529, 7927
Quiroga Ochoa, Ovidio, 3597
Quirós, Rodrigo, 7138
Quiroz Paz-Soldán, Eusebio, 3231

Raat, William Dirk, 2650-2652
Rabassa, Clementina, 7382
Rabassa, Gregory *trans.*, 6530, 6989, 7883, 7890, 7897-7898, 7900, 7902, 7908-7909, 7919, 7945
Rabell Romero, Cecilia Andrea, 2104, 2517
Rabossi, Eduardo A., 9633, 9670
Rachum, Ilan, 4156
Radell, David R., 2833
Los radicales, 3840
Raffo Magnasco, Benito, 9559
Raja Gabaglia, Marisa. *See* Gabaglia, Marisa Raja.
Rama, Carlos M., 2219, 3558, 9520
Ramayón, Eduardo E., 3841
Ramírez, Fausto, 330
Ramírez, Sergio, 6646-6649
Ramírez Estrada, Alsino, 6770
Ramírez Farías, Carlos, 7299
Ramírez Necochea, Hernán, 3658
Ramón, Armando de, 3254
Ramón, David, 1028, 1030
Ramón, Gonzalo, 6771
Ramón Medina, José. *See* Medina, José Ramón.
Ramón y Rivera, Luis Felipe, 7383
Ramos, Donald, 4042
Ramos Gómez, Luis J., 282, 2518, 4043
Ramos Gonçalves, Alice. *See* Gonçalves, Alice Ramos.
Ramos Pérez, Demetrio, 2321, 2369, 2974, 3116
Ramos R., Antonio, 3910-3911
Randall, Laura, 2440
Rangel, Leyla Castello Branco, 76
Rangel Pestana, Francisco. *See* Pestana, Francisco Rangel.
Rapoport, Mario, 3842
Rasco y Bermúdez, José Ignacio, 2220
Rasgos de la vida pública de Juan Manuel de Rosas, 3843

Rasi, Humberto M., 6990
Rasmussen, Jorgen Nybo, 2006
Rato de Sambuccetti, Susana, 3844
Rau, Wolfgang Ludwig, 4157
Raudales Soto, Julio, 2909
Ravera, Rosa María, 9728
Raworth, Tom *trans.*, 7832
Real Cuesta, Javier, 2105
Real de Azúa, Carlos, 9521-9522
Real Díaz, José Joaquín, 2462
Reale, Miguel, 9481
Rebello, Edgardo de Castro, 4009
Reber, Vera Blinn, 334
Rébula, Angela María Amaral, 54
Recalde A., Sergio, 3912
Recaséns Siches, Luis, 9701-9702
Recent Latin American drawings, 1969-1976: lines of vision, 313
Rector, John, 3395
Recuperación de Julián Bautista, 9029
Redmond, Walter Bernard, 9482
Rees, Peter W., 2441
Rego Neto, Hugo Napolião do, 4010
Reich, Peter L., 985
Reig Satorres, José, 3095
Reid, Alastair *trans.*, 6821, 7868, 7870-7871, 7874
Reinecke, John E., 6131
Reis, Arthur Cesar Ferreira, 4011
Reis, Jaime, 4158
Reis, Marcos Konder, 7578
Reis Júnior, Pereira, 4159
Reisler, Mark, 2763
Reixach Vilá, Pedro, 3117
Relación sacada de la probanza fecha por parte de Pedro Lozano en el plieto que trata con Melchor Verdugo sobre el Prencipal Guaman e sus sujetos, 3232
Remmer, Karen L., 3659
Renault, Delsa, 4160
Renault, Delso, 4012
Rendón, Silvia P., 2007
René-Moreno, Gabriel, 3598-3599
Renga: a chain of poems, 7879
Rengifo, César, 400, 7300
Rengifo, Diana, 3118
Renique C., José Luis, 2106
Rens, Ivo, 6842
El Repertorio Americano: Londres, 1826-1827, 2370
Resnick, Melvyn C., 6056
Resor, Randolph R., 4161
Rest, Jaime, 6991-6992
Restrepo Canal, Carlos, 3435

Restrepo Ricaurte, Inés, 3152
Restrepo Tirado, Ernesto, 3153
Retamal Avila, Julio, 3084
Retana, Marco, 6650
Reunión de Estudio Centro Catalográfico Centroamericano, *San José, 1976*, 55
Reverón, Armando, 401
Revilla, Angel, 6057
Revista Biblioteca Nacional, 7384
Revista Chilena de Literatura, 6888
Revista de Antropofagia, 7753
Revista de Costa Rica, 2806-2807
Revista de Filosofía de la Universidad de Costa Rica, 9634
Revista de la Academia Hondureña de Geografía e Historia, 2808
Revista de la Biblioteca Nacional, 7212
Revista de la Facultad de Derecho de México, 9703
Revista de la Junta de Estudios Históricos de Mendoza, 3845
Revista de la Universidad de México, 1028
Revista de Literaturas Hispánicas, 6822
Una revista de música, 9117
Revista de Teatro, 7642
Revista del Archivo Nacional, 2834, 3085
Revista del Instituto Ecuatoriano de Historia Eclesiástica, 3476
Revista do Instituto do Ceará, 77
Revista do Instituto Histórico e Geográfico, 434
Revista Histórica, 3947
Revista Lotería. See *Lotería*.
Revista Mexicana de Ciencia Política, 9704
Revueltas, José, 6585
Rey, Agapito, 2560
Rey, José Antonio León, 6058
Rey Fajardo, José del, 3119, 3154
Reyes, Alfonso, 6531
Reyes, Aurelio de los, 1028-1030
Reyes, Jaime, 7139
Reyes Abadie, Washington, 3410, 3948
Reyes Nevares, Beatriz, 7213
Reyna, María del Carmen, 2653
Reynaga Burgoa, Ramiro. See Wankar.
Rezende, Carlos Penteado de, 9058
Rial, José Antonio, 7301
Ribamar Ferreira, José. See Gullar, Ferreira [*pseud. for* José Ribamar Ferreira].
Ribeiro, Antonia Mota de Castro Memória, 78
Ribeiro, Antônio Carlos, 7484

Ribeiro, Darcy, 2221, 9428
Ribeiro Costa, Joaquim. See Costa, Joaquim Ribeiro.
Ribeiro Neto, Pedro Antônio de Oliveira, 435-436
Ribeiro Uchôa, Célia. See Uchôa, Célia Ribeiro.
Ribera, Nicolas Joseph de, 2952
Ribeyro, Julio Ramón, 6782, 6843, 7302
Ribeyrolles, Charles, 449
Ricci, Julio, 6957
Richards, Katharine C., 7385
Richardson, Ruth, 7386
Richmond, Douglas W., 2764-2765
Ridings, Eugene W., 4162
Riese, Berthold, 1985
Riismandel, John N., 2835
Riley, James D., 2519-2521
Riley, Michael, 2522
Rincón, Carlos, 6735
Río, Ignacio del., 2442
Rio, João do [*pseud. for* Paulo Barreto], 7643
Río, Marcela del, 6586
Rionda Arreguín, Luis, 9716
Ríos, Julian, 6702
Ríos Velazco de Caldi, Ramona Luisa, 107
Rípoda Ardanaz, Daisy, 3241
Ripoll, Carlos, 7303
Rippy, J. Fred, 2222
Riquelme de Molinas, Yula, 7140
Riquelme García, Benigno, 3913
Riva-Agüero, José de la, 3559
Riva Buglio, Hugo, 7387
Rivas de Domínguez, Celia Ruiz. See Ruiz Rivas de Domínguez, Celia.
Rivera, José Eustasio, 6532-6533
Rivera, Pedro, 1033
Rivera, Rodolfo, 1030
Rivera Cusicanqui, Silvia, 2107
Rivera Echenique, Silvia, 3846
Rivera Saavedra, Juan, 6783
Rivero, Mario, 371
Riz, Liliana de, 3660
Robalino Dávila, Luis, 3476a
Roberts, Gemma, 6823
Robins, Robert S., 3525
Robinson, Cecil, 6617
Robinson, David J., 2029, 3120, 3299
Robles, Humberto E., 6827
Robles, José A., 9635
Roca, C. Alberto, 3413
Rocha, Carlos Eduardo da, 437, 500
Rocha e Silva, M. See Silva, M. Ro-

cha e.
Rocha Nogueira, Arlinda. *See* Nogueira, Arlinda Rocha.
Rocha Peres, Fernando da. *See* Peres, Fernando da Rocha.
Roche, Jean, 4163, 7754
Roche, Mercel, 2322
Rockland, Michael A., 6534
Rocque, Carlos, 4164
Roda, Juan Antonio, 372
Rodman, Selden, 509
Rodrigues, Ermínio, 6118
Rodrigues, Geraldo Pinto, 7579
Rodrigues, José Honório, 4013, 4044
Rodrigues, José Mário, 7580
Rodrigues, José Wasth, 501
Rodrigues dos Anjos, Augusto de Carvalho. *See* Anjos, Augusto [de Carvalho Rodrigues] dos.
Rodrigues dos Santos, Paulo. *See* Santos, Paulo Rodrigues dos.
Rodríguez, Augusto G., 3847
Rodríguez, Celso, 2293, 2461, 3208
Rodríguez, Iraida, 6737
Rodríguez, Luis Felipe, 6696
Rodríguez, Marco Antonio, 6772
Rodríguez, Mario, 2223-2224, 2836
Rodríguez, Victor Manuel, 6651
Rodríguez Alcalá de González Oddone, Beatriz, 7009
Rodríguez Almodóvar, Antonio, 6535
Rodríguez Araujo, Octavio, 2766
Rodríguez Avellaneda, Antonio José, 3365
Rodríguez Ayestas, Julio, 2911
Rodríguez B., Orlando, 7388
Rodríguez Becerra, Salvador, 2837
Rodríguez Campos, Manuel, 3458
Rodríguez Castelo, Hernán, 6536
Rodríguez Castillos, Osiris, 7141
Rodríguez Coronel, Rogelio, 6618
Rodríguez Cruz, Agueda María, 2323
Rodríguez de Montes, María Luisa, 6051
Rodríguez Leal, Edgard, 3121
Rodríguez Losa, Salvador, 2008
Rodríguez-Monegal, Emir, 6537-6538, 6738, 6993
Rodríguez O., Jaime E., 3477
Rodríguez Objío, Manuel, 3023
Rodríguez Pérez, Elena, 3014
Rodríguez Plata, Horacio, 3155
Rodríguez Ramos, Esther, 6739
Rodríguez S., Juan Agustín, 3396
Rodríguez-Sardiñas, Orlando, 7214
Rodríguez Vallejo, José, 2523
Rodríguez Varela, Alberto, 3850
Rodríguez Villegas, Hernán, 3086
Roetti, Jorge Alfredo, 9656
Roffe, Alfredo, 1047
Roffe, Ambretta, 1047
Roggiano, Alfredo, 6432
Roig, Arturo Andrés, 9483, 9523
Rojas, Armando, 3330
Rojas, Elena M., 6059
Rojas, Gonzalo, 7142
Rojas, Jorge, 7032
Rojas, Manuel, 6871
Rojas, Waldo, 7025, 7143
Rojas Garcidueñas, José, 6453
Rojo, Grínor, 6889, 7389
Roldán, Washington, 9137
Roldán Oquendo, Ornán, 2654
Rolón, Raimundo, 3914
Roman, Richard, 2767-2768
Romano, Ruggiero, 2225
Romano de Sant' Anna, Affonso. *See* Sant' Anna, Affonso Romano de.
Romano-V., Octavio Ignacio, 7850
Romay, Francisco J., 3848
Romero, Armando, 6763
Romero, Elvio, 7144
Romero, Florencia B. de, 3385
Romero, José Luis, 2371
Romero, Luis Alberto, 3849
Romero, Mario Germán, 6009
Romero Carranza, Ambrosio, 3850
Romero Galván, José Rubén, 2009
Romero Quiroz, Javier, 290-291
Romero Vargas, Germán, 2820
Romualdo, Alejandro, 7145-7146
Ron, José, 9429
Roncari, Luiz, 4036
Roque da Silva, Rolando. *See* Silva, Rolando Roque da.
Ros, Rafael G., 402
Rosa, F. Affonso Santa. *See* Santa Rosa, F. Affonso.
Rosa, João Guimarães, 6539
Rosa, Joaquim, 4165
Rosa, José María, 3851
Rosado Maia, Jerônimo Vingt-Un. *See* Maia, Jerônimo Vingt-Un Rosado.
Rosales, Alberto, 9733
Rosario, Rubén del, 133, 6060
Rosas Marcano, Jesús, 3357
Rose, Juan Gonzalo, 7147
Rosebury, Theodor, 2324
Rosell, Avenir, 7390
Rosen, Keith S., 2183
Rosenblat, Angel, 6010-6011, 6061

Rosengarten, Frederic, Jr., 2912
Ross, Claudio, 7148
Ross, Delmer G., 2913-2914
Ross, Stanley R., 2769-2770
Ross, Waldo, 6433
Rossi, Iris, 41
Rossignol, Jacques, 3661
Rostworowski de Diez Canseco, María, 2108-2112, 3233-3234
Rotella, Oscar S., 9636
Rouillon D., Guillermo, 9524
Rouquié, Alain, 6540
Rouse, John E., 2226
Rout, Leslie B., Jr., 2227
Rovinski, Samuel, 7304-7305
Rowe, Leo Stanton, 3560
Rowe, William *trans.*, 7860
Roys, Ralph Loveland, 2010
Rubinstein Moreira, 7215
Rubio, Norma, 3134
Rubio Mañé, J. Ignacio, 2372
Rubio Sánchez, Manuel, 2838
Rudder, Robert S., 7854
Rueda, Manuel, 7149
Ruffinelli, Jorge, 6619-6620
Ruibal Corella, Juan Antonio, 2655
Ruiz, Ramón Eduardo, 2771
Ruiz Carvalho de Baqueiro, Eloisa, 9118
Ruiz Castañeda, María del Carmen, 2656
Ruiz Rivas de Domínguez, Celia, 9130
Ruiz Rivera, Julián Bautista, 2113, 3156-3157
Rumazo González, Alfonso, 3087
Ruscalleda Bercedóniz, Jorge María, 7216
Russell, D.E.H., 2228
Russell-Wood, A.J.R., 4045
Rutledge, Ian, 2156, 3852
Ruz Menéndez, Rodolfo, 56

Sá, Carlos A. de, 7581
Sá Menezes, Jayme de. *See* Menezes, Jayme de Sá.
Sabat de Rivers, Georgina, 6434
Sábato, Ernesto, 6964
Sabino, Carlos, 9415
Sabino, Fernando, 7485
Sabogal, José, 381
Sabóia de Carvalho, Margarida. *See* Carvalho, Margarida Sabóia de.
Sacheri, Carlos A., 9560, 9705
Sachs, Ignacy, 2229
Saco López, José Antonio, 2986
Sadeek, Sheik M., 7812-7813
Saeger, James S., 3300

Sáenz, Carlos Luis, 6662a
Sáenz, Jimena, 3853
Sáenz de Santa María, Carmelo, 6435
Saes, Décio Azevedo, *marquês de*, 4166
Safir, Margery A., 6994
Sagrera, Martín, 2230
Sahagún, Bernardino de, 2011
Saia, Luis, 502
Said Ali, Manuel, 6101
Saint John, Ronald Bruce, 3561, 3600
St. Martin, Hardie *trans.*, 7892, 7907, 7923
Saint-Phalle, Thibalut de, 2389
Saint Vil, Jean Claude, 7789
Sainz, Gustavo, 7907
Salamanca, Daniel, 3601
Salame, Paulo J., 4086
Salame, Pedro A., 4086
Salão Global de Inverno, V, *Belo Horizonte, Brazil*, 479
Salarrué [*pseud. for* Salvador Salazar Arrué], 6652-6653
Salas, Eugenio Pereira. *See* Pereira Salas, Eugenio.
Salas, Horacio, 7033, 7217
Salazar, Braulio, 403
Salazar Valiente, Mario, 2915
Salcedo-Bastardo, J.L., 3331
Saldaña, José P., 2657
Saldías, Adolfo, 3854
Saldívar, Julio P.M., 3915
Sales, Artur de, 7582
Sales, Herberto, 7423
Salés, Luís, 7583
Salgado, J.A. César, 6541
Salgado, José Eusebio, 2443
Salgado Loureiro, María Amélia. *See* Loureiro, María Amélia Salgado.
Salgado Martins, José. *See* Martins, José Salgado.
Salinas Mariaca, Ramón, 3602
Salinas Meza, René, 3255
Salles, David, 7729
Salles, José Bento Teixeira de, 4167
Salles, Waldemar Batista de, 7486
Salles Gomes, Paulo Emílio. *See* Gomes, Paulo Emílio Salles.
Salmerón, Fernando, 9444
Salom Becerra, Alvaro, 6764
Salterain y Herrera, Eduardo de, 3949
Saltor, Jorge E., 9445
Salum-Flecha, Antonio, 3916
Salvador (city), *Brazil*. Diretoria do Arquivo. Divulgação e Estatística, 4046
Salvador (city), *Brazil*. Secretaria Mu-

nicipal de Educação. Departamento de Cultura, 450
Salvat Monguillot, Manuel, 3397
Salzedo y Pineda, Manuel de, 3256
Samaniego, Marcial, 3917
Samayoa Guevara, Héctor Humberto, 2839
Sampaio, Dorian, 108
Sampaio, José da Silveira, 7644
Sampaio, Walter M., 7584
Sampay, Arturo E., 9484
Sanabria, José Rubén, 9734
San Antonio Bicentennial Heritage Committee, *San Antonio, Texas*, 2571
Sánchez, Florencio, 7306
Sánchez, Jean-Pierre, 2012, 6454
Sánchez, Joseph P., 2572
Sánchez, Luis Alberto, 3562
Sánchez, Luis Rafael, 6697, 7307-7309
Sánchez Albornoz, Nicolás, 2114, 2231
Sánchez Bella, Ismael, 2325
Sánchez Domínguez, Enrique, 3918
Sánchez Espinar, Luis Felipe, 6784
Sánchez-Fabrés Mirat, Elena, 2573
Sánchez Flores, Ramón, 2524
Sánchez Gómez, María del Pilar, 2444
Sánchez Lamego, Miguel A., 2772
Sánchez Mármol, Manuel, 6542
Sánchez Martínez, Guillermo, 342
Sánchez Sorondo, Fernando, 6939
Sánchez Vasquez, Adolfo, 9706
Sander, Reinhard W., 7827
Sanders, G. Earl, 2326, 3158, 3606
Sanders, William T., 2525
Sandoval, Armando M., 109
Sandoval Rodríguez, Isaac, 2232
Sandstrom, Alan R., 9115
San Esteban, Ricardo, 3855
Sanguinetti, Horacio, 3856
Sanjinés, Jorge, 978-979
Sanjinés Goitia, Julio, 3604
Sanlés Martínez, Ricardo, 2272
Santa Cruz, Domingo, 9088
Santa María, Carmelo Sáenz de. *See* Sáenz de Santa María, Carmelo.
Santamaría, Daniel J., 3242
Santana, Alberto, 1007
Santana, Francisco, 7174
Santana Cardoso, Ciro Flamarion, 2327, 2916-2917
Santander, Carlos, 6890
Santander, Francisco de Paula, 3345
Sant' Anna, Affonso Romano de, 7585
Sant' anna Moraes, Maia Augusta de. *See* Moraes, Maia Augusta de Sant' anna.
Santa Rosa, F. Affonso, 7586
Santiago, 520
Santiago, Silviano, 7755
Santiago, Théo Araujo, 2328
Santisteban, Jorge, 3563
Santos, Célia Regina Ferreira, 451
Santos, Corcino Medritos dos, 4047
Santos, Francisco Alves dos, 996
Santos, José de Almeida, 535
Santos, José Martins dos, 510
Santos, Paulo Rodrigues dos, 4014
Santos, Silvio Coelho dos, 4015
Santos Filho, Lycurgo de Castro, 4016
Santos Guterres, Sérgio dos. *See* Guterres, Sérgio dos Santos.
Santos Jota, Zélio dos. *See* Jota, Zélio dos Santos.
Santos Neves, Guilherme. *See* Neves, Guilherme Santos.
Santos Titara, Ladislau dos. *See* Titara, Ladislau dos Santos.
Sañudo, José Rafael, 3332
Sanz, Carlos, 2233
Sanz, Pablo R., 3857
Sanz-Pastor, Consuelo, 263
Sánzio de Azevedo, Rafael. *See* Azevedo, Rafael Sánzio de.
São Paulo (state), *Brazil*. Secretaria da Cultura, Ciência e Tecnologia. Pinacoteca do Estado, 480
Saraví, Mario Guillermo, 3858-3859
Sarduy, Severo, 6740-6741
Sargent, David H., 9030
Sarmiento, Domingo Faustino, 6543-6544
Sarmiento, Domingo Fidel, 3860
Sarti, Sergio, 9485
Sarubi, Valdir, 481
Sashin, G.Z., 3605
Sater, William F., 3662
Sauer, Carl Ortwin, 2526
Saunders, John *trans.*, 7942
Savaiano, Eugene, 6083
Savelle, Max, 2329
Saxe Fernández, Eduardo, 9561
Sayles, Stephen, 2658
Scenna, Miguel Angel, 2330, 3861-3862
Schaedel, Richard P., 2175
Schaefer, Jürgen, 2401
Schallhorn, E., 3257
Schinca, Milton A., 3950
Schindler, Helmut, 3863
Schirato, Sérgio José, 9430
Schmeling, Gila do Amaral von, 4168
Schmidt, Augusto Frederico, 7587

Schmidt, Donald L., 2773
Schmidt, Steffen W., 2402
Schmidt Osmanczik, Ute, 9562
Schmitt, Jack *trans*., 7944
Schnaith, Nelly, 3713
Schneider, Jürgen, 2187
Scholes, France V., 2840
Schóo, Ernesto, 6940
Schoonover, Thomas, 2659, 2918
Schopf, Federico, 7218
Schorer Petrone, Maria Theresa. *See* Petrone, Maria Theresa Schorer.
Schubert, Guilherme, 4048
Schulman, Ivan A., 7219
Schulte, Rainer, 7851
Schumann, Peter, 964
Schvartzman, Celia de, 7150
Schwab, Artur, 6102
Schwartz, Stuart B., 2256, 4049
Schwatz, Roberto, 7730
Science and Society, 2403
Scliar Zilberknop, Lúbia. *See* Zilberknop, Lúbia Schliar.
Seal-Coon, F.W., 2953
Seba Patrón, Francisco, 2660
Segarra Iñiguez, Guillermo, 3183
Segreti, Carlos S.A., 3301, 3864
Segundo tomo de recopilación de cédulas despachadas en diferentes tiempos por su Majestad y Señores de su real Consejo de Indias para la Audiencia y Cancillería Real de la ciudad de San Francisco del Quito del Perú, 3184
Seiguerman, Osvaldo, 6941
Selección documental del período bolivariano, 3377
Seluja Cecín, Antonio, 3951
Semana de Estudos Históricos, *I, Ponte Nove, Brazil, 1972*, 4050
Seminario Nacional de Filosofía, *I, Bogotá, 1975*, 9707
Semo, Enrique, 2445, 2473, 2661
Sempat Assadourian, Carlos, 2104, 2234
Sena Madureira, Pedro Paulo de. *See* Madureira, Pedro Paulo de Sena.
Senna Pereira, Maura de. *See* Pereira, Maura de Senna.
Sepich-Lange, Juan R., 9708
Seproni, Marta, 7355
Sepúlveda, César, 2446
Sepúlveda, Mélida Ruth, 6674
Serrano, A.E., 9709
Serrano, Eduardo, 373-375
Serrano Caldera, Alejandro, 9601
Serrão, Joel, 4169

Serrera, Ramón María, 2527
Setúbal, Carmelita, 7472
Setzekorn, William David, 2919
Seward, John H., 2662
Seyferth, Giralda, 4170
Seymour, Arthur J., 7821-7822
Shapira, Yoram, 2774
Sharon, Douglas, 2115
Sharp, William Frederick, 3159
Sharpless, Richard E., 3436
Shaw, Donald L., 6545, 7391
Shaw, R. Paul, 2404
Shea, Daniel E., 2116
Shelby, Barbara *trans*., 7938
Sheppard, Jill, 2954
Sherman, William L., 2841
Shur, Leonid Avelevich, 2373
Sibellino, Antonio, 353
Siegel, Bernard J., 4171
Sierra Mefía, Rubén, 9637
Sieveking, Alejandro, 7310
Siles Guevara, Juan, 6546
Silié, Rubén, 2975, 2987
Silva, Alberto, 997
Silva, [Antônio Francisco] da Costa e, 7588
Silva, Aristides Monteiro de Carvalho e, 7756
Silva, Deonísio da, 7447
Silva, Desiderio Macías, 7151
Silva, Domingos Carvalho da, 7589
Silva, Euclides Carneiro da, 6119
Silva, Francisco Pereira da, 7645
Silva, Hélcio Pereira da, 7646
Silva, Hélio, 4172
Silva, Jorge, 1015
Silva, Ludovico, 9710
Silva, M. Rocha e, 9661
Silva, Maria Beatriz Nizza da, 4051
Silva, Orlando da, 421
Silva, Paulo Augusto da. *See* Paulo Augusto [*pseud. for* Paulo Augusto da Silva].
Silva, Ricardo, 6547
Silva, Rolando Roque da, 7590-7591
Silva, Zander Campos da, 6120
Silva Acevedo, Manuel, 7152
Silva Brito, Mário da. *See* Brito, Mário da Silva.
Silva Carneiro, Newton I. da. *See* Carneiro, Newton I. de Silva.
Silva de Rodríguez, Cecilia, 6548
Silva G., Osvaldo, 3089
Silva Herzog, Jesús, 2775-2778
Silva Olival, Moema de Castro e. *See*

Olival, Moema de Castro e Silva.
Silva V., Fernando, 3089
Silveira, Valdomiro, 7448
Silveira de Souza, Sara Regina. *See* Souza, Sara Regina Silveira de.
Silveira Sampaio, José de. *See* Sampaio, José de silveira.
Silveira Soares Cardozo, Manoel da. *See* Cardozo, Manoel da Silveira Soares.
Silvert, Kalman H., 2405
Simmons, Merle E., 2374
Simmons, Ruth F.S., 7805
Simposio Nacional sobre la Obra Narrativa de Ciro Alegría, *Arequipa, Perú, 1974*, 6844
Simposio Pablo Neruda, *Columbia, S.C., 1974*, 7220
Simposium [sic] Conmemorativo de 150 Aniversario de la Independencia de Panamá de España, *Panamá, 1971*, 2842
Sims, Robert L., 6824
Sinclair, John H., 2235
Singer, Paul, 4173
Siqueira Cavalcanti, Homero Homem de. *See* Homem [de Siqueira Cavalcanti], Homero.
Sistema de prefabricaciones de viviendas en Venezuela, 404
Skármeta, Antonio, 6872
Skell, Otto, 7153
Slade, James J., III, 2779
Slomp Giron, Loraine. *See* Giron, Loraine Slomp.
Smith, Clifford T., 3550
Smith, Hubert, 965
Smith, Octavio, 2976
Smith, Peter Seaborn, 4174
Smith, Robert S., 438
Smith, Steven, 3454
Smith, T. Lynn, 2406
Smith Fernández, Alberto, 2843
Soaje Ramos, G., 9671
Soares, Luiz Eduardo, 521
Soares, Murilo César, 7449
Sobel, Lester A., 2407
Sobrevilla, David, 7221
Sociedad Argentina de Escritores, *Buenos Aires*, 6942
Sodré, Nilson Werneck, 134
Soeiro, Susan A., 2236
Sofer, Eugene F., 3865-3866
Sola, José Vicente, 3302
Solano, Francisco de, 2117, 2331, 3122
Solano y Pérez Lila, Francisco de, 2528
Solari, Juan Antonio, 3867-3870
Soldán y Unanué, Pedro Paz. *See* Arona, Juan de [*pseud. for* Paz Soldán y Unanué, Pedro].
Soler, Rafael, 6698
Soler, Ricaurte, 2375, 2920, 9431, 9662
Soler Cañas, Luis, 6084
Soley Güell, Tomás, 2809
Sologuren, Javier, 7154
Solomon, Denis, 6132
O Som do Pasquim: grandes entrevistas com os astros da música popular brasileira, 9059
Sommers, Joseph, 6621
Soons, Alan, 6436
Sordi Sodi, Carmen, 9119
Sorel, Andrés, 6699
Soriano, Graciela, 9711
Soriano Badani, Armando, 6752
Soriano G., José, 9602
Sorrentino, Fernando, 6943, 6995
Sosa Miatello, Sara, 106
Sosnowski, Saúl, 6996-6998
Soto, Pedro Juan, 7928
Soto Badilla, José Alberto, 9603
Soucougnan, 7790
Sousa, Afonso Felix de, 7592
Sousa, J. Galante de, 7757
Sousa Gaioso, Raimundo José de. *See* Gaioso, Raimundo José de Sousa.
Sousa Mauá, Irineu Evangelista de. *See* Mauá, Irineu Evangelista de Sousa.
Souza, Antônio Cândido de Melo e, 7758
Souza, Eudoro de, 9563
Souza, Hugo de A., 7450
Souza, José Ingacio de Melo, 998
Souza, Luiz de Castro, 4175
Souza, Raymond D., 6742
Souza, Sara Regina Silveira de, 439
Souza Barros, Manoel. *See* Barros, Manoel Souza.
Souza Queiroz, Paulo Edmur de. *See* Queiroz, Paulo Edmur de Souza.
Sovereign, Marie F., 7731
Spain. Ministerio de Educación y Ciencia. Dirección General del Patrimonio Artístico y Cultural. Comisaría Nacional de Archivos. Secretaría General Técnica. Centro de Proceso de Datos, 2237
Spalding, Hobart A., Jr., 2408
Spalding, Tassilo Orpheu, 7424
Speck, Paula, 6999
Spencer, B., 3052
Speratti Piñero, Emma Susana, 7000

Sperber, Suzi Frankl, 7732
Spix, Johann Baptist von, 4052
Spores, Ronald, 2013
Spota, Luis, 6587-6589
Spranz, Bodo, 2014
Squirrú, Rafael F., 354-358
Stagg, Albert, 2574
Stahl, Gerold, 9663
Stahringer de Caramuti, Ofelia I., 3871
Stan, E. Jeffrey, 3459
Stang, Gumund, 2238
Stansifer, Charles L., 2921
Starr, Frederick, 2015
Stawinski, Alberto Victor, 4176
Stegmaier Rodríguez, Juan L., 2376
Stein, Ernildo, 9735
Stein, Stanley J., 2386
Steiner, Stan, 7846
Stenzel, Werner, 2016
Stepan, Nancy, 4017
Stephens, Doris T., 7222
Stephenson, Elie, 7791
Sterne, Richard C., 7392
Stevenson, Robert, 9015-9020, 9031, 9075, 9098, 9120, 9127, 9133-9135
Stiehm, Bruce G., 6023
Stimson, Frederick S., 6549
Stoel-Gammon, Caroline, 6103
Stolk, Gloria, 6700
Stols, Eddy, 2409, 4177
Storni, Hugo, 3303
Strand, Mark, 7839
Street, James H., 2410
Street, Jorge L., 3269
Stuardo Ortiz, Carlos, 3663
Suárez, Diego, 2377
Suárez, Hebert, 3952
Suárez, Santiago Gerardo, 2232
Suárez Altmairano, Modesto, 2575
Suárez Figueroa, Naudy, 3460
Suárez Molina, Víctor M., 79
Suárez Radillo, Carlos Miguel, 7393
Suassuna, Ariano, 536
Suber, Howard, 973
Subercaseaux, Benjamín, 9686
Subercaseaux, Bernardo, 9089
Subero, Efraín, 36, 6012, 7034, 7223-7224
Sucre, Antonio José de, 3333
Sucre, Guillermo, 7225
Sugawara H., Masae, 2529
Sullivan, Thelma D., 2017
Sullivan, William M., 37
Sulmont, Denis, 3564
Summers, William, 9128
Sundiata, I.K., 3040

Suñer, Margarita, 6024-6025
Super, John C., 2530
Sutulov, Alexander, 3664
Swietlicki, Alain *trans*., 7921
Szászdi, Adám, 3096, 3185-3187
Szekely, Alberto, 2411
Szewczyk, David M., 80, 2531
Szichman, Mario, 7001
Szuchman, Mark D., 3866, 3872
Szyszlo, 382

Taboada Terán, Néstor, 6753, 6773
Takaoka, Yoshiya, 482
Talaia O'Donnell, Francisco. *See* O'Donnell, Francisco Talaia.
Talayer, Felipe, 7155-7156
Talesnik, Ricardo, 7311
Tamayo Vargas, Augusto, 6550
Tancer, Shoshana B., 2239
Tanzi, Héctor José, 2333, 2378, 3304
Tapia-Videla, Jorge, 3665
Tapia y Rivera, Alejandro, 6551
Tarn, Nathaniel, 7840, 7874
Tatum, Charles, 7345
Taussig, Michael, 3437
Tavares, Luis Henrique Dias, 4018, 4053
Tavares, Odorico, 7593
Tavares Barbosa, Cláudio. *See* Barbosa, Cláudio Tavares.
Tavares-Neto, José, 4019
Távora, Araken, 522
Taylor, Douglas, 6133
Taylor, Gerald, 2118
Taylor, Hallie D., 7920
Taylor, Julie M., 9032
Taylor, William B., 2487, 2532-2533, 2780
Teatro paulista 1968, 7657
Teatro puertorriqueño. Décimo festival, 7312
Teatro puertorriqueño. Undécimo festival, 7313
El teatro puertorriqueño dentro del nuevo teatro latinoamericano: Colectivo Nacional de Teatro de Puerto Rico, 7394
Teatro 70, 7314
Teffé Hermas Fonseca, Nair de. *See* Fonseca, Nair de Teffé Hermas.
Teixeira, Hindemburgo Dobal. *See* Dobal [Teixeira], H[indemburgo].
Teixeira de Salles, José Bento. *See* Salles, José Bento Teixeira de.
Teixeira Monteiro, Duglas. *See* Monteiro, Duglas Teixeira.

Tejada Gómez, Armando, 7157
Tejerina Carreras, Ignacio G., 3873
Teles, Gilberto Mendonça, 7594
Tellería Toca, Evelio, 3063
Telles, Sérgio, 483
Téllez, Freddy, 9486
Téllez, Germán, 274
Téllez, Hernando, 6552
Tello, Jaime, 6062, 7158
Tello, Pilar León, 2379
Temple, Ella Dunbar, 3378
Le temps et la morte dans la philosophie contemporaine d' Amérique Latine, 9487
Tena Ramírez, Felipe, 2534
Tena Reyes, Jorge, 3024
Tenen Ortega, Guillermo, 6774
Tenenbaum, Barbara H., 2663
Te Paske, John J., 2535
Terán, Ana Enriqueta, 7159
Terán, Oscar, 2922
Terán Mata, Juan Manuel, 9488
El tercer cine: el actor en la revolución, 1016
Terminología en percepción remota: documento de trabajo, 6085
Terrell, Tracy D., 6063
Terzaga, Alfredo, 3874
Teschner, Richard V., 6013
Texas Studies in Literature and Language, 6845
Théberge, Pedro, 4178
Theisen, Gerald, 2664
Thomas, Mary Elizabeth, 2988
Thomas, Teresa, 3299
Thompson, Donald, 9069
Thompson, Eric, 2840
Thompson, George Alexander, 2844
Thompson, Gerald, 2576
Thompson, Lawrence A., 2341
Thompson, Nora B., 2923
Thompson, Buchanan Parker, 2577
Thouvenot, Marc, 2018
Tichauer, Werner Guttentag, 9040
Timmons, Wilbert H., 2578, 2665
Tinajero, Fernando, 9723
Tipton, David, 7828, 7860
Tirado Mejía, Alvaro, 3438-3439
Tisnés Jiménez, Roberto María, 3366
Titara, Ladislau dos Santos, 4179
Titiev, Janice Geasler, 7226
Tito, A., 7658
Tizón, Héctor, 6944
Tjarks, Germán O.E., 3919
Tobin, Patricia, 6825

Tobis, David, 2890
Tobler, Hans Werner, 2754-2755
Toĉilovac, Goran, 6846
Todaro Williams, Margaret. *See* Williams, Margaret Todaro.
Todo es Historia, 3875
Togno, María Elena, 6945
Tolman, Jon M., 7759-7760
Tomlins, Jack E. *trans*., 7934
Tomlinson, Charles *trans*., 7879
Tord Nicolini, Javier, 3213, 3235
Torelly Meurer, Carmen. *See* Meurer, Carmen Torelly.
Tormo Sanz, Leandro, 3243
Toro, Alfonso, 2781
Toro González, Carlos del, 3064
Torquemada, Juan de, 2334
Torre, Toribio de la, 2447
Torre Villar, Ernesto de la, 2536, 2666
Torres, Antônio, 7425
Torres, Hernán, 7227
Torres, Ivo, 7595
Torres de Araúz, Reina, 2924
Torres Fierro, Danubio, 7014
Torres-García, Joaquín, 7160
Torres Wilson, José A. de, 3953
Torretti, Roberto, 9417
Torriente, Loló de la, 343
Tosta, Virgilio, 3123
Tovar A., Romeo, 2845
Tovar Pinzón, Hermes, 2537
Traba, Marta, 359, 376
Traboulay, David M., 2335
Trautmann, Wolfgang, 2538
Trejo Delarbe, Raúl, 2782
Trelles A., Efraín, 2106
Trelles Plazaola, Luis, 1041-1042
3 [i.e. Tres] obras de teatro vanguardia nicaragüense, 7315
Trevisan, Armindo, 7596
Trevisan, Dalton, 7451, 7945
Trevisan, João Silvério, 7452
Trias, Rolando A. Laguarda, 4054
Trías, Vivian, 3920
Troconis de Veracoechea, Ermila, 3124-3126
Troiano, James J., 7395-7396
Troncoso, Rosa Coralia, 3876
Tross, Sérgio, 7453
Troupe, Quincy, 7851
Trueblood, Felicity M., 2385
Truyol y Serra, Antonio, 9604
Tulchin, Joseph S., 2412
Tupinambá da Frota, José. *See* Frota, José Tupinambá da.

Turner, Clorinda Matto de. *See* Matto de Turner, Clorinda.
Turovsky, Paul, 2416
Turró, Ricardo, 9033
Tutino, John M., 2539
Tzitsikas, Helene, 6553

Uchôa, Célia Ribeiro, 4020
Ugarte Corcuera, Francisco, 9638
Ulibarri, George S., 2240
Ulloa, Daniel, 2540
Ulloa, Juan, 6654
Ulloa, Justo C., 6743
Ulloa, Leonor A. de, 6743
Ulloa Barrenechea, Ricardo, 335
Las últimas experiencias del Teatro Experimental de Cali, 7397
Unger, Edyla Mangabeira, 7597
United Nations. Food and Agriculture Organization (FAO), 27
United Nations Educational, Scientific, and Cultural Organization (UNESCO), *N.Y.* Oficina Regional de Cultura para América Latina y el Caribe. Comisión Nacional Cubana de la UNESCO, 81
United States. Department of State, 2241
Universidad de Antioquia, *Medellín, Colombia*. Centro de Investigaciones Económicas, 110
Universidad de Buenos Aires, *Arg*. Facultad de Filosofía y Letras. Instituto de Historia del Arte, 255
Universidad de Chile, *Santiago*. Facultad de Arquitectura y Urbanismo, 268
Universidad de Costa Rica, *San José*. Servicios de Biblioteca, Documentación e Información, 82
Universidad de Oriente, *Cumaná, Ven*. Biblioteca Central. Núcleo de Sucre, 83
Universidad de Puerto Rico, *Río Piedras*. Centro de Investigaciones Sociales, 8
Universidad Nacional del Sur, *Bahía Blanca, Arg.*, 57, 84
Universidade de São Paulo. Escola Superior de Agricultura Luis de Queiroz. Departamento de Ciências Sociais Aplicadas, 111
Universidade de São Paulo. Faculdade de Arquitetura e Urbanismo. Biblioteca, 503
University of Miami, *Coral Gables, Fla*. Library, 85
University of the West Indies, *Cave Hill, Barbados*. Institute of Social and Economic Research (East Caribbean), 9
Upton, John *trans*., 7891
Urbaneja Achelpohl, Luis Manuel, 6800
Urbanski, Edmund Stephen, 2242
Ureña, Pedro Henríquez, 6744
Uriarte, Carlos Enrique, 360
Uribe Echevarría, Juan, 7175
Uribe-Villegas, Oscar, 6026
Uricoechea, Fernando, 4180
Uriz, Francisco, 7258
Urquiza, Concha, 7161
Urquiza-Almande, Oscar F., 7398
Urquizo Sossa, Carlos, 3387
Urra Veloso, Pedro, 2925
Urrello, A., 6554
Urrutia Blondel, Jorge, 9090
Urton, Gary, 2119
Uruguay, Biblioteca Nacional, 38, 7399
Uruguay. Poder Legislativo. Biblioteca. Departamento Selección y Registro de Material Bibliográfico. Sección Bibliografía Uruguaya y Depósito Legal, 10
Usher de Herreros, Beatriz, 6064
Usigli, Rodolfo, 7400
Uslar-Pietri, Arturo, 2336-2337, 6555, 6853, 7162

Val, Chagas, 7598
Valades, José C., 2667
Valcárcel, Carlos Daniel, 3236
Valcárcel, Luis E., 9525
Valdano Morejón, Juan, 3478
Valdelomar, Abraham, *Conde de Lemos*, 6556
Valderrama, Mariano, 3565
Valdés, Enrique, 6873
Valdés Acosta, Gema, 6086
Valdespino, Andrés, 7303
Valdivia, Manuel Rafael, 7035
Valdman, Albert, 6134-6135
Valencia, Tita, 6590
Valenti Ferro, Enzo, 9021
Valentino Ramírez, Pablo, 86
Valenzuela, Luisa, 6946, 7929
Vallaça, Antonio Carlos, 7426
Valladares, Clarival do Prado, 7659
Valladares Rubio, Manuel, 2846
Valle, Dinorath do., 7454
Valle, Roberto do., 7455
Vallejo, César, 7163, 7235, 7880-7881
Vallejos, M. A. Raúl, 9639

Valverde y Téllez, Emeterio, 112
Van Cleve, John V., 3566
van Oss, Adrian, 113
Van Steenberghe de Dourmont, Roberto, 3877
Vance, Joel, 9022
Vanden, Harry E., 9526
Vanderwood, Paul J., 2668-2669
Vangelista, Chiara, 2413
Vanzo, Julio, 361
Vargas, Carlos Alonso, 6065
Vargas, Francisco Alejandro, 3334
Vargas, Germán, 6826
Vargas, Jorge A., 28
Vargas, José María, 3188
Vargas, Túlio, 4181
Vargas Cariola, Juan Eduardo, 3666
Vargas Llosa, Mario, 6847, 7908-7909
Vargas Ugarte, Rubén, 301
Varini, César M., 256
Varona, Alberto J., 3667
Vasco de Escudero, Grecia, 3189
Vasconcellos, Sylvio de, 440
Vasconcelos, José, 6591
Vasques, Edgar, 523
Vásquez, Emilio, 3567
Vaughan, Mary Kay, 2783
Vaughan Ricaurte, Mary Jane, 3160
Vaz, Henrique C. de Lima, 9605
Vázquez, Eduardo, 9717
Vázquez, José Antonio, 3921
Vázquez Machicado, José, 87, 3244
Vázquez Machicado, Humberto, 3388
Vázquez Pérez, Eduardo, 7401
Veblen, Thomas T., 2847
Vebr, Ludomír, 2314
Vedoya, Juan Carlos, 3878-3879
Vega, Pastor, 966
Vega B., Wenceslao, 2977
Veiga, José J., 7427
Veiga, Manuel, 9060
Veitia Linaje, Joseph de, 2338, 2978
Velasco Ibarra, José María, 3479
Velasco Mackenzie, Jorge, 6775
Velasco Márquez, Jesús, 2670
Velázquez, José Francisco (El Viejo), 9147
Velázquez, María del Carmen, 2579-2580
Velázquez, Rafael Eladio, 3305-3307
Vélez de Escalante, Silvestre, 2581
Véliz, Claudio, 3668
Vendramini, Maria do Carmo, 9061
Venezuela. Academia Nacional de la Historia. Departamento de Investigaciones, 3127
Venezuela. Academia Nacional de la Historia. Sociedad Venezolana de Historia de la Medicina, 3345a
Venezuela. Biblioteca Nacional, 58
Venezuela. Biblioteca Nacional. Centro Bibliográfico Venezolano, 42
Venezuela. Biblioteca Nacional. Fondo No Bibliográfico, 9148
Ventura, Zuenir, 999
Vera, Gustavo Adolfo, 3568
Vera, Pedro Jorge, 6776
Vera y Cuspinera, Margarita, 9489
Veracoechea, Ermila de, 3358
Verani, Hugo J., 7015
Verdaguer, María Graciela, 387
Vergara Arias, Gustavo, 3379
Vergara y Vergara, José María, 6455
Vergitsky, Bernardo, 7002
Veríssimo, Luís Fernando, 524, 7487
Veríssimo de Mattos, José, 7700
Verniory, Gustave, 3669
Versiani, Ivana, 7709
Versiani Velloso, Arthur, 9432
Vianna, Hildegardes, 4021
Vicente, José, 7647
Vicente do Salvador, *brother*, 4055
Vico, Horacio J., 3954
Vicuña Mackenna, Benjamín, 3670
La vida y obra del Mariscal Andrés Santa Cruz, 3088
Vidal, Hernán, 6622, 7402-7403
Vidal, Luis Fernando, 6848
Vidaurre Retamoso, Enrique, 3606
Vieira, Emanuel Medeiros, 7456
Vieira Ferreira, Fernando Luiz. See Ferreira, Fernando Luiz Vieira.
Viel, Benjamin, 2243
Viel Temperly, Héctor, 7164
Viggiano, Alan, 7457
Vigneras, Louis-André, 2339, 3097
Vigness, David M., 2784
Vignolo, Griselda, 7355
Vila, Pablo, 3128
Vila Vilar, Enriqueta, 3005
Vilalta, Maruxa, 7316
Vilhena, Maria da Conceição, 7761
Villaça, Alcides, 7599
Villaça, Antonio Carlos, 4182
Villacres Moscoso, Jorge W., 3480
Villalobos R., Sergio, 3089, 3671
Villamarín, Juan A., 2120, 2340, 3161
Villamarin, Judith E., 2340
Villanueva, Víctor, 3569-3570
Villanueva Urteaga, Horacio, 3380-3381
Villarino, Ciro, 2541

Villarroel Triveño, Augusto, 3389
Villasana, Angel Raúl, 11
Villate S., German, 6456
Villaverde, Cirilo, 6557
Villavicencio, Laura N. de, 7228
Villegas, Alfredo G., 3411
Villegas, Juan, 7229
Villoro, Luis, 9640
Viñas, David, 7003
Viñuales, Graciela María, 3295
Virgin Islands of the United States. Bureau of Libraries, Museums and Archaeological Services. Virgin Islands Information & Referral Service, 59
Viscarra Fabre, Guillermo, 6754
Visconti, Eliseu, 484
Visita de Camaná: 1789, 3237
Vitale, Ida, 7225
Vitier, Cintio, 6745
Vittone, Luis, 3922
Vivanco, Alejandro, 6066
Vodanovic, Sergio, 7404
Volpi, Alfredo, 485
Von Hagen, Victor Wolfgang, 2244
Votre, Sebastião Josué, 6104
Vozes, 7762
Vrhel, Frantisek, 2019

Wachowicz, Romão, 4183
Wachowicz, Ruy Christovam, 4184-4185
Waciuma, Wanjohi, 2582
Waidatt Herrera, Domingo, 3880
Walker, John, 6891
Walsh, Donald *trans.*, 7867, 7873
Walsh, María Elena, 7165
Walter, Richard J., 3881
Wanderley, Jaime dos G., 7660
Wankar [*pseud.* for Ramiro Reynaga Burgoa], 2121
Wanke, Eno Teodoro, 7763
Warman, Arturo, 2785
Warner, Keith Q., 6136, 7806
Warren, J. Benedict, 2542
Wasserstrom, Robert, 2926
Waterbury, Ronald, 2786
Watson Espener, Maida, 7405
Watts, A. Faulkner, 2810
Weaver, Frederick Stirton, 2245
Webb, Walter Prescott, 2671
Weber, David J., 2583, 2672-2673
Weber, Francis J., 2584
Weber, João Hernesto, 7701
Wegmann H., Osvaldo, 3672
Weidman, Harold E., 2310

Weilbauer, Arthur, 3090
Weinberger, Eliot *trans.*, 7877, 7901
Weischet, W., 3257
Weiss, Judith A., 3018, 6746
Weistein, Michael A., 9490
Welch, Claude E., Jr., 2414
Weller, Hubert P., 7230
Werk, Alcides, 7600
Werneck Sodré, Nelson. *See* Sodré, Nelson Werneck.
Whitaker, Arthur P., 2246, 3882
White, David H., 2585
Whitecotton, Joseph W., 2020
Whittaker, William G., 2787
Wicke, Charles R., 2021
Wiercinski, Andrzej, 2022
Wilgus, A. Curtis, 12, 2247
Wilhite, John F., 3162
Wilkie, Edna Monzón de, 2415
Wilkie, James W., 2248, 2415-2416, 2788
Wilkinsin, J.B., 2448
Willeke, Venâncio, 4022-4023
Willey, Gordon R., 2023
Williams, Frederick G., 7764
Williams, Gail W., 2389
Williams, Glyn, 3883-3884
Williams, John Hoyt, 3091, 3923-3924
Williams, Lorna V., 7807
Williams, Margaret Todaro, 4186
Williams, Miller, 7851a, 7876
Williams G., Roberto, 9129
Williman, José Claudio, 3308
Wilner, Norberto, 3885
Wilson, Larman C., 2387
Winford, Donald, 6137
Winget, Lynn W., 6083
Winn, Peter, 3955-3956
Winston, Joe Bacchus, 7823
Wirth, John D., 4187
Wistrand Robinson, Lila, 9136
Witherup, William *trans.*, 7866
Wolf, Eric R., 2417
Wolff, Egon, 4188, 7932
Wolff, Frieda, 4188
Woll, Allen, 3673
Woodbridge, Hensley C., 2341, 6014
Woodward, Ralph Lee, Jr., 2811
Woodyard, George W., 7353, 7855a
World Literature Today, 6849
Wortman, Miles, 2674, 2848
Wrigg, Ivan, 7601
Wyers Weber, Frances, 6892

Xavier, Ismail, 967

Xavier, Livio, 4189, 7702
Xirau, Ramón, 9564

Yáñez, Agustín, 7910
Yates, Donald A., 6413
Yauri Montero, Marcos, 6785
Yeager, Gene, 2675
Yedra, Elena, 6747
Yepes, J.M., 2249
Yero Pérez, Luis, 6748
Ygobone, Aquiles D., 3309
Yurkievich, Saul, 7225
Yurrieta Valdés, José, 292

Zagonel, Carlos Albino, 4190
Zalduendo, Eduardo A., 3886
Zanini, Mário, 486
Zantwijk, R. van, 2024
Zapata Arellano, Rodrigo, 6066a
Zapata Olivella, Manuel, 2342
Zapatero, Juan Manuel, 267, 275
Zárate, Dora P. de, 9076
Zarlenga, Ethel Gladys, 7317
Zarza, Idalia Flores G. de, 3887
Zavala, Lorenzo de, 2676-2678
Zavala, Silvio, 6437
Zavaleta, Carlos Eduardo, 6786
Zea, Leopoldo, 9433-9435, 9491, 9527
Zélio, 525
Zeno Gandía, Manuel, 6701
Zentner, Federico, Jr., 2927
Zerecero, Anastasio, 2679
Zevallos Paz-Soldán, Carlos Ortiz de, 3571
Zevallos Quiñones, Jorge, 2122
Zide's fifty drops of blood, 7824
Zierer, Ernesto, 6008
Zilberknop, Lúbia Scliar, 6099
Zimmerman Zavala, Augusto, 3572
Zinsser, Christian, 2928
Zokner, Cecilia Teixeira de Oliveira, 7010
Zorrilla, Juan Fidel, 2449, 2586
Zotter, Hans, 29
Zubatsky, David S., 6014a
Zuccolotto, Afrânio, 7602
Zuidema, R.T., 2123-2124
Zuleta Alvarez, Enrique, 3888
Zúñiga, Neptalí, 3098
Zúñiga Guardia, Carlos Iván, 2929
Zuvekas, Clarence, Jr., 30
Zwetsch, Valdir, 7458